# A HISTORY

OF

# CLASSICAL SCHOLARSHIP

CAMBRIDGE UNIVERSITY PRESS

C. F. CLAY, Manager

LONDON : FETTER LANE, E.C. 4

NEW YORK : THE MACMILLAN CO.
BOMBAY ⎫
CALCUTTA ⎬ MACMILLAN AND CO., Ltd.
MADRAS ⎭
TORONTO : THE MACMILLAN CO. OF
CANADA, Ltd.
TOKYO: MARUZEN-KABUSHIKI-KAISHA

SCENES FROM THE SCHOOLS OF ATHENS EARLY IN THE FIFTH
CENTURY B.C.

Vase-painting by Duris on a Cylix, with red figures on black ground, found at
Caere, and now in the Berlin Antiquarium.

*Frontispiece*, described on p. 42.

# A HISTORY

## OF

# CLASSICAL SCHOLARSHIP

### VOL. I

*FROM THE SIXTH CENTURY B.C.*
*TO THE END OF THE MIDDLE AGES*

BY

Sir JOHN EDWIN SANDYS, Litt.D., F.B.A.,

FELLOW OF ST JOHN'S COLLEGE, ORATOR EMERITUS, AND HON. LL.D. CAMBRIDGE;
HON. LITT.D. DUBLIN; HON. D.LITT. OXFORD; HON. LL.D. EDINBURGH AND ATHENS;
COMMANDER IN THE HELLENIC ORDER OF THE SAVIOUR

**THIRD EDITION**

**WITH TWENTY-FOUR ILLUSTRATIONS**

## CAMBRIDGE
### AT THE UNIVERSITY PRESS
1921

*Quid est aetas hominis, nisi ea memoriâ rerum veterum cum superiorum aetate contexitur?*

Cicero, *Orator*, § 120.

PRINTED IN GREAT BRITAIN

# PREFACE TO FIRST EDITION.

THE present work owes its origin to the fact that, some nine years ago, at the kind suggestion of my friend Professor Jebb, I was invited by the editor of *Social England* to prepare a brief survey of the History of Scholarship, which was included in the volumes published in 1896 and 1897. In course of time I formed a plan for a more comprehensive treatment of the History of Classical Scholarship in general, which should begin with its birth in the Athenian age, should trace its growth in the Alexandrian and Roman times, and then pass onwards, through the Middle Ages, to the Revival of Learning, and to the further developements in the study of the ancient Classics among the nations of Europe and in the English-speaking peoples across the seas. I was already familiar with the *Outlines of the History of Classical Philology* by Professor Gudeman of Philadelphia; and I may add that, if, in place of the eighty pages of his carefully planned *Outlines*, the learned author of that work had produced a complete History on the same general lines, there might have been little need for any other work on the same subject in the English language. But, in the absence of any such History, it appeared to be worth my while to endeavour to meet this obvious want, and, a few years ago, my proposal to prepare a general History of Classical Scholarship was accepted by the Syndics of the University Press. My aim has been, so far as practicable, to produce a readable book, which might also serve as a work of reference. I confess that the work has grown under my hands to a far larger bulk than I had ever contemplated; but, when I reflect that a German 'History of Classical Philology', which does not go beyond the fourth century of our era, fills as many as 1900 large octavo pages, I am disposed to feel (like Clive) 'astonished at my own moderation '. I had hoped to complete the whole of my task in a single volume, but this has proved impossible, owing mainly to the vast extent and the complexity of the literature connected with the history of classical learning in the West of Europe during the eight centuries of the Middle Ages. In studying this part of my subject, I have found myself compelled to struggle with a great array of texts, in various volumes of the *Rolls Series*, the *Monumenta Germaniae Historica*, and Migne's *Patrologia Latina* ; and to master the contents of a multitude of scattered monographs in French, German and Italian, as well as English, publications. With these and other resources I have endeavoured to trace the later fortunes of the Latin Classics, to deal with all the more important indications of the mediaeval knowledge of Greek, and to give an outline of the Scholastic Philosophy. Without taking some account of the latter, it is impossible to have an adequate understanding of the literature of the Middle Ages. And it is a necessary part of my subject, in so far as it arose out of the study of translations of Greek texts, and was inextricably bound up with the successive stages in the gradual expansion of the mediaeval knowledge of the works of Aristotle. But, in tracing the general course of a form of philosophy, which, however valuable as a kind of mental gymnastic, was on the whole unfavourable to the wide and liberal study of the great masterpieces of Classical Literature, I have mainly confined myself to the points of immediate contact with the History of Scholarship ; and thus (if I may give a new turn to a phrase in Seneca), *quae philosophia fuit, facta philologia est*[1]. In the work in general I have studied the History of Scholarship in connexion with the literary, and even, to some slight extent, the political history of each period. But the treatment of the principal personages portrayed in the course of the work has not been on any rigidly uniform scale. Thus, among the three great authors of far-reaching influence, who stand on the threshold of the Middle Ages, there is necessarily far less to be said about the personality of Priscian than about that of Boëthius or of Cassiodorus. Many names of minor importance, which are only incidentally mentioned in the text, have been excluded from the final draft of the Index, and space has thus been found for

[1] *Ep.* 108 § 23.

fuller references to far more important names, such as those of
Aristotle and Plato, Cicero and Virgil. The study of the subject
will, I trust, be further facilitated by means of the twelve chronological tables. A list of these will be found on page xi.

Of the several divisions of my subject (set forth on page 14),
the first six are included in the present volume, which aims at
being complete so far as it extends, and, in point of time, covers
as many as nineteen of the twenty-five centuries, with which those
divisions are concerned. In continuation of this work, I hope to
produce, at no distant date, a separate volume on the History of
Scholarship from the time of Petrarch to the present day[1]. The
first draft of a large part of that volume has already been prepared, and, in the Easter Vacation of last year, I was engaged in
the further study of the literature of the Renaissance, as well as of
certain portions of the Middle Ages, in the hospitable libraries of
Florence. In the spring of the present year I visited the homes
of mediaeval learning on the Loire, and also studied the sculptured
and the written memorials of the mediaeval system of education,
which still survive as a visible embodiment of the influences that
moulded the mind of John of Salisbury in 'the classic calm of
Chartres'.

It is a pleasure to conclude this preface by offering the tribute
of my thanks to all who in any way have helped towards the
completion of what has unavoidably proved a very laborious
undertaking. My gratitude is due, in the first place, to the
Syndics of the University Press, and to the staff of the same,
not forgetting the ever-attentive Reader, who (besides more
important corrections) has endeavoured to reduce the spelling
of mediaeval names to a uniformity little dreamt of in the
Middle Ages themselves. If, in the next place, I may here record
my thanks to those under whose influence this volume has been
prepared, I cannot forget the friend who (as I have stated in
the opening words of this preface) gave the first impulse which
led to the ultimate production of the present work. If, again, I
may give a single example of all that I owe to two other scholars—
one of whom I have happily known for forty years, the other,
alas! for too few—a hint from the late Lord Acton gave me my
first clear impression of the erudition of Vincent of Beauvais;

[1] Published in two volumes in 1908.

first clear impression of the erudition of Vincent of Beauvais; a word from Professor Mayor set me at work on Joannes de Garlandia. Among the Fellows of Trinity, Dr Henry Jackson has been good enough to supply me with a clear statement of his views on Plato's *Cratylus*, and Mr James Duff has kindly tested and confirmed my opinion as to a point connected with the mediaeval study of Lucretius[1]. The College catalogues and other works of Dr James have brought to my knowledge not a few points of interest in the mediaeval manuscripts of Cambridge. I have thus been led to include among the *facsimiles* an autograph of Lanfranc, an extract from a copy of the works of John of Salisbury, which once belonged to Becket, and the colophon of an early transcript of a translation by William of Moerbeke. Four of the *facsimiles* are here published for the first time. To Sir Edward Maunde Thompson, and to his publishers, Messrs Kegan Paul and Co., I am indebted for the use of five of the many *facsimiles* which adorn his well-known *Handbook of Greek and Latin Palaeography*. I have also borrowed two short extracts from the three hundred *facsimiles* in Chatelain's *Paléographie des Classiques Latins*, and one from those in Wattenbach and von Velsen's *Exempla Codicum Graecorum*. I have to thank the Registrary of the University for the use of a single illustration (and the offer of more) from his important volume on the *Care of Books*; and I gratefully recall the trouble taken on my behalf by the Librarian and the staff of the University Library; by the Librarians of Peterhouse, Gonville and Caius, Corpus Christi, Magdalene, and Trinity Colleges; by the Librarian and Assistant Librarian of my own College; and by one of my former pupils, Professor Rapson, of the British Museum. My debt to the published works of scholars at home and abroad is fully shown in the notes to the following pages.

[1] p. 535 n. 3.

*October*, 1903.

# PREFACE TO SECOND EDITION.

A DEMAND for a new edition of this volume having arisen at an unexpectedly early date, the illustrations, as well as the text and notes, have been submitted to a careful revision. In the course of that revision all the suggestions made by reviewers both at home and abroad have been duly considered. Almost all the references printed in the text of the first edition have been transferred to the notes of the second. In the illustrations of the 'Athenian Age', an ancient representation of a *rhapsode* has been prefixed to the chapter on the early study of epic poetry, and the 'masks of comedy and tragedy' and the so-called 'Aristotle' of the Spada Palace have given place to *facsimiles* from the MSS of Aristotle and Aristophanes. Certain pages on the Roman study of Greek have been removed from the beginning of Book IV to a more convenient place at the end of the first chapter of Book III. Under the 'Byzantine Age' there are many additional references to the recent literature of the subject, including Professor Krumbacher's valuable contribution to the encyclopaedic work entitled *Die Kultur der Gegenwart* (1905). Under the 'Middle Ages in the West' there are similar references to standard works, such as Gaston Paris' *Littérature française au Moyen-Age* (1888), to the bibliographical survey of mediaeval Latin literature in the second volume of Gustav Gröber's *Grundriss der romanischen Philologie* (1902), to Professor Ker's *Dark Ages* (1904), and to M. Roger's *Enseignement des lettres classiques d'Ausone à Alcuin* (1905). The brief account of St Patrick has been revised in the light of the *Life* by Professor Bury (1905), and the notice of Peter of Blois supplemented with the aid of an unpublished work by the Rev. W. G. Searle. In the notes in general many references to the recent literature of each subject have been inserted. The new matter in the notes and text amounts in all to about 28 pages....

*October*, 1906.

S.

*b*

# PREFACE TO THIRD EDITION

IN this third edition the author has submitted the whole volume to a careful revision. Apart from corrections of accidental oversights, he has thought it best to allow the text to remain substantially the same. Here, however, as in the revised summary of the complete work published in 1915 under the title of *A Short History of Classical Scholarship*, he has more clearly recognised the part played by Varro, in one particular point, as a link between the Alexandrian and the Roman grammarians (p. 140); he has also assigned 'Virgil,' the eccentric grammarian of Toulouse, to no earlier date than the middle of the seventh century of our era (p. 450); and he has found sufficient reason for modifying his views as to the 'early knowledge of Greek in Ireland' (p. 451).

On at least one hundred and fifty pages, the notes have been brought up to date by the addition of references to the recent literature of the subject. That literature includes the two volumes of the eminently suggestive Lectures of the great authority on the mediaeval fortunes of the Latin Classics, Ludwig Traube of Munich (1861—1907), posthumously published at that place in 1909 and 1911, and the elaborate and comprehensive History of the Latin Literature of the Middle Ages by the Saxon scholar, Max Manitius, published at the same place in 1911.

The researches of Remigio Sabbadini of Milan are mainly concerned with the story of the recovery of classical manuscripts during the Revival of Learning, but the second part of his *Scoperte dei codici Latini e Greci* (1914) supplies us with a retrospect of some of the early humanists of Italy, who died before the death of Petrarch in 1374. It is accordingly quoted, in a note on Italian 'precursors of the Renaissance,' on p. 611, and also on p. xviii of the Bibliography of the present volume. On the other hand, Sabbadini's early humanists of France and Germany died in the next century, and therefore belong to the second volume, which begins with the Revival of Learning, and was published with the third and concluding volume in 1908.

*June*, 1920.

# CONTENTS.

---

# CONSPECTUS OF CHRONOLOGICAL TABLES.

## ABBREVIATIONS.

In the notes and index MA stands for *Mittel-Alter*, *Moyen-Age*, and *Middle Ages*.

A smaller numeral added to that of the volume or page, *e.g.*, ii[2] or 123[4], denotes the edition to which reference is made.

# LIST OF ILLUSTRATIONS.

(21)   Altar-piece by Francesco Traini (1345) in the Church of S. Caterina, Pisa.   From the 'Christ in Glory' a single ray of light falls on each of the six figures of Moses and St Paul and the four Evangelists, here represented as bending forward from the sky, and holding tablets inscribed with passages from the books of the Scriptures which bear their names.   In addition to the rays that proceed from each of these figures, three from the 'Christ in Glory' may be seen descending on the head of the seated form of St Thomas Aquinas, who displays an open book with the first words of his *Summa contra Gentiles* :—*Veritatem meditabitur guttur meum, et labia mea detestabuntur impium* (Proverbs, viii 7), while some of his other works are lying on his lap. The figure is stated by Vasari to have been copied from a portrait lent by the abbey of Fossanuova (North of Terracina), where Thomas Aquinas died in 1274.   Two other rays are represented as coming from the open books displayed by Aristotle on the left and Plato on the right, and described by Vasari as the *Ethics* and *Timaeus* respectively.   Another ray, not a beam of illumination, but a lightning-flash of refutation, falls from the *Summa contra Gentiles*, striking the edge of a book lying on the ground beside the writhing form of its author, Averroës.   Many other rays may be seen descending from the several works of St Thomas on the two crowds of admiring and adoring Dominicans below.   In the original, among the rays on the left, may be read the text, *hic adinvenit omnem viam disciplinae* (Baruch, iii 32), and, among those on the right, *doctor gentium in fide et veritate* (1 Tim. ii 7).   Cp. Vasari, *Vite, Organga*, ad fin., i 612 f Milanesi; Rosini, *Storia della Pittura Italiana* (1840), ii 86 f, 93; Renan, *Averroës*, 305–8[1]; Hettner, *Italienische Studien* (1879), 102–8; and Woltmann and Woermann, *History of Painting*, i 459 E.T.          *facing* p. 582

(22)   Colophon of the 'Theological Elements' of Proclus, from a XIII cen ury copy of the translation finished at Viterbo by William of Moerbeke, 18 May, 1268.   *Procli Dyadochi Lycii, Platonici philosophi, elementatio theologica explicit capitulis* 211.   *Completa fuit translatio hujus operis Viterbii a fratre G. de Morbecca ordinis fratrum praedicatorum* xv *Kalendas Junii Anno Domini* M°C°C° *sexagesimo octauo*.   Reproduced from a photograph taken from the original in *Peterhouse Library, Cambridge*   .     .     .     .     . 588

(23)   Simon, Abbot of St Albans, seated at his book-chest, from Cotton MS in the *British Museum*   .     .     .     .     .     .     .     . 623

(24)   Grammar and Priscian, from the figures of the Seven Liberal Arts and their ancient representatives in the right-hand doorway of the West Front of *Chartres Cathedral*.   .     .     .     .     .     .     . 672


For the sources from which this and certain of the other cuts are derived, see letterpress under the several cuts.

# TITLES OF CERTAIN WORKS OF REFERENCE.

The following list is limited to those works of reference which are most frequently quoted in the present volume, either by the author's name alone, or by a much abbreviated title. It has no pretensions to being a complete bibliography of the subject, or indeed of any part of it. The leading authorities on all points of importance are cited in the notes, *e.g.* on pp. 524, 666. For the bibliography in general, the best book of reference is that of Hübner, which is placed at the head of the list. In the case of literature later than 1889, this may be supplemented from other sources, such as Bursian's *Jahresbericht*, the *Bibliotheca Philologica Classica*, and the summaries in the principal Classical periodicals of Europe or the United States of America.

HÜBNER, E. *Bibliographie der klassischen Alterthumswissenschaft, Grundriss zu Vorlesungen über die Geschichte und Encyklopädie der klassischen Philologie*, ed. 2, 8vo, Berlin, 1889.

## On the Athenian, Alexandrian or Roman Ages.

CHRIST, W. *Geschichte der griechischen Litteratur bis auf die Zeit Justinians* (1889[1], 1890[2], 1898[3], 1905[4]) [references to the sections of ed. 4, which are the same as those of ed. 3], ed. 5, pp. 1319; 1908–13; ed. 6, 1912–; large 8vo, München.

CROISET. *Histoire de la Littérature Grecque*, in five vols. (1887–99), esp. vol V pp. 1—314 (*Période Alexandrine*) by Alfred Croiset; and pp. 315—1067 (*Période Romaine*) by Maurice Croiset; 8vo, Paris, 1899.

EGGER, É. *Essai sur l'Histoire de la Critique chez les Grecs* (1849); ed. 3, pp. 588; small 8vo, Paris, 1887.

GRÄFENHAN, A. *Geschichte der klassischen Philologie im Alterthum*, to 400 A.D.; four vols., pp. 1909; large 8vo, Bonn, 1843–50.

NETTLESHIP, H. (i) *Lectures and Essays on subjects connected with Latin Literature and Scholarship*, pp. 381; and (ii) *Lectures and Essays*, pp. 269; crown 8vo, Oxford, 1885–95.

SAINTSBURY, G. (1) *A History of Criticism and Literary Taste in Europe from the earliest texts to the present day*, vol. I pp. xv+499 (Classical and Mediaeval Criticism); 8vo, Edinburgh and London, 1900. (2) *Loci Critici*, pp. 439, Boston, 1903.

SCHANZ, M. *Geschichte der römischen Litteratur bis zum Gesetzgebungswerk des Kaisers Justinian*; three editions of parts i—ii, in 4 vols., two edd. of part iii, and one ed. of first half of part iv, large 8vo, ending with St Jerome (d. 420). München, 1890—1904; completed by Hosius and Krüger, 1920.

STEINTHAL, H.. *Geschichte der Sprachwissenschaft bei den Griechen und Römern* (1863), 2 vols. 8vo; ed. 2, Berlin, 1890–1.

SUSEMIHL, F. *Geschichte der griechischen Litteratur in der Alexandrinerzeit*, two vols. 8vo, pp. 907 + 771 ; Leipzig, 1891–2.

TEUFFEL, W. S. *History of Roman Literature* (to about 800 A.D.), revised and enlarged by L. Schwabe, translated from the fifth German ed. (1890) by G. C. W. Warr, 2 vols. 8vo, pp. 577 + 615 ; London and Cambridge, 1900; sixth German ed. revised by W. Kroll and F. Skutsch, Leipzig, in 3 vols. completed 1913.


## On the Middle Ages.

BURSIAN, C. *Geschichte der classischen Philologie in Deutschland*, 2 vols. 8vo, vol. 1 pp. 1—90, München, 1883.

CRAMER, <Joannes> Fredericus. *De Graecis Medii Aevi Studiis*, sc. *De Graecis per Occidentem Studiis* (1) *usque ad Carolum Magnum*, pp. 44 ; (2) *usque ad expeditiones in Terram Sanctam susceptas*, pp. 65 (the pages in both cases are those of the *complete* editions), small 4to pamphlets, Sundiae (Stralsund), 1849–53.

EBERT, A. *Geschichte der Litteratur des Mittelalters im Abendlande bis zum Beginne des XI Jahrhunderts*; 3 vols. 8vo, 1874–87 ; ed. 2 of vol. 1, Leipzig, 1889.

GASPARY, A. *History of Italian Literature*, chapters i–xi (to the death of Dante), with a brief sketch of mediaeval Latin literature in Italy, during cent. iv–xiii, in pp. 1—49 of E.T. by H. Oelsner, crown 8vo, London, 1901.

GIDEL, C. *Les Études grecques en Europe* (fourth cent.—1453), pp. 1—289 of *Nouvelles Études*, 8vo, Paris, 1878.

GRADENIGO, G. *Ragionamento Istorico-Critico intorno alla Letteratura Greco-Italiana*, pp. 176, 8vo, Brescia, 1759.

GRAF, Arturo. *Roma nella Memoria e nelle Immaginazioni del Medio Evo*, two vols. small 8vo ; esp. vol. II 153—367 (quoted in notes to pp. 629-50); Torino, 1882–3.

GRÖBER, G. *Grundriss der romanischen Philologie*, Survey of Mediaeval Latin Literature from 550 to 1350 A.D. in vol. II i 97—432, divided into three periods, (1) 550—800 A.D. Decline of Literature (pp. 101—118); (2) 800—1000 A.D. Ecclesiastical Renaissance (pp. 118—181); (3) 1000—1350 A.D. Golden Age of Mediaeval Latin Literature (pp. 181—427); large 8vo, Strassburg, 1902.

HAURÉAU, B. *La Philosophie Scolastique* (1850); ed. 2, vols. I, and II (parts i and ii), 8vo, Paris, 1872–80.

HEEREN, A. H. L. *Geschichte der classischen Litteratur im Mittelalter*, 2 vols. small 8vo ; vol. I, Book i, pp. 10—170 (*c*. 330—900 A.D.); Book ii, pp. 171—376 (900—1400 A.D.), Göttingen, 1822.

*Histoire Littéraire de la France*, begun at Saint-Germain-des-Prés by the Benedictines of the Congregation of Saint-Maur (vols. I—XII, 1733–63); and continued, as the *Hist. Littéraire etc.* (vols. XIII—XXXII, 1814–98) by the Institut of France. (Victor Le Clerc's survey of cent. xiv in vol. XXIV 1—602 is quoted from the separate 8vo ed. of 1865.) 4to, Paris, 1733—1898.

JOURDAIN, Amable. *Recherches critiques sur l'âge et l'origine des traductions latines d'Aristote, et sur les commentaires grecs ou arabes employés par les docteurs scolastiques* (1819); ed. 2 (Charles Jourdain), 8vo, Paris, 1843.

KÖRTING, G. *Die Anfänge der Renaissance-litteratur in Italien*, nominally vol. III but really introductory to vols. I (Petrarch) and II (Boccaccio) in the unfinished *Geschichte der Litteratur Italiens im Zeitalter der Renaissance* (1878-80); 8vo, Leipzig, 1884.

KRUMBACHER, K. (1) *Geschichte der byzantinischen Litteratur von Justinian bis zum Ende des Oströmischen Reiches* (527—1453 A.D.), ed. I, pp. 495, 1890; ed. 2, pp. 1193; large 8vo, München, 1897. (2) *Die griechische Literatur des Mittelalters* (324—1453 A.D.), pp. 237—282 of *Die Kultur der Gegenwart* I viii; large 8vo, Berlin and Leipzig, 1905.

LEYSER, Polycarp (of Helmstadt). *Historia Poëtarum et Poëmatum Medii Aevi* (400—1400 A.D.), pp. 1132; small 8vo, Halle, 1721 and (with new title-page) 1741.

MAITLAND, S. R. *The Dark Ages* (1844), 1853[3], 1890[5]. 8vo, London.

MAÎTRE, Léon. *Les Écoles Épiscopales et Monastiques* (768—1180 A.D.); 8vo, Paris, 1866.

MANITIUS, Max. *Geschichte der lateinischen Literatur des Mittelalters.* Part i, Justinian to 950 A.D.; large 8vo with index, pp. 766, München, 1911.

MIGNE, L'Abbé J. P. *Patrologiae Cursus Completus; Series Latina;* 217 vols. royal 8vo, including a large part of the poetic, epistolary, historical and philosophical (as well as the 'patristic') Latin Literature of the 1000 years from Tertullian (d. 240) to Innocent III (d. 1216), Paris, 1844-55; followed by four vols. of Indices, 1862-4.

*Monumenta Germaniae Historica.* folio series of *Scriptores* etc. edited by Pertz and others (Hanover), 1826-91; continued in quarto series, the latter including (for the later Roman Age) the best editions of Ausonius, Symmachus, Sidonius, and the *Variae* of Cassiodorus, and (for the Middle Ages) Gregory of Tours, the *Letters* of Gregory the Great, and the works of Venantius Fortunatus, with four vols. of *Poëtae Latini*, vols. I and II edited by Dümmler, III by Traube, and IV i by Winterfeld. Berlin, 1877- (in progress).

MULLINGER, J. B. *The Schools of Charles the Great* (quoted mainly in chap. xxv), pp. xx + 193; 8vo, London, 1877.

MULLINGER, J. B. *History of the University of Cambridge*, vol. I, esp. pp. 1—212 (containing the introductory chapters on the Middle Ages); pp. 686; 8vo, Cambridge, 1873.

NORDEN, E. *Die Antike Kunstprosa vom VI Jahrhundert v. Chr. bis in die Zeit der Renaissance*; two vols. 8vo, pp. 969; esp. pp. 657—763 (*Das Mittelalter...*). Leipzig, 1898, reprinted 1909.

PARIS, Gaston. *La Littérature française au Moyen-Age*, Paris, 1888; ed. 2, 1890; ed. 3, 1905.

POOLE, Reginald Lane. *Illustrations of the History of Medieval Thought*, pp. 376; 8vo, London, 1884, ed. 2, 1920.

PRANTL, Carl von. *Geschichte der Logik im Abendlande*, esp. vol. II (1861); ed. 2, Leipzig, 1885; four vols. Leipzig, 1855-70.

RASHDALL, Hastings. *Universities of Europe in the Middle Ages*, vol. I, and II (in two Parts); 8vo, Oxford, 1895.

RENAN, E. *Averroès et l'Averroisme* (1852) ; ed. 4 ; 8vo, pp. 486, Paris, 1882.

'*Rolls Series*' ; *Rerum Britannicarum Medii Aevi Scriptores*, or *Chronicles and Memorials of Great Britain and Ireland during the Middle Ages*, published under the direction of the Master of the Rolls, 244 vols. royal 8vo. The vols. quoted are mainly those containing the works of William of Malmesbury, Alexander Neckam, Giraldus Cambrensis, Grosseteste, Matthew Paris, Roger Bacon, and the ' Satirical Latin Poets of cent. XII ', I and II. London, 1858–96.

SABBADINI, R. *Le Scoperte dei Codici Latini e Greci....* Vol. II, Firenze, 1914, includes notices of early humanists in England (Richard of Bury), Germany (Amplonius Ratinck, and Nicolas Cusanus), France (Jean de Montreuil, and Nicola Clémangis), and Italy (Dionigi da S. Sepolcro, Giovanni Colonna, Mussato, Benzo, Giovanni d' Andrea, etc.), with a detailed list on pp. 199—265 bearing on the survival of the several Classical authors in the Middle Ages. The two volumes of Sabbadini's *Scoperte* (1905-14) are partly summarised in his *Storia e Critica di Testi Latini*, Catania, 1914.

Of the above humanists, all the Italians and Richard of Bury (d. 1345) died before Petrarch (d. 1374) ; all the rest, in the next century.

STEINSCHNEIDER, M. *Die hebräischen Uebersetzungen des Mittelalters, und die Juden als Dolmetscher, ein Beitrag zur Literaturgeschichte des Mittelalters*, pp. xxxiv + 1077, large 8vo, Berlin, 1893.

TIRABOSCHI, G. *Storia della Letteratura Italiana* (ed. 1, Modena, 1772– ); esp. vols. III—V (476—1400 A.D.) of ed. 2, Modena, 1787-94.

TOUGARD, L'Abbé A. *L'Hellénisme dans les Écrivains du Moyen-Age du septième au douzième siècle*, pp. 70 ; large 8vo, Paris, 1886.

TRAUBE, L. *Vorlesungen und Abhandlungen*, I, *Zur Paläographie und Handschriftenkunde*, ed. P. Lehmann, 1909 ; II, *Lat. Philologie des Mittelalters*, ed. P. Lehmann, 1911 ; III, *Kleine Schriften*, 1920 (Beck, München).

TRAUBE's *Quellen und Untersuchungen zur lat. Philologie des Mittelalters*, continued by P. Lehmann, includes *inter alia* Hellmann's *Sedulius Scottus*, and Rand's *Johannes Scottus*, 1906, J. Becker's *Textgeschichte Liudprands von Cremona*, and K. Neff's *Gedichte des Paulus Diaconus*, 1908 ; C. H. Beeson's *Isidor-Studien*, 1913 ; and P. Lehmann, *Vom Mittelalter und von lat. Philologie des Mittelalters*, 1914 (Beck, München).

UEBERWEG, F. *Grundriss der Geschichte der Philosophie*, vol. 1 (1864) ; ed. 8 Heinze, 1894 ; ed. 11 Praechter (Berlin), 1920 ; E. T. London, 1872 etc.

WATTENBACH, W. *Das Schriftwesen im Mittelalter* (1871[1], 1875[2]) ; ed. 3, Leipzig, 1896.

WATTENBACH, W. *GQ*, i. e. *Deutschlands Geschichtsquellen im Mittelalter*, ending *c.* 1250 (ed. 1, 1858) ; ed. 6, Berlin, 1893-4 ; ed. 7 of vol. i, 1904.

On Greek in the Twelfth Century, cp. C. H. Haskins in *Harvard Studies in Classical Philology*, xxi (1910), 75—102, xxiii (1912), 155—166 (Sicilian Translations), and in *American Historical Review*, 1920, 603—615, with the literature there quoted.

# OUTLINE OF PRINCIPAL CONTENTS.

*Es tu scolaris? Sum. Quid est scolaris? Est homo discens virtutes cum solicitudine....Qualis substantia est scolaris? Est substantia animata sensitiva scientiae et virtutum susceptibilis.*

From *Es tu scolaris?*, a mediaeval
catechism of Grammar printed in
Bäbler's *Beiträge* (1885), pp. 190 f.

# CHAPTER I.

## INTRODUCTORY.

THE term 'scholar', in its primary sense a 'learner', is applied
in its secondary sense to one who has learned
thoroughly all that 'the school' can teach him, one Definition of<br>'Scholar'
who through his early training and his constant
self-culture has attained a certain maturity in precise and accurate
knowledge. Thus Shakespeare says of Cardinal Wolsey:—'he
was a *scholar*, and a ripe and good one'[1]. The term is specially
applied to one who has attained a high degree of skill in the
mastery of language, as where Ruskin says in *Sesame and Lilies*:—
'the accent, or turn of expression of a single sentence, will at once
mark a *scholar*'[2]. It is often still further limited to one who 'has
become familiar with all the very best Greek and Latin authors',
'has not only stored his memory with their language and ideas,
but has had his judgment formed and his taste corrected by living
intimacy with those ancient wits'[3]. The true scholar, though in
no small measure he necessarily lives in the past, will make it his
constant aim to perpetuate the past for the benefit of the present
and the future. He will obey the bidding of George Herbert:—
'If studious, copie fair what Time hath blurr'd'[4]. Even if he has
long been in the position of a teacher of others, he will never
cease to be a learner himself; his motto will be *discendo docebis,
docendo disces*; like the 'Clerk' in Chaucer's *Prologue*, 'gladly
wolde he lerne, and gladly teche'; as he advances in years, he
will still endeavour to say with Solon:—γηράσκω δ' αἰεὶ πολλὰ
διδασκόμενος; and, when he dies, he may well be content if his
brother-scholars or his pupils pay him any part, however small, of

---

[1] *Henry VIII*, IV ii 51.        [2] p. 24 (1888).
[3] Donaldson's *Classical Scholarship and Classical Learning*, 1856, p. 150.
[4] *The Church Porch*, xv.

the honour paid to a votary of learning by a Robert Browning, and deem him not unworthy of *A Grammarian's Funeral*.

'Scholarship' may be defined as 'the sum of the mental attainments of a scholar'. It is sometimes identified with 'learning' or 'erudition'; but it is often contrasted with it. Nearly half a century ago this contrast was clearly drawn by two eminent contemporaries at Oxford and Cambridge. 'I maintain', says Donaldson, 'that not all learned men are accomplished scholars, though any accomplished scholar may, if he chooses to devote the time to the necessary studies, become a learned man'[1]. 'It is not a knowledge', writes Mark Pattison, 'but a discipline, that is required; not science, but the scientific habit; not erudition, but scholarship'[2]. 'Classical Scholarship' may be described as being, and in the present work is understood to be, 'the accurate study of the language, literature, and art of Greece and Rome, and of all that they teach us as to the nature and the history of man'.

*Definition of 'Scholarship'*

As compared with the term 'philology', often borrowed in English from the languages of France and Germany, the term 'scholarship' has the advantage of being a more distinctively English word, and of having the terms 'scholar' and 'scholarly' in exact correspondence with it, whereas 'philology' is in England a borrowed word of ambiguous meaning, while 'philologer' and 'philologist' are apt to be used in a linguistic sense alone. Thus, Scott in the *Antiquary* makes one of his characters say of the question whether a particular word is Celtic or Gothic:—'I conceive that is a dispute which may be easily settled by *philologists*, if there are any remains of the language'[3]. We may also recall the memorable words of Sir William Jones :—'No *philologer* could examine the Sanskrit, Greek, and Latin without believing them to have sprung from some common source'[4]. 'Philologer' is hardly ever used in any wider sense; even in the linguistic sense, the word we generally prefer is 'scholar'. 'When I speak contemptuously of *philology*', says Ruskin, 'it might be answered me, that I am a bad *scholar*'[5].

*Scholarship and 'Philology'*

[1] *Classical Scholarship and Classical Learning*, p. 149 (1856).

[2] *Essays*, i 425 (written in 1855).    [3] c. vi p. 61 of Centenary ed.

[4] *Works*, iii 34, ed. 1807.           [5] *Modern Painters*, IV xvi § 28 n.

The present confusion in the English use of the word 'philology' may be illustrated by the fact that in a standard work bearing the title of a 'Manual of Comparative Philology', the term 'Philology' is frequently used in the same sense as ' *Comparative* Philology ', and as a synonym for ' the Science of Language '. The author, I need hardly add, is fully conscious of the confusion between the English and German senses of the word. " In Germany " (as he justly observes) " the word *Philologie* means only the body of knowledge dealing with the literary side of a language as an expression of the spirit and character of a nation, and consequently the department dealing with language as language forms but a subordinate part of this wide science. But in England the study of language as such has developed so largely in comparison with the wider science of Philology under which it used to rank, that it has usurped for itself the name of ' Comparative Philology ' and in recent years of ' Philology ' without any limitation "[1]. Similarly, in the article on ' Philology ' in the latest edition of the *Encyclopaedia Britannica* :—" Philology is the generally accepted comprehensive name for the study of the word; it designates that branch of knowledge which deals with human speech, and with all that speech discloses as to the nature and history of man. Philology has two principal divisions, corresponding to the two uses of 'word' or 'speech', as signifying either what is said, or the language in which it is said, as either the thought expressed— which, when recorded, takes the form of literature—or the instrumentality of its expression : these divisions are the *literary* and the *linguistic*.... Continental usage (especially German) tends more strongly than English to restrict the name ' philology ' to " the *literary* sense. Meanwhile, in England, it is unfortunately the fact that 'philology' and 'comparative philology' are constantly confounded with one another. Yet, some forty years ago, Max Müller insisted that *comparative philology* has really nothing whatever in common with *philology* in the wider meaning of the word, ' *Philology*...is an historical science. Language is here treated simply as a means. The classical scholar uses Greek or Latin... as a key to the understanding of the literary monuments which bygone ages have bequeathed to us, as a spell to raise from the

[1] P. Giles, *Manual of Comparative Philology*, p. 3 f.

tomb of time the thoughts of great men in different ages and
different countries, and as a means ultimately to trace the social,
moral, intellectual, and religious progress of the human race....
In *comparative philology* the case is totally different. In the
science of language, languages are not treated as a means;
language itself becomes the sole object of scientific inquiry "[1].

The above reasons are sufficient to justify the choice of the
title 'History of Classical Scholarship' for a work appealing
primarily to students and scholars who, in England or elsewhere,
claim English as their mother-tongue. But, whether, in this
connexion, we prefer to use the English word 'Scholarship',
or the foreign word 'Philology', in either case the history of the
latter term is part of the history of our subject, and a few preliminary paragraphs may well be devoted to a brief examination
of the ancient Greek originals from which that term and also the
terms 'philologer', 'grammarian' and 'critic' are directly derived.
The variations in the meanings of the ancient terms themselves,
as compared with those of their modern derivatives, are not
uninteresting or unimportant.

The word φιλολογία has a somewhat varied history[2]. It is
first found in Plato, where it means the 'love of dialectic' or 'of
scientific argument'[3]. The corresponding adjective φιλόλογος is

φιλόλογος     applied to 'a lover of discourse'[4], as contrasted with
a 'hater of discourse'[5]. It is applied to Athens
as a city 'fond of conversation', in contrast with Sparta and Crete
with their preference for brevity of speech[6]. Socrates applies it to
himself in a studiously ambiguous sense, either 'fond of talking',
or 'fond of speeches' (like those of the orator Lysias)[7]. Elsewhere, when added to φιλόσοφος, it means a 'lover of reason'[8].
Thus its uses in Plato are as varied as the meanings of the word
λόγος, 'speech', 'discourse', 'conversation', 'argument', 'reason'.

[1] *Lectures on the Science of Language*, i 24, ed. 1866.

[2] Lehrs, *De vocabulis* φιλόλογος, γραμματικός, κριτικός (Königsberg, 1838);
reprinted in Appendix to *Herodiani scripta tria*, pp. 379—401, 1848; cp.
Boeckh, *Encyklopädie...der philologischen Wissenschaften*, pp. 22—24.

[3] *Theaet.* 146 A.        [4] *ib.* 161 A.        [5] *Laches* 188 C.

[6] *Laws* 641 E; cp. Isocr. *Antid.* 296, where φιλολογία and εὐτραπελία are
characteristic of Athens.

[7] *Phaedrus* 236 E.        [8] *Rep.* 582 E.

Aristotle describes the Spartans as having made Chilon, one of
the 'Wise Men' of Greece, a member of their Council, although
they were ἥκιστα φιλόλογοι, 'the least literary of all people'[1];
and in the 'Aristotelian' writings we find included under the
general phrase, ὅσα περὶ φιλολογίαν, questions of reading, rhetoric,
style and history[2]. Thus far, the word has not yet acquired any
narrower signification. When Stobaeus (in the fifth century of
our era), in telling an anecdote of Pericles, uses φιλόλογος in one
of its later senses, that of 'educated', in contrast to 'uneducated'
(ἀπαίδευτος), he is not really quoting the language of Pericles
himself, but is only reflecting the usage of a later age[3].

The first to assume the title of φιλόλογος at Alexandria was
the learned and versatile scholar, astronomer, geographer, chronologer, and literary historian, Eratosthenes (c. 276—195 B.C.). The
same title was assumed at Rome by a friend of Sallust and Pollio,
a Roman freedman of Athenian birth, Lucius Ateius Praetextatus
(fl. 86—29 B.C.)[4]. The term is applied by Plutarch to those who,
in reading poetry, are attracted by its beauty of expression[5]. In
late Greek it is mainly found in two senses (1) 'studious', 'fond
of learning', (2) 'learned', 'accomplished'[6]. The first is approved
by the Atticist Phrynichus; the second is condemned[7].

The word is frequent in the familiar Latin of Cicero's Letters,
philologia is there applied to the 'study of literature'[8], and philologus means 'learned' or 'literary'[9]. Vitruvius calls Homer
poëtarum parens philologiaeque omnis dux, 'the father of poetry and
the foremost name in all literature', and describes the Pergamene
princes as prompted to found their famous Library by the delights

[1] Rhet. ii 23, 11.			[2] Probl. xviii, p. 916 b.
[3] Stobaeus, O 17.
[4] Suetonius, De Grammaticis, 10.
[5] De Audiendis Poëtis, c. 11.
[6] Lehrs, l.c., p. 380, (1) eruditionis amicus, studiosus; (2) eruditus, litteratus.
[7] p. 483, Rutherford, φιλόλογος· ὁ φιλῶν λόγους καὶ σπουδάζων περὶ
παιδείαν· οἱ δὲ νῦν ἐπὶ ἐμπειρίαν τιθέασιν οὐκ ὀρθῶς.
[8] Ad Att. ii 17, 1; (Cicero filius) ad Fam. xvi 21, 4; συμφιλολογεῖν = una
studere, ib. § 8.
[9] Ad Att. xiii 12, 3; 52, 2; xv 15, 2; used as a Subst. in xv 29, 1 and ad
Quint. fr. ii 10, 3.

of *philologia*, or 'literature'[1]. In Seneca's Letters *philologus* is
contrasted with *grammaticus* in the lower sense of the latter: the
*philologus* (he observes) will notice points of antiquarian interest;
the *grammaticus*, matters of expression[2]. Lastly, in the fanciful
allegory *de nuptiis Philologiae et Mercurii*, written by Martianus
Capella in the fifth century, the bride Philologia appears as
the goddess of speech, attended by seven bridesmaids personifying
the seven liberal Arts. In modern Latin the meaning of *philologus*
had been made much more comprehensive. It is now used in the
sense of a 'scholar', thus including all that ancient writers understood by *grammaticus* in the higher sense of the term, and much
more besides,—not only a knowledge of the languages of Greece
and Rome but also a knowledge of all that contributes to the
accurate understanding of their literature and their art. Those
who in modern Latin are called *philologi* were in ancient times
known either as *grammatici* (in its higher sense), or as *critici*.

Having briefly traced the history of the word φιλόλογος, we
may now deal no less briefly with the two terms which in modern
Latin, and in French and German, it has ultimately superseded,
the terms γραμματικός and κριτικός.

In the golden age of Greek literature the common meaning of
γραμματικός    γράμματα is 'letters of the alphabet', and γραμματικός is applied to one who is familiar with those
letters, knows 'their number and their nature'[3]; one in short who
has learnt to read[4]. In the same age τέχνη γραμματική is simply
the art of γράμματα[5], the art of reading[6]. Not in the same age
only, but in all later ages, γραμματιστής is a teacher of γράμματα,
a teacher of reading and writing[7]. The corresponding Latin term
to γραμματιστής is *litterator*[8].

[1] vii *Praef.* § 8 and § 4.

[2] *Ep.* 108 § 29.

[3] Plato, *Philebus* 17 B; cp. *Theaet.* 207 B; Xen. *Mem.* iv 2, 20.

[4] Plato, *Rep.* 402 B.

[5] *Philebus* 18 D, *Cratylus* 431 E; *Soph.* 253 A; cp. ἡ τῶν γραμμάτων μάθη-
σις (*Theaet.* 206 A, 207 D; *Protag.* 345 A).

[6] Aristotle, *Pol.* 1337 *b* 25 f; *Categ.* c. 9; *Top.* vi 5, 142 *b* 31 f.

[7] Plato, *Euthydemus* 279 E, περὶ γραμμάτων γραφῆς τε καὶ ἀναγνώσεως οἱ
γραμματισταί, cp. *Protag.* 326 D, *Laws* 812 A.

[8] Suetonius, *De Grammaticis*, 4.

In the earlier time γράμματα seldom means 'literature'[1]; but
it is to this sense of the word that we owe the new meaning given
to its derivative γραμματικός in the Alexandrian age. That new
meaning is a 'student of literature', especially of poetical literature; and similarly γραμματική now comes to mean the 'study of
literature', especially of poetry. γραμματική in this new sense of
the term is sometimes said to have begun with Theagenes of
Rhegium (*fl.* 525 B.C.), who was the earliest of the allegorical
interpreters of Homer[2]. When Plato is described as the first who
speculated on the nature of γραμματική[3], we may assume that the
reference is to the *Cratylus*, a dialogue in which he discusses the
nature of words. Aristotle is similarly described as the founder
of the art of γραμματική in that higher sense which implies the
learned study of poetic literature[4]. But this is only the language
of *later writers*, and we may be sure that neither Theagenes nor
Plato nor Aristotle would have described *himself* as γραμματικός,
except in the sense applicable to all who could read and write.

The first who was called γραμματικός in the new sense of the
term was a pupil of Theophrastus, the Peripatetic Praxiphanes of
Rhodes (*fl.* 300 B.C.), the author of certain works on history and
poetry. According to another tradition, the first who received
this designation was Antidorus of Cumae, who wrote a treatise on
Homer and Hesiod, and also a work on Style, and may be placed
very early in the Alexandrian age. After the time of Antidorus, we
find Eratosthenes giving the title γραμματικά to a work in two
books, but their contents are unknown[5]. Dionysius Thrax (born

---

[1] It seems to bear this meaning in Plato, *Apol.* 26 D, ἀπείρους γραμμάτων,
though this is denied by Kaibel in *Hermes*, xxv (1890) 102 f.

[2] Schol. on Dionysius Thrax, p. 729, 22, (γραμματικὴ) ἀρξαμένη μὲν ἀπὸ
Θεαγένους, τελεσθεῖσα δὲ παρὰ τῶν Περιπατητικῶν Πραξιφάνους καὶ Ἀριστοτέλους.

[3] Diogenes Laertius, iii 25, πρῶτος ἐθεώρησε τῆς γραμματικῆς τὴν δύναμιν.

[4] Dion Chrysostom, *Or.* 53, 1, ἀφ' οὗ φασι τὴν κριτικήν τε καὶ γραμματικὴν
ἀρχὴν λαβεῖν. Cp. Susemihl, *Geschichte der Gr. Litt. in der Alexandrinerzeit*,
ii 663—5.

[5] Clemens Alexandrinus, *Stromateis* i p. 309, Ἀντίδωρος (Ἀπολλόδωρος MS)
ὁ Κυμαῖος πρῶτος τοῦ κριτικοῦ εἰσηγήσατο (παρῃτήσατο Usener) τοὔνομα καὶ
γραμματικὸς προσηγορεύθη. ἔνιοι δὲ Ἐρατοσθένη τὸν Κυρηναῖόν φασιν, ἐπειδὴ
ἐξέδωκεν οὗτος βιβλία δύο, γραμματικὰ ἐπιγράψας. ὠνομάσθη δὲ γραμματικός, ὡς
νῦν (*c.* 200 A.D.) ὀνομάζομεν, πρῶτος Πραξιφάνης (*c.* 300 B.C.).

about 166 B.C.), in the earliest treatise on Grammar now extant, defined γραμματική as being 'in general the practical knowledge of the usage of writers of poetry and prose'[1]. He divided it into six parts :—(1) accurate reading, (2) explanation of poetic figures of speech, (3) exposition of rare words and of subject-matter, (4) etymology, (5) statement of regular grammatical forms. These five parts form the 'minor' or 'imperfect' art of Grammar, the 'perfect' art including: (6) 'the criticism of poetry, which is the noblest part of all'[2]. A better subdivision gives us only four parts, (1) correction of the text, (2) accurate reading, (3) exposition, (4) criticism[3]. Dionysius of Halicarnassus twice describes τὴν γραμματικήν as including the art of reading and writing and the art of grammar, without extending its meaning to literary criticism[4].

In the Roman age the Alexandrian meaning of γραμματικός is noticed by Suetonius who makes the borrowed word *grammaticus* synonymous with the Latin *litteratus*[5]. He adds that Cornelius Nepos agrees with this view, and regards *litterati* and *grammatici* as equivalent to *poëtarum interpretes*. Similarly Cicero treats *grammatica* (neuter plural) as synonymous with *studium litterarum*[6], and includes in its province *poëtarum pertractatio, historiarum cognitio, verborum interpretatio, pronuntiandi quidam sonus*[7]. Elsewhere he describes *grammatici* as *interpretes poëtarum*[8]. Just as Cicero identifies the science with *studium litterarum*, so Quintilian describes it as sometimes translated by *litteratura*[9], and as including disquisitions on style and subject-matter, the explanation of difficulties and the interpretation of poetry[10]. He divides it into two parts, (1) 'the science of correct language', (2) 'the

---

[1] ἐμπειρία ὡς ἐπὶ τὸ πολὺ τῶν παρὰ ποιηταῖς τε καὶ συγγραφεῦσι λεγομένων (Iwan Müller's *Handbuch*, i 130[1], 152[2]).

[2] Cp. Philo, p. 348 B C and 462 G ; and Sext. Emp. pp. 224, 226, quoted by Classen, *De Gram. Gr. primordiis*, p. 12 f.

[3] Schol. on Dion. Thrax in Bekker's *Anecd.* 736, (μέρος) διορθωτικόν, ἀναγνωστικόν, ἐξηγητικόν, κριτικόν.

[4] *De Dem.* p. 1115 R., *De Comp. Verb.* p. 414 Schaefer (c. 14).

[5] *De Grammaticis*, 4.          [6] *De Or.* i § 10.          [7] *ib.* § 187.

[8] *De Div.* i § 34 ; cp. *ib.* 116 and *Orator* § 72. Cp. *ad Att.* vii 3, 10, quoniam grammaticus es, si hoc mihi ζήτημα persolveris, magna me molestia liberaris.

[9] II i 4.                              [10] I ii 14.

interpretation of poetry'[1]; the former, he adds, must include 'correct writing', and the latter must be preceded by 'reading aloud with correctness'. It thus embraces correct reading and correct writing, and, beside these, criticism, which detects spurious lines or spurious works, and draws up select lists of approved authors[2]. Seneca, as an adherent of the Stoic philosophy, which had paid special attention to Grammar, uses *grammaticus* in a somewhat narrower sense[3]. He also compares the different lights in which Cicero's treatise *de Republica* is viewed by a *philosophus*, a *philologus* and a *grammaticus*. While the *philosophus* wonders that so much can be argued on the side contrary to that of Justice, the *philologus* notices that, of two kings of Rome, the father of the one (Ancus) and the mother of the other (Numa) were unknown; also that Romulus is said to have perished during an eclipse of the sun, that the *dictator* was formerly called the *magister populi*, and that there was a *provocatio ad populum* even in the time of the kings, 'as Fenestella also holds'. But the *grammaticus* (he continues) notices (1) verbal expressions, such as *reapse* for *re ipsa*, (2) changes in the meaning of words, as the use of *calx* for *creta*, of *opis pretium* (in Ennius) for *operae pretium*, (3) the phrase *caeli porta*, borrowed by Ennius from Homer, and itself borrowed in turn by Virgil[4]. Lastly, when Aulus Gellius (*fl.* 150 A.D.) wished to ascertain the meaning of the phrase *ex iure manum consertum*, he applied to a *grammaticus*, who professed to expound Virgil, Plautus and Ennius, but (as it happened) was quite unaware that this legal phrase was actually found in Ennius[5]. Thus it appears that, in and after the Alexandrian age, γραμματικός mainly implied aptitude in the study and interpretation of poetry, and γραμματική included not only Grammar but also (in its higher sense) the criticism of the poets.

---

[1] I iv 2.

[2] I iv 3, (iudicium) quo quidem ita severe sunt usi veteres grammatici, ut non versus modo censoria quadam virgula notare et libros, qui falso viderentur inscripti, tanquam subditos summovere familia permiserint sibi, sed auctores alios in ordinem redegerint, alios omnino exemerint numero.

[3] *Ep.* 88 § 3, grammaticus circa curam sermonis versatur, et, si latius evagari vult, circa historias, iam ut longissime fines suos proferat, circa carmina.

[4] *Ep.* 108 §§ 30—34.

[5] Gellius, xx 10.

The Alexandrian use of γραμματικός in the above sense was
apparently somewhat later than the use of κριτικός
in the same general sense.   The word κριτικός is
found in a pseudo-platonic dialogue of uncertain date, in a passage
in which the Greek boy, on reaching the age of seven, is humorously described as 'suffering much at the hands of tutors and
trainers, and teachers of reading and writing' (γραμματισταί), and
as 'passing, as he grows up, under the control of teachers of
mathematics, tactics and criticism' (κριτικοί)[1].   There is reason to
believe that, just as this use of κριτικοί probably preceded that of
γραμματικοί in its Alexandrian sense, similarly the term κριτική
was earlier than the corresponding term γραμματική[2].

κριτικός

Criticism was regarded as founded by Aristotle, and among
its foremost representatives in the Alexandrian and Pergamene
age were Aristarchus at Alexandria and Crates at Pergamon[3].
Crates and his pupils of the Pergamene School subordinated
γραμματική to κριτική, and preferred to be called κριτικοί[4].  Criticism was among the higher functions of the γραμματικός.  Thus
Athenaeus (fl. c. 200 A.D.) describes the authorship of certain
poems as a matter for the critical judgement (κρίνειν) of the best
γραμματικοί[5]; and Galen (c. 130—200 A.D.) wrote a treatise on the
question whether any one could be κριτικός and also γραμματικός,
implying a certain distinction between these terms.

Meanwhile, more than two centuries before Galen, Cicero in
one of his letters, after alluding to Aristarchus, describes himself

---

[1] *Axiochus* 366 E.   Cp. P. Girard, *l'Éducation Athénienne*, p. 224—7.

[2] Schol. on Dionysius Thrax, p. 673, 19, ἐπιγέγραπται γὰρ τὸ παρὸν σύγγραμμα κατὰ μέν τινας περὶ γραμματικῆς, κατὰ δὲ ἑτέρους περὶ κριτικῆς τέχνης·
κριτικὴ δὲ λέγεται ἡ τέχνη ἐκ τοῦ καλλίστου μέρους.  Bekker, *Anecdota*, p. 1140,
τὸ πρότερον κριτικὴ ἐλέγετο (ἡ γραμματική), καὶ οἱ ταύτην μετιόντες κριτικοί.  Cp.
Usener in Susemihl, *l.c.*, ii 665.

[3] Dion Chrysostom, *Or.* 53, 1, Ἀρίσταρχος καὶ Κράτης καὶ ἕτεροι πλείους τῶν
ὕστερον γραμματικῶν κληθέντων, πρότερον δὲ κριτικῶν, καὶ δὴ καὶ αὐτὸς ὁ
Ἀριστοτέλης, ἀφ' οὗ φασι τὴν κριτικήν τε καὶ γραμματικὴν ἀρχὴν λαβεῖν.

[4] Sextus Emp., *Math.* i 79, (Κράτης) ἔλεγε διαφέρειν τὸν κριτικὸν τοῦ γραμ-
ματικοῦ· καὶ τὸν μὲν κριτικὸν πάσης, φησί, δεῖ λογικῆς ἐπιστήμης ἔμπειρον εἶναι·
τὸν δὲ γραμματικὸν ἁπλῶς γλωσσῶν ἐξηγητικὸν καὶ προσῳδίας ἀποδοτικὸν κτλ.,
and 248, Ταυρίσκος ὁ Κράτητος ἀκουστής, ὥσπερ οἱ ἄλλοι κριτικοί, ὑποτάσσων
τῇ κριτικῇ τὴν γραμματικὴν κτλ.

[5] p. 116.

as about to decide, *tamquam criticus antiquus*, whether a certain
document is genuine or spurious[1]. The term is also used by
Horace, in a passage in which he calls Ennius an *alter Homerus*,
*ut critici aicunt*, where Varro is probably meant[2]. It also occurs
repeatedly in the Commentary on Virgil by Servius, in the frequent
phrase *notant critici*[3]. Lastly, κριτικός is found as a designation of
Dionysius of Halicarnassus; also of Munatius of Tralles (the
tutor of Herodes Atticus) in the second century, and of Cassius
Longinus in the third[4]. Thus it appears that, owing to a certain
ambiguity in the term γραμματικός with its lower sense of 'grammarian' and its higher sense of 'scholar', and a corresponding
ambiguity in the term γραμματική with its lower sense of 'grammar'
and its higher sense of 'scholarly criticism', the term κριτικός
was generally applied to those of the γραμματικοί who excelled in
the higher branch of γραμματική, that of literary criticism. We
may conclude on the whole that one who in modern times is in
English called a 'scholar', in French a *philologue*, and in German
a *philolog*, would in ancient times have been called either a *grammaticus* or a *criticus*, according to his degree of distinction, the
latter being the higher term of the two; while the term *philologus*
in general designated a lover of learning, or a learned student of
varied accomplishments and especially of antiquarian tastes[5].

In modern times the first who called himself *studiosus philologiae* was F. A. Wolf, the founder of the modern
German school of scholarship, who thus described Modern 'Philology'
himself in the matriculation-book of the University
of Göttingen on 8 April 1777, a date which has accordingly been
designated as the 'birthday of Philology'[6]. In after years Wolf
himself was dissatisfied with the term *Philologie* because its
Alexandrian associations confined it to the study of Literature
alone, to the exclusion of Art, and also because in modern times
it was apt to be regarded as synonymous with the Science of

[1] *ad Fam.* ix 10, 1.                    [2] *Ep.* II i 51.
[3] Servius on *Aen.* i 71, viii 731, xi 188 etc. (ap. Lehrs, *l.c.*, p. 397 note).
[4] Usener on Dionysius Hal. *de Imitatione*, p. 133 note; and Lehrs, *l.c.*,
p. 395.
[5] Lehrs, *l.c.*, p. 379.
[6] F. Haase in Ersch und Gruber, *s.v.* 'Philologie,' p. 383 n. 29.

Language. He therefore preferred the term *Alterthums-wissen-schaft*, ' the Science of Antiquity '[1]. Other terms have been suggested at various times[2], but in France and Germany the term *Philologie* still holds its own.

' Philology' was for a long time limited to linguistic studies, and was regarded as only including grammar, lexicography, exegesis, and textual and literary criticism; but, since the time of Wolf, it has been generally understood in a wider sense, as including the study of ancient life in all its phases, as handed down to us in the literature, the inscriptions, and the monuments, of Greece and Rome[3]. It has thus been interpreted by scholars such as Ast and Bernhardy, Boeckh and Otfried Müller, Ritschl and Haase[4]. In contrast to the comprehensive definition given by these, we have the narrower view best represented by Gottfried Hermann, who saw in ' Philology' a science of language alone[5].

The varied studies included within the province of ' Philology' have been grouped and classified in different ways by Wolf and Bernhardy, Boeckh and Müller, Ritschl, Reichardt and Haase[6]. The tendency in the later classifications of the subject has been to make Grammar not a merely instrumental means towards the

[1] *Kleine Schriften*, ii 814 f.

[2] *e.g.* 'classical learning,' *studia humanitatis*, and the unclassical term *humaniora* (criticised by Boeckh, *Encyklopädie der philologischen Wissenschaften*, p. 24 f).

[3] *Kleine Schriften*, ii 826.

[4] Ast, *Grundriss der Philologie* (1808), p. 1 ; Bernhardy, *Grundlinien zur Encyklopädie der Philologie* (1832), pp. 48—53 ; Boeckh, *Rheinisches Museum* (1827), i 41 ; Müller, *Göttingen gel. Anzeiger* iii (1836), p. 1682 ; Ritschl (1833), in *Opuscula*, v 7 ; and Haase in Ersch u. Gruber, iii 23 p. 390 ; Usener, *Philologie u. Geschichtswissenschaft*, Bonn, 1882, p. 14 ; Wilamowitz, *Philologie u. Schulreform*, Göttingen, 1892, p. 8 (all quoted in Freund's *Triennium Philologicum*, i p. 9[3] f). Cp. Hermann Paul's *Grundriss der Germanischen Philologie*, i 1—7.

[5] Hermann's view was attacked by Boeckh and Müller, *l.c.* In the preface to the *Acta Societatis Graecae* he had spoken with contempt of the Comparative Philologists 'qui ad Brachmanas et Ulphilam confugiunt atque ex paucis non satis cognitarum linguarum vestigiis quae Graecorum et Latinorum verborum vis sit explanare conantur' (cp. Freund, p. 20[3]).

[6] Wolf, *Kleine Schriften*, ii 894 ; Bernhardy, *Grundlinien*, p. xi ; Boeckh, *Encyklopädie*, pp. 54—64 ; Müller, *l.c.*; Ritschl, *l.c.*; Reichardt, *die Gliederung der Philologie* (1846) ; and Haase, *l.c.* (transcribed in Freund, *l.c.* pp. 15—18[3]).

study of 'Philology', but one of the main subjects of study in
itself. It has also become increasingly necessary to include
among the introductory studies, the general and also the comparative Science of Language. Inscriptions, which were classed by
Wolf under the heading of Art, are now rightly regarded as part
of the written records of antiquity, and as supplying, side by
side with Literature, part of the documentary evidence for the
history and the antiquities of the Greek and Roman world[1].

The history of Classical Scholarship corresponds to the last
of the four and twenty subdivisions of 'Philology'     History of
suggested by Wolf; and is the first of the studies    Classical
                                      Scholarship
introductory to 'Philology' in the scheme proposed
by Haase, and also in that elaborately carried out in the encyclopaedic work known as Iwan Müller's *Handbuch der klassischen
Altertumswissenschaft* (1886 f). A knowledge of the general course
of the history of Classical Scholarship in the past is essential to
a complete understanding of its position in the present and its
prospects for the future. Such a knowledge is indispensable to the
student, and even to the scholar, who desires to make an intelligent use of the leading modern commentaries on classical authors
which necessarily refer to the labours of eminent scholars in
bygone days. And the study of that history is not without its
incidental points of interest, in so far as it touches on themes of
such variety, and such importance, as the earliest speculations on
the origin of language, the growth of literary and dramatic criticism
at Athens, the learned labours of the critics and grammarians of
Alexandria and Rome, and of the lexicographers of Constantinople.
It also has its points of contact with the Scholastic Philosophy of
the Middle Ages, with the Revival of Learning and the Reforma-
tion of Religion, and with the foundations of the educational
systems of the foremost nations of the modern world.

The volume now offered to the public is the first instalment of
a History of Classical Scholarship from the sixth    Subdivisions
century B.C. to the present day. That history, so   of the proposed
                                            work
far as it is included in this volume, may be most

---

[1] Boeckh, Introd. to *Corp. Inscr. Gr.* vol. vii.

conveniently distributed over the following six divisions of the subject, but the dates of the limits assigned to each division must be regarded as only approximate.

I.    The Athenian Age, from 600 to 300 B.C.

II.   The Alexandrian Age, from 300 B.C. to the beginning of the Christian era.

III.  The Roman Age of *Latin* Scholarship, from 168 B.C. to 530 A.D.

IV.   The Roman Age of *Greek* Scholarship, from the beginning of the Christian era to 530 A.D.

V.    The Byzantine Age, or the Middle Ages in the East, from 530 to 1350 A.D.

VI.   The Middle Ages in the West, from 530 to 1350 A.D.

The remainder of the work will include the Revival of Learning in Italy from 1350 A.D. to the death of Leo X in 1521, with the subsequent history of scholarship in Italy; and a survey of the modern history of scholarship in France, Holland, England, and Germany, as well as the other nations of Europe and the United States of America.

The time to be traversed will ultimately extend to as much as two thousand five hundred years, and in the sequence of the centuries the narrative will pass from one home of learning to another, from Athens to Alexandria and Pergamon, from Pergamon and Alexandria to Rome, and from Rome to Constantinople. It will also range over the vast expanse of the Middle Ages in the West, as well as in the East of Europe, pausing for a time in Italy at the date of the death of Dante (1321). On some future day it may invite us to visit the studious haunts of Petrarch at Vaucluse and Arqua; to linger for a while in Florence and in other famous cities of Italy; and then to turn to the chief centres of scholarship in the northern lands which were successively reached by the Revival of Learning. For three centuries of this survey our interest will be mainly fixed on Athens, for three on Alexandria, for more than five on Rome; then, for eight centuries, it will be first concentrated on Constantinople, and afterwards diffused over the West of Europe. Rather less than six centuries will thus await our study at some not far distant time. In any future review of the period of exactly two centuries that divides the death of

Dante from the death of Leo X, our attention will be almost
exclusively confined to Italy, and, in the final period of little more
than 380 years, we shall look forward to tracing the progress of
scholarship in Italy and in other lands from the close of the
Italian Renaissance down to the present day.

In that final period, even more than in the far earlier 'Ages'
of the present volume, a history of scholarship must necessarily
to a large extent consist of notices of the lives and works of
individual scholars. In the case of the more important names,
some estimate of the value of their services will naturally be
expected. In the case of names of minor importance, the briefest
mention must suffice; and, in a work so limited in compass as
compared with the wide extent of the subject, many will unavoidably be omitted altogether. Every endeavour will however be made
to give accurate details as to the dates connected with those who
are mentioned in these pages. Names of special importance in
the annals of literature or scholarship will also find a place in the
chronological tables, in which an attempt will be made to give a
brief conspectus of the more than nineteen centuries over which
the present volume extends. The reader may remember that Cicero,
in his *Orator*, tells us that his friend Atticus, in composing a
comprehensive work extending over seven centuries, had succeeded
'by a strict observance and specification of dates, without omitting
any notable event, in including within the compass of a single
volume the annals of seven hundred years'. Elsewhere he makes
the author modestly ask, 'what his work could possibly contain,
that was either new or particularly useful to Cicero', and himself
vouchsafes a reassuring reply as to its 'utility', and as to its
containing 'much that was new to him'. I trust that the reader,
whether in using the present work he finds much or little that is
new to him, will at any rate find in its chronological tables,
unpretentious as they are, the same kind of utility that Cicero
found in the *liber annalis* of Atticus :—*ut explicatis ordinibus
temporum uno in conspectu omnia viderem*[1].

---

[1] Cicero, *Orator* 120, *Brutus* 14 f. For a conspectus of the periods covered
by these tables, and the pages on which they will be found, see p. xi *supra*.

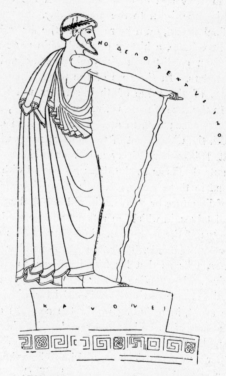

RHAPSODE RECITING AN EPIC PASSAGE

beginning ὧδέ ποτ' ἐν Τύρινθι (sic)....

From an amphora from Vulci, published in *Monumenti dell' Istituto*, v (1849) pl. 10; now in the British Museum (E 270 in *Catalogue of Vases*, iii p. 202, ed. Cecil Smith). See pp. 19, 30 *infra*.

# BOOK I

## *THE ATHENIAN AGE*

---

ξυνελὼν λέγω τὴν πᾶσαν πόλιν τῆς Ἑλλάδος παίδευσιν εἶναι.

THUCYDIDES, ii 41 § 1.

τοσοῦτον δ᾽ ἀπολέλοιπεν ἡ πόλις ἡμῶν περὶ τὸ φρονεῖν καὶ λέγειν τοὺς ἄλλους ἀνθρώπους, ὥσθ᾽ οἱ ταύτης μαθηταὶ τῶν ἄλλων διδάσκαλοι γεγόνασι, καὶ τὸ τῶν Ἑλλήνων ὄνομα πεποίηκε μηκέτι τοῦ γένους ἀλλὰ τῆς διανοίας δοκεῖν εἶναι, καὶ μᾶλλον Ἕλληνας καλεῖσθαι τοὺς τῆς παιδεύσεως τῆς ἡμετέρας ἢ τοὺς τῆς κοινῆς φύσεως μετέχοντας.

ISOCRATES, *Panegyric*, § 50.

| Epic Poets | Lyric Poets | Dramatists | Philosophers | Historians | Orators &c. |
|---|---|---|---|---|---|
| *floruit* <br> Homer <br> *c.* 700 Hesiod <br> Before 700 <br> earlier Cyclic Poets, Stasinus, *Cypria*, Arctinus, *Aethiopis, Iliupersis*, and Agias, *Nostoi* <br> **700** | | | | | |
| Intermediate Cyclic Poets; <br> *c.* 660 Lesches, *Little Iliad* <br> *c.*645 Peisander <br><br> **600** | 690 Callinus*e* <br> 676 Terpander <br> 657 Alcman <br> 650 Archilochus*ei* <br> 640 Tyrtaeus*e* <br> 640 Semonides of Amorgos*i* <br> 620 Mimnermus*e* <br> 620 Stesichorus <br> 612 Alcaeus <br> 612 Sappho <br> 600 Arion | | | | |
| Later Cyclic Poets; <br> *c.* 566 Eugammon, *Telegonia* <br><br> Homeric Hymns <br> **500** | 594 Solon*ei* <br> *c.* 639—559 <br> 544 Ibycus <br> 542 Hipponax*i* <br> 540 Theognis*e* <br> 537 Phocylides*e* <br> 530 Anacreon | 580 Susarion*c* <br><br><br> 534 Thespis | 585 Thales <br> *c.* 624—548 <br><br> 575 Anaximander <br> *c.* 611—547 <br> 550 Anaximenes <br> *c.* 588—524 <br> 530 Pythagoras <br> *c.* 580—*c.* 500 <br> 530 Xenophanes <br> *c.* 576—480 | 550 Cadmus of Miletus <br><br><br> 500 Hecataeus | |
| 489 Panyâsis <br><br> Antimachus <br> *fl. c.* 464—410 <br><br><br><br><br><br><br> 404 Choerilus <br> **400** | Simonides of Ceos 556—468 <br> Pindar 518—*c.* 443 <br> Bacchylides *c.* 507—430 | Epicharmus*c* <br> 540—450 <br> Phrynichus <br> *fl.* 512—476 <br> Aeschylus <br> 525—456 <br> Sophocles <br> 495—405 <br> 449 Cratinus*c* <br> Euripides <br> 480—406 <br> 429 Eupolis*c* <br> 429 Phrynichus*c* <br> Aristophanes*c* <br> *c.* 450—385 | 500 Heracleitus <br> *c.* 535—475 <br> 495 Parmenides <br><br> 455 Empedocles <br> 450 Anaxagoras <br> *c.* 500—428 <br> Socrates <br> 469—399 <br> 420 Democritus <br> 460—357 | Herodotus <br> *c.* 484—*c.* 425 <br> 430 Hellanicus <br> Thucydides <br> *c.* 460—*c.* 400 | 466 Corax <br> Tisias <br> 427 Gorgias <br> *c.* 485—380 <br> Pericles <br> 493—429 <br> 447 Protagoras <br> *c.* 480—411 <br> 435 Prodicus <br> 435 Hippias <br> Antiphon <br> 480—411 <br> Thrasymachus <br> *c.* 457—400 <br> Andocides <br> *c.* 440—390 <br> Lysias <br> *c.* 445—378 |
| **Critics** <br><br> (525 Theagenes) <br><br> Zoïlus <br> *fl.* 365—336 <br> 340 Heracleides Ponticus <br> Chamaeleon <br><br><br><br> Praxiphanes <br> **300** | **Musicians** <br><br> (676? Terpander) <br> (508 Lasus) <br> Melanippides <br> d. 412 <br> Philoxenus <br> 435—380 <br> Timotheus <br> d. 357 <br><br> 310 Aristoxenus | *Middle Comedy* <br> 390—320 <br> Antiphanes*c* <br> Anaxandrides*c* <br> Alexis*c* <br><br> *New Comedy* <br> 320—250 <br> Philemon*c* <br> *c.* 350—263 <br> Menander*c* <br> 344—292 <br> Diphilus*c* | 400 Antisthenes <br><br> Plato 420—348 <br> Aristotle <br> 384—322 <br> Theophrastus <br> 372—287 <br> Zeno <br> *c.* 364—263 <br> Epicurus <br> 341—270 | Ctesias <br> *fl.* 415—398 <br> Xenophon <br> *c.* 430—*c.* 355 <br> 360 Cleidemus <br> Ephorus <br> *c.* 405—330 <br> 352 Theopompus <br> 346 Androtion <br> Dicaearchus <br> 347—287 <br> Timaeus <br> *c.* 350—*c.* 260 <br> Philochorus <br> *c.* 306—261 | Isocrates <br> 436—338 <br> Isaeus 420—348 <br> Demosthenes <br> 384—322 <br> Aeschines <br> 389—314 <br> Lycurgus <br> *c.* 390—324 <br> Hypereides <br> *fl.* 344—322 <br> Deinarchus <br> *fl.* 342—291 <br> Demetrius of Phaleron <br> *fl.* 317—307 |

*e elegiac, i iambic, c comic poets.*

# CHAPTER II.

## THE STUDY OF EPIC POETRY.

THE earliest poems of Greece supplied the Greeks with their earliest themes for study, for exegesis, and for literary criticism. From about 600 B.C. we have definite proof of the recitation of the Homeric poems by rhapsodes in many parts of the Greek world,—at Chios, at Delos, at Cyprus, at Syracuse, at Sicyon, and in Attica. The recitations in Attica were probably connected with the festivals of Dionysus at Athens and with a similar festival at Brauron[1]; and, by an ordinance of Solon, the date of whose archonship is 594 B.C., the rhapsodes were required to recite consecutive portions of the Homeric poems, instead of selecting isolated passages[2]. The effect of this ordinance would be not

Homer and the rhapsodes

Solon

---

[1] Clearchus in Athen. vii 1, ἡ τῶν ῥαψῳδῶν (ἑορτή), ἣν ἦγον κατὰ τὴν τῶν Διονυσίων. Hesychius, Βραυρωνίοις τὴν Ἰλιάδα ἦδον ῥαψῳδοὶ ἐν Βραυρῶνι τῆς Ἀττικῆς. Cp. Welcker, *Der epische Cyclus*, i p. 391 f; A. Mommsen, *Heortologie*, pp. 122, 138. For a representation of a rhapsode reciting, see p. 16 *supra*.

[2] Diogenes Laertius, *Life of Solon*, i 2, 57, τά τε Ὁμήρου ἐξ ὑποβολῆς γέγραφε ῥαψῳδεῖσθαι, οἷον ὅπου ὁ πρῶτος ἔληξεν, ἐκεῖθεν ἄρχεσθαι τὸν ἐχόμενον. I here understand ἐξ ὑποβολῆς not as the exact equivalent, but as the *correlative* of ἐξ ὑπολήψεως in [Plato], *Hipparchus*, 228 B (quoted on p. 21), ἐξ ὑποβολῆς, 'by the giving of a cue', referring to the *first* of two successive reciters, who *ends at a given cue* and leaves the second to take it up (ὑποβάλλει), and ἐξ ὑπολήψεως, 'by the taking up of a cue', to the *next* reciter, who *takes up the cue* (ὑπολαμβάνει). ἐξ ὑποβολῆς has been much discussed. The various interpretations may be stated thus: (1) '*se invicem excipiendo*' 'in continuous (or alternate) succession' (Wolf, Boeckh, Wilamowitz); (2) *ex praecepto*, 'according to a prescribed rule', the rhapsodes omitting what they were told to omit, but reciting the rest unaltered (Nitzsch); similarly (3) *ex exemplari praescripto*, '*ad fidem exemplaris probati*', 'from an authorised

merely to cause the competition to be more severe, but also to promote on the part of the audience, no less than on that of the reciters, a more consecutive and more complete knowledge of the contents of the poems themselves. Moreover, the competitions between rhapsode and rhapsode, like the contests between poet and poet in an earlier time, would excite in the audience a faculty for discriminating not only between the competing reciters but also between their competing recitations, and would thus give an early impulse to a widely diffused and popular form of literary criticism.

The above tradition regarding the Athenian legislator Solon has its counterpart in a legend relating to the Spartan legislator Lycurgus. The date of Lycurgus is uncertain, one account placing him in 776 B.C., at the beginning of the Olympic era, and another a century earlier. According to Plutarch[1], Lycurgus met with the Homeric poems in Crete, and brought a copy back with him to Greece. Plutarch's authority for this may possibly have been Ephorus, a historian of the fourth century B.C. Even on

**Peisistratus** Attic soil, Solon has a rival in Peisistratus, whose rule at Athens began in 560 and ended in 527 B.C. According to the well-known story, he is said to have been the first to collect the scattered poems of Homer and to arrange them in order. The story is not found in any earlier author than Cicero, or in any extant Greek writer earlier than Pausanias (*fl.* 174 A.D.)[2]; but the question whether it was Solon or Peisis-

---

text' to be exactly followed by the reciter (Gräfenhan, *Gesch. d. kl. Phil.* i 268; Bernhardy, *Gr. Litt.* i 330[4]); (4) *praesente aliquo qui verba subiceret,* 'with prompting' (Hermann, Monro, and others), omitting οἶον ὅπου—τὸν ἐχόμενον. Part of the extensive literature of the controversy may be seen in Wolf, *Proleg.* c. xxxii; Boeckh, *Corpus Inscr. Gr.* ii 676 ff; Nitzsch, *Quaestio Homerica* iv (1828), *De Hist. Homeri* ii 132 (1837), *Sagenpoesie,* p. 413 (1852); Hermann, *Opusc.* v 300—311, vii 65—87 (1834—9); Wilamowitz, *Homerische Untersuchungen,* p. 263—6 (1884). Cp. Ritschl, *Opusc.* i 56; Sengebusch, *Diss.* ii 111; A. Mommsen, *Heortologie,* p. 138; Bergk, *Gr. Lit.* i 499, Christ, *Gr. Litt.* § 37[4]; Jebb's *Homer,* p. 77; Andrew Lang's *Homer and the Epic,* p. 36; and Monro's *Odyssey* xiii—xxiv, p. 395.

[1] *Lycurgus,* c. 4, discussed by Wilamowitz, *Hom. Unt.* pp. 267—285.

[2] Cicero, *De Or.* iii 137, qui primus Homeri libros, confusos antea, sic disposuisse dicitur, ut nunc habemus; Pausanias, vii 26, Πεισίστρατος ἔπη τὰ Ὁμήρου διεσπασμένα τε καὶ ἄλλα ἀλλαχοῦ μνημονευόμενα ἠθροίζετο. Cp. Wolf's

tratus who did a signal service to the Homeric poems was apparently familiar to a Megarian historian of the fourth century B.C.[1] The story about Peisistratus, it need hardly be added, has been much discussed. Accepted unreservedly by some eminent scholars and rejected entirely by others, it has sometimes been accepted in a limited sense by those who hold that the story need only imply the restoration of a unity which in process of time had been gradually ignored[2]. The festival of the Panathenaea, at which the Homeric poems were in after times usually recited[3], was celebrated with special splendour by Peisistratus, who is even sometimes called the founder of the festival[4]; and, according to a dialogue attributed to Plato, it was one of the sons of Peisistratus, namely Hipparchus (527—514 B.C.), who 'was the *first* to bring into this land the poems of Homer, and who compelled the rhapsodes to recite them successively, in regular order, at the Panathenaea, as they still do at the present day'[5]. The story is inconsistent with the statement that the poems of Homer were recited at Athens in the time of Solon, but it is

Hipparchus

---

*Prolegomena*, c. xxxiii; Egger, *Histoire de la Critique* (ed. 1887), pp. 9—18; Wilamowitz, *l.c.*, pp. 235—266; Flach's *Peisistratos und seine litterarische Thätigkeit* (1885); and E. Meyer, *Gesch. des Alterthums*, ii 388—391; also Jebb's *Homer*, p. 114, A. Lang, *Homer and the Epic*, p. 37, T. W. Allen in *Classical Review*, xv (1901) p. 7 f, and Monro, *Od.* xiii—xxiv, p. 402 f.

[1] Diogenes Laertius, i 2, 57, μᾶλλον οὖν Σόλων Ὅμηρον ἐφώτισεν ἢ Πεισίστρατος, <Dr Leaf, *Iliad*, 1900, p. xviii, here inserts ἐκεῖνος γὰρ ἦν ὁ τὰ ἔπη εἰς τὸν κατάλογον ἐμποιήσας καὶ οὐ Πεισίστρατος, > ὥς φησι Διευχίδας ἐν πέμπτῳ Μεγαρικῶν. On the date of Dieuchidas, cp. Wilamowitz, *l.c.*, p. 240 f.

[2] Jebb's *Homer*, p. 114 f. It is accepted in this sense by Ritschl, but rejected altogether by Ludwich, Wilamowitz and Flach. It had been accepted by Wolf and Lachmann, both of whom regard the written Homer as dating from Peisistratos. This view has recently been gaining ground. Dr Leaf (*Iliad*, 1900, p. xix) believes that 'an official copy of Homer was made in Athens in the time of Solon and Peisistratus'.

[3] Lycurgus, *c. Leocr.* 102, οὕτω γὰρ ὑπέλαβον ὑμῶν οἱ πατέρες σπουδαῖον εἶναι ποιητήν, ὥστε νόμον ἔθεντο καθ' ἑκάστην πεντετηρίδα μόνον τῶν ἄλλων ποιητῶν ῥαψῳδεῖσθαι τὰ ἔπη.

[4] Scholiast on Aristeides, *Panath.* p. 323 Dindorf. The athletic contests of the Great Panathenaea had however been instituted in 566 B.C. (Busolt, *Gr. Gesch.* ii² 344), six years before Peisistratus became tyrant.

[5] [Plato], *Hipparchus* 228 B, ἠνάγκασε τοὺς ῥαψῳδοὺς Παναθηναίοις ἐξ ὑπολήψεως ἐφεξῆς αὐτὰ διιέναι. Cp. note 2 on p. 19.

possibly true that the recitations at the *Panathenaea* in particular
were introduced by Hipparchus. It was on the invitation of
Hipparchus[1] that Simonides of Ceos lived at Athens from about
522 to 514 B.C., and it is interesting to notice that it is in
Simonides that we find the earliest extant quotation from Homer
in a line which he ascribes to 'the man of Chios',—οἵηπερ φύλλων
γενεή, τοιήδε καὶ ἀνδρῶν[2].

There are some dubious stories of early interpolations in the
Homeric poems. Thus Peisistratus is said to have
introduced into the *Odyssey* a line in honour of the
Attic hero, Theseus[3]; and both Solon and Peisistratus are credited
with the insertion of a line referring to Ajax, for the supposed
purpose of proving that Salamis was an ancient possession of
Athens[4]; but, as the recovery of Salamis took place in Solon's
time, while Peisistratus was still a boy, Solon alone should have
been mentioned in this connexion[5]. Onomacritus, who is said to
have been one of the four who put together the Homeric poems
under the authority of Peisistratus[6], was, according to Herodotus,
caught in the act of interpolating the oracles of Musaeus, and was
banished by the tyrant's son, Hipparchus[7].

*Early inter-*
*polations*

Meanwhile Homer had been frequently imitated by Hesiod[8]
(*fl. c.* 700 B.C.), had been described by the early
elegiac poet Callînus (*c.* 690) as the author of an
epic called the *Thebais*[9], and had been copied
in various ways by the earliest of the iambo-
graphers Archilochus (*fl.* 650), whom ' Longinus '[10] describes as

*Influence of*
*Homer on*
*early Greek*
*poets*

[1] *ib.* 228 C, and Aristotle's *Constitution of Athens*, c. 18 § 1, where
Hipparchus is also called φιλόμουσος.

[2] *Iliad* vi 146.

[3] *Od.* xi 631, Θησέα Πειρίθοόν τε, θεῶν ἐρικυδέα τέκνα. Plutarch, *Theseus*
20; cp. Flach, p. 27.

[4] *Il.* ii 558, στῆσε δ' ἄγων, ἵν' Ἀθηναίων ἵσταντο φάλαγγες. Strabo,
p. 394; cp. Flach, p. 29.

[5] Cp. Diog. Laert. i 2, 57, and see Busolt, *Gr. Gesch.* ii² 220.

[6] Tzetzes, *Proleg. in Aristoph.* τεσσάρων ὄντων <τῶν> ἐπὶ Πεισιστράτου
συνθέντων τὸν Ὅμηρον. Cp. La Roche, *Hom. Textkr.* p. 10, and Jebb's *Homer*,
p. 115 n.

[7] Her. vii 6.

[8] Sihler, in *Proc. Amer. Phil. Assoc.* 1902, xxvii—xxxi.

[9] Pausanias, ix 9, 5.                    [10] περὶ ὕψους, c. 13 § 3.

'most Homeric', and by melic poets such as Alcman (about 657),
and Stesichorus (640—555)[1].

In the age succeeding the expulsion of the Peisistratidae,
Pindar, with a conscious reference to the origin of
the word *Rhapsodos*[2], describes the Rhapsodes as
'the sons of Homer, singers of deftly woven lays'[3].   He also
alludes to the laurel-branch that they bore as an emblem of poetic
tradition.   Homer himself (he tells us) had 'rightly set forth all
the prowess of Ajax, leaving it as a theme for other bards to sing,
by the laurel-wand of his lays divine'[4].   Pindar's praise of Amphi-
araüs is a clear reminiscence of a Homeric line in praise of
Agamemnon[5].   He describes the 'fire-breathing Chimaera' in a
phrase like that of Homer[6], but differs from him in minor details
as to Bellerophon, Ganymede and Tantalus[7].   He shows a similar
freedom in giving a new meaning to a phrase borrowed from his
own countryman the Boeotian poet, Hesiod, by applying to the
athlete's toilsome training a proverbial admonition originally
referring to the work of the farm[8].   In the age of Pindar, and in
the Athenian age in general, the poet and his audience were alike
saturated with the study of the old poets, Homer and Hesiod, and
a touch alone was wanted to awaken the memory of some long-
familiar line.

Pindar.

---

[1] Mahaffy, *Gr. Lit.* i 31.  Cp. for Hesiod, Christ, § 65[4]; for Archilochus
and Stesichorus, Bergk ii 191 and 293, and (in general) i 483.

[2] ῥαψῳδός, from ῥάπτειν ἀοιδήν (Hesiod, frag. 227), *contexere carmen, pan-
gere versus.*  Cp. Bergk, *Gr. Lit.* i 490.

[3] *Nem.* ii 1, Ὁμηρίδαι, ῥαπτῶν (lit. 'stitched') ἐπέων ἀοιδοί.

[4] *Isth.* iii 55, Ὅμηρος...πᾶσαν ὀρθώσαις ἀρετὰν κατὰ ῥάβδον ἔφρασεν θεσπε-
σίων ἐπέων λοιποῖς ἀθύρειν.  Cp. Bergk, *Gr. Lit.* i 492.

[5] *Ol.* vi 17, ἀμφότερον μάντιν τ' ἀγαθὸν καὶ δουρὶ μάρνασθαι, and *Iliad* iii
179, ἀμφότερον, βασιλεύς τ' ἀγαθὸς κρατερός τ' αἰχμητής.  The reminiscence is
far less clearly marked when he says that Homer ἄγγελον ἐσλὸν ἔφα τιμὰν
μεγίσταν πράγματι παντὶ φέρειν (*Pyth.* iv 278), a phrase which has no nearer
parallel in our own Homer than the line,—ἐσθλὸν καὶ τὸ τέτυκται ὅτ' ἄγγελος
αἴσιμα εἰδῇ (*Iliad* xv 207).  Cp. *Isth.* iv 37 with *Il.* vii 198 f; also *Nem.*
vii 20.

[6] Pindar, *Ol.* xiii 90 and *Il.* vi 182.

[7] *Ol.* xiii 67 (Gildersleeve's n.) : i 43, 57 (Fennell's n.).

[8] *Isth.* v 67, μελέταν ἔργοις ὀπάζων, and Hesiod, *Works and Days*, 411, με-
λέτη δέ τοι ἔργον ὀφέλλει.

The influence of the Homeric poems on the tragic poets of
Athens was very considerable.  Notwithstanding
Aristotle's statement that 'the *Iliad* and the *Odyssey*
each furnish the theme of one tragedy, or of two,
at the most'[1], we find that they supplied Aeschylus with the theme
of at least six tragedies and one satyric drama, Sophocles with
that of three tragedies (*Nausicaa*, and the *Phaeacians*, and possibly
the *Phrygians*), and Euripides with that of one satyric drama, the
*Cyclops*.  The unknown author of the *Rhesus* derived his theme
from the *Iliad*; and Achilles and Hector, with Laertes, Penelope
and her Suitors, were among the themes of the minor tragic poets
of the fifth and fourth centuries.  Aristotle's statement is practically true of Sophocles and Euripides, but not of Aeschylus,
whom he almost ignores in his treatise on Poetry.  It is however
the fact that, among the tragic poets in general, a far larger
number of their subjects were suggested by other poems of the
Epic Cycle, namely the *Cypria*, the *Aethiopis*, the *Little Iliad*,
the *Iliupersis*, the *Nostoi* and the *Telegonia*[2].

The Tragic poets

Aeschylus himself probably regarded 'Homer' as the author
of all the poems of the Epic Cycle, when he
described his dramas as 'slices from the great
banquets of Homer'[3].  In the *Frogs* of Aristophanes, he is made
to confess that it was from 'Homer the divine' that his mind
took the impress of noble characters like those of the 'lion-hearted'
heroes, Teucer and Patroclus[4].  The influence of Homer shows
itself in many of his picturesque epithets, and in the use of not a
few archaic nouns and verbs, as well as in Homeric phrases and
expressions, and Homeric similes and metaphors[5].

Aeschylus

Sophocles is described by Greek critics as the only true
disciple of Homer, as the 'tragic Homer', and as
the admirer of the Epic poet[6].  His verbal indebt-

Sophocles

---

[1] *Poet.* 23 § 4.

[2] See Nauck, *Tragicorum Graecorum Fragmenta*, pp. 963—8, or Haigh,
*Tragic Drama of the Greeks*, pp. 473—6.

[3] Athen. 347 E, τεμάχη τῶν Ὁμήρου μεγάλων δείπνων.

[4] *Frogs*, 1040.

[5] For details, see Haigh, *l.c.*, p. 85.

[6] Ion, *in vita Sophoclis*, μόνον...Ὁμήρου μαθητήν.  Polemo, ap. Diog
Laert. iv 20, Ὅμηρον τραγικόν.  Eustathius on *Iliad*, pp. 440, 605, 851, 902

edness to Homer is less than that of Aeschylus, though, like
other dramatists, he borrows certain epic forms and epithets, as
well as certain phrases and similes.    His dramas reproduce the
Homeric spirit.    He is also Homeric in the ideal, yet human,
conception of his characters[1], and in the calm self-control, which
characterises him even in scenes of violent excitement.    Here, as
elsewhere, 'he has caught the impress of Homer's charm'[2].
While very few of his dramas were directly suggested by the *Iliad*
or *Odyssey*, he is described as 'delighting in the Epic Cycle'[3].
The extant plays connected with that Cycle are the *Ajax* and
*Philoctetes*.

Of the extant plays of Euripides, the *Cyclops* alone is directly
taken from Homer's *Odyssey*, while the Epic Cycle        Euripides
is represented by the *Iphigeneia in Aulide, Hecuba,*
*Troades, Andromache, Helen, Electra, Iphigeneia in Tauris* and
*Orestes.*    The plot of no extant play that was certainly written by
Euripides is inspired by the *Iliad*, but the opening scene of the
*Phoenissae*, where Antigone and her aged attendant view from the
palace-roof the movements of the Argive host outside the walls of
Thebes, is clearly a reminiscence of the memorable scene in the
*Iliad*, where Helen and Priam watch the Greek heroes from the
walls of Troy[4].

Turning from the tragic poets to the historians, we find
Herodotus speculating on the date of Homer.   He        Herodotus
places Hesiod, as well as Homer, about four hun-
dred years before his own time, *i.e.* about 400 years (or exactly
12 generations[5]) before 430 B.C.[6]   He assumes that other poems
beside the *Iliad* and *Odyssey* were generally attributed to Homer,
namely the *Cypria* and the *Epigoni*.   He doubts the Homeric
authorship of the *Epigoni*[7], and denies that of the *Cypria*[8]; but

etc., φιλόμηρος.  Cp. Lechner, *De Sophocle poeta* Ὁμηρικωτάτῳ (1859); Schneidewin's *Sophokles*, p. 27; Bergk, *Gr. Litt.* i 830, iii 369 f; and Haigh, *l.c.*,
p. 202 f.

[1] Arist. *Poet.* 3 § 2.
[2] *Vita Soph.* Ὁμηρικὴν ἐκματτόμενος χάριν.
[3] Athen. 297 D, ἔχαιρε...τῷ ἐπικῷ κύκλῳ.  Cp. Christ, *Gr. Litt.* § 175 p. 258[4].
[4] *Il.* iii 139—244.
[5] Her. ii 142; E. Meyer's *Forschungen*, i 152 f; Mahaffy, *Gr. Lit.* i 24.
[6] Her. ii 53.        [7] Her. iv 32.        [8] Her. ii 117.

his denial of the latter is founded on the fact that, in the form in which he knew the poem, it implied that Paris, on leaving Sparta, sailed for Troy, and not for Sidon, as stated in the *Iliad*[1]. As Professor Jebb has aptly observed, 'this suggests how little these attributions probably regarded the evidence of style, language, or spirit. Unless there was some contradiction on the surface, the attribution could pass current, or could be left an open question'[2].

Thucydides regards the Phaeacians as a historical people and the Homeric catalogue as a historical document[3].

**Thucydides**

But he makes the story of the siege of Troy a theme for rationalising criticism. In this spirit he suggests that the Greek chiefs were compelled to go to Troy, not by the obligations of their oath to Helen's father, but by the superior power of Agamemnon; and that the long duration of the siege was due to the Greeks being forced to spend part of their time in keeping up their supply of provisions[4]. In a far different spirit to that of the earlier age which interpolated lines in Homer to the credit of Athens, he makes Pericles proudly declare in his funeral oration that Athens needs no Homer to praise her[5].

Among the earliest treatises on Homer was that ascribed to Democritus (460—357 B.C.), though we know nothing of its purport[6]. But, if he really wrote such a work,

**Democritus**

it may have contained some of the sayings on Homer attributed to him by later writers, who quote Democritus as speaking of Homer's divine genius, the varied beauty of his epic verse, and the happy union of order and variety which marked the composition of his poems[7]. It was possibly his study of Homer that inspired him with the lofty and often poetical language for which he is eulogised by Cicero[8].

For the three centuries between 600 and 300 B.C. the Homeric

---

[1] *Il.* vi 290.          [2] *Homer*, p. 86.          [3] *ib.* p. 85.

[4] Thuc. i 9 and 11.          [5] ii 41, 4.

[6] Diog. Laert. IX vii 13 § 48, περὶ Ὁμήρου ἢ (?) ὀρθοεπείης καὶ γλώσσεων. Cp. Egger, *l.c.*, p. 107[3], and Saintsbury's *History of Criticism*, i 15.

[7] Dion Chrysostom, *Or.* 53 *init.*, Ὅμηρος φύσεως λαχὼν θεαζούσης ἐπέων κόσμον ἐτέκτηνατο παντοίων· ὡς οὐκ ἐνὸν ἄνευ θείας καὶ δαιμονίας φύσεως οὕτω καλὰ καὶ σοφὰ ἔπη ἐργάσασθαι, and Clemens Alexandrinus, *Stromat.* vi 18.

[8] *De Or.* i 49; *Orator*, 67.

poems were the subject of a considerable amount of uncritical study. Homer was 'the educator of Hellas'[1]; and, during the fifth century B.C., the Sophists, who were among the most active educators of their age, had naturally much to say of one whose poems formed the foundation of all education at Athens. Thus Protagoras (*c.* 480—411 B.C.), who classified the modes of expression under the heads of question, answer, prayer and command, ventured to criticise the opening words of the *Iliad*, for expressing what was meant as a *prayer* to the Muse in the form of a *command*, μῆνιν ἄειδε θεά ; but Aristotle, who quotes this criticism, justly observes that it is not of any special value as applied to poetry[2]. A specimen of his criticism of Simonides is given in the *Protagoras* of Plato, and it is probably this specimen alone that has prompted an enthusiastic student of Plato and Aristotle in the fourth century A.D. to describe Protagoras as 'expounding the poems of Simonides and other poets'[3].

Homer and the Sophists

Protagoras

Hippias of Elis, so far as we can infer from the two Platonic dialogues which bear his name, was interested, not only in the accurate study of letters and syllables, and rhythms and harmonies[4], but also in discussing the characters of the Homeric heroes, holding the 'frank and straightforward' Achilles superior to the 'wily and false' Odysseus[5]. He probably agreed with the father of one of the interlocutors in the *Lesser Hippias* in considering the *Iliad* a finer poem than the *Odyssey*, Odysseus being the central figure of the one poem, and Achilles of the other[6]. Like the historian Ephorus, in the following century, he supposed that Homer was a native of Cumae[7]. He collected parallel passages from Homer, Orpheus, Musaeus and Hesiod[8]; and he observed with truth that the term τύραννος did not belong to the Homeric age, but came into use in

Hippias

---

[1] Plato, *Rep.* 606 E, τὴν Ἑλλάδα πεπαίδευκεν.

[2] *Poet.* c. 19 § 5.

[3] Themistius, *Or.* 23, τὰ Σιμωνίδου τε καὶ ἄλλων ποιήματα ἐξηγούμενος.

[4] *Hippias Major*, 285 B ; *Minor*, 368 D.

[5] *Hippias Minor*, 365 B.          [6] *ib.* 363 B.

[7] *The Sixth Life of Homer* in Westermann's Βιόγραφοι, p. 30 f.

[8] Possibly in a work entitled συναγωγή, quoted in Athen. 609 A.

the time of Archilochus, whereas in Homer even the lawless king Echetus is called a βασιλεύς[1].

His namesake, Hippias of Thasos, gave a new sense to two passages of Homer by proposing an emendation in each. He altered the indicative δίδομεν into the infinitive διδόμεν in the words δίδομεν δέ οἱ εὖχος ἀρέσθαι, 'we grant him to obtain his prayer', which appear to have been introduced from *Iliad* xxi 297 in place of the words Τρώεσσι δὲ κήδε' ἐφῆπται occurring thrice in *Iliad* ii 15, 32, 69. The objection to the indicative is that it implies that Zeus himself was intentionally deceiving Agamemnon in sending the Dream-god on his errand to the hero, but the infinitive only removes the charge of deception one step further, as the Dream-god, who is prompted to deceive the hero, is undoubtedly sent by Zeus. The difficulty, such as it is, seems only to have been founded on a mistake, as it is only by misplacing the phrase of *Iliad* xxi that any difficulty arises. In the other passage (*Iliad* xxiii 328) an ambiguous ov is supposed to have been misunderstood as οὗ, 'of it', in which case the lines in question would have run as follows :—

ἕστηκε ξύλον αὖον, ὅσον τ' ὄργυι', ὑπὲρ αἴης,
ἢ δρυὸς ἢ πεύκης· τὸ μὲν οὐ καταπύθεται ὄμβρῳ.

> 'There stands a withered trunk, some six feet high,
> Of oak, or pine, *half*-rotted by the rain'[2].

Hippias appears to have proposed to change οὐ into οὐ ('*half*-rotted' into '*un*-rotted'), which is the reading in our present text[3].

Lastly, Gorgias (*c.* 485—380 B.C.) probably composed a Eulogy of Achilles[4]. He is the author of two extant speeches connected with the tale of Troy,

*Gorgias*

---

[1] *Od.* xviii 84 ; see Argument to Soph. *O.T.*, and cp. Friedel, *De Hippiae Sophistae studiis Homericis*, Halle, 1872; and *De Sophistarum studiis Homericis* in *Dissert. Philol. Halenses*, i (1873) pp. 130—188.

[2] Lord Derby's rendering, except so far as 'half-rotted' is here substituted for his translation of the ordinary text, 'unrotted.'

[3] Aristotle, *Poet.* c. 25 § 11 and *De Soph. El.* iv 8, with Wolf's *Proleg. ad Homerum*, c. xxxvii p. 102 Wagner; also Vahlen, *Beiträge zu Aristoteles Poetik*, iii 368, and ed. 3, p. 69 f. On the other hand, Ritter on *Poet. l.c.* supposes that οὐ was the old text, read by Hippias as οὗ.

[4] Aristot. *Rhet.* iii 17.

namely the 'Encomium of Helen' and the 'Defence of Palamedes'. Among the pupils of Gorgias, Licymnius may perhaps be
identified with an expositor of Homer mentioned in the Homeric
*scholia*[1]; while Alcidamas appears to have written a declamation
on the *Odyssey*, which he describes as 'a fair mirror of human
life'[2].

The Homeric representations of the gods roused a protest on
the part of the founder of the Eleatics, Xenophanes
of Colophon (*fl.* 530 B.C.), who says that 'Homer
and Hesiod have imputed to the gods all that is
blame and shame for men'[3]. It was on other

Protests
against the
Homeric
mythology

grounds that his younger contemporary, Heracleitus, declared that
'Homer and Archilochus deserved a sound thrashing'[4], nor did
he spare Hesiod. He apparently held that the first two poets
were wrong in regarding happiness as dependent on the will of
Heaven, and the third, in distinguishing between lucky and un-
lucky days[5]. Another great contemporary, Pythagoras, is said to
have descended to the world below, and to have seen the soul of
Hesiod bound to a brazen column, squeaking and gibbering;
and that of Homer hanging from a tree and encircled by serpents,
in punishment for all that he had said concerning the gods[6].

In reply to protests such as these, some of the defenders of
Homer maintained that the superficial meaning
of his myths was not the true one, and that there
was a deeper sense lying below the surface. This
deeper sense was, in the Athenian age, called the

Homer
defended by
allegorical
interpretation

ὑπόνοια[7], and the ὑπόνοιαι of this age assumed the name of
'allegories' in the time of Plutarch[8]. Theagenes of Rhegium
(*fl.* 525 B.C.), who suggested a two-fold form of allegory, moral

---

[1] On *Il.* ii 106.  [2] Aristot. *Rhet.* iii 3 § 4; cp. §§ 1, 3.

[3] Sextus Emp., *Math.* ix 193, πάντα θεοῖς ἀνέθηκαν Ὅμηρός θ᾽ Ἡσίοδός τε |
ὅσσα παρ᾽ ἀνθρώποισιν ὀνείδεα καὶ ψόγος ἐστίν (Zeller's *Pre-socratic Philosophy*,
i 561, and Jebb's *Homer*, p. 88 n.). Cp. Xenophanes, in Herodian, ii 16, 20
Lentz, ἐξ ἀρχῆς καθ᾽ Ὅμηρον ἐπεὶ μεμαθήκασι πάντες. Cp. in general Gräfenhan,
*Gesch. d. kl. Phil.* i 202 f, 211 f, and Egger, *l.c.*, p. 96³ f.

[4] Diog. Laert. ix 1.  [5] Zeller, *l.c.*, i 10, 32, 102 f.

[6] Diog. Laert. viii § 21. Cp. Geffcken, *Antike Kulturkämpfe*, in *Neue
Jahrb.* xv 593—611.  [7] Xen. *Symp.* 3 § 6; cp. Plato, *Rep.* 378 D.

[8] *De audiendis poetis*, c. 4 p. 19 E.

and physical, regarded the names of the gods as expressing either
the mental faculties of man or the various elements of nature.
Thus Apollo was, in his view, opposed to Poseidon, as fire to
water; Pallas to Ares, as wisdom to folly; Hera to Artemis, as
the air to the moon; Hermes to Leto, as reason, or intelligence,
to forgetfulness[1]. Anaxagoras of Clazomenae (*fl.* 450 B.C.) saw
the rays of the sun in the arrows of Apollo. Not content with
this obvious anticipation of Solar Mythology, he is said (whether
truly or not) to have found in the web of Penelope an emblem
of the rules of dialectic, the warp being the premises, the woof
the conclusion, and the flame of the torches, by which she
executed her task, being none other than the light of reason[2].
Though he is stated to have been the first to interpret the
Homeric myths in a moral sense[3], this is probably true of his
pupils only, especially of Metrodorus of Lampsacus (d. 464 B.C.),
who maintained that Hera, Athene and Zeus were the elements
of nature[4], and that Agamemnon[5] represented the air. Such
interpreters as these may well have been in Aristotle's mind, when
he mentions the 'old Homerists, who see small resemblances,
but overlook large ones'[6].

In the *Memorabilia* of Xenophon the rhapsodes are described
as 'very precise about the exact words of Homer, but very foolish
themselves'[7]. Among the rhapsodes who were also celebrated as
*interpreters* of Homer, were Stesimbrotus of Thasos[8], a contemporary of Pericles, and Ion of Ephesus, a contemporary of Socrates. Ion, who gives his name
to one of the most interesting of the shorter
dialogues of Plato, was not only a reciter, but also an interpreter of Homer. He comes to recite Homer to more than 20,000
Athenians at the Panathenaea. He wears a golden crown and is
arrayed in a magnificent robe[9]. He is 'possessed' with an enthusiasm for Homer, and he transmits his enthusiasm to his audience.

**Homer in Plato's *Ion***

---

[1] Schol. Venet. on *Il.* xx 67. Cp. Monro, *Od.* xiii—xxiv, p. 410.

[2] Schol. on *Od.* ii 104.

[3] Diog. Laert. ii 11. Cp. Monro, 411.

[4] Tatian, *c. Graecos*, 202 D (Zeller, *l.c.*, ii 372).        [5] Hesychius, *s.v.*

[6] οἱ ἀρχαῖοι Ὁμηρικοί, *Met.* xiii 6, 7, p. 1093 *a* 27.

[7] *Mem.* iv 2, 10.        [8] Xen. *Symp.* 3, 6; Monro, 411.

[9] Cp. 'rhapsode reciting' on p. 16 *supra*.

It is through him that the magnetic influence, which has passed from the Muse to the poet, passes from the poet to the listener, who is the last link in the magnetic chain[1]. Ion was also the author of a commentary on Homer. He declares that he 'can speak about Homer better than anyone else',—better than Metrodorus or Stesimbrotus; and it may fairly be assumed that the fluent rhetorical exposition, with which he 'embellishes' Homer, was in the main a fanciful allegorical interpretation of the poet's meaning.

But no apologetic interpretation of the Homeric mythology was of any avail to save Homer from being expelled with all the other poets from Plato's ideal Republic. Plato insists that the stories of gods and heroes told

*Homer in Plato's Republic*

by Homer and Hesiod give a false representation of their nature[2]. The poet is a mere 'imitator', and 'we must inform him that there is no room for such as he in our State'[3]. 'The awe and love of Homer', of which Plato had been conscious from his childhood, 'makes the words falter on his lips; but the truth must be spoken'[4]. 'All the poets, from Homer downwards, are only imitators; they copy images of virtue, but the truth they never reach'[5]. 'We are ready to admit that Homer is the greatest of poets.., but we must remain firm in our conviction that hymns to the gods and eulogies of famous men are the only poetry which ought to be admitted into our State'[6]. Homer's expulsion from Plato's Republic called forth a considerable controversial literature[7]. Athens, notwithstanding this expulsion, continued to learn Homer by heart[8], and this ancient custom was continued far beyond the Athenian age. Even at the close of the first century of our era there were Greeks in the Troad who taught their children Homer from their earliest years[9]. In fact, from the Athenian age to the present day, the study of Homer has never ceased.

[1] *Ion* 533 D—E.
[2] *Rep.* 377 D—378 E.   Hesiod is also clearly meant, though not mentioned, in *Laws* 886 B—C.
[3] *Rep.* 398 A.      [4] 595 B.      [5] 600 E.      [6] 607 A.
[7] Sengebusch, *Diss.* i 119 (Mahaffy, *Gr. Lit.* i 33).
[8] Xen. *Symp.* 3 § 5.
[9] Dion Chrysostom, *Or.* 11 p. 308 R.

In connexion with the use of Homer as a text-book, we may recall two anecdotes of some little interest in Plutarch's *Life of Alcibiades*[1]. We are there told that when Alcibiades 'was just emerging from boyhood, he went to a schoolmaster and asked him for a book of Homer; and, on the master's replying that he had nothing whatsoever of Homer's, Alcibiades struck him with his fist, and went on his way'. Another schoolmaster told him that he 'had a copy of Homer, emended by himself'. 'What?' said Alcibiades, 'are you really content to teach reading and writing, when you are capable of emending Homer? Why are you not instructing young men?' The first of these anecdotes shows that a young Athenian held he had a right to expect even an elementary teacher to possess part at least of the poems of Homer; the second presents us with an early example of amateur textual criticism; and both imply that Homer was really better suited as a text-book for young men than for mere children.

In the earliest play of Aristophanes there was a scene in which
Aristophanes
a father, who believed in the old-fashioned style of poetic education, is represented as examining his son as to the meaning of certain 'hard words in Homer'[2]: the son, who has a preference for the prose of practical life, retorts by asking his father the meaning of obsolete terms in the laws of Solon. In the *Frogs*, 'the divine Homer' is counted among the nobler poets, because he is preeminently the poet of the art of war[3]. He is also quoted or parodied in several passages[4].

Turning from the comic poet to one of the gravest of the
Isocrates
ancient rhetoricians, we find Isocrates, in his letter of exhortation to Nicocles, expressing his own admiration for Homer and for the early tragic poets[5], and rebuking his contemporaries for preferring the most paltry comedy

[1] Plut. *Alcib.* 7.

[2] Aristoph. Δαιταλεῖς, quoted by Galen *in praef. lexici Hippocratici*, p. 404 Franz, πρὸς ταῦτα σὺ λέξον Ὁμηρείους γλώττας, τί καλοῦσι κόρυμβα..., τί καλοῦσ' ἀμενηνὰ κάρηνα.

[3] *Frogs* 1036.

[4] *Birds* 575, 685, 910, 914, *Peace* 1089 ff, *Clouds* 1056. Cp. Monro, *Od.* xiii—xxiv, p. 415 f, and Sherrans, *De poëtarum comicorum Atticorum studiis Homericis*, 1893.

[5] Isocr. 2 § 48.

to the poems of Hesiod and Theognis and Phocylides [1]. In his *Panegyric* he describes the fame of Homer as enhanced by the fact that 'he pronounced a splendid eulogy on those who fought against the foreign foe', adding that this was the reason why he had been honoured by Athens in the instruction of her youth [2]. In his pamphlet *Against the Sophists* he points out why it is that Homer, who 'is deemed the wisest of men', describes the gods as deliberating. It is because he desires to teach mortal men that even the gods cannot discern the future [3]. Lastly, in his *Panathenaic*, written in the 95th year of his age, he speaks of the frequenters of the Lyceum as reciting the poems of Homer and Hesiod, and as 'talking twaddle' about them; but he defers his own remarks on those poets to a more convenient season, which never came [4].—It was probably in the time of the pupils of Isocrates that Homer became the theme of the paltry criticisms of Zoïlus [5].

The quotations from the 'Homeric poems' in the Athenian age sometimes differ from our present texts. Thucydides [6] quotes two passages from the 'Homeric' hymn to Apollo [7] in a form slightly different from
*Quotations from Homer*

that handed down to us in the MSS of the hymns, while he identifies with Homer the 'blind man' there described as 'dwelling in rocky Chios'. Similar divergences may be noticed in Plato's quotations. Some of these are clearly intentional, while others are almost certainly due to mistakes of memory [8]. Aeschines quotes a passage of fifteen lines from the *Iliad* [9], the longest quoted by any classical writer, with at least four variations; and Lycurgus a shorter passage with very slight changes [10]. Further, about twenty-one of Aristotle's quotations from Homer differ from our ordinary text [11], and there are also five passages in which he refers

[1] Isocr. 2 §§ 43, 44.
[2] *Paneg.* 159.
[3] 13 § 2.
[4] 12 §§ 33, 34.
[5] On his date, see p. 108 f.
[6] Thuc. iii 104.
[7] *Homeric Hymn*, i 145—150 and 165—172.
[8] *Rep.* 379 D (Monro, *Od.* p. 429 note), 388 A, 389 E, 405 E, 424 B.
[9] *Il.* xxiii 77—91, quoted by Aeschin. i 149.
[10] *Il.* xv 494—9; Lyc. § 103.
[11] *Iliad* ii 32, 196, 391 f, iv 125, vi 200, vii 63, viii 18 f, 84, ix 385 f, 538 f, 592 f, x 1, 12, 457, xi 542, xiv 217, xv 245; *Odyssey* iv 567, xi 598, xv 399,

very loosely to the language of the Homeric poems[1]. All these variations may be due to errors of memory, and they appear to throw little (if any) light on the state of the Homeric text in the fifth and fourth centuries B.C. On the whole, the evidence of quotations shows that the text of those centuries was practically the same as ours[2].

The epic poet Antimachus, of Colophon in Ionia (*fl.* 464—410), who was among the older contemporaries of Plato, prepared a text of Homer, which is mentioned about twelve times in the Venetian Scholia on Homer[3]. This text was supposed by Mr F. A. Paley to be perhaps the first publication of the *Iliad* and *Odyssey* in their present form[4]. An 'edition' of Homer is also attributed to Aristotle by Plutarch and Strabo. The former in his life of Alexander quotes Onesicritus as stating that Alexander constantly kept under his pillow, with his dagger, a copy of the *Iliad*, which Aristotle had corrected for him, called 'the casket copy'[5]. Strabo calls Alexander an admirer of Homer (φιλόμηρος), adding that there was a recension of Homer called 'that of the casket'; that Alexander had perused and annotated certain parts of it with the help of men like Callisthenes and Anaxarchus; and that he kept it in a casket of costly workmanship which he had found in the Persian treasure[6]. On the eve of his victorious career in Asia,

**Early 'editions' of Homer**

---

xix 121. Cp. R. Wachsmuth, *De Aristotelis Studiis Homericis Capita Selecta*, pp. 1—19, and on the variations in Plato and Aeschines, as well as in Aristotle, Laroche, *Homerische Textkritik* (1866), pp. 23—36, with Wilamowitz, *Hom. Unt.*, p. 299. Cp. Römer, *Die Homercitate und die Homerischen Fragen des Aristoteles*, in Transactions of Munich Academy, xvii (1884) 264—314, 639 ff; and Vahlen, *S. Ber.* of the Berlin Academy, 1902, (1) 168 f.

[1] *Eth.* ii 9, iii 11 ; *Pol.* viii 3, p. 1338 *a* ; *Rhet.* iii 4 ; *Poet.* 8.

[2] A. Ludwich, *Die Homer-vulgata als voralexandrinische erwiesen*, 1898 ; Monro, *Od.* 426—430.

[3] ἡ Ἀντιμάχου (*sc.* ἔκδοσις), ἡ κατὰ Ἀντίμαχον, ἡ Ἀντιμάχειος. Schol. on *Il.* i 298, 424, 598; v 461; xiii 60; xxiii 870; and *Od.* i 85. Cf. Monro, *Od.* 413.

[4] *Homeri quae nunc exstant an reliquis Cycli carminibus antiquiora iure habita sint* (1878), p. 39, quis ille fuerit qui Homerum nostrum litteris primum mandavit, si non fuit Antimachus, ego ignoro.

[5] Plut. *Alex.* 8, ἡ ἐκ τοῦ νάρθηκος.

[6] Strabo, p. 594. 'The *Iliad of the Casket* may safely be dismissed as a picturesque legend' (Monro, *Od.* 418).

he visited the plains of Troy, and placed a garland on the
tomb of Achilles, declaring him happy in having had, in his
life, a faithful friend, and in his death a mighty herald of his
fame[1].

Aristotle, in his treatise on Poetry, describes Homer as
'representing men as better than they are'[2], and as
'pre-eminent in the serious style of poetry'[3], as   Aristotle on
'the earliest and the most adequate model' of all   Homer
the excellences of epic poetry, and as 'unequalled in diction and
thought'[4]. The poet keeps himself in the background, leaving
his characters, which are clearly marked, to speak for themselves[5].
He has taught all other poets the true art of illusion[6]. In
'unity of plot', as in all else, he is of surpassing merit; he has
made the *Iliad*, as well as the *Odyssey*, centre round a single
action[7]. These two poems 'have many parts, each with a certain
magnitude of its own; yet they are as perfect as possible in
structure'[8]. In the *Rhetoric* Aristotle, in explaining what he
means by 'bringing things before the eye', or vividness of
expression, cites a series of metaphors from Homer :—the stone of
Sisyphus 'remorseless' in its bounding down into the valley, the
flying arrow 'yearning' for its mark, the javelins 'thirsting' for the
foeman's blood, and the 'passionate' spear-point, speeding
through the hero's breast. The same vivid effect, he adds, is
produced by the similes, in which Homer gives life and movement
and animation to things inanimate, as in the line where he says of
the 'waves of the bellowing ocean ',—'Arch'd and crested with
foam, they sweep on, billow on billow'[9].

Aristotle's interest in Homer led him to draw up a collection
of *Homeric Problems*, a subject which he approaches in the
chapter on 'critical difficulties and their solutions' towards the
close of his treatise on Poetry[10]. These Problems are only preserved in a fragmentary form[11]. For most of our knowledge of

[1] Plut. *Alex.* 15.

[2] 2 § 3.          [3] 4 § 9.          [4] 24 §§ 1, 2.

[5] § 7.          [6] § 9.          [7] 8 § 3.

[8] 26 § 6. Cp. Jebb's *Homer*, p. 4 f; Monro, 417 f.

[9] *Rhet.* iii 11 §§ 3, 4.

[10] *Poet.* 25, περὶ προβλημάτων καὶ λύσεων, esp. §§ 10, 11.

[11] ἀπορήματα, προβλήματα or ζητήματα (originally in either 6, 7 or 10

their purport we are indebted to the *scholia* on the MSS of Homer,
especially in the Venice MS B (cent. xi). They are there quoted
in twenty-one places, not to mention isolated passages of Strabo,
Plutarch and Athenaeus; they were also familiar to the Neo-
platonist Porphyry, the author of a similar work in the third
century of our era. The points raised concern the ethical and
dramatic sense of the poems, rather than verbal or literary
criticism[1]. For example, 'Why does Agamemnon tempt the
army to return to Greece?'[2] 'When the Greeks are fleeing to
their ships, why is it that Odysseus flings off his cloak, when he
runs at the bidding of Athene to stay their flight?'[3] 'Why does
Homer assign to Crete one hundred cities in the *Iliad*, and only
ninety in the *Odyssey*?'[4] 'Why are we told in the *Iliad* that the
sun-god sees and hears everything, and yet in the *Odyssey* he
needs a messenger to tell him of the slaughter of his oxen?'[5] 'If
the gods drink nothing but nectar, why is Calypso described as
*mixing* a draught for Hermes, *mixing* implying the addition of
water?'[6] "What is meant by '*more* of the night than two of the
three parts is gone, and (yet) the third part still remains'?[7]" 'Why
are two talents of gold (an *apparently* large amount) given as a
fourth prize in a chariot-race?'[8] Part of Aristotle's reply to this
last question is to the effect that the Homeric talent was smaller
than the Attic talent; and, so far, modern scholars are in entire
accord with Aristotle. Once we seem to reach the region of
textual criticism when the question is asked, "why is the epithet
αὐδήεσσα 'voiceful', 'speaking with human voice', applied to the
'goddesses' Circe and Calypso[9], as well as to the once mortal

books), Aristot. frag. 142—179 Rose. In one of these fragments we find the
verb ἠπόρησεν (159), in five the corresponding verb λύειν (149, 160, 161, 164,
174) and in one (179) the title Ἀρ. Ὁμηρικοῖς ἀπορήμασιν. Cp. Mitchell
Carroll, *Aristotle's Poetics, c. 25, in the light of the Homeric Scholia* (Baltimore,
1895).

[1] Cp. Egger, *l.c.*, pp. 188—194[3], and Saintsbury, *l.c.*, pp. 49 f.

[2] *Il.* ii 73.

[3] *Il.* ii 305.          [4] *Il.* ii 649; *Od.* xix 173.

[5] *Il.* iii 277; *Od.* xii 374.     [6] *Od.* v 93.          [7] *Il.* x 253.

[8] *Il.* xxiii 269; Arist. *Frag.* 164 Rose.

[9] Each of these is called a θεὸς αὐδήεσσα in *Od.* x 136 etc., and xii 449.

Ino?"[1]  Here it is strangely proposed in the first two cases to read αὐλήεσσα, which can only mean 'apt at playing on the flute', and yet is described as a synonym for μονῴδης, 'apt in singing a solo'; and, in the case of Ino, to read οὐδήεσσα, 'earthly'.  These fragmentary *Homeric problems*, as a whole, are very disappointing; and it may well be doubted whether Aristotle himself is really responsible for them, any more than for much that has come down under his name in the varied contents of the general *Problems*[2]. It is refreshing to turn from these to the passage in his treatise on Poetry, where he quotes the Homeric phrase, describing the comrades of Diomede as sleeping with their spears standing upright on their butt-ends, 'their spears stood upright on the spike'[3], instead of being laid level with the ground, in which case (as observed by the scholiast) there would have been no risk of a spear falling, and raising an alarm.  Aristotle solves the difficulty caused by the exceptional position of the spear, by simply suggesting that 'this was the custom then, as it is now among the Illyrians'[4].  It was probably in one of his lost chapters on Poetry that Aristotle observed that 'the most striking thing in Homer' was the passage describing the effect produced on the Trojans when they first see Patroclus, gleaming in the armour of Achilles, and fancy for the moment that Achilles has laid aside his 'wrath', and has been reconciled to the Greeks:—'each several man *peered round*[5] to seek escape from sheer destruction'.  This, adds Aristotle, is characteristic of barbarians[5].

We have seen thus far that, from the days of Solon to those of Aristotle, Homer was constantly studied and quoted, and was a favourite theme for allegorizing interpretation and for rationalistic or rhetorical treatment.  He was also the subject of a very limited amount of *verbal* criticism.  Of any *literary* criticism of his poems, we have scanty evidence, with the important exception of Aristotle's treatise on Poetry.  The criticism of his *text* was in the main reserved for the Alexandrian age.

---

[1] *Od.* v 334, βροτὸς αὐδήεσσα.          [2] Zeller, *Aristotle*, i 96, 104.
[3] *Il.* x 152 f, ἔγχεα δέ σφιν | ὄρθ' ἐπὶ σαυρωτῆρος.          [4] *Poet.* 25 § 7.
[5] Townley Schol. on *Il.* xvi 283 (Aristot. *Frag.* 130 Rose) πάπτηνεν: δεινότατον τῶν ἐπῶν Ὁμήρου τοῦτό φησιν Ἀριστοτέλης ἐν ᾧ πάντες φευκτιῶσι, καὶ οἰκεῖον βαρβάρων.

Apart from Homer, the epic poets studied in the Athenian age included those of the 'Epic Cycle' (*c.* 776—566 B.C.) which (as we have already seen) supplied the tragic poets with many of their themes. The *Theogony* of Hesiod (who flourished

Hesiod

about 700 B.C.) was also studied as a text-book of mythology, and the questions which it raised may well have been embarrassing to instructors who had to deal with exceptionally precocious pupils. We are told that Epicurus, before the age of fourteen (*c.* 328 B.C.), asked certain schoolmasters and sophists some puzzling questions about Hesiod's account of Chaos , and that, dissatisfied with their replies, he resolved on devoting himself to the study of philosophy[1]. Still more popular was Hesiod's poem on *Works and Days*, which with its moral maxims and its precepts of farming is the prototype not only of Tusser's *Points of Good Husbandrie* but also of Tupper's *Proverbial Philosophy* Aristophanes makes Aeschylus name Hesiod among the 'noble poets', because he tells of 'tilling the soil and times for ploughing and seasons of harvest'[2]. One passage from this poem, that on Fame or Rumour, is quoted by Aristotle, as well as twice by Aeschines[3], who also quotes on two occasions a passage of political import[4], and in the second of these last occasions introduces the lines by observing that 'the reason why we learn the precepts of the poets by heart in our boyhood is in order that we may obey them when we arrive at man's estate'. Hesiod was also the reputed author of a versified form of the precepts of reverence and obedience, which Achilles learnt from the centaur Cheiron ; and the fame of Cheiron's precepts is attested not only by Pindar[5] and Plato[6], but also by that unknown artist who on a vase in the Berlin Museum represents two boys standing and listening with rapt attention to a boy seated between them who is reading from a scroll, with a box before him on which rests a second scroll bearing in archaic

---

[1] Diog. Laert. x 2.                    [2] *Frogs*, 1034.

[3] *Works and Days*, 761 ; Aeschin. 1 § 129, 2 § 144 (cp. Dem. 19 § 243); Aristot. *Eth.* vii 13, 5.

[4] *ib.* 240 f; Aeschin. 2 § 158, 3 § 135.

[5] *Pyth.* iv 102.

[6] *Rep.* 391 B—C.

characters the title + IRONEIA[1]. The Hesiodic authorship of this work was first denied in the Alexandrian age, by Aristophanes of Byzantium[2].

Only two more epic poets need here be mentioned. The first of these, Antimachus of Colophon (*fl. c.* 464 —410), the author of a prolix poem called the *Antimachus* *Thebais*, is said to have begun the story of the return of Diomede with the death of Meleager, and to have reached the end of Book XXIV before getting the Seven heroes before the gates of Thebes[3]. Nevertheless he appears to have been approved by Plato, who is said to have been present on the occasion when the poet recited his voluminous work. One by one the company slipped away, till Plato alone remained. 'I shall go on reading', said the poet unperturbed, 'Plato alone in my opinion is worth a thousand'[4]. The philosopher is also said to have sent to Colophon for a complete collection of his poems, and to have preferred him to Choerilus[5], an opinion which was afterwards opposed in the Pergamene School by Crates of Mallos[6]. In the Alexandrian age the diffuseness of his epic poem was condemned by Callimachus[7], whose condemnation is echoed by Catullus[8]. Nevertheless he was awarded a high place in the Canon of the epic poets[9], and was even preferred to Homer by the emperor Hadrian[10], possibly because he was easier to imitate. Mention has already been made of his 'edition' of Homer, some of the readings of which are recorded in the Homeric *scholia*[11].

The second of these epic poets, Choerilus of Samos (*fl.* 404 B.C.), who was regarded by the Spartan general, Lysander, and by the Macedonian king, Arche- *Choerilus*

---

[1] See cut in Klein, *Euphronios*, 283[2]; Daremberg and Saglio, *s.v. Éducation*, p. 469; or P. Girard, *Éd. Ath.*, p. 149.

[2] Quint. i 1, 15 (cp. Kinkel, *Ep. Gr. Frag.*, i p. 148 f).

[3] Porphyrion on Horace, *A.P.* 146.　　　　[4] Cic. *Brutus*, 191.

[5] Proclus on Plato, *Tim.* i p. 28 C (Kinkel, *l.c.*, p. 274).

[6] *Anth. Pal.* xi 218.　　　　[7] Frag. 441.

[8] *C.* 95, 10.　　　　[9] Quint. x i 53.

[10] Dio Cass. lxix 4 (cp. Hist. Aug. *Hadr.* 15).

[11] *Supra*, p. 34, note 3. Cp. A. Ludwich, *Aristarchs Homerische Textkritik*, i 18; ii 432, 383.

laus, as one of the foremost poets of his time[1], was the author
of an important Epic on the Persian wars. Choerilus broke
new ground by abandoning the old mythological themes in
favour of a national and historical subject. He attained the
unique honour of a decree providing apparently for the public
recitation of his poems together with those of Homer[2]. Aristotle in the *Topics*[3] considers the Homeric similes clearer than
those of Choerilus. In the *Rhetoric*[4] he quotes what is obviously part of the exordium of his Epic, immediately after the
first phrase of the *Iliad* and the *Odyssey*.

From another passage early in this poem Aristotle quotes
a single phrase as an example of an apologetic exordium:—
νῦν δ' ὅτε πάντα δέδασται, 'now that all has been apportioned'.
His readers were doubtless familiar with the context, which has
fortunately been preserved in an ancient *scholium*, and in the
form of the following paraphrase may fitly close the present
chapter :

> Oh! the bards of olden ages, blessed bards in song-craft skill'd,
> Happy henchmen of the Muses, when the field was yet untill'd.
> All the land is now apportion'd; bounds to all the Arts belong;
> Left the last of all the poets, looking keenly, looking long,
> I can find no bright new chariot for the race-course of my song[5].

---

[1] Plutarch, *Lysand.* 18; Athen. 345 D.
[2] Suidas, σὺν τοῖς Ὁμήρου ἀναγινώσκεσθαι ἐψηφίσθη (Kinkel, *l.c.*, p. 265).
[3] viii 1.
[4] iii 14.
[5]
> ἆ μάκαρ, ὅστις ἔην κεῖνον χρόνον ἴδρις ἀοιδῆς,
> Μουσάων θεράπων, ὅτ' ἀκήρατος ἦν ἔτι λειμών·
> νῦν δ' ὅτε πάντα δέδασται, ἔχουσι δὲ πείρατα τέχναι,
> ὕστατοι ὥστε δρόμου καταλείπομεθ', οὐδέ πη ἔστι
> πάντη παπταίνοντα νεοζυγὲς ἄρμα πελάσσαι.

# CHAPTER III.

## THE STUDY OF LYRIC POETRY.

AN interesting picture of the normal course of education at Athens is drawn by Protagoras in the dialogue of Plato which bears that name. In the picture in question special stress is laid on the study of the poets.

The study of poetry. Plato's Protagoras

> When the boys have learned their letters, and are beginning to understand the sense of what is written,...their teachers set beside them the works of excellent poets, and compel the boys, while seated on the benches, to read them aloud and learn them by heart. In these are contained many admonitions, many detailed narratives and eulogies and laudations of brave men of old. These are learnt by heart, in order that the boy may emulate and imitate those brave men, and be eager to become like them.... Then, again, the teachers of the *cithara*, as soon as their pupils have learned to play on that instrument, instruct them in the works of other excellent poets, the composers of songs[1], which they set to music, forcing the very souls of the boys to become familiar with their rhythms and their melodies, in order that they may be more gentle, and be better fitted for speech and action by becoming more beautifully 'rhythmical' and 'melodious'; for the whole of man's life has need of beauty of rhythm and of melody. Besides all this, their parents send them to the master of gymnastic, in order that they may have their bodies in better condition and able to minister to the virtue of their minds, and not be compelled by the weakness of their bodies to play the coward either in war or in any other action[2].

The study of the poets is also emphasised in the references to the ordinary course of education contained in Plato's *Laws*:

> We have very many poets (says 'the Athenian' in that dialogue), writing in hexameter verse, and in (iambic) trimeters, and in all other kinds of

---

[1] μελοποιῶν.　　　　　[2] Plato, *Protag.* 325 c—326 E.

'metres,' some with a serious purpose, others aiming merely at raising a laugh. With these the many myriads of Athens say that young men, who are being rightly educated, should be nurtured and saturated, by being made to have much to hear at recitations, and much to learn, and by getting whole poets by heart; while others select choice passages out of all the poets and make a collection of certain complete set-speeches, and say that these are what should be committed to memory by anyone who is to be made good and wise by a variety of experience and a variety of learning[1].

The artistic counterpart of these pictures is to be found in the scenes from an Athenian school which adorn the outside of an Attic vase executed by Duris in the early part of the fifth century B.C. In the centre of one of the two scenes the master, seated on a chair, holds a scroll half open, and listens to a boy standing before him, who may either be saying by heart the lesson that he has learnt, or committing it to memory under the master's prompting. The open part of the scroll bears a rather inaccurate copy of a line from some ancient Hymn :—Μοῖσά μοι ἀμφὶ Σκάμανδρον εὔρροον ἄρχομαι ἀείδειν. To the left is a bearded master playing a seven-stringed lyre, face to face with a pupil who is playing on a smaller instrument of the same kind; both of these are seated on stools. To the right, seated on another stool, is a bearded man with a staff in his hand, probably the boy's tutor or supervisor, the παιδαγωγός. In the centre of the second scene a youthful teacher sits holding a tablet in his left hand and a stylus in his right. He is apparently correcting an exercise written by the boy who stands before him. To the left another youthful teacher is playing the double flute as a lesson to a second boy standing before him. To the right, as in the first scene, sits a bearded man with a staff, watching the giving of the lesson. A variety of articles are suspended on the walls, including a scroll tied up, a pair of writing-tablets fastened together by a string, a wicker-basket, two flat drinking-cups, a cross-like object consisting of two intersecting pieces (possibly for drawing angles and straight lines), and lastly a flute-case, and three lyres[2].

*Vase-painting by Duris*

---

[1] Plato, *Laws*, 810 E.

[2] Published (with red figures on black ground) in *Mon. d. Inst.* ix pl. 54; also, with article by Michaelis, in *Arch. Zeitung*, xxxi p. 1. See *Frontispiece*.

The stringed instrument of the Homeric poems is the
*phorminx* or *cithara* or *citharis.* The *citharis* and      The cithara
the 'lyre' are synonymous in the Hymn to Hermes,      and the lyre
where the 'lyre' is first mentioned. But a distinction is sometimes drawn between the 'lyre' and the *cithara.*
While the 'lyre' (with projecting 'horns' and with a simple
equivalent for the original tortoise-shell body) is the instrument
depicted in the vase-painting, and also mentioned in the context
of the passage from the *Laws*[1], it is the 'cithara' (in which the
'shell' is replaced by a wooden case and the 'horns' superseded
by a prolongation of the case on either side of the strings) that is
mentioned in the passage from the *Protagoras.* Elsewhere, both
the instruments are mentioned together[2]. But, although the lyre
and the 'cithara', and especially the former, were the instruments
ordinarily used in education, the poets, whose songs were set to
the music of these instruments, were never known
in the Athenian age as the 'lyric' poets, but as      'lyric' or
                                                       'melic' poets
μελοποιοί, 'makers of μέλη' or 'songs'[3]. For the
earliest use of the term 'lyric' we have to wait until the Alexandrian age, in which a pupil of Aristarchus, the grammarian
Dionysius Thrax[4], refers to 'lyric poetry'; while, for the first
mention of a 'melic' poet, we have to wait still longer, even until
the time of Plutarch[5] (*fl.* 80 A.D.).

In contrasting the old and the new style of education
Aristophanes, in a play whose date is in or after
423 B.C., describes the master of the good old days      Lamprocles
                                                          and Phrynis
as making his pupils learn the song of 'Pallas,
dread sacker of cities', composed by Lamprocles (*c.* 476 B.C.), the
fellow-pupil of Pindar and the instructor of Damon[6], or the

---

[1] 809 E, λύρας ἅψασθαι.                    [2] Plato, *Rep.* 399 D.

[3] Also as κιθαρῳδοί (Bergk, *Gr. Litt.* ii 117).

[4] *Ars Gramm.* p. 6 *l.* 10 Uhlig, λυρικὴ ποίησις (cp. Smyth's *Greek Melic
Poets,* p. xvii n.). Cp. Varro's *Relliquiae,* p. 187 Wilmanns, and Cicero's
*Orator,* 183.

[5] ii 120 C, τοῦ μελικοῦ Πινδάρου, cp. Plin. *N.H.* vii 89, 192; *poëmatis melici*
is found as early as Cicero, *De Opt. Gen. Or.* 1.

[6] Παλλάδα περσέπολιν, δεινὰν θεὸν ἐγρεκύδοιμον,
ποτικλῇ͂ζω πολεμαδόκον, ἀγνὰν
παῖδα Διὸς μεγάλου δαμάσιππον (cp. Smyth, *l.c.,* p. 340).

'loudly sounding strain' of Cydides (or Cydias of Hermione),—
songs marked by the grave and severe melody of the olden
time, as contrasted with the difficult and complicated turns and
flourishes of the modern style of the Lesbian Phrynis[1]. Elsewhere he frequently denounces the dithyrambic poet, Cinesias,
who with the foreigners Phrynis, Melanippides and Timotheus
is also attacked by Pherecrates in a celebrated passage preserved
by Plutarch[2].

The study of the 'melic' poets in the Athenian age may be
partly inferred from citations. A line of Alcaeus

*Alcaeus and Sappho*

(*fl.* 612—580 B.C.) addressed to Sappho (*fl.* 612),
and four lines of her reply are preserved by
Aristotle[3]; and the famous palinode of Stesichorus is quoted
in the *Phaedrus* of Plato[4]. Anacreon of Teos (*fl.*

*Anacreon. Simonides*

530 B.C.) and Simonides of Ceos (556—468 B.C.)
were both invited to Athens by Hipparchus. As
the singer of love and wine, Anacreon does not lend himself
either for purposes of education, or for quotation by grave
philosophers or orators. He is the poet of the *symposium*. The
sweetness of his melodies is mentioned by Aristophanes[5], who
couples his name with that of Ibycus of Samos (*fl.* 544 B.C.). A
much more serious poet is Simonides. A popular definition of
justice as 'paying one's debts', ascribed to Simonides, is criticised
in the *Republic*[6]. In the *Protagoras*, one of his poems is selected
by Protagoras as a thesis for discussion[7]. In that poem the
Sophist professes to find a contradiction. The poet first says,
'hard it is for a man to become good'; and then inconsistently
reproaches Pittacus for saying, 'hard it is to be good'. The
solution offered by Socrates, who draws a distinction between
*being* and *becoming*, is probably 'a caricature of the methods of
interpretation' practised by the Sophists, and the discussion on
the passage as a whole may be 'regarded as Plato's satire on the

[1] Ar. *Clouds*, 966—972.
[2] *De Musica*, p. 1141 § 30 (on Phrynis, cp. Smyth, p. lxvi, on Melanippides
and Timotheus, *ib.* 454, 462).
[3] *Rhet.* i 9 (cp. Smyth, p. 239).
[4] 243 A; cp. *Rep.* 586 C.
[5] *Thesm.* 161.
[6] i p. 331 D—E.
[7] p. 339 (Smyth, pp. 54, 309).

tedious and hypercritical arts of interpretation which prevailed in
his own day"[1]. His elegiac epigram on those who fell at Marathon
is quoted by Lycurgus[2], who also quotes one of his two epigrams
on the heroes of Thermopylae, both of which are quoted by
Herodotus[3]. In none of these cases is the name of the author
mentioned, though the epigram on the seer Megistias is expressly
ascribed to Simonides. The opening line of his ode in honour of
the victory in the mule-race won by Anaxilas of Rhegium, or
possibly by his son, is quoted by Aristotle as an example of the
use of epithets to lend elevation to a subject:—" When the victor
in the mule-race offered him a small fee, he declined to compose
the ode in honour of the victory on the ground that he was
shocked at the thought of writing on the subject of semi-asses;
but when the victor actually gave him sufficient pay, he wrote:—
'Hail to the brood of the storm-footed coursers'"[4].

The Theban Pindar (518—c. 443 B.C.) must have been popular
at Athens, not because he celebrated the Pythian
victory of Megacles the Alcmaeonid[5], but because          Pindar
he recognised Salamis as the glory of the Athenians[6], and Athens
herself as 'the gleaming city of the violet crown' and 'the
bulwark of Hellas'[7]. It is said that in consequence of these
praises of Athens, Pindar was fined by his countrymen, but that
the Athenians paid the poet twice the amount of the fine and set
up a statue of bronze in his honour[8]. Pindar is repeatedly
quoted by Plato, for example in the *Meno*, where he is counted as
one of the 'divine poets', and a splendid passage is cited from his
dirges[9]. The lines on the reign of Law seem to have been
Plato's favourite quotation, for he refers to them in the *Protagoras*,
the *Gorgias* and the *Symposium*, and also in the *Laws*[10]. The

---

[1] Jowett's *Plato*, i 113[1], 124[3].

[2] *Leocr.* 109.                              [3] vii 228.

[4] *Rhet.* iii 2, 14, χαίρετ' ἀελλοπόδων θύγατρες ἵππων.

[5] *Pyth.* vii.                              [6] *Pyth.* i 75.

[7] Frag. 46, αἴ τε λιπαραὶ καὶ ἰοστέφανοι καὶ ἀοίδιμοι, Ἑλλάδος ἔρεισμα,
κλειναὶ Ἀθᾶναι, δαιμόνιον πτολίεθρον, cp. *Nem.* iv 18, *Isth.* ii 20, and Aristoph.
*Ach.* 636—640.

[8] [Aeschin.] *Ep.* iv (Donaldson's *Pindar*, p. 346); cp. Isocr. *Antid.* 166.

[9] *Meno*, p. 81 B.

[10] Frag. 151, νόμος ὁ πάντων βασιλεὺς κτλ. Cp. Schröder in *Philologus*,
1918 (*Amer. Journ. Phil.* 1919, 218 ff).

same passage is cited by Herodotus[1], and by the rhetorician Alcidamas[2]. Pindar was held in honour all over the Greek world. He was early known in Thessaly, as well as in his native Thebes and in Orchomenus; one at least of his odes was familiar to Tenedos; he was still more famous in Aegina; he was not unknown at Argos and Sicyon and Corinth; his name must have lived on the lips of men at the scenes of the celebration of the great Greek games, at the Isthmus and at Nemea, at Delphi and Olympia. He was bound by the ties of hospitality with the Achaeans dwelling above the Ionian sea on the Thesprotian border of Epirus[3], where 'the mountain-pastures sweep downwards from Dodona to the Ionian main'[4]. His fame extended to the western as well as the eastern Locrians; in the south-east to distant Cyrene, and in the west, as far as Himera and Camarina and Acragas and Syracuse. The lines of the Sixth Olympian ode bidding men 'remember Syracuse and Ortygia, where Hieron ruleth with unsullied sceptre and with perfect counsel, while he tendeth not only the worship of Demeter with her ruddy feet, and the festival of her daughter, Persephone, with her white horses, but also the might of Zeus, the lord of Aitna', have been found stamped on an ancient brick at Syracuse, possibly by Hieron's own order[5]; and the Seventh Olympian in honour of the most famous of Greek boxers, Diagoras of Rhodes, was inscribed in golden letters in the temple of Athene in the Rhodian town of Lindos[6]. Pindar composed an encomium in honour of the Macedonian king, Alexander 'the Philhellene'[7]; and, one hundred and fifty years afterwards, at the sack of Thebes (335 B.C.), it was in memory perhaps of that encomium that another Alexander,

[1] Her. iii 38.                    [2] Arist. Rhet. iii. 3 § 3.

[3] Nem. vii 64 f.

[4] Nem. iv 52 f.

[5] Ol. vi 93—96; Zeitschr. f. Alterth. 1846, p. 616; Bergk ad loc.; and Freeman's Sicily, ii 539.

[6] Gorgon ap. Schol. Cp. A. Croiset, La poésie de Pindare, p. 18. C. Graux, Rev. de Phil. v 117 (= Notices Bibl. 302), supposes that the ode was written in gold ink on the inner surface of a little roll of parchment or fine leather (Gildersleeve's Pindar, p. 184).

[7] Frag. 121 [86].

'The great Emathian conqueror, bid spare
The house of Pindarus, when temple and tower
Went to the ground'[1].

Of the rest of the nine principal 'melic' poets of Greece neither the earliest, Alcman of Sparta (*fl.* 657 B.C.), nor the latest, Bacchylides of Ceos (*c.* 507—430), is quoted by any of the authors of the Athenian age. Bacchylides, however, and his uncle, Simonides, are supposed to have been in Pindar's mind in a well-known passage of the Second Olympian, in honour of Theron :—'many swift arrows have I beneath my bended arm within my quiver, arrows vocal to the intelligent (φωνάεντα συνετοῖσιν), though for their full meaning they need interpreters. Wise is he that knoweth much by nature; but, when men have merely learnt their lore, they are turbulent and intemperate of tongue, even as a pair of crows idly chattering (γαρύετον) against the divine bird of Zeus'[2]. But time has brought some compensation to Bacchylides. We now know that, in the ode in honour of an Olympian victory of Hieron won in the same year as that of Theron (476 B.C.), Pindar's rival compared his own range of flight to that of an eagle[3]; and that, in celebrating another victory of Hieron eight years afterwards (468 B.C.), he too could say : 'I utter words intelligible to the prudent'[4].

In Aristotle's treatise on Poetry[5], mention is made of 'dithyrambic poetry', and 'the music of the flute and the *cithara*'; but in that treatise, in its present form, lyric poetry is never discussed. The author, however, was not necessarily unsympathetic towards this kind of composition. We still possess a grave and dignified ode to Virtue written by Aristotle himself[6].

The lyric poetry of Greece may be conveniently regarded as including not only the 'melic' but also the 'elegiac' and 'iambic' poets. All alike were associated with song, and were generally accompanied by music, the instrument, in the case of 'melic' poets, being the lyre or the *cithara*, and in the case of 'elegiac'

[1] Milton, *Sonnet* 8 ; cp. Pliny, vii 109; Aelian, *Var. Hist.* xiii 7.
[2] *Ol.* ii 91—97.  Cp. Jebb's *Bacchylides* (1905), 13—23.
[3] v 16—27.        [4] iii 85, φρονέοντι συνετὰ γαρύω.          [5] 1 § 2.
[6] ap. Athen. 695 A (Smyth, pp. 142, 468).

and 'iambic' poets the flute[1]. Of the elegiac poets, one of the
earliest (in the ordinary view) is Tyrtaeus (*fl.* 640

**Elegiac poets.**
**Tyrtaeus**
B.C.). His poem on *Good Government* (Eunomia)
is specially mentioned by Aristotle, while not
less than thirty-two lines from his spirited and stirring *Exhortations* are quoted in court by the orator Lycurgus. Two other
portions of the same poem are embodied in passages in the
*Laws* of Plato, where their author is called a 'most divine poet',
though Plato regrets that personal bravery in battle is the only

**Mimnermus**
kind of virtue that wins his praise[2]. Mimnermus
of Smyrna (*fl.* 620 B.C.) is partly a political and
still more a sentimental poet. He sighs as he prays:—'Ah!
that from sickness safe and bitter cares, Death may o'ertake me,
e'en at *sixty* years'[3]. The sentiment meets with a protest
from the sturdy good sense of Solon who, addressing Mimnermus,
says:—"But, if, even now, you will take my advice, erase this;
nor bear me any ill-will for having thought on this theme better
than you; emend the words, Ligyastades, and sing: 'May death

**Solon**
o'ertake me, e'en at *eighty* years'"[4]. In Solon's
case, the prayer was apparently answered, for he
seems to have died at the age of eighty (*c.* 639—559). In his
poems elegiac and iambic verse are alike represented. Among
his elegiacs are some forty lines of a vigorous and patriotic poem
on Athens, which Demosthenes calls upon the clerk of the court
to read aloud in the course of the speech for the prosecution of
Aeschines, and also two or three passages, probably from the
same poem, which Aristotle quotes in his *Constitution of Athens*,
together with thirty-five iambic lines on his political reforms, and
nine trochaic lines on the same topic. In his *Rhetoric* he quotes
a single line of admonition to Critias. Plato cites a couplet in
the *Lysis*, without the author's name, and elsewhere mentions
Solon and his contemporaries[5].

---

[1] Cp. Jebb's *Growth and Influence of Classical Greek Poetry*, pp. 108, 117,
122.

[2] Arist. *Pol.* v 6, **2**; Lycurg. *Leocr.* 107; Plato, *Laws*, 629 A, E, 660 E.

[3] Frag. 6.                    [4] Frag. 20.

[5] Dem. 19 § 255; Arist. *Const. Ath.* c. 5 and 12; *Rhet.* i 15; Plato, *Lys.*
212 E, *Charmid.* 157 F, *Tim.* 20 E and esp. 21 B—C.

In the *Timaeus* in particular Critias (who died in 404 B.C.) recalls an incident which happened when he was a boy of about ten years of age. It was on the day of the Apaturia set apart for the registration of boys; and, in accordance with the custom of that festival, parents gave prizes for recitation (ῥαψῳδία), many poems were recited, and among them ' many of us boys sang the poems of Solon, which were new at the time ' (*i.e.* recently introduced into public recitations). Someone said to the boy's grandfather, a contemporary and relation of Solon's, that, in his judgement, Solon was ' not only the wisest of men, but also the noblest of poets '. The old man smiled and said that, ' if Solon had only made poetry the business of his life,…he would have been as famous as Homer or Hesiod, or any poet '.

The elegiac epigrammatists Demodocus of Leros and Phocylides of Miletus (*fl.* 537 B.C.) are cited by Aristotle in     Phocylides. the *Ethics*[1] and *Politics*[2] respectively, the former    Theognis passage describing the character of the Milesians, and the latter the advantage of belonging to the middle classes. Theognis of Megara (*fl.* 540 B.C.) is commended in Plato's *Laws* for eulogising political loyalty, and is paraphrased in the *Meno*, while his proverbial sayings are quoted by Xenophon and Aristotle[3]. Most of his verses are of a political, and indeed intensely aristocratical, type, and they could hardly be expected to be popular in democratic Athens. The only evidence adduced to show that he was one of the standard school-authors is the proverbial line :—' *That* indeed I knew before Theognis was born '[4]. All that this proves is that his moral maxims were often quoted and had long been very trite. They seem to have inspired much of the worldly wisdom of Isocrates, who names Theognis (with Hesiod and Phocylides) as a wise counsellor who was neglected in comparison with the comic poets of the day[5]. His lighter verses were expressly meant to be sung at the

---

[1] vii 9.            [2] iv 11, 9.

[3] Plato, *Laws*, 630, *Meno*, 95 E; Xen. *Mem.* i 2, 20, *Symp.* ii 5; Arist. *Eth.* i 8, x 9.

[4] τουτὶ μὲν ᾔδειν πρὶν Θέογνιν γεγονέναι (Dousa ad Lucil. frag. incert. 102, quoted by Gräfenhan, i 71); Plut. *Mor.* ii 777. Cp. Schömann, *Op.* iv 25 f.

[5] Isocr. 2 § 43.

*symposium* to the strains of flutes, and a phrase from one of them has actually been found inscribed on a wine-cup of Tanagra[1].

The foremost of the early iambic poets, Archilochus of Paros

**Iambic poets. Archilochus**

(*fl.* 650), though ranked with Homer by the ancients, is described by Pindar, at a distance of two centuries, as 'the bitter-tongued Archilochus, who fell full often into distress by battening on virulent abuse of his enemies '[2]. Pindar also mentions 'the chant of Archilochus, vocal at Olympia, even the song of victory, swelling with its thrice-repeated refrain', which, in the absence of any special ode, was sung as the ancient counterpart of our modern strain of victory:—'See the conquering hero comes'. Archilochus is twice imitated by Aristophanes[3], twice quoted by Aristotle[4], and twice in the Platonic dialogues[5]. His poems were recited by rhapsodes, and sung to music like those of Homer and Hesiod, Mimnermus and Phocylides[6]. The other 'iambic' poets, Semonides of Amorgos and Hipponax of Ephesus, are not quoted in the Athenian age. The 'iambics' of Solon have been already noticed[7].

It must not be inferred from the limited range of the quotations from the elegiac, iambic and melic poets in the Athenian age, that those poets were comparatively unknown. Almost all of their poetry was 'occasional'; much of it was ephemeral; and few besides Pindar could say:—'longer than deeds liveth the word '[8]. Many however of their poems played a part in the private life of Athens, either in the school, or at the *symposium*, or both. Elegiac poetry lasted for sixteen centuries, beginning with Callînus (*c.* 690 B.C.) and ending with the Greek Anthology of Constantinus Cephalas (*c.* 920 A.D.). In the Greek drama this metre is only used once, in the lament of Andromache[9]; but iambic poetry found a fresh lease of life in the dialogue, and melic in the chorus, of the drama; while the epic poetry of narration survived in the messenger's speeches of Greek tragedy.

---

[1] 1365, ὦ παίδων κάλλιστε, cp. 241 f; Christ, *Gr. Litt.* § 100[4].

[2] *Pyth.* ii 55.                    [3] *Ranae,* 704, *Pax,* 603.

[4] *Pol.* vii 6, 3, *Rhet.* iii 17.            [5] *Rep.* 365 C, *Eryx.* 397 E.

[6] Athen. 620.                      [7] p. 48.

[8] *Nem.* iv 6.                      [9] Eur. *Andr.* 103—116.

The canon of Greek lyric poetry closes in 452 B.C., the date of the last known odes of Pindar and Bacchylides. Meanwhile the personal and reflective interest, which lyric poetry had excited in the individual, had begun to abate in the presence of the public enthusiasm aroused in vast audiences by the drama. Aeschylus had won his first tragic prize in 484 B.C.; Sophocles in 468, about the time of the death of Simonides; and Euripides in 442, about the time of the death of Pindar; while the year 450 is the approximate date of the successes gained in the Old Attic Comedy by Crates and Cratinus, and also of the birth of Aristophanes.

From the Codex Ravennas (cent. xi) of Aristophanes.
Size about ¾ of original published in complete *facsimile* (Leyden, 1904).

Criticism of Aeschylus in *Ranae*, 1126—1136 :—

> ΑΙ.  Ἑρμῆ χθόνιε, πατρῷ’ ἐποπτεύων κράτη,
> σωτὴρ γενοῦ μοι σύμμαχός τ’ αἰτουμένῳ.
> ἥκω γὰρ ἐς γῆν τήνδε καὶ κατέρχομαι.
>
> ΔΙ.  τούτων ἔχεις ψέγειν τι;  ΕΥ.  πλεῖν ἢ δώδεκα.
> ἀλλ’ οὐδὲ ταῦτα πάντα γ’ ἔστ’ ἀλλ’ ἢ τρία. ·
> ἔχει δ’ ἕκαστον εἴκοσίν γ’ ἁμαρτίας.
>
> ΔΙ.  Αἰσχύλε, παραινῶ σοι σιωπᾶν· εἰ δὲ μή,
> πρὸς τρισὶν ἰαμβείοισι προσοφείλων φανεῖ.
>
> ΑΙ.  ἐγὼ σιωπῶ τῷδ’;  ΔΙ.  ἐὰν πείθῃ γ’ ἐμοί.
> εὐθὺς γὰρ ἡμάρτηκεν οὐράνιόν γ’ ὅσον.
>
> ΑΙ.  ὁρᾷς ὅτι ληρεῖς;  ΔΙ.  ἀλλ’ ὀλίγον γέ μοι μέλει.

# CHAPTER IV.

## THE STUDY AND CRITICISM OF DRAMATIC POETRY.

LITERARY criticism was promoted at Athens not only by the epic recitations of the rhapsodes[1], but also by the contests for the prizes offered for lyric, and much more by those for dramatic, poetry. But such criticism was purely of a popular and unprofessional kind. The contests of the drama were at first decided by acclamation, and the voice of the people awarded the prize. Subsequently the decision was made by five judges in comic, and probably the same number in tragic, contests. This small number of judges was appointed by lot, out of a large preliminary list elected by vote. It speaks well for the general competence of the judges that Aeschylus and Sophocles were usually successful; but, strange to say, at the presentation of the *Oedipus Tyrannus*, Sophocles was defeated by a minor poet, Philocles, a nephew of Aeschylus. Euripides won the prize on five occasions only, while Aeschylus is credited with thirteen victories, and Sophocles with at least eighteen. The decisions pronounced by the judges on such occasions were not without their effect in leading to the improvement of plays which were unsuccessful at their first presentation. The revision and reproduction of unsuccessful plays was not an uncommon practice[2].

*Dramatic poetry and literary criticism*

Dramatic criticism occasionally found its way into the plays themselves. Euripides, in his *Electra* (l. 526—544), openly criticises the means adopted by Aeschylus in the *Choëphoroe* for

---

[1] p. 20.

[2] Egger, *Hist. de la Critique*, p. 26 f.

bringing about the recognition of Orestes by his sister. Such criticism, singularly out of place in tragedy, was more frequent and more appropriate in comedy. More than sixty years after the memorable occasion, when the contest between Aeschylus and Sophocles had been decided for the first time in favour of the latter by the verdict of Cimon and his colleagues (468 B.C.), the comic poet, Phrynichus, represented the nine Muses themselves as assembled in court to decide on the respective merits of the tragic poets, and passed an encomium on the dramatic career of Sophocles[1].

*Criticism in Attic Comedy*

*The Muses of Phrynichus*

On the above occasion the *Muses* of Phrynichus competed with the play familiar to ourselves under the name of the *Frogs* of Aristophanes (405 B.C.). In that play, it will be remembered that Sophocles takes no part in the contest for the throne of Tragedy. Aeschylus and Euripides enter the lists and criticise passages in one another's plays. These criticisms extend over nearly three hundred lines (1119—1413), but a very brief analysis will here suffice.

*The Frogs of Aristophanes*

Euripides begins by taking Aeschylus to task for his bombastic style, while Aeschylus criticises his rival's prologues. Euripides next claims credit for making Tragedy more familiar, more domestic; Aeschylus, for inspiring his countrymen with a patriotic spirit by means of martial plays, such as the *Seven against Thebes* and the *Persae*. He also taunts his opponent with bringing on to the stage not only women with strange passions, but also fallen kings in rags and tatters. Thereupon Euripides attacks the opening lines of the *Choëphoroe*, finding fault (among other things) with one or two tautological phrases, 'listen' and 'hear,' and 'I have come,' and 'I revisit'[2]. (In the latter case Aeschylus triumphantly retorts that the second verb is rightly added, being particularly appropriate to return from *exile*.) Aeschylus rejoins with an attack on Euripides for the monotony of his prologues, and ridicules the too frequent recurrence of the pause after the fifth syllable of the iambic line, adding to all the verses in which this pause occurs, and in which the grammatical construction allows, a burlesque and trivial conclusion,—'lost his little flask of oil' (ληκύθιον ἀπώλεσεν), by which the poet's tragic phrase is

---

[1] Egger, *l.c.*, p. 38 f; cp. *Fragmenta Comicorum Graecorum*, ii 592 Meineke, μάκαρ Σοφοκλέης, ὃς πολὺν χρόνον βιοὺς | ἀπέθανεν, εὐδαίμων ἀνὴρ καὶ δεξιός, | πολλὰς ποιήσας καὶ καλὰς τραγῳδίας· | καλῶς δ' ἐτελεύτησ', οὐδὲν ὑπομείνας κακόν.

[2] 1128, ἥκω γὰρ εἰς γῆν τήνδε καὶ κατέρχομαι. See *facsimile* on p. 51.

made to end in bathos. Euripides in reply attacks the choruses of Aeschylus, stringing together a number of pompous phrases, and criticising their obscurity, their ponderous metres, and their monotonous refrains. Aeschylus returns the compliment with a series of affectedly pretty verses from the choruses of Euripides, exemplifying (among other things) his innovations in choral music and metre. He next parodies his rival's monodies, in choral lines combining the false sublime with the vulgar pathetic, and both with impertinent appeals to the help of Heaven. Lastly, the two poets put their verses to the test of the balance. A large pair of scales is produced; Aeschylus stands beside one of the scales and Euripides by the other; each in turn repeats a single line from one of his own plays, and the scale is supposed to rise or fall, according as the sense of the line is light or heavy. In the end Aeschylus, weary of competing line against line, challenges Euripides to a final and comprehensive contest. With the challenge he combines a sly allusion to the help that Euripides was supposed to derive from his slave Cephisophon in the composition of his plays, and to the book-learning already noticed in a line describing him, as 'from learned scrolls distilling the essence of his wit' (943) :—

> Come! no more line for line! Let him bring *all*,—
> His wife, his children, his Cephisophon,
> And mount the scale himself, with all his books.
> I shall outweigh them with two lines alone.

Dionysus, the arbiter of this conflict of wits, finally decides in favour of Aeschylus, who is accordingly brought back to the upper world. In the ensuing chorus (1482—1499) Aristophanes dwells on the triumphant recall of Aeschylus as a tribute to the good taste and sound sense characteristic of the true poet, while the fate of Euripides is a warning that it is not well to sit and chatter with Socrates, denouncing the art of poetry and neglecting the noblest aims of the tragic art.

The passing attack on Socrates does not fairly apply to the Socrates whom we know in Plato; but, in the controversy as a whole, we feel that, although the author is clearly prejudiced against Euripides, the points selected for criticism on each side are both interesting and instructive. The criticism of Aristophanes (as has been well observed) " rests upon a reasoned view of art and taste as well as of politics and religion. He disapproves the sceptical purpose, the insidious sophistic, the morbid passion of his victim; but he disapproves quite as strongly the tedious preliminary explanations and interpolated narratives, the 'precious' sentiment and style, the tricks and the trivialities ". Yet he 'is far too good a critic and far too shrewd a man not to allow a pretty full view of the Aeschylean defects, as well as to put in the mouth of Euripides himself a very fairly strong defence of his own merits'. Notwithstanding this signally effective dramatic example of the 'direct criticism of actual texts', it is remarkable that 'formal criticism in prose' was long in making its appearance, and when it appeared showed 'much less mastery of method'[1].

The traces of literary criticism preserved in the fragments of Attic Comedy are far more numerous than has been sometimes supposed[2]. Hesiod was quoted and parodied in the *Cheiron* of Pherecrates, a play in which Music complains of the maltreatment she has received from some of the lyrical composers of the day[3]. In the *Hesiodi* of Telecleides we have some references to contemporary poets, and a passage on Euripides, referring to his being aided in his tragedies by Mnesilochus and Socrates, possibly comes from this play[4]. Other plays of the Old Comedy, like the *Tragedians* of Phrynichus and the *Poets* of Plato, were possibly concerned with literary criticism. The lovers of Euripides were satirised in the *Phileuripides* of Axionicus[5], and of Philippus or Philippides[6]. *Sappho* was the title of six plays; of four of these we know next to nothing; but in that of Antiphanes[7] she was represented as propounding and solving riddles; and in that of Diphilus[8], as having among her admirers Archilochus, who flourished forty years before her time, and Hipponax, seventy years after it. In the case of Sappho in particular, any inference that we may draw from the mere titles of such plays must necessarily be uncertain.

---

[1] Saintsbury's *History of Criticism*, i p. 22 f. See also Jebb's *Classical Greek Poetry*, pp. 230—3, and H. M. Reynolds in *Proc. Amer. Phil. Assoc.* xxi (1890), xvii f. The terseness of Euripides was appreciated by Aristophanes (frag. 397 D).

[2] See esp. Baker, *De Comicis Graecis litterarum iudicibus*, in *Harvard Studies*, xv (1904), 121—240.

[3] Athen. 364 A, B ; Plut. *De Musica*, § 30 ; cp. Meineke, *Fr. Com. Gr.* II 334 f ; Egger, *l.c.*, 39 ; Baker, *l.c.*, 153.

[4] Meineke, I 88, II 371 ; Baker, 156.

[5] Athen. 175 B (Meineke, I 417) ; Baker, 211.

[6] Meineke, I 341, 474 ; Baker, 221.

[7] Meineke, I 277 f ; Baker, 196.      [8] Meineke, I 447 ; Baker, 217.

There is a passage in the comic poet Timocles, humorously
describing the consolations enjoyed by the spectator of a tragedy
who finds his own troubles lightened by the contemplation of
the troubles of others in the play.   There is also a passage from
the *Poïēsis* of Antiphanes, insisting that Tragedy is far easier
to write than Comedy because in Tragedy the story is already
familiar to the audience[1].   But neither of these passages really
contains any literary criticism.   It is far otherwise with the very
striking fragment ascribed to Simulus (a comic poet about 355
B.C.), which is welcomed with enthusiasm by an excellent judge
of literary criticism, as advancing 'not only a theory of poetry
and poetical criticism, but one of such astonishing completeness
that it goes far beyond anything that we find in Aristotle, and
is worthy of Longinus himself at his very happiest moment'[2].
Of this fragment I offer the following rendering:

> Nature of Art bereft will not suffice
> For any work whate'er in all the world;
> Nor Art again, devoid of Nature's aid.
> And, e'en if Art and Nature join in one,
> The poet still must find the ways and means,
> Passion, and practice; happy chance and time;
> A critic skilled to seize the poet's sense.
> For, if in aught of these he haply fail,
> He cannot gain the goal of all his hopes.
> Nature, good will, and pains, and ordered grace
> Make poets wise and good, while length of years
> Will make them older men, but nothing more[3].

[1] Athen. vi 222 A, 223 B; Baker, *l.c.*, 199, 212.

[2] Saintsbury's *History of Criticism*, i 25.

[3] Stobaeus, 60, 4, οὔτε φύσις ἱκανὴ γίγνεται τέχνης ἄτερ | πρὸς οὐδὲν ἐπιτή-
δευμα παράπαν οὐδενί, | οὔτε πάλι τέχνη μὴ φύσιν κεκτημένη. | τούτων ὁμοίως τῶν
δυοῖν συνηγμένων | εἰς ταὐτόν, ἔτι δεῖ προσλαβεῖν χορηγίαν, | ἔρωτα, μελέτην,
καιρὸν εὐφυῆ, χρόνον, | κριτὴν τὸ ῥηθὲν δυνάμενον συναρπάσαι. | ἐν ᾧ γὰρ ἂν
τούτων τις ἀπολειφθεὶς τύχῃ, | οὐκ ἔρχετ' ἐπὶ τὸ τέρμα τοῦ προκειμένου. | φύσις,
θέλησις, ἐπιμέλει', εὐταξία, | σοφοὺς τίθησι κἀγαθούς· ἐτῶν δέ τοι | ἀριθμὸς οὐδὲν
ἄλλο πλὴν γῆρας ποιεῖ.   In l. 6—7 Meineke on Stob. (omitting χρόνον as superfluous) aptly suggests καιρόν, εὐφυῆ κριτήν, ἅπαν τὸ ῥηθὲν κτλ. ; but εὐφυῆ
καιρόν occurs in Polybius i 19, 12.   In *Frag. Com. Gr.* I xiii he considers πάλι
and τέχνη in l. 3, and τὸ before ῥηθέν in l. 7, foreign to Attic Comedy, and
identifies the author of this and two partly similar passages with a didactic poet
named Simulus little earlier than the Augustan age.   The passage is partly
parallel to Horace, *A. P.*, 408—413.

The philosopher Xenocrates, when attacked by Bion, declined to defend himself; 'Tragedy' (he said), 'when satirised by Comedy, does not deign to reply'[1]. There is in fact very little evidence that the attacks of the Comic poets led to any changes in the text of the Tragic writers. It is possible that a line in the *Medea* may owe its present form to a jest in the *Clouds* of Aristophanes[2]. The prologues of the *Meleager* and *Oeneus* of Euripides, which were ridiculed in the *Frogs*, were apparently altered by Euripides the younger before those plays were again put on the stage[3]. That of the *Iphigenia in Aulide* is not attacked by Aristophanes; in fact the play was not produced until after the *Frogs*[4]; but it has two alternative openings:—(1) a dialogue in anapaests, (2) an ordinary Euripidean prologue. Possibly the latter was superseded by the former owing to the gibes of Aristophanes against the poet's prologues in general. A line from a scene in the *Telephus* of Euripides representing Achilles playing at dice, 'Achilles has thrown twice—Twice a deuce ace', quoted in the *Frogs* (1400), is said to have been afterwards omitted by the poet, with the whole of the context; but the omission cannot have been due to the *Frogs*, as Euripides died shortly before that play was produced. Hence it was either omitted by Euripides the younger, or, if by the poet himself, the omission may have been suggested by a possibly earlier attack by Eupolis.

The plays of Aeschylus were frequently reproduced after his death, but in the fourth century Sophocles was more popular, and finally Euripides was left without a rival. In process of time, alterations made by actors and copyists led to uncertainties as to the true text. A decree was accordingly carried by the eminent Athenian statesman and orator, Lycurgus (*c.* 390—324 B.C.), providing, not only for the erection of bronze statues of the three great tragic poets, but also for the preservation of a copy of their tragedies in the public archives. The town-clerk was to collate the actors' copies with this text, and no departure

[1] Diog. Laert. iv § 10.
[2] Eur. *Med.* 1317, τί τάσδε κινεῖς κἀναμοχλεύεις πύλας (with Porson's and Verrall's notes), Ar. *Clouds*, 1397, σὸν ἔργον ὦ καινῶν ἐπ ὦν κινητὰ καὶ μοχλευτά.
[3] Fritzsche on Ar. *Ranae*, 1206.
[4] Introd. to my ed. of Eur. *Bacchae*, p. xliii.

therefrom was to be allowed in acting[1].  Possibly the manuscript included only those of the plays which continued to be acted after their authors' death.  It is said to have been this manuscript that was borrowed for the Alexandrian Library by Ptolemy Euergetes (247 or 146 B.C.), who deposited the sum of fifteen talents as a pledge for its safe return, but instead of returning it, forfeited his pledge, kept the original, and sent the Athenians a sumptuous copy in its place[2].  If it ever reached Alexandria at all, it does not appear to have been regarded as a final authority.  Otherwise we should not find mere conjectures on the part of the Alexandrian critic, Aristophanes, carefully mentioned in the Scholia on the Tragic poets.  It is probable that the object of Lycurgus was not so much to restore the original text of the plays, as to record the current acting-version, so as to prevent unauthorised departures from the form which long experience had approved. The official copy thus supplied a test for rejecting alterations due to actors of later date than the time of Lycurgus[3].

The leading tragic poets are quoted as authorities by orators and (not without occasional criticism) by philoso-

**Quotations from tragic poets**

phers.  Lycurgus cites no less than 55 lines from the *Erechtheus* of Euripides, with two shorter passages from unnamed tragic poets[4]; Aeschines[5] two short passages from Euripides, and Demosthenes[6] 16 lines from the *Antigone* of Sophocles, as illustrating maxims of political conduct which Aeschines had violated.  Plato quotes from Aeschylus three passages of the *Septem Contra Thebas*[7], but protests against the

---

[1] [Plutarch], *Lives of the Ten Orators*, p. 841 F, τὰς τραγῳδίας αὐτῶν ἐν κοινῷ γραψαμένους φυλάττειν, καὶ τὸν τῆς πόλεως γραμματέα παραναγιγνώσκειν τοῖς ὑποκρινομένοις, οὐκ ἐξεῖναι γὰρ <παρ' added by Grysar> αὐτὰς (*al.* ἄλλως) ὑποκρίνεσθαι.

[2] Galen, *in Hippocratis Epidem.* III 2.  See below, p. 111.

[3] p. 15 of Korn, *De publico Aeschyli Sophoclis Euripidis fabularum exemplari Lycurgo auctore confecto*, Bonn (1863), pp. 34; cp. Wilamowitz in *Hermes*, xiv 151, and in Eur. *Herakles*, i 130[1]; also Peterson on Quintilian, x 1, 66, 'correctas (Aeschyli) fabulas in certamen deferre.'

[4] *Leocr.* §§ 100, 92, 132.

[5] 1 § 154.

[6] 19 § 247; *Antigone*, 175—190.

[7] *S. C. T.* 1 (*Euthyd.* 291 D), 451 (*Rep.* 551 C), 592 f (*Rep.* 361 B, 362 A).

language respecting Apollo, which, in another play, the poet puts in the lips of Thetis[1]. He never quotes a line from Sophocles, while he ascribes to Euripides a line which also occurred in the *Aias Locrus* of the former[2]. In this connexion he says that 'people regard tragedy on the whole as wise, and Euripides as a master therein'. He also quotes Euripides twice in the *Gorgias*[3]. Of Aristotle it is enough to say that his citations from Aeschylus are very few, those from Sophocles more numerous, while those from Euripides are taken from as many as ten of his extant plays, not to mention fourteen others[4]. Aristophanes is one of the persons who take part in Plato's *Symposium*, but the language of the comic poets is very rarely quoted by the philosophers, and never by the orators.

To the Athenian the theatre was mainly a place of amusement, but it was also to some extent a means of education. Aristophanes makes Aeschylus say to Euripides: 'What the master is to childhood, the poets are to youth; therefore we poets are bound to be strictly moral in our teaching'[5]. The teaching of Euripides may not have been entirely sound, but it was widely popular. His popularity throughout the Greek world is partly attested by Plutarch. In the *Life of Nicias*[6], we are told that, at the disastrous close of the Sicilian expedition (413 B.C.), some of the Athenian prisoners at Syracuse owed their liberty to the fact that they were able to recite passages from Euripides; and that, at Caunus, on the Carian coast, opposite to Rhodes, a vessel pursued by pirates was not allowed to enter the port, until it was found that some of those on board knew by heart the songs of Euripides, —stories which have supplied Browning with the theme of *Balaustion's Adventure*. Similarly, in the *Life of Lysander*[7] we learn that, nine years later, when Athens had been conquered by Sparta, and a Theban proposed that the city should be destroyed and its site left desolate, the Spartan captains were

*The study of the dramatists*

---

[1] *Rep.* 383 B.   Cp. 380 A, 563 C, *Phaedo*, 180 A, *Symp.* 383 B.

[2] σοφοὶ τύραννοι τῶν σοφῶν συνουσίᾳ (*Rep.* 568 A with schol.; *Theag.* 125 B).

[3] 484 E, 492 E.   *Melanippe* in *Symp.* 177 A.

[4] See the *Index* of Bonitz or of Heitz.

[5] *Frogs*, 1055.          [6] *c.* 29.          [7] *c.* 15.

deeply moved by a Phocian who sang before them the opening
chorus of the *Electra* of Euripides. But, whatever compunction
may have been caused by this pathetic incident, the walls between
Athens and the Peiraeus[1] were undoubtedly demolished, though,
to the fancy of Milton,

> 'the repeated air
> Of sad Electra's poet had the power
> To save the Athenian walls from ruin bare'[2].

In and after the times of Euripides, selections from the tragic
poets were probably learnt by heart in the schools of Athens.
Such may have been the set speeches (ῥήσεις), mentioned in
Plato's *Laws*[3]. The study of 'tragedy', as an alternative subject
at school, is implied by the comic poet Alexis, who represents the
legendary musician Linus as setting before the youthful Hercules
a number of volumes and telling him to look carefully at their
titles and choose the one that strikes his fancy most. The volumes
include a *tragedy* (author not named), as well as Orpheus, Hesiod,
Choerilus, Homer, Epicharmus and 'all kinds of books'; but
the choice of Hercules characteristically falls on a manual of
cookery[4].

In the midst of the dramatic contest between Aeschylus and
Euripides, Aristophanes pays his audience the compliment of
assuming that 'each has got his little book, to prompt him to be
clever'[5]; and he is generous enough towards Euripides to make
Dionysus confess that reading a copy of the poet's *Andromeda* on
board ship has smitten him with a sudden desire to see Euripides
once more[6]. But Aristophanes himself, and the poets of the Old
Attic Comedy, with their unbridled license of personal attack on
public characters, were unsuited for the purposes of education,
though the plays of their Sicilian precursor Epicharmus (d. 450)
appear to have been rich in moral maxims[7]. The later Attic
Comedy was more appropriate for this purpose; and 'Comedy'
as well as 'Tragedy' was among the subjects for which prizes
were given to junior boys at a school in Teos in the second

---

[1] Xen. *Hell.* ii 2, 20—23, popularly called 'the walls' in Dem. *Lept.*
§§ 69, 72.

[2] Milton, *Sonnet* 8.                    [3] 811 A.

[4] Athenaeus, 164 B.                    [5] *Frogs*, 1114.

[6] *ib.* 54.                    [7] Diog. Laert. viii 78, γνωμολογεῖ.

century B.C.[1]   In the Roman age an alphabetical list of some 850 sententious sayings was collected from the plays of Menander. As in Comedy, so also in Tragedy.  Early in the Christian era the Tempter might appropriately represent Athens as the place for hearing and learning all that

> 'the lofty grave tragedians taught
> In Chorus or Iambick, teachers best
> Of moral prudence, with delight receiv'd,
> In brief sententious precepts, while they treat
> Of fate, and chance, and change in human life,
> High actions and high passions best describing'[2].

Dramatic criticism in Plato is represented mainly by certain important passages of the *Republic*, and also by some incidental references in other dialogues.  In the *Phaedrus*[3] a person coming to Sophocles or Euripides, and saying that he 'knows how to compose very long speeches about a small matter and very short speeches about a great matter, and also pathetic or terrible and menacing speeches', is described as 'knowing only the preliminaries of Tragedy'[4], while Tragedy itself is the 'arranging of all these elements in a manner suitable to one another and to the whole'[5].   Tragedy, in brief, must be an organic whole.   In the *Philebus*[6] the passions excited by Tragedy and Comedy are described as producing a feeling of pleasure mixed with pain.  In the *Gorgias*[7] the aim of 'that grave and august personage, Tragedy,' is narrowly scrutinised.  Her aim is merely to please the spectators, and her creations are denounced as only another form of flattery.   At the close of the *Symposium*, in the early morning, when the rest of the company have either withdrawn or have fallen asleep, we find Socrates still discoursing with the comic poet, Aristophanes, and the tragic poet, Agathon, and pressing both of them to admit 'that the genius of comedy was the same as that of tragedy, and that the truly artistic writer of tragedy ought also to be a writer of comedy', but the two poets (we are assured) were 'getting very sleepy, and did not quite understand his meaning'[8].   That

[1] Boeckh, *C. I. G.* 3088 (=no. 913 in Michel's *Recueil*).
[2] Milton, *P. R.* iv 261—6.            [3] 268 C.            [4] 269 A.
[5] 268 D.            [6] 48 A.            [7] 502 B.            [8] 223 D.

meaning may possibly have been that the object of tragedy as well as comedy is to influence men's hearts ; tragic, as well as comic effect, if it is to be attained by means of true art, must 'presuppose a scientific knowledge of mankind, and this knowledge will fit its possessor equally for either capacity'[1]. Tragedy and Comedy, not as they *might* be, but as they *were*, find very scanty appreciation in the *Republic* and the *Laws*. Plato urges that the 'imitation', or (as we should say) representation, of what is bad and unworthy, which plays so prominent a part in music and in poetry, and especially in the drama, imperceptibly familiarises both artists and the public with thoughts and acts which are reprehensible[2]. Further, the effect, which Tragedy produces on the audience, depends on the excitement of pity and grief; that of Comedy, on the excitement of laughter and (ultimately) exultation over the misfortunes of others. The poets (he continues) claim our sympathy for the passions of love, anger, fear, jealousy, and the rest,—all of them unworthy passions, which we do not approve in ourselves, and the representation of which ought not to afford us any pleasure[3]. The excitement of pity and fear by means of Tragedy is, according to this view, relaxing and enfeebling, these emotions being apt to degenerate into sentimentality and to make men unmanly. For these and similar reasons Plato banishes dramatic poetry from his ideal Republic.

While Plato thus objects to Tragedy as tending to make men cowardly and effeminate by the excitement of their sympathies, Aristotle tacitly opposes this view in his famous definition of Tragedy. The closing words of that definition imply that Tragedy presents us with noble objects for the exercise of the feelings of pity and fear, and affords relief by removing them from our system:—'through pity and fear accomplishing' (not the *purification* but) 'the *purgation* of those emotions'[4]. That the latter is the true meaning of *katharsis* was seen by Milton in his preface to *Samson*

and in
Aristotle

[1] Zeller, *Plato and the Older Academy*, p. 509 n. 66.

[2] *Rep.* 395 C f, 401 B ; *Laws*, 816 D (Zeller, *l.c.*, p. 510).

[3] *Rep.* 603 C—608 A, 387 C f, *Laws*, 800 C f (Zeller, *l.c.*, p. 511).

[4] *Poet.* 6 § 2.

*Agonistes* (1671). Milton's interpretation had been anticipated
in Italy by Scaino (1578) and Galuzzi (1621)[1]: and the exact
sense of the term has since been discussed by Twining (1789), by
Weil[2] (1847) and Bernays (1857), and by many others[3].

The treatise on Poetry includes a slight sketch of the historical
development of Tragedy.   In the fuller form of the treatise, or in
some other work, Aristotle may have mentioned Thespis as introducing the 'prologue and the set speech'[4].   The treatise, in its
present form, tells us that Aeschylus was the first to introduce
a second actor, that he made the chorus more subordinate and
gave greater prominence to the dialogue; also that Sophocles·
introduced a third actor, and added scene-painting[5].   In the only
other reference to Aeschylus, apart from a passing mention of his
*Niobe*[6], it is noticed that Euripides had improved on a line in
Aeschylus by altering an ordinary word into one that was rarer,
thus producing a beautiful instead of a trivial effect[7].   Sophocles
and Euripides are twice contrasted, firstly, when Aristotle insists
that the chorus 'should be regarded as one of the actors and be
an integral part of the whole and join in the action, in the manner
of Sophocles but not of Euripides'[8]; and secondly, when he tells
us that 'Sophocles said that he drew men as they *ought* to be (or
'to be drawn'), but Euripides as they *are*'[9].   There are at least four
references to the *Oedipus*[10], a play which Aristotle obviously admires.
Euripides is defended against the criticism of those, who 'censure
him for making many of his plays end unhappily'; this (says
Aristotle) is 'the right ending'; such plays 'have the most tragic
effect', and in this respect Euripides, 'faulty as he is in the

---

[1] Bywater, *Journ. of Philol.* xxvii 266—275 (1900); ed. 1909, 152 f, 361 f.

[2] *Versammlung deutscher Philol.* x (Basel) 131 f.

[3] *e.g.* Egger, *l.c.*, pp. 267—300; Susemihl and Hicks, *Politics of Aristotle*,
pp. 641—656; and Butcher's *Aristotle's Theory of Poetry*, pp. 236—268. The
relations between Aristotle's *Poetic* and Plato are discussed by Chr. Belger, *De
Aristotele etiam in Arte Poetica componenda Platonis discipulo* (Berlin), 1890,
and by G. Finsler, *Platon und die aristotelische Poetik* (Leipzig), 1900.

[4] Themistius, *Or.* 26, 316 D. Cp. Rose, *Ar. Pseudepigraphus*, 79.

[5] 4 § 13.                     [6] 18 § 5.

[7] 22 § 7, θοινᾶται for ἐσθίει.          [8] 18 § 7.

[9] 25 § 6, cp. Butcher, *l.c.*, p. 361², and Seaton in *Class. Rev.* xi 300 f.

[10] c. 14, 15, 16, 26; afterwards known as the *Oedipus Tyrannus*.

management of the rest, is recognised as the most tragic of the poets'[1]. His *Medea*, his *Iphigeneia in Tauris* and his *Orestes* are noticed. Poets who have 'dramatised the whole story of the Fall of Troy, instead of selecting portions, like Euripides, have been unsuccessful'[2]. In the *Rhetoric*[3] Euripides is described as having set an example to others by the skilful selection of his vocabulary from the language of ordinary life. The only actual mention of Aristophanes in the treatise on Poetry is where Sophocles is described as 'from one point of view, an imitator like Homer, both imitating higher types of character'; from another, like Aristophanes, both being dramatic poets[4]. The chapters on Comedy have not come down to us; but, even from the treatise as it stands, it has been surmised that Aristotle preferred the poets of the Middle Comedy, with its growing preference for generalised types of character, to the personal satire and rude invective of the Old Attic Comedy. A 'lampooner' is the label which Aristotle, by implication, attaches to its foremost extant representative, Aristophanes[5].

Aristotle's interest in the Drama led to his laying the foundation of its history in the form of a collection of abstracts of the archives recording the dates of the several plays. From the term (διδάσκειν), applied to the teaching and training of the chorus and actors and the general rehearsal of a play, the play itself, or the connected group of plays produced by a poet at a single festival, was called a *didascalia*. The same designation would naturally be given to the public record of the result, and hence the title of Aristotle's work. Such a work was doubtless largely founded on the various records of success in the dramatic contests. These records were of five kinds: (1) the documents preserved by the State in the public archives; (2) the inscriptions on the monuments erected at private expense by the citizen, who as *chorêgus* had borne the cost of the production of the play; (3) public lists of victors in all the contests at one particular festival; (4) similar lists of the victors at one particular kind of contest at such a festival; (5) lists of tragic and comic actors and tragic and comic poets,

*Aristotle's didascaliae*

---

[1] 13 § 6.        [2] 18 § 5.        [3] iii 2 § 5.

[4] 3 § 2.        [5] 5 § 3; 9 § 5; Butcher, *l.c.*, p. 370 f.

with numerals denoting the total number of their victories.
Plutarch has preserved an early example of (2), commemorating
a victory won in 476 B.C., when the *chorêgus* was Themistocles[1].
As an example of (3) we have the list of the victors' names,
including that of Aeschylus, for 458 B.C., the year in which he
produced the trilogy of the *Oresteia*. Aristotle's work, founded
on records like these, is the ultimate source of our knowledge
of the results of the dramatic contests in which poets such as
Aeschylus, Sophocles, Euripides and Aristophanes were competi-
tors. It was the foundation of a similar work by Callimachus
(*c.* 260 B.C.), which in its turn supplied the facts embodied by
Aristophanes of Byzantium (*c.* 200 B.C.) in a work which survives in the fragments quoted from it by the Scholiasts in
the Arguments to Greek plays still extant. There are thirteen
fragments of Aristotle's *didascaliae*, five of them with Aristotle's
name and the rest without it[2]. The accuracy of the tradition beginning with the public records of Athens and passing
through the works of Aristotle, Callimachus, and Aristophanes of
Byzantium down to the Scholiasts who transcribed the Arguments
which ultimately reach us in the MSS of the Greek dramatists,
has in one important particular received a striking confirmation.
Though some fourteen or fifteen centuries had elapsed between
the date of the Medicean MS of Aeschylus (tenth or eleventh
century), and the date of the first performance of the *Agamemnon*
(458 B.C.), the copyist's written record of the name of the *chorêgus*
and the archon of the year and the fact that the first prize was
won by Aeschylus, was confirmed by an inscription found on the
Acropolis in 1886, giving a complete list of the victors at the
City Dionysia of the year in question[3].

---

[1] Plutarch, *Them.* 5 § 3, Θεμιστοκλῆς Φρεάρριος ἐχορήγει, Φρύνιχος ἐδίδασκεν,
'Αδείμαντος ἦρχεν. Cp. Dittenberger's *Sylloge*, 694-5[2], and Gercke in *Jahresb.*
vol. 124, p. 480 f.

[2] Aristot. Frag. 618—630 Rose. Cp. Trendelenburg, *Grammaticorum
Graecorum de arte tragica iudicia*, pp. 3 f; A. Müller's *Bühnenalterthümer*
p. 375 f; Haigh's *Attic Theatre*, pp. 59—64, 319—328; and Jebb in Smith's
*Dict. Ant.* ii 865 A.

[3] Haigh, *l.c.*, pp. 18, 64, 319. The only point in which the copyist has
gone wrong is in writing *Olympiad* 28 ($\overline{\kappa\eta}$) by mistake for 80 ($\overline{\pi}$).

Aristotle is also said to have written a work on *Dionysiac Victories*, but it is never quoted and is probably only another name for his *Didascaliae*.  Lastly, he drew up lists of victors in the Olympian and Pythian games[1].  One of these Olympian victors he mentions in the *Ethics*[2], in illustration of a particular kind of ambiguity of designation.  Notwithstanding the statement made by an ancient commentator on Aristotle, Alexander of Aphrodisias, that Ἄνθρωπος was here a proper name, the name in fact of a successful boxer at Olympia, the editors have generally rejected this explanation and printed the word with a small initial letter, ἄνθρωπος.  But a *papyrus* found at Oxyrhynchus, and first published in 1899, shows that the Greek Commentator was right, for we there find the name Ἄνθρωπος as that of the winner of the Olympian boxing-match for 456 B.C.[3]

[1] Diog. Laert. v 21, Ὀλυμπιονῖκαι and Πυθιονῖκαι (Frag. 615–7 Rose).

[2] vii 4, Ἄνθρωπος ὁ τὰ Ὀλύμπια νικῶν.

[3] Grenfell and Hunt, *Oxyrhynchus papyri*, ii p. 93, and *Classical Review*, xiii 290.

FROM THE CODEX PARISINUS, Aᶜ, no. 1741 (cent. xi), OF
ARISTOTLE'S *Rhet.* and *Poet.*

λόγου· τελευτὴ δὲ τῆς λέξεως ἁρμόττει ἡ ἀσύνδετος, ὅπως ἐπίλογος ἀλλὰ μὴ λόγος ᾖ, εἴρηκα, ἀκηκόατε, ἔχετε, κρίνατε.

τέλος Ἀριστοτέλους τέχνης ῥητορικῆς.

Ἀριστοτέλους περὶ ποιητικῆς.

περὶ ποιητικῆς αὐτῆς τε καὶ τῶν εἰδῶν αὐτῆς, ἥν τινα δύναμιν ἕκαστον ἔχει, καὶ πῶς δεῖ συνίστασθαι τοὺς μύθους εἰ μέλλει καλῶς ἕξειν ἡ ποίησις, ἔτι δὲ ἐκ πόσων καὶ ποίων ἐστὶ μορίων, ὁμοίως δὲ καὶ περὶ τῶν ἄλλων ὅσα τῆς αὐτῆς ἐστι μεθόδου, λέγωμεν ἀρξάμενοι κατὰ φύσιν πρῶτον ἀπὸ τῶν πρώτων.

# CHAPTER V.

## THE CRITICISM OF POETRY IN PLATO AND ARISTOTLE.

THE earliest Greek theory of poetry is that which we find in the Homeric poems. In the *Odyssey* the source of poetry is found in 'inspiration'  The blind bard Demodocus is 'beloved by the Muse', who gave him the gift of 'sweet song'; he is 'prompted to sing the glorious deeds of heroes' by the Muse, who 'loves the race of bards' and has 'taught them all the ways of song'; he is 'taught by the Muse, the child of Zeus, or by Apollo'; and, when he begins to sing, he is 'impelled by a god'[1]. Similarly, the bard Phemius, the unwilling servant of the suitors of Penelope, says in pleading for his life before Odysseus :—'self-taught am I ; but it was a god that inspired my mind with all the varied ways of song'[2].

The Theory of Poetry in Homer

A belief in the divine inspiration of the poet is one of the doctrines of Democritus, whose recognition of the inspiration of Homer has been already noticed[3]. Of poets in general he says :—'all that a poet writes under the influence of enthusiasm and of holy inspiration is exceedingly beautiful'[4]. He 'denies that any one can be a great poet, unless he is mad'[5]. 'Poets who are sober', he excludes from the haunts of Helicon[6].

Democritus

---

[1] *Od.* viii 63–5, 73 ἀνῆκεν, 481 οἴμας, 488, 499 ὁρμηθεὶς θεοῦ.

[2] *Od.* xxii 347.          [3] p. 26.

[4] Clemens, *Strom.* 698 B, ποιητὴς δὲ ἅσσα μὲν ἂν γράφῃ μετ᾽ ἐνθουσιασμοῦ καὶ ἱεροῦ πνεύματος καλὰ κάρτα ἐστί.

[5] Cicero, *Divin.* i 80.

[6] Horace, *A. P.*, 295.

The theory of 'inspiration' is also prominent in Plato.   In
Plato's view, the source of all artistic and poetic
creation, as also of philosophy, is a higher inspiration.   In the *Phaedrus* he describes the 'state of being possessed
by the Muses' as a kind of 'madness, which, on entering a
delicate and virgin soul, arouses and excites it to frenzy in odes
and other kinds of poetry, with these adorning the myriad exploits
of ancient heroes for the instruction of posterity.   But he that is
without the Muses' madness when he knocks at the doors of
Poesy, fancying that *art* alone will make him a competent poet,—
he and *his* poetry, the poetry of sober sense, will never attain
perfection, but will be eclipsed by the poetry of inspired madmen'[1].
In the *Apology* Socrates consults the poets—'tragic, dithyrambic
and the rest', asks them the meaning of their finest passages, and
finds that there was hardly any one of the bystanders who could
not have talked better about their poetry than they did themselves.
He soon concludes that it was not by wisdom that poets wrote
poetry, but (like diviners and soothsayers) by a kind of genius and
inspiration[2].   In the *Laws* it is 'an old story', which has been an
immemorial tradition at Athens and is accepted everywhere else,
that 'whenever a poet is enthroned on the tripod of the Muse, he
is not in his right mind'[3].   In the *Meno* the epithet 'divine' is
applied to poets and statesmen, as well as to 'diviners and
prophets, who say much that is true without knowing what they
say'[4].   But the fullest expression of this thought is to be found in
the *Ion*, a dialogue whose genuineness has been doubted or denied
by some critics (including Ast, Schleiermacher, Susemihl and
Zeller), while others (such as K. F. Hermann, Stallbaum, Steinhart and Grote) accept it as one of Plato's earliest works :—

It is not by art, but by being inspired and possessed, that all good epic
poets produce their beautiful poems; and similarly with all good melic poets,
—just as the Corybantic revellers are not in their right mind when they are
dancing, even so the melic poets are not in their right mind when they are
composing their beautiful strains.   On the contrary, when they have fallen
under the spell of melody and metre, they are like inspired revellers, and on
their becoming possessed,—even as the Maenads are possessed and not in their
right senses, when they draw honey and milk from the rivers,—the soul of

[1] 245 A.          [2] 22 B.          [3] 719 C.          [4] 99 D.

the melic poets acts in like manner, as they themselves admit. For the poets tell us (as you remember) that they cull their sweet strains from 'fountains flowing with honey', 'out of the gardens and dells of the Muses', and bring them to us like bees; for, like bees, they are ever on the wing. And what they say is true; for the poet is a light and winged and holy being; he cannot compose until he becomes inspired and out of his senses, with his mind no longer in him; but, so long as he is in possession of his senses, not one of them is capable of composing, or of uttering his oracular sayings. Many as are the noble things that they say about their themes of song, like your own sayings, Ion, about Homer, yet, inasmuch as it is not by Art that they compose but by the gift of God, all that the poet can really succeed in composing is the theme to which he is impelled by the Muse. Thus, one of them composes dithyrambs, and another hymns of praise, and another epic or iambic verses; and each of them succeeds in one kind of composition only, for it is not by Art that they produce these poems but by a power divine ...And the reason why God takes away their senses, when he uses them as his ministers, even as he uses the ministrations of soothsayers and prophets divine, is in order that we who hear them may know that, since they are out of their senses, it is not these poets who utter the words which we prize so highly, but it is God himself who is the speaker, and it is *through* them that he is speaking to us[1].

Elsewhere, Plato uses far more sober language, when he calmly analyses the process by which the art of poetry comes into being. Poetry is then described not as an 'inspiration', but as a kind of 'imitation'[2]. 'Imitation' is the characteristic of all art, and of the poetic art in particular. In the third book of the *Republic* the question is started whether 'all imitation is to be prohibited', 'whether tragedy and comedy are to be admitted into the State', and it is contended that the same person cannot play a serious part in life and also imitate many other parts; and that, even in forms of imitation that are closely connected, as in Tragedy and Comedy, the same persons cannot succeed in both. All imitative poetry is accordingly rejected[3]. In the tenth book the attack on poetry as an imitative art is renewed. All poetic imitations are there denounced as dangerous to those who have not discerned their true nature[4]. Just as the painter makes only a superficial likeness of a thing, and not the actual thing itself, much less the ideal thing, so the whole tribe of imitators, including the poet and the tragic poet in

[1] *Ion*, 533 E—534 D.    [2] Zeller's *Plato*, p. 509—513.
[3] *Rep.* 394-5.    [4] 595 B.

particular, are 'in the third degree removed' (or, as we should say, 'twice removed') 'from the truth'[1].

Plato's description of art as a kind of 'imitation' has not unnaturally met with a considerable amount of criticism. Thus it has been justly observed, that 'in modern times we should say that art is not merely imitation, but rather the expression of the ideal in forms of sense'[2]. Poets and painters are more than mere imitators, as Plato himself admits elsewhere in the case of the painter. 'How', he asks, 'would a painter be in any less degree a good painter who having painted a perfect pattern of the highest human beauty, and left nothing lacking in the picture, is unable to prove that such a man might possibly exist?' and the answer is, 'He would not'[3]. 'No theory', it has been remarked, 'can be more erroneous than that which degrades art into mere imitation, which seeks for beauty in the parts and not in the whole....The requirement of composition in a work of art is alone an evidence that mere imitation is not art'[4]. Of the passage from the *Gorgias*, above cited, it has been frankly said that 'the censure...is too sweeping even from Plato's point of view, for Euripides at any rate aimed at a moral purpose of one sort or other, and sacrificed to his zeal as an instructor much of the popularity and much also of the poetic beauty of his plays. As a criticism on Sophocles and Aeschylus it is, to modern apprehension, still more deplorable'. One of the passages already quoted from the *Phaedrus*[5] 'proves that Plato had a thorough perception of poetic excellence whenever it suited him to forget his political theories'[6].

Even when we pass from Plato to Aristotle, we are still
Aristotle     pursued by the description of Poetry as one of the 'imitative' arts, and of Poetry and Music in particular as 'modes of imitation'[7]. But there is a change in the point of view corresponding to the difference between the philosophy of Plato and the philosophy of Aristotle. Plato,

---

[1]  597 E.          [2] Jowett's *Plato*, ii 130 ed. 1871.          [3] *Rep.* 472 D.
[4] Jowett and Campbell on *Rep.* 596 D.          [5] 268 C.
[6]  W. H. Thompson on *Gorg.* 502 B.—See also Saintsbury's *History of Criticism*, i 17—20. Cp. p. 61 *supra*.
[7] *Poet.* 1 § 2.

'starting from the notion of pure being', and regarding the world of 'ideas' as the world of true existence, and sensible phenomena as merely copies of a suprasensuous archetype, in the domain of art has apparently but a small opinion of the earthly counterparts of the celestial originals.  In Plato's view the poet and the painter (as we have seen) make an imperfect copy of the actual, while the actual in its turn is only a distant adumbration of the ideal.  Plato accordingly regards a work of art, whether a poem or a picture, as in the degraded position of a copy of a copy, and therefore twice removed from the truth.  Poets and painters alike are superficial in their knowledge of the things which they 'imitate' or represent, and the result of such imperfect knowledge cannot be worthy of admiration[1].  The contrast between Plato and Aristotle is thus summed up by Zeller[2]:—
'While Plato and Aristotle agree in regarding art as a species of imitation, they draw very different conclusions from this account of it.  Plato thinks of it only as the imitation of sensible phenomena and accordingly expresses the utmost contempt for the falsity and worthlessness of art; Aristotle, on the other hand, looks upon artistic presentation as the sensible vehicle to us of universal truths and thus places it above the empirical knowledge of individual things'.  Here and elsewhere, Aristotle, in whose philosophy the fundamental doctrine was not Being but Becoming, has a higher regard for the processes of growth and development and for the phenomena of the visible world.  Hence his greater regard not only for the study of physical science but also for the appreciation of the products of imitative art, whether in painting or in poetry.  In short, while 'imitation' is a term common in this connexion to Aristotle and to Plato, the suggestion of contempt implied in Plato's use of the term has disappeared[3].

The impression given to a modern reader by the somewhat narrow term 'imitation' with its suggestion of a slavishly mechanical copy, is sufficiently corrected by the hints supplied by Aristotle himself.  While art is traced by Aristotle to the natural

[1] Cp. *Timaeus*, 19 D.     [2] *Aristotle*, ii 307.
[3] This is fully set forth by Professor Butcher, *l.c.*, pp. 121—162[2], esp. pp. 158—160; see also esp. Zeller's *Aristotle*, ii 300—324, and Belger and Finsler, quoted on p. 63 n.

love of 'imitation', and to the pleasure felt in recognising likenesses[1], art is not confined to mere copying. Art not only imitates Nature, but also completes its deficiencies[2]. Art endeavours to seize the universal type in the individual phenomena. Poetry (as compared with history) represents things in their universal aspect[3]. Immediately after speaking of 'imitation', Aristotle recognises that the poet, in particular the tragic poet, may represent men as better than they are, just as Polygnotus depicted men as nobler than they were[4]. He also allows room for the play of genius and even for the transport of phrensy, when he says that 'poetry demands either a natural quickness of parts, or a touch of madness', adding that poets of the former type can mould themselves to the characters which they represent, while those of the latter are transported out of themselves[5]. But, while Aristotle recognises the workings of poetic phrensy, he has no term to express 'imagination', in the sense of a 'creative faculty'. In the *Rhetoric*[6] he describes *phantasia* as 'a kind of feeble sensation'; elsewhere he defines it as 'a movement resulting from the actual operation of the faculty of sense'[7], *i.e.* as 'the process by which an impression of sense is pictured and retained before the mind'[8]. Even among the most imaginative of peoples, the workings of the 'imagination' had not yet been analysed. For *phantasia* in the sense of 'creative imagination' we have to wait for more than five centuries till we find it in Philostratus[9].

---

[1] *Poet.* 2 § 1; 15 § 8.

[2] *Phys.* ii 8, ἡ τέχνη τὰ μὲν ἐπιτελεῖ ἃ ἡ φύσις ἀδυνατεῖ ἀπεργάσασθαι, τὰ δὲ μιμεῖται.

[3] *Poet.* 9 §§ 1—3.          [4] 1 § 4.

[5] 17 § 2. Cp. *Rhet.* iii 7, 11, ἔνθεον ἡ ποίησις, *Probl.* xxx 1, Μάρακος... ἀμείνων ἦν ποιητής, ὅτ' ἐκσταίη, and Plato's *Ion*, quoted on p. 68; also Finsler, *l.c.*, 172—191.

[6] i 11, 6.

[7] *De Anima*, iii 3, 429 a 1, κίνησις ὑπὸ τῆς αἰσθήσεως τῆς κατ' ἐνέργειαν γιγνομένη (ed. E. Wallace, p. 153).

[8] E. Wallace, *Outlines of the Philosophy of Aristotle*, p. 90[3]; cp. Cope on *Rhet.* i p. 205; Freudenthal, φαντασία bei Arist.; Bonitz, *Index, s.v.*

[9] *Vita Apollonii*, vi 19 (cp. Saintsbury, *l.c.*, i 120); of the images of the gods carved by a Pheidias or a Praxiteles, φαντασία ταῦτ' εἰργάσατο, σοφωτέρα μιμήσεως δημιουργός. μίμησις μὲν γὰρ δημιουργήσει ὃ εἶδεν, φαντασία δὲ

Aristotle's Theory of Poetry is partially unfolded in his treatise on that subject, a most suggestive work which has come down to us in an unsatisfactory condition, imperfect in some of its parts and interpolated in others. Its general outline (omitting interpolations) is as follows :—

The arts of Poetry, Music, Dancing, Painting and Sculpture rest on a common principle of 'imitation'; but they differ in the means, objects and manner of imitation. In Poetry, the *means* are rhythm, language, and melody (c. 1). The *objects* of imitation are persons in action, either persons of a higher type as in Tragedy, or of a lower type as in Comedy (c. 2). The *manner* of imitation may be either a combination of direct and dramatic narrative, as in Homer, or direct narrative alone[1], or pure drama, as in Tragedy and Comedy (c. 3).

Poetry originated in the instinct of imitation, and of melody and rhythm. It soon parted in two directions, as is proved by the *Iliad* and *Odyssey*, as compared with the *Margîtes*, a satirical poem (here ascribed to Homer), and by Tragedy, as compared with Comedy. Then follows a sketch of the history of Tragedy (c. 4) and Comedy. Epic poetry agrees with Tragedy in being an imitation, in verse, of characters of the higher type, but epic action has no limits of time, and Tragedy has some constituent parts peculiar to itself (c. 5). Tragedy is then defined as 'an imitation of an action that is serious, complete, and of a certain magnitude ; in language embellished with each kind of artistic ornament, the several kinds being found in separate parts of the play; in the form of action, not of narrative ; through pity and fear effecting the proper purgation of these (*lit.* 'such') emotions'[2]. It has six elements ; three external, scenic presentment, lyrical song (μελοποιία), and diction; and three internal, plot, character, and thought (c. 6). The plot must be a whole, complete in itself, and of adequate magnitude (c. 7). It must have a unity of action (c. 8). Dramatic unity can be attained only by the observance of poetic truth (c. 9). The plot may be either simple, when the turning-point is reached without reversal of fortune (περιπέτεια), or without recognition (ἀναγνώρισις) ; complicated, when it is reached by either or both (c. 10). Reversal of fortune and dramatic incident (πάθος) are next

---

καὶ ἃ μὴ εἶδεν· ὑποθήσεται γὰρ αὐτὸ πρὸς τὴν ἀναφορὰν τοῦ ὄντος.   καὶ μίμησιν μὲν πολλάκις ἐκκρούει ἔκπληξις, φαντασίαν δ' οὐδέν· χωρεῖ γὰρ ἀνέκπληκτος πρὸς ὃ αὐτὴ ὑπέθετο.   Cp. chap. xix *init.*

[1] *i.e.* either 'as in some of the later epic poets', cp. 24 § 7 (Bywater, *Journal of Philology*, xiv 42), or 'as in certain types of lyric poetry', cp. with ἀπαγγέλλοντα Plato *Rep.* 394 C, δι' ἀπαγγελίας τοῦ ποιητοῦ (of dithyrambs).   But Ritter and Vahlen rightly hold that only *two* kinds of poetry are here noticed, epic and dramatic, not *three* as in Plato *l.c.*   Cp. Belger, pp. 34—44, and Bywater's ed., p. 118 f.

[2] Butcher's *transl.* Cp. p. 62.

defined (c. 11). A perfect tragedy should imitate actions which excite pity and fear. Pity is excited by unmerited misfortune; fear, by the misfortunes of men like ourselves (c. 13). These emotions should spring from the plot itself (c. 14). The character represented must be good, appropriate, true to life, consistent; it should also be idealised (c. 15). Recognition may be brought about in various ways (c. 16). The tragic poet should follow certain rules: (i) with a view to a perfect and consistent realisation of the *dramatis personae*, he must place the scene before his eyes, and in imagination act the parts himself; (ii) he must first draw the outline of the play, and then fill in the episodes (c. 17). He must be careful about the complication (δέσις) and especially about the disentangling or *dénouement* (λύσις) of the plot. He should combine varied forms of poetic excellence. He must not overload a Tragedy with details suitable to an Epic poem. He must make the choral odes an organic part of the whole (c. 18). Thought (διάνοια), or the intellectual element in Tragedy, may be expressed by dramatic speeches or by dramatic incidents. Diction mainly belongs to the province of declamation, rather than that of poetry (c. 19). Various kinds of words are next distinguished, and metaphor, in particular, defined and exemplified (c. 21). Elevation of language may be combined with perspicuity by a certain infusion of rare, or metaphorical, or ornamental words, with those that are common; or by the use of words which have been extended, contracted, or otherwise altered (c. 22).

Epic poetry *agrees* with Tragedy in unity of action (c. 23), also in being either simple or complicated, 'ethical' or 'pathetic', in having the same parts (with the exception of song and scenery), and in requiring artistic thought and diction. It *differs* in scale, and in metre, and in the art of giving an air of reality to fictions which are really incredible (c. 24). The principles on which critical objections brought against Poetry should be met, are then set forth (περὶ προβλημάτων καὶ λύσεων). Poetic truth, as distinguished from ordinary reality, is next elucidated (c. 25). Epic poetry is sometimes supposed to be superior to Tragedy, because it appeals to a cultivated audience, which has no need of gesture. Tragedy, however, is really the higher art: it has all the elements of Epic poetry, with the addition of music and scenic accessories; it also attains its end within narrower limits of time, and it has more unity of action (c. 26)[1].

Of the 'Three Unities' of Action, Time and Place, popularly ascribed to Aristotle, it will be observed that Unity of Action is the only one which he actually enjoins[2]. As a treatise on poetry the work is obviously incomplete, Lyric poetry being

---

[1] For a more detailed analysis see Butcher, *l.c.*, pp. 1—3; cp. Saintsbury, *l.c.*, pp. 32—39; and Prickard's Lecture on *Aristotle on the Art of Poetry*, pp. 9—18.

[2] Egger, *l.c.*, 265³; Butcher, *l.c.*, 283—295².

practically ignored, and Comedy noticed only in a slight sketch
of its origin. In the sixth chapter the author undertakes to treat
of Comedy, but his treatment of the subject has not reached us.
He defines 'the ludicrous'[1], but the 'different kinds of the
ludicrous', which, as we know from the *Rhetoric*[2], were once discriminated in the treatise on Poetry, doubtless in connexion with
Comedy, are not to be found in the present text[3]. In the *Politics*[4],
while briefly treating of *katharsis*, he promises to express himself
more clearly on this point in his treatise on Poetry (ἐν τοῖς περὶ
ποιητικῆς), but this part of the definition of Tragedy[5] is unfortunately not explained in our text[6]. In the complete work he also
treated of synonyms, as stated in the *Rhetoric*[7]; and he possibly
made mention of Thespis[8]. His dialogue *On Poets*[9], probably in
three books, was a popular treatment of the same theme as his
treatise on Poetry, which in its original form probably consisted
of two. Even in its present condition it is an invaluable work.
Severely scientific and masterly in method, unadorned in style,
and almost entirely destitute of literary grace and charm, it
nevertheless stands out conspicuously in Greek literature as the
earliest example of a systematic criticism of Poetry; and, in our
present survey of the critical literature of the past, we shall find
nothing in Greek literature to rival it as a model of literary criticism
until, in the Roman age, we ultimately reach the celebrated treatise
*On the Sublime.*

[1] c. 5 § 1.                                   [2] iii 18.
[3] Cp. Vahlen's 3rd ed. (1885), pp. 77—80.
[4] 1341 *b* 39.                              [5] 6 § 2.
[6] See Frag. 5 (Vahlen and Bywater).
[7] iii 2, 7. Cp. Frag. 4 Vahlen, = 1 Bywater.        [8] p. 63 *supra.*
[9] *Vita Aristotelis Marciana*, ὁ περὶ ποιητῶν διάλογος (Rose, *Ar. Fragmenta,*
1886, p. 76, with the eight fragments there quoted).

# CHAPTER VI.

## THE RISE OF RHETORIC AND THE STUDY OF PROSE.

THE greater part of the materials for the early history of Greek rhetoric has been collected by Spengel in his *Artium Scriptores* (1828), by Westermann in his *Geschichte der Beredtsamkeit* (1833-5), and by Cope in his articles on the Sophistical Rhetoric in the *Cambridge Journal of Classical and Sacred Philology* (1855-7). The history itself has been fully set forth by Professor Blass in the first volume of his *Attische Beredsamkeit* (1868), and has been brilliantly sketched by Sir Richard Jebb in his *Attic Orators* (1876)[1], while it has also been briefly traced in the Introduction to the *De Oratore* of Cicero, as edited by Professor Wilkins (1879) and in that to the *Orator,* as edited by the present writer (1885)[2]. All that is here attempted is a very short survey of the subject, so far as it concerns our immediate purpose.

In the heroic age some of the foremost heroes are described
Homeric orators
in the Homeric poems as orators as well as warriors. Achilles is trained to be 'a speaker of words, as well as a doer of deeds'[3]; Nestor is the clear-voiced orator, from whose lips 'sweeter than honey flowed the stream of speech'[4]; Menelaus touches only on salient points 'in words though few, yet clear'[5]; while Odysseus, though awkward in action, is beyond compare with his 'deep voice' and with his 'words that fall like flakes of wintry snow'[6].

---

[1] vol. I, pp. cviii—cxxxvii.

[2] pp. ii—xi. Cp. Volkmann, *Die Rhetorik der Griechen u. Römer in system. Uebersicht*, ed. 2, 1885; and in Iwan Müller's *Handbuch*, II D, 455—489.

[3] *Il.* ix 443.                    [4] i 249.

[5] iii 214.                    [6] iii 222.

In historic times Athens was the only city of Greece where eloquence found a home. The eloquence of Pericles is said to have been singularly persuasive.

Pericles

We are told by Eupolis that 'a power persuasive rested on his lips; such was his charm; alone among the speakers, he ever left his sting in them that heard him'[1]; while Aristophanes describes him as, like the Olympian Zeus, 'lightening and thundering and confounding Greece'[2]. But his eloquence was of a purely practical kind, uninfluenced by the theoretical treatment of the art, which had sprung into being in Sicily, but apparently made little, if any, impression on Athens until after the beginning of the Peloponnesian war.

Greek rhetoric had risen in Sicily with the establishment of democracy at Acragas in 472 B.C., and at Syracuse in 466. Its earliest professors had been Corax and Tisias, and Pericles had passed away two years before Gorgias,

Gorgias

the famous pupil of Tisias, made his first appearance in Athens in 427. He came as an envoy to invite Athens to aid his native town of Leontini against the encroachments of Syracuse. The embassy is described by Thucydides[3]; but, although the speech delivered by Gorgias made a singular sensation, the name of Gorgias is not mentioned. It is a Sicilian historian, Diodorus[4], who tells us that 'the Athenians, clever as they were and fond of oratory (φιλόλογοι), were struck by the singular distinction of the style of Gorgias, with its pointed antitheses, its symmetrical clauses, its parallelisms of structure and its rhyming endings, which were then welcomed owing to their novelty'. These figures of speech are most simply classified as follows :—

ἀντίθεσις     = contrast of sense.
παρίσωσις    = parallelism of structure.
παρομοίωσις = parallelism of sound.

The last is subdivided into ὁμοιοκάταρκτον, ὁμοιοτέλευτον and παρονομασία, according as the 'parallelism of sound' affects the beginning, or the end, or the whole, of the two contrasted words. Gorgias was the founder of an artificial or semi-artistic type of

---

[1] Pliny, *Ep.* i. 20, 17.          [2] *Ach.* 531.
[3] iii 68.                          [4] xii 53.

Greek prose.  His style had a strongly poetical colouring[1]; even at the close of his life he observed in a poetic vein : ' At last Sleep lays me with his brother Death'; and another of his last sayings finds its parallel in Waller's line describing the body in old age as 'the soul's dark cóttage, battered and decayed'.  His sentences were broken up into short symmetrical clauses, which had a general effect very similar to that of actual metre ; and his example was closely followed by certain writers of artificial prose in later ages, especially among the adherents of ' Asianism ' in the third and following centuries B.C., who had their counterpart in the ' Euphuism' of our own 16th century[2].

The figures of speech characteristic of Gorgias were retained by his pupil, the eminent rhetorician, Isocrates (436—338 B.C.).  Isocrates, however, unlike the later 'Asiatic' adherents of Gorgias, with their cramped and jerky sentences, succeeded in expanding the unduly concise and monotonous clauses of his master by moulding them into an ampler and more varied periodic form, in which metrical and symmetrical effects were diversified by meandering melodies of rhythm and subtle harmonies of cadence.  A very short specimen of his prose may here be quoted from the latter part of his *Panegyric* (§ 186) :—φήμην δὲ καὶ μνήμην καὶ δόξαν | πόσην τινὰ χρὴ νομίζειν, | ἢ ζῶντας ἕξειν, | ἢ τελευτήσαντας καταλείψειν, | τοὺς ἐν τοῖς τοιούτοις ἔργοις ἀριστεύσαντας ; The style of Isocrates was in the main the foundation of the style of Cicero ; and the style of Cicero has in its turn supplied the languages of Europe with a model for some of the most highly finished forms of the ampler types of modern prose.

While rhetoricians of the Sicilian school of Gorgias, in culti-vating a semi-poetic type of prose, aimed mainly at 'beauty of language' (εὐέπεια), the Greek school of certain other Sophists, such as Protagoras, Prodicus and Hippias, aimed at 'correctness of language' (ὀρ-θοέπεια)[3].  Protagoras classified the modes of speech ; Prodicus, whose style is parodied in Plato's *Protagoras*[4],

Isocrates

Protagoras.
Prodicus.
Hippias

---

[1] Arist. *Rhet.* iii 1, 9.
[2] Norden, *Die Antike Kunstprosa*, pp. 25 f, 134 f, 786 f.
[3] Plato, *Phaedrus*, 267 C ; Spengel, *Artium Scriptores*, pp. 40 f.    [4] 337 A—C.

dwelt on distinctions between synonyms; while Hippias aimed
at a correct and elevated style of expression.    Two
more names may be briefly noticed.  Thrasymachus      Thrasyma-
                                                      chus and
of Calchedon (*c.* 457—400 B.C.) marked an epoch      Theodorus
in Greek prose by forming a style intermediate
between the 'elaborately artificial' style of Thucydides and the
'simple and plain' style of Lysias, and became in this respect a
precursor of Plato and Isocrates[1]; while Theodorus of Byzantium
(*fl.* 412 B.C.), who is regarded as a prominent rhetorician both by
Plato and Aristotle, introduced some novel terms for the subdivisions of a speech, and is described in the *Phaedrus*[2] as a 'cunning
speech-wright' (λογοδαίδαλος), a phrase implying mastery in
rhetorical artifice.

The two dialogues of Plato specially concerned with rhetoric
are the *Gorgias* and the *Phaedrus*.    In the former
it is described, not as an art, but as a happy knack         Plato's
                                                             *Gorgias* and
acquired by practice and destitute of scientific             *Phaedrus*
principle[3].    In both dialogues Plato casts ridicule
on the writers of the popular rhetorical treatises; but, in the
*Phaedrus*, instead of denouncing rhetoric unreservedly, he draws
up an outline of a new rhetoric founded on a more philosophic
basis, resting partly on dialectic, which aids the orator in the
invention of arguments, and partly on psychology, which enables
him to distinguish between the several varieties of human character in his audience and to apply the means best adapted to produce
that persuasion which is the aim of his art[4].

The hints which Plato throws out in the *Phaedrus* are
elaborately expanded in the *Rhetoric* of Aristotle,
especially in the first two books, which deal with        Aristotle's
                                                          *Rhetoric*
the modes of producing persuasion.    In the first
book these are classified; while the second includes (1) 'a careful
analysis of the affections of which human nature is susceptible,
and also of the causes by which such affections are called forth;
(2) a descriptive catalogue of the various modifications of the
human character, and the sort of arguments adapted to each'[5].

---

[1] Dion. Hal. *de adm. vi dicendi Dem.* c. 1—3.

[2] 266 E.                          [3] 463 B, 501 A.

[4] Thompson's *Phaedrus*, p. xiv.           [5] *ib.* p. xx.

The first two books, which thus deal with the invention of
arguments (εὕρεσις), are followed by a third occupied with the
two other parts of rhetoric, style (λέξις) and arrangement (τάξις).

The third book includes criticisms on the poetic style of Gorgias (c. 1),
defines the main merits of style as perspicuity and propriety (c. 2), touches on
'metaphors' and 'epithets', gives examples of bad taste in the use of compound
or foreign words, or of redundant epithets, in prose (c. 3), and distinguishes
between 'similes' and 'metaphors', with examples of the latter (c. 4). Purity
of Greek depends on the proper use of connecting words or clauses (σύνδεσμοι),
on the avoidance of periphrasis and ambiguity, and the proper use of gender
and number. As a general rule, every written composition should be easy to
read, and easy to deliver. Therefore it must avoid all excess of connecting
words or clauses, and everything that is difficult to punctuate (ἃ μὴ ῥᾴδιον
διαστίξαι). It must also avoid zeugma and parenthesis (c. 5). Amplitude of
style may be produced by the use of periphrasis; conciseness by its avoidance.
We must make our meaning clear by the use of metaphors and epithets, but
we must avoid the poetical. Amplitude may also be produced by the use of
the plural for the singular, by the repetition of the article before the epithet as
well as before the noun, and by the enumeration of negative characteristics
(c. 6). Propriety of style may be attained by making it expressive of the emotions, true to character, and appropriate to the subject (c. 7). Prose must have
rhythm, without metre. The first paean (–◡◡◡) supplies an appropriate
rhythm for the beginning; the fourth (◡◡◡–) for the end of a sentence. It
is best to end with a long syllable; and the conclusion must be made clear,
not by the transcriber or by any marginal mark of punctuation (παραγραφή),
but by the rhythm (c. 8). Prose style may either be the continuous style (λέξις
εἰρομένη), which runs on with a continuity supplied by connecting particles
alone, a style like that of Herodotus, or the compact and periodic style (λέξις
κατεστραμμένη). The period must be neither too short nor too long; if it
consists of several clauses, it must be easily pronounced in a single breath.
The clauses may either be simply parallel to one another, or antithetically
contrasted; ten examples of these are added from the *Panegyric* of Isocrates.
Besides ἀντίθεσις or 'contrast of sense', there is also παρίσωσις, where the
two parallel clauses are equal in length, and παρομοίωσις, where there is a
resemblance either in the beginning or in the end of the contrasted words
(c. 9). Among graces of style may be mentioned 'metaphor' (c. 10) and vivid
personification (c. 11). The written style is different from the style of debate,
whether deliberative (*i.e.* parliamentary) or forensic. The written style is
precise; that of debate lends itself to effective delivery. Delivery must not be
monotonous, but appropriately varied. Deliberative speaking is like scene-
painting: before a large audience minute details are useless. The forensic
style is more precise. The 'epideictic' style (that of encomium) lends itself
best to writing; its aim is to be read; next to this is the forensic.—The rest of
the book is concerned with the arrangement of the several parts of the

speech :—exordium (προοίμιον, c. 14), narrative (διήγησις, c. 16), proofs (πίστεις, c. 17), and peroration (ἐπίλογος, c. 19).

Aristotle was born at Stageirus in 384, lived at Athens from 367 to 347, was tutor to Alexander from 343 to 340, returned to Athens from 335 to 323, and died at Chalcis in 322. The *Rhetoric* was not completed before 338 B.C.[1], probably not before 336[2]. If 336 was the date of its completion, the author was then 48 years of age, and a new interest is added to his own statement that the mind is in its prime '*about* the age of 49'[3]. Possibly, while *Aristotle's relations to Isocrates and Demosthenes* writing these very words, the author was himself conscious for a moment that he had approximately reached the prime of his own intellectual life. The year 338 B.C. is the date not only of the battle of Chaeroneia, but also of the death of 'that old man eloquent', Isocrates, who eight years previously had urged Philip to levy war on Persia (*Or.* 5 ; 346 B.C.) ; and, after the battle, wrote to the victor rejoicing that many of his own hopes were already fulfilled. Notwithstanding the traditional feud between Isocrates and Aristotle, which has been assigned to the latter part of Aristotle's first residence in Athens, both were inspired with Macedonian sympathies. Moreover, the artificial style of Isocrates lent itself readily to citations illustrating rhetorical forms of expression. Hence we are not surprised to find that there is no author from whom Aristotle quotes more frequently in the *Rhetoric* ; there are as many as ten citations from him in a single chapter[4]. While Isocrates was 52 years older than Aristotle, Demosthenes was his exact contemporary. But, although Aristotle was at Athens during the delivery of the *First Philippic* (351) and the *Three Olynthiacs* (349), he never illustrates a single rule of rhetoric from any of the speeches of the great orator. To Demosthenes he ascribes an isolated simile, which is not to be found in his extant speeches[5], while he cites the saying of a minor orator, that the policy of Demosthenes was the cause of the disasters of Athens, as an example of fallacious reasoning[6]. He mentions the 'orators at Athens, and Isocrates'[7], and (in a passage open to suspicion) describes *hyperbole* as a favourite

---

[1] ii 23, 6.     [2] ii 23, 18.     [3] ii 14, 4.
[4] iii 9.     [5] iii 4, 3.     [6] ii 24, 8.     [7] iii 17, 10.

figure with the 'Attic orators'[1]. He quotes striking metaphors
from speakers such as Iphicrates, Leptines, Cephisodotus, Peitho-
laüs, Moerocles and Polyeuctus, but his quotations are apparently
not derived from any published works, being rather of the nature
of 'parliamentary' anecdotes from the everyday talk of the
Lyceum[2]. He illustrates the metaphorical use of βοῆσαι from an
obscure contemporary of Demosthenes[3], though he might have
illustrated it better from Demosthenes himself[4]. It is not entirely
fanciful to suppose that Aristotle, who lived as a foreigner at
Athens, and had close relations with Philip and Alexander, may
have felt a sense of delicacy in exemplifying the precepts of rhetoric
from the speeches of the great opponent of Macedonia. He
never quotes the other anti-Macedonian orators, Lycurgus and
Hypereides, but he also makes no mention of the Macedonian
orator, Aeschines. In relation to the foreign policy of Athens,
he apparently deemed it best, as a foreigner, to remain neutral.
Of the Ten whom a later age recognised as the 'Attic orators',
Isocrates is the only one whom he quotes by name ; while a
passage, which has come down to us in the funeral oration
wrongly ascribed to Lysias[5], is quoted by Aristotle without the
name of any author whatsoever[6], being probably written by an
unknown imitator of Isocrates.

The study of the style of prose in the Athenian age was
mainly connected with the study of rhetoric. The
prose of public speech was the first to attain an
artistic form, but other kinds of prose had a closer
connexion with it than they have in modern times.
In the domain of history, the style of Thucydides shows the
influence of the Sicilian rhetoric ; and the historian readily resorts
to *speeches* as a means of expressing the political opinions of the
day, while he employs the medium of a *dialogue* to give a
dramatic representation of the controversy between Athens and
Melos. In the next century, two prominent historians, Ephorus
and Theopompus, were both of them pupils of that trainer of
rhetoricians, Isocrates. The criticisms in the *Rhetoric* are not
confined to the criticism of speeches. A particular kind of prose-

*Relations of
rhetoric to
prose in
general*

---

[1] iii 11, 16.          [2] Cp. Wilamowitz, *Aristoteles und Athen*, i 350.
[3] iii 10, 7.     [4] 19 §§ 92, 129.     [5] 2 § 60.     [6] *Rhet.* iii 10, 7.

style is there[1] exemplified from Herodotus, while many of the
precepts apply to prose in general, and not a few to poetry as
well.  From the time of Aristotle downwards literary criticism
forms part of the province of rhetoric.

The earliest complete work in Greek prose now extant is that
of Herodotus (484—c. 425 B.C.), who, according to
the Chronicle of Eusebius, read his ' books ' aloud        The study of
                                                            prose authors
to the Council at Athens about 446–4 B.C.  Ac-
cording to Lucian[2], he recited his history to an enraptured
audience at Olympia, and his books, which were nine in number,
were thenceforth known by the names of the nine Muses.  The
biographers of Thucydides have added that the future historian of
the Peloponnesian war was himself present and was moved to tears
by the recital ; but the story is generally regarded as unworthy of
credit[3].  Some of the statements of Thucydides on early Greek
navies may have been derived from Herodotus, whom he appears
to be tacitly correcting in his account of the affair of Cylon and
the prerogatives of the Spartan kings[4].  He claims that his own
conclusions on the early state of Hellas are more trustworthy than
those derived from his predecessors, whether ' poets ' or ' writers
of prose '[5], but the only historian whom he mentions by name is
Hellanicus[6].  Similarly the only historian named by Herodotus is
Hecataeus[7], who had already been criticised by Heracleitus in the
celebrated saying : ' much learning does not teach sense ; else it
would have taught Hesiod and Pythagoras, and also Xenophanes
and Hecataeus '[8].  Thucydides in turn was studied by Demosthenes, as is clear from the style[9] as well as from the matter[10] of
his speeches, however little we may credit Lucian's statement that
the orator transcribed the work of the historian eight times over[11].
The style of Demosthenes, again, is studied and criticised by

---

[1] iii 9, 2.                       [2] *Aëtion*, 1.

[3] Dahlmann's *Life of Herodotus* (G. V. Cox, 1845); and Stein's ed., p. xxi.

[4] Thuc. i 126 and i 20.              [5] i 21.

[6] i 97.   On ' Prose Writings in Thucydides' time ', see Thuc. i, ed. Forbes,
p. xli—lxxx.            [7] ii 143 etc.              [8] Fragment 16.

[9] Dion. Hal. *Thuc.* 53, 54 (Dem. 14 § 13); cp. Blass, *Att. Ber.* III i[2] 19, 37.

[10] *Phil.* iii 47—51, *Ol.* iii 21, *Lept.* 73.

[11] *Adv. Indoctum*, 4.

Aeschines[1], who quotes a series of harsh metaphors, which he ascribes to his opponent. Lastly, the dialogues of Plato were studied and quoted by his great pupil, Aristotle. The citations fall under four heads : either (*a*) the name of Plato, or Socrates, is added to the title of the dialogue ; or (*b*) the title alone is given ; or (*c*) the name of Plato is mentioned without specification of any particular work ; or (*d*) the reference is in general terms and in the plural number, introduced by phrases such as 'certain persons say' or 'think', where some particular work of Plato's is either certainly or probably meant[2]. The evidence of these citations is of some importance in determining the genuineness of the dialogues ascribed to Plato[3].

While the place of poetry in Athenian education was due partly to a belief in the poet as a teacher and as an inspired being, partly to the fact that poetry attained an artistic form at an earlier date than prose (besides being easier to commit to memory), the place of prose was distinctly subordinate. In elementary education prose appears to have been partly represented by the traditional fables of Aesop[4]. In Plato's *Phaedrus*[5] Socrates is described as disparaging reading and writing in comparison with talking and memory; but in Xenophon's *Memorabilia*[6] we find him unrolling and perusing, with his friends, 'the treasures of the wise men of old, which they wrote down in books and left behind them'. As a young man, he had 'heard someone reading aloud' a book of Anaxagoras, and hastened to obtain it[7]. 'Strains written in prose', and 'compositions in prose, without rhythm or harmony', are discussed, as well as poetry, in the scheme of education in Plato's *Laws*[8], but the 'works handed down by many writers of this class' (whether in prose or verse) are deemed 'dangerous', while a discourse like that in the *Laws* is described as 'inspired of heaven' and 'exactly like a poem', and as in fact an appropriate pattern for other discourses to be used in the education of youth[9].

*Place of Prose in education*

[1] iii 166.

[2] See the Index of Bonitz, and of Heitz.

[3] Zeller's *Plato*, 54—77.

[4] Ar. *Birds*, 471.     [5] 274 C.          [6] i 6, 14.

[7] *Phaedo*, 97 B.       [8] 809 B, 810 B.   [9] 811 C—E.

After the death of Plato the original manuscripts of his dialogues were possibly preserved in the school of the Academy. For eight years the school was under the care of his nephew and successor, Speusippus, and afterwards for twenty-five under that of Xenocrates, who was succeeded by Polemon and others. Copies of the original MSS were doubtless made at an early date, and some of these may have been transmitted from Athens to Alexandria, possibly through the agency of Demetrius of Phaleron[1]. The earliest extant MS of any part of Plato has been found in Egypt. It is the Petrie papyrus from Gurob in the Faiyûm, containing about 12 columns of the *Phaedo*, being portions of a neatly written trade-copy assigned to the middle of the third century B.C.[2]

*Early transmission of the works of Plato and Aristotle*

On the death of Aristotle, the school of the Lyceum, with the library of its founder, remained for more than 34 years under the control of his successor Theophrastus. During this time Aristotle's pupil, Eudemus of Rhodes, wrote to Theophrastus for a transcript of a passage in the *Physics* which was missing in his own copy of that work[3], and doubtless other copies of the master's manuscripts were in circulation during his successor's life-time[4]. Theophrastus, on his death in or about 287 B.C., left his own library with that of Aristotle to his pupil Neleus, who removed it to his home at Scepsis in the Troad. A few years later the town passed into the possession of the Kings of the Attalid dynasty, who from about 230 B.C. began to found a great Library at Pergamon to vie with that of the Ptolemies at Alexandria. The heirs of Neleus prudently concealed the MSS in a cellar, awaiting an opportunity for sending them safely out of

[1] Grote's *Plato*, i 122, 135, 169; criticised in Zeller's *Plato*, 51–3, and esp. in Gomperz, *Platonische Aufsätze*, ii 1899.

[2] See p. 87; the original is exhibited in the British Museum, Case A, 1. Cp. Mahaffy's *Petrie Papyri* (1891) pl. viii—x; E. M. Thompson's *Palaeography*, p. 120; Kenyon's *Palaeography of Gk papyri*, p. 59—63; Blass in *S. Ber. sächs. Gesellsch.* l. 197 f; Gomperz, *S. Ber. Wiener Akad.* cxxvii (1892); and Usener, *Gött. Nachr.* (1892).

[3] Zeller's *Aristotle*, i 136; Grote's *Plato*, i 140.

[4] Stahr, *Aristotelia*, ii 1—166, 294 f; Susemihl, *Gr. Litt. Alex.*, ii 299 f, note 324.

the country. The MSS had thus remained in their possession for more than 150 years, when, about 100 B.C., they were bought by Apellicon of Teos, and restored to Athens. After the capture of Athens by Sulla in 86 B.C., they were transported from Athens to Rome, where they were consulted by scholars such as Tyrannion, Andronicus[1], and others; but, owing to long neglect, many of them had become illegible, and the copies made after they had passed into the hands of Apellicon were disfigured with unskilful conjectures and restorations. The above story of their fortunes is told us by Tyrannion's pupil, Strabo, who adds that Aristotle was the first to 'collect books', thus setting 'an example afterwards followed by the Kings of Egypt'[2]. The story is partly confirmed in one passage of Athenaeus[3], but contradicted in another[4] carelessly asserting that *all* the books of Aristotle in the possession of Neleus were purchased for the Alexandrian library by Ptolemy II, who is elsewhere described as possessing more than 1000 books or rolls of the Aristotelian writings[5]. The earliest extant manuscript is the papyrus containing Aristotle's *Constitution of Athens*, found in Egypt in 1890 and ascribed to about 100 A.D.[6]

Apart from Aristotle's library we hear of no important collection of books in the Athenian age, though books are said to have been collected by Polycrates of Samos, by Peisistratus and Euripides[7], and by a pupil of Plato and Isocrates, the 'tyrant' Clearchus who founded a library at the Pontic Heraclea in Bithynia before 364 B.C.[8], while in 400 B.C. 'many books' are mentioned by Xenophon[9] as found in the cargo of some vessels wrecked on the coast of the Euxine. In or after the first century B.C. an incomplete title of a speech of Demosthenes and titles of portions of Hellanicus appear by the side of Aeschylus, Sophocles, Crates, Diphilus, and the *Meleager* and *Alcmaeon* of Euripides, in

[1] Added in Plutarch's *Sulla*, 26.

[2] Strabo, pp. 608–9; *Ethics*, ed. Grant, *Essay* i 5–8; Grote's *Plato*, i 138 f.

[3] 214 D—E.                              [4] 3 B.

[5] Schol. Arist. 22 *a* 12. Cp. Zeller's *Aristotle*, c. iii, and Shute's *History of the Aristotelian Writings*, pp. 29—45.

[6] Complete facsimile edited by Kenyon (1891); specimen given by E. M. Thompson, *l.c.*, p. 140.                    [7] Athen. p. 3.

[8] Photius, *Bibl.* 222 *b*.                    [9] *Anab.* vii 5, 14.

an inscription conjecturally supposed to contain a list of books
presented by Athenian youths to the library of their *gymnasium*[1].
We know for certain that 100 volumes were annually presented by
the youth of Athens to the library of the *gymnasium* called the
*Ptolemaion*, which was founded at Athens early in the Alexandrian
age (probably by Ptolemy Philadelphus) and was visited in the
Roman age by Cicero[2] and Pausanias[3]. But in the Athenian age
itself, it was not so much the books that the Athenian read as
the words that he heard, in the theatre, in the law-courts, in the
groves of Academe and in the walks of the Lyceum, that served
to complete his education. In the language of John Henry
Newman, 'it was what the student gazed on, what he heard, what
he caught by the magic of sympathy, not what he read, which
was the education furnished by Athens'[4].

[1] *C. I. A.* ii 992.          [2] *De Finibus*, v 1, 1.

[3] i. 17, 2 (with Frazer's note). Cp. *C. I. A.* ii 465, 468, 478, 480, 482,
ἔδοσαν καὶ βιβλία εἰς τὴν ἐν Πτολεμαίῳ βιβλιοθήκην, and Dittenberger, *De
Ephebis*, p. 51; Curtius, *Stadtgeschichte von Athen*, lxxxii 238, 282; and
P. Girard, *l'Éducation Athénienne*, p. 159 f.

[4] *Historical Sketches*, p. 40.

From the earliest extant ms of the Phaedo of Plato,
p. 83 A (*c.* 250 B.C.); p. 85 *supra*.

(Sir E. M. Thompson's *Palaeography*, Handbook, p. 120;
cp. *Introduction*, 1912, p. 110.)

$<$αισθη$>$σεων πειθουσα δε εκ τουτωμ
$<$με$>$ν αναχωρειν οσομ μη αναγκη
χρησ$<$θ$>$αι αυτην δ' εις εαυτην συλ-
λεγεσθαι και αθροιζεσθαι παρακε-
λευεσ$<$θ$>$αι πιστευειν δε μηδενι αλλωι

# CHAPTER VII.

## THE BEGINNINGS OF GRAMMAR AND ETYMOLOGY.

WE are told by Herodotus[1] that the Phoenicians who came

**Herodotus** with Cadmus brought with them the letters of the Phoenician alphabet, and that in course of time they adapted the method of writing them to the requirements of the Greek language. In the temple of the Ismenian Apollo at Thebes, Herodotus had himself seen three tripods inscribed with 'Cadmeian' letters, 'for the most part resembling those of the Ionians'. He assigns the three inscriptions to the age of Laïus in the third, and to those of Oedipus and Laodamas in the fourth and sixth generations from Cadmus[2]. We are also told by Herodotus that the Ionians who lived nearest to the Phoenicians (*e.g.* in Cyprus and Rhodes) borrowed the Phoenician alphabet, with a few changes, and that they habitually called them the 'Phoenician' letters[3],—a statement confirmed by an inscription found near the Ionian town of Teos[4].

Spelling was taught by means of a series of syllables combining the consonants with all the vowels in succession. Fragments of a tile have been found in Attica bearing the syllables αρ βαρ γαρ δαρ, ερ βερ γερ δερ etc.[5] The comic poet Callias wrote a 'letter-play' (γραμματικὴ τραγῳδία) in which the *dramatis personae* were the letters of the alphabet, all of which were enumerated in the prologue, with a separate enumeration of the vowels at a later point. The play included a spelling-chorus, βῆτα ἄλφα βα etc., and some of its choral arrangements are said to have been

---

[1] v 58.        [2] v 59—61.        [3] v 58.

[4] *C. I. G.* 3044 = *I. G. A.* 497 B 37 (*c.* 475 B.C.), ὃς ἂν...φοινικήϊα ἐκκόψει (Roberts, *Greek Epigraphy*, p. 170).

[5] *Philistor*, iv 327.

imitated in the *Medea* of Euripides (431 B.C.),—a statement of no value except as an indication of the probable date of the play[1]. In the *Theseus* of Euripides a slave who could not read was represented as describing the shape of each of the characters in the name of ΘΗΣΕΥΣ, and the same device was adopted in the case of the same name by Agathon and Theodectes, while Sophocles is said to have represented the shapes of various letters of the alphabet, in one of his satyric dramas, by means of the attitudes assumed by a dancer[2]. In the archonship of Eucleides (403 B.C.) it was ordered at Athens on the proposal of Archinus that all *public* documents should be written in the Ionic characters[3]; and the 'treaty with the barbarian' (commonly called the 'peace of Cimon' or 'Callias', after 466 or 449 B.C.) is denounced by Theopompus as a fabrication, on the ground that the characters used in the inscription recording it were those of the Ionic instead of the Attic alphabet[4]. The fact that Euripides, who died three years before the archonship of Eucleides, recognises H as the second letter of 'Theseus' (as above noticed) is part of the proof that the Ionic alphabet was in *literary* and *private* use at Athens before 403 B.C.

The current division of letters (στοιχεῖα), as may be inferred from three passages of Plato, was as follows :    Plato
(1) 'voiced' or 'vocal' letters (φωνήεντα, *vocales*), our 'vowels'; (2) 'voiceless' letters (ἄφωνα), our 'consonants'. The latter were divided into (*a*) letters not only 'voiceless' but also 'without sound' (ἄφωνα καὶ ἄφθογγα), our 'mutes'; and (*b*) letters that are 'not vocal', but 'not without sound' (φωνήεντα μὲν οὔ, οὐ μέντοι γε ἄφθογγα), *i.e.* λ, μ, ν, ρ, ς, afterwards known as 'semivowels' (ἡμίφωνα)[5]. A passage in the *Timaeus*[6] mentions the 'teeth', 'tongue' and 'lips' as producing 'the river of speech', which is 'the fairest and noblest of all streams'. In the *Cratylus*[7] Plato notices that the only letters which have no special names are E, Y, O, Ω, thus showing that the names *epsilon, upsilon,*

---

[1] Cp. Verrall's *Medea*, p. xxiii.
[2] Athen. p. 453-4.    [3] Suïdas, *s.v.* Σαμίων δῆμος.
[4] Harpocration, *s.v.* Ἀττικοῖς γράμμασιν.
[5] *Cratylus*, 424 C; *Philebus*, 18 B, C (where τὰ μέσα are the 'semivowels'); *Theaet.* 203 B.    [6] 75 D.    [7] 394 D.

*omicron* and *omega* are of later origin, the Greeks in this age
calling these letters εἰ, υ, ου, and ω.  The name *epsilon*, or 'simple'
ε, was afterwards introduced to distinguish that letter from the
diphthong αι, and similarly *upsilon*, or 'simple' υ, to distinguish
that letter from the diphthong οι, and both these names belong to
the late Byzantine age, when ε and αι, and υ and οι respectively,
were pronounced alike.  The name *omega* is also late: ἄλφα and
Ω (not *omega*) are recognised in the best MSS of the Greek Testament, ἐγώ εἰμι τὸ ἄλφα καὶ τὸ ὦ[1], and in Prudentius:—'ἄλφα et ὦ
cognominatus'[2].

The earliest trace of any classification of words is to be found
in Plato.  'Grammar' was at first regarded mainly as the art of
reading and writing[3]; but it also included the theory of the nature
of sounds and of accent, with questions of quantity and rhythm,
and in these respects it was closely connected with Music.
With the classification of words grammar entered on a new stage.
It is traditionally held that Plato was the first to distinguish
between the Noun and the Verb, calling the former ὄνομα and the
latter ῥῆμα.  But the correspondence between these terms is
incomplete[4], and the distinction drawn by Plato between ὄνομα
and ῥῆμα does not answer to the *grammatical* distinction between
Noun and Verb, but to the *logical* distinction between Subject
and Predicate[5].  This is true even of the passage in the *Sophistes*[6],
which is the main support of those who ascribe to Plato the first
distinction between Noun and Verb as parts of speech.  He
there says:—'There are two kinds of intimations of being which
are given by the voice', 'one of them called ὀνόματα and the
other ῥήματα'; 'that which denotes action we call ῥῆμα', 'the
articulate sign set on those who do the actions we call ὄνομα'; 'a
succession of ὀνόματα or ῥήματα alone is not discourse'; 'it is only
when they are mingled together that language is formed'[7].  ῥῆμα

[1] *Revelation*, i 8.
[2] Mayor's *First Greek Reader*, p. lii; Blass, *Pronunciation of Ancient Greek*, p. 20.          [3] p. 6 *supra.*
[4] Classen, *De Gram. Gr. primordiis* (1829), p. 45 f.
[5] Deuschle, *Die Plat. Sprachphilosophie* (1852), p. 8 f.
[6] 261 E.
[7] Cp. *Theaet.* 206 D, *Symp.* 198 B, 199 B, *Rep.* 340 E, 462 C, 464 A, 474 A, 562 C, *Tim.* 49 E; also *Crat.* 425 A, 431 B (Deuschle, p. 9).

in Plato includes every kind of predicate. Thus, in the *Cratylus*[1], Διὰ φίλος (being predicated of a person) is called a ῥῆμα, while its derivative Δίφιλος is an ὄνομα. In later times Plato's ὄνομα and ῥῆμα were regarded as grammatical parts of speech, and the question whether this division was meant by Plato to be exhaustive, or whether the other parts of speech were only omitted because they were comparatively unimportant, was discussed by Plutarch in his *Platonic Questions*[2], and decided in the latter sense. In Plato we find suggestions of the distinction afterwards drawn in grammar between the Substantive and the Adjective[3]; he also recognises Number[4], Tenses of Verbs[5], and 'Active and Passive'[6].

Moods are not yet mentioned, but Protagoras had already distinguished in rhetoric some of the various modes of expression which correspond to the Moods of grammar[7]. He had also divided nouns into three classes, male, female, and inanimate (σκεύη), a classification apparently founded on a real or natural, and not on a grammatical basis, 'male' and 'female' nouns denoting male and female persons, or distinctions in sex, whether in mankind or among animals in general, and things inanimate including the names of all other objects, natural and artificial, real and abstract. This last class contains many words which are grammatically masculine or feminine, but the classification of Protagoras can hardly be identified with a classification of nouns as masculine, feminine and neuter. Protagoras uses in the sense of 'classes' the same term (γένη) which was afterwards adopted in grammar to denote 'genders'[8].

In the earlier Greek philosophers we find a few traces of speculation on the origin of language. Thus Pythagoras (*fl.* 540 —510 B.C.) held that, next to 'number', the highest wisdom belonged to 'him who gave things their names'[9]. Heracleitus

---

[1] 399 B.      [2] *Moralia*, ii 1008.

[3] Cp. ἐπωνυμία in *Parm.* 131 A, *Soph.* 225 D, *Phaedr.* 238 A.

[4] *Soph.* 237 E.      [5] *Parm.* 151 E, 156 A; *Soph.* 262 D.

[6] *Soph.* 219 B; *Philebus* 26 E. Cp. Deuschle, pp. 10, 17, 18; Schömann, *Die Lehre von den Redetheilen* (1862), p. 2; and Steinthal, *Sprachwissenschaft*, i[2] 137 f.      [7] p. 27.

[8] Cope in *Journ. of Cl. and S. Phil.* iii 48 f., and on Arist. *Rhet.* iii 5, 5 and *Introd.* p. 293. Ar. *Clouds* 659 ff. may be a satire on Protagoras.

[9] ὁ τὰ ὀνόματα τοῖς πράγμασι θέμενος, Proclus on Plato's *Cratylus*, p. 6; Cicero, *Tusc. Disp.* i 25; Steinthal, p. 157 f.

(*fl.* 500 B.C.), though celebrated for the obscurity of his language, appears to have laid stress on linguistic expression, but we know of no scientific enunciation of his on this subject. He is, however, known to have held that words existed naturally (φύσει). Words, he said, were not like the artificial, but like the natural images of visible things; they resembled shadows, and reflexions in water, or images seen in mirrors[1]. Democritus (460—357 B.C.) described the names of the gods as their 'vocal images'[2]. His contemporary Hippocrates (*c.* 460—359 B.C.) called names 'ordinances of nature' (φύσιος νομοθετήματα); and Antisthenes (*fl.* 400 B.C.) wrote on names and on language in connexion with his dialectical theories[3]. But our knowledge of these speculations is very imperfect. In the case of Plato we have more material for forming an opinion, but even here there is much that is confused and perplexing. It was said of Plato that he was the first to speculate on the nature of 'grammar'[4]; and some of the passages on language in his dialogues have been collected by Stobaeus[5], but all these are of less importance than the dialogue known as the *Cratylus*.

In the *Cratylus* there are three interlocutors holding different views as to the nature and origin of language. (1) HERMOGENES holds that language is *conventional*, and that all names have their origin in convention and mutual agreement (ξυνθήκη καὶ ὁμολογία, 384 D); like the names of slaves, they may be given and altered at pleasure. (2) CRATYLUS, a follower of Heracleitus, holds that language is *natural*, and that every name is either a true name or not a name at all; he cannot conceive of degrees of imitation; a word is either the perfect expression of a thing or a mere inarticulate sound. (3) SOCRATES takes up an intermediate position, holding that language is founded on *nature*, but modified by *convention*[6]. In his view 'language is conventional and also natural, and the true conventional-natural is also the rational; it is a work not of chance but of art; the dialectician is the artificer of words, and the legislator

---

[1] Ammonius on Aristotle, *de Interp.* p. 24 B Ald., quoted by Lersch, *Sprachphilosophie*, i 11 f; cp. Plato, *Theaet.* 206 D; Steinthal, pp. 171, 173.
[2] ἀγάλματα φωνήεντα, Olympiodorus on Plato, *Philebus*, p. 242; Steinthal p. 182.
[3] Zeller's *Plato*, p. 211 f.
[4] Favorinus ap. Diog. Laert. III i 19, 25, πρῶτος ἐθεώρησε τῆς γραμματικῆς τὴν δύναμιν.
[5] 81 §§ 14—16 (*Philebus*, p. 186; *Theaet.* 202 B; *Sophist*, 261 D).
[6] Lewis Campbell, *Encycl. Brit.* ed. 9, s.v. *Plato*.

gives authority to them'[1]. Words are the expressions or imitations of things by means of sound. In the extravagance of some of his etymologies, Socrates is regarded by Jowett as 'ridiculing the fancies of a new school of sophists and grammarians[2]; but, 'when the fervour of his etymological enthusiasm has abated', he ends, as he began, with 'a rational explanation of language'. 'Having explained compound words, by resolving them into their original elements, he proceeds to analyse simple words into the letters of which they are composed'. He 'supposes words to be formed by the imitation of ideas in sounds; he also recognises the effect of time, the influence of foreign languages, the desire of euphony...; and he admits a certain element of chance'[3]. He says, apparently in irony, 'my notion is, that we may put in and pull out letters at pleasure and alter the accents, and we may make words into sentences and sentences into words' (399 A). The name ἄνθρωπος (he adds) is a case in point, for a letter has been omitted and the accent changed; the original meaning being ὁ ἀναθρῶν ἃ ὄπωπεν—'he who looks up at what he sees'. He observes in a more serious mood that, in speaking of the gods, we are only speaking of our names for them :—'the truest names of the gods are those which they give themselves, but these are unknown to us' (400 E). Inquiring about the *human* names of the gods, he makes many fanciful suggestions, the only one which can be accepted being his derivation of the name of Pallas ἀπὸ τοῦ πάλλειν τὰ ὅπλα (407 A). He suspects that certain words, which cannot be explained with the help of Greek alone, must be of foreign origin, 'for the Greeks, especially those who were under the dominion of the barbarians, often borrowed words from them. Consider whether this word πῦρ is not foreign; for it is not easily brought into relation with Greek, and the Phrygians may be observed to have this same word slightly inflected, just as they have ὕδωρ and κύνες, and many other words' (409 D, 410 A). κακόν (416 A) and ὀφέλλειν (417 C) he considers 'foreign' words; but 'the idea that the Greek language and that of the barbarians could have had a common source never entered his mind'[4]. After proposing some far-fetched etymologies, he excuses himself by adding 'you must remember that all language is in a process of disguise or transition; and letters are taken out and put in at pleasure, and twisted and twirled about in the lapse of ages—sometimes for the sake of euphony' (414 C). Again, 'mere antiquity may often prevent our recognising words, after all their complications; and we must remember that, however far we carry back our analysis of words, there must be some ultimate elements which can be no further analysed' (421 D, E). 'Secondary names derive their significance from the primary; how, then, do the primary indicate anything?' (422 A). 'The only way in which the body can express anything is by *imitation*; and the tongue or mouth can *imitate* as well as the rest of the

---

[1] Jowett's *Plato*, i 622[1]= 257[3].

[2] *ib.* p. 624[1], 259[3].

[3] *ib.* p. 625[1], 259[3].

[4] Max Müller's *Lectures*, i 132 (1866).

body. What, then, is a name? A name is not a musical or pictorial imitation, but an imitation of that kind which expresses the nature of the thing;
and is the invention not of a musician, or of a painter, but of a namer' (423
A–E). "The way to analyse names will be by going back to the *letters*, or
primary elements of which they are composed. First, we classify the letters
of the alphabet, and, when we have learnt the letters singly, we shall learn to
know them in their various combinations. We may apply letters to the
expression of objects, and form them into syllables; and these again into
words (424 C–E). I mean that this was the way in which the *ancients* formed
language. Whether the primary and secondary elements are rightly given, is
a question which we can answer by conjecture alone. But still we hold that
the method which we are pursuing is the true and only method of discovery.
Otherwise we must have recourse to a *Deus ex machina*, and say that 'the
gods gave the first names, and therefore they are right'; and this will perhaps
be our best device, unless indeed we say that the barbarians are older than we,
and that we learnt of them, or that the lapse of ages has cast a veil over the
truth" (425 A–E). Primary words which do not admit of derivation from
foreign languages 'must be resolved into the letters of which they are composed, and therefore the letters must have a meaning. The framers of language
were aware of this: they observed that $a$ was adapted to express size; $\eta$
length; $o$ roundness; $\nu$ inwardness; $\rho$ rush or roar; $\lambda$ liquidity; $\gamma\lambda$ the detention of the liquid or slippery element; $\delta$ and $\tau$ binding; $\phi$, $\psi$, $\sigma$, $\xi$, wind and
cold, and so on' (426 C–427 D).

'Plato's analysis of the letters of the alphabet', says Jowett[1], 'shows a
wonderful insight into the nature of language'. 'In passing from the gesture
of the body to the movement of the tongue', he "makes a great step in the
physiology of language. He was probably the first who said that 'language is
imitative sound', which is the greatest and deepest truth in philology". But
*convention* has its influence no less than *imitation*. '*Imitation*', says Plato,
'is a poor thing, and has to be supplemented by *convention*, which is another
poor thing; although I quite agree, that if we could always have a perfect
correspondence of sound and meaning, that would be the most perfect form of
language' (435 C–D).

Plato, it will be observed, is a supporter of what has since been called the
onomatopoetic theory of language. 'He was probably also the first who made
a distinction between simple and compound words...; but he appears to have
been wholly unaware of the difference between a root and a termination'[2].
The dialogue *may* have been in part 'a satire on the philological fancies of the
day'[3]; the author *may* have been ridiculing 'the arbitrary methods...which
were in vogue among the philologers of his time'[4], but this is uncertain.

The etymological speculations of Plato in the *Cratylus* were regarded with

---

[1] Jowett's *Plato*, i p. 646[1], 283–4[3].

[2] *ib.* p. 646[1], 284[3].                          [3] *ib.* p. 62₀[1], 260[3].

[4] *ib.* p. 627[1], 262[3].

respect by Dionysius of Halicarnassus and by Plutarch, but they are now generally treated as too absurd to be taken seriously. Schleiermacher describes as 'a valuable discovery of modern times' the view that Plato meant all or most of his etymologies as mere parody and caricature. This view is accepted by Stallbaum, Brandis, Zeller[1] and others; but is opposed by Grote[2], who here (as elsewhere) appears to take an unduly literal and prosaic view of the flights of fancy and the play of humour which are among the most constant characteristics of Plato's manner. But, if we do not accept Plato's etymologies as intended to be taken seriously, it does not necessarily follow that he meant them as mere caricatures of the etymological speculations of his day. 'The position which he takes up in the *Cratylus* is' (as suggested to me by Dr Henry Jackson) 'a definite one, and seriously maintained. He holds that, whereas the significance of names is determined by custom and convention, the names themselves have their origin in attempts to represent vocally the things signified by them. For, secondary names are derived from primary names, and primary names are constructed out of rudimentary sounds, which, in virtue of the action of the organs used in producing them, are naturally suitable for the representation of certain rudimentary processes and states: *e.g.* the letter $\rho$, in virtue of the movement of the tongue in producing it, appropriately represents movement. But, to all appearance, he wishes to suggest (1) that, partly because from the beginning there was in names an arbitrary element, partly because in the course of time names have been corrupted and disguised, their origins are lost in obscurity; and (2) that, inasmuch as names could at best represent the views of their makers, they cannot be, as the Heracleiteans seem to have thought them, guides to truth. It would appear then that Plato attaches no value whatever to the particular etymologies offered; and, as in his wilder flights he ironically appeals to the authority of Euthyphro (396 D), it may well be that in this part of the exposition there is a satirical element. Moreover, Plato's interest in the general question about the origin of language is subordinate to his interest in the theory of ideal unities, which at the end of the dialogue he opposes to the dogma of Cratylus, that things are to be studied in their names'[3].

The dialogue has been discussed by Steinthal, who maintains that Plato begins by assuming that words exist as a product of *nature*, but ends by holding that they exist as the result of *convention*[4]. This view is confessedly opposed to the scholiastic tradition, as represented by Proclus, who makes Plato a supporter of the *natural* origin of language[5]; but the views may be reconciled by regarding Plato as holding an intermediate position between the adherents of *nature* and *convention*. It has also been discussed by many others[6],

---

[1] *Plato*, p. 213 n.				[2] *Plato*, ii 519—529.
[3] See also Dr Jackson's Praelection on the *Cratylus*, 1906.
[4] *Sprachwissenschaft*, i[2] 107, 150.			[5] *ib.* 168.
[6] *e.g.* Dittrich (Berlin) 1841; Schaarschmidt, *Rheinisches Museum*, xx 321—356, Alberti, *ib.* xxi 180—209, xxii 477—499, Lehrs, *ib.* xxii 436—440;

best perhaps by Deuschle[1], and (from the comparative philologist's point of view) by Benfey[2]. It is a dialogue of enduring interest as the earliest attempt at a philosophy of language, but language is here (as elsewhere) in Plato's view subordinate in importance to dialectic. Its general teaching seems, in Zeller's opinion, to be summed up in the conclusion that 'we must give up seeking in words a knowledge of things' (435 D–436 D, 438 C); 'we must turn our attention not to names, but to the things themselves' (439 A, 440 C), and 'acknowledge the dialectician to be superior to the maker of language' (389 A–390 E)[3]. Similarly, it has been shown by Mr D. D. Heath in the *Journal of Philology* (xvii 192–218) that Plato's sketch of the theory of nomenclature, and his discussion and criticism of the Heracleitean school, is entirely 'subordinate to the clearly expressed conclusion':—'A scientific nomenclature as perfect as possible *might* suffice for teaching the truths of nature. But, inasmuch as names are but images, and therefore necessarily imperfect representations of things, the surest way is the study of the things themselves; and therefore...*a knowledge of the truth of things, independently acquired, is a necessary preliminary to the formation of such an approximately perfect nomenclature*' (p. 193). On the question how far Plato is serious in his etymologies taken in detail Mr Heath holds that 'Plato had no thought of propounding an elaborate history and analysis of the Greek language', and that this part of the dialogue may be compared to the myths in other dialogues, described by Grote as 'fanciful illustrations invented to expand and enliven general views' (p. 201).

The controversy as to the origin of language long continued. Aristotle rejected the opinion that words existed naturally, and held that their meaning was purely conventional (*De Interp.* c. 2 and 4); Epicurus, that words existed at first naturally, and afterwards conventionally (θέσει)[4]. The Megarian philosopher, Diodorus, took the side of convention, and, by way of asserting his right to invent a language of his own, himself called one of his slaves ἀλλὰ μήν, and gave the others arbitrary names from other Greek particles[5]. The Stoics on the other hand traced the origin of language to nature[6]; and the same view was held by the Roman grammarian Nigidius Figulus (d. 45 B.C.), as we learn from Aulus Gellius (x 4), who describes the question as one which was much debated.

Luckow (Treptow) 1868; Hayduck (Breslau) and Dreykorn (Zweibrücken) 1869; also by Steinhart in his *Prolegomena*, Susemihl in his *Genetische Entwickelung*, i 144—174, and Ch. Lenormant in his *Commentaire* (Athens), 1861.

[1] *Die Platonische Sprachphilosophie* (Marburg), 1852, p. 83.
[2] *Göttingen Abhandlungen*, xii (1866), 189—330.
[3] Zeller's *Plato*, p. 214.
[4] Diog. Laert. x 75; Lucr. v 1027 f.
[5] Ammonius on Arist. *de Interp.* p. 103, ap. Lersch, i 42.
[6] Origen, *contra Celsum*, i 24 (Lersch, i 46).

Aristotle's treatise on Poetry includes an analysis of the parts of speech and other grammatical details (c. 20), and a passage on the gender of nouns (c. 21).   Probably   Aristotle both of these passages are interpolations.   In the former a 'letter' is defined, and letters divided into vowels, semivowels and mutes (φωνήεντα, ἡμίφωνα and ἄφωνα); a noun, a verb, and a 'connecting word' (σύνδεσμος) are also defined; and 'inflexion' (πτῶσις) is described as belonging to the noun and the verb, and expressing 'of', 'to', or the like, or the relation of number, or that of 'mode of address'[1].   In the *De Interpretatione* the verb in the present tense is the ῥῆμα, and the other tenses are its πτώσεις, and elsewhere the πτωσεις of a noun include even adjectives and adverbs. In contrast with πτῶσις, the nominative is called κλῆσις[2].   Various cases are distinguished by Aristotle, but their number and their names are still undetermined[3].   In addition to 'Active and Passive' Verbs, those subsequently known as 'Neuter' and 'Deponent' are now recognised for the first time[4].   The symbol of the rough breathing distinguishing ΟΡΟΣ 'boundary' from ΟΡΟΣ 'mountain' is called by Aristotle a παράσημον[5], the former word being probably written as ⊦ΟΡΟΣ.   The writings of Heracleitus are described as hard to punctuate (διαστίξαι)[6], but the only mark of punctuation actually mentioned by Aristotle is the παραγραφή[7], a short horizontal dash drawn below the first word of the line in which the sentence is about to end.   It is from this ancien-symbol, which marks the close of the sentence, that we give to the sentence itself, or to a connected group of sentences, the name of a 'paragraph'.

The only parts of speech that Aristotle recognises in the first chapter of the *Categories* are ὄνομα and ῥῆμα, the Noun and the Verb.   In the *Rhetoric*[8] and the *Problems*[9] he makes incidental mention of σύνδεσμοι, a term including conjunctions, connecting particles and even connecting clauses.   In the treatise on Poetry[10] he is also made to mention ἄρθρα (Pronouns and Articles), but we

---

[1] Classen, *l.c.*, 52—58; Steinthal, *l.c.*, i[2] 253–9.

[2] Steinthal, i[2] 266 f.                    [3] Classen, 64 f.

[4] Schwalbe's *Beitrag* (1838), p. 92.        [5] *Soph. El.* 177 *b* 3.

[6] *Rhet.* iii 5.          [7] *Rhet.* iii 8.        [8] iii 5 and 12.

[9] xix 20.                  [10] c. 20.

are assured by Dionysius of Halicarnassus [1] that only three parts of speech were recognised by Aristotle, and, for this and other reasons, the chapter in question is best regarded as an inter polation.

In the controversy as to the origin of language Aristotle, as already observed[2], is an adherent of 'convention' and not of 'nature'. The terms constituting a Proposition are declared by Aristotle to be a Noun in the nominative case as Subject, and a Verb as Predicate[3]; and the Verb is distinguished from the Noun as connoting time[4]. While Plato[5] regards the Proposition as composed of the ὄνομα and the ῥῆμα (having no other terms than these for Subject and Predicate), and expresses affirmation by φάσις and negation by ἀπόφασις, Aristotle has a technical term not only for affirmation (κατάφασις) and negation (ἀπόφασις) and for negative Noun and Verb, but also for Subject (τὸ ὑποκείμενον) and for Predicate (τὸ κατηγορούμενον)[6]. 'Subject' is in fact the modern form of *subjectum*, the late Latin rendering in Martianus Capella[7] of the term first found in Aristotle.

The further developement of the terminology of Grammar was reserved for the Stoics of the third and following centuries B.C.[8] Meanwhile, the Peripatetic School carried on the Aristotelian tradition by the special study of the history and the criticism of Literature. Our survey of the Athenian age may here conclude with a brief mention of a few of the members of that School.

**The Peripatetic School**

Heracleides Ponticus of Heraclea (*fl.* 340 B.C.) had been a pupil of Plato before he became a pupil of Aristotle. While his philosophical works were soon forgotten, his grammatical and literary writings long survived. He wrote on Rhetoric and Music, and also on Poetry and Poets, on Homeric problems, on the age of Homer and Hesiod, on Homer and Archilochus, and on Sophocles and Euripides. One of his works, entitled γραμματικά, may have touched on questions of literary criticism. The excerpts ἐκ τῶν Ἡρακλείδου περὶ

**Heracleides Ponticus**

---

[1] *De Comp.* c. 2.     [2] p. 96 *supra*.     [3] Grote's *Aristotle*, i 156.
[4] *De Interp.* 16 *b* 2.     [5] *Soph.* 261 f.
[6] *ib.* 194 f; cp. Steinthal, i² 183 f, 235 f.     [7] iv 361.     [8] p. 146 f.

πολιτειῶν are portions of an abridgement of the πολιτεῖαι of
Aristotle, now ascribed to Heracleides *Lembos*, an Alexandrian
'grammarian' who lived under Ptolemy Philometor (182–146 B.C.)[1].
A fellow-countryman and a rival of Heracleides Ponticus, named
Chamaeleon, wrote on Homer, Hesiod, Stesichorus,    Chamaeleon
Sappho, Anacreon, Lasus, Pindar, Simonides,
Thespis and Aeschylus; also on the early history of Tragedy
and on Ancient Comedy[2]. The Peripatetic School included
Aristoxenus of Tarentum, the leading authority in    Aristoxenus
the ancient world on Rhythm and Music (*fl.* 318
B.C.), who wrote on the History of Music, and on Tragic dancing
and Tragic poets, besides biographies of Pythagoras, Archytas,
Socrates and Plato[3].

The critical study of prose style was continued by Aristotle's
successor, Theophrastus of Eresos in Lesbos (372–    Theophrastus
287). Among the ten works on rhetoric ascribed to
him by Diogenes Laërtius[4] was a treatise *On Style* (περὶ λέξεως),
still extant in the time of Cicero. He is expressly named in
Cicero's *Orator* in connexion with the style of Herodotus and
Thucydides (§ 39), the four points of excellence in style (79), the
rhythm of prose (172, 228), and the use of the paean (194, 218);
while several passages may probably be traced to him, e.g. that on
delivery and its effect on the emotions (55), on beauty of diction
(80) and on moderation in the use of metaphor (81). To Theophrastus we also owe the division of style into the 'grand', the
'plain', and the 'mixed' or 'intermediate', adopted by Cicero in
§§ 20, 21. In the Augustan age his treatise on style is either
expressly quoted or otherwise noticed in several passages of
Dionysius of Halicarnassus[5], and is possibly the source of other

[1] Gräfenhan, *l.c.*, i 63 f, 360; Classen, *l.c.*, p. 8; Müller, *F. H. G.* ii
197—207; Christ, *Gr. Litt.* § 420[4]; also Unger, *Rhein. Mus.* xxxviii 481 ff;
Cohn, Breslau, 1884; Schrader, *Philol.* xliv 236 ff; Holzinger, *Philol.* liv, lvi;
Voss, Rostock, 1897; Susemihl, *Lit. Alex.* i 501–5.

[2] Athen. 406 E; Christ, § 420[4]; Köpke, Berlin, 1856.

[3] Müller, ii 262—292; Christ, § 422[4]; Hübner, *Bibliographic*, p. 12.

[4] v 46—50. Cp. Rabe's Bonn Diss. 1890.

[5] *De Comp.* 16, *De Lysia*, 14, *De Dem.* 3, *De Isocr.* 5; cp. Theophr.
*Fragm.* iii 93—96 Wimmer, and the present writer's ed. of Cic. *Orator*, p. lxx
and note on § 79; also A. Mayer, *Theophr.* περὶ λέξεως (Leipzig), 1910.

passages where his name is not mentioned[1]. Theophrastus also wrote a work on Comedy[2]. He and his school appear to have discussed the question whether by parts of speech ὄνομα and ῥῆμα alone were meant, or whether they also included ἄρθρα and σύνδεσμοι[3].

Among the younger pupils of Aristotle was Dicaearchus of Messana (347–287 B.C.), the author of an important work entitled βίος τῆς Ἑλλάδος. It was the first attempt at a history of civilisation, tracing the 'Life of Greece' from the dawn of history to the age of Alexander. It included an account of the geography and history, as well as the moral and religious condition of the country, besides embracing music and poetry in its extensive range. Treatises on Constitutions, such as those of Pellene, Corinth and Athens, mentioned by Cicero[4], may have either formed part of this work or served as materials for it; while that on 'musical competitions' may have belonged to a larger treatise on 'Dionysiac contests'. His name is assigned to certain Arguments to the plays of Sophocles and Euripides ; and those on the *Alcestis* and *Medea* are still extant. He also wrote biographies of the Seven Wise Men, and of Pythagoras and Plato, besides treating of the leading poets in the course of his great work on Greece. He did much for the study of Greek geography, and his maps were known to Cicero[5]; but he was much more than a mere student. He measured the altitudes of the mountains of the Peloponnesus, and he appeared as a public speaker at the Panathenaic festival at Athens, and at the Panhellenic festival at Olympia[6].

A pupil of Theophrastus, Praxiphanes of Rhodes or Mytilene (*fl.* 300 B.C.), was one of the first to pay special attention to 'grammatical' studies in the *literary* sense of the term[7]. His interests included history, poetry, rhetoric, and the criticism and interpretation of literature. He

---

[1] Usener (*D. H. de Imitatione*, 1889, p. 141) says of Dionysius : 'normas elocutionis aestimandae Theophrasto plerumque debet '.

[2] Athen. 261 D.          [3] Simplicius on Arist. *Categ.* fol. 8, ed. Ven.

[4] *Ad Atticum*, ii 2.          [5] *ib.* vi 2.

[6] Müller, *F. H. G.* ii 225 –253; Christ, § 421[4]; Hübner, p. 13.

[7] p. 7 *supra*.

was the first to suggest the spuriousness of the beginning of the
ordinary text of Hesiod's *Works and Days* on the ground of its
omission in the earlier MSS; and he also criticised the opening
words of Plato's *Timaeus*. His work on poetry was in the form
of a dialogue between Plato and Isocrates; and, probably between 291 and 287 B.C., he counted among his pupils Aratus and
Callimachus[1].

All the members of the Peripatetic School, whose names have
hitherto been mentioned, belonged by birth to other lands than
Attica. They had come from Italy and Sicily, from the shores of
the Euxine and from the islands across the Aegean, to find a
philosophic training of the most varied kind in the city which was
the school not of Greece alone but also of the Greek world in its
widest sense. We now turn in conclusion to the name of one
who, although he was the son of a freedman only, was nevertheless of Attic birth, and rose to the highest political position in
Athens, and even in his fall was a most appropriate intermediary
for the transmission of the learning of Athens to the new city,
which Alexander, the victorious advancer of Greek civilisation in
the distant East, had founded early in 330 B.C. on the western
verge of the Delta of the Nile.

Demetrius of Phaleron, who was born about 354–348 B.C. and
died after 283, was a pupil of Theophrastus, and
began his public career about 324. For a period of    Demetrius of
                                                      Phaleron
ten years (317—307) he ruled with distinction at
Athens as Regent for Cassander. As an incident of literary
interest, it may be mentioned that he was the first to introduce
recitations by rhapsodists into the *theatre* of Athens[2]. After his
fall in 307 he fled to Thebes, and, ten years later, in 297, left
for Egypt, where he attained great influence at the court of
Ptolemy I, and gave the first impulse towards the founding of the
Alexandrian Library. Having urged Ptolemy I not to appoint
Ptolemy Philadelphus as his successor, Demetrius was naturally
banished from Alexandria when Philadelphus became sole ruler in

---

[1] Susemihl, i 144 f; cp. Preller, *De Praxiphane* (1842) in *Ausgewählte
Aufsätze* (1864); also articles in *Hermes* xii 326 f (Wilamowitz), xiii 46 f
(Hirzel) and 446 f (Schöll).     [2] Athen. 620 B.

283.   Besides his numerous political and oratorical works, he wrote on the *Iliad* and the *Odyssey*, collected the Fables of Aesop, and drew up a chronological list of the Arcnons of Athens.   In his treatise on Rhetoric he told the story he had heard from Demosthenes himself, on the way in which the orator had in his youth corrected the defects of an indistinct delivery[1]; the work also included details as to the birth of Isaeus and the death of Isocrates, and as to the masterly manner in which the architect Philon described the construction of his naval armoury in the presence of the people[2].   The treatise περὶ ἑρμηνείας which bears his name belongs to a later age.   His public speeches are only represented by inadequate fragments ; we have therefore to rely mainly on Cicero for our knowledge of his oratorical charac-teristics.   He is described as the leading representative of the 'intermediate' style, which combines the minimum of force with the maximum of charm ; his diction was marked by a placid smoothness, and 'lit up by the stars of metaphor and metonymy'[3]. More florid than Lysias and Hypereides[4], he marks the beginning of the decline in Attic eloquence which followed the death of Demosthenes[5].   In the history of Scholarship he marks the close of the Athenian and the beginning of the Alexandrian age, serving as a link between the first capital of Greek culture and the second, in so far as, after holding a prominent position in the oratorical and political world of Athens, he prompted the founding of the famous Library of Alexandria.

[1] Plut. *Dem.* c. 11.                    [2] Cic. *de Or.* 1 62
[3] *Orator*, §§ 91 f.                      [4] *Brutus*, 285.
[5] *Introd.* to Cic. *Orator*, p. xxxiii.   Cp. Christ, § 424[4]; Susemihl, 1 135—144.

ALEXANDER THE GREAT.
Silver tetradrachm of Lysimachus, king of Thrace.
(From the British Museum.)

# BOOK II

## *THE ALEXANDRIAN AGE*

-----

πολλοὶ μὲν βόσκονται ἐν Αἰγύπτῳ πολυφύλῳ
βιβλιακοὶ χαρακῖται ἀπείριτα δηριόωντες
Μουσέων ἐν ταλάρῳ.

Timon of Phlius, ap. Athen. 22 D.

*In the thronging land of Egypt,*
*There are many that are feeding,*
*Many scribblers on papyrus*
*Ever ceaselessly contending,*
*In the bird-coop of the Muses.*

On the Alexandrian Museum, *c.* 230 B.C.

| Rulers of Egypt | Rulers of Pergamon, &c. | Poets | Scholars and Critics, &c. | Chronologers, Historians &c. | Philosophers |
|---|---|---|---|---|---|
| 330 foundation of Alexandria<br>323 d. of Alexander<br>Ptolemy I (*Soter*)<br>322 satrap<br>305 king<br>285 Ptolemy II (*Philadelphus*)<br>270 d. of Arsinoe II<br><br>247 Ptolemy III (*Euergetes* I)<br><br>238 decree of Canopus<br><br>222 Ptolemy IV (*Philopator*)<br>205 Ptolemy V (*Epiphanes*)<br>**200**—— | 283 Philetaerus<br>278 Antigonus Gonatas, king of Macedonia, d. 239<br>263 Eumenes I<br><br>241 Attalus I<br><br>222 Antiochus the Great, king of Syria, d. 187 | *floruit*<br>300 Philetas<br>*c.* 340—*c.* 285-3<br>290 Hermesianax<br>285 Alexander Aetolus b. *c.* 315<br>285 Lycophron b. *c.* 330—325<br>276 Aratus<br>276 Timon of Phlius *c.* 315—*c.* 226<br>272 Theocritus b. *c.* 324<br>Leonidas of Tarentum<br>260 Callimachus *c.* 310—*c.* 240<br>250 Apollonius Rhodius b. *c.* 283<br>250 Rhianus<br>*c.* 250 Herondas<br>220 Euphorion b. *c.* 276 | 285 Zenodotus *c.* 325—*c.* 234<br><br>234 Eratosthenes *c.* 275—*c.* 195<br><br>200 Hermippus | 295 Sosibius *c.* 280 Craterus<br>280 Berosus<br>277 Manetho<br>272 Hieronymus of Cardia<br>264 *Marmor Parium*<br>240 Antigonus of Carystos 295-0—*c.* 220 | 322 Theophrastus *P*<br>320 Pyrrhon *c.* 360—270<br>317-07 Demetrius of Phaleron *P*<br>314 Polemon *a*<br>308 Zeno *s* 364—263<br>306 Epicurus 341—270<br>304 Crantor *a*<br>300 Praxiphanes *P*<br>287 Straton *P*<br>276-0 Crates *a*<br>270 Arcesilas *a* *c.* 315—241<br>264 Cleanthes *s* 331—232<br>241 Lacydes *a*<br>232 Chrysippus *s* *c.* 280—*c.* 208-4 |
| 196 Rosetta stone<br>182 Ptolemy VI (*Eupator*)<br>182 Ptolemy VII (*Philometor*)<br>146 VIII (*Philopator Neos*)<br>146 IX (*Euergetes* II, or *Physcon*)<br>117 Cleopatra III and her sons X (*Philometor Soter* II, or *Lathyrus*) and XI (*Alexander*)<br>**100**—— | 197 Eumenes II<br><br>159 Attalus II<br><br>138 Attalus III<br>133 d. of Attalus, who makes Rome his heir | 150? Moschus<br>150 Nicander<br><br>Antipater of Sidon | 195 Aristophanes of Byzantium *c.* 257—*c.* 180<br>180 Aristarchus *c.* 220—145<br>168 Crates of Mallos<br><br>*c.* 145 Ammonius<br>*c.* 130 Dionysius Thrax | 197 Neanthes<br>191 Heracleides<br>*c.* 185 Polemon of Ilium<br><br>170 Demetrius of Scepsis b. *c.* 214<br>170 Polybius *c.* 205—*c.* 123<br>144 Apollodorus | 176 Aristobulus *P*<br>155 Carneades *a* *c.* 219—129<br>140 Panaetius *s* *c.* 181—*c.* 109<br>121 Cleitomachus *a* *c.* 175—*c.* 105<br>105 Philo of Larissa *a* *c.* 147—80 |
| 81 Ptolemy XII (*Alexander* II)<br>81 Ptolemy XIII (*Auletes*)<br><br>51 *Cleopatra* VI and Ptol. XIV, (47) Ptol. XV, and (45) *Caesarion*<br>30 Egypt becomes a Roman province | | 100? Bion<br>80? *Bionis epitaphius anon.*<br><br>60 Meleager<br><br>12 Antipater of Thessalonica | Ptolemy of Ascalon<br>Philoxenus<br>45 Apollodorus (rhetor) of Pergamon, 105-23<br>30 Didymus *c.* 65 B.C.—10 A.D.<br>Aristonicus<br>Tryphon<br>30—8 Dionysius of Halicarnassus<br>Caecilius<br>25 Juba d. 20 A.D.<br>Apollonius | 70 Castor of Rhodes<br>60 Diodorus (*c.* 90—*c.* 30) visits Egypt<br><br>24 Strabo (*c.* 63 B.C.—*c.* 24 A.D.) visits Egypt | 80 Antiochus *a* d. 68<br>80 Poseidonius *s* *c.* 135—*c.* 45<br>60 Andronicus *P*<br>55 Philodemus<br><br>Q. Sextius b. *c.* 70<br>Philo Judaeus b. 20 B.C. d. after 40 A.D. |

# CHAPTER VIII.

## THE SCHOOL OF ALEXANDRIA.

GREEK Scholarship was fostered in Alexandria under the rule of the earlier Ptolemies. It was during the reign of Ptolemy Soter, who had been satrap of Egypt from 322 to 305 B.C., and was king from 305 to 285, that Demetrius of Phaleron gave the first impulse towards the founding of public libraries in the Egyptian capital (*c.* 295 B.C.)[1]. Ptolemy Soter, who had in vain invited Theophrastus and Menander to settle in Alexandria, entrusted the education of his son and successor Ptolemy Philadelphus (285–247) to the poet and scholar, Philetas of Cos, and to the philosopher, Straton, the successor of Theophrastus; and the monarchical city of Alexandria took the place of democratic Athens as the literary centre of the Greek world. Early in the Alexandrian age literary institutions of the highest importance were founded in the city of the Ptolemies. The foundation of the Great Library in particular was probably due in the first instance to Ptolemy Soter, acting under the advice of Demetrius[2], but the credit is often assigned to Philadelphus, who may have continued and completed his father's designs[3], though he was himself mainly interested in zoology[4]. Philadelphus[5] is also credited with the foundation of the splendid shrine of learning known as the Μουσεῖον, 'the temple, or home, of the Muses', which is described by Strabo,

The Museum

---

[1] Susemihl, *Geschichte der griechischen Litteratur in der Alexandrinerzeit* (1891), i 6, 138.

[2] Wilamowitz, *Antigonos von Karystos*, p. 291, and Kuiper (Utrecht) 1894 (Mahaffy's *Empire of the Ptolemies*, 1895, p. 92).

[3] Susemihl, i 6—7.

[4] Diodorus, iii 36, 3 f (Mahaffy, *l.c.*, p. 128 f).

[5] Athen. 203 C, E.

who visited Alexandria in 24 B.C., as forming part of the royal
quarter of the city, and as including a covered walk, an arcade
furnished with recesses and seats, and a large building containing
a common hall, in which the Scholars who were members of the
Museum met for their meals. This learned body had endowments;
and its president, nominated by the government, was called 'the
priest of the Museum'[1]. The provision for the maintenance of
these Scholars was apparently on so liberal a scale that a satirical
poet of that age, Timon of Phlius (writing about 230 B.C.),
humorously called it a 'bird-coop of the Muses'[2]. It is among
the attractions of Alexandria mentioned by Herondas[3], immediately
after the θεῶν ἀδελφῶν τέμενος, the precinct of the temple of
Philadelphus and his sister and wife, Arsinoe II, who (as we now
know)[4] died in 270 B.C.[5] It had some points of contact with
the Academy and the Lyceum. The name recalls the Platonic
brotherhood, or *thiasos*, with its common cult of the Muses in the
'groves of Academe', as well as the 'Museum' mentioned in the
will of Theophrastus[6]; while its covered walk, or *peripatos*, is no
less suggestive of still earlier memories of the Peripatetic School.
But we may realise its character still better by regarding it as a
kind of prototype of a College at Oxford or Cambridge, with its
common hall for dining and its cloisters and grounds, and with
some provision for the endowment of research. The members of
the Museum probably received annual stipends; but whether the
Library, as in an English College, was part of the buildings of the
Museum, is unknown, though it was probably very near them.
We are also unaware whether there were any arrangements for
instruction. Even 500 years after its foundation it is eulogised by
Philostratus as a society of celebrities[7]; in the following century

[1] p. 793 f, τῶν δὲ βασιλείων μέρος ἐστὶ καὶ τὸ Μουσεῖον, ἔχον περίπατον
καὶ ἐξέδραν καὶ οἶκον μέγαν, ἐν ᾧ τὸ συσσίτιον τῶν μετεχόντων τοῦ Μουσείου
φιλολόγων ἀνδρῶν κτλ.

[2] Quoted on p. 103.                    [3] i 31.

[4] Mahaffy's *Ptolemaic Dynasty*, p. 79. Cp. *Rhein. Mus.* liii 464.

[5] For portraits of Ptolemy Soter (and Berenike I) and also of Ptolemy
Philadelphus and Arsinoe II, see coin inscribed ΘΕΩΝ ΑΔΕΛΦΩΝ
on p. 145.                               [6] Diog. Laert. v 51.

[7] *Vit. Soph.* i 22, 5 τράπεζα Αἰγυπτία ξυγκαλοῦσα τοὺς ἐν πάσῃ τῇ γῇ
ἐλλογίμους.

the quarter of the city where it lay is described by Ammianus Marcellinus as 'having long been the home of eminent men'[1], while the last who is actually named as a member of the Museum is the celebrated mathematician and neo-platonist Theon (*fl.* 380 A.D.), the father of the noble-hearted and ill-fated Hypatia (d. 415 A.D.). It is in connexion with the pathetic story of her life that the old associations of this memorable haunt of Alexandrian scholars and poets have been happily characterised by Kingsley :—'School after school, they had all walked and taught and sung there, beneath the spreading planes and chestnuts, figs and palm trees. The place seemed fragrant with all the riches of Greek thought and song'[2].

The other literary institutions of the earlier Ptolemies were the two libraries. The larger of these is stated to have been in the *Brucheion*, the N.E. quarter of Alex-
    The Library
andria, and was probably very close to the Museum[3]. It has however been conjecturally placed in the *western* half of the city, S.E. of the Heptastadion, about 400 yards from the Great Harbour, and to the north of the main street, which was lined with shady colonnades[4] and extended for nearly four miles from the N.E. to the S.W. of Alexandria[5]. 'There it towered up, the wonder of the world, its white roof bright against the rainless blue; and beyond it, among the ridges and pediments of noble buildings, a broad glimpse of the bright sea'[2].

The smaller Library, sometimes called the 'daughter-library', was in the *Rhakôtis*, the S.W. quarter, near the temple of Serapis

---

[1] xxii 16, diuturnum praestantium hominum domicilium. The Museum and the Libraries of Alexandria have been the theme of several monographs, by Ritschl (*Opuscula*, i 1 f), Parthey, and Klippel, all in 1838, and by Göll 1868, Weniger 1875, and Couat 1879; they have also been discussed by Clinton, *Fasti*, iii 380 f; Bernhardy, *Gr. Litt.* i 527—542[4]; Susemihl, *l.c.*; Holm, *Gr. Hist.* iv, c. 14; Mahaffy's *Empire of the Ptolemies*, 91—99; and Dziatzko in Pauly-Wissowa, s.v. *Bibliotheken*, 409—414.

[2] *Hypatia*, c. 2.         [3] Susemihl, i 336.

[4] Aristides, ii 450 Dind., ἐν τῷ μεγάλῳ δρόμῳ τῷ κατὰ τὰς στοάς.

[5] Cp. Dziatzko, in Pauly-Wissowa, s.v. *Bibliotheken*, p. 412. Similarly Botti's map of 1898, reproduced in Mahaffy's *Egypt under the Ptolemaic Dynasty*, puts the Museum in the middle of the Neapolis, and south of the Emporium, with the Public Gardens between the Museum and the main street; but this seems too far west from the Brucheion and the Royal Palace.

and 'Pompey's Pillar', and not far from the Mareotic lake,
The Library<br>of the<br>Serapeum which extends behind the spit of land on which
Alexandria was built. It is this Library which is
doubtless intended by the rhetorician Aphthonius
(end of cent. iv), when he mentions it in the course
of his glowing description of the 'acropolis' of Alexandria. The
description has a twofold interest, firstly, because it appears to
imply that, by the time when it was written, an 'acropolis' had
been formed on the rising ground surrounding the Serapeum[1],
and secondly, because the Library is stated to have been closely
connected with a temple and with certain colonnades, and both
of these are among the characteristics of ancient libraries[2]

The completion of the Library of the *Serapeum*, like that of
the Great Library of the *Brucheion*, may be ascribed to Ptolemy
Philadelphus. It was also Philadelphus who, according to the
'Letter of Aristeas', quoted by Josephus[3], caused the Law of
Moses to be translated into Greek by a commission of learned
Jewish elders, thus beginning the version known as the *Septuagint*,
probably projected in the reign of Ptolemy Soter[4]. To the reign
of Philadelphus, and to about the year 255 B.C., belongs the
settlement of a Greek colony in the newly reclaimed and greatly
enlarged oasis of Lake Moeris, now known as the Faiyûm. The
Hellenic culture of that district is attested by the numerous *papyri*
there discovered by Mr Flinders Petrie in 1889-90, including
portions of the *Phaedo* and *Laches* of Plato, and of the *Antiope* of
Euripides, ascribed to the 3rd century B.C.[5]

It may here be observed that Zoïlus of Amphipolis, whose
name is proverbial for the bitterness of his criticisms on Homer,
is wrongly assigned to the age of Philadelphus, who is described

---

[1] Cp. Clem. Alex. *Protrep.* p. 14 Sylburg.

[2] Aphthonius, *Progymnasmata*, c. 12 (i 107 Walz), παρῳκοδόμηνται δὲ
σηκοὶ τῶν στοῶν ἔνδοθεν, οἱ μὲν ταμίαι γεγενημένοι τοῖς βίβλοις, τοῖς φιλοπονοῦσιν
ἀνεῳγμένοι φιλοσοφεῖν, καὶ πόλιν ἅπασαν εἰς ἐξουσίαν τῆς σοφίας ἐπαίροντες, οἱ δὲ
τοὺς πάλαι τιμᾶν ἱδρυμένοι θεούς.

[3] *Ant. Jud.* xii 2.

[4] Susemihl, i 6 (note) and Swete's *Introduction to the Greek Old Testament*,
pp. 9—28, 520.

[5] Mahaffy's *Empire of the Ptolemies*, pp. 156, 180 ; Kenyon, *Palaeography
of Greek papyri*, p. 6 f. Cp. *Facsimile* on p. 87 *supra*.

in Vitruvius[1] as having listened to his criticisms with silent
contempt, and also as having caused him to be crucified for his
pains.  Zoïlus the critic is now regarded as identical with Zoïlus
the rhetorician, and his true date is determined by the fact that
the rhetorician was a pupil of Polycrates, an earlier contemporary
of Isocrates, that his rhetorical writings are said to have been
studied by Demosthenes in his youth (c. 365 B.C.), and that he
composed a historical work ending with the death of Philip
(336 B.C.).  He accordingly flourished between the above dates.
The description of his person in Aelian[2], his short cloak, his long
beard and his closely shaven crown, are suggestive of a Cynic.
His pupil Anaximenes was also a pupil of Diogenes the Cynic ; it
was probably in sympathy with the Cynics that he attacked Plato;
like Antisthenes, the founder of the Cynics, he also attacked
Isocrates ; and above all he signalised himself by attacking
Homer.  His criticisms on Homer filled nine books, and the
designation *Homeromastix*, said by Suïdas to have been a nickname of the anthor, may possibly have been the title of the work.
It included an encomium on the ill-used Cyclops, Polyphemus, in
the course of which the critic remarked that, as soon as Odysseus
had been cursed by the Cyclops, he was abandoned even by
his guardian-goddess Athene[3].  The companions of Odysseus,
described by the poet as 'weeping' when turned into swine by
Circe, he ridiculed as 'whining porkers'[4]; he satirised the
perfect symmetry with which Odysseus, in his contest with the
Cicones, lost exactly six men from each of his ships[5]; he criticised
the poet for describing Achilles as bidding Patroclus 'mingle
stronger drink' for the Achaean envoys[6]; Apollo, as making the
innocent mules and dogs of the Achaean camp the first victims of
his pestilential arrows[7]; and Zeus himself, as weighing the Fates
in a pair of scales[8].  Like Plato[9], he found fault with the
inordinate grief of Achilles over the death of Patroclus[10].  He
also carped at the description of Athene causing 'the fire to blaze

---

[1] *Praef.* vii.
[2] *Var. Hist.* xi 10.
[3] Schol. on 'Plato's' *Hipparchus*, p. 229 D.
[4] χοιρίδια κλαίοντα (περὶ ὕψους, 9 § 14).
[5] *Od.* ix 60.
[6] *Il.* ix 203.
[7] *Il.* i 50.
[8] *Il.* xxii 209.
[9] *Rep.* 388 A.
[10] *Il.* xviii 22.

from the head and shoulders' of Diomedes[1], to the peril of that
hero's life, and of Idaeus '*leaving* his stately chariot'[2], when he
might have escaped more easily (if that indeed had been his
object) by remaining in it.   He attacked the statement that 'the
spirit fled away *beneath* the ground, like smoke'[3], whereas smoke
rises upwards.  Like Chrysippus, he charged Homer with combining a plural verb with a singular noun in *Il.* i 129, Ζεὺς δῶσι, and
was refuted by Aristarchus, who pointed out that the right reading
was δῷσι (the contracted form of the 3rd Person Singular of the
Subjunctive Aorist δώῃσι), as in *Od.* i 168, πατὴρ ἀποδῷσιν[4]  But,
in comparison with the attacks on the poet's invention, the attacks
on his grammar are rather rare.   A confused legend preserved by
Suïdas makes the assembled Greeks at *Olympia* indignantly drive
him from the festival and fling him down from the crest of the
Scironian cliffs,—which are not far from the scene of the *Isthmian*
games.   One or two of his criticisms on Homer (those on *Il.* i 50
and ix 203) happen to be identical with those to which Aristotle
replies in his treatise on Poetry (c. 25).   In the Alexandrian age
the first to answer his attack on Homer was Athenodorus, the
brother of the poet Aratus[5], while in Roman times he is described
by Ovid as owing his name and fame solely to his envious detrac-
tion of the merits of Homer :

> 'ingenium magni livor detrectat Homeri :
> quisquis es, ex illo, Zoïle, nomen habes'[6].

To return to our immediate subject, the number of MSS
comprised in the two Alexandrian Libraries is variously stated.
We are informed that, in reply to a royal inquiry, it was stated by
Demetrius of Phaleron (about 285 B.C.), that it was already
200,000, and that he would soon bring it up to 500,000[7].   In
the time of Callimachus (*c.* 310—*c.* 240 B.C.), the larger Library
contained 400,000 volumes, including several works in each

---

[1] *Il.* v 7.                                    [2] *Il.* v 20.
[3] *Il.* xxiii 100.                          [4] Cobet, *Misc. Crit.* 339.
[5] Susemihl, i 293, note 39.
[6] *Remed. Amoris*, 365 (cp. Pope's *Essay on Criticism*, 465 f, and the
sequel to l. 124 in the first draft of the poem).  On Zoïlus see esp. Lehrs, *De
Aristarchi studiis*, 200-7[3], and Blass, *Att. Ber.* ii[2] 373-8; and cp. Clinton's
*Fasti*, iii 380 f, 485.
[7] 'Aristeas' ap. Euseb. *Praep. Ev.* viii[2] p. 350 a.

volume, and also 90,000 separate works[1]. In the middle of the first century B.C. the number is said to have been 700,000[2]. The smaller Library comprised 42,800 volumes[3], which were probably comparatively modern MSS with each roll complete in itself[4].

The Ptolemies are said to have resorted to many ingenious devices with a view to adding to the treasures of their Libraries. We are told by Galen[5] that the numerous vessels which entered the harbour were compelled to surrender any MSS which they had on board, and that the owners of these MSS had to rest content with copies of the same; these MSS were known as τὰ ἐκ πλοίων, and among them (according to one version of the story) was a MS of a book of Hippocrates brought to Alexandria by the physician Mnemon of Side in Pamphylia[6]. Galen is also the authority for the story already quoted[7] as to the way in which the official text of the three great tragic poets of Athens was secured for Alexandria by Ptolemy Euergetes, *i.e.* either the first of that name (247—222 B.C.), or the second[8], also known as Ptolemy Physcon (146—117 B.C.). The keenest rivalry arose between the royal patrons of learning at Alexandria and Pergamon. It is even stated that one of the Ptolemies, probably Philadelphus, prohibited the export of paper made from the Egyptian *papyrus*, and thus led to the use of skins of animals as materials for writing in the reign of the Pergamene prince, Eumenes (I, 263—241 B.C.)[9]. But such materials had been long in use, so that we can only infer that improvements in their preparation were introduced at Pergamon. In process of time skins were made smooth for writing on *both* sides, instead of only one, and the material thus manufactured was called *charta pergamena*, or 'parchment'; but the word is not found earlier than the Edict of Diocletian (301 A.D.)[10]. Eumenes II (197—159 B.C.) is said to have invited the Alexandrian Librarian, Aristophanes of Byzantium, to leave Alexandria for Pergamon, and the mere suspicion that the

[1] Tzetzes, ap. Susemihl, i 342.
[2] Gellius vi 17; Amm. Marc. xxii 16, 13.            [3] Tzetzes, *u.s.*
[4] Dziatzko, *l.c.*, p. 411.            [5] xvii *a*, p. 606.
[6] Susemihl, i 815, ii 681.            [7] p. 58 *supra*.
[8] Usener in Susemihl, ii 667.            [9] Pliny, *N. H.* xiii 70.
[10] Birt, *Antike Buchwesen*, p. 51.

Librarian was ready to accept such an invitation prompted Ptolemy Epiphanes (205—182 B.C.) to put him in prison[1]. The royal passion for collecting MSS at Alexandria and Pergamon naturally led to the fabrication of many spurious works[2]; and to various devices for giving recent copies a false appearance of antiquity[3]; it also led to careless transcription for the mere sake of rapidity of production[4].

It will be remembered that the Library has been conjecturally placed at a distance of about 400 yards from the harbour of Alexandria[5]. In 47 B.C., shortly after the death of Pompey, the conflicts between the Roman soldiers and the Egyptians in the streets of the city compelled Caesar to set the royal fleet on fire to prevent its falling into the hands of the Egyptians. The naval arsenal was also burnt[6]. According to the historian Orosius (*c.* 415 A.D.), the flames spread to the shore, where 40,000 volumes *happened* to be stored up in the adjacent buildings[7] The phrase used by Orosius has led to the conjecture that these volumes, having been removed by Caesar from the Library, were temporarily stacked in certain buildings near the harbour, with a view to their being shipped to Rome as part of the spoils of conquest: and that the burning of these books led to the legend of the burning of the Library[8]. It is not at all probable that the Library itself was at this time consumed by fire. The author of the *Bellum Alexandrinum*[9] expressly states that, as even the private houses of the citizens, including the very floors and roofs, were built entirely of stone, Alexandria was in general safe from the risk of a conflagration. Writing about 80 A.D., Plutarch in

[1] Suïdas, ap. Susemihl. i 431; cp. ii 667.

[2] Galen, xv p. 105, πρὶν γὰρ τοὺς ἐν Ἀλεξανδρείᾳ καὶ Περγάμῳ γενέσθαι βασιλεῖς ἐπὶ κτήσει βιβλίων φιλοτιμηθέντας, οὐδέπω (!) ψευδῶς ἐπεγέγραπτο σύγγραμμα· λαμβάνειν δ' ἀρξαμένων μισθὸν τῶν κομιζομένων αὐτοῖς σύγγραμμα παλαιοῦ τινος ἀνδρός, οὕτως ἤδη πολλὰ ψευδῶς ἐπιγράφοντες ἐκόμιζον, and *ib.* p. 109.

[3] David (or Elias) in Schol. on Aristot. 28 *a* 13 f (Susemihl, ii 413, note 367).      [4] Strabo, 609 (Susemihl, ii 667 f).

[5] p. 107 *supra.*      [6] Caesar, *B. C.* iii 111.

[7] Orosius, vi 15, 31, quadraginta milia librorum proximis *forte* aedibus condita exussit.

[8] Parthey *Museum Alex.* p. 32.      [9] i 2.

his *Life of Caesar*[1] implies that the flames spread from the
fleet to the docks and from the docks to the Library; and, early
in the 3rd century, Dio Cassius[2] describes the arsenal and the
stores of corn and of books as having perished in the flames;
but these accounts seem less probable than the suggestion that it
was not the Library itself, but only those of the books which had
been transferred to buildings near the harbour, that suffered
destruction. The Court Journals at Alexandria were consulted
not only by Diodorus Siculus[3], before Caesar's visit, but also by
Appian[4] long after (*c.* 160 A.D.). The story of the burning of the
Library is not mentioned either by Cicero, who shortly afterwards
induced Cleopatra, during her stay in Rome, to promise to get
him some books from Alexandria[5], or by Strabo, who visited
Alexandria only 22 years later. The earliest mention of the
disaster which befell the MSS is in Seneca[6]. 'The Pergamene
Libraries', containing 200,000 separate volumes, were presented
to Cleopatra by Antonius in 41 B.C.[7], and Domitian is said to
have supplemented the deficiences of the libraries in Italy by
means of transcripts from the Alexandrian MSS[8]. In the time of
Aurelian (272 A.D.) the larger part of the region of Alexandria in
which the Library was situated was laid waste[9], and it may be
conjectured that this was the date when the Library suffered most
damage; for, late in the following century, we find a rhetorician
of Antioch, Aphthonius, assigning a special importance to another
Library, identified as that of the *Serapeum*[10]. Under Theodosius I
(391 A.D.) the temple of Serapis, which had been partly burnt in
183 A.D., was demolished, and transformed into a church and
monastery, by Theophilus, the patriarch of Alexandria, and the
lesser Library of the Serapeum can hardly have survived this
destruction. Orosius, at the time of his visit, saw only empty
book-cases in 'the temples' of the city[11], but his evidence is very

[1] c. 49.                                    [2] xlii 38.
[3] iii 38.                                   [4] *Praef.* 10.
[5] *Ad Att.* xiv 8, xv 15 (Mahaffy, *l.c.*, 461).
[6] *De Tranq. An.* 9, quadraginta milia librorum Alexandriae arserunt.
[7] Plut. *Ant.* 58.                          [8] Suet. *Dom.* 20.
[9] Amm. Marc. xxii 16, 5.
[10] Aphthonius, quoted on p. 108.
[11] Orosius, vi 15, 32, quamlibet hodieque in templis exstent, quae et nos

vague[1]. In 642 A.D., when Amrou, the general of Omar, Caliph
of the Saracens, captured Alexandria, it is stated that Johannes
Philoponus, the commentator on Aristotle, asked the conqueror
for the gift of the Alexandrian Library, that the conqueror felt
constrained to consult the Caliph, and that the Caliph made the
well-known reply:—'if these writings of the Greeks agree with
the book of God, they are useless and need not be preserved; if
they disagree, they are pernicious and ought to be destroyed'.
It is added that the contents of the Library were consigned to the
flames, and that they served for six months as fuel for the 4000
baths of Alexandria. The authority for this story is Abul-
pharagius[2]; but it has been urged by Gibbon[3] that his account,
written in a distant province six centuries after the event, is
refuted by the silence of two annalists of an earlier date and of
a direct connexion with Alexandria, the more ancient of whom,
the patriarch Eutychius, has minutely described the destruction
of the city. The destruction of books, the historian adds, is
contrary to the principles of Mohammedanism. In any case it
may well be doubted whether any large number of ancient MSS
were still to be found in Alexandria at the date of its capture by
the general of the Saracens[4].

The first four Librarians of Alexandria were Zenodotus
(c. 285—c. 234 B.C.); Eratosthenes (c. 234—195);
The Librarians      Aristophanes of Byzantium (195—180); and Aristarchus (180 or 172—146). It has sometimes been
supposed that Callimachus was Librarian between the time of
Zenodotus and that of Eratosthenes; and Apollonius Rhodius,
between that of Eratosthenes and Aristophanes; but chrono-

---

vidimus, armaria librorum, quibus direptis exinanita et a rusticis hominibus
nostris temporibus memorant, etc.

[1] Gibbon, iii 495 Bury.

[2] *Dvnast.* p. 114, vers. Pocock (cp. Gibbon, v 453, 515, Bury).

[3] c. 51.

[4] Cp. Susemihl, i 344. The modern writers agreeing or disagreeing with
Gibbon on this point are quoted by Parthey, *Mus. Alex.* p. 106. Cp. notes in
Bury's ed. of Gibbon, v 454, and 452 (where it is observed that Philoponus
lived more than a century before the conquest of Alexandria). Cp. p. 377
*infra.*

logical considerations make this view improbable[1]. Nearly a
century after the appointment of Aristarchus, an inscription from
Paphos shows that the office was given, after 89 B.C., to a kinsman
and priest of Ptolemy Soter II (Lathyrus), named Onesander,
who is otherwise unknown[2].

Of the names above mentioned Callimachus and Apollonius
Rhodius are celebrated in the history of Literature as well as in
that of Scholarship; we may therefore cast a passing glance on
the literature of the Alexandrian age before giving a more detailed
account of the representatives of Scholarship in the same period.

The literature of this age was slavishly imitative rather than
spontaneously creative; it was inspired not by the
immediate impulse of true genius, but by the       Alexandrian
reflected reminiscences of a golden age that was       literature
gone for ever; it appealed not to the general body of free citizens,
but to the cultivated few, who formed a separate class of men of
learned and critical tastes, either actually enjoying or attempting
to attract the favour of the court, amid the multitudinous popula-
tion of a vast commercial city. In this age poetry was produced
by men of learning, who may be described as professional men of
letters. Parody and Satire are represented by Timon of Phlius
(c. 315—c. 226), who lived at Calchedon and Athens, cultivating
his garden to the age of nearly ninety, and using the vehicle of
hexameter verse for those criticisms on the dogmatic schools of
philosophy, which incidentally supply us with an early satirical
allusion to the Alexandrian Museum[3]. Pastoral Poetry is admirably represented by Theocritus of Syracuse (*fl.* 272 B.C.). Of
his idylls, the 17th (273–1 B.C.) is an *encomium* on Ptolemy
Philadelphus, celebrating his extensive empire, his extraordinary
wealth, and his generosity towards priests and poets; the 14th
(after 269 B.C.) is on the soldiers in his service; the 15th, the
*Adoniazusae* (before 270 B.C.), paints a graphic picture of the
thronging crowds of Alexandria at a festival attended by two

[1] Busch, *De bibliothecariis Alex. qui feruntur primis*, 1884; Dziatzko in
Pauly-Wissowa, s.v. *Bibliotheken*, p. 412; Gercke in *Jahresb.* vol. 150,
p. 484 f.

[2] *Journ. Hell. St.* ix 240.

[3] p. 103 *supra*.

ladies from Syracuse; while, for the dwellers amid the dust and din and glare of Alexandria, there was a peculiar charm in his inimitable pastoral poems, with their glimpses of the idyllic life of shepherds and herdsmen resting beside the fountains beneath the plane-trees, or amid the pine-woods and the upland pastures that look down on the Sicilian sea. With Theocritus we associate the two other idyllic poets, Moschus of Syracuse, the author of the *Runaway Eros* (*c.* 150), and Bion of Smyrna, the author of the *Lament for Adonis* (*c.* 100 B.C.)[1]. The *Mimes* of Herondas, first published in 1891, may be as early as the latter part of the reign of Philadelphus. Theocritus and Herondas alike found a model in the *Mimes* of Sophron, which must have remained in existence till late in the first or early in the second century A.D., as the label of a MS of that date has been found in Egypt[2]. Didactic Poetry is represented by Aratus of Soli, who lived at the court of Pella (276 B.C.), and imitated Hesiod in his extant astronomical poem entitled the *Phaenomena*, paraphrased from Eudoxus, concluding with *Prognostics of the Weather*, paraphrased from Theophrastus. It was a work that won the praises of Callimachus[3], and, in the Roman age, the compliment of repeated translation by Varro Atacinus, Cicero, Germanicus and Avienus. Didactic poetry is also represented by the extant epics on venomous bites (*Thêriaca*) and on antidotes (*Alexipharmaca*) composed by Nicander (150 B.C.), one of whose lost poems was imitated in the *Metamorphoses* of Ovid. Other learned types of verse are represented by the elegiac Hymns and Epigrams of Callimachus (*c.* 310—*c.* 235), by the epic poem of Apollonius Rhodius (*fl. c.* 250—200) on the Argonauts, and by the iambic drama of Lycophron (*c.* 295). In the same age mathematical and other kindred sciences were represented by Euclid (*fl.* 300 B.C.)[4], and Archimedes of Syracuse (*c.* 287—212 B.C.); by those masters of Mechanics, Heron of Alexandria and Philon of Byzantium; by the earliest writer on Conic Sections, Apollonius of Perga, and by

---

[1] On Bion's date, cp. Bücheler, in *Rhein. Mus.* xxx 33—41; Knaack, in Pauly-Wissowa, *s.v.*; and Christ, § 365[4], p. 547, n. 3.

[2] *Oxyrhynchus Papyri*, ii p. 303.          [3] *Anth.* ix 507.

[4] It was Ptolemy I who was informed by Euclid that there was no royal road to geometry (Proclus, *in Eucl.* p. 68).

the astronomer, Hipparchus of Nicaea; Geography, by Eratosthenes; the Chronology of Chaldaea by Berôsus (280), that of Egypt by Manetho (277), and that of Greece by the unknown author of the Parian Marble, now in Oxford, with its summary of Greek history beginning from the earliest times and originally ending with 264 B.C.[1] The important trilingual inscriptions, in hieroglyphic and demotic Egyptian and in Greek, which are known as the 'decree of Canopus', discovered by Lepsius in 1865, and the 'decree of Memphis' or the 'Rosetta Stone', found by the French near the Rosetta mouth of the Nile in 1798, belong to the years 238 and 196 respectively[2]. The 'Rosetta Stone' was placed in the British Museum in 1802, and the Greek text restored by Porson early in the following year; it afterwards supplied Young and Champollion with the key to the deciphering of Egyptian hieroglyphics. The great age of Alexandrian criticism is drawing to its end with the death of Aristarchus about 145 B.C., when we reach an important representative of History in the person of Polybius (c. 205—c. 123), who in 146 B.C. witnessed the destruction of Carthage and the burning of Corinth, closing with that year his record of Roman conquest, which throws light on the history of Egypt, especially between the accession of Ptolemy Philopator (222 B.C.) and that of Ptolemy Physcon (146). Though he is the first great historian since Herodotus and Thucydides, he is little interested in the earlier Greek literature, quoting Herodotus only twice, and Thucydides and Xenophon only once. His historic vision rests far less on Alexandria than on Rome; and, in the history of Scholarship, his work is mainly interesting as the earliest and best example, now extant, of the 'common dialect' founded on Attic Prose,

---

[1] ed. Flach, 1884, and F. Jacoby, 1904, and in *Rhein. Mus.* lix. The fall of Troy is here assigned to 1208 B.C. (It had previously been assigned to 1171 B.C. by Sosibius, a member of the Alexandrian Museum under Ptolemy II, and the author of a chronological work, in which Homer is described as having flourished *c.* 865 B.C. The fall of Troy was afterwards placed by Eratosthenes in 1184, and this has become the traditional date.) A new fragment published in *Ath. Mitt.* 1897, p. 183, covering the years 336—299, shows that the first prize was won by Menander in 316 (not in 322), and by Philemon in 328, the life of the latter thus probably extending from *c.* 350 to 263—2.

[2] Texts in Mahaffy, *l.c.*, pp. 226—239, and 316—327.

which prevailed in the Greek world from about 300 B.C.[1]   In the century after Polybius we find in Diodorus Siculus (*c.* 40 B.C.) a historian who took Ephorus, the pupil of Isocrates, for his model, and who, in compiling a history which ended with Caesar's Gallic Wars, consulted the Libraries and the public archives of Rome, visited Alexandria and parts of Upper Egypt about 60 B.C., and, in relating the early history of Egypt, paused over the name of the ancient king, Osymandyas, who placed above the portal of a library of sacred books in Thebes an inscription describing it as a 'sanatorium for the soul'[2].   Of Alexandria at the date of his own visit he tells us, as an eye-witness, that a Roman who had accidentally killed a cat was mercilessly put to death by the populace[3].   The incident is of some importance for our present purpose.   It proves that the mob of Alexandria was 'no longer Greek, as it professed to be', but was 'deeply saturated with Egyptian blood'[4], thus showing that, towards the close of the Alexandrian age, as at the beginning, Greek civilisation in Alexandria was confined to a very limited circle.

The Alexandrian age is in the main an age of erudition and

Philetas

criticism.   Even its poets are often scholars.   The earliest of the scholars and poets of this age is Philetas of Cos[5] (*c.* 340—*c.* 285–3), the preceptor not only of Ptolemy Philadelphus (about 295–2 B.C.), but also of Zenodotus and of the elegiac poet Hermesianax.   He was remarkable for the extreme delicacy of his frame; it is even stated that he was compelled to wear leaden soles to prevent his being blown away by the wind[6].   He was the author of a glossary of unusual poetic words, quoted as ἄτακτα or ἄτακτοι γλῶσσαι or simply γλῶσσαι[7]. The readings which he preferred in the Homeric text are mentioned in several of the *scholia*[8], while those preferred by a greater Homeric scholar, Aristarchus, were noted by the latter in a work

---

[1] Cp. O. Cuntz, *Polybios und sein Werk*, 1902.

[2] Diod. Sic. i 49, 3, ψυχῆς ἰατρεῖον.   The king has been identified with Ramses (II) Miamun (cent. 14 B.C.).

[3] Diodorus, i 14.

[4] Mahaffy, *l.c.* 440.        [5] Strabo, 657 ult., ποιητὴς ἅμα καὶ κριτικός.

[6] Athen. 552 B; Aelian, *V. H.* ix 14.        [7] Cp. Athen. 383 B.

[8] *Il.* ii 269, xxi 126, 179, 252 (Susemihl, i 179, n. 26).

entitled πρὸς Φιλητᾶν¹. About 292 he returned to Cos, where
he apparently presided over a brotherhood of poets including
Theocritus and Aratus². Cos had been 'liberated' from Antigonus
by Ptolemy Soter in 310; in that island his son Philadelphus had
been born in 308; and from this time onwards it was closely
connected with Alexandria. It was a place of safety for royal
exiles; and, with its lofty mountains and its verdant slopes, it was
also a favourite retreat for men of letters weary of the heat and
turmoil of the great commercial city³. It is doubtful whether it
was a 'place of education for royal princes'; it seems more
probable that Philetas was summoned to Alexandria than that
Philadelphus was sent to Cos. As a poet, Philetas was a writer
of amatory elegiacs of simple form, but without any special power.
At Alexandria his fame was soon superseded by that of Callimachus, though Roman writers regard them as nearly equal in
repute. They are linked together in a well-known couplet of
Propertius:

> 'Callimachi manes et Coi sacra Philetae,
> 　in vestrum, quaeso, me sinite ire nemus'⁴.

His pupil Zenodotus of Ephesus (c. 325—c. 234 B.C.) was
made the first Librarian of the great Alexandrian
Library early in the reign of Ptolemy Philadelphus.　　Zenodotus
As Librarian, Zenodotus classified the epic poets, while Alexander
Aetolus dealt with the tragic and Lycophron with the comic
drama⁵. He compiled a Homeric glossary, in which he was

---

¹ Didymus on *Il.* i 524, ii 111.

² Susemihl, i 175, and in *Philologus*, 57 (1898). The identification of
Aratus the friend of Theocritus (*Id.* vi) with the astronomical poet is doubtful
(cp. Wilamowitz in *Göttingen Nachrichten*, 1894, 182 f).

³ Mahaffy, *l.c.* 54. Cos is the scene of the second poem of Herondas.
It was off Cos that Philadelphus was defeated by Antigonus *c.* 258, thus
losing for a time the mastery of the sea which he recovered off Andros in 247
(*ib.* 150).

⁴ iv 1, 1. Cp. iii 26, 31; iv 3, 52; v 6, 3; Quint. x 1, 58.

⁵ Scholium II of Tzetzes on Greek Comedy: § 19 in Studemund's article
in *Philologus*, 46 (1888) p. 10, ἱστέον ὅτι Ἀλέξανδρος ὁ Αἰτωλὸς καὶ Λυκόφρων ὁ
Χαλκιδεὺς ὑπὸ Πτολεμαίου τοῦ Φιλαδέλφου προτραπέντες τὰς σκηνικὰς διώρθωσαν
βίβλους· Λυκόφρων μὲν τὰς τῆς κωμῳδίας, Ἀλέξανδρος δὲ τὰς τῆς τραγῳδίας, *ib.*
§ 21 τὰς δέ γε σκηνικὰς Ἀλέξανδρός τε...καὶ Λυκόφρων διωρθώσαντο· τὰς δέ γε
ποιητικὰς Ζηνόδοτος πρῶτον καὶ ὕστερον Ἀρίσταρχος διωρθώσαντο.

apparently content with merely guessing at the meaning of difficult words[1]. Shortly before 274 he produced the first scientific edition of the *Iliad* and *Odyssey*. It was about that date that Timon of Phlius, when consulted by the poet Aratus about a proposed edition of Homer, replied that it must be founded on ancient MSS and not on those that had already been revised (τοῖς ἤδη διωρθω-μένοις)[2]. Zenodotus is described as the earliest editor (διορθωτής) of Homer[3]; his edition was founded on numerous MSS; each of the two poems was probably now for the first time divided into 24 books, and spurious lines marked with a marginal obelus. His reasons for condemning such lines were mainly because he deemed them inconsistent with the context, or unsuited to the persons, whether deities or heroes, whose action is there described. Thus he rejected *Iliad* iii 423–6 on the ground that it was un-becoming for Aphrodite 'to carry a seat' for Helen; and similarly he altered a passage in iv 88, because it is out of character for a goddess to *endeavour* to find the object of her search. In both cases a later critic in the Venetian *scholia* (probably Aristarchus) triumphantly replies that the goddess is for the time disguised in human form, and the supposed impropriety vanishes[4]. Himself an epic poet, he occasionally inserted verses of his own to complete the sense, or blended portions of several verses into one. He deserves credit, however, for making the comparison of MSS the foundation of his text. Our knowledge of his criticisms rests almost entirely on statements recorded in the *scholia* on the Venice MS (A) of Homer. He sometimes confuses σφῶι (2d person) and σφωέ (3d person), νῶι (Nom. and Acc.) and νῶιν (Gen. and Dat.)[5], makes the dual interchangeable with the plural, regards -αται as a singular as well as a plural termination, and -ιω instead of -ιων as a termination of the Comparative; but he clearly recognises the fact that ἑός is not confined to the third person, and the readings preferred by him are not unfrequently

---

[1] Knaack, s.v. *Alexandrinische Litt.* in Pauly-Wissowa, p. 1404.

[2] Diog. Laert. ix 113.

[3] Suïdas, *s.v.*

[4] Lehrs, *De Aristarchi Studiis Homericis*, p. 333[3]; cp. Cobet, *Misc. Crit.* 225–39 (esp. 227, 234) and 251, and p. 133, n. 2 *infra*.

[5] Cobet, *l.c.* 250.

important[1]. He is sometimes right, when his great successors, Aristophanes and Aristarchus, are wrong[2]. His recension of Homer was the first recension of *any* text which aimed at restoring the genuine original. It was succeeded by a recension executed with taste and judgement by the epic poet Rhianus[3]. Zenodotus also produced a recension of Hesiod's *Theogony*, and made conjectures on the text of Pindar and Anacreon[4]. His merits as a Homeric critic are well summed up by Sir Richard Jebb. 'In the dawn of the new scholarship, he appears as a gifted man with a critical aim, but without an adequate critical method. He insisted on the study of Homer's style; but he failed to place that study on a sound basis. The cause of this was that he often omitted to distinguish between the ordinary usages of words and those peculiar to Homer. In regard to dialect, again, he did not sufficiently discriminate the older from the later Ionic. And, relying too much on his own feeling for Homer's spirit, he indulged in some arbitrary emendations. Still, he broke new ground; his work had a great repute; and to some extent, its influence was lasting'[5].

Alexander Aetolus (born *c.* 315, *fl.* 285—276 B.C.) was responsible for the classification of the tragic and satyric dramas in the Alexandrian Library. It is probably owing to this fact that he is called a γραμματικός by Suïdas. His work at Alexandria lasted from *c.* 285 to 276 B.C., at which date he withdrew to the Macedonian capital of Antigonus Gonatas. In his youth he was probably a companion of Theocritus and Aratus in Cos, and he was also associated with the latter in Macedonia. As a tragic poet, he was included among the seven known as the Alexandrian Pleias. He also wrote in epic verse, and in anapaestic tetrameters. Among the latter were some notable lines on Euripides :—

*Alexander Aetolus*

---

[1] See Index to Dr Leaf's *Iliad*, s.v. *Zenodotus.*

[2] Römer in *Abhandl. Münch. Akad.* I Cl. xvii 639—722.

[3] Mayhoff, *De Rhiani Cretensis Studiis Homericis*, 1870, ap. Susemihl, i 399 f.

[4] Düntzer, *De Z. Studiis Homericis*, 1848; Römer, *l.c.*; Christ, § 428[4]; Susemihl, i 330–4, and Hübner's *Bibliographie*, § 7.

[5] Jebb's *Homer*, p. 92 f; cp. Monro, *Od.* 436 f.

ὁ δ' Ἀναξαγόρου τρόφιμος χαιοῦ στριφνὸς μὲν ἔμοιγε προσειπεῖν,
καὶ μισογέλως, καὶ τωθάζειν οὐδὲ παρ' οἶνον μεμαθηκώς,
ἀλλ' ὅ τι γράψαι, τοῦτ' ἂν μέλιτος καὶ σειρήνων ἐτετεύχει[1].

Lycophron of Chalcis in Euboea (born *c.* 330—325 B.C.) was
Lycophron    summoned to Alexandria *c.* 285 B.C., and entrusted
with the arrangement of the comic poets in the
Alexandrian Library. Either in his Euboean home (*c.* 295), or
more probably in Alexandria (*c.* 284), he wrote his *Alexandra*,
a very lengthy tragic monologue consisting of a strange combination of mythological, historical and linguistic learning, grievously
wanting in taste and deliberately obscure in expression. He was
one of the tragic Pleias of Alexandria. He also wrote the earliest
treatise on Comedy in at least eleven books, the extant fragments
of which give an unfavourable impression of his attainments as
a scholar[2].

Callimachus of Cyrene (*c.* 310—*c.* 240), and his somewhat earlier
contemporary Aratus, studied at Athens under the Peripatetic
Praxiphanes (*c.* 290). In his youth he was invited to Alexandria,
Callimachus    where he spent the rest of his life. His *Coma
Berenices*, written in 246 B.C., and only preserved in
the translation by Catullus, incidentally refers to the famous sister
and second wife of Ptolemy Philadelphus, Arsinoe II, who died
in 270 B.C.[3], and was worshipped as Aphrodite Zephyritis, while
the poem as a whole is intended as a compliment to Berenice,
the newly-wedded queen of Ptolemy Euergetes I. His literary
feud with Apollonius Rhodius has left its mark on the poems
of both[4]. Even in his old age he was still conscious of this
feud, when he described himself as having 'sung strains which
envy could not touch', ὃ δ' ἤεισεν κρέσσονα βασκανίης[5]. In
contrast to the vast and diffuse epic of Apollonius, he preferred

---

[1] In Gellius, xv 20, 8. Cp. Meineke, *Analecta Alexandrina*, 215—251;
Couat, *Poésie Alex.* 105—110; Susemihl, i 187—190; Christ, § 353[4].

[2] Strecker, *De Lycophrone etc.*, ap. Susemihl, i 274; Lycophron's *Alexandra*, ed. Holzinger, 1895; Christ, § 375[4]; and Hübner, *Bibliographie*, § 7.

[3] p. 106 *supra*.

[4] Apollonius in *Anth. Pal.* xi 275, Καλλίμαχος· τὸ κάθαρμα, τὸ παίγνιον,
ὁ ξυλινὸς νοῦς. | αἴτιος· ὁ γράψας ' αἴτια Καλλιμάχου' (Croiset, *Litt. Gr.* v 211);
*Argonautica*, iii 932 f; and Callimachus in *Hymn to Apollo*, 105—114.

[5] *Epigr.* 21, 4.

composing hymns and epigrams, and treating heroic themes on
a small scale, expressing his aim in a phrase that has become
proverbial :—μέγα βιβλίον μέγα κακόν[1]. He is sometimes supposed to have succeeded Zenodotus as head of the Alexandrian
Library. Whether he actually held that official position or not,
he was certainly a most industrious bibliographer. He is said
to have drawn up lists of literary celebrities in no less than
120 volumes described as πίνακες τῶν ἐν πάσῃ παιδείᾳ διαλαμψάντων
καὶ ὧν συνέγραψαν. This vast work was far more than a mere
catalogue. It included brief lives of the principal authors, and,
in the case of the Attic drama, the dates of the production of the
plays. It was divided into eight classes :—(1) Dramatists, (2) Epic
and Lyric poets, (3) Legislators, (4) Philosophers, (5) Historians,
(6) Orators, (7) Rhetoricians, (8) Miscellaneous Writers. In the
Drama, the order was that of date ; in Pindar and Demosthenes,
that of subject ; in Theophrastus and in the Miscellaneous
Writers, the order was alphabetical. If the authorship was
disputed, the various views were stated. In these lists, as well
as on the label (σίλλυβος) attached to each roll in the Library,
the opening words and the number of lines contained in each
work were given, in addition to the author and the title[2]. Legends
of the origin and foundation of various cities were included
not only in the four books of his poem known as the Αἴτια, but
also in one of his prose-works. Among the latter was a list of
the writings and of the provincialisms of Democritus. His works
in prose and verse extended to over 800 volumes[3]. To his school
belonged some of the most celebrated scholars and poets, such as
Eratosthenes, Aristophanes of Byzantium, his own rival Apollonius
Rhodius, with Hermippus, Istrus, and Philostephanus of Cyrene.
His monograph on the different names given to the same thing in
different nations, and a work on dialects by Dionysius Iambos,
had a considerable effect on linguistic research in the next
generation. This may be traced not only in the remains of

[1] Athen. 72 A, Καλλίμαχος ὁ γραμματικὸς τὸ μέγα βιβλίον ἴσον ἔλεγεν εἶναι
τῷ μεγάλῳ κακῷ.

[2] O. Schneider's *Callimachea*, ii 297—322 ; Susemihl, i 337—340.

[3] On Callimachus, see Couat, *Poésie Alex.* 111—284; Christ, § 349[4]; Susemihl, i 347—373; and Hübner's *Bibliographie*, § 8.

Aristophanes and Istrus, but also in those of Neoptolemus of Parion and Philemon of Athens. Neoptolemus wrote on 'glosses', and also composed a treatise on poetry, which was one of the authorities followed by Horace in his *Ars Poetica*[1]; while Philemon wrote on 'Attic nouns and glosses', and was the precursor of the purists who in later times maintained the integrity of Attic Greek against foreign corruption[2].

While the evidence in favour of describing Callimachus as head of the Alexandrian Library is very far from conclusive, and indeed depends mainly on *a priori* probabilities, it is certain that that high office was actually filled by his pupil and fellow-countryman, Eratosthenes of Cyrene, who is now generally regarded as the second of the Alexandrian Librarians.

Eratosthenes (*c.* 275—*c.* 195 B.C.)[3] spent some years in Athens, whence he was recalled to Alexandria by Ptolemy Euergetes (*c.* 235 B.C.), and placed at the head of the Library. He remained in that important position during the reigns of Ptolemy Euergetes (d. 222 B.C.), and Philopator (222—205). The tastes of the former were scientific, those of the latter literary and aesthetic. Philopator was not only the author of a tragedy, but also honoured the memory of Homer by building a temple which was adorned with a seated statue of the poet, surrounded by emblems of the cities which claimed his birth[4]. The building of this temple has been regarded as an indication of a change of attitude towards Homer. While Zenodotus had allowed his personal caprice to introduce fanciful alterations into the poet's text, the influence of Callimachus and Eratosthenes inspired a feeling of greater reverence for Homer as the Father of Greek poetry, and also led to a more sober treatment of his text by Aristophanes and Aristarchus, as well as to a careful imitation of his manner in the epic poems of Rhianus[5].

Eratosthenes bore among the members of the Museum the singular designation of βῆτα, which is supposed to be due either

*Eratosthenes*

---

[1] Porphyrion, ap. Susemihl, i 405.

[2] Susemihl, i 372–3.

[3] Gercke in *Jahresb.* vol. 124, p. 486, suggests *c.* 284—204.

[4] Aelian, *Var. Hist.* xiii 22.

[5] Usener ap. Susemihl, ii 671.

to some physical peculiarity (such as the bowed back of old age)
or (far more probably) to his attaining the second place in many
lines of study[1]. The more complimentary designation of πένταθλος implied his high attainments in more than one kind of
mental gymnastics, while (like the second sense of βῆτα) it
suggested that he was inferior to those who confined themselves
to a single line of study[2]. We can easily imagine each of the
specialists of the Museum proudly conscious of his supremacy
in his own department, and enviously depreciating his widely
accomplished and versatile colleague, who was really 'good all
round', as a 'second-rate' man. But it is only in his minor epics
and elegiacs and in his philosophical dialogues that he seems
actually to have deserved a place lower than the very highest.
In other respects he attained the foremost rank among the most
versatile scholars of all time. It was this wide and varied learning
that prompted him to be the first to claim the honourable title of
φιλόλογος[3]. He was the first to treat Geography in a systematic
and scientific manner[4]. He also wrote on Mathematics, Astronomy and Chronology[5], and, in connexion with the latter, we
may mention his work on the Olympian victors. But the
masterpiece of his many-sided scholarship was a work in at least
twelve books, the first of its kind, on the Old Attic Comedy (περὶ
τῆς ἀρχαίας κωμῳδίας). He there corrected his predecessors,
Lycophron and Callimachus, dealing with his theme, not in the
order of chronology, but in a series of monographs on the authorship and date of the plays, and on points of textual criticism,
language and subject-matter. He was less strong in his knowledge of Athenian antiquities[6] than in that of the Attic dialect in

---

[1] β, γ, δ, ε, ζ, θ, λ were all used as nicknames; cp. Photius, *Bibl.* p. 151,
7—28, and Parthey, *Mus. Alex.* p. 53 n. In Rostand's *L'Aiglon*, I iii, we
find the phrase, *je fais donc le bêta*.

[2] In [Plato] *Anterastae*, 135 E, οἱ πένταθλοι are described as δεύτεροι as
compared with the best runners and wrestlers. Cp. ὕπακρος, 136 A, and περὶ
ὕψους, c. 34 § 1, (of Hypereides) σχεδὸν ὕπακρος ἐν πᾶσιν ὡς ὁ πένταθλος.

[3] p. 5 *supra.*

[4] Tozer's *History of Ancient Geography*, p. 182.

[5] Mendelssohn, *De Eratosthenis Chronographi fontibus et auctoritate,*
Göttingen, 1871.

[6] p. 163.

its historical development. His encyclopaedic learning was not
incompatible with poetic taste. In opposition to the prosaic
opinion that the battles of the warriors in the *Iliad*, and the
wanderings of the hero of the *Odyssey*, were a precise description
of actual events, he maintained that the aim of every true poet is
to charm the imagination and not to instruct the intellect[1]. 'The
scenes of the wanderings of Odysseus will be found' (said Eratosthenes), 'when you find the cobbler who sewed up the bag of the
winds, and not before'[2].

His successor as Librarian (*c.* 195 B.C.) was Aristophanes of
Byzantium (*c.* 257—*c.* 180[3]), the pupil of Zenodotus, Callimachus and Eratosthenes. He was the
first of the Librarians who was not a poet as well
as a scholar; but in Scholarship he holds, with Aristarchus, one
of the foremost places in the ancient world. He reduced
accentuation and punctuation to a definite system. Some sort
of punctuation had already been recognised by Aristotle[4]. To
Aristophanes are attributed the use of the mark of elision, the
short stroke (ὑποδιαστολή) denoting a division in a word (such as
the end of a syllable), the hyphen (‿ below the word), the comma
(ὑποστιγμή), the colon (μέση στιγμή) and the full-stop (τελεία
στιγμή); also the indications of quantity, ‿ for 'short' and – for
'long', and lastly the accents, acute ´, grave `, and circumflex ^ or
˜[5]. These accents were invented with a view to preserving the
true pronunciation, which was being corrupted by the mixed

*Aristophanes
of Byzantium*

---

[1] Strabo, p. 7, ποιητὴς πᾶς στοχάζεται ψυχαγωγίας, οὐ διδασκαλίας (an
opinion criticised by Strabo).

[2] *ib.* p. 24. On Eratosthenes, cp. Christ, § 429[4], Susemihl, i 409—428;
and Hübner's *Bibliographie*, § 9.

[3] Gercke in *Jahresb.* vol. 124, p. 486, suggests 266–5—189-8.

[4] p. 97 *supra*.

[5] Pseudo-Arcadius, pp. 186—190, ap. Nauck, *Aristophanis Byz. frag.*
(1848) p. 12 f; this epitome of Herodian has been ascribed to Theodosius
(end of cent. 4, Christ, § 628, p. 870[4]). Cp. Steinthal, *l.c.*, ii 79 n. See also
Blass on *Gr. Palaeogr.* in Iwan Müller's *Handbuch*, vol. i, C § 6. It is contended by K. E. A. Schmidt, *Beiträge zur Gesch. d. Gr.* p. 571 f, that accents
and marks of punctuation existed before Aristophanes. The account in Pseudo-
Arcadius may possibly have been fabricated by Jacob Diassorinus (cent. 16;
see Cohn in Pauly-Wissowa, s.v. *Arkadios*). Cp. Lentz, *Herodiani rell.* I xxxvii.

populations of the Greek world. Aristophanes was certainly the
originator of several new symbols for use in textual criticism.
To the short horizontal dash called the ὄβελος or 'spit' —, which
had already been used by Zenodotus to denote a spurious line, he
added the asterisk ✳ to draw attention to passages where the
sense is incomplete, and, in lyric poets, to indicate a change
in the metre; also the κεραύνιον Τ, to serve as a collective
obelus where several consecutive lines are deemed to be spurious;
and, lastly, the ἀντίσιγμα, or inverted sigma, Ɔ, to draw attention
to tautology[1]. These symbols were used in his edition of the
*Iliad* and *Odyssey*, which marked an advance on that of Zenodotus and the next editor, Rhianus. He agreed with Zenodotus
in obelising many lines, but he also reinstated, and obelised,
many which had been entirely omitted by his predecessor. Thus
he appears to have had some regard for manuscript evidence, or
at least for the duty of faithfully recording it, even if he dis-
approved it. In rejecting certain lines, he acted on independent
grounds; in this he showed considerable boldness, but was often
right. A good example of his acuteness is his rejection of the
conclusion of the *Odyssey*, from xxiii 296 to the end[2]. Like
Zenodotus, however, he is apt to judge the picture of manners
presented in the Homeric poems by the Alexandrian standard,
and to impute either impropriety, or lack of dignity, to phrases
that are quite in keeping with the primitive simplicity of the
heroic age[3].

Besides his Homeric labours, he edited the *Theogony* of
Hesiod, and the lyric poets, Alcaeus, Anacreon and Pindar. In
the case of Pindar he produced what was probably the first
collected edition. He divided the odes into sixteen books, eight
on divine, and eight on human themes (εἰς θεούς and εἰς ἀνθρώπους). Each of these groups had further subdivisions, viz. I
(on divine themes), *hymns, paeans, dithyrambs, prosodia, parthenia*
(the last three in 2 books each); II (on human themes), *hypor-*

---

[1] Nauck, *.c.*, pp. 16—18; Lehrs, *De Aristarchi Studiis Homericis*, p. 332³,
note 240; Reifferscheid, *Suetoni Reliquiae*, pp. 137—144. Cp. Monro, *O..* 421³,
and Susemihl, i 435 ¹, n. 28.     [2] Nauck, *l.c.*, p. 32.

[3] *Od.* xv 19, 82, 88; xviii 281 etc., quoted by Cobet, *Misc. Crit.* 225—7.
Cp. Ruskin's *Modern Painters*, iii 83.

*chemata* (in 2 books), *encomia, threnoi, epinikia* (in 4 books). A book of ceremonial odes was added to 1 as an appendix to the *parthenia* (τὰ κεχωρισμένα τῶν παρθενίων), and similarly, at the end of the book of Nemean odes, which was probably the last of the four books of *epinikia*, an appendix of poems unconnected with Nemean victories (probably under the name of τὰ κεχωρισμένα τῶν Νεμεονίκων)[1].

The general outline of this arrangement assumes that the titles of the various books in the poet's *Life* in the Breslau MS are ultimately due to Aristophanes. Further, there is reason to believe that it was Aristophanes who divided the texts of the lyrical poets into metrical κῶλα[2]. The test of metre was thus easily applied, and interpolations detected[3]. The *scholia* on Pindar, unlike those on Homer, assume a fixed text, and it seems probable that this text was practically settled by Aristophanes[4]. In the lyric poets, his erudition enables him to defend readings which Zenodotus had condemned. Thus 'Anacreon[5] describes a fawn as forsaken κεροέσσης...ὑπὸ ματρός. Zenodotus wrote ἐροέσσης ('lovely') on the ground that only the males have horns. Aristophanes vindicated the text by showing that poets (Pindar, Sophocles and Euripides) ascribe horns to hinds as well as to stags'[6].

It may fairly be inferred from the *scholia* on Euripides and Aristophanes that he prepared a recension of both of those poets. It is probable that he also edited Aeschylus and Sophocles. He wrote introductions to the plays of all the three

---

[1] Cp. Thomas Magister, *Vita Pindari*; Wilamowitz, Eur. *Her.* i 139[1], and *Textgeschichte der griechischen Lyriker* in Göttingen *Abhandl.* 1900, 1—121.

[2] Dion. Hal. *De Comp. Verb.* 22, κῶλα...οὐχ οἷς 'Αριστοφάνης, ἢ τῶν ἄλλων τις μετρικῶν, διεκόσμησε τὰς ᾠδάς (of Pindar); cp. *ib.* 26 (of Simonides). The MS of Bacchylides is written in κῶλα.

[3] Thus, in Pindar, *Ol.* ii 26, φιλεῖ δέ μιν Παλλὰς αἰεί is followed in many MSS by φιλέουσι δὲ Μοῖσαι, but the Scholiast remarks:—ἀθετεῖ 'Αριστοφάνης, περιττεύειν γὰρ αὐτό φησι πρὸς <τὰς> ἀντιστροφάς.

[4] Wilamowitz, *l.c.*, p. 142 f.        [5] 52 [49] Bergk.

[6] Lehrs, *De Aristarchi Stud. Hom.* p. 352[3], quoted in Jebb's *Homer*, p. 93. The authority for the opinion of Aristophanes on this point is Aelian *Hist. An.* vii 39; and, for that of Zenodotus, the *scholium* of Didymus on Pindar, *Ol.* iii 29=52, χρυσοκέρων ἔλαφον θήλειαν (identified as a reindeer by Professor Ridgeway, *Early Age of Greece*, i 360-3).

tragic poets, as well as to Aristophanes, and these have survived in an abridged form in the Arguments (ὑποθέσεις) prefixed to their plays[1], which are ultimately founded on the researches of Aristotle and others of the Peripatetic School[2]. Aristophanes also divided the works of Plato into trilogies, viz. (1) *Republic, Timaeus, Critias*; (2) *Sophistes, Politicus, Cratylus*; (3) *Laws, Minos, Epinomis*; (4) *Theaetetus, Euthyphron, Apologia*; (5) *Crito, Phaedo, Letters*[3]; but an arrangement which separates the *Crito* and *Phaedo* from the *Apologia* cannot be regarded as satisfactory.

He further compiled an important lexicographical work entitled λέξεις[4], in the course of which he treated of words supposed to be unknown to ancient writers, or denoting different times of life, forms of salutation, terms of relationship or civic life or of Attic or Laconian usage[5]. The work showed a wide knowledge of dialects, and marked a new epoch by tracing every word to its original meaning, thus raising 'glossography' to the level of lexicography[6]. He probably wrote a work on *Analogy* or grammatical regularity, as contrasted with *Anomaly* or grammatical irregularity[7]. In this work he apparently endeavoured to determine the normal rules of Greek declension, by drawing attention to general rules of regular inflexion rather than irregular and exceptional forms. Among his other works was a great collection of proverbs, an article on a phrase in Archilochus (ἀχνυμένη σκυτάλη), a treatise on comic masks, and a list of

---

[1] Schneidewin in Göttingen *Abhdl.* vi 3—37; and Trendelenburg, *Grammaticorum Graecorum de arte tragica iudiciorum reliquiae* (Bonn, 1867).

[2] Wilamowitz, p. 144 f (see *supra*, p. 64 f).

[3] Diog. Laert. iii 61, ap. Nauck, *l.c.*, p. 250; cp. Christ, p. 429[3], and *Platon. Stud.* p. 5 f.

[4] A fragment of this work, preserved in a MS of Mount Athos, is published in Miller's *Mélanges*, 427—434; cp. Cohn, in *Jahrb. f. Phil.*, *Suppl.* xii 285, and Fresenius, *De λέξεων...excerptis Byzantinis*, Wiesbaden, 1875.

[5] His articles on πρόξενοι, ἰδιόξενοι, δορύξενοι and ξένοι are clearly the source of the 3rd scholium on Lucian's *Phalaris*, ii 1.

[6] Nauck, pp. 69—234; Susemihl, i 439 f.

[7] Varro, *L. L.* x 68, tertium (analogiae) genus est illud duplex quod dixi, in quo et res et voces similiter proportione dicuntur, ut *bonus malus, boni mali*; de quorum analogia et Aristophanes et alii scripserunt; and ix 12, Aristophanes ...qui potius in quibusdam veritatem (=analogiam) quam consuetudinem secutus. Cp. Nauck, pp. 264—271; Steinthal, ii 78—82; Susemihl, i 441.

passages borrowed by Menander[1]. He also wrote a work on the
πίνακες of Callimachus[2]. Lastly, there is reason to believe that
he drew up lists of the ancient poets who were foremost in the
various forms of poetry. This is inferred from a passage of
Quintilian (x i 54) stating that Apollonius Rhodius is not included
in the *ordo a grammaticis datus*, 'because Aristarchus and Aristophanes did not include any of their own contemporaries'. In
the same chapter (§ 59) he states that Archilochus was one of the
three iambic poets approved by Aristarchus; elsewhere (1 4, 3)
he describes the ancient *grammatici* not only as obelising lines
and rejecting certain works as spurious, but also as including
certain authors in their list and entirely excluding others; and
from the first chapter of his tenth book (§§ 46—54) we infer that
the four leading epic poets were Homer, Hesiod, Antimachus and
Panyasis. These passages are almost all the foundation for the
discussions on the Alexandrian canon from the time of Ruhnken[3]
downwards. Ruhnken regarded it as a classified list of writers of
*prose*, as well as verse. Bernhardy[4] and others limited it to poets
alone, while the canon of the orators has since been regarded
either as the work of the Pergamene school (*c.* 125 B.C.)[5], or as
due to Didymus, or still more probably to Caecilius of Calacte[6],
the friend of Dionysius of Halicarnassus. Between the age of
Aristarchus and that of Strabo, Philetas and Callimachus were
added to the canon of the elegiac, and Apollonius, Aratus,
Theocritus and others, to that of the epic poets. The most
important document bearing on the Alexandrian canon is a list

[1] His indication of Menander's debt to others was combined with a marked
admiration for the poet expressed in the words, ὦ Μένανδρε καὶ βίε, | πότερος
ἄρ' ὑμῶν πότερον ἀπεμιμήσατο; Syrianus *in Hermogenem*, ii 23 Rabe.

[2] Athen. 408 F, τὸ πρὸς τοὺς Καλλιμάχου πίνακας, 336 E, ἀναγραφὴ δραμάτων.

[3] *Hist. Crit. Orat. Gr.*, pp. 94—100 = *Opusc.* i 385—392; cp. Wolf's
*Kleine Schriften*, ii 824. (The term 'canon' is due to Ruhnken, who also
uses the phrase τῆς πρώτης τάξεως, and quotes *ordo* from Quintilian.)

[4] *Gr. Litt.* i[4] 185-8.

[5] Brzoska, *De canone decem oratorum Atticorum*, 1883.

[6] Suïdas mentions among his works χαρακτῆρες τῶν ι' ῥητόρων. Cp. Meier,
*Opusc.* i 120 f, esp. 128; P. Hartmann, *De canone decem oratorum*, 1891;
Susemihl, i 444, 521, ii 484 and esp. 694 f; and Kroehnert, *Canonesne
poëtarum scriptorum artificum per antiquitatem fuerunt?* 1897; also Heydenreich's *Erlangen Dissertation*, 1900.

published by Montfaucon from a MS of the tenth century from Mount Athos, and (with some variations) by Cramer from a late MS in the Bodleian. The following are the names included in this list, as revised by Usener[1], who omits late additions. The last in the list is Polybius, who died more than 50 years after Aristophanes of Byzantium.

*(Epic) Poets* (5): Homer, Hesiod, Peisander, Panyasis, Antimachus.

*Iambic Poets* (3): Semonides, Archilochus, Hipponax.

*Tragic Poets* (5): Aeschylus, Sophocles, Euripides, Ion, Achaeus.

*Comic Poets, Old* (7): Epicharmus, Cratinus, Eupolis, Aristophanes, Pherecrates, Crates, Plato.  *Middle* (2): Antiphanes, Alexis.  *New* (5): Menander, Philippides, Diphilus, Philemon, Apollodorus.

*Elegiac Poets* (4): Callinus, Mimnermus, Philetas, Callimachus.

*Lyric Poets* (9): Alcman, Alcaeus, Sappho, Stesichorus, Pindar, Bacchylides, Ibycus, Anacreon, Simonides.

*Orators* (10): Demosthenes, Lysias, Hypereides, Isocrates, Aeschines, Lycurgus, Isaeus, Antiphon, Andocides, Deinarchus[2].

*Historians* (10): Thucydides, Herodotus, Xenophon, Philistus, Theopompus, Ephorus, Anaximenes, Callisthenes, Hellanicus, Polybius[3].

Aristophanes of Byzantium was probably nearly 60 when he counted among his pupils his successor Aristarchus of Samothrace (*c.* 220—145 B.C.), who lived in Alexandria under Ptolemy Philometor (181—146), and, on the murder of his pupil Philopator Neos and the accession of Euergetes II (146), fled to Cyprus, where he died soon after. His continuous commentaries (ὑπομνήματα) filled no less than 800 volumes, partly as notes for lectures, partly in finished form. These were valued less highly than his critical treatises (συγγράμματα) on such subjects as the *Iliad* and *Odyssey*, on the naval camp of the Achaeans[4], and on Philetas and on Xenon (one of the

[1] *Dion. Hal. de Imitatione,* p. 130, reprinted in Peterson's Quintilian x, p. xxxvi.

[2] Deinarchus, omitted by Usener, is restored by Kroehnert.

[3] On the Canon, see Steffen, *De canone qui dicitur Aristophanis et Aristarchi,* 1876; Kroehnert, *l.c.* (who rejects all 'canons' except that of the Orators); Susemihl, i 444–7 and the strictures of Wilamowitz, in Göttingen *Abhandl.* 1900, 5 f, 63—71. (Cp. in general Radermacher, *s.v. Kanon,* in Pauly-Wissowa, 1919.) On Aristophanes in general, see Susemihl, i 428—448; Christ, § 435[4]; Wilamowitz, *Eur. Her.* i. 137—153[1]; Cohn *s.v.* in Pauly-Wissowa; and Hübner's *Bibliographie,* § 11.

[4] Cp. Goedhart's Dissertation (Utrecht, 1879).

9—2

earliest of the *chorizontes*, who ascribed the *Iliad* and the *Odyssey*
to different poets). As a commentator he avoided the display of
irrelevant erudition, while he insisted that each author was his
own best interpreter. He also placed the study of grammar on a
sound basis; he was among the earliest of the grammarians who
definitely recognised eight parts of speech, Noun, Verb, Participle,
Pronoun, Article, Adverb, Preposition and Conjunction[1]. As a
grammarian he maintained the principle of *Analogy*, as opposed
to that of *Anomaly*. He produced recensions of Alcaeus,
Anacreon and Pindar[2]; commentaries on the *Lycurgus* of Aeschylus, on Sophocles and Aristophanes, and even on Herodotus[3];
and recensions, as well as commentaries, in the case of Archilochus
and Hesiod. He had a profound knowledge of Homeric
vocabulary, and was the author of two recensions of the *Iliad* and
the *Odyssey*, with critical and explanatory symbols in the margin of
each. These symbols were six in number: (1) the *obelus* — to
denote a spurious line, already used by Zenodotus and Aristophanes[4]; (2) the *diplê* (διπλῆ) >, denoting anything notable either
in language or matter; (3) the *dotted diplê* (διπλῆ περιεστιγμένη) ⸖,
drawing attention to a verse in which the text of Aristarchus
differed from that of Zenodotus; (4) the *asterisk* (ἀστερίσκος) ✳,
marking a verse wrongly repeated elsewhere; (5) the *stigmê* or
dot (στιγμή), used by itself as a mark of *suspected* spuriousness,
and also in conjunction with (6) the *antisigma* ⊃, in a sense
differing from that of Aristophanes, to denote lines in which the
order had been disturbed, the dots indicating the lines which
ought immediately to follow the line marked with the *antisigma*[5].

[1] ὄνομα, ῥῆμα, μετοχή, ἀντωνυμία, ἄρθρον, ἐπίρρημα, πρόθεσις, σύνδεσμος
(ὄνομα included the Adjective). Quint. i 4, 20, alii ex idoneis...auctoribus
octo partes secuti sunt, ut Aristarchus. Cp. Ribbach (Naumburg, 1883).

[2] Cp. Feine's Dissertation (Leipzig, 1883).

[3] Grenfell and Hunt, *Amherst papyri*, ii (1901), no. 12, Ἀριστάρχου <εἰς
τὸ> Ἡροδότου α′ ὑπόμνημα (the only known proof that he ever commented on
writers of prose).

[4] p. 127 *supra*. *Codex Venetus* (of Aristarchus), τὸν δὲ ὀβελὸν ἔλαβεν ἐκ
τῆς Ζηνοδότου διορθώσεως.

[5] Cp. p. 142 *infra*; also Lehrs and Reifferscheid, quoted on p. 127;
Ludwich, *Aristarchs Homerische Textkritik*, i 19—22; and Jebb's *Homer*, p. 94.
Similar symbols were used in an edition of Plato (Diog. Laert. iii 66) some-
times identified with that of Aristophanes of Byzantium, mentioned on p. 129

In his criticisms on Homer three points have been noticed.
(1) His careful study of Homeric *language*. Thus he observes
that in Homer ὧδε never means 'here' or 'hither', but always
'thus'; that βάλλειν is used of missiles, οὐτάζειν of wounding at
close quarters; φόβος of 'flight', and πόνος of the 'stress' of
battle. (2) His strong reliance on *manuscript authority*, and, in
cases of conflicting readings, on the poet's usage. In contrast
with Zenodotus, he abstained from merely conjectural readings,
and was even censured by later critics for excess of caution.
(3) His comments on the *subject-matter*, comparing the Homeric
versions of myths with those in other writers, and noticing characteristic points of Homeric civilisation. His interest in topography
led him to make a plan of the Trojan and the Greek camp; and
to notice that Ἄργος Πελασγικόν denotes Thessaly, and Ἄργος
Ἀχαϊκόν the Peloponnesus[1]. As a critic he is more sober and
judicious than Zenodotus and Aristophanes, but he sometimes
lapses, like his predecessors, into an over-fondness for finding
'improprieties' of expression in the plain and unaffected style of
Homer[2].

The Homeric MSS accessible to Aristarchus mainly fall into
two groups, those bearing the names of (1) *persons*, or (2) *places*.
The former are known as αἱ κατ᾽ ἄνδρα (ἐκδόσεις); the latter as αἱ
κατὰ πόλεις, or αἱ ἀπὸ (or ἐκ, or διὰ) τῶν πόλεων, or αἱ τῶν πόλεων.
The former are often cited by the name of the editor:—Antimachus, Zenodotus, Rhianus, Sosigenes, Philemon, Aristophanes;
the latter, by the names of the places from which they came:—
Massilia, Chios, Argos, Sinope, Cyprus, Crete and Aeolis; but
the Cretan edition was probably not used by Aristarchus, and the
Aeolian is cited only for some variants in the *Odyssey*. Besides
these groups there were other texts denoted as 'common' or

---

(Gomperz, *Plat. Aufsätze*, ii). On Aristarchus see also Lehrs, *De Aristarchi
Studiis Homericis* (1833), ed. 3, 1882; Ludwich, *l.c.*, 2 vols. (1885); Steinthal,
*Gesch. der Sprachwissenschaft*, ii 100[2]f; Wilamowitz, *Eur. Her.* p. 138[1];
P. Cauer's *Grundfragen*, 11—35; Susemihl, i 451—463; Christ, § 436[4];
Cohn *s.v.* in Pauly-Wissowa; Monro, *Od.* 430f, 439—454; and Hübner's
*Bibliographie*, § 12 ; also Roemer, *Aristarchs Athetesen* (1912), and *Philologus*,
LXX, 321-52.

[1] Jebb's *Homer*, p. 94 f.

[2] Cobet, *Misc. Crit.* 229 ; W. Bachmann, *Die ästhetischen Anschauungen
Aristarchs*, Nürnberg, 1902-4.

'popular' (κοιναί, δημώδεις), representing the 'vulgate' of the day, described as 'the more careless' (εἰκαιότεραι) as contrasted with the 'more accurate' or 'scholarly' (χαριέστεραι)[1].

The extant evidence for the text of Homer is to be found mainly in the two MSS in Venice, A and B, belonging to the 10th and 11th century respectively, together with statements in the *scholia* in the earlier of these MSS, and quotations in ancient authors. From these materials what may be called the 'vulgate' text of Homer has been formed, and down to the year 1891 the evidence of Homeric *papyri*, going back as far as the Christian era, was in agreement with this text. In contrast with this text were the readings of the Alexandrian critics, and certain of the quotations in ancient authors. In 1891 fragments of an earlier papyrus of *Iliad* xi 502—537, found by Mr Flinders Petrie among dated documents belonging to 260—224 B.C. and published by Professor Mahaffy, supplied indications of a text differing from the vulgate and including four more lines in a passage consisting of 39 lines. Similar phenomena were noticed in the fragment published by M. Nicole at Geneva in 1894, and by Messrs Grenfell and Hunt in 1897. Two suggestions arose from these discoveries. The first was that these Ptolemaic *papyri* represented a prolix prae-Alexandrian text, before it was cut down into the current text by the criticisms of Zenodotus, Aristophanes and Aristarchus. But this suggestion is opposed to the evidence of the *scholia*, which record the readings preferred by the Alexandrian critics and show that the Alexandrian school had hardly any effect on the traditional text. The second suggestion was that the remarkable additions to the Homeric text found in nearly all the few Ptolemaic *papyri* proved that the vulgar text of the present day could not have been in existence in the Ptolemaic age, but must have come into being at a later date. But (1) the statements in the *scholia* relating to the Alexandrian critics, Didymus and Aristonicus, who distinguish between the editions of their Alexandrian predecessors, especially those of Aristarchus,

---

[1] La Roche, *Hom. Textkritik*, p. 45 f; Ludwich, *l.c.*, i 3—16; Jebb's *Homer*, p. 91 f; and Mr T. W. Allen in *Class. Rev.* 1901, pp. 241–6, *The eccentric editions and Aristarchus*. On the history of the Homeric poems in the Alexandrian age cp. Monro, *Od.* 418—454.

and certain other editions, known as 'common' or 'popular', show that a vulgar text of some sort or other was in existence in Alexandrian times. (2) The evidence of quotations in prae-Alexandrian writers shows that their text of Homer was substantially the same as ours. 152 portions of the Homeric text are quoted by 29 writers from Herodotus downwards, and the 480 lines (or thereabout) thus quoted do not include more than 9 to 11 lines in addition to the ordinary text. It may thus be inferred that the ordinary Homeric text preceded the Alexandrian age and that it existed as early as the fifth century B.C. The Ptolemaic *papyri* may therefore be regarded simply as a few stray examples of eccentric texts of Homer, and texts no less eccentric may have been not unknown to the author of the *Second Alcibiades*[1], and to Aeschines and Plutarch, who occasionally quote from a text including lines not found in the ordinary text of Homer[2].

Notwithstanding the very slight impression which Aristarchus produced on the current text of Homer, later writers had a profound respect for his authority as a critic. In the Venice MS (A) of Homer the scholiast on *Il.* ii 316 knows that the accent of πτέρυγος is normally proparoxytone, but accepts the paroxytone πτερύγος solely on the *authority* of Aristarchus[3]; and on *Il.* iv

---

[1] 149 D. 'The fact that this spurious quotation is found in a spurious Platonic dialogue only emphasizes the fact that to the real Plato Homer is our Homer, neither more nor less' (Leaf[2] on *Il.* viii 548 f).

[2] See esp. Ludwich, *Die Homer-vulgata als voralexandrinische erwiesen*, 1898, rev. by Mr T. W. Allen in *Class. Rev.* 1899, pp. 39—41. In the same volume, p. 334 f, Mr Allen shows that the modern Homeric text is identical with the ancient vulgate to the extent of about 60 per cent. of the passages where its readings are noticed, and further that in about 20 per cent. the ancient vulgate was in *conflict* with another text, and in about 20 per cent. had been *dislodged* by that text. On p. 429 f he shows that, of the known readings of **Aristarchus** (664 in number), between one-fifth and one-sixth have left no trace whatever in our MSS, and only one-tenth are found in all MSS hitherto collated. In *Class. Rev.* 1900, p. 242 f, he shows that of the known readings of **Zenodotus** (385 in number) 259 survive in none of our MSS, and the rest in all or some, only 4 being found in all; also that of the readings peculiar to **Aristophanes of Byzantium** (81), 46 are found in none of our MSS, and the rest in some or all, only two being found in all. [Ludwich's views are criticised by Grenfell, in *J. H. S.* 1919, p. 17 ff.]

[3] πειθόμεθα αὐτῷ ὡς πάνυ ἀρίστῳ γραμματικῷ

235 he follows Aristarchus in preference to Hermappias, 'even although the latter appears to be in the right'[1]. His power of critical divination is recognised by Panaetius, who calls him a 'diviner'[2]; and with Cicero[3] and Horace[4] his name is a synonym for a great critic, and it has so remained ever since. He was the founder of scientific Scholarship. He was also the head of a School, and Apollodorus, Ammonius and Dionysius Thrax were among the most famous of his forty pupils. Even the king (Euergetes II), whose accession in 146 was the signal for a persecution of his Hellenic subjects from which men of letters, like Aristarchus, were not exempt, discussed points of Homeric criticism with his courtiers far into the night, and himself proposed an ingenious emendation of a line in the *Odyssey*[5].

Next to Aristarchus, the most important pupil of Aristophanes
Callistratus    was Callistratus, whose admiration for his master led to a bitter feud with Aristarchus. He wrote criticisms on the passages in Homer attacked by the latter, as well as a commentary on the *Iliad*, and on Pindar, Sophocles, Euripides and Aristophanes[6].

Before turning to the pupils of Aristarchus[7], we must mention
Hermippus    a pupil of Callimachus, Hermippus of Smyrna, the author of an extensive biographical and biblio- graphical work, connected with his master's *Pinakes* and including lives of literary celebrities and lists of their writings, so far as they were preserved in the Alexandrian Library. The work is cited under its various subdivisions, On the Legislators, On the Seven Wise Men, On Pythagoras, Gorgias, Isocrates, Aristotle and Chrysippus (d. *c.* 208–4 B.C.). It was one of the chief authorities

---

[1] εἰ καὶ δοκεῖ ἀληθεύειν. This grammarian is also quoted on xi 326, xiii 137, but is otherwise unknown.

[2] μάντις, Athen. 634 C.        [3] *Ad Att.* i 14, 3.        [4] *A.P.* 450.

[5] *Od.* v 72. Plut. *de adul.* 17, 60 A, Πτολεμαίῳ φιλομαθεῖν δοκοῦντι περὶ γλώττης καὶ στιχιδίου καὶ ἱστορίας μαχόμενοι μέχρι μέσων νυκτῶν ἀπέτεινον. Athen. 61 C, Πτολ. ὁ δεύτερος Εὐεργέτης παρ' Ὁμήρῳ ἀξιοῖ γράφειν, 'ἀμφὶ δὲ λειμῶνες μαλακοὶ σίου ἠδὲ σελίνου'. σία (a marsh plant) γὰρ μετὰ σελίνου φύεσθαι ἀλλὰ μὴ ἴα (Susemihl, i 9).

[6] R. Schmidt, *De Callistrato Aristophaneo*, reprinted with Nauck, *Aristoph. Byz.*; cp. Susemihl, i 449 f.

[7] Blau, *De Aristarchi Discipulis*, 1883.

followed by Diogenes Laërtius, and by Plutarch in his *Lives* of Lycurgus, Solon and Demosthenes[1].

Apollodorus of Athens (*fl.* 144 B.C.) was a pupil of Aristarchus in Alexandria, which he left *c.* 146 B.C. After 144 B.C. he dedicated to Attalus II of Pergamon a great work on Chronology, beginning with the fall of Troy and ending with the above date. The work was afterwards brought down to 119 B.C. It was written in comic trimeters, possibly as an aid to the memory; it unfortunately superseded the probably far greater chronological work of Eratosthenes, and took its place as a great storehouse of chronological facts. Apollodorus is named in one of Cicero's *Letters*[2] as likely to throw light on the date of an Epicurean philosopher and of certain politicians at Athens. Where the exact date of the birth and death of any personage was unknown, he used some important date in that personage's active life to determine the time at which he flourished; this was called his ἀκμή and was regarded as corresponding approximately to the age of 40[3]. Following in the track of Eratosthenes and of Demetrius of Scepsis, he wrote a commentary in 12 books on the Homeric catalogue of ships, often quoted by Strabo[4]; also on Sophron and Epicharmus, and on Etymology, and further a geographical compendium in iambic verse, and an important work in 24 books on the Religion of Greece (περὶ θεῶν)[5]. Some of the numerous fragments of this work are inconsistent with the corresponding passages in the mythological *Bibliotheca*, which bears the name of the same author. Between 100 and 55 B.C. a handbook of mythology was compiled, which became the source from which Diodorus, Hyginus and Pausanias drew their information on this subject; this was also the source of the extant *Bibliotheca* (possibly of the time of Hadrian) bearing the name of Apollodorus[6].

Apollodorus

---

[1] Christ, §432[4]; Susemihl, i 492–5.

[2] *Ad Att.* xii 23, 2.　　　　[3] Diels in *Rhein. Mus.* xxxi 1 f.

[4] B. Niese in *Rhein. Mus.* xxxii 306.

[5] Christ, § 438[4]; Susemihl, ii 33—44; Schwarz in Pauly-Wissowa, *s.v.* pp. 2857–75; and Hübner's *Bibliographie*, § 14, p. 21.

[6] Christ, §576[4]; Susemihl, ii 50 f; cp. F. Jacoby, *Apollodors Chronik*; and Schwarz, *l.c.*, pp. 2875–86.

Aristarchus was succeeded by his pupil Ammonius, who
devoted himself mainly to the exposition and the
defence of his master's recensions of Homer. He
wrote 'on the absence of more than two editions of the Homeric
recension of Aristarchus', 'on Plato's debt to Homer', and also
'on Prosody', probably in the course of his criticisms on Homer.
He was one of the main authorities followed by Didymus in his
work on the recension of Homer by Aristarchus. Lastly, he
wrote a commentary on Pindar, in which he appears to have
followed in his master's footsteps[1].

Another eminent pupil of Aristarchus was Dionysius Thrax
(born c. 166 B.C.). In his admiration for his
master's apparently perfect familiarity with all the
tragedies in existence, he painted his master's
portrait with a figure representing Tragedy (possibly on a breast-
plate) near his heart[2]. He afterwards taught in Rhodes, where he
made a model of Nestor's cup[3], the material for which was
provided by means of a subscription on the part of his pupils.
But his main title to fame is that he was the author of the earliest
Greek Grammar. This is still extant. It is a work of less than
16 printed pages[4]. It begins by defining Grammar[5], and stating
its six parts (ἀνάγνωσις, ἐξήγησις, γλωσσῶν καὶ ἱστοριῶν ἀπόδοσις,
ἐτυμολογία, ἀναλογίας ἐκλογισμός, κρίσις ποιημάτων). It next deals
with Accentuation (τόνος), Punctuation (στιγμή), Letters and
Syllables (στοιχεῖα καὶ συλλαβαί), and, after enumerating the
Parts of Speech (ὄνομα, ῥῆμα, μετοχή, ἄρθρον, ἀντωνυμία, πρόθεσις,
ἐπίρρημα, σύνδεσμος), ends with Declension and Conjugation,
without including either Syntax or precepts on Style. In this
Grammar ὄνομα includes not only the Noun, but also the Adjective
and the Demonstrative and Interrogative Pronouns; and ἄρθρον,

---

[1] Susemihl, ii 153; Pauly-Wissowa, s.v. p. 1865.

[2] Aristarchus, however, was sometimes criticised severely by his pupil, as
appears from the *scholia* on *Il.* ii 262, xiii 103.

[3] *Il.* xi 632–5.

[4] Bekker's *Anecdota Gr.* (1816), pp. 629—643; Engl. trans. by T. Davidson
(reprinted from *Journal of Speculative Philosophy*, St Louis, U.S.A.), 1874:
the best text is that of Uhlig, 1883. It was apparently written at Rhodes,
under Stoic influence.

[5] p. 8 *supra*.

not only the Article but also the Relative Pronoun; while ἀντωνυμία ('Pronoun') is limited to the Personal and Possessive Pronouns[1]. It remained the standard work on grammar for at least 13 centuries. It was known to the great grammarians of the imperial age, Apollonius and Herodian. Among its many commentators may be mentioned Choeroboscus (end of cent. 6), Stephanus (early in cent. 7), and (not much later) Heliodorus and Melampus[2]. It became the source of the grammatical catechisms (ἐρωτήματα) of the Byzantine age, e.g. that of Moschopulos, and also of the manuals introduced into Italy during the Renaissance by Byzantine refugees such as Chrysoloras, Gaza, Constantine Lascaris and Chalcondylas. The Greek terms of this treatise thus survived for many centuries, e.g. ὄνομα, γένος, ἀριθμός, κλίσεις ('Declensions'), πτώσεις ('Cases'), πτῶσις ὀνομαστικὴ καὶ εὐθεῖα (Nom.), γενική (Gen.), δοτική (Dat.), αἰτιατική (Acc.), κλητική (Voc.); ῥῆμα, συζυγίαι ('Conjugations'), διαθέσεις ('Voices'), ἐγκλίσεις ('Moods'), χρόνοι ('Tenses'), πρόσωπα ('Persons'). With a strict adherence to Attic usage the Active and Passive Voices are here exemplified by τύπτω and τύπτομαι, the Numbers by τύπτω, τύπτετον and τύπτομεν, and the Persons (in inferior MSS) by τύπτω, τύπτεις, τύπτει. It was apparently in the Canons of the late Alexandrian grammarian Theodosius (probably a friend of Synesius of Cyrene, fl. 400 A.D.), that this verb appeared for the first time with the complete paradigm of all its imaginary moods and tenses. Before the end of the fifth century the paradigm was included in the Armenian and Syriac versions of the supplements to Dionysius Thrax[3]; and, through the Manuals of the Renaissance, it has found its way into modern Grammars, although, as is now well known, the Present and Imperfect, Active and Passive, were the only tenses actually used in Attic prose of the Athenian age[4].

Among the Romans, Varro was indebted to the Grammar of Dionysius Thrax for his definition of the 'Persons' of the Verb, and for that of Grammar itself. It was also the authority followed by Suetonius, by Remmius Palaemon (the teacher of Quintilian),

---

[1] Classen, De Gram. Gr. prim., p. 85.
[2] Susemihl, ii 173 note. Cp. A. Hilgard's ed. of the Scholia, 1901.
[3] ed. Uhlig, pp. liii, 49, 51.
[4] Cp. Dem. Select Private Orations, ii, Excursus to Speech against Conon.

and (probably at second hand) by later Roman grammarians, such as Donatus, Diomedes, Charisius and Dositheus. The original text was known to Priscian.

Dionysius Thrax was also the writer of two or three rhetorical works, together with a critique on Crates, and commentaries on the *Works and Days* of Hesiod, and on the *Odyssey* and the *Iliad*. In this last he followed Aristarchus in actually regarding Homer as a native of Athens[1].

His pupil, Tyrannion the elder, a native of Amisus, who was

Tyrannion

taken to Rome by Lucullus in 67 B.C., and was a teacher there in the time of Pompey the Great, was among the first to recognise the value of the Aristotelian MSS transported to Rome by Sulla in 86 B.C.[2]. He has been identified as the learned adviser of Atticus in his editions of Greek authors, such as Aristotle and Theophrastus. While Dionysius Thrax had divided Grammar into six parts, it was probably his pupil, Tyrannion, who, more logically, divided it into four :—(1) accurate recitation, (2) exposition, (3) correction of the text, and (4) criticism. It was through Varro that this division was first transmitted to the Roman grammarians[3]. Tyrannion wrote on the connexion between the Greek and Latin languages, and on the parts of speech. A commentary on the latter work was written by his pupil, Tyrannion the younger, who reached Rome as a prisoner and owed his freedom to Terentia, the wife of Cicero[4].

The most versatile and industrious of all the successors of

Didymus

Aristarchus was Didymus (*c.* 65 B.C.—10 A.D.), who taught at Alexandria, and perhaps also in Rome[5]. To his prodigious industry he owed the notable name of *Chalcenterus*[6]. He is said to have written between 3500 and 4000 books, and we are not surprised to learn that he sometimes forgot in one book what he had himself written in another[7]. He is

---

[1] Christ, § 439[4]; Susemihl, ii 168—175 ; Cohn in Pauly-Wissowa ; and Hübner's *Bibliographie*, § 14, p. 20.          [2] p. 86 *supra*.

[3] Usener, *Ein altes Lehrgebäude der Philologie*, in *S. Ber. bayer. Akad.* 1892, 582 f.          [4] Christ, § 442[4]

[5] Susemihl, ii 195, note 264 ; and esp. Wilamowitz, *Eur. Her.* 157—168.

[6] Χαλκέντερος, cp. Amm. Marc. xxii 16, 16, multiplicis scientiae copia memorabilis.

[7] Quint. i 8, 19, cp. Athen. 130 C ; also Quintilian, i 8, 19, and Seneca, *Ep.* 88 § 37.

described by Macrobius[1] as *grammaticorum facile eruditissimus omniumque quique sint quique fuerint instructissimus*. His lexicographical labours included treatises on 'metaphors,' on 'words of doubtful meaning', on 'names corrupted by change of spelling', and two vast works on the language of Comedy, and on the language of Tragedy (λέξεις κωμικαί and τραγικαί). The last two (and especially the second of these) may be regarded as the ultimate source of most of the lexicographical learning which has come down to us in Athenaeus and the *scholia*, and in the lexicons of Hesychius and Photius. The 28th book of the work on the language of Tragedy is cited by Harpocration[2]; and one of the longer fragments is preserved by Macrobius[3]. Turning to his labours as an editor, textual critic and commentator, we have first to mention his elaborate attempt to restore the Homeric recension of Aristarchus in his work περὶ τῆς Ἀρισταρχείου διορθώσεως. Aristarchus had produced two recensions of the text; but both were lost, and Didymus had to restore their readings with the help of transcripts together with such evidence as could be derived from the critical monographs and the continuous commentaries of Aristarchus. At the end of each book of the *Iliad* in the Venice MS of Homer known as A, Didymus is mentioned, together with his younger contemporary, Aristonicus, and Herodian, the author of a treatise on the prosody and accentuation of the *Iliad* (*c.* 160 A.D.), and Nicanor, the writer on Homeric punctuation (*c.* 130 A.D.), as one of the sources of the *scholia* in that MS. The following is a simple example of a *scholium* on *Il.* x 306, in which the readings preferred by Zenodotus, Aristophanes and Aristarchus are all recorded:—

> δώσω γὰρ δίφρον τε δύω τ' ἐριαύχενας ἵππους,
> οἵ κεν ἀριστεύωσι θοῇις ἐπὶ νηυσὶν Ἀχαιῶν,

οὕτως Ἀρίσταρχος, οἵ κεν ἄριστοι ἔωσι· ὁ δὲ Ζηνόδοτος αὐτοὺς οἳ φορέουσιν ἀμύμονα Πηλείωνα (cp. l. 323)· Ἀριστοφάνης καλοὺς οἳ φορέουσιν.

In the following passage (*Il.* viii 535—541) we have critical symbols in the margin, with a *scholium* giving the statement by Aristonicus of the views of Zenodotus and Aristarchus, and adding

[1] v 18.    [2] *s.v.* ξηραλοιφεῖν.
[3] v 18 §§ 9, 12, on the use of Ἀχελῷος for water in general.

that the statement of those views by Didymus was identical with
that of Aristonicus :—

$$a$$

⊃ αὔριον ἦν ἀρετὴν διαείσεται, εἴ κ' ἐμὸν ἔγχος
⊃ μείνηι ἐπερχόμενον· ἀλλ' ἐν πρώτοισιν, ὀίω,
⊃ κείσεται οὐτηθείς, πολέες δ' ἀμφ' αὐτὸν ἑταῖροι,
• ἠελίου ἀνιόντος ἐς αὔριον. εἰ γὰρ ἐγὼν ὣς
• εἴην ἀθάνατος καὶ ἀγήρως ἤματα πάντα,
• τιοίμην δ' ὣς τίετ' Ἀθηναίη καὶ Ἀπόλλων,
ὡς νῦν ἡμέρη ἥδε κακὸν φέρει Ἀργείοισιν.

ὅτι ἢ τούτους δεῖ τοὺς τρεῖς στίχους μένειν, οἷς τὸ ἀντίσιγμα παράκειται, ἢ
τοὺς ἑξῆς τρεῖς, οἷς αἱ στιγμαὶ παράκεινται· εἰς γὰρ τὴν αὐτὴν γεγραμμένοι εἰσὶ
διάνοιαν. ἐγκρίνει δὲ μᾶλλον ὁ Ἀρίσταρχος τοὺς δευτέρους διὰ τὸ καυχηματικω-
τέρους εἶναι τοὺς λόγους· ὁ δὲ Ζηνόδοτος τοὺς πρώτους τρεῖς οὐδὲ ἔγραφεν. τὰ
αὐτὰ δὲ λέγει περὶ τῶν στίχων τούτων ὁ Δίδυμος ἃ καὶ ὁ Ἀριστόνικος· διὸ οὐκ
ἐγράψαμεν τὰ Διδύμου. (In the MS the third στιγμή should have been prefixed
to the last line, and not to the last but one, which was apparently absent from
the recension of Aristarchus[1].)

Didymus also wrote commentaries on Hesiod, Pindar and
Bacchylides, and on Aeschylus, Sophocles and Euripides. Many
of the *scholia* on Pindar and Sophocles, as well as the extant
Lives of the three tragic poets, are probably in the main due to
Didymus. He further commented on the comic poets, Eupolis,
Cratinus, and Aristophanes, the extant *scholia* on the last being
traceable through Symmachus to Didymus, and ultimately to
Aristophanes of Byzantium[2]. Extending his industry to prose, he
produced an edition of Thucydides, whose life by Marcellinus
is, either entirely, or at least so far as regards §§ 1—45, taken from
Didymus[3]; also of the Attic orators Antiphon, Isaeus, Hypereides,
Aeschines and Demosthenes[4], besides at least ten books of
rhetorical memoranda on the orators, and a monograph περὶ τοῦ

[1] Aristophanes, Aristarchus and his successor Ammonius, as well as
Didymus and Aristonicus, are mentioned in the interesting *scholia* on *Il.* x
398, partly quoted in Leaf's n. Cp. *facsimile* in H. Browne's *Handbook of
Homeric Study* (1905), p. 54.

[2] Symmachus *fl.* 100 A.D. (Wilamowitz, *Eur. Her.* i 179[1]); cp. O. Schneider,
*De veterum in Ar. scholiorum fontibus*, pp. 59—63.

[3] Susemihl, ii 203, note 314.

[4] *De Demosthene commenta*, ed. Diels and Schubart (1904), including
many quotations from Philochorus and Theopompus, with fragments of a
lexicon to Dem. *contra Aristocratem*. See also Foucart's *Mémoire* (1907).

δεκατεῦσαι. His grammatical works included a treatise on inflexions (περὶ παθῶν), and on orthography; his literary and antiquarian works, a treatise on myths and legends (ξένη ἱστορία), on the birthplace of Homer, on the death of Aeneas, on Anacreon and Sappho[1], on the lyric poets, on the ἄξονες of Solon[2], on proverbs, and even on the *De Republica* of Cicero.

Notwithstanding his restoration of the Aristarchic recension of Homer, he appears to have had an imperfect sense of the requirements of systematic textual criticism. His younger contemporary, Aristonicus of Alexandria, wrote a treatise on the critical signs used by Aristarchus; and, wherever the views of Didymus differ from those of Aristonicus, the latter are as a rule to be preferred[3]. The work of Aristonicus was probably written before that of Didymus on the same general subject[4], and appears to have given a more complete account of the passages criticised by Aristarchus[5]. In the comments of Didymus on Pindar and Aristophanes, and on Sophocles and Euripides, there is little trace of any exceptional acumen; but he deserves our gratitude for gathering together the results of earlier work in criticism and exegesis, and transmitting these results to posterity. The age of creative and original scholars was past, and the best service that remained to be rendered was the careful preservation of the varied stores of ancient learning; and this service was faithfully and industriously rendered by Didymus[6].

Among the younger contemporaries of Didymus was a specialist in grammar and pure scholarship, who flourished under Augustus, named Tryphon, son of Ammonius, probably not the pupil of Aristarchus bearing that name[7]. Fragments of his works are preserved by writers such as Apollonius Dyscolus, Herodian, Athenaeus, and a third Ammonius

Tryphon

---

[1] Seneca, *Ep.* 88 § 37.				[2] Plut. *Solon*, 1.

[3] Cp. Christ, § 443, p. 635[4]; Wilamowitz, *l.c.*, 161.

[4] Lehrs, *l.c.*, 28[3]; Ludwich, *Aristarchs Homerische Textkritik nach den Fragmenten des Didymos*, i 51.

[5] Ludwich, i 60 f.

[6] Wilamowitz, *Eur. Her.* i 157—166[1]; cp. Christ, § 443[4]; Susemihl, ii 195—210; M. Schmidt, *Did. fragm.* (1854); Ludwig, *l.c.*; and Hübner's *Bibliographie*, § 14, p. 22.

[7] p. 138 *supra*.

(c. 389 *A.D.*) who abridged a work on Synonyms by Herennius Philon (c. 100 A.D.).    It appears from these fragments that, besides dealing with points of orthography and prosody, and with various parts of speech, he wrote on the local and the literary dialects of Greece, on terms of music, and on names of plants and animals.    Late abridgements of his works on letter-changes and on tropes and metres are still extant, but many of them now survive in their titles alone, *e.g.* those on the dialect of Homer and the lyric poets, and on Doric and Aeolic Greek.    The titles of several show that he was a strict adherent of 'Analogy'[1].

Theon the 'grammarian', of Alexandria, who flourished under
**Theon**    Tiberius, wrote a commentary on the *Odyssey*, and possibly also on Pindar; and apparently produced from the materials collected by Didymus a lexicon of tragic and of comic diction.    Besides completing the commentary of his father, Artemidorus, on the Αἴτια of Callimachus, he was himself a commentator on Lycophron, Theocritus, Apollonius Rhodius, and Nicander.    To the poets of the Alexandrian age his relation was the same as that of Didymus to the great writers of the classical age of Athens.    He has accordingly been aptly described as 'the Didymus of the Alexandrian poets'[2].

The scholars of Alexandria were (as we have seen) mainly but not exclusively concerned with the verbal criticism of the Greek poets, primarily with that of Homer, and secondarily with that of Pindar and the dramatists.    They were the earliest examples of the professional scholar, and they deserve the gratitude of the modern world for criticising and classifying the literature of the golden age of Greece and handing it down to posterity.    From the verbal critics of Alexandria we now turn to the more varied studies cultivated in the school of Pergamon, and to the system of grammar connected with that school.

---

[1] Christ, § 554[4]; Susemihl, ii 210–3; Fragments collected by Velsen (Berlin) 1853; supplemented in Schwabe's *Dionysius et Pausanias*, p. 69. Τρύφωνος τέχνη, published by the British Museum in 1891.

[2] Christ, § 555[4]; Susemihl, ii 215–7.    Cp. Maass in *Phil. Unt.* iii 33, and cp. Wilamowitz, *l.c.*, i 156, 161, 186.

In this brief notice of Tryphon and Theon, we have already passed the chronological limits of this Book.    Later Alexandrians, beginning with Pamphilus and Apion, are reserved for the Roman age (p. 295 *infra*).

Ptolemy I
and Berenike I.

Ptolemy II
and Arsinoe II.

GOLD OCTADRACHM OF PTOLEMY II AND ARSINOE II
inscribed ΘΕΩΝ ΑΔΕΛΦΩΝ.

(From the British Museum.)

For other portraits of Ptolemy I, Berenike I and their son Ptolemy II see
the sard from the Muirhead collection figured in Mr C. W. King's *Antique
Gems and Rings*, I p. ix and II pl. xlvii 6, and supposed by Mr King to have
been engraved for the Signet of Ptolemy II.

# CHAPTER IX.

## THE STOICS AND THE SCHOOL OF PERGAMON.

GRAMMAR was studied by the Stoics, not as an end in itself,
but as a necessary part of a complete system of
dialectics. Much of their terminology has become
a permanent part of the grammarian's vocabulary,
and some of their views on matters of language
may seem to the modern reader very far from novel. They
distinguished between the inarticulate cries of animals, and the
articulate voice of man (φωνὴ ἔναρθρος). The latter might be
either reduced to writing (ἔγγραμμος) or not (ἄγραμμος). When
reduced to writing, it became a λέξις, having for its elements the
24 letters. They further distinguished between the sound (στοι-
χεῖον) of the letter, and its written character (χαρακτὴρ τοῦ
στοιχείου), and the name of the character (e.g. ἄλφα). They
regarded the letters as consisting of seven vowels and six consonants (β γ δ, π κ τ), the rest being perhaps loosely regarded as
semivowels. From these letters words (λέξεις) were formed,
either conveying sense (σημαντικαί) or not. The former became
a λόγος; λέγειν was the expression of reason in words, while προ-
φέρεσθαι was merely the utterance of a sound. Speech might be
either in Prose or Verse; it was also of a twofold nature, appealing
to the ear and to the mind[1]. While the earlier Stoics recognised
four parts of speech, ὄνομα, ῥῆμα, σύνδεσμος, ἄρθρον, Chrysippus
distinguished between ὄνομα as 'a proper name' (e.g. Σωκράτης),
and ὄνομα προσηγορικόν, nomen appellativum (e.g. ἄνθρωπος). Under

The
Grammar of
the Stoics

---

[1] Diog. Laert. vii 55—58; cp. R. Schmidt, Stoicorum Grammatica (Halle,
1839), p. 18 f; Gräfenhan, Gesch. der Philologie, i 441, 505; Steinthal, Sprachwissenschaft, i² 291-3, and Egger, l.c., p. 349 f.

ἄρθρον was included the pronoun as well as the article, and it was noticed that, while the ἄρθρον was inflected, the σύνδεσμος was not. The definition of the ῥῆμα is identical with that of the κατηγόρημα, or predicate. Predicates may be active (ὀρθά), passive (ὕπτια), or neuter (οὐδέτερα). A special variety of the verbs passive in form, but not in sense, are the 'reflexive causative' verbs (ἀντιπεπονθότα) now generally called 'middle'. The term πτῶσις or 'inflexion' is applied by the Stoics to the noun and the ἄρθρον (pronoun and adjective), not to the verb. While Aristotle calls the nominative ὄνομα, and the oblique cases πτώσεις, the Stoics apply πτῶσις to the nominative as well, but they do not (like Aristotle) call an adverb a πτῶσις of the corresponding adjective[1]. In fact they confine πτῶσις to the four cases, the nominative (ὀρθὴ πτῶσις or εὐθεῖα, *casus rectus*) and the three oblique cases (πτώσεις πλάγιαι), the genitive (γενική), the dative (δοτική) and the accusative (αἰτιατική). The original meaning of these oblique cases was soon forgotten; the accusative did not originally mean the case that denotes the object of an accusation, but the case that denotes the effect of (τὸ αἰτιατόν, 'that which is caused by') an action; so that its original meaning is best expressed by the epithet *effectivus* or *causativus*. Again, γενική to the Stoics could only mean the case that denotes the γένος or kind or class (as in the 'partitive' genitive), although Priscian afterwards translated it by *generalis*[2]. A verb, when used with a nominative subject, is called by the Stoics a σύμβαμα (*e.g.* περιπατεῖ); when used with an oblique case a παρασύμβαμα (*e.g.* μεταμέλει). A verb with a nominative subject needing an oblique case to complete the sentence is called ἔλαττον ἢ σύμβαμα (*e.g.* Πλάτων φιλεῖ Δίωνα); a verb with an oblique case needing another oblique case to complete the sentence is called ἔλαττον ἢ παρασύμβαμα (*e.g.* Σωκράτει μεταμέλει Ἀλκιβιάδους)[3]. In other words, we have two kinds of verb, personal and impersonal, and each of these kinds may be either transitive or intransitive. Time past, present and future was distinguished as (χρόνος) παρῳχημένος, ἐνεστώς and μέλλων. The Stoics named the present and past tenses as follows:

---

[1] *Supra*, p. 97. Steinthal, i 297—303.
[2] Zeller's *Stoics etc.* p. 94.      [3] Steinthal, i 306.

Present:    (χρόνος) ἐνεστὼς παρατατικός (or ἀτελής).
Imperfect: παρῳχημένος παρατατικός (or ἀτελής).
Perfect:    ἐνεστὼς συντελικός (or τέλειος).
Pluperfect: παρῳχημένος συντελικός (or τέλειος).

The above four tenses, whether τέλειοι or ἀτελεῖς, are all ὡρισμένοι, (*tempora*) *finita*; the other tenses, whether future or past, are ἀόριστοι; but, while the future is called ὁ μέλλων (χρόνος), the term ἀόριστος is only used of the past[1].

The Stoics also paid special attention to Etymology. They regarded language as a product of nature, and 'onomatopoeia' as the principle on which words were first formed. This is definitely stated by Origen[2], and the statement is confirmed in a treatise bearing the name of St Augustine[3]; while, before the time of either, the fanciful etymologies of the Stoics had been singled out for attack by Galen[4]. Apart from Diogenes Laërtius and certain ancient commentators on Aristotle, our chief authority for the views of the Stoics on questions of language is the treatise of St Augustine above mentioned[5]. Their grammatical theories were known to Varro, who (as he tells us) combined the study of Cleanthes with that of Aristophanes of Byzantium[6].

The founder of the Stoics, Zeno of Citium (364–263)[7], is said to have written περὶ λέξεων, and as, in Stoic termi-
Zeno       nology, λέξις is defined as 'voice in written form', it has been conjectured that the work dealt mainly with definitions of terms, while it included passages in which the author gave an

---

[1] Steinthal, i 309, 314; T. Rumpel, *Casuslehre*, 1845, pp. 1—70.

[2] *Contra Celsum*, i p. 18, ...ὡς νομίζουσιν οἱ ἀπὸ τῆς Στοᾶς φύσει (ἐστὶ τὰ ὀνόματα), μιμουμένων τῶν πρώτων φωνῶν τὰ πράγματα καθ' ὧν τὰ ὀνόματα, καθὸ καὶ στοιχεῖά τινα ἐτυμολογίας εἰσάγουσιν.

[3] *Principia Dialecticae*, c. 6, haec quasi cunabula verborum esse crediderunt, ut sensus rerum cum sonorum sensu concordarent.

[4] *De Platonis et Hippocr. Dogm.* ii 2, ἀλαζών ἐστι μάρτυς ἡ ἐτυμολογία..., (Chrysippus appeals to the evidence of poets and) τὴν βελτίστην ἐτυμολογίαν ἢ τι ἄλλο τοιοῦτον, ἃ περαίνει μὲν οὐδέν, ἀναλίσκει δὲ καὶ κατατρίβει μάτην ἡμῶν τὸν χρόνον.—On the subject in general cp. R. Schmidt, *Stoicorum Grammatica*; also Steinthal, i 271—374; Christ, § 426[4], and Susemihl, i 48—87.

[5] Steinthal, i 293 f; Teuffel, *Rom. Lit.*, § 440, 7 Schwabe.

[6] Varro, *L. L.* v 9, non solum ad Aristophanis lucernam, sed etiam ad Cleanthis lucubravi.

[7] Gomperz, in *S. Ber.* Vienna Acad. cxlvi (1903), 6.

extended meaning to the term 'solecism'[1]. He also wrote on
'poetry', and produced five books on 'Homeric problems', full of
allegorical interpretations, which were justly attacked by Aristarchus[2]. Like Aristotle, he accepted the *Margites* as a work of
Homeric authorship, and in *Od.* iv 84 he introduced by emendation a reference to the 'Arabians'[3]. He regarded Zeus, Hera
and Poseidon as representing aether, air and water respectively;
and, in interpreting Hesiod's *Theogony*, he gave free play to his
etymological fancy[4]. The allegorical interpretation of myths in
general, and of the Homeric poems in particular, was in fact one
of the characteristics of the Stoic school[5].

Zeno's successor, Cleanthes of Assos (331—232), wrote on
grammar, and was the first of the Stoics to write on
rhetoric[6]. In his work περὶ τοῦ ποιητοῦ he treated          Cleanthes
of Homer, applying playful etymologies and fanciful allegories to
the interpretation of the poet. In the allegorical sense which he
applies to the herb 'moly' we find the earliest known example of
the word ἀλληγορικῶς[7]. With Cleanthes 'the Eleusinian mysteries are an allegory; Homer, if properly understood, is a witness
to truth; the very names given to Zeus, Persephone, Apollo, and
Aphrodite are indications of the hidden meaning which is veiled
but not perverted by the current belief, and the same is true of
the myths of Heracles and Atlas'[8]. He described poetry as the
best medium for expressing the dignity of divinity[9]; and his grave
and dignified *Hymn to Zeus* is still extant[10].

As a representative of the grammatical as well as the general
teaching of the Stoics he was less famous than Chry-
sippus (*c.* 280—*c.* 208-4), who is proverbially known          Chrysippus
as the Pillar of the Stoic Porch[11], εἰ μὴ γὰρ ἦν Χρύσιππος, οὐκ ἂν

---

[1] A. C. Pearson, *Fragments of Zeno and Cleanthes*, pp. 27, 81, 82.

[2] Diog. Laert. vii 4; Dion Chrys. *Or.* 53, 4.

[3] Pearson, *l.c.*, pp. 31, 218, 219.

[4] Pearson, *l. c.*, pp. 13, 155.          [5] Zeller's *Stoics*, 334—348.

[6] Cic. *de Fin.* iv 7; Quint. ii 15, 35; Striller, *De Stoicorum studiis rhetoricis.*

[7] Pearson, pp. 287, 293.          [8] *ib.* p. 43.

[9] Philodemus, *De Musica*, col. 28; cp. Seneca, *Ep.* 108, 10 (*ib.* p. 279 f).

[10] Stobaeus, *Ecl.* i 1, 12 (*ib.* p. 274).

[11] Cic. *Acad.* ii 75, qui fulcire putabatur porticum Stoicorum.

ἦν Στοά[1]. He showed his independence of character by declining an invitation to the court of Alexandria, and by never dedicating to royalty any of his numerous works. They exceeded the number of 700, and it was said of him that no one ever was a clearer dialectician or a worse writer[2]; accordingly his writings have not survived. Himself a native of Soli in Cilicia, he wrote several works on 'Solecisms', a term which then had no connexion with the dialect of the inhabitants of Soli, but implied faults of logic, as well as offences against good taste and correct pronunciation[3]. He also wrote a series of works on 'ambiguity' (ἀμφιβολία), with treatises 'on the five cases', 'on singular and plural terms', 'on rhetoric', and 'on the parts of speech'[4]. To the five parts of speech recognised by Chrysippus (ὄνομα, προσηγορία, ῥῆμα, σύνδεσμος and ἄρθρον), his pupil, Antipater of Tarsus, added a sixth (μεσότης, the participle). Chrysippus agreed with Zeno in holding that not only justice, but also law, and language in its correct form (ὀρθὸς λόγος), exist by nature. He wrote four books on 'anomaly'[5], being (so far as is known) the first to use the term in a grammatical sense, as the opposite of 'analogy'[6], the adherents of 'analogy' insisting on the *rules* applicable to the forms of words, and the adherents of 'anomaly' on the *exceptions*. The cause of 'analogy' was maintained by the Alexandrian critic, Aristarchus, while among the most conspicuous adherents of 'anomaly' was the Stoic Crates of Mallos, who, like Chrysippus and Antipater, was a native of Cilicia, and (about 168 B.C.) was the head of the Pergamene school.

Pergamon, the literary rival of Alexandria, was a town of

Pergamon
and its rulers

ancient origin in a lofty situation looking down on the valley of the Caïcus, about 15 miles from the Mysian coast. Early in the Alexandrian age a dynasty was there founded by Philetaerus, treasurer of Lysimachus, king of Thrace. Throwing off his allegiance to Lysimachus (c. 283), he appropriated the vast treasure of 9000 talents entrusted

---

[1] Diog. Laert. vii 183.        [2] Dion. Hal. *De Comp. Verb.* c. 4.

[3] Gräfenhan, i 508 f.        [4] Classen, *De Gram. Gr. Prim.* 73 f.

[5] Diog. Laert. vii 192, περὶ τῆς κατὰ τὰς λέξεις ἀνωμαλίας πρὸς Δίωνα, δ′; Varro, *L. L.* ix 1 (Susemihl, ii 8).

[6] Lersch, *Sprachphilosophie*, i 51.

to his care, and bequeathed his power to his nephews Eumenes I
(263—241) and Attalus I (241—197).   Eumenes I was not only a
generous patron of Arcesilaus, a native of the neighbouring town
of Pitane, the first president of the Middle Academy at Athens,
and the writer of epigrams in honour of Attalus I; he also
invited to his court the Peripatetic philosopher, Lycon[1].  His
famous successor, Attalus I, claimed the title of king after his
early victories over the Gallic invaders, and celebrated those
victories by a splendid series of sculptures in bronze, the most
famous of which is familiar to us in the marble copy now known
as the 'Dying Gaul' of the Capitoline Museum.  Among the
sculptors employed on these works was Antigonus, who also wrote
treatises on the toreutic art and on famous painters, and is once
called Antigonus of Carystos[2].  The sculptor and writer on art
has accordingly been identified with the author of that name and
place, who died later than 226 B.C., after writing lives of philosophers founded on his personal knowledge and frequently quoted
by Diogenes Laertius, and also a work on the wonders of nature,
which is still extant.  In literature he is the leading representative
of the earlier Pergamene School[3].  Attalus I was himself an
author, and his description of a large pine-tree in the Troad is
preserved in Strabo[4].  He invited to his court Lacydes, the
successor of Arcesilaus, as the head of the Academy at Athens,
but Lacydes declined with the apt reply that pictures should
be seen from a certain distance.  He nevertheless laid out for
Lacydes a special garden in the grounds of the Academy[5].  He
was more successful in inviting the future historian of his reign,
the younger Neanthes, and the eminent mathematician, Apollonius of Perga, who dedicated to the king his celebrated work
on Conic Sections.  It was probably under his rule that books
began to be collected for the Pergamene Library,    The Library
but the credit of actually building the fabric is
expressly assigned by Strabo[6] to his successor Eumenes II
(197—159 B.C.), the elder son of Attalus I by Apollonis, whose

---

[1] Diog. Laert. iv 30, 38.            [2] Zenobius, *Paroem.* v 82.

[3] Cp. the brilliant and suggestive work of Wilamowitz, *Antigonos von
Karystos*, in *Phil. Unt.* iv ; also Christ, § 430[4]; and Susemihl, i 468 f.

[4] p. 603.          [5] Diog. Laert. iv 60.          [6] p. 624.

beautiful head may still be seen figured on the coins of Cyzicus[1].
Eumenes II strove to bring the Library to the same level as that
of Alexandria, and apparently endeavoured to induce Aristophanes
of Byzantium to leave Alexandria for Pergamon[2]. He adorned
his capital with magnificent structures, including a great altar of
Zeus. The frieze represented the battle of the Gods and Giants
in a perfect pantheon of highly animated mythological figures,
whose varied attributes possibly owed part of their inspiration to
the learned mythologists of the Pergamene Library[3]. The altar
has been assigned to about 180—170 B.C., and our knowledge of
its sculptures, as well as of the architecture and topography of
Pergamon in general, has been vastly increased by the German
excavations of 1878 to 1886[4]. Along a lower level than the
precinct of the altar, ran the vast terrace of the theatre, with the
theatre itself above it, to the left of the altar. Above the theatre
and the altar was the precinct of the temple of Athena Polias
Nicephorus, with the acropolis rising beyond it, 1000 feet above
the level of the sea. The precinct of Athena, a quadrangle of
about 240 feet by 162, was bounded on the east by a single
colonnade, about 19 feet in breadth, and by a double colonnade,
twice as broad, to the north. These colonnades were in two
stories, and to the north of the upper storey of the double
colonnade the remains of four large rooms have been discovered.
The largest of these is 42 feet in length and 49 in width; the rest
vary in length, and are 39 feet wide. Along the eastern, northern
and western sides of the largest room are the foundations of a
narrow platform or bench, and in the centre of the northern side
a mass of stonework identified as the pedestal of a statue. In
front of this pedestal, and facing the south-east entrance, was
found a colossal statue of Athena, the tutelar divinity of libraries[5];
and, in adjacent portions of the ruins, pedestals of statues bearing
the names of Homer, Alcaeus, Herodotus and Timotheus of

[1] Head's *Coins of the Ancients*, Plate 48, 6. For portrait of Eumenes II,
see p. 166 *infra*.

[2] Suïdas (*s.v.* Ἀριστοφ.) ὡς βουλόμενος πρὸς Εὐμένη φυγεῖν, *supra*, p. 111.

[3] E. A. Gardner's *Handbook of Gr. Sculpture*, ii 462.

[4] Cp. the official reports; also Baumeister's *Denkmäler*, pp. 1201—1287;
and Holm, iv c. 21, n. 1 etc.

[5] Juv. iii 219; Plin. *N. H.* vii 210.

Miletus (d. 357 B.C.), besides two Macedonian historians (Apollonius and Balacrus) who are less known to fame[1]. A block of stone inscribed with a couplet in honour of Sappho, identical with that assigned in Anth. vii 15 to Antipater of Sidon (c. 150 B.C.), had been seen at Pergamon early in the fifteenth century. Such portrait-statues are characteristic of libraries[2]. In the largest room were observed two rows of holes in the north wall, and the lower of these two rows was continued along the east wall. These holes may have served to receive supports for brackets or shelves. There is every probability that the ruins of these four rooms are all that remains of the famous Pergamene Library[3]. The small adjacent rooms may have been used by copyists and attendants, while the upper floor of the colonnade in front of the Library may have served as a place of either transit or lounge. In any case it had a sunny outlook towards the S.E., thus commanding an immediate view of the temple of the 'Victorious Athena' and the sculptured memorials of victory or of gratitude in the court below, and, beyond the latter, a wide prospect of the valley of the Caïcus.

The inscriptions above the colonnades and on the literary statues already mentioned are sometimes assigned to the reign of Attalus II (159—138)[4], who, like both of his predecessors, was a patron of art and learning. It was to Attalus II that Apollodorus of Athens dedicated his great work on Chronology after leaving Alexandria for Pergamon (c. 146 B.C.)[5]. As a pupil of the Stoic Seleucus, and, for a still longer time, of Aristarchus, Apollodorus forms a link between the school of Alexandria and that of Pergamon, which was closely connected with the Stoic philosophy.

Attalus II was succeeded by Attalus III (138—133), a sanguinary tyrant, who failed to follow the great example set by his

[1] Fränkel, nos. 198—203.          [2] Plin. N. H. xxxv 10.

[3] Conze, *Monatsber. d. Berlin. Akad.* 1884, pp. 1259—1270; Baumeister's *Denkmäler*, p. 1222 with general plan on p. 1215 and restoration of the precinct of Athena on p. 1219; Pauly-Wissowa, s.v. *Bibliotheken*, p. 414; Pontremoli and Collignon's *Pergame*, pp. 135—152; and J. W. Clark, *The Care of Books* (1901), pp. 7—11, where there is a plan of the Library reduced from Plate iii in vol. II of the *Altertümer von Pergamon*, 1885.

[4] Urlichs, *Perg. Inschr.* (1883), p. 20 f.

[5] See p. 137.

predecessors either as patrons of learning or as promoters of the arts of sculpture and architecture.   He was apparently, however, the theme of an encomium by Nicander (c. 202—c. 133), already mentioned[1] as the author of didactic poems on venomous bites and on antidotes, who possibly had some sympathy with the king's pursuits.   Neglecting his royal duties, he amused himself with gardening, taking special interest in the cultivation of poisonous plants.   He also had a fancy for making models in wax and casting figures in bronze[2].   Such was the degenerate form in which the patronage of art expired in the last of the Attalids. The inscriptions of Pergamon[3] credit him however with military prowess in some victory (possibly involving a slight extension of territory) which is otherwise unknown.   In his brief reign of five years there appears to have been nothing more notable than the bequest of his property to the Roman people (133 B.C.).   His family had then been in power for exactly 150 years[4].

Antigonus of Carystos has already been mentioned as the leading representative of the early Pergamene school[5].

**Polemon of Ilium**   Among other scholars who owed allegiance to the rulers of Pergamon, was Polemon of Ilium, a contemporary of Aristophanes of Byzantium (fl. 200—177 B.C.). He is known to have addressed a letter to Attalus, probably the first of that name.   It was doubtless in recognition of his work on the treasures of Delphi that he was made a *proxenus* of that place in 177 B.C.   He lived for some time at Athens, of which he became a citizen, and also probably at Pergamon; but he was specially famous for his extensive travels in all parts of Greece, and in Italy and Sicily.   He was a prolific writer on Greek topography, and his diligence in copying, collecting and expounding inscriptions led to his receiving from an adherent of Crates in a later age the title of *stelokopas*, or 'the tapper of tablets'[6], a title reminding us of the itinerant antiquary whose

---

[1] p. 116 *supra*.                [2] Justin xxxvi 4, 3 (ap. Susemihl, ii 415).

[3] Fränkel, nos. 246, 249.

[4] On the history of Pergamon, cp. Fynes-Clinton, *Fasti Hell.*, iii 400—410; Holm's *History of Greece*, iv c. 13, n. 6, and c. 21; and Wilcken in Pauly-Wissowa, s.v. *Attalus*.   On the 'will' of Attalus III cp. Mommsen, *History of Rome*, Bk iv c. 1, and Mahaffy in *Hermathena*, ix (1896), pp. 389—405.

[5] p. 151 *supra*.                [6] Herodicus ap. Athen. 234 D.

care in tending the moss-grown memorials of the names of the
Covenanters led to his being known as 'Old Mortality'.  Polemon
was however more widely famous as the *periegetes*.  His works
were quoted by Didymus and Aristonicus, and by Strabo and
Plutarch, the latter of whom eulogises his learning and his vivid
interest in Hellenic matters[1].  He devoted four books to the
Votive Offerings on the Athenian Acropolis alone.  The question
how far Pausanias is directly or indirectly indebted to Polemon
has been much discussed, but his indebtedness is conclusively
disproved by Mr Frazer[2].  His interests were not limited to
topography.  His antiquarian researches led him to the study of
Greek Comedy, and we owe to Polemon nearly all that is known
on the subject of Greek parodies[3].

Antiquarian research was represented about 150 B.C. by
Demetrius of Scepsis in the Troad (born *c.* 214 B.C.),
who wrote a discursive work in 30 books on the      Demetrius of
list of the Trojan forces comprised in only 60 lines        Scepsis
of the second book of the *Iliad*.  In the language of Professor
Jebb, 'this work appears to have been one of the most wonderful
monuments of scholarly labour which even the indefatigable
erudition of the Alexandrian age produced.  The most complete
examination of every point which the subject raised or suggested
was supported by stores of learning drawn from every province of
ancient literature, from every source of oral or local tradition.
Mythology, history, geography, the monographs of topographers,
the observations of travellers, poetry of every age and kind,
science in all its ancient branches, appear to have been laid under
contribution by this encyclopaedic commentator'[4].  He is quoted
by Strabo in more than 25 passages, particularly in connexion
with the topography of the Troad, where his local knowledge is
described as especially valuable[5].  In agreement with the views
of Hellanicus of Miletus, Polemon of Ilium had with local

---

[1] *Qu. Symp.* v 2, 675 B, πολυμαθοῦς καὶ οὐ νυστάζοντος ἐν τοῖς Ἑλληνικοῖς
πράγμασιν ἀνδρός.

[2] *Pausanias*, I lxxxiii—xc.

[3] Athen. 698 B.  Preller, *Polemonis periegetae fragmenta* (1838); Susemihl,
i 665—676; Christ, 434[4].

[4] *J. H. S.* ii 34 f.              [5] p. 602, §43.

patriotism identified the Greek Ilium in the Trojan plain as the
site of Homeric Troy. The Greek Ilium corresponds to *Hissarlik*,
or Schliemann's 'Troy,' which lies only 3 miles from the Hellespont. The pretensions of the Ilians were rejected by Demetrius
of Scepsis in favour of a lofty site about 3¾ miles further inland,
corresponding to the village of *Bunárbashi*[1].

From Polemon of Ilium and Demetrius of Scepsis, who
belonged to the district of the Troad subject to the rulers of
Pergamon, we pass to the name of one who was closely connected
with Pergamon itself. The head of the Pergamene school during
the reign of Eumenes II (the builder of the Library)
was Crates of Mallos. He was a strong opponent
of his somewhat earlier contemporary, the great
critic Aristarchus of Alexandria, being (like Chrysippus) an
adherent of 'anomaly' as opposed to 'analogy'[2]. He was also
an opponent of Aristarchus in the allegorical treatment of Homer
which (as we have seen[3]), was characteristic of the Stoic school
to which Crates belonged. His views were expounded in an
allegorical commentary on Homer, and also in a critical commentary, entitled Ὁμηρικά and διορθωτικά respectively[4]. Fragments of these are preserved in the *scholia*, which also contain
traces of a 'life of Homer'. Besides these we have some stray
remarks on Hesiod, and fuller proof of the existence of commentaries on Euripides and Aristophanes, with a work on the Attic
dialect. Whether he produced any 'edition' of Homer, as
distinguished from critical remarks on the text, is uncertain[5].

*Crates of Mallos*

---

[1] Jebb's *Homer*, p. 148; cp. *J. H. S.* ii 33, iii 185—217; and (in favour of
*Hissarlik*) Mahaffy, *ib.* iii 69 f. On Demetrius, cp. Susemihl, 681–5; Christ,
§ 392[4]; Leaf's *Troy*, 1912, 135 f.

[2] Varro, *L. L.* ix 1, Crates nobilis grammaticus qui fretus Chrysippo
homine acutissimo, qui reliquit περὶ ἀνωμαλίας IIII libros, contra analogiam
atque Aristarchum est nixus. Gellius, ii 25, ἀναλογία est similium similis decli-
natio, quam quidem Latine proportionem vocant. ἀνωμαλία est inaequalitas
declinationum, consuetudinem sequens. Duo autem Graeci Grammatici illus-
tres, Aristarchus et Crates, summo opere ille ἀναλογίαν, hic ἀνωμαλίαν deien-
sitavit.

[3] p. 149 *supra*.

[4] He appears to have proposed δίς for τρίς in *Od.* xii 106 (Ludwich's
*Homervulgata*, p. 193 f).

[5] C. Wachsmuth, *De Cratete Mallota* (1860), p. 31; Ludwich, i 43; Maass,

Among his Homeric readings several deserve mention, as in *Il.*
xxi 323, τυμβοχόης (for τυμβοχοῆσ(αι), preferred by Aristarchus),
*ib.* 558, πρὸς πεδίον Ἰδήϊον (for Ἰλήϊον), and xxiv 253, κατηφέες
(for κατηφόνες). In xi 754 he preferred διὰ σπιδέος to δι᾽ ἀσπιδέος
πεδίοιο[1]. He agreed with Zenodotus and Eratosthenes, against
Aristarchus, in allowing Homer to combine the dual with the
plural[2]. He endeavoured to bring Homer into accord with the
Stoic views on geography. The stream of Oceanus was supposed
to flow through the torrid zone, sending forth two branches
towards each of the poles. The scene of the voyage of Odysseus
was accordingly laid in the outer and not (as Aristarchus thought)
in the inner (or Mediterranean) sea[3]. Menelaus in his voyage of
seven years was deemed to have sailed from Gadeira to India[4].
In the description of the land of the Laestrygones, where 'the
courses of the night and day are near together'[5], Crates saw a
reference to the short northern nights[6]. His interest in geography
was further shown by the fact that he constructed a terrestrial
globe, mentioned by Strabo[7].

The controversy on 'analogy' and 'anomaly', in which Crates
was interested as a grammarian of the Stoic school, turned
mainly on matters of declension and conjugation. Aristophanes
of Byzantium had endeavoured to classify words by the application
of five tests. If two words were of the same 'kind', *e.g.* both
of them nouns or verbs, in the same 'case' or 'inflexion', and
identical in termination, number of syllables and sound, they were
'analogous' to one another; *i.e.* they belonged to the same
declension or conjugation. Aristarchus added a sixth test, by
which both the words compared were to be simple or both of
them compound. Crates appears to have regarded all the trouble
spent on determining the laws of declension and conjugation as
idle and superfluous, and preferred simply to accept the phenomena of language as the arbitrary results of custom and usage.

---

*Aratea*, pp. 167—207; Helck, 1905. Maass (p. 172) holds that he produced three
Homeric works, (1) διόρθωσις, (2) περὶ διορθώσεως or διορθωτικά, (3) Ὁμηρικά.

[1] Wachsmuth, 28 f.      [2] *ib.* 20 f.      [3] Gell. xiv 6, 3.

[4] Strabo, p. 38; cp. Gudeman, in *Johns Hopkins University Circulars*,
Dec. 1902.

[5] *Od.* x 86.      [6] Schol. on Aratus, *Phaen.* 61.

[7] p. 116. Cp. *Vol. Hercul.* xi 147[2], τὰ περὶ τῆς σφαιροποΐας ὁ Κρ[ά]της
(Usener, ap. Maass, *l.c.*, p. 169).

But he was wrong in denying all 'analogy', and in practically opposing the accurate grammatical scholarship of the Alexandrian school[1].

Crates was probably responsible for drawing up the classified lists (πίνακες) of authors in the Pergamene Library, in which (as is sometimes held) the leading writers of prose, especially the orators, had a prominent place, just as the poets had in the lists of the Alexandrian grammarians[2]. It is true that Dionysius of Halicarnassus mentions the Pergamene lists in connexion with a speech of Deinarchus[3]; but he also states that he had found no detailed account of that orator written either by Callimachus, or by the Pergamene scholars[4]. This shows that the critic was equally prepared to find what he wanted in the lists of the Alexandrian as in those of the Pergamene school, and that the orators were not necessarily excluded from the former. Again, Athenaeus[5] says of a play ascribed to Alexis, that it was not included in the lists of Callimachus or Aristophanes, or even in those drawn up by the scholars in Pergamon. It will be observed that poets were not excluded from the Pergamene lists. The poet Alcman is the subject of the only notice which has been conjecturally identified as a fragment of the lists of Crates[6]; and the only epigram attributed to Crates[7] describes the epic poet Choerilus as far inferior to Antimachus.

Crates was sent as an envoy to the Roman Senate 'shortly after the death of Ennius'. Now, Ennius died in 169 B.C., and Suetonius[8], who connects the visit of Crates with that event, also

---

[1] Susemihl, ii 7—10; cp. Steinthal, ii 121—126. On Crates in general cp. Lübbert, *Rhein. Mus.* xi (1857), 428—443; C. Wachsmuth, *l.c.*, and Hübner's *Bibliographie*, § 13.

[2] Reifferscheid, Breslau, 1881–2; Brzoska, *ibid.* 1883 (Susemihl, i 343, 521, ii 12, 484, 694).

[3] *De Dein.* 11, οὗτος ἐν τοῖς Περγαμηνοῖς Πίναξι φέρεται ὡς Καλλικράτους.

[4] *ib.* 1, ὁρῶν οὐδὲν ἀκριβὲς οὔτε Καλλίμαχον οὔτε τοὺς ἐκ Περγάμου γραμματικοὺς περὶ αὐτοῦ γράψαντας.

[5] 336 E, οἱ τὰς ἐν Περγάμῳ ἀναγραφὰς ποιησάμενοι.

[6] Suïdas, Ἀλκμὰν Λάκων ἀπὸ Μεσσόας, κατὰ δὲ τὸν Κράτητα πταίοντα (?) Λυδὸς ἐκ Σάρδεων. [7] *Anth.* xi 218.

[8] *De Grammaticis*, c. 2, primus...studium grammaticae in urbem intulit Crates Mallotes, Aristarchi aequalis, qui missus ad senatum ab Attalo rege inter secundum ac tertium Punicum bellum *sub ipsam Ennii mortem*, cum regione Palatii prolapsus in cloacae foramen crus fregisset, per omne legationis

states that Crates was sent to Rome by Attalus, *i.e.* Attalus II,
who came to the throne in 159 B.C. Hence it is sometimes
assumed (*e.g.* by Fynes-Clinton) that the visit of Crates belongs
to the year 159. But it appears probable that, while Suetonius
is right in connecting it closely with the death of Ennius, he is
wrong in assigning it to the reign of Attalus. Attalus was repeatedly in Rome as the envoy of his elder brother Eumenes II
when the latter was on the throne. Of the five years in which he
was in Rome (192, 181, 168, 163, 160), one was 168 B.C., the
year immediately after the death of Ennius, when, after fighting
on the side of Aemilius Paulus at Pydna, he was sent to congratulate the Romans on their victory. On this occasion he was
certainly accompanied by the physician Stratius[1], and it appears
probable that he was also accompanied by Crates. It would thus
appear that Crates was really sent *ab Eumene rege cum Attalo*,
and not *ab Attalo rege*. By a curious accident the visit of Crates
had a remarkable effect on literary studies in Rome. While he
was wandering on the Palatine, he accidentally stumbled over
an opening in a drain and broke his leg. He passed part of
the time during which he was thus detained in giving lectures,
which aroused among the Romans a taste for the scholarly study
of literature, with results which will be mentioned as soon as
we reach the Roman age[2]. It may here, however, be suggested
that, in the course of his conversations with leading Romans, he
could hardly have failed to mention the halls and colonnades of
the Pergamene Library and the adjacent temple, the building of
which is assigned to Eumenes II, whose envoy he seems to have
been. As Attalus whom he apparently accompanied to Rome
had fought at Pydna, and as Quintus Metellus was one of the
three selected to carry to Rome the despatches announcing the
victory[3], Metellus doubtless met Crates in Rome. In this connexion it is interesting to remember that in 146 B.C. Metellus
built the colonnades of the *Porticus Metelli* and one of the
temples which they enclosed, and that the *Porticus Octaviae*, built
by Augustus on its site (after 33 B.C.), included within its colon-

---

simul et valetudinis tempus plurimas acroasis subinde fecit assidueque disseruit,
ac nostris exemplo fuit ad imitandum. Cp. Scioppius, Introd. to *Grammatica
Philosophica* (1628), quoted in Max Müller's *Lectures*, ii 110[5].

[1] Livy, xlv 19.　　　[2] p. 172 *infra*.　　　[3] Livy, xliv 45.

nades a library of Greek and also a library of Latin books, which succeeded that of Asinius Pollio in the *Atrium Libertatis* (37 B.C.), and preceded the Palatine Library (28 B.C.)[1]. Thus the visit of Crates may have ultimately had some influence on the structural arrangements of the public libraries of Rome.

The most famous pupil of Crates was the Stoic philosopher

The School of Crates

Panaetius (*c.* 185—110)[2], who nevertheless abandoned his master's allegorical method of interpretation for the natural method of Aristarchus[3]. To his school also belonged Artemon of Pergamon, the author of a commentary on Pindar's Odes in honour of Sicilian princes; Zenodotus of Mallos, who defended certain Homeric passages obelised by Aristarchus; Asclepiades[4] of Myrleia in Bithynia (born between 130 and 80 B.C.), who wrote a learned monograph on Nestor's cup, with commentaries on Homer and Theocritus, a history of Bithynia and a history of 'grammarians'; and Heracleon of Tilotis in Egypt, the author of a commentary on the *Iliad* and *Odyssey*[5].

While there is no evidence as to any direct connexion between Pergamon and the 'Asiatic' style of oratory represented (*c.* 250 B.C.) by Hegesias, a native of the city of Magnesia ad Sipylum, about 40 miles distant, we have certainly a point of contact between Pergamon and the Attic reaction in the first century B.C., and

Apollodorus of Pergamon

also between both and Rome. Pergamon was the birthplace of the rhetorician Apollodorus (*c.* 102— *c.* 20 B.C.), who, after counting 'the Attic Dionysius' among his pupils in his native place, left Pergamon for Rome, where he was selected by Julius Caesar as an instructor of the young Octavian (45 B.C.), and where he founded a flourishing school of rhetoric[6]. Another point of contact between Pergamon

Athenodorus

and Rome may be found in the person of the Stoic Athenodorus of Tarsus, who abused his position as

---

[1] Cp. Middleton's *Ancient Rome*, ii 200 f; and J. W. Clark, *The Care of Books*, pp. 12—14.

[2] The friend of the younger Scipio, and the authority followed by Cicero in the *De Officiis*. Cp. Susemihl, ii 63—80, 704 f.

[3] Schmekel, p. 207 f (ap. Susemihl, ii 705).

[4] Pauly-Wissowa, *s.v.* 1628—30; B. A. Müller, Leipzig, 1903.

[5] Susemihl, ii 13—27; Schanz, in *Hermes*, xxv (1890), 36—54.

[6] Susemihl, ii 504 f.

head of the Pergamene Library by attempting to tamper with passages in the works of the earlier Stoics differing from the views of their successors[1]. He is perhaps in part responsible for the story respecting the Peisistratean redaction of the Homeric poems[2]. He was already an old man in 70 B.C. when Cato visited Pergamon, and invited him to become an inmate of his house in Rome, where he died[3]. The school of Crates claims another learned Greek who settled in Rome, Alexander Polyhistor (*c.* 105—*c.* 35 B.C.). Taken prisoner in the time of Sulla, he was made a citizen of Rome by the Dictator, after he had served as a teacher in the house of Lentulus. His writings, which were more remarkable for their quantity than their quality, were mainly uncritical compilations on historical and geographical subjects. His legendary history of Rome was followed in certain points by Livy[4], Tibullus[5] and Virgil[6]; and his list of the Sibyls and his early history of Delphi, by Pausanias. He was interested in the nations of the East and especially in the Jews. He appears to have aimed at supplying the imperfectly educated Roman public with a variety of information which would enable them to understand the learned poets of the day, and would foster a belief in the legendary connexion between the kings of Rome and the heroes of Troy. Among his pupils was the freedman Hyginus, who was appointed by Augustus to preside over the Palatine Library[7]. Demetrius Magnes, a contemporary of Cicero, besides dedicating to Atticus a work on Concord[8], was the author of two lost works of a historical and philological character, (1) on cities, and (2) on authors, bearing the same name. The greater part of the account of Deinarchus in the latter has been quoted and criticised by Dionysius of Halicarnassus[9], while other portions of the work found their way into the 'Lives of Philosophers' compiled by Diogenes Laërtius[10].

*Alexander Polyhistor*

*Demetrius Magnes*

---

[1] Diog. Laert. vii 34.
[2] Susemihl, ii 246.
[3] Plut. *Cato Minor*, 10, 16.
[4] i 3.
[5] ii 5.
[6] *Aen.* x 388.
[7] Susemihl, ii 356—364; Pauly-Wissowa, i 1449 f.
[8] *Ad Att.* viii 11, 7; 12, 6.
[9] *De Dinarcho*, c. 5.
[10] Susemihl, i 509 f.

In comparing the scholarship of Alexandria with that of Pergamon, we must remember that the former passed through several phases. Under the first Ptolemy, Hecataeus of Abdera, who was a historian as well as a scholar, wrote a history of Egypt representing it as the home of wisdom from time immemorial[1]. Under the first three Ptolemies, whose combined rule extended over a century (323—222 B.C.), scholarship of the first rank flourished at Alexandria and left its mark on all later ages, while the poetry of that time, which found imitators in Rome, was of the second rank, except in the case of Theocritus, who was not very closely connected with Alexandria. In the first age of Alexandrian scholarship Philetas, Zenodotus, Callimachus and Eratosthenes were 'poets' as well as scholars. In the second, Aristophanes and Aristarchus were scholars alone: the scholar had now narrowed into the specialist, but had gained a new power in the process. This second age closes with the accession of Ptolemy Physcon (146), and the death of Aristarchus (c. 143). Physcon played at textual criticism, and yet persecuted the Greeks of Alexandria, including the great critic himself[2]. The Alexandrian Greeks are described by Polybius[3], who visited their city about 136 B.C., as less uncivilised than the mercenary soldiers, while, in comparison with both, the native Egyptians were 'clever and civilised'. Physcon set his mercenaries upon the Alexandrians of Greek descent with the result that this class was almost extinct when Polybius visited the place. This persecution of the Greeks made the Jews, who had been influenced by Greek culture, and were regarded with suspicion by Physcon, an increasingly important element in the intellectual life of Alexandria. It also 'filled the islands and cities with grammarians, philosophers, geometricians, musicians, painters, trainers, physicians and many other professional persons, whose poverty impelled them to teach what they knew, and thus to turn out many notable pupils'[4]. In the third age of Alexandrian scholarship, a pupil of Aristarchus, Apollodorus of Athens, preferred Athens and Pergamon to Alexandria, while Dionysius the Thracian left Alexandria for Rhodes, and Didymus, a century later, possibly resided in Rome.

[1] Holm, iv c. 20, n. 8.    [2] On Physcon (Euergetes II), see *supra*, p. 136, n. 5.
[3] xxxiv 14.    [4] Menecles ap. Athen. 184 c.

But in all its phases the school of Alexandria was in the main a school of *verbal criticism*. Even the versatile and widely-accomplished Eratosthenes laid himself open to the attacks of a representative of the Pergamene school, Polemon of Ilium, who exposed his mistakes in matters connected with Attic antiquities, drawing from them the ironical inference that Eratosthenes, who was actually educated at Athens, could never have visited Athens at all[1]. This is one of the earliest indications of the literary rivalry between Alexandria and Pergamon. The conflict between Aristarchus, the adherent of 'analogy', and Crates, the adherent of 'anomaly', is another. The feud descended to the successors of both: pupils of Aristarchus, such as Dionysius Thrax and Parmeniscus, attacked the opinions of Crates, while a pupil of Crates, Zenodotus of Mallos, attacked those of Aristarchus[2]. It found an echo even in distant Babylon. A follower of Crates, of uncertain date, named Herodicus of Babylon, doubtless recalling the disputes of the Alexandrian critics on the epic forms of the personal pronouns, and especially the fact that Aristarchus had proved that Homer used only μιν, not νιν, describes the followers of Aristarchus as 'buzzing in corners, and busy with mono-syllables' :—

> γωνιοβόμβυκες μονοσύλλαβοι, οἷσι μέμηλεν
> τὸ σφὶν καὶ σφωΐν καὶ τὸ μὶν ἠδὲ τὸ νίν[3].

While the school of Alexandria was mainly interested in verbal scholarship, the school of Pergamon found room for a larger variety of scholarly studies. In that school art and the history of art were represented by Antigonus of Carystos; learned travel and the study of inscriptions, by Polemon of Ilium ; topography, by Demetrius of Scepsis ; chronology, by Apollodorus

[1] περὶ τῆς Ἀθήνησιν Ἐρατοσθένους ἐπιδημίας. Cp. Strabo, p. 15, with Wilamowitz, *Antigonos von Karystos*, p. 164 f; and Susemihl, i 670 f.

[2] C. Wachsmuth, *l.c.* 7.

[3] Athen. p. 222 A, cp. Cobet, *Misc. Crit.*, p. 250, and Susemihl, ii 24 f. Similarly Philip of Thessalonica (probably in the time of Trajan) satirically describes grammarians as belonging to the pack of Zenodotus and the troops of Callimachus, as hunters of wretched particles, who delight in μὶν and σφὶν (*Anth.* xi 321), and as bookworms of the school of Aristarchus ; and prays that an inglorious night may descend on the followers of Callimachus (*ib.* 347); cp. xi 142, and Virgil, *Catal.* ii 4.

of Athens; the philosophy of the Stoics, combined with grammar and literary criticism, by Crates of Mallos. The cosmopolitan Stoics were readily induced to settle in Pergamon, while philosophers of the Academic school remained true to Athens. Attalus I and Eumenes I showed a special interest in that school, and in Athens in general. The former commemorated his conquest of the Gauls by dedicating famous works of sculpture on the acropolis of Athens, as well as on the lofty terraces of Pergamon; and, in the time of the latter, Pergamon had its own festival of the Panathenaea. The Attalid dynasty was also strongly attracted towards Rome. While the Alexandrian Aristophanes suggested the possible spuriousness of the lines in which Poseidon foretells the rule of Aeneas[1], a belief in the legend of Aeneas was prudently fostered by the school of Pergamon[2].

As compared with Pergamon and Alexandria, few of the cities of the Greek world were of special importance as seats of learning during the Alexandrian age. Under the spell of its olden associations, Athens continued to be frequented as a school of philosophy. Of the foremost representatives of the New Comedy, which flourished there from the death of Alexander to about 250 B.C., Philemon alone visited Alexandria. Athens was also the home of historians. It was there that Philochorus was engaged on the study of the history of Attica until he met a violent end as a supporter of the cause of Ptolemy Philadelphus against Antigonus Gonatas (261). It was there that the half-brother of Antigonus, Craterus (321—c. 265), the son of Alexander's general of the same name, collected and elucidated the historic decrees preserved in the public archives. It was there also that Apollodorus composed his great works on chronology and mythology. Among natives of other lands, Timaeus of Tauromenium (c. 350—c. 260) spent the last 50 years of his life at Athens, and Polemon of Ilium found a centre of his travels in the world-famous city which had made him one of her honorary citizens. In the Alexandrian age, Pella, the capital of the Macedonian kings, was a place of literary resort under Antigonus Gonatas alone (275—239), when the king, who was himself a pupil of a Megarian philosopher (Euphantus),

_Athens_

_Pella_

----
[1] *Il.* xx 306-8.          [2] Wilamowitz, *l.c.*, p. 158 f, esp. 161.

and a friend of Zeno, attracted to his court two of Zeno's pupils;
probably also the philosopher and poet, Timon of Phlius; and
certainly the poets Alexander Aetolus and Aratus, who is said to
have been indebted to the king himself for the theme of his great
astronomical poem.   Aratus also visited the Syrian court in the
time of Antiochus Soter (287–262).   Under Antiochus the Great
(224—181), Antioch, the newly founded capital of
Syria, was adorned with a theatre and a circus, and            Antioch
with works of art and a library, which in 220 B.C. was placed
under the care of the learned epic poet, Euphorion of Chalcis,
who there remained until his death, and in the following century
became a favourite model with poets such as Tibullus, Propertius,
and Cornelius Gallus, besides being the theme of a passing
reference in Virgil[1].   Antioch is described as a home of learning
and culture in the youth of Cicero's client the poet Archias, who
was born c. 119 B.C.[2]   A library, with a temple of the Muses, was
also founded there by the last of the Antiochi (after 69 B.C.).
Antioch thus received from the last of the Seleucids the gift of a
'Museum', which Alexandria had received from the first of the
Ptolemies.   Tarsus was celebrated for its schools,         Tarsus
but only her own citizens resorted to them, and
even these finished their education elsewhere[3].   Cos, as has been
already noticed[4], was a literary retreat closely connected with
Alexandria, while Rhodes, which welcomed from
Alexandria the poet of the Argonautic expedition      Cos and
and the author of the earliest of Greek grammars,        Rhodes
was a school of rhetoric not only in the last few years of the life
of Aeschines, but also in the early part of the first century B.C.,
when the eclectic school of Molon contributed its share to the
training of the eloquence of Cicero.   Rhodes was also the scene
of the studies of Castor, the author of an important chronological
work, quoted by Varro[5] and by Julius Africanus, beginning with
Ninus, king of Assyria, and ending with Pompey's triumph in 61 B.C.[6]
It was further famous as the birth-place of the Stoic Panaetius (c.
185—110)[7], and as the school of his pupil Poseidonius (138—45),
whose lectures were attended by Cicero in 78, and by Pompey in

---

[1] *Ecl.* x 50.        [2] *Pro Archia*, 4.        [3] Strabo, p. 673.
[4] p. 119 *supra*.        [5] Augustine, *De Civ. Dei*, xxi 8, 2.
[6] Susemihl, ii 365—372.        [7] E. Schwartz, *Charakterköpfe*, 1903.

67 and 62 B.C.   His extensive travels in Italy, Gaul and Spain, resulted in a continuation of Polybius from 144 to 86 B.C., a work inspired by a keen interest in geography, ethnography and the historical development of human society at large.   Its influence has been traced in Diodorus and Strabo ; in Lucretius, Livy, Caesar and Sallust; in Varro and Cicero, and, recently, even in the *Germania* of Tacitus [1].   Lastly, it was the birth-place of Andronicus, who presided over the Peripatetic school at Athens shortly before the middle of the first century B.C., and produced a new edition of the 'systematic' works of Aristotle and Theophrastus, with classified lists of their writings, copies of their wills, and paraphrases of the *Categories* and commentaries on certain other works of Aristotle [2].   As a Peripatetic he thus rendered at least as great a service to literature as any that had been rendered at Athens in the Alexandrian age by Academic philosophers such as Polemon, whose favourite poets were Homer and Sophocles [3]; or Crantor, the admirer of Homer and Euripides [4], and the writer not only of the first commentary on the *Timaeus* or on any part of Plato [5], but also of a work on consolation, afterwards imitated by Cicero and Plutarch; or Clitomachus, who was destined to be one of the main authorities followed by Cicero in the *De Divinatione* as well as in the *De Natura Deorum*.

[1] Gudeman, *Trans. Amer. Phil. Assoc.* xxxi (1900) 107 f; cp. Christ, § 405[4], and Susemihl, ii 128 f.　　　　　[2] Susemihl, ii 301-5.

[3] Diog. Laert. iv 20.　　[4] *ib.* 26.　　[5] Proclus on *Tim.* 24 A.

SILVER TETRADRACHM OF EUMENES II
Founder of the Pergamene Library (see p. 151 f).
(From the British Museum.)

# BOOK III

## *LATIN SCHOLARSHIP IN THE ROMAN AGE*

---

*Grammatica Romae ne in usu quidem olim, nedum in honore ullo erat, rudi scilicet ac bellicosa etiam tum civitate, necdum magnopere liberalibus disciplinis vacante.*

SUETONIUS, *De Grammaticis*, § 1.

*Je treuve Rome plus vaillante avant qu'elle feust sçavante.*

MONTAIGNE, *Essais*, i 24.

| Political Events | Literary Events | Poets | Historians | Orators | Scholars and Critics &c. |
|---|---|---|---|---|---|
| **300** | | | | | |
| Third Samnite War 298—290<br>272 Tarentum taken<br>First Punic War 264—241 | | 272 Andronicus reaches Rome | | 280 Appius Claudius Caecus | |
| | 240 the first Latin play exhibited at Rome | 240 Andronicus c. 284—c. 204<br>235 Naevius c. 264—194<br>Plautus 254-1—184 | | | |
| Second Punic War 218—202 | | 204 Ennius 239—169 | 216 Q. Fabius Pictor[g] b. c. 254<br>210 L. Cincius Alimentus[g] | | |
| **200** | | | | | |
| First Macedonian War 200—197<br>Syrian War 192—190 | | 179 Caecilius d. 168 | 195 Cato 234—149 | 195 Cato 234—149 | |
| Second Macedonian War 171—168 | Cato, *De Agri Cultura*, the *earliest extant work in Latin Prose* | Pacuvius 220—132 | | 167 L. Aem. Paulus<br>147 Scipio Africanus minor | |
| Third Punic War 149—146<br>Numantine War 143—133 | 161 expulsion of Greek rhetoricians and philosophers | 166 Terence 185—159<br>Lucilius 180—103<br>L. Accius 170—c. 90 | 151 A. Postumius Albinus[g]<br>142 C. Acilius[g] | 144 Ser. Sulp. Galba<br>140 C. Laelius<br>137 M. Lepidus Porcina | 168 Crates of Mallos visits Rome |
| 123 *Leges Semproniae*<br>Cimbrian War 113—102<br>Jugurthine War 111—106 | 155 Critolaus, Carneades and Diogenes at Rome | | 115 L. Coelius Antipater | 133 Tib. Gracchus 163—133<br>123 C. Gracchus 154—121<br>115 M. Aemilius Scaurus<br>105 P. Rutilius Rufus | 133 Valerius Soranus b. c. 154<br>Porcius Licinus<br>Volcatius Sedigitus<br>100 L. Ael. Stilo c. 154—c. 74 |
| **100** | | | | | |
| Marsian War 90—88<br>82 Sulla dictator | 92 schools of Latin rhetoric closed<br>c. 88 school of Latin grammar opened by Sevius Nicanor, and of Latin rhetoric by L. Plotius Gallus | Laberius 105—43<br>Lucretius 97—53<br>Catullus c. 84—54<br>Bibaculus c. 83—c. 24<br>Varro Atacinus 82—37 | Cl. Quadrigarius<br>Valerius Antias<br>78 Sisenna<br>73 Macer<br>Nepos 99—54<br>Sallust 86—34<br>A. Hirtius d. 43 | 99 M. Antonius 143—87<br>95 L. Licinius Crassus 140—91<br>88 P. Sulp. Rufus 124—88<br>c. 85 *auctor ad Herennium* 124—74<br>75 C. Aur. Cotta 124—74<br>69 Hortensius 114—50<br>63 Cicero 106—43<br>59 Caesar 100—44<br>Calvus 82—47 | Servius Clodius d. 60<br>Staberius Eros<br>Varro 116—27<br>Orbilius 114—c. 17<br>Atticus 109—32<br>Santra<br>Tiro c. 104—c. 4<br>Valerius Cato b. c. 100<br>58 Nigidius Figulus 98—45<br>Ateius Praetextatus |
| 60 First triumvirate<br>Gallic War 58—51<br>Civil War 49—45<br>44 d. of Caesar<br>43 Second triumvirate | 39 first public library founded by Pollio<br>28 *bibliotheca Palatina* | 45 Publ. Syrus<br>Gallus 70—27<br>Virgil 70—19<br>Horace 65—8<br>Tibullus 54—19<br>Propertius 49—15 | | 40 Pollio 76 B.C.—5 A.D.<br>31 Messala 64 B.C.—8 A.D. | 28 Hyginus 64 B.C.—17 A.D.<br>Fenestella 52 B.C.—19 A.D.<br>12 Q. Caecilius Epirota<br>10 Verrius Flaccus |
| 31 battle of Actium<br>30 Augustus<br>63 B.C.—14 A.D. | 22 *Aen.* ii, iv and vi recited<br>18 *Carmen Saeculare*<br>14 Vitruvius *De Architectura*<br>9 close of Livy's History | Ovid 43 B.C.—18 A.D. | Livy 59 B.C.—18 A.D. | | |

# CHAPTER X.

## ROMAN STUDY OF GREEK BETWEEN
### 169 B.C. AND 14 A.D.

THE Latin alphabet was (either directly or indirectly) borrowed at an early date from the Greek colonists of Magna Graecia; and Latin literature, which is best regarded as beginning with the close of the First Punic War (241 B.C.), was founded mainly on Greek models. Its earliest writers were not natives of Rome; they were not even natives of Latium. Thus the first of Latin poets was the Greek Andronicus (*c.* 284—*c.* 204), afterwards known as L. Livius Andronicus, who taught Greek and Latin in Rome, and produced in rude Saturnian verse a rendering of the *Odyssey* which was still in use as a text-book in the youth of Horace[1]. He also translated Greek plays into Latin, in metres approximating to those of the Greek originals, and with a special preference for plays connected with the tale of Troy. The first of these plays was exhibited about 240 B.C. Next in order is Naevius (*c.* 264—194), a native of Campania, but of Latin descent, who exhibited in 235 B.C. the first of many plays of Greek origin. Late in life he produced in the old Saturnian measure an important poem on the First Punic War, parts of which were imitated in the *Aeneid* of Virgil. In the four Saturnian lines of his epitaph, he is so conscious of his position as a Latin poet, and so forgetful of his debt to Greece, that he describes his loss as lamented not by the foreign 'Muses'

*Greek influence before 169 B.C.*

---

[1] *Ep.* ii 1, 65.

but by the native Italian *Camenae*, adding that on his death the old Latin tongue ceased to be spoken in Rome.

> 'Inmortales mortales si foret fas flere,
>   Flerent Divae Camenae Naevium poetam;
>   Itaque, postquam est Orchi traditus thesauro,
>   Obliti sunt Romae loquier lingua Latina'[1].

Naevius is followed by Ennius (239—169), the native of a small town in Calabria, who was as familiar with Greek and Oscan as with Latin[2]. By a curious irony of fortune it was Cato, the pertinacious opponent of Greek influence, who prompted Ennius to settle in Rome (204 B.C.), where he gave lessons in Latin and Greek. In his tragedies he was largely indebted to Greek originals. In his great epic poem on the history of Rome, known as the *Annales*, he discarded the old Saturnian measure for the Greek hexameter, casting contempt on the rude versification of his predecessors :—

> Others have told the tale
> In verses sung of yore by Fauns and Bards,
> Ere my own time, when none as yet had climbed
> The Muses' cliffs or learnt the lore of song[3].

The new metre was further elaborated by Lucretius, who pays his predecessor the noble tribute of having been 'the first to bring down from lovely Helicon a crown of leaf unfading, destined to flourish in fame amid the nations of Italy'[4]; and it was tuned to new harmonies of cadence by Virgil, who in his *Aeneid* not merely borrows here and there from the earlier poet, but is also imbued throughout with his national spirit. It was characteristic of Ennius to write an inscription for his own bust, not in the Saturnian measure of old Rome but in the elegiac couplet lately imported from Greece.

> 'Nemo me lacrimis decoret, nec funera fletu
>   Faxit. Cur? Volito vivu' per ora virum'[5].

The poet who had done Latin literature the great service of supplying it with a new epic metre, also took an interest in minor

---

[1] Gellius, i 24, 2 (Hertz). Gudeman, in *Trans. Amer. Phil. Assoc.* xxvi (1896) 140 f, suggests that this epitaph (with those on Plautus and Pacuvius) was composed by Varro.

[2] Gellius, xvii 17.　　　　　　[3] Cic. *Brutus* 71, 76; *Orator* 171.

[4] Lucr. i 117.　　　　　　[5] Cic. *Tusc. Disp.* i 34.

points of scholarship, such as grammar and spelling, and is said to
have invented a system of shorthand[1].   All the three early poets
above mentioned, Andronicus, Naevius and Ennius, wrote comedies
as well as tragedies, but their comedies were exclusively of the
kind called *palliatae*, plays 'dressed in the *Greek* mantle'.   The
school of Ennius claims Pacuvius, his sister's son, the author of
twelve tragedies founded on the legends of Greece, and modelled
in one case on Sophocles and in another on Euripides.   Greek
originals belonging to the New Attic Comedy of Philemon, Diphilus and Menander, were the models followed by Plautus (254—
184) and by Terence (185—159).   Intermediate in time between
Plautus and Terence is Caecilius, who died in 168 B.C. (one year
after the death of Ennius, and two years before the production of
the *Andria*), leaving to the literature of his country some forty
comedies, the titles of all of which are suggestive of Greek originals[2].
The debt of Latin literature to Greek in epic and dramatic poetry
was also extended to history.   The earliest of Roman historians,
Q. Fabius Pictor (born *c.* 254 B.C.), who belonged to the age of
Naevius and Ennius, wrote in Greek, and the same is said
(whether truly or not) of his younger contemporary, L. Cincius
Alimentus (praetor in 210 B.C.)[3].   Greek was certainly the language in which A. Postumius Albinus wrote the History of Rome
which he dedicated to Ennius[4].   Foremost among the Roman
nobles in the study of Greek was C. Sulpicius Galus, who presided as praetor at the performance of a play of Ennius in the
year of the poet's death[5], and who fought in the battle of Pydna
and predicted the eclipse of the moon which immediately preceded it[6].

[1] Teuffel's *History of Roman Literature*, ed. Schwabe, trans. by G. C. W.
Warr, ed. 1900, p. 127 and § 104, 5.   Two books *de litteris syllabisque* and *de
metris* are attributed to a later Ennius (Suet. *Gram.* 1), who may also be the
author of the system of shorthand mentioned by Isidore, *Orig.* i 22, vulgares
notas Ennius primus mille et centum invenit.   Cp. M. Schanz, *Geschichte der
Römischen Litteratur* (in Iwan Müller's *Handbuch*), § 39 ult.

[2] On Plautus, Caecilius, Andronicus, Ennius, and Terence, as translators,
cp. Leo, *Plautinische Forschungen* (1895), 77—89.

[3] Dion. Hal. *Ant. Rom.* i 6 (cp. H. Nettleship, *Essays*, i 341, Mommsen,
*Hist. of Rome*, Book iii c. 14 note, and Schanz, § 64, 2).

[4] Teuffel, § 127, 1.

[5] Cic. *Brutus*, 78.            [6] Liv. xliv 37.

The defeat of the Macedonian king, Perseus, by Lucius Aemilius Paullus at the battle of Pydna (168 B.C.) marks the beginning of a new epoch, and several incidents of literary interest are connected with that event. The conqueror of Pydna, on his visit to Olympia, standing before the Zeus of Pheidias, knew enough of the Homeric poems to declare that the sculptor must have derived his inspiration from Homer; and Aemilius Paullus was apparently the theme of the only truly Roman play mentioned among the works of Pacuvius (220—132), the nephew of Ennius. Again, the battle of Pydna and the consequent predominance of Rome in the Greek world led to the expatriation of 1000 men of mark among the Achaeans, who were scattered among the Etruscan towns. After dwindling in seventeen years to 300, they were restored to their native land with Polybius, the foremost of the exiles, who afterwards returned to Rome to renew his friendship with the younger Scipio, and ultimately to tell the story of the victories of Rome from the beginning of the Second Punic War to the fall of Carthage and of Corinth in 146. Further, the Greek library of the king defeated at Pydna was reserved for the use of the conqueror's sons, the second of whom was the future conqueror of Carthage, famous in literature as the centre of the 'Scipionic circle'. And, finally, the victory of Pydna led to a further expansion of Greek influence in Latin literature by bringing to Rome in the person of Crates of Mallos (and probably in the train of those who came to congratulate the Romans on their victory), the foremost representative of the school of Pergamon.

Our authority for the visit of Crates and its consequences is the treatise of Suetonius *De Grammaticis*. He begins that treatise with the remark that in earlier times, while Rome was still uncivilised and engrossed in war, and was not yet in the enjoyment of any large amount of leisure for the liberal arts, the study of literature (*grammatica*) was not in use, much less was it in esteem. The beginnings of that study, he adds, were unimportant, as its earliest teachers, who were poets and half-Greeks (namely Livius Andronicus and Ennius, who were stated to have taught in both languages at Rome and elsewhere), limited themselves to translating Greek authors or reciting anything which they happened

Crates<br>of Mallos

to have composed in Latin.   After adding that the two books on letters and syllables and also on metres ascribed to Ennius were justly attributed to a later writer of the same name, he states that, in his own opinion, the first to introduce the study of literature into Rome was Crates of Mallos, who, during his accidental detention in Rome, gave many recitations and lectures which aroused an interest in the subject[1].   We are further informed that the example set by Crates led to the publication in seven books of a new edition of the epic of Naevius on the First Punic War, and to the public recitation of the *Annals* of Ennius ; and also (two generations later) to the recitation of the satires of Lucilius.   The text of Ennius was emended not long after his death by Octavius Lampadio[2].

The Roman study of Greek is strikingly exemplified by the fact that, about 164 B.C., Tiberius Sempronius Gracchus[3] addressed the Rhodians in a Greek speech that was still extant in the time of Cicero[4].   Greek influence was stoutly resisted by the elder Cato (234—149), and it was probably at his instance that the Greek philosophers and rhetoricians were expelled from Rome in 161.   The philosophers returned in 155 in the persons of the Academic

Cato the elder

Carneades, the Peripatetic Critolaus, and the Stoic Diogenes, who aroused the interest of the young Romans, and the indignation of the aged Cato, by the sophistry of the arguments with which they defended the seizure of Oropus by Athens[5].   In his old age Cato warned his son against Greek physicians and also against Greek literature, adding that the latter was worthy of inspection but not of study[6].   He is said to have learnt Greek late in life[7], and to have derived some advantage, as an *orator*, from the reading of Thucydides and still more from that of Demosthenes ; but Plutarch, in recording this tradition, is careful to add that, even as a *writer*, Cato showed the influence of Greek

[1] See p. 159.   It is assumed by Mommsen (Bk iv c. 12) that the Homeric poems were the theme of these lectures.   On this there is no evidence, but Homer was certainly a main subject of the literary studies of Crates.

[2] Gellius, xviii 5, 11.

[3] The father of the Gracchi.

[4] *Brutus*, 79.

[5] Plut. *Cato*, i 22.

[6] Plin. *N. H.* xxix 14.

[7] Cic. *De Sen.* 26.

literature, and that many of his apophthegms were translated from Greek[1].   Toward the end of his days, as he looked forward to the conquest of Carthage by the younger Scipio, he expressed his sense of the contrast between that leader and the rest of the Roman generals by quoting a line from Homer :—οἶος πέπνυται, τοὶ δὲ σκιαὶ ἀΐσσουσι[2].   Among the Greek friends of the younger Scipio were the Stoic Panaetius and the future historian Polybius, who, while Carthage was in flames, saw his former pupil musing on the fate of Empires, and heard him murmuring the lines of the *Iliad* :—ἔσσεται ἦμαρ ὅταν ποτ᾽ ὀλώλῃ Ἴλιος ἱρὴ καὶ Πρίαμος καὶ λαὸς ἐϋμμελίω Πριάμοιο.   The fall of Corinth, in the same year as that of Carthage (146), made Rome the master of the Hellenic world; but Greece, though conquered in arms, continued victorious in the field of letters : *Graecia capta ferum victorem ceperat*, is more true than *cepit*[3].

Among the first of the Romans who travelled in Asia Minor

**Accius**

was L. Accius (170—*c.* 90 B.C.), who was famous as the author of numerous tragedies on the tale of Troy.   In the history of Scholarship he concerns us only as the author of a history of Greek and Roman poetry, especially that of the drama, written in Sotadean verse, under the name of *Didascalica*, a title probably suggested by the διδασκαλίαι of Aristotle[4].   He was the first to discuss the genuineness of certain plays wrongly assigned to Plautus[5].   Among the peculiarities of his orthography we are told that he never used the letters Y and Z, and that, when A or E or U was long, he denoted the fact by writing it double[6].   His interest in these subjects is proved by the fact that Varro dedicated to him the treatise *de antiquitate litterarum*[7].   The innovations in language and

**Lucilius**

spelling introduced by Accius are ridiculed by Lucilius (180—103 B.C.), who, besides discussing

[1] *Cato*, i 2.                    [2] *ib.* 27.

[3] Horace, *Ep.* II i 156.

[4] Madvig, *Opusc.* i 87 f (p. 70 f, ed. 1887); Hermann, *Opusc.* viii 390; Lachmann, *Kl. Schriften*, ii 67; Norden, in *Rhein. Mus.* xlviii (1893) 530 f; and Hendrickson, *Amer. Jour. Phil.* xix (1898) 285 f, esp. 303 f.

[5] Gellius, iii 3, 9.

[6] Mar. Vict. *Gram. Lat.* 6, 8; Ritschl, *Opusc.* iv 142.

[7] Teuffel, § 134, 7 and 11 ; Schanz, §§ 49, 50.

points of orthography and prosody, satirises the bombastic language of the Latin tragedians, criticises even Homer and Euripides, and takes his contemporaries to task for their provincialisms and also for their affected imitation of Greek phraseology[1]. Lucilius himself, while he banters the Roman Epicurean, Titus Albucius, on his fancy for being saluted in Greek, is (like the rest of the Scipionic circle) himself familiar with the master-pieces of Greek literature. Gaius Acilius, who had interpreted to the Senate the speeches of the Greek envoys of 155, produced in 142 a Greek history of Rome; and Greek was the language of another lost history, written by the son of the elder Africanus. P. Licinius Crassus Dives Mucianus, consul in 131, was so familiar with Greek, that as governor of Asia he delivered his decisions either in ordinary Greek or, if the case required, in any of the four dialects of that language[2].

*Histories of Rome written by Romans in Greek*

Lucilius was succeeded by an epigrammatic poet less known to fame, Porcius Licinus, the author of a trochaic poem on the history of Roman literature, in the course of which he insisted on the lateness of the origin of Roman poetry in the oft-quoted lines:

> 'Poenico bello secundo Musa pinnato gradu
> Intulit se bellicosam in Romuli gentem feram'[3].

Among the younger contemporaries of Accius and the precursors of Varro was Q. Valerius of Sora (born *c.* 154), a man of distinction in linguistic and antiquarian research. When Varro was asked the meaning of *favisae Capitolinae*, he admitted that he knew nothing of the origin of the word *favisae* and took refuge in quoting the opinion of Valerius to the effect that *favisae* was a corruption of *flavisae* and meant the same as *thesauri*[4].

*Q. Valerius*

The foremost scholar of this age was L. Aelius Stilo Praeconinus (*c.* 154—*c.* 74 B.C.) of Lanuvium, a Roman knight, who read the plays of Plautus and others with younger men such as Varro and Cicero. He owed the name of *Praeconinus* to his father's occupation as a *praeco*, and that

*Stilo*

---

[1] Teuffel, § 143, 7.          [2] Quint. xi 2, 50.

[3] Gellius, xvii 21, 45.          [4] *ib.* ii 10, 3 (Teuffel, § 147, 1).

of *Stilo* (or 'Penman') to his skill in writing speeches for members
of the Roman aristocracy.  In 100 B.C. he left Rome for Rhodes,
where he spent two years[1].  Dionysius Thrax, the head of the
Aristarchean school, was then in Rhodes, and it was probably
owing to his influence that Stilo introduced the symbols of
Aristarchus into the criticism of the Latin poets[2].  We find
Stilo designated *litteris ornatissimus* by Varro, as quoted by
Gellius[3], who himself describes him as *doctissimus eorum temporum*,
adding that Varro and Cicero followed his example in refraining
from the use of *novissimum* in the sense of *extremum*[4].  He is
characterised by Cicero in the *Brutus* (205) as a man of the
profoundest learning in Greek and Latin literature, and as an
accomplished critic of ancient writers and of Roman antiquities
in their intellectual as well as in their historical and political
aspects.  His legal and antiquarian pursuits are noticed in the
*De Oratore*[5].  His grammatical and especially his etymological
inquiries were partly inspired by his devotion to the Stoic
philosophy.  He appears to have been an industrious writer,
and much of his lore passed into the pages of Varro and of
Verrius Flaccus, of Pliny the elder and of Gellius.  His writings
included a commentary on the *Carmina Saliorum*[6]; a critical list
of the plays of Plautus, in which he recognised 25 plays as
genuine, and in connexion with which he possibly passed the
encomium on the style of Plautus quoted by Varro, to the effect
that, had the Muses wished to speak in Latin, they would have
used the language of Plautus[7].  He also wrote a treatise on
axiomatic statements (περὶ ἀξιωμάτων) apparently connected with
the Syntax of the Stoics, which Gellius[8] found after diligent search
in the Library in the temple of Peace; an edition of the works
of Q. Metellus Numidicus, whom he accompanied into exile in

---

[1] Suet. *Gram.* 3.

[2] Gellius, vi 9, 11—12 ; Marx, *Proleg. ad Herennium*, 138 f.

[3] i 18, 2.

[4] x 21, 2.  Varro quotes Aelius Stilo in *De L. L.* v 18, 21, 25, 66, 101 ;
vi 7, 59 (cp. Reitzenstein, *M. Ter. Varro*, 1901, 31 f, 37 f, 43, 52).

[5] i 193, Aeliana (Madvig for *aliena*) studia.

[6] Varro, *L. L.* vii 2 ; cp. Festus s.v. *manuos, molucrum, pescia*, quoted by
Suringar, *Historia Critica Scholiastarum Latinorum*, i 29.

[7] Quint. x 1, 99.                    [8] xvi 8, 2.

100 B.C.; probably also an antiquarian work on the laws of
the XII Tables, and lastly a glossary including articles on etymological, antiquarian and historical subjects[1]. The Satires of
Lucilius and the Annals of L. Coelius Antipater were dedicated
to Stilo. Among the scholars who succeeded Stilo[2] were L. Plotius
Gallus and Saevius Nicanor, early teachers of Latin rhetoric and
literature respectively; Aurelius Opilius, a student of Plautus;
Antonius Gnipho, a commentator on the Annals of Ennius;
M. Pompilius Andronicus, who wrote criticisms on the Annals,
published by Orbilius; Servius Clodius, who married the daughter
and stole some of the papers of Stilo, and is described as the
author of a catalogue of the genuine plays of Plautus[3]; and
lastly Staberius Eros, the instructor of Brutus and Cassius, whom
Pliny the elder[4] calls with some exaggeration *conditor grammaticae*.

Stilo's most famous pupil, M. Terentius Varro (116—27 B.C.),
is characterised by Cicero[5] as *diligentissimus investi-*
*gator antiquitatis*, by Quintilian[6] as *vir Romanorum*                    Varro
*eruditissimus*, and by St Augustine as one who had read so much
that one wondered he had any time left for writing, and had
written so much that one might well believe that scarcely any one
could have read the whole of his works[7]. His books numbered
as many as 620, belonging to 74 separate works. They included
XLI books *Antiquitatum rerum humanarum et divinarum*, with
other antiquarian works *de vita* and *de gente populi Romani*, a
book of 'origins' called *Aetia* (like the Αἴτια of Callimachus), and
a treatise on Trojan families and on the Roman tribes. His
writings on literary history comprised works on Plautus[8] and on

---

[1] Goetz in Pauly-Wissowa, i 532 f. Cp. Mommsen, *Hist. of Rome*, Bk iv
c. 12 and 13; Teuffel, § 148; Schanz, § 76.

[2] Suet. *Gram.* 3, 5—8 etc. Teuffel, § 159; Schanz, §§ 194—6.

[3] Gellius, iii 3, 1. Cp. Cic. *ad Fam.* ix 16, 4 (to Paetus), Servius, frater
tuus, quem litteratissimum fuisse iudico, facile diceret 'hic versus Plauti non
est; hic est', quod tritas aures haberet notandis generibus poëtarum et consuetudine legendi.

[4] xxxv 199.              [5] *Brutus*, 60.              [6] x 1, 95.

[7] *De Civ. Dei*, vi 2. Much the same was afterwards said of St Augustine
by Isidore (vii 179 ed. 1803), 'mentitur qui te totum legisse fatetur'.

[8] The 21 plays recognised by Varro were called the *Fabulae Varronianae*
(Gellius iii 3, 3), which may safely be identified with the 20 extant plays and

the drama, on poetry and on style, with three books on Libraries;
but unhappily they have not survived, and there is nothing to
show that they were seriously concerned with literary criticism.
His grammatical writings included xxv books *de Lingua Latina*,
of which v—x (published before 43 B.C.) are extant; II—VII were
on etymology; vīii—xvi on inflexion, analogy and anomaly; and
xvii—xxv on syntax; also a book on the origin of the Latin
language, three books on analogy (*de similitudine verborum*), and
four *de utilitate sermonis*. Further he was the author of the first
encyclopaedic work in Latin on the 'liberal arts.' Under the
name of *disciplinarum libri novem*, it comprised (1) grammar,
(2) logic, (3) rhetoric, (4) geometry, (5) arithmetic, (6) astronomy,
(7) music, (8) medicine, (9) architecture, the first seven of which
were the seven liberal arts of Augustine[1] and Martianus Capella,
afterwards represented by the *trivium* and the *quadrivium* of the
educational system of the Middle Ages. His poetical works included certain *saturae Menippeae*, a new type of satirical composition in which verse was blended with prose, of which fragments
remain. His model in these was the Greek Cynic, Menippus of
Gadara (*c.* 250 B.C.). In his *Imagines* he collected 700 portraits
of famous Greeks and Romans. Lastly there were his three
books *de Re Rustica*[2]. A large portion of all this varied literary
activity is the theme of Cicero's glowing eulogy in the *Academica*[3].

But (apart from fragments) the only works which have survived
are the books *de Re Rustica*, and six books *de Lingua Latina*.
Books v—xxv of the latter were dedicated to Cicero, who had
waited impatiently for the fulfilment of Varro's promise to dedicate
to him an important work, and who thus received a recognition of
the handsome compliment paid by himself in dedicating to Varro

the *Vidularia*, of which fragments only have survived in the Ambrosian
Palimpsest (cent. v). Cp. Leo, *Plautinische Forschungen*, 17 f, 45 f.

[1] *Retract.* i 6, where however 'philosophy' is substituted for 'astronomy'.

[2] Teuffel, §§ 164—9; Schanz, §§ 182—193. Cp. Ritschl, *Opusc.* iii
419—505; Mommsen, *Hist. of Rome*, Bk v c. 12; Wordsworth's *Early Latin*,
pp. 356—8; and Nettleship, ii 146 f; also Schanz, §§ 183—193; Wilmanns,
*De Varronis libris grammaticis*, pp. 226, 1864; Usener, *Ein altes Lehrgebäude
der Philologie*, in *S. Ber. bayer. Akad.* 1892, 582—648; and Reitzenstein,
*Varro und Johannes Mauropus von Euchaita, eine Studie zur Geschichte
der Sprachwissenschaft*, 97 pp., 1901.          [3] i § 9.

the second edition of his *Academica* (45 B.C.). Varro's treatise is
the earliest extant Roman work on grammar. This great work,
which was finished before Cicero's death in 43 B.C., owed much
to the Stoic teaching of Aelius Stilo, and also to that of a later
grammarian who combined the Stoic and the Alexandrian traditions[1]. Varro even derived his definition of grammar from that of
Dionysius Thrax[2], probably through the medium of Stilo, and he
was directly indebted to Dionysius' pupil, the elder Tyrannion[3].
The first three of the surviving books are on Etymology, book v
being on names of places, vi on terms denoting time, and vii on
poetic expressions. To ourselves the value of these books lies in
their citations from the Latin poets, and not in their marvellous
etymologies. But Varro is right in regarding *meridies* as standing
for *medius* (and not *merus*) *dies*, and in connexion with this word
he records the interesting fact that he had himself seen the form
in D carved on a sun-dial at Praeneste[4]. The next three books
are concerned with the controversy on Analogy and Anomaly:
viii on the arguments against Analogy, ix on those against
Anomaly, and x on Varro's own view of Analogy.

In the first of these books we have arguments and illustrations in favour of
the charm of variety : *ex dissimilitudine plus voluptatis, quam
ex similitudine, saepe capitur ;* hence it may be inferred *verbo-*      Analogy and
*rum dissimilitudinem, quae sit in consuetudine, non esse vitan-*      Anomaly in
*dam* (31—32). In speech, it is urged by the anomalist, there      Varro
is no rule; the inflexions of similar words are sometimes similar, as, from
*bonum* and *malum*, *bono* and *malo ;* sometimes dissimilar, as, from *lupus* and
*lepus*, *lupo* and *lepori ;* again the inflexions of dissimilar words are sometimes
dissimilar, as *Priamus*, *Paris*, and *Priamo*, *Pari ;* sometimes similar, as
*Iuppiter*, *ovis*, and *Iovi*, *ovi.* If analogy is not universal, argues the anomalist,
there is no such thing as true analogy. The book ends with many examples

---

[1] Reitzenstein, *M. Ter. Varro* (1901).

[2] Varro, frag. 91, grammatica est scientia eorum quae a poëtis historicis
oratoribusque dicuntur ex parte maiore; cp. p. 8 *supra.* Varro supplies us with
the earliest example of the use of *lyricus* in Latin, if Wilmanns, *De Varronis
Libris Grammaticis*, p. 187, is right in assigning to Varro the passage in Serv.
*de accentibus*, 17, 'Dionysius...Aristarchi discipulus, cognomento Thrax, domo
Alexandrinus, qui Rhodi docuit, *lyricorum* poetarum longe studiosissimus...'

[3] p. 140 *supra.* On various other Greek authorities cp. Kroll in *Jahresb.*
vol. 124, p. 29; also F. Muller, De veterum, imprimis Romanorum studiis
etymologicis, pp. 262 (Utrecht, 1910).

[4] *L. L.* vi 4.

of irregularity in declension, in the degrees of comparison, and in diminutives and proper names.  The next book (IX), in arguing against anomaly, begins with the suggestion that that *nobilis grammaticus*, Crates, in accepting the view of Chrysippus, and in attacking that of Aristarchus, had misunderstood both. When Chrysippus wrote on anomaly, he meant to show that similar things are often denoted by dissimilar words, and dissimilar things by similar words, which is true.  Again, when Aristarchus wrote on analogy, he held that we must accept the inflexion or derivation of certain words as a pattern (or paradigm) for the rest, *so far as custom admits* (§ 1).  Varro is probably wrong in describing Crates as having mistaken the meaning of Chrysippus and Aristarchus, and, when he himself admits the claims of *consuetudo*, he virtually gives up the case for strict analogy.  All that the anomalist maintained was that analogy very often broke down, and he accordingly concluded that it was not analogy but *consuetudo* that was the guiding principle of language.  As Varro was reluctant to call himself an anomalist, he takes refuge in the expedient of bringing forward a third party, consisting of those who *in loquendo partim sequi iubent nos consuetudinem, partim rationem*.  So long as *partim* remains undefined, this description comes to nothing, as either of the two contending parties might claim it as representing their views.  Varro regards this third party as approximating to his own view of analogy; at the same time he regards that party as open to the same objection as the anomalists :—*consuetudo et analogia coniunctiores sunt inter se, quam ii credunt* (ix 2)[1].

Cicero's view agrees with that of Varro.  He is an analogist, who nevertheless respects *consuetudo*.  As a practical orator it would
**Cicero** have been impossible for him to disregard it.  So he keeps to himself his knowledge of the scientifically correct forms, and is content to follow popular usage.  He knew that in earlier Latin there had been no aspirate in *pulcros, Cetegos, triumpos, Kartaginem*, but he followed popular usage in introducing the aspirate (*Orator*, 160).  He uses *confidens* in the sense of 'shameless', although he knows it is wrong (*Tusc. Disp.* iii 14); he finds no fault with *scripsere*, although he holds that *scripserunt* alone is right (*Orator*, 157).  *Usum loquendi populo concessi, scientiam mihi reservavi* (*ib.* 160). Cicero does not follow euphony for its own sake, but simply as part of popular usage : *consuetudini auribus indulgenti libenter obsequor* (*ib.* 157)[2].

Analogy was the theme of a work by Caesar, written while he was crossing the Alps[3], probably in 55 B.C.  It was dedicated to Cicero[4],
**Caesar** and consisted of two books (1) on the alphabet and on words, and (2) on irregularities of inflexion in nouns and verbs.  It was in this work that Caesar laid down the memorable rule : *ut tamquam scopulum, sic fugias inauditum atque insolens verbum*[5].  He thus admitted the claim of *consuetudo*

[1] Steinthal, *Sprachwissenschaft*, ii 130—136[2].  Cp. Reitzenstein, *l.c.*, pp. 44—65 and F. H. Colson, in *Cl. Quarterly*, 1919, 24—36.

[2] Steinthal, ii 154.                    [3] Suet. *Caes.* 56.

[4] *Brutus*, 253 ; Gellius, xix 8, 3.

[5] Gellius, i 10, 4.  Cp. Hendrikson, in *Cl. Philol.* i 97—120.

even in a work characteristic of his ruling passion for reducing everything to law and order and uniformity. Similarly the decay and the revival of words is made by Horace to depend on *usus, quem penes arbitrium est et ius et norma loquendi* (*A. P.* 71 f).

The conflict between the analogists and the anomalists continued beyond the limits of time assigned to this chapter. To complete our survey of the subject, it may here be added that Pliny the elder (25—    **Pliny** 79 A.D.), among whose works were *dubii sermonis libri octo*[1], was an analogist, but he allowed *consuetudo* its full rights (*consuetudini et suavitati aurium censet summam esse tribuendam*), holding *esse quidem rationem, sed multa iam consuetudine superari*[2]. Although originally language may have been entirely guided by analogy, *consuetudo* is the natural enemy of *ratio* and often drives it from the field. Pliny thus recognises the rights of *consuetudo* far more openly than Varro. He also recognises the force of *authority*, and accepts forms sanctioned *veteri dignitate*. Authority and antiquity are the constant allies of anomalous *consuetudo*, and against these three forces analogy must struggle in vain[3].

Quintilian (*c.* 35—95 A.D.) is also an analogist, but he limits the province of analogy to deciding in cases of doubt (i 6, 4). With Quin-    **Quintilian** tilian analogy rests not on reason but on precedent; it does not legislate on language, but simply observes and notes its laws (*ib.* 16).

A century later in Greek literature the sceptical physician, Sextus Empiricus, who flourished between 180 and 200 A.D., was a spirited champion of anomaly. He ridicules the extreme analogists of    **Sextus Empiricus** his day as 'scholars who, although scarcely able to string two words together, wanted to convict of barbarism all the ancient writers who were conspicuous for correctness of language (εὐφράδεια) and excellence of Greek (Ἑλληνισμός), *e.g.* Thucydides, Plato and Demosthenes' (*adv. Math.* i 98).

The struggle, however, between the two principles was mainly limited to rather more than one century before and one century after our era. Under the influence of the Aristarchic school of analogists, grammatical forms were investigated with great accuracy. The paradigms of grammar were the result of this struggle, which gave 'the necessary impulse to a complete analysis of the forms of language'[4]. In the first effort to reduce the facts of the Greek language to order, the observation of the vast mass of regular forms led to their classification, and tempted the grammarian to endeavour to reduce all irregularities into agreement with the normal types. Such was the work of the earlier analogists. We may say of them that they held a brief for the 'rule'; while the anomalists showed cause for the 'exception'. The net result of the struggle was the ultimate recognition of the fact that in the realm of language, as in the world of nature, uniformity and variety are inextricably intermingled with one another.

---

[1] Plin. *Ep.* iii 5, 5.          [2] Charisius, i p. 99.          [3] Steinthal, ii 155.
[4] Cp. J. Wordsworth's *Early Latin*, pp. 653–4.

Cicero began his study of Greek philosophy under the Epicu-

**Cicero**       rean Phaedrus, but was soon attracted more strongly
             to the Stoic Diodotus (who ended his days as an in-
mate of Cicero's house) and to the Academic Philo, the pupil of
Clitomachus. In resuming and completing his education in Greece
(79–77 B.C.), he studied at Athens the Stoicised Academic philosophy of Antiochus of Ascalon ; and rhetoric, partly at Athens, but
mainly at Rhodes, where he formed a close friendship with the
Stoic Poseidonius. So deeply imbued was he with Greek learning
that, on his return to Rome, he was even reproached as 'a Greek
and a pedant'[1]. His vague and distant interest in Greek art is
indicated in the *Fourth Verrine* (69 B.C.) ; his closer interest in
Greek literature, in the *Pro Archia* (62 B.C.)[2] ; and his familiarity
with the Paradoxes of the Stoics, in the work of that name, and in
the *pro Murena*. About 60 B.C. we find him enthusiastically
studying Dicaearchus[3] and Theophrastus[4], and writing historical
memoirs in the manner of Theopompus[5]. Poseidonius has
apparently suggested the opening passage in the earliest of his
rhetorical treatises, the *De Inventione*[6], while other portions are
borrowed from Hermagoras. A far higher degree of originality
is shown in his maturer works, the *De Oratore* (55 B.C.) and the
*Brutus* (46), but the former of these gives proof of his familiarity
with Greek philosophy, while the *Orator* (46), in which he attacks
the narrow Atticists of the day, is inspired in part by Plato,
Isocrates, Demosthenes, Aristotle and Theophrastus[7]. The *De
Optimo Genere Oratorum* is a short preface to Cicero's lost
translation of the speeches of Aeschines and Demosthenes 'On
the Crown'. He also translated the *Oeconomicus* of Xenophon,
and the *Protagoras* and *Timaeus* of Plato, part of this last being
still extant. His *Topica*, written on board ship without books
(in July, 44), is not really a translation of the corresponding work
of Aristotle. In connexion with his philosophical dialogues, he
was specially studying Aristotle in 54 B.C.[8] The titles of his

[1] Plut. *Cic.* 5.                      [2] p. 192 *infra*.
[3] *Ad Att.* ii 2.          [4] *ib.* ii 7, 4 ; i 16, 3.        [5] *ib.* ii 6, 2.
[6] Philippson in *Neue Jahrb.* 133, p. 417.
[7] Cp. the present writer's ed., pp. lxvii—lxxi.
[8] *Ad Quint.* iii 5 and 6.

earliest philosophic writings, the *De Republica* (54) and the *De Legibus* (52), are suggested to him by Plato, and the *Dream of Scipio*, related in the last book of the former, is the counterpart of the *Vision of Er* at the close of the *Republic*.  In 51 B.C. he revisited Athens (staying with Aristus, the brother of Antiochus), and succeeded in preventing the destruction of the house of Epicurus by the patron of the great Epicurean poet, Lucretius. At Mitylene he met the Peripatetic Cratippus ; and, on his return from Cilicia, he once more stayed with Aristus at Athens (49). During the Civil War we find him appropriately studying Demetrius Magnes, *On Concord*.  In the fourth and fifth books of the *De Finibus*, and in the *Academica* (45), his main authority is Antiochus.  In the *Tusculan Disputations* (44) he follows either Philo or Poseidonius, Panaetius and Antiochus.  A letter to Atticus[1] implies that, in connexion with this work, he studied certain treatises of Dicaearchus.  In the first book of the *De Natura Deorum* (44), he probably follows the Epicurean Zeno ; certainly Poseidonius[2] and possibly Philodemus ; in the second, Poseidonius (amongst others) ; and in the third, certainly Clitomachus.  The last two are among the sources of the *De Divinatione* (44), while §§ 87—89 of the second book are, according to Cicero himself, taken from Panaetius.  In the *De Senectute* (44) he is perhaps inspired by the Peripatetic Aristo of Ceos ; in the *De Amicitia* (44) his main authority is Theophrastus.  The first two books of the *De Officiis* (44) are confessedly founded on Panaetius, with additions from Poseidonius, and possibly from Athenodorus Calvus, who certainly supplied Cicero with the general scheme of the third book[3].  Even in his lost *Consolatio* in memory of Tullia, he closely followed Crantor περὶ πένθους, while his lost *Hortensius* was modelled on the *Protrepticus* of Aristotle and of Poseidonius[4].  Writing to Atticus[5] in 45 B.C., the year in which he composed the *De Finibus* and the *Academica*, he frankly

---

[1] xiii 32, 2.          [2] i §.123.          [3] *Ad Att.* xvi 11, 4 and 14, 4.

[4] For further details on the Greek authorities followed by Cicero in his philosophical works, cp. Hirzel's *Untersuchungen*, 1877–83 ; Thiaucourt's *Essai*, 1885 ; Schanz, §§ 158—172 ; and the current editions of the several works, esp. Dr Reid's *Academica*, pp. 1—9, and Prof. J. B. Mayor's *De Nat. Deorum*, i p. xlii f.

[5] xii 52, 3.

disclaims originality, calling the works on which he was then engaged merely 'copies':—ἀπόγραφα *sunt : minore labore fiunt ; verba tantum affero, quibus abundo*. Early in life he had translated into Latin verse the astronomical poem of Aratus, and in 60 B.C. had lavished all the resources of Greek rhetoric on a memoir of his consulship, which excited the admiration and the despair of Poseidonius, who had been requested to write on the same subject[1]. In his *Letters*, especially in those addressed to a Greek scholar like Atticus, he readily resorts to Greek. However inadequate and inaccurate may have been his transcripts from Greek philosophical texts, he deserves the credit of having enlarged the vocabulary of Latin and of the modern languages derived therefrom, by his admirably adequate renderings of Greek philosophical terms[2]. εἶδος, ποιότης and ποσότης have attained 'a much longer life and a far more extended application' in Cicero's *species, qualitas* and *quantitas*, and their modern derivatives. His renderings of the later Greek writers like Epicurus, Chrysippus and Philodemus are in point of style better than the originals. In his opinion as to the comparative merits of Greek and Latin he is not always consistent. At one time 'he gives to Greek the preference over Latin[3], at another to Latin over Greek[4]; in reading Sophocles or Plato he would acknowledge their unrivalled excellence; in translating Panaetius or Philodemus he would feel his own immeasurable superiority'[5].

Cicero's early translation of Aratus is repeatedly imitated by
**Lucretius** an incomparably greater poet, Lucretius (97—53 B.C.). In massive and majestic verse that poet unfolds in fairly lucid form his exposition of the physical system of Epicurus, the writer of 'a harsh jargon that does not deserve to be called a style'[6]. The Roman poet has carefully studied Democritus, Anaxagoras and Heraclitus. Incidentally he borrows from Empedocles, and perhaps from Poseidonius (v); also from

---

[1] *Ad Att.* i 19, 10; ii 1, 1.

[2] Cp. Bernhardt, *De Cicerone Graecae philosophiae interprete*, Berlin, 1865; and Clavel, *De Cicerone Graecorum interprete*, Paris, 1868 (in part a reproduction of H. Estienne's *Ciceronianum Lexicon Graeco-latinum*, 1557).

[3] *Tusc.* ii 35.          [4] *De Fin.* i 10.

[5] Munro's *Lucretius*, Introd. p. 306–7³.          [6] Munro, *u. s.*, p. 306.

Thucydides, whom he repeatedly misrepresents, and once abandons for Hippocrates[1]. He translates Homer[2], and imitates Hesiod[3], and Euripides[4]. In one passage only he gives a close rendering of Antipater of Sidon[5], an epigrammatist of the second half of the second century, whose versification is in strict accord with the best Alexandrian models. In this isolated and tacit rendering of a minor Alexandrian poet, and in his openly avowed admiration for Ennius[6], Lucretius stands in strong contrast with the poets of the new school, the *poëtae novi*[7] or νεώτεροι[8], the *cantores Euphorionis*, who regarded the grand old poet with contempt[9]. Discarding the drama and the ampler forms of epic poetry, this new school aimed at reproducing the legendary lore and the artificial versification of the 'Alexandrian' poets with their minor epics, and their amatory, satirical or mythological elegies and epigrams. Its leaders were Valerius Cato and Calvus (82—47), and its greatest poet was Catullus (84—54), whose Alexandrian affinities are especially marked in his *Attis*[10] and his *Coma Berenices*, both of them translated from Callimachus, also in his *Peleus and Thetis*, and in the elegiacs addressed to M'. Allius, with their many examples of the art of mythological digression. His study of earlier Greek models is shown in his rendering of an ode of Sappho, and in his adoption of her most characteristic metre. Among his companions in Bithynia (57– 6 B.C.) was C. Helvius Cinna, who there obtained a copy of Aratus[11]; it was apparently Parthenius of Nicaea whom he imitated in two elaborate poems which were so obscure as to need a scholiast. Varro Atacinus (born in 82 B.C.), who began his career with an epic on Caesar's conquest of the Sequani, and with satires lightly esteemed by Horace[12], at the age of 35 threw himself with great enthusiasm into the study of Greek literature, producing a geo-

*Marginal notes:* Cantores Euphorionis · Catullus · Cinna · Varro Atacinus

---

[1] vi 1180–95.  [2] ii 24, 324; iii 21, 1000, 1025; v 905 f; vi 971.
[3] v 1289.  [4] i 101; ii 991—1006; v 805.
[5] iv 181 f.  [6] i 117.  [7] Cic. *Orator*, 161.
[8] *ad Att.* vii 2, 1.  [9] *Tusc.* iii 45.  [10] Wilamowitz (1879).
[11] Isidore, vi 12 (Merry's *Fragments of Roman Poetry*, p. 254).
[12] *Sat.* i 10, 46.

graphical poem apparently in imitation of Alexander of Ephesus,
Prognostics after the model of Aratus, and a Latin version of the
Argonautics of Apollonius Rhodius.   His skill as a translator is
proved by his rendering of the following lines :—

> οὐδὲ κυνῶν ὑλακὴ ἔτ᾽ ἀνὰ πτόλιν, οὐ θρόος ἦεν
> ἠχήεις· σιγὴ δὲ μελαινομένην ἔχεν ὀρφνην (iii 749).

> 'Desierant latrare canes urbesque silebant;
> Omnia noctis erant placida composta quiete'.

These two lines are preserved by the elder Seneca[1], who records
the fact that Ovid wanted to strike out the last three words;
he also refers to the still finer treatment of the same theme
in Virgil[2].

Turning from the poets to the historians of the last few
decades of the Republic, we note that Caesar
(100—44), like Cicero, studied rhetoric at Rhodes;
and that, in his account of the early state of Gaul,
he is probably following the Rhodian Poseidonius.   Cornelius
Nepos may have modelled on Apollodorus the great chronological
work mentioned in the dedication of the poems of Catullus
(52 B.C.); he also wrote lives of 'grammarians', which have unhappily perished.   Sallust (86—35·4), in the lengthy introductions
to his 'Catiline' and 'Jugurtha', and in the Speeches and almost
all the Letters interspersed in those works, is an imitator of
Thucydides, whom he further resembles in the brevity and conciseness of his style[3].

*Caesar.*
*Nepos.*
*Sallust*

Among the poets of the Augustan age Virgil (70—19 B.C.)
was early directed by Asinius Pollio to the study
of Theocritus, whom he imitates in at least 17
passages of his *Eclogues*[4].   The lines in Eclogue viii 37—41,
regarded by Voltaire as the most beautiful passage in Virgil, and
by Macaulay as 'the finest lines in the Latin language', are simply
translated, and in one particular mistranslated, from Theocritus[5],

*Virgil*

---

[1] p. 313 K.                    [2] *Aen.* viii 26 f.

[3] Cp. Peterson on Quintilian, x 1, 101, and A. F. West in *Proc. Amer.
Phil. Assoc.* 1902, xxiii—xxv. Sallust's 'introductions' are possibly due in part
to Poseidonius (C. Wachsmuth, *Einleitung in das Stud. d. alt. Gesch.* 662).

[4] For details see Kennedy's notes, Conington's *Introduction*, Sellar's
*Virgil*, c. IV i, or Schanz, § 224, and P. Jahn (1897-9).

[5] xi 25 f; ii 82.   Sellar's *Virgil*, p. 150.

whose meaning is also missed when πάντα δ' ἔναλλα γένοιτο is rendered *omnia vel medium fiant mare*[1]. In general, however, his imitations and adaptations are admirably true to his original. In the *Georgics* he borrows from Homer and Hesiod, and from 'Alexandrian' poets such as Aratus, Apollonius Rhodius, Callimachus, Theocritus, Bion, Nicander[2], and Parthenius[3]. The passage on the zones came from the *Hermes* of Eratosthenes[4]; but there is no warrant for the statement of Servius[5] that Virgil borrowed largely from the closing passage on agriculture in the *Oeconomicus* of Xenophon. The first half of the *Aeneid* is mainly founded on the *Odyssey*, and the second on the *Iliad*. The account of the Fall of Troy is partly inspired by the cyclic poet, Pisander[6]; the passion of Dido by that of Medea in Apollonius Rhodius[7]; the description of Camilla possibly by that of Penthesilea in the lost *Aethiopis* of Arctinus. Homer and Apollonius are the source of not a few of the similes; the happy comparison suggested by the play of light reflected on the ceiling from a brazen bowl of water being derived from the latter of these poets[8]. Lastly, there are some fine reminiscences of the great tragic poets of Greece[9].

Horace (65—8 B.C.) imitates Archilochus in his early *Epodes*[10], and not Archilochus alone but also Alcaeus and Sappho in the metres of his maturer *Odes*, which (in Book iv 2) supply proof of the poet's familiarity with works of Pindar that have since perished. In his *Ars Poetica* he is said to have included the most notable of the precepts of the Alexandrian critic, Neoptolemus of Parium[11], and he there insists

Horace

---

[1] *Ecl.* viii 58.

[2] Quint. x 1, 56. B. O. Foster in *Proc. Amer. Phil. Assoc.* xxxiii (1902), xcvi f.

[3] Gellius, ix 9, 3; Macrobius, v 2, 4; Morsch, *De Graecis in Georgicis a Vergilio expressis* (1878), p. 39; and Conington's *Introduction*, and on *G.* i 437. Cp. P. Jahn in *Hermes* xxxvii, 161—172, *Rhein. Mus.* lviii, *Philologus*, N.F. xvii.     [4] *Georg.* i 233; Probus on Virg. *Georg.* p. 42 K.

[5] On i 43.          [6] Macrobius, v 2, 4.          [7] *ib.* v 17, 4.

[8] *Aen.* viii 22, and Ap. R. iii 755; cp. Heinze's *Virgils Epische Technik*, 1903.

[9] *e.g.* iv 469—473. Cp. Nettleship, i 121–5, and Schanz, § 233–4; also Kroll in *Jahresb.* vol. 124, p. 32.

[10] *Epist.* i 19, 23.                    [11] p. 190 *infra*.

on the constant study of the great Greek models of style[1]. Poets

Gallus  of the Alexandrian age were studied by Virgil's contemporary, Cornelius Gallus (70—27 B.C.), who
probably imitated Parthenius in his *Lycoris*, and certainly produced translations and imitations of Euphorion[2]. The learned
Alexandrian type of Elegy was abandoned by Tibullus (d. 19 B.C.),

Propertius  while it was closely followed by Propertius (d. 15 B.C.),
who openly avows his veneration for Philetas and
Callimachus[3]. The Αἴτια of the latter is the precursor not only
of the last book of Propertius, but also of the *Fasti* of Ovid

Ovid  (43 B.C.—18 A.D.), which, in its antiquarian details
and in all points connected with the Calendar,
follows the *Fasti* of Verrius Flaccus, which we possess in an
abridged form in the *Fasti Praenestini*[4]. The poet was prevented
by his banishment in 8 A.D. from finishing the *Fasti*. The same
disaster led to his flinging his *Metamorphoses* into the fire; and
the text was only recovered by means of copies already made by
the poet's friends. A Greek poem on the same subject had been
composed by Parthenius under the same title, and by Nicander
under that of ἑτεροιούμενα. In one of his stories of transformation
he gives two divergent accounts in different parts of his poem.
The legend of the halcyon existed in two forms, one preferred
by Nicander, another by Theodorus[5]: Ovid follows the former
in xi 270, the latter in vii 401. He imitates Homer, the Greek
tragedians[6] and Euphorion. He must have known the Greek
Argument to the *Medea* of Euripides, as he makes the same
mistake that is there made of connecting the revival of the nurses
of Bacchus with the revival of Aeson[7]. It may here be suggested
that he probably had his attention drawn to this Argument while
preparing his own early play on Medea. It need hardly be added

---

[1] 268-9.

[2] Probus on Virg. *Ecl.* x 50, and Servius on *Ecl.* vi 72 and x 1.

[3] iv 1, 1; v. 6, 3. On his Greek models cp. Otto (1882-6), and introd.
to Rothstein's ed. 1898.

[4] Winther, *De fastis Verrii Flacci ab Ovidio adhibitis* (1885). Hülsen
(1880) and Willers (1898) emphasise the influence of Varro.

[5] Probus on Virg. *Georg.* p. 44 K.; Bethe (1903).

[6] F. Beyschlag in *Berl. Phil. Woch.* 1903, 1372 f.

[7] vii 294. Robert, *Bild und Lied*, p. 231, 5.

that his *Metamorphoses* and his *Heroides* display a wide familiarity with the legendary lore of Greece[1]. One of his obscurer works, the *Ibis*, is an imitation of the vituperative poem of that name in which Callimachus attacked Apollonius Rhodius[2].

The first Universal History written in Latin, a work completed by Pompeius Trogus in 9 A.D., was probably founded on that of the Alexandrian Timagenes. It has only survived in the abridgement (probably of the third century) drawn up by Justin, from which it may be inferred that the original authorities were Dinon, Ephorus, Theopompus, Timaeus, Phylarchus, Polybius and possibly Poseidonius[3]. The way in which Livy (59 B.C.—17 A.D.), the foremost historian of the Augustan age, deals with his authorities, may be best studied in his fourth and fifth decades. While he there follows the Roman annalists, Cl. Quadrigarius and Valerius Antias, in his narrative of exclusively Roman events, his authority for the relations between Rome and the Hellenic States is Polybius. He does not however copy his Greek original too closely, but apparently aims at giving his version a Roman tone and a rhetorical colouring[4]. In the narrative of the operations closing with the battle of Cynoscephalae (xxx 5—10) we can minutely compare the copy with the original (xviii 18—27); and can feel (with Munro) 'how satisfying to the ear are the periods of Livy when he is putting into Latin the heavy and uncouth clauses of Polybius'[5].

*Pompeius Trogus*

*Livy*

---

[1] G. Lafaye, *Les Métamorphoses...et leurs modèles grecs* (Paris, 1904).

[2] *Ibis*, 58 f.          [3] Schanz, §§ 328—330.

[4] Nissen's *Untersuchungen*, 1863; Schanz, § 325.

[5] Lucretius, *Introd.* p. 306[3].

# CHAPTER XI.

## LITERARY CRITICISM AND GRAMMAR IN THE FIRST CENTURY B.C.

LITERARY criticism in the Roman age was partly borrowed from Greek sources such as the *Poetic* and *Rhetoric* of Aristotle, and the lost treatise *On Style* by Theophrastus. It may also have been influenced by critics such as Aristophanes and Aristarchus, the reputed founders of the Alexandrian 'canon'[1], while the *Ars Poetica* of Horace included among its sources of inspiration a lost treatise on poetical composition by Neoptolemus of Parium[2], whose date is probably between that of Callimachus and Aristophanes[3].

Early in the first century B.C. we find a 'canon' of ten Latin comic poets drawn up by Volcacius Sedigitus; the names included are Caecilius, Plautus, Naevius, Licinius, Atilius, Terence, Turpilius, Trabea, Luscius and Ennius[4]. A threefold variety of style was recognised by Varro (as by Theophrastus); and Pacuvius was taken by him as a type of *ubertas*, Lucilius of *gracilitas*, Terence of *mediocritas* in the good sense of the term[5]. Literary criticisms also appeared incidentally in his *saturae*, where he says, in one passage, that the palm is claimed by Caecilius for his plots, by Terence for his delineation of character, and by Plautus for his dialogues; and, in another, that truth to character is the special merit of Titinius, Terence and Atta; while the excitement of the emotions is that of Trabea, Atilius and Caecilius[6]. The

---

[1] p. 130 f.

[2] Porphyrio ('in quem librum congessit praecepta Neoptolemi τοῦ Παριανοῦ de arte poëtica, non quidem omnia, sed eminentissima'), discussed by Nettleship, *Essays*, i 173, ii 46—48.    [3] Susemihl, i 405.

[4] Gellius, xv 24; cp. Reich's *Mimus*, i 337—353.    [5] *ib.* vi (vii) 14, 8.

[6] Nettleship, ii 50–3; cp. Saintsbury's *History of Criticism*, i 240 f.

criticisms on ancient poets current in the youth of Horace[1] have
been attributed to Varro[2]

Literary criticism in Cicero (106—43 B.C.) has a conventional
and *borrowed* element, as in the frequent comparison
between literature and the arts of painting and
sculpture[3].   In this he had been preceded by Neoptolemus and
others, and he was succeeded by Dionysius[4] and Quintilian[5].
The late Greek criticism also produced many new technical terms,
several of which passed into the Latin of the Ciceronian and
Augustan ages[6].   The critical vocabulary of the Latin language
was largely extended by Cicero, who shows a special fondness for
discriminating between varieties of style by means of metaphors
borrowed either from moral qualities or from the physiology of
the human body[7].   Whenever he is *original* in his criticisms on
poetry, he has a marked preference for the grand and free style
of the older poets, such as Accius, Ennius and Pacuvius.   In his
criticisms on oratorical prose, in the *Brutus* and the *Orator*, he
vindicates his own literary principles against a new school, that
of the Roman Atticists, comprising orators like Calvus, whose
models were Lysias and Thucydides.   As a test of the truth of
these divergent views he lays down the principle that, 'given time
and opportunity, the recognition of the many is as necessary a
test of excellence in an artist as that of the few'[8].   A great style
must therefore 'combine *all* the elements of excellence'[9].   Cicero's
genius as a critic is revealed in his review of the styles of Galba
and Gaius Gracchus, of Antonius, Crassus and Scaevola, of Cotta
and Sulpicius; of Caesar, Calidius and Hortensius[10].   In a few
terse phrases he summarises the literary qualities of the speakers
whom he passes in review, displaying a fulness of insight, a
perfect mastery of thought, and a power of self-controlled expres-

Cicero

---

[1] *Ep.* ii 1, 55.                                      [2] Nettleship, ii 52.

[3] *Brutus*, §§ 70, 75, 228, 261, 298; *Orator*, § 36 (with the present writer's
*Introduction*, pp. lxxi—lxxiii); and Nettleship, ii 54 f.

[4] *De Comp.* 21, *De Isocr.* 2, *De Isaeo*, 4.

[5] xii 10, 1—10.                                         [6] Nettleship, ii 56.

[7] Cp. the present writer's notes on Cic. *Orator*, §§ 25, 76; also Causeret's
*Étude* (1886), pp. 155–8, and Saintsbury, i 220.

[8] *Brutus*, § 183 f (Nettleship, ii 58 f).             [9] *De Or.* iii 96 f, 101.

[10] *Brutus*, §§ 93, 125, 139, 143, 148, 201, 261, 274, 301.

sion standing in strong contrast with his usual prolixity.  In the
*De Legibus*[1], as in the *De Oratore*[2], history, in accordance with
the traditional Greek view dating from the time of Ephorus and
Theopompus, the pupils of Isocrates, is regarded as a branch of
oratory.  The idea of a painful study of authorities undertaken
with the simple purpose of ascertaining the truth, is unfamiliar to
his age.  It might have been developed among the philosophers
or the scholars of the time, but philosophy turned towards
'problems of speculative ethics, while scholarship satisfied itself
with verbal and textual criticism'[3].  In the *De Republica*[4] Cicero
happily describes Comedy as the *imitatio vitae*, the *speculum consuetudinis*, the *imago veritatis*.  In the *De Oratore*[5] he touches
on the varied excellences of Greek and Roman poets and orators,
and[6] unfolds a detailed theory of beauty of speech depending
either on words themselves and their combinations or on figures
of speech and thought.  In the *Pro Archia* he shows a personal
interest in eulogising literature in the presence (as we know from
the scholiast) of his brother Quintus.  He also supplies us with
valuable evidence as to the state of Greek culture in Southern
Italy, and also in Latium and Rome, shortly before 102 B.C.[7]
In the *Letters* the only important piece of literary criticism is the
much discussed phrase in which Cicero expresses his agreement
with his brother as to the 'poems' of Lucretius :—'Lucretii
poemata, ut scribis, ita sunt; multis luminibus ingenii, multae
tamen artis', where it has unnecessarily been proposed to insert
a *non* either before *multis* or before *multae*[8].  It is disappointing
to find in Cicero so vague a criticism of the merits of a poet who
had done him the honour of studying and imitating his own
translation of Aratus[9].

The *Orator*, which supplies some of the best examples of

---

[1] i 5.                [2] ii 51 f.              [3] Nettleship, ii 56—68.
[4] iv 13.              [5] iii 27 f.             [6] *ib.* 149—207.

[7] *Pro Archia*, § 5, erat Italia tum plena Graecarum artium ac disciplinarum,
studiaque haec et in Latio vehementius tum colebantur quam nunc isdem in
oppidis, et hic Romae propter tranquillitatem rei publicae non neglegebantur.

[8] *Ad Quintum*, ii 11.  Introd. to Munro's *Lucr.* vol. i pp. 313–5, ed. 1873;
cp. Saintsbury, pp. 214–7.

[9] Munro on *Lucr.* v 619; cp. Mackail's *Latin Literature*, p. 50, and Sihler,
in *Trans. Amer. Phil. Assoc.* 1897 (xxviii).

Cicero's taste as a literary critic, also affords us valuable evidence
as to the nature and extent of his knowledge of the philology of
the Latin language.   In the course of an excursus on the proper
collocation of words, in accordance with the laws of euphony[1],
we find him regarding *vexillum* as the earlier form of *velum*[2],
while it is really a diminutive of it; *capsis* as standing for *cape
si vis*[3], an opinion rightly rejected by Quintilian; and the compound words *ignoti, ignavi* and *ignari,* as preferred for reasons of
euphony to *innoti, innavi* and *innari*[4], whereas *gnoti, gnavi* and
*gnari* are obviously the original forms of the simple words.

Asinius Pollio (76 B.C.—5 A.D.) wrote a severe criticism on
the archaisms of Sallust[5], who in this respect was
regarded as having imitated and even plagiarised            Pollio
from the elder Cato[6].   It was only with reluctance (according to
the elder Seneca) that Pollio expressed a very high opinion of
Cicero :—'huius viri tot tantisque operibus mansuri in omne
aevum praedicare de ingenio atque industria supervacuum est'[7].

An account of the consulship of Cicero was written in Greek
during his life-time by his friend Atticus[8] (109—32),
whose *liber annalis,* a chronological work covering      Atticus and
seven centuries of Roman history[9], is probably the      Tiro
source of the *Fasti Capitolini* and of the 'Chronograph' of
354 A.D.[10]   He also played an important part in literature as the
head of an establishment of learned slaves engaged as copyists[11].
We still possess the Life of Atticus by Cornelius Nepos, while
that of Cicero is unfortunately lost.   Cicero's Life was also written
by his freedman Tiro, and it is to Atticus and Tiro that we are
doubtless mainly indebted for the survival of his works.   Tiro is
specially named in connexion with the Letters and the Speeches[12].
He wrote several works on the Latin language[13], and invented a
system of shorthand, which was carried further by Philargyrus, a

---

[1] §§ 146—162.            [2] § 153.            [3] § 154.            [4] § 158.
[5] Suet. *Gram.* 10.            [6] Suet. *Aug.* 86; Quintilian, viii 3, 29.
[7] Seneca, *Suas.* vi 24.            [8] *Ad Att.* ii 41; Nepos, *Atticus,* 18.
[9] Nepos, *l.c.*; Cic. *Orator,* § 120, *Brutus,* §§ 14, 19.            [10] Schanz, § 116.
[11] Nepos, *l.c.,* 13, 3; Cic. *ad Att.* xiii 21, 3; 44, 3; Fronto, *Ep.* 10.   Hul-
leman's *Atticus,* p. 173.
[12] *Ad Att.* xvi 5, 5; Gellius, i 7, 1; xiii 21, 16; cp. Quint. x 7, 30.
[13] Gellius, xiii 9, 2.

freedman of Agrippa, and Aquila, a freedman of Maecenas, and also by Seneca[1]. After flourishing in the Carolingian age, it became less common at the beginning of the tenth century, and vanished after the twelfth[2].

Among the younger contemporaries of Cicero, the Neo-
Pythagorean P. Nigidius Figulus (*c.* 98—45 B.C.),
the praetor of 58 B.C., was ranked by a later age
as second to Varro in learning[3]. His *commentarii grammatici* dealt with grammar in general, and especially with orthography, synonyms, and etymology. They are often quoted by Gellius, who complains of their being more obscure and less popular than the corresponding works of Varro[4]. He was perhaps the inventor of the method of denoting the long vowel by an apex[5]. L. Ateius Praetextatus, who was born at Athens and became a Roman freedman, assumed (like Eratosthenes) the name of *Philologus*. He was a student of style and of Roman history, and a friend of Sallust and Asinius Pollio[6]. Valerius Cato, who had a great reputation as a teacher of young noblemen with a taste for poetry, closed his life in extreme poverty; but even the satirical lines of Bibaculus unconsciously do him honour by comparing him as a *summus grammaticus* with the scholars of Alexandria and Pergamon :—*en cor Zenodoti, en iecur Cratetis*[7].

Latin grammar owes its terminology, in the first instance, to Varro; and, in the next, to Nigidius Figulus. In the middle of the first century B.C. the Gender or *genus* of a noun or *nomen substantivum* was distinguished by the terms *virile, muliebre* and *neutrum* (*masculinum* and *femininum* not occurring earlier than the second century A.D.)[8]. The Number or *numerus* was described by Varro as either *singularis* or *multitudinis,* while *pluralis* is found later in Quintilian (who represents the teaching of Remmius Palaemon),

*Margin notes:* Nigidius Figulus · L. Ateius Praetextatus · Valerius Cato · Grammatical terminology

---

[1] Isidore, *Orig.* i 21.                [2] Schanz, § 178, ult.

[3] Gellius, iv 9, 1.                [4] xvii 7, 5; xix 14, 3.

[5] Teuffel, § 170; Hübner, *Römische Litt.* § 45[5] (p. 44 Mayor); Mommsen, *Hist. of Rome*, Bk v c. 12; also Schanz, § 181.

[6] Suet. *Gram.* 10; Schanz, § 195, 6.

[7] *ib.* 11; Teuffel, § 200; Schanz, § 98.

[8] First found in Caesellius Vindex (Gellius vi (vii) 2).

and *plurativus* in Gellius. A Case (as with the Stoics) might be
either *rectus* or *obliquus*; the *casus rectus* was also known to Varro
as the *casus nominandei* or *nominativus*; the Genitive was called
by Varro the *casus patricus*, by Nigidius the *casus interrogandi*;
the Dative was described by both as the *casus dandi*, while *gene-
tivus* and *dativus* occur in Quintilian; the Accusative is in Varro
the *casus accusandei* or *accusativus*; the Vocative the *casus vocan-
dei*, while *vocativus* is found in Gellius; the Ablative, recognised
by Quintilian, possibly owes its name to Caesar, Varro's name for
it being the *sextus* or *Latinus casus*, as it was not found in Greek.
The Declensions and Conjugations are unrecognised by Varro.
He divides each of the three times, past, present and future, into
a *tempus infectum* and a *tempus perfectum*; but he knows nothing
of any technical sense of *modus*[1].

The earliest of the literary criticisms of Horace (65—8 B.C.)
are those of the fourth and tenth of his first book
of *Satires* (35 B.C.). He there asserts his own principles under the guise of a polemic against Lucilius.    *Literary
criticism in
Horace*
His predecessor's style, he says, is too hasty and too slovenly,
while the Old Attic Comedy is too narrow in its scope to serve
as a model for his own *satura*. Poetry, he insists, is not a matter
for the crowd; it is the gift and privilege of the few[2]. About
19 B.C. we have the criticisms of his *Ars Poetica*, founded in part
on Greek originals and prompted apparently by a desire to recall
his countrymen from the critical principles of the Ciceronian and
the Alexandrian ages, to those on which the great works of Hellas
were founded. Mr Saintsbury, who justly describes it as 'the
only complete example of literary criticism that we have from any
Roman', criticises its desultoriness and its arbitrary convention-
ality, while he fully recognises its brilliancy, its typical spirit, and
its practical value[3]. In the two Epistles of the Second book
Horace discards the framework of Greek words and Greek texts,
and relies on his own genius. In poetry he insists on the worthlessness of mere antiquity, and on the importance of perfect finish.

---

[1] Cp. Lersch, *Sprachphilosophie*, ii 223—256; Gräfenhan, ii 291—306;
and L. Jeep, *Zur Geschichte von den Redetheilen bei den Lateinischen Gramma-
tikern*, pp. 124—259.

[2] i 4, 40 and 71: Nettleship, ii 70.     [3] *Hist. of Criticism*, i 221-8.

The older Latin poets, admired by Varro and Cicero, are more coldly regarded by Horace, while they meet with a warmer appreciation in Ovid[1]. Virgil and Horace became classics soon after their death, driving out the taste for the older poets, and finding admirers and imitators in Lucan and Persius respectively.

While Virgil's *Eclogues* and *Georgics* were published during his life-time, the *Aeneid* was first edited by Varius and Tucca after his death (19 B.C.). He was attacked by Carvilius Pictor in his *Aeneidomastix*; his *vitia*, or supposed faults of style, were collected by Herennius; his *furta*, or alleged plagiarisms, by Perellius Faustus; and his translations from the Greek, by Octavius Avitus; while his detractors were answered by Asconius, better known as the earliest commentator on Cicero[2]. The first to expound Virgil in the schools of Rome was a freedman of Atticus, named Q. Caecilius Epirota, who opened a school after the death of his second patron, the poet Cornelius Gallus (27 B.C.)[3]. Virgil was criticised by Hyginus, the librarian of the Palatine Library, and by Cornutus, the friend of Persius. In the time of Quintilian[4] and Juvenal[5] he shared the fate, which Horace[6] had feared for himself, of being a textbook for use in schools. The first critical edition of Virgil was that of Probus in the time of Nero. Among his interpreters were Velius Longus, under Trajan; Q. Ter. Scaurus, under Hadrian; Aemilius Asper (towards the end of the 2nd century), and Aelius Donatus (*fl.* 353 A.D.). The earliest *extant* commentaries are those in the Verona *scholia*, including quotations from Cornutus, Velius Longus, Asper, and Haterianus (end of 3rd cent.): that on the *Eclogues and Georgics* bearing the name of Probus (*fl.* 56—88 A.D.); that on the *Aeneid* by Tib. Claudius Donatus (end of 4th century), which is simply a prose paraphrase exhibiting the rhetorical connexion of the successive clauses; and that on the whole of Virgil by Servius (late in 4th century), which includes references to the lost commentary by *Aelius* Donatus, who appears to have been deficient in knowledge and judgement

*Early study of Virgil*

---

[1] *Amores*, i 15—19, *Tristia*, ii 423; Nettleship, ii 70—73. See also Sellar's *Horace* etc., pp. 102—117.

[2] Nettleship in Conington's *Virgil*, i[4] pp. xxix—cix.   [3] Suet. *Gram.* 16.

[4] i 8, 5—6.          [5] vii 226 f.          [6] *Ep.* i 20, 17.

and far too fond of allegorising interpretations, and in these
respects inferior to the learned and sober Servius[1].   The earliest
MSS of Virgil belong to the 4th or 5th century.

The first critical edition of Horace was that of Probus; the
first commentary that of Q. Terentius Scaurus,
followed (late in the 2nd century) by Helenius      **Early study of Horace**
Acro, who also expounded Terence and Persius.
The only early commentaries now extant are the *scholia* collected
by Pomponius Porphyrio (3rd cent.), and by Pseudo-Acro, and
those compiled from various MSS by Prof. Cruquius of Bruges.   It
is only through Cruquius (1565) that we know anything of the
*codex antiquissimus Blandinius*, borrowed from the library of a
Benedictine monastery in Ghent[2], and burnt with the monastery
after it had been returned to the library.   It represented a recension earlier than the date of Porphyrio, as, in Sat. i 6, 126, instead
of *fugio rabiosi tempora signi* (recognised by Porphyrio), it had the
true text :—*fugio campum lusumque trigonem*.   The only MS which
retains the latter is the *codex Gothanus* (cent. 15).   In this, and
seven other MSS, we find a record at the end of the *Epodes* showing
that, at the close of the Roman age, there was a recension of
Horace produced, with the assistance of Felix, *orator urbis Romae*,
by Vettius Agorius Basilius Mavortius (the consul of 527)[3].   The
earliest extant MS belongs to the eighth or ninth century.

In the next chapter we shall turn to the Grammarians and
Scholars of the Augustan age.

---

[1] Nettleship, *l.c.* ; cp. Schanz, § 248.

[2] Codices 'in monte Blandinio', 'Roma Gandavum perlati' refers to the
monastery of St Peter on the Blandenberg in Ghent (J. Gow, in *Cl. Rev.*
1909, p. 204).     [3] Cp. Schanz, §§ 263-5 ; and Teuffel, § 240, 6 and 477, 3.

IDALIAELVCOSVBIM
FLORIBVSETDVLCIAD
IAMQ·IBATDICTOPAR

# Conspectus of Latin Literature &c., 1—300 A.D.

| Roman Emperors | Poets | Historians, Biographers | Orators, Rhetoricians | Scholars, Critics &c. | Other Writers of Prose |
|---|---|---|---|---|---|
| **A.D.** | | | | | |
| | | 9 Pompeius Trogus | L. Ann. Seneca I 54 B.C.—39 A.D. | | |
| 14 Tiberius | Germanicus 15 B.C.—19 A.D. c. 14 Manilius | | | | c. 14 Celsus |
| | | 30 Velleius Paterculus | P. Rutilius Lupus | | |
| 37 Caligula | 30—40 Phaedrus | 31 Valerius Maximus | | | 43-4 Pomponius Mela |
| 41 Claudius | L. Ann. Seneca II 4 B.C.—65 A.D. | 41 Q. Curtius | | 35—70 Palaemon | L. Ann. Seneca II 4 B.C.—65 A.D. |
| 54 Nero | 54 Calpurnius Persius 34—62 Lucan 39—65 | | | 54-7 Asconius 3—88 56—80 Probus | Petronius d. 6. 64-5 Columella |
| 68 Galba | | | 68-88 Quintilian c. 35—95 | | |
| 69 Otho | | | | | |
| 69 Vitellius | | | | | |
| 69 Vespasian | Valerius Flaccus d. c. 90 | | | | |
| 79 Titus | Statius d. c. 95 | | | 76 Elder Pliny 23—79 | |
| 81 Domitian | Silius 25—101 | Tacitus c. 55—120 | | | |
| 96 Nerva | Martial c. 40—104 | | 100 Younger Pliny 61—c.113 | | 70-97 Frontinus d. c. 103 |
| 98 Trajan | | | | | |
| **100** | Juvenal c. 55 or 60—140 | | | | |
| 117 Hadrian | | 120 Suetonius c. 75—160 137 Florus | | L. Caesellius Vindex Q. Ter. Scaurus Velius Longus | |
| 138 Antoninus Pius | *poetae neoterici* | Justin | 143 Fronto c. 90—168 | c. 150 C. Sulp. Apollinaris d. c. 160 | Gaius 110—180 |
| 161 M. Aurelius (161-9 L. Verus) | | | 158 Apuleius | 169 Gellius b. c. 130 Aemilius Asper Flavius Caper Statilius Maximus | |
| 180 Commodus | | | | | |
| 193 Pertinax | | | | Terentianus Maurus | |
| 193 Julianus | | | | Helenius Acro | Tertullian |
| 193 Septimius Severus | | | | Festus | c. 150—230 |
| **200** | | | | | |
| 211 Caracalla | | | | Porphyrio | |
| 217 Macrinus | | | | | 218? Solinus |
| 218 Elagabalus | | | | | |
| 222 Alexander Severus | | 223 Marius Maximus | | C. Julius Romanus | Cyprian c. 200—255 |
| 235 Maximin | | | | | |
| 238 Gordian I,II | | | | 238 Censorinus | |
| 238 { Pupienus { Balbinus | | | | | |
| 238 Gordian III | | | | | |
| 244 Philippus | | | | | |
| 249 Decius | 249 Commodianus | | | | |
| 251 Gallus | | 250 Junius Cordus | | | |
| 253 Aemilianus | | | | | |
| 253 Valerian & Gallienus | | | | | |
| 268 Claudius II | | | | | |
| 270 Aurelian | | | | | |
| 275 Tacitus | | | | | |
| 276 Florianus | | | | | |
| 276 Probus | | Spartianus | Aquila Romanus | | |
| 282 Carus | | Capitolinus | | | |
| 283 Carinus & Numerian | | Vulcatius Gallicanus | 295 Arnobius | | |
| 284 Diocletian | 284 Nemesianus | Trebellius Pollio | 297 Eumenius Lactantius | Mar. Plotius Sacerdos | |
| (286 Maximian) | | | | | |
| **300** | | | | | |

*Continued from page* 168.

# CHAPTER XII.

## LATIN SCHOLARSHIP FROM THE AUGUSTAN AGE TO 300 A.D.

THE Temple of the Palatine Apollo, founded in memory of the victory of Actium, was dedicated by Augustus in 28 A.D. Like the Temple of the 'Victorious Athena' at Pergamon, it was surrounded by colonnades giving access to a Library. The Library consisted of two apartments, one for Greek and the other for Latin books, with a spacious hall between; and we are informed that the books were collected by Pompeius Macer[1], and that the Head Librarian was C. Julius Hyginus[2].

Hyginus (c. 64 B.C.—17 A.D.), the pupil of Alexander Polyhistor (p. 159) and the friend of Ovid, was one of the foremost scholars of the Augustan age. In his studies he followed the traditions of Varro as well as those of Nigidius Figulus. Among the most important of his multifarious works were (1) his commentary on Virgil, and (2) his treatise on the *Urbes Italiae*, repeatedly cited by Servius[3]. Hyginus was succeeded by his own freedman Modestus, who is mentioned in Quintilian[4] and Martial[5]; and by M. Pomponius Marcellus, who began life as a boxer and ended it as a pedant. During a discussion in court as to whether a word used by the emperor Tiberius was good Latin or not, he had the courage to say to

Hyginus

---

[1] Suet. *Caesar*, 56.  [2] Suet. *Gram.* 20.

[3] Teuffel, § 262; Schanz, §§ 342—6; he is not the author of the extant works on Astronomy and Mythology which bear his name (Schanz, §§ 347—350). For most of the scholars mentioned in this chapter and the next, cp. Gräfenhan, iv 57—94.

[4] i 6, 36.  [5] x 21, 1.

the emperor: 'civitatem dare potes hominibus, verbo non potes'[1].
Varro was the model set up by Fenestella (52 B.C.—19 A.D.), the

Fenestella
author of more than 22 books of Annals, which
became the source of a vast variety of later erudition connected with Roman antiquities and literary history. He
is described by Lactantius as a 'diligentissimus scriptor'[2]. In the

Verrius
Flaccus
same age Verrius Flaccus (*fl.* 10 B.C.) produced his
great work *De Verborum Significatu*, the first Latin
lexicon ever written. This survives in the incomplete and fragmentary abridgement by Pompeius Festus (2nd cent.
A.D.)[3], which in its turn was further abridged by Paulus, who
dedicated his epitome to Charles the Great. We learn from
Suetonius that Verrius Flaccus introduced among his pupils the
principle of competition. He was made tutor to the grand-children of Augustus and died as an old man in the reign of
Tiberius. The remains of his work may still be traced in
Quintilian, Gellius, Nonius, Macrobius and other writers[4]. It
appears to have been of the nature of an encyclopaedia, including
'not only lexicographical matter, but much information on points
of history, antiquities, and grammar, illustrated by numerous
quotations from poets, jurists, historians, old legal documents,
and writers on religious or political antiquities'[5]. Much of his
treatise *De Orthographia* can be recovered from the works on
the same subject by Terentius Scaurus and Velius Longus, who
wrote under Trajan and Hadrian, and from Quintilian i 4 and 7[6].
At Praeneste, a statue was erected in his honour with a semi-circular marble recess inscribed with his *Fasti*[7], partially preserved
in the *Fasti Praenestini*[8].

A name of note in the history of Latin Grammar is that of

Palaemon
Q. Remmius Palaemon (*fl.* 35–70 A.D.) of Vicentia.
By birth a slave, and by trade a weaver, he learnt
the elements of literature while accompanying his master's son
on his way to school: and, after obtaining his freedom, he held

---

[1] Suet. *Gram.* 22.

[2] *Inst. Div.* i 6, 14, ap. Teuffel, § 243, 2.  Cp. Schanz, § 331.

[3] Reitzenstein (1887); Willers (1898).          [4] Nettleship, i 201—247.

[5] *ib.* p. 205.      [6] *ib.* ii 151–8.      [7] Suet. *Gram.* 17.  Teuffel, § 74, 3.

[8] Teuffel, § 74, 3 and § 261; Schanz, §§ 340-1; Bursian's *Jahresb.* 113, 128 f.

the foremost place among teachers of Grammar in Rome.  He
was born towards the end of the reign of Augustus, and lived
under Tiberius and Claudius, both of whom declared that morally
he was the last man to whom the education of youth ought to be
entrusted.  His popularity was due to his marvellous memory, his
readiness of speech, and his power of improvising poetry.  His
*Ars Grammatica*, probably published between 67 and 77 A.D.,
was the first exclusively scholastic treatise on Latin Grammar
We infer from Juvenal[1] that it contained rules for correct speaking,
examples from ancient poets, and chapters on barbarism and
solecism.  The *scholia* on Juvenal[2] inform us that Palaemon was
the preceptor of Quintilian, and it is highly probable that, in
i 4 and 5 §§ 1—54, Quintilian is paraphrasing from his preceptor's treatise.  He was the first to distinguish four declensions,
and part of his grammatical teaching is preserved by Charisius
(4th century).  Palaemon humorously regarded his own advent
as an arbiter of poetry as predicted by Virgil in the phrase, *venit
ecce Palaemon;* and he vaingloriously asserted that letters had
been born at his birth, and would die at his death[3].

   The elder Seneca, L. Annaeus Seneca of Corduba (*c.* 54 B.C.—
39 A.D.), is a link between the republican and the
imperial times.  In the first half of his life he was        Seneca the
an admirer of the style of Cicero and of Pollio and     elder
Messala, while in his old age he recorded his earlier recollections
in works which illustrate the history of oratory under Augustus
and Tiberius, and are interesting in connexion with matters of
rhetorical criticism[4].  He mentions Apollodorus of Pergamon
(who included Augustus among his pupils), and he supplies some
reminiscences of Ovid as a declaimer[5].  In the latter part of his
life we may place P. Rutilius Lupus, the author of an abridgement
of a work on the figures of speech by the younger Gorgias (44 B.C.)
containing well-chosen examples translated from speeches of Attic
orators which are no longer extant[6].

----

   [1] vi 452 f, vii 215.                         [2] vi 452.
   [3] Suetonius, *Gram.* 23; Teuffel, § 282; Nettleship, ii 149, 163–9; Schanz,
§ 475; also K. Marschall, *De Q. Remmii Palaemonis libris grammaticis*, 1887;
Bursian's *Jahresb.* vol. 68 (1891 ii), p. 132 f; and Jeep's *Redetheile*, p. 172 f.
   [4] Cp. Saintsbury, i 230–9.                   [5] *Controv.* ii 2, 8.
   [6] Teuffel, § 270; Schanz, § 480; Halm, *Rhet. Lat. Min.* 3—21.

The younger Seneca[1] (*c.* 4 B.C.—65 A.D.) is absorbed in the philosophy of the Stoics[2], but does not share their interest in Grammar. He criticises Cicero and Virgil for their admiration of Ennius[3], and notes the obsoleteness[4] of the language of Ennius and Accius, and even of that of Virgil, whom he nevertheless cites very frequently, calling him a 'vir disertissimus'[5] and a 'maximus vates'[6]. He quotes Horace occasionally, especially the *Satires*, and Ovid far oftener, especially the *Metamorphoses*, describing their author as 'poëtarum ingeniosissimus, ad pueriles ineptias delapsus'[7]. He casts contempt on those who are wholly engaged in the study of 'useless letters', and satirises the craze of the Greeks for inquiring as to the number of the oarsmen of Ulysses, and whether the *Iliad* was written before the *Odyssey*, and whether the same poet was the author of both[8]. In the 88th of his *Letters*, he sneers at the 'grammatici'[9]; he justly ridicules the attempts to make out Homer to have been a Stoic, an Epicurean, a Peripatetic or a Platonist[10]; he does not even care to inquire whether Homer or Hesiod was the earlier poet[11]; and he pities the 'superfluous' learning contained in the 4000 volumes of Didymus, with their discussions on the birthplace of Homer, and the moral character of Sappho and Anacreon[12]. In his 108th *Letter* he complains that the spirit of disputatiousness has turned 'philosophy' into 'philology'[13], and also points out that the 'grammarian' examines Virgil and Cicero from a point of view different from that of the 'philologer' or the 'philosopher'[14]. He is almost afraid of taking an undue interest in such matters himself[15], though elsewhere he is generous enough to describe the 'grammarians' as the *custodes Latini sermonis*[16]. Lastly, in making the earliest mention of the alleged destruction of 40,000 MSS at Alexandria[17], he leaves it to Livy to praise the Alexandrian Library as 'a noble monument of

---

[1] Cp. Saintsbury, i 246 f; Teuffel, §§ 287—290 ; Schanz, §§ 452—472.

[2] His debt to Epicurus, and other Greek philosophers, has been traced in detail by Usener, and by Thomas (1891).

[3] Gellius, xii 2 (Seneca, *Frag.* 110–3) and *Dial.* v 37, 5.

[4] *Ep.* 58, 1—6.　　　　[5] *Dial.* viii 1, 4.　　　　[6] *ib.* x 9, 2.

[7] *Nat. Q.* iii 27, 13.　　　　[8] *Dial.* x 13, 1—9; cp. *Nat. Q.* iv 13, 1.

[9] § 3.　　　[10] § 5.　　　[11] § 6.　　　[12] § 37.　　　[13] § 23.

[14] §§ 24—34 ; p. 9 *supra*.　　[15] § 35.　　[16] *Ep.* 95 § 65.　　[17] *Supra*, p. 112 f.

royal taste and royal foresight', himself regarding it as a monument of learned extravagance, and even withdrawing the epithet
'learned'; for the books (he maintains) had been bought for mere
show and not for real learning[1].

Much more interest in literature seems to be shown by another
victim of Nero, a far less moral writer, Petronius       Petronius
(d. 66 A.D.).  His extant work is in form a *satura*
*Menippea*, in which prose is interspersed with verse in various
metres parodying the style of Seneca, Lucan and Nero[2].  Literary
criticism is here incidentally represented in the opening protest
against the bombastic language which results from the practice of
declamation[3].  It is also exemplified in a later passage warning
the poet against allowing any particular sentence to be too ob-
trusive for its context, insisting on the use of choice language
and the avoidance of vulgarity, and justifying this view by
appealing to Homer and Virgil, as well as the Greek Lyric
poets, and Horace with (what Petronius happily describes as) his
*curiosa felicitas*[4].  Literary criticism also finds its place in the
Satires of Persius (34—62 A.D.) who touches on the       Persius
interest felt by the descendants of Romulus for the
after-dinner discussion of literary topics[5].  His highly satirical
and allusive prologue is followed by a satire on the professional
poet and on the mania for poetic recitation, with parodies of the
'precious' style affected by the poetasters of the day.  There is
also a critical element in the opening passages of the fifth and
sixth Satires, his general attitude being a protest against a fantastic
pursuit of Greek themes, and a preference for a manly Roman style[6].

One of the most competent commentators of the first century
was Q. Asconius Pedianus (*c.* 3—88 A.D.), who was       Asconius
certainly acquainted with Livy, and was probably,
like Livy, born at Patavium.  He was the author of a lost work in
vindication of Virgil[7], but is best known as the writer of a learned
historical commentary on Cicero's speeches.  All that has survived
is certain portions of the commentary on the Speeches *in Pisonem*,

---

[1] *Dial.* ix 9, 5.                   [2] Teuffel, § 305, 4; Schanz, §§ 393–6.
[3] §§ 1, 2.                           [4] § 118.  Saintsbury, i 242–5.
[5] i 31.                              [6] Saintsbury, i 248—253.
[7] *Contra obtrectatores Vergilii*, quoted by Donatus in his Life of Virgil.

*pro Scauro*, *pro Milone*, *pro Cornelio*, and *in toga candida*. It abounds in historical and antiquarian lore, and shows familiarity with even the unpublished works of Cicero, and the speeches of his partisans and his opponents. Its method is modelled on that of Didymus[1]. It was composed about 55 A.D., and is only preserved in transcripts of the MS found by Poggio at St Gallen in 1417[2].

Grammar was one of the many subjects which attracted the attention of the elder Pliny (23—79 A.D.), who, in the Preface to his *Naturalis Historia*[3], mentions what he modestly calls certain *libelli* which he had written on this subject. His nephew, Pliny the younger[4], names in the list of his uncle's works eight *libri* on *dubius sermo* (or Irregularities in Formation), written in the time of Nero. It is probably this work that is the source of a large part of Quintilian i 5, 54 to i 6, 287[5]. It is also probably the same work that is meant by the *Ars Grammatica* attributed to Pliny by Priscian and by Gregory of Tours. Pliny, as we have already noticed[6], is an analogist. Little else is known of his views, but there is reason to believe that the work by Valerius Probus *de nomine* is founded on the grammatical writings of the elder Pliny[7]. The books of his encyclopaedic *Naturalis Historia* which deal with Ancient Art are (with all their imperfections) the foundation of our knowledge of that subject[8]. The work has survived in many MSS, having been very popular in the Middle Ages. Extracts from the geographical portions appear in Solinus, and other excerpts in the *Medicina Plinii*.

M. Valerius Probus of Beyrut (*fl.* 56–88 A.D.) was the foremost grammarian of the first century A.D. Weary of the career of a soldier, he resolved on becoming a

Pliny the elder

Probus

---

[1] Leo (1904).

[2] Madvig (1828); Teuffel, § 295, 2—3; Wissowa in Pauly-Wissowa, *s.v.*; ed. in Orelli's *Cicero* v 2 pp. 1—95, and by Kiessling and Schöll (1875). Cp. Suringar, *Hist. Critica*, i 117—146; Voigt, *Humanismus*, i 239—240[3]; also Schanz, § 476, esp. p. 337[2].

[3] § 28.    [4] iii 5, 5.    [5] Nettleship, ii 158—161.    [6] p. 181.

[7] O. Froehde, *Valerii Probi de nomine libellum Plinii Secundi doctrinam continere demonstratur*, 1892; cp. Nettleship, ii 146, 150; Schanz, § 494, 5.

[8] On Pliny's authorities, cp. F. Münzer, *Quellenkritik der Naturgeschichte* (1897), and Kroll in *Jahresb.* vol. 124, p. 47 f.

scholar. His interest in literature was first excited by certain
ancient Latin authors which he had read before arriving in Rome,
and here he continued his studies and gathered round him a number of learned friends, with whom he spent several hours a day in
discussing the Latin literature of the past[1]. Martial, in sending
into the world his third book of epigrams, bids it farewell with
the words: *nec Probum timeto*[2]. Gellius, among several eulogistic
references, describes him as an 'illustrious grammarian'[3], and
Sidonius Apollinaris calls him 'a pillar of learning'[4]. He published a few unimportant criticisms, besides leaving behind him a
*silva observationum sermonis antiqui*. Specimens of his conversational teaching on this subject are preserved by Gellius, who cites
at second-hand his remarks on Plautus, Terence, Virgil, Sallust
and Valerius Antias, mentions some of his writings, *e.g.* on the
Perfect form *occecurri*, and also states that he made the penulti-
mate of the Accusative of *Hannibal* and *Hasdrubal* long, on the
ground that it was so pronounced by Plautus and Ennius (whose
pronunciation of these forms has not been followed by Horace
or Juvenal). He produced recensions of Plautus (?), Terence,
Lucretius, Virgil, Horace and Persius[5], with critical symbols like
those used by the Alexandrian Scholars. These symbols, which
were 21 in number, had already been used by Vargunteius and
by Aelius Stilo[6]. He also wrote a work on the ancient contrac-
tions used in legal Latin. In settling the text of Virgil, he went
back to the earliest authorities. We are told that he had himself
examined a MS of the *First Georgic* corrected by Virgil's own
hand[7], and traces of some of his critical signs survive in the
Medicean MS of Virgil, while we may ascribe to him the nucleus
at least of the extant commentary on the *Bucolics* and *Georgics*,
which bears his name. Among the grammatical works assigned
to Probus is one on anomaly (*de inaequalitate consuetudinis*),
another on tenses, and on doubtful genders. Two treatises have
come down to us under his name: (1) *Catholica*, dealing with the
noun and the verb; (2) a prolix and feeble treatise on Grammar

---

[1] Suet. *Gram.* 24.   [2] iii 2, 12.   [3] i 15, 18.
[4] *Carm.* ix 334.   [5] Cp. Leo, *Plautinische Forschungen*, 21—41 *passim.*
[6] Reifferscheid, *Suetoni Reliquiae*, p. 137 i. Teuffel, § 41, 2. Gräfenhan,
iv 372, 380.   [7] Gellius, xiii 21, 4.

(to which the title *Instituta Artium* has been given) with an
appendix *de differentiis* and *de nomine excerpta*. It is supposed
that these are ultimately founded on the remains of the teaching
of Probus which may have been reduced into the form of a
text-book in two parts:—(1) the *Instituta Artium*, dealing with
letters, syllables and the eight parts of speech; and (2) the
*Catholica*, dealing with nouns and verbs[1]. Pliny and Probus are
probably responsible for most of the remarks on irregularities of
declension and conjugation found in the later grammarians. To
these two writers, and to Palaemon, may be ascribed the main
outlines of the traditional Latin Grammar[2].

From Probus we turn to a name of far greater note. Fabius
　　　　　　　　Quintilianus (*c* 35—95 A.D.), born at Calagurris
**Quintilian**　　on the Ebro, was the pupil of Palaemon and the
preceptor of Tacitus and the younger Pliny His father was a
teacher of rhetoric in Rome, where he himself passed the greater
part of his life as a pleader in the law-courts and as a professor of
rhetoric. In 68 A.D. he was placed at the head of the first State-
supported school in Rome, and probably twenty years afterwards
he began his great work, the *Institutio Oratoria*. His views on
education ultimately come from Chrysippus. The study of
literature (*de grammatica*) is the theme of chapters 4—8 of his
first book, while c. 9 is *de officio grammatici*. There is reason
to believe that c. 4 and c. 5 §§ 1—54 are founded on Palaemon;
c. 5 § 54 to c. 6 § 27 on Pliny, and c. 7 §§ 1—28 on Verrius
Flaccus[3]. In the controversy between analogists and anomalists,
Quintilian, as we have seen[4], was on the side of the former without adhering to them very strictly. In the first chapter of the
tenth book he suggests a course of reading suitable for the future
orator, including (1) the Greek and (2) the Latin classics arranged
under the heads of poetry, the drama, history, oratory and philosophy. In (1) he virtually admits that he is giving the criticism
of others, not his own. These criticisms have so much in
common with those of Dionysius of Halicarnassus that it is
practically impossible to dispute Quintilian's indebtedness to that

---

[1] Teuffel, § 300; Schanz, §§ 477–9; Aistermann, lxxiv + 156, Bonn, 1910.

[2] Nettleship, ii 170 f; Schanz, §§ 494–5. Cp. Bursian's *Jahresb.* 113
(1903), 133–6.　　　　　[3] Nettleship, ii 169.　　　　[4] p. 181 *supra*.

author, though an attempt has been made to show that the
identity is due to both having borrowed from the same earlier
authority[1]. In part of his criticisms on the Greek poets, historians
and philosophers, he appears to be indebted to Theophrastus
and the Alexandrian critics, such as Aristophanes and Aristarchus[2].
In (2) his aim throughout is to make canons of classical Latin
authors corresponding as closely as possible with the canons of
Greek authors. He gives no independent opinion on Pacuvius
and Accius, and hardly notices Plautus, Caecilius, and Terence;
he misconceives Lucretius; and although his criticisms on post-
Ciceronian writers are sound and well-expressed, they are generally
brief. It is clear that literature before and after Cicero has
comparatively little attraction for Quintilian. His refined and
carefully written criticism on Cicero is a monument of trained
insight, grounded on manly and sober sense. While Quintilian
is concerned with the literary and professional aspects of the
question as to the reading which is best suited for the formation
of a good oratorical style, Tacitus (*c.* 55—120 A.D.)
in his Dialogue *De Oratoribus* (81 A.D.), a work of    Tacitus
the highest originality, profundity and historic insight, takes a
loftier view, seeing clearly that literature must be 'judged as the
expression of national life, not as a matter of form and of
scholastic teaching'[3]. The doubts as to the Tacitean authorship
of the Dialogue have been partly met by the fact that a phrase
there found[4] is mentioned as expressing the opinion of Tacitus
in a letter addressed by Pliny the younger (61—*c.* 113 A.D.) to
Tacitus himself[5]. The criticism of oratory has also
an attraction for the younger Pliny. He writes a    The younger
long letter to Tacitus, in the course of which he    Pliny
refers to the typical orators in Homer, and quotes the ancient

[1] Usener, *Dion. Hal. de Imitatione*, p. 132. Heydenreich, *De Quintiliani
...libro X* (1900), maintains that Quintilian was directly indebted to Dionysius.

[2] Nettleship, ii 76—83; and Peterson's *Quintil. X*, pp. xxviii—xxxvii. For
a *facsimile* from a MS of Quintilian (X 1, 87), see p. 215.

[3] Nettleship *l.c.* p. 87 ff. Teuffel, § 325 (Quintilian); § 334 (Tacitus); cp.
Schanz, § 483 f and § 428 f; ed. Orelli-Andresen, 1877; Peterson, 1893;
Gudeman, 1894.    [4] cc. 9 and 12; in nemora et lucos; nemora et luci.

[5] ix 10, 2; poëmata...quae tu inter nemora et lucos commodissime perfici
putas.

eulogies on the style of Pericles[1]. He also refers to the *De Corona* and the *Meidias* of Demosthenes[2], and quotes several passages from his public speeches as examples of happy audacity of phrase[3].

Pliny was born in about the same year as Juvenal, and died

Martial

about nine years later than his earlier contemporary Martial. Of these two poets, Martial (*c.* 40— *c.* 102–4 A.D.) shows a high appreciation of Catullus[4], who was beyond the reach of the flattery which he lavishes on his own contemporary Silius Italicus[5]. In criticising another contemporary, whose verses were so obscure as to call for a scholiast, he expresses a hope that his own poems may give pleasure to grammarians, but may be intelligible without their aid[6]. In many other epigrams, as has been fully shown by Mr Saintsbury[7], 'we have a very considerable number of pronouncements on critical points or on points connected with criticism'. Early in the sixth century Martial was imitated by the African poet, Luxorius, who is sometimes regarded as the compiler of the poems of the 'Anthologia Latina' preserved in the *Codex Salmasianus*[8].

In Juvenal (*c.* 55–60—140 A.D.) there is much mention of

Juvenal

literature, but literary criticism is hardly to be found. He satirises the learned ladies who prefer talking Greek to Latin[9], and weigh the merits of Homer and Virgil[10]. In the seventh Satire he describes the ideal poet, and pays a passing compliment to Quintilian[11]; in the tenth[12] he 'points a moral' as to the perils of a political career by referring to the fate of Demosthenes and Cicero, but he does not permit any of these themes to tempt him into the criticism of literature[13].

Statius

Juvenal is the only contemporary of Statius (*c.* 40— *c.* 96 A.D.) who mentions that poet[14], and there are some fine touches of criticism in the poem by Statius on the

---

[1] i 20.                              [2] ii 3, 10; vii 30, 4.

[3] ix 26,8—12. Cp. Teuffel, § 340; Schanz, § 444 f. Literary criticism in Pliny, Tacitus and Quintilian is fully treated by Saintsbury, i 270—321.    [4] x 78 etc.

[5] iv 14; vii 63.        [6] x 21, grammaticis placeant, sed sine grammaticis.

[7] i 256—268.        [8] Teuffel, § 476.        [9] vi 185–7.

[10] vi 435–6.        [11] 53 f, 186 f.        [12] 114—132.

[13] Saintsbury, i 253–6.        [14] Juv. vii 82–7.

birthday of Lucan, where Ennius and Lucretius (amongst others) are briefly characterised :—

> 'Cedet Musa rudis ferocis Enni,
> Et docti furor arduus Lucreti'[1].

From this group of poets we turn to the name of a writer of prose, who is our main authority on the history of Latin Scholarship from 168 B.C. to the time of Probus, and whose varied erudition made him a favourite author in the early Middle Ages. C. Suetonius Tranquillus (*c.* 75—160 A.D.), who was an advocate under Trajan, and private secretary to Hadrian, spent the latter part of his life in preparing encyclopaedic works on the history of language and literature. Apart from his extant work *de vita Caesarum,* he wrote an important series of biographies entitled *de viris illustribus* under the headings of 'poets', 'orators', 'historians', 'philosophers', 'scholars' (*grammatici*), and 'rhetoricians'. Of the early part of this work we possess excerpts alone. From the book on 'poets', we have short lives of Terence, Horace, Lucan, Virgil and Persius[2]; from that on 'historians', a few remains of a life of the elder Pliny. Of his 36 biographies of 'scholars and rhetoricians', no less than 25 have survived. Among the numerous subjects of his lost works were the games of the Greeks and Romans, varieties of raiment, terms of abuse, and Roman institutions and customs. It was probably in another lost work entitled *Pratum* or *Prata* that (among many other topics) he treated of various notations of time in connexion with the Roman year, being one of the authorities followed on this point by Censorinus and Macrobius[3], besides being one of the main sources of the erudition of Isidore of Seville. The works of Suetonius included a defence of Cicero against the attacks of the Alexandrian Scholar, Didymus, and a treatise on the critical signs used in the margins of MSS[4]. Most

[1] *Silvae,* ii 7, 75 f; cp. Saintsbury, i 268 f.

[2] The view that Borgius' *vita Lucreti,* published by J. Masson in the *Academy,* no. 1155 (1894), and discussed in *Journal of Philology,* xxiii 220—237, comes from Suetonius, has been refuted by Fritsche in *Berl. Phil. Woch.* 1895, 541, and by Woltjer, *ibid.* 317, and *Mnemosyne,* xxiii 222.

[3] Reifferscheid, *Suetoni Reliquiae,* p. 149 f.

[4] περὶ τῶν ἐν τοῖς βιβλίοις σημείων (Suïdas). Cp. Bergk, *Kl. Philol. Schr.* i 593; Reifferscheid, p. 135 f; Traube, *Comment. Woelfflin.* 200, and *Archiv f. Stenographie,* 1901, 53 (Schanz, § 532, 4).

of our knowledge of the meanings of these symbols is due to
Suetonius[1].

Among the Scholars of the second century A.D. were Caesellius
Vindex, a learned analogist[2]; Q. Terentius Scaurus,
who wrote on orthography as well as Grammar and
Poetry, and was also a commentator on Plautus and
Virgil, and probably on Horace[3]; Velius Longus and Flavius
Caper[4], both of whom wrote on orthography; and
Aemilius Asper, the learned and acute commen-
tator on Terence, Sallust and Virgil[5]. A special interest attaches
to M. Cornelius Fronto of Cirta (*c.* 90—168 A.D.), the tutor of
M. Aurelius and the admirer of the earlier Roman
literature as represented by Plautus, Ennius, Cato,
Gracchus, Lucretius, Laberius and Sallust. He never mentions
Terence or Virgil, though he betrays occasional reminiscences, not
of Virgil only, but also of Horace and Tacitus[6]. He depreciates
Seneca, but bestows frequent encomiums on Cicero, though he
cares more for his letters than for his speeches, in which he finds
very few of those rare words for which Fronto himself had an
excessive partiality[7]. In literary criticism ' his utterances do not
go beyond neatly formulated criticisms of the old
scholastic type '[8]. Mention may here be made of
C. Sulpicius Apollinaris of Carthage, the teacher of
Pertinax and of Gellius, and the author of the *quaestiones episto-
licae*, and of metrical summaries of Plautus, Terence
and the *Aeneid*[9]; and Arruntius Celsus, an anno-
tator on Plautus and Terence[10].

More important than either of these is Aulus Gellius[11] (born

Marginal notes (left column):
*Scaurus.*
*Velius Longus*
*Caper. Asper*
*Fronto*
*C. Sulpicius Apollinaris*
*Arruntius Celsus*

---

[1] On Suetonius in general, cp. Teuffel, § 347, Schanz, §§ 529—536; and
Macé, *Sur Suetone*, 1900.

[2] Teuffel, § 343; Schanz, § 593.          [3] *ib.* § 352; Schanz, § 594 f.

[4] *ib.* § 343; Schanz, §§ 596, 599.          [5] *ib.* § 328; Schanz, § 598.

[6] p. 144 Naber, 'novissimum homini sapientiam colenti amiculum est
gloriae cupido' (cp. Tac. *Hist.* iv 6).

[7] Teuffel, § 355, 5; Schanz, §§ 549 f, esp. § 552; R. Ellis, *Lecture*, 1904.

[8] Nettleship, ii 91.          [9] Teuffel, § 357, 1—2; Schanz, § 597.

[10] *ib.* 357, 3; Schanz, § 605, 5.

[11] *ib.* 365; Schanz, § 607—9; Nettleship, i 248—276; cp. Boissier, *Fin du
Paganisme*, ed. 3, 1898, i 178—180; and Saintsbury, i 322—9; also Hertz,
*Renaissance und Rococo in der römischen Litteratur*, 1865.

*c.* 130 A.D.), the author of the *Noctes Atticae*, an interesting
and instructive compilation of varied lore on the
earlier Latin Language and Literature, and on Law        Gellius
and Philosophy, deriving its name from the fact that the author
began it, about the age of thirty, in the winter evenings near
Athens.  Its main importance is due to its large number of
citations from works which are now no longer extant.  At Athens
the author became acquainted with the mysterious philosopher,
Peregrinus Proteus[1], and was often invited to the country-house
of that distinguished patron of learning, Herodes Atticus[2]; he
attended the monthly meetings of the students[3], and made excursions to Aegina and Delphi[4].  In his extant work he shows
himself a most industrious student and a typical Scholar.  He
frequents Libraries, whether in the *domus Tiberiana* on the
Palatine, or in the Temple of Peace founded by Vespasian, in
the Temple of Trajan, or in that of Hercules at Tibur, or even
at Patrae in Greece, where he finds a 'really ancient MS' of
Livius Andronicus[5].  The reading aloud of a passage on melted
ice or snow from a MS of Aristotle, borrowed by a friend from
the Temple at Tibur[6], leads him to forswear cold drinks for
the rest of his life.  He has pleasant memories of his teacher
Antonius Julianus, who paid a large sum for the purpose of
verifying a single reading in an ancient MS of Ennius[7]; he refers
to good MSS of Fabius Pictor, Cato, Catullus, Sallust, Cicero and
Virgil, but in these references it is possible that he may be really
borrowing from Probus who, according to Suetonius, 'gave an
immense amount of attention to the collection of good MSS of
classical authors'[8].  In matters of style, he has some general
remarks accompanying a short comparison between Plato and
Lysias, also between Menander and Caecilius, and C. Gracchus
and Cicero[9].  He tells the story of the meeting at Tarentum
between the aged Pacuvius and the youthful Accius, when Pacu-

---

[1]  xii 11, 1.        [2] i 2, 1; xix 12.        [3] xv 2, 3.        [4] ii 21; xii 5.
[5]  xiii 20, 1; xvi 8, 2; xi 17, 1; ix 14, 3; xviii 9, 5.
[6]  xix 5, 4; cp. ix 14, 3.
[7]  xviii 5, 11.  It was Julianus who, in the summer holidays, took Gellius
and his other pupils to hear a recitation from the Annals of Ennius in the
theatre of Puteoli (xviii 5, 1—5).
[8]  Suet. *Gram.* 24 (Nettleship, i 274).        [9] ii 5, ii 23, x 3.

vius, after hearing Accius read his *Atreus*, pronounced it grand
and sonorous, but perhaps harsh and crude, and Accius replied
that he hoped his poems would improve in time, like apples that
were harsh and crude at first, but afterwards became sweet and
mellow[1]. He quotes a comparison between the eruption of Aetna
as described by Pindar and by Virgil[2]. He also defends Sallust
and Virgil against their detractors, and discusses the style of
Seneca[3]. More than a fourth of his work is concerned with
Latin lexicography, *e.g.* the singular use of *mille*[4], with notes on
*pedarii senatores*[5], on the different senses of *obnoxius*[6], on *proletarii* and *adsidui*[7], on the exact meaning of the phrase in Ennius,
*ex iure manum consertum*[8], and on Cicero's use of *paenitere*[9]. He
also discusses synonyms, words of double meaning, derivations,
and moot points of Grammar, such as the pronunciation of H and
V[10], the quantity of IN and CON in composition[11], the question
whether one should say *tertium* or *tertio*, *curam vestri* or *vestrum*[12],
and the difference between *multis hominibus* and *multis mortali-
bus*[13]. He quotes a large variety of Greek and Latin authors,
taking a special interest in the earlier Latin Literature and in
Latin 'grammarians'. But he rejects a friend's suggestion that
he should discuss (among many other minor matters) the question
what was the name of the first 'grammarian'[14]. Among the more
miscellaneous contents of his work, readers of *Sandford and
Merton* may be interested to find the original text of the story
of 'Androclus and the Lion,' here quoted from the Alexandrian
'grammarian' Apion[15]. In a history of *Classical* Scholarship it
may be worth noticing that, while Cicero[16] describes Cleanthes
and Chrysippus as *quintae classis* in comparison with Democritus,
Gellius contrasts a 'scriptor *classicus*' with a 'scriptor *proletarius*'[17],
obviously deriving his metaphor from the division of the Roman
people into *classes* by Servius Tullius, those in the first class being
called *classici*[18], all the rest *infra classem*, and those in the last
*proletarii*. As *infra classem* and *classici testes* are explained by
Paulus[19] in his abridgement of Festus (the epitomiser of Verrius

---

[1] xiii 2.     [2] xvii 10.     [3] xii 2.     [4] i 16.     [5] iii 18.     [6] vi 17.
[7] xvi 10.     [8] xx 10.     [9] xvii 1.     [10] ii 3; x 4.     [11] ii 17.
[12] x 1; xx 6.     [13] xiii 28.     [14] xiv 6, 3.     [15] v 14, 10—30.     [16] *Acad.* ii 73.
[17] xix 8, 15, classicus adsiduusque (=locuples) scriptor, non proletarius.
[18] vi (vii) 13, 1 where Cato is quoted.     [19] pp. 113 and 56 (Nettleship, i 269).

Flaccus), it is probable that Verrius is also the authority followed by Gellius. In any case it is from this rare use of *classicus* that the modern term 'classical' is derived.

To the close of the 2nd century may be assigned Terentianus Maurus, the writer of a manual in verse on 'letters, syllables and metres', the metrical portion of which is founded on a work by Caesius Bassus, the friend of Persius[1]; also Acro, the commentator on Terence and Horace; and Festus, the author of the abridgement of Verrius Flaccus just mentioned. Porphyrio, whose *scholia* on Horace are still extant, probably belongs to a later date than Acro, whom he quotes on *Sat.* i 8, 25, and whose name is wrongly given to a number of miscellaneous *scholia* on Horace founded partly on Acro and Porphyrio with some additions from the *Roma* of Suetonius[2]. Statilius Maximus is known to have revised a MS of the Second Agrarian speech of Cicero with the aid of the text edited by Cicero's freedman, Tiro[3], whose *libri Tironiani* are mentioned by Gellius[4] in connexion with the Verrine orations. Statilius, who is also known to have commented on peculiarities in the diction of Cato, Sallust and Cicero, falls between the time of Gellius, who never quotes him, and that of Julius Romanus, who quotes him repeatedly.

The Scholars of the 3rd century include the learned grammarian, C. Julius Romanus, extensively quoted by Charisius[5]; and the writer of several grammatical works, Censorinus[6], whose extant but incomplete treatise *De die natali* (238 A.D.), mainly compiled from a lost work of Suetonius, contains much valuable information on points of history and chronology. In the second half of this century we may place Aquila Romanus, the author of a work on figures of speech, adapted from Alexander Numenius[7]; and Marius Plotius Sacerdos, the author of an *Ars Grammatica* in three books, the second of which is mainly identical with the *Catholica* ascribed to Probus[8].

*Terentianus.*
*Acro. Festus.*
*Porphyrio*

*Censorinus*

---

[1] Teuffel, § 373ᵃ; Schanz, § 514.  [2] Teuffel, § 374; Schanz, § 601–2.

[3] Statilius Maximus rursus emendavi ad Tyronem etc. (A. Mai, *Cic. cod. Ambros.* p. 231, ap. Jahn, *Sächs. Berichte*, 1851, 329).

[4] i 7, 1; xiii 21, 16.  [5] Teuffel, § 379, 1; Schanz, § 603.

[6] *ib.* 6—8; Schanz, § 632.  [7] *ib.* § 388; Halm, *Rhet. Lat. Min.* 22 f.

[8] p. 205 *supra*. Teuffel, § 394; Schanz, § 604 f; Jeep, *Redetheile*, pp. 73—82.

A characteristic product of this age is the epitome of Pliny bearing the name of Solinus, which afterwards became popular in a new form and under the pretentious title of *Polyhistor*. Just before the last quarter of this century the emperor Tacitus (275–6) provided for the preservation of the works of his 'ancestor' the historian by causing a copy to be placed in each of the public libraries and by arranging for the transcription of further copies in the future[1].

As we glance over the three centuries from the age of Augustus to that of Diocletian, which have been rapidly traversed in this chapter, we are bound to recognise that, in the first century A.D., grammatical studies are more systematic, but at the same time more narrow, than in the last century of the republic. The preparation of practical manuals for educational purposes has superseded the scientific and learned labours of a Varro, and has ultimately led to the actual loss of the greater part of his encyclopaedic works; but we may well be thankful to the grammarians of the first century for all the lore that they have preserved[2], and we cannot forget that in that century learned comment on Cicero, who is already a Classic, is represented by the sober sense of an Asconius, and literary criticism by the sound judgement and good taste of Cicero's admirer, Quintilian.

The second century, in which Suetonius with all his varied learning must be regarded as little more than a minor counterpart of Varro, was in matters of Scholarship an age of epitomes and compilations. Learning became fashionable, but erudition often lapsed into triviality, and the ancient classics were ransacked for phrases which ill assorted with the style of the time. In the domain of Scholarship the most interesting personalities in this century are those of Cornelius Fronto and Aulus Gellius. It is characteristic of this age that, when Gellius calls to inquire after Fronto, who has been kept at home by the gout, the question as to the 'approximate' cost of the construction of a new bath for the relief of the learned patient leads to a scholarly discussion, in the course of which it is shown that the supposed vulgarism *praeterpropter* ('thereabout', 'more or less') was actually used by Varro and Cato and was really as old as Ennius[3].

[1] Vopiscus, *Tac.* 10.        [2] Nettleship, ii 171.        [3] Gellius, xix 10.

In the third century the only scholar worthy of consideration
has been Censorinus, yet even he owes his learning mainly to
Suetonius, the inheritor of the traditions of Varro. But while
Varro, who did not condescend to sacrifice to the Graces, has
been punished for his lack of style and for his prolixity by the
loss of by far the larger part of all his learned works, and while
Suetonius, with his wide range of scholarly research, scarcely
survives except in his biographies, the diminutive work of
Censorinus, a mere birthday gift with its borrowed erudition,
and its second-hand citations, has succeeded in descending to
posterity, thanks in part to its brevity and perhaps to its saving
grace of style. The great argosies have foundered, but the tiny
skiff has suffered little damage in drifting down the stream of
time.

*(aequalita)te pensamus. ceteri omnes longe sequentur. nam Macer et Lucre-*
*tius legendi quidem, sed non ut phrasin, id est corpus eloquentiae faciant;*
*elegantes in sua quisque materia sed alter humilis alter difficilis. Atacinus*
*Varro in his, per quae nomen est adsecutus, interpres operis alieni, non sper-*
*nendus quidem, verum ad augendam facultatem dicendi parum locuples.*

# Conspectus of Latin Literature &c., 300—600 A.D.

| Roman Emperors | Poets | Historians & Biographers | Orators and Rhetoricians | Scholars and Critics | Other Writers of Prose |
|---|---|---|---|---|---|
| 305 Constantius I<br>306 Constantine I | | Vopiscus<br>Lampridius | | 323 Nonius | |
| | 330 Juvencus | | | | |
| 337<br>–40 {Constantine II<br>–61 {Constantius II<br>–50 {Constans I | | | | | |
| 361 Julian<br>363 Jovian<br>364–75 Valentinian I<br>367–83 Gratian<br>375 Valentinian II | 350 Avienus | 360 Aurelius Victor<br>363 Eutropius | 362 Claudius Mamertinus | 353 Marius Victorinus<br>353 Aelius Donatus<br><br>Charisius<br>Diomedes | 350 Hilary of Poitiers d. 367 |
| 392 Theodosius I<br>395 Honorius | 379 Ausonius<br>c. 310—c. 393<br><br>395—404 Claudian | 390 Ammianus<br>c. 330—400 | 389 Pacatus<br>391 Symmachus<br>c. 345—405 | Servius<br>Ti. Claudius Donatus<br>Macrobius | 373 Ambrose<br>c. 340—397<br>386 Jerome<br>331—420<br>395 Augustine<br>354—430 |
| **400** | | | | | |
| 423 John<br>425 Valentinian III | 404 Prudentius 348—c. 410<br>409 Paulinus 353—431<br>416 Namatianus<br>Cl. Marius Victor, d. 425–450<br>435 Merobaudes<br>c. 440 Sedulius | Vegetius<br>Sulp. Severus c. 365—425<br>417 Orosius b. c. 390<br><br>439—451 Salvian | Chirius Fortunatianus<br>C. Julius Victor | 401 Torq. Gennadius revises text of Martial<br><br>Nicomachus Flavianus and his son Nicomachus Dexter revise text of Livy | 415 Cassianus c. 360—435<br>Martianus Capella<br>429 Hilary of Arles d. c. 450<br>434 Vincentius Lerinus<br>440 Leo I 395—461 |
| 455 Petronius Maximus<br>455 Avitus<br>457 Majorian<br>461 Libius Severus<br>467 Anthemius<br>472 Olybrius<br>473 Glycerius<br>474 Julius Nepos<br>475–6 Romulus Augustulus | 470 Apollinaris Sidonius c. 430—480<br>484–96 Dracontius | 455 Prosper c. 400—463 | | Consentius<br>Phocas | 470 Claudianus Mamertus |
| *Gothic Kings*<br>476 Odoacer<br>493 Theodoric | 490 Avitus 460—c. 525 | Gennadius | | 494 Asterius revises text of Virgil | |
| **500** | | | | | |
| | Cyprianus c. 475—550 | 511 Eugippius *vita Severini* | 507 Ennodius 473—521<br>514 Cassiodorus c. 480—c. 575 | Fulgentius c. 480—550<br>512 Priscian | 510 Boëthius c. 480—524 |
| 526 Athalaric<br>534 Theodahad<br>536–9 Vitiges<br>541–52 Totila | | | | 527 Vettius Agorius Mavortius revises text of Horace | 529 Benedict 480—543<br>529 *Monte Cassino founded* |
| 527 Justinian I | Maximianus<br>Arator<br>550 Corippus | | | | |
| 565 Justin II | | 551 Iordanis<br>Gildas 516—573 | | | |
| 578 Tiberius II<br>582 Mauricius | Fortunatus c. 535—600 | 573 Gregory of Tours 538—593 | | | 580 d. Martin of Bracara<br>590 Gregory I c. 540—604 |
| | | Isidore of Seville c. 570—636 | | | |
| **600** | | | | | |

*Continued from page* 198.

# CHAPTER XIII.

## LATIN SCHOLARSHIP FROM 300 TO 500 A.D.

EARLY in the third century (212 A.D.) Caracalla had extended the title and the obligations of Roman citizenship to all the free inhabitants of the empire; and throughout that century (though in no connexion with this important constitutional change) the most memorable contributions to Latin literature had come, not from Rome, but from the provinces; not from pagans, but from Christians. The first half of the century had included the closing years of Tertullian (*c.* 150—230) and nearly the whole of the life of Cyprian (*c.* 200—258), both of them closely connected with Carthage; while, towards the end of the century, Numidia had been represented in Latin literature by Arnobius, and Bithynia by Lactantius, who had been summoned from Africa by Diocletian to teach Latin rhetoric in his new capital of Nicomedia. Under the rule of Diocletian (285—305) Rome ceased to be the residence of the emperor and its importance was for a time still further diminished by the transfer of the imperial capital to Constantinople (330). But it continued to be a centre of world-wide interest during the struggle between the adherents of a gradually receding paganism and a slowly but surely advancing Christianity. In 362, by a decree of Julian the Apostate, which is denounced even by a pagan historian as deserving perpetual oblivion[1], Christians were forbidden to teach grammar and rhetoric, on the ground of their disbelief in the gods of Homer, Thucydides and Demosthenes. The decree

*The third century*

*The fourth century*

---

[1] Amm. Marc. xxii 10, 7, obruendum perenni silentio.

resulted in the resignation of an eminent teacher, Victorinus, and in the short-lived production of purely Christian text-books. Twenty years later, in the conflict that raged round the question as to the emperor Gratian's removal of the Altar of Victory from its immemorial position in the Senate House, the old order was represented by Symmachus and Praetextatus, and the new by St Ambrose and Pope Damasus, and, shortly afterwards, by Prudentius. Towards the end of the fourth century (392) the ruin of the ancient religion of Rome was completed by the decree of Theodosius, by which death was the penalty for offering sacrifice. About the same year, a Greek of Antioch, Ammianus Marcellinus, was completing in Rome itself, and in a strange variety of Latin, blended with many reminiscences of the 'sayings of Cicero', his continuation of Tacitus, the extant portion of which is invaluable as an authority for the years 353 to 378, besides including interesting glimpses of contemporary life in Rome, as where he writes of certain leisurely Romans who 'hated learning like poison'[1], and whose 'libraries were closed for ever like the tomb'[2]. A little later (395—405) in the first decade of the division of the empire of Theodosius between his two sons, Arcadius in the East and Honorius in the West, Claudian of Alexandria, the last representative of paganism[3] among the greater Latin poets, was living in Italy, at Rome and Milan. The latest date to which any of his poems can be assigned is 404 or 405. The former of these years saw the publication of the first collected edition of the poems of one who had been born in Spain and had only recently arrived in Rome, the great Christian poet, Prudentius; and the latter was the date of the completion at Bethlehem of St Jerome's Latin version of the Bible, which he had begun in Rome more than twenty years before.

Meanwhile the study of Grammar in the fourth century begins in northern Africa with the name of the Numidian tiro, Nonius Marcellus, and culminates at Rome about the middle of the century with the far greater name of Donatus, the commentator on Terence and the preceptor of St Jerome. It was continued at

---

[1] xxviii 4, 14, detestantes ut venena doctrinas.

[2] xiv 6, 18, bybliothecis sepulcrorum ritu in perpetuum clausis.

[3] Claudian was possibly a *nominal* Christian (Pauly-Wissowa, iii 2656).

an uncertain date by less original grammarians, such as Charisius and Diomedes, who have the modest merit of preserving for posterity the grammatical teaching of an earlier age.   The general state of learning in this century is best illustrated by the names of Ausonius (himself a teacher of grammar and rhetoric) and his distinguished friend, Q. Aurelius Symmachus; also by those unwearied expositors of Virgil, Servius and Macrobius; and, lastly, by St Jerome and St Augustine, whose lives extended to the twentieth and thirtieth years respectively of the following century.

In the fifth century the controversy as to the religious causes that led to the capture of Rome by the Goths under Alaric in 410 inspired the greatest of the works of St Augustine, the *De Civitate Dei*; and St Augustine in his turn prompted a young Spanish priest, Orosius, who reached Hippo about 414, to supplement that work by writing a history of the world, which barely mentions Pericles and refers to Demosthenes only as the recipient of Persian bribes, and is founded mainly on the Bible, Livy, Tacitus, Suetonius, Justin, Eutropius, and possibly St Jerome's rendering of the Chronicle of Eusebius.   Before the end of the fourth century, owing to an impulse first given by St Athanasius at Trier in 336, monasteries had been established in Gaul in 360 and 372 by St Martin of Tours (d. 400); before 410 the monastery of Lérins (off Cannes) was founded by St Honoratus: and, about 415, monastic discipline was introduced into Gaul from the East by Cassian, the founder of the monastery of St Victor at Marseilles. In his *Monastic Institutes* he recognises manual labour as a remedy for *ennui*, quoting with approval the saying sanctioned by the 'ancient fathers' in Egypt, that 'a monk who works is troubled by one devil only, but a monk who is idle by many'[1]; but he mentions the copying of MSS only once, and that in the case of an Italian monk, who confessed he could do nothing else[2].   In a sequel[3] to this treatise he reports his conversations with the

The fifth century

---

[1] *De institutis coenobiorum et de octo principalium vitiorum remediis*, Lib. x (on *acedia* or *taedium sive anxietas cordis*) 23, operantem monachum daemone uno pulsari, otiosum vero innumeris spiritibus devastari.

[2] *ib.* v 39 (Ebert, i² 351).   [3] *Collationes Patrum* (Ebert, 352-4).

hermits of the Thebaid, dwelling on the ideal of the monastic life and, though himself far from friendly towards classical literature[1], nevertheless supplying that incentive towards intellectual studies which led to the monasteries of the West becoming the homes of learning and literature and even of classical scholarship in the Middle Ages. The Vandals had not yet invaded Africa in 429, when a work whose influence lasted throughout the Middle Ages had been there composed by Martianus Capella. Between the capture of Carthage by the Vandals in 439 and the inroad of Attila and his Huns into Gaul in 451, Salvian, the presbyter of Marseilles, who attained a hale old age in 480, was prompted by the calamities of his country to compose the memorable treatise *De Gubernatione Dei* with its gloomy presage of the approaching end of the constitution, the civilisation and the learning of Rome[2]. The quarter of a century that elapsed between the defeat of Attila by Aëtius on the Catalaunian plains in 451, and the extinction of the Western Empire by Odoacer, the son of one of Attila's officers, in 476, corresponds in Latin literature to the active life of the Gallic poet and letter-writer, the accomplished bishop of Auvergne, Apollinaris Sidonius, who saw his diocese annexed by the Visigoths in 475, and died less than nine years later.

In the history of Scholarship the fourth century opens with
Nonius        the name of Nonius Marcellus of Thubursicum in
              Numidia (*fl.* 323 A.D.), the author of an encyclo-
paedic work compiled for the benefit of his son, and entitled *De Compendiosa Doctrina*. It is divided into three parts, lexico-graphical, grammatical and antiquarian. In the grammatical portion the compiler is largely indebted to Probus, Caper and Pliny; and, in the lexicographical, to the scholars and antiquarians from the reigns of Nero and Vespasian to those of Trajan and Hadrian, and especially to Verrius Flaccus[3]. Nonius frequently copies Gellius, but never mentions his name. The value of his

---

[1] *Collationes Patrum*, xiv 12, 13 (Roger, *L'Enseignement des Lettres Classiques d'Ausone à Alcuin*, 146).

[2] ed. Halm, 1877.

[3] Nettleship, i 228—232, 277—321; Teuffel, § 404[a]; Schanz, § 826.

work lies mainly in its numerous quotations from early Latin
literature[1]. All who have studied it speak of the compiler with
the utmost contempt. He is so ignorant, or (more probably) so
careless, as to imply that *M. Tullius* was not the same person
as *Cicero*[2].

During this century Latin Scholarship flourished far less
vigorously in Africa than in Gaul, where it is well
represented by Ausonius and his circle, who had
a direct and intimate knowledge of the Latin Classics. The life
of Ausonius (*c.* 310—*c.* 393)[3] extends from near the beginning
to near the end of the century; so that in Latin literature the
fourth century may be described as the century of Ausonius.
Born at Bordeaux, he there went through the early stages of
a 'grammatical' education which included Greek, though he
admits that in that language he had been a dull pupil[4]. His
education was continued under his uncle at Toulouse (*c.*320–328);
about 334 he became professor, first of 'grammar', and afterwards
of rhetoric, in his native town; and, thirty years later, he was
summoned to Trier to teach 'grammar' and rhetoric to the
youthful Gratian. After his pupil had ascended the throne (late
in 375), Ausonius was appointed to several high offices, becoming
*praefectus Galliarum* in 378 and consul in the following year. On
the death of Gratian (383) he returned to Bordeaux, where he
was actively engaged in a variety of literary work. It is to this
period that nearly all his extant writings belong. Most of his
poems are marked less by poetic power than by skill in versification. He is well described by M. Boissier[5] as 'an incorrigible
versifier', and his verses are usually of a trivial type. But they
present us with a graphic and varied picture of the personalities
and the general circumstances of his time, with eulogistic accounts

Ausonius

---

[1] See esp. W. M. Lindsay, *Nonius Marcellus*, 1901, and ed. 1903.

[2] P. Schmidt (1868), p. 92, ap. Teuffel, § 404[a], 4.

[3] Teuffel, § 421; Schanz, § 786; chronology in Peiper's ed. pp. 90—114.

[4] *Commem. Prof. Burdigalensium*, viii 13—16:—

> 'Obstitit nostrae quia, credo, mentis
> Tardior sensus neque disciplinis
> Adpulit Graecis puerilis aevi
> Noxius error'.

[5] *La Fin du Paganisme* (1891), i 205 = 175[3].

of his own relations, and his former instructors or colleagues at
Bordeaux, whether professors of Rhetoric, wholly concerned with
Prose, or 'grammarians', *i.e.* professors of Literature, mainly
concerned with Verse. One of these, 'a second Quintilian', is
famous for his marvellous memory, and rivals Demosthenes in
delivery[1]; a second, we are assured, will (apparently by his
literary works) add to the fame of the emperor Julian, and to
that of Sallustius, his colleague as consul in 363 A.D.; a third
is compared to Aristarchus and Zenodotus; a fourth knows
Scaurus and Probus by heart; a fifth is familiar not only with
these grammarians, but also with Livy and Herodotus, and the
whole of Varro[2]. In the verses addressed by Ausonius to
his young grandson, who is just going to school, his motto is
*disce libens*; by a quotation from Virgil, *degeneres animos timor
arguit*, he encourages his grandson not to be afraid of his master;
he exhorts him to read, in the first place, Homer and Menander,
also Horace and Virgil, Terence and Sallust[3]. Writing to his
younger contemporary, the celebrated Symmachus, he flatteringly describes him as combining the merits of Isocrates, Cicero
and Virgil[4]; he similarly assures Tetradius that his satires
will rival those of Lucilius[5]; he invites the rhetorician Axius
Paulus to come with haste 'by oar or wheel', bringing with him
his own poems of every kind, to some quiet country-place on
the estuary of the Garonne, to which Ausonius proposes to escape
after he has visited the crowded streets of Bordeaux on Easter
Sunday. On New Year's day he sends the same friend a
macaronic epistle in a strange mixture of Greek and Latin[6];
and, in a third letter beginning in Latin and ending in Greek,
tells him this time to leave all his own poems at home, as
he will find at his host's every variety of verse, not to mention
Herodotus and Thucydides and other works in prose[7]. This
last letter closes with the happy ending :—'vale; valere si voles
me, iam veni'. But the only poem of Ausonius that rises to
a distinctly high level is his *Mosella* with its fascinating description of the crystal waters and the vineclad banks of the river
between Berncastel and Trier, where the poem was written

---

[1] *Commem.* 1.     [2] *ib.* 2, 13, 15, 20.     [3] *Idyl.* iv 46—63.
[4] *Ep.* ii.     [5] *Ep.* xi.     [6] *Ep.* viii.     [7] *Ep.* ix.

about the end of 370 A.D.  The poet's correspondent, Symmachus,
while he makes merry over the minute description of the fishes
of the stream (a description which has proved sufficiently precise
to enable a Cuvier to identify the fifteen species enumerated by
the poet), goes so far as to rank the poem with those of Virgil[1].
As a specimen we may here quote (and render) four lines alone,
marking in italics the phrase especially admired by Edward Fitz-
Gerald[2], who owed to Professor Cowell his first knowledge, not of
Omar Khâyyam only, but also of Ausonius :—

> ' Quis color ille vadis, seras cum propulit umbras
> Hesperus, et viridi perfundit monte Mosellam!
> Tota natant crispis iuga motibus, et *tremit absens*
> *Pampinus*, et vitreis vindemia turget in undis '.  (192–5.)

What a glow was on the shallows, when the shades of Evening fell,
And the verdure of the mountain bathed the breast of fair Moselle!
In the glassy stream reflected, float the hills in wavy line,
Swells the vintage, sways the trembling tendril of the absent vine.

Apart from its purely original passages, which are inspired with a
love of Nature striking a new note in Latin literature, the poem
abounds in happy reminiscences not of Virgil only but also of
Horace, Lucan and Statius[3]; and (as we know from the *Cento*) it
is far from being the only proof of its author's intimate knowledge
of the text of Virgil.  As a teacher of ' grammar', he had neces
sarily been long familiar with Latin literature.  Among his great
precursors as ' grammarians ' he mentions men like Aemilius
Asper, Terentius Scaurus, and Probus[4].  He even compares a
now unknown ' grammarian' of Trier with Varro and Crates and
the grammarians of Alexandria[5], among whom he elsewhere names
Zenodotus and Aristarchus and the symbols which they used in
the criticism of Homer[6].  He states that his father, who was
eminent as a physician, knew Greek better than Latin[7].  His
own epigrams include several in Greek, and also (as already
noticed) in Greek and Latin combined, with Latin renderings

---

[1] *Ep.* i 14, ego hoc tuum carmen libris Maronis adiungo.

[2] *Letters* (1846), i 205 (ed. 1894).  The original is obviously imitated in
Pope's *Windsor Forest*, 211-6.

[3] See ref. in Peiper's ed. pp. 457—466.          [4] *Praef.* i 20.

[5] *Ep.* xiii 27—30.                    [6] *Ludus Sept. Sap.* i 12.

[7] *Id.* ii 9.

from the Greek Anthology. As a specimen of these last the
following epigram on the Greek games may be quoted:

> 'Quattuor antiquos celebravit Achaïa ludos;
>    Caelicolum duo sunt et duo festa hominum.
>  Sacra Iovis Phoebique, Palaemonis Archemorique
>    Serta quibus pinus, malus, oliva, apium'[1].

He is the one Latin poet who has exactly imitated the 'greater
Sapphic' metre, which is only approximately copied by Horace[2].
Many of his verses, especially those comprised in his *Technopaegnion*, are mere efforts of technical skill. Among these we
have a long series of lines ending with a monosyllable, including
a useful couplet distinguishing *vas* and *praes* :—

> 'Quis subit in poenam capitali iudicio? *vas.*
>  Quid si lis fuerit nummaria, quis dabitur? *praes*'.

Of his lines on the letters of the alphabet the following are perhaps
the most interesting :—

> 'Cecropiis ignota notis, ferale sonans V.
>  Pythagorae bivium ramis pateo ambiguis Y'.

It is difficult to imagine that a man capable of writing such
trifles as these (not to mention his lines on the Caesars and on
celebrated cities) had some ten years previously (in 378 A.D.)
filled the splendid position of praetorian praefect of the provinces
of Gaul (an official whose sway extended even over Spain and the
opposite coast of Africa, and over the southern part of Britain),
and, in the four years between 376 and 380, had seen his father
honorary praefect of Illyricum, his son and son-in-law proconsuls of
Africa, and his nephew praefect of Rome[3]. It seems as if, on his
return to the scenes of his early work as a professor at Bordeaux,
the praefect relapsed into the 'grammarian', spending his time on
learned trifles, which are among the least important products of
scholarship, and consoling himself in his tedious task by recalling
Virgil's famous phrase :—'in tenui labor, at tenuis non gloria'[4].

---

[1] *Anth. Gr.* ix 357.

[2] Sappho, *frag.* 60; Horace, *Carm.* i 8; and Auson. *Id.* vii, p. 116 Peiper,
Bissula, nomen tenerae rusticulum puellae.

[3] Seeck's Introd. to *Symmachus* (in *Mon. Germ. Hist.*), p. lxxix f.

[4] *Georg.* iv 6, loosely quoted in *Praef.* to *Technopaegnion.*

We may regret that Ausonius does not appear to havé used his great opportunities for reforming the educational system which prevailed in the schools of the Western Empire, and thus rendering a lasting service to the cause of learning[1]; but we may allow him the credit of having possibly inspired the memorable decree promulgated by Gratian in 376, which improved the status of public instructors by providing for the appointment of teachers of rhetoric and of Greek and Latin 'grammar' in the principal cities of Gaul, and fixing the amount of their stipends[2].

Whatever doubts may be felt as to the religion of Ausonius, who was apparently a heathen at heart, though a Christian by profession, there are none as to that of either of his younger contemporaries and correspondents, Paulinus[3] and Symmachus[4]. Paulinus (353—431), a man of noble birth, a favourite pupil of Ausonius, gave early proof of his metrical skill in a poetic version of a work of Suetonius, *De Regibus*, and a fragment of that version is still extant[5].    He was consul and governor of a province before the age of thirty.   His conversion to Christianity (*c.* 390) prompts his former instructor to pray the 'Muses of Boeotia' to restore his friend to the poetry of Rome[6]; but Paulinus firmly replies that hearts consecrated to Christ are closed to Apollo and the Muses[7].   He became

Paulinus

[1] Mullinger's *Schools of Charles the Great*, pp. 13—16.

[2] Cod. Theodos. xiii 3, 11, ...frequentissimis in civitatibus...praeceptorum optimi quique erudiendae praesideant iuventuti, rhetores loquimur et grammaticos Atticae Romanaeque doctrinae (printed in full in Peiper's Ausonius, p. c). On Ausonius cp. also Schenkl's ed. (in *Mon. Germ. Hist.*); also Boissier's *Fin du Paganisme*, i 175[3] f, ii 66—78[3]; Roger, *L'Enseignement des Lettres Classiques d'Ausone à Alcuin* (1905), 2—18 etc.; Dill's *Roman Society in the Last Century of the Western Empire*, pp. 159, 402, with pp. 167—188, 'The Society of Ausonius': and T. R. Glover's *Life and Letters in the Fourth Century*, pp. 102—124.   The best of the earlier accounts is in the *Histoire Littéraire de la France*, i 2 (1733), pp. 281—318.   Trans. Evelyn-White, 1919 f.

[3] ed. Hartel, Vienna, 1894-5; Peiper's Ausonius, pp. 266—309; Ebert, *Lit. d. Mittelalters*, i[2] 293—311; Teuffel, § 437, Schanz, § 876, and Boissier, ii 49—103[3]; also Dill, p. 396 f.

[4] ed. Seeck in *Mon. Germ. Hist.*; Teuffel, § 425; Schanz, § 816; Boissier, ii 267[3] f; Dill, pp. 143—166; T. R. Glover, pp. 148—170.

[5] Ausonius, *Ep.* xix (p. 267 Peiper).

[6] *Ep.* xxv (p. 289) Latiis vatem revocate Camenis.

[7] *Carm.* x 22, negant Camenis, nec patent Apollini | dicata Christo pectora.

bishop of Nola in 409, but even his Christian poems retain the traces of his early training in their reminiscences of Horace and Virgil. He is especially fond of the Sapphic stanza and the metres of the Epodes, and the second Epode in particular is obviously imitated in his paraphrase of the first Psalm:—

> 'Beatus ille qui procul vitam suam
> Ab impiorum segregarit coetibus'.

His attitude towards pagan literature is clearly shown in a letter to his friend Jovius, whom he rebukes for attributing the unexpected recovery of a large sum of money to the favour of Fortune instead of the over-ruling of Divine Providence. He regretfully observes that his friend had found time for the study of Xenophon, Plato and Demosthenes, and for the pursuit of philosophy, but had no leisure for being a Christian. He compares the charms of literature to the fruit of the lotus and the songs of the Sirens, which made men forget their true home. He would not, however, have his friend lay aside his philosophy, but season it with faith and religion. Like St Augustine and St Jerome, he would have him regard the powers of language, that he had gained from the study of pagan literature, as spoils won from the enemy to be used to lend fresh force to the cause of truth. In the course of the letter Paulinus himself quotes Virgil, and the pleadings of his prose for the recognition of Divine Providence are reinforced in a set of 166 lines of verse[1].

Q. Aurelius Symmachus[2] (c. 345—405), praefect of Rome in 384–5, and consul in 391, was a devoted adherent of the old order. It was in this spirit that, in 384, he addressed to Valentinian II in his third *Relatio*[3] a dignified appeal for the restoration of the Altar of Victory to its place in the Senate House, impressively pleading for religious toleration on the ground that 'the great mystery might well be approached in more ways than one'. His general character resembles that of Cicero, while

Symmachus

---

[1] *Ep.* 16 and *Carm.* 22. Cp. *Ep.* 5; also Boissier, *Fin du Paganisme*, ii 83–5[3]; J. E. B. Mayor, *Latin Heptateuch*, p. liv note.

[2] Teuffel, § 425; Schanz, § 816; also Norden in *Kultur der Gegenwart*, I viii 378 f.

[3] Bury's Gibbon, iii 192 (c. 28); cp. Boissier's *Fin du Paganisme*, ii 274[3], and abstract in T. R. Glover, p. 154 f.

his letters are modelled on those of the younger Pliny, whose
*genus dicendi pingue et floridum* was regarded by Macrobius[1] as
surviving in the 'luxuriance' of his own earlier contemporary,
Symmachus. 'But the *luxuriancy* of Symmachus' (says Gibbon)
'consists of barren leaves, without fruits, and even flowers; few
facts, and few sentiments, can be extracted from his verbose
correspondence'. As he is apparently restrained by the fear of
dulness from relating incidents of the day, which would have
been interesting to posterity, his letters are in fact rather colourless
compositions[2]; but in the times of the Renaissance they were
much admired by Politian and Pomponius Laetus. Eminent as
a scholar, a statesman, and an orator, he aims in general at a
correctly classical style, though he sometimes lapses into such
words as *genialitas* and *optimitas*, and into such constructions as
*fungi officium* and *honoris tui delector*. But almost every page of
his letters betrays his familiarity with the great writers of the past.
He describes himself as 'always loving literature'[3]. He gives
a Latin rendering of a sentence in Demosthenes[4]. He quotes
repeatedly from Cicero, Terence and Virgil, once from Plautus
and Horace, and twice from Valerius Maximus[5]. His father
mentions Varro as 'the parent of Roman erudition'[6], and
assumes that the son is familiar with Varro's epigrams. After
369 A.D., Symmachus sends Ausonius a copy of part at least
of Pliny's 'Natural History'[7]; in 396, he proposes to find for

---

[1] *Saturnalia*, v 1, 7.

[2] In writing to his brother (iii 25) he says (apparently of a postscript,
which has not been preserved):—'subieci capita rerum, quia (quae?) complecti
litteris *fastidii fuga* nolui'. Elsewhere he relegates the news of the day to an
*index* or *indiculus* or *breviarium*, which is unhappily lost.

[3] iv 44.

[4] *Ol.* 3 § 39, parvis nutrimentis quamquam a morte defendimur, nihil tamen
ad robustam valetudinem promovemus (*v. l.* promovemur), *Ep.* i 23 p. 14
Seeck.

[5] Seeck's *Index*. Cp. Kroll, *De Symmachi studiis Graecis et Latinis* (1891).

[6] *Ep.* i 2.

[7] *Ep.* i 23, Si te amor habet naturalis historiae, quam Plinius elaboravit,
en tibi libellos, quorum mihi praesentanea copia fuit. In quis, ut arbitror,
opulentae eruditioni tuae neglegens veritatis librarius displicebit. Sed mihi
fraudi non erit emendationis incuria. Malui enim tibi probari mei muneris
celeritate, quam alieni operis examine. Vale.

his distinguished friend Protadius a copy of Pliny's 'German Wars', and offers him Caesar's 'Gallic War', if he is not satisfied with the account of Caesar in the last book of Livy[1]. It is clear that, in the time of Symmachus, the whole of Livy was still extant. In 401 he presents his friend Valerianus with a complete transcript[2]; and the interest in Livy, which was inspired by Symmachus and his family, is still attested by the subscriptions to all the books of the first decade[3]. Three of them bear the further subscription of one of the Nicomachi, and three that of the other[4], both of these revisers of the text being connexions of Symmachus by marriage. About the same time, and inspired perhaps by his example, other aristocratic Romans interested themselves in the revision of Latin MSS. In 401 Torquatus Gennadius revised the text of Martial[5]; in 402 Fl. Julius Tryfonianus Sabinus, that of Persius[6] at Barcelona, and even that of Nonius Marcellus at Toulouse[7]. Symmachus also lives in literature as one of the principal interlocutors in the *Saturnalia* of Macrobius, and their friendship descended to the third generation, for we find the great-grandson of Symmachus revising at Ravenna a copy of the commentary of Macrobius on the 'Dream of Scipio', in the company of another Macrobius, doubtless a descendant of the author[8].

---

[1] *Ep.* iv 18 p. 104.

[2] *Ep.* ix 13, munus totius Liviani operis, quod spopondi, etiam nunc diligentia emendationis moratur.

[3] Victorianus v. c. emendabam domnis Symmachis.

[4] Nicomachus Dexter v. c. emendavi ad exemplum parentis mei Clementiani (end of Books iii, iv, v): Nicomachus Flavianus v. c. iii praefect. urbis emendavi apud Hennam (end of Books vi, vii, viii). Teuffel, § 256, 11; § 428, 2; Schanz, § 806. See *facsimile* from the Medicean MS on p. 250.

[5] Teuffel, § 322, 8 and Friedländer's ed. i 69.

[6] Teuffel, § 302, 5.

[7] Teuffel, § 404[a], 5; cp. Gräfenhan, iv 383 f.

[8] Teuffel, § 444, 8. On *subscriptiones* in general, see Jahn in *Sächs. Berichte*, 1851, pp. 327—372, and the Breslau programs of Haase (1860) and Reifferscheid (1872); also Spengel in *Philologus*, xvii 555, Mommsen and Studemund's *Analecta Liviana* (1873), and B. A. Müller, *Codicum Latinorum Subscriptiones* (announced 1906). Cp. Marx, *ad Herennium*, p. 1 f. A MS of Apuleius was revised by one Crispus Salustius in 395 at Rome, and again in 397 at Constantinople (Jahn, p. 331).

To the age of Symmachus are assigned the rhetorical treatises
of (1) Chirius Fortunatianus, the author of a        Rhetoricians
catechism of rhetoric founded on Quintilian, with
illustrations from Cicero[1]; (2) Sulpicius Victor, a practical jurist
rather than a scholastic rhetorician; (3) Julius Victor, who closely
follows Quintilian; and (4) Julius Rufinianus, the author of a
supplement to Aquila Romanus, in which figures of speech are
exemplified from Ennius and Lucilius, as well as from Cicero and
Virgil[2].

But Virgil was not exploited by rhetoricians alone.    After the
first quarter of the fourth century Virgil (to a far
greater degree than Lucretius, Ovid, Lucan and        Study of
Horace) was imitated by the sacred poet Juvencus        Virgil
(c. 330), who was highly popular in the time of Petrarch as well
as in that of Charles the Great[3].    He was tortured into a sacred
cento by Proba, the 'incomparable wife' of a praefect of Rome,
about the middle of the century[4], and into a profane cento by
Ausonius towards its close.    He was the theme of commentaries
(as we shall shortly see) by Servius and Macrobius.    He was the
favourite poet of the schoolmaster; and fathers of the Church,
like St Jerome and St Augustine, confess how deeply they had
been interested in him in their youthful days[5].    A pleasant picture
of the interest in Virgil, which was felt in Gaul late in this century,
is presented to us in a letter written by Rusticus (possibly the
bishop of Narbonne from c. 430 to 461) to Eucherius, bishop of
Lyons from 435 to 450 A.D.    The writer recalls what he had read
as a boy (probably about 400 A.D.) in the library of a student of
secular literature.    The library, he tells us, was adorned with
'portraits of orators and poets, worked in mosaic, or in wax of
different colours, or in plaster; and under each the master of the
house had placed inscriptions noting their characteristics; but,
when he came to an author of acknowledged merit' (as for in-

---

[1] Saintsbury, i 346.

[2] Teuffel, § 427; Schanz, §§ 838—842; texts of all these in Halm, *Rhet.
Lat. Min.*

[3] Ebert, i[2] 117.

[4] *Corp. Inscr. Lat.* vi 1712.    Ebert, i[2] 125.

[5] Comparetti, *Virgilio nel Medio Evo*, i cap. 1—5; Schanz, § 247 (*Vergils
Fortleben im Altertum*).

stance, Virgil) 'he began as follows' (adding three lines from
Virgil himself) :—

> Virgilium vatem melius sua carmina laudant;
> 'In freta dum fluvii current, dum montibus umbrae
> Lustrabunt convexa, polus dum sidera pascet,
> Semper honos nomenque tuum laudesque manebunt'.

> Virgil is lauded best in Virgil's lays:—
> 'As long as rivers run into the deep,
> As long as shadows o'er the hillside sweep,
> As long as stars in heaven's fair pastures graze,
> So long shall live your honour, name, and praise'[1].

The middle of the fourth century marks the date of a grammarian and rhetorician of African origin, C. Marius
Victorinus[2], the author of several philosophical and
rhetorical works (including a prolix commentary on Cicero *De
Inventione*[3]), and also of a treatise on metre in four books, founded
mainly on the Greek of Aphthonius. He received the literary
distinction of a statue in the forum of Trajan. It is interesting to
remember that the study of his Latin rendering of certain 'Platonic'
works had an important influence on the religious development of
St Augustine[4], who records the fact that late in life their translator
became a convert to Christianity[5]. The illiberal decree of Julian
(as already mentioned) led to the resignation of his appointment
as a Christian teacher in 362[6].

Among his distinguished contemporaries was the grammarian
and rhetorician Aelius Donatus, the author of a
Grammar, which has come down to us in a shorter
and in a longer form[7]; also of a valuable commentary on Terence[8],

*(marginal note: Victorinus)*

*(marginal note: Donatus)*

---

[1] Conington's rendering of *Aen.* i 607 f. Cp. Migne, lviii 489; Lanciani's
*Ancient Rome* (1888), p. 196; and J. W. Clark's *Care of Books*, p. 43.

[2] Teuffel, § 408, 1; Schanz, § 828; Jeep's *Redetheile*, pp. 82–9.

[3] Halm, *Rhet. Lat. Min.* 155—304; cp. Saintsbury, i 348.

[4] *Conf.* vii 9.        [5] *ib.* viii 2.        [6] *ib.* viii 5.

[7] Jeep, pp. 24–8. It is the theme of extant commentaries by Servius and
others (*ib.* 28—56); and continued to be a text-book throughout the Middle
Ages. Cp. *Registres du Châtelet*, ii 103, 'Il avait apprins jusqu'à son *Donnet*
et *Catonnet*' (Madame Duclaux, *Fields of France*, 260). In old French, and in
the English of Langland and Chaucer, *Donat* or *Donet* is synonymous with
'grammar', or indeed with any kind of 'lesson' (Warton's *English Poetry*,
sect. viii).        [8] ed. Wessner, 1902.

which has been combined with one or two others in the extant
*scholia* on Terence, and of a commentary on Virgil, frequently
cited by Servius[1]. Two other grammarians, who were contemporaries with one another, and had much in common, are Charisius
and Diomedes, the former of whom transcribed
large portions of the works of Julius Romanus[2],　Charisius.
Cominianus, and Palaemon, and thus preserved for　Diomedes
us much of the earlier grammatical teaching, while the latter
borrowed largely from the lost work of Suetonius, *de poëtis*[3]. Passages from the grammatical treatises of Varro are included in the
works of both[4].

In the latter half of the fourth century Maurus (or Marius)
Servius Honoratus (born *c.* 355) was famous as a
Virgilian commentator, whose work owes much of　Servius
its value to its wealth of mythological, geographical and historical
learning. It has come down to us in two forms, a longer and a
shorter. The longer was regarded as the genuine commentary by
Scaliger and Ribbeck; the shorter by Otfried Müller and Thilo[5].
It has been shown by Nettleship that Servius and Isidore used
the same original authorities, especially Suetonius, and that
passages in which Servius seems to be copying from Donatus are
probably copied from an earlier authority, Nonius, and ultimately
from Verrius Flaccus[6]. His commentary is further founded on
materials borrowed, possibly at second or third hand, from Cato,
Varro, Nigidius and Hyginus. It is a vast treasure-house of
traditional lore. The author displays great erudition, as well as
a certain aptitude for verbal exposition, and perhaps an over-
fondness for pointing out the rhetorical figures used by the poet;
but he supplies practically nothing that is worth calling literary
criticism. He tells us that the fourth *Aeneid* is borrowed from
Apollonius Rhodius; and, in the introduction to the *Georgics*,

---

[1] Teuffel, § 409; Schanz, § 832; Nettleship in Conington's *Virgil*, i[4] p. c.

[2] Froehde in *Jahrb. f. Philol.* 18 Suppl. (1892), 567—672; cp., however,
Jeep ap. Bursian's *Jahresb.* vol. 113, 158 f.

[3] Teuffel, § 419.

[4] Wilmanns, *De Varronis libris grammaticis*, pp. 152-5, 172. Cp.
Bursian's *Jahresb.* vol. 113, 157—164.

[5] ed. Thilo and Hagen, 1878—1902.

[6] *Essays*, i 322—340, and in Conington's *Virgil*, i[4] pp. ciii—cvii.

notes that Virgil has followed Homer at a distance in the *Aeneid*, has proved himself second to Theocritus in the *Eclogues*, and has greatly surpassed Hesiod in the *Georgics*[1].

In the same century the most scholarly representative of
St Jerome          Christianity was Hieronymus, commonly called St Jerome (331—420 A.D.), who is celebrated as the unwearied translator and expositor of the Old and New Testaments.   As a youth he was sent to Rome, where he became a pupil of Donatus[2].   He has himself recorded in his commentary on the book of Ecclesiastes[3] that his teacher, in expounding the line in Terence, *nullum est iam dictum, quod non dictum sit prius*[4], used the words which have since passed into a proverb: *pereant qui nostra ante nos dixerunt.*   He also studied the Greek philosophers, and laboriously[5] formed for himself a library.   From Rome he went to Trier, where he studied theology, and felt himself called to a new life.   After continuing his studies at Aquileia, he embarked for the East, where he lay ill for a long time in Syria, reflecting with remorse on the past, but finding some respite in reading his favourite authors, such as Plautus and Cicero, while he cared little (as he confesses) for the uncouth Latin of the Psalms.   At last he fell into a fever and dreamt that he was dead, and that he was being dragged before the tribunal of the Judge of all men.   Falling on his face to hide himself from the brightness of the vision, he heard an awful voice demanding, 'Who art thou?'   On his answering, 'A Christian', he heard with trembling the terrible reply :—'It is false ; thou art no Christian ; thou art a Ciceronian ; where the treasure is, there is the heart also'[6].   From that hour (in the year 374 A.D.) he renounced the reading of the ancient classics, buried himself in the desert between Antioch and the Euphrates, leading a hermit's life for five years and engaging after a while in manual labour and

---

[1] Cp. Suringar, ii 59—92; Thomas, *Essai* (1880); Teuffel, § 431; and Schanz, §§ 248, 835; also Saintsbury, i 334—340.

[2] *Apol. adv. Rufinum*, i 16, puto quod puer legeris...commentarios...in Terentii comoedias *praeceptoris mei* Donati, aeque in Vergilium; *Chron.* 356-7 A.D., Victorinus rhetor et Donatus *praeceptor meus* Romae insignes habentur.

[3] i 9.                              [4] *Eunuchus*, prol. 41.

[5] *Ep.* 22, c. 30, Migne, summo studio et labore.          [6] *Ep.* 22, c. 30.

ultimately in the transcription of MSS. As a further means of
self-discipline, he devoted himself to the study of Hebrew.
Returning to Antioch, he went to Constantinople (380), where
he studied under Gregory of Nazianzus, and also completed his
knowledge of Greek. One of the most important fruits of this
study was his translation of the Chronicle of Eusebius, which,
in its original Greek, now survives in fragments alone. Two
years afterwards he returned to Rome, where he lived for three
years as the Secretary of pope Damasus (382–5). Near the
theatre of Pompey in the Campus Martius that pope had built a
library for the archives of the Latin Church, and this building,
which is called by Jerome the *chartarium ecclesiae Romanae*[1], is
supposed by some[2] to have been connected with colonnades after
the manner of the great pagan libraries of Rome, which had been
modelled on that of Pergamon (p. 159 f.). At the instance of the
pope, Jerome now began his revision of the Latin Bible, and in
due time completed his rendering of the Gospels and the Psalms.
In 385 he left for Palestine, where he founded a monastery at
Bethlehem (386). There, as in the desert, he set the example of
a monastic life mainly devoted to literary labour. In his cell at
Bethlehem (a subject which has caught the fancy of Dürer[3]) he
was constantly adding to his store of books. He lectured his
monks on theology, and gathered round him a school of boys,
whom he instructed in grammar and in the classical authors,
especially in Plautus, Terence and, above all, in Virgil. Here
the learned scholar was in his true element; the 'Ciceronian'
and the 'Christian' were reconciled with one another. He
resumed his study of Hebrew and worked at his Latin rendering
of the Old Testament, his treatise *de viris illustribus* (in imitation
of that of Suetonius), and much besides. His monastery was
attacked by Pelagians in 416, and his last years at Bethlehem
(where he died in 420) were embittered by the incursions of
barbarians[4].

---

[1] *Apol. adv. Rufinum*, iii c. 20 (J. W. Clark's *Care of Books*, p. 42).

[2] De Rossi and Lanciani (*ib.* p. 43).

[3] For its treatment by other artists, cp. J. W. Clark, *Care of Books*, figs.
140, 149, 153.

[4] Ebert, i[2] 184—192; Schanz, §§ 972—999, who places his birth in 348.

His *Letters*, extending from 370 to 419, were very popular during the Middle Ages and the Renaissance. They abound in quotations from his favourite classical authors, and from Virgil in particular. The suicide of Judas, the wiles of the Tempter, the inroads of the barbarians, the enmity of the monks, and the gloom of the catacombs, are all of them suggestive of quotations from Virgil[1]. He also cites Ennius and Naevius, Plautus and Terence, Cicero and Sallust, Horace and Juvenal. In the very letter[2] in which he regrets an excessive use of rhetoric, and is penitent for an undue partiality for scholastic learning, he lapses into references to Greek philosophers such as Pythagoras, Democritus, Xenocrates, Plato, Zeno and Cleanthes; Greek poets such as Homer, Hesiod, Simonides, Stesichorus and Sophocles; Hippocrates and Isocrates; not to mention Roman writers such as Cato the Censor[3]. In one of his letters[4] he justifies his frequent citations from secular literature; in another[5] he shows himself fully conscious of the merits of the famous generals, 'whose manly virtues illuminate the history of Rome'; in a third[6] he discusses the best method of translation, defending his own plan of rendering the Scriptures according to their sense rather than in the slavish spirit of a merely verbal literalism. 'In his fearless determination to ascertain the precise meaning of the sacred text, he offers a splendid example of rare candour and patient industry'[7]. In sacred literature his most famous achievement is the Latin *Vulgate*. In the Middle Ages an interest in textual criticism was stimulated by the existence of his three successive versions of the Psalter:—(1) his revision of the *Itala*, called the *Psalterium Romanum*, (2) the version founded on Origen's *Hexapla*, known as the *Psalterium Gallicanum*, and (3) his rendering of the Hebrew original[8]. In general scholarship his most celebrated work was his translation and continuation of the Chronological

[1] *Epp.* 58, 60 Migne.                [2] *Ep.* 52.

[3] Boissier, i 327—334[3]; Lübeck, *Hieronymus quos noverit scriptores et ex quibus hauserit*, 1872. He often quotes Seneca and Persius.

[4] *Ep.* 70.          [5] *Ep.* 60, 5.          [6] *Ep.* 57.

[7] Dill's *Last Century of the Western Empire*, p. 125.

[8] Cp. Schanz, § 980; and Traube in *Deutsche Literaturzeitung*, 1904, 134 f; also *Vorlesungen*, 1911, 48 f.

Canons of Eusebius, with large additions from Suetonius, *de viris
illustribus*, and his successors down to 325, and from his own
researches between that date and 378 A.D.   These additions can
be identified with the aid of the Armenian translation of Eusebius,
discovered in 1787[1].   We catch a glimpse of the literary methods
of the age in the preface to Jerome's translation, which he
describes as a hasty production very rapidly dictated to a shorthand writer.   He concludes his treatise *de viris illustribus* by translating from Irenaeus[2] a solemn adjuration requiring every future
copyist to compare[3] his transcript with the MS from which he
makes his copy, and to correct[4] it, and also to transcribe the form
of adjuration.   A similar form, described as the *obtestatio Eusebii*,
appears at the beginning of certain MSS of Jerome's translation of
the Canons[5].

St Augustine (354—430) must here be noticed very briefly, and
solely in connexion with the subject of the present
work.   The story of his life is unfolded to us in his       St Augustine
immortal *Confessions*.   He there tells us that, as a boy, he liked
Latin, as soon as he had got beyond the elements; while he hated
Greek, though he could assign no sufficient reason for his hatred[6].
He admits, and regrets, his early fondness for Virgil, lamenting
(above all) the tears that he had shed over the death of Dido, and
recalling with penitence his boyish delight in the story of the
'wooden horse' and the burning of Troy and the ghost of
Creusa[7].   Homer he hated, apparently because the language
(unlike his native Latin) was strange to him[8].   At the age of

---

[1] A. Schöne, *Eusebi chronicorum libri duo*, 1866–75; A. Schöne, *Die
Weltchronik des Eusebius*, 1900.—Cp. Teuffel, § 434, 9; Schanz, § 977;
and Ebert, i[2] 207—210; also p. 349 n. 1 *infra*.

[2] ap. Euseb. *Hist. Eccl.* v 20.

[3] ἀντιβάλῃς is the word used by Irenaeus; cp. Strabo, 609.

[4] *emendes* (in the lower sense); cp. *Ep.* 52; Suet. *Dom.* 20; Symmachus,
i 18.                                    [5] Jahn, in *Sächs. Berichte*, 1851, p. 367.

[6] *Conf.* i 13, 20, Quid autem erat causae cur Graecas litteras oderam,
quibus puerulus imbuebar, ne nunc quidem satis exploratum est. Adamaveram
enim Latinas, non quas primi magistri, sed quas docent qui grammatici
vocantur.                          [7] *Conf.* i §§ 20—22.

[8] *ib.* 23, Cur ergo Graecam grammaticam oderam talia cantantem? Nam
et Homerus peritus texere tales fabellas, et dulcissime vanus est, et mihi tamen
amarus erat puero etc.

19 he received his first serious impressions from the *Hortensius* of Cicero[1], an eloquent call to the study of philosophy, which is now lost with the exception of a few fragments. At 20 he studied for himself the *Categories* of Aristotle[2], and a series of works on the 'liberal arts'[3]. In 383 he left Carthage for Rome, and, half a year later, on the recommendation of Symmachus, then praefect of Rome, was appointed teacher of rhetoric at Milan. He there found a friend in Ambrose. At the age of 31 we see him studying, in the quest of truth, certain 'Platonic' works translated into Latin by Victorinus[4]. In the autumn of the following year he resigned his appointment, and withdrew with his mother and son and a few friends to a country-house (Cassiacum) near Milan, there to prepare himself for his baptism, which took place at Easter, 387. Part of his time during this period of retirement was occupied in the study of Virgil and in a general survey of the 'liberal arts', and the literary work, which he had thus begun, was resumed on his return to Milan. But we are here concerned only with the cyclopaedia of the liberal arts, which he now began in imitation of Varro's *Disciplinae*. It was intended to be a survey of all the arts, viz. grammar, logic, rhetoric, music, geometry, arithmetic and philosophy (this last taking the place of astronomy); but only the part on grammar was then completed, while a portion of that on music, and introductions to the rest, were finished at a later date[5]. All that has survived is the dialogue on music, and abridgements of the work on grammar, with parts of the introductions to rhetoric and logic, though the authorship of the last two has been disputed. The work on rhetoric[6] is founded on Hermagoras, the Rhodian instructor of Cicero, and on Cicero himself; it is only preserved in MSS of Fortunatianus[7]; while the work on logic (*Principia Dialecticae*), in the course of which Augustine is mentioned as the author, is one of our authorities on the Grammar of the Stoics[8].

---

[1] *Conf.* iii 4, 7, viii 7, 17.          [2] *ib.* iv 16, 28.

[3] *ib.* iv 16, 30.                         [4] *ib.* vii 9, 13; viii 2, 3 (*supra*, p. 230).

[5] *Retract.* i c. 6.                       [6] Halm, *Rhet. Lat. Min.* 137—151.

[7] *Supra*, p. 229.

[8] *Supra*, p. 148. The work must have been founded either on the corresponding part of Varro's *Disciplinae*, or on the first book of the *De Lingua Latina* (Wilmanns, *De Varronis libris grammaticis*, pp. 16—19); and, in

In 388 Augustine returned to Africa, where he became Presbyter
of Hippo in 391 and Bishop from 396 to his death in 430.
He lives in general literature as the author of the *Confessions*
(a favourite book with Petrarch and many since his time), and the
*De Civitate Dei*, which was finished in 426 A.D.    In the latter he
quotes largely from Varro's *Antiquitates* (especially the account of
the distinctively Roman divinities[1]), and from Cicero's treatise
*De Republica*.   He has thus preserved for us considerable portions
of both of those important works[2].

To the end of the fourth and the beginning of the fifth century
belongs Macrobius, the author of an extant commentary on Cicero's *Dream of Scipio* (in the sixth
book of the *De Republica*), and of a miscellaneous work in seven
books under the name of *Saturnalia*.   The latter is in the form
of a dialogue dealing with a vast number of topics connected
with the earlier Roman literature and religion.   The scene of the
dialogue is the house of Vettius Agorius Praetextatus, an expert
in augural and pontifical law, who died in 384.   As statesman,
scholar, antiquarian, philosopher and mystic, he was then one of
the most eminent in the heathen world of Rome.   He translated
the *Analytics* of Aristotle, and spent part of his leisure in emending
the text of the ancient Classics[3].   He is now best known as the
restorer in 367 of the *Porticus Deorum Consentium*, still to be
seen near the Clivus Capitolinus.   He also lives in the interesting
inscriptions addressed by himself to his wife, and by his wife to
her husband, which present us with a pleasant picture of their
devotion to each other and to the varied religious rites of their
time[4].   Among the interlocutors are the scholar and statesman

---

either case, Varro's own authority was probably a grammarian writing under
Stoic influence, possibly Philoxenus, who may well have been a contemporary
of Varro (Reitzenstein, *M. Ter. Varro*, p. 87).

[1] Francken's *Fragmenta Varronis* (1836).   Cp. S. Angus (Princeton, 1906).

[2] Teuffel, § 440, 7 and 10; Ebert, i[2] 212—251.   On St Augustine's attitude
towards literature, cp. Saintsbury, i 378 f; and on his *Confessions*, Harnack,
*Reden und Aufsätze* i (1904) 49 f; T. R. Glover's *Fourth Century*, 194—213.
S. Angus, *Sources of De Civitate Dei*, i—x, pp. 279, Princeton, 1906.

[3] 'meliora reddis quam legendo sumpseras' (Bücheler's *Anth. Lat.* no.
111, l. 12).

[4] *Corp. Inscr. Lat.* vi 1778–9 (Bücheler, *l.c.*).   Cp. Dill's *Last Century of
the Western Empire*, pp. 17, 18, 77, 154 f; and Glover, pp. 162–4.

Symmachus[1], and Servius, here represented as a modest student of Virgil, who naturally takes an important part in the lengthy discussions on that poet. The author is sometimes identified with Macrobius the *Praefectus praetorio Hispaniarum* (399), the proconsul of Africa (410), the *vir illustris* and the *praepositus sacri cubiculi* of 422 A.D.[2] The first of these dates is connected with an edict forbidding the destruction of the treasures of art in the temples of Spain and Gaul, and the praefect of that date may well have been a pagan. But the holder of the office named in 422 must have been a Christian; whereas, at the dramatic date of the *Saturnalia* (*c.* 380), its author was an admirer of Symmachus and others of the pagan party, and a devout worshipper of the gods of polytheism, with a strong inclination towards Neo-platonic views. Thus, unless we assume either a complete change of belief or a merely nominal acceptance of Christianity at a later date than that of the composition of the *Saturnalia*, there are great difficulties in the proposed identification. The fact remains that the extant works of Macrobius contain no mention of any person or thing connected with Christianity. Their author was not a native of Rome; he may have been born in Africa or (more probably) in Greece. At any rate his name is Greek, he has some knowledge even of recondite portions of Greek literature, and he is the writer of a grammatical treatise on the differences between the verb in Latin and the verb in Greek[3].

In the *Saturnalia* he deals largely with matters of mythology and grammar, including etymology (naturally of a prae-scientific type); but the discussion turns mainly on the varied and comprehensive merits of Virgil. This discussion is started in an interesting passage at the end of the first book, and is continued (after an interval) throughout books III to VI. The first of these books proves the poet's accurate knowledge of religious ritual; the next gives examples of his command of the resources of rhetoric; book V compares him with Homer and includes (as in Gellius) a parallel between Pindar's description of

---

[1] p. 226 *supra*.          [2] Teuffel, § 444, 1 and 7.

[3] *ib.* 9; Glover, pp. 171–2. Erasmus, *Ciceronianus*, p. 148 (p. 65, ed. 1621), regards Macrobius as a *Graeculus*. The treatise on the Greek Verb was abridged by Joannes Scotus (Tillemont, *Emp.* v 664).

Aetna and Virgil's, while book vi dwells on Virgil's indebtedness
to the earlier Latin poets, and concludes with a long series of
verbal criticisms assigned to the character of Servius[1].   Book vii,
which owes much to the *Convivial Questions* of Plutarch, includes
(among many other matters) a lengthy account of the Roman
calendar.

The author once borrows tacitly from Seneca[2] and far more
frequently from Gellius and Suetonius, and certain ancient commentators on Virgil, besides citing Plutarch and Athenaeus, and
adding extracts from Didymus.   He also has a number of references
to Cicero, but only two to Catullus and Horace, one to Persius,
three to Juvenal and many to minor grammarians, his main
interest being reserved for Virgil and his predecessors.   But 'it is
Virgil's learning that appeals to him rather than his poetry, and
while there is much truth in what he says of Virgil's felicity in
using his knowledge of antiquity and literature, it is absurd to
make it, as he does, Virgil's chief claim to distinction'[3].   The
*Saturnalia*, notwithstanding its misconception of Virgil's poetry,
has naturally been largely quoted by modern editors of the poet[4].
At the dramatic date of the dialogue Servius was a young man
who had not yet written his Commentary on Virgil, but he may
have written it before the composition of the *Saturnalia*[5].   Between the *Saturnalia* and the Commentary there are some points
in common[6], and it is questioned whether Macrobius is borrowing
from Servius, or whether our text of Servius has been interpolated
from that of Macrobius[7].   As a point of modern interest we may

---

[1] vi 6—9.  Cp. Saintsbury, i 329—334, and Glover, 173—185.

[2] *Ep.* 47 § 5, in *Sat.* i 11, 13.                    [3] Glover, p. 181.

[4] Cp. Nettleship on Virgil and his ancient critics in Conington's *Virgil*,
i[4] pp. xxix—lvi.

[5] His oral teaching alone is mentioned by Macrobius:—i 2, 15, Servius
inter grammaticos doctorem recens professus; vi 6, 1, nunc dicat volo Servius
quae in Vergilio notaverit...; *Cotidie* enim *Romanae indoli enarrando eundem
vatem* necesse est habeat huius adnotationis scientiam promptiorem.

[6] *Sat.* iii 10—12, and Servius on *Aen.* iii 21, iv 57, viii 279, 285; also *Sat.*
i 15, 10 and 17, 14, and Servius on *Aen.* viii 654 and i 8.

[7] It seems most probable that 'both Macrobius and Servius were drawing
upon older commentaries and criticisms', such as the *Aeneidomastix* of Carvilius Pictor, the *vitia* of Herennius, the *furta* of Perellius Faustus, and the *liber
contra obtrectatores Vergilii* o. Asconius (Nettleship, in Conington, i[4] li—liii).

remember that Dr Johnson, at the age of 19 and on the evening
of his arrival as a freshman in Oxford, sat silent in the presence
of his father and his tutor, but, in the course of their conversation,
'suddenly struck in and quoted Macrobius'[1]. Whether it was
a precept of conduct in social life, or an appropriate anecdote, or
a criticism on Virgil which was then quoted, we cannot tell; but
we may be certain that on that occasion the future commentator
on Shakespeare could not have been better described than in the
words applied by Macrobius to the future commentator on Virgil,
who is characterised in the *Saturnalia* as *iuxta doctrina mirabilis
et amabilis verecundia*[2].

The Commentary on the *Dream of Scipio* is many times
longer than the text, which it has happily preserved. It includes
not a few digressions on Neo-platonic topics, as well as on myths
and matters of astronomy, including the 'music of the spheres'[3].
Here, as in the *Saturnalia*, the author is not original, but admits
his obligations to Plotinus and others[4]. His general aim is to
support Plato and Cicero in maintaining the existence of a life
beyond the grave, and incidentally he sees in Homer's 'golden
chain' suspended between heaven and earth a series of links
successively descending from the supreme God to the lowest of
his creatures. We are not here concerned with the rest of the
contents of the Commentary[5]. It may be added, however, that
the treatise was much admired in the Middle Ages. Its author is
described as 'no mean philosopher' by Abelard, and is quoted as
an authority on Neo-platonism by St Thomas Aquinas[6]. He is
mentioned by Guillaume de Lorris, who borrows from the *Dream
of Scipio* the framework for the first part of the *Roman de la Rose*[7].
He is also familiar to Chaucer[8].

---

[1] Boswell (31 Oct. 1728), i 32 ed. Napier.

[2] i 2, 15.                 [3] ii 3, 7, 11.

[4] He owes much to Porphyry *On the Timaeus* (Linke, *Abh. f. M. Hertz*).

[5] They are well analysed in Dill, 106—112, and in Glover, 186—193.

[6] Petit, *De Macrobio Ciceronis Interprete* (1866), c. ix and pp. 72, 79
(Glover, p. 187 note 1).

[7] Gaston Paris, *Litt. Fr. au MA*, § 111.

[8] *Parlement of Foules*, l. 19 f; cp. E. P. Anderson in *Proc. Amer. Phil.
Assoc.* xxxiii (1902), xcviii.

In northern Africa, before its conquest by the Vandals,
Martianus Capella produced (c. 410—427)[1] an encyclopaedia of the seven liberal arts in the form of       Martianus
                                                          Capella
an allegory representing the marriage of Mercury
and Philologia, who is attended by seven bridesmaids personifying
the liberal arts. The work is chiefly founded on Varro's *Disciplinae*; the book on Rhetoric (v) is mainly taken from Aquila
Romanus; that on Geometry and Geography (vi), from Solinus
and Pliny; and that on Music (ix), from Aristides Quintilianus.
As in Varro's *Satura Menippea*, the prose is often varied with
verse; and the verse, in spite of certain 'false quantities', is
pleasanter reading than the prose, which oscillates between the
two extremes of being, at one time tame and jejune, at another
over-florid and bombastic. The story of the allegory is introduced
in the first two books. Mercury, having resolved on wedding
a wife, consults Apollo, who speaks in the highest terms of a
*doctissima virgo* named Philologia. The bride is raised to divine
rank and, after she has been compelled, with some reluctance, to
abjure all her learning, is carried off to heaven amid the songs of
the Muses. The seven following books are devoted to a description of the persons and attributes of the seven bridesmaids,
Grammar, Logic, Rhetoric, Geometry, Arithmetic, Astronomy,
and Music. The order is the same as in Varro, and the number
of the books is also the same, the only difference being that
whereas Varro devotes two further books to Medicine and Architecture, Martianus Capella omits these and uses the first two
books to introduce his allegory. In the heavenly Senate of the
second book, Homer, Virgil, and Orpheus are described as
sounding the lute, while Archimedes and Plato are turning
spheres of gold; Thales is in a watery mist, Heraclitus aglow
with fire, and Democritus wrapped in a cloud of atoms, while
Pythagoras threads the mazes of certain celestial numbers,
Aristotle is in constant quest of Entelecheia, and Epicurus
is adorned with roses and violets[2]. In the book on Rhetoric the

---

[1] 'Roma quam diu viguit' (vi 637) suggests a date later than Alaric's capture of Rome in 410; 'Carthago nunc felicitate reverenda' (vi 669) a date
earlier than the Vandal invasion of Africa in 429.

[2] ii 212 (Dill, p. 415).

examples are mainly from Cicero, also from Terence and Virgil, and, to a less extent, from Ennius and Sallust. But the author adds fantastic touches of his own; for example, the kiss with which Rhetoric salutes Philologia is heard throughout the assembly, *nihil enim silens, ac si cuperet, faciebat*[1]. The Arts in general, and Grammar in particular, are allowed to talk undiluted and unmitigated text-book, and the dramatic form of the work as a whole is often lost in dull and dry detail.

The work is probably later in date[2] than the *disciplinarum libri* of St Augustine which belong to 387. In the earlier Middle Ages it was the principal, often the only, text-book used in schools, and it exercised a considerable influence on education and on literary taste. The Christian rhetorician, Securus Memor Felix, Professor of Rhetoric in Rome (who took part in the Mavortian recension of Horace in 527), revised the text with the aid of his pupil, the grammarian Deuterius, either in 498 or more probably in 535[3]. It is once quoted in the *Expositio Sermonum Antiquarum* of Fulgentius (*c.* 480—550), who imitates it in his *Mythologicon*[4]. It is also mentioned by Gregory of Tours (d. 595)[5], is often quoted by John of Salisbury (d. 1180), and is represented by many MSS, including one at Cambridge of the eighth century, and others

---

[1] Liber v, *prope finem*.

[2] Discussed by H. Parker, 'The Seven Liberal Arts', *English Historical Review*, 1890, pp. 417—461. Mr Parker, while rightly opposing the late date 470, seems to make far too much of the mention of 'Byzantium' in vi 657 as denoting a date earlier than 330.

[3] Jahn, in *Sächs. Berichte*, 1851, p. 351. Denk, p. 209, assigns Deuterius to Pisa. Deuterius *may* have taught at Milan (note on Ennodius, lxiii 279 Migne). On the strength of a subscription to a MS of Martianus Capella, where ARV is written instead of R, Wiltheim (cp. Roger, 99) connects Felix with Clermont. Similarly Tillemont, *Emp.* v 665, and Denk, *l.c.*; but the *Hist. Litt. de France*, iii 173, admits that his native place is unknown.

[4] Fulgentius is better known as the author of an allegorical exposition of the *Aeneid* (Teuffel, § 480).

[5] *Hist. Franc.* x ad fin., si te...Martianus noster septem disciplinis erudiit. It was expounded by Joannes Scotus (d. *c.* 875), Alexander Neckam, and Remigius of Auxerre, and is mentioned in 1149 by Wilibald (Jaffé, *Mon. Corbeiensia* i 275—9). It is also followed in a poem by Theodulphus, Bp of Orleans under Charlemagne, entitled *De septem liberalibus artibus in quadam pictura depictis*, Migne, cv 333, and *Mon. Hist. Germ., Poëtae Latini*, i 544.

once belonging to the monasteries of Bamberg and Reichenau
at the beginning and the end respectively of the tenth[1]. The
last seven books (as has been recently observed) 'are strictly
instructive, and sapless as the rods of mediaeval schoolmasters.
The allegory of the first two books is pleasingly pedantic and the
whole work presents the sterile union of fantasy and pedantry,
so dear to the closing years of pagan scholarship, when the old
straw was thrashed, re-tied in queer-shaped bundles, and then
thrashed again. The process produced *pabulum* for coming
generations'[2]. But its influence on mediaeval poetry and art
must not be forgotten. That influence may be traced in the *Anti-
claudianus* of Alanus ab Insulis in the twelfth century[3], in the
*Hortus Deliciarum* of Herrad of Landsberg, in the sculptured
representations of the seven liberal arts in the thirteenth[4], and
in Attavante's illuminations of the MS of Martianus in the Library
of St Mark's at Venice, executed for Matthias Corvinus, king of
Hungary (*c.* 1460).

The year 450 marks the death of Theodosius the younger,
the emperor of the East who condescended to be
a copyist and was celebrated for his calligraphy.    Recensions
                                                      of Solinus,
Even while he was presiding over the races of the    Vegetius etc.
Circus, he passed the time in producing specimens of beautiful
handwriting. The record of his having copied a MS of Solinus is
still preserved in transcripts of that copy bearing the subscription:—*opera et studio* (or *studio et diligentia*) *Theodosii invictissimi
principis*. In the same year we have a recension of Vegetius at
Constantinople by one Eutropius, while, in the subsequent half-
century, we have recensions of Pomponius Mela and of abridgements of Valerius Maximus, produced at Ravenna by Rusticius
Helpidius Domnulus, either the correspondent of Ennodius and

---

[1] Teuffel, § 452; Ebert, i 482—5. Cp. Mullinger's *Univ. of Cambridge*,
i 23—26, 100; Saintsbury, i 349—354, and Dill, 412 f.

[2] H. O. Taylor, *The Classical Heritage of the Middle Ages* (1901), p. 51.

[3] Migne, ccx.

[4] Mâle, *l'art religieux du xiii^e siècle*, pp. 102—121 (1898). The *earliest*
sculptured representations of the liberal arts are found on the façades of
Chartres (1145 A.D.) and Laon (Viollet le Duc, *Dict. de l'Arch.*, s.v. *Arts
Libéraux*).

Cassiodorus, or that of Apollinaris Sidonius, who will next engage our attention[1].

In the latter half of the fifth century the foremost representative of Scholarship in Gaul was Gaius Sollius Apollinaris Sidonius (*c.* 431—*c.* 482-4). He was born at Lyons, where he was educated in poetry, rhetoric and philosophy. His father and grandfather were Christians, and held high office in the State. His wife's father, Avitus, became emperor of Rome in 455, and caused a statue of Sidonius to be placed among those of literary celebrities in the library of Trajan[2]. Similarly, in recognition of his panegyrics, he was honoured with a laurelled bust by Majorian (461), and with a second statue by Anthemius (467), who made him praefect of Rome. From about 472 to his death, about 484, he was bishop of the *urbs Arverna*, now known as Clermont Ferrand. He was a layman of high estate when he was unanimously elected bishop; in times of trouble due to the aggressions of the Visigoths under Euric, who annexed Auvergne and imprisoned its bishop in 475, he discharged the duties of his office in an exemplary manner; and, when he lay a dying in his cathedral church, a vast crowd of men, women and children was heard lamenting and exclaiming: *cur nos deseris, pastor bone, vel cui nos quasi orphanos derelinquis?*[3] He survives in his poems and his letters. His poems are written in hexameters, elegiacs and hendecasyllables, a favourite metre in this age. One of these last[4] shows a wide, though possibly superficial, familiarity with classical literature. In his hexameter poems the mythological element is predominant. On becoming a bishop he professed to give up writing verses[5], but he not infrequently relapsed into that form of amusement. He mainly imitates Virgil and Horace, Statius and Claudian[6], and he was himself imitated by learned poets in the Middle Ages, but in the dawn of the Renaissance he was deemed a difficult writer by Petrarch[7]. His letters are modelled on those of the younger

<Apollinaris Sidonius>

---

[1] Jahn, in *Sächs. Berichte*, 1851, 342-7.

[2] *Carm.* vii.            [3] Greg. Tur. *Hist. Franc.* ii 23.

[4] *Carm.* ix.            [5] *Ep.* ix 12, 2; 16, 3, ll. 45—64.

[6] Cp. Geisler, *Loci similes auctorum Sidonio anteriorum* in Luetjohann's ed., pp. 351 f, 384—416.

[7] *Epp. Fam.*, *Praef.* p. 21 (1859), 'illius stili obice.'

Pliny, resembling in this respect the letters of Symmachus, but
far excelling them in vivid colouring and varied interest. Like
Pliny's, they include elaborate descriptions of several country-
houses[1]. Above all, they supply us with many graphic details as
to the state of society and of learning in Gaul, and as to the
literary tastes of the writer himself, which are also suggested in
his poems. He quotes from Virgil and Horace, from Cicero and
Tacitus; he is an admirer of Sallust[2]; with his son he reads
Menander and Terence[3]; in his youth he has studied the *Categories* of Aristotle[4]; one of his friends is devoted to the study of
Plato[5]; but the only dialogue named by himself is the *Phaedo*,
and that in the Latin translation of Apuleius[6]. He tells us of the
Latin authors in the library of a noble friend near Nîmes, which
included Varro and Horace, as well as Augustine and Prudentius
and a Latin translation of Origen[7]. His friend Lampridius of
Bordeaux (whom he has special reasons for humouring) is described as declaiming with equal facility in Greek and in Latin[8];
another friend, Consentius of Narbonne, composes in Greek as
well as Latin verse[9], while Magnus, the father of Consentius, is
flatteringly compared with Homer and Herodotus[10], with Sophocles,
Euripides and Menander, and with a series of Latin authors from
Plautus to Martial[11]. When he hears of a monk, who has passed
through the town, carrying off to Britain, the native land of
Faustus (the semi-pelagian bishop of Riez in Provence), a mysterious MS written by Faustus himself, he drives after him with all
speed and does not rest until he has had the MS copied by his
secretaries at his dictation[12]. A treatise, in which Faustus maintained the corporeal nature of the soul, was answered by Mamertus
Claudianus, who translates large portions of the dialogues of Plato,
besides referring to Thales, Pythagoras, Zeno, Epicurus, Porphyry,

---

[1] *Epp.* ii 2 and 9.                [2] *Carm.* ii 190, xxiii 152.

[3] *Ep.* iv 12.                       [4] iv 1.

[5] iv 11.                             [6] ii 9; *Carm.* ii 178.

[7] ii 9, 4. Other libraries are mentioned in viii 4 and 11 § 2, *Carm.* xxiv 92,
and a *bybliopola* in *Ep.* v 15.

[8] ix 13.                             [9] ix 15, l. 21.

[10] C. xxiii 134, primos vix poterant locos tueri | torrens Herodotus, tonans
Homerus.

[11] *Carm.* xxiii.                    [12] ix 9, 16.

and other philosophers[1]. This reply he dedicated to Sidonius,
who exhausts the vocabulary of literary allusion in acknowledging
the compliment, but never approaches the point at issue between
his friends[2]. It is Sidonius who preserves for us the familiar
example of a 'recurrent' verse, which is the same whether read
backwards or forwards, *Roma tibi subito motibus ibit amor*[3]. He
sends to a friend the 'logistoric' works of Varro, and the chronology of Eusebius[4]. He regrets that literature is held in esteem
by few, *pauci studia nunc honorant*[5]; but he rejoices that the
literary spirit, 'now dying out', has found a refuge in the noble
heart of a friend[6]. He laments the inroad of barbarisms into the
classical idioms of the Latin language[7]. In contrast with Latin,
he regards Celtic and German with contempt[8]. He is not attracted even by the best of his German neighbours[9]. His Muse
falters in the presence of barbarous Burgundians; 'how', he asks,
'can I write six-feet hexameters when surrounded by seven-feet
barbarians?'[10] We cannot part with Sidonius better than in the
terms of grateful appreciation recently applied to himself and his
literary contemporaries. He fully deserves to be called the foremost of those who 'in a period of political convulsion and literary
decadence, softened the impact of barbarism, and kept open for
coming ages the access to the distant sources of our intellectual
life'[11].

---

[1] ed. Engelbrecht, 1885.          [2] iv 3.

[3] ix 14, 4.          [4] viii 6, 18.

[5] v 10, 4.          [6] iv 17.

[7] ii 10, 1, tantum increbruit multitudo desidiosorum, ut, nisi vel paucissimi
quique meram Latiaris linguae proprietatem de trivialium barbarismorum robi-
gine vindicaveritis, eam brevi abolitam defleamus interemptamque.

[8] iii 2; v 5, 1.          [9] iv 1; vii 14.          [10] *Carm.* xii.

[11] Dill's *Last Century of the Western Empire*, p. 451. On Sidonius, cp.
Luetjohann's ed. (in *Mon. Germ. Hist.*); also the Benedictine *Histoire Littéraire
de France*, vol. ii; Teuffel, §§ 466, 1 and 467; Ebert, i[2] 419 f; the works of
Germain (1844), Kaufmann (1864–5), and Chaix (1866), and Mullinger's *Schools
of Charles the Great* (1877), pp. 16—20; Denk's *Gallo-Fränkisches Unterrichts-
und Bildungswesen* (1892), pp. 141—153, 160–3; Mommsen, *Reden und
Aufsätze* (1905), 132 f; Roger, *L'Enseignement des Lettres Classiques d'Ausone
à Alcuin*, 60—81; Saintsbury, i 383–9; and Dill, 187—223, 410 f, 434—451.
Cp. Hodgkin's *Italy and her Invaders*, ii 298—374.

The interest in Latin literature survived longest in Gaul, where
schools of learning were flourishing as early as the       Schools of
first century at Autun, Lyons, Toulouse, Nîmes,       learning in
Vienne, Narbonne and Marseilles; and from the       Gaul
third century onwards, at Trier, Poitiers, Besançon and Bordeaux[1].
In the schools of Gaul three tendencies may be traced[2]: (1) that
of Sidonius, whose relations to the Classics have been already
reviewed; of Ennodius (c. 474—521), who was born in Gaul, and
in his earlier years regarded the pursuits of literature as the cure
for the troubles of his time[3], but, after becoming bishop of Pavia,
detested the very name of 'liberal studies'[4]; and of Venantius
Fortunatus (c. 535—600), an Italian by birth, who became presbyter of Poitiers and wrote an epic on St Martin of Tours,
modelled on Virgil and Claudian. This tendency may be described as 'essentially heathen, with a veneer of churchmanship'.
(2) The second tendency is that of men like Paulinus of Nola,
which, while introducing into the Church 'a new Pantheon' of
locally important saints (such as Felix of Nola), 'jealously guards
its pupils from the contagion of the gentile Classics'. (3) The
third tendency is 'that of the wiser, more truly catholic teachers',
such as Hilary of Poitiers (d. 367), who, as noticed by Jerome[5],
is an imitator of Quintilian; Sulpicius Severus (d. 425), who, in
his *Chronica*, imitates Sallust, Tacitus and Velleius, and, in his
works on St Martin of Tours, while he depreciates the Classics[6],
nevertheless makes Cicero his model, and has reminiscences of

---

[1] Denk, 82—93; Roger, 2 f, 81 f, 91 f. The celebrated school at Augus-
todunum (*Autun*) is noticed by Tacitus, *Ann.* iii 43 (21 A.D.); its decline
began in 270; and, after its destruction by the barbarous Bagaudae, its
restoration was warmly urged in 297 by the rhetorician Eumenius, who gives
an interesting account of its position in the midst of the finest buildings of the
city, with its class-rooms for the teaching of Grammar, Rhetoric and Philosophy,
its colonnades adorned with illustrations of History and Geography, and its
baths, gymnasium and palaestra (Or. iv in *Panegyrici Latini*, ed. Bährens).

[2] J. E. B. Mayor, *Latin Heptateuch*, 1889, p. liv f.

[3] *Eucharist. de vita sua*, vi 394.

[4] *Ep.* ix 1, ed. Hartel, 1882; ed. Vogel, 1885; cp. Dubois, *La Latinité
d'Ennodius*, 1903; Ebert, i² 432 f; Roger, 191—3.

[5] *Ep.* 83 (cp. Roger, 150 f).

[6] *Vita Martini*, c. 1 (Roger, 144).

Virgil; Claudius Marius Victor (d. *c.* 425—450), who ascribes all the disasters of his time to the rhetorical education of the day with its abandonment of Paul and Solomon for Terence, Virgil, Horace and Ovid[1]; Hilary of Arles (d. *c.* 450), who succeeded Honoratus as bishop of Arles and wrote his life, and found his chief delight in expounding difficult passages to his pupils[2]; Alcimus Avitus[3], bishop of Vienne (d. *c.* 525), who imitates Virgil, Horace, Juvencus, Claudian, Sedulius and Sidonius; and lastly Cyprianus, bishop of Toulon (*c.* 475—550), the author of a rendering of the Heptateuch in Latin verse. These last, 'while borrowing from the Roman models their language, their taste and their examples of primitive virtue, endeavour to create a reformed literature, not ashamed to draw its inspiration and topics from Hebrew and Christian tradition'[4]. In the same spirit Ambrose (d. 397), who was the son of a *Praefectus Galliarum* and was probably born at Trier, but completed his education at Rome, borrows the substance of large parts of his *Hexaëmeron* from Basil, and is specially fond of quoting Virgil; while his model in the *De Officiis Ministrorum* is obviously the *De Officiis* of Cicero. In his Latin hymns his precursor was Hilary of Poitiers, who was inspired by the hymns of the Greek Church.

To the age of Sidonius may be ascribed two treatises by a Gallic Grammarian bearing the same name as (and possibly identical with) his poetical friend, Consentius[5]. To the same age, but to other lands, may be assigned certain commentaries on the Grammar of Donatus, one of which (that of the Mauretanian Pompeius) was popular in the Middle Ages; also a glossary, with quotations from Plautus and Lucilius, by Luctatius Placidus, probably a native of Africa; and expositions of the *Eclogues* and *Georgics* of Virgil by Philargyrius and others[6]. About ten years after the death of Sidonius

**Grammarians and Commentators**

---

[1] Denk, p. 224. His own models include Virgil, and also Lucretius and Ovid.

[2] Denk, p. 191 (quoting *Hist. Litt.* iii 23).

[3] ed. Peiper (*Mon. Germ. Hist.* 1883); Teuffel, § 474, 5.

[4] J. E. B. Mayor, *l.c.*

[5] *De nomine et verbo*, and *De barbarismis et metaplasmis* (Keil, *Gr. Lat.* v 2, 338).

[6] Philargyrius in Thilo and Hagen's *Servius*, iii 2 (1902); Teuffel, § 472.

we find the consul of 494, Turcius Rufius Apronianus Asterius, who was the first to publish the *Carmen Paschale* of the Christian poet Sedulius, revising a text of Virgil in Rome, as is proved by a 'subscription' in the Medicean MS at the end of the *Eclogues*.

The 'subscription,' written out in full, runs as follows :—

'Turcius Rufius Apronianus Asterius, uir clarissimus et inlustris, ex comite domesticorum protectorum, ex comite priuatarum largitionum, ex praefecto urbi, patricius et consul ordinarius, legi et distincxi codicem fratris Macharii, uiri clarissimi, non mea fiducia set eius cui si et ad omnia sum deuotus arbitrio, XI Kalendas Maias Romae.

PUBLI            UERGILI            MARONIS

us
Quisque legis relegas felix, parcasque benigne,
    Si qua minus uacuus praeteriit animus;
Distinxi emendans, gratum mihi munus amici
    Suscipiens, operi sedulus incubui.

BUCOLICON        LIBER        EXPLICIT'[1].

Sidonius describes one of his friends as a happy Tityrus who had recovered the lands which he had lost to the barbarians[2]. Their ever-threatening incursions might well have tempted him in his latter days to say with Virgil :—*impius haec tam culta novalia miles habebit? barbarus has segetes?* But the 'barbarians' of his own day were soon to be superseded by victorious invaders, who were ultimately to change the name of Gaul into that of France. Only a few years after his death, the Franks under Clovis defeated Syagrius and his Belgians at Soissons (486); ten years later the defeat of the Alemanni[3] was immediately followed by the baptism of Clovis (496); and the subsequent victories over the Armoricans, Burgundians (500) and Visigoths (507) led to the practical termination of the Roman power and the establishment of the Merovingian dynasty in Gaul, a change formally ratified by Justinian in 536. Meanwhile Odoacer, who had put an end to the Western Empire in 476, was himself superseded in 493 by Theodoric, king of the Ostrogoths, who ruled over Italy till his death in 526. In the years covered

---

[1] Jahn, in *Sächs. Berichte*, 1851, p. 348 f; Teuffel, § 231, 9; *facsimile* in Ribbeck, *Vergili Opera*, iv 206. In the original, the first couplet is written by mistake at the end of the *subscriptio*, with marks denoting its proper place.

[2] *Ep.* viii 9, 5 l. 12.

[3] Assigned to 492 in Bury's *Later Roman Empire*, i 284.

by the reign of Theodoric, which may be regarded as a time
of transition between the Roman Age and the Middle Ages,
Scholarship is represented by the great names of Boëthius and
Cassiodorus in the West, and Priscian in the East.   These names
are reserved for the following chapter.

FROM CODEX LAURENTIANUS LXIII 19 (Cent. X) OF LIVY viii ULT.

(Chatelain's *Paléographie des Classiques Latins*, pl. cx.)  See p. 228.

# CHAPTER XIV.

## LATIN SCHOLARSHIP FROM 500 TO 530 A.D.

In the first quarter of the sixth century, which is the close of
the Roman period and the prelude of the Middle
Ages in the West, no name is more eminent in
Latin literature than that of Anicius Manlius Severinus Boëthius
(*c.* 480—524). He was the head of the noble Anician house,
which had been famous for six centuries; of his four names, the
second recalled a hero of the Roman Republic, and the third a
saintly hermit of Noricum[1]; while his wife was the daughter of the
senator Symmachus, the great-grandson of the orator of that
name[2]. A student from his early years and renowned for the
wide range of his learning, which included an intimate knowledge
of Greek, he formed the ambitious resolve of rendering and expounding in Latin the whole of Plato and Aristotle, with a view to
proving their substantial agreement with each other[3]. Though
only a part of this vast scheme was completed, his success in that
part was immediately recognised. One of his correspondents,
Ennodius, bishop of Pavia, assured him that 'in his hands the
torch of ancient learning shone with redoubled flame'[4]; while
Cassiodorus, writing about 507 A.D., as the secretary of Theodoric,
paid homage to his high services as an interpreter of the science
and philosophy of Greece:—'through him Pythagoras the musician, Ptolemy the astronomer, Nicomachus the arithmetician,
Euclid the geometer, Plato the theologian, Aristotle the logician,
Archimedes the mechanician, had learned to speak the Roman

---

[1] Bury, *Later Roman Empire*, i 285 f.   [2] p. 226.
[3] Boëthius on Aristotle, *De Interpr.* ii 2, 3 p. 79 Meiser (= Migne, lxiv
433).
[4] *Ep.* vii 13.

language"[1]. So varied were his accomplishments that he was requested by Theodoric to construct a sundial and a water-clock for the king of the Burgundians[2], to nominate a musician for the court of Clovis, 'the king of the Franks'[3], and to detect a fraud in the currency of the realm[4]. When he received these requests he already bore the designation of *illustris* and *patricius*. He became sole consul in 510, and, even in the year of his consulship, he was inspired by patriotic motives to continue to instruct his fellow-countrymen in the wisdom of Greece[5]. He reached the height of his fame in 522, when the consulship was held by his two sons, and their father pronounced in the Senate a panegyric on Theodoric. Not long afterwards, he and his father-in-law, Symmachus, were charged with the design of liberating Rome from the barbarian yoke. The grounds of the charge are obscure[6]; he was condemned by the Senate unheard; and the student of philosophy, who had unfortunately been prompted by Plato to take part in the affairs of the State, found himself compelled to bid farewell to the scene of his studies, leaving his library, with its walls adorned with ivory and glass[7], for the gloom of a prison between Pavia and Milan, where, after some delay, he was put to a cruel death in 524. His fate was shared in the following year by Symmachus; and, a year later, the dying hours of Theodoric are said to have been troubled with remorse for these deeds of wrong (526). In 722 a tomb was erected in his memory by Luitprand, king of the Lombards, in the same century he was venerated as a 'martyr', and this ancient local cult was formally approved in 1883[8].

[1] *Variae*, i 45 (Milman, *Hist. Lat. Christ.* i 413, ed. 1867).

[2] *Var.* i 45.          [3] ii 40.          [4] i 10.

[5] *Comm. in Ar. Categ.* ii (Migne, lxiv 201), Etsi nos curae officii consularis impediunt quominus in his studiis omne otium plenamque operam consumamus, pertinere tamen videtur hoc ad aliquam reipublicae curam,...cives instruere etc.

[6] His own account of the charge is given in *Phil. Cons.* i 4 *prose* 66, senatum dicimur salvum esse voluisse etc. The whole question is discussed in Hodgkin's *Italy and her Invaders*, III iv c. 12.

[7] *Phil. Cons.* i 5 *pr.* 20, bybliothecae comptos ebore ac vitro parietes.

[8] *Acta Sanctae Sedis*, xvi 302–3; the decree is headed:—'Servo Dei Severino Boëtio, philosopho martyri sancto nuncupato'.

Boëthius holds an intermediate position between the ancient
world and the Middle Ages. He was the last of the learned
Romans who understood the language and studied the literature
of Greece; and he was the first to interpret to the Middle Ages
the logical treatises of Aristotle. His *philosophical works*[1] include
a commentary on Porphyry's Introduction to the *Categories* as
translated by Victorinus; a translation of that Introduction by
Boëthius himself, with a still more extensive commentary; a
translation of the *Categories*, with a commentary in four books
(510 A.D.); a translation of the *De Interpretatione*, with a commentary in two, and another in six (507–9 A.D.); renderings of
the first and second *Analytics*, the *Sophistici Elenchi* and the
*Topics* of Aristotle; fragments of a commentary on the *Topics* of
Cicero, with several original works on division, definition, and on
various kinds of syllogisms. We also possess his treatise on
Arithmetic (which is highly esteemed), on Geometry (a Latin
transcript from parts of Euclid), and on Music (which is held to
have even retarded the scientific development of the art by re-
verting to the Pythagorean scale[2]).

In the history of Scholarship the main importance of Boëthius
lies in the fact that his philosophical works on Aristotle gave the
first impulse to a problem which continued to exercise the keenest
intellects among the schoolmen down to the end of the Middle
Ages. The first signal for the long-continued battle between the
Nominalists and the Realists was given by Boëthius. Porphyry,
in his 'Introduction to the Categories', had propounded three
questions: (1) 'Do *genera* and *species* subsist', *i.e.* really exist, 'or
do they consist in the simple conception of the subject?' (2) 'If
they subsist, are they corporeal or incorporeal?' (3) In either
case, 'are they separate from sensible objects, or do they reside
in these objects, forming something coexistent with them?'[3].
These questions Porphyry had set aside as requiring deeper

---

[1] Migne, lxiv 1—1215.

[2] Macfarren in *Enc. Brit.* quoted by Hodgkin, iii 529.

[3] *In Porph. Comment.* i 82 Migne (de generibus et speciebus), sive subsistant,
sive in solis nudis intellectibus posita sint, sive subsistentia corporalia sint an
incorporalia, et utrum separata a sensibilibus an in sensibilibus posita. Cp.
Hauréau, *Histoire de la Philosophie Scolastique*, i 47—52, with H. F. Stewart's
*Boëthius*, c. vii, esp. p. 248 f.

investigation. Boëthius in his first commentary on Porphyry, in which he had accepted the translation by Victorinus, stated that it was impossible to doubt the real existence of *genera* and *species*[1]; but, towards the close of the first book of his second commentary, founded on his own translation of Porphyry, we find him weighing and comparing the opinions of Plato and Aristotle:— 'according to Plato, *genera* and *species* are not merely conceptions, in so far as they are universals; they are real things existing apart from bodies; according to Aristotle, they are conceived as incorporeal, in so far as they are universals, but they have no real existence apart from the sensible world'[2]. He now inclines towards the opinion of Aristotle, whereas formerly he had preferred that of Plato; but, like Porphyry himself, he leaves the question undetermined, deeming it unbecoming to decide between Plato and Aristotle. A rhymer of the twelfth century, Godefroi de Saint Victor, has happily described Boëthius as remaining silent and undecided in this conflict of opinions:—

> 'Assidet Boethius, stupens de hac lite,
> Audiens quid hic et hic asserat perite,
> Et quid cui faveat non discernit rite,
> Nec praesumit solvere litem definite'[3].

But this vacillating judgement could not satisfy the keen intellects of the schoolmen, and we find the Aristotelian tradition resolutely maintained in the eighth century by Rabanus Maurus, and no less resolutely opposed in the ninth by Joannes Scotus, the champion of Plato and Realism, and the opponent of the vaguely Aristotelian teaching of Boëthius[4]. The conflict continued in various forms (in discussions whether universals are *realia ante rem*, or *nomina post rem*, or *realia in re*) down to the end of the Middle Ages.

The interests of Boëthius were primarily philosophical and secondarily theological; and his study of dialectic was combined with some attention to abstruse points of theoretical theology. The MSS credit him with five brief theological treatises[5], and the

---

[1] Migne, lxiv 19 C, si rerum veritatem atque integritatem perpendas, non est dubium quin verae (vere?) sint. Cp. F. D. Maurice, *Mediaeval Philosophy*, p. 11.          [2] Migne, lxiv 86 A; Stewart, p. 253.

[3] *Fons Philosophiae* (Hauréau, i 120).

[4] Hauréau, i 144, 173.          [5] Migne, lxiv 1247—1412.

question whether they can be ascribed to the same authorship as the *Philosophiae Consolatio* has long been debated. A fragment of Cassiodorus discovered in 1877 supports the genuineness of four of the five, including the *De Trinitate* addressed to his father-in-law Symmachus. All the four treatises appear to belong to his early life, and his interest in his theme is mainly dialectical[1]. While his translation of the *Categories* did not supersede 'St Augustine's' until the end of the tenth century[2], and his renderings of the *Analytics*, *Topics* and *Sophistici Elenchi* were apparently unknown until the twelfth[3], his theological treatises were familiar to Alcuin (*c.* 735—804) and to Hincmar, bishop of Rheims (850), to Joannes Scotus (d. *c.* 875) and to Remigius of Auxerre (d. 908)[4]. The fact that they were expounded by Gilbert de la Porrée, bishop of Poitiers from 1141, is another link connecting Boëthius with the Middle Ages.

The crowning work of his life, the *Philosophiae Consolatio*, was composed in prison not long before his death. It is in the form of a dialogue, and includes 39 short poems in 13 different metres, intermingled with prose after the Menippean manner, which had been applied to lighter themes by Varro, by Seneca and Petronius, and by Martianus Capella, but is here raised to a far higher dignity. The work begins with an elegiac poem inspired by the Muses who are described as actually present in the prisoner's cell, when the queenly form of Philosophia appears, and, bidding them depart, herself consoles the prisoner's sorrows. In the phraseology of the poetical passages Seneca is the author mainly imitated, but there are some reminiscences of Virgil and Horace, Ovid and Juvenal[5]. One of the poems[6] ends with the Platonic doctrine of reminiscence; another[7] is entirely inspired by Plato's *Timaeus*, which is repeatedly quoted in the prose passages, with obvious echoes of the *Gorgias*[8]. There are also

---

[1] H. Usener on the *Anecdoton Holderi* (Pauly-Wissowa, s.v. *Boëthius*, p. 600). Cp. Hodgkin's *Cassiodorus*, pp. 73—84, and Stewart, pp. 11—13, 108—159; and, on the other side, C. Jourdain's *Excursions Historiques*, p. 19 f. Ed. E. K. Rand, trans. H. F. Stewart (with *Cons. Phil.*) in Loeb Library, 1918.

[2] Hauréau, i 97.     [3] Prantl, *Gesch. der Logik*, ii 4.

[4] The Commentaries of the last two edited by E. K. Rand (1906).

[5] Pp. 228—231 ed. Peiper.     [6] iii 11.     [7] iii 9.     [8] iv 2 and 4.

indications of indebtedness to the lost *Protrepticus* of Aristotle[1];
and direct quotations from Aristotle's *Physics* and *De Caelo*, and
from the *De Divinatione* and the *Somnium Scipionis* of Cicero.
As an eclectic philosopher, the author also borrows from the
Stoics. Throughout the work there is no evidence of distinctively
Christian belief, but there are a few phrases of apparently Christian
origin. Neo-platonism and Christianity are respectively implied
in the mention of human destiny as influenced either *daemonum
variâ sollertiâ*, or *angelicâ virtute*[2]. The utterances of Philosophia
are described as *veri praevia luminis*[3]; the world is under the
beneficent rule of a *rerum bonus rector*[3]; the writer regards heaven
as his 'home', his *domus*[3] and his *patria*[4], and as the realm where
the sceptre is held by the *dominus regum* and all tyrants are
banished. Biblical reminiscences are suggested by passages such
as the description of the *summum bonum, quod regit cuncta
fortiter, suaviterque disponit*[5], by *vasa vilia et vasa pretiosa*[6] and
by *huc omnes pariter venite*[7]. But the absence of all reference to
the consolations of religion is much more remarkable than the
presence of a few phrases such as these. The author's belief in
prayer and in providence implies that his mind was tinged by
Christian influence, and is probably due to a Christian education.
In fact he could hardly have held public office in this age without
having been a Christian, at least by profession. He does not
oppose any Christian doctrine, but his attitude is that of a Theist
and not that of a Christian. He supplied the Middle Ages with
an eclectic manual of moral teaching severed from dogma and
endued with all the charm of exquisite verse blended with lucid
prose ; and, as the latest luminary of the ancient world, he remained
long in view, while the sources of the light which he reflected
were forgotten. The masterpiece which was his last legacy to
posterity was repeatedly translated, expounded and imitated in
the Middle Ages, and these translations were among the earliest

[1] Bywater in *Journ. Phil.* ii 59; Usener, *l.c.*, 51; 2 *pr.* 4, 38, and 4 *pr.*
6, 20 (Peiper).

[2] iv 6 *pr.* 51. But 'angels play a prominent part in the systems of Iamblichus and Proclus' (E. K. Rand, *Harvard Studies*, xv 18).

[3] iv 1.        [4] iv 1 and v 1.        [5] iii *pr.* 12, and *Wisdom*, viii 1.
[6] iv *pr.* 1.        [7] iii *m.* 10.

literary products of the vernacular languages of Europe,—English,
French, German, Italian and Spanish, among the translators
being names of no less note than king Alfred, Chaucer and
queen Elizabeth. It was also translated into Greek by Maximus
Planudes (d. 1310). The emperor Otho III, who died in 1002, a
hundred years after Alfred, placed in his library a bust of
Boëthius, which was celebrated by the best Latin poet of the age,
the future pope Silvester II[1]. Three centuries later, he is quoted
more than 20 times in the *Convito* and elsewhere by Dante[2],
whose best-known lines, *Nessun maggior dolore Che ricordarsi del
tempo felice Nella miseria*[3], are a reminiscence of Boëthius[4]:—*in
omni adversitate fortunae infelicissimum est genus infortunii fuisse
felicem*[5]. Dante places him in the Fourth Heaven among the
twelve 'living and victorious splendours' which are the souls
of men learned in Theology:—

> Here in the vision of all good rejoices
> That sainted soul, which unto all that hearken
> Makes manifest the treachery of the world.
> The body, whence that soul was reft, is lying
> Down in Cieldauro[6], but the soul from exile
> And martyr's pain hath come unto this peace[7].

Two hundred years after Dante, the book of Consolation composed by Boëthius in the 'Tower of Pavia' brought solace to
Sir Thomas More in the Tower of London. It has since won the
admiration of the elder Scaliger[8] and Casaubon, and has been
described as a 'golden volume' by Gibbon, who eulogises its

---

[1] Peiper's *Boëthius*, p. 40.

[2] Moore's *Studies*, i 282–8; R. Murari, *Dante e Boezio*, Bologna, 1905.

[3] *Inf.* v 121.                    [4] II iv 4.

[5] Boëthius had been anticipated by Synesius, *Ep.* 57, lxvi 1392 Migne,
συνεπιτίθεται δή μοι τῇ πικρᾷ τῶν παρόντων αἰσθήσει μνήμη τῶν παρελθόντων
ἀγαθῶν, ἐξ οἵων ἄρα ἐν οἵοις γεγόναμεν.

[6] The (now desecrated) Church of San Pietro of the *Golden Ceiling*, in
Pavia.

[7] *Paradiso*, x 124.

[8] *Poëtices liber vi*, Quae libuit ludere in poesi divina sane sunt; nihil illis
cultius, nihil gravius, neque densitas sententiarum venerem, neque acumen
abstulit candorem. Equidem censeo paucos cum illo comparari posse. Cp.
Blount's *Censura*, 746, and Migne, lxiii 573, where Lipsius and G. J. Vossius
are also quoted.

author as 'the last of the Romans whom Cato or Tully could
have acknowledged for their countryman'[1].

While the life of Boëthius was prematurely cut short by a
violent death, that of his contemporary Cassiodorus,
Cassiodorus
the skilful and subservient Minister of the Ostrogothic dynasty, was prolonged beyond the age of ninety. He
was born between 480 and 490 B.C. at Scyllacium (*Squillace*) in
southern Italy. His full name was Flavius Magnus Aurelius
Cassiodorus *Senator,* the last of these names alone being used by
himself in his official correspondence. *Cassiodorus* is there the
designation of his father, and is not applied to the son before the
eighth century, when it is found in Paulus Diaconus[2], and also in
Alcuin's list of the library at York :—' *Cassiodorus* item, Chryso-
stomus atque Ioannes'[3], a line supplying evidence against the
form *Cassiodorius,* which once found favour with certain scholars.
His father, as Praetorian Praefect in 500, conferred on him the
post of Consiliarius, or Assessor in his Court. A brilliant oration
in honour of Theodoric led to his being appointed Quaestor, and
thereby becoming, in accordance with the new meaning of that
office, the Latin interpreter of his sovereign's will and the drafter
of his despatches. The duties of the office are thus described in
the ' Formula of the Quaestorship' drawn up by himself on behalf

[1] Bury's Gibbon iv 197—204 (c. 39). Cp. also Hodgkin's *Italy and her
Invaders,* III iv c. 12; A. P. Stanley in Smith's *Dict.*; Hartmann in Pauly-
Wissowa; Teuffel, § 478; Ebert, i² 485—497; Zeller, *Phil. der Griechen,* iii (2)
927 f; *Boëthii Opera* in Migne, vols. lxiii, lxiv; *Comm. in Arist.* περὶ ἑρμηνείας,
ed. Meiser (1877–80); *Philosophiae Consolationis libri V,* ed. Peiper (1871);
Anglo-saxon trans. by king Alfred, ed. Sedgefield (1899 f); good English
trans. by H. R. James (1897) and W. V. Cooper (1902). On mediaeval trans-
lations, and on Boëthius in general, cp. H. F. Stewart's (Hulsean) *Essay* (1891).
On his relation to Christianity, Nitzsch (1860); Usener's *Holderi Anecdoton*
(1877); Hildebrand (1885); P. Giovanni Semeria, *Il Cristianesimo di Severino
Boezio rivendicato* (Rome, 1900); E. K. Rand, *On the Composition of Boëthius'
Cons. Phil.,* in *Harvard Studies,* xv (1904) 1—28; and, on his relation to the
Middle Ages, Hauréau, *Histoire de la Philosophie Scolastique,* i 112 f (1872);
Prantl's *Geschichte der Logik,* ii 4 ; Mullinger's *Univ. of Cambridge* i 27–9 ; and
H.O. Taylor's *Classical Heritage of the Middle Ages,* 51–6. Cp. Manitius, 22–36.

[2] *Hist. Langob.* i 25 (Justiniani) temporibus Cassiodorus apud urbem
Romam tam saeculari quam divina scientia claruit.

[3] Migne, ci 843.

of the king :—'the Quaestor has to learn our inmost thoughts, that he may utter them to our subjects...He has to be always ready for a sudden call, and must exercise the wonderful powers which, as Cicero has pointed out, are inherent in the art of an orator...He has to speak the King's words in the King's own presence'. He has to set forth every subject on which he has to treat, 'with suitable embellishments'. He has to receive and to answer the petitions of the Provinces[1]. The extant letters written by Cassiodorus as Quaestor extend from 507 to 511 A.D. Like his father, he became governor of Lucania and the region of the Bruttii, the land of his birth. He was sole consul in 514, published his *Chronicon* in 519, and, at the death of Theodoric in 526, was holding (probably not for the first time) the high position of *Magister Officiorum*, or 'head of the Civil Service', which he continued to hold as virtually Prime Minister to Theodoric's daughter, Amalasuentha, while she acted as regent for her son Athalaric. Though formally *Magister* only, he also acted as Quaestor :—*erat solus ad universa sufficiens*[2]; 'whenever eloquence was required, the case was always put into his hands'[3]. Between 526 and 533 he wrote his *History of the Goths*. From 533 to 536, under the three short-lived successors of Theodoric, he was Praetorian Praefect, as his father had been before him ; and we still possess the Letter in which he informs himself of his own elevation to that high office[4]. At the end of 537 he published, under the title of *Variae*, the vast collection of his official Letters. In 540, when Belisarius, the victorious general of the ungrateful Justinian, entered Ravenna, Cassiodorus had apparently already withdrawn from the world and had returned to spend the evening of his days on his ancestral estate among the Bruttii. He there wrote an account of his ancestors and a treatise *On the Soul*. He also founded two Monasteries, and, for the instruction of 'his monks', wrote an exceedingly lengthy *Commentary on the Psalms*; a comparatively short *Commentary on the Epistles*; an ecclesiastical history (from 306 to 439) called the *Historia Tripartita*, combining in a single narrative the translations of the Greek historians

---

[1] *Variae*, vi 5, p. 300 f of Hodgkin's (condensed translation of the) *Letters of Cassiodorus*.

[2] ix 25, 7.            [3] ix 24, 6.            [4] ix 24.

Socrates, Sozomen and Theodoret, executed at his request by Epiphanius; and an educational treatise entitled the *Institutiones Divinarum et Humanarum Lectionum* (begun about 543). In the 93rd year of his age his monks surprised him by asking for a treatise on spelling: he accordingly produced a compilation *De Orthographia*, borrowed from the works of twelve grammarians, beginning with Donatus and ending with Priscian. He survived the final fall of the Ostrogothic kingdom in 553, and even the invasion of Italy by Alboin, king of the Lombards, in 568; and died between 575 and 585, in the 96th year of his age[1].

The *Chronicon*[2] of Cassiodorus, which closes its abstract of the history of the world with 519 A.D., is mainly an inaccurate copy of Eusebius and Prosper, while towards its close it is unduly partial to the Goths. The charge of partiality has also been brought against his *Gothic History*, in which he had aimed at giving an air of legitimacy to the dominion of the Goths in Italy. It only survives in the abridgement by Iordanes[3]. The *Commentary on the Psalms* and the *Historia Tripartita* were widely known in the Middle Ages. His other works have points of contact with our present subject. His official Letters, arranged in twelve books, to which he gave the name of *Variae,* are undoubtedly addressed to a vast variety of persons, from the emperor Justinian down to the chief of the shorthand writers; but, so far from being marked by the corresponding variety of style which their writer claims for them[4], they are apt to strike a modern reader as almost uniformly inflated, florid, tawdry and unduly grandiloquent[5]. A certain degree of elevation of manner may fairly be expected of a minister who proudly recalls his protracted conversations with his king,—those *gloriosa colloquia*[6],

---

[1] Trithemius, *De Scriptoribus Ecclesiasticis*, 1494, f. 35, claruit temporibus Iustini senioris [518—527] et usque ad imperii Iustini iunioris paene finem [565—578], annos habens aetatis plus quam xcv anno domini DLXXV.

[2] Migne, lxix 1214-48; first edited by Cochlaeus, who dedicated it (in 1528) to Sir Thomas More, while he dedicated to Henry VIII the first ed. of some of the *Variae* (1529).

[3] Ed. Mommsen, 1882 (*Mon. Germ. Hist.*).          [4] *Praef.* § 15.

[5] Cp. R. W. Church, *Miscellaneous Essays*, p. 169 f, 191-8, ed. 1888; Bury, *Later Roman Empire*, ii 187.

[6] *Praef.* § 8.

in which, besides discoursing on affairs of State, the monarch
would inquire concerning the sayings of wise men of old[1]; but it
must be confessed that, in the Letters in general, the thought is
'often a piece of tinsel wrapped up in endless folds of tissue-
paper'[2]. He is specially fond of beginning and ending his letters
with 'wise saws', and interspersing them with 'modern instances'.
There is often a 'lack of humour'[2] in the incongruous way in
which documents otherwise not deficient in dignity are studded
with stories about birds, such as thrushes, doves and partridges,
storks, cranes and gulls, hawks, eagles and vultures; or beasts,
like the chameleon, the salamander and the elephant; or fishes,
for example, the sucking-fish and torpedo, the pike and the
dolphin, the *murex* with its purple dye, and the *echinus*, 'that
dainty of the deep'. 'The wandering birds love their own nests;
the beasts haste to their own lodgings in the brake; the vo-
luptuous fish, roaming the fields of ocean, returns to its own
well-known cavern: how much more should Rome be loved by
her children!'[3] This last is actually from a letter on the em-
bellishment of Rome. Elsewhere we read of the repair of its
walls, its temples and its aqueducts[4], and of the structure, as well
as the factions, of the *Circus Maximus*[5]. In the diploma for the
appointment of a public architect in Rome, some of the future
characteristics of Gothic architecture, the 'slender shafts of
shapely stone', compared by Sir Walter Scott to 'bundles of
lances which garlands had bound', seem almost to be anticipated
in the graceful phrases of the secretary of the Ostrogothic
dynasty:—*quid dicamus columnarum iunceam proceritatem? moles
illas sublimissimas fabricarum quasi quibusdam erectis hastilibus
contineri?*[6] Marbles and mosaics are ordered for Ravenna[7]; in a
letter of 537 we have the first historic notice of Venice[8]; we also
come across delightful descriptions of Como, of the baths of
Bormio, Abano and Baiae[9], and of the milk-cure for consumption
among the mountain-pastures south of the Bay of Naples[10]. We

---

[1] ix 24, 8.          [2] Hodgkin's *Cassiodorus*, p. 17.
[3] i 21 (p. 156 Hodgkin).          [4] i 25, 28; ii 34; iii 31.
[5] iii 51 etc.          [6] vii 15, 3, and Scott's *Lay*, ii 9 and 11.
[7] i 6; iii 9.          [8] xii 24.          [9] xi 14; x 29; ii 39; ix 6.
[10] xi 10.

read of a present of amber from the dwellers on the Baltic[1], and of the arrival at Rome of a water-finder from Africa[2]. An order for the supply of writing-material for the public offices transports us to the Nile, and prompts a discourse on the invention of paper, 'which has made eloquence possible'[3]. To the historian the great interest of the letters of 'this last of Roman statesmen'[4] lies in the way in which they illustrate in detail the working out of the broad principles of law and administration embodied in the Edict of Theodoric[5], and the promotion of peaceful, orderly and civilised relations between his Gothic and his Roman subjects[6]. They justify the ascription to the king of the high merits of wisdom[7] and toleration[8], and the noble resolve implied in the phrase:—*nos quibus cordi est in melius cuncta mutare*. They describe the Burgundians[9] and Pannonians[10] as barbarians in comparison with the Goths. In a document drawn up for the successor of Theodoric, which is interesting to scholars as well as to historians, a broad distinction is drawn between the barbarian kings and the legitimate Gothic lords of Italy. The subject is the increase of the salaries of grammarians.

'Grammar is the noble foundation of all literature, the glorious mother of eloquence......The grammatical art is not used by barbarous kings: it abides peculiarly with legitimate sovereigns. Other nations have arms: the lords of the Romans alone have eloquence...The Grammarian is a man to whom every hour unemployed is misery, and it is a shame that such a man should have to wait the caprice of a public functionary before he gets his pay'...Such men 'are the moulders of the style and character of our youth. Let them..., with their mind at ease about their subsistence, devote themselves with all their vigour to the teaching of liberal arts'[11].

Cassiodorus recommends Felix, a native of Gaul, for the consulship of 511 on literary as well as other grounds, because he is a *verborum novellus sator*[12]. He cannot refer to Rhegium without

---

[1] v 2.                    [2] iii 53.                              [3] xi 38.

[4] Ugo Balzani's *Early Chronicles of Italy*, p. 12.

[5] R. W. Church, *Miscellaneous Essays*, p. 158, ed. 1888; Hodgkin's *Italy and her Invaders*, iii 280.

[6] On *civilitas* (defined in Mommsen's Index as *status reipublicae iustus*) see Hodgkin's *Cassiodorus*, p. 20 and index.

[7] xi 1, 19 sapientia (*v.l.* patientia).

[8] ii 27, nemo cogitur ut credat invitus.                    [9] i 45 f.

[10] iii 23 f.           [11] ix 21, p. 406 Hodgkin.           [12] ii 3.

reminding the recipients of a State-document that the place is 'so
called from the Greek ῥήγνυμι'[1]. He oddly supposes that *Cir-
censes* stands for *circum* and *enses*[2]. Writing to one of his
subordinates in the law-court, the holder of the then very humble
office of *Cancellarius*, he makes the following interesting reference
to the origin of the name :—

> Remember your title, *Cancellarius*. Ensconced behind the lattice-work
> (*cancelli*) of your compartment, keeping guard behind those windowed doors,
> however studiously you may conceal yourself, it is inevitable that you should
> be the observed of all observers[3].

It is only once (in his Preface) that he alludes to Horace
(*nonumque prematur in annum*) ; but he has several reminiscences
or adaptations of Virgil, including the phrase often cited since in
speeches of eulogy :—*primo avulso non deficit alter aureus*[4]. He
quotes Cicero's rhetorical works alone[5], and Tacitus solely to
inform the dwellers on the Baltic of the supposed origin of
amber[6]. Throughout the Letters he exhibits (though in an
infinitely lower degree) 'the encyclopaedic culture of a Cicero or
the elder Pliny'[7].

In the last book of the *Variae*, he paints a pleasant picture of
the first city of the Bruttii, Scyllacium, the place of his birth. He
describes it as 'hanging like a cluster of grapes upon the hills,
basking in the brightness of the sun all the day long, yet cooled
by the breezes from the sea, and looking at her leisure on the
labours of the husbandmen in the cornfields, the vineyards, and
the olive-groves around her'[8]. Such was the region to which he
withdrew, after spending thirty years in the service of the Ostrogothic dynasty, there to devote himself for the rest of his long life
to a work destined to have a lasting influence on the learning of
the Middle Ages. He had already been corresponding with
Agapetus, the Pope of 535–6, on a scheme for founding by
subscription at Rome a theological school on the model of those

---

[1] xii 14.          [2] iii 51.          [3] xi 6, pp. 112, 463 Hodgkin.

[4] *Var.* v 4; cp. ii 40, 7; v 21, 42 § 11, and xii 14 (*intuba* is not *amara*
among the Bruttii).

[5] *De Or.* i 30; *Brutus* 46.

[6] *Germ.* 45 (*Var.* v 2, 'quidam Cornelius').

[7] R. W. Church, *l.c.*, p. 160.          [8] xii 15, p. 8 Hodgkin.

of Alexandria and Nisibis[1]. Agapetus selected a house on the
Caelian hill, afterwards connected with the Church of San Gregorio
Magno, and there built a library:—a line from an inscription, seen
in the ninth century by a pilgrim from Einsiedeln, says of this
Pope:—*codicibus pulchrum condidit arte locum*[2]. The wider
scheme for a theological school at Rome had been rendered
impossible by the conflicts which arose on the invasion of Italy
by Belisarius; but Cassiodorus was now able to carry out his plan
on a suitable site in the region of his birth. While he was still
Praetorian Praefect, he had formed a series of *vivaria*, or preserves
for fishes, at the foot of the Moscian mount overlooking the bay
of Squillace[3]; and here he founded one of his two monasteries,
which (like the modern College of *Fishponds* near Bristol) obtained
from these *vivaria* the name of the *monasterium Vivariense*[4].
We read of its well-watered gardens, and its baths for the sick by
the banks of the neighbouring stream of Pellena[5], while 'at the
foot of the hills and above the sand of the sea' there was a
'fountain of Arethusa', fringed with a crown of rustling reeds,
making a green and pleasant place all round it[6]. For those who
preferred a more unbroken solitude, there was another monastery,
or rather hermitage, in the 'charming seclusion of the Castle Hill',
a lonely spot surrounded by ancient walls, possibly of some
deserted fort[7]. Such are the descriptive touches preserved mainly
in his *Institutiones*, a partly theological and partly encyclopaedic
work which he composed for the benefit of 'his monks' between
543 and 555[8]. In the first part of this work, bearing the separate

[1] *Inst. Praef.* Migne lxx 1105 f; cp. Hodgkin, p. 56; Boissier, *Fin du
Paganisme*, i 216[3].

[2] Einsiedeln MS (De Rossi, quoted in J. W. Clark's *Care of Books*, p. 44).

[3] *Var.* xii 15, 14.

[4] Mr A. J. Evans places the Roman *Scyllacium* at Roccella, 6 miles N.E.
of the modern *Squillace*, and the monastery between *Squillace* and the shore,
Virgil's *navifragum Scylaceum* (Hodgkin, pp. 9, 68—72). *Roccella* is described
as 'a little world of scenic splendour' and is the subject of a fine illustration in
Lear's *Calabria*, p. 104.

[5] *Inst.* i 29.                        [6] *Var.* viii 32 (p. 380 Hodgkin).

[7] *Inst.* i 29, montis Castelli secreta suavia...muris pristinis ambientibus
inclusa.

[8] Mommsen's Pref. to *Variae*, p. xi. A later revision is implied in the
reference in c. 17 to the end of Justinian's reign (565).

title *De Institutione Divinarum Litterarum*, he describes the contents of the nine *codices* which made up the Old and New Testaments; warns his monks against impairing the purity of the sacred text by merely plausible emendations; only those who have attained the highest learning in sacred and secular literature could be allowed to correct the sacred texts. Revisers of other texts must study the works of the ancients, *libros priscorum*, and correct those texts with the aid of those who are masters in secular literature[1]. He notices the Christian historians, and some of the principal Fathers, incidentally mentioning as a colleague in his literary labours the monk Dionysius (Exiguus), who settled the date of our present era, the earliest use of which occurs in the year 562 A.D.[2] He urges his monks to cultivate learning, not however as an end in itself, but as a means towards the better knowledge of the Scriptures[3]. After dealing with secular literature and recommending the study of the Classics, he exhorts those of his readers, who have no call towards literary work, to spend their efforts on agriculture and gardening; and in this connexion to read the ancient authors on these subjects:— Gargilius Martialis, Columella and Aemilianus Macer, manuscripts of which he had left for their perusal[4]. It has been surmised that, but for Cassiodorus, the treatise of Cato *De Re Rustica* would have perished[5]; but it may be remarked that he does not actually mention that work. He spent large sums on the purchase of MSS from northern Africa and other parts of the world[6], and encouraged his monks to copy them with care. He mentions a certain division of the books of the Bible found *in codice grandiore littera grandiore (clariore?) conscripto* containing Jerome's version. This MS he had presumably brought from Ravenna, and it has been conjectured that part of it survives in the first and oldest quaternion of the *codex Amiatinus* of the Vulgate, now in the Laurentian Library in Florence. The frontispiece of the latter represents Ezra writing the Law, and the press with open doors

[1] 1130 B, ubicumque paragrammata in disertis hominibus reperta fuerint, intrepidus vitiosa recorrigat.

[2] *Computus Paschalis* in Migne, lxix 1249, first ascribed to Cassiodorus by Pithoeus.

[3] *Inst.* i 28, p. 1142 A—B.

[4] *ib.* p. 1142-3.

[5] Norden's *Kunstprosa*, p. 664.

[6] *Inst.* i c. 8.

in the background has a general resemblance to that containing the four Gospels among the mosaics of the mausoleum of Galla Placidia at Ravenna (440)[1]. The books in the monastic library of Cassiodorus were preserved in presses (*armaria*), nine of which contained the Scriptures, and works bearing on their study, the few Greek MSS being in the eighth *armarium*. The arrangement in general was not by authors but by subjects. The biographical works of St Jerome and Gennadius were combined in a single *codex*, and similarly with certain rhetorical works of Cicero, Quintilian and Fortunatianus[2].

He is specially interested in those of his monks who are careful copyists. In describing the *scriptorium* he dwells on the special privileges of the *antiquarius*, who, 'by copying the divine precepts, spreads them far and wide, enjoying the glorious privilege of silently preaching salvation to mortals by means of the hand alone, and thus foiling with pen and ink the temptations of the devil; every word of the Lord written by the copyist is a wound inflicted on Satan'[3]. The art of the copyist had been practised by the younger monks alone in the monastery of St Martin's at Tours[4]; and, in the rules laid down by Ferreolus in Gaul, *c.* 550 A.D., reading and copying were considered suitable occupations for monks who were too weak for severer work[5]. But these arts receive a far stronger sanction from Cassiodorus. He himself set the example of making a careful copy of the Psalms, the Prophets and the Epistles[6].

Some precepts of spelling are included in the *Institutiones*, from which it appears that Cassiodorus approved of *in* in composition being assimilated to the following consonant for the sake of euphony[7]. For the same reason he prefers *quicquam* to *quidquam*.

---

[1] H. J. White, in *Studia Biblica*, 1890, ii 273—308; J. W. Clark's *Care of Books*, frontispiece, and pp. 39—41.

[2] i 8, 17; ii 2. Franz, *Cass.* pp. 80—92, gives a list of books either certainly or probably included in the Library.

[3] *Inst.* i 30.     [4] Sulp. Severus, *Vita S. Martini*, c. 7.

[5] c. 28, *paginam pingat digito*, qui terram non praescribit aratro (Franz, *Cass.* p. 56).     [6] *Praef.* p. 1109 B.

[7] i 15 (p. 1129 A, Migne), multa etiam respectu euphoniae propter subsequentes litteras probabiliter immutamus, ut *illuminatio, irrisio, immutabilis, impius, improbus.*

To avoid mistakes the copyist must read the works of ancient authors on orthography, Velius Longus, Curtius Valerianus, Papyrianus, 'Adamantius Martyrius'[1] on V and B, Eutyches on the rough breathing, and Phocas on genders. These works he had himself collected to the best of his ability. He adds that biblical MSS should be bound in covers worthy of their contents, and that he had supplied a pattern volume, including specimens of different kinds of binding. For use by night he had provided lamps so skilfully contrived that they never ran short of oil and never needed trimming, while he had also constructed a sundial for bright days and a water-clock for the night and for days that were overcast[2].

In the ninth century, the first part of the *Institutiones* was imitated by Rabanus Maurus in his treatise *De Institutione Clericorum*, and was used as a text-book at the monastery of Reichenau[3]. In the second part, which is a brief manual *De Artibus ac Disciplinis Liberalium Litterarum*[4], Cassiodorus gives a succinct account of the seven liberal arts, half the work being devoted to Dialectic alone, and the rest about equally divided between the six other arts, with a somewhat fuller treatment of Rhetoric in particular. The allegory of Martianus Capella on the liberal arts is not mentioned by Cassiodorus, but it can hardly be doubted that, by emphasising the sanctity of the number 'seven', by giving a new meaning to the saying that 'Wisdom hath builded her house, she hath hewn out her seven pillars', and by connecting the seven arts with the education of his monks, he unconsciously increased the popularity of that pagan work[5]. The short chapter on Music mentions a work by Albinus, which the author remembers reading in Rome, but it had possibly been lost, *gentili incursione sublatus*. The long chapter on Dialectic includes

---

[1] Teuffel, § 472, 6.                    [2] i 30.

[3] Franz, *Cass.* p. 124.                [4] Migne, lxx 1150—1213.

[5] H. Parker, in *Historical Review*, v 456. Cp. Hauréau, *Hist. de la Phil. Scol.* i 25, and Mariétan, *Problème de la Classification des Sciences* (Thèse de Fribourg en Suisse), 1901, pp. 61, 83 (Roger, *Ausone à Alcuin*, 181 n. 3). 'The old pagan learning was never destroyed, notwithstanding the complete victory of Christianity'; and Cassiodorus was one of those who, 'by Christianizing it to a certain extent, made it more popular to later generations' Ugo Balzani, p. 5).

an abstract of a large part of the *Organon* of Aristotle, in the
course of which the reader is referred to Porphyry's *Introduction*,
and to the six books of the commentary on the *De Interpretatione*
by Boëthius (*viro magnifico*), a MS of which is left to the monks.
The quaint saying that Aristotle, in writing the *De Interpretatione*,
*calamum in mente tingebat*, is here quoted. A chapter on logical
fallacies is added, besides some matter more closely connected
with Rhetoric than Dialectic. At the close of this part of the
work, Plato and Aristotle are oddly described as *opinabiles
magistri saecularium litterarum*, a phrase which, considering the
author's powers of rhetorical expression, is faint praise indeed.
It may be noticed, however, that the highly artificial style of the
*Variae* is somewhat simplified in the *Institutiones*, where (in the
author's own language) *plus utilitatis invenies quam decoris*[1].
Erasmus, while fully appreciating the high character and the
piety of Cassiodorus, does not approve of his attempting in
the *Institutiones* to cover the whole field of sacred and secular
learning[2]. But the work was doubtless useful to the unlearned
monks for whom it was mainly intended. The chapter on
Rhetoric was imitated by Isidore of Seville, and by Alcuin, who
also owes much to that on Dialectic[3].

The treatise *De Orthographia*[4] gives rules of spelling to enable
the copyist to avoid certain common mistakes. The four chapters
extracted from the treatise of 'Adamantius Martyrius' on V and
B show that those letters must have been constantly confounded
in the pronunciation of imperfectly educated persons, who drew
little (if any) distinction between *vivere* and *bibere*[5]. Among the
lost works of Cassiodorus were some compilations from Donatus
and Sacerdos[6]. By his careful attention to the training of
copyists he did much towards preventing the earlier Latin
literature from perishing. He knew Greek, but preferred to
read Greek authors in Latin translations[7]. He caused a Latin

---

[1] p. 1240 C.          [2] *Ep.* 1038.          [3] Franz, *Cass.* p. 125.
[4] Keil, *Gram. Lat.* vii 127.
[5] Migne, p. 1261 C, *bibo*...a vita per v, a potu per b scribendum est.
Mistakes, such as *vibamus* for *bibamus*, and *fobeas* for *foveas*, actually occur
in MSS of the Vulgate (Franz, *Cass.* p. 61).          [6] p. 1123 D.
[7] *Praef.* 1108 A, dulcius enim ab unoquoque suscipitur, quod patrio sermone
narratur.

rendering to be made of the *Jewish Antiquities* of Josephus[1].
St Jerome in his cell at Bethlehem had set the first great example
of isolated literary labour.   Cassiodorus appears to have been the
first to have applied this principle in a wider and more systematic
manner to the organisation of the convent.   As has been well
observed by Dr Hodgkin, 'the great merit of Cassiodorus, that
which shows his deep insight into the needs of his age and
entitles him to the eternal gratitude of Europe, was his determination to utilise the vast leisure of the convent for the preservation
of Divine and human learning, and for its transmission to later
ages'.   Similarly it has been remarked by Prof. W. Ramsay that
'the benefit derived from his precepts and example was by no
means confined to the establishment over which he presided, nor
to the epoch when he flourished.   The same system was gradually
introduced into similar institutions, the transcription of ancient
works became one of the regular and stated occupations of the
monastic life, and thus, in all probability, we are indirectly
indebted to Cassiodorus for the preservation of a large proportion
of the most precious relics of ancient genius'[2].   In fact it is
generally agreed that the civilisation of subsequent centuries, and,
in particular, the institution of monastic libraries and monastic
schools, where the light of learning continued to shine in the
'Dark Ages', owed much to the prescience of Cassiodorus[3].

Boëthius and Cassiodorus have been happily described as the
'great twin-brethren', and have been compared to a 'double-
headed Janus'[4].   While the gaze of Boëthius looks back on the
declining day of the old classical world, that of Cassiodorus looks
forward to the dawn of the Christian Middle Ages; but both
alike, in their different ways, prevented the tradition of a great
past from being overwhelmed by the storms of barbarism.
Cassiodorus, who had devoted the first half of his life to Politics,
and the second to Religion, stands in more than one sense on the
confines of two worlds, the Roman and the Teutonic, the Ancient

---

[1]  *Inst.* i 17.

[2]  W. Ramsay in Smith's *Dict. Biogr.* s.v.

[3]  Cp. Ebert, i 500[2], and Norden's *Kunstprosa*, p. 663—5; also A. Olleris,
*Cassidore conservateur des livres de l'antiquité*, 1841.

[4]  Ebert, i 486[2], *einen Januskopf bildet dieses Dioskurenpaar.*

and the Modern. It has even been observed that the very word *modernus* is first used with any frequency by Cassiodorus[1].

Apart from the *Institutiones* he does not appear to have drawn up any written Rule for the guidance of his monks, and we know nothing of the fortunes of his monastery after the death of the founder. He recommends his monks to read the Institutes of Cassian, the founder of Western Monasticism; while he warns them against that writer's views on free will[2]. Of Benedict and the Benedictine Rule we have no mention in his extant writings. His precepts are indeed consistent with that Rule, but there is nothing to show that they were suggested by it. He is first claimed as a Benedictine by Trithemius (d. 1516)[3], but the silence of Cassiodorus is considered by Baronius[4] to be a sufficient reason for rejecting this claim, and Baronius is not really refuted by Garet in his lengthy dissertation on this subject (1679)[5]. The Benedictine monastery on Monte Cassino was founded in 529, more than ten years before that of Cassiodorus on the bay of Squillace; but it was the latter which set the first example of that devotion to literary labour which afterwards became one of the highest distinctions of the Benedictine order[6].

Benedict, who belonged to the same Anician *gens* as Boëthius,
**Benedict** was born at Nursia, north of the old Sabine region, in 480, the year (either actually or approximately) of the birth of Boëthius and Cassiodorus. Among those whom he gathered round him, when, *despectis litterarum studiis*[7], he had

---

[1] Hodgkin, pp. 1—2. Cp. *Var.* iv 45 (Symmachus) antiquorum diligentissimus imitator, modernorum nobilissimus institutor; iii 5, 3, modernis saeculis moribus ornabatur antiquis; 8, 1; 31, 4; viii 14, 2; 25, 1; xi 1, 19. The word is found in Cassiodorus's slightly older contemporary, Ennodius, lxiii 54 A, 232 B, and in a diploma of 499 (Wölfflin, *Rhein. Mus.* xxxvii 92).

[2] *Inst.* i 29.        [3] *De viris illustribus ord. Ben.* i c. 6 and iii c. 7.

[4] *Annales*, ad ann. 494 (no. 77).        [5] Migne, lxix 483—496.

[6] Cassiodori *Opera* in Migne, lxix, lxx; *Variae*, ed. Mommsen (in *Mon. Hist. Germ.*) 1894; Bury's Gibbon, iv 180 f, 522; Hodgkin's *Italy and her Invaders*, 1885, iii 274—7, 310—328, and *Letters of Cassiodorus*, 1886, with the literature there quoted, esp. A. Franz, *M. Aur. Cassiodorus Senator*, pp. 137, 1872, and R. W. Church, in *Ch. Quarterly*, 1880 (*Misc. Essays*, 1888, pp. 155—204); also V. Mortet, in *Revue de Philologie*, 1900, 1903 (1904); Roger, 175—187; and Ker's *Dark Ages*, 117—9. Cp. Traube, *Vorlesungen*, i 106, ii 127—131, 145; Manitius, 36—52.

[7] Gregorii *Dialogi*, ii *init.*

fled from the delights and the dangers of Rome to the solitudes
near Subiaco, was the young Roman noble, Maurus, afterwards
known as St Maur.    After a time he went some 50 miles south-
ward to Monte Cassino, where a temple of Apollo was still
standing with a sacred grove which was a centre of superstition
among the surrounding peasants.    The people were persuaded to
destroy the altar and burn the grove[1]; and higher up the hill
the last stronghold of paganism was superseded in 529 by a
monastery, which, notwithstanding many changes, still looks
down from a height of more than 1700 feet on a wild mountain
district to the north, on the rocky summits of the Abruzzi to the
east, and to the west and south on the long reaches of the silent
stream that winds through the broad valley of the Garigliano,—
the *rura, quae Liris quieta mordet aqua taciturnus amnis*.    Near
the foot of the hill were the ruins of a Roman amphitheatre, and
hard by was the site of the villa of 'that pagan Benedictine'[2],
Varro.    The three virtues inculcated in the Benedictine discipline
were silence in solitude and seclusion, and humility and obedience;
the three occupations of life which were enjoined, the worship of
God, reading, and manual labour.    Chapter 48 of the 'Rule of
St Benedict' after declaring that 'idleness is the enemy of the
soul', prescribes manual labour, combined with the setting apart
of certain hours (nearly two hours before noon in summer, and
until 8 or 9 a.m. in other parts of the year) for sacred reading,
*lectio divina*.    During Lent each of the monks is to receive a
book from the library and to read it straight through.    One of
the monks is also chosen in each week to read aloud to the
rest during their meals[3].    No one is to presume to have either
a book or tablets, or even a pen (*graffium*) of his own[4].    Thus
the learned labours of the Benedictines were no part of the
original requirements laid down by the founder of their order.

[1] Gregorii *Dialogi*, ii 8 ; cp. Dante, *Paradiso*, xxii, 37—45.

[2] Montalembert, *Monks of the West*, i 434, ed. 1896.

[3] c. 38.

[4] c. 33.   *Benedicti Regula Monachorum*, ed Wölfflin, 1895 ; and in his
article in *Archiv*, ix (1896) 493 ; Traube's *Textgeschichte*, 1898.  Cp. Hallam's
*Lit. of Europe*, i 4 ; Harnack's *Mönchtum*, 42[4]; Norden, p. 665, note ; Grütz-
macher, *Die Bedeutung Benedikts von Nursia* ; Roger, 171—5 ; Manitius, 88—
91 ; Cuthbert Butler, *Benedictine Monachism*, pp. 23, 160—183, 332—352.

Before the death of the founder (*c.* 542), his faithful disciple, Maurus, had crossed the Alps; had been welcomed at Orleans; and at Glanfeuil on the Loire, near Angers, had founded the first Benedictine monastery in France, on the site afterwards known as St Maur-sur-Loire[1]. The name of St Maur still survives in the English surname of Seymour; and it is associated for ever with the learned labours of the French Benedictines of the 'Congregation of St Maur', whose headquarters from 1630 to the French Revolution were the Abbey of Saint-Germain-des-Prés in the south of Paris[2].

It is said that, late in life, Benedict foresaw that the lofty buildings of Monte Cassino would fall in ruins before the ravages of the spoiler[3], a foreboding fulfilled by the Lombards in 583, and the Saracens in 857. Towards the end of 542 he was visited by Totila, king of the Goths, who came not to destroy the fabric but to consult its founder, and departed impressed with the lessons of humanity which he had learnt from Benedict[4]. It is also said that the closing years of the founder's life were brightened with a vision of the splendid future which awaited his Order. Such at least was the interpretation which tradition assigned to the story of his once seeing the darkness of the dawn suddenly dispelled by a light more dazzling than that of day[5]. The fulfilment of his hopes, so far as it is connected with our immediate subject, will attract our attention at later points in this work.

The last of the grammarians from whom Cassiodorus compiled his treatise *De Orthographia* was Priscian, *qui nostro tempore Constantinopoli doctor fuit*[6]. Almost all that is further known of his date is that he composed (about 512) a poetic panegyric on Anastasius, emperor of the East from 491 to 518[7]; and that a transcript of his great work on grammar was completed at Constantinople by one of his pupils, the

Priscian

---

[1] Mabillon's *Acta Sanctorum Ordinis S. Benedicti*, i 290.

[2] Plans showing site of library in J. W. Clark's *Care of Books*, pp. 115 f.

[3] Gregorii *Dialogi*, ii 17 (with Preface of Mabillon, *l.c.*).

[4] *ib.* ii 15; Mrs Jameson's *Monastic Orders*, i 7—13, and Milman's *Lat. Christianity*, ii 80—96. Cp. Hodgkin's *Italy and her Invaders*, iv 462—498.

[5] Gregorii *Dialogi*, ii 34; Montalembert, *l.c.*, i 435 f.

[6] c. 12.                    [7] Bährens, *Poët. Lat. Min.* v 264.

calligrapher Theodorus, in 526–7[1]. Three of his minor works,
(1) on numerals, weights, and measures, (2) on the metres of
Terence, and (3) some rhetorical exercises, are almost entirely
derived from Greek originals. They were dedicated to Symmachus (possibly the consul of 485), who was known to the
author by his high repute before he met him (probably on some
occasion, otherwise unknown, when Symmachus visited Constantinople). Priscian was a native of Caesarea in Mauretania, and
there is no proof that he ever lived in Rome. His *Grammar* is
divided into XVIII books; I—XVI on Accidence; XVII and XVIII
on Syntax. In the dedication he states that he proposes to
translate from the Greek of Apollonius (Dyscolus) and Herodian;
but that his work would be of small extent compared with the
*spatiosa volumina* of the former and the *pelagus* of the latter. He
follows Apollonius very closely, as may be seen from those
portions of his work in which the corresponding books of
Apollonius are almost completely preserved, viz. the parts on the
Pronoun, Adverb, and Conjunction, and on Syntax. Most of
Priscian's Latin learning comes from Flavius Caper; much is also
due to Charisius, Diomedes, Donatus (with Servius on Donatus),
and Probus; and to an earlier list of grammatical examples from
Cicero. The work is remarkably rich in quotations from Cicero
and Sallust; also from Plautus, Terence, Virgil, Horace, Ovid,
Lucan, Persius, Statius and Juvenal. There are fewer from Cato,
and from Accius, Ennius and Lucretius; very few from Catullus
and Propertius, Caesar, and the elder Pliny; and none from
Tibullus or Tacitus. The Greek examples are mainly from
Homer, Plato, Isocrates and Demosthenes. His own style is
very prolix, and he seems to have little consciousness of the
importance of the order of words in Latin prose. His fame in
after times was great. His pupil, Eutyches, calls him ʻRomanae
lumen facundiae' and ʻcommunis...hominum praeceptor'. A MS
of Priscian had reached England in the life of Aldhelm (d. 709).
He is quoted by Bede, and is described as ʻLatinae eloquentiae

---

[1] ...scripsi artem Prisciani eloquentissimi grammatici doctoris mei manu
mea in urbe Roma (*v.l.* Romana) Constantinopoli...Olybrio v. c. consule, *i.e.*
Mavortio Olybrio, cons. 526–7 (Jahn, *Sächs. Berichte*, 1851, p. 354).

decus' by Alcuin, who mentions his name in the list of the library at York. He is copied in a grammatical treatise by Alcuin's pupil, Rabanus Maurus, and minutely studied by the latter's pupil, Servatus Lupus (d. 862). His grammar was one of the great text-books of the Middle Ages and is accordingly still represented by more than 1000 MSS. Early in the Renaissance, in a poem on the reported death of Petrarch, Priscian appears as the foremost representative of Grammar (1343)[1]; and, after the middle of the fourteenth century, it was either Priscian or Donatus whose portrait was placed beneath the personification of Grammar among the Seven Earthly Sciences in the chapter-house (afterwards called the Spanish chapel) of Santa Maria Novella at Florence, while among the representatives of the Seven Heavenly Sciences, the central figure has sometimes been identified as Boëthius (c. 1355).

It was only two years after Boëthius was consul in Rome (510) that Priscian eulogised an emperor of the East in Constantinople (512). Between these dates is the death of Clovis (511), for whom Boëthius had some seven or eight years previously selected a skilled harper at the request of Theodoric's minister, Cassiodorus. Two years after the death of Boëthius (524) falls the death of Theodoric (526), and within a year of that event the copy of Priscian's Grammar, from which all our extant MSS are ultimately descended, was being transcribed in Constantinople. The close of the Roman age is marked by the death of Boëthius; and the fact that the great work of Priscian was copied by his pupil, not in Rome, but in Constantinople, foreshadows the beginning of the Byzantine age of scholarship. Two years after the archetype of Priscian had been transcribed, the Schools of Athens were closed in the early part of the reign of Justinian, probably at the very time when in the West the monastery of Monte Cassino was rising above the ruins of the altar of Apollo. As we pass in fancy from the ruins of Apollo's altar to the Castle Hill that looks down on the Vivarian monastery and the

---

[1] Antonio Beccaria, *Grammatica era prima in questo pianto | E con lei Prisciano* (Priscian, I xxxi Hertz).—Best ed. of Priscian, that of Hertz (with minor works by Keil), 1855-9. Cp. Teuffel, § 481; and Jeep's *Redetheile*, 89—97.

bay of Squillace, and think of Cassiodorus spending the last thirty-three years of his life among his monks, training them to become careful copyists, and closing the latest work of his long life by making extracts for their benefit from the pages of Priscian, we feel that we have left the Roman age behind us, and that we are already standing within the confines of the Middle Ages.

abol enet· Naturerzoe
utquaeprimumfecer
creanetquiaperenno
montuautfernpenin

FROM THE BIBLICAL COMMENTARY OF MONTE CASSINO
written before 569 B.C.

(E. M. Thompson's *Palaeography*, p. 202.)

# BOOK IV

## *GREEK SCHOLARSHIP IN THE ROMAN AGE*

---

ὁ καθ᾽ ἡμᾶς χρόνος...ἀπέδωκε τῇ μὲν ἀρχαίᾳ καὶ σώφρονι ῥητορικῇ τὴν δικαίαν τιμήν, ἣν καὶ πρότερον εἶχε, καλῶς ἀπολαβεῖν·...αἰτία δ᾽ οἶμαι καὶ ἀρχὴ τῆς τοσαύτης μεταβολῆς ἐγένετο ἡ πάντων κρατοῦσα Ῥώμη.

Dionysius Halicarnassensis, *De Oratoribus Antiquis*, c. 2—3.

ἡμεῖς οὐ πρὸς τὰ διημαρτημένα ἀφορῶμεν, ἀλλὰ πρὸς τὰ δοκιμώτατα τῶν ἀρχαίων.

Phrynichus, *Eclogae Dedicatio.*

| A.D. | | | | | |
|---|---|---|---|---|---|
| 14 Tiberius | | *c.* 24 d. Strabo | Theodorus of Gadara | Theon Seleucus | |
| 37 Caligula | Philippus of Thessalonica | | | Apion / Heliodorus / 40 ? Anonymus περὶ ὕψους | 40 Philo Judaeus (b. 20 B.C.) visi Rome |
| 41 Claudius | | | | | |
| 54 Nero | | | | 50 Pamphilus / Pamphila / Erotianus | |
| | Lucillius | 63 Josephus 37—*c.* 98 | | | |
| 68 Galba | | | | | |
| 69 Otho | | | | | |
| 69 Vitellius | | | | | |
| 69 Vespasian | | | 75 Nicetes of Smyrna | Epaphroditus | |
| 79 Titus | | Plutarch *c.* 46—*c.* 125 | Dio Chrysostom *c.* 40—*c.* 114 | | |
| 81 Domitian | | | | | Dioscorides |
| 96 Nerva | | | | Demetrius περὶ ἑρμηνείας | |
| 98 Trajan | | | | | |
| **100** | | | | | |
| 117 Hadrian | Dionysius Periegetes / Mesomedes | Herenn. Philon *c.* 64—*c.* 141 / Phlegon / Aelian, *Tacticus* / Arrian *fl.* 130—171 | Favorinus / Alexander / Aelius Theon | 110 Aspasius / Ael. Dionysius / Nicanor / Apollonius Dyscolus | |
| 138 Antoninus Pius | | | 143 Herodes Atticus 103—179 | | 151 Albinus / Lucian *c.* 125—*c.* 192 / Alciphron |
| | | 160 Appian | | | |
| 161 M. Aurelius (161-9 L. Verus) | 169 Oppian, *Halieutica* | 161-9 Polyaenus, *Poliorcetica* | | Herodian Pausanias, *Atticista* | Galen 131—201 |
| 180 Commodus | | Ptolemaeus | Demetrius | Hephaestion | 175 Atticus Numenius |
| 193 Pertinax | | 173 Pausanias | 176 Aristides | Harpocration | Sextus Empiricus |
| 193 Julianus | Babrius | | 129—*c.* 189 Maximus Tyrius | 180 Phrynichus | Clemens Alexandrinus *c.* 160—*c.* 215 |
| 193 Septimius Severus | | | Hermogenes | 180 Pollux / Alexander Aphrodisiensis | 193 Athenaeus |
| **200** | | | | | |
| 211 Caracalla | 211 Pseudo-Oppian, *Cynegetica* | 211-21 Dion Cassius *c.* 155—230-40 | 215 Philostratus I, *Lives of the Sophists*, b. *c.* 170, *fl.* 215-45 | 207 Pseudo-Dositheus | Xenophon Eph Diogenes Laertius (Ammonius Saccas) |
| 217 Macrinus | | | | | |
| 218 Elagabalus | | | 235 Apsines *c.* 190—250 | | 203 Origen 185—254 |
| 222 Alexander Severus | | 221 Julius Africanus | 235 Philostratus II, *Heroicus* and earlier *Eikones*, b. *c.* 190 | | 222 Aelian *c.* 170—230 |
| 235 Maximin | | | | | |
| 238 Gordian I,II | | | | | |
| 238 { Pupienus { Balbinus | | | | | |
| 238 Gordian III | | | | | |
| 244 Philippus | | 250 Herodian *c.* 165—*c.* 255 | 260 Minucianus | | 244 Plotinus 204—270 |
| 249 Decius | | | | | |
| 251 Gallus | | | | | |
| 253 Aemilianus | | | | | |
| 253 Valerian & Gallienus | | | Longinus *c.* 220—273 | | 262 Porphyry 233—*c.* 301-5 |
| 268 Claudius II | | | | | |
| 270 Aurelian | | | 273 Menander | | |
| 275 Tacitus | | | | | |
| 276 Florianus | | | | | |
| 276 Probus | | | | Timaeus | |
| 282 Carus | | | | | |
| 283 Carinus & Numerian | | | | Aristides Quintilianus | |
| 284 Diocletian (286 Maximian) | | | | | Heliodorus |
| **300** | | | | | |

*Continued from p.* 104.

# CHAPTER XV.

## GREEK LITERARY CRITICISM IN THE FIRST CENTURY OF THE EMPIRE.

In the Augustan age Rome was in a preeminent degree a centre of attraction to the leading representatives of Greek literature. It was visited by Strabo about 20 B.C., forty years before the completion of his great work on Geography with its frequent citations from the older Greek literature, beginning with Homer, and from writers in the Alexandrian age, such as Eratosthenes and Hipparchus, Demetrius of Scepsis, and Apollodorus. Ten years earlier is the approximate date of the publication of the History of Diodorus, partly founded on researches in the libraries of Rome. It is also the date of the arrival in Rome of Dionysius of Halicarnassus, who lived in Rome for at least 22 years, from 30 to 8 B.C. He had learnt Latin, and had become familiar with Latin literature, before producing in the latter year his extant work on Early Roman History[1]. We are here, however, concerned with his rhetorical writings alone. It was in the time of Dionysius that the struggle between Atticism and Asianism, which had continued from the days of Demosthenes to those of Cicero, was to all appearance decided in favour of the former; and Dionysius ascribes the victory of Atticism to the commanding influence of the mistress of the world, and to the critical as well as practical instincts of her statesmen[2]. The writings of Dionysius contributed much towards the revival and the maintenance of a true standard of Attic prose. The exact date of their production is unknown; but the author's

*Dionysius of Halicarnassus*

---

[1] On the study of Latin among the Greeks, cp. Egger, *Mémoires de l'histoire ancienne et de la philologie*, 259—276, and Gudeman, in *Proc. Amer. Phil. Assoc.* XXI (1890) vii—x.

[2] *De Oratoribus Antiquis*, 2—3; see p. 277.

own references to certain of his works as already published occasionally supply data for an approximate chronological order, which will here be followed in a brief notice of each :—

(1) *The First Letter to Ammaeus.* The aim of this short treatise is to refute the opinion of an unknown Peripatetic, that Demosthenes owed his success as an orator to the precepts laid down in the *Rhetoric* of Aristotle. Dionysius shows that twelve important speeches of Demosthenes were delivered before the end of the Olynthian war (348 B.C.) mentioned in the Third Book of the *Rhetoric*; and twelve others between the Olynthian war and 339 B.C., *i.e.* before the completion of the *Rhetoric*, which he would even assign to a later date than the *De Corona* (330 B.C.). In connexion with the Olynthian war he quotes several important passages from Philochorus. He also supplies us with a partial chronology of the life of Aristotle, and of the speeches of Demosthenes; but he includes among the latter the *Speech on Halonnesus*, the *Fourth Philippic*, and the *Speech in reply to the Letter of Philip*; and his order of the *Olynthiacs* (II, III, I) is open to very grave dispute. He justly observes that Greek rhetoric is indebted not to the Peripatetic school alone, but also to orators such as Antiphon, Isocrates, Isaeus, Demosthenes, Aeschines, Lycurgus and Hypereides; to Thrasymachus and Theodorus; to Alcidamas (the pupil of Gorgias); to Theodectes and other disciples of Isocrates; and to Anaximenes, the contemporary of Philip and Alexander[1]. This is the only extant work of Dionysius which deals solely with a question of literary *history* as contrasted with literary *criticism*.

(2) The treatise *On the Arrangement of Words* (περὶ συνθέσεως ὀνομάτων, *De Compositione Verborum*), dedicated to the writer's pupil, Rufus Melitius, is a more extensive and a maturer work. It begins by distinguishing between thoughts and words, between 'the sphere of subject-matter' (ὁ πραγματικὸς τόπος) and 'the sphere of expression' (ὁ λεκτικὸς τόπος). This last includes *choice* of words, and *arrangement* of words, but the latter alone is here treated. Then follows a brief review of the history of the 'parts of speech'. Nouns, verbs and connecting-particles (σύνδεσμοι) were recognised by 'Theodectes and Aristotle'. The article (ἄρθρον) was added by the Stoics. Later writers successively separated the adjective (τὸ προσηγορικόν) and the pronoun (ἀντωνυμία) from the noun; the adverb (ἐπίρρημα) from the verb; the preposition (πρόθεσις) from the connecting-particle; the participle (μετοχή) from the adjective, and so on. The proper combination of these parts of speech makes a κῶλον, and the proper combination of κῶλα makes a 'period' (c. 2). The art of arrangement in verse and prose is next illustrated (c. 3) from Homer (*Od.* xvi 1—16) and Herodotus (i 8—10), and shorter passages in both are rewritten to show the superiority of their original form. Among those who had neglected the art, were Polybius, Hegesias and Chrysippus (c. 4). At a later point, the due arrangement of words and clauses, and figures of thought, are discussed (c. 6—9). Beauty (or 'nobility') of style (τὸ καλόν) is exemplified by

---

[1] *Ad Ammaeum*, i 2 (W. Rhys Roberts, p. 41).

Thucydides and Antiphon; charm of style (ἡ ἡδονή) by Ctesias and Xenophon; and both by Herodotus (c. 10), for whom his countryman, the Halicarnassian critic, has an unbounded admiration. These results are mainly attained by means of melody, rhythm, variety, and propriety (τὸ πρέπον). In connexion with melody we have an examination of a few lines of the *Orestes* (c. 11). But, in the use of all these means, much must depend on tact (καιρός), and no manual of tact had been hitherto mapped out by any rhetorician or philosopher (c. 12)[1]. Euphony (as an element of 'melody') is next illustrated by the sounds of the letters of the alphabet, here divided into vowels (φωνήεντα, φωναί) and consonants (ψόφοι); and the latter into semivowels (ἡμίφωνα) and mutes (ἄφωνα). Long vowels are more euphonious than short vowels. The descending order of euphony is for the vowels, ᾱ, η, ω, υ, ι, ο, ε; and for the semivowels, λ and ρ, next μ and ν, and lastly s, which is denounced as a disagreeable letter. The nine mutes are next classified firstly as ψιλά (*tenues*) κ, π, τ; δασέα (*aspiratae*) χ, φ, θ; and μέσα (*mediae*) γ, β, δ; and secondly as gutturals (κ, χ, γ), labials (π, φ, β) and dentals (τ, θ, δ); and in the former classification the aspirates are regarded as superior to the *mediae*, and the *mediae* to the *tenues* (c. 14). The effect produced by apt combination of letters and syllables is happily illustrated (c. 15) by Homer's ἠϊόνες βοόωσιν (*Il.* xvii 265) and χερσὶ ψηλαφόων (*Od.* ix 416). Further, the *sense* of the word must be suggested by the *sound*, as in Homer's descriptions of the scream of the eagle, the rush of arrows, and the breaking of waves on the shore. In this connexion it is noticed that aptitude for imitation, and for invention of names, is a natural instinct; and Plato is mentioned as having been the first to discuss etymology, in the *Cratylus* and elsewhere. '*That* diction' (he continues) 'must necessarily be beautiful in which there are beautiful words; and beautiful words are caused by beautiful syllables and letters'[2]. Then follow further illustrations from Homer, the 'poet of the many voices' (ὁ πολυφωνότατος ἁπάντων τῶν ποιητῶν), whether he is describing the grace of Penelope, the growth of the palm-tree, the beauty of Chloris, the ugliness of Gorgo, the meeting of the mountain-torrents, the conflict between Achilles and the Scamander, or the fate of the comrades of Odysseus in the den of Polyphemus. Beauty of language had been defined by Theophrastus as depending on the beauty of individual words; but much may be attained by skilful combinations of sound. In the Catalogue of the ships (*Il.* ii 494—501) even the uncouth names of Boeotian towns had been invested with beauty by the skill of Homer (c. 16). The various metrical feet are next enumerated and distinguished (c. 17); and metrical effects illustrated from masters of style, such as Homer, Thucydides, Plato and Demosthenes, as contrasted with the Asiatic orator, Hegesias (c. 18). In the sequel, the charm of variety is exemplified by the metres of Stesichorus and Pindar, and by the periods of Herodotus, Plato and Demosthenes (c. 19); apt propriety by Homer's effective description of the stone of Sisyphus, where the sound is an echo to the sense (*Od.* xi 593-8). The three ἁρμονίαι, or modes of composition, are next distinguished as (1) the 'austere' (αὐστηρὰ ἁρμονία or σύνθεσις), represented by

---

[1] Rhys Roberts, p. 46 n.　　　　[2] Cp. Saintsbury, i 130.

Antimachus and Empedocles in epic poetry, Pindar in lyric, Aeschylus in tragic; Thucydides in history, and Antiphon in oratory (c. 22); (2) the 'smooth or florid' (γλαφυρά, ἀνθηρά), by Hesiod, Sappho, Anacreon, Simonides, Euripides, Ephorus, Theopompus and Isocrates (c. 23); and (3) the 'intermediate' (κοινή), by Homer, Stesichorus, Alcaeus, Sophocles, Herodotus, Democritus, Plato, Aristotle and Demosthenes (c. 24). In connexion with the question how far a composition in prose may resemble a beautiful poem, the brief rule in Aristotle's *Rhetoric* (iii 8, 3), that prose must have rhythm without metre, is expanded into the precept that prose should be metrical, rhythmical and melodious without actually becoming metre, rhythm or poem. This precept is illustrated by passages from Demosthenes; and, in reply to the objection that it is incredible that so great an orator could have spent such pains on these minor matters, the critic urges that there is no cause for wonder, if one who surpassed all his predecessors in oratorical fame should, in fashioning works for all future ages, and in submitting himself to the inexorable test of Envy and of Time, never use a thought or a word at random, but should pay no small regard to the order of his thoughts, and the grace of his language. If Isocrates spent at least ten years on his *Panegyric*, and the first eight words of Plato's *Republic* were found on the author's tablet arranged in several different ways, we cannot wonder if Demosthenes also took pains to attain euphony and harmony, and to avoid employing a single word, or a single thought, which he had not carefully weighed[1]. The work concludes with the inquiry how far poetry can resemble fine prose. This is less possible in heroic and iambic than in lyric verse, where the measures are more free, as is shown in Simonides' famous *Ode on Danaë*, which (like Pindar's dithyramb in c. 22, and Sappho's *Ode to Aphrodite* in c. 23) is here fortunately transcribed and thus transmitted to posterity.

(3) *On the Ancient Orators* (περὶ τῶν ἀρχαίων ῥητόρων ὑπομνηματισμοί). This treatise was originally in two parts, comprising (1) three earlier orators, Lysias, Isocrates, Isaeus, (2) three later orators, Demosthenes, Hypereides, Aeschines, the first three being distinguished as having invented eloquence, and the second three as having brought it to perfection. (1) alone is extant; the account of Demosthenes in (2) may possibly survive in an expanded form in the special treatise on that orator (No. 4). Here the critic aims at establishing a standard for Greek prose, not in oratory alone, but in every variety of composition. Hence he treats the orators less as individual writers than as types. In the Essays on Lysias, Isocrates and Isaeus, he gives a life of each followed by a critique on his style, and a series of illustrative extracts from his works. The style of Lysias is praised for purity of diction, moderation in the use of metaphor, clearness, conciseness, terseness, vividness, truth to character, perfect appropriateness, winning persuasiveness and inimitable charm (c. 13); Isocrates is commended for his patriotic spirit, as well as for a smoothness and amplitude of style, which is marred however by a certain tameness and pro-

---

[1] This celebrated passage, with its context, is translated in Jebb's *Attic Orators*, I lxxvi f.

lixity; Isaeus, who is less natural and more obtrusively clever than Lysias, is extolled as the source of the oratorical power of Demosthenes. The three orators are contrasted in several happy phrases: *e.g.* 'Isocrates *strives* to attain the charm which, with Lysias, is a gift of nature' (*Isocr.* 3). Lysias is so natural that 'even if he states what is *false*, you believe him'; Isaeus so clever that 'even if he is telling the *truth*, you suspect him' (*Is.* 3). Lysias 'does not arouse his audience, as Isocrates or Demosthenes' (*Lys.* 28).—Dionysius deals with Demosthenes and Deinarchus in later works (Nos. 4 and 6), but on a different scale and with a different aim.

(4) *On the Eloquence of Demosthenes.* The original title and the beginning are lost; the current titles, περὶ τῆς λεκτικῆς Δημοσθένους δεινότητος and *De admiranda vi dicendi in Demosthene*, come from Sylburg's ed., 1586. At the end the author promises a treatise περὶ τῆς πραγματικῆς αὐτοῦ δεινότητος, which is not extant. The present work, even in its mutilated form, is justly regarded as a masterpiece of criticism[1]. Demosthenes is here described as having formed his style on a happy combination of all that was best in the three typical varieties of diction, (1) the *elevated and elaborate* (λέξις, ὑψηλή, περιττή, ἐξηλλαγμένη), represented by Thucydides; (2) the *smooth and plain* (λιτὴ καὶ ἀφελής), by Lysias; (3) the *mixed and composite* (μικτὴ καὶ σύνθετος), by Isocrates (c. 1—3, 33, 34, 36). The distinction between these three types is probably due to Theophrastus (c. 3). In the latter part of the treatise the three *modes of composition* (as contrasted with the three *varieties of diction* above mentioned) are (as in *De Comp.* 22—24) carefully discriminated, (1) the *austere*, represented by Aeschylus, Pindar and Thucydides; (2) the *smooth*, by Hesiod, Sappho, Anacreon and Isocrates; and (3) the *mixed*, by Homer, Herodotus, Plato and Demosthenes (c. 36—42)[2]. Demosthenes, in all his multiform variety, is compared to the fabled Proteus (c. 8). His speeches are remarkable for their effect on the emotions, which may still be felt even by the reader. 'When I am reading any of the speeches of Isocrates, I become sober and calm..., but, when I take up one of those of Demosthenes, I am roused to enthusiasm, and driven hither and thither..., and I share in all the emotions that sway the mind of man' (c. 22).

(5) *The Letter to Gnaeus Pompeius* (possibly a Greek freedman of Pompey) is in reply to a correspondent who is dissatisfied with the writer's criticisms on Plato. Dionysius protests that he has really fallen under the spell of Plato's marvellous powers of expression, and adds that, although he happens to prefer Demosthenes to Plato and Isocrates, he does no wrong to either of the latter (c. 1). He quotes from his *Ancient Orators* a passage on Plato describing him as combining the *elevated* style with the *plain*, and as being less successful in the former, whereas the *plain* style in Plato is 'mellowed by the tinge of antiquity', it 'remains radiant in beauty', and is 'like a balmy breeze blowing from meadows of surpassing fragrance'. He cites examples of both of these styles from the *Phaedrus*, adding that, whereas, in Plato, 'elevation of style sometimes lapses into emptiness and dreariness', this is never, or hardly ever,

---

[1] Blass, *Gr. Bereds.*, p. 180.  [2] Cp. *supra*, p. 281 f.

the case in Demosthenes (c. 2). He has also been asked for his views on Herodotus and Xenophon. In reply he quotes, from the Second Book of his lost treatise *On Imitation* (περὶ μιμήσεως), a long passage on these historians, and also on Thucydides, Philistus and Theopompus. This is almost all that survives of the treatise in question. The First Book (Dionysius tells us) was on the general nature of Imitation (not as a principle underlying all the fine arts, but as a process of copying existing models of style); the Second, on the authors who ought to be imitated; the Third (not then finished), on the proper mode of imitation. Fragments of an epitome of the Second Book are extant under the title of τῶν ἀρχαίων κρίσις, *De Veterum Censura*[1]. It is these fragments that enable us to compare the criticisms of Dionysius with those of Quintilian (x i).

(6) *On Deinarchus.* Dionysius here deals with the life and style of Deinarchus, but his main object is to draw up a critical list of that orator's speeches. He distinguishes 60 as genuine and more than 27 as spurious. Some of them are rejected on grounds of either style or chronology, as in the case where he triumphantly shows that, at the date of the delivery of a certain speech, its supposed author, Deinarchus, 'had not yet attained the age of ten' (c. 13).

(7) *On Thucydides,* addressed to Q. Aelius Tubero, probably the jurist and historian of that name. This is a critique (*a*) on the historian's treatment of his subject-matter, and (*b*) on his style. Under (*a*) Dionysius discusses the historian's choice of his theme, and his mode of handling it, objecting to his annalistic method (c. 9), his unsatisfactory statement of the causes of the war (10), and his abrupt conclusion (12). He ought (says Dionysius) to have begun with the *true* cause, the growth of the Athenian power; and the most effective ending (as he says elsewhere) would have been the return of the exiles from Phyle and the restoration of the constitution (*ad Pomp.* 3). Dionysius also finds fault with the insignificance of the occasion selected for the delivery of the famous Funeral Oration (18), and with the want of proportion in various parts of the work (13—15). Under (*b*) he quotes the account of the last battle in the great harbour of Syracuse (vii 69—72) and the reflexions on the factions of Greece (iii 81—2) for praise and blame respectively (c. 26—33). In the second passage he is specially severe on the sentence, ῥᾷον δ' οἱ πολλοὶ κακοῦργοι ὄντες δεξιοὶ κέκληνται ἢ ἀμαθεῖς ἀγαθοί, καὶ τῷ μὲν αἰσχύνονται, ἐπὶ δὲ τῷ ἀγάλλονται (iii 82, 7) and his remarks (c. 32) compel one to conclude that he could not construe the passage. He also finds fault with the Melian Dialogue (37—41), but in the next chapter (42) adds a list of those of the speeches that he deems worthy of imitation. On the whole, however, he has an unfavourable opinion of the speeches, while he regards the narrative portions of the history as (with few exceptions) admirable. Here and elsewhere (c. 25 and *ad Pomp.* c. 3, *de Deinarcho* c. 23) Dionysius clearly contemplates the case of his contemporaries actually trying to write like Thucydides. The case was not imaginary, as we may infer from earlier evidence in Cicero's *Orator*

---

[1] Usener, *Dion. Hal. de Imitatione* (*supra*, p. 207, n. 1).

(30, 32). It is in this connexion that Dionysius insists in conclusion that Thucydides had been imitated by no ancient writer except Demosthenes, who had assimilated his merits, while he had avoided his faults (c. 53).[1]

(8) *The Second Letter to Ammaeus* deals more minutely with the *style* of Thucydides. It begins with a summary of the characteristics of that style, quoted from *De Thucydide*, c. 24. It exemplifies each of those characteristics in turn, viz. his use of obscure, archaic and poetic words (c. 3), of periphrasis and brachylogy (4), of noun for verb (5) and verb for noun (6), of active for passive (7) and passive for active (8), of singular for plural and plural for singular (9 and 13); of persons for things and things for persons (14); also his confusion of genders (10), his peculiar uses of cases (11) and tenses (12), his use of parenthesis (15), his involved expressions (16), and his affected figures of speech (17). In the criticism of historians in general Dionysius is unsatisfactory; like other ancient writers, he regards history as a branch of rhetoric, and he is far less conscious of the intellectual greatness than of the stylistic obscurity of Thucydides. He tells us that 'there are very few who can understand *everything* in Thucydides, and there are *some* things which even *they* cannot understand without a commentary' (51). Even apart from the textual evidence supplied by his extensive quotations from the historian, such a statement incidentally confirms the belief that in the days of Dionysius the historian's text was not very different from that which we now possess. If all the clauses recently rejected as 'ascripts', on the ground of their interfering with perfect lucidity of expression, had been really absent from the text of that time, we should not have found in Dionysius so many complaints as to the difficulty of Thucydides.

Thus far for the genuine works of Dionysius. The *Art of Rhetoric*, ascribed to him, is quite unworthy of his name, and is (in part at least) demonstrably later than his time. It falls into three sections: (1) on the various types of epideictic speeches (c. 1—7), in which mention is made of an orator Nicostratus, who lived under Marcus Aurelius (d. 180 A.D.); (2) on oratorical figures of thought (περὶ τῶν ἐσχηματισμένων λόγων), treated in c. 8 and more fully in c. 9, possibly a very early work of Dionysius and including in both chapters one of his favourite quotations, οὐκ ἐμὸς ὁ μῦθος; (3) on the faults to be avoided in oratorical exercises (c. 10), and on the criticism of speeches (c. 11). These two chapters have many points of similarity, and probably a common author-ship. The author's promise of a treatise *On Imitation* at the end of c. 10 must have led to the whole work being assigned to Dionysius, though it is unlike him either in matter or manner[2].

In the undoubtedly genuine works of Dionysius we may regret a certain want of appreciation of the real merits of Thucydides and of Plato; but we must recognise the fact that, in the minute and technical criticism of the art and craft of Greek literature,

---

[1] The views of Dionysius on Thucydides are criticised in a commentary on Thuc. ii found at Oxyrhynchus (*Times*, 14 May, 1906).

[2] Cp. Christ, § 464, p. 666[4] note 3.

these works stand alone in all the centuries that elapsed between the *Rhetoric* of Aristotle and the treatise *On the Sublime*. Their author is called by an anonymous writer the 'canon of rhetorical criticism'[1], and is described by Doxopatres (cent. xi) as 'the great Dionysius, the excellent exponent and indeed the father of our art'[2]. Among modern writers, he is recognised by Gräfenhan[3] as, 'in point of learning and insight, one of the best critics of his time'. M. Egger[4] less generously observes that 'apart from industry in the accumulation of materials and a certain acumen in grammatical analysis, he is destitute of all that marks a true critic'. Mr Saintsbury, necessarily placing him below Aristotle in authority, method and traditional importance, and below 'Longinus' in critical inspiration, accepts him 'as a critic who saw far, and for the most part truly, into the proper province of literary criticism—that is to say, the reasonable enjoyment of literary work and the reasonable distribution of that work into good, not so good, and bad'[5]. Lastly, Professor Rhys Roberts, in an admirable edition of the 'Three Literary Letters', has noticed that 'his critical writings form a golden treasury of extracts from the best writers of Greece'; that he repeatedly 'reminds us of the often-forgotten truth that the excellence of the ancient authors was the result of ingenious and elaborate art'. 'A studied simplicity is the ideal he upholds'. 'His own style of writing…is at least eminently lucid and unaffected'. 'He was at once a scholar and a critic', and 'he furnishes us with one of the earliest and best examples of the systematic exercise of the art of literary criticism'. He dwells, 'at perhaps disproportionate length, on matters of style and purely verbal criticism; but for the modern world' this has 'not been altogether a disadvantage; he has helped where help was most needed'[6]. In that modern world he has inspired Boileau (1674) and Pope (1711)[7] with some of their precepts on the art of poetry, and (in 1834) Tennyson was quoting from the extant epitome of a lost work of Dionysius[8] when he said in a letter to

---

[1] Spengel, *Rhet. Gr.* i 460.        [2] Walz, *Rhet. Gr.* vi 17.        [3] iii 344.
[4] p. 395.        [5] pp. 127, 137.        [6] pp. 46–9.
[7] Cp. *Essay on Criticism*, 175–8 (*De Comp.* c. 12), and 665, 'See Dionysius Homer's thoughts refine, And call new beauties forth from ev'ry line'.
[8] Ἀρχαίων κρίσις.

Spedding: 'I have written several things since I saw you, some
emulative of the ἡδὺ καὶ βραχὺ καὶ μεγαλοπρεπές of Alcaeus, others
of the ἐκλογὴ τῶν ὀνομάτων καὶ τῆς συνθέσεως ἀκρίβεια of
Simonides'[1].

With the name of Dionysius of Halicarnassus we naturally
associate that of his friend Caecilius of Calacte on
the northern coast of Sicily. Dionysius describes
his friend as agreeing with him in the view that it
was 'the enthymemes of Thucydides' which 'had been specially
imitated and emulated by Demosthenes'[2]; and the two critics are
often linked together by Quintilian[3] and the unknown writer of the
*Lives of the Ten Orators*. Caecilius was the author of a work on
the characteristics of the Ten Orators[4], but the only important
fragment of this work which has reached us is a criticism on
Antiphon, noticing that he seldom, if ever, uses the 'figures of
thought'[5]. The title is, however, of interest as the earliest trace
of that canon of the Ten, which is recognised by Quintilian, but
not by Dionysius, and which cannot with any certainty be ascribed
to Didymus. As Caecilius was a pupil of the Pergamene scholar
Apollodorus, it has been proposed to trace this canon to the
school of Pergamon[6], but it is quite as likely to have had an
Alexandrian origin[7]. In either case it is important to notice that
the very form of the title shows that the canon was already recognised and was not invented by Caecilius. His rhetorical writings
included a comparison between Demosthenes and Aeschines
and between Demosthenes and Cicero ; also a lexicon, an art of
rhetoric and a work on figures of speech[8]. His lost treatise περὶ

Caecilius of Calacte

---

[1] *Memoir*, i 140.—On the rhetorical works of Dionysius, cp. Blass, *De
Dion. Hal. Scriptis Rhetoricis*, 1863, *Gr. Bereds.* (1865) c. vi ; Christ, § 464[4];
Croiset, v 356—370; also Egger, 396—406; Saintsbury, 127—137; and esp.
W. Rhys Roberts' ed. of the 'Three Literary Letters,' *ad Ammaeum* i, ii and
*ad Pompeium* (Cambridge Univ. Press), 1901, and the literature there quoted ;
also Max. Egger's *Denys d'Halicarnasse*, 306 pp. (1902); Teubner text, ed.
Usener.

[2] *Ad Pomp.* 3.    [3] iii 1, ix 3.

[4] περὶ χαρακτῆρος τῶν δέκα ῥητόρων.    [5] Photius, p. 485 b 15.

[6] Brzoska (1883), refuted by R. Weise, *Quaestiones Caecilianae* (1888).

[7] p. 129.

[8] On Caecilius, cp. Blass, *Gr. Ber.* 191—221; Christ, § 465[3]; Croiset v

ὕψους ('on elevation of style') is described by the author of the extant treatise bearing the same title, as falling short of the dignity of the subject, as giving innumerable examples to illustrate the *nature* of 'the sublime', but stating nothing as to the *means* whereby it may be attained. It is also criticised for omitting 'passion' as one of the sources of 'the sublime'[1], and for preferring Lysias to Plato[2].

The extant treatise περὶ ὕψους was regarded as the work of 'Dionysius Longinus' by all editors from 1554 to 1808, when Amati pointed out that in a Vatican MS it was ascribed to 'Dionysius *or* Longinus'.

**Anonymus περὶ ὕψους**

The same alternative is offered in the *index* to two Paris MSS; but, in the *superscription* of this treatise in both, the two names are set side by side, with a considerable space between them. Lastly, a Florence MS of the treatise bears the inscription ἀνωνύμου περὶ ὕψους. In this last description we must for the present acquiesce, as there are very grave difficulties in ascribing the treatise either to Dionysius of Halicarnassus or to Cassius Longinus (d. 273), or to any other known author, such as Plutarch or Theon of Alexandria. The latest writers quoted in the treatise itself are Amphicrates (*fl.* 90 B.C.), Cicero, Caecilius and Theodorus of Gadara (*fl.* 30 B.C.), and it may very well be assigned to the first century of our era[3]. In any case it is convenient to notice it here in close connexion with Dionysius and his friend Caecilius, whose own work on the same subject appears to have prompted its publication. Its general aim is to point out the essential elements of an impressive style, which, avoiding all tumidity, puerility, affectation and bad taste, finds its inspiration in grandeur of thought and intensity of feeling, and its expression in nobility of diction and in skilfully ordered composition. It deals not merely with 'the Sublime'; it is a survey of literary criticism in general, with special reference to the

---

374–8; also Rhys Roberts in *Am. Journ. Phil.* xviii 302–12, and in his ed. of 'Longinus' *On the Sublime* (Camb. Univ. Press), 1899, pp. 7, 220–2; and Pauly-Wissowa, v (1897) 1174–88.

[1] c. 8.   [2] c. 32 § 8.

[3] See Rhys Roberts, pp. 1—17, and Kaibel in *Hermes*, 1899, 107—132 (in refutation of F. Marx in *Wiener Studien*, xx, 1898, 169—204, who supported the authorship of Cassius Longinus). Wilamowitz places it *c.* 40 A.D. (*Gr. Lit.* 1905, 148).

elements which invest style with a certain elevation or distinction. (In the following abstract the few *lacunae* in the text are indicated by asterisks.)

After noticing the defects of the treatise of Caecilius on the same subject (*supra*, p. 287), the author defines 'the Sublime' as consisting in 'a certain distinction and excellence of language' (c. 1); and, in answer to the inquiry whether there is such a thing as 'an *art* of the Sublime,' he replies that a lofty type of style may be the gift of Nature, but it is controlled by Art (c. 2). * * *

The faults of style which are inconsistent with the Sublime are (1) tumidity, (2) puerility, (3) misplaced emotion, and (4) bad taste (τὸ ψυχρόν). These faults are described: tumidity is exemplified from Aeschylus, and bad taste from Timaeus (c. 3—4). They are all caused by the fashionable craze for novelty of expression (c. 5).

To avoid these faults we must acquire a clear knowledge of the true Sublime. This is difficult owing to the fact that *a just judgement on style is the final fruit of much experience* (ἡ τῶν λόγων κρίσις πολλῆς ἐστι πείρας τελευ-ταῖον ἐπιγέννημα). The true Sublime is that which pleases all and always (c. 6—7).

It has five sources: (1) grandeur of conception, (2) intensity of emotion, (3) appropriate employment of figures of thought and speech, (4) nobility of verbal expression, and (5) dignity and elevation of composition (c. 8).

The first of these holds the foremost place, and can only be attained by (so far as possible) 'nourishing a soul sublime' (τὰς ψυχὰς ἀνατρέφειν πρὸς τὰ μεγέθη). '*Sublimity*' (as I have said elsewhere) *is the echo of greatness of soul* (ὕψος μεγαλοφροσύνης ἀπήχημα). This is illustrated from Homer, in contrast with Hesiod; also from 'the legislator of the Jews'..., who wrote in the beginning of his Laws, 'God said, Let there be light, and there was light; let there be land, and there was land.' As compared with the *Iliad*, the *Odyssey*, which was clearly the author's later work, shows a decline in several respects, in its love of the marvellous and in its subordination of action to narrative and to delineation of character. The Homer of the *Odyssey* is like the sinking sun, which is still a glorious orb, but is less intense in its brightness; it is also like the ebbing-tide of greatness, drawing us into a region of shallows strewn with myth and legend. 'If I am here speaking of old age, it is still the old age of *Homer*' (c. 9).

Grandeur of conception is also shown in choosing the most striking points, and in grouping them into a consistent whole. This is best exemplified in Sappho's *Ode* (*to Anactoria*), where the most varied sensations are combined in one perfect picture (c. 10).

It is also shown by Amplification (c. 11) as is seen in Demosthenes, as compared with Plato and with Cicero. Plato has less of ' the glow of a fiery spirit ' than Demosthenes. Demosthenes again is like a sudden tempest, or a thunderbolt, while Cicero resembles a widespread conflagration, fed by a vast and inexhaustible store of flame (c. 12)[1].

It is further attained by imitating great writers of prose or poetry, even as Homer was imitated by Archilochus, Stesichorus, Herodotus and Plato. In composing anything that calls for loftiness of thought or language, it is well to ask ourselves how the same thought would have been expressed by Homer or Thucydides or Plato or Demosthenes; or how our own sayings would be likely to strike Homer or Demosthenes in the past, or each succeeding age in the future (c. 14).

It is also produced by vivid imagery which stirs the emotions, as in Euripides, who spends the utmost pains on giving a tragic effect to the emotions of love and madness, besides invading all the other regions of the imagination. Images of a fine type are found in Aeschylus and Sophocles, and in Demosthenes and Hypereides (c. 15).

'Intensity of emotion' is here left untouched, as it is reserved for another treatise. The true Sublime also finds expression in Figures of speech, such as *Adjuration*, which is well illustrated by the famous oath in Demosthenes, by those who fell at Marathon, Salamis, Artemisium and Plataea (*De Cor.* 208), where the orator, conscious of the defeat at Chaeroneia, does not allow the passion of the moment to betray him into calling any of the earlier engagements victories, but forestalls all possible rejoinder by promptly adding:—'*all* of whom had the honour of a public funeral, and not the *victorious* only' (c. 16). The use of a Figure is most effective when the fact that it *is* a Figure is unobserved, as in the oath by the men of Marathon, where the 'Figure' is concealed by the splendour of the context (c. 17). Figures include *rhetorical question*, exemplified in the orator's questions about Philip in the First Philippic (§§ 10, 44); also *asyndeton*, illustrated from Homer's *Odyssey* (x 251-2), the *Meidias* of Demosthenes (§ 72) and the *Hellenica* of Xenophon (iv 3, 19, ἐωθοῦντο ἐμάχοντο ἀπέκτεινον ἀπέθνῃσκον), as contrasted with the accumulation of connecting particles, characteristic of the school of Isocrates (c. 19—21); also *hyperbaton* (or inversion of order). It is by the use of this last Figure in the best writers that imitation approaches the effects of nature; for Art is then perfect, when it seems to be Nature, and Nature again is most effective when she is pervaded by the unseen presence of Art. Many illustrations of this Figure may be found in Herodotus, Thucydides and Demosthenes (c. 22). Figures in which several cases are combined, as well as accumulations, variations and gradations of expression, are very effective, as also interchanges of cases, tenses, persons, numbers and genders. The interchange of singular and plural, and the use of the present for the past, are next illustrated; and it is added that a

---

[1] Cp. Tacitus, *Dial.* 36, 'magna eloquentia, sicut flamma, materia alitur et motibus excitatur et urendo clarescit', and Pitt's famous rendering: 'It is with eloquence as with a flame; it requires fuel to feed it, motion to excite it, and it brightens as it burns' (Samuel Rogers' *Recollections*, p. 178, and Stanhope's *Life of Pitt*, iii 413, ed. 1879).

vivid effect is produced by addressing the reader, and also by suddenly changing from the third person to the first (c. 27). The last Figure mentioned is *peri-phrasis*, which must be handled with great discrimination (c. 28—29).

The fourth source of the Sublime is a careful choice of striking words used in their normal sense (c. 30), on the effect of which it is needless to dilate, *for beautiful words are in very truth the peculiar light of thought* (φῶς γὰρ τῷ ὄντι ἴδιον τοῦ νοῦ τὰ καλὰ ὀνόματα). * * * As to the number of Metaphors which may properly be used in a single passage, the true standard is Demosthenes (e.g. *De Cor.* 296). Excessive boldness of metaphor may be subdued by the apologetic devices suggested by Aristotle and Theophrastus. An accumulation of meta-phors may be allowed in passionate passages. It may also be exemplified from Plato's *Timaeus* (65 C—85 E) and elsewhere, though Plato is often criticised for this, and Lysias is preferred by Caecilius (c. 32).

Here follows an interesting digression (c. 33—36) on the question whether we should prefer grandeur of style with some attendant faults to a perfectly faultless mediocrity, and a greater *number* of merits to merits that are higher in kind. The critic decides that Homer is to be preferred to the comparatively faultless Theocritus and Apollonius Rhodius; Archilochus to Eratosthenes; Pindar to Bacchylides; Sophocles to Ion (c. 33); Demosthenes to Hypereides (c. 34)[1]; Plato to Lysias (c. 35).

Closely related to Metaphors are *Comparisons and Similes* (c. 37), but the discussion of these is lost. * * * Then follow illustrations of *Hyperbole* from Herodotus and Isocrates (c. 38).

Dignity or elevation of composition consists in the careful arrangement of words, as in the sentence of Demosthenes (*De Cor.* 188) closing with ὥσπερ νέφος; and in the proper collocation of phrases, as in Euripides, whose poetic quality is due to his power of composition rather than his invention.

Among faults destructive of the Sublime are excess of rhythm, broken and jerky clauses (c. 41), undue conciseness and undue prolixity (c. 42), and lastly triviality of expression (c. 43).

A philosopher has inquired, why the present age does not produce great authors, and whether this is due to a despotic government. The writer suggests that it is due rather to human passions, such as the love of money, and the love of pleasure; and asks how we can imagine, in such an age, the survival of an unbiassed critic of great works that are destined to descend to posterity. He concludes by promising a separate treatise on the Passions in connexion with discourse in general and the Sublime in particular (c. 44).

Strange to say, this remarkable work is never mentioned by any extant classical writer. In modern times, beginning with 1554, it has been frequently edited and still more frequently

---

[1] In c. 34, 1 the text runs: εἰ δ' ἀριθμῷ μὴ τῷ ἀληθεῖ κρίνοιτο τὰ κατορθώ-ματα. I may here suggest εἰ δ' ἄρα μὴ τῷ μεγέθει ἀλλὰ τῷ πλήθει. In 33, 1 we have πλείους contrasted with μείζους; and in 35, 1 μεγέθει with πλήθει.

translated, notably by Boileau (1674), whose preface prompted the tribute paid to the supposed author of the treatise in the closing couplet of the following passage in Pope's *Essay on Criticism* :—

> 'Thee, bold Longinus! all the Nine inspire,
> And bless their critic with a poet's fire.
> An ardent judge, who zealous in his trust,
> With warmth gives sentence, yet is always just :
> Whose own example strengthens all his laws ;
> And is himself that great sublime he draws'.

Fénelon preferred it to Aristotle's *Rhetoric*, commending it for the way in which it kindles the imagination while it forms the taste[1]. Gibbon, who used Boileau's translation and notes, found the Greek, 'from the figurative style and bold metaphors, extremely difficult' (12 *Sept.* 1762). Macaulay inadequately describes its author as 'rather a fancier than a critic'[2]. In recent times it has been characterised by Egger[3] as 'the most original Greek essay in its kind since the *Rhetoric* and *Poetic* of Aristotle'. Of its unknown author it has been well said by Mr Andrew Lang :—'he traces dignity and fire of style to dignity and fire of soul';...'he proclaims the essential merits of conviction and of selection'; 'he sets before us the noblest examples of the past'; 'he admonishes and he inspires'[4]. The work was eulogised by Casaubon[5] and Ruhnken[6] as a 'golden book'; and similarly Mr Saintsbury, while describing 'almost all the book' as deserving 'to be written in letters of gold', would write 'in precious stones' the author's 'admirable descant' on 'beautiful words' : *for beautiful words are in deed and in fact the very light of the spirit*[7]. The latest English editor[8] aptly closes his Introduction by characterising the author as one whose 'deep humanity and broad sympathies have helped him to interpret the spirit of antiquity to the modern mind, and have given him a permanent place in the history of literature as

[1] *Premier Dialogue sur l'Éloquence*, quoted by Egger, p. 427.

[2] *Works*, vii 662 (ed. 1866). [3] p. 426.

[4] *Introduction* to Mr H. L. Havell's translation (1890), p. xxx f.

[5] Quoted in Boileau's *Préface*.

[6] *Dissert.* p. 24 (*Opusc.* p. 525). [7] p. 167.

[8] W. Rhys Roberts, p. 37.

the last great critic of ancient Greece and (in some sense) the first international critic of a wider world'[1].

The treatise of Demetrius on Verbal Expression[2], wrongly attributed to Demetrius of Phaleron, certainly belongs to the Roman age[3], and probably to the first century of our era. The author frequently quotes from the *Rhetoric* of Aristotle, and has many interesting remarks on oratorical style and rhythm. Thus he happily compares the ' disjointed' style to a number of stones lying near one another, loose, scattered and uncombined, and the 'periodic' style to the same stones when bound compactly in the self-supporting cohesion of a vaulted dome[4]. He contrasts the clauses (κῶλα) of Prose with the metres of Verse, illustrates these clauses from Hecataeus and from the *Anabasis* of Xenophon, and expresses a general preference for short clauses. He also discusses periods, and parallel clauses (including *homoeoteleuta*). His main subject is well described by Mr Saintsbury[5] as the ' Art of Prose Composition '.

Demetrius

---

[1] On the treatise in general, cp. Christ, § 551[4]; Croiset, v 378—383; Egger 425—439; Saintsbury, i 152—174; Churton Collins, *Studies in Poetry and Criticism* (1905), 204—262; also the editions of Weiske (1809), Egger (1837), Jahn (1867, ed. Vahlen 1887[2], 1905[3]), and esp. Rhys Roberts (1899), with the literature quoted in the two editions last mentioned; English translations by H. L. Havell (1890), and A. O. Prickard (1906).

[2] περὶ ἑρμηνείας, Sp. iii 259—328; ed. Radermacher, 1901, and Rhys Roberts, 1902, who ascribes it to the first century A.D. Cp. Christ, § 424[4].

[3] § 108 refers to the patrician *laticlave*.      [4] § 13.      [5] i 104.

# CHAPTER XVI.

## VERBAL SCHOLARSHIP IN THE FIRST CENTURY OF THE EMPIRE.

TURNING from literary criticism to lexicography, we have to
record, among early lexicographers and compilers
of collectanea, the royal name of Juba II, king
of Mauretania (*fl.* 25 B.C.). The son of Juba I, who (like Cato)
put an end to his life after his defeat at Thapsus (46 B.C.), he was
taken to Rome, where he received a careful education. As a
reward for fighting on the side of Octavian against Antony and
Cleopatra, he was permitted to marry the daughter of the latter,
and was restored to his kingdom (29 B.C.). Four years later
he was allowed to extend his dominion from Numidia on the
East to the Pillars of Hercules on the West, placing his capital
at Iol, to which he gave the name of Caesarea (the modern
*Cherchel*). After a tranquil reign he died under Tiberius about
20 A.D. He is praised for his historical research by Plutarch,
who calls him the most accomplished of kings[1], while his varied
learning is similarly lauded by Pliny[2] and Athenaeus[3]. He wrote
on the history of Rome, and on Assyria, Arabia, and Libya,
besides a work in at least eight books on the Art of Painting,
with biographies of eminent artists, and another in at least seventeen on the History of the Theatre. The latter dealt with the
instruments of music used in the Drama, with choral songs and
dances, and the distribution of the several parts among the actors.

*Juba*

---

[1] *Sertor.* 9, ὁ πάντων ἱστορικώτατος βασιλέων, and *Anton.* 87 ὁ χαριέστατος
βασιλέων.

[2] *N. H.* v 1, studiorum claritate memorabilior quam regno.

[3] 83 B, ἀνὴρ πολυμαθέστατος.

It is quoted by Athenaeus[1] and Photius[2], and large parts of it have probably passed without the author's name into our *scholia* on the dramatists and especially into the *Onomasticon* of Pollux[3]. A manual on metre ascribed to Juba was really founded on the work of a later writer, Heliodorus[4].

Pamphilus of Alexandria (*fl.* 50 A.D.) was the compiler of a vast work in 95 books on rare or difficult words

Pamphilus

(περὶ γλωσσῶν ἤτοι λέξεων), which was superseded by abridgements and ultimately lost.   An abridgement of Pamphilus was regarded by C. F. Ranke, M. Schmidt, Ritschl and Naber as the source of the lexicon of Hesychius, and this abridgement was identified by Ranke and Schmidt with the Περιεργοπένητες (the 'poor students' lexicon') of Diogenianus, mentioned by Hesychius himself in his preface.   But it has since been contended by Weber that the work of Diogenianus was an abridgement not of Pamphilus alone but of a large number of other lexicons[5]. The original work of Pamphilus was known to Athenaeus, who quotes it under various titles and often by the author's name alone.

Among the contemporaries of Pamphilus was his namesake Pamphila, who lived for 23 years at Epidaurus

Pamphila

collecting materials for a miscellaneous work in 33 books on facts and anecdotes connected with the history of literature.   It is often quoted by Aulus Gellius[6].   Homer, Euripides and Menander were studied in her home, but it is uncertain whether the works on those authors, noticed by Suïdas and others, were written by her father Soteridas or her husband Socratidas.

A far less quiet life was led by the 'grammarian' Apion, an Alexandrian Greek of Egyptian origin, who

Apion

succeeded Theon[7] as head of the Alexandrian

[1] 175 D.                                        [2] *Bibl.* 161.

[3] Rohde, *De Pollucis fontibus* (1870); Bapp, *Leipz. Stud.* viii 110 f.—Christ, § 553[4]; Croiset, v 402.

[4] Schanz, *Lat. Lit.* § 606.

[5] Hugo Weber, *Philol. Suppl.* iii (1878), 454 f; cp. Bursian's *Jahresb.* xvii 125 (1881).  Cp. Christ, §§ 556[4], 631[4].

[6] *e.g.* xv 17 and 23.  Cp. Croiset, v 407.  It is Pamphila who has preserved the tradition that, at the beginning of the Peloponnesian war, the age of Hellanicus was 65, of Herodotus 53, and of Thucydides 40 (he was more probably 30).                                        [7] p. 144 *supra*.

school, and taught at Rome in the times of Tiberius and Claudius. His unwearied industry caused him to be regarded as one of the sons of toil under the nickname of Μόχθος, while his unbounded vanity and his noisy self-assertion prompted Tiberius to call him 'the cymbal of the world', and Pliny[1] to improve on this phrase by describing him as 'the drum of his own fame', or (as we should say) 'the blower of his own trumpet'. With the aid of the writings of Aristarchus, he compiled a Homeric glossary which is frequently quoted by Hesychius and Eustathius[2]. He pretended that he had summoned from the grave the shade of Homer, with a view to inquiring as to the names of the poet's parents, and the place of his birth; but he refused to impart to others the information which he had received[3]. His historic work on Egypt supplied Gellius with the story of Androclus and the Lion[4]. It also included certain charges against the Jews of Alexandria, which were brought to the notice of Caligula, and answered by Josephus (37—c. 100 A.D.) in a work still extant. The cause of the Jews also found an able advocate under Caligula and Claudius in the person of the aged Philo Judaeus (from 20 B.C. till after 40 A.D.), who thus emerged for a while from a life of study mainly spent on Plato and on the allegorical interpretation of the Book of Genesis and the exposition of the Law of Moses.

Among the minor grammarians of this (and the immediately preceding) age, may be mentioned Ptolemy of Ascalon, who appears to have taught in Rome in the time of Caesar, and was the author of works on the correct pronunciation of Greek, on Homeric accentuation and on the Aristarchic recension of Homer; Apollonius, son of Archibius, who produced under Augustus a Homeric lexicon, an abridgement of which is still in existence; Seleucus of Alexandria, a commentator on Homer, who was invited to the table of Tiberius with a view to discussing points which had arisen in the emperor's daily reading, and who, to prepare himself for such discussions, took the imprudent precaution of asking the attendants what the emperor had been reading, with the result

Minor grammarians

---

[1] N. H. Pref. 25.

[2] Gräfenhan, iii 58, 226, 254; Christ, § 557; Croiset, v 405.

[3] Josephus, contra Apionem, ii 2.     [4] p. 212 supra.

that he was first disgraced and then compelled to put himself
to death[1]; Philoxenus of Alexandria, who similarly devoted his
attention to Homer, and to accentuation, and is often quoted
in the *scholia*; Erotianus, who composed under Nero a lexicon
to Hippocrates, which is still extant; and Epaphroditus of
Chaeroneia (probably the patron of Josephus), who (according
to Suïdas) lived at Rome under Nero, Vespasian, Titus and
Domitian, and applied the resources of his large library of 30,000
books to the exposition of Homer, Hesiod, Pindar, Cratinus and
Callimachus[2]. It may here be added that the only extant Greek
work of L. Annaeus Cornutus, the friend and preceptor of Persius,
is a survey of the popular mythology as expounded in the etymological and symbolical interpretations of the Stoics[3]. His
Latin works on 'figures of thought', on 'pronunciation and
orthography', and his 'commentaries on Virgil', have not survived; while the commentaries on Persius and Juvenal, which
bear his name, belong to the Middle Ages[4].

[1] Suet. *Tib.* 56.
[2] Gräfenhan, iii 65 f; Croiset, v 352 f.
[3] *Cornuti Theologiae Graecae compendium*, ed. C. Lang, 1881.
[4] Croiset, v 418.

# CHAPTER XVII.

## THE LITERARY REVIVAL AT THE END OF THE FIRST CENTURY A.D.

In the revival of Greek literature towards the close of the first century, our attention is claimed by two authors of special interest, who supply us with incidental evidence on the state of learning in their time.

The first of these is Dion Chrysostom (*c.* 40—*c.* 114 A.D.), who was born at Prusa in Bithynia, and was exiled from Bithynia and from Italy during the fifteen years of the reign of Domitian (81—96). In all the three periods of his life, before and during and after his exile, he was a great traveller; and, in the many places which he visited, he gave ample proof of the eloquence which gained him the name of Chrysostom. We still possess, in different degrees of completeness, some eighty of his discourses, which, however, resemble essays rather than orations. In one of these[1] he professes to prove to the citizens of New Ilium 'that Troy was not captured'. For his proof he relies on an Egyptian priest whom he does not name, and on inscriptions which had disappeared; also on points of improbability, or impropriety, in the Homeric narrative. The composition as a whole is conceived in a vein of irony, and is simply a rhetorical exercise which is not intended to be taken seriously[2]. Far more interesting than the prolixities of his argument is the incidental mention of the striking fact that in his day the inhabitants of New Ilium learnt the *Iliad* by heart from their earliest years. In another[3] we have an instructive comparison between the *Philoctetes* of Sophocles

---

[1] *Or.* 11.     [2] Von Arnim's *Dio von Prusa*, p. 166 f.     [3] *Or.* 52.

Dion Chrysostom

(409 B.C.) and the plays of Aeschylus and Euripides (431 B.C.) on the same subject. The preliminaries to the perusal of the three plays are not without their interest. The writer tells us that he rose about the first hour of the day in the cool and almost autumnal air of a midsummer morning; he made his toilette and said his prayers, took a quiet drive followed by a walk and a short rest; after this, when he had bathed and anointed himself, he had a slight breakfast, and then set to work on the plays. He states that he was in delicate health at the time, and it has been suggested that he was recruiting at the country-house of a friend and wrote his essay for the entertainment of a house-party of persons interested in classical literature[1].

He describes his delight in comparing the different ways in which the three great tragic poets had dealt with the same theme. The work of Aeschylus was marked by his customary grandeur, his antique simplicity, his audacity of thought and expression[2]; that of Euripides by precision, acumen, and rhetorical skill[3]; while that of Sophocles was in the happy mean between the two, with its noble and elevated composition[4], at once tragic and harmonious, charming and sublime. Incidentally we learn that, in the play of Euripides, Odysseus foreshadowed the approach of envoys from Troy; that, in Aeschylus and Euripides alike, the person of Odysseus was artfully disguised by Athena, and the chorus was composed of natives of Lemnos and not (as in Sophocles) of the Greek companions of Odysseus. The choruses of Sophocles were full of charm and dignity, and did not contain so many moral sentiments as those of Euripides. But Dion would prefer to abolish the chorus altogether[5].

In a third piece[6] we have a short summary of the opening of the *Philoctetes* of Euripides; in another[7], an essay on the indebtedness of Socrates to Homer. In his Rhodian oration[8], in which he rebukes the Rhodians for dishonouring their benefactors by placing new names on the pedestals of their statues, he is clearly imitating the *Leptines* of Demosthenes. All the above belong to the *literary* group of his discourses. The *political* group (on the affairs of Bithynia) does not here concern us; while the *moral* dis-

---

[1] Von Arnim, p. 162.

[2] ἡ μεγαλοφροσύνη καὶ τὸ ἀρχαῖον, ἔτι δὲ τὸ αὔθαδες τῆς διανοίας καὶ φράσεως, and τὸ αὔθαδες καὶ ἁπλοῦν.

[3] τὸ ἀκριβὲς καὶ δριμὺ καὶ πολιτικόν.

[4] σεμνήν τινα καὶ μεγαλοπρεπῆ ποίησιν.

[5] See also Jebb's *Philoctetes*, pp. xv—xxi.

[6] *Or.* 59.        [7] *Or.* 55.        [8] *Or.* 31.

courses of the third period of his life, which are mainly inspired by the teaching of the Stoics, include grave denunciations of the vices and follies of the inhabitants of the Phrygian town of Celaenae, and of Tarsus and Alexandria. But, fortunately, they also include an idyllic picture of the happy and contented life of the poor herdsmen and huntsmen of Euboea, which is almost unique in ancient literature[1]; and a discourse on the blessings of an intelligent monarchy, purporting to have been addressed to the semi-civilised inhabitants of Olbia, near the mouth of the Borysthenes, most of whom knew Homer by heart, while some of them had even studied Plato[2]. Above all, they include the *Olympic* oration[3], in which Pheidias is described as expounding to the Greeks assembled at Olympia the principles which had guided him in the composition of his colossal image of the Olympian Zeus. The discourse appears to have been prompted by the tradition that Pheidias had derived his inspiration from the three famous lines in which the nod of Zeus is described in Homer[4]. There is a striking passage pointing out some of the contrasts between poetry and sculpture.

The art of the poets (says Pheidias) is free and unfettered. Homer in particular has not confined himself to a single dialect, but he has blended the Doric and even the Attic with the Ionic, combining all these varieties with as much care as the colours in dyeing, and not even limiting himself to the dialects of his own day but going back to the past and giving fresh currency to some archaic word, like an antique coin recovered from a long-lost hoard; not disdaining even the language of barbarians, or neglecting any word endued with sweetness or strength. Homer's metaphors and his modifications of ordinary words are also eulogised. He has proved himself a creative poet in his diction, in his metre, and in his varied imitations of all manner of sounds, whether of rivers and forests, of wind and fire and sea, of stone or bronze, of beasts or birds, of flutes or shepherds' pipes. Hence he is never at a loss for words expressing every shade of thought, and, by the fertility of his fancy, he can inspire the mind with any emotion he pleases. But we, poor artists (says Pheidias), are far from enjoying any such freedom. We must use a material

---

[1] *Or.* 7. Abridged translation in Mahaffy's *Greek World under Roman Sway*, pp. 276—290. Cp. Otto Jahn's *Populäre Aufsätze*, 58—74 (*Eine antike Dorfgeschichte*). Incidentally we learn from this discourse that, at Thebes, all but the Cadmea was now in ruins, while a votive Hermes, dedicated of old for some victory in flute-playing, had been set up anew amid the ruins of the ancient agora.

[2] *Or.* 36.  [3] *Or.* 12.  [4] *Il.* i 528—530.

that is solid and durable, a material hard to find and hard to work ; and to each image of a god we can only impart a single form which has to express all the fulness of the nature and power of the Deity. Poets, on the other hand, can easily comprise in their verse many varied forms of beauty ; they can at will represent these forms either at rest or in motion ; they can represent acts and words, and the effect of illusion, and the lapse of time. With the poet, a single inspiration, a single impulse of the soul, suffices to cause an infinite number of words to flow forth from their source, before the image and the thought, which he has seized, escape him. *Our* art, on the contrary, is painful and difficult ; it spends its effort on hard and obdurate stone, and its progress must needs be slow. But the greatest obstacle is that the artist must keep the same image in his mind, it may be for years, until he has completed his work. It is said, perhaps truly, that the eyes are more trustworthy than the ears ; but they are more difficult to convince and they insist on clearer and more vivid evidence. The eyes remain fixed on the objects which they are contemplating, while the ears may easily be excited and led astray, when they are thrilled with words endued with all the magic of metres and of sounds. (i 234–6 Dindorf.)

This passage has sometimes been regarded as the germ of Lessing's *Laocoon* ; but it is very doubtful whether it was even known to Lessing, who, as his readers will remember, takes as the starting-point of his famous Essay the criticism of the dictum ascribed by Plutarch[1] to Simonides, to the effect that Painting is silent Poetry, and Poetry is Painting endued with language.

The Olympic discourse also contains some interesting remarks on Plato and on myths. As a philosopher, Dion clearly took for his model the Socrates whom he knew in the pages of Plato and Xenophon. In the introduction to that discourse he ironically assumes a Socratic ignorance as a means towards stimulating reflexion in others. Addressing the Alexandrians in *Or.* 32, he describes himself (like Socrates in Plato's *Apology*) as sent to them to forget himself and solely to attend to their moral good[2]. As a writer, Dion is characterised by a certain smooth and fluent charm combined with complete absence of emphasis[3]. His turns of phrase not unfrequently remind us of Plato or Demosthenes, both of whom were among his favourite authors. When he went into exile (as we are assured by Philostratus[4]) the only two books which he took with him were the *Phaedo* of Plato, and the speech of Demosthenes, *De Falsa*

[1] *De Gloria Ath.* 3.			[2] i pp. 404, 407 Dind.
[3] Croiset, v 483.			[4] *Vit. Soph.* i 7.

*Legatione.* In drawing up a course of study for a distinguished friend, who had asked his advice, he names Menander and Euripides, and (above all) Homer, among the poets (leaving melic, elegiac, iambic and dithyrambic poets to men of leisure); among prose authors, Herodotus and Thucydides and, in the second rank of historians, Theopompus rather than Ephorus; and among orators, Hypereides, Aeschines and Lycurgus, as easier to understand and to imitate than the great masters, Demosthenes and Lysias. Beside the ancient Attic orators, notwithstanding the opinion of the rigid Atticists of the day (τῶν πάνυ ἀκριβῶν), even recent rhetoricians might be studied with advantage. Lastly, among the 'Socratics', he specially recommends Xenophon, adding that Xenophon's harangues in the *Anabasis* sometimes moved him to tears[1].

From Dion Chrysostom we turn to one of the most versatile and prolific of his literary contemporaries. Plutarch,

Plutarch

who was born at Chaeroneia between 45 and 50 A.D., was already familiar with the poetry of Greece, when, after attaining the age of 19, he left his Boeotian home to spend several years in Athens. He there studied rhetoric, mathematics and, above all, philosophy, especially that of Plato, under the guidance of Ammonius. He afterwards visited Egypt, and (under Vespasian) spent a considerable time in Rome, where his lectures on philosophy were attended by leading Romans, such as Arulenus Rusticus. He also explored various parts of Italy, including the battle-field of Bedriacum in the North[2]. After his travels he returned to his home and there passed the remainder of his long life, only leaving it occasionally for Athens or Delphi, or for the warm baths of Thermopylae or of Aedepsus in Euboea. He died, probably under Hadrian, about 125 A.D.

---

[1] *Or.* 18. On Dion in general, cp. von Arnim's critical ed. (1893–6), and his *Leben und Werke des Dio von Prusa* (1898); also E. Weber in *Leipz. Stud.* (1887); Christ, § 520[4]; Croiset, v 466—483; Egger, 440—455; and Saintsbury, i 109—113.

[2] *Otho*, 14. His guide on this occasion was an archaeologist of consular rank, Mestrius Florus,—the same who, at the table of Vespasian, urged the emperor to say *plaustra* instead of *plostra*, and on the following day was accordingly greeted by the emperor as *Flaurus* (φλαῦρος) instead of *Florus* (Suet. *Vesp.* 22).

As a strong adherent of the Platonic philosophy, he discusses[1] the origin of the soul as described in the *Timaeus*, and deals with minor points connected with Plato, in the ten chapters of his 'Platonic Questions'. The vision of Er at the close of the *Republic* has its counterpart at the close of the *De Sera Numinis Vindicta*. The fact that 'no infant smiles in the waking moments of its first few weeks, but only when it falls asleep', is explained in one of the fragments of his *De Anima* 'by the Platonic doctrine that the transplanted soul is disturbed and terrified by the aspect of this world, which it regards with displeasure, while in sleep it recalls its happier state with God and smiles at the glorious vision'[2]. He often attacks the views of the Stoics and Epicureans, though he not unfrequently borrows from the Stoics and disagrees with Plato. Of the strictly philosophical works of Aristotle he seems to have read little; but, in the collection and classification of facts and in the encyclopaedic pursuit of knowledge, he shows the influence of the Peripatetic school; he certainly quotes many details from Aristotle, Theophrastus and Straton. His religion finds its natural centre in Delphi; he discusses the mysterious letter **E** inscribed above the portal of the Delphian temple, concluding with the explanation given by his own master, Ammonius, that the symbol of the letter stands for its name (εἶ) and thus means 'Thou art',—the worshipper's tribute to the Being of the God whose temple he approaches. In the 'Pythian Oracles' he inquires into the reason why Apollo, who of old was wont to respond in verse, now uttered his oracles in prose alone. The dialogue on the 'Cessation of Oracles' includes much on the subject of demons, as beings intermediate between gods and men, and is lit up with a strange light by the simple yet mysterious legends of the old prophet of the Erythrean Sea, of the genii of the British Isles, and of the death of Pan, a theme which has since been made memorable by the Muse of Milton and also by a later Muse.

The Miscellanies of Plutarch, commonly called the *Moralia*, include several works not unconnected with literary criticism; but, even in literary criticism, Plutarch is apt to aim mainly at

[1] p. 1012 f.
[2] p. 736. Mahaffy's *Greek World under Roman Sway*, p. 292 f.

moral edification. His comments on Homer (Ὁμηρικαὶ μελέται) survive in fragments only; those on the Boeotian Hesiod's *Works and Days*, as may be inferred from the passages preserved by Proclus and Tzetzes, must have been a medley of minute observation and moral disquisition. Some of his notes on the didactic poems of Aratus and Nicander may be seen in the *scholia* on those authors, but they are solely on matters of natural science[1]. Of the works which have reached us in a more complete form, the tract 'On the Education of Children', which was probably not written by Plutarch, is very interesting, but is only slightly connected with literature. 'How a young man should study poetry' is a title full of promise, which only ends in disappointment. The author is oppressed by the consciousness that, in matters of morality, the old Greek poets are not entirely safe guides for young persons; but, instead of pointing out that the Homeric poems represent a primitive and undeveloped stage of moral and religious thought, he struggles to find in the old poets salutary examples of conduct and precepts of action, and only succeeds in this effort by means of fanciful interpretations[2]. 'You cannot prevent clever boys from reading poetry, so you must make the best of it. It is like the head of an octopus, very nice to eat, nourishing enough, but apt to give restless and fantastic dreams[3]. So you must be careful to administer paedagogic correctives, and to put the right meaning on dangerous things'[4]. Plutarch has in fact no pretensions to literary criticism; he is simply a moralist bent on compelling all literature to minister to edification. He is, however, entitled to our gratitude for preserving here and elsewhere many passages from the poets, which would otherwise have been lost to posterity[5]. As a native of Boeotia, Plutarch takes a special interest in citations from the Theban poet, Pindar. But even the merit of preserving for us

[1] Plutarch, v 20—36 Dübner.

[2] Cp. J. Oakesmith's *Religion of Plutarch*, pp. 69, 176 (Longmans, 1902). Plutarch is here borrowing from the Stoics and Peripatetics (A. Schlemm, *De fontibus Plutarchi De Audiendis Poetis*, 1893).

[3] p. 15 B.            [4] Saintsbury, i 140.

[5] Cp. F. M. Padeford, *On the Study and Use of Poetry by Plutarch...*, New York, 1892.

the relics of early Greek poetry is absent from the treatise 'On
Study' (περὶ τοῦ ἀκούειν), which merely inculcates a calm and
dispassionate attentiveness, and even warns the student against
taking any special pleasure in style.  'A man who will not attend
to a useful statement, because its style is not Attic, is like a man
who refuses a wholesome medicine because it is not offered him
in a jar of Attic manufacture'[1].  Literature is to Plutarch a wholesome medicine, and not a source of enthusiasm, a fountain of
refreshment, a well-spring of delight.

It is uncertain whether the treatise *On the Malignity of
Herodotus* was written by Plutarch.  It begins and ends with
commendations of Herodotus as a ready writer, and the possessor
of a charming and graceful style.  It also praises him as a good
judge of character, but it repeatedly sets him below Thucydides
as a historian, and cites a large number of passages to prove what
the writer regards as his bad temper, spite and uncharitableness.
In the centuries that had passed since the Persian wars, orators
and rhetoricians had diffused a kind of glamour over the memories
of the glorious days of Greece, and the historian whose picture of
the past included shade as well as light, was unpopular with those
who had deceived themselves into the belief that an undimmed
and unbroken splendour rested on the victorious conflict between
the Greeks and the Barbarians.  Even in Plutarch's own days
the victory of Plataea, in which the Thebans had no part, was
still commemorated on the spot where it had been won[2].

In a treatise, which has reached us in an imperfect form[3],
Plutarch shows a high appreciation of the merits of Menander,
while he is shocked at the occasional coarseness of Aristophanes,
whom he refuses to regard as a moral teacher.  He considers
Aristophanes as vulgar (φορτικός, βάναυσος) and theatrical (θυμε-
λικός); Menander as graceful, sententious and sensible.  The latter
is compared to a breezy and shady meadow, brightened with
flowers, on which the eye can rest with a sense of repose.
Plutarch is quite unconscious of the genius of Aristophanes, and
can find no cause for the poet's great reputation for 'cleverness'
(δεξιότης).  If passages from the old Attic Comedy are recited

---

[1] c. 9 ; Saintsbury, i 141.      [2] *Aristides*, 19, 21.
[3] p. 853.

at a banquet, every guest must be attended by a grammarian to explain the personal allusions[1].

In the nine books of his *Convivial Questions* the literary element is but slightly apparent. In arranging your guests at table, he would have you place 'the eager learner beside the distinguished scholar'[2]. He inquires why A is the first letter of the alphabet[3]. He discusses the number of the Muses[4] and the three kinds of Dances[5], the custom of wearing garlands at dinner, the material of the victor's crown in the Isthmian games[6], the question whether prizes for poetry were of ancient date[7], and why it was that the dramatic and artistic representation of things painful was pleasant[8]. In discoursing on the art of conversation, he draws many of his illustrations from Homer[9]. In connexion with Homer, he inquires why it was that, in the order of the games, boxing came before wrestling and running[10]; and what was the exact meaning of $\zeta\omega\rho\acute{o}\tau\epsilon\rho\sigma\nu$[11] and $\dot{a}\gamma\lambda\alpha\acute{o}\kappa\alpha\rho\pi\sigma s$; and of $\dot{v}\pi\acute{\epsilon}\rho$-$\phi\lambda\sigma\iota\alpha$, as an epithet of apple-trees in Empedocles[12]. In the letter of consolation addressed to his wife, he finds fault with critics who 'collect and gather together all the lame and defective verses of Homer, which are but few in number, and in the meantime pass over an infinite sort of others, which were by him most excellently made'[13]. In the introduction to the dialogue *De Defectu Oraculorum* points of grammar, such as the question whether $\beta\acute{a}\lambda\lambda\omega$ loses a $\lambda$ in the future, and what is the positive of $\chi\epsilon\hat{\iota}\rho\sigma\nu$ and $\beta\acute{\epsilon}\lambda\tau\iota\sigma\nu$, are described as causing the disputants to contract their brows and contort their features; while other topics can be discussed with a calm and unruffled mien[14].

Plutarch is mainly a moralist, not only in his so-called *Moralia*, but also in his *Lives*, with their vivid moral portraiture, which made Montaigne call them his 'breviary', and Madame Roland 'the pasture of great souls'[15]. Several of his *Lives*, e.g. his *Pericles* and his *Caesar*, his *Demosthenes* and his *Cicero*, have

---

[1] *Quaest. Conv.* vii 8, 3 § 5.

[2] i 2, 6.          [3] ix 2.          [4] ix 14.          [5] ix 15.

[6] v 3.          [7] v 2.          [8] v 1.          [9] ii 1.

[10] ii 5.          [11] v 4.          [12] v 8.

[13] p. 611. Trench, *Plutarch*, p. 27.          [14] p. 412 F.

[15] Trench, p. 34 f.

a literary as well as a historical interest; but it is disappointing
to find that, at the moment when we expect some literary criticism
in the comparison between the two greatest orators of Greece
and Rome, Plutarch (notwithstanding the interest in Latin rites
and customs shown in his *Roman Questions*) shirks the task on
the ground of his imperfect knowledge of Latin[1]; he actually
rebukes Caecilius for instituting such a comparison[2]; and, even
in the case of the Greek orator, offers no criticism on his style.
His *Life of Cicero*[3] implies some acquaintance (either direct or
indirect) with Cicero's philosophical works. His knowledge of Latin
has been discussed by Weissenberger[4], who defends him from
some of the attacks of Volkmann. His *Lives of Galba and Otho*
were founded either on Tacitus or on some authority common to
both[5]. In his *Life of Lucullus*[6] we find a possibly indirect quotation from Latin literature[7], while his description of Rome as τῶν
ἀνθρωπίνων ἔργων τὸ κάλλιστον[8] is perhaps a reminiscence of
Virgil's *rerum pulcherrima Roma*[9]. His *Roman Questions*, in
which Ovid's *Fasti* are never quoted, are partly founded on Varro
and Juba; and his *Greek Questions* on Aristotle.

On the whole, Plutarch cannot be seriously regarded as a
literary critic, but he fully deserves the credit of being a lover
of literature. Literature is fully recognised in his fragmentary
discourse on the question whether the Athenians were more
glorious in war or in wisdom; and, in attacking the Epicureans,
he warmly defends the cause of letters. His treatise on the
profit which a young man may obtain from the writings of the
poets supplied Basil with many hints for his treatise on the gain
to be derived from the study of heathen authors. Montaigne
'can hardly do without Plutarch'. In Southey's *Doctor* the
translation of the *Moralia* by Philemon Holland is one of the
few books for which Daniel Dove finds room on his shelves.
He is the theme of more than 250 allusions or direct references

---

[1] *Dem.* 2.                              [2] *Dem.* 3.
[3] 24, 40.                            [4] *Die Sprache Plutarchs*, 1895.
[5] Schanz, § 438 ; E. G. Hardy's *Studies in Roman History*, 294 f.
[6] c. 39, described, as a 'palpable interpolation', by Gudeman, *Trans.
Amer. Phil. Assoc.* xx 149 n. 16.
[7] Horace, *Ep.* i 6, 45.            [8] *De Fortuna Rom.* 316 E.
[9] *Georg.* ii 534. Oakesmith's *Religion of Plutarch*, p. 84 n.

on the part of Jeremy Taylor; his *Moralia* occupied 24 years
of the life of Daniel Wyttenbach, and had an important influence
on the career of Neander[1]. 'Plutarch', says Emerson[2], 'will be
perpetually rediscovered from time to time as long as books last'[3].

Plutarch and Dion Chrysostom have points of contact with
Favorinus of Arles (born *c.* 75 A.D.), who was a
pupil of Dion and a friend of Fronto and Plutarch.

Favorinus

He visited Ephesus, but lived mainly in Rome, where his lectures
were attended by Herodes Atticus. He is much admired by
Gellius. He was one of the most learned men of the age of
Hadrian, whose favour he enjoyed for a time; and he appears
to have died under Antoninus Pius. He vied with Plutarch in
the number and variety of his writings, which included philosophy,
history, philology and rhetoric; but he was more of a rhetorician
than a philosopher. In philosophy he was a Sceptic. Besides
several semi-philosophical works, he wrote at least five books of
*Memoirs*, and twenty-four of *Miscellanies*. The latter is described
by Photius as a store-house of erudition, and both are among the
authorities followed by Diogenes Laërtius[4]. He survives in fragments only; but he may here serve to mark the transition from
Dion and Plutarch to the Sophists and the Atticists of the age
of the Antonines, who will be briefly noticed in the next chapter.

[1] Trench, pp. 74, 108 f, 121.

[2] Essay prefixed to translation of Plutarch's *Morals*, revised by Prof.
W. W. Goodwin (1870); see also Essay on *Books* in *Society and Solitude*,
p. 451 of *Prose Works*, ed. 1889.

[3] On Plutarch, cp. the monographs by Gréard (1866) and Volkmann (1869),
R. C. Trench's *Four Lectures* (1873) and J. Oakesmith's *Religion of Plutarch*;
also Christ, §§ 470—485[4]; Croiset, v 484—538; Egger, 409—425; and Saints-
bury, i 137—146. On 'Plutarch as Philologist' see Gudeman in *Trans. Amer.
Phil. Assoc.* 1895; and on his quotations from early Greek philosophers,
A. Fairbanks, *ib.* 1897. Cp. R. Hirzel, *Der Dialog*, ii 124—237, 1895.

[4] Christ, § 510[4]; Croiset, v 539 f.

# CHAPTER XVIII.

## GREEK SCHOLARSHIP IN THE SECOND CENTURY.

For nearly two-thirds of the second century the Roman Empire was under the beneficent rule of Hadrian (117—138) and the Antonines (138—180). Hadrian, the patron of Greek literature in general and of rhetoric in particular, was specially devoted to Athens, where he had distinguished himself as archon under the rule of Trajan. After he had ascended the throne, he completed the magnificent temple of the Olympieum, which had been begun by Peisistratus 650 years before. In the region north of the Acropolis, he built the 'Stoa' which bore his name, with its walls and colonnades of Phrygian marble, its roof glittering with gold and alabaster, and its chambers stored with books, and beautified with paintings and statues[1]. The bust of Sophocles, and the marble personifications of 'the Iliad' and 'the Odyssey', found in the neighbourhood, may once have adorned the Library in these buildings. M. Aurelius established at Athens a school of Philosophy, with a professorial chair for each of the four sects, the Academics, Peripatetics, Stoics and Epicureans; and a school of Rhetoric with two chairs, the 'political' and the 'sophistical', the holder of the latter being appointed by the emperor and set over the whole of the University. The selection of the four professors of Philosophy was assigned to Herodes Atticus (103—179), who, like Hadrian, was one of the greatest benefactors of Athens. His lavish liberality caused the Panathenaic Stadium on the Ilissus to gleam with marble from the quarries of Pentelicus, and (about the time when Pausanias was writing his

The second century. Hadrian

Herodes Atticus

---

[1] Pausanias, i 18, 9.

*Description of Greece*) raised a new Odeum with a roof of cedar
to the south of the ascent to the Acropolis. He was the most
brilliant of the Sophists of the age ; he could refute the pretended
Stoic by means of appropriate passages from Epictetus ; and, in
giving alms to a Cynic impostor, who had only 'the beard and
the staff' of his profession, he could quote an effective precedent
from Musonius[1]. His house at Athens and his villa, amid the
olive-groves and water-courses of Cephisia, were frequented by
statesmen, philosophers and rhetoricians[2]; and among these last
was the eminent rhetorician Aristides. In the age of the Antonines
a remarkable proof of proficiency in Greek was given by M.

**M. Aurelius**     Aurelius, the 'Stoic on the throne', in the famous
*Meditations* (τὰ εἰς ἑαυτόν), which (as it happens)
include a single chapter on the moral effect of Attic tragedy and
comedy[3], while they represent in general the highest standard
of morality attained prior to Neo-Platonism and apart from
Christianity. The author of the *Meditations* gave early encourage-
ment to the precocious genius of the rhetorician Hermogenes ;
among the preceptors of the adoptive brother of M. Aurelius,
L. Verus, were Hephaestion and Harpocration ; while the tutor
of Commodus was the grammarian Pollux, whom his former pupil
appointed professor of Rhetoric at Athens. During this century
there was no lack of patronage for Scholarship at Athens and
Rome ; but, meanwhile, the greatest grammarian of the age,
Apollonius Dyscolus, was living in poverty in Alexandria. His
son, Herodian, lived in Rome, and dedicated to M. Aurelius his
great work on accentuation.

In the second century an interest in the ancient epics of

**Poets, His-**     Greece is attested by a composition in prose pur-
**torians, etc.**     porting to give an account of a poetic competition
between Homer and Hesiod[4]. Verse is represented
by the didactic poems of Dionysius Periegetes and Oppian, by
the hymn to Nemesis by Mesomedes and the fables of Babrius ;

---

[1] Gellius, i 2, 3—13; ix 2.          [2] *ib.* i 2, 2.          [3] xi 6.

[4] ἀγών, printed in Goettling's *Hesiod*, pp. 241—254, and in Rzach's. Cp.
Christ, § 72[4]. Part of the original poetic form of this ἀγών, ascribed to Lesches,
has been discovered in a papyrus of cent. III B.C. (Gercke in *Jahresb.* vol. 124,
1905, p. 476).

history, by Appian (*fl.* 160) and by Arrian (*fl.* 130), the modern
Xenophon, who, with his 'chameleon-like'[1] style, imitates Herodo-
tus and Thucydides as well as Xenophon and Ctesias; military
history, by Polyaenus (*fl.* 161–9); geography and astronomy, by
Claudius Ptolemaeus of Alexandria; while topography and biography were combined in the 'cities and their celebrities' of
Philon of Byblus (*c.* 64—141), and the chronology of the Olympic
Games was studied by Phlegon of Tralles.  In the age of Trajan
and Hadrian (if not at an earlier date) Ptolemaeus Chennus of
Alexandria, besides writing a historical drama called the *Sphinx*,
and an epic poem in twenty-four books entitled *Anthomerus*,
compiled a vast collection of miscellaneous anecdotes which was
known to Photius[2].  He has acquired a new importance from
the fact that he is now regarded as the author of a lost treatise on
the *Life and Works of Aristotle*, dedicated to one Gallus, and
ascribed to 'Ptolemaeus' in an Arabic list of the *Works*, which
is derived from a Syriac rendering of the Greek original[3].

In the time of the Antonines Archaeology and Topography
were the theme of Pausanias, who was still engaged on
his *Description of Greece* in 173 A.D.[4], having written
**Pausanias**
his account of Attica before, and that of Achaia after, the
building of the Odeum of Herodes Atticus.  From his home
in Asia Minor, near the river Hermus and mount Sipylus, he
travelled over Greece, Italy and Sardinia, and even visited Syria,
and the oracle of Ammon in the Libyan desert.  His work is
invaluable for its varied information on the mythology, topography,
sculpture and architecture of ancient Greece; and its utility has
been recognised in the archaeological exploration of Athens and
Argolis, of Delphi and Olympia.  It is neither a manual of
archaeology, nor a guide-book, but a volume of reminiscences
of travel.  It cannot reasonably be doubted that it is founded
largely on the author's own experience; but there has been much
discussion as to the degree of his indebtedness to authorities such

---

[1] Kaibel in *Hermes*, xx (1875) 508.

[2] *Cod.* 190, καινὴ ἱστορία.

[3] Christ, § 559[4], and esp. A. Baumstark, *Aristoteles bei den Syrern*, 1900.
The list is given in Arist. *Frag.* pp. 18—22 Rose.

[4] v 1, 2.

as Polemon of Ilium in archaeology[1], Artemidorus of Ephesus
(*fl.* 100 B.C.) in topography, and Istrus of Paphos (a pupil of
Callimachus) in history. He cites Euripides far less often than
the ancient epic poets; and almost all that we know (or think we
know) of the Messenian wars is due to his having preserved for us
the substance of the lost epic of the Alexandrian poet, Rhianus[2].

Of the Sophists who lived under the Antonines, one of the
most celebrated was Aelius Aristides (129—189),
who studied oratory at Pergamon and Athens, besides visiting Rhodes and travelling in Egypt. The
storms, which he encountered on his voyage to Italy in 155,
shattered his health and compelled him to live as a valetudinarian
for many years at Pergamon and Smyrna. When Smyrna was
ruined by an earthquake (178), he obtained the aid of M. Aurelius
for its restoration. At Athens he delivered his Panathenaic discourse, with its rhetorical review of Athenian history. History
he regards as holding a position intermediate between poetry and
rhetoric[3]; rhetoric he defends from Plato's attacks in the *Phaedrus*
and *Gorgias*, while he shields Miltiades, Themistocles, Cimon
and Pericles from the contempt with which they had been
treated in the latter of those dialogues. He is also the author of
several fictitious discourses on events in Greek history, and of a
prose paraphrase of the speech of Achilles in the ninth *Iliad*.
Lastly, he has left us a pleasant picture of a learned and accomplished lecturer on the ancient Classics in the person of a teacher
of M. Aurelius named Alexander of Cotyaeum, whose countrymen
are assured that he will be gratefully welcomed by the authors of
old in the world below, where he will be assigned an enduring
throne as the best of their interpreters[4]. Unhappily, the only
work of Alexander mentioned by Aristides is vaguely stated to
be on the subject of Homer, and he is now represented solely by
a fragment on a point of textual criticism in Herodotus[5]. In

*Rhetoricians.*
*Aristides*

---

[1] p. 154 *supra.*

[2] Christ, § 501[4]; Croiset, v 679—683; Kalkmann, *P. der Perieget* (1886);
Gurlitt and Bencker (1890); Heberdey, *die Reisen des P.* (1894); Frazer's
*Pausanias* (1898); ed. Hitzig et Blümner, 1896—1910; trans. W. H. S.
Jones, 1918— .

[3] ii 513.          [4] *Or.* 12.          [5] Quoted by Porphyry, p. 288, Schrader.

editions of Aristides we find two compositions inspired by the
*Leptines* and proving an intimate acquaintance with the text of
Demosthenes; but their authorship is not quite certain[1].   In
style Aristides is one of the strictest Atticists of his time, his
favourite models being Thucydides, Plato, Xenophon, Isocrates
and Demosthenes.   To rival Demosthenes was his main ambition,
and he had the satisfaction of seeing in a dream the apparition of
a philosopher who assured him that he had even surpassed that
orator[2].   As a successful imitator of the Attic writers he is highly
praised by Phrynichus[3]; his copiousness and force are lauded by
Longinus[4]; by later rhetoricians, such as Libanius and Himerius,
he is regarded as a classic; his fame descended to the Byzantine
age, in which Thomas Magister classes him alone with Homer,
Thucydides, Demosthenes and Plato; and the study of his
speeches in the schools is still attested by the extant *scholia* and
*prolegomena*.   His love of literature on its rhetorical side is frank
and outspoken; 'speeches' (he tells us) 'are his sole delight',
'the whole gain and sum of life is oratorical occupation'[5].   In his
apology for the blunder of commending himself in the course of
an address to a deity[6], he justifies himself by many quotations
from orators and poets, and from Solon in particular; but he
shows no taste for literary criticism.   In a history of Scholarship
his main claim to notice rests on his successful study of the
ancient models of Attic prose, and also on the fact that he has
preserved for us[7] the longest passage from the iambic poems of
Solon which was known to us until the recovery of Aristotle's
*Constitution of Athens*[8].

   Inferior to Aristides is the 'Platonic philosopher', Maximus
of Tyre (*fl.* 180), who lectured in many lands (including Phrygia and Arabia), and paid several visits     Maximus
to Rome.   All his forty-one discourses are written     Tyrius

   [1] They are not found in the MSS of Aristides, and are only attributed to him
on the ground of a passage in his Speech against Capito, p. 315 (H. E. Foss,
1841).              [2] i 325.              [3] ap. Photium, p. 101 A 18.

   [4] Dindorf's *Aristides*, iii 741.

   [5] Canter in Dindorf's *Aristides*, iii 779, quoted by Saintsbury, i 114 f.

   [6] *Or.* 49.              [7] *Or.* 49.

   [8] On *Aristides*, see the editions of Dindorf (1829) and Keil (1899); and cp.
Christ, § 521[4] f; Croiset, v 572—581; and Saintsbury, i 113—6.

in the affected and over-symmetrical style of Gorgias, with an inordinate fancy for the accumulation of synonyms.  As a Platonist of eclectic tastes, while he opposes the Epicureans, he borrows at will from the Peripatetics, Stoics and Neo-Pythagoreans; and, like Plutarch, he may be regarded as a precursor of the Neo-Platonists. But, while Plutarch is a genuine philosopher and a wise counsellor on the conduct of life, Maximus is merely a rhetorician, who happens to write by preference on philosophic subjects.   The subjects themselves are not uninteresting : *e.g.* 'Does Homer represent any special philosophic school ?'[1]; 'On Plato's God'[2]; 'On the *Daimonion* of Socrates'[3]; 'On Socratic Love'[4]; 'Was Plato justified in banishing Homer from his Republic ?'[5]; 'Have poets or philosophers discoursed better concerning the Gods ?'[6]; 'Are the liberal arts conducive to virtue?'[7].   He discusses the influence of music and geometry; he is fond of quoting from Homer and Sappho[8], and has contributed to the restitution of the fair fame of the Lesbian poetess[9]; he eulogises Homer for his breadth of view and his varied knowledge, but describes Aratus as no less famous[10]; he sees little difference between poetry and philosophy; he favours the allegorical interpretation of poetry; has a high admiration for Plato[11]; and, in discussing Plato's attitude towards Homer, insists that an admiration for Plato is quite compatible with an admiration for Homer.   On the whole, we are bound to admit that, so far as regards literary criticism, the high expectations raised by the titles of his lectures only end in disappointment[12].

The brilliant and versatile satirist, Lucian of Samosata (*c.* 125—*c.* 192), who includes rhetoricians and sophists among the many themes of his satire, is himself a product of the sophistical and rhetorical education of his time.   Born in northern Syria, and educated in Ionia, he travelled and lectured in Asia Minor, Greece and Macedonia, and even in Italy and Gaul; resided for some twenty years

Lucian

---

[1] 32.                  [2] 17.                  [3] 14, 15.              [4] 24—27.

[5] 23.                  [6] 10.                   [7] 37.                  [8] *e.g.* 24, 9.

[9] Welcker's *kl. Schriften*, ii 97.                                   [10] 30.

[11] 17, 1; 27, 4.

[12] Christ, §511[4]; Croiset, v 581–2; Saintsbury, i 117–8.

(*c.* 165—185) at Athens; and, towards the end of his life, held
a Government appointment in Egypt.

A history of Scholarship is only concerned with a few of the
four-score writings that bear his name. His *Judgement of the
Vowels* (δίκη φωνηέντων), which throws some light on the Attic
Greek of his day, describes a lawsuit brought before the court
of the vowels by the letter Sigma against the letter Tau, complaining of violent ejectment from various words such as σήμερον,
θάλασσα and Θεσσαλία, which the Atticists of the time pronounced
τήμερον, θάλαττα and Θετταλία. His satire *On the proper manner
of writing History* (πῶς δεῖ ἱστορίαν συγγράφειν), which was once
much admired, is an attack on the incompetent historians, who
were preparing to describe the Parthian War (which ended in 165)
in the style of Herodotus and Thucydides. This attack on contemporary historians is veiled under the disguise of advice to the
historians of the future. The two great requirements of the true
historian (says Lucian) are intelligence (σύνεσις) and power of
expression (ἑρμηνεία). His *Parasite* is a parody of the discussions
held by rhetoricians and philosophers, from Plato downwards, on
the subject of rhetoric. In his *Lexiphanes* we have a playful
satire on the Atticists of the day, and on their fancy for interspersing their compositions with obsolete phrases borrowed from
the old Attic authors. A specimen of this kind of patch-work is
produced by Lexiphanes himself, who is severely criticised, and
is solemnly admonished to reject the miserable inventions of
modern rhetoricians, to emulate the great classical writers such
as Thucydides and Plato, and the ancient masters of tragedy and
comedy, and, above all, to sacrifice to the Graces and to perspicuity.
Lexiphanes has been supposed[1] to be a satirical representation of
Pollux, the lexicographer; but the latter was not appointed professor of rhetoric at Athens until the reign of Commodus, whereas
the *Lexiphanes* was apparently one of Lucian's earlier works[2].
His *Pseudologistes* (or Solecist) is directed against grammarians
who lapsed into solecisms, in spite of a pedantic attention to
correctness of style. Elsewhere, he writes an amusing satire
(*Adversus Indoctum*) on a collector of books in handsome bind-

---

[1] By the Scholiasts and C. F. Ranke, *Pollux u. Lucian* (1831).

[2] § 26. Christ, § 539[4].

ings, including copies of Archilochus and Hipponax, Eupolis and
Aristophanes, Plato, Antisthenes and Aeschines, which he could
neither read nor understand.    In the *Teacher of Orators* (ῥητόρων
διδάσκαλος) Lucian attacks the prevailing type of instruction in
the person of one of its most conspicuous representatives, sometimes identified (as in the *Lexiphanes*) with the lexicographer
Pollux.   In the same spirit as in that dialogue, Lucian distinguishes
between the two paths which lead to the attainment of rhetorical
skill, (1) the long and laborious imitation of the great authors
of old, such as Plato and Demosthenes ; (2) the collection of
fashionable phrases for ordinary use and affected archaisms for
occasional adornment[1].   Rhetoric is also represented in his *Bis
Accusatus*, where Lucian is accused by 'Rhetoric' of having
deserted her, and by 'Dialogue' of having disgraced her.   In
his *Conversation with Hesiod*, he ridicules the ancient poets for
pretending to be inspired interpreters of the will of heaven.
Lastly, in his dialogue *On Dancing*, he states that, as an interpreter of the poets, an accomplished dancer of pantomime ought
to know Homer and Hesiod, and (above all) the tragic poets,
by heart.

Lucian singles out, in the literature of his age, the defects
which were due to an affected imitation of ancient models ; he
ridicules the frivolity of the rhetoricians, and the pretentiousness
of the historians of his day ; and rallies the Atticists for their
superstitious cult of an obsolete phraseology.   He is himself an
Atticist of a higher though far from perfect type, and Cobet has
abundantly shown, *quanto opere a Graecitatis antiquae dicendi
sinceritate desciverit*[2].   His verbal familiarity with Greek literature
is attested by his constant quotations from Homer, Hesiod and
Pindar[3], and his frequent reminiscences of Thucydides, Xenophon,
Plato and Demosthenes[4].   The *encomium* on that orator found
among his writings, shows a just appreciation of the patriotism of
Demosthenes, but is wanting in wit, and is probably spurious.

---

[1] Saintsbury, i 151.                    [2] *Var. Lect.* 300 f; cp. 75 f.
[3] Ziegeler, *De Luciano poëtarum iudice et imitatore* (1872).
[4] Brambs, *Citate und Reminiscenzen bei Lucian* (1888).   On Lucian's
Atticism, cp. Du Mesnil (1867), W. Schmid, *Attikismus*, i 221–5, and
Chabert (1897).

The legend of the Olympic recitation of the history of Herodotus
is found in the writing which bears that historian's name.   Traces
of Horace[1] and Juvenal have been detected in Lucian, and a
passage in the *Germania* of Tacitus[2] finds its parallel in the
*Method of writing History*[3].   His skill as a critic of art is proved
by his *Portraits* (Εἰκόνες) and his *Zeuxis*.   In his management of dialogue he exhibits the influence of Plato, while his genius has much
in common with that of Aristophanes, to whom he repeatedly
refers.   He owes something also to the comedies of Cratinus, and
to the satires of Menippus[4].   In his *Prometheus es* he admits that
he has 'attempted to adjust the philosophical dialogue to something like the tone of the comic poets', and to avoid the faults
and combine the excellences of both[5].   In the Byzantine age[6] he
was often imitated ; he was also a favourite author during the
Renaissance[7]; and the travellers' tales of his *True History* have
been told anew in various forms by Rabelais, Cyrano de Bergerac,
and Swift.   His interest in the great writers of Attic prose is
clearly marked ; but he has not sufficient seriousness of purpose
or stability of principle to be a really great critic of classical
literature[8].

With Lucian we may associate a slightly later writer, Alciphron,
represented in the fictitious letters of Aristaenetus[9]
as one of the correspondents of Lucian, whom he          Alciphron
undoubtedly imitates[10].   His own imaginary *Letters* are inspired
by the Attic Comedy of Philemon, Diphilus and Menander.

The Greek of Lucian was imitated in Latin by Apuleius of
Madaura in Africa, who wrote in the times of
Antoninus Pius and M. Aurelius.   It was Lucian's          Apuleius
*Ass* that inspired the satiric novel known as the *Metamorphoses* of

---

[1] A. Heinrich, *Lukian u. Horaz* (1885).          [2] § 3.          [3] § 60.

[4] Rabasté, *Quid comicis debuerit Lucianus* (1867).

[5] Saintsbury, i 149.

[6] Krumbacher, *Gesch. d. Byz. Lit.* §§ 194, 198, 211, p. 756[2], and Hase,
*Notices et Extraits*, ix 2, 129.

[7] Förster, *Lucian in der Renaissance* (1886).

[8] Cp. Saintsbury, i 146—152; also Egger, 464–9; Christ, §§ 533—542[4];
and esp. M. Croiset, v 583—616, and his *Essai* (1882).

[9] i 5 and 22.

[10] Cp. iii 55 with Lucian's *Symposium*.

Apuleius, which includes the celebrated myth of *Cupid and Psyche.* The author's title to the name of *philosophus Platonicus* rests on his minor works :—(1) *De Deo Socratis,* a prolix exposition of the Platonic doctrine on the subject of God and the daemons ; (2) *De Platone et eius dogmate,* a treatise on the natural and moral philosophy of Plato, followed by a spurious book on the logic of Aristotle. He also wrote *De Mundo,* a free translation of the περὶ κόσμου, bearing the name of Aristotle, and probably written by Nicolaus of Damascus[1].

Greek rhetoric includes the criticism of literature and the study of models of style, and in these respects

Technical
rhetoricians

has points of contact with the general history of Scholarship. All that was essential in the previous teaching of rhetoric was summed up in the time of Hadrian by Alexander[2], son of Numenius. His treatise on Figures[3] was

Alexander

the authority mainly followed by later writers, such as Tiberius[4] on the figures of Demosthenes; Phoebammon[5] on 'rhetorical figures' (which he classifies and reduces in number); and Herodian[6], who introduces examples from the poets. The age of Hadrian may perhaps also claim Aelius Theon

Aelius Theon

of Alexandria, who wrote commentaries on Xenophon, Isocrates and Demosthenes, and whose *Progymnasmata* or 'preliminary exercises' are still extant[7]. Theon's work deals with the art of writing under twelve divisions : —maxims, fables, narration, confirmation and refutation, commonplaces, description, encomium, comparison, prosopopoeia (or character-drawing), thesis (or abstract question), and proposal of a law; and it includes many illustrations from ancient literature. It was superseded by a similar work composed towards the end of the fourth century by Aphthonius, the pupil of Libanius ; but, in the mean time, it continued to hold its own

---

[1] All these *Opuscula de Philosophia* have been edited by Goldbacher (1876).

[2] Fragments in Spengel, *Rhet. Gr.* iii 1—6.

[3] Sp. iii 9—40.                    [4] Sp. iii 59—82.

[5] Sp. iii 43—56.                   [6] Sp. iii 60—104.

[7] Sp. ii 59. Cp. Saintsbury, i 93 f, who rightly inclines to place him before Aphthonius. The name of Aelius given him by Suïdas suggests the age of Hadrian.

beside the work of Hermogenes.  Hermogenes of Tarsus, who
lived under M. Aurelius and was already dis-
tinguished at the age of fifteen, failed to fulfil the          Hermogenes
high promise of his early years.  His *Progymnasmata*[1] are less
interesting than those of Theon; his works on legal issues[2], on
rhetorical invention (with examples from the Attic orators)[3], and
on eloquence[4], are more remote from the history of Scholarship than his treatise defining the different varieties of style
and suggesting methods for imitating them, with critical remarks
on some of the best prose writers[5].

In this century rhetoric, as the art of literary expression, was
in close alliance with grammar and lexicography.
To the age of Hadrian we may assign the eminent          Grammarians
grammarian Apollonius Dyscolus, who lived and died in poverty
in what was once the royal quarter of Alexandria.  He appears to
have spent a short time in Rome, under Antoninus
Pius.  His name of Dyscolus ('crabbed') is said to          Apollonius
have been due to a sourness of temper, caused by          Dyscolus
extreme poverty[6]; but it is far more probable that it was suggested
by the difficulty of his style.  Apollonius and his son, Herodian,
are the most important grammarians of the imperial age.  He was
the founder of scientific grammar, and the creator of Greek Syntax.
Of his numerous writings a large portion was lost at an early date.
The fact that Priscian founded his great grammatical work on
that of Apollonius, has suggested the view that the writings of
Apollonius (most of which are now known by their titles alone)
formed part of a complete 'art of grammar', treated under thirteen
heads.  This view (which is that of Dronke[7] and Uhlig) is not, however, generally accepted.  The existence of a complete art of grammar
cannot be inferred either from Priscian, or from the *scholium* on
Dionysius Thrax[8], which is quoted for this purpose.  Apollonius

---

[1] Sp. ii 3—18; cp. Saintsbury, i 90–2.

[2] περὶ στάσεων, Sp. ii 133—174.

[3] περὶ εὑρέσεως, Sp. ii 177—262.

[4] περὶ μεσόδου δεινότητος, Sp. ii 426–56.

[5] περὶ ἰδεῶν ii 265—425, esp. 410-25.  Cp. Croiset, v 629—634.

[6] Anonymous life (ap. Flach, *Hesychius Miles.*, p. 243).  Cp. Gräfenhan,
iii 70 f.

[7] *Rhein. Mus.* xi 549 f.                    [8] Preller, *Aufsätze*, p. 89.

must therefore be regarded as the author, not of a systematic treatise, but of a series of special studies on important points[1]. The subjects of his principal works were, the parts of speech in general, also nouns and verbs in particular, and syntax. The parts of speech, in his view, were eight in number, arranged in the following order:—noun, verb, participle, article, pronoun, preposition, adverb and conjunction. His works on nouns and verbs were extensively quoted, not only by Priscian, but also by Georgius Choeroboscus (c. 600) and the scholiasts on Dionysius Thrax. But only four of his writings have survived—those on the pronoun, adverbs[2], conjunctions and syntax[3]. This last is in four books, the first of which determines the number and order of the parts of speech (assigning precedence to the noun and verb), and next discusses the syntax of the article; the second deals with the syntax of the pronoun; the third begins with the rules of 'concord' (καταλληλότης) and their exceptions, followed by the general syntax of the verb; the fourth includes the syntax of prepositions, adverbs and conjunctions, but only a small portion of this is still extant[4].

While Dionysius Thrax was, as we have seen, the first to make a special study of grammar[5], it was Apollonius who placed that study on a scientific basis. He analysed the true nature of language and of its component parts; set aside certain fantastic theories current in his day, and introduced scientific explanations in their place. Thus he refutes those who supposed that 'the article served to distinguish the genders', and insists that each part of speech has its origin in a conception characteristic of itself[6]. The characteristic of the article is 'the retrospective reference to a person already mentioned'; such a retrospect takes place, when we speak either of a known person, or of a

---

[1] Cp. Matthias, in *Fleckeis. Jahrb.*, *Suppl.* xv, quoted in Jeep's *Redetheile*, p. 94.

[2] First printed in Bekker's *Anecd. Gr.* ii 630—646.     [3] *ib.* ii 479—525.

[4] ed. R. Schneider and Uhlig (1878 f). Cp. L. Lange, *Das System der Syntax des Apollonios Dyskolos* (1852), and Egger, *Ap. Dyscole* (1854); also Steinthal, ii 220—347; Christ, § 564[4]; Cohn in *Pauly-Wissowa*, II i 136—9; and Croiset, v 635 f.

[5] p. 138 *supra*.

[6] *Syntax*, i. p. 23 Bekker, ἕκαστον δὲ αὐτῶν ἐξ ἰδίας ἐννοίας ἀνάγεται.

definitely recognised class[1]. He was the only ancient grammarian
who wrote a complete and independent work on Syntax, and his
opinions continued to be recognised as authoritative throughout
the Middle Ages, and down to the time of Theodorus Gaza and
Constantinus Lascaris inclusive. His definitions of the parts of
speech show a marked advance on those of his predecessors, and
are adopted by Priscian and by subsequent grammarians[2]. Priscian[3]
calls him 'maximus auctor artis grammaticae', and refers to him
and his son as 'maximis auctoribus'[4]. The vast extent of their
works is implied in Priscian's mention of the 'spacious volumes'
of Apollonius, and the *pelagus* of the writings of Herodian[5].

Aelius Herodianus, the son of Apollonius Dyscolus, lived at
Rome under M. Aurelius. His principal work,
entitled καθολικὴ προσῳδία, was in 21 books, the       Herodian
first 19 treating of accentuation in general, book 20 on quantities
(χρόνοι) and breathings (πνεύματα), and book 21 on enclitics,
*diastole* and *synaloephe*. It was mainly founded on Aristarchus
and Tryphon, and the nature of its subject left little (if any) room
for originality. It is now represented only by excerpts preserved
by Theodosius and 'Arcadius'. Herodian also wrote on orthography; on barbarisms and monosyllabic words; on nouns and
verbs; on inflexions, declensions and conjugations. Our knowledge of these works depends entirely on extracts in later
grammarians, *e.g.* in the Homeric *scholia*, and in Stephanus of
Byzantium. His only extant work is a treatise 'on peculiar
diction' (περὶ μονήρους λέξεως), consisting of a series of articles
on exceptional or anomalous words. The close of the preface
skilfully leads up to the first article in the list, that on Zeus[6].
We have also an abstract of his teaching on syllables 'common'
in quantity (περὶ διχρόνων), and numerous excerpts from his work
on the accentuation of the *Iliad* and the *Odyssey*. These excerpts
are mainly preserved in the Homeric *scholia*[7]. Herodian generally

---

[1] *ib.* p. 26 (Croiset, *l.c.*).

[2] Cp. Gräfenhan, iii 109—132.              [3] xi 1.

[4] vi 1. Cp. xiv 1, xvii 1.                     [5] *Proëm.* §4.

[6] πρῶτος ἡμῖν θεὸς παρέστω· δίκαιον γὰρ τὴν ἀρχὴν ἀπ᾽ αὐτοῦ ποιήσασθαι,
ὡς καὶ ὁ Σολεὺς (Aratus) ἀρχόμενος ἔφη ἐκ Διὸς ἀρχώμεσθα.

[7] Lehrs, *Herodiani scripta tria* (1848).

agrees with Aristarchus, while he often discusses the views of
Tryphon and others less known to fame[1]. By grammarians of
later ages he is generally called ὁ τεχνικός[2].

Another of the sources of the above *scholia* was the work of
Nicanor (περὶ στιγμῆς), written by an Alexandrian
grammarian rather earlier than Herodian, probably
in the reign of Hadrian. Nicanor distinguished eight varieties of
punctuation[3], viz. three forms of the full stop[4]; two of the colon[5];
and three of the comma[6]. His interest in punctuation led to his
being known as 'the punctuator' (ὁ στιγματίας)[7].

In the second century lexicography received a new impulse
from the prevailing fancy for imitating the great
Attic models of the past. The *study* of those
models had been begun in the days of Dionysius
of Halicarnassus, while their *imitation* was the characteristic of
the new Sophists, who came into existence towards the close of
the first century, and flourished during the age of the Antonines[8].
This new type of imitative literature stimulated the production of
lexicographical works prepared by compilers claiming the name of
'Atticists'. Their aim was partly to collect words and phrases
sanctioned by Attic usage, partly to explain unfamiliar terms
found in Attic authors. Lists of such words had already been
drawn up, in the Alexandrian age, by Aristophanes and Crates;
and, early in the imperial age, by Demetrius Ixion and Caecilius
of Calacte; also, in the first century A.D., by minor grammarians
such as Dorotheus and Epitherses, Nicander and Irenaeus[9]. But
it was in the time of Hadrian, at the beginning of a new age of

*Margin notes: Nicanor; Lexico-graphers*

[1] Lehrs, *De Aristarchi Studiis Homericis*, p. 30³; cp. Ludwich, *Aristarchs Hom. Textkr.* i 75—80.

[2] Cp. in general Hiller, *Quaestiones Herodianae* (1866); Lentz, *Herodiani technici reliquiae* (1867); Gräfenhan, iii 72, 99; Christ, § 565⁴; Croiset, v 637.

[3] Bachmann, *Anecd.* ii 316.

[4] ὑπερτελεία, τελεία, ὑποτελεία.       [5] ἄνω πρώτη, ἄνω δευτέρα.

[6] ἀνυπόκριτος, ἐνυπόκριτος, and ὑποστιγμή. This last is a 'stop put after a protasis', an apodotic comma.

[7] Friedländer, *Nicanoris...reliquiae* (1850); cp. Gräfenhan, iii 67, 94; Christ, § 563⁴; Croiset, v 637 f.

[8] Cp. Bernhardy, *Gr. Litt.* i 630—642⁴.

[9] Croiset, v 639.

Greek Scholarship[1], that lexicography made its first important advance.

In that age the chief representative of lexicography is the 'Atticist', Aelius Dionysius, described by Suïdas as a descendant of Dionysius of Halicarnassus. He *Aelius Dionysius* compiled a lexicon of Attic words in five books with a supplement in five more, both parts including many examples of each word. Photius[2] describes it as equally useful to imitators of Attic style and students of Attic writers. His own copy included a similar lexicon, of equal bulk, but containing fewer examples, compiled by another 'Atticist', Pausanias, who lived under Antoninus Pius and *Pausanias the 'Atticist'* possibly also under M. Aurelius. Photius[3] suggests the desirability of recasting and combining the lexicons of both of these 'Atticists' in a single work with all the items in a single alphabetical order[4]. For most of our knowledge of both, we are indebted to Eustathius. The sources of their learning are Aristophanes of Byzantium and Didymus, Pamphilus and Diogenianus, Tryphon and Herodian[5]. In the age of Hadrian, Julius Vestinus of Alexandria com- *Vestinus* piled collections of words from Thucydides, and from Isaeus, Isocrates, Demosthenes and other orators[6]; while his fellow-townsman, Valerius Pollio, made a selection of Attic phrases, mainly from the poets. Pollio's son, Diodorus, confined himself to explaining difficult terms in the Attic orators[7].

Of the 'Atticists' the most interesting to ourselves are Phrynichus and Moeris, some of whose works are *Phrynichus* still extant. Phrynichus (*fl.* 180) appears to have taught Rhetoric in Bithynia under M. Aurelius and Commodus. He was a passionate purist, and, in spite of feeble health,

---

[1] Wilamowitz, *Eur. Her.* i 173.

[2] *Cod.* 152.    [3] *Cod.* 153.

[4] *Cod.* 152-3. Cp. Rindfleisch, *De Pausaniae et Aelii Dionysii lex. rhet.* (1866).

[5] E. Schwabe, *Aelii Dionysii et Pausaniae Frag.* (1890), combined in alphabetical order.

[6] Suïdas, Οὐηστῖνος.

[7] Phot. *Cod.* 149 f. Cp., in general, Christ, § 571[4]; Croiset, v 640 f.

composed a vast lexicon of Attic terms in 37 books, under the
title of σοφιστικὴ προπαρασκευή, 'the rhetorical magazine'. All
that we know of this great work is the selection published in
Bekker's *Anecdota*[1], and the summary in Photius[2], who describes
the work as at least five times too long, and the author as failing
to illustrate by example that beauty of style which he commends
by precept. It was partly founded on the work of Aelius
Dionysius. As authorities Phrynichus recognised, in prose, Plato
and the ten Attic orators, also Thucydides, Xenophon, Aeschines
Socraticus, Critias and Antisthenes (with a special preference for
Plato, Demosthenes and Aeschines Socraticus); and, in verse,
Aeschylus, Sophocles, Euripides and Aristophanes[3]. He composed
(probably in his youth) a far shorter work which has come down
to us, known to Suïdas as the Ἀττικιστής, with an alternative title
ἐκλογὴ ῥημάτων καὶ ὀνομάτων Ἀττικῶν. It consists of a long list of
rules and prohibitions, telling the student what expressions to
avoid, and what to use instead[4]. Throughout the work the author
keeps his attention fixed on the general usage of the best Attic
writers, without regard to exceptional or mistaken divergencies
from the strict Attic rule[5]. Those whom Phrynichus specially
singles out for animadversion, among recent writers who had
departed from the Attic standard, are two of the age of
Hadrian:—Lollianus, who was himself a Greek and taught at

---

[1] i pp. 1—74.　　　　　　　　[2] *Cod.* 158.

[3] Photius, *cod.* 158, p. 101 *b*. This lexicon was probably originally arranged
according to subjects (Kaibel's *Göttingen Diss.*, 1899).

[4] You must say not ἑκοντήν, but ἐθελοντήν; not ὄπιθεν, but ὄπισθεν; not
ἱκεσία, but ἱκετεία; not ὑπόδειγμα, but παράδειγμα; not ὠνάμην, but ὠνήμην;
not μέχρις and ἄχρις, but μέχρι and ἄχρι; not ἀπίναι, but ἀπιέναι; not εἰσιέτω,
but εἰσίτω; not εὐχαριστεῖν (which has survived in modern Greek), but χάριν
εἰδέναι. ἄρτι must not be constructed with the Future; τέμαχος must be used
only of fish. You must not say ἀποτάσσομαι, but ἀσπάζομαι; not σημᾶναι, but
σημῆναι; not φλεγμᾶναι, but φλεγμῆναι; not περιέσσευσε, but ἐπερίσσευσε; not
πιοῦμαι, but πίομαι; not ἤλειπται, but ἀλήλειπται; not ὤμοκε, but ὀμώμοκε; not
ἀπελεύσομαι, but ἄπειμι; not πεινᾶν and διψᾶν, but πεινῆν and διψῆν; not κακο-
δαιμονεῖν, but κακοδαιμονᾶν. 'To answer' is not ἀποκριθῆναι, but ἀποκρίνασθαι;
ἐπίδοξος must not be used in the sense of ἐπίσημος; you must not use ἐωνησάμην,
but ἐπριάμην; not ἤμην, but ἦν, and so on, through more than 400 items. Ed.
Lobeck (1820); Rutherford (1881).

[5] Cp. Dedication to Cornelianus, quoted on p. 277.

Athens; and Favorinus, a native of Gaul, who was not unknown in Rome[1].

The views of Phrynichus on points of Attic usage were controverted by Orus, a grammarian of uncertain   *Orus* date, who is sometimes placed shortly after Phrynichus[2]. Orus is possibly one of the authorities followed in the short anonymous lexicon called the *Anti-Atticist* (Ἀντιαττικιστής)[3]. The latter gives ancient authorities for words condemned by Phrynichus and others. Thus Phrynichus[4] condemns the use of ἀκμήν for ἔτι, though he knew that it is once found in Xenophon. The *Anti-Atticist* records this use, and justifies it by adding a reference to Hypereides. Of the life of Aelius   *Moeris* Moeris we know nothing; but we possess his collection of Attic terms (λέξεις Ἀττικαί), which, like one of the works of Phrynichus, is sometimes called the Ἀττικιστής[5].

The date of Valerius Harpocration, the author of an important lexicon to the Attic orators (λέξεις τῶν δέκα ῥητόρων),   *Harpocration* is uncertain. He is described by Suïdas as a rhetorician of Alexandria. According to various modern views, he was a contemporary of either Tiberius[6], or Hadrian[7], or Libanius[8]. It is perhaps best to place him in the second century[9], and to identify him with the Harpocration mentioned by Julius Capitolinus[10] among the *grammatici Graeci* charged with the education of L. Verus; he would thus belong to the age of the Antonines. He cites no grammarian or lexicographer later than the time of Augustus, and it is this fact that has led to his

[1] p. 308 *supra*.

[2] E. Hiller, *Die Zeit des Gram. Oros*, Jahrb. f. cl. Phil., 1869, p. 438 f, agrees with Ritschl, *Opusc.* i 582, in placing him shortly after Phrynichus. But Reitzenstein, *Etymologika*, pp. 287 f and 348, makes him a contemporary of Orion (*c.* 425 A.D.).

[3] Bekker, *Anecd.* i 75—116.      [4] no. 100.

[5] ed. Bekker, 1833; cp. Christ, § 571[4]; Croiset, v 641.

[6] E. Meier, *de aetate Harp.* in *Opusc. Acad.* ii.

[7] Bernhardy, *Quaestionum de Harp. aetate specimen*.

[8] Valesius, ed. 1682; Libanius (*Ep.* 371) reproaches Themistius for attracting 'the Egyptian Harpocration' to the inclement climate of Constantinople (*c.* 353).

[9] So Dindorf.            [10] Jul. Capitol., *Verus*, c. 2.

being placed as early as Tiberius ; but it is also consistent with a
later date, as it is doubtful whether the first two centuries saw
the publication of any work on the Attic orators which it was
possible for him to cite. His lexicon has come down to us in
two forms, the complete work and an abridgement; but the MSS
of the former are far inferior to those of the latter. One of the
MSS of the complete work (P) is in the Library of Trinity College,
Cambridge : another (Q) in that of the University (Dd 4, 63). In
the margin of the second is a series of articles (including a passage
from Philochorus on the subject of ostracism), first published by
Dobree (1822) under the name of *Lexicon rhetoricum Canta-
brigiense.* The work of Harpocration himself is of special value
in connexion with the language of the Attic orators and the
institutions of Athens. Besides quotations from the tragic and
comic poets, it preserves for us a number of passages from the
Atthidographers Hellanicus, Androtion, Phanodemus, Philochorus,
and Istrus, from the *Constitutions* of Aristotle, from the *Laws* of
Theophrastus, from historians such as Hecataeus, Ephorus and
Theopompus, Anaximenes and Marsyas, also from Craterus, the
collector of Attic decrees, from travellers such as Polemon and
Diodorus (*On Demes*), and from scholars such as Callimachus,
Eratosthenes and Didymus of Alexandria, Dionysius of Halicarnassus and his namesake, the son of Tryphon. These two
last are apparently his latest authorities. In five passages he
mentions certain MSS of Demosthenes known as 'Αττικιανά,
which are also mentioned in two of our Demosthenic MSS (the
Munich and Venice MSS, B and F respectively) at the end of the
*Speech on Philip's Letter*[1], and are probably connected with the
person of that name noticed by Lucian[2], who is sometimes
identified with Atticus, the friend of Cicero[3]. Harpocration
seldom goes so far astray as in the article on the phrase ὁ κάτωθεν
νόμος[4], where he actually records three erudite but erroneous

---

[1] διώρθωται ἐκ δύο 'Αττικιανῶν. Cp. Galen, *fragm. comm. in Tim. Plat.*
p. 12 Daremberg, κατὰ τὴν τῶν 'Αττικῶν ἀντιγράφων ἔκδοσιν, and Bernhardy
*Gr. Litt.* i 634[4].

[2] *Adv. Indoctum*, 2, 24.

[3] Cp. Dziatzko in Pauly-Wissowa, *s.v.* 'Αττικιανά.

[4] Dem. 23 § 28.

explanations proposed by Didymus, instead of stating that it simply means 'the law next below', 'the following law'[1].

Another lexicographer, Julius Pollux (Πολυδεύκης) of Naucratis (*fl.* 180 A.D.), is the author of an *Onomasticon*[2] of Attic words and phrases in ten Books, dedicated to his imperial pupil, Commodus[3], who appointed him to a professorship at Athens, which he held until his death at the age of 58. The arrangement is according to subjects. Among the most valuable portions are Book IV, on music, dancing and the Greek theatre, probably partially borrowed from Juba[4]; Book VIII, on the Athenian tribunals and officers of State, founded partly on Aristotle's *Constitution of Athens*[5]; and Book IX, § 51 f, on coins. His primary authorities are the lexicons of Didymus, Tryphon and Pamphilus; in Book II he partly relies on a medical writer named Rufus; and, from Book IX onwards (as he himself tells us), he has made use of the *Onomasticon* of Gorgias the younger. His biographer, Philostratus, informs us that, while in matters of criticism he was fairly competent, his declamations were marked by more spirit than skill[6]; and, as already observed[7], the scholiast on the *Lexiphanes* and *Rhetorum Praeceptor* of Lucian informs us that both of those works, with their ridicule of those who affected an ultra-Attic phraseology, were intended as a satire on Pollux. But, on the whole, there seems to be good reason for agreeing with Hemsterhuis[8], the editor of both, that Pollux is *not* attacked by Lucian, though Lucian, who is himself an Atticist, remorselessly attacks the affected Atticism of his day.

Pollux

---

[1] ὁ μετὰ τοῦτον νόμος (Bekker's *Anecd.* 269). Cp. Cobet, *De auctoritate et usu Grammaticorum veterum* (1853); Blass in I. Müller's *Handbuch*, i B 4, p. 155[2].—On Harpocration, cp. Christ, § 572[4]; Croiset, v 646 f.

[2] ed. Dindorf (1824); Bekker (1846); Bethe (1900— ). Cp. Christ, § 573[4]; Croiset, v 645 f.

[3] Ἰούλιος Πολυδεύκης Κομμόδῳ Καίσαρι χαίρειν. 'The young Commodus received the title of Caesar in 166, but the higher title of Augustus in 177' (Jebb in *Companion to Gk Studies*, p. 148).

[4] p. 294 *supra*. Rohde, *De Pollucis in apparatu scaenico enarrando fontibus* (1870).

[5] See *Introduction* p. xxv, and *Testimonia*, in present writer's ed.

[6] *Vit. Soph.* ii 12, τὰ μὲν κριτικὰ ἱκανῶς ἠσκεῖτο κτλ.    [7] p. 315 *supra*.

[8] Lucian, *Proleg.* p. 31 f, and v 175 ed. Bipont.

In this age the leading authority on metre was Hephaestion of
Alexandria, probably identical with the grammarian
of that name who, together with Telephus of Pergamon, and Harpocration, was charged with the education of
L. Verus[1]; if so, he belongs to the middle of the second century.
His work on metre (originally in no less than 48 books) has only
survived in the epitomised form of his own *Encheiridion*. Of the
three best MSS one is in Paris and two in Cambridge, while the
*scholia* (including extracts from an earlier authority, Heliodorus,
and from the unabridged work of Hephaestion) are preserved in
two MSS in Oxford[2]. It long remained the standard work on the
subject. We also possess part of his treatise on poetry, the most
important portion of which is the passage on the *parabasis* in
Attic Comedy.

Early in the second century the study of Aristophanes was
facilitated by Symmachus (*c.* 100), whose extant
*scholia* prove that he commented on the plays in
the following order:—*Plutus, Nubes, Ranae, Equites, Acharnians,
Vespae, Pax, Aves, Thesmophoriazusae, Ecclesiazusae* and *Lysis-
trata.* He apparently produced the first edition of select plays
of Aristophanes[3]. The metres of that poet had already been
studied by Heliodorus, who preceded Hephaestion, and is sometimes placed in the first half of the first century A.D.

Among commentators on Plato, in the age of the Antonines,
we may mention Albinus, who was one of the instructors of Galen in 151, and wrote a considerable work
on the dogmas of Plato, the two surviving fragments
of which include a discussion on the order of the dialogues, and a summary of Plato's teaching (under the
slightly altered name of Alcinous)[4]. A commentary on Plato was
also written by one Atticus (*fl.* 175), and extracts from his exposition
of the *Timaeus* are preserved by Proclus. The mathematical

*Marginal notes:*
Hephaestion

Symmachus

Commenta-
tors on Plato;
Albinus.
Atticus.
Theon.
Numenius

---

[1] Jul. Capitol., *Verus*, c. 2.

[2] ed. Gaisford (1855[2]), and Westphal (1866); also ed. Consbruch (Leipzig,
1906). Cp. Christ, § 567[4]; Croiset, v 649 f.

[3] Wilamowitz, *Eur. Her.* i[1] 179 f; and literature quoted in Christ, § 214[4],
p. 315. The above order of plays is opposed by Dr Rutherford, *Schol.
Aristoph.* iii 38, 43; see, however, *Cl. Rev.* xx 116 f.

[4] Printed in K. F. Hermann's text of Plato, vol. vi (Croiset, v 691).

passages in Plato were expounded in a Neo-pythagorean spirit
by Theon of Smyrna, and part of this exposition has survived[1].
Lastly, the Neo-pythagorean Numenius, who wrote on the divergencies between the teaching of Plato and that of the later
Academy, is among the precursors of Neo-platonism.

A varied training in the principles of the Platonists, Peripatetics, Stoics and Epicureans, fell to the lot of Galen      Galen
(131—201), who was born at Pergamon in the reign
of Hadrian, and studied medicine in Pergamon, Smyrna and
Alexandria before settling for a while in Rome.   On the death of
M. Aurelius (180), he returned to Pergamon and there ended his
days.  Besides being a prolific writer on medical and philosophical
subjects (including ethics and logic), he wrote on matters connected
with grammar and literary criticism.   Of ten such works that he
names in the list of his own writings[2], five were on Ancient
Comedy.  Some of the rest dealt with questions of Atticism,
including a lexicon in 48 books comprising words used by the
early Attic writers.   In the treatise *On the order of his own works*[3]
he shows that he had no sympathy with the Atticism of the day;
he even ridicules those who criticised errors of pronunciation.
The aim of his lexicon was simply to determine the exact sense of
the words used by ancient writers, which, as he found, were often
misunderstood by his contemporaries.  He is practically repeating
a precept of Aristotle's *Rhetoric*[4], when he says that the greatest
merit of style is perspicuity[5], and the excellence of his own style
is due to his using ordinary language free from the affectations
of Atticism and archaism[6].  He wrote commentaries on Plato's
*Timaeus* and *Philebus*, on Aristotle's *Categories* and *Analytics*,
and on Theophrastus and Chrysippus ; but, with the exception of
fragments of the first, they have not survived.   His 118 genuine
extant works include one on sophistical expressions[7], and another
on the dogmas of Hippocrates and Plato.

---

[1] ed. Hiller, 1878.         [2] c. 17.        [3] c. 5.        [4] iii 2, 1.

[5] *De Facultatibus Nat.*, c. 1, ἡμεῖς γε μεγίστην λέξεως ἀρετὴν σαφήνειαν
εἶναι πεπεισμένοι.

[6] Croiset, v 721, 725; cp. Christ, § 645[4], and W. Herbst, *Galeni—de
Atticissantium studiis testimonia* (Leipzig, 1911).

[7] *Libellus de Captionibus quae per dictionem fiunt*, Gabler, 1903 (*Cl. Rev.*
xviii 50).

Towards the close of the second century the empiric school
of medicine was represented by Sextus Empiricus,
whose writings are our principal authority on the
Greek Sceptics. The shorter of his two extant
works, the *Pyrrhonean Sketches*, is an outline of the views of the
founder of the Sceptics, in the form of a refutation of the logical,
physical and moral doctrines of the dogmatists; the longer, the
*Sceptical Commentaries*, consists of eleven Books, i—v being
directed against the dogmatists, and the remaining six against
teachers of the sciences (πρὸς μαθηματικούς), viz. the grammarians
(vi), rhetoricians (vii), geometricians (viii), arithmeticians (ix),
astrologers (x), and musicians (xi)[1]. He endeavours to demolish
all the liberal arts[2] in turn, with a view to proving that nothing
whatever can really be taught: much of his work, though marked
by considerable acumen, is puerile and pedantic; but his poetic
quotations are of some interest; and, happily, in attacking the
arts, he preserves some important facts about them. Thus his
attack on the grammarians is of special value for certain items of
evidence connected with the history of Scholarship[3]. It may be
added that he approves the division of Grammar into three parts,
(1) *technical*, including the study of diction; (2) *historical*, including
the explanation of mythological and antiquarian allusions; (3) *exegesis, criticism* and *emendation* (i 4). He is here probably following
Apollonius[4].

The close of the century is marked by a name of note
among Christian scholars. Clement of Alexandria
(*c.* 160—*c.* 215), probably an Athenian by birth,
sought in the philosophic schools of Greece and
Italy, of Syria and of Palestine, the teaching which he found at
last at Alexandria (*c.* 180) in the lectures of the Stoic Pantaenus,
who had become a convert to Christianity. Clement himself
taught at Alexandria (*c.* 190—203), first as the colleague and next
as the successor of Pantaenus, counting Origen among his pupils.
About 203 he left Alexandria for ever, passing the rest of his life

[1] In the MSS the second group of Books is wrongly placed first, and the
whole work is often quoted by the title of that group, *Adv. Mathematicos*.

[2] ἐγκύκλια μαθήματα, p. 600, l. 23.          [3] *e.g.* p. 10 n. 4 *supra*.

[4] Christ, § 512[4]; Croiset, v 701-3.

at various places in Asia Minor, and also at Antioch.  The three principal works, in which his teaching is successively unfolded, are (1) his *Exhortation* (λόγος προτρεπτικὸς πρὸς Ἕλληνας), a learned and systematic attack on paganism, dealing almost entirely with Greek mythology and Greek speculation; (2) his *Paedagogus*, a course of instruction resting on reason as well as revelation, and partly borrowed from the Greek philosophers, and from the Stoic Musonius Rufus[1]; (3) his *Miscellanies*[2], in which he aims at giving precision of form to precepts of moral perfection, and reconciling faith with reason, Christian truth with pagan philosophy.  That philosophy he regards as originally derived from the Hebrew Scriptures and as leading up to Christianity by promoting habits of serious thought and purifying the mind from unreasoning prejudice[3].  In the spirit of an eclectic[4], he borrows freely from the Greek philosophers, and above all from Plato, sometimes expressly acknowledging his obligations, sometimes tacitly leaving them to be detected by readers familiar with the original[5].  He regards Greek philosophy as given by God for the training of the nations, while it supplies the Christian philosopher with a recreation only, as compared with the serious objects of his study[6].  He has been well described as 'a born orator and friend of the Muses, delighting in apt anecdotes and fine sayings, loving everything in the shape of literature'[7].  There is no doubt as to the vast variety of his learning, however imperfectly it may be assimilated.  It is from the Pythagorean Numenius[8] that he borrows his famous simile comparing Truth to the body of Pentheus, torn asunder by fanatics, each seizing a limb and fancying he has the whole[9]. He describes the mount of God as the true Cithaeron, and applies to the mysteries of the Christian Church phrases borrowed from

---

[1] Wendland, *Quaest. Muson.* (1886); *Musonii Reliquiae*, ed. Hense (1905). On Clement's quotations from Plato, cp. C. P. Parker in *Harvard Studies*, xii (1901) 191—200.

[2] κατὰ τὴν ἀληθῆ φιλοσοφίαν γνωστικῶν ὑπομνημάτων στρωματεῖς (parti-coloured bundles); such fanciful titles were fashionable in this age; cp. Pref. to Gellius.  Cp. Hort and Mayor's ed. of Book vii (1902), pp. xi f.

[3] Croiset, v 746—53.          [4] *Strom.* i p. 124.

[5] F. L. Clark in *Proc. Amer. Phil. Assoc.* 1902, xii—xx.

[6] *Strom.* vi 149—168.          [7] Bigg's *Neoplatonism*, p. 162.

[8] ap. Euseb. *Praep. Ev.* xiv 5, 7.          [9] *Strom.* i 13, 57.

the *Bacchae* of Euripides[1]. The Gospel is to him 'the New Song more powerful than that of Orpheus or Arion'[2]. His style is deeply tinged with phrases from Homer, whom he sometimes interprets allegorically; he also shows a marked familiarity with Attic usage[3]. For modern scholars the *Miscellanies* are by far the most important of his works. The varied learning there displayed has some resemblance to that accumulated in the nearly contemporaneous work of Athenaeus. The author himself compares its variety to that of a flowery meadow or a wooded mountain diversified with every kind of growth[4]. But, in all this diversity, there is the leading thought that all the objects of knowledge are brought into unity in the perfect Christian philosopher. To Clement, all the philosophy, and indeed all the learning, of the Greeks was more recent than that of other nations, and most of it borrowed from the Jews. In the same spirit, Numenius had already asked: 'What is Plato but Moses expressing himself in Attic Greek?'[5]. Such opinions may be traced to the learned Jews of Alexandria, to Philo Judaeus (20 B.C.—40 A.D.), and to Aristobulus (176 B.C.), who says as much in commenting on the *Timaeus* of Plato[6]; and one of the links between Aristobulus and Clement may perhaps be found in Alexander Polyhistor, who was interested in the Jews[7]. In connexion with Greek Scholarship the most important passages in the *Miscellanies* are I 21 (a comparison between Hebrew and Greek chronology); v 14 (on the debt of Greek to Hebrew literature); and VI 2 (on plagiarisms of Greek authors from one another)[8]. The second of these passages is partly compiled from Tatian.

Clement of Alexandria is the earliest of the Greek Fathers who were specially conspicuous for learning. He has preserved a large number of details respecting the Orphic and Eleusinian mysteries; and, from the knowledge of the mysteries displayed

---

[1] ll. 470–7; *Strom.* iv 25.        [2] *Exhort.* c. 1.

[3] Bigg's *Christian Platonists*, p. 45 n; cp. (on his allegories) Hatch's *Hibbert Lectures*, p. 70.

[4] *Strom.* vi 1; vii 111.        [5] *Strom.* i 22, 150.

[6] Cp. *Strom.* v 14, 97.

[7] *Supra*, p. 161. Cp. Cobet, Ἑρμῆς, i 170.        [8] Christ, § 681[4].

in his *Exhortation*[1], it might even be inferred that he had
himself been initiated.   Readers of Lobeck's *Aglaophamus* may
remember that, in these matters, he is there cited as a most
important witness[2].

[1]  2 and 12.   Cp. G. W. Butterworth, trans., Heinemann, 1919.
[2]  *Aglaophamus*, p. 140.

From Codex Parisinus (914 A.D.) of Clemens Alexandrinus
(*Protrept.* §48), copied by Baanes for Arethas, abp of Caesarea (p. 404 *infra*).

(E. M. Thompson's *Palaeography*, p. 164.)

<παραστησά>μενον ἐθνῶν· ἐπανελθόντα εἰς Αἴγυπτον ἐπαγαγ<έσθαι τεχ-
νί>τας ἱκανούς· τὸν οὖν Ὄσιριν, τὸν προπάτορα <τὸν αὐτοῦ>, δεδαλθῆναι ἐκέ-
λευσεν αὐτὸς πολυτελῶς· κ<ατασκευά>ζει δὲ αὐτὸν Βρύαξις ὁ δημιουργός· οὐχ
ὁ Ἀθην<αῖος· ἄλλος> δέ τις ὁμώνυμος ἐκείνωι τῶι Βρυάξιδι· ὃς ὕλη <ι>

# CHAPTER XIX.

## GREEK SCHOLARSHIP IN THE THIRD CENTURY.

In turning from the second to the third century, which
approximately begins with the accession of Septimius Severus in 193 and ends with the abdication
of Diocletian in 305, we feel conscious of a sense
of decline. We leave the age of Aristides and Lucian for that of
the Philostrati, and Aelian and Athenaeus. In science we have
no longer any names to compare with those of Ptolemy of
Alexandria and Galen of Pergamon. In history, however, we
note a decided advance in authors such as Dion Cassius and
Herodian, both of whom made Thucydides their model. In
philosophy, the high level reached in the previous century by
M. Aurelius is fully maintained by the earliest of the Neo-
platonists. The decline of poetry, represented in the early part
of the century by the *Cynegetics* of Pseudo-Oppian, is compensated
by the rise of romance in the writings of Xenophon of Ephesus,
and of Heliodorus.

The Sophists of this century include Philostratus 'the Athenian'
(b. *c.* 170; *fl.* 215—245) who, before the year 217,
dedicated his *Life of Apollonius of Tyana* to the
empress Julia Domna, the wife of Severus, the
mother of Caracalla, 'the patroness of every art, and the friend
of every man of genius'[1]. Perhaps the most memorable passage
is that in which Apollonius, in connexion with the art of Sculpture,
identifies φαντασία with 'the *creative* imagination'[2], thus giving
the term a new meaning unknown to Aristotle. A few years

---

[1] Gibbon, c. 6 (i 127 Bury). Philostr. *Vit. Apoll.* i 3; *Vit. Soph.* ii 30;
*Ep.* 73.

[2] vi 19 (quoted on p. 72); cp. περὶ ὕψους, xv 1, and Egger, p. 484.

later (*c.* 230–7) Philostratus wrote the *Lives of the Sophists*, Book I including the ancient Sophists, such as Gorgias; Book II, the modern, among whom Herodes Atticus is prominent. These *Lives* are neither real biographies nor critical studies, but are rhetorical portraits drawn in an exaggerated style. Incidentally we here learn that, during the life of Herodes Atticus, a purer Greek was spoken in Attica than in Athens itself[1]; and that, even after the death of Aristides, the study of rhetoric flourished at Smyrna[2]. His *Gymnasticus*, written after 219, is not without interest in connexion with the history of the Olympic games and the various kinds of athletic contests. His *Letters* are mainly inspired by the New Comedy of Athens and by the elegiac poets of Alexandria[3]. They also supply an interesting link between Greek and English poetry; for it is here that we find the source of Ben Jonson's well-known *Song to Celia* :—

'Drink to me only with thine eyes,
    And I will pledge with mine;
Or leave a kiss but in the cup
    And I'll not look for wine....
I sent thee late a rosy wreath,
    Not so much honouring thee,
As giving it a hope that there
    It could not wither'd be.
But thou thereon didst only breathe
    And sent'st it back to me;
Since when it grows, and smells, I swear,
    Not of itself but thee !'[4]

Bentley's grandson, Cumberland, found fault with Jonson for thus borrowing a 'parcel of unnatural, far-fetched conceits' from a 'despicable sophist's' 'obscure collection of love-letters'; and Cumberland's criticism was in turn denounced by Gifford[5].

[1] ii 1, 13.          [2] ii 26, 1.

[3] Croiset, v 764—770. *Gymnasticus*, ed. Jünther, 1909.

[4] *Ep.* 33, ἐμοὶ δὲ μόνοις πρόπινε τοῖς ὄμμασιν...μόνου δ' ἐμβαλοῦσα ὕδατος καὶ τοῖς χείλεσι προσφέρουσα πλήρου φιλημάτων τὸ ἔκπωμα (cp. Aristaenetus, i 25, and Agathias in *Anth. Pal.* v 261). 2, πέπομφά σοι στέφανον ῥόδων, οὐ σὲ τιμῶν, καὶ τοῦτο μὲν γάρ, ἀλλ' αὐτοῖς τι χαριζόμενος τοῖς ῥόδοις, ἵνα μὴ μαρανθῇ. 46, *ult.*, τὰ λείψανα (τῶν ῥόδων) ἀντίπεμψον μηκέτι πνέοντα ῥόδων μόνον ἀλλὰ καὶ σοῦ.

[5] Ben Jonson, viii (1875) 259 note. Cp. Saintsbury, i 119.

Philostratus, 'the Athenian', is surpassed in poetic imagination,

Philo-<br>stratus II,<br>of Lemnos and in a certain affectation of literary simplicity, by his nephew, 'Philostratus of Lemnos' (born *c.* 190). The *Heroicus* of the latter comprises a series of portraits of the heroes of the Trojan war, purporting to be derived from the manifestations vouchsafed by the spirit of Palamedes to a vine-dresser of scholarly tastes on the shore of the Hellespont. Homer's description of those heroes is here corrected, and made more ethical and more dramatic. The work has some little interest in a history of Scholarship, in so far as it mentions certain Greek tragedies that are no longer extant, viz. the *Oeneus*[1] and the *Palamedes*[2] of Euripides, while it also attests a continued interest in the study of Homer. In his *Eikones* he professes to give a description of sixty-four pictures in a gallery at Naples. The question whether actual works of art are here described has been much discussed, the opinion that the descriptions are derived from passages in the ancient poets being maintained by K. Friederichs (1860), and opposed by Brunn (1861, 1871), while an intermediate view is suggested by F. Matz (1867).

One of the imitators of the *Eikones* of Philostratus II was

Philo-<br>stratus III his grandson, Philostratus III. Seventeen of his descriptions are still extant. They are preceded by a brief discourse on the relations between painting and poetry. The *Eikones* are also imitated by Calli-

Callistratus stratus in his fourteen descriptions of statues, including three by Praxiteles and one by Lysippus[3].

Among writers of miscellanies we may mention Aelian

Aelian (*c.* 170—230), who was a priest at his native place, Praeneste. A Roman in spirit, he spoke Greek 'like an Athenian', his preceptor being Pausanias, the 'Atticist'[4]. He is the author of seventeen books *On Animals*, mainly borrowed from Alexander of Myndos (first century A.D.), and of fourteen books of *Historical Miscellanies* (ποικίλη ἱστορία). In both of these works he exhibits wide and varied learning, and

---

[1] i 5.                                   [2] xii 2.

[3] Christ, §§ 524–6[4]; Croiset, v 761—773. Schmid, *Atticismus*, iv 7, however, assigns the above works of Philostratus II to Philostratus I. See also K. Münscher, *Die Philostrati*, in *Philologus*, Suppl. x (1907).

[4] Philostr. *Vit. Soph.* ii 31.

a certain industry in collecting facts tending towards moral and
religious edification. The *Rustic Letters*, which bear his name,
are probably of Athenian origin ; they are idyllic in tone, and are
inspired by the Middle and New Attic Comedy[1].

A vast variety of erudition has been preserved by Athenaeus
of Naucratis, who lived at Rome under Commodus
and his successors. His comprehensive work, en-   **Athenaeus**
titled Δειπνοσοφισταί or ' Doctors at dinner', originally consisted
of thirty books. It was abridged into fifteen ; and it is this
abridgement that has survived in an incomplete form in a single
MS. The scene is laid at the house of the Roman pontiff
Larentius ; and all kinds of accomplishments,—grammar, poetry,
rhetoric, music, philosophy and medicine,—are represented among
the many interlocutors, some of whom bear famous names, such
as Plutarch, Arrian, Galen and Ulpian. The contemptuous
reference to Commodus[2] implies that the work was produced
after that emperor's death (193)[3]. It is an encyclopaedia under
the disguise of a dialogue. Food and drink, cups and cookery,
stories of famous banquets, scandalous anecdotes, specimens of
ancient riddles and drinking songs, and disquisitions on instruments of music, are only part of the miscellaneous fare which is
here provided. To the quotations in Athenaeus we are indebted
for our knowledge of passages from about 700 ancient writers
who would otherwise be unknown to us, and, in particular, for
the preservation of the greater part of the extant remains of the
Middle and New Attic Comedy. We also owe to him the
preservation of the celebrated *scolion* of Callistratus on Harmodius
and Aristogeiton[4].

Rhetoric is represented in this age by Apsines of Gadara
(*c.* 190—250), who taught at Athens *c.* 235–8, and
was a friend of Philostratus ' the Athenian ', and a   **Rhetoricians.**
rival (*c.* 244–9) of Fronto of Emesa. His speeches   **Apsines**
have perished, but part of his teaching survives in his *Rhetoric*[5],
which contains nothing essentially new. Its aim is purely

---

[1] Christ, § 529[4]; Croiset, v 774–7.   [2] 537 F.
[3] Dittenberger, Halle *Apophoreton* (1903), assigns the work to 193–7.
[4] p. 695, ed. Kaibel, 1887–90 ; cp. Christ, § 532[4]; Croiset, v 778—780.
[5] Spengel's *Rhet. Gr.* i 331—414.

practical; it gives few rules, but it happily illustrates them by
many examples. The author appears also to have written a
commentary on Demosthenes[1]. The *Rhetoric* of Minucianus[2]
Minucianus   was regarded as a classic and was expounded by
          Porphyry. It was also expounded by Menander
of Laodicea, probably the Menander mentioned in the *scholia* to
Demosthenes and Aristides. The name of Menander is also
Menander   borne by two treatises still extant[3], the first of
          which is ascribed by Bursian[4] to Menander and
the second to Genethlius, while these ascriptions are reversed by
Nitsche[5]. In the first the various types of epideictic discourse
are distinguished; and the sources from which they derive their
material, classified. Hymns to the gods are divided into nine
classes, and poets named as examples of each. The 'Praises of
Cities', 'Harbours' and 'Bays', and the proper method of composing an encomium on an Acropolis, are among the many
matters treated in this work. The second treatise deals with
forms of compliment, condolence etc.[6]

The most eminent rhetorician of the third century was Cassius
Longinus   Longinus (*c.* 220—273), the nephew and heir of
          Fronto of Emesa, the pupil of Origen, the admirer
of Plotinus, the preceptor of Porphyry, and the minister of Queen
Zenobia. He studied at Alexandria, taught for thirty years at
Athens, and ended his days at Palmyra as the counsellor of
Zenobia, whom he nobly supported in her resistance to Aurelian,
who put him to death in 273. Of his treatise *On the Chief End*
(περὶ τέλους) only an extensive fragment remains[7]. He also wrote
a Neo-Platonic treatise (περὶ ἀρχῶν), but Plotinus, after reading it,
remarked that Longinus was a scholar (φιλόλογος), but not a
philosopher[8]. As a rhetorician, he composed several works; and
we still possess part of his treatise on *Rhetoric* imbedded in that
of Apsines, and first identified by Ruhnken as the work of

---

[1] *Schol.* on Dem. *Lept.* p. 458, 9; and on Hermogenes, v 517 Walz. Cp.
Pauly-Wissowa, *s.v.* and Croiset, v 781 f.

[2] Spengel, i 415—424.                    [3] *ib.* iii 329—446.

[4] *Bayer. Akad.* 1882, *Abt.* 3.

[5] Berlin (1883); Bursian's *Jahresb.* xlvi 98 f.

[6] Croiset, v 782 f; Saintsbury, i 104 f.

[7] Porphyry, *Vit. Plotini*, § 20.          [8] *ib.* § 14.

Longinus¹. It is little more than a collection of practical observations on 'invention', arrangement, style, delivery, and the art of memory². It owed its reputation to the fact that it was found simple, short and easy to remember, as compared with the earlier *Rhetoric* of Hermogenes³. The studies of Longinus ranged over philosophy, rhetoric and criticism; in the opinion of Porphyry, he was the first of critics⁴, while Eunapius describes him as a 'living library and a walking museum'⁵. He produced two editions of a treatise on Attic phrases, and several works on Homer⁶; and his Homeric problems had their influence on a similar work by his pupil, Porphyry. It was his high renown as a critic that led to the conjecture of the copyists that he was the author of the treatise *On the Sublime*⁷; and there are some points of coincidence with that treatise in the fragments of his *Philological Discourses*⁸.

Materials for a history of Philosophy existed at an early date in the form of documents preserved by certain schools. These had been utilised in the *lives* written by authors such as Aristoxenus, Speusippus, Hermippus and Antigonus of Carystos; in the *lists* of the successive heads of each school drawn up by Sotion and Heracleides Lembus; and in the summaries of the *opinions* held in one or other school, as stated by Theophrastus, Areius Didymus, and Aëtius⁹. But the history of Philosophy had still to be written, and it is only an uncritical compilation that is supplied by Diogenes Laërtius (of Laërte in Cilicia), who may be placed early in the third century. He ends his account of the Sceptics with the immediate successor of Sextus Empiricus¹⁰, and he says

---

¹ *Opusc.* 183–5; Wyttenbach's Life of Ruhnken, p. 169, quoted in Walz, *Rhet. Gr.* ix p. xxiii f.

² Spengel, i 299—320.            ³ *ib.* p. 321.

⁴ *Vit. Plotini* 20, κριτικωτάτου καὶ ἐλλογιμωτάτου, and 21, ἐν κρίσει πρῶτος.

⁵ *Vita Porphyrii*, p. 456a 2 in *Eunapii Vitae*, ed. Boissonade (Didot, 1849).

⁶ Suïdas mentions ἀπορήματα and προβλήματα Ὁμηρικά, εἰ φιλόσοφος Ὅμηρος etc.

⁷ p. 288 *supra*.

⁸ φιλόλογοι ὁμιλίαι, Walz, *Rhet. Gr.* vi 225 (on Sophocles); vii 963 (περὶ λέξεως στομφώδους, cp. περὶ ὕψους iii 1, xxxii 7).

⁹ Diels, *Doxographi*.            ¹⁰ ix 116.

nothing of Neo-Platonism. His work is dedicated to a lady of
high rank, interested in philosophy[1]. It aims at enumerating
the chief representatives of each school, with brief biographical
sketches of an anecdotic character, a list of their works and a
popular statement of their views. The first two books include
the 'Seven Wise Men of Greece', the earliest philosophers down
to Anaxagoras and Archelaus, and Socrates and his pupils with
the exception of Plato, who is reserved for book iii. Book iv is
on the Academics, v on Aristotle and the Peripatetics, vi on the
Cynics, and vii on the Stoics from Zeno to Chrysippus. In viii
we return to the earlier age, to the school of Pythagoras, with
Empedocles and Eudoxus; in ix we have a confused jumble
including Heracleitus, the Eleatics, the Atomists and the Sceptics,
while x is entirely on the School of Epicurus, to which the
compiler himself appears occasionally to incline. Even in the
case of Epicurus, the author has been convicted of gross carelessness in the use of his authorities[2], while, in his list of the
works of Aristotle, he follows the old Alexandrian catalogue,
ignoring the fact that they had subsequently been edited in a
fuller form by Andronicus of Rhodes, in the time of Cicero. The
work appears to have been partly founded on the works of
Diocles of Magnesia (ἐπιδρομὴ φιλοσόφων, first century B.C.), and
Favorinus of Arles (παντοδαπὴ ἱστορία), with literary items from
the forgeries[3] of Lobon of Argos (περὶ ποιητῶν)[4].

Late in the second and early in the third century is the age
of the most important of the ancient commentators on Aristotle, Alexander of the Carian town
of Aphrodisias. He flourished under Septimius
Severus, having been called to Athens *c.* 198, and having dedicated
to Severus and Caracalla (not later than 211) his work *On Fate*,
which is an inquiry into Aristotle's opinions on Fate and Free-
will. His works, which are of special value in connexion with
the text of Aristotle and the history of Greek philosophy, are

*Alexander
of Aphrodisias*

---

[1] iii 47, ix 20.                              [2] Usener, *Epicurea*, xxi f.

[3] Hiller in *Rhein. Mus.* xxxiii 518 f.

[4] F. Nietzsche, in *Rhein. Mus.* xxiii—xxv, and Wilamowitz, *Phil. Unt.* iv
330–49. Favorinus alone is regarded as his original by Maass, *Phil. Unt.*,
*Heft* 3 and Rudolph, *Leipz. Stud.* vii 126 (Christ, § 514[4]; Croiset, v 818—820).

largely quoted by later writers, such as the Neo-Platonists Syrianus and Simplicius. Holding aloof from the mystical tendencies of the Academics of his time, he mainly confined himself to the interpretation of Aristotle. His extant commentaries deal with the First Book of the *Analytics*[1], the *Topica*[2], the *De Sensu*[3] and the *Metaphysics*[4]. He is also the author of several independent treatises[5]. About half of his voluminous writings were edited and translated into Latin at the revival of learning; and his genuine works have been recently published, mainly by the Berlin Academy[6].

The only original product of Greek genius in the third century was Neo-Platonism, which necessarily involved a renewed study of the teaching of Plato, though it attempted to combine that teaching with the tenets of other schools of Greek philosophy. The doctrines of those earlier schools had already been partially merged into one another, and had also been blended with old and new varieties of belief. This tendency had shown itself in Philo Judaeus, in Plutarch and Numenius and (early in this century) in Alexander of Aphrodisias, the commentator on Aristotle. In the same century the verbal study of Plato's text was exemplified in the Platonic lexicon of the sophist Timaeus[7], which is later than Porphyry unless the extract from that Neo-Platonist[8] is an interpolation.

Neo-Platonism is generally regarded as having been founded by Ammonius Saccas, who taught at Alexandria during the first half of the third century, but did not reduce his teaching to a written form. Among his many pupils (*c.* 205—211) was the Christian philosopher Origen[9] (185—254), who in 203 succeeded Clement as head of the Christian School of Alexandria. He was the first great scholar among the

Origen

---

[1] ed. Wallies (1883).      [2] *id.* (1891).

[3] ed. Thurot (1875); Wendland (1901).

[4] Latest ed. Hayduck (1891).

[5] *Scripta Minora*, ed. Bruns in *Suppl. Ar.* ii.

[6] Gerke in Pauly-Wissowa, i 1453 f.

[7] ed. Ruhnken, 1789.      [8] *s.v.* οὐχ ἥκιστα.

[9] Porphyry ap. Euseb. *H. E.* vi 19, 7. Zeller, *Phil. d. Gr.* iii 2, 459, suggests that the Christian philosopher has been confounded with a pagan pupil of Ammonius bearing the same name.

Greek Fathers. With his own hand he supplied himself with transcripts of the Greek Classics, but sold them all for a small sum in order to be enabled to teach others without receiving any remuneration. The work of Origen most closely connected with Scholarship was his *Hexapla*, an edition of the Old Testament exhibiting in six parallel columns the Hebrew text and the same in Greek characters, with the four translations by Aquila, Symmachus, the 'Seventy' and Theodotion. Seven shorthand writers and as many copyists took part in it, and the work filled fifty large rolls of parchment; but it is now represented by fragments alone. He also devoted much time and labour to the text of the New Testament. As a commentator he holds that Scripture has in general three senses, the literal, the moral, and the spiritual; and, with a view to eliciting the last of these, he specially favours the allegorical method of interpretation. These three senses he regards as corresponding to the body, soul and spirit, which he fancifully describes as figured in the water-pots of Cana 'containing two or three firkins a-piece'[1]. This weakness for allegorising was combined with a wide variety of learning. According to a discourse delivered in his presence in 239 by his pupil, Gregory Thaumaturgus, the range of his teaching at Caesarea included dialectics, physics, geometry, astronomy, ethics, metaphysics and theology; while he is described by Jerome as finding in Plato and Aristotle, in Numenius and Cornutus, support for the doctrines of Christianity[2]. Origen spent the last twenty years of his life at Caesarea. Copies of the greater part of his works were made by Pamphilus (d. 309) for the famous library which he founded in that city[3].

The principles of Neo-Platonism were reduced to writing by Plotinus (204—270), who studied under Ammonius Saccas at Alexandria from 232 to 243, and spent the remaining twenty-six years of his life at Rome. He may justly be regarded as the true founder of Neo-Platonism, in so far as he perpetuated its principles in a written form. In his

**Plotinus**

---

[1] Origen's *Philocalia*, c. 12, p. 19, J. A. Robinson.

[2] Jerome, *Ep.* 70. Cp. Croiset, v 845–55; cp. Christ, § 682[4], Bigg's *Christian Platonists*, and Westcott in *Dict. Chr. Biogr.*

[3] Hieron. *De scriptoribus eccl.* c. 75.

class-room 'the later Platonic and Aristotelian commentators were read[1]; but everywhere an original turn was given to the discussions, into which Plotinus carried the spirit of Ammonius'[2]. The teaching of Plotinus has been preserved with the aid of his pupil, Porphyry (233—c. 301–5), in six groups of nine books called the *Enneades*[3]. Porphyry had, in his youth, known Origen at Alexandria; and had been a pupil

Porphyry

of Cassius Longinus at Athens. It was from Longinus that he received the name of 'Porphyrius', as a rendering of his Tyrian name of Malchus, or 'King'. In 263 he became the pupil of Plotinus in Rome. He was a scholar and a mathematician, as well as a philosopher and a historian. From Porphyry to Julian one of the principal aims of Neo-Platonism was the philosophic defence and maintenance of paganism. Porphyry's attacks on Christianity, which were mainly concerned with historical criticism, and had an important influence on Julian 'the Apostate', were answered by Eusebius and others. His *History of Philosophy* was mainly confined to Plato, but it included a *Life of Pythagoras*, which is extant. He was among the last of the writers on philosophy who had a first-hand knowledge of the writings of his predecessors; and he quotes Longinus[4] as saying that, with the exception of Plotinus and Amelius (a pupil of Plotinus), philosophers had ceased to do anything more than collect and expound and expand the opinions of their predecessors. In extreme old age he wrote the *Life of Plotinus*; and his own expositions of his master's teaching are still represented in his *Sententiae*[5]. He also compiled a work on Chronology, which is among the authorities followed by Eusebius[6]. In the domain of Scholarship he produced a treatise on 'philological research' (φιλόλογος ἱστορία), and on 'grammatical questions' (γραμματικαὶ ἀπορίαι), as well as an 'introduction' to Thucydides, and to the

---

[1] Porph. *V. Plot.* 3.

[2] T. Whittaker, *The Neo-Platonists*, p. 33; cp. Bigg's *Neoplatonism*, p. 187, and R. Eucken, *Die Lebensanschauungen der grossen Denker*, 1902[4].

[3] ed. Creuzer (Oxford, 1835), (Paris, 1855); Kirchhoff, 1856; H. F. Müller, 1878; Volkmann, 1883. E.T. by S. MacKenna, 1908—; cp. W. R. Inge, *The Philosophy of Pl.*, 1919.     [4] *Frag.* 5, 5.

[5] T. Whittaker, pp. 112–4.     [6] *Frag. Hist. Gr.* iii 688 f.

*Categories* of Aristotle. His *Eisagoge*, or introduction to the
latter, as translated by Boëthius[1], had an important influence
on the thought of the Middle Ages; his commentary on the
*Categories* exists in fragments only[2]. He also wrote on 'the
philosophy of Homer', and on the profit which kings might
derive from his poems. This department of his literary activity
is now represented only by some fragments of his *Homeric
Questions* (Ὁμηρικὰ ζητήματα)[3], which have several points of
contact with Aristotle's *Homeric Problems*[4], and by his work *On
the Cave of the Nymphs*[5]. In the latter, the Cave in Ithaca,
which is the theme of the beautiful description in *Od.* xiii 102—112,
is treated as an allegory of the universe; the cave itself and the
nymphs, the two entrances into the cave, the vessels of stone
and the bees, are all of them allegorically interpreted in a highly
imaginative composition marked with superabundant learning
and (happily) enriched with numerous citations. Many moral
sentences borrowed from Sextus and Epicurus are imbedded in
his *Letter to Marcella*[6]; while his treatise *De Abstinentia* (περὶ
ἀποχῆς ἐμψύχων), in which vegetarianism is recommended to those
alone who lead a philosophic life[7], has preserved for us the substance of the treatise of Theophrastus *On Piety*[8], besides many
quotations from the poets, *e.g.* the important fragment of the
*Cretes* of Euripides. The work on Homer's *Life and Poems*,
preserved in Plutarch's *Moralia*, is sometimes ascribed to Porphyry. The pleasing effect there recognised in the figure *homoeo-*

[1] p. 253 *supra*.

[2] *Porphyrii Isagoge et in Aristotelis Categorias commentarium*, ed. Busse
in *Comm. Arist.* iv, with Boëthius' translation of the *Isagoge* (1887). The
*Isagoge* was also translated into Syriac, and the work of a Hellenised Syrian
was thus the means of introducing his countrymen to the study of Aristotle
(A. Baumstark, *Aristoteles bei den Syrern*).

[3] ed. H. Schrader (1880). Cp. Gräfenhan, iii 298 f.

[4] Ar. *frag.* 142, 164, 178, Rose.

[5] Nauck, ed. 2 (1886), with *Vita Pythag.*, *De Abstinentia* and *Ad
Marcellam*. Cp. Heraclitus, *Allegoriae Homericae*, 1851, *Quaestiones Hom.*,
1910.

[6] Usener's *Epicurea*, p. lviii f; cp. A. Zimmern, *Porphyry to Marcella*
(1896).

[7] T. Whittaker, pp. 114—122.            [8] Bernays, *Theophrastos* (1866).

*teleuton*, has led to its being credited with an early recognition of
the charm of rhyme[1].

The theory of Music was treated by Aristides Quintilianus,
who is certainly later than Cicero[2], and probably
later than Porphyry.  His description of the descent    **Aristides**
of the Soul from the region of the Ether, and of        **Quintilianus**
its passing through that of the Moon[3], is distinctly Neo-Platonic,
and can be closely paralleled by a passage in Porphyry[4].  The
value of his work depends mainly on its indebtedness to Aristoxenus of Tarentum, and to still earlier authorities, such as
Damon of Athens, the friend of Plato[5].

[1] Trench, *Sacred Latin Poetry*, p. 30[2] (Saintsbury, i 68 f).—On Porphyry
in general, see Lucas Holstenius, *De vita et scriptis Porphyrii* (1655), and
Croiset, v 831—841, and cp. Christ, § 621[4].

[2] περὶ μουσικῆς, ii 6.

[3] περὶ μουσικῆς, ii 17.

[4] *Sententiae*, 32.

[5] von Jan in Pauly-Wissowa, ii 894.

FROM CODEX PARISINUS OF A STUDENT'S COPY OF A COMMENTARY ON
PORPHYRY'S INTRODUCTION TO ARISTOTLE'S CATEGORIES (1223 A.D.).

(E. M. Thompson's *Palaeography*, p. 172.)

τούτων, ἐκεῖ εἰσίν, καὶ αἱ ὑπόλοιποι· ὅπου δὲ μία ⟨ἐκλείπεται⟩, ἐκεῖ καὶ
πᾶσαι ἐκλείπουσι. εἰρηκότες τὰς κοινωνί⟨ας χωρή⟩σωμεν καὶ ἐπὶ τὰς διαφοράς.
δευτέρα δὲ διαφορὰ αὐτῶν ⟨ὑπέρχεται⟩, ὁ τρόπος τῆς κατηγορίας· αἱ μὲν γὰρ ἐν
τῶι τί ἐστιν κατηγο⟨ροῦντες⟩ ὥσπερ τὸ γένος καὶ τὸ εἶδος· αἱ δὲ ἐν τῶι ὁποῖον
⟨τί ἐστιν⟩ ὥσπερ ἡ διαφορά, καὶ τὸ ἴδιον καὶ τὸ συμβεβηκός.

*David the Armenian.*

# Conspectus of Greek Literature, &c., 300—600 A.D.

| Roman Emperors | Poets | Chronologers & Historians | Orators and Rhetoricians | Scholars and Critics | Other Writers of Prose |
|---|---|---|---|---|---|
| 305 Constantius I<br>306 Constantine I | | 313 Eusebius 265—340 | | | Iamblichus c. 280—c. 330<br>326 Athanasius 295—373 |
| 337 -40 { Constantine II<br>-61 { Constantius II<br>-50 { Constans I | | | 335 Philostratus III Later *Eikones* ? Callistratus<br>340 Proaeresius 276—368<br>Libanius 314—c. 393<br>Themistius 310-20—c. 394 | Ulpian<br>335 Dexippus<br>365 Theon<br>Olympiodorus I | 367 Epiphanius 315—403<br>Gregory Nazianzen c. 330—c. 390<br>371 Basil 331—379<br>Gregory of Nyssa c. 343—c. 396 |
| 361 Julian<br>363 Jovian<br>364 Valens<br>378 Theodosius I<br>395 Arcadius | 362 Apollinaris of Laodicea, d. c. 383-92<br>Quintus Smyrnaeus | | Himerius c. 315—386<br>Aphthonius | 391 { Ammonius<br>{ Helladius<br>Theodosius | 381 Chrysostom 344-7—404<br>394 Theodore of Mopsuestia c. 350—403 |
| **400** | | | | | |
| 408 Theodosius II | Palladas<br>c. 410 Nonnus<br>Eudocia | 405 Eunapius, *Lives of Philosophers and Sophists*<br>429 Theodoret 386—c. 458<br>439 Socrates | Troilus<br>Syrianus | Stephanus Byzantinus<br>425 Orus<br>425 Orion | 406 Synesius c. 370—c. 413<br>Isidore of Pelusium c. 370—450<br>412 Cyril of Alexandria 380—444<br>415 d. of Hypatia<br>431 d. of Plutarchus |
| 450 Marcian<br>457 Leo I<br>474 Leo II<br>474 Zeno | Anatolius, bp of Constantinople 449-58 | 443 Sozomen<br>450 Zosimus | | Hesychius Alexandrinus<br>Stobaeus | 415-50 Hierocles<br>431-38 Syrianus<br>438-85 Proclus 410—485<br>c. 450 *Syriac Commentators on Aristotle* |
| 491 Anastasius I | Tryphiodorus<br>Colluthus<br>Musaeus | John of Antioch | Procopius of Gaza<br>Marcellinus | Hermeias<br>Timotheus of Gaza | 485 Marinus<br>480—520 'Dionysius Areopagita'<br>Aristaenetus |
| **500** | Christodorus | | | | |
| 518 Justin I<br>527 Justinian I | Paulus Silentiarius<br>Romanus<br>*fl.* 527—565<br>Agathias c. 536—582 | 518 Zachariah of Mytilene<br>533-6 Procopius *fl.* 527—562<br>Petrus Patricius *fl.* 534—562<br>533 Nonnosus Agathias c. 536—582<br>551 John Lydus | Sopater<br>Choricius<br>Agapetus | Ammonius son of Hermeias<br>Simplicius<br>Joannes Philoponus<br>c. 550 Hesychius of Miletus | Isidorus<br>Hegias<br>520 Damascius<br>529 *The School of Athens closed* |
| 565 Justin II<br>578 Tiberius II<br>582 Mauricius | | 563 John Malalas c. 500-73<br>581 Theophanes<br>582 Menander Protector<br>593 John of Epiphania<br>593 Evagrius | | Joannes Charax<br>564 Olympiodorus II<br>? David the Armenian<br>? Choeroboscus | 559 Anastasius of Antioch d. 599 |
| **600** | | | | | |

Continued from p. 278.

# CHAPTER XX.

## GREEK SCHOLARSHIP IN THE FOURTH CENTURY.

THE fourth century begins a few years before the abdication of Diocletian (305). By the end of its first quarter (324), Christianity was recognised as the religion   The fourth century of the State, and Byzantium chosen as the site of the new capital, which was henceforth to become a new centre of Greek learning. Before two-thirds of the century had passed, a pagan reaction had intervened during the brief reign of Julian (361–3). A historian of the eleventh century, who assigns to his reign the last of the pagan oracles, informs us that the emperor sent envoys to restore the temple of Apollo at Delphi, but the work was no sooner begun than the envoys were bidden to return with the following response :—

> εἴπατε τῷ βασιλῆι, χάμαι πέσε δαίδαλος αὐλά.
> οὐκέτι Φοῖβος ἔχει καλύβαν, οὐ μάντιδα δάφνην,
> οὐ παγὰν λαλεοῦσαν· ἀπέσβετο καὶ λάλον ὕδωρ[1].

Tell ye the king : to the ground hath fallen the glorious dwelling ;
Now no longer hath Phoebus a cell, or a laurel prophetic ;
Hushed is the voiceful spring, and quenched the oracular fountain.

By the end of the fourth century, the Serapeum of Alexandria had been destroyed (391), the Senate of Rome had (nominally at least) become Christian (394), the Olympian festival had been abolished, the overthrow of paganism completed under Theodosius I, and the rule of the Roman Empire divided on his death between his two sons, Arcadius, who ruled in the East, and Honorius in the West (395).

---

[1] Cedrenus, *Hist. Comp.* i 304, p. 532 Bonn.

In this time of transition from paganism to Christianity, the
principal Greek authors on the Christian side were Eusebius,
Athanasius, Epiphanius, Basil, Gregory of Nazianzus, Gregory of
Nyssa, Chrysostom, and Theodore of Mopsuestia. Of these,

Eusebius          Eusebius (265—340), the devoted pupil of Pamphilus (d. 307), in whose library he laid the
foundation of his vast erudition and whose name he gratefully
assumed by calling himself Eusebius Pamphili, was bishop of
Caesarea in Palestine (313—340). Jerome[1] describes Pamphilus
as emulating the zeal of a Peisistratus or a Demetrius Phalereus in
the collection of mss from all parts of the world. His pupil and
friend Eusebius is best known as a historian and chronologer.
In the previous century a sketch of the comparative chronology
of the history of the Jews and Gentiles had been drawn up by
Sextus Julius Africanus, ending with 221 A.D. This was one of the
principal works incorporated by Eusebius in his *Chronicle*. The
latter was in two parts, (1) an epitome of universal history, and
(2) chronological tables, the whole constituting the greatest
chronological work produced by the ancient world. It is the
foundation of most of our knowledge of the dates of Greek and
Roman history, down to 325 A.D. In part (1), the first authority
quoted for Greek history is Castor of Rhodes (60 B.C.), who
supplies the lists of the kings of Sicyon, Argos and Athens. Next
comes a list of Olympian victors, doubtless taken from Sextus
Julius Africanus, ending with the Olympic victor of 220 A.D.;
the kings of Corinth and Sparta from Diodorus; of Macedonia,
Thessaly and Syria from Porphyry, who had previously been
followed in the list of the Ptolemies. The epitome of Roman
history begins with excerpts from Dionysius of Halicarnassus,
Diodorus and Castor, and mentions Cassius Longinus, Phlegon
of Tralles and Porphyry among the authorities followed. The
author's object was to show that the Books of Moses were earlier
than any Greek writings, but scholars may be grateful to him for
having carried his work far beyond the narrow limits necessary to
prove that point. The Greek of Eusebius survives in excerpts
only; for our knowledge of the rest we have to rely on the Latin
version by Jerome, and the Armenian translation, first published

[1] *Ep.* 34, vol. i p. 155.

in 1818[1]. The *Ecclesiastical History* of Eusebius (ending with
324 A.D.) was the first of its kind; while his *Praeparatio
Evangelica*[2] includes a survey of the various forms of religious
belief, with numerous citations from the philosophers of Greece,
as many as twenty-three of the dialogues of Plato being quoted,
and more than fifty passages from the *Laws* alone[3].

Athanasius of Alexandria (295—373), the champion of orthodoxy, with all his subtlety of dialectic, is more interesting as a
man of action than as an orator and an author. Epiphanius
(315—403), the head of a school of learning near Jerusalem from
335 to 367, and, for the rest of his life, bishop of Constantia
(the ancient Salamis in Cyprus), gives in his *Refutation of Heresies*
a brief account of the various forms of Greek philosophy[4]. Basil
(331—379), bishop of Caesarea in Cappadocia,
and Gregory of Nazianzus in the same region       Basil
(*c.* 330—*c.* 390), were pupils at Athens of the Christian teacher
Proaeresius and of the pagan Himerius. Both alike protest
against the prejudice with which the ancient Greek literature was
regarded by many Christians, the former devoting a special discourse to proving by numerous citations that that literature is
full of precepts and examples calculated to elevate the mind and
to prepare it for Christian teaching[5]. Basil describes his retreat
on the river Iris in Pontus, where he spent five years in founding
the earliest monasteries of the East and in making selections from
the works of Origen, as more beautiful than the island of Calypso[6].
When the envoy sent by Basil to Pope Damasus for aid in
contending against the semi-Arians of the East returned without

---

[1] *Eusebi Chronicorum libri duo*, ed. Schoene 1866–75; Schoene, *Die
Weltchronik des Eusebius* (1900); *Facsimile* of the Bodleian MS of Jerome's
Version, with introduction by J. K. Fotheringham (1905), and of *fragmenta
Leidensia Parisina Vaticana* by Traube (Leiden, 1902). Cp. Salmon in *Dict.
Chr. Biogr.* ii 348–55.

[2] ed. E. H. Gifford, 1903.        [3] Lightfoot in *Dict. Chr. Biogr.* ii 331 *b*.

[4] Printed separately by Diels in his *Doxographi*, pp. 587—593, and severely
criticised on pp. 175-7.

[5] πρὸς τοὺς νέους ὅπως ἂν ἐξ ἑλληνικῶν ὠφελοῖντο λόγων, ed. Sommer (1894),
Bach (1901). Cp. *De Studio S. S. ad Greg. Ep.* ii, and Gregor. Naz. *Funeral
Sermon on Basil*, p. 323 c Morell, on profane education, ἣν οἱ πολλοὶ Χριστιανῶν
διαπτύουσιν, ὡς ἐπίβουλον καὶ σφαλερὰν καὶ Θεοῦ πόρρω βάλλουσαν, κακῶς εἰδότες
(Croiset, v 937).                              [6] *Ep.* 14; 358 A.D.

result, Basil expressed in a quotation from Homer[1] his regret that
he had ever approached so proud a personage[2]. In his *Hexaëmeron*
he imitates Philo Judaeus, and in his turn is imitated by
Ambrose. The Funeral Sermon on Basil, a masterpiece of
sacred eloquence, was preached by his friend Gregory of Nazianzus.
The latter is best known as an eloquent preacher ; but he was also
a skilful writer of hexameter, elegiac, iambic and ionic verse of
the ordinary classical type, varied twice by metres of a new kind
depending not on quantity but on accent. In his verses he
occasionally borrows from Empedocles and frequently imitates
Hesiod[3]. The cento from the *Bacchae* and other plays of
Euripides, once ascribed to him, is now recognised as a production of the Middle Ages[4]. Basil's brother, Gregory of Nyssa
(*c.* 343—*c.* 396), while he incidentally shows us that Christian
youth still continued to be instructed in pagan poetry[5], is mainly
a theologian animated in exegesis by Origen's partiality for the
spiritual, figurative and allegorical form of interpretation, which
was strongly opposed by Theodore of Mopsuestia (*c.* 350—403)
and by Chrysostom. Chrysostom (344-7—404), who exhibits the

**Chrysostom**  art of a Demosthenes and an Isocrates superadded
to a great natural genius, was a pupil of Libanius at
Antioch, where for sixteen years (381—397) he wielded by his
extraordinarily eloquent discourses a far wider influence than he
ever attained during his brief and troubled tenure of the patriarchate
of Constantinople (398—403). Theodore of Mopsuestia (*c.* 350—
428) is highly esteemed as a biblical expositor and a theological

**Theodore of Mopsuestia**  controversialist. His opposition to the allegorical
method of interpretation is noticed by Photius[6].
He prefers the grammatical and historical method
which he had inherited from Chrysostom's master and his own,
Diodorus of Antioch ; and in the exegesis of the New Testament,
he shows the instincts of a scholar in noticing minor words which
are often overlooked, in attending to niceties of grammar and
punctuation, and in keenly discussing doubtful readings[7].

---

[1] *Il.* ix 698 f.  [2] *Ep.* 239.  [3] Rzach in *Wiener Studien*, xxi (1899) 98—215.
[4] ed. Brambs (1885). Its merit is much exaggerated in A. Baumgartner's
*Gesch. der Weltlitteratur*, vol. iv (1900).
[5] ii p. 179.  [6] *Cod.* 3.  [7] H. B. Swete in *Dict. Chr. Biogr.* iv 947 *a*.

The mystic and Neo-Platonist, Iamblichus, died about 330 A.D.
This enables us to infer the approximate date of the Neo-Platonist
Dexippus, who refers to Iamblichus in the introduction to his
extant Commentary on the *Categories* of Aristotle[1].

Dexippus

Dexippus is also the author of a dialogue on the
criticisms of Plotinus on the *Categories*[2].   Apart from Neo-
Platonists, the principal writers of prose, on the pagan side, were
Himerius, Themistius, Libanius and Julian.   Himerius, born at
Prusa (*c.* 315), was for nearly forty years a teacher

Himerius

at Athens.   Of his seventy-one *Declamations* only
thirty-four have survived.   Some of these are rhetorical exercises
on themes such as the defence of Demosthenes by Hypereides,
or the plea of Demosthenes for the recall of Aeschines.   Others
are of the nature of inaugural orations at the beginning of an
Academic course.   One of the latter is as solemn a discourse
as that of a hierophant at Eleusis :—' Before the ceremony opens
which is to give you access to the sanctuary, let me distinctly
warn you what you should do, and what you should avoid'[3].   In
another he tells his 'freshmen' that, to lead his flock, he has
no occasion to resort to the rod, but is content to rely on melody
alone : 'what blended sound of flute and pipes can touch your
souls like the simple accents of this Chair ?'[4]   In an earlier age
he might have been an elegant poet instead of a semi-poetical
rhetorician.   He is far from being a profound student of Thucydides and Demosthenes ; he shows a much deeper interest in
poetry.   He borrows largely from the ancient lyric poets, supplying
us with prose paraphrases of some of the lost odes of Alcaeus[5],
Sappho[6] and Anacreon[7], and also showing his familiarity with
Stesichorus, Ibycus, Simonides and Pindar[8].

---

[1] ed. Busse, 1888.

[2] ed. Spengel, 1859.

[3] xxii 7; xv 3. (Capes, *University Life in Ancient Athens*, p. 80 f); cp.
Bernhardy, *Gr. Litt.* i 660[4]; Juleville's *L'École d'Athènes* ; and Hertzberg,
*Geschichte Griechenlands*, iii 311–57.

[4] xv 2 ; Capes, p. 114 f.          [5] xiv 10.

[6] Frag. 133, 147 Bergk.          [7] Frag. 124–6 Bergk.

[8] xxii 5 ; xiii 7 ; Teuber, *Quaest. Himerianae* (1882) ; ed. Dübner (1849) ;
cp. Christ, § 602[4], and Croiset, v 869 f.

Themistius (born *c.* 310–20) declined important appointments
**Themistius** in Rome and Antioch, and spent most of his life
at Constantinople, where he had a high reputation
as an eloquent teacher. He enjoyed the favour of the emperors
Constantius II, Julian, Jovian, Valens and Theodosius, and was
entrusted with the education of Arcadius, but probably did not
live to see his pupil ascend the throne of the East (395). We
possess part of his early work, his *Paraphrases of Aristotle*, the
portion still extant being a somewhat prolix exposition of the
*Later Analytics*, the *Physics*, the *De Anima*, and some minor
treatises[1]. His paraphrase of the *Metaphysics*, Book Λ, was
translated into Arabic (in century IX), and thence into Hebrew
(1255), and Latin (1576)[2]. In his teaching he appears to have
assigned a prominent place to the *Categories*. When he is
charged with making his pupils presumptuous and conceited, he
inquires : ' have you ever heard of any of my friends speaking
proudly or behaving haughtily on the strength of synonyms or
homonyms or paronyms ?'[3] His original work consists mainly
of official harangues. Under several successive emperors he was
practically the public orator of Constantinople, and the noblest
use which he made of that position was to plead repeatedly for
toleration in matters of religious belief and worship. He was
highly esteemed by Christians and pagans alike[4]. His Christian
correspondent Gregory Nazianzen calls him 'the king of eloquence'[5]. He names, as the five Classics studied in Constantinople,
Thucydides, Isocrates, Demosthenes, Plato and Aristotle[6]; as a
sixth, he mentions Aristophanes[7]. He shows us his general
relation to the ancient Classics in a composition addressed to his
father[8], where we find him vaguely referring to the 'golden Menander,
and Euripides, and Sophocles, and fair Sappho and noble Pindar',
while he quotes and actually discusses various authors in his
*Basanistes*[9]; but he supplies us with nothing of the nature of

[1] ed. Spengel, 2 vols. (1866); also *Anal. Pr.* i, ed. Wallies (1884), and
*De Caelo*, ed. Landauer (1902).

[2] Steinschneider, *Hebr. Uebersetzungen*, § 89.

[3] *Or.* xxiii p. 351 (Grote's *Ar.* i 81).

[4] Christ, § 601[4]; Croiset, v 871–6; ed. Dindorf, 1832.

[5] *Ep.* 140.        [6] *Or.* iv p. 71.        [7] *Or.* xxiii p. 350.        [8] *Or.* 20.

[9] *Or.* 21.

definite literary criticism. 'To Themistius...the great writers of
old are persons worthy of infinite respect, to be quoted freely, but
to be quoted...for the substance only'[1]. In another of his
discourses[2] he complains of the length of time spent by teachers
on the exposition of a single author, 'wasting as much time on
one poor book as the Greeks spent in the siege of Troy'. He
holds himself aloof from the Sophists of the day: 'the Sophists
might dwell contentedly in the unrealities of dreamland, but
eternal verities alone engaged the attention of his class'[3].

Another leading teacher of the day was Libanius (314—c. 393).
He was born at Antioch. At the age of fifteen he
showed his first eagerness for literary learning, sold     Libanius
all his favourite pigeons, and turned with enthusiasm to the
ancient Classics. The authors then most read were Homer and
Hesiod, Herodotus and Thucydides, Lysias and Demosthenes;
but others, such as the dramatists, and Pindar and Aristophanes,
Plato and Aristotle, were not neglected, as is proved by quotations
in Libanius and his contemporaries. At the age of twenty he
read the *Acharnians* during a terrific storm of thunder and
lightning, which almost blinded him and made him deaf, and
even left him liable to headaches for the rest of his life[4]. At
the age of twenty-two, though his kinsmen wished to keep him
at home, and his friends offered him rich heiresses in marriage,
he insisted on completing his education at Athens: 'he would
have declined the hand even of a goddess, if he could only see
the smoke of Athens'[5]. At Athens he at once became the victim
of a party of students who insisted on his attending the lectures
of their favourite professor alone, whom he soon deserted for
the private study of the ancient Attic authors[6]. He was a student
for about four years, during which he visited Corinth, Argos
(where he was initiated in the local mysteries) and Sparta (where
he attended the primitive ceremony of scourging at the altar
of Artemis Orthia)[7]. But his time at Athens passed swiftly
by: 'he saw it only as in a dream, and then went on his way'[8].
Soon afterwards, however, he became a public teacher at Athens,

---

[1] Saintsbury, i 125.         [2] *Or.* 23.         [3] Capes, p. 90.
[4] i 9 f, Reiske; *Ep.* 639.    [5] i 11 (Capes, p. 66).
[6] i 13 (*ib.* 99 f).          [7] i 18.           [8] Capes, p. 67.

Constantinople, Nicaea and Nicomedeia, where he spent five years (344—349), which long remained in his memory as the very 'flower' and 'spring-time of his life'[1]. It was there also that he was visited by a friend who brought with him the welcome gift of a whole waggon-load of books[2]. From Nicomedeia he returned to Constantinople and Athens, and finally, at the age of forty, after sixteen years' absence, reached his old home at Antioch, where he remained as a public teacher for the rest of his life. Among the Greek rhetoricians of the Roman age he mentions Favorinus, Adrianus and Longinus[3], and he takes special pains to obtain a bust of Aristides[4]. Like Themistius at Constantinople, he was a devoted adherent of the pagan cause at Antioch, but his most famous pupil was Chrysostom. We are told that, on his death-bed, he would have named Chrysostom as his successor, 'if he had not been carried off by the Christians'[5]. The genuineness of the correspondence between Libanius and Basil is doubtful, and there is no certain proof that the Christian bishop ever became the pupil of the pagan rhetorician.

Libanius was a prolific writer. Among his purely scholastic works[6] are his *Declamations* ($\mu\epsilon\lambda\dot{\epsilon}\tau\alpha\iota$), and his *Rhetorical Exercises* ($\pi\rho o\gamma\upsilon\mu\nu\alpha\sigma\mu\acute{\alpha}\tau\omega\nu\ \pi\alpha\rho\alpha\gamma\gamma\acute{\epsilon}\lambda\mu\alpha\tau\alpha$), the latter including speeches composed in the characters of Achilles and Medea, and a somewhat dull and formal comparison between Demosthenes and Aeschines. He is also the author of certain critical works on Demosthenes, including a *Life* of that orator and *Arguments* to his speeches. These are preserved in the MSS, and printed in most of the editions, of Demosthenes; he rightly declines to accept the Speech on Halonnesus as the work of Demosthenes, and is inclined to ascribe to Hypereides the Speech on the treaty with Alexander. Among his rhetorical works are an Apology for Socrates and a Speech against Aeschines, both in the artificial manner of Aristides. When he bitterly reproaches the gods in his *Monodies* on the destruction of Nicomedeia and on the death of Julian, his composition is in strict accord with the precepts

---

[1] i 38.    [2] i 39.

[3] *Epp.* 1313, 546, 998.    [4] *Ep.* 1551.

[5] Sozom. viii 2.    [6] ed. Reiske (1784—97); Förster, 1903– .

of the rhetorician Menander[1].   Many of his other speeches are
much more interesting owing to the light which they throw on
the academic life and on the general culture of the time.   We
learn that he had assistants to copy all his speeches, and a slave
in charge of the complete collection[2].   In one of his discourses
he describes two of the pictures (scenes of country life) that
adorned the Senate-House of Antioch[3]; in another, he defends
the pantomime of his day against the attacks of Aristides[4].   As
a widely popular teacher, he is proud of the number of his pupils;
he is 'too modest to aver that he has filled the three continents
and all islands, as far as the pillars of Hercules, with rhetoricians',
but he avows that he has 'spiritual children' in Thrace and
Bithynia, in Ionia and Caria, in Galatia and Armenia, in Cilicia
and Syria[5].   He represents a student complaining to himself:
'what shall I gain from all this ceaseless work, from reading
through so many poets, so many rhetoricians, and writers of
every style of composition?'[6]   He complains of the inattentive-
ness of his class: 'some of them stand like statues, with their
arms folded; others vacantly count the numbers of those who
come in late, or stare at the trees outside...; they forget all
about Demosthenes, the latest comments as completely as the
first'[7].   He exhorts the idlers to 'pay less attention to the races
and more to their books'[8].   His life and times are also reflected
in his *Letters*, of which more than 1600 have survived[9].   Here
we incidentally learn that he was ignorant of Latin[10]; he reproaches
a Roman friend for not writing to him in Greek, although his
correspondent had thoroughly studied Homer and Demosthenes[11];
and he tells Demetrius[12] that, having been much bored by the
recitations of his pupils, he had, instead of lecturing in person,
read them parts of the 'artificial epistolary discourse' of his
correspondent.   He is familiar with Attic comedy[13], and no

---

[1] iii 435 Sp.

[2] *Ep.* 656.

[3] iv 1048 and 1057.

[4] iii 345.

[5] iii 444 (Capes, p. 79 f).

[6] iii 438 (*ib.* p. 81 f).

[7] i 200-2 (Bernhardy, *Gr. Litt.* i 663[4]; Sievers, p. 29; Capes, p. 111 f).

[8] *Or.* xxxiii (ii 294 f); Saintsbury, i 123.

[9] ed. J. C. Wolf (1738).

[10] *Epp.* 923, 1241.

[11] *Ep.* 956.

[12] *Ep.* 128 (Saintsbury, *l.c.*).

[13] Förster, *Rhein. Mus.* 32, 86 f.

writer of that age is more thoroughly imbued with the language
of Demosthenes and the other Attic orators. Four centuries
later he was regarded by Photius as, on the whole, maintaining
a true standard of Attic style[1]. In the most recent criticism
of Demosthenes, his reminiscences of the orator's language supply
part of the materials for determining the original text; and a
permanent value attaches to his *Arguments* to the orator's
speeches[2]. Probably his only contact with modern literature
is to be found in the fact that his sixth *Declamation*[3] has been
imitated in the character of Morose in Ben Jonson's *Silent
Woman*[4].

Some of the extant *scholia* on Demosthenes bear the name
of Ulpian. They are of little value[5], and probably
belong in part alone to this eminent Sophist, the
author of a number of lost rhetorical treatises and declamations,
who taught rhetoric at Emesa and Antioch, under Constantine,
counting among his pupils the Christian Proaeresius, and possibly
the pagan Libanius[6].

Ulpian

Three of the discourses of Libanius, not to mention many
incidental remarks in the rest of his writings, are
on the life and character of the emperor Julian,
with whom he had much in common. Blinded by the beauty
and the power of the ancient Classics, both alike 'loved to dwell
in a world of gods, goddesses, and heroes'[7]. When Libanius
heard of Julian's death, we are assured that nothing but the
principles of Plato, and the duty of writing an encomium on

Julian

---

[1] *Cod.* 90, κανὼν...καὶ στάθμη λόγου Ἀττικοῦ. He is often called Δημοσθένης
ὁ μικρός. Cp. Bielski, *De aetatis Dem. studiis Libanianis*, 1914; G. Middleton,
*Studies in the Orations of Lib.*, Aberdeen, 1919, pp. 8—12.

[2] Cp. Index to present writer's *First Phil. and Olynthiacs* of Demosthenes.

[3] δύσκολος γήμας λάλον γυναῖκα ἑαυτὸν προσαγγέλλει (separately edited by
F. Morell, Paris, 1593-7).

[4] *Works*, iii (1875) 341 note; Hallam's *Lit.* iii 97[4]. On Libanius in
general, cp. Sievers, *Das Leben des Libanius* (1868); Juleville, *Sur la Vie et
la Correspondance de Libanius*; Christ, § 599[4]; Croiset, v 876-83; Egger,
502-9; Saintsbury, i 121-4; also Petit, *Libanius*, and A. Harrent, *Les
écoles d'Antioche*, 1898.

[5] Boeckh, *Staatshaushaltung*, ed. Fränkel, p. 535 'der unwissende Ulpian',
cp. 399, 412, 549, 612, 641; better appreciated on p. 624.

[6] Müller and Donaldson, *Gk Lit.* iii 290 f.

[7] J. R. Mozley in *Dict. Chr. Biogr.* iii 710 *b*.

the emperor, prevented the rhetorician from falling on his sword[1].
Julian, the son of the half-brother of Constantine, had owed his
Greek training to a Hellenized Scythian, Mardonius, an admirer
of Plato, Aristotle, Theophrastus, and (above all) of Homer.
When the lad was longing for races and dances and other delights,
his tutor gravely referred him to Homer's admirable descriptions
of the races in memory of Patroclus, to the dances of the Phaeacians, the lays of Phemius and Demodocus, the palm-tree of
Delos, the isle of Calypso, the cave of Circe and the garden
of Alcinoüs[2]. After spending six years in the seclusion of Cappadocia, he attended lectures at Constantinople and Nicomedeia.
At the latter place, at the age of fourteen, he was not allowed to
hear Libanius, but he privately obtained reports of his lectures[3].
He spent a short time as a student at Athens (355), counting
among his companions the future bishops Basil and Gregory
of Nazianzus. Writing afterwards to two of his fellow-students,
he urged them not to despise light literature or to neglect rhetoric
and poetry, but to pay more attention to mathematics, and to
Plato and Aristotle[4]. His own studies, however, were soon
interrupted by affairs of state. Summoned by his cousin
Constantius to take the command in Gaul, he left Athens with
regret, stretching out his hands to the Acropolis and imploring
Athena, with tears in his eyes, to grant him the boon of death[5];
and, reluctantly assuming the purple robe of a Caesar at Milan,
he expressed his foreboding of his future fate by murmuring to
himself the ill-omened line of Homer: ἔλλαβε πορφύρεος θάνατος
καὶ μοῖρα κραταίη[6]. When the news of his victories in Gaul
arrived at Constantinople, the wits of the court derided him
as a 'dabbler in Greek'[7]; but the Gallic soldiers soon hailed
him as emperor at Paris, while he mused on the *Odyssey*[8], and
prayed Zeus 'to send him a token'. Constantius died on his
march against him, and Julian ascended the throne.   The pagan

[1] i 91 f, 521.

[2] *Misopogon*, 351 D.

[3] Libanius, i 527.          [4] *Ep.* 55.

[5] *Ep.* p. 275 A.          [6] *Il.* v 83; Amm. Marc. xv 8, 17.

[7] *ib.* xvii 11, 1, litterionem Graecum.

[8] iii 173; *Ep.* p. 284 C.

and the Neo-Platonist, the believer in magic and the worshipper of the Sun-god, who had been a heathen at heart for the last ten years, now flung off the mask and appeared in his true colours. Thenceforth his great aim was the preservation of 'Hellenism', or Hellenic civilisation, of which the ancient religion was an expressive symbol[1]. He proclaimed toleration for all religions; wrote admonitory letters to pagan priests forbidding them to read Archilochus or Hipponax, or the old Attic comedy, or amatory novels, or infidel writings, such as those of Epicurus, 'most of which the gods' (he is glad to say) 'have permitted to perish'[2]. He also published a decree forbidding Christian teachers, who did not believe in the gods of Homer and Hesiod, Herodotus and Thucydides, Lysias, Isocrates and Demosthenes, to give any instruction in pagan literature[3]. It was probably owing to this edict that Apollinaris, formerly a grammarian at Alexandria and now a priest of the church at Laodicea, prepared a series of Christian poems, while his son, of the same name, composed in the metre of Homer twenty-four books on biblical history down to the time of Saul, imitated Pindar, Euripides and Menander in sacred verse, and turned the Psalms into Greek hexameters[4]. Julian attempted a religious revival at Antioch, where he became exceedingly unpopular, avenging himself by writing, under the title of *Misopogon*, a severe satire on that city. From Antioch he started on a punitive expedition against the Persians; at an early stage of his march, he wrote to Libanius, whom he had lately described as that 'citizen of Antioch, that excellent artificer of speeches, who is dear to Hermes and to me'[5], stating that at Beroea all good omens were sent by Zeus, to whom he had royally sacrificed a white bull[6]; but the expedition ended in the death of Julian, who was fatally wounded in a skirmish near the Persian capital of Ctesiphon on the Tigris. His brief reign

---

[1] Whittaker, *Neo-Platonists*, p. 144.

[2] p. 386 c; T. R. Glover, p. 64.

[3] *Ep.* 42, p. 423 A; Greg. Naz. *Or.* iii 51.

[4] The last alone has survived, Migne xxxiii 1313.

[5] *Misopogon*, 354 c.

[6] *Ep.* 27, p. 399 D.

was not forgotten: 124 years afterwards, the votaries of the
ancient gods still reckoned their years from his death[1].

His writings teem with proofs of his familiarity with the old
Greek Classics. From a child he had been passionately fond
of possessing books[2]. When he visits Ilium as emperor, he finds
a bishop of pagan sympathies protecting from profanation the
temple of Athena, the shrine of Hector and the tomb of Achilles[3].
The mere enumeration of the passages which he quotes from
Homer would fill three pages of print[4]. He also cites Hesiod
and Pindar, Euripides and Aristophanes, Theocritus and Babrius.
He was fond of reading Bacchylides[5]. His numerous quotations
from Euripides are mainly confined to the *Bacchae*, *Phoenissae*
and *Orestes*[6]. He never cites Aeschylus; he lived in a time
when Sophocles was evidently read no longer; for he actually
quotes a proverbial line from *Oed. Tyr.* 614 without knowing
its source. He had been taught by Mardonius to emulate Plato
and Socrates, Aristotle and Theophrastus[7]; he often mentions
Aristotle, but quotes more frequently from Plato; he urges his
former fellow-students to study both[8]. His favourite speeches
in Demosthenes are the *First* and *Second Olynthiacs*, and the
*De Corona*, but he also knows the *Leptines* and the *De Chersoneso*.
In Isocrates, he quotes oftenest from the *Evagoras* and the
*Panegyricus*, and also from the *ad Demonicum* and *ad Nicoclem*.
By far the largest amount of indebtedness to Isocrates and
Demosthenes is (not unnaturally) found in his earliest extant
oration, the encomium on Constantius, composed at the age of
twenty-four[9]. During his stay in Cappadocia, he borrowed 'many
philosophical and rhetorical works' from George, afterwards bishop
of Alexandria, who was slain by the mob of that city, leaving
behind him a valuable library, which Julian caused to be sent
to Antioch for his own use[10]. He founded a public library in

[1] Mar. *vit. Procli*, 36.
[2] *Ep.* 9; *Misopogon*, p. 347 A.
[3] *Ep.* 78.
[4] Brambs, *Studien* i (1897), pp. 41-3.
[5] Amm. Marc. xxv. 4, 3.
[6] Brambs, i 54.
[7] *Misopogon*, 353 B.
[8] *Ep.* 55.
[9] Brambs, *Studien* ii (1899).
[10] *Epp.* 9, 36.

Constantinople and placed his own collection in it[1]. This library was destroyed by fire 128 years after his death[2].

It was probably in, or shortly after, the time of Julian, that
Quintus Smyrnaeus
Quintus of Smyrna composed the epic poem which serves to fill the gap between the story of the *Iliad* and that of the *Odyssey*. The versification of his hexameters suggests an earlier date than that of Nonnus, who flourished *c.* 410. Quintus is an imitator of Homer, Hesiod and Apollonius Rhodius. He is true to the Homeric tone, and he adopts Homer's vocabulary without borrowing his conventional phrases. Just as Hesiod, early in the *Theogony*, tells of the Muses 'who on a day taught him a beautiful song, while he was feeding his lambs under divine Helicon', so Quintus avers that the Muses had inspired him when, as a boy, he was 'tending his fine flocks on a lowly hill in the plain of Smyrna, thrice as far from the Hermus, as a shout would carry'[3]. He is familiar with the legendary scenes near Smyrna, with Niobe turned to stone on the cliff of Sipylus[4], with the Phrygian haunt of Endymion[5], and with the storied islands and headlands and tombs of the Troad[6]. He is probably independent of the Cyclic poets, and the attempt to prove his indebtedness to Virgil has not succeeded[7]. Modern critics have praised the way in which he relates the stories of Penthesilea and Deidameia; and the tale of Oenone, which Quintus 'somewhat lazily handled of old', has been retold in a fresh form by Tennyson. His work, as a whole, is characteristic of an age which 'could admire but not create'. Even the tale of Oenone is believed to be of Alexandrian origin[8]; and throughout the work there are many proofs of special indebtedness to the Alexandrian poet, Apollonius Rhodius[9].

[1] Zosimus, iii 11, 5.

[2] On Julian, cp. J. Wordsworth in *Dict. Chr. Biogr.* and the literature there quoted, including G. H. Rendall's *Hulsean Essay* (1879); also A. Gardner (1895), G. Negri (1901), and T. R. Glover's *Fourth Century*, pp. 47—76; with Christ, § 603[4]; and Croiset, v 893—902.

[3] xii 308—313.                              [4] i 294—306.

[5] x 126—137.                                [6] vii 400—416.

[7] Refuted by Koechly in his ed., p. xiii f.

[8] Rohde's *Gr. Roman*, p. 118[2].

[9] Kemptzow, 1891.—On Quintus in general, cp. T. R. Glover's *Fourth*

The grammarian Theodosius of Alexandria may possibly be
identified with the 'wonderful grammarian Theodosius', to whom Synesius sends his greetings near    Theodosius
the close of his fourth Letter. If so, he may be placed about
the end of the fourth century. His name is wrongly assigned
to a collection of commentaries[1] on the Grammar of Dionysius
Thrax, consisting of two parts, the first including extracts from
the Greek version of Priscian by the Byzantine monk Planudes
(end of cent. xiii), with *scholia* by Melampus and Stephanus, and
the second being the work of Theodorus Prodromus (cent. xii)[2].
Theodosius is probably the author of the epitome of Herodian's
work on accentuation (κανόνες τῆς καθολικῆς προσῳδίας) attributed
to Arcadius, a celebrated grammarian of Antioch (before 600 A.D.)[3].
He is undoubtedly the author of certain 'introductory rules on the
inflexions of nouns and verbs'[4]. This work was often appended
to that of Dionysius Thrax and was formerly ascribed to the
latter. But there is a marked difference between them. Thus,
while Dionysius Thrax confines himself to quoting only those
tenses of τύπτω which were in actual use, Theodosius sets forth
all the imaginary aorists and futures of that verb, regardless of
ancient usage. He is the earliest grammarian who does so; and
his work transmitted this misleading teaching to later ages, in
which it was expounded by Joannes Charax and Georgius Choeroboscus (cent. vi), through whom it descended to the grammars
of the Renaissance, and even to those of modern Europe. These
monstrous and portentous forms have shown a wonderful vitality,
notwithstanding the fact that they have been virtually slain by
Cobet, who vigorously denounces them as 'monstra et portenta

---

*Century*, 77—101 ; G. W. Paschal's *Study* (Chicago, 1904); Christ, § 584[4];
Croiset, v 903-5.

[1] *Theodosii Alex. grammatica*, ed. Göttling (1822).

[2] Uhlig, *Dion. Thrax*, page xxxvii; Hilgard in *Gram. Gr.* iv page
cxxvii f.

[3] ed. M. Schmidt, 1860.

[4] εἰσαγωγικοὶ κανόνες περὶ κλίσεως ὀνομάτων καὶ ῥημάτων, Bekker *Anecd. Gr.*
974—1061 ; ed. Hilgard with the *Scholia* of Choeroboscus in *Gram. Gr.*
iv 1889-94.

formarum,...quae in magistellorum cerebris nata sunt, in Graecorum libris nusquam leguntur'[1].

Near the close of the century (391), among those of the
pagan party who resisted the destruction of the
Serapeum at Alexandria, were the grammarians
Ammonius and Helladius[2]. The work on synonyms
bearing the name of the former is only a Byzantine edition of
the work of Herennius Philon[3], while the lexicon of Helladius
was known to Photius[4] and was one of the authorities followed
by Suïdas. Ammonius and Helladius fled from Alexandria to
Constantinople, where they became the instructors of the ecclesiastical historian, Socrates[5].

*Ammonius and Helladius*

---

[1] *Variae Lectiones*, p. 330. On Theodosius in general, cp. Christ, § 628[4],
and Cohn in Pauly-Wissowa. Cp. *supra*, p. 139.

[2] Rufinus, *Hist. Eccl.* ii 22 ; Socr. v 16—17.

[3] Cohn in Pauly-Wissowa, ii 1866.

[4] *Cod.* 145.

[5] Photius, *cod.* 28.

# CHAPTER XXI.

## GREEK SCHOLARSHIP FROM 400 TO 530 A.D.

IN this chapter, which closes our survey of the Roman age, the time to be traversed begins in the brief and ineffective reign of Arcadius, and ends in the first few years of the long and fruitful reign of Justinian.
Under the successor of Arcadius, the skilled calligrapher Theodosius II, a University was founded at Constantinople, as a counterpoise to the School of Athens; and the literary interests of the day are further illustrated by the fact that his consort, Eudocia, a native of Athens, won the applause of Antioch for a Greek speech closing with the Homeric line: ὑμετέρης (for ταύτης τοι) γενεῆς τε καὶ αἵματος εὔχομαι εἶναι[1]. Early in the fifth century we find evidence of a revival of interest in Greek poetry in northern Egypt. It is the age of Nonnus, who was born at Panopolis in the Thebaid, and probably lived at Alexandria. His vast and diffuse epic in forty-four books on the adventures of Dionysus is an immense repertory of mythological lore. After his conversion to Christianity he wrote a free and flowing paraphrase of the Gospel according to St John. The versification of both is marked by the predominance of dactyls, the strict avoidance of consecutive spondees, an almost invariable preference for the trochaic caesura in the third foot, and the constant use of the acute accent on one of the last two syllables,—generally the last but one. These innovations, which are better suited to the idyll than to the epic, are unknown to Quintus Smyrnaeus; and the

Poets.
Nonnus

[1] *Il.* vi 211, xx 241; Evagrius, i 20; Bury's *Later Roman Empire*, i 131.

last of them forms a prelude to the accentual versification of
the Byzantine age[1]. The school of Nonnus includes the Egyptian
grammarian and poet, Tryphiodorus, the author of an elegant

Tryphiodorus.
Collûthus.
Musaeus.
Christodorus

but uninteresting poem on the *Fall of Troy*; Collûthus, of Lycopolis in the Thebaid (*fl.* 491—518),
the writer of a short epic on *Helen*; and (the only
true poet of the three) Musaeus, whose *Hero and
Leander*, with its echoes of the Alexandrian age of Callimachus,
is the most charming product of Greek literature at the close
of the Roman age[2]. During the transition from the fifth to the
sixth centuries Christodorus of Coptus distinguished himself by
his rhetorically poetical description of the seventy-three statues
of the poets, philosophers, historians and heroes of Greece, which
adorned the gymnasium of Zeuxippus at Constantinople until its
destruction by fire in 532[3].

In the fifth century general history is best represented by

Historians

Zosimus, an imitator of Polybius[4], and ecclesiastical
history by Socrates, who continues Eusebius from
306 to 439, and Sozomen and Theodoret, who cover part of the
same period. All four of these historians belong to the middle
of the fifth century.

In the same century the philosophers devoted their attention

Philosophers

mainly to the *Timaeus* of Plato, and to certain
pseudo-orphic poems and a collection of oracles,
which had already been expounded by Porphyry. The light
of Neo-Platonism grows dim after the death of Proclus (485),
and it slowly disappears in the course of the sixth century. The
Syrian school of Iamblichus (*c.* 280—*c.* 330), which had been
so brilliant in the first half of the fourth century, fell into obscurity
after the death of Julian. Early in the fifth century a new centre
of Neo-Platonism was formed at Alexandria, and in that school
the most interesting personality was that of Hypatia. Her father

Hypatia

was the philosopher and mathematician, Theon,
the commentator on Aratus, Euclid and Ptolemy,

[1] Christ, § 585[4]; Croiset, v 994—1000; cp. Bury, i 317—320.

[2] Christ, § 586[4]; Croiset, v 1003. On Tryphiodorus and Collûthus cp.
Weinberger in *Wiener Studien*, 18 (1896) 116—179.

[3] *Anth. Pal.* ii.          [4] Zosimus imitates Xenophon's use of σύν.

the compiler of a list of consuls from 138 to 372, and the last known member of the Alexandrian Museum (365). She studied the Platonic philosophy at Athens, and lectured at Alexandria on mathematics, as well as on Plato and Aristotle; in her philosophic teaching she followed the tradition of Plotinus[1]. As recorded in the ecclesiastical history of the time, her brilliant career was cut short by the fanaticism of the Alexandrian mob in the spring of 415[2].

The most distinguished of her pupils was Synesius, who in his *Letters* shows a very high regard for his teacher, even after he had become bishop of Ptolemais, the metropolitan see of the Cyrenaic Pentapolis. He was born at Cyrene (*c.* 370), being descended from the Dorian founders of his native city, which, as he proudly recalls, was also the birthplace of Carneades and Aristippus. In his boyhood he led a healthy life in the open air, thus acquiring that love of the chase which never left him. His youthful education under Hypatia at Alexandria included mathematics and philosophy (*c.* 390–5). He describes himself as united to one of his friends, Hesychius, by the sacred bond of their common study of geometry[3]; he presents to another, Paeonius (an important personage at Constantinople), an astrolabe of his own invention[4]; and, in one of his *Letters*, he tells a third that he fancies the very stars look down with kindly influence on himself, as the only man in Libya who could look up to them with the eyes of knowledge[5]. His father, a senator of Cyrene, left him his library; Synesius himself had many more books to bequeath than he had thus inherited; and, during his whole life, his sympathies were thoroughly Greek. From about 400 to 402 (during the patriarchate of John Chrysostom) he stayed at Constantinople as the special envoy of Cyrene at the court of Arcadius, before whom he delivered on his country's behalf a courageous[6] plea for a

Synesius

---

[1] W. A. Meyer, quoted by Bury, i 208.

[2] There are monographs on Hypatia by Hoche (*Philologus*, xv 435 f), and W. A. Meyer (1886).

[3] *Ep.* 92.  [4] Migne, lxvi 1577.

[5] *Ep.* 100, p. 1470 D.

[6] 1310 A, τῶν πώποτε Ἑλλήνων θαρραλεώτερον.

remission of taxation. The speech owes much to reminiscences of Dion Chrysostom, whose style, however, is more simple than that of Synesius[1]; and, besides including passages from the *Gorgias* and *Republic*, it is interspersed with some sixteen quotations from the poets. In one of the phrases which he borrows from Homer, he even describes the emperors as having, by their robes of purple and gold and their barbaric gems, brought on themselves 'that Homeric curse—the coat of stone'[2]. At Constantinople or elsewhere, he had apparently been bored by people who gave themselves airs on the strength of having seen the groves of Academe, the Lyceum of Aristotle and the porch of Zeno[3]. He accordingly paid a visit to Athens, writing to his brother from Anagyrus to tell him that he had been to Sphettus and Thria, to Cephisia and Phaleron, and that he had seen the Academy and the Lyceum, and all that remained of the 'Painted Porch', which a Roman proconsul had robbed of the masterpieces of Polygnotus. The splendour of Athens (he adds) only survived in places bearing famous names; Hypatia of Alexandria far surpassed the 'brace of Plutarchean Sophists' (either Plutarchus and Syrianus, or a son and son-in-law of the former), who attracted their pupils to their lecture-rooms, not by the fame of their discourses but by the bribe of jars of honey from Hymettus; for Athens, once the home of the wise, derived the last remnant of her glory from her bee-keepers alone[4].

He left Constantinople during an earthquake, and reached the Cyrenaic coast during a terrific storm. After his return, he spent two years at Alexandria (402–4), married a Christian wife and in 404 settled down at his old home as a country gentleman delighting in his horses and dogs, dividing his time between 'books and the chase'[5], and suppressing local bands of brigands, when to his surprise and embarrassment he found himself called by the voice of the people to be bishop of Ptolemais (406). After seven months of uncertainty, he allowed himself to be consecrated by the Alexandrian patriarch, Theo-

---

[1] Theodorus Metochita, in Dindorf's *Dion*, ii 367. Cp. *Byz. Zeitschr.* 1900, 85—151.

[2] *Il.* iii 57; 1080 A.     [3] *Ep.* 54.     [4] *Ep.* 136.

[5] 1307 D, 1388 C; cp. 1484 A, 1488 C.

philus, early in 407. He was soon very active in the discharge
of his duties, but his tenure of office must have been brief, for
we find no trace of him beyond 413. It therefore seems probable
that he died one or two years before the tragic end of Hypatia.
Seven of his *Letters* are addressed to her; he regards her as 'his
mother and sister, and his preceptor'; and, when he has lost all
his three sons and is trembling for the fate of Cyrene, he confides
to her his woes, and (quoting Homer) assures her that, 'if men
forget the dead that dwell in Hades, yet even there' he will
remember Hypatia[1]. His *Dion*, an *Apologia pro vita sua*, written
*c.* 405, is a treatise on education and moral discipline, composed
for the benefit of a son who was yet unborn, and suggested by
the teaching of Dion Chrysostom, whose later writings he regards
as models of simple and natural elegance. He tells Hypatia
how he had come to write it[2]. Certain philosophers had accused
him of pretending to opinions about Homer, and of caring for
beauty and rhythm of language. He accordingly holds up Dion
as an example of a rhetorician who had become a philosopher
without losing the charm of a classic style. In the treatise itself
he insists that the true philosopher must be a thorough Greek;
must be initiated into the mysteries of the Graces, and familiar
with everything that is important in literature; all this he will
*know* as a scholar (φιλόλογος) and will *judge* as a philosopher[3].
'These rigid critics, who profess a contempt for rhetoric and
poetry, do so not of their own choice, but owing to poverty
of nature'[4]. 'Beauty of language is *not* an idle thing; it is a
pure pleasure, which looks away from matter to real existence'[5].
'A man may be well-equipped in speech, and, at the same time,
a master of philosophy.' Synesius aims at being both, notwithstanding the criticisms of philosophers who are illiterate, and of
grammarians who criticise philosophical works, syllable by syllable,
without producing anything of their own[6]. He also answers those
of his critics who had reproached him with using incorrect and

---

[1] *Ep.* 124; also 10, 15, 16, 33, 80, 153; cp. *Ep.* 4, 1342 B (to his brother
at Alexandria), ἄσπασαι τὴν σεβασμιωτάτην καὶ θεοφιλεστάτην φιλόσοφον, καὶ
τὸν εὐδαίμονα χορὸν τὸν ἀπολαύοντα τῆς θεσπεσίας αὐδῆς, and *Epp.* 132, 135 f.

[2] *Ep.* 153.　　　　　[3] 1125 A, C.　　　　　[4] 1125 D.

[5] 1129 B.　　　　　[6] 1152 A.

faulty texts; 'what does it matter' (he replies) 'if one syllable is
put for another?' 'The very necessity for making emendations
is itself an excellent training.' 'The whole end of books is to
call out ability into active exercise; to make us think, and think
clearly'[1]. In conclusion he refers with charming candour to his
own skill in improvising the sequel of any passage which he
happened to be reading, and to his own imitations of ancient
tragedies and comedies, possibly dating from his Alexandrian
days;—adding that, in these compositions, the reader would have
taken him for a contemporary, now of Cratinus and Crates, now
of Diphilus and Philemon. The influence of Porphyry is apparent
in the *Dion*; and that of Plotinus in his treatise *On Dreams*
(which he regards as a means of divine revelation). In this
hastily written work he incidentally remarks that thoughts revealed
to him in the visions of the night had helped him not merely
in the pursuits of the chase, but even in the cultivation of his
style[2].

His *Letters*, 159 in number, ranging in time from *c.* 399 to
413, are full of the news of the day, full too of grace and point
and literary interest. They are praised by Evagrius, Photius and
Suïdas[3]. We here find, now the traveller, now the man of action,
absorbed in his country's good; now the meditative student, and
now the active administrator. Throughout them all, the writer's
literary proclivities are most strongly marked. He tells us that
he has been asked for some of his poems, but that he 'has not
had time even to take them out of their boxes'[4]. In the same
*Letter* he quotes from the *Odyssey*[5] and from Archilochus. In
a few lines full of idyllic charm, written to his brother at the
seaside, he describes the birds and trees and flowers that surround
him at Cyrene, adding that the cave of the Nymphs calls for
a Theocritus to sing its praises[6]. In a violent storm between
Alexandria and the Cyrenaic coast he recalls the *Ajax* of
Sophocles and the tempests in the *Odyssey*[7]. He assures one
of his friends, half in fun, that the rustics south of Cyrene regard

[1] 1160 C–D; 1556 A; cp. Nicol, p. 109; Crawford, p. 163 f.
[2] c. 9.          [3] Volkmann's *Synesius*, p. 113.
[4] *Ep.* 129.      [5] ix 51.
[6] *Ep.* 114.      [7] *Ep.* 4.

Odysseus and the Cyclops as still in the land of the living, and
suppose that the emperor, whom they have never seen, is the
same as a certain Agamemnon who once sailed to Troy[1].  To
Synesius himself, Menelaus is the type of the true philosopher
who can extort the truth even from the evasive Proteus[2].
Throughout the whole of his writings his references to Greek
literature are very numerous.  He refers most frequently to Plato
(*c.* 133 times), Homer (*c.* 84) and Plutarch (*c.* 36); less often
to Aristotle (20) and Herodotus (16), and to Hesiod, Pindar,
Euripides, Aristophanes, Xenophon and Plotinus (*c.* 10 each);
while the smallest number of quotations comes from Archilochus,
Empedocles, Aeschylus, Sophocles, Thucydides and Demosthenes[3].
A far greater familiarity with Demosthenes is shown by his
correspondent, the monk and scholar Isidore of Pelusium
(*c.* 370—*c.* 450), whose reminiscences of Demosthenes, scattered
up and down his 2000 Letters, are sometimes of value for
purposes of textual criticism[4].  Once, when Dion quotes a
passage, which is really to be found in *Il.* xxii 401, Synesius
actually ventures to assert that Dion must have invented it[5].
His writings happily illustrate the extent and the character of
the study of Greek literature which prevailed in his age[6], while
they also embody the opinions of a man of singular versatility,
a student as well as a sportsman, a man of genuine cultivation
but not entirely free from pedantry, one who stood on the border-
land between Neo-Platonism and Christianity, and filled at one
time the position of a pagan orator and philosopher, and at
another that of an active patriot and a Christian bishop.  His
*Hymns* have won high praise from Mrs Browning, who translated
two of them, while the tenth and last and simplest of them all
has found its way into *Hymns, Ancient and Modern*[7].  Even
in an abstruser poem of portentous length, a passage where he
bids all the sounds of inanimate Nature be silent while he sings

---

[1] *Ep.* 147.          [2] 1128 D.

[3] Crawford, pp. 522–79; Hauck's Friedland Program, 1911.

[4] Cp. index to present writer's ed. of *First Philippic and Olynthiacs*.

[5] 1200 A.

[6] Cp. Volkmann's *Synesius*, p. 135.

[7] No 185, 'Lord Jesus, think on me' (trans. by A. W. Chatfield, 1876).

the Father and the Son, supplies us with a strain of not ungraceful simplicity :—

> Let heaven and earth awed silence keep,
> Let air and sea be still,
> Let rushing winds and waters sleep,
> Hushed be the river, hushed the rill[1].

Touches of poetry are not wanting even in his prose. In contrasting the freedom of his life at Cyrene with the slavery endured by the orators in the law-courts of Alexandria, he says in his *Dion* :—'I sing to these cypresses ; and this water here runs, rushing along its course, not measured off, or dealt out by the water-clock... And, even when I have ceased, the stream flows on, and will flow on, by night and by day, and till next year, and for ever'[2].

In contrast with the Neo-Platonic and Christian hymns of

Palladas

Synesius we may briefly glance at the 150 epigrams of one of the latest of the pagan poets, Palladas. We there see him sighing over the gods of the ancient world, whose days are gone for ever[3]; studying the old poets, but finding himself so poor that he is compelled to sell his Pindar and his Callimachus[4]; writing witty verses on the scholastic uses of the *Iliad*[5]; discovering that, in the *Odyssey* as well as the *Iliad*, Homer is a misogynist[6]; and revealing himself as in general a gloomy pessimist, whose only enthusiasm is for Hypatia :—

> Thee when I view, thyself and thy discourse
> I worship, for I see thy virgin-home
> Is in the stars, thy converse is in heaven,
> Adorable Hypatia, Grace of speech,
> Unsullied Star of true philosophy[7].

[1] iii 72—81.

[2] *Dion*, c. 11, 1149 A ; Crawford, p. 195.—On Synesius in general, see *Opera* in Migne, lxvi 1021—1616 ; Tillemont, *Mémoires*, xii ; Clausen (1831) ; Druon's *Études* (1859) ; Volkmann (1869) ; Lapatz (1870) ; A. Gardner (1886) ; J. C. Nicol (1887) ; Halcomb in *Dict. Chr. Biogr.*; Nieri in *Rivista di filologia* xxi (1892) 220 f ; Seeck in *Philologus* lii (1893) 458–83 (where the chronology of the *Letters* is revised) ; W. Fritz (*Die Briefe*), pp. 230 (1898) ; W. S. Crawford (1901) ; and T. R. Glover's *Fourth Century*, pp. 320—356 ; also Christ, § 654[4], Croiset, v 1043–9 ; and c. 21 of Kingsley's *Hypatia*.

[3] *Anth. Pal.* ix 441.          [4] ix 175.

[5] ix 173–4.          [6] ix 166.

[7] ix 400.    Cp. Alfred Franke, Leipzig Diss., pp. 101 (1899), and T. R. Glover, pp. 303–19.

The murder of Hypatia, as we are assured by Socrates[1],
brought no small discredit on the patriarch Cyril and the Church
of Alexandria.   Cyril (380—444) had succeeded
Theophilus as patriarch in 412.   Apart from hom-    Cyril.
ilies and commentaries, the extant works of Cyril    Theodoret
include a defence of Christianity against Julian, and against the
Arians and Nestorians.   He was opposed by the friend of
Nestorius, Theodoret (386—c. 458), bishop of Cyrrhus in northern
Syria (428).   Theodoret, in his examination of Christian truth
in the light of Greek philosophy, written soon after his appointment as bishop, institutes a comparison between the various
schools of philosophy.   His statement of the opinions of the
Greek philosophers is of value in so far as it has been proved
to be founded on Aëtius, who lived in the first century B.C.[2]

The study of Greek in this age is illustrated by the fact that,
at the synod held in 415 at Diospolis (the ancient
Lydda), Pelagius, who was born of a Roman family    Pelagius
in Britain (c. 370—c. 440), made a great impression owing to his
perfect familiarity with Greek, which was an unknown tongue to
the historian Orosius, the emissary of St Augustine at preceding
conferences in Palestine[3].   On the side of St Augustine in the
Pelagian controversy was a good Greek scholar, Marius Mercator
(fl. 418—449), who wrote in Greek against the Nestorians.   The
decline of Greek scholarship at Rome at this time is indicated
by the fact that, when Nestorius sent a Greek letter and other
documents to Pope Celestine (430), the latter was compelled to
invite Cassianus to come from Marseilles to translate them[4].

Athens was the scene of the latest phase of Neo-Platonism[5].
The mystic teaching of the Syrian pupil of Porphyry, Iamblichus (d. c. 330), author of a life of    Neo-
Pythagoras and an exhortation to the study of    Platonists.
philosophy, including excerpts from Plato and Aristotle, was    Plutarchus
introduced into Athens by one Nestorius.   At the end of the
fourth century a new school was engrafted on the old by the son

---

[1] vii 15.

[2] ἡ περὶ τῶν ἀρεσκόντων ξυναγωγή, Diels, Doxographi, pp. 45 f.

[3] C. Gidel, Nouvelles Études sur la litt. Gr. moderne (1878), p. 61 f.

[4] ib. 64–5.       [5] Cp. F. Schemmel, in Neue-Jahrb. 1908, 494—513.

of this Nestorius, Plutarchus (d. 431), who restored the authority
of dialectic, besides devoting himself to mystic speculation, and
to the Neo-Platonic exposition of Aristotle as well as Plato.  He
wrote an important commentary on Aristotle's treatise *De Anima* ;
little, however, of his work has survived except the passages
quoted by Olympiodorus (the younger) and other commentators
on Aristotle.  His successors as heads of the School of Athens
were Syrianus (431–8), Proclus (438–85), Marinus, Isidorus,
Hegias, and lastly Damascius (529).

A pupil of Plutarchus, Hierocles of Alexandria, who succeeded
Hypatia, and flourished between 415 and 450,
produced a commentary on the 'golden verses' of
'Pythagoras', which is still extant[1].  A pupil of
Hierocles, the Christian Neo-Platonist Aeneas, is the author of a
dialogue called *Theophrastus*, on the immortality of the soul and
the resurrection of the body, which is praised for its brilliant
style and its successful imitation of Plato.  Of the successor of
Plutarchus, Syrianus of Alexandria, we are told that he was in
the habit of introducing his pupils to the 'lesser mysteries' of
Aristotle before initiating them in Plato.  He is said to have written
commentaries on the *Phaedo*, *Republic* and *Laws*.  His commentary on three books of the *Metaphysics* has been published[2]; his
comments on the rhetorician Hermogenes have also survived[3].
All our knowledge of the Neo-Platonism of Syrianus is due to
his distinguished pupil, Proclus, who declares that he owes
everything to that inspired teacher.  Proclus (410—
485), who was born in Constantinople, and studied
grammar under Orion, and Aristotle under Olympiodorus the
elder at Alexandria, went to Athens shortly before 430.  The
first place, at which he sat down or drank water, was close to a
temple dedicated to Socrates.  At Athens he read with Syrianus the
whole of Aristotle, and afterwards Plato ; and there he remained,
living a laborious life in the practice of severe abstinence, and
continuing to preside over the School for forty-seven years.  We
are assured that he was a deep thinker, a fluent lecturer and a

*Hierocles.*
*Syrianus*

*Proclus*

[1]  ed. Gaisford in *Stobaei Eclogae*, ii (1850) ; Mullach, *Frag. Fhil.* i 408.

[2]  ed. Usener, in Berlin Aristotle, v (1870) ; ed. Kroll (1902).

[3]  ed. Rabe, 1892–3.

man of great personal charm. His pupils deemed him divinely
inspired, and on one occasion a casual attendant at his lectures
declared that his head was illumined with a celestial splendour[1].
In accordance with his principle that 'all things sympathise with
all'[2], he held that the philosopher should observe the religious
rites of all nations and be 'the hierophant of the whole world';
he also practised the cult of the dead, visiting in the first instance
the tombs of the ancient Attic heroes[3]. He reduced Neo-
Platonism to a precise and systematic form, but was incapable
of restoring life to theories which had long lost touch with reality.
He wrote rapidly, and wrote much, mainly in the form of
comments on Plato. To the teaching of Plato he adhered more
closely than Plotinus; and Plato is the source of his system of
triads. Among his extant works are commentaries on the *Republic*, *Timaeus* and *Parmenides*, also his 'Theological Elements'
and a treatise on Plato's 'theology'[4]. In the course of his
commentary on the *Republic* he defends Homer against the
attacks of Plato. Seven of his Hymns to the Gods have survived.
They are inspired with the breath of an 'immortal longing', like
that of Plato or Plotinus; and the poet is ever pressing toward
the 'path sublime', while he prays to the Sun and Athene and
the Muses for the pure and 'kindly light that leads upwards ($\phi\hat{\omega}_S$
$\dot{\alpha}\nu\alpha\gamma\dot{\omega}\gamma\iota o\nu$), the means of attaining thereto being the study of
books that awaken the soul'[5]. His pupil, Marinus, describes
him as having sounded all the depths of the theology and
mythology of the Greeks and barbarians, and as having reduced
them to perfect harmony[6]. Proclus (says Zeller) is really a
'scholastic': all his genius is devoted to the interpretation of
texts, which he accepts unreservedly without caring to criticise
them[7]. It is stated that he often said that 'if it were in his
power, he would withdraw from the knowledge of men, for the
present, all ancient books except the *Timaeus* and the Sacred

[1] Marinus, *Proclus*, c. 23.         [2] *Elements of Theology*, no. 140.
[3] Whittaker, p. 160.               [4] V. Cousin, ed. 2, 1864.
[5] Bury's *Later Roman Empire*, i 316.         [6] Marinus, c. 22.
[7] See, however, Whittaker, p. 162. Proclus (with other followers of
Plotinus) is discussed in E. von Hartmann's *Gesch. der Metaphysik*, 1899,
176—202. For his Commentaries on Plato, cp. Whittaker, ed. 2, 231—314.

Oracles'[1]. He was not thinking of the Scriptures, but his aspiration as to Plato was not long afterwards fulfilled in the Western world, by the fact that 'along with the few compendia of logic and the liberal arts, which furnished almost the sole elements of European culture for centuries, there was preserved' a Latin translation of a large portion of the *Timaeus*[2].

After Proclus, Neo-Platonism lived on for about a century. Among its representatives were Hermeias (end of cent. v), who taught at Alexandria, and whose diffuse *scholia* on the *Phaedrus* are still extant[3]; many extracts from them are quoted in the edition of Dr Thompson, who observes that, 'amidst a heap of Neoplatonic rubbish, they contain occasional learned and even sensible remarks'[4]. He agrees with Synesius[5] in supposing that beauty of every kind is the theme of this dialogue. He was succeeded at Alexandria (early in cent. vi) by his son Ammonius, who is still represented by his commentaries on the logical treatises of Aristotle[6], and is the earliest of the extant expounders of the *Eisagoge* of Porphyry[7]. Among the pupils of Ammonius were Simplicius, Asclepius[8], Olympiodorus the younger, and Joannes Philoponus. The last of these wrote (among other works) a commentary on Aristotle's *Physics*[9]. His commentary on Porphyry's *Introduction* to the *Categories* was much studied by the Syrians[10].

After languishing under the successors of Proclus (Marinus,

[1] Marinus, c. 38.

[2] By Chalcidius; cp. Whittaker, p. 160. On the same writer's *commentary* on the *Timaeus* (*c.* 300 A.D.) cp. Switalski (Münster, 1902), who holds that it is possibly a translation from the work of an eclectic Platonist of the second century, who borrowed from Numenius, and who derived from Adrastus and Albinus the substance of the commentary of Poseidonius on the *Timaeus*.

[3] Published in Ast's ed., 1810, and by Couvreur, 1902.

[4] Thompson's *Phaedrus*, pp. ix, 92, 136.

[5] Volkmann's *Synesius*, p. 148.

[6] ed. Busse, *Categ.* 1895, *De Interpr.* 1897.

[7] Busse's ed. (1891), and Berlin program (1892), cp. Bursian's *Jahresb.* lxxix 88.

[8] *Comm. on Ar. Metaphysics* A–Z, ed. Hayduck (1888), largely founded on Alexander of Aphrodisias.          [9] ed. Vitelli (1887–8).

[10] Baumstark, *Ar. bei den Syrern*, 1900.

Isidorus and Hegias) the School of Athens revived for the last
time under Damascius, who studied at Alexandria and was a
pupil of Marinus at Athens.   He was not merely a
mystic, like Iamblichus ; he was also a dialectician,    **Damascius**
like Proclus.  His 'Life of Isidorus' (disfigured by many puerilities)
and his 'Problems and Solutions on First Principles' have survived[1]: his commentaries on Aristotle have perished.   He was
the head of the School in 529, when the 'golden chain' of the
Platonic succession was broken by the edict of Justinian, which
put an end to the teaching of Neo-Platonism at
Athens.   The public payments to the professors    **The School
of Athens**
had long ceased ; even their private endowments    **closed by
Justinian**
were now suppressed, and the closing of the School
was the natural consequence[2].   Its teachers lingered for a short
time in their Athenian home, and, in 532, seven of them, namely
Diogenes and Hermeias, Eulalius and Priscianus, Damascius,
Isidorus and Simplicius, left for the court of Chosroes, the enlightened monarch who had recently ascended the Persian throne
and who proved his interest in Greek philosophy by promoting
the translation of certain Platonic and Aristotelian writings.
Their high expectations were bitterly disappointed and they soon
entreated permission to return.   In 533 Chosroes concluded a
treaty with Justinian, which ensured the protection of the philosophers from persecution for their opinions[3].   They returned to
the dominions of the empire, to settle, not at Athens, but at
Alexandria.   Among those who had left Athens for Persia was
a pupil of Damascius and Hermeias, Simplicius of Cilicia, whose
commentaries on the *Categories*[4], [5]*Physics*, *De Caelo*
and *De Anima*[5] of Aristotle are still extant ; and    **Simplicius**
whose 'moral interpretation of Epictetus is preserved in the

---

[1] ἀπορίαι καὶ λύσεις, ed. Ruelle (1889).

[2] Bury's Gibbon, iv 266 n ; cp. Finlay's *History of Greece*, i 277-87 Tozer ;
Herzberg's *Geschichte Griechenlands*, iii 488—545 ; and Gregorovius, *Stadt
Athen im Mittelalter*, i 54-7 ; also L. Friedländer in *Deutsche Rundschau*,
1899, 421 f.

[3] Agathias (*fl.* 570) ii 30 (Ritter and Preller, *ult.*).

[4] Basel, 1551.

[5-5] ed. Diels, Heiberg, Hayduck (1882-95).

library of nations, as a classic book'[1].  This last is popular in
style, while the main value of the rest lies not in their exegesis
but in their citations from early Greek philosophers.  After 564
we find at Alexandria the younger Olympiodorus, who has left

Olympiodorus
the younger

us a life of Plato and commentaries on the *First
Alcibiades, Gorgias, Phaedo, Philebus,* and Aristotle's
*Meteorologica.*  They unfortunately exhibit no
originality, either literary or philosophic.  David the Armenian,
probably a pupil of Olympiodorus[2], produced a commentary on
the *Organon* and on Porphyry's *Introduction* to the *Categories*[3].
The Neo-Platonic School, and, with it, the study of Greek
philosophy, practically ceased towards the end of the sixth
century[4].

Shortly after the close of the School of Athens, we find (in

'Dionysius
the Areopagite'

532) the first mention of the writings of 'Dionysius
the Areopagite'.  Their many coincidences with
the teaching of Proclus and Damascius have led to
their author being identified as a Christian Neo-Platonist, and
to their date being assigned to *c.* 480—520.  The works on the
heavenly and on the ecclesiastical hierarchy (with the triple triads
in each), and those on the divine names and on mystical theology,
had their influence on the 'angelology', the mysticism, and (in
the case of Joannes Scotus) the pantheism of the Middle Ages[5].
Their author has been called the father of Scholasticism.  He
was specially studied by John of Damascus in the Eastern, and
by Aquinas in the Western Church ; while the effect of his
teaching may be traced not only in Dante[6], in Savonarola, Ficino

[1] Gibbon, c. xl (iv 267 Bury).

[2] So Rose, *De Ar. libr. ordine* (1854), 244 f, and Busse, *Praef. in
Porphyrium,* xli–iv.  Neumann (1829) regarded him as a pupil of Syrianus
and placed him at the end of the *fifth* century.

[3] See *facsimile* on p. 345.

[4] On Neo-Platonism in general, cp. Zeller, *Phil. d. Gr.* iii 2 (and the
literature there quoted) ; also T. Whittaker's *Neo-platonists* (1901) ; and Bigg's
*Neoplatonism* (1895).

[5] Milman, *Lat. Chr.* ix 57 f ; Westcott, *Religious Thought in the West,*
pp. 142–93 ; T. Whittaker, p. 188 ; H. Koch, *Pseudo-Dionysius* (1900) ; later
literature reviewed by Leimbach in *Philos. Jahrb. der Görres-gesellschaft,*
x (1897) 90 f.

[6] *Par.* x 115–7 ; xxviii 97—132.

and Pico della Mirandola, but also in the 'trinall triplicities' of Spenser[1], and in the magnificent line in which Milton enumerates more than half the orders of the heavenly hierarchy :—

'Thrones, Dominations, Princedoms, Virtues, Powers'[2].

While Plato and Aristotle were being expounded at Athens and Alexandria, grammar and lexicography were not neglected. With the grammarians the main source of inspiration was Herodian.   Grammarians
It was from Herodian that Timotheus of Gaza (*c.* 500) derived the substance of his treatise on combinations of vocal sounds[3]; on the same model, Joannes Philoponus (early in cent. vi), already mentioned as a pupil of Ammonius, wrote a work on dialects and accentuation, including an alphabetical list of words differing according to their accent[4], which was widely used in the Middle Ages; and, similarly, Joannes Charax (in the first half of cent. vi) compiled an abstract of Herodian's work on Orthography, part of which (a fragment on enclitics) is still extant[5].

In lexicography the labours of the Atticists of the second century were continued in a series of mechanical compilations.   Lexico-graphers. 'Ammonius' A treatise on Synonyms[6], attributed in the MSS to 'Ammonius', who left Alexandria for Constantinople in 391[7], appears to be only a revised edition of that of Herennius Philon on the same subject[8]. A more important work is that of Orion, who was born at the Egyptian Thebes, and was one of the teachers of Proclus   Orion at Alexandria (*c.* 430), and of Eudocia, the consort of Theodosius II, at Constantinople. This was an Etymological Lexicon, the extant portions of which prove that it was founded on

---

[1] *Hymne of Heavenly Love*, 64; cp. *Hymne of Heavenly Beautie*, 85—98.

[2] *P. L.* v 601. The ultimate source of these terms is the Vulgate trans. of *Rom.* viii 38; *Col.* i 16. Cp. Lupton in *Dict. Chr. Biogr.* i 847–8.

[3] κανόνες καθολικαὶ περὶ συντάξεως, Cramer, *Anecd. Par.* iv 239.

[4] ed. Egenolff (1880).

[5] Bekker's *Anecd.* 1149–56. Krumbacher, *Byz. Litt.* § 242[2] f.

[6] περὶ ὁμοίων καὶ διαφόρων λέξεων, ed. C. F. Ammon (1787). Christ, § 629[4]. Cohn in Pauly-Wissowa, *Ammonios* (no. 17), ascribes the work to the Byzantine age.

[7] Socr. *Hist. Eccl.* v 16.       [8] p. 362 *supra*.

the researches of Heracleides Ponticus, Apollodorus, Philoxenus, Apollonius Dyscolus, Herodian, and Orus of Miletus, who has often been confounded with Orion[1]. The work of Orion in its original form was one of the sources of the etymological compilations of the Byzantine age.

Hesychius of Alexandria, who probably belongs to the fifth century, is the compiler of the most extensive of our ancient Greek lexicons. It is not so much a 'lexicon' as a glossary. In the preface it is described as a new edition of the work of Diogenianus[2], with additions from the Homeric lexicons of Apion and Apollonius (the son of Archibius). Whether the lexicon of Diogenianus was an independent work, or only an abstract of that of Pamphilus[2], is still a matter of controversy. Hesychius is of special value in connexion with the emendation of classical authors. His work has often enabled Ruhnken and later critics to restore the original word in ancient texts where its place has been taken by an explanatory synonym. The existing lexicon, large as it is, is an abridgement only; in its original form, it apparently included the names of the authorities for each statement[3].

In the next century another scholar of the same name, Hesychius of Miletus, who lived under Justinian, was the author of a lexicon of special importance in connexion with the history of Greek literature[4]. He owed much to Aelius Dionysius and Herennius Philon. Our knowledge of his lexicon is solely due to the citations of Suïdas, who describes his own work as an epitome of that of Hesychius of Miletus.

*Hesychius of Alexandria*

*Hesychius of Miletus*

---

[1] Ritschl, *De Oro et Orione, Opusc.* i 582—673; Christ, § 630⁴. Orus and Orion were probably contemporaries; both of them taught first at Alexandria, and afterwards at Constantinople (cp. Reitzenstein's *Etymologika*, pp. 287 f, and 348).

[2] p. 295 *supra*.

[3] Ruhnken's *Praefatio*, in *Opusc.* pp. 192—219. See also Wentzel's *Hesychiana*, in *Hermes*, 1898, 275—312.

[4] ὀνοματολόγος ἢ πίναξ τῶν ἐν παιδείᾳ ὀνομαστῶν. *Hesychii Milesii Onomatologi quae supersunt*, ed. Flach (1882). Cp. Krumbacher, *Byz. Litt.* § 139².

The reign of Justinian saw an abridgement of the great geographical lexicon of Stephanus of Byzantium. The original work was produced after 400 A.D.; and its extent may be inferred from the fact that the articles before Σ filled as many as fifty books. The only part of the original which has been preserved is the article on Ἰβηρία and those from Δύμη to Δώτιον. It must ·have included many extracts from ancient authors, with notices of historical events and famous personages. In grammar Stephanus follows Herodian; and, in geography, Hecataeus, Ephorus, Eratosthenes, Artemidorus (*fl.* 100 B.C.), Strabo, Pausanias, and especially Herennius Philon[1].

Stephanus of<br>Byzantium

Among the earliest of compilers of chrestomathies was Proclus, who is regarded by Gregory of Nazianzus[2] and by Suïdas as identical with Proclus the Neo-Platonist[3], and this opinion is accepted by Wilamowitz[4], though the character of the work is totally different from that of the extant writings of that philosopher. Earlier scholars[5] had identified him with Eutychius Proculus of Sicca (instructor of M. Aurelius), who, however, is a *Latin*[6] grammarian. He is possibly the Proclus, whose 'enumeration of festivals' is mentioned by Alexander of Aphrodisias[7]. For almost all our knowledge of the 'grammatical (*i.e.* literary) chrestomathy' of Proclus we are indebted to Photius[8], who states that, in the first two books, the author, after distinguishing between poetry and prose, dealt with

Chresto-<br>mathies.<br>Proclus

---

[1] Christ, § 597[4]; ed. Dindorf (1825), Westermann (1839), Meineke (1849). P. Sakalowski, *Fragmente von Steph. von Byz.* (1891), holds that the work was finished before 530. Cp. Stemplinger's *Studien*, in *Philologus*, 1904, 615—630.

[2] Migne, xxxvi 914, Πρόκλος ὁ Πλατωνικὸς ἐν μονοβίβλῳ περὶ κύκλου γεγραμμένῃ.

[3] p. 372 *supra*.

[4] *Phil. Unt.* vii 330; supported by Imnisch, *Festschrift für Gomperz*, 1903.

[5] Valesius, and Welcker, *Ep. Cycl.* i 3 f.

[6] Capitolinus, *M. Aurelius*, c. 2.

[7] On Aristot. *Soph. El.* p. 4. Kaibel, who regards it as an anonymous work, determines its date and character (Göttingen *Abhandl.* 1898), and, in his *Proleg. περὶ κωμῳδίας*, shows that much of the Byzantine learning on poetry came from this source. The 'sources' of 'Proclus' are discussed by Zielinski, in *Woch. kl. Phil.* 1898, 1331 f. Cp. F. Stein, *Gram. Quaestiones*, Bonn, 1908.

[8] *Cod.* 239.

epic, elegiac, iambic and melic poetry, naming the leading
representatives of each; and that he described the epic cycle in
particular as a consecutive series of poems by various authors.
This account is confirmed by the fragments of Proclus preserved
in the *codex Venetus* of the *Iliad* and in some other MSS.  They
include a short life of Homer, and a list of the authors of the
Trojan part of the cycle, viz. the *Cypria*, the *Iliad*, the *Aethiopis*
(Arctinus), the *Little Iliad* (Lesches), the *Iliupersis* (Arctinus), the
*Nosti* (Agias), the *Odyssey*, and the *Telegonia* (Eugammon), with
an abstract of the contents of all except the *Iliad* and the *Odyssey*.
Our knowledge of the contents of the lost epics of Greece comes
almost entirely from this source[1].  The two other books probably
dealt with dramatic poetry, and prose.

The *Readings in History* by Sopater of Apamea, and the
sources from which they were derived, are known to us solely
through the account in Photius[2].  The only chrestomathy which
has come down to us in an approximately complete form is that

**Stobaeus**

of Joannes Stobaeus (of Stobi in Macedonia), who
is probably not much later than Hierocles (*c.* 450),
the latest author whom he cites.  In its original form it was in
four books, (1) on philosophy, theology and physics, (2) on
dialectic, rhetoric, poetry and ethics, (3) on virtues and vices,
(4) on politics and domestic economy.  The work is divided into
206 sections, each denoted by a short motto under which all the
extracts are grouped, first those in verse, and then those in prose.
The number of writers thus represented is no less than 500[3].  In
the Middle Ages the four books were treated by copyists as
belonging to two separate works, (1) and (2) being entitled
'Extracts on Physics and Ethics' (ἐκλογαί), and (3) and
(4) the 'Anthology', a name that really belongs to the whole
work[4].

---

[1] Monro's *Appendix* to Homer's *Od.* (1901), pp. 343—383.  Christ,
§ 637[4]; Croiset, v 978.  Text in Gaisford's *Hephaestion*, Westphal's *Scr.
Metr. Gr.*, and Kinkel's *Fragmenta Epicorum Gr.* i 1, 2, 16 f, 32 f, 36 f, 49,
52, 57, 63, 69.

[2] *Cod.* 161.       [3] Photius, *cod.* 167 ; Meineke's *praef.* xxxvii.

[4] ed. Gaisford (1822); Meineke (1857); Wachsmuth and Heyse (1884-95);
cp. Christ, § 639[4]; Croiset, v 979.

The study of rhetoric still survived as part of a general education and as a necessary preparation for public life. We may here briefly notice Aphthonius, who, as a pupil of Libanius, belongs to the end of the fourth and the beginning of the fifth centuries. He is celebrated for his small manual of preliminary exercises (προ-γυμνάσματα), a work remarkable for its simplicity and clearness, and for the variety of its examples[1]. It follows the tradition of Hermogenes, but the number of the exercises is here extended from twelve to fourteen by the separation of 'refutation' from 'confirmation', and the introduction of a new section on 'blame'. It was the theme of several commentaries, and continued to be used as a text-book not only in the Byzantine age[2], but even as late as the seventeenth century. It is happily described by Mr Saintsbury[3] as 'one of the most craftsmanlike cram-books that ever deserved the encomium of the epithet and the discredit of the noun'. After Aphthonius, the writers on rhetoric are only commentators on their predecessors. Thus Troilus (c. 400), Syrianus (430), Marcellinus (c. 500) and Sopater (early in cent. vi) all wrote commentaries on Hermogenes. Marcellinus was also the author of an extant life of Thucydides, probably founded on the labours of Didymus[4].

Early in the sixth century the principal schools of ancient learning in the East were those of Athens, Alexandria and Constantinople[5]. Of these, Athens was the last stronghold of paganism ; Alexandria, 'the centre of the widest culture', the home (especially in the fourth and fifth centuries) of pagan poetry and philosophy, as well as of Christian theology ; and Constantinople, the seat of a university since the time of Theodosius II[6], and, to a large extent, a school of Christian learning[7]. The secular library there

*Rhetoricians*

*Aphthonius*

*Schools of learning*

---

[1] Spengel, ii. Cp. Christ, § 546[4]; Croiset, v 982 f.

[2] Commentaries by Joannes Geometres (first half of cent. x) and Joannes Doxopatres (first half of cent. xi) are mentioned by Krumbacher, *Byz. Litt.* 452, 462 and esp. 735[2].

[3] i 92.                              [4] Susemihl, *Gr. Litt. Alex.* ii 203 n.

[5] Himerius, vii 13 ; Themistius, xxiii p. 355. Cp. Ch. Diehl, *Justinien et la civilisation byz. au* vi *s.* (1901), livre iii.

[6] Bury, i 128.                       [7] Bury, i 212, 317.

founded by Julian (with its marvellous MS of Homer, forty yards
long) had been destroyed by fire in 491, but there was a library
of ecclesiastical literature in the patriarchal palace[1]. The best
days of Nicomedeia and Antioch were in the fourth century,
in the times of Libanius. The Greek and Syriac school of
Edessa in Western Mesopotamia had been finally closed in 489.
Apart from these, the eastern shores of the Mediterranean could
boast of Berytus, which, from the third century till its destruction
by an earthquake in 551, was a great school of Roman law,
besides being (as described by Eusebius) a school of Greek
secular learning[2]. Further to the south was the school of
Caesarea, which had counted Origen among its teachers, and
the historians Eusebius and Procopius (*fl.* 527—562) among its
students. There was even a home of culture in the former land
of the Philistines. Towards the close of the fifth century, Gaza[3]
produced a grammarian in Timotheus, and rhetoricians such as
Procopius of Gaza (*fl.* 491—527), whose paraphrases of Homer
were admired by Photius[4], and his pupil and successor, Choricius[5],
who held the office of orator under Justin and Justinian. The
speeches of Choricius were among the models studied in the
Byzantine age, and they are even now of value in the textual
criticism of Demosthenes[6].

All the rhetoricians, lexicographers and grammarians, whom
we have now passed in review, belong to the age that ended
with 529 A.D., the eventful year in which the School of Athens
was closed in the East, and the Monastery of Monte Cassino
founded in the West. Three years later (532) the rebuilding

[1] Bernhardy, *Gr. Litt.* i 664[4]; Bury, i 252.

[2] *De Mart. Palaest.* iv 3; cp. Liban. *Ep.* 1033; and Bernhardy, *Gr. Litt.*
i 664[4]. Nonnus, *Dion.* xli 396, calls it 'the nurse of tranquil life', and Agathias,
ii 15, 'the pride (ἐγκαλλώπισμα) of Phoenicia'.

[3] Seitz, *Die Schule von Gaza* (1892); Roussos, τρεῖς Γαζαῖοι (1893);
Wilamowitz, *Gr. Lit.* (1905) 215.

[4] p. 103 *a*. His *Letters* are published in the *Epistolographi Graeci* (ed.
Didot). Cp. Eisenhofer (Freiburg in B., 1897); also *Byz. Zeitschr.* vi 55 f,
viii 263 f.

[5] ed. Boissonade, 1846; Förster in *Philol.* liv 93—123 &c.

[6] See index to present writer's *First Philippic and Olynthiacs* of
Demosthenes.

of the Church dedicated to the Eternal Wisdom by the founder
of Constantinople was begun by Justinian, who adorned that
Christian Church with columns from the pagan temples of
Ephesus and Heliopolis, and left behind him, in the many-tinted
marbles, the deeply-carved capitals, the lofty dome and the
spacious splendour of Santa Sophia, the last of the great religious
buildings of the ancient world.  Between 529, the date of the
publication of Justinian's *Code*, and 533, that of the completion
of the *Digest* and the *Institutes*, the legal learning of the past
was summed up and reduced to a systematic form, while the
old Roman Law of the Twelve Tables was finally superseded.
In the following year, the emperor who had suppressed the
School of Athens, put an end to the consulship of Rome, thus
virtually closing the Roman age in the West, as he had already
closed it in the East[1].

[1] If, in the transitional reign of Justinian, any further event should be sought
to mark the end of the old order and the beginning of the new, it may be
found perhaps (with Prof. Bury) in the plague of 542, which raged for four
months in Constantinople and for four years in the Roman Empire.  'When
the plague has ceased, we feel in 550 that we are moving in a completely
other world than that of 540 ' (Bury's *Later Roman Empire*, i 400).

The beginning of the last dialogue in the Bodleian Plato (Leyden Facsimile, 1898–1899), copied by John the Calligrapher for Arethas, deacon of Patrae, Nov. 895 A.D. (p. 403 f. *infra*).

Ἔχεις μοι εἰπεῖν, ὦ Σώκρατες, ἆρα διδακτὸν ἡ ἀρετή; ἢ οὐ διδακτὸν ἀλλ' ἀσκητόν; ἢ οὔτε ἀσκητὸν οὔτε μαθητόν, ἀλλὰ φύσει παραγίγνεται τοῖς ἀνθρώποις ἢ ἄλλῳ τινι τρόπῳ; (ΣΩ.) Ὦ Μένων, πρὸ τοῦ μὲν Θετταλοὶ εὐδόκιμοι ἦσαν ἐν τοῖς Ἕλλησιν καὶ ἐθαυμάζοντο ἐφ' ἱππικῇ τε καὶ πλούτῳ, νῦν δέ, ὡς ἐμοὶ δοκεῖ, καὶ ἐπὶ σοφίᾳ, καὶ οὐχ ἥκιστα οἱ τοῦ σοῦ ἑταίρου Ἀριστίππου πολῖται Λαρισαῖοι. τούτου δὲ ὑμῖν αἴτιός ἐστι Γοργίας· ἀφικόμενος γὰρ εἰς τὴν πόλιν ἐραστὰς ἐπὶ σοφίᾳ εἴληφεν Ἀλευαδῶν τε τοὺς πρώτους, ὧν ὁ σὸς ἐραστής ἐστιν Ἀρίστιππος.

# BOOK V.

## THE BYZANTINE AGE.

---

ἐστερήθημεν καὶ βιβλίων, καινὸν τοῦτο καὶ παράδοξον, καὶ νέα καθ' ἡμῶν ἐπινενοημένη τιμωρία.

PHOTIUS, *ad Imperatorem Basilium, Ep.* 218, ed. Valettas.

μὴ θαυμάσῃς, εἰ φίλος Ἀθηναίων καὶ Πελοποννησίων καθέστηκα ...δεῖ γὰρ τοὺς παῖδας ἀγαπᾶσθαι διὰ τοὺς πατέρας.

PSELLUS, *Ep.* 20, ed. Sathas.

τί δή ποτε, ὦ ἀγράμματε, τὴν μοναστηριακὴν βιβλιοθήκην τῇ σῇ παρεξισάσεις ψυχῇ; καὶ ὅτι μὴ σὺ κατέχεις γράμματα, ἐκκενοῖς καὶ αὐτὴν τῶν γραμματοφόρων σκευῶν; ἄφες αὐτὴν στέγειν τὰ τίμια. ἐλεύσεταί τις μετὰ σέ, ἢ γράμματα μαθών, ἢ ἀλλὰ φιλογράμματος.

EUSTATHIUS, *De emendanda vita monastica,* c. 128, ed. Tafel.

| Emperors | Poets | Historians, Chroniclers | Rhetoricians | Scholars | Ecclesiastic Writers |
|---|---|---|---|---|---|
| **600**— | | | | | |
| 602 Phocas | | | | | |
| 610 Heraclius | | 610-31 John of Antioch | | 610 Stephanus of Alexandria | |
| | 626 Sergius | 610-40 Theophylact Simocattes | | | 630 Maximus Confessor |
| | 629 Sophronius | | | | 580—662 |
| 641 Heraclius, Constantinus, and Heracleonas | 610-41 Georgius Pisides | 630 *Chronicon Paschale* | | | |
| 642 Constans II | | | | | *Barlaam and Josaphat* |
| 668 Constantine IV | | | | Jacob of Edessa *fl.* 651—719 | Anastasius Sinaites *fl.* 640—700 |
| 685 Justinian II | Andreas of Crete | | | | |
| 695 Leontius | *c.* 650—720 | | | | |
| 697 Tiberius III | | | | | |
| **700**— | | | | | |
| 705 Justinian II (restored) | | | | | |
| 711 Philippicus | | | | | |
| 713 Anastasius II | | | | | |
| 715 Theodosius III | | | | | |
| *House of Leo* | | | | | |
| 717 Leo III | 736 John of Damascus *c.* 699—*c.* 753 | | | | 736 John of Damascus |
| 741 Constantine V | 743 Cosmas of Jerusalem | | | | |
| | Stephen of St Sabas | | | | |
| 775 Leo IV | 725—794 | | | | |
| 780 Constantine VI | Theodorus Studites | Georgius Syncellus | | | |
| 797 Eirene of Athens | 759—826 | *fl.* 784—*c.* 810 | | | |
| **800**— | | | | | |
| 802 Nicephorus I | | Nicephorus Patriarches d. 829 | | Theognostus *fl.* 813-20 | 806 Nicephorus Patriarches d. 829 |
| 811 Stauracius | | 813 Theophanes Confessor d.817 | | Michael Syncellus *fl.* 829-42 | |
| 811 Michael I | | | | | |
| 813 Leo V | | *Theophanes continuatus* | | 830-76 *Syriac and Arabic translations of Aristotle* | |
| 820 Michael II | | 813—961 | | | |
| 829 Theophilus | 830 Josephus Studites d. 883 | | | | |
| 842 Michael III | | | | 857 Photius *c.* 820—*c.* 891 | 857 Photius *c.* 820—*c.* 891 |
| *Macedonian Dynasty* | | | Nicolaus, *Epistolae* 852—925 | 863 Cometas | |
| 867 Basil I | | 867 Georgius Monachus | | 870 d. Alkendi | |
| 886 Leo VI | | | | 870 Ignatius | |
| | | | | 882 *Etymologicum parvum* | |
| **900**— | | | | | |
| 912-59 Constantine VII | 917 Constantinus Cephalas, editor of *Anthologia Palatina* | | | 907 Arethas *c.* 860—932+ | |
| 920-44 Romanus I | | Constantine Porphyrogenitus 905—959 | | | |
| 959 Romanus II | | | | | |
| 963 Nicephorus II | | 963 Symeon Magister | *Philopatris* 965 or 969 | 950 d. Alfarabi | |
| 969 John I, Zimisces | 961 Theodosius, Ἅλωσις Κρήτης | | | 950-76 Suïdas | Symeon Metaphrastes, *Lives of Saints* |
| 976 Basil II | John Geometres *fl.* 963—986 | 992 Leo Diaconus *c.* 950—992 | | | |
| **1000**— | | | | | |

*Continued from p.* 346.

# CHAPTER XXII.

## BYZANTINE SCHOLARSHIP FROM 529 TO 1000 A.D.

IN the history of Greek Literature the Byzantine age, in the broadest sense of the term, may be said to begin with the founding of Constantinople in 330 and to end with its fall in 1453. It may be divided into three parts: (1) the *early* Byzantine period, of about three centuries, from 330 to the death of Heraclius in 641; (2) the *intervening* period of two centuries, which, so far as secular learning at Constantinople is concerned, may be described as a dark age extending from about 641 to about 850; (3) the *later* Byzantine period of six centuries from 850 to 1453[1]. In the history of Scholarship this third period extends over five centuries only, beginning in 850 with the great revival of Byzantine learning heralded by the auspicious name of Photius, and ending about 1350, when, a full century before the fall of Constantinople, the interest in Scholarship passes westward to the cities of Northern Italy which caught the first rays of the new light that came to them from the East.

In our survey of the history of Scholarship, we have found it convenient to treat the first two centuries (330—529) of the first of the above periods as the last two centuries of the Roman age, leaving a period of little more than a century (529—641) for the opening pages of the present Book. In this century, history is represented by

Period I, 529—641. Historians

---

[1] Krumbacher, *Geschichte der Byzantinischen Litteratur*, ed. 2, 1897, pp. 11 f; and *Die griechische Literatur des Mittelalters*, in *Die Kultur der Gegenwart*, 1905, I viii 237—285. Cp. Wilamowitz, on *Welt-perioden*, Göttingen, 1897.

the 'statesman and soldier' Procopius of Caesarea (*fl.* 527—562), the secretary of Belisarius and the historian of his campaigns, who resembles Herodotus in his love of the marvellous, Thucydides in his diction, and Polybius in his subordination of the course of events to the influence of Fortune[1]; by the 'poet and rhetorician'[2] and student of the ancient classics, Agathias (536—582), who, in relating the end of the Gothic war, the Perso-Colchian wars (541—556) and the invasion of the Huns (558), recognises a divine Being (τὸ θεῖον) as the author of retribution[3]; by Menander Protector (582), the imitator and continuator of Agathias; and by the Egyptian Theophylactus Simocattes, the euphuistic historian who describes the reign of Maurice (582—602) in a style rich in metaphors borrowed from the Hebrew Scriptures and the Greek Romances.    Antiquarian research is the province of Joannes Laurentius Lydus (*c.* 490—570), who studied Aristotle and Plato under a pupil of Proclus, and in his work *On Offices* gave a full account of the Roman civil service and the causes of its decline[4].    In poetry we have an imitator

Poets

of Callimachus and of Nonnus in the person of Paulus Silentiarius (the gentleman-usher who preserved silence in the palace of Justinian), the author of nearly 100 elegant epigrams in the *Palatine Anthology*[5], and also of a celebrated *Description of the Church of Santa Sophia*[6], in which he incidentally betrays his contempt for the Athenians, and at the same time flatters the emperor who closed their philosophic School, by stating that his verses will be judged, not by 'beaneating Athenians,' but by men of piety and indulgence, in whom God and the Emperor find pleasure'[7].    George of Pisidia (*Georgius Pisǐdes*), besides celebrating the campaigns of Heraclius, wrote a poem on the Creation, with a view to refuting Aristotle and Plato, Porphyry and Proclus.    Except in a single poem, in which

---

[1] Bury's *Later Roman Empire*, ii 178.    Ed. Haury (Leipzig), and Comparetti, 1895–8.  Cp. Felix Dahn, *Procopius von Caesarea* (1865), and Krumbacher, *Gr. Lit. des MAs*, 263 f.

[2] Gibbon, c. 43 (iv 420 Bury).        [3] Bury, ii 254 f.

[4] *ib.* ii 183 f.        [5] *e.g.* v 266, 270, 301.

[6] ed. Graefe (1822); Bekker (1837); German trans. Salzenberg (1854).

[7] Bury, ii 185 f.

he imitates the hexameters of Nonnus, he uses the iambic measure alone, and is generally strict in observing its rules; but he departs from the standard of the ancient poets in breaking the law of the final Cretic, and in never allowing the accent to fall on the last syllable of the line[1]. Psellus, the foremost representative of the Byzantine literature of the eleventh century, did him the honour of devoting a long letter to answering the question 'whether Euripides or Pisides wrote better verses'[2]. The historian Agathias, who in his youth was addicted to heroic verse and 'loved the sweets of poetic refinement', allows reminiscences of the poets to colour his prose. He contributes about 100 epigrams to the *Palatine Anthology*[3], with a preface[4] written in the style of the New Comedy and including a quotation from the *Knights* of Aristophanes[5]. He assures us that 'poetry is really a thing divine and holy', and that 'its votaries (as Plato would say) are in a state of fine phrenzy'[6]. The sacred poets of this age are Sergius, patriarch of Constantinople (626), and Sophronius, patriarch of Jerusalem (629).

Late in the sixth century is the earliest date that can be assigned to Georgius Choeroboscus, who played an important part in Byzantine education by his lectures on Grammar at the university of Constantinople[7]. The chronological order of his principal works was: (1) a treatise on prosody, followed by lectures on (2) Dionysius Thrax, (3) Theodosius, (4) orthography, (5) Hephaestion, and (6) Apollonius and Herodian. His grammatical learning is derived from the above authors, and from Orus, Sergius, Philoponus and Charax, the last three of whom belong to the sixth century. He is himself first quoted in the *Etymologicum Florentinum*, a MS of cent. x, representing a work prepared under the direction of Photius,

Choeroboscus

---

[1] *ib.* ii 256 f; Krumbacher, *Gr. Lit. des MAs*, 266 f.

[2] Leo Allatius, *De Georgiis*, reprinted in Fabricius, *Bibl. Gr.* x 7 f; Bouvy, *Poètes et Mélodes* (1886), p. 169; Krumbacher, p. 710².

[3] *e.g.* v 237, 261; vi 76.          [4] iv 3.

[5] 55 f.          [6] Bury, ii 185.

[7] Certain MSS of his *scholia* on Theodosius describe him as διάκονος and οἰκουμενικὸς διδάσκαλος. He was also the University Librarian, χαρτοφύλαξ. Cp. Hilgard, in *Gram. Gr.* iv p. lxi f. Papadopulos-Kerameus places him after 750 (*Byz. Zeitschr.* viii 212 f).

with the aid of authorities which followed Choeroboscus, who accordingly cannot well be placed *later* than 750[1]. His prolix lectures on the rules of Theodosius of Alexandria on nouns and verbs have come down to us in a complete form, part of them having been taken down by dictation (ἀπὸ φωνῆς)[2]. He appears to have had comparatively little influence on the later Byzantine grammarians, who preferred to study the great original writers on grammar, but in the age of the Renaissance he is closely followed in the text-books of Constantine Lascaris (Milan, 1476) and Urbanus of Belluno (Venice, 1497)[3].

Early in the seventh century (610) Aristotle was being ex-
Stephanus pounded by Stephanus of Alexandria, the author of commentaries on the *Categories*[4], *De Interpretatione*, *De Caelo, de Anima, Analytics, Sophistici Elenchi*, and *Rhetoric*[5].

The ecclesiastical writers of this age include Anastasius, patriarch of Antioch (559, d. 599), a precursor of Scholasticism, and an opponent of Justinian's opinion that the body of Christ was incorruptible; and Maximus Confessor (580—662), the private secretary of Heraclius and the opponent of his views on monotheletism. The latter is among the persons conjectured as possible authors of the anonymous *Chronicon Paschale*, an
Chronicon Paschale epitome of the history of the world from the Creation to 630 A.D., containing lists of consuls first published by Sigonius (1556), and many other chronological details first communicated by Casaubon to Scaliger and published by the latter in his edition of the *Chronicon* of Eusebius (1606)[6]. Among the authorities on which it is founded are Sextus Julius Africanus and Eusebius, the Consular *Fasti* and the Chronicle of John Malalas. This last in its present form
Malalas ends with the year 563; its author was a native of Antioch, who aimed at supplying the public of his day with a handbook of chronology written in the language of

[1] Reitzenstein, *Etymologika*, p. 190, n. 4.

[2] ed. Hilgard, *Gram. Gr.* iv 1 (1889) 101—417 and iv 2 (1894) Proleg. and 1—371.

[3] Krumbacher, § 244[2].          [4] ed. Hayduck (1885).

[5] ed. Rabe, *Comm. Arist.* xxi 2.

[6] Salmon in *Dict. Chr. Biogr.* i 510; Graux, *Fonds grec de l'Escurial*, 346f.

ordinary life.  The only MS is in the Bodleian ; the name of the author was identified by John Gregory (d. 1646), and the work published by John Mill (1691), with an appendix consisting of the famous 'Letter to Mill', which revealed to Europe the critical skill and the scholarship of Bentley.  In this 'Letter' the passages quoted by Malalas from the Greek poets are emended and explained, the laws of the anapaestic metre laid down, and the blunders in proper names corrected, the 'earliest dramatists' Themis, Minos and Auleas being shown to be mistakes for Thespis, Ion of Chios and Aeschylus[1].  Malalas regards Herodotus as a successor of Polybius, and Cicero and Sallust as Roman poets[2].  To the first half of the seventh century may be assigned the legend of the monk Barlaam and the Indian prince Josaphat, the most famous and most widely-known romance of the Middle Ages.  The discovery of a Syriac version of the lost Greek original of the *Apology of Aristides* in the monastery of mount Sinai shows that sixteen printed pages of *Barlaam and Josaphat* are borrowed directly from Aristides[3].

Barlaam and Josaphat

Our second period of two centuries (641—850) includes the hundred years of the iconoclastic emperors, Leo the 'Isaurian' having issued in 727 the decree against images, which was revoked by the empress Eirene in 802, and Leo the Armenian having in 816 promulgated a similar decree, which was finally set aside by the empress Theodora in 843.  The chief opponent of the iconoclasm of Leo the 'Isaurian' was the Syrian John of Damascus (*c.* 699—753)[4], who held high office at the court of the Saracens, and sent forth from Damascus three celebrated discourses in defence of the worship of images. He had been educated by Cosmas, an Italian monk familiar with Plato and Aristotle, who had been brought by Arab pirates,

Period II, 641—850

John of Damascus

---

[1] Jebb's *Bentley*, pp. 12—16; Prof. G. T. Stokes, in *Dict. Chr. Biogr.* s.v. ; Krumbacher, § 140[2].

[2] Krumbacher, *Gr. Lit. des MAs*, 265.

[3] J. Armitage Robinson, *Cambridge Texts and Studies*, 1891 ; Krumbacher, § 392[2]; Bury, ii 532—4.

[4] Krumbacher, §§ 16, 275[2]; *Gr. Lit. des MAs*, 268.

probably from the shores of Calabria, to the slave-market of Damascus. John is also celebrated as the author of the *Fons Scientiae* (πηγὴ γνώσεως), an encyclopaedia of Christian theology beginning with brief chapters on the *Categories* of Aristotle, together with extracts from the *Eisagoge* of Porphyry, for his knowledge of both of which he was indebted to Leontius of Byzantium (485—*c.* 542). Elsewhere, he describes certain of his opponents as seeing in Aristotle 'a thirteenth apostle'[1]. In applying to Christian theology the logical system of Aristotle, he became, through Peter Lombard and Thomas Aquinas, a name familiar to the Schoolmen of the West. He has been assigned 'the double honour of being the last but one of the Fathers of the Eastern Church, and the greatest of her poets'[2].

At the convent of St Sabas, which looks down on the Dead Sea from a rocky ravine S.E. of Jerusalem, he composed those hymns, three at least of which have, in their English renderings, become widely

Greek hymns    known in modern times :—'Those eternal bowers'; 'Come, ye faithful, raise the strain'; and the Golden Canon of the Greek Church, ''Tis the Day of Resurrection'[3]. His adoptive brother, Cosmas of Jerusalem, was the most learned of the Greek Christian poets[4], while to his nephew, Stephen of St Sabas (725—794), is assigned the original of the hymn 'Art thou weary, art thou languid?'[5] All of these were preceded by Anatolius, bishop of Constantinople 449—458, the author of the evening hymn of the Greek islanders, 'The day is past and over'[6]; by Romanus, who is regarded as 'the greatest poet of the Byzantine age' (*fl.* 527—565)[7], and by his imitator Andreas, archbishop of Crete (*c.* 650—720), the author of the Great Canon of 250 stanzas, and of the hymn beginning, 'Christian! dost thou see them?'[8] The monastery of Studion in Constantinople was the retreat of Joseph of Sicily (*fl.* 830), who inspired the hymn, 'O happy band of pilgrims'[9], and of Theodore of Studion (759—826), the author of the Canon, which, for the four centuries preceding the *Dies Irae*, remained the 'grandest Judgment-hymn of the Church'[10]. Among other writers of hymns were the

---

[1] *Contra Jacobitas*, c. 10.

[2] J. M. Neale's *Hymns of the Eastern Church*, p. 33 (ed. 1863).

[3] *ib.* 38, 55, 57.          [4] *ib.* 64—83.

[5] *ib.* 84–6.          [6] *ib.* 2—12.

[7] Krumbacher, § 272[2], p. 663, and *Gr. Lit. des MAs*, 259—262. P. Maas, *Byz. Zeitschr.* xv (1906) 1 f, has proved that Romanus belongs to the reign of Justinian.

[8] Neale, pp. 17, 18.

[9] *ib.* 122—152.          [10] *ib.* p. 112.

historian Theophanes (d. *c.* 817), and Methodius, patriarch of Constantinople (843–7), who called the Synod which in 843 restored the worship of images[1].

In this second period, apart from sacred poetry, works in prose have been left not only by John of Damascus, who has been already noticed, but also by Anastasius Sinaites (*fl.* 640—700), who begins his principal work, the Ὁδηγός or ' Guide to the true way', with a number of definitions clearly taken from Aristotle; and by Theodore of Studion (759—826), who is still represented by his theological writings and by a large collection of letters which throw light on the social life of the ninth century[2]. He was famous for his calligraphy and for his services in promoting the preservation and multiplication of mss[3]. Under Leo the Armenian (813—820) the grammarian Theognostus compiled a work on orthography comprising more than a thousand rules, mainly founded on Herodian's great work on accentuation. The vowels and the diphthongs which, in Byzantine Greek, have the same pronunciation as those vowels, are here grouped together, ε with αι, and υ with οι, the vowel being called ε ψιλόν, or υ ψιλόν, to distinguish it from the diphthong[4]. In the first half of the ninth century Michael Syncellus (*fl.* 829–42) wrote a popular manual on Syntax. The other prose-writers of the first half of that century include George Syncellus (d. *c.* 810), who brought his Chronicle of the world down to the reign of Diocletian; Theophanes (d. *c.* 817), who carried it on to his own day, to be succeeded by others who continued the work to 901; and the patriarch Nicephorus (d. 829), who wrote a short history of the empire from 602 to 769, and was, with Theodore of Studion, one of the main opponents of the ico-noclastic emperor Leo the Armenian. Among the emperor's supporters was John the Grammarian, patriarch from 832 to 842, who to great literary attainments added a wide knowledge of

*Theognostus*

*Chroniclers etc.; George Syncellus, Theophanes, Nicephorus*

---

[1] *ib.* pp. 89, 119. The Greek texts of some of the above hymns are printed in Moorsom's *Companion to Hymns Ancient and Modern*, pp. 79—91[2].

[2] Migne, xcix.

[3] Krumbacher, § 61, 6[2]; G. A. Schneider (Münster, 1900), 112 pp.; and A. Gardner, *Theodore of Studium* (1905).

[4] Krumbacher, § 245[2]; cp. *supra* p. 90.

science which led to his being accused by the ignorant of studying magic[1]. But, on the whole, the iconoclastic age was singularly barren in secular learning.

It was, however, during the two centuries described as the dark age of secular literature at Constantinople

Aristotle
among the
Syrians and
Arabians

that the light of Greek learning spread eastwards to Syria and Arabia. The philosophy of Aristotle had already found acceptance, in the fifth century, among the Syrians of Edessa, and, about the middle of that century, Syriac commentaries on the *De Interpretatione*, the *Analytica Priora* and the *Sophistici Elenchi* had been produced by Probus. The School of Edessa, closed by Zeno in 489 owing to its sympathy with Nestorianism, was succeeded by that at Nisībis[2], which attracted the notice of Cassiodorus, and that at Gandisapora[3] (between Susa and Ecbatana), which sent forth Syrian students to instruct the Arabians in philosophy and medicine respectively. In the sixth century works of Aristotle had been translated into Syriac by Sergius of Resaina[4]; and, in the seventh, the *De Interpretatione*, *Categories* and *Analytics* were produced in the same language, together with a *Life* of Aristotle, by Jacob, bishop of Edessa (*fl.* 651—719). Under the rule of the Abbāsidae (which lasted from 750 to 1258, and whose capital of Bagdad was founded in 762) the medical science of the Greeks became known to the Arabs through the medium of the Syrians; and, in the reign of the son of Harun-al-Raschid, the calif Almamun (813—833), whose request for the temporary use of the services of Leo the mathematician was resolutely refused by the emperor Theophilus (*c.* 830)[5], philosophical works were translated by Syrian Christians from Greek into Syriac, and from Syriac into Arabic. It was under Almamun that Aristotle was first translated into Arabic under the direction of Ibn al Batrik

---

[1] Finlay, ii 117, 143, 207 f.

[2] καὶ Συρίης πέδον εἶδα καὶ ἄστεα πάντα Νίσιβίν [τ'], | Εὐφράτην διαβάς. Inscr. in Ramsay's *Cities etc. of Phrygia*, ii 723. Cp. Lightfoot's *Ignatius*, i 497. See p. 264 *supra*. On the statutes of the School in 496 and 590 A.D. cp. Nestle, in *Zeitschr. für Kirchengesch.* 1897, 211—229.

[3] Gondi Sapor in Gibbon, c. 42 (iv 361 Bury).

[4] A. Baumstark, *Lucubr. Syro-Graecae*, 358—438.

[5] Cedrenus, p. 549; Gibbon, c. 52 (vi 34 Bury).

('Son of the Patriarch'). The Nestorian Honein Ibn Ishak, or Johannitius (d. 876), who was familiar with Syriac, Arabic and Greek, presided over an important school of interpreters at Bagdad; and (besides versions of Plato, Hippocrates and Galen)[1] Greek commentaries on Aristotle were, in his name, translated by his sons and his disciples into Syriac and Arabic. In the tenth century new translations of Aristotle, Theophrastus, Alexander of Aphrodisias, Themistius, Syrianus, Ammonius etc. were produced by the Nestorian Syrians. Of the Arabian philosophers in the East the most important were Alkendi of Basra (d. *c.* 870), who commented on the logical writings of Aristotle; Alfarabi of Bagdad (d. 950), who in logic followed Aristotle unreservedly, and accepted the Neo-Platonic doctrine of emanation; Avicenna (980—1037), who taught in Ispahan, combining instruction in medicine with the exposition of Aristotle, analysing the *Organon* and writing commentaries on the *De Anima* and *De Caelo*, and on the *Physics* and *Metaphysics*[2]; and Algazel (1059—1111), who began his teaching at Bagdad and opposed (on religious grounds) the doctrines of Aristotle[3]. The Arabic translations of Aristotle passed from the East to the Arabian dominions in the West, Spain having been conquered by the Arabs early in the eighth century. The study of Aristotle in Spain in the twelfth century, and the influence of the Latin translations of the Arabic versions of Aristotle, is reserved for our review of the Middle Ages in the West[4].

At the beginning of the two centuries which are regarded as

[1] *ib.* vi 29 n. For Arabic works on Plato's *Republic*, cp. Wenrich, 124.

[2] cp. Carra de Vaux (Paris, 1900).

[3] Ueberweg's *Grundriss*, ed. 8, ii § 28 (pp. 402—417 of *History of Philosophy*, E. trans.) with the literature quoted there, and in Hübner, § 35, and Krumbacher, p. 1098[2] f, esp. G. Flügel, *De Arabicis scriptorum Graecorum interpretibus* (1841), J. G. Wenrich, *De auctorum Graecorum versionibus et commentariis Syriacis Arabicis Armenicis Persicisque* (1842), A. Müller, *Die griechischen Philosophen in arabischer Ueberlieferung*, Halle, 1873, J. Lippert's *Studien* (1894), E. Sachau, *Zu den Aristoteles-Studien im Orient*, in γενεθλιακὸν *zum Buttmannstage* 1899, pp. 50—64, and Steinschneider, in *Centralbl. f. Bibl.* 1889, 51—81, and Virchow's *Archiv*, 124 (1891) 115—136; also A. Baumstark, *Aristoteles bei den Syrern vom v—viii Jahrhundert* (1900). Cp. Hauréau, *Histoire de la Philosophie Scolastique*, ed. 2, II i 15—29. On Theophilus of Edessa, translator of Homer, see *Berl. Phil. Woch.*, 1910, 444 f.

[4] c. xxx.

the darkest portion of the Byzantine age, Leo the 'Isaurian', who repelled the last great effort of the Saracens to destroy Constantinople and ably reformed the military defences and the civil administration of the empire, did no service whatsoever to the cause of learning. He actually disendowed the imperial academy in the quarter between the palace walls and Santa Sophia, and ejected the Ecumenical Doctor at its head and the 12 learned men who assisted him in giving instruction in arts and theology[1]. He is even stated by Zonaras, and by George the Monk, to have burnt the Academy with its library of 33,000 volumes of sacred and secular literature,—an act which (considering the position of the building) would have been so indiscreet that it is absolutely incredible. It is probable, however, that the schools of theology were alone suppressed, as we know that learned divines such as Theodore of Studion and the patriarch Nicephorus 'received an excellent secular education in grammar, language, science and philosophy'[2]. Towards the end of this dark period, Leo the Byzantine received permission from Theophilus (829–42) to teach in public; under his successor, Caesar Bardas, who ruled on behalf of Michael the Drunkard, iconoclasm was abolished (through the influence of Michael's mother, Theodora), and the university of Constantinople restored (863). In 857 the

Period III,
850—1350

patriarch Ignatius, a man of the highest integrity, whose father (Michael I) and grandfather (Nicephorus I) had filled the imperial throne, was banished; and a man of equal integrity and greater learning, Photius, whose brother had married the sister of the empress Theodora, and whose grand-uncle Tarasius had been patriarch in his day, was, like Tarasius, raised as a layman from the position of chief Secretary of State to that of the head of the Eastern Church[3]. The appointment of Photius led to a serious conflict with the papacy; and Ignatius was restored in 863. Basil I (867—886), the founder of the Macedonian dynasty, appointed Photius tutor to the emperor's son, afterwards known as Leo the Wise; and the two sets of moral exhortations, which have come down to us under the name of Basil and are founded largely on

[1] Finlay, ii 44; Bury, ii 433 f.
[2] Bury, ii 435, 519.          [3] Finlay, ii 175 f.

the work on the duties of princes dedicated by Agapetus to
Justinian, and also (like Photius' letter[1] to the king of the
Bulgarians) on the moral precepts of Isocrates, may possibly
have been really composed by Photius[2]. On the death of Ignatius
in 878, Photius was reinstated by Basil, to be exiled by his pupil,
Leo the Wise, in 886, and to die in exile in 891.

Photius, who was born *c.* 820–7, had scarcely completed his
own education when he was seized by his life-long
passion for instructing others. He displayed an          Photius
almost pedantic partiality for correcting the grammatical mistakes
of his friends, and this passion pursued him not only during his
tenure of the patriarchate, but even in the time of his exile[3].
His house was the constant resort of eager youths to whom he
interpreted the *Categories* of Aristotle, and the controversies
respecting *genera* and *species*, and 'mind' and 'matter'[4]. He
composed text-books of dialectic, and discussed with his pupils
points of theology and scholarship. Even when he had risen
to high office, his activity as a teacher did not cease. His house
continued to be frequented by the most inquisitive members of
the intellectual society of the capital[5]. Books were read aloud
in the master's presence and were criticised by the master himself,
who stated his opinion on their substance and their form. From
all who listened to his lectures he exacted the most implicit
submission, even demanding written promises of adhesion to his
views[6]. The wide range of his attainments was admitted even
by his opponents; and, in his many-sided erudition, he not only
surpassed his contemporaries, but even rivalled the most learned
of the ancients. In his philosophical studies he showed a special
partiality for Aristotle, while he had less capacity for appreciating
Plato, and was indeed strongly opposed to the Platonic doctrine

[1] *Ep.* 6, pp. 224–48, ed. Valettas.

[2] Krumbacher, § 191[2].

[3] e.g. *Ep.* 236 Valettas, ...οὔτε σολοικίζουσι...συνήθης εἰμὶ πείθεσθαι.

[4] *Quaest. Amphil.* 77 c. 1 (Hergenröther, iii 342).

[5] *Ep.* 3, *ad Papam Nicolaum* (p. 149 Valettas), οἴκοι...μένοντι χαρίεσσα
τῶν ἡδονῶν περιεπλέκετο τέρψις, τῶν μανθανόντων ὁρῶντι τὸν πόνον, τὴν σπουδὴν
τῶν ἐπερωτώντων, τὴν τρίβην τῶν προσδιαλεγομένων κτλ. Cp. Hergenröther, i
322–35.

[6] Hergenröther, i 335, note 118.

of Ideas[1]. In his dialectical treatises he generally followed the methods adopted by Porphyry, Ammonius and John of Damascus[2].

The two works of Photius which are of special importance in the history of Scholarship, are (1) his *Bibliotheca* and (2) his *Lexicon*. In dedicating his *Bibliotheca* or *Myriobiblon* to his brother Tarasius, he states that it was written in compliance with his brother's request for information as to the books which had been read aloud and discussed in the circle of Photius during his brother's absence. Photius himself was at the time preparing for his journey as envoy to the Assyrian court, *i.e.* to the seat of the calif at Bagdad. From the letter of dedication it has been sometimes inferred that this vast work was compiled during the embassy itself[3]; but, whatever ambiguity there may be in the dedication, the most natural interpretation of the conclusion is that it was completed before the author departed for Assyria[4]. The work, which must have been finished before 857 A.D., while the author was still a layman, consists of 280 chapters, corresponding to the number of separate volumes (*codices*) read and reviewed, and it fills altogether 545 quarto pages in double columns in Bekker's edition. Some of these reviews contain lengthy extracts, with criticisms on the style or subject-matter. Among the prose writings are the works of theologians, historians, orators and rhetoricians, philosophers, grammarians and lexicographers, physicists and physicians, and even romances, acts of councils, and lives of saints and martyrs. Next to the theologians, the historians fill the largest space; and, among the historical writings here preserved for posterity, are important notices of, or extracts from, Hecataeus, Ctesias, Theopompus, Diodorus Siculus, Memnon of Heraclea, Arrian, Phlegon of Tralles, and the chronologist Sextus Julius Africanus, besides later historians

---

[1] Hergenröther, iii 342.        [2] Krumbacher, § 216[2].

[3] *e.g.* Nicolai in Brockhaus, *Encykl.* part 87 p. 359; Saintsbury, i 176. Gibbon, c. 53 (vi 105 Bury) is rather vague.

[4] p. 545, εἰ μὲν ταύτην τὴν πρεσβείαν διανύοντα (διανοοῦντα MS) τὸ κοινὸν καὶ ἀνθρώπινον καταλάβοι τέλος, ἔχεις τὴν αἴτησιν τῆς ἐλπίδος οὐ διαμαρτοῦσαν... εἰ δ' ἐκεῖθεν ἡμᾶς ἀνασωσάμενον τὸ θεῖόν τε καὶ φιλάνθρωπον νεῦμα εἰς τὴν ἀλλήλων θέαν...ἀποκαταστήσει (he will send his brother a fresh series of reviews).

such as Olympiodorus of Thebes, Nonnŏsus of Byzantium, and
Candidus the Isaurian. We are also supplied with excerpts from
the chrestomathies of Proclus and Helladius, and brief reviews of
the lexicon of the latter, as well as similar works by Diogenianus,
and the Atticists Aelius Dionysius, Pausanias and Phrynichus.
The author is particularly happy in his literary criticisms. He
notes the charm of Herodotus, the monotonously balanced clauses
of Isocrates, the clear, simple and pleasant style of Ctesias.
Josephus in his view is rich in argument, and in sententiousness
and pathos; Appian, terse and plain; and Arrian, masterly in
his capacity for succinct narration. Lucian spends all his pains
on producing a prose comedy in a style that is brilliant and
classical. Phrynichus has collected excellent linguistic materials
for the use of others, without making any use of them himself.
Philostratus is lucid and graceful; Synesius has dignity of phrase,
but is apt to become over-poetical, though his *Letters* are full
of charm; Cyril of Alexandria writes in a poetical variety of
prose; Libanius is a canon and standard of Attic style. Lastly,
in writing the earliest extant review of any novel, the critic
describes the *Aethiopica* of Heliodorus as abounding in pathetic
situations and hairbreadth escapes[1]. The work, as a whole, is
such as to prove, in the language of Gibbon, that 'no art or
science, except poetry, was foreign to this universal scholar, who
was deep in thought, indefatigable in reading and eloquent in
diction'[2].

In his *Lexicon* (λέξεων συναγωγή), which belongs to a later
date than the *Bibliotheca*, he makes use of excerpts from the
vocabularies of Aelius Dionysius and Pausanias, both of them
partly founded on Diogenianus; he also uses the abridged Harpocration, with the Platonic lexicons of Timaeus and Boëthus[3].
For Homeric words he depends on Pseudo-Apion, Heliodorus
and Apollonius. This Lexicon has been preserved solely in the
*codex Galeanus* (*c.* 1200), formerly in the possession of Dr Thomas
Gale (d. 1702), and now in the Library of Trinity College, Cam-

[1] Cp. Saintsbury, i 176—183.

[2] c. 53 (vi 104 Bury). The work is unduly depreciated by A. Solari, in
*Riv. di storia antica*, ix 456—465. Edgar Martini, *Textgeschichte* (Teubner,
Leipzig), 1911. [3] Naber's *Proleg.*

bridge. It was twice transcribed by Porson, and published from his second transcript by Dobree (1822)[1]. The explanations of certain words given by Photius in the learned Letters addressed during his first exile (867–77) to Amphilochus, bishop of Cyzicus, agree with those of the *Lexicon*[2].

The above was not the only *Lexicon* executed under the superintendance of Photius. In the *Etymologicum Florentinum*[3], preserved in a MS of cent. x, and now called the *Etymologicum genuinum*, Photius is cited in five passages, once in the form οὕτως ἐγώ, Φώτιος ὁ πατριάρχης[4]. But (curiously enough) he is not named in the numerous extracts derived from his earlier *Lexicon* and described as taken ἐκ τοῦ ῥητορικοῦ. In his *Amphilochian Questions*[5], he quotes a passage on the magnet which we find in the *Etymologicum*, and which ultimately comes from the chrestomathy of Helladius quoted by Photius in the *Bibliotheca*[6]. At the end of one of the articles of the *Etymologicum* the poor scholar who originally transcribed the work laments his poverty and describes himself as impelled by the love of language (τῷ τῶν λόγων ἔρωτι) to spend sleepless nights over his task, in the hope of deriving great advantage from it and leaving to posterity something worthy of remembrance[7]. The authorities here quoted include Methodius, Orus and Orion, Zenobius (the commentator on Apollonius), Herodian, Choeroboscus, Theognostus (*fl.* 820), and many *scholia* on the ancient poets. It would appear that the explanations of Homeric words current early in the sixth century were supplemented from Choeroboscus and reduced to a lexicographical form; that interpolations were then introduced, and that, in this last stage, the work was taken up by Photius, who thus became the founder of the Greek Etymological Lexicons. The *Etymologicum genuinum* was followed by the *Etymologicum parvum*, which was also drawn up under the orders of Photius, and,

---

[1] Previously edited (from another transcript) by Hermann (1808); and since, by Naber (1864–5).

[2] Hergenröther, iii 10.

[3] Printed (with *Et. parvum*) in E. Miller's *Mélanges* (1868), pp. 11—340.

[4] Reitzenstein's *Etymologika* (summarised in *Berl. Phil. Woch.* 1898, p. 902 f), pp. 58—60 f.

[5] 131.    [6] p. 529. Reitzenstein, 63–5.    [7] *ib.* 66.

according to the statement at its close, was completed on Sunday
13 May, the date of 'the opening of the great church' (of Santa
Sophia) in a year identified as 882, when the church was repaired
and the western apse rebuilt by the emperor Basil the Macedonian[1].
Even on the day of the opening of his great cathedral church, the
patriarch was doubtless not uninterested in the completion of the
least of his three Lexicons.

His extant *Letters*[2] are mainly on points of dogmatic theology
or exegesis, though many of them deal with exhortation and
admonition, condolence or reproof.  In a letter addressed, during
his exile, to the emperor Basil I, he bitterly complains that he has
even been deprived of the use of his books[3].  In another he
expresses his surprise that the bishop of Nicomedeia regards
St Peter's use of ἐγκομβώσασθε[4] as a barbarism, and justifies it from
Epicharmus and Apollodorus of Carystos[5].  In a third, he writes
to the bishop of Cyzicus, eulogising the epistles of Plato in
preference to those of Demosthenes and Aristotle, and recommending his correspondent to study those 'ascribed to Phalaris,
tyrant of Acragas', and those of Brutus and of the royal philosopher
(probably M. Aurelius) and Libanius, together with those of Basil,
Gregory Nazianzen, and Isidore[6].  He tells the bishop of Laodicea
to cultivate a pure Attic style[7]; and, lastly, he corrects a composition by the monk and philosopher, Nicephorus, and offers to make
a collection of rhetorical works on his behalf, as soon as he is
definitely informed as to the books which he requires[8].  The
second part of his long letter to Michael, king of the Bulgarians[9],
is borrowed largely from the *Nicocles* of Isocrates.  The style of
his *Letters* varies from the extreme of an excessive redundancy to
that of an almost laconic terseness.  One of the most beautiful
passages in his longer letters is that in the first letter to Pope

---

[1] *ib.* 69.  Papadopulos-Kerameus prefers identifying the year as 994, the
date of the restoration of Santa Sophia by Basil II (*Byz. Zeitschr.* viii 212 f).

[2] 260 in the ed. of Valettas; 45 more published by A. Papadopulos-
Kerameus, 1896.

[3] p. 531 ed. Valettas, quoted on p. 385.    [4] 1 Pet. v 5.    [5] p. 541.

[6] p. 545.  It is possibly owing to the influence of Photius that the letters
of 'Phalaris' and Brutus have been preserved in so many mss (Hergenröther,
iii 230).

[7] p. 547.         [8] p. 551.         [9] *Ep.* 6.

Nicholas (861), where he describes the loss of a life of peaceful calm which befell him on his ceasing to be a layman, and regretfully dwells on the happiness of his home in the days when he was surrounded by eager inquirers after learning by whom he was always welcomed on his return from court[1].

Among the minor contemporaries of Photius were Cometas, a professor of Grammar (863), who prepared a recension of Homer which is the theme of two epigrams written by himself[2]; and Ignatius, the 'master of the grammarians' (870—880), who describes himself as the restorer of Grammar :—

Ἰγνάτιος τάδε τεύξεν, ὃς ἐς φάος ἤγαγε τέχνην
γραμματικήν, λήθης κευθομένην πελάγει[3].

But the waves of oblivion have rolled over the Grammar of Ignatius, as well as the Homeric recension of Cometas.

The absence of all notice of the classical Greek Poets in the *Bibliotheca* of Photius has often been observed. Possibly its learned author was more partial to prose. His pupil, Leo the philosopher, whom Caesar Bardas appointed Professor of Mathematics at the University of Constantinople, describes himself as bidding farewell to the Muses, as soon as he becomes a pupil of Photius in the 'diviner lore' of rhetoric[4]. The prose of Photius is certainly better than his scanty contributions to sacred verse; and, apart from this, his omission of poetry in a work professing to record only a portion of his reading in his maturer years is quite consistent with his having studied the usual classical poets in the days of his youth. In the ninth century the authors studied at school, and familiar to the general public in Constantinople, included Homer, Hesiod, Pindar; certain select plays of Aeschylus (*Prometheus, Septem, Persae*), Sophocles (*Ajax, Electra, Oedipus Tyrannus*), and Euripides (*Hecuba, Orestes, Phoenissae,* and, in the second degree, *Alcestis, Andromache, Hippolytus, Medea, Rhesus, Troades*)[5];

Study of
the Classics

[1] p. 149 Valettas, ἐξέπεσον εἰρηνικῆς ζωῆς, ἐξέπεσον γαλήνης γλυκείας κτλ. On Photius, cp. Milman's *Latin Christianity,* iii 156—170; Hergenröther's *Photius,* 1867-9; Krumbacher, § 216[2], and *Gr. Lit. des MAs,* 270 f.

[2] *Anth. Pal.* xv 37, 38.          [3] *ib.* 39.  Krumbacher, p. 720[2].

[4] *Anth. Gr.,* Appendix iii 255.

[5] The κωλομετρία of Eugenius (*fl.* 500) was confined to 15 plays of the three tragic poets.  Cp. Bernhardy, *Gr. Litt.* i 694[4]; and Wilamowitz, *Eur. Her.* i 195[1].

also Aristophanes (beginning with the *Plutus*), Theocritus, Lycophron and Dionysius Periegetes. The prose authors principally
studied were Thucydides, parts of Plato and Demosthenes, also
Aristotle, Plutarch's *Lives*, and especially Lucian, who is often
imitated in the Byzantine age[1]. Among rhetoricians, the favourite
authors were Dion Chrysostom, Aristides, Themistius and Libanius;
among novelists, Achilles Tatius and Heliodorus. The geographer
Strabo is hardly noticed before the Byzantine age. In sacred
literature, the books chiefly read were, apart from the Scriptures,
certain of the Greek Fathers, such as Basil, Gregory of Nazianzus
and of Nyssa, Chrysostom, Johannes Climax (525—600, author
of a devotional work on the *Scala Paradisi* ending with the
*Liber ad Pastorem*), and John of Damascus, together with lives
of saints and martyrs[2]. The predominance of sacred literature
is obvious in the catalogues of the great Greek libraries, such as
those on Mount Athos[3]. But the fact that so large a body of
secular literature has been preserved at all is mainly due to the
learning and enlightenment of eminent ecclesiastics such as Photius
and Arethas.

Arethas was one of the many distinguished pupils of Photius.
He was born at Patrae about 860–5, was Arch-    **Arethas**
bishop of Caesarea in Cappadocia in or before 907,
and died in or after 932 (the date of a Moscow MS copied on his
behalf). Although his residence in Cappadocia kept him far
removed from the chief centres of learning, he devoted himself
with remarkable energy to the collection of classical as well as
ecclesiastical writings, and to commenting on the same. Certain
of his annotations on Plato[4], Dion Chrysostom[5], Pausanias[6],

[1] *e.g.* in the *Philopatris* (965 or 969), *Timarion* (*c.* 1150) and *Mazaris*
(*c.* 1416). Cp. Krumbacher, §§ 459, 467, 492[2]; and, on the above date of the
*Philopatris*, Rohde's *Kleine Schriften*, i 411, and S. Reinach in *Rev. Archéol.*
(1902) i 79—110 (rev. by Krumbacher in *Byz. Zeitschr.* xi 578 f). It was
placed *c.* 602–10 by Gutschmid and Crampe (followed by R. Garnett in
*Cornhill*, 1901, 616 f).

[2] Krumbacher, § 215[2], p. 505.

[3] ed. Lambros (Camb. Univ. Press), 2 vols., 1895 f.

[4] M. Schanz in *Philol.* 34 (1874) 374 f; E. H. Gifford in *Class. Rev.*
1902, p. 16; J. Burnet, *ib.* p. 276.

[5] A. Sonny, Kiev, 1896, esp. pp. 85—94.

[6] F. Spiro, in *Valla-Festschrift*, 1900, 129—138.

Lucian[1], Tatian, Athenagoras, Clement of Alexandria, and Eusebius are still extant; and he happens to be the author of three indifferent epigrams in the Palatine Anthology[2]. His interest in classical literature is attested by important MSS copied under his orders and at his own expense. Among these are MSS of Euclid (888); the Apologists, Clemens Alexandrinus[3], Eusebius (914); Aristides (917); possibly also of Dion Chrysostom, and certainly of Plato (895)[4]. Arethas was one of the earliest commentators on the Apocalypse, and his own copy of Plato found its way to the scene of the apocalyptic vision at Patmos. This famous MS was brought from Patmos to Cambridge by the traveller, Dr Edward Daniel Clarke, afterwards Professor of Mineralogy in that University. It is now in the Bodleian at Oxford, and is known as the *codex Bodleianus Clarkianus* 39. At the end of the volume it bears an inscription stating that it was 'written by John the calligraphist, for Arethas, Deacon of Patrae, in the month of November 895'. In October 1801, when Clarke discovered the MS in the midst of a disordered heap of volumes lying on the floor of the monastic library, 'the cover was full of worms, and falling to pieces'[5]. Its value was fully appreciated by Porson at Cambridge (in 1802)[6] and by Gaisford at Oxford (1812). Its readings were published by the latter in 1820, and it has since been reproduced in facsimile (1898 f). It was acquired by Arethas when he was already a deacon. The Oxford MS of Euclid (888), which was acquired before he held any ecclesiastical office, is almost the earliest dated example of the Greek minuscule writing of the Middle Ages[7].

The patriarch Photius had been finally deposed on the accession of his former pupil Leo the Wise (886). The next eighty years were entirely taken up with the reigns of the son and the

---

[1] Rabe, in *Göttingen Nachrichten*, 1903, 643—656; and ed. *Scholia*, 1906.

[2] xv 32–4.          [3] *Facsimile* on p. 333.          [4] *Facsimile* on p. 384.

[5] Clarke's *Travels*, vi 46 (ed. 4, 1818).

[6] Luard's *Correspondence of Porson*, p. 80.

[7] E. M. Thompson, *Palaeography*, p. 163. On Arethas, cp. Krumbacher, § 217[2], E. Maass in *Mélanges Graux*, pp. 749–66, and Jülicher in Pauly-Wissowa, iii 675–7. Dräseke has suggested that he may have been the 'Aretas' described by Andronicus of Rhodes as having edited the *Letters* of Aristotle (*Zeitschr. f. wiss. Theologie*, xliv (1901), 589 f).

grandson of Basil the Macedonian, Leo the Wise and Constantine Porphyrogenitus, both of whom were chiefly distinguished for their literary productions. Leo          Leo VI,
(886—911) was the author of certain homilies and    Constantine VII
epigrams, with a book of oracles which gained him the name
of 'the Wise'[1]. The treatise on Tactics bearing his name was
probably written by Leo the 'Isaurian'[2]. Constantine Porphyrogenitus, so called because he was born in the porphyry chamber
in the imperial palace, was kept in the background from the age
of seven to that of forty (912—945), and consoled himself meanwhile by writing books and painting pictures[3]. He produced
a biography of Basil I, treatises on the military subdivisions and
the administration of the empire[4], and a vast work on the cere-
monies of the court[5]. He also rendered considerable service
to Greek literature by organising the compilation of a series of
encyclopaedias of History, as well as Agriculture and Medicine.
The encyclopaedia of History was drawn up under 53 headings,
such as On Embassies[6], Virtues and Vices, Conspiracies, Strata-
gems, and Military Harangues. It included numerous extracts
from earlier historians, beginning with Herodotus and ending with
Theophylact Simocattes. The most important of these extracts
are those from Polybius. They were published by Fulvius Ursinus
at Antwerp in 1582 under the title *Selecta de Legationibus*, and,
with additions by Hoeschel, in 1603[7]. Further extracts from
Polybius and others were included in the *Excerpta de Virtutibus et
Vitiis* published by Henricus Valesius[8] (1634), from a MS found
in Cyprus and acquired by Peirescius[9], and hence known as the
*Excerpta Peiresciana*. A third series of extracts was included in
the *Excerpta de Sententiis*, published by Mai in 1827[10].

---

[1] Krumbacher, pp. 168, 628, 721[2].          [2] *ib.* p. 636[2].

[3] Gibbon, c. 48 (v 208 f Bury) and c. 53 (vi 62-6). Cp. A. Rambaud,
*L'empire grec au dixième siècle; Const. Porph.* (1870).

[4] Migne, cxiii 63—422.          [5] *ib.* cxii 74—1416.

[6] *ib.* cxiii 605—652; *Excerpta Historica*, ed. De Boor etc. (Berlin,
1903- ).

[7] ed. De Boor, 1903.          [8] Henri de Valois (1603-76).

[9] Nicolas Claude Fabre de Peiresc (1580—1637).

[10] Krumbacher, §§ 107—144, esp. § 112[2].

To the early part of the tenth century we may ascribe the
Greek Anthology compiled by Constantine Cephalas, who held office at the Byzantine court in 917.
He included in his collection the earlier Anthologies
of Meleager, Philippus and Agathias, whose prefatory poems he
preserves in his fourth book, and whose epigrams may be found
in books v—vii and ix—xi.  The Anthology of Cephalas consists
in all of xv books, contained in a *Codex Palatinus* of century xi,
so called because it belonged to the Library of the Palatinate
at Heidelberg.  In 1623, on the capture of Heidelberg by Tilly,
this MS was among the 3500 presented to the Pope and transported to the Vatican.  It was divided into two parts, and after
the treaty of Tolentino in 1797 was taken to Paris (with 37 other
Palatine MSS) as part of the Italian spoils of Napoleon Bonaparte.
After the Peace of Paris (1815) the first part, consisting of
Books i—xii, was (with the 37 other MSS) restored to Heidelberg,
which also possesses a photographic facsimile of the 48 leaves
still retained in Paris.  The MS was first made known to scholars
by Salmasius, who transcribed the whole at Heidelberg in 1607[1].
Up to that time the Greek Anthology had only been known in
the form of the *Anthologia Planudea* (cent. xiv), which will be
noticed in the sequel[2].

It is only the literary epigrams of the *Anthology* that are
connected by their subject with the history of Scholarship.  Some
of them contain the very essence of ancient literary criticism.
Among the poets here criticised we find Homer, Hesiod and
Antimachus ; Alcman, Archilochus, Stesichorus, Alcaeus, Sappho,
Ibycus, Hipponax, Anacreon and Pindar ; Aeschylus, Sophocles
and Euripides ; Aristophanes and Menander ; Lycophron and
Callimachus ; Aratus and Nicander[3].  All the nine lyric poets
are skilfully discriminated in a single epigram[4]; all the three
bucolic poets described as gathered into one flock and one fold[5];
and, in the dedicatory verses by Meleager and Philippus, each of
the poets whose verses are entwined in the garland of the

The Antho-
logy of
Cephalas

---

[1] Christ, § 357, p. 534[4]; Krumbacher, pp. 727–9[2].        [2] p. 428.

[3] vii 1—75; 405–9; 709; 745; ix 24—26; 64; 184—213; 506, 575 etc.;
cp. J. A. Symonds, *Greek Poets*, 359–66 ; and Saintsbury, i 81–6.

[4] ix 184.                    [5] ix 205.

*Anthology* is distinguished by the name of an appropriate flower. The writers of prose criticised by these poets are comparatively few; but they include Herodotus and Thucydides, Xenophon and Plato, and some other philosophers[1]. A Byzantine epigrammatist, Thomas Scholasticus, who recognises 'three stars in rhetoric', admires Aristides and Thucydides no less than Demosthenes[2]. Lastly, the verbal critics of Alexandria are the theme of several satirical epigrams, the best known of which are those of Herodicus (preserved by Athenaeus), and of Antiphanes[3] and Philippus[4].

In the latter half of the tenth century the expulsion of the Arabs from Crete (961) is commemorated by Theodosius Diaconus in a long iambic poem of some
historical interest[5]. In the same age we have the prolific poet, John the Geometer (*fl.* 963–86), whose best work is to be found in his epigrams on the old poets, philosophers, rhetoricians and historians[6]. Historical studies are meanwhile represented (1) by the Chronicle bearing the name of 'Symeon Magister' who is probably identical with the cele-
brated Hagiographer, Symeon Metaphrastes[7]; and (2) by the history of the third quarter of the tenth century by Leo Diaconus, whose style is influenced by Homer as well as Procopius[8].

*Poets*

*Historians*

To the third quarter of the tenth century (950–76)[9] we may assign the great Lexicon of Suïdas (Σουΐδας), which
is a combination of a lexicon and an encyclopaedia,
the best articles being those on the history of literature. It is founded (1) on earlier lexicons, such as the abridged Harpo-
cration, Aelius Dionysius, Pausanias and Helladius; (2) on *scholia* on Homer, Sophocles, Aristophanes and Thucydides, and on commentaries on Aristotle; (3) on histories, especially those

*Suïdas*

---

[1]  vii 93—135; 676; ix 188, 197.

[2]  xvi 315. This, however, is from the *App. Planudea* and is later than Cephalas.

[3]  xi 322.          [4]  xi 321. *Supra*, p. 163 n.

[5]  Migne, cxiii 987 f.          [6]  *ib.* cvi 901 f; Krumbacher, §§ 305–6[2].

[7]  Krumbacher, § 149[2].

[8]  *ib.* § 117[2]. Cp. *Byz. Zeitschr.* vi 106, 285.

[9]  The list of emperors, *s.v.* 'Αδάμ, ends with Joannes Tzimiskes (d. 976); but this may be a later addition, and the lexicon as a whole may be of earlier date.

included in the Excerpts of Constantine Porphyrogenitus ; (4) on
biographical materials collected by Hesychius of Miletus, and by
Athenaeus ; and (5) on other writers especially popular at Constantinople in the tenth century, such as Aelian, Philostratus
and Babrius. Its numerous coincidences with the lexicon of
Photius are best explained by regarding both as having borrowed
from the same originals. The earliest extant reference to the
lexicon is found in Eustathius (latter part of cent. xii). The learned
Greeks of the Renaissance, *e.g.* Macarius, Michael Apostolius,
Constantine Lascaris and 'Emmanuel' (probably Chrysoloras),
compiled many extracts from its pages[1]. A minor lexicon, the
*Violarium* ('Ιωνιά) bearing the name of Eudocia (1059—1067),
the consort of Constantine Ducas, is partly composed of excerpts
from Suïdas, and is now ascribed to Constantine Palaeokappa
(*c.* 1543)[2], who was actually indebted to printed books for some
of the learning which he palmed off on the world under the
name of an empress of the eleventh century.

[1] On Suïdas, cp. Christ, § 633[4] ; Krumbacher, § 233[2] ; Wentzel, *Beiträge
zur Geschichte der griechischen Lexikographen* (*S. Ber. Berlin Akad.* 1895,
477—487) ; J. Bidez, *La tradition manuscrite—de Suidas* (*ib.* 1912).

[2] Christ, p. 844[4] ; Krumbacher, § 240[2].

# Conspectus of Greek Literature, &c., 1000—c. 1453 A.D.

| Emperors | Poets | Historians, Chroniclers | Rhetoricians, &c. | Scholars | Ecclesiastical Writers |
|---|---|---|---|---|---|
| **1000** | | | | | |
| 976 Basil II | | | | | |
| 1025 Constantine VIII | | | | | |
| 1028 Romanus III | Christophorus of Mytilene *fl.* 1028-43 | | John Doxopatres 'Siceliotes' | Avicenna 980—1037 | |
| 1034 Michael IV | John Mauropus *fl.* 1042-55 | | | | |
| 1042 Michael V | | | | | |
| 1042 Constantine IX | | | | Psellus 1018—78 | |
| 1054 Theodora | | | | | Symeon c. 1025—c. 1092 |
| 1056 Michael VI | | | | | |
| 1057 Isaac I Comnenus | | 1071 John Xiphilinus | | 1057-9 Isaac Porphyrogenitus | |
| 1059 Constantine X Ducas | | 1080 John Scylitzes | | Algazel 1059—1111 | |
| 1067 Romanus IV | | 1080 Michael Attaliates | | John Italus | |
| 1071 Michael VII Ducas | | 1080 Nicephorus Bryennius 1062—c. 1138 | Michael Andreopulus, translator of 'Syntipas' | Michael of Ephesus | 1078 Theophylact |
| 1078 Nicephorus III | *Christus Patiens* | Cedrenus | | Eustratius of Nicaea c. 1050—1120 | Euthymius Zigabenus *fl.* 1081—1118 |
| 1081 Alexius I | | | | | |
| **1100** | | | | | |
| 1118 John II Comnenus | Theodorus Prodromus d. c. 1159 | Constantine Manasses | | '*Etymologicum Gudianum*' | |
| 1143 Manuel I Comnenus | | 1145 Zonaras | Michael Italicus *fl.* 1147-66 | | 1143 Nicholaus of Methone d. c. 1165 |
| 1180 Alexius II Comnenus | | 1148 Anna Comnena 1083—1148 | *Timarion* | Tzetzes 1110—1180+ | |
| 1183 Andronicus I Comnenus | | 1176 John Cinnamus 1143—c. 1186 | 1155 Nicephorus Basilakes | 1175 Eustathius d. c 1192-4 | |
| 1185 Isaac II Angelus | | Michael Glykas c. 1130—c. 1190 | 1175 Michael Acominatus 1140—1220 | | |
| 1195 Alexius III | | | | Gregorius Corinthius | |
| **1200** | | | | | |
| 1203 Isaac II & Alexius IV | | 1206 Nicetas Acominatus c. 1150—c. 1211 | | '*Etymologicum Magnum*' between 1100 and 1250 | |
| 1204 Alexius V Ducas | 1204 *Loss of Constantinople Latin Emperors* | | | | |
| *Nicaean Emperors* | 1204 Baldwin I | | | | |
| 1204 Theodore I Lascaris | 1206 Henry | | | | |
| 1222 John III Ducas | 1217 Peter | | | | |
| | 1219 Robert | | | | |
| 1254 Theodore II Lascaris | 1228 Baldwin II -61 | | Blemmydes c. 1197—1272 | | |
| 1258 John IV Lascaris | | | | | |
| 1259 Michael VIII Palaeologus | | | Georgius (Gregorius) Cyprius 1241—c. 1290 | | |
| 1261 *Recovery of Constantinople* | | | Nicephorus Chumnus c. 1261—c. 1328 | 1296 Maximus Planudes 1260—1310 | 1275 Joannes Beccus d. c. 1293 |
| 1282 Andronicus II | *Anthologia Planudea* | 1261 Acropolites 1217—1282 | | | |
| **1300** | | | | | |
| | Manuel Philes c. 1275—1345 *Iliad* of Const. | 1308 Pachymeres 1242—c. 1310 | | Moschopulus *fl.* 1295—1316 | |
| 1328 Andronicus III | Hermoniacus c. 1323-35 | Xanthopulus 1295—c. 1360 | | Thomas Magister *fl.* 1283—1328 | 1349 Gregorius Palamas |
| 1341-76 John V | | | | Theodorus Metochites *fl.* 1283—1328 | Barlaam *fl.* 1339-48 |
| 1341-55 John VI Cantacuzenus | | | Demetrius Cydones c. 1325—c. 1396 | Triclinius | Nicolaus Cabasilas (*Mystic*) d. 1371 |
| 1376 Andronicus IV | | 1356 John Cantacuzenus c. 1295—1383 | | John Pediasimus *fl.* 1328-41 | |
| 1379 John V (restored) | | 1359 Nicephorus Gregoras 1350—1425 | 1391 Manuel II | Andreas Lopadiotes, *Lexicon Vindobonense* | 1438 Bessarion c. 1395—1472 |
| 1391 Manuel II | | 1462 Ducas | 1416 *Mazaris* | 1397 Chrysoloras c. 1355—1415 | |
| 1425 John VIII | | 1463 Laonicus | 1450 Matthaeus Camariotes | | |
| 1448 Constantine XI | | 1467 Critobulus | | | |
| 1453 *Fall of Constantinople* | | 1477 Phrantzes | | | |

*Continued from p.* 386.

# CHAPTER XXIII

## BYZANTINE SCHOLARSHIP, 1000—1350 A.D. AND AFTER

THE consolidation of Byzantine legislation and despotism, which had continued for a century (867—963) under the first four emperors of the Basilian dynasty, was followed by a shorter period of conquest and military glory (963—1025) under John Tzimiskes and Basil 'the slayer of the Bulgarians', and ended in a still shorter period of conservatism and stationary prosperity (1025—1057) under Constantine VIII and the three successive husbands of his daughter Zoë[1]. Shortly before this last period falls the birth of Psellus (1018—1078), the most notable personage in the Byzantine literature of the eleventh century.

Psellus

Born at Nicomedeia, he learnt law at Constantinople from the future patriarch Xiphilinus, whom he imbued with an interest in philosophy. According to his own account, his study of inferior philosophers led him at last to Aristotle and Plato, and thence to Plotinus, Porphyry, Iamblichus and Proclus[2]. He also tells us that in his time learning flourished no longer at Athens or Nicomedeia, at Alexandria or in Phoenicia, or in either Rome, the Old or the New[3]. Under the second of the three husbands of Zoë, Michael the Paphlagonian (1034–41), he held a judicial appointment at Philadelphia; and under the third, Constantine Monomachus (1042–55), he became Professor of Philosophy in the newly founded Academy of law, philosophy

---

[1] On this period cp. Carl Neumann, *Die Weltstellung des byz. Reichs* (1894) 81 f, and Schlumberger's *Épopée Byzantine*, part iii (1025–57).

[2] *History of Psellus* (vi 37 f) p. 108, ed. Sathas 1899.

[3] *ib.* p. 110.

and philology at Constantinople. In that capacity he aroused
a new interest in the philosophy of Plato, which he preferred
to that of Aristotle, the favourite philosopher of the Church, thus
exposing himself to the imputation of heresy. As a public
teacher, he did much for the revival of Greek literature, and
particularly for the study of Plato; and students even from Arabia
and the distant East sat at his feet. He rose to the high position
of Secretary of State; but, when (in 1054) the friend of his youth,
Xiphilinus, withdrew to the famous monastery on the slopes of
the Mysian Olympus, he became a monk, and, on the death
of the emperor (1055), entered the monastery of his friend. It
was not long, however, before he returned to public life; and,
after the overthrow of the last of the Basilian dynasty (Michael VI)
in 1057, he held high office under Isaac Comnenus and both
of his successors. He became Prime Minister under the next
emperor, his own pupil Michael VII, who proved 'a worthless
sovereign', spending his time in composing rhetorical exercises
and sets of iambic or anapaestic verse, instead of attending to
public business[1]. In 1075 he delivered the funeral oration over
his friend Xiphilinus, the third of the patriarchs whom he thus
commemorated; and, not long after the fall of his imperial pupil,
he died (1078).

His attainments as a scholar were most varied. In his speech
in memory of his mother[2], he describes himself as lecturing on
Homer and Menander and Archilochus, on Orpheus and Musaeus,
on the Sibyls and Sappho, on Theano and 'the wise woman
of Egypt', meaning probably Hypatia. By Menander he perhaps
intends proverbial lines from that poet, for, elsewhere, he mentions
Μενάνδρεια, and not Menander, immediately after the tragic poets
and Aristophanes[3]. In his high-flown eulogy of Constantine
Monomachus, the eloquence, wit and wisdom of the emperor
remind him of the great orators, lyric poets and philosophers
of old[4] His voluminous writings include not only a history
of the century (976—1077) preceding the close of his life, but
also an iambic poem on Greek dialects and on rules of grammar,
and a brief description of the surroundings of Athens. In his

---

[1] Finlay, iii 38.                           [2] Sathas, *Bibl. Gr. Medii Aevi*, v 59.
[3] *ib.* 538; Krumbacher, p. 504[2] n.                    [4] Sathas, *l.c.*, v 110.

*Letters*, in which the Greek Classics are often mentioned, he pays honour to the Athenians and Peloponnesians for the sake of their ancestors[1], and laments that the Academy and the Stoa have fallen into obscurity and that the Lyceum has become nothing more than a name[2]. In a Letter on Gregory Nazianzen he has many interesting criticisms on the style of the ancient writers[3]. His list of the forensic phrases of Athens includes a passage on the reforms of Cleisthenes, with regard to the distribution of the demes among the new tribes, which we now know to have been ultimately derived from Aristotle's *Constitution of Athens*[4]. Psellus has been well described as the Photius of the eleventh century. His general model in style is Plato, while the short rhythmical and antithetical clauses of his *Letters* resemble the sacred poetry of the Byzantine age. He exercised a considerable influence on the writers of the next generation[5].

The successor of Psellus as Professor of Philosophy was John Italus, a keen student of dialectic, who (without neglecting Plato and the Neo-Platonists) mainly devoted himself to the exposition of Aristotle, and especially to the *De Interpretatione* and Books II—IV of the *Topica*[6]. A pupil of Psellus, Michael of Ephesus, commented on part of the *Organon* (adding excerpts from Alexander of Aphrodisias) and also on the *Ethics*[7]; while Eustratius of Nicaea (*c.* 1050—*c.* 1120) expounded the *Ethics*[8] as well as the Second Book of the *Later Analytics*[9].

Commentators on Aristotle

---

[1] *Ep.* 20, quoted on p. 385; Gregorovius, *Stadt Athen*, i 177.

[2] *Ep.* 186, p. 472, Sathas.

[3] First letter to Pothos printed in H. O. Coxe, *Cat. Bodl.* i 743—751.

[4] 21 § 4 with *Testimonium* in present writer's ed. Psellus may have derived his quotation from Vestinus, the epitomator of Pamphilus (Bursy, *De Arist. πολ. Ἀθ.*, 1897).

[5] Krumbacher, § 184[2], and *Gr. Lit. des MAs*, 272 f; cp. Bury's Gibbon, v 504. Psellus is satirised in the *Timarion* as 'the sophist of Byzantium' (*Byz. Zeitschr.* vi 483). His comment on Plato's *Phaedrus* is printed in *Hermes*, 1899, 315–9.

[6] Krumbacher, § 185[2].

[7] ed. Heylbut in Berlin *Ar. Comm.* xx 461—620; on *Ethics* v, ed. Hayduck (1901).

[8] Krumbacher, pp. 1—406.

[9] Venice, 1534. Cp. Krumbacher, pp. 430[2] f.

Among the published works of Psellus we find an encomium of more than 25 pages in honour of Joannes

Joannes
Maurŏpus

Mauropus who, besides passing through the ordinary education of his day, had made a special study of Latin, had modelled his Greek on that of Isocrates, and not unfrequently lit up the sombre style of his Letters with some glowing phrase 'like a rose in winter'[1]. Not long after the accession of Constantine Monomachus (1042) he became Professor of Philosophy at Constantinople; but we soon afterwards find him in 1047 bishop of Euchaita, which lies between the Iris and the Halys, a day's journey beyond Amasia in Pontus. He was the founder of the annual festival which is still celebrated by the Eastern Church in memory of Chrysostom, Basil and Gregory Nazianzen; and he sets a noble example of Christian toleration in an epigram in honour of Plato and Plutarch[2]. In the history of Scholarship he deserves mention as the author of an etymological work in iambic verse. The words selected are suggested by the Greek text of the Scriptures and they are arranged in order of subjects, beginning with words such as $\Theta\epsilon\acute{o}s$, $\check{a}\gamma\gamma\epsilon\lambda os$, $o\dot{v}\rho\alpha\nu\acute{o}s$, $\dot{a}\sigma\tau\acute{\eta}\rho$, $\check{\eta}\lambda\iota os$, $\sigma\epsilon\lambda\acute{\eta}\nu\eta$, and with the names of the winds and the four elements. Plato in the *Cratylus* had conjectured that $\pi\hat{v}\rho$ was an old 'barbaric' word, but had attempted to supply a derivation for $\gamma\hat{\eta}$. Later etymologists had added $\gamma\hat{\eta}$ to the list of primary words; and Joannes Mauropus agrees with them, protesting against a contemporary who excluded $\gamma\hat{\eta}$ from the primary words, and adding that, for monosyllables, we are not bound to discover etymologies. The authority followed by Mauropus was apparently Jacob, bishop of Edessa (701), who produced a Christian version of an earlier work on 'etymology' or 'Hellenism', ultimately founded either on Seleucus or some contemporary grammarian in the age of Augustus and Tiberius[3].

We have already noticed the *Etymologicum genuinum* and the

Etymological
Lexicons

*Etymologicum parvum* as having been prepared under the direction of Photius. Next in date to these works is the *Etymologicum* (*c.* 1100) deriving

---

[1] Psellus in Sathas, *l. c.*, v pp. 148—150.    [2] Krumbacher, § 308[2].

[3] Reitzenstein, *Etymologika* (1898), 173—189, and *Varro und Johannes Mauropus*, 1901.

the epithet of *Gudianum* from the former owner of an inferior MS
of the same (1293), the Dane Marquard Gude (d. 1689), whose
collection was presented by Peter Burman to the Library of
Wolfenbüttel. Many items in this *Etymologicum* are borrowed
from the *Et. genuinum* and the *Et. parvum*, and their source is
denoted in the best MS, the *codex Barberinus* I 70 (hardly later
than cent. xi), by a monogram for Φώτιος[1]. Some of the items so
marked are not to be found in our MSS of the two *Etymologica*
edited by Photius, but all of them were probably taken from less
imperfect copies of the same works[2]. In general, the compiler
fails in judicious selection, while he attempts to combine divergent
views, and copies from his different authorities the same opinion
in varying forms[3]. For the preservation of the old lexicons the
ninth and tenth centuries were as fatal as they were fruitful.
Photius and his circle diffused a wider interest in lexicography,
but the value of the works produced was constantly deteriorating,
the originals being abridged or expanded at the copyist's caprice.
In the twelfth century industrious scholars appear to have gone
back to the works of the age of Photius. Hence arose the
so-called *Etymologicum Magnum*, which was founded mainly on
the *Et. genuinum* with additions from the *Et. Gudianum* and
from Stephanus of Byzantium and Tryphon 'on breathings',
while it dealt very freely with the *Et. gen.* by altering the headings
and the phraseology, suppressing quotations, adding passages
from Homer, and in general aiming at something more than an
expanded recension of its original[4]. It was compiled between
1100 and 1250. It was first printed (with many interpolations)
by Callierges (1499) who was the first to give the work the name
of *Et. magnum*. It was afterwards edited by Sylburg (1594) and
Gaisford (1848). The *Etymologicum* of 'the great grammarian'
Symeon[5] is an abridged edition of the *Et. genuinum* with additions

---

[1] Reitzenstein, *l. c.*, p. 138. The publisher of that work (B. G. Teubner)
has kindly supplied me with a *facsimile* of the symbol, ⲫ. Leopold Cohn
(*Deutsche Litteraturzeitung*, 1897, p. 1417) demurs to accepting ⲫ as a
monogram for Φώτ(ιος), but gives no other explanation. Mr T. W. Allen,
who has examined the MS, assures me that this monogram has several forms.
In one of them, φ combined with Τ rises from the middle of ω.

[2] *ib.* 152 f.          [3] *ib.* 155.          [4] *ib.* 241 f.

[5] Studemund, *Anecd. Var. Gr.* i 113 f.

from the *Et. Gudianum*, Stephanus of Byzantium and a lost 'rhetorical lexicon'. It is later than 1100 and earlier than 1150, the approximate date of the lexicon of 'Zonaras'[1], which derives its etymological glosses from this source. An expansion of Symeon's work is described as the 'great grammar'[2].

The *Lexica Segueriana* are so called because they are preserved in a MS of cent. xi formerly belonging to Pierre Séguier (1588—1672, President of the French Academy), now in the Paris Library (*Coislinianus* 345). This MS, which contains a number of minor lexicons and treatises on syntax, presents us with a vivid picture of the general range of grammatical studies in Constantinople during the tenth and eleventh centuries. It includes lexicons to Homer (that of Apollonius), Herodotus and Plato (that of Timaeus), the lexicons of Moeris and Phrynichus, and five anonymous lexicons, generally called the *Lexica Segueriana*, (1) an anti-atticist work directed against Phrynichus; (2) a lexicon on syntax with examples going down as far as Procopius (*fl.* 527—562) and Petrus Patricius (*c.* 500—562); (3) a list of forensic terms; (4) rhetorical terms with notes on Greek antiquities, derived from a lexicon to the Orators; (5) a συναγωγὴ λέξεων χρησίμων, in which the treatment of words beginning with A is very lengthy owing to numerous additions from Phrynichus, Aelius Dionysius and others[3]. The glossaries of Philoxenus and Cyril, and the *lexicon technologicum* of Philemon, were not produced by the persons whose names they bear[4].

The *Lexicon Vindobonense* was the work of one Andreas Lopadiotes (first half of cent. xiv). Almost its only value rests on the fact that it has preserved lines from Sophocles[5] and Pherecrates not found elsewhere. It is mainly founded on the abridged Harpocration[6].

---

[1] Probably compiled by Antonius Monachus (see Stein's Herodotus, ed. maior, ii 479 f).

[2] Reitzenstein, 254 f. Cp. Krumbacher, § 237[2].

[3] The *Lex. Seg.* are printed in Bekker's *Anecd. Gr.* pp. 75—476, including A of (5); the rest of which has since been published in Bachmann's *Anecd. Gr.* i 1—422. Cp. Christ, § 635[3]; Krumbacher, § 236[2].

[4] Krumbacher, §§ 561, 571[2].

[5] Nauck 738, ζημίαν λαβεῖν ἄμεινόν ἐστιν ἢ κέρδος κακόν.

[6] Krumbacher, § 238[2].

The eleventh century claims one of the best of the Byzantine poets, Christophorus of Mitylene (*fl.* 1028–43), who writes occasional verses and epigrams in the iambic metre[1]. The tragic cento called the *Christus Patiens*, once ascribed to Gregory Nazianzen, is now assigned to the eleventh or twelfth century[2].

*Poets*

History is represented not only by Psellus, the friend of the patriarch John Xiphilinus, but also by that patriarch's nephew and namesake, who, at the prompting of Michael VII (1071–8), produced an epitome of books 36 to 80 of Dion Cassius and thus preserved for us the substance of the last twenty books, which would otherwise have been completely lost[3]. The year 1080 approximately marks the close of three other historical works, (1) the Chronicle (811—1079) of John Scylitzes who carries on the works of 'George Syncellus and of Theophanes; (2) the history (1034–79) of Michael Attaliates; and (3) the materials for the life of Alexius Comnenus collected by Nicephorus Bryennius who makes Xenophon his model, and whose work is continued and completed by his wife, the daughter of Alexius, Anna Comnena. Late in this century, or early in the next, we may place the Chronicle compiled by Cedrenus, which begins with the Creation and ends with 1057 A.D.[4]

*Historians*

One of the foremost Byzantine rhetoricians is John Doxopatres, also known as John Siceliotes, an important commentator on Hermogenes and Aphthonius[5]. He belongs to the first half of the eleventh century[6]. At the close of the same century a widely popular collection of oriental stories, which had been translated from Sanskrit into all the languages of the East, was rendered from Syriac into Greek under the name of 'Syntipas' by Michael Andreopulus, a Christian subject of the Armenian prince Gabriel of Melitene. Through this Greek rendering the stories passed to the West, where they reappeared in the romances of the Seven Sages and of Dolo-

*Rhetoricians*

---

[1] ed. Rocchi (1887) ; Krumbacher, § 307².

[2] Krumbacher, § 312².        [3] *ib.* § 153².        [4] *ib.* § 152².

[5] Walz, *Rh. Gr.* ii and vi.   Cp. Saintsbury, i 187 f.

[6] Krumbacher, § 195².

pathos, and even had their influence on the *Gesta Romanorum* and on the *Decameron* of Boccaccio[1].

The ecclesiastical writers of the century include Symeon, the head of the Monastery of St Mamas in Constanti-
nople, one of the greatest mystics of the Eastern Church and the precursor of the fanatic quietists of the fourteenth century[2]; and the eminent biblical commentator, Theophylact, archbishop of Bulgaria, who owes much to Chryso-stom and Gregory Nazianzen[3]. His *Exhortation*, addressed to his royal pupil, Constantine, son of Michael VII, is founded on Xenophon, Plato, Polybius, Diogenes Laërtius, Synesius, and especially on Dion Chrysostom and Themistius. It also shows a striking absence of prejudice in its quotations from Julian 'the Apostate'. His *Panegyric* on the emperor Alexius Comnenus closes with an impressive appeal for the protection of learning[4]

*Ecclesiastical writers*

The twelfth century is marked by the name of Tzetzes (*c.* 1110—*c.* 1180), the author of a didactic poem on literary and historical topics extending over no less than 12,674 lines of accentual verse, and displaying a vast amount of miscellaneous reading. The name of *Chiliades* is due to its first editor, the author's own name for it being simply βίβλος ἱστορική. The work is in the form of a versified com-mentary on his own *Letters*, which are full of mythological, literary and historical learning. The following lines on the seven liberal arts, founded on a passage in Porphyry, are a very favour-able example of his style :—

*Tzetzes*

> δευτέρως δὲ ἐγκύκλια μαθήματα καλοῦνται
> ὁ κύκλος, τὸ συμπέρασμα πάντων τῶν μαθημάτων,
> γραμματικῆς, ῥητορικῆς, αὐτῆς φιλοσοφίας,
> καὶ τῶν τεσσάρων δὲ τεχνῶν τῶν ὑπ' αὐτὴν κειμένων,
> τῆς ἀριθμούσης, μουσικῆς, καὶ τῆς γεωμετρίας,
> καὶ τῆς οὐρανοβάμονος αὐτῆς ἀστρονομίας[5].

The contents of this prodigious work show that its author's reading included, in verse, Homer, Hesiod, Pindar, the tragic poets, Aristophanes, Theocritus, Apollonius Rhodius, Lycophron,

---

[1] *ib.* § 393[2], and Gaston Paris, *Litt. Fr. au MA*, § 71, bibliogr. on p. 255 f.
[2] Krumbacher, § 63[2].   [3] *ib.* § 52[2].
[4] *ib.* § 196[2].   [5] xi 525 f.

Nicander, Dionysius Periegetes, Oppian, the Orphica, Quintus Smyrnaeus and the Greek Anthology.  In prose, he was familiar with historians, such as Herodotus, Diodorus, Josephus, Plutarch, Arrian, Dion Cassius and Procopius; with orators, such as Lysias, Demosthenes and Aeschines; with philosophers, such as Plato and Aristotle; with geographers, such as Strabo and Stephanus of Byzantium; and, lastly, with the satirist Lucian.  The total number of authors quoted exceeds 400[1].  His other works include *Allegories*[2] on the Iliad and the Odyssey in 10,000 lines (*c.* 1145–58); a Commentary on the Iliad (*c.* 1143); hexameter poems on *Antehomerica*, *Homerica* and *Posthomerica*; *scholia* on Hesiod (before 1138)[3] and on Aristophanes, with important *prolegomena* giving valuable information on the Alexandrian Libraries[4]; *scholia* on Lycophron, Oppian, and probably Nicander; a versified epitome of the *Rhetoric* of Hermogenes; and, lastly, a poem on Prosody (after 1138).  We learn much about Tzetzes from his own writings; he often complains of his poverty and his misfortunes and of the scanty recognition of his services.  He was once reduced to such distress that he found himself compelled to sell all his books, except his Plutarch; and he had bitter feuds with other scholars.  His inordinate self-esteem is only exceeded by his extraordinary carelessness.  He calls Simonides of Amorgos the son of Amorgos, makes Naxos a town in Euboea, describes Servius Tullius as 'consul' and 'emperor' of Rome, and confounds the Euphrates with the Nile.  He is proud of his rapid pen and his remarkable memory; but his memory often plays him false, and he is, for the most part, dull as a writer and untrustworthy as an authority[5].

The patrons of Tzetzes included Isaac Comnenus, brother of the best of the Byzantine emperors, John II (d. 1143); also the latter's son and successor, Manuel I (d. 1180), and Manuel's

---

[1] Cp. H. Spelthahn, Munich Diss. 1904.      [2] Cp. Saintsbury, i 187.

[3] On the Byzantine study of Hesiod, cp. M. R. Dimitrijevíc, *Studia Hesiodea* (Leipzig, 1899), 234 pp.

[4] *Supra*, p. 119 n.  On his notes on the *Aves*, cp. J. W. White in *Harvard Studies*, xii 69—108.

[5] Krumbacher, § 219[2].  His own authorities are discussed by Zielinski in *Woch. f. kl. Phil.* 1898, 1331 f.

first wife the German princess Bertha (Eirene). Anna Comnena, the sister of John, may here be mentioned as the
Anna<br>Comnena writer of a life of her father Alexius I, which supplemented and continued in 1148 the materials collected by her husband, the distinguished soldier and diplomatist, Nicephorus Bryennius (d. 1137). She is familiar with Homer, Aristophanes, and the tragic poets, as well as with Herodotus, Thucydides and Polybius, and her work is the earliest monument of the literary revival inspired by the example of Psellus[1]. John II and Manuel were among the
Theodorus<br>Prodromus patrons of Theodorus Prodromus (d. after 1159), a poverty-stricken poet, who writes in colloquial as well as classical Greek, and is specially successful in prose, as an imitator of Lucian[2].

The most memorable name among the scholars of the twelfth century is that of Eustathius, whose philological
Eustathius studies at Constantinople preceded his tenure of the archbishopric of Thessalonica from 1175 to c. 1192. Of his *Commentary on Pindar*, written while he was still a deacon, the only part preserved is a valuable preface on lyrical and Pindaric poetry, on the poet's life, and on the Olympic games and the pentathlum[3]; but there is nothing to show that he possessed any more of the Epinician Odes than ourselves. His next work is his *Paraphrase and scholia to Dionysius Periegetes*[4], followed by an important *Commentary on the Iliad and Odyssey*[5]. That on the Iliad is twice as long as that on the Odyssey; both are preceded by literary introductions in which the commentator dwells with enthusiasm on the abiding influence of Homer on the literature of Greece[6]. Both of them comprise many excerpts from earlier writers, including Herodian's work on accentuation.

---

[1] Krumbacher, §§ 120, 121[2]. Translated by Schiller in *Allgemeine Sammlung historischer Memoires*, Jena, 1790. Cf. Carl Neumann, *Gr. Geschichtsschreiber...im* 12 *Jahrh.* (1888) 17 f.

[2] *ib.* §§ 313, 333[2]; p. 361 *supra*.

[3] Printed in Dissen and Schneidewin's *Pindar*, 1843.

[4] ed. Bernhardy (1828), and C. Müller in *Geogr. Gr. Min.* ii 201 f.

[5] ed. Stallbaum, 7 vols. 1825-30.

[6] In another work he refers to dramatic representations of Homeric scenes at Thessalonica; *Opuscula*, p. 81, Tafel.

The title παρεκβολαί implies incidental extracts made in the course of general reading, and is specially appropriate to what is primarily a compilation. Eustathius makes much use of the Homeric glossary of Apion and Herodorus, which is partly founded on the same materials as the *scholia* to the Venice MS of Homer and has thus preserved some of the criticisms of Aristarchus. Among his other authorities are Athenaeus, Strabo, and Stephanus of Byzantium; also Heracleides of Miletus and two Greek works of Suetonius, together with the lexicons of Aelius Dionysius and Pausanias, the original *Etymologicum magnum* (*i.e.* the complete text of the imperfectly preserved *Et. genuinum*)[1], and Suïdas, who is not quoted by any earlier commentator. These are only a few of his text-books: 'from his horn of plenty' (in the phrase of Gibbon) he 'has poured the names and authorities of four hundred writers'[2].

His great commentary on Homer has led modern scholars to regard him as one of the most instructive of the Byzantines. But he is much more than a mere scholiast; while in learning he stands high among all his contemporaries, he is also a man of political insight, and a bold and far-seeing reformer. His *Commentaries* belong to his earlier life at Constantinople, when his house was the chief literary centre in the capital and was comparable with the Academies of ancient Athens[3]. His works on the history of his own times refer to the years after he had become archbishop of Thessalonica (1175). During the disastrous invasion by the Normans from Sicily in 1185 he remained at the post of peril, conciliated the Sicilian generals and induced them to restrain the excesses of their troops[4], and afterwards wrote a narrative of the causes and the result of the invasion[5]. He also did much towards raising the general intellectual and moral standard among the Greek monks of his diocese. He protests against their reducing their monastic libraries to the level of their own ignorance by parting with their books, and implores them to allow those libraries to retain their precious stores for

[1] Reitzenstein, *Et.* p. 252 n.          [2] c. 53 (vi 105 Bury).
[3] Euthymius, ap. Tafel, *De Thessal.* p. 399.
[4] Finlay, iii 215.
[5] ed. Tafel (1832); Bekker (1842); also in Migne, cxxxv.

the sake of those who at some future time might be inspired with
a greater love of learning than themselves[1].

On the death of Eustathius (*c.* 1192–4) an eloquent panegyric
on that 'last survivor of the golden age' was pro-
**Michael
Acominatus**   nounced by his former pupil, Michael Acominatus,
who apparently became archbishop of Athens in
the same year as that in which Eustathius was called to Thessalonica (1175).   His brother, Nicetas Acominatus, distinguished
himself as a statesman and as the historian of the years 1180
to 1206, while his own tenure of the see of Athens is the brightest
page in the mediaeval history of Greece.   On reaching his see,
he writes of the ruined condition of Athens and the desolation
of Attica ; but, on taking up his official residence on the platform
of the Acropolis, he must have felt that few bishops in Christendom had such a glorious cathedral as the Parthenon.   In his
inaugural discourse, he describes his audience as the genuine
descendants of the Athenians of old, eulogises Athens as the
mother of eloquence and wisdom, and as indebted for her fame
not to the memorials of bygone times (among which he describes
the choragic monument of Lysicrates as the 'Lantern of Demosthenes'), but to the virtue of her citizens.   But he soon becomes
conscious that his eloquent discourse has been imperfectly understood by the Athenians of his day; and, as time goes on, he
is oppressed by the contrast between the Athens of the past and
of the present ; he sees the sheep feeding amid the scanty ruins
of the Painted Porch.   The charm of the Attic landscape still
remains, and, from the height of Hymettus, he can view, in
one direction, the whole of Attica, and, in the other, the Cyclades,
spread out like a map before him ; but he feels that the ancient
race of orators and philosophers has vanished ; he composes the
only extant poem of lamentation over the downfall of Athens[2] ;
and he consoles himself with the books which he has brought
from Byzantium, with Homer and Thucydides, with Euclid,
Nicander and Galen, all the volumes that he finds in the official
library of his see being contained in two chests beside the altar

---

[1] *De emendanda vita monastica*, c. 128 (quoted on p. 385).   Krumbacher,
§ 221[2], and *Gr. Lit. des MAs*, 274.

[2] Boissonade, *Anec. Gr.* v 374 ; Sp. Lampros, ii 397.

in the Parthenon. On the capture of Constantinople during the Fourth Crusade in 1204, Athens was handed over to the Franks and became a see of the Latin Church, and Michael withdrew to the neighbouring island of Ceos, where he died in 1220 within sight of the shores of Attica[1].

Michael Acominatus had not yet ceased to be archbishop of Athens, when certain 'Greek philosophers of grave aspect' are stated by Matthew Paris to have arrived from Athens at the court of King John (*c.* 1202)[2]. They were doubtless monks from the East, but they were not allowed to remain in England. Matthew Paris[3] elsewhere assures us that his older contemporary, John of Basingstoke, archdeacon of Leicester, informed Robert Grosseteste, the learned bishop of Lincoln, that, while he was studying at Athens, he had seen and heard certain things unknown to the Latins. He had there found a copy of the *Testament of the Twelve Patriarchs*, which the bishop of Lincoln caused to be translated into Latin by a monk of St Albans ; and he had himself translated into that language a Greek Grammar. During his visit, he had also learnt much from Constantina, the daughter of the archbishop of Athens, a girl of less than twenty, who (besides being familiar with the *trivium* and *quadrivium*) could predict pestilences and earthquakes as well as eclipses. As the archdeacon died in 1252, the only Greek archbishop of Athens, who could have been the father of this learned lady, was obviously Michael Acominatus. But the latter assures us that he had no children ; and, while we may well believe that John of Basingstoke really visited Athens and brought some Greek MSS to England, we must conclude that there is some mistake as to the identity of the learned lady of whom he had often spoken to Matthew Paris[4].

Athens and England

[1] Krumbacher, § 199[2], and esp. Gregorovius, *Stadt Athen*, i 204—227, 240-4. The first complete ed. is that of Sp. Lampros, 2 vols. (Athens, 1879 f).          [2] *Hist. Anglorum (Minor)*, ed. Madden, iii 64.

[3] *Chronica Maiora*, ed. Luard, v 285.

[4] Gregorovius, *l. c.*, i 231-4. Cp. Hopf, *Geschichte Griechenlands vom Beginn des MAs*, in Ersch u. Gruber (1867) vol. 85, 175-7. John of Basingstoke's visit is assigned to 1240 in Cantor's *Gesch. d. Math.* ii 100[2]; if this date is correct, the 'girl of less than twenty' could not have been the daughter of an archbishop who died in 1220.

Another learned ecclesiastic of this age is Gregorius, archbishop of Corinth (*c.* 1200), author of an extant
work on *Greek Dialects*. This is founded partly
on Tryphon (cent. i B.C.) and Joannes Philoponus
(cent. vi A.D.), on *scholia* and glossaries to Pindar, Aristophanes
and especially Theocritus, and probably also on the author's
independent reading of Herodotus, as well as Pindar and Theocritus. It aims at completeness but is defective in arrangement;
its popularity is, however, abundantly proved by its preservation
in numerous manuscripts[1].

Gregorius<br>Corinthius

History in the twelfth century is represented by the three
Chroniclers, Constantine Manasses, whose 6733
lines of accentual verse begin with the Creation
and end with the year 1081; and Zonaras and Glykas, both of
whom close their prose chronicles in 1118[2]. The two principal
historians of this time are Cinnamus, whose work has survived
in an abstract extending from 1118 to 1176; and Nicetas
Acominatus, whose great history in 21 books covers the years
between 1180 and 1206 and thus includes the Latin conquest
of Constantinople[3].

Historians

His brother Michael, the archbishop of Athens, may be
classed among the rhetoricians of this century,
which also claims Michael Italicus (*fl.* 1147–66),
many of whose *Letters* are addressed to members of the imperial
house and to the leading men of the time. In one of them
he pulls to pieces a work composed by an unnamed patriarch
of Constantinople, pointing out that nearly the whole of it is
copied from Chrysostom, Basil and Gregory of Nyssa. In another
he writes to the poor scholar, Theodorus Prodromus, who hand-
somely calls his correspondent a second Plato[4]. Another prolific
rhetorician of this age is Nicephorus Basilakes, whose lament
over his brother who fell in the Sicilian war probably belongs
to the year 1155[5].

Rhetoricians

---

[1] ed. G. H. Schaefer (1811); cp. Krumbacher, § 248[2].

[2] Krumbacher, §§ 154–6[2].            [3] *ib.* §§ 122–3[2].

[4] *ib.* § 197[2]. Theodorus (like Theophylactus Simocattes, and Thomas
Magister) was himself familiar with the Pseudo-Platonic *Axiochus* (Brinkmann
in *Rhein. Mus.* li (1896) 441—455).            [5] *ib.* p. 473[2].

Among ecclesiastical writers, Nicolaus of Methone (*fl.* 1143–
80) throws a considerable amount of light on the
theological controversies of the time, but his reputa-    Nicolaus
                                                          of Methone
tion has suffered since the repeated discoveries of
his unacknowledged indebtedness to Photius and others.    His
critical examination of Proclus is borrowed almost *verbatim* from
Procopius of Gaza; but, although it is destitute of originality,
it shows that, owing to the renewed interest in ancient philosophy
which arose in the twelfth century, there was a special call for
defending the plain teaching of the Church against the subtleties
of Neo-Platonism[1].

During the time of the Empire of Nicaea, and the rule of
the house of Lascaris, *i.e.* from the loss of Constantinople in 1204 to its recovery in 1261, the       Empire of
                                                        Nicaea;
most notable name in literature is that of Nice-        Blemmydes
                                                        and Acro-
phorus Blemmydes (*c.* 1197—1272), who is a            polites
philosopher, as well as a theologian, geographer,
rhetorician and poet. His manual of Logic and Physics has
been preserved in many MSS[2]. The contemporary historian of
this age is Georgius Acropolites (1217—1282), a dignified personage, who avoids vulgarisms, and, instead of condescending to
the use of γάδαρος (γαΐδαρος), the vulgar Greek word for an ass,
prefers its grander etymological counterpart ἀείδαρος, 'the ever-
beaten one'[3]. But the Greek Empire of Nicaea presents us with
nothing of importance in the history of Scholarship, and the same
is true of the contemporary Latin Empire of Constantinople
(1204–61). Learned men in the West had long      Constanti-
regarded the capital of the East as the treasure-  nople and
                                                    the West
house of ancient literature. In the tenth century, .
the arch-priest Leo of Naples had brought back with him a MS
of the legend of Alexander by Pseudo-Callisthenes, and had
translated it into Latin[4]. In 1167, one Guillaume of Gap, a

---

[1] Krumbacher, § 22[2].

[2] *ib.* § 186[2]; *Curriculum vitae et Carmina*, ed. Heisenberg, 1897.

[3] *ib.* p. 287[2].

[4] Zacher, Pseudo-Callisthenes (1867); Krumbacher, § 374 p. 850[2]. A
rendering of the Greek had already been made before 340 by Julius Valerius
(Schanz, § 374).

student of medicine who became a monk, was sent to Constantinople by the Abbé of St Denis in search of Greek MSS, but it is
probable that the MSS with which he returned were only connected with 'Dionysius the Areopagite'[1]. When the Normans
took Thessalonica (1185), the collections of books, which they
sold for a mere trifle, found Italians ready to purchase them[2].
Even before the Latin conquest of Constantinople, the Italians
are said to have bought up MSS and sent off whole ship-loads
of them[3]. Great havoc was doubtless inflicted by that conquest,
and by the three conflagrations by which it was attended. On
19 August, 1203, the second of these conflagrations, which
originated in the wilful act of a few Flemish soldiers, lasted for
two days, when 'splendid palaces, filled with works of ancient
art and antique classic manuscripts, were destroyed'[4]. 'Without
computing the extent of our loss, we may drop a tear' (says
Gibbon) 'over the libraries that have perished in the triple fire
of Constantinople'[5]. After the capture of the city (13 April,
1204), when the Franks passed in procession through the streets,
they showed their contempt for a people of scribes and scholars
by displaying a pen and an ink-horn and a sheet of paper, but
the Greek historian of these events had his revenge when he
denounced the conquerors as 'ignorant and utterly illiterate
barbarians'[6]. During the seven and fifty years of the Latin
emperors, there was probably a certain amount of literary intercourse between the East and the West. In 1205, Pope Innocent III exhorted the 'Masters and Scholars of the University
of Paris' to go to Greece and revive the study of literature in
the land of its birth[7]. Philip Augustus founded a college on the
Seine where the Greeks of Constantinople might study the Latin

---

[1] Jourdain, *Recherches*, p. 46; Delisle in *Journal des Savants*, 1890,
725—739.

[2] Eustathius, *De Thess. a Latinis capta*, c. 135.

[3] Michael Acominatus, i 17 (Gregorovius, *l. c.*, i 286).

[4] Finlay, iii 261, after Nicetas, 356, and Villehardouin, 82.

[5] c. 60 *ult.*

[6] Nicetas, ἀγραμμάτοις βαρβάροις καὶ τέλεον ἀναλφαβήτοις, Gibbon, c. 60
(vi 409 Bury).

[7] '...in Graeciam accedentes, ibi studeretis literarum studia reformare,
unde noscitur exordium habuisse' (Jourdain, *Recherches*, p. 48).

language[1]. Lastly, in 1209, according to Guillaume le Breton, certain works on Metaphysics, composed (it was said) by Aristotle, had recently been brought from Constantinople and translated into Latin, but these *libelli* (he adds) were ordered to be burnt as likely to foster heresy[2].

The Byzantine age ends with the Palaeologi, who held sway between the recovery of Constantinople from the Franks in 1261 and its capture by the Turks in 1453. The scholars who lived under that dynasty are the precursors of a new era. They differ widely from those who lived under the Macedonian (867—1057) and Comnenian (1057—1185) dynasties, in their treatment of classical texts. While most of the MSS from the ninth to the twelfth centuries (such as the Laurentian MS of Aeschylus, Sophocles and Apollonius Rhodius, and the Ravenna MS of Aristophanes) maintain the tradition of the Alexandrian and the Roman ages, those of the thirteenth and following centuries show that Byzantine scholars were beginning to deal with old Greek texts in a capricious manner, and to tamper with the metres of ancient poets with a view to bringing them into conformity with metrical systems of their own invention[3]. The scholars of these centuries have less in common with Photius, Arethas and Eustathius than with the earliest representatives of the revival of learning in the West, who are the inheritors of the latest traditions of the Byzantine age[4].

Scholars under the Palaeologi

Among the late Byzantine scholars who had much in common with the precursors of the Renaissance the first in order of time is the monk Maximus Planudes (*c.* 1260—1310). He had an exceptionally good knowledge of Latin, having possibly been led to acquire that language by the constant controversies between the Greek and Latin Churches. It was probably owing to his knowledge of Latin that he was

Planudes

---

[1] Jourdain, p. 49.    [2] Or the *Physics, ib.* p. 187 f.

[3] Wilamowitz, *Eur. Her.* i 194[1], 'Diese Byzantiner sind eigentlich gar nicht als Schreiber, sondern als Emendatoren aufzufassen; sie sind nicht die Collegen der braven stupiden Mönche, die treufleissig nachmalten, was sie nicht nur nicht verstanden, sondern auch nicht zu verstehen meinten, sondern sie sind unsere Collegen...Sie haben so manchen Vers für immer geheilt, und noch viel öfter das Auge von Jahrhunderten geblendet.'

[4] Krumbacher, p. 541[2] f.

sent as envoy to Venice in 1296. Among the many Latin works, which he introduced to his countrymen by translating them into Greek, were Caesar's *Bellum Gallicum*, Cicero's *Somnium Scipionis*, Ovid's *Metamorphoses* and *Heroides*, the smaller grammar of Donatus, and Boëthius, *De Consolatione Philosophiae*, where even the poetical passages are skilfully rendered in the corresponding Greek metres. His translation of the *Heroides* was founded on a MS now lost, which must have been superior to our existing MSS.

The value of this translation has been signally proved. In vi 47, *quid mihi cum Minyis, quid cum Tritonide pinu*, the version of Planudes alone has preserved the true reading *Dodonide* which is confirmed by Δωδωνίδος...φηγοῦ, used to describe the material of the cutwater of the Argo by Apollonius Rhodius, i 527 and iv 583[1].

His independent works included a dialogue on Grammar with a treatise on Syntax[2]; a collection of Letters, of special interest in connexion with the writer's studies[3]; a life of Aesop, with a prose paraphrase of the 'Fables'[4]; *scholia* on Theocritus and Hermogenes; a work on Indian mathematics, and (probably) the *scholia* on the first two books of the Arithmetic of Diophantus. Among his compilations were historical and geographical excerpts from Plato, Aristotle, Strabo, Pausanias, Dion Cassius, Synesius, Dion Chrysostom and Joannes Lydus, some of them important in connexion with textual criticism. He also abridged and rearranged (with a few additions) the Anthology of Constantine Cephalas[5], thus forming the collection of Greek epigrams called the *Anthologia Planudea*, the only Greek Anthology known to scholars before the recovery of the Anthology of Cephalas in 1607. The Planudean Anthology, still preserved in the Library of St Mark's at Venice, is in the hand of Planudes himself. It ends with his name, and with the date, Sept. 1302 (*i.e.* 1301 A.D.)[6].

Among his eminent contemporaries was John Beccus, patriarch

---

[1] Gudeman, *De Heroidum Ovidii codice Planudeo*, Berlin, 1888 (quoted by Arthur Palmer, ed. 1898).

[2] Bachmann, *Anecd. Gr.* ii 1—166.

[3] ed. M. Treu, Breslau (1890).

[4] *ed. princeps*, Milan, *c.* 1479 (*A. J. P.* 1903, 304—317); Krumbacher, § 395[2]; A. Hausrath in *Neue Jahrb. für kl. Alt.*, 1898, 305 f; and *Die Aesop-studien des Maximos Planudes* in *Byz. Zeitsch.* x (1901) 91.

[5] p. 406 *supra*.          [6] Krumbacher, § 223[2].

from 1275 to 1282, who strongly supported the union of the
Eastern and Western Churches, even dying in prison for that
cause in 1293[1]. The chief opponent of Beccus was Gregory
of Cyprus, patriarch from 1283 to 1289, whose *Life* and *Letters*
supply a pleasing picture of his times, while his interest in
education is proved by his mythological stories and by his prose
paraphrases of Aesop[2]. Gregory's devoted pupil and strong
adherent, Nicephorus Chumnus (*c.* 1261—*c.* 1328),
was connected with the royal house, his daughter     Nicephorus
                                                      Chumnus
having been married to the son of Andronicus II.
He left public life for the retirement of the monastery in 1320.
His literary works were mainly directed against Plato and the
Neo-Platonists, and especially against Plotinus; but he also attacks
the Aristotelian philosophy. It thus appears that the controversy
on Plato and Aristotle, which was one of the characteristics of
the Renaissance, had its counterpart as early as the Byzantine
age. In this respect, amongst others, Nicephorus Chumnus is
a precursor of the Renaissance. In his rhetorical writings he
insists on the maintenance of the Attic standard of style, finding
his own models in Isocrates and Aristides, and also in his master,
Gregory of Cyprus. His rhetorical manner often mars the effect
of his *Letters*, some of which are professedly written in the
Laconic and others in the Attic style; while a certain monotony
results from the frequent recurrence of the same construction and
the same combination of connecting particles[3].

Maximus Planudes counted among his pupils and friends
Manuel Moschopulus (*fl.* 1300), the nephew of
an archbishop of Crete[4]. The reputation of Mos-     Moschopulus
chopulus is largely due to his having extracted from the two
volumes of an anonymous grammatical work a catechism of
Greek Grammar, which had a considerable influence during the
early Renaissance[5]. He also compiled a school-lexicon of Attic

---

[1] Krumbacher, § 29[2].        [2] *ib.* §§ 30, 202[2].        [3] *ib.* § 203[2].

[4] On his life, cp. M. Treu, *Planudis Epp.* 208—212; five of his *Letters* in
*Studi Ital. di filol. cl.* x (1902) 55—72.

[5] On its relation to the *Erotemata* of Chrysoloras, Chalcondyles etc., cp.
Voltz, in Jahn's *Jahrb.* 139 (1889) 579-99; and Hartfelder's *Melanchthon*
(1889), p. 255.

Greek, besides brief notes on the first two books of the *Iliad*, as well as on Hesiod[1], Pindar's *Olympian Odes*, Euripides and Theocritus[2]. His influence on the Byzantine text of Pindar was unsatisfactory. Among the MSS of Pindar a 'family' of forty-three, most of them containing the *Olympian Odes* alone, is regarded as representing the 'badly interpolated edition of Moschopulus'[3].

Among his contemporaries was Thomas Magister, secretary to Andronicus II (1282—1328). After becoming a monk, and assuming the name of Theodulus, he devoted himself to the special study of the ancient Classics. He was the author of several school-books, the chief of which is a 'selection of Attic nouns and verbs'[4] founded on Phrynichus, Ammonius, Herodian, Moeris and others[5], with many additions from his own reading, especially in Herodotus, Thucydides, Aristides and Synesius. He also wrote *scholia* on Aeschylus, Sophocles and Euripides, and on three plays of Aristophanes (*Plutus, Nubes, Ranae*). The *scholia* on Pindar, which bear his name, are ascribed by Lehrs[6] to Triclinius.

*Thomas Magister*

Another scholar of the same age was Theodorus Metochites (d. 1332), who, like his eulogist Thomas Magister, was in the service of Andronicus II. Though inferior to the foremost scholars of former generations, such as Photius and Psellus, he was one of the most learned men of his time. His works include *Philosophical and Historical Miscellanies*, with excerpts from more than seventy philosophers and historians, which are often of textual importance. His erudition is praised in the highest terms by his pupil, Nicephorus Gregoras[7], a man of encyclopaedic learning, who is best known as a historian, though he is also the writer of a commentary on the wanderings of Odysseus, and of many works

*Theodorus Metochites*

---

[1] *Facsimile* on p. 439.          [2] Krumbacher, § 224[2].

[3] Seymour's *Selected Odes*, p. xxiii; Tycho Mommsen's ed., p. xxiv f.

[4] ed. Ritschl, 1832.

[5] *e.g.* the Atticist Philemon, the author of a lost lexicon in iambic verse, probably of the second century, fragments of which are found in Eustathius (L. Cohn in *Philol.* 1898, 353—367).

[6] *Pindarscholien*, 97–9. Krumbacher, § 225[2].

[7] vii 11 p. 272 ed. Bonn, βιβλιοθήκη γὰρ ἦν ἔμψυχος καὶ τῶν ζητουμένων πρόχειρος εὐπορία (Krumbacher, § 226[2]).

still remaining in manuscript, including a treatise on Grammar and Orthography[1].

The foremost textual critic of the age of the Palaeologi was Demetrius Triclinius (early in cent. xiv). He ex- **Triclinius** pounded and emended (and not unfrequently corrupted) the texts of Hesiod, Pindar, Aeschylus, Sophocles, Euripides (*Hecuba, Orestes, Phoenissae*)[2] and Theocritus. His *scholia* on Aeschylus and Hesiod (*c.* 1316–20) still exist in his own handwriting in Naples and Venice respectively[3]. His transcript of Hesiod bears the date 1316[4]; that of Aphthonius (at New College, Oxford) is dated 1298. His MS of Aeschylus was allied to a Venice MS of cent. xv, while that of Pindar was copied from the Florentine MS D (cent. xiii—xiv)[5]. He acquired a considerable knowledge of metre, but was misled to some extent by the changes of pronunciation which had come over the Greek language in the course of the Byzantine age. His textual emendations differ widely in value. In the case of Pindar in particular, 'he altered the text to conform to his crude rules of grammar and metric. His notes are full of conceit and self-assertion. Their value has been said to be chiefly negative; any text is suspicious which contains the readings recommended by him'[6]. His edition is now represented in a family of twenty-eight MSS[7]

Early in the fourteenth century the monk Sophonias wrote paraphrases of Aristotle's *Categories, Prior Analytics,* **Sophonias** *Sophistici Elenchi, De Anima*[8], *De Memoria* and *De Somno*, which were once attributed to Themistius and owe their value solely to their excerpts from the best of the earlier commentaries. In the same century *scholia* on the whole of the *Organon* were compiled by Leon Magentinus, **Leon** metropolitan of Mitylene[9]. The rhetorician and **Magentinus** grammarian, John Glykys, who was highly esteemed

---

[1] Krumbacher, § 128[2].

[2] Wilamowitz, *Eur. Her.* i 194[1], 'Triklinios ist in Wahrheit eher als der erste moderne Tragikerkritiker zu führen denn als ein zuverlässiger Vertreter der Ueberlieferung.'  [3] Krumbacher, § 227[2].

[4] *Facsimile* on p. 439.  [5] Wilamowitz, *l. c.*

[6] Seymour's *Selected Odes*, p. xxii.  [7] Tycho Mommsen's ed. p. xxx f.

[8] ed. Hayduck, 1883.  [9] Krumbacher, § 182[2].

by his pupil, the historian Nicephorus Gregoras, and was for a
short time patriarch of Constantinople (1319), wrote
a Syntax more remarkable for its lucidity than for
its learning, in which he quotes largely from Homer, Thucydides,
Plato and Demosthenes, as well as from the Septuagint[1].

Glykys

Among the miscellaneous works of John Pediasimus
(*fl.* 1282—1341), professor of philosophy at Constantinople, were some *scholia* on Hesiod's *Theogony* and *Shield
of Hercules*, and on the *Syrinx* of Theocritus[2].   Our list of late
Byzantine scholars may here close with the name
of Manuel Chrysoloras, who was born a century
before the fall of Constantinople, and died forty
years before that event, having meanwhile played a leading part
in the revival of Greek learning in Italy.

Pediasimus

Manuel
Chrysoloras

Among the late Byzantine poets, the counterpart of Theodorus
Prodromus in the twelfth century is Manuel Philes
in the fourteenth (*c.* 1275—1345).   The favourite
metre for his dialogues, and for his writings on zoology and on
works of art, is the iambic trimeter, in his use of which he never
allows the accent to fall on the final syllable[3].   While Philes
remains true to the classical types of metre and language, his
contemporary Constantine Hermoniacus was prompted by a
despot of Epirus (1323-35) to produce in the language of daily
life a new version of the *Iliad* written in short trochaic lines
consisting of only four accentual feet[4].   Philes wrote a poem
in memory of his patron Pachymeres (1242—*c.* 1310), whose
great historical work continues from 1261 to 1308
the ample narrative of Acropolites, while his minor
writings include a treatise on the *quadrivium* and an abstract
of the philosophy of Aristotle[5].   Half a century later we have
the ecclesiastical historian, Xanthopulus (1295—*c.* 1360), whose
history practically ends with 610 A.D.   He was coeval with the
emperor John Cantacuzenus (1295—1383), who, on his abdication
in 1355, withdrew to a monastery, where he composed a history
of the years 1320 to 1356, in which he records 'not a confession,

Poets

Historians

---

[1] Krumbacher, § 249[2].          [2] *ib.* § 228[2].
[3] *ib.* § 324[2].          [4] *ib.* § 371[2].
[5] *ib.* § 126[2].

but an apology, of the life of an ambitious statesman'[1]. He was also coeval with Nicephorus Gregoras (1295—c. 1360), who was educated under Theodorus Metochites, and (like Pachymeres) showed a special partiality for controversial theology while writing, in a style modelled on that of Plato, the history of the period between the Latin conquest of Constantinople and the end of his own life (1204—1359)[2]. After these historians a whole century elapses before we reach the Athenian Laonicus Chalcondyles (fl. 1446—63), a brother of the first modern editor of the Iliad and an imitator of Herodotus and Thucydides, who begins with 1298 and ends in 1463 his account of the expansion of the Ottoman power; Ducas, who describes, in a literary form of popular Greek, the period from 1341 to 1462; Phrantzes (1401—c. 1477), who writes, in a style intermediate between that of Chalcondyles and Ducas, the history of the years 1258—1476; and Critobulus of Imbros, an imitator of Thucydides, who, in sharp contrast with Ducas and Chalcondyles, avowedly takes the Turkish point of view in tracing the victorious career of the conqueror of Constantinople[3].

The rhetoricians of this age include the essayist Demetrius Cydones (c. 1325—c. 1396), who studied Latin at Milan, and imitated Plato not only in his lament over those who fell in the civil feuds of Thessalonica (1346), but also in his appeal to the Greeks to be at unity among themselves and with the Latin Church (1369)[4]. They further include the emperor Manuel Palaeologus (1350—1425), who vainly visited Italy, France and England (1399—1402) in quest of aid against the Turks. In the precepts addressed to his son, he imitates Isocrates; and, in one of his Letters, we find him thanking Demetrius Cydones for a copy of the lexicon of Suïdas, which, arriving at a time when the emperor was short of funds, is humorously described as having made him rich in words, but not in wealth[5]. Lastly, we have the 'rhetorical epitome' of

Rhetoricians

---

[1] Gibbon, c. 63 (vi 489 Bury).

[2] Krumbacher, § 128[2], and Gr. Lit. des MAs, 277.

[3] Krumbacher, §§ 132-5[2].

[4] ib. § 207[2] (cp. G. Jorio, in Studi Ital. di filol. cl. 1897, 257—286).

[5] ib. § 210[2].

Matthaeus Camariotes, who continued to teach Philosophy, Rhetoric and Grammar, even when the Turks were threatening Constantinople (1450), and who begins his rhetorical monody on the troubles of his time by sighing with the Psalmist for 'the wings of a dove'[1].

The ecclesiastical writers of this age are mainly absorbed in the controversy with the *Hesychastae*, or Quietists, as represented primarily by Gregorius Palamas (d. 1349), who, in quest of a life of contemplation, left the court of Constantinople for the monasteries of Mount Athos. His opponents continued the attack on the Quietists begun by the Calabrian monk, Barlaam (*fl.* 1339–48). Nicolaus Cabasilas, the last of the great Greek mystics, died in 1371. A century later saw the death of Bessarion, who meanwhile had transferred his allegiance from the Eastern to the Western Church, and had done much for the promotion of Greek Scholarship in Italy as a patron of learning, as an enthusiastic student of Plato, and as founder of the Library of St Mark's at Venice.

*Ecclesiastical writers*

Of the extant remains of Byzantine literature, apart from theological works, nearly half belong to the domain of Scholarship in the widest sense of the term. The scholars of the Byzantine, and of the latter part of the Roman age, are unsystematic and diffuse, are deficient in originality of thought and independence of character, and are only too ready to rest satisfied with a merely mechanical reproduction of the learning of the past. In matters of Scholarship they seldom show a real advance, or even display a sound and impartial judgement. But, if they are themselves to be judged in a spirit of fairness and candour, they cannot be compared with the great Alexandrian critics, from whom they are parted by a thousand years, in the course of which the cultivation of Scholarship was attended with ever increasing difficulty and discouragement. A Planudes or a Triclinius cannot reasonably be judged by the same standard as an Aristophanes or an Aristarchus; and a Moschopulus has as little as a Melanchthon in common with the great Alexandrians. Even the Byzantine scholars of

*Byzantine Scholarship*

[1] Krumbacher, pp. 451, 498[2].

the ninth and eleventh centuries did not enjoy the advantages
of the Alexandrian age, or of our own; but they served to
maintain a continuity of tradition by which the learning of
Alexandria has been transmitted to Europe.   They must be tried
by the standard of their own contemporaries in other lands:
a Photius must be compared with an Alcuin; a Psellus with
an Anselm.   The erudite Byzantines who lived under the dynasty
of the Palaeologi, men like Planudes, Moschopulus, and Theodorus Metochites, will be seen in their true light, if they are
regarded as among the earliest precursors of the Renaissance.
For it must be remembered that, for the revival of Greek learning,
we are indebted not only to the Greek refugees who in the middle
of the fifteenth century were driven from Constantinople to the
hospitable shores of Italy, or even to the wandering Greeks of
the previous century.   The spirit of the Renaissance was at work
in Constantinople at a still earlier time.   In the ninth century,
that spirit is embodied in the brilliant personality of Photius,
which illuminates an age of darkness and barbarism.   In the
tenth, the intelligent knowledge of antiquity and the aspiration
after its continued preservation appear to decline, while the
despotic will of Constantine Porphyrogenitus threatens to bury
the remains of earlier Greek literature under a mass of encyclopaedic works projected on a magnificent scale but executed in
a most mechanical manner.   But, in the same age, we may
gratefully acknowledge the efforts made by intelligent custodians
and expositors of the treasures of the past, such as Arethas the
*bibliophile*, and Suïdas the lexicographer.   In the eleventh century
the comprehensive intellect of a Psellus is attracted to the study
of antiquity as a whole, in the way that was afterwards characteristic of the foremost humanists of the Renaissance; while, under
the Comneni (1057—1185) and the Palaeologi (1261—1453), the
humanistic spirit is unmistakably prominent.   It has accordingly
been well observed, that historians of the Renaissance must in
the future go back as far as Moschopulus and Planudes, and,
even further still, to a Eustathius and a Psellus, an Arethas and
a Photius.   To obtain a continuous view of the course of
grammatical tradition, we must remember that the works, which
enabled Theodorus Gaza, Constantine Lascaris and Manuel

Chrysoloras to promote the study of the Greek language and literature in Italy, were directly derived from Greek and Byzantine sources, from the canons of Theodosius, and the catechism of Moschopulus, while the ultimate originals of both of the latter were the works of Dionysius Thrax in the Alexandrian, and Apollonius and Herodian in the Roman age.

Although it was mainly by the preservation and transmission of ancient literature that Byzantine scholarship had an important influence on the learning of the West, there was no lack of original and independent scholars who applied their powers to the emendation and interpretation of the old Greek Classics, and even to the elaboration of new metrical systems. Their weakest side was Grammar. They laid little stress on Syntax and not much more on Accidence, while they paid special attention to Accentuation and Orthography, the latter subject deriving a peculiar importance from the changes which had affected the pronunciation of the Greek language. But the scientific study of Grammar was set aside for the preparation of mere manuals for the use of beginners. The innumerable treatises on Accidence, Syntax, Prosody, and Metre, which abound in most collections of mediaeval MSS, cannot be regarded as works of Scholarship but merely as commonplace text-books and exercise-books for use in the schools of Constantinople. These treatises seldom agree with one another, every teacher and transcriber having in turn applied the processes of combination or interpolation to altering his copy at his own caprice[1].

It would be interesting to ascertain what portions of ancient literature were in the actual possession of the Byzantines, and which were their favourite works. In and after the ninth century they possessed little more than ourselves of the remains of classical Greek literature, such as Homer, Hesiod, Pindar, the Attic dramatists, the prae-Alexandrian historians and orators, and Plato and Aristotle[2]. But they were better provided with the works

*The Greek Classics in and after Century IX*

---

[1] Abridged from Krumbacher, pp. 499—502[2]. Cp. *Gr. Lit. des MAs*, 275 f; also Carl Neumann, *Byz. Kultur und Renaissance-Kultur* (1903), with the criticisms in *Byz. Zeitschr.* xiii (1904) 275 f, 710 f.

[2] pp. 402-3 *supra*.

of the learned specialists and of the later historians. The compilers of excerpts in the time of Constantine Porphyrogenitus
(912–59) had before them complete copies of many of the latter
(such as Dexippus, Eunapius, Priscus, Malchus, Petrus Patricius,
Menander Protector and John of Antioch), now surviving in
fragments only. Considerable portions of Polybius were unknown
to them, but many fragments of that historian have been preserved
to us through these excerpts alone. It was only in an imperfect
form that Dion Cassius was known to Zonaras and Xiphilinus.
Late in the thirteenth century we have an incomplete list of
authors recommended for study, in which 'Rhetoric' is represented
by Lysias, Demosthenes, Aeschines, and also by Herodotus and
Thucydides, and, among later writers, Plutarch, Lucian, Libanius,
Himerius, Choricius, Procopius of Gaza, and Procopius of
Caesarea[1].

The loss of a large part of Greek literature may be ascribed
to the general cessation of literary activity from the middle of
the seventh (the age of Theophylact Simocattes) to the middle
of the ninth century (the age of Photius). In the tenth, many
prose works may have perished owing to the compilation of
excerpts under Constantine Porphyrogenitus. There was probably
a considerable destruction of ancient literature in the three fires
of Constantinople which attended its capture by the Franks in
1204. But its capture by the Turks in 1453 probably did
comparatively little damage to the surviving remains of ancient
libraries. By that time Greek MSS had already been recognised
as a valuable commodity. Possibly in the first storming of the
city much was destroyed, but it is expressly stated by a contemporary writer that, on the fall of Constantinople, the Turks
made money of the MSS which they found, and that they
despatched whole cart-loads of books to the East and the West[2].

---

[1] *Anecdoton Hierosolymitanum*, in *Comm. in Aristot. Graeca*, III i (1901)
p. xv, where Byzantine writers are also mentioned, including Psellus, ὅστις
ἐστὶν ἀναγκαῖος. The *Anecdoton* ends with the works of Aristotle and the
Commentaries on each.

[2] Ducas, c. 42 (p. 312 ed. Bonn), τὰς δὲ βίβλους ἀπάσας, ὑπὲρ ἀριθμὸν
ὑπερβαινούσας, ταῖς ἁμάξαις φορτηγώσαντες ἀπανταχοῦ ἐν τῇ ἀνατολῇ καὶ δύσει
διέσπειραν· δι' ἑνὸς νομίσματος δέκα βίβλοι ἐπιπράσκοντο, Ἀριστοτελικοί, Πλατω-
νικοί, θεολογικοὶ καὶ ἄλλο πᾶν εἶδος βίβλου. Krumbacher, § 213², pp. 503–6.

Another historian, who writes as a friend of the Turks, notices the destruction of books sacred and profane, stating that some were destroyed, but 'the greater number' were sold for a mere trifle[1]. There is probably a good deal of exaggeration in the statement made by a Venetian, Laurus Quirinus, who, writing to Pope Nicholas V, on 15 July, 1453, says, on the authority of a cardinal, that more than 120,000 volumes had been destroyed[2].

The debt of modern Scholarship to the Byzantine age cannot be better summed up than in the following extract from Mr Frederic Harrison's Rede Lecture of 1900 :—

'The peculiar, indispensable service of Byzantine literature was the preservation of the language, philology, and archaeology of Greece. It is impossible to see how our knowledge of ancient literature or civilisation could have been recovered if Constantinople had not nursed through the early Middle Ages the vast accumulations of Greek learning in the schools of Alexandria, Athens, and Asia Minor; if Photius, Suidas, Eustathius, Tzetzes, and the Scholiasts had not poured out their lexicons, anecdotes, and commentaries; if the *Corpus Scriptorum historiae Byzantinae* had never been compiled; if indefatigable copyists had not toiled in multiplying the texts of ancient Greece. Pedantic, dull, blundering as they are too often, they are indispensable. We pick precious truths and knowledge out of their garrulities and stupidities, for they preserve what otherwise would have been lost for ever. It is no paradox that their very merit to us is that they were never either original or brilliant. Their genius, indeed, would have been our loss. Dunces and pedants as they were, they servilely repeated the words of the immortals. Had they not done so, the immortals would have died long ago'[3].

When the Byzantine age, in the fullest sense of the term, ended in 1453 with the conquest of Constantinople by the Turks, the attention of the youthful conqueror, Mohammed II, was arrested, as he rode through the hippodrome, by the brazen column composed of three serpents intertwined, which is still to be seen on the *Atmeidan*. More than nineteen centuries had passed since the heads of those serpents had first supported the historic tripod which the Greeks had dedicated at Delphi in memory of their victory over the barbarians at Plataea. A

---

[1] Critobulus, c. 62, 3 (Bury's Gibbon, vii 194 n).

[2] Letter in Cotton MSS quoted in Hodius, *De Graecis Illustribus*, 1742, p. 192. Cp. Pastor's *History of the Popes*, ii 209 E.T., and Document 22 (Dec. 1453).

[3] *Byzantine History in the Early Middle Ages*, p. 36.

blow from the conqueror's mace shattered part of one of the serpents' heads, and that shattered head was an expressive emblem of the fact that the power of the Greeks to resist the barbarians was now at an end. But we may gratefully remember that the capital of the Eastern Empire had, with all its elements of weakness, proved strong enough to stand for centuries as the bulwark of Europe against the barbarians of the East, thus sheltering the nascent nations of the West, while they slowly attained the fulness of their maturity, and, at the same time, keeping the treasures of the old Greek literature in a place of safety, until those nations were sufficiently civilised to receive them. From our survey of the history of Scholarship in the Byzantine age, we now turn to the story of its fortunes during the corresponding period of the Middle Ages in the West of Europe.

END OF SCHOLIA ON HESIOD'S WORKS AND DAYS BY MANUEL MOSCHOPULUS, COPIED BY DEMETRIUS TRICLINIUS 1316 A.D.

Codex S. Marci Venetus 464, fol. 78; Wattenbach et von Velsen, *Exempla Codicum Graecorum*, xxi (pp. 430 f *supra*).

# BOOK VI.

## THE MIDDLE AGES IN THE WEST.

------

*semper aut discere aut docere aut scribere dulce habui.*
> BEDE, *Historia Ecclesiastica*, v 24.

*mihi satis apparet propter se ipsam appetenda sapientia.*
> SERVATUS LUPUS, *Ep.* 1.

*in otio, in negotio, et docemus quod scimus et addiscimus quod nescimus.*
> GERBERT, *Ep.* 44.

*claustrum sine armario <est> quasi castrum sine armamentario.*
> GEOFFREY of Sainte-Barbe-en-Auge (*c.* 1170), in Martène, *Thesaurus novus Anecdotorum*, i 511.

*notitia linguarum est prima porta sapientiae.*
> ROGER BACON, *Opus Tertium*, c. 28, p. 102 Brewer.

*On peut dire que la philosophie scolastique est née à Paris et qu'elle y est morte. Une phrase de Porphyre, un rayon dérobé à l'antiquité, la produisit; l'antiquité tout entière l'étouffa.*
> VICTOR COUSIN, *Ouvrages Inédits d'Abélard*, p. lx (1836).

| Italy | Spain | 'France' W. Frankland | 'Germany' E. Frankland | British Isles |
|---|---|---|---|---|
| **600** | | | | |
| 604 d. Gregory I | 570–636 Isidore of Seville | 535–600 Venantius Fortunatus | | 602–5 Augustine abp of Canterbury |
| 612 f. Bobbio | | 613 Frank kingdoms united under Clothar II | 614 f. St Gallen | ?Hisperica famina |
| 615 d. Columban | | 620 f. Fleury | | |
| Greek monasteries founded in Rome by Martin I (649–55) | 657 Eugenius III bp of Toledo | 625 f. St Riquier | | 651 d. Aidan bp of Lindisfarne |
| | | 630 f. Ferrières | | 668–90 Theodore of Tarsus abp of Canterbury |
| | | 634 f. Rébais | | |
| | | 'Virgilius Maro' | 645 d. Gallus | |
| | | 650 f. Péronne | | 673 b. Bede |
| | | 656 f. Stavelot | | 675 b. Boniface |
| | | 658 Fredegarius | | 688–726 Ina, king of Wessex |
| 690 Greek declines in Italy | 690 d. Julian bp of Toledo | 662 f. Corbie | | 690 d. Benedict Biscop |
| | | 688 d. St Wandrille | | |
| **700** | | | | |
| 715–31 Gregory II | 714 Arab Conquest of Spain | 721 f. Prüm | | 650–709 Aldhelm |
| 726 f. Novalesa | | | 724 f. Reichenau | 732 Egbert abp of York |
| 730–80 Greek refugees in Italy | | 732 Saracens defeated by Charles Martel | 727 f. Murbach | |
| 731–41 Gregory III | | | | 734 d. Tatwine abp of Canterbury |
| | | 752 end of Merovingian & beginning of Carolingian line | | 735 d. Bede, b. Alcuin |
| 770 Petrus Pisanus | | | | |
| 774 end of Lombard kingdom | | 742–66 Chrodegang abp of Metz | 744 f. Fulda | |
| 786 end of Greek rule in central Italy | | | 754 d. Boniface | |
| | | | 763 f. Lorsch | |
| 725–97 Paulus Diaconus | | 772–814 Sole rule of Charles the Great | 743–84 Virgil bp of Salzburg | 778–81 Alcuin head of the school of York |
| 795–817 Leo III | | 796–804 Alcuin at Tours | | |
| **800** | | | | |
| Charles the Great crowned at Rome | | 810 Dungal at St Denis | 822 f. Corvey | 810–5 b. Joannes Scotus |
| 817–24 Pascal I | | 814–40 Louis the Pious | 770–840 Einhard | |
| 818–50 Greek refugees in Italy | | 821 d. Theodulfus bp and founder of school of Orleans | 843 Treaty of Verdun | |
| 823 Dungal at Pavia | | 826 Ermoldus Nigellus | 776–856 Rabanus Maurus | |
| | | 837 Thegan | 809–49 Walafrid Strabo | |
| | | 840–77 Charles the Bald | 830 f. Hirschau | |
| | | 805–62 Servatus Lupus | 850 Ermenrich of Ellwangen | |
| 846 d. Pacificus of Verona | | 845 Joannes Scotus (d. 875) | 852 Rudolf, Ann. Fuld. | |
| | | 850 d. Freculphus | 856 f. Gandersheim | |
| 858–67 Nicholas I | | 840–60 Sedulius at Liège | 874 Agius, Poeta Saxo | 871—c. 900 Alfred |
| | | 865 d. Radbertus | | |
| | | 877 d. Eric of Auxerre | 890 Salomo III, abbot of St Gallen | |
| | | 881–8 Charles the Fat | | |
| **900** | | | | |
| | | 908 d. Remi of Auxerre | 911 end of E. Carolingians | |
| | | | 912 d. Notker Balbulus | |
| 916–24 Gesta Berengarii | | 910 f. Cluni | 918–36 Henry of Saxony | |
| | | 915 d. Regino of Prüm | | |
| 924 d. Berengar | | 923 d. Abbo Cernuus | 925 Lotharingia recovered for Germany | |
| | | 930 d. Hucbald | | |
| | | | 936 Ecbasis Captivi | |
| 961–2 Otho I crowned at Rome king of Italy and emperor | | 942 d. Odo of Cluni | 936–73 Otho I | 942–58 Odo abp of Canterbury |
| | | 950 b. Gerbert of Aurillac | 965 d. Bruno abp of Cologne | 959–88 Dunstan abp of Canterbury |
| 967 d. Gunzo of Novara | | | 973 d. Ekkehard I | c. 955—1030 Ælfric of Eynsham |
| 972 d. Luitprand bp of Cremona | | 987 end of W. Carolingians & beginning of line of Hugh Capet | 973–83 Otho II | |
| | | | 983 Walther of Speier | 969 f. Ramsey |
| 974 d. Ratherius bp of Verona | 980 Cordova the centre of Arabic learning | | 984 Hroswitha of Gandersheim | 985–7 Abbo of Fleury at Ramsey |
| 999–1003 Silvester II (Gerbert) | | 991–6 Gerbert abp of Rheims | 990 d. Ekkehard II | |
| **1000** | | | 996–1002 Otho III | |

*Continued from page* 216.
b. *born*; d. *died*: f. *founded*.

# CHAPTER XXIV.

## FROM GREGORY THE GREAT (*c.* 540—604)
## TO BONIFACE (675—754).

THE Roman age has already been described as coming to an end in the memorable year 529, when the Monastery of Monte Cassino was founded in the West and the School of Athens closed in the East. The history of Scholarship during the Middle Ages in the West, to which we now turn our attention, covers a period of rather more than eight centuries, extending from about 530 to about 1350 A.D. Shortly after the beginning of this period, we have the birth of the biographer of Benedict, Gregory the Great (540), the father of mediaeval Christianity; and, shortly before its end, the death of Dante (1321), who embodies in his immortal poem much of the scholastic teaching of the Middle Ages. In our survey of this period, we propose to pass in review the names of special interest in the world of letters, so far as they have definite points of contact with the history of classical learning. The present chapter begins with the biographer of Benedict, and ends with Boniface.

Gregory the Great (*c.* 540—604), who became Pope in 589, belonged to a senatorial family and received a liberal education which made him second to none in Rome[1]. He had already filled the high office of Praetor, when he withdrew from a secular life and devoted his ancestral wealth to the founding of six monasteries in Sicily, and a seventh in Rome, which he selected for his own retreat. As papal envoy in Constantinople (584-7), notwithstanding his ignorance of Greek, he entered into a controversy with the Patriarch himself.

Gregory I

[1] Greg. Tur. *Hist. Franc.* x 1; Paulus Diaconus, *Vita Greg.* c. 2.

In one of his *Letters*[1] he complains that there were none in Constantinople who were capable of making a good translation from Latin into Greek, an expression implying, on his own part, some slight acquaintance with the latter language, although, in another letter, he disclaims all such knowledge, adding that he had never written any work in that language[2]. In his *Magna Moralia* he sets forth an allegorical interpretation of the Book of Job, which he was not capable of studying either in Hebrew or in Greek, but only in the earlier and the later Latin versions.   It was his own influence that led to the general recognition and acceptance of the Latin Vulgate.   Towards the close of the long letter prefixed to the *Moralia*, he confesses his contempt for the art of speech, and admits that he is not over-careful in the avoidance of barbarisms or inaccurate uses of prepositions, deeming it 'utterly unworthy to keep the language of the Divine Oracles in subjection to the rules of Donatus'[3]; and this principle he applies to his own commentary, as well as to the sacred text. His attitude towards the secular study of Latin literature is well illustrated in the letter to Desiderius, bishop of Vienne.   He is almost ashamed to mention the rumour that has reached him, to the effect that the bishop was in the habit of instructing certain persons in grammatical learning.   'The praises of Christ cannot be pronounced by the same lips as the praises of Jove'[4].   He hopes to hear that the bishop is not really interested in such trifling subjects[5].   Elsewhere, however, the study of Grammar and the knowledge of the liberal arts are emphatically commended on the ground of the aid they afford in the understanding of the Scriptures; but the genuineness of the work, in which this opinion is expressed[6], is doubtful.   Later writers record the tradition that Gregory did his best to suppress the works of

[1] *Epp.* vii 27, ed. Ewald and Hartmann.

[2] *Epp.* xi 55, nos nec Graece novimus, nec aliquod opus aliquando Graece conscripsimus (cp. vii 32, quamvis Graecae linguae nescius).

[3] *Epp.* v 53.

[4] *Epp.* xi 34, 'in uno se ore cum Iovis laudibus Christi laudes non capiunt'; a reminiscence of Jerome's *Ep. ad Damasum*, 21 § 13, 'absit ut de ore Christiano sonet Iupiter omnipotens', xxii 386 Migne (R. L. Poole's *Medieval Thought*, 8).

[5] nugis et secularibus litteris ; *Epp.* xi 34.

[6] Book v of *Comm.* on *I Kings* 3, 30, Migne lxxix 356.

Cicero, the charm of whose style diverted young men from the
study of the Scriptures[1], and that he burnt all the books of Livy
which he could find, because they were full of idolatrous
superstitions[2]. It was even stated that he set the Palatine
Library on fire, lest it should interfere with the study of the
Bible, but the sole authority for this is John of Salisbury[3]
(d. 1180), and the statement is unworthy of credit[4].

In the same century we have an interesting group of three
historians, all of whom exemplify the prevailing
decline in grammatical knowledge. The first of                Iordanes
these is Iordanes, the author of a universal chronicle, who, in his
abridgement (551) of the *History of the Goths* by Cassiodorus,
borrows his preface from Rufinus and his opening words from
Orosius, and confesses his debt to others in delightfully ungram-
matical Latin[5]. The justice with which he describes himself as
*agrammatus*[6] is apparent on every page of his work. He makes
*dolus* and *fluvius* neuter, and *flumen*, *gaudium* and *regnum*
masculine ; and abounds in errors of declension and conjugation;
but even his blunders in grammar, gross as they are, cannot
conceal the debt which he obviously owes to the rhetorical
phraseology of Cassiodorus, to whom he is also indebted for all
his learned quotations[7].

The interval between the consulship and the death of
Cassiodorus corresponds to the life of Gildas of
Bath (516—573), the first native historian of Britain.       Gildas

---

[1] In Edict of Louis XI (1473) ; P. Lyron, *Singularitates Historicae*, i 167
(Tiraboschi, *Letteratura Italiana*, ii 2, 10, vol. iii, p. 118 ed. 1787).

[2] S. Antoninus, *Summa Theol.* iv 11, 4 (*ibid.*). Cp. Leblanc, *Utrum
Gregorius Magnus litteras humaniores et ingenuas artes odio persecutus sit*
(1852), criticised by Roger, 156.

[3] *Policraticus*, ii 26, viii 19.

[4] On Gregory, cp. Tiraboschi, *Lett. Ital.* iii 109—123 (ed. 1787) ; Bayle's
*Dict.*, s.v. ; Gibbon, c. 45 ; Heeren, *Cl. Litt. im Mittelalter*, i 78—81 ;
Milman, *Lat. Christ.* ii 97—145; Ebert, *Lit. des Mittelalters*, i² 542–6;
Roger, 187—195; Ker's *Dark Ages*, 132–8; F. H. Dudden (1905), i 153 f,
282—294 ; and Teuffel, § 493 ; *Epp.* ed. Ewald and Hartmann in *Mon. Germ.
Hist.* 1891-99. Cp. Manitius, 92—106.

[5] Scito me maiorum secutum scriptis ex eorum latissima prata paucos flores
legisse.

[6] *Get.* 265.       [7] Teuffel, § 485; Manitius, 210-5; Ker's *Dark Ages*, 130.

The learning he had derived from St Iltud, the 'teacher of the Britons', was enlarged by a visit to Ireland; and he even founded a monastery in Brittany. Brendan of Clonfert found him in possession of a missal written in Greek characters[1]. Much of the earlier part of his 'lament on the ruin of Britain' is derived from St Jerome's *Letters* and from a Latin version of the *Ecclesiastical History* of Eusebius. It includes several reminiscences of Virgil[2]. The work as a whole is written in a verbose, florid, fantastic and exaggerated form of monastic Latin, and its prolix periods often tend to obscurity[3].

It was in the year of the death of Gildas (573) that Gregory, the historian of the Franks (*c.* 538—594), became bishop of Tours. In the preface to his *History* he refers to the decay of literature in Gaul[4]. His works in general show a certain familiarity with Virgil, especially with the first book of the *Aeneid*, but he cannot quote three lines of verse without making havoc of the metre[5]. Yet he ventures to criticise the versification of king Chilperic[6], who, besides writing Latin poetry, had (like Claudius) attempted to add several new letters to the Latin alphabet[7]. He is familiar with the preface to the *Catiline* of Sallust; but his quotations from Cicero are borrowed from Jerome, and those from Pliny and Gellius are probably second-hand. He repeatedly apologises for his imperfect knowledge of grammar[8]. He combines the plurals *haec* and *quae*

*Gregory of Tours* (margin note)

---

[1] G. T. Stokes, *Proc. Irish Acad.* 1892, 193.

[2] *Aen.* ii 120, 497; ix 24.

[3] ed. Mommsen in *Mon. Germ. Hist.* 1892. Cp. Ebert, i[2] 562–5; Teuffel, § 486, 1; Ker's *Dark Ages*, 131 f; Roger, 225 f; Manitius, 208 f.

[4] Decedente atque immo potius pereunte ab urbibus Gallicanis liberalium cultura litterarum...Vae diebus nostris, quia periit studium litterarum a nobis.

[5] *H. F.* iv 30 and *Mart.* i 40.

[6] *H. F.* v 44, 'scripsit alios libros idem rex versibus, quasi Sedulium secutus; sed versiculi illi nulla paenitus metricae conveniunt ratione'. Nevertheless, posterity placed the statue of Chilperic over the S.W. door of Notre-Dame, with a lyre in his hand in the attitude of Apollo (Montfaucon, *Mon. de la Monarchie*, t. i). Mâle, however, *L'Art Religieux*, 438, identifies this as David.

[7] Cp. Schmid, *Gesch. der Erziehung*, II i 333.

[8] *H. F.* iv 1, veniam precor, si aut in litteris aut in syllabis grammaticam artem excessero, de qua adplene non sum imbutus. *Vit. Patr.* 2, *praef.*, non me artis grammaticae studium imbuit neque auctorum saecularium polita lectio

with a singular verb; he writes *antedictus cives* for *antedictos*, and *percolibantur* (i.e. *perculebantur*) for *percellebantur*; and one of his favourite constructions is the accusative absolute. The study of his works shows that, in his day, the pronunciation of Latin differed from the spelling; *e* was confounded with *i*, and *o* with *u*; many of the consonants were pronounced feebly or suppressed altogether; aspiration was little observed, and a sibilant sound was introduced into *ci* and *ti*. Meanwhile, the vocabulary was being enlarged by the addition of words borrowed from Greek and Hebrew and even from barbarous languages, and by the use of old words in new senses. The departure from classical usage is most striking in matters of syntax, while there is comparatively little change in the inflexions. Gregory of Tours is primarily an authority for the history of the Franks during the century preceding his own death; but he also supplies important evidence on the characteristics of the Latin language in the days of its decline[1]. The decay of letters is lamented in the next century by Fredegarius Scholasticus (*fl.* 658), who, in the preface to a Chronicle written in a Burgun-   Fredegarius dian monastery, complains that the world is on the wane, intellectual activity is dead, and the ancient writers have no successors[2].

Among the older contemporaries of Gregory, bishop of Tours, was Martin, archbishop of Bracara, whom he describes in general as second to none of his own   Martin of age in the world of letters, and in particular as the   Bracara, d. 580

erudivit. *Liber in gloria confessorum, praef.*, timeo, ne, cum scribere coepero, quia sum sine litteris rethoricis et arte grammatica, dicatur mihi a litteratis: 'O rustice et idiota...qui nomina discernere nescis; saepius pro masculinis feminea...commutas; qui ipsas quoque praepositiones...loco debito plerumque non locas'...sed tamen respondebo illis et dicam, quia : 'opus vestrum facio et per meam rusticitatem vestram prudentiam exercebo'.

[1] Max Bonnet, *Le Latin de Grégoire de Tours* (1890). *Opera*, ed. Arndt and Krusch, in *M. G. H.*; Migne, lxxi; *Hist. Fr.* ed. Omont, 1886. Cp. Ebert, i[2] 566—79; Teuffel, § 486, 3—9; Kurth, *Grégoire de Tours et les études classiques au vi[e] s.*, in *Rev. des Quest. hist.* ii (1878) 588; Manitius, 216, *Neues Archiv*, xxi 553; Ker's *Dark Ages*, 125—130; and Roger, 102-9.

[2] *Script. rer. Merov.* ii 557, nec quisquam potest huius temporis nec presumit oratoribus precedentibus esse consimilis; cp. Haase, *De Medii Aevi Stud. Philol.* 28; Wattenbach, *GQ*, i[7] 114-8; Gröber, *Grundriss*, II i 102.

author of the Latin verses over the south door of the church of
St Martin at Tours. In his ethical works, and especially in his
treatise *de ira* and the *formula honestae vitae* (on the four
cardinal virtues)[1], he makes much use of Seneca, and these works
were long ascribed to Seneca himself[2]. A French translation of
the second was dedicated to Philip II[3].

The decline in Scholarship which has been traced in the
historians is also to be noticed in the poets of this
age. The poets of the middle of the sixth century
include the Tuscan Maximianus, who spent his
youth in Rome, and wrote in his later years the six elegies which
had a singular fascination for students in the Middle Ages[4]. He
is a Christian who poses as a pagan. Familiar with Virgil,
Catullus, and the elegiac and lyric poets of the Augustan age, he
is not always correct in points of prosody, his metrical mistakes
including *verĕcundia* and *pĕdagogus*[5]. Irregularities of prosody are
also frequent in the metrical version of the *Acts of the Apostles*
produced by Arator, who studied at Milan and Ravenna. In
the same age the African Corippus (550) writes epic poems on
historical subjects in a fluent style inspired by Virgil and Claudian,
while he also imitates Ovid, Lucan and Statius, being, in point
of prosody, the most correct of all the poets of his time[6]. His
contemporary, Venantius Fortunatus (*c.* 535—*c.* 600),
was educated at Ravenna, left Italy for Gaul,
where he found a friend in Gregory of Tours, and, towards the
end of his life, became bishop of Poitiers. He is a devoted
adherent of Radegunde (the widow of king Clothar I) and her
foster-daughter. He tells us that Radegunde was a profound
student of St Gregory, St Basil and St Athanasius, and that
Gertrude, abbess of Nivelle, had sent messengers to Rome and
to Ireland for the purchase of books[7]. He also mentions the

*Margin notes:* Poets;
Maximianus,
Arator,
Corippus

Fortunatus

---

[1] Included in Supplement to Haase's ed. of Seneca.

[2] Teuffel, § 494, 2 ; Schanz, § 470; Manitius, 109 f. On his Latinity, Haag,
*Rom. Forschungen* x (1888) 835 f ; and index to Krusch, *Script. rer. Merov.*

[3] Gaston Paris, *Saint Alexis*, 213 ; *Romania*, viii 476.

[4] Reichling in *Mon. Germ. Paed.* XII pp. xx, xxxvii f.

[5] Manitius in *Rhein. Mus.* xliv 540; R. Ellis in *A. J. P.* v 1—15 and
*Cl. Rev.* xv 368 ; ed. Petschenig (1890), Webster (1900).

[6] Manitius, 162–170.          [7] viii 1 ; cp. Roger, 126 note.

custom of giving recitations from Virgil and other poets in the
Forum of Trajan[1]. His elegiacs and hexameters include many
reminiscences of Virgil and Ovid, Claudian and Sedulius, Prosper
and Arator, while he is himself imitated by later versifiers such as
Alcuin and Theodulfus, Rabanus Maurus and Walafrid Strabo[2].
He describes a castle on the Mosel, and a voyage from Metz to
Andernach[3], without attaining the charm of the *Mosella* of
Ausonius. He addresses the bishop of Tours in a generally
correct set of Sapphics after the Horatian model, unhappily
ending with *care Grĕgōri*. In the same poem he mentions
Pindar (*Pindarus Graius*), and, in the prose preface to his *Life
of St Martin*, he even quotes four rhetorical terms in the original
Greek[4]. He flatters the poets and orators of his day with the
assurance that they found their inspiration in Homer and
Demosthenes[5]; but his own study of his classical predecessors
does not prevent his perpetrating such mistakes as *ādhuc, īnitium,
idŏlum, ecclĕsia* and *trĭnitas*; and he succeeds in making four
false quantities in the six Greek names included in the single
line, *Archȳta, Pythagoras, Arătus, Cato, Plāto, Chrȳsippus*[6].
Three, however, of his sacred poems are widely known. Ambrose
is his model in *Vexilla regis prodeunt*, while the triumphant
trochaic tetrameter of the Roman soldiers, and of Prudentius, is
the type followed in *Pange lingua gloriosi proelium certaminis.*
The ordinary elegiac couplet is used in the description of Spring
(*Salve festa dies*) written for Felix, bishop of Nantes, whom he
belauds as a perfect Greek scholar and as 'the light of Armorica'.
It is only in these three poems, and in the modern hymns
translated from them[7], that Fortunatus may be said to have
survived to the present day[8]. St Jerome[9] describes a certain

---

[1] iii 20 ; vi 8.

[2] Manitius, Index iii and iv to ed. by Leo and Krusch in *Mon. Hist. Germ.*
(1881–5).

[3] iii 12 ; x 9.     [4] ἐπιχειρήματα, ἐλλείψεις, διαιρέσεις, παρενθέσεις.

[5] viii 1.     [6] vii 12, 25 ; cp. *index rei metricae* in Leo's ed.

[7] Moorsom's *Companion to Hymns A. and M.*, pp. 58—66[2].

[8] Cp. Ampère, *Hist. Litt.* ii 312 f ; Ozanam, *La Civilisation Chrétienne
chez les Francs*, pp. 412–9 (ed. 1855) ; Ebert, i[2] 533 ; Teuffel, § 491 f ; Leo in
*Deutsche Rundschau*, 1882, 414 f ; W. Meyer, *Der Gelegenheitsdichter Venantius
Fortunatus* (1901) ; Saintsbury, i 396–9 ; Ker's *Dark Ages*, 119—124 ; and
Roger, 100–2 ; also Manitius, 170—181.     [9] *Ep.* 125.

richness and splendour as characteristic of the Latin style of Gaul, and such a style is said to have been attained by St Desiderius, bishop of Cahors, who died in 665[1].

The decadence of Latin in the seventh century (one of the darkest ages in Latin literature) is exemplified in the person of the grammarian Virgilius Maro, who may perhaps be assigned to the middle of that century[2]. He assures us that his master Aeneas gave him the name of Maro, 'quia in eo antiqui Maronis spiritus redivivit'. He describes certain grammarians as wrangling for a fortnight over the vocative of *ego*[3], and as drawing their swords after an equally long discussion on inchoative verbs[4]. His only value lies in the way in which he illustrates the transition from Latin to its Provençal descendant, and from quantitative to rhythmical forms of verse. He is once described as belonging to the school of Toulouse[5]. He records the custom of having two separate Libraries (1) of Christian, (2) of pagan literature[6]. He also tells us that his preceptor 'Virgilius Assianus' wrote a work on the twelve kinds of Latin[7]. With the help of Greek, he coins new words: *scribere* becomes *charaxare*, *rex* appears as *thors* (from θρόνος), and a cryptic form of Latin comes into use, which has points of similarity with that of the *Hisperica famina* (cent. vii), where, amid much that is singularly obscure, it is a relief to find so clear a phrase as :—'*pantes* solitum elaborant agrestres *orgium*'[8]. The scene is laid in a land where the language is Irish, and it is characteristic

'Virgil', the grammarian

Hisperica Famina

---

[1] Migne, lxxxvii 220 (Norden, 635).

[2] His only extant works are his fifteen *Epitomae ad Fabianum puerum*, and his eight *Epistolae ad Julium germanum diaconum* (Mai, *Cl. Auct.* v 1); cp. Hümer (Wien, 1882), and ed. Hümer, 1886; Roger, 110—126; Manitius, 119—127. Zimmer, *S. Ber.* Berlin Acad. 1910, p. 1067, places him *c.* 460 A.D. But his etymologies are apparently derived from Isidore (636), though this is denied by Kuno Meyer, *Learning in Ireland in the Fifth Century* (1913), p. 22 n. 7.

[3] *Epist.* ii p. 123.        [4] *Epist.* iii p. 138.

[5] Abbo of Fleury (d. 1004), *Quaest. Gr.* ed. Mai, *Cl. Auct.* v 349, Virgilius Tolosanus. He quotes the dialect of Bigorre, N. of the Pyrenees.

[6] *Epist.* iii p. 135.  Cp. Roger, 124 n. 4.        [7] *Ep.* v 2, pp. 124–6.

[8] Mai, *l. c.*, v 479 f; Ozanam, *La Civilisation Chrétienne chez les Francs* (1855), 423–51, 483 f, and *Études Germ.* ii 479 f; Ernault (Paris, 1886);

of the possibly Irish origin of this strange composition that we
here find two words borrowed from Greek.

During the sixth and seventh centuries in Ireland we find
a few traces of Greek.   Thus we find *antropi* (for
ἄνθρωποι) in Muirchu's *Life of St Patrick* (written      Greek in
before 698), *anthleta* (for *athleta*) in the 'Antiphonary      Ireland
of Bangor' (*c.* 680—691), and *onomata* in codex A of the 'Life of
St Columba' by Adamnan (d. 704)[1].

The Hellenisms which have been discovered in the Irish, as
well as the British, writers of the sixth and seventh centuries
supply no proof of any real knowledge of the language, many of
them being simply Greek terms that had already been borrowed
in ordinary ecclesiastical Latin, while the rest were probably
derived mainly from glossaries.   Among these was probably the
Greek and Latin glossary and conversation-book known as the
*Hermeneumata Pseudo-Dositheana*[2].

In and after the ninth century, the classical culture exhibited
by a few Irish scholars such as Sedulius and John the Scot,
was due to their residence abroad, in lands that came under
the influence of the Caroline revival of learning[3].

Teuffel, § 497, 7; *Hisperica Famina*, ed. Stowasser (1887), and Stowasser
and Thurneysen in *Archiv Lat. Lex.* 1886, 168, 526; ed. Jenkinson (1908);
R. Ellis in *Journ. Philol.* xxviii (1903) 209 f.  Zimmer, *Nennius vindicatus*
(1893), 291 f, assigns it to S.W. Britain (first half of cent. vi); cp. Roger,
238—256; Manitius, 156-9; Traube, *Vorlesungen*, ii, 91, 173.

[1] Roger, 268—273; and Gougaud, *Les Chrétientés Celtiques* (1911), 247 f.
Exaggerated views were formerly held as to the early knowledge of Greek in
Ireland.

Cp. Cramer, *De Graecis Medii Aevi Studiis* (1849), i 42; Ozanam, *l.c.*
475-82; Hauréau, *Singularités Historiques et Littéraires* (1861), pp. 1—36;
G. T. Stokes, *Ireland and the Celtic Church* (1886), Lect. xi, and in *Pro-
ceedings of Royal Irish Acad.* 3rd Series, ii 179—202, esp. 193; D. Hyde,
*Literary History of Ireland* (1899), 217; and H. Zimmer, *Keltische Kirche in
Britannien u. Irland*, in *Realencyclopädie f. prot. Theol.* (1901), abstract in
*Eng. Hist. Rev.* 1901, p. 757 f.  Jubainville believed that Greek was intro-
duced into Ireland from Gaul in century v (Roger, 203, n. 2).

[2] Goetz, *Corpus Glossariorum Lat.* iii (1892).

[3] Cp. Traube, *Vorlesungen*, ii (1911), 39 f, 84; M. Esposito, *The knowledge
of Greek in Ireland during the Middle Ages*, in 'Studies', Dublin, 1912,
i pp. 665—683.

On 'Scots on the Continent', see A. W. Haddan's *Remains* (1876),

St Patrick's 'nephew', Sechnall, or Secundinus, is said to have produced at Dumshaughlin, S. of Tara, the first Latin hymn that was composed in Ireland. Its 23 stanzas are written in a trochaic rhythm, with an almost complete disregard of metrical quantity, *e.g.*

> 'Dominus illum elegit ut doceret barbaras
> Nationes, ut piscaret per doctrinae retia,
> Ut de seculo credentes traheret ad gratiam
> Dominumque sequerentur sedem ad etheriam'[1].

The Irish monk, Columban, born in Leinster about 543, had received an excellent education on one of the many islands of Lough Erne before he entered the monastery of Bangor on the Eastern coast of Ulster. The monastery was then at the height of its fame, and it was doubtless owing to the classical training he had there received, that he was able at the age of 68 to address a friend in a lengthy poem of Adonic verse, from which the few following lines are taken:—

Columban

> 'Inclyta vates,          Doctiloquorum
> Nomine Sappho,          Carmina linquens,
> Versibus istis          Frivola nostra
> Dulce solebat          Suscipe laetus'.
> Edere carmen.                          Migne, lxxx 291.

Elsewhere he quotes Juvenal, and recommends the reading of the ancient poets as well as the ancient fathers[2]. About 585, he was suddenly smitten with a longing for foreign travel. Attended by twelve companions, he left for Gaul; and, having been invited to settle in Burgundy, he founded in the woodland solitudes of the Vosges the three monasteries of Anegray, Luxeuil (*c.* 590) and Fontaines[3]. It was about this time that he composed his Rule,

---

258—294; cp. H. Zimmer's *Irish Element in Mediaeval Culture* (E. T., 1891); Greith, *Geschichte d. altirischen Kirche in ihrer Verbindung mit Rom, Gallien u. Alemannien* (Freiburg in B., 1867); W. Schultze, in *Centralblatt f. Bibliothekswesen*, 1884, 185, 233, 281.

[1] Bury, *Life of St Patrick*, 1905, 117, 247.

[2] Ussher, *Ep. Hib. Syll.* p. 11 f. His letters (ed. Gundlach) include reminiscences of Sallust, Virgil, Horace, Ovid, and Persius.

[3] *Life* by Jonas, cc. 9, 10. Cp. Margaret Stokes, *Three Months in the Forests of France* (1895), and Roger, 406—415.

which has much in common with that of Benedict, and prescribes
the copying of MSS, besides teaching in schools and constant toil
in field and forest[1]. He was banished from Burgundy about 610,
and, after withdrawing to Nantes, returned towards the Rhine,
passing from Zürich to Zug and ultimately to the Lake of
Constance, where he spent two or three years in preaching to
the heathen. When he left for Italy (c. 612), he was welcomed
by the king of the Lombards and his queen Theodolinda; and,
S.E. of the Lombard capital of Pavia, he founded on the stream
of the Trebbia the monastery of Bobbio[2] (c. 613). In a cavern,
high above the opposite bank of the stream, he died in 615[3].
His life was written in the same century by Jonas, a monk of
Bobbio, who quotes Virgil and Livy, and has evidently formed
his style on the study of the Classics. Columban's 'belt, chalice
and knife' are still shown in the *sacrarium*[4].

The monastery founded by the Irish monk became a home of
learning in northern Italy. In course of time its library received
gifts of MSS of the fourth and fifth centuries, originally transcribed
for men of letters in Rome, and others of later date, presented by
wandering countrymen of the founder, such as Dungal[5], the Irish
monk who presided over the school at Pavia in 823. The first
catalogue, which contained 666 MSS, including Terence, Lucretius,
Virgil, Ovid, Lucan, Persius, Martial, Juvenal and Claudian, with
Cicero, Seneca and the elder Pliny, was drawn up in the tenth

---

[1] Migne, lxxx 209. Margaret Stokes, *Six Months in the Apennines, a
Pilgrimage in search of vestiges of the Irish Saints in Italy* (1892).

[2] On the spot it is pronounced *Bobio*, according to the old spelling of the
name. The epitaph on Bp Cummian (d. 730) has *Ebovio* (Margaret Stokes,
*Six Months in the Apennines,* p. 152).

[3] In the same year died Aileran, an Irish monk who borrows from Origen,
Philo and Josephus the best part of a brief explanation of certain Biblical
names (Migne, lxxx 327–34).

[4] M. Stokes, pp. 14, 178 f. On Columban, cp. Ozanam, *Civ. Chrét.* c. iv;
Ebert, i[2] 617 f; Milman, ii 284—295; Dr Moran, *An Irish Missionary and
his Work* (1869); G. T. Stokes, *Ireland and the Celtic Church*, Lect. vii; and
M. Stokes, *l. c.*; also Roger, 230–2, 269 n. 5, 433 n. 2; and Manitius, 181–7.

[5] Wattenbach, *Schriftwesen im MA*, p. 489. Gottlieb, however, maintains
that the work of the elder Dungal against Claudius of Turin was given by a
later Dungal in cent. xii (Traube, *Abhandl. bayr. Akad.* 1891, 332–7).

century, and has been printed by Muratori[1]. It is arranged
according to the authors and the donors of the MSS. The
second, 'restored' in 1461 and including 280 volumes, was
discovered and published in 1824 by Peyron[2]. The library was
explored by Giorgio Merula (1493)[3], Tommaso Inghirami (1496),
and Aulo Giano Parrasio (1499)[4]. Many valuable MSS were removed
by Cardinal Borromeo, some of them being placed in the Ambrosian
Library, which he was founding at Milan (1606), while others were
sent to the Vatican at the instance of Paul V (1618). In 1685
the monastery was visited by the learned Benedictine, Mabillon[5].
During the 18th century a number of the remaining volumes
were transported to Turin[6]. The greater part have thus been
dispersed through the libraries of Rome, Milan and Turin, while
some have found their way to Naples and Vienna[7]. It is
practically certain that the Ambrosian palimpsest of Plautus[8]
and those of several of Cicero's Speeches (cent. iv) and of the
Letters of Fronto[9], discovered in the Ambrosian Library early in

---

[1] *Ant. Ital.* iii 809—880, esp. p. 818; cp. G. Becker's *Catalogi Bibliothe-
carum Antiqui* (1885), p. 64; and Léon Maître's *Écoles*, p. 297.

[2] *Fragmenta Orat. Cic.* p. iii f.

[3] O. von Gebhardt, in *Centralbl. f. Bibl.* v (1888) 343 f; and Sabbadini,
*Scoperte* (1905), 156 f.

[4] Sabbadini, *Scoperte*, 159.

[5] *Iter Italicum*, 215. He describes it as 'the *Bobian* (called by the ancients
the *Ebobian*) monastery'.

[6] Of the 70 MSS from Bobbio, 12 were destroyed in the fire of 26 Jan. 1904,
including the palimpsest fragments of Cicero's Speeches (cent. ii—iii) and of
the Theodosian Code (vi), and the fragments of Cassiodorus (vi). Cp.
Gorrini, *L'Incendio della Biblioteca Nazionale* (Torino, 1905), p. 41 n. Catalogue of the surviving MSS in *Riv. di filol. cl.* xxxii 436 f.

[7] M. Stokes, 281–2. On the MSS in Turin, cp. Ottino (1890), and
catalogue quoted in note 6; on those in Rome and Milan, Seebass in
*Centralbl. f. Bibl.* xiii; on others, Gottlieb, *ib.* iv 442 f, and Gebhardt,
*ib.* v 343–62, 383—431, 538. Cp. W. M. Lindsay, *ib.* xxvi 293 f; and
R. Beer in *S. Ber.* Vienna Acad. 1911, 78—104.

[8] Studemund, *Apographum*, p. v f, Neque unde neque quo tempore codex
in bibliothecam Ambrosianam pervenerit, certo constat...Ubi sacer codex
conscriptus sit nescimus. Bobbii eum conscriptum esse et vulgo credunt et
inde probabile fit, quod rude ac parum elegans scripturae genus......amanuensem
non Italum fuisse persuadet; itemque genus scripturae Anglo-saxonicum quo
supplementa illa insignia sunt, vix amanuensi ex Italia oriundo tribuerim.

[9] E. Hauler, *Wiener Studien*, xxxi 2; C. R. Haines, E. T., Heinemann, 1919–.

the 19th century, all came from the monastery founded by the
Irish monk at Bobbio; but the monks of that monastery, while
they deserve our gratitude for preserving these MSS at all, have
made the task of deciphering them needlessly difficult by inscribing
on these ancient scrolls later copies of works so easily accessible
as the Vulgate, and the Acts of the Councils and the works of
St Augustine.  Among other MSS, which once belonged to Bobbio,
may be mentioned fragments of Symmachus (in Milan) and the
Theodosian Code (formerly in Turin); *scholia* on Cicero[1] (cent. v),
MSS of St Luke (v–vi), St Severinus (vi), Josephus (vi–vii),
St Ambrose, St Augustine and St Maximus (vii), Gregory's
*Dialogues* (*c.* 750), and St Isidore (before 840)[2].  Lastly we cannot
forget the 'Muratorian fragment' (cent. viii or earlier), the earliest
extant list of the books of the New Testament.

When the founder of Bobbio left for Italy, one at least of his
companions, Gallus by name, remained on the shore
of the Lake of Constance.  Accompanied by several         Gallus and
                                                          St Gallen
of the other Irish monks, he founded on a lofty site
in the neighbourhood (614) the monastery which has given the
name of St Gallen to the town which surrounds it.  The founder
died in extreme old age about 645.  The monastery of St Gallen
has proved no less important than that of Bobbio as a treasure-
house of Latin as well as Irish literature[3].  As we shall see in the
sequel, at least three important MSS of Valerius Flaccus, Asconius,
and an anonymous commentator on the Verrine Orations were
there discovered in 1416 by Poggio, together with a complete copy
of Quintilian[4].  The Library still possesses a few leaves of a MS
of Virgil belonging to the fourth or fifth century[5].  Another

---

[1] First published by Mai (Milan, 1815, and Rome, 1828) from palimpsest
partly in Vatican and partly in Ambrosian Library; ed. Orelli, V ii 214—369;
recent literature in Bursian's *Jahresb.* cxiii (1902) 192 f.

[2] *Facsimiles* from all the nine MSS here dated are published by the Palaeographical Society.  The Medicean Virgil (v) and the sole MS of Charisius
(vii—viii), now at Naples, also came from Bobbio.

[3] Cp. F. Weidmann, *Gesch. d. Bibliothek von St Gallen* (1842); Catalogues
of the MSS in G. Becker's *Catalogi* (1885); cp. Léon Maître's *Écoles*, p. 278 f;
and Ozanam's *Civ. Chrét.* p. 487 f.

[4] Sabbadini, *Scoperte*, 77—79.

[5] *Facsimile* on p. 197.

pupil of Columban, Agilius (St Aile), was the first abbot of the
monastery founded at Resbacus (Rébais, E. of Paris) in 634[1], and
the MSS there copied included Terence, Cicero, Virgil, Horace,
Donatus, Priscian and Boëthius[2].

Within less than 25 years after the Irish monks had founded
Bobbio and St Gallen, and thus unconsciously
promoted the preservation of some of the most
important remains of Latin literature, Isidore, bishop
of Seville (c. 570—636), produced an encyclopaedic work which
gathered up for the Middle Ages much of the learning of the
ancient world. The work is known as the *Origines*, and is
remarkable for the great variety of its contents and for its
numerous citations from earlier authorities. The friend, for
whom it was composed, divided it into 20 Books, describing the
whole as a vast volume of 'etymologies' including everything that
ought to be known. Books I—III are on the liberal arts, grammar
(including metre) filling a whole Book; IV, on medicine and on
libraries; V, on law and chronology; VI, on the books of the
Bible; VII, on the heavenly and the earthly hierarchy; VIII, on
the Church and on sects (no less than 68 in number); IX, on
language, on peoples, and on official titles; X, on etymology;
XI, on man; XII, on beasts and birds; XIII, the world and its
parts; XIV, physical geography; XV, political geography, public
buildings, land-surveying and road-making; XVI, stones and
metals; XVII, agriculture and horticulture; XVIII, the vocabulary
of war, litigation and public games; XIX, ships and houses, dress
and personal adornment; and XX, meats and drinks, tools and
furniture. The work is mainly founded on earlier compilations,
Book II being chiefly taken from the Greek texts translated by
Boëthius; the first part of IV from Caelius Aurelianus; XI from
Lactantius; and XII—XIV, XV etc., from Pliny and Solinus;

[1] Jonas, *Vita S. Columbani*, 26.

[2] Greith, *Altirische Kirche*, p. 291 (Denk, *Gallo-Fränkisch. Unterricht*,
257 f). *Perrona Scottorum* (Péronne, near Corbie) was founded by Irish
monks *c.* 650; its abbot, Cellanus (d. 706), was an admirer of Aldhelm; and
the three monasteries on the Somme, Corbie, Péronne and St Riquier, served
as links between the insular and the continental literature (Traube, in *S. Ber.*
of Munich Acad. Dec. 1900, *Perrona Scottorum*, p. 493).

while its plan, as a whole, and many of its details, appear to have
been borrowed from the lost *Prata* of Suetonius[1]. The author
also makes use of Lucretius, Sallust, and an epitome of Vitruvius,
with Jerome, Augustine, Orosius and others[2]. The work was so
highly esteemed as an encyclopaedia of classical learning that, to
a large extent, it unfortunately superseded the study of the classical
authors themselves[3]. Among its compiler's other writings is a
Chronicle founded on Sextus Julius Africanus and on Jerome's
rendering of Eusebius (ending with 615), a History of the Goths,
a continuation of Gennadius *De Viris Illustribus*, and a treatise
*De Natura Rerum*, widely known in the Middle Ages. We gain
a vivid impression of his own surroundings from the verses written
by himself for the 14 presses (*armaria*), which composed his
library and were adorned with the portraits of 22 authors
Theology is represented by Origen, Hilary, Ambrose, Augustine,
Jerome, Chrysostom and Cyprian; poetry by Prudentius, Avitus,
Juvencus and Sedulius; ecclesiastical history by Eusebius and
Orosius; law by Theodosius, Paulus and Gaius; medicine by
Cosmas, Damian, Hippocrates and Galen; and, besides these 20,
we have Gregory the Great and Isidore's elder brother, Leander.
Each of these is commemorated in elegiac verse, beginning with
three couplets on the library in general, implying that it contained
secular as well as sacred literature :—

> 'sunt hic plura sacra, sunt hic mundalia plura:
>     ex his si qua placent carmina, tolle, lege.
> prata (vides) plena spinis, et copia florum;
>     si non vis spinas sumere, sume rosas...'

The series ends with some lines addressed " To an Intruder', the
last couplet of which runs as follows :—

> 'non patitur quenquam coram se scriba loquentem;
>     non est hic quod agas, garrule, perge foras'[4].

Though Isidore was himself familiar with many portions of pagan
literature, the only authors which he permitted his monks to read

---

[1] Nettleship, i 330 f; Schanz, § 534.
[2] Dressel, *De Isidori Originum Fontibus*, Turin (1874).
[3] Cp. Norden, *Kunstprosa*, 398.
[4] Migne, lxxxiii 1107; cp. J. W. Clark's *Care of Books*, p. 46.

were the Grammarians.   He held it safer for them to remain in
humble ignorance than to be elated with the pride of knowledge,
or led into error by reading dangerous works[1].   In support of
this narrow view, he even appeals to the Vulgate rendering of
Psalm lxxi, where, by combining the end of verse 15 (as translated
from an inferior variant in the LXX) with the beginning of the
following verse, he obtains the singular text :—*quia non cognovi
litteraturam*[2], *introibo in potentias Domini*[3].   Had he referred to
Cassiodorus, he might there have found a better motto in the
prayer :—*praesta, Domine, legentibus profectum*[4].

Isidore has the reputation of having been 'learned in Greek
and Latin and Hebrew'[5].   He distinguished between
five varieties of Greek, *i.e.* the four dialects and the
κοινή, and eulogised it as excelling all languages in
euphony[6].   But his knowledge of the language was very slight.
Acquaintance with Greek is attested in Spain at a still earlier date
in the person of the 'world-renowned Spaniard' who took a
prominent part in the Council of Nicaea, Hosius, bishop of
Cordova (d. 357), who is said to have brought a Greek teacher
back with him from the East to aid him in the study of Plato.
John, the Gothic bishop of Gerona (590), had in his youth spent
seven years in Constantinople with a view to perfecting himself in
Greek and Latin[7]; and, about the time of Isidore's death, some
knowledge of Greek is shown by Julian, bishop of Toledo (d. 690),
who gives Greek titles to two of his works[8], and touches twice on
the beauty of the style of Demosthenes[9]; while, in 657, another
bishop of that see, Eugenius III, declares that it would need the

[1] *ib.* 877, *Isidori Regula*, c. 8, gentilium libros vel haereticorum volumina
monachus legere caveat ; melius est enim eorum perniciosa dogmata ignorare
quam per inexperientiam in aliquem laqueum erroris incurrere.  Cp. *Sentent.*,
pp. 685-7.

[2] γραμματείας *v.l.* for πραγματείας.         [3] *Sententiarum Liber*, iii 13.

[4] *Inst.* i 33.  On Isidore in general, cp. Ebert, i² 588—602; Teuffel,
§ 496; Gröber, II i 110; Ker's *Dark Ages*, 138; Roger, 195–201; Saintsbury,
i 400 f; Manitius, 52—70; Traube, *Vorlesungen*, ii 157—162.  *Etymologiae*,
ed. Lindsay, Oxford, 1910; facsimile of Toledo MS (Leyden, 1909); Beeson,
*Isidor-Studien* (München, 1913).

[5] Migne, lxxxi 53 D, 86 B.         [6] *Ep.* ix 1, 4.

[7] Isidore, *De Viris Ill.*, c. 44.

[8] προγνωστικῶν and ἀντικειμένων; Migne, xcvi 453, 495.         [9] *ib.* 727.

powers of a Socrates or a Plato, a Cicero or a Varro, to do justice
to the memory of Gregory the Great[1].

In the South of Gaul, Greek was to a large extent the language
of commerce; and, even in the Roman town of
Arles, Greek was commonly spoken by the Jews     Gaul
in the early part of the sixth century[2]. In the North, in 659,
we find St Ouen, archbishop of Rouen, urging the superiority of
sacred over secular writings by asking what was the worth of philosophers such as Pythagoras, Socrates, Plato and Aristotle, or the
'sad strains of those wicked poets', Homer, Virgil and Menander,
or the histories of Sallust, Herodotus and Livy, or the eloquence
of Lysias, Gracchus, Demosthenes and Tully, or the acumen of
Horace, Solinus, Varro, Democritus, Plautus and Cicero[3]. The
odd juxtaposition of some of these names excites suspicion, and
the mention of Tully and Cicero, Democritus and Menander,
suggests a doubt whether St Ouen had really read the secular
writings on which he casts such profound contempt. About
a century before his death, two celebrated Graeco-Latin MSS, the
*Codex Bezae* of the Gospels and Acts, and the *Codex Claro-
montanus* of St Paul's Epistles, had been copied in Western
Europe, possibly in Gaul itself; and Gaul may also claim
a Graeco-Latin glossary of the seventh century[4]. In the same
century the library at Ligugé contained 'nearly all the Greek and
Latin Fathers'[5].

While the evidence for a knowledge of Greek at this time is
slight indeed in Gaul, it is even slighter in Germany,
where there is no proof of any interest in Greek     Germany
before the revival of learning under Charles the Great. Literary
interests were, however, partially revived in the northern monasteries under the influence of the Benedictine Chrodegang,
archbishop of Metz (742—766), who had been Chancellor to
Charles Martel from 737 to 741. The rules which he framed

---

[1] Migne, lxxxvii 415 C.
[2] Papon, *Hist. gén. de Provence*, i 113; Gross, in *Monatschr. f. Gesch. u. Wiss. des Judenthums*, xxvii (1878) 68.
[3] Migne, lxxxvii 479; cp. Roger, 413.
[4] Harley MS 5792; Palaeographical Society's *Facsimiles*, ii 25.
[5] *Hist. Litt. de la France*, ii 429. Cp. Traube, *Vorlesungen*, ii 83 f.

for the restoration of discipline[1] were adopted in the monasteries of France, Italy, Germany and England, and a certain uniformity was thus secured in the singing, the language and the script of the monastic schools which continued until the time of Alcuin[2].

Italy

Meanwhile, in Italy, there had been a decline in the knowledge of Greek during the fifth and sixth centuries; the Greek and Latin Churches failed to come to an understanding because they no longer understood one another's language. The decline was followed by a partial revival in the seventh and eighth centuries[3]. Four of the popes of the seventh and eighth centuries were actually Greeks by birth[4]. In 648, Maurus, archbishop of Ravenna, writes in Greek[5] to Pope Martin I (649—655), who sends to personages in the East a number of letters written in Greek[6], but there is no proof that the Greek was his own, though in the Lateran Council, which condemned the Monothelites (649), we have many references to the Greek Fathers. It is supposed that it was under Martin I that the first Greek monasteries were founded in Rome[7]. Such monasteries would serve as places of refuge to those of the Greek monks who were driven from the East by the Monothelite heresy (622–80). The reply sent by Pope Agatho (c. 679) to a Byzantine emperor is preserved in Greek as well as in Latin, together with the Greek original of another letter. The Acts of the third Council of Constantinople, which finally confirmed the condemnation of the Monothelites, were translated from Greek into Latin by Pope Leo II (683), who rebuilt the basilica of *S. Giorgio in Velabro* in memory of the recent reconciliation of the Greek and Latin Churches[8]. But Greek must have been still

---

[1] D'Achery's *Spicilegium*, i 564 f; Migne, lxxxix 1053—1126; *Life* in Pertz, *Mon.* xii 552–72; Roger, 427.

[2] Denk, *Gallo-Fränkisch. Unterricht*, 271-6; cp. Putnam's *Books in the Middle Ages*, i 128 f.

[3] Steinacker, in *Gomperz-Festschrift* (1902), 324—341; cp. Harnack, *Altchrist. Lit.* p. lix, and *Dogmengeschichte*, II i 31 f; and Krumbacher, in *Rhein. Mus.* xxxix 353 f.  [4] Theodorus, John VI, VII, Zacharias.

[5] Migne, lxxxvii 103.  [6] *ib.* 119—198.

[7] Hardouin, *Conciles*, iii 719; Gidel, *Nouvelles Études*, p. 150.

[8] Battifol, in *Mélanges d'archéol. et hist.* vii (1887) 419—431, and, on Byzantine book-shops in Rome, viii 297 f.

on the decline, as the year 690 is regarded as the date of the
temporary extinction of that language in Italy[1]. In the following
century the iconoclastic decrees of 727 and 816 drove many of
the Greek monks and their lay adherents from the Empire in the
East to the South of Italy and even to Rome itself. The Syrian
Pope, Gregory III (731—741), built them a monastery dedicated
to St Chrysogonus[2]. In Rome, during the two centuries of the
Exarchate of Ravenna (554—750), 'Greek officials, Greek clergy,
Greek monks, Greek residents, continued to form, as it were,
a Byzantine army of occupation; they invaded the churches, and
even the Papal Chair, and naturally they brought with them the
language and the culture of Constantinople'[3]. In 750 the Greek
Pope, Zacharias, received the Greek nuns who brought from the
convent of St Anastasia a celebrated image of the Virgin and
the relics of St Gregory Nazianzen; Paul I (761) was equally
hospitable to the monks, who probably procured for him the
Greek MSS which he sent to Pepin-le-Bref[4]; while Hadrian I (780)
enlarged for the benefit of the Greeks the church which had been
known since the end of the sixth century as that of *S. Maria in
schola Graeca*, but was thenceforth called *S. Maria in Cosmedin*,
the new name being taken (as at Ravenna) from the quarter
of Constantinople named *Kosmedion*. In 818 the existing
monasteries were too few to contain all the Greek monks that
flocked to Rome, and Pascal I gave the fugitives the monastery
of St Praxedis, while other popes in the same century, *e.g.*
Stephen IV (817) and Leo IV (850), founded monasteries for them
in Rome and in Southern Italy[5]. The South of Italy continued
to be politically connected with Constantinople from the time
of the recovery of Italy by the generals of Justinian (553)[6] to its
capture by the Normans (1055), and, in the extreme South,

---

[1] Martin Crusius, *Annales Suevici*, 274 (Gidel, p. 156).

[2] Leo II and Gregory III are the only Popes described in the *Liber
Pontificalis* as *Graeca Latinaque lingua eruditi*.

[3] Rushforth, in *Papers of British School in Rome*, i (1902) 11; cp. Diehl's
*Exarchat de Ravenne*, 241 f.

[4] Cp. Roger, 431 f.

[5] Muratori, *Script. Ital.* III i 215, 234. Cp. Gardthausen, *Gr. Paläographie*,
p. 418.

[6] Bury, *Later Roman Empire*, ii 439 f, 447 f.

Greek monks of the Basilian order were still in existence in the age of the Renaissance. Even at the present day there are villages in the ancient Calabria near the 'heel', and in the modern Calabria near the 'toe' of Italy, where Greek continues to be spoken with slight varieties of dialect, while the tradition of Greek as a living language lingers in other parts of those regions[1]. The decline of learning in Northern Italy, at the time when the Greek monks were flocking to her Southern shores, is attested by Lothair I, who, in his decree of 823, deplores the general extinction of learning and reorganises education throughout his Italian dominions by instituting central schools at nine important places,—Pavia, Ivrea, Turin, Cremona, Florence, Fermo, Verona, Vicenza and Friuli[2]. The head of the school at Pavia was an Irishman.

Early indications of a knowledge of Greek in Britain have been traced in certain Latin renderings from the Old Testament apparently taken directly from the LXX. These are contained in the anonymous work *De Mirabilibus Sacrae Scripturae* (*c.* 660), and in a MS of Irish Canons (early in cent. viii)[3]. Three Greek letters (εις) may be seen on an ancient block of tin, now in the Penzance Museum[4]; and some slight knowledge of Greek is implied in an Irish Canon of the end of the seventh century, where a monk is thus defined:—

Britain
and Ireland

[1] Morosi, *Studi sui dialetti greci della terra d' Otranto*, Lecce (1870), and *Dialetti...in Calabria* (1874), and Zambelli, Ἰταλοελληνικά, pp. 23, 202 ; cp. Roger Bacon, *Opus Tert.* 33 ; Cramer, i 26 ; Gidel, *Nouvelles Etudes*, 145—156, and Tozer in *J. H. S.*, x 11—42, esp. 38 f ; also A. Dresdner, *Kultur- u. Sittengeschichte der italienischen Geistlichkeit im* 10. *u.* 11. *Jahrhundert* (1890), p. 195 f ; and A. Palmieri, *Les Études Byzantines en Italie*, in *Viz. Vremennik*, x (1903) 281—303. Cp. Traube, *Vorlesungen*, ii 85 f.

[2] Muratori, *Script. Rer. Ital.* I ii 151 ; *Antiq. Medii Aevi*, iii 815 ; Tiraboschi, iii 179 f ; *Mon. Germ. Legg.* i 248.

[3] J. R. Lumby, *Greek Learning in the Western Church during the seventh and eighth centuries*, Cambridge (1878), p. 3. 'In the AS church the Greek creed was sung in service, as at St Gallen and Reichenau'. 'King Athelstan's psalter' includes the Lord's prayer and the apostles' creed in AS characters, but in the Greek language. See esp. Caspari's *Quellen zur Gesch. des Taufsymbols*, iii (Christiania, 1875) 188—99, 219—34, 466—510 (Mayor on Bede, p. 298 f).

[4] Haddan and Stubbs, *Councils* etc. i 699.

*monachus Graece, Latine unalis, sive quod solus in eremo vitam solitariam ducat, sive quod sine impedimento mundiali mundum habitet*[1]. In the Book of Armagh (*c.* 807) the Lord's Prayer is written in Latin words but in Greek characters[2]; and, down to the days of archbishop Ussher, a church at Trim was called the 'Greek church'[3], while its site was still known in 1846 as the 'Greek park'[4]. The Irish monk, Virgil the geometer, who became the first bishop of Salzburg towards the end of the eighth century (767–84), was charged by Boniface with believing in the existence of the antipodes[5]; and, half a century later, an Irish monk of Liège, named Sedulius, was copying a Greek Psalter, writing Latin verses[6], making extracts from Origen and expounding Jerome[7]. He has been identified as the compiler of the *Collectaneum* in the Library at Cues on the Mosel that once belonged to Nicolaus Cusanus, who in 1451 bought some of his MSS at Liège, the former home of Sedulius[8]. The *Collectaneum* includes extracts from the *ad Herennium* and from Cicero, *De Inventione*, *pro Fonteio*, *pro Flacco*, *in Pisonem*, *Philippics*, *Paradoxa* and *Tusculan Disputations*; also from Frontinus, Valerius Maximus, the *Scriptores Historiae Augustae*, Vegetius, Macrobius, Orosius, Cassiodorus and Bede; and, further, a series of moral sayings from Terence and Publilius Syrus, and 74 Greek 'proverbs' in a Latin form. Many of the above extracts are imbedded in his *liber de rectoribus Christianis* (855–9), a work in Latin prose varied with passages in elegiac, sapphic, and other

---

[1] Haddan and Stubbs, *Councils* etc. i 170 f.

[2] See, however, Roger, 269.        [3] Ussher, *Ep. Hibern. Syll.* note 16.

[4] G. T. Stokes, *Ireland and the Celtic Church*, p. 218 n.

[5] *ib.* 224; Ozanam, 133 f. Boniface, *Ep.* lxvi, Jaffé iii 191. Cp. Wattenbach, *GQ,* i[7] 136; Krabbo, *Mittheil. des Instituts f. österr. Geschichtsforschung*, xxiv (1902), 1 f; Andrew D. White's *Warfare of Science with Theology*, 1 105–6; also Roger, 263.

[6] *Poëtae Latini Aevi Car.* iii 151—237 Traube. He often borrows from Virgil, Ovid and Fortunatus.

[7] G. T. Stokes, pp. 225–8; cp. Ebert, ii c. 6; Pirenne, *Sedulius de Liège* (Bruxelles, 1882); Traube, *Abhandl. bayr. Akad.* 1891, 338—346; Ker's *Dark Ages*, 160. His comm. on Eutyches, founded on Macrobius and Priscian, shows a knowledge of Greek (Hagen, *Anecd. Helv.* 1—38).

[8] Traube, *l. c.* 364–9.

kinds of lyric verse[1]. The 'Greek proverbs' of the *Collectaneum*
were probably of Irish origin, and possibly earlier than the seventh
century[2], while Sedulius may have borrowed his Vegetius from the
Irish colony at Laon[3]. Another Irish monk, the grammarian
Dicuil (*c.* 825), in a short treatise on Geography[4] ranging from
Iceland to the pyramids of Egypt, gives an impression of very wide
attainments by naming the following Greek authors:—Artemidorus,
Clitarchus, Dicaearchus, Ephorus, Eudoxus, Hecataeus, Herodotus,
Homer, Onesicritus, Philemon, Pytheas, Thucydides, Timosthenes
and Xenophon of Lampsacus. His work is mainly founded on
Caesar, Pliny and Solinus and includes quotations from Pomponius
Mela, Orosius, Priscian and Isidore of Seville[5]. Macrobius and
Priscian are his authorities on grammar[6].

While Ireland sent forth Columban to found monasteries in
Eastern France and Northern Italy in 585 and 612 respectively,
Rome, in the person of Gregory, sent Augustine to Britain in the
interval between the above dates. Augustine arrived in Kent
in 597 and died archbishop of Canterbury in 605. Some sixty
years later, the archbishopric was offered by Pope Vitalian first to
Hadrian, who is described as 'most skilful in both the Greek and
Latin tongues'[7], and finally to Theodore, who was born at Tarsus
and educated at Athens, and therefore familiar
with Greek[8]. This Greek archbishop (668—690)
founded a school at Canterbury for the study of
Greek, and bestowed upon his foundation a number of books
in his native language. Nine hundred years later, archbishop
Parker showed an antiquarian at Canterbury copies of 'Homer
and some other Greek authors, beautifully written on thick paper
with the name of this Theodore prefixed in the front, to whose
library he reasonably thought (being led thereto by show of great

Theodore
of Tarsus

[1] ed. S. Hellmann, *Sedulius Scottus*, 1906, pp. 19—91; on the *Collectaneum*, *ib.* pp. 92—117.

[2] *ib.* 121 f, 135.   [3] 104.

[4] *De Mensura Orbis Terrae.*

[5] *ib.* 214–6; Ebert, ii 392–4; cp. Letronne, *Recherches*, ii 3, vi 8, and Beazley's *Dawn of Modern Geography*, p. 317 f.

[6] Teuffel, § 473, 9.   [7] Bede, *H. E.* iv 1.

[8] Described by the Greek Pope Zacharias in *Bonifatii Epp.*, 185 Jaffé, as 'Greco-Latinus ante philosophus et Athenis eruditus'.

antiquity) that they sometime belonged'[1]; but there is no doubt
that this MS of Homer, which is still preserved among the Parker
MSS in the Library of Corpus Christi College, Cambridge, belonged
not to Theodore of Tarsus (who had died eight centuries before it
was written), but to Linacre's friend, William Selling[2]. With the
help of Hadrian, who had declined the archbishopric, Theodore
made many of the monasteries of England schools of Greek and
Latin learning, so that, in the time of Bede (673—735), some
of the scholars who still survived, such as Tobias, bishop of
Rochester (d. 726)[3], were as familiar with Latin and Greek as
with their mother-tongue[4]. The Worcestershire monk, Tatwine,
who became archbishop of Canterbury (d. 734), besides writing
riddles in Latin verse, was the author of a Latin grammar founded
on Donatus and his commentators[5]; and the tradition of Greek
descended to the early days of Odo (875—961), archbishop of
Canterbury[6].

Among the pupils of the school at Canterbury in 670 was
Aldhelm (c. 650—709), who had been previously       **Aldhelm**
educated under the Irish scholar, Maidulf, the
founder of the monastery of Malmesbury, of which Aldhelm after-

---

[1] Lambarde, *Perambulation of Kent*, p. 233 ed. 1576; Milman, *Lat. Christ.*, ii 272.

[2] M. R. James, *Abp Parker's MSS* (1899), p. 9.

[3] Bede, *H. E.* v 8, 20, 23.

[4] *ib.* iv 2 (with Mayor's note on p. 298). Cp. J. Gennadius, in the *Times*, 1 Sept. 1896, and Roger, 286–8. Immediately before the riddles of Aldhelm, in a Leyden MS of Adémar de Chabannes, a monk named Gautbert gives on p. 147 f. a far from accurate account of the chronological succession of grammarians in the West from the end of cent. vii to the middle of cent. x. He subsequently recapitulates the names as follows :—' Theodorus monacus et abbas Adrianus Aldelmo instituerunt grammaticam artem. Aldhelmus Bedam. Beda Rhabbanum. Rhabbanus Alcuinum. Alcuinus Smaragdum. Smaragdus Theodulphum. Theodulphus Iohannem et Heliam reliquit, sed non imbuit. Elias Heiricum, Heiricus Hucbaldum et Remigium. Remigius Gerlannum episcopum. Gerlannus Guidonem episcopum Autisioderensium'. He notes that a name is missing between 'Beda' and 'Rhabbanus', but he is unaware that 'Rhabbanus' was the pupil, and not the teacher, of Alcuin. The latest edition of Gautbert's account is by Delisle, in *Notices et Extraits*, xxxv (1), 1896, 311 f. Cp. also Traube, *Vorlesungen*, ii 164 f.

[5] *De octo partibus orationis*; Teuffel, § 500, 4 ; Roger, 332–4; Manitius, 203.

[6] Migne, cxxxiii 934 B—C.

wards became abbot (675). Most of his literary labours were
associated with Malmesbury, which continued to be a seat of
learning down to the later Middle Ages. Aldhelm visited Rome
about 692 and was bishop of Sherborne from 705 to his death.
The church that he built at Bradford on Avon is still standing.
In the records of his life we are told that 'he had mastered all the
idioms of the Greek language, and wrote and spoke it, as though
he were a Greek by birth'. 'King Ina had hired the services of
two most skilful teachers of Greek from Athens'[1]; and under
Hadrian[2], abbot of St Augustine's, Canterbury, Ina's kinsman,
Aldhelm, 'made such rapid strides in learning that ere long he
was thought a better scholar than either his Greek or Latin
teachers'[3]. He often introduces Greek words into his Latin letters,
an affectation censured by William of Malmesbury[4]; he alludes to
Aristotle and the Stoics, and employs Greek terms in defining
Greek metres. His dialogue on Latin prosody (which fills forty-
five columns in Migne) is enlivened with a number of ingenious
riddles in verse, which the pupil is expected to solve and to scan.
In writing on Latin metres, he naturally quotes Latin poets, such
as Terence, Virgil, Horace, Juvenal and Persius. His principal
prose work, *De Laudibus Virginitatis*[5], ends with a promise (which
was duly fulfilled) of treating the same theme in verse:—'the
rhetorical foundations being laid and the walls of prose constructed,
he would roof it with dactylic and trochaic tiles'[6]. His Latin prose
is unduly florid[7]. His prose and verse alike are marked by a love

---

[1] Migne, lxxxix 66.

[2] William of Malmesbury, *Gesta Pontificum*, v § 189.

[3] *ib.* 85. His familiarity with Greek and Latin is mentioned by the
'Scottus ignoti nominis' who wants to borrow a book for a fortnight and
offers himself as a pupil:—dum te praestantem ingenio facundiaque Romana
ac vario flore litterarum, etiam Graecorum more, non nesciam, ex ore tuo,
fonte videlicet scientiae purissimo, discere malo, quam ex aliquo (alio ?)
quolibet potare turbulento magistro; Bonif. *Ep.* 4 (Mayor's *Bede*, p. 298).

[4] *Gesta Pontificum*, v § 196, p. 344; Warton's *Eng. Poetry*, *Diss.* II,
p. cxxxv (ed. 1824); Cramer, i 41.

[5] *Facsimile* (with portrait) in *Social England*, i 307[2].

[6] H. Morley's *English Writers*, ii 135.

[7] 'Angli pompatice dicere solent', and 'ex pompa Anglum intelliges', says
William of Malmesbury on Aldhelm, *Gesta Pontificum*, *l.c.* Cp. *Ep. ad
Eahfridum* (after 685), lxxxix 94 Migne,...'Hiberniae rus, discentium opulans

of Greek idioms and of alliteration[1]. His main claim to distinction is that 'he was the first Englishman who cultivated classical learning with any success, and the first of whom any literary remains are preserved'[2].

While Aldhelm has been justly called the father of Anglo-Latin verse, his younger and far more famous con-

Bede

temporary, Bede (673—735), has left his mark in literary history almost exclusively in the field of prose. He spent his whole life in the monastery of Jarrow, dividing his time between the duties of religion and learning[3]. He began his literary work at the age of 30, finding copious materials in the books which had been brought from Rome and elsewhere by his own teachers, Benedict Biscop and Ceolfrid. Even on his death-bed he was working still, and the last hours of his life saw the completion of his translation of St John's Gospel into Anglo-Saxon[4].

In the *Historia Ecclesiastica gentis Anglorum* (731) we have interesting references to the generosity with which Irish professors received English pupils (in 614) and furnished them gratis with books and teaching[5], the diffusion of learning by Theodore and Hadrian and their pupils[6], the studies of the English in Rome[7], and the collection and circulation of books in England[8]. The author appears throughout as a master of the learning of his times, as (in Fuller's phrase) 'the most general scholar of his age'[9]. His

vernansque (ut ita dixerim) pascuosa numerositate lectorum, quemadmodum poli cardines astriferis micantium ornantur vibraminibus siderum'. 'The flowers of his eloquence are reserved for Irish friends or Irish pupils' (Haddan's *Remains*, 267). One of his Irish correspondents was Cellanus, abbot of *Perrona Scottorum* (cp. Traube, *S. Ber. bayr. Akad.* 1900, 469—538). His metrical studies are mentioned in his letter to Hedda, bp of Winchester (676—705), Jaffé iii 32. Cp. Manitius, 134—141.

[1] Ebert, i[2] 622—34; Milman, ii 279 f; Teuffel, § 500, 2; Mayor's *Bede*, p. 201; L. Bonhoff (Dresden, 1894); Traube, *l.c.*, 477—9; Manitius, *S. Ber. Wien. Akad.* cxii 535 f; Roger, 288—301; Bp Browne (1903); Gaskoin's *Alcuin*, 20—23; Ker's *Dark Ages*, 139 f; W. B. Wildman (1905).

[2] Stubbs in *Dict. Chr. Biogr.* Cp. Ozanam, *Civ. Chrét.* p. 493-7.

[3] *H. E.* v 24 (quoted on p. 441).

[4] Cuthbert quoted in Mayor's *Bede*, p. 179, and Fuller, *ib.* 192.

[5] iii 27.　　　　　　　　　　　　　[6] iv 18; v 20.

[7] v 19.　　　　　　　　　　　　　　[8] v 15, 20.

[9] Fuller's *Worthies*, p. 292, ed. 1662.

diction, which is clear, natural and comparatively pure, gives the surest proof of mental discipline won by the study of the ancients and of the chief Fathers of the Church.

Of Benedict Biscop he tells us that, from each of his five visits to Rome, he returned with great store of books[1] and pictures. Bede's chronological works are founded on Jerome's edition of Eusebius, and on Augustine and Isidore. His skill in Latin verse is shown in his elegiacs on queen Etheldrida[2], and in his hexameters on the miracles of St Cuthbert. He also wrote a treatise on metre, with an appendix on the figures of speech used in the Scriptures. Some knowledge of Greek is shown in this treatise and in the references to a Greek MS of the *Acts*[3] which are to be found in his *Liber Retractionum*. The Latin authors most frequently quoted by him are Cicero, Virgil and Horace, and (doubtless at second-hand) Lucilius and Varro. The decline of learning at his death is lamented by William of Malmesbury in the brief tribute paid to his memory :—*sepulta est cum eo gestorum omnis paene notitia usque ad nostra tempora* (cent. xii)· *adeo nullus Anglorum studiorum eius aemulus, nullus gloriarum eius sequax fuit*[4].

It was not until long after the death of Bede that his *Historia Ecclesiastica* became known to his contemporary Boniface, or Winfrid (675—754), who was born two years after the birth of Bede and died twenty years after his death. A native of Crediton, he was educated at Exeter and Nursling. With the sanction of Gregory II (719) he preached

Boniface
and Fulda

---

[1] *Vitae Abbatum*. Of his fourth journey it is stated 'eum innumerabilem librorum omnis generis copiam apportasse'. He also obtained books at Vienne; and his sixth journey (685) was almost entirely devoted to the collection of books, including classical works.

[2] *H. E.* iv 20.

[3] The Bodleian Greek and Latin *codex Laudianus* F 82, according to Berger, in *Notices et Extraits*, xxxv (1) 176. Cp. Roger, 390.

[4] *Gesta Regum*, i 62 (Mayor's *Bede*, 187). On Bede, cp. Teuffel, § 500, 3; and Ebert, i[2] 634—650, translated (with other authorities) in Mayor and Lumby's *Bede*; Manitius, 70—87; Ozanam, *Civ. Chrét.* 498 f; Wattenbach, *GQ*, i[7] 146; Roger, 304—310; Ker's *Dark Ages*, 141–6; and H. Morley's *English Writers*, ii 140—157. The Latin poets known to Aldhelm and Bede are enumerated by Manitius, *S. Ber. d. Wien. Akad.* 1886, 535—634.

in Thuringia and Friesland, converted the Saxons and Hessians, became a bishop in 723 and archbishop of Maintz in 745, resigning that dignity to return to Friesland in 753 and to die a martyr's death in the following year. His devoted follower, Sturmi of Noricum, had already founded a settlement in the woodland solitudes of Hersfeld, and, penetrating still further into the depths of the vast forest of beech-trees, had tracked the stream of the Fulda for nearly 30 miles to the South, until he reached a still more lonely place, where a plot of land extending four miles every way was given to God by the pious Carloman and a notable monastery (that of Fulda) built with the approval of Boniface (744)[1]. Boniface is best known as 'the apostle of Germany'. In literature his works are of slight importance. They include two text-books on metre and on grammar (founded on Donatus, Charisius and Diomedes)[2], a set of acrostic hexameters on the virtues and vices, and some sermons and letters written in an inelegant type of Latin[3]. Among these last we find letters from English abbesses written in the florid style of Aldhelm, in which he is addressed, *amantissime frater*[4], while his own letters are described as *dulcissimae*[5]. One of his relatives, a nun who afterwards presided over the convent of Bischofsheim, sends him with much misgiving a short set of Latin hexameters[6]. He writes to his friends in England for books, and asks a learned abbess to make him a copy of St Peter's Epistles 'in letters of gold'[7]. The only trace of any knowledge of Greek in his letters is to be found in a few Greek words written in Latin characters[8]. His sense of grammatical accuracy is so deeply shocked, when he hears of an ignorant priest administering the rite of baptism *in nomine Patria et Filia et Spiritus sancti*, that he almost doubts the validity of the rite[9]. At the age of 60 he was

---

[1] Bonifacii *Ep.* 79 (751 A.D.) in Jaffé's *Bibl. Rerum Germ.* iii 218; Pertz (ii 368), *Vita Sturmii* (Milman, *Lat. Christ.* ii 304 f).

[2] Bursian, i 15, and in *Bayer. Akad.* 1873, 457 f, and *Jahresb.* i 8.

[3] *Epp.* ed. Dümmler, in *Epp. Merov. et Kar. Aevi*, i 231; *Carmina*, ed. Dümmler, in *Poët. Lat. Aevi Car.* i 1.

[4] *Ep.* 14 Jaffé, in *Bibl. Rerum Germ.* iii.          [5] *Ep.* 16 Jaffé.

[6] *Ep.* 23.                                            [7] *Ep.* 32.

[8] *Apo ton grammaton agiis* (= a litterarum sacris) and *cata psalmistam thesaurizat*, *Ep.* 9.

[9] *Ep.* 58 Jaffé, lxxxix 929 Migne.

still capable of writing elegant hexameters congratulating the Greek Zacharias on his elevation to the papacy[1]. When he died in Friesland, his body was conveyed to the monastery which had been founded under his sanction at Fulda. The monastery adopted the Benedictine Rule, and soon rivalled St Gallen as a school of learning, numbering among its inmates Einhard, the future biographer of Charles the Great, and Rabanus Maurus, the earliest *praeceptor Germaniae*. In 968 it was deemed the most important in all Germany. It has since been converted into a Seminary, while the abbey-church hard by has become a Cathedral; but the bones of the founder still rest in the ancient crypt, and, in the midst of the many towers of the town that has gathered round the monastery, a statue of bronze continues to perpetuate the memory of Boniface[2].

[1] *Ep.* 42 Jaffé, p. 748 Migne.

[2] On Boniface, cp. Ozanam, *Civ. Chrét.* c. v, 170—219, 503–6; Ebert, i[2] 653–9; Teuffel, § 500, 5; Bursian, *Cl. Philol. in Deutschland*, i 14 f; Norden, *Kunstprosa*, 669; Roger, 310—313, 334–6; and on the School of Fulda, Specht, *Unterrichtswesen in Deutschland*, 1885, 296—306.

Cp. also Manitius, 142—152; Bp. G. F. Browne, *Boniface of Crediton and his companions*, with 17 illustrations, 1910.

# CHAPTER XXV.

## FROM ALCUIN (c. 735—804) TO ALFRED (849—900).

In the present chapter we are mainly concerned with the interest taken in the study of the Classics from the age of Charles the Great to that of Alfred. As a scholarly adviser, the Welsh monk Asser was to Alfred what the English deacon Alcuin was to Charles the Great.

Among the pupils of Bede was Egbert, archbishop of York, and among the pupils of Egbert in the cathedral school of that city was Alcuin (c. 735—804), who was probably born in the year of Bede's death. He owed less, however, to the general supervision of archbishop Egbert than to the direct teaching of his master Ælbert, who (in 766) succeeded Egbert as archbishop. More than once his master went abroad in search of new books or new studies[1]; and, on one of these occasions, his pupil accompanied him to Rome. In 778 Alcuin was himself placed at the head of the School and Library of York. We still possess the Latin hexameters, in which he gives us an enthusiastic description of the Library and a list of the authors which it contained[2]. Among prose authors he mentions Jerome, Hilary, Ambrose, Augustine, Athanasius, Orosius; Victorinus and Boëthius; Gregory and Leo; Basil and Chrysostom; Cassiodorus and Fulgentius; Aldhelm and Bede; among earlier writers, in prose or verse, Pompeius (Trogus) and Pliny; Aristotle (doubtless

Alcuin

---

[1] *De Sanctis Euboricae urbis*, 1455. He also sent for the books of certain 'cosmographers' (Jaffé, *Bibl. Rer. Germ.* iii 291).

[2] *De Pont. Eccl. Ebor.* 1535—1603, ci 843 Migne, and in *Poetae Lat. Aevi Car.* i 203 f; well rendered in West's *Alcuin*, p. 34.

in Latin[1]) and Cicero; Virgil, Lucan and Statius; among later poets, Sedulius and Juvencus, and, among grammarians, Donatus and Priscian. His enumeration of all these and other authors shows that, in the last quarter of the eighth century, the Library at York far surpassed any, even in the twelfth century, in England or France, whether at Christ Church, Canterbury, or at St Victor's in Paris, or at Bec in Normandy[2]. Alcuin himself had copied text-books at York in his youth, and scribes were afterwards sent there to copy MSS for his monastery at Tours[3].

Alcuin paid a second visit to Rome in 780; and, on his return in the following year, met Charles the Great at Parma, and was thus led to take part in the revival of learning which marks that monarch's reign[4]. He had already visited the Frankish court at Aachen on his return from Rome, twelve years before, in the year of Charles' accession (768). He was now invited to become the head of a school attached to the court; and, after obtaining the consent of his king and his archbishop, was installed as master of the school in 782, and continued to preside over it for eight years. The school is best regarded as a migratory institution attached to the court, whether at Aachen or elsewhere[5]. Charles was as familiar with colloquial Latin as with his native German; he seems also to have understood Greek, though he spoke it imperfectly[6]. His instruction in Latin and Greek appears to have been derived from an elderly grammarian, Peter of Pisa, while Greek was taught at his court (782–6) by Paulus Diaconus (c. 725—797), a Benedictine monk, who had learnt his Greek at Pavia, and had lived at Beneventum (which was closely connected with the Greeks), and who wrote his celebrated *History of the Lombards* at

---

[1] Possibly the abridgement of the *Categories* bearing the name of Augustine (Hauréau, *Hist. de la Philosophie Scolastique*, i 93–7).

[2] Léon Maître's *Écoles*, pp. 290, 295; Mullinger's *Schools of Charles the Great*, p. 61; Roger, 313—321.

[3] *Ep.* 38.

[4] So completely had the tradition of learning been broken in Gaul that a contemporary states that before his reign 'nullum studium fuerat liberalium artium' (Monachus Engolismensis, ap. Duchesne, ii 76). Cp. Monach. Sangall. i 1 (*Mon. Carolina*, p. 631).

[5] Léon Maître, p. 39.

[6] Einhard's *Vita Caroli*, c. 25.

Monte Cassino, after his final retirement from the world[1]. He shows his knowledge of Greek in his *History*, in his summary of the abridgement of Verrius Flaccus by Pompeius Festus[2], and in his revision of the Homilies which were issued by Charles in 782 with the following memorable pronouncement:—'We impose upon ourselves the task of reviving, with the utmost zeal, the study of letters well-nigh extinguished through the neglect of our ancestors. We charge all our subjects, as far as they may be able, to cultivate the liberal arts, and we set them the example'[3]. The revision of all the church books enjoined in 789 stimulated a high degree of activity in the *scriptoria* of Frankland[4].

After a short absence in England (790–3), Alcuin, who had already been appointed abbot of St Loup near Troyes and of Ferrières near Orleans, was in 796 made abbot of St Martin's at Tours, which he soon restored to a commanding position among the schools of the land. He taught his monks to use the pen instead of the spade and hoe, telling them that copying MSS was better than cultivating the vine[5]. Under his rule the clear and precise hand known as the Caroline Minuscule was developed at Tours[6]; and 'the script, which was accepted as the standard in the imperial schools, served seven centuries later as a model for the first type-founders of Italy and France'[7]. Alcuin sent some of his

---

[1] ed. Waitz, in *Mon. Germ. Hist.* 1878; *Poëmata* and *Epistolae*, ed. Dümmler; cp. F. Dahn (1876); Wattenbach, *GQ*, i[7] 177—186; and Ker's *Dark Ages*, 164—171; also Ebert, ii. 36—56; Teuffel, § 500, 6; Balzani's *Early Chroniclers of Italy*, 66—90; Manitius, 257—272; *Gedichte*, ed. Karl Neff in Traube's *Quellen*, III iv, pp. 231 (1908).

[2] Nettleship, i 202; Teuffel, § 261, 6; p. 200 *supra*.

[3] Pertz, *Leg.* i 44 (Mullinger's *Schools of Charles the Great*, p. 101).

[4] Wattenbach, *Schriftwesen im MA*, 327[3]; E. M. Thompson, *Palaeography*, 233, and in *Comp. to Latin Studies*, Cambridge, 1920, 783.

[5] Fodere quam vites melius est scribere libros (*ad Musaeum*).

[6] Delisle, *Mém. de l'Acad. des Inscr.* (1885), xxxii 29—56, with 5 *facsimiles*; Traube, *S. Ber. bayr. Akad.* 1891, 427 f; E. M. Thompson, *l.c.*, 233 f.

[7] Putnam, *Books and their Makers in the Middle Ages*, i 107 (after Delisle, *l.c.*). Alcuin's direct share in the formation of the script, which became characteristic of Tours, has, however, been disputed by Prof. K. Menzel of Bonn in his contribution to the fine folio volume entitled *Die Trierer Ada-Handschrift* (Leipzig, 1889), 3—5. Prof. Menzel there assigns the credit to Alcuin's successors, (1) Fridugis of York (804–34), and (2) Adelard (834–45), under the former of whom Adalbaldus was active as a skilful copyist (Watten-

monks to England for books[1], and continued in constant correspondence with scholars in the land of his birth and the land of
his adoption. He was himself a scholar and a teacher to the last:
'in the morning of his life' (in the language of one of his letters)
'he had sowed in Britain; and now, in the evening of that life,
he ceased not to sow in France'[2]. He died in 804, four years
after Charles had been crowned Emperor in Rome.

Among Alcuin's prose works a prominent place is here due to
his dialogues on Grammar, Rhetoric, and Dialectic. He is mainly
a grammarian[3]. In his first dialogue *On Grammar*[4], the seven
liberal arts are compared to the seven pillars of the house of
Wisdom[5], and are described as the seven steps by which the
student ascends to the heights of Theology. The substance of his
second dialogue is taken from earlier grammarians, among whom
Donatus and Priscian are mentioned, while the definitions are
borrowed from Isidore. The interlocutors are a well-informed
English youth of fifteen, who answers the inquiries of an eager
Frank who is one year younger, while the master himself presides
over the disputation. Grammar is here somewhat narrowly
defined as the science of written sounds, the guardian of correct
speaking and writing. In the dialogues *On Rhetoric* and *Dialectic*

---

bach, *GQ*, i[7] 187). He also points out that the semi-uncial variety of that
script (*facsimile* in E. M. Thompson's *Palaeography*, 234) hardly survived the
year 900, while the Caroline minuscules lived on (*ib.* 235). The 'Ada MS'
(a celebrated *codex aureus* of the Latin Gospels, prepared by command of
Charles the Great, and presented to the abbey of St Maximin, at Trier, by the
emperor's sister Ada, d. 817? or 823?) is written in exceedingly beautiful
minuscules by two scribes, (A) *c.* 790–9, and (B) *c.* 800–20. The external
and internal splendour of the MS suggests that it was probably prepared in the
imperial city of Aachen itself; and the date of its completion is presumably
after the death of Alcuin (804). On the other hand, the ordinary script of
Alcuin's own time at Tours may be regarded as well represented by a mixed
MS of certain works of Alcuin and Bede, now at Cologne (no. cvi; *facsimile* in
Arndt's *Schrifttafeln*, 37–40). Cp. Traube's *Vorlesungen*, ii (1911), 25 f, and
E. K. Rand and G. Howe, *The Vatican Livy and the Script of Tours*, in
'Mem. of American Academy in Rome', 1917. [1] *Ep.* 38.

[2] *Ep.* 43 (78 Jaffé), c. 209 Migne. [3] Cp. Hauréau, i 126.

[4] Cp. J. Frey, *De Alcuini arte grammatica commentatio* (Münster, 1886);
also Freundgen in *Sammlung Pädagog. Schriften*, Paderborn (1889); Roger,
336—341. [5] *Prov.* ix 1.

the persons concerned are Charles and Alcuin, and the principal
authorities followed in the former are Cicero *De Inventione* and
Julius Victor[1], and, in the latter, Boethius, Isidore and the
Pseudo-Augustinian *Categories*[2]. The importance of *Dialectic* is
also urged in the dedication of the treatise *On the Trinity*, while
the fragment *On the Seven Arts* shows that Cassiodorus was
studied in the age of Alcuin. The tract *On Orthography*
discusses in alphabetical order a number of Latin words which
were apt to be wrongly spelt, and is useful in connexion with the
pronunciation of Latin and the criticism of the texts of the time.
The student is here told to distinguish between *alvus* and *albus*,
*vellus* and *bellus*, *acervus* and *acerbus*; also between *vel* and *fel*,
*quod* and *quot*[3]. It may be noticed with regret, that, in the course
of this tract, the author strangely derives *hippocrita* (*simulator*)
from *hippo* 'falsum' and *chrisis* 'judicium'[4].

His *Life of St Willibrord*, the precursor of Boniface, supplies
evidence as to the flourishing state of learning in Ireland :
Willibrord left Northumbria, *quia in Hibernia scholasticam erudi-
tionem viguisse audivit*[5]. The 1657 hexameters of his patriotic
poem *On the Kings, Bishops and Saints of York* contain many
reminiscences of Virgil and Prudentius. His *Epigrams* consist
partly of inscriptions for various monastic buildings, or for the
beginning or end of MSS. The epigram *ad Musaeum libros
scribentium*[6] includes a couplet of some interest in connexion
with Alcuin's letter urging Charles to require copyists to attend to
matters of punctuation[7]:—

> 'per cola distinguant proprios et commata sensus,
>     et punctos ponant ordine quisque suo'.

Of his 300 *Letters*[8] (all written in France, and five-sixths of them
at Tours, during the last eight years of his life), the most interesting are those addressed to his friends in England or to

---

[1] Halm, *Rhet. Lat. Min.* 521.

[2] Severely criticised by Hauréau, i 26 f ; cp. Prantl, *Logik*, ii 14 f.

[3] Keil, *Gram. Lat.* vii 295 ; Mullinger, 78 f ; Roger, 346–9.

[4] Migne, ci 910 B.          [5] c. 4.

[6] 67.          [7] *Ep.* 112 Jaffé, 101 Migne.

[8] *Alcuiniana* (1873) ; cp. Sickel's *Alcuinstudien* in Vienna Acad. 1875,
461—550.

Charles the Great or to his former pupil Arno, bishop of Salzburg. They are well written, and clear and natural in expression, the best in point of style being those addressed to the king[1]. But the restoration of correct Latinity under Charles the Great, as exemplified in these *Letters*, led to a separation between the Latin of scholars and the Latin of the people; and at the Council of Tours in 812 it was found necessary to require the employment of the popular language for the purposes of religious instruction[2].

Alcuin's Greek quotations are mainly borrowed from Jerome, and his knowledge of the language (illustrated in a letter to Angilbert[3] where he quotes from the LXX version of the Psalms) is obviously very slight[4]. In the School of the Palace Angilbert was known as Homer, another as Macharius[5] and Alcuin himself as Flaccus. He is familiar with Horace. Virgil he had studied with enthusiasm in those early days at York when, in the language of his biographer, he was *Vergilii amplius quam Psalmorum amator*[6]; but, in after-life, when he had become celebrated as a teacher, he is described as saying to his students :—'The sacred poets are sufficient for you, and there is no reason why you should be corrupted by the luxuriance of Virgil's language'[7]. The library at Bern, however, possesses a MS of Virgil in Caroline minuscules (cent. ix), which is believed to be either written in Alcuin's hand or at least transcribed from his own copy[8], and which certainly once belonged to his monastery at Tours[9]; and there is no prejudice against the poet in his own verses to his brethren at York[10] :—

[1] Separately edited by H. Schütze (1879).

[2] Gaston Paris, *Litt. Fr. au MA*, p. 14.

[3] *Ep.* 27 (252 Jaffé).

[4] Alcuin's Greek scholarship (like that of many others) is much exaggerated by Tougard, *L'Hellénisme dans les écrivains du Moyen-Age du vii au xii s.* (1886), p. 23. Cp. Hauck, *Kirchengeschichte*, ii 134 n. 4.

[5] Richbod abbot of Lorsch, archbishop of Trier, 795—804 (Wattenbach, *GQ*, i[7] 308).

[6] *Alcuini vita*, c. 1.

[7] *ib.* c. 10, sufficiunt divini poëtae vobis, nec egetis luxuriosa sermonis Virgilii vos pollui facundia; cp. Maitland's *Dark Ages*, 182[3], Wattenbach, *GQ*, i[7] 190, and Mullinger, 112.

[8] C. G. Müller, *Analecta Bernensia*, iii 23 f (Comparetti, *Virgilio*, i 122).

[9] Chatelain, *Pal. des Cl. Lat.* pl. 67.          [10] 260 f.

    'Moenibus Euboricae habitans tu sacra iuventus,
    fas idcirco, reor, comprendere plectra Maronis,
    somnigeras subito te nunc excire Camenas,
    carminibusque sacris naves implere Fresonum'.

Yet even here, he seems to regard Virgil mainly as a model for sacred verse. Elsewhere he regrets that one of his friends is less familiar with the four Gospels than with the twelve *Aeneades* (*sic*)[1]. But, notwithstanding his 'timid mistrust of pagan learning', 'he loved the temple of the Muses, and was at once their high-priest and their apostle in the days when the worshippers at their shrine were few'[2].

Alcuin has been described in the Benedictine History of the Literature of France[3] as 'the most learned man of his age', while recent writers have credited him with 'ability as an administrator', and with 'a certain largeness of view, in spite of his circumscribed horizon'. He was conscious 'of the continuity of the intellectual life of man', and 'of the perils that beset the transmission of learning from age to age'. 'In every way that lay in his power, he endeavoured to put the fortunes of learning for the times that should succeed him in a position of advantage, safeguarded by an abundance of truthfully transcribed books, sheltered within the Church and defended by the civil power'[4]. The tradition of learning had descended from Benedict Biscop, Bede and Egbert to Alcuin; and the influence of Alcuin, which passed from York to Tours, was transmitted through Rabanus to Fulda and thence to Auxerre and Ferrières, to Old and New Corbie[5], and Reichenau, St Gallen and Rheims, while part of that influence finally reached Paris[6]. Alcuin marks the beginning of the period in the history

---

[1] *Ep.* 34 (*Alcuiniana*, p. 714).

[2] Mullinger, p. 127.         [3] iv 344.

[4] A. F. West, *Alcuin*, 122 f.      [5] p. 490 *infra*.

[6] *ib.* 165, and Monnier, 264—8[2]. On Alcuin's life and works (Migne, c, ci), see Lorenz (1829, E. T. 1837); Monnier (1853; ed. 2, 1864); Hauréau, i[2] 123 f, and *Charlemagne et sa Cour* (1880[5]) 198—224; Werner (1881[2]); Dümmler in *Neues Archiv*, xviii 51—70, and *Alg. D. Biogr.*, also *Poëtae Lat.*, i 160—351 (1881); Jaffé's *Alcuiniana* (1873); Ebert, ii 12—36; Wattenbach, *GQ*, i[7] 186—190; Hauck, *Kirchengeschichte*, ii 119—145; Mullinger (1877), and West (1893); also H. Morley's *English Writers*, ii 158—172; Gaskoin, *Alcuin, his Life and his Work*, 1904; Ker's *Dark Ages*, 151-3; Roger, *Ausone à Alcuin*, 313-8, 321-4, 336—349, 394-9, 440-6; Manitius, 273—88; with the

of European education which is described as the Benedictine
Age, the age extending from the brief revival of learning under
Charles the Great to the rise of the University of Paris (*c.* 1170)[1].

Among the monasteries founded by Charles was that of Lorsch,
E. of the Rhine, near Worms (763); while among those that
witnessed a revival of learning in his time was that founded near
Caudebec, to the W. of Rouen, by St Wandrille (d. 668), a pupil
of Columban. Part of the building is still in use, while the rest
remains beautiful even in its ruins. A school was there established
by the abbot Gervold (d. 806), and a *scriptorium* instituted by a
priest named Harduin, who himself copied the four Gospels
*Romana litera*[2], *i.e.* apparently in uncial characters[3]. In a
fragment of its Chronicle we find many words borrowed from the
Greek such as *scema, onomata, paralisis, tirannidem, anaglificus,*
while *curia* is explained by *bouleuterion* and *turricula* by *pyr-
giscos*[4]. A knowledge of Greek is also shown in the Chronicle of
Freculphus, a pupil of Rabanus Maurus and bishop of Lisieux
(d. 850)[5].

In the age of Charles the study of Greek was incidentally
promoted by intercourse between the West and the East, whether
in the form of diplomacy in general, or in the way of overtures for
the intermarriage of members of the two imperial houses. Thus
there were negociations for a marriage, first between Charles and
the empress Eirene (d. 803), and next between a daughter of the
former and a son of the latter (the ill-fated Constantine VI).
In this second case the daughter, and the priests who were to
accompany her, learnt Greek in view of a project that ended in
nothing[6]. Late in 804 Charles is said to have founded a school
at Osnabrück, where Greek as well as Latin was studied, partly
for the purpose of training envoys capable of speaking Greek at
Constantinople[7]. Hatto, bishop of Basel, gave a Greek name

---

literature there quoted. For the whole of the period between 768 and 1180,
cp. Léon Maître, *Les Écoles Épiscopales et Monastiques* (1866).

[1] Léon Maître, 173; Rashdall's *Universities*, i 26, 293.

[2] *Gesta abb. Fontanell.* c. 16 in Pertz, *Mon.* ii 292.

[3] Wattenbach, *Schriftwesen*, 370[2].            [4] Migne, cv 741 b—c.

[5] Migne, cvi 1128, 1147, 1162 (Tougard, 26); Wattenbach, *GQ*, i[7] 237 f.

[6] Cedrenus, ii 21 Bonn.

[7] Migne, xcviii 894 b. The genuineness of the 'capitular' for the founda-

(*hodoeporicum*) to the narrative of his fruitless journey to Constantinople, and Greek words occur in his writings. The envoys subsequently sent by the emperor of the East greeted the emperor of the West as '*imperatorem* καὶ βασιλέα'. Near the close of his life, Charles is said to have carefully compared the Latin text of the Gospels with the Greek and the Syriac[1].

Among the friends of Alcuin and the advisers of Charles was Theodulfus, who practically succeeded Alcuin as head of the palace school, and in 798 became bishop of Orleans and abbot of Fleury. He is memorable not only as the initiator of free education, but also as an accomplished Latin poet. In one of his poems he mentions his favourite authors; they include the Fathers and Isidore, the 'pagan philosophers' with Prudentius and other Christian poets, the grammarian Donatus and his commentator Pompeius, together with Virgil and Ovid. In reference to these last he favours the mystic or allegorical interpretation of mythology[2]. In another poem he supplies us with the earliest poetic description of the seven liberal arts[3]. Under Louis the Pious he was suspected of disloyalty and imprisoned from 818 to his death in 821. In his prison he composed the famous hymn beginning *Gloria laus et honor tibi*[4], which continued to be sung in France during the procession on Palm Sunday for nine and a half centuries, down to the outbreak of the Revolution[5].

Theodulfus

tion of Osnabrück, quoted by Prantl, Léon Maître, and others, has been disputed by Launoi and Rettberg (Bursian, *Cl. Philol. in Deutschland*, i 28; cp. Cramer, ii 17) and disproved by R. Wilmans, *Kaiserurkunden d. Provinz Westfalen*, p. 368, and by Sickel, *Acta Carol.* ii 428 (Wattenbach, *GQ*, i⁷ 176, n. 3).

[1] Thegan, *De gestis Ludovici*, c. 7; Gidel, *Nouvelles Études*, 157—161. His care in the correction of MSS is lauded by the copyist Winidharius, *Poëtae Car.* i 89, Non passus sentes mendarum serpere libris.

[2] *Carm.* 14, 19, i 543 Dümmler's *Poëtae Lat. Aevi Carol.*, In quorum dictis quamquam sint frivola multa, Plurima sub falso tegmine vera latent.

[3] *Carm.* 46, i 544 Dümmler.

[4] *Carm.* 69, i 558 Dümmler; Moorsom's *Historical Companion*, 'All glory, laud, and honour'.

[5] Ebert, ii 70—84; K. Lersch (Halle, 1880); Hauréau, *Sing. Hist.* 37 f; Wattenbach, *GQ*, i⁷ 170; Ker's *Dark Ages*, 153 f; Manitius, 537-43.

Among the Irish monks who represented learning under
Charles the Great were Clement and Dungal. The
*Acts of Charles*, written by a monk of St Gallen
late in the ninth century, tells us of 'two Scots
from Ireland', who 'lighted with the British merchants on the
coast of Gaul', and cried to the crowd, 'if any man desireth
wisdom, let him come unto us and receive it, for we have it for
sale'[1]. They were soon invited to the court of Charles. One of
them, Clement, partly filled the place of Alcuin as head of the
palace school[2]. The other 'was sent into Italy, to the monastery
of St Austin at Pavia'. In the MSS the name of the second
Irishman is either wrongly given as *Albinus* (*i.e.* Alcuin) or is
left blank. It may here be suggested that the missing name is
obviously that of Dungal. That learned Irishman was asked by
Charles to explain the double eclipse of 810, and his letter in
reply proves his familiarity with Greek and Latin poets, and with
Virgil in particular[3]. Under the emperor's grandson, Lothair
(823), Dungal was placed at the head of the school at Pavia[4].
Another Irish monk, Donatus (*c.* 800—876), who, in his early
wanderings in North Italy, was welcomed in 829 as bishop of
Fiesole, alludes, in the latest prayer of his life, to the 'prophetic'
lines in the *Fourth Eclogue*, and tells us in his own epitaph that
he had 'dictated to his pupils exercises in Grammar, and schemes
of metre, and Lives of Saints'[5].

*Clement, Dungal, Donatus*

The life of Charles the Great was written in admirable Latin
by Einhard (*c.* 770—840), a layman educated at
Fulda, who, from about 795, did good service at the
court of Aachen as architect as well as diplomatist. He had an
excellent library, and was a diligent student of the ancient Classics.
After the death of Charles in 814 he withdrew from the court and
built two churches in the Odenwald, living at the place afterwards

*Einhard*

---

[1] Pertz, *Mon.* ii 731; *Mon. Carolina*, 631; Ebert, iii 214 f; Ker's *Dark Ages*, 175.

[2] Mullinger, 121 f.　　　　[3] Migne, cv 447—458; *Mon. Carolina*, 396.

[4] pp. 453, 462 *supra*. The possible identity of Dungal of Pavia with the recluse of St Denis (810) is admitted by Traube, *Abhandl. bayr. Akad.* 1891, 332 f (also published separately as *O Roma nobilis*).

[5] *Poëtae Lat. Aevi Car.* iii 692 Traube; M. Stokes, *Six Months in the Apennines*, 206, 247 f.

known as Seligenstadt from 830 till his death ten years later[1]. His *Life of Charles*[2], which was finished shortly after his hero's death, has been justly described as a 'classic monument of historic genius'[3], as 'one of the most precious bequests of the early Middle Ages'[4], as the 'ripest fruit of that revival of humane and secular learning, which had been brought about by Charles himself'[5]. In comparison with the ancient Romans, its author describes himself as a *homo barbarus*, and all the tribes between the Rhine and Weser, the Baltic and the Danube, as 'barbarians'. But it marks the highest point attained in the classical studies of the Caroline age. To Einhard Charles is a new Augustus, and the culmination of his hero's connexion with old Rome is his coronation in Rome itself (800). Einhard's model in Latin style is the *Life of Augustus* by Suetonius[6], and he also gives proof of a careful study of Caesar and Livy. 'His book has a modern character, because it has learned the ancient rules of construction'[7]. In his preface he quotes the *Tusculan Disputations*, and he also imitates the rhetorical works of Cicero and certain of his speeches,— the *Second Verrine*, the *First Catilinarian*, and the *Pro Milone*[8]. It was probably owing to the architectural tastes of Einhard that the work of Vitruvius became first known in Germany and was preserved for other lands and later ages. The oldest extant MS, the Harleian, once belonged to Goderamnus of Cologne, abbot of Hildesheim (1022–30); but it is little later than Einhard. Einhard writes to a student at Fulda, asking him to make inquiries as to

---

[1] Wattenbach, *GQ*, i[7] 198—206.

[2] Jaffé-Wattenbach, *Einharti Vita Caroli Magni*, 1876[2]; E.T. by W. Glaisher.

[3] Mullinger, 126.

[4] Hodgkin, *Charles the Great*, 222.

[5] Ebert, ii 94; cp. Wattenbach, *GQ*, i[7] 198—209.

[6] See parallel passages in Preface and notes to cc. 18—27 in Jaffé-Wattenbach's ed.; also F. Schmidt (Bayreuth, 1880), and (on his other models) Manitius in *Neues Archiv*, vii 517—68. 'He is really more classical than his model (Suetonius), because he puts more thought into his work and is more seriously interested in his subject....Out of the common accessible culture of the time, the learning and scholarship, he selects those elements and learns those principles which are suitable for his own genius—like every other scholar in any other age' (Ker's *Dark Ages*, 172–3).

[7] Ker's *Dark Ages*, 172.          [8] Manitius, *l.c.*, 565 f; *Lat. lit.* 639–46.

the meaning of certain technical terms in Vitruvius[1]. The copy
of that author formerly preserved at Fulda appears to have been
subsequently sent to Reichenau[2].

Except in the case of Einhard, the revival of learning promoted by Charles the Great, with the aid of Alcuin, was mainly
concerned with sacred literature, and it was of no long duration[3].
After the death of Charles literary interests soon began to decline
under his feeble son, Louis the Pious (d. 840), though Louis
himself (like his father) 'knew Latin and understood Greek'[4].
His early conquest of Barcelona (801), and his alliances with the
Bretons (818) and the Danish king Harold (826), were sung in
6000 elegiac verses by a student of Virgil, Ovid, Lucan, and
Horace, the monk of Aquitaine, Ermoldus Nigellus[5]. Thegan,
the high-born bishop, who wrote the *Life of Louis*, declares that
a poet would need the united powers of Homer, Virgil and Ovid
to describe the guilt of the low-born bishops who opposed their
emperor (833)[6]. In 829 the prelates of Gaul were compelled to
urge him to 'cause public schools to be established in at least
three fitting places' of his realm, in accordance with the canon of
826 enjoining the appointment of 'masters and doctors to teach
the study of letters and of the liberal arts'[7]. During his reign the
school of the monastery at Tours lost its recent importance, while
the school of the palace was under the Irish monk, Clement, who
compiled a grammar for the son of Louis, the future emperor
Lothair (d. 855)[8]. Charles the Bald, the son of Louis the Pious
by his second wife, the accomplished Judith, was king of France
in 840—877 and emperor of the West for the last two years of his
life. At the head of his school he placed the foremost philosopher
of the early Middle Ages, John the Scot (to whom we shall return
in the sequel), and he is praised for inviting teachers of philosophy
not only from Ireland but also from Greece[9].

[1] *Ep.* 56 Jaffé.        [2] Vitruvius, ed. Müller-Strübing, p. iii f.

[3] Bartoli, *I Precursori del Rinascimento* (1876), 10—16.

[4] Thegan, *Vita Ludov.* 19.

[5] Pertz, *Mon.* ii 464 f; *Poëtae Lat. Aevi Car.* ii 1—93 ; Ebert, ii 170–8 ;
Wattenbach, *GQ*, i[7] 228 ; Ker's *Dark Ages*, 155–8 ; Manitius, 552–7.

[6] *Vita Ludov.* 44 (Milman, iii 141) ; Wattenbach, 229.

[7] R. L. Poole's *Medieval Thought*, 24 f.

[8] Wattenbach, 253.        [9] Eric, p. 496 *infra*.

The ancient and important school of Fulda, which had been founded under the sanction of Boniface[1], was the scene of the learned labours of the most proficient of the pupils of Alcuin. Hraban or Rabanus, born at Mainz in 776, was educated at Fulda, and (after 801) at Tours under Alcuin, who gave him the name of Maurus, the favourite pupil of Benedict. Rabanus himself became a teacher at Fulda, where he treasured the notes he had taken of Alcuin's lectures at Tours[2]. He continued to teach as abbot in 822, among his pupils being Servatus Lupus and Walafrid Strabo. At Fulda he founded the Library, and part of his teacher Alcuin's epigram *ad Musaeum* was inscribed over the door of the *Scriptorium*[3]. In 842 he retired to a lonely hill a few miles from Fulda, and there composed his encyclopaedic work *De Universo*. He became archbishop of Mainz in 847 and died in 856[4].

Apart from extensive biblical commentaries, he wrote several educational works. In one of these he was the first to introduce Priscian into the schools of Germany. He also wrote a short treatise on alphabets and abbreviations; and a chronological work founded on Boëthius, Isidore and Bede. His treatise on clerical education ends with a few chapters on pagan learning, which he describes as helpful towards the understanding of the Scriptures[5]. He also reviews the liberal arts, especially Grammar, which he defines as the 'science of interpreting the poets and historians; and the art of correct writing and speaking'[6], thus recognising the *literary* side of Grammar more strongly than Alcuin. Dialectic[7] and the other arts are to be carefully studied for ecclesiastical purposes. The former is the 'disciplina disciplinarum; haec docet docere, haec docet discere'[8]. Rabanus recognises that the writings of the Platonists in particular contain many useful moral precepts, and

---

[1] p. 469 *supra*.

[2] Ne vaga mens perdat cuncta dedi foliis; | hinc quoque nunc constant glossae parvique libelli. Migne, cxii 1600.

[3] Wattenbach, *Schriftwesen*, 432[3]. On the library cp. Dümmler, *Ostfränk. Reich*, ii 652, n. 13.

[4] Wattenbach, *GQ*, i[7] 256—261; Hauck, *Kirchengeschichte*, ii 555 f.

[5] *De Cleric. Inst.* iii c. 16 f.

[6] c. 18; cp. Freundgen, in *Sammlung Pädagog. Schriften*, Paderborn, 1889.

[7] c. 20.                        [8] c. 26.

much that is true on the worship of the one God. A large part of
this work is compiled from Augustine and Cassiodorus, and from
Gregory's *Cura Pastoralis*. His vast encyclopaedia *De Universo*
is practically a theological edition of Isidore. His latest work,
*De Anima*, founded on Cassiodorus, is strangely followed by a few
chapters on the military discipline of the Romans, copied from
Vegetius for the benefit of Lothair II. Certain glosses on Aristotle
and Porphyry implying an adherence to Nominalism are accepted
by their discoverer, Cousin, as the work of Rabanus, though they
are attributed by others[1] to one of his pupils. Rabanus has the
reputation of knowing Greek, and in his writings we have passages
assuming some slight knowledge of that language. Thus, in discussing the derivation and meaning of *syllaba*, after quoting
Priscian, he has recourse to Greek :—' *nam syllaba dicta est ἀπὸ
τοῦ συλλαμβάνειν τὰ γράμματα* '[2]. He appears to have no direct
knowledge of Homer, although he mentions the *Iliad* and *Odyssey*,
as well as the *Aeneid*, as examples of a mixed kind of poetry
(*coenon* vel *micton*)[3]. He is said to have held that Latin was
derived from Greek, and that a knowledge of Greek was an aid to
the more accurate knowledge of Latin[4]. At Fulda twelve monks
were regularly employed as copyists, and down to the seventeenth
century there was a large collection of MSS, most of which were
unfortunately scattered during the Thirty Years' War. The
library of the Westphalian monastery of Corvey (founded 822) is
mentioned in the ninth century, and learning also flourished at
Regensburg (652) on the Danube, and at Reichenau (724) on an
island of the Untersee, W. of the Lake of Constance[5].

[1] Prantl and Kaulich (Seth, in *Enc. Brit.* xxi 420 *b*).

[2] *Op.* i 29 ; Migne, cxi 617 ; from Isidore, *Etym.* i 16, 1.

[3] i 203 ; Migne, cxi 420 ; from Suetonius, *De Poëtis* (p. 5 Reifferscheid),
ap. Diomedem, lib. iii 482 Keil. In cvii 408 *quidam eloquens* is his authority
for a passage nearly identical with Cic. *Orator*, § 69 ; this quotation (which I
have not seen noticed elsewhere) must have ultimately come from a writer who
had a complete MS of the *Orator*. The *codices mutili* begin with § 91.

[4] Trithemius (Migne, cvii 84 B), ap. Cramer, ii 23. Cp. Köhler's *Hrabanus
Maurus*, 13 f. On Rabanus, cp. Ebert, ii 120 ; Mullinger's *Schools*, 138—151 ;
West's *Alcuin*, 124—164 ; and Ker's *Dark Ages*, 160 ; *Opera* in Migne,
cvii—cxii. Cp. also Manitius, 288—302.

[5] Ziegelbauer, *Hist. Litt. Ord. S. Ben.* i 487, 569, ap. Heeren, *Cl. Litt.
im MA*, i 162 f.

The most important pupil of Rabanus was Walafrid Strabo
(*c.* 809—849).   Unlike his master, he had a genuine
gift for poetry ; he studied Christian and pagan   Walafrid<br>Strabo
poets, and wrote on sacred as well as secular
themes.   Of his sacred poems the most striking is that on the
*Visions* of Wettin, an early precursor of Dante's *Divina Commedia*.
His two great secular poems are (1) *On the statue of Theodoric*,
and (2) his *Hortulus*, a description of the plants in the monastic
garden of Reichenau, which was widely read during the Middle
Ages and the Renaissance.   Its charm and freshness are not im-
paired by frequent reminiscences of Virgil and Ovid, or by a few
quotations from Serenus Sammonicus[1].   In his other poems his
principal model is Prudentius.   He is also the author of the
original form of the *Glossa Ordinaria* (subsequently revised by
Gilbert de la Porrée and Anselm of Laon), which occupies the top
and side margins of MSS of the Vulgate.   He brought out a new
edition of the *Life of Gallus* and of Einhard's *Life of Charles the
Great*.   His only independent work in prose was connected with
Ecclesiastical History, being written at the request of the librarian
of his monastery.   He died in the prime of life (849), being
accidentally drowned in crossing the Loire.   He was certainly a
man of singular literary versatility ; and his influence, as tutor to
Charles the Bald and as abbot of Reichenau, was always healthy
and bore lasting fruit[2].

A remarkable picture of the varied learning of the time is
presented by a letter written (*c.* 850) by a pupil of
Walafrid, Ermenrich of Ellwangen[3], to Grimold,   Ermenrich<br>of Ellwangen
abbot of Weissenburg and St Gallen.

After discussing the difference between the mind and the soul, he passes
on to points of Grammar, dealing particularly with accent, quantity and
pronunciation, and naming as authorities, not only Alcuin and Bede, Priscian
and Donatus, but also Consentius, Sextus Pompeius and Servius.   He next

[1] See Dümmler's notes on pp. 335—350.   In l. 106, *Aut arbustivum vitis
genus* comes from Columella, *De Arbor.* 4.

[2] Migne, cxiii—cxiv ; poems in *Poëtae Lat. Aevi Car.* ii 259—423 Dümmler ;
Ebert, ii 145—166 ; Wattenbach, *GQ*, i[7] 277—280 ; Hauck, ii 661 ; Specht,
310 ; Ker's *Dark Ages*, 159 ; Manitius, 302—314.

[3] Edited (from a MS at St Gallen) by Dümmler (1873) ; cp. Bursian in
*Jahresb.* i 10 f ; Wattenbach, 281 f ; Manitius, 497 f.

introduces a specimen of the allegorical interpretation of Scripture, with a digression on the nature of the soul. With the aid of Virgil and his commentators, he adds some remarks on pagan mythology, incidentally expressing his contempt for the pagan poets, whose works he condescends to regard as of the nature of manure, useful for fertilising the fields of sacred literature. He knows that Virgil has imitated Theocritus in the *Eclogues*, Hesiod in the *Georgics* and Homer in the *Aeneid*, but his knowledge of these facts is clearly due to Servius alone[1]. He refers in conclusion to the monastery of St Gallen, adding a specimen of his proposed poetic life of the founder, with some sets of verses in praise of his own preceptor, and on the sacred theme of the Trinity.

In the course of this letter he quotes Lucretius[2], Virgil and Servius, Ovid, Prudentius, Juvencus, Arator, the Latin Homer, the epitaph on the son of Cato the Censor, the *Mosella* of Ausonius, Priscian's translation of Dionysius Periegetes, and lastly Pliny, Boëthius and Fulgentius[3]. The letter also displays some slight knowledge of Greek vocabulary (as well as ignorance of Greek Accidence and Prosody) by the introduction of isolated words or single lines, sometimes in Greek and Latin combined. But, as a whole, it is a specimen of superficial learning rather than of true taste. The writer's erudition was, however, recognised by his being made bishop of Passau in 865, nine years before his death[4].

A far more agreeable picture is presented to us in the 130 *Letters* of Servatus Lupus, born of a noble family in the diocese of Sens, educated at Ferrières and at Fulda, and abbot of the former from 842 to his death, little more than twenty years later. At Fulda he had not only been educated for six years under Rabanus, the most learned theologian of the day, but had also obtained literary advice and instruction from Einhard, the ablest scholar of the time. While Alcuin, the instructor of Rabanus, was exceedingly narrow in his literary interests, Lupus, the pupil of Rabanus, has a far wider range. In his literary spirit he is a precursor of the humanists of the Renaissance. To one of his correspondents he expresses his regret that the pursuits of literature are almost obsolete[5]; to another, his delight at their revival in his own neighbourhood[6].

*Servatus Lupus*

---

[1] p. 232 *supra*.　　　　　　　　[2] i 150–6.

[3] Gottlieb, *Bibliotheken*, p. 441.　　　　[4] Ebert, ii 179—184.

[5] 34, nunc litterarum studiis paene obsoletis.

[6] 35, reviviscentem in his nostris regionibus sapientiam.

In writing to Einhard he confesses that a love of letters had been implanted in him almost from his very boyhood, and contrasts the revival of letters in Einhard's own time, under Charles the Great, with their decline in the days when 'men scarcely tolerate any who attempt to acquire knowledge'[1]. He is himself an eager borrower, and a wary lender, of books. He asks one of his relations to send a capable monk to Fulda and borrow from the abbot a copy of Suetonius 'in two moderate-sized volumes, which he can either bring himself, or send by a trusty messenger'[2]. He begs the archbishop of Tours to send him a copy of the commentary of Boëthius on the *Topica* of Cicero[3]. He writes to the abbot of York to ask for the loan of the Questions on the Old and New Testaments ascribed to St Jerome by Cassiodorus, also those of Bede, the seventh and following books of St Jerome on Jeremiah, and the twelve books of the *Institutions* of Quintilian[4]. Not content with borrowing from Fleury in his own neighbourhood and from other monasteries in France, and from Fulda and York, he even writes to Rome. Thus he applies to pope Benedict III (855–8) for the above books of St Jerome, and for certain MSS of Cicero *de Oratore*, and of Quintilian, which he had seen in Rome (849), the latter being 'in a single volume of moderate size'. He adds that his monastery already possessed parts of the last two works, and concludes by begging for the loan of the commentary on Terence by Donatus[5]. He is himself so cautious about lending a MS which is in constant demand, that he has almost resolved on despatching it to some place of security for fear of losing it altogether[6]. In the same letter he answers a number of minor questions on points of spelling and prosody by appealing to the grammarian Caper, and by quoting thrice from Virgil, twice from Martial, and once from Prudentius, Alcuin and Theodulfus. He lends the bishop of Auxerre St Jerome's commentary on the Prophets before he has had time to read it himself, and (doubtless in answer to some inquiry) informs him that Caesar had not really written a *History of Rome*, but only the *Commentaries on the Gallic War*, of which the bishop had doubtless heard, and a copy of which would be

[1] *Ep.* 1.   [2] 91.   [3] 16.
[4] 62.   [5] 103.   [6] 20.

sent as soon as possible, adding that the continuation was the work of Caesar's secretary, Hirtius[1]. With a view to correcting his own texts, he borrows extra copies of works already in his possession. He thanks a friend for revising his copy of Macrobius and for sending a MS of the commentary of Boëthius; he inquires about a MS of Cicero's *Tusculan Disputations*, and, in the same letter, answers questions on prosody by quoting Virgil and Juvencus as well as Servius and Priscian[2]. He informs a monk of the Benedictine monastery at Prüm that he intends to compare his own copy of Cicero's *Letters* with the text which he has just received, and thus arrive at the truth; he also asks for his friend's copy of Cicero's translation of Aratus, with a view to filling up some *lacunae* in his own[3]. He declines to send a MS to a monk at Sens, because his messenger will be exposed to the perils of a journey on foot[4]. He cannot lend Hincmar the *Collectaneum* of Bede on the Epistles of St Paul, because 'the book is too large to be concealed in the vest or the wallet, and, even if either were possible, it might be a prey to robbers tempted by the beauty of the MS'[5]. He is prevented from sending Gellius to Einhard because the abbot has once more kept it in his own possession[6]. He is interested in obtaining, through Einhard, carefully copied specimens of uncial characters[7]; and it may be remembered that it was in this age that Charles the Bald caused a MS of the Gospels to be copied in letters of gold for the abbey of St Denis[8], with the donor's portrait as frontispiece, and that he received a MS of

[1] 37.  [2] 8.  [3] 69.
[4] 20.  [5] 76.  [6] 5.

[7] 5 (cxix 448 C, Migne), 'scriptor regius Bertcaudus dicitur antiquarum litterarum, duntaxat earum quae maximae sunt, et *unciales* a quibusdam vocari existimantur, habere mensuram descriptam. Itaque, si penes vos est, mittite mihi eam per hunc, quaeso, pictorem, cum redierit, schedula tamen diligentissime sigillo munita'. *Unciales* is doubtless a reminiscence of St Jerome's Preface to Job: 'uncialibus (ut vulgo aiunt) litteris' (F. Madan in *Cl. Rev.* xviii (1904) 48). Cp. *Commentarium Einsiedlense*, attributed by Traube (*S. Ber.* Munich, 1900, 533–5) to Remigius, *the pupil of Servatus Lupus*, 'quaedam enim (litterae) *unciales* dicuntur, quae et maximae sunt et in initiis librorum scribuntur' (Hagen's *Anecd. Helv.* 221 f).

[8] *Hist. Litt. de la France*, iv 282 f. S. Berger (*Hist. de la Vulgate*, 277) ascribes the 'chrysograph' MSS to the Palace School.

the Bible in Caroline minuscules[1] from the abbot of Tours, where
that hand had been formed under the rule of Alcuin.

His attitude towards the Classics may be partly illustrated by
a letter in which he good-humouredly describes a presbyter of
Mainz, named Probus, as charitably including Cicero and Virgil
(whose works he is copying) in the number of the elect[2]. His own
literary tastes are more clearly shown in his first letter to Einhard,
where, after saying that, in his judgement, 'learning should be
sought for its own sake'[3], he adds that he had found the authors
of the day far removed from the dignity of the Ciceronian style
emulated by the foremost of the Latin Fathers, until at last he
lighted on Einhard's admirably written *Life of Charles the Great*[4].
A wide knowledge of Latin literature is displayed in his frequent references to Latin authors. Among historians, we find Livy[5], Sallust,
Caesar, Suetonius, Justin and Valerius Maximus[6]; in rhetoric,
Cicero and Quintilian; among poets, Terence, Virgil, Horace
and Martial; and, among grammarians, Caper, Gellius, Donatus,
Servius, Macrobius and Priscian. He describes a knowledge of
German as 'most necessary at the present day'[7]; at the same
time, he protests against the rumour that he had himself gone to
Fulda to learn that language; it would not have been 'worth his
while to go so far for such a purpose'; he had really spent his
time there in copying MSS, *ad oblivionis remedium et eruditionis
augmentum*[8]. There is hardly any sign that he knew Greek. He
consults Einhard about certain Greek words in Servius[9]; and,
when he is himself consulted on similar points by Gotteschalk, he
hints that the niceties of the language are best ascertained from
the Greeks themselves[10]. He states that *blasphemus* is obviously a
Greek word, because of the collocation of *p* and *h*, and he proves

---

[1] Specimen in Lecoy de la Marche, *Les Manuscrits* (Quantin), p. 69. It
was written (*c.* 845–50) by a monk of Marmoutier. Cp. p. 473 *supra*.

[2] 20 *ad finem*.                    [3] Quoted on p. 441.

[4] p. 434 A.

[5] 34, illud quod sequitur tangere nolui donec in Livio vigilantius inda-
garem.

[6] Cp. Traube in *Abhandl. bayer. Akad.* xix (2) 370 f, and *S. Ber.* 1891,
p. 402 f; Schnetz, *Ein Kritiker des Val. Max.* im 9 Jahrhundert, 1901.

[7] 70.                                [8] 6.

[9] 5 *ad fin*.                        [10] 30 *ad fin*.

from Prudentius that the second syllable is long, but he adds that
he is informed by a Greek that, 'among the Greeks' (who in this
case clearly allowed the accent to supersede the quantity), 'it was
always pronounced short',—an opinion shared by Einhard[1]. Even
in his treatise on the tenets of the Latin Fathers, written in answer
to an inquiry from Charles the Bald[2], he cannot refrain from
quoting Cicero and Virgil[3].

The importance of the age of Servatus Lupus, in regard to the
preservation and transmission of MSS, may be inferred from the
large number of MSS of the ninth century and the first half of the
tenth, which are recorded as having belonged to the monastic
libraries of France[4]. It was also about this time that classical MSS
first found their way into Germany, the writers of the golden age
being scantily represented by Virgil, Lucan, Livy and portions
of Cicero, while later authors were more frequent, especially
Macrobius, Martianus Capella and Isidore.

While the monastery of Ferrières, near Sens and the Upper
Seine, was the home of Lupus, that of Corbie on
the Somme, near Amiens, is similarly associated
with his contemporary Radbertus, who also bears
the name of Paschasius (c. 790—865). He joined in founding
the New Corbie in Westphalia (822)[5]. His familiarity with Latin
literature is shown by the passages which he tacitly borrows from
Cicero, Seneca, Virgil and Horace, and there is some slight
evidence that he was acquainted with Greek[6].

**Paschasius Radbertus**

In the reign of Charles the Bald (840—877), whom Lupus
describes as 'doctrinae studiosissimus'[7], there is a certain revival

---

[1] 20 p. 467 C—D.                    [2] 128.

[3] Migne, cxix 633. For the *Letters* see Migne, cxix 431—610, and cp.
Nicholas, *Étude* (1861); De la Rochéterie, in *Mémoires* i (1865-72) 369—466
of the *Acad. de Sainte Croix d'Orléans*; Mullinger's *Schools of Charles the
Great* (1877) c. 4; Sprotte's *Biographie* (1880); and ed. by Du Dezert (Paris,
1888); also Ebert, ii 203—9; Manitius in *Rhein. Mus.* (1893) 313—320; and
Norden's *Kunstprosa*, 699 f. Cp. Manitius, 483—490.

[4] Norden, 704 f.

[5] Corvey, founded by Louis the Pious; Wattenbach, *GQ*, i[7] 301 n. 1.

[6] Migne, cxx; Tougard, *L'Hellénisme*, p. 30; Ebert, ii 230 f. His four
poems (including an 'egloga') are printed in *Poëtae Lat. Aevi Car.* iii 45—53
Traube.                    [7] *Ep.* 119.

of interest in literature, but it resembles the final flicker of an
expiring flame rather than 'a light that rises to the stars'. This
last is the flattering phrase used by Eric of Auxerre (d. *c.* 877) in
a letter addressed to the king. He even describes Greece as
lamenting the loss of those of her sons whom the liberality of the
king has attracted to Gaul, and nearly all Ireland, with the band
of her philosophers, as disdaining the perils of the sea and
embracing a voluntary exile in answer to the summons of one
who was a Solomon in wisdom[1].

The chief representative of Ireland and philosophy at the
court of Charles the Bald was Joannes Scotus, or
John the Scot[2] (*c.* 810–5—*c.* 875), who, from about
845, was the head of the palace school and thus
took part in a temporary revival of learning. In his person the
Greek Scholarship of Ireland found a welcome in France in the
days when England was being overrun by the Danes. His
favourite manual was Martianus Capella. He was also familiar
with the Greek Fathers, such as Basil, Chrysostom and Gregory
Nazianzen (whom he oddly identifies with his namesake of
Nyssa), he had a special admiration for Origen[3], and he borrowed
largely from Maximus Confessor (d. 662)[4]. In the phrase of
William of Malmesbury, his mental vision was 'concentrated on
Greece'[5]. While his Latin style is recognised as correct and
even elegant, he is fully conscious of the inadequacy of his
Greek scholarship. He is familiar with Plato's *Timaeus*[6], and it
has been supposed[7] that he knew the original text; at any rate,

Joannes
Scotus
(Erigena)

---

[1] Migne, cxxiv 1133.

[2] Known to his contemporaries as *Joannes Scotus, Scottus,* or *Scotigena*;
and called by himself, in his translation of 'Dionysius', *Joannes Ierugena*
(changed in later MSS into *Erugena* and *Eriugena*). *Erigena* appears later
still, and *Joannes Scotus Erigena* not earlier than cent. xvi (Christlieb, 15 f,
ap. R. L. Poole's *Medieval Thought*, 55; and Traube in *Poëtae Lat. Aevi
Car.* iii 518).

[3] Cp. Baur's *Lehre von der Dreieinigkeit*, ii 263—344 (Poole, 60).

[4] J. Dräseke, *Scotus Erigena u. dessen Gewährsmänner*, Leipzig 1902,
and in *Z. f. wiss. Theol.* xlvi (1903) 563—580.

[5] *Gesta Regum Angl.* ii § 122, in Graecos acriter oculos intendit.

[6] In *De Div. Nat.* i 31 he quotes in Latin 30 D f. In iii 27 he refers to the
planets, 'quae semper circulos suos circa solem peragunt, sicut Plato in Timaeo
edocet'.                              [7] Hauréau, i[2] 152.

his Latin quotations from the *Timaeus* are independent of the translation by Chalcidius. His general familiarity with Greek is fully proved by the fact that he was chosen to execute a Latin translation of 'Dionysius the Areopagite'. Certain works of 'Dionysius' had been sent by pope Paul I to Pepin-le-Bref between 758 and 763[1], and a splendid MS of his mystical writings had subsequently been presented to Louis the Pious by the Byzantine emperor, Michael the Stammerer (827). The author was regarded as the patron-saint of France, and Hilduin, the abbot of St Denis, had in vain attempted to produce a satisfactory version. Thus it fell to the lot of an Irishman of the West to introduce the works of a Greek mystic of the East to the knowledge of a Franco-Roman king. The faithful and literal rendering executed by Joannes Scotus was regarded as an interpretation which itself needed an interpreter. Such was the opinion of the papal librarian, Anastasius, who had himself learned Greek at Constantinople, and wondered how 'this barbarian living on the confines of the world, who might have been deemed to be as ignorant of Greek as he was remote from civilisation, could have proved capable of comprehending such mysteries and translating them into another tongue'[2]. The influence of 'Dionysius' is apparent in many parts of the great work of Joannes Scotus, *De Divisione Naturae*, and particularly in the last book, with its doctrine of the final absorption of the perfected soul into the Divine Nature[3], where, by a fusion of Neo-Platonism and Christianity, he forms a 'theory of the Eternal Word as containing in Himself the exemplars of created things', a theory implying the formula *universalia ante rem*. Another important work, his *Liber de Praedestinatione*, was written at the request of Hincmar, archbishop of Rheims, and a man of some pretensions to a knowledge of Greek[4], in criticism of the Augustinian doctrine as stated by Gotteschalk (840). In his

[1] *Codex Carolinus*, 24 ; Roger, 431 f.

[2] Migne, cxxii 93 C—D. The date of the translation is 858-60. The original was found in France and not brought from Ireland ; and the same is true of his later translation of Maximus on Greg. Naz.

[3] Abstract in R. L. Poole, 60—73.

[4] Migne, cxxv 538 A—B. Cp. Carl von Noorden's *Hinkmar* (1863); Schroers (1884); Traube, in *Poëtae Lat. Aevi Car.* iii 406–20, and Munich *Abhandl.* xix 2 (1891), 362 f (Hincmar's Irish colony at Laon).

reply (851) he constantly resorts to the aid of Dialectic. He also anticipates the doctrine of the Schoolmen by insisting that true philosophy and true religion are identical with one another[1]. He describes the course of his argument as passing through the four stages of 'division, definition, demonstration and analysis', adding the Greek name of each[2]. When the Latin Fathers fail him, he appeals to the Greek, and, when the Fathers desert him, he takes refuge in the philosophers. The mistakes of his opponents he compassionately describes as mainly due to their ignorance of the Greek language. His treatise was opposed by theologians at Lyons and Fulda, and by Prudentius, bishop of Troyes, who traces in its pages 'the folly of Origen' and the trickery of an unsanctified sophistry, and meets his opponent's 'assumption of superiority on the ground of his classical learning' by appealing to Jerome's abjuration of Cicero. Jerome had maintained that the Scriptures should be understood in their simplicity instead of serving as a battle-ground of the rhetoricians; while Joannes Scotus had dragged his readers back to Greek sources for all that he had failed to find in Latin. Lastly, Prudentius attacks the work of Martianus Capella, which was deemed to have been mainly responsible for leading the author into this labyrinth of error, and tempting him to prefer the teaching of Varro, which was supported by that of Capella, although it had been refuted by St Augustine. The close attention paid to Capella by Joannes Scotus is further exemplified by the Commentary discovered by Hauréau among the MSS of the ninth century which once belonged to the great Benedictine monastery of Saint-Germain-des-Prés[3].

The controversy between Joannes Scotus and his opponents

---

[1] *De Div. Naturae*, i 1; Hauréau, i[2] 153 n. 1.

[2] *De Praedestinatione*, i 1 (Migne, cxxii 358 A), (μέθοδος) διαιρετική, ὁριστική, ἀποδεικτική and ἀναλυτική. Cp. Ammonius, *in Porphyrii Isagogen*, p. 34, 24 ed. Busse (1891), quoted by me in *Hermathena*, xxix 431, and David the Armenian's *Prolegomena* to Porphyry's *Isagoge*: εἰσὶ δὲ τέσσαρες αἱ διαλεκτικαὶ μέθοδοι· εἰσὶ γὰρ διαιρετική, ὁριστική, ἀποδεικτική, ἀναλυτική (J. A. Cramer's *Anecd. Paris.* iv 442); also Fr. Cramer, *De Gr. Medii Aevi Studiis*, ii 34 n. 156.

[3] *Notices et Extraits*, xx (2) pp. 1 f (Hauréau, i 152). Cp. R. L. Poole, 76, n. 25, and E. K. Rand, *Johannes Scottus*, 11, 81.

may well be regarded as a turning-point in the history of mediaeval scholarship[1]. The mechanical tradition handed down by Bede and Alcuin is now superseded by a spirit of inquiry and discussion, and the claims of reason, as contrasted with those of authority, are eagerly maintained[2].

It is probable that Joannes Scotus remained in Frankland, even after the death of Charles the Bald (877)[3]. An English tradition makes him end his days at Malmesbury, where he is said to have been stabbed to death by the pens of his pupils[4], and where the traveller, Leland[5], afterwards saw 'an image set up in the abbey church' in his honour.

The Latin authors quoted by him include Virgil and Horace, Pliny and Boëthius[6]. His knowledge of Greek was quite exceptional for the age in which he lived. His partiality for that language is proved by his selecting a Greek title for his principal work, περὶ φύσεως μερισμοῦ, *id est De Divisione Naturae*, in the course of which he is constantly quoting 'Dionysius' and Gregory, and frequently referring to the *Categories* of Aristotle. "If anyone wishes to know more about the 'possible' and the 'impossible', *legat* περὶ ἑρμηνείας, hoc est, *De Interpretatione Aristotelem* "[7]. In the dedicatory preface to his translation of the 'Areopagite', he praises the king for prompting him not to rest satisfied with the literature of the West, but to have recourse to the 'most pure and copious waters of the Greeks'. In approaching his task, he modestly describes himself as a mere tiro in Greek ; and although, in a work extending over 160 columns of print, he succeeds in presenting a closely literal rendering of his original, the general truth of his description of his own attainments, when put to the test of original composition, is clear enough in the few Greek

[1] Mullinger, p. 189.

[2] *De Div. Nat.* i 69 p. 513 B, ratio immutabilis nullius auctoritatis adstipulatione roborari indiget.

[3] The commentary on Boëthius, *Opusc. Sacra*, is later than 867 (Rand, 3, 18, 27).

[4] William of Malmesbury, *Gesta Regum Angl.* ii § 122, discussed in R. L. Poole's *Medieval Thought*, 313—329, and Traube, *l. c.* iii 522.

[5] *Itinerary*, ii 26[2].

[6] Migne, cxxii 498.  Cp. Dräseke (quoted on p. 491), and Rand, *l. c.*, 84.

[7] *ib.* 597 C.

hexameters which he addresses to the king of France and the archbishop of Rheims[1]. They are sufficiently bad to discredit bishop Bale's story[2] that their author had studied Greek at Athens. Even his Latin elegiacs he occasionally intersperses *sacro Graecorum nectare*, *i.e.* with Greek words written in Greek characters. It was probably in connexion with his own study of Greek that he drew up a Latin abstract of the treatise of Macrobius on the differences between the Greek and Latin verbs[3]. Aristotle who, in his judgement, is 'the acutest of the Greeks in the classification of all created things', is specially quoted in connexion with the ten Categories, which 'apply to things created, and not (as St Augustine has shown) to the Creator'[4]. Plato, however, had seen that all inquiries as to the nature of the existence of things created had for their aim the knowledge of the Creator; he therefore follows Plato. His Platonism makes him a Realist, and his extreme Realism ends in Pantheism. 'John the Irishman' has been happily characterised by a countryman of his own as 'an erratic genius', 'brilliant, learned, heretical'[5]. His principal work was regarded as the source of certain heresies in the early part of the thirteenth century. It was accordingly committed to the flames by the orders of pope Honorius III (1226), and the *editio princeps*, published by Thomas Gale at Oxford in 1681, was placed in the index of prohibited books a few years after its publication[6].

---

[1] *ib.* 1237; also in Traube, *l. c.*, iii 518–56, with other *Carmina Scottorum Latina et Graecanica, ib.* 685—701. The *Versus Romae* are there (p. 554) placed later than 878, and the allegorical treatment of Ovid's *Met.*, in the *Integumenta*, not earlier than cent. xiii (p. 526). Both were once ascribed to Joannes Scotus.

[2] R. L. Poole, 311 f.

[3] Ussher, *Ep. Hib.* p. 135; Teuffel, § 444, 9; Keil, *Gr. Lat.* v 595 f; p. 238 *supra*.　　　　　　　　　　　[4] *De Div. Nat.* i 14.

[5] G. T. Stokes, *Ireland and the Celtic Church*, p. 218.

[6] On Joannes Scotus, see *Opera* ed. Floss (Migne, cxxii) and the literature there quoted; also Guizot's *Civilisation en France*, iii leçon 29, pp. 137—178; Maurice, *Mediaeval Philosophy*, 45—79; Hauréau, i 148—175; Ebert, ii 257—267; Wattenbach, *GQ*, i[7] 323 f; Milman, *Lat. Christ.* iv 330 f; Mullinger's *Schools of Charles the Great*, c. 5; R. L. Poole's *Medieval Thought* (1884), 53—78; H. Morley's *English Writers*, ii 250–9; A. Gardner (1900); and Ker's *Dark Ages*, 161 f. Cp. Manitius, 323—339. Autograph *mar-*

Two of the contemporaries of John the Scot may here be
briefly mentioned, both of them natives of Auxerre.
The elder of these, Eric (841—877 ?), was educated
under Servatus Lupus at Ferrières. Among the
fruits of his studies which he sent with a set of elegiacs to the
bishop of Auxerre, we find a series of extracts from Suetonius and
Valerius Maximus, copied under the direction of Lupus. The
six books of his metrical Life of St Germanus of Auxerre show
a familiarity with Virgil, and some slight knowledge of Greek[1].
He is also the author of a number of notes on the translation of
Aristotle *De Interpretatione* by Boëthius, the *Eisagoge* of Porphyry,
and the *Categories* of Aristotle, as 'translated from Greek into
Latin by St Augustine'[2]. This last, however, is not really a
translation from Aristotle, and it must therefore be inferred that
in the tenth century the text of the *Categories* was still unknown[3].
Eric's distinguished pupil, Remi of Auxerre, taught at Rheims
(*c.* 893), and was the first to open a school in Paris (900 ; d. 908).
His commentaries on Donatus[4] and Martianus Capella[5] are still
extant. Greek words occur in his treatise on Music and in his
commentary on Genesis and on Donatus. In the latter, which
remained in use to the times of the Renaissance, his chief Latin
authority is Virgil. He also commented on the *Disticha* of Cato[6],

*ginalia* in MS of περὶ φύσεων, Reims 875, and commentary on St John's Gospel,
Laon 81, and in MSS at Bamberg (Traube, in *Quellen und Untersuchungen*, I ii
(1906) p. viii f). E. K. Rand, in Traube's *Quellen, l. c.*, 106 pp., edits and
assigns to John the Scot a commentary on the *Opuscula Sacra* of Boëthius.

[1] Ebert, ii 285—292 ; Traube, *l. c.*, iii 422. He has also some knowledge
of Caesar, the *Odes* and *Epodes* of Horace, and of Persius and Petronius,
*ib.* 424 ; and *Heiricus magister* is quoted in *scholia* on Juvenal, ix 27. Cp.
Traube, *l. c.*, iii 424—5, and in *Neues Archiv*, xviii 71—105, and *Rhein.
Mus.* xlviii 558—568 ; and Wattenbach, i 332 f ; also Rand, *Johannes Scottus*,
16, 97.

[2] Prantl, *Logik*, ii 41—44 ; Rand, *l. c.*, 83.

[3] Hauréau, 188 and 196.

[4] ed. W. Fox (1902) ; cp. Haase, *De Medii Aevi Stud. Philol.* 26 f note ;
Thurot, in *Notices et Extraits*, xxii (2) ; Bursian, *Cl. Philol. in Deutschland*,
i 27 and note ; Traube, *S. Ber. bayer. Akad.* 1900, 532 f.

[5] Hauréau, i 203—5 ; cp. Ebert, iii 234 f.

[6] Mancini, *Rendiconti Accad. Lincei*, ser. v, xi 175 f, 369 f ; and Traube,
in *Berl. Phil. Woch.* 1903, 261.

the *Carmen Paschale* of Sedulius[1], and the *Opuscula Sacra* of Boëthius[2].

The Irish monk Dungal[3] (d. 826) is not only a student of Cicero and Macrobius, but he also shows some slight knowledge of Greek by using the word μήνη and the phrase κατὰ ἀντίφρασιν, and by explaining the term *apologia* 'secundum proprietatem Graeci sermonis'[4]. Half a century later, we find traces of classical studies not only in Dungal's school at Pavia, but also at Modena. While the Franks on their march tò rescue Louis II at Beneventum (871) sang rude rhymes regardless of inflexions and abounding in biblical citations only[5], the citizens who guarded the walls of Modena chanted far more elegant lines of accentual Latin verse recalling the ancient sieges of Troy and Rome:—

*Classics at Pavia, Modena and St Gallen*

> 'O tu, qui servas armis ista moenia,
> Noli dormire, moneo, sed vigila:
> Dum Hector vigil extitit in Troïa,
> Non eam cepit fraudulenta Gretia', etc.[6]

Towards the close of the ninth century there is evidence of the study of the Classics at St Gallen, which possessed Irish translations from Hippocrates and Galen, and the Greek Grammar of Dositheus (cent. iv)[7]. Among the MSS added to its library by Hartmund (c. 841—883) were a (Latin) Josephus, Justin, Solinus, Orosius, Martianus Capella, Priscian and Isidore[8]; and Latin verse was written (and forms of deeds and letters drawn up) by the versatile abbot Salomo III (890)[9]. A learned monk of St Gallen, Notker

---

[1] Hümer in Vienna Akad. April 1880.

[2] Rand, *l. c.*, 87—106; ed. H. F. Stewart, in prep.    [3] p. 480 *supra*.

[4] Migne, cv 455, 473, 467.

[5] Traube, *l. c.*, 403–5.

[6] Muratori, *Ant. Ital.*, diss. 40 (Hallam, *Lit.* i[4] 26 f); cp. Ebert, iii 174 f; Traube, *O Roma nobilis* (1891), p. 9; *Poëtae Lat. Aevi Car.* iii 702–5; and Gröber's *Grundriss*, II i 168.

[7] Bursian, i 28 f; Teuffel, § 431, 7; Schanz, § 836.

[8] Bursian, i 33 n.

[9] *ib.* i 39.  Ebert, iii 150 f, 154 f.  On his encyclopaedia cp. G. Meier, *Die sieben freien Künste*, i 16 *b*.  It was founded on an abridgement of the *Liber Glossarum* (Goetz, in *Abhandl. sächs. Ges.* xiii 226 f, 244 f).  On his

the Stammerer[1] (c. 830—912), laboriously copied out for the
episcopal chancellor of Charles the Fat a Greek MS of the Canonical
Epistles which had been lent by the bishop of Vercelli[2].   Notker
intersperses Greek words in his Latin[3]; he ends a letter explaining
certain musical symbols with the words : *Salutant te ellinici fratres*,
implying that some at least of his brother-monks were students of
Greek[4].   But his desire for a translation of Origen suggests that
he was unfamiliar with that language.   The words of his profoundly
pathetic anthem, *Media vita in morte sumus*, suggested by the
sudden death of a workman engaged in building a bridge over
the gorge of the Goldach at Martinstobel[5], continued to be sung
at compline during part of Lent, and have found their way into
the English Order for the Burial of the Dead.   About the
same time another monk, vaguely described as 'Poëta Saxo', was
composing his Latin epic on Charles the Great, beginning with
four books of hexameters (partly founded on Einhard) and ending
with a book of elegiacs lamenting the death of Charles and the
invasions of the Normans[6].   The part of the Chronicle of Regino,
abbot of Prüm, which relates to the year 889, is written in the
style of Justin[7].   A Graeco-Latin Glossary was copied at Laon[8]
before 869 by the Irish hellenist Martin[9]; a similar work existed

life cp. Dümmler, *Mitth. d. antiq. Ges.*, Zürich, xii 262; for his poems, see
*Poëtae Lat. Medii Aevi*, iv 296 f.  Cp. Manitius, 594–8.

[1] *Balbulus.*  Cp. Meyer von Knonau, in *Mitth. der antiq. Ges.* xix (Zürich, 1877); and Manitius, 354—367.

[2] Pertz, *Mon.* ii 101; Migne, cxxxi 989 C.

[3] Migne, 1025 A—B.

[4] Ekkehart minimus, in H. Canisius, *Thesaurus*, ii 3 p. 198 (ed. 1725). On St Gallen in c. ix and x cp. Wetzel (1877), and Specht (1885), 109, 313–28.

[5] Von Arx, *St Gallen*, i 93–5; Scheffel's *Ekkehard*, note 186; on his *Sequences* cp. Ker's *Dark Ages*, 219.

[6] Pertz, *Mon.* i 227 f; Jaffé's *Carolina*, 542 f; Ebert, iii 125 f. *Poëtae Lat. Medii Aevi*, iv 1—71 Winterfeld.  He has been identified with the poet Agius (of Corvey), author of a fine elegiac poem in memory of Hathumoda, the first abbess of Gandersheim (d. 874); Traube, *Poëtae Lat. Aevi Car.* iii 368–88; Hüffer, *Korveier Studien* (1898); Wattenbach, *GQ*, i[7] 307 f; Manitius, 583 f.

[7] Bursian, i 40.  Cp. Wattenbach, *GQ*, i[7] 311–4; Manitius, 695 f.

[8] ed. E. Miller in *Notices et Extraits*, xxix 2, 1—230; cp. P. Piper, *die älteste deutsche Literatur*, 338 f.

[9] Traube, in Munich *Abhandl.* xix 362.

in the library of Corbie, and Greek MSS in those of St Riquier
and of Rheims.[1]   In century viii or ix, an unknown
'monk of Einsiedeln' visited Pavia and Rome,   The 'monk of Einsiedeln'
made a plan of the latter, and returned with copies
of Latin and even of Greek inscriptions[2].   There is evidence of the
ecclesiastical use of Greek (especially in the chanting
of the Creed) in the dioceses of Münster, Rheims   Ecclesiastical use of Greek
and Poitiers, and at the Cathedral of Vienne[3];
and, in the rite for the consecration of churches, the bishop was
required to write in the dust with his staff the letters of the Greek
alphabet, the evidence for this custom extending over centuries viii
to xv[4].   Greek was the language used in the fourteenth century
in chanting the *Gloria in excelsis* at the midnight Mass at Tours,
and also, from the thirteenth century to the Revolution, in the
annual Mass at St Denis on the octave of the patron Saint of
France[5].

But Greek studies, on the whole, fell into decline during the
two centuries after the death of Joannes Scotus.   They survived,
to some slight extent, among those who had been trained in his
school, such as Hucbald (d. 930)[6], who celebrated   Hucbald
Charles the Bald in 146 hexameters, in which
every word begins with the letter C[7], and also sang of the victory

---

[1] Appendix to Léon Maître, *Écoles*; Tougard, *L'Hellénisme*, 36 f.

[2] *Anon. Einsiedlensis*, first published by Mabillon, *Analecta*, p. 358;
see Mommsen in *Ber. d. sächs. Ges.* 1850, p. 287 f.  Cp. p. 264 *supra*.
The author was probably a monk of Reichenau (Wattenbach, *GQ*, i[7] 280;
Specht, 311).  *Corpus Inscr. Lat.* vi (1) p. ix f, nos. 1—80.

[3] Martène, *De Antiquis Ecclesiae Ritibus*, i 88, 102, 114, 117 (ed. 1736);
Tougard, 20.

[4] Martène, ii 679; cp. Roger Bacon's *Gk Gr*. pp. 25, 83, 195, and *Opus
Majus*, i 94 (=iii 117) Bridges.

[5] Martène, i 279; Tougard 21; cp. Gardthausen, *Gr. Pal.* 422, and
esp. Omont, in *Études d'histoire du MA dédiés à Gabriel Monod* (1896)
177—185 (*Byz. Zeitschr.* vi 461 f).  The 'Greek Mass in honour of St Denys'
was printed in 1658 and 1777 (cp. Egger, *Hellénisme en France*, i 49).

[6] Wattenbach, *GQ*, i[7] 335 f; Manitius, 588–94.

[7] *Carmina clarisonae calvis cantate Camenae* &c; Migne, cxxxii 1042 f;
Ebert, iii 167; *Poëtae Lat. Medii Aevi*, iv 267 f.

of Louis the Stammerer over the invading forces of the Normans.
Some of Hucbald's verses are varied with Greek words, which
also occur in his treatises on music[1]. Louis himself gave the
name of *Alpha* to a monastery which he had founded in
Burgundy, and that of *Carlopolis* to Compiègne[2]. The Latin

**Abbo** poëm on the siege of Paris by the Normans
(885–7), written by Abbo 'Cernuus', monk of
Saint-Germain-des-Prés (d. 923)[3], abounds in Greek words ; and
in 'book iii' of his poëm, all such words are explained by
interlinear glosses in Latin[4].

The ninth century closes in England with the name of Alfred

**Alfred** (849—*c.* 900). He was taken to see Rome at the
age of five, and again at the age of seven. Notwithstanding the general decay of learning, and the disquiet
caused by the Danish invasions, he led a studious life in his
youth, and, after succeeding to the throne in 871, began a series
of translations from Latin authors with the aid of the Welsh
monk, Asser. In English literature Alfred is 'our first translator'
In his rendering of Boëthius (*c.* 888) he does not hesitate, in the
interests of his people, to add to the original whenever he thinks
fit. Thus in one case he expands three lines of Latin into nearly
thirty. He also translated the *Universal History* of Orosius,
adding or omitting, as he deemed best. A third translation
(in which his own name does not appear) is that of Bede's
*Ecclesiastical History* ; and a fourth, that of Gregory's *Cura
Pastoralis*[5]. It is only in this last that the king states his general
design as a translator. He laments that there were but few south
of the Humber, and none south of the Thames, who could
understand the Divine Service, or even explain a Latin epistle
in English. He had therefore thought it good to translate into

---

[1] Tougard, 40.

[2] Gidel, 189 f.

[3] Pertz, *Mon.* ii 776—805 ; Migne, cxxxii 722 ; *Poëtae Lat. Medii Aevi*, iv 72 f.

[4] Tougard, 39 ; Ebert, iii 129 f ; Freeman, *Historical Essays*, i 225–34 ; Wattenbach, *GQ*, i[7] 329 f ; Ker's *Dark Ages*, 159 ; Manitius, 585–8.

[5] Hatton MS (cent. ix) lines 1—15 in plate i of Skeat's *XII Facsimiles*, 1892.

English the books that were most necessary to be known. At the king's request, the bishop of Worcester produced an abridged translation of Gregory's *Dialogues*. A similar translation of St Augustine's *Soliloquies* is ascribed to Alfred himself. In the introduction to the latter he refers to his previous works under the parable of the wood 'from which he and his friends had brought the fairest trees and branches they could bear away, leaving many remaining for those who should come after them'[1].

[1] H. Morley's *English Writers*, ii 266—292, and the rest of the literature *ib.* p. 294, with that produced at the 'Millenary' of 1901, esp. Plummer's *Ford Lectures*; also Pauli's *Life*; Schmid's *Gesch. der Erziehung* (1892) II i 210—223. Asser's *Life of Alfred* (ed. W. H. Stevenson, 1904) is an example of 'florid Latin encasing much good plain sense' (Ker's *Dark Ages*, 177).

# CHAPTER XXVI.

## THE TENTH CENTURY.

THE six centuries extending from the beginning of the sixth to the end of the eleventh are proverbially known as the Dark Ages; and, of all these centuries, the tenth is held in lowest esteem. It is the age of gloom, the age of iron, the age of lead[1]. England was being repeatedly overrun by the Danes, and the monastic reforms of Dunstan only incidentally promoted the interests of learning. The Normans had definitely established themselves in France (912), where the line of Charles the Great came to an end in 987, to be succeeded by the House of Capet. Hordes of Hungarians had meanwhile been ranging over the whole of Germany, the South of France, and the North of Italy; in the last year of the ninth century they had set on fire the monastic library of Nonantola, near Modena[2], and, on their return to the North, they inflicted the same fate on the monasteries of St Gallen and Fulda[3]. In Germany, the line of Charles had been followed in 911 by that of the Saxon kings, the second of whom, Henry the

[1] Baronius, *Annales*, 900 A.D., 'saeculum...ferreum...plumbeum...obscurum'; 'obscurum' is the epithet selected by Cave. Leibnitz, *Introd. in Script. Rerum Brunsvic.* § 63 (1707), paradoxically regards it as (in Germany at any rate) a 'golden age', compared with cent. xiii; while Guizot and Hallam (*Lit.* i 4⁴) agree in describing cent. vii, rather than cent. x, as the *nadir* of the human intellect in Europe, and similarly W. P. Ker, *The Dark Ages* (1904), 99. In contrast to Leibnitz, Charles, *Roger Bacon*, 97, considers it generally agreed that cent. xiii is the 'golden age' of the Middle Ages. Cp. Muratori, *Antiq.* iii 831; Mabillon, *Acta SS.*, *saeculum* v, *praef.* ii; *Hist. Litt. de la France*, vi 18 f, and Mosheim's *Eccl. Hist.* i 590 (1863).

[2] Muratori, *Annali*, ann. 899. Mabillon (*Voy. Lit.* 252) found only two MSS there.

[3] Milman, *Lat. Christ.* iii 280.

Fowler, was the first to check the Hungarian inroads (933), which were finally quelled by his son Otho the Great (955), who was crowned emperor of the West in Rome (962) and was succeeded by Otho II and Otho III. When the third Otho received the imperial crown in Rome from the German pope, Gregory V (996), the sixty years of the abasement of the papacy came to an end. Three years later, Gerbert, the foremost scholar of the age, became pope of Rome. The century closed with the youthful emperor's impressive visit to the vaulted chamber where Charles the Great still sat enthroned beneath the dome of Aachen[1]; and, within the next three years, the emperor and the pope had both passed away.

In this century learning flourished at the ancient capital of Aachen, under the guidance of Bruno, brother of Otho I and archbishop of Cologne from 953 to 965. It also flourished further to the South, in the region of the Meuse and Mosel at Toul and Verdun, which were occupied by colonies of monks from Greece and Ireland[2]. It was in the same region that an abbot of Prüm, Regino, who died at Trier in 915, produced a chronicle displaying its author's acquaintance with Justin[3], and a treatise on harmony in which Greek terms are correctly explained[4]. John of Vandières (between Metz and Toul), afterwards abbot of Gorze (near Metz), studied the current *Introductions* to the logical works of Aristotle with a view to understanding the references to the *Categories* in the *De Trinitate* of Augustine[5]; and Ratherius of Liège (d. 974), thrice bishop of

*Regino*

*John of Vandières*

*Ratherius*

---

[1] Otho of Lomello, in *Chron. Noval.* in Pertz, *Mon., Scr.* vii 106 (discussed by Lindner, and Hodgkin, *Charles the Great*, 250).

[2] Pertz, *Mon., Scr.* iv 501, *Widrici Vita S. Gerardi Episcopi Tullensis* (963—994), 'Coetum quoque Grecorum ac Scottorum agglomerans non modicum, propriis alebat stipendiis commixtum diversae linguae populum'; cp. Mabillon, *Annal.* iv 90 ; Martène, *Thesaur.* iii 1066 ; Calmet, *Hist. Lorr.* i, *Hist. Episc. Tull.* c. 52 ; *Hist. Litt. de la France,* vi 57 ; Cramer, *De Graecis Medii Aevi Studiis,* ii 37 ; Gidel, *Nouvelles Études,* 195 ; Haddan's *Remains,* 286.

[3] Wattenbach, *GQ,* i[7] 311–4 ; Bursian, *Cl. Phil. in Deutschland,* i 40.

[4] Migne, cxxxii 491–9 (Tougard, *Hellénisme,* 38 f) ; Ebert, iii 326—331.

[5] Mabillon, *Acta SS. O. S. B.* vii 393.

Verona, quotes Greek and also Latin authors, among the latter being Plautus, Phaedrus, and Verona's poet, Catullus[1]. In his treatise *De Contemptu Canonum* he introduces a quotation from Horace with the words :—*perlepide Flaccus cantitat noster* ; and he declines to ordain any except those who give proof of proficiency in literature[2]. Among his lost works may be noticed a Latin Grammar, which recalls the usual penalty for boyish neglect of grammatical rules by its quaint title of *Sparadorsum*[3].

In the first quarter of the century (916–24) Verona was apparently the home of the unknown grammarian,

Panegyricus Berengarii

who composed the epic poem called the *Gesta* or *Panegyricus Berengarii*, in which he borrows from Virgil and the Latin 'Homer', and Statius and Juvenal. Considerable knowledge of the grammarians is displayed in a contemporary commentary intended to facilitate the study of this poem in the grammar-schools of the day[4].

Early in the same century, in France, the monastery of Cluni[5] was founded by William, duke of Aquitaine (910), to be ruled by

Odo of Cluni

Berno, its first abbot (d. 927), and reformed by his successor, Odo (d. 942) ; and these reforms infused new life into the schools connected with the Order at Metz and Rheims, at Liège and Paris[6]. Odo, in the early days which he had spent as a youth of high birth in the monastery of St Martin at Tours, had taken delight in the study of Virgil, when he was warned in a dream to abandon that perilous occupation. In his dream he saw a beautiful vase teeming with poisonous serpents ; the beautiful vase (he felt assured) was the poet's verse, while the serpents were his pagan sentiments[7]. He went to Paris and attended the lectures on Logic and the liberal arts delivered by Remi of Auxerre, but retained little of Remi's philosophic teaching.

---

[1] R. Ellis, *Catullus*, p. viii[2].

[2] Migne, cxxxvi 564 ; Ozanam, *Documents Inédits*, 14 ; cp. A. Vogel, *Ratherius von Verona* (1854) ; Ebert, iii 373 f, 383.

[3] *Spara* (=*Serva*) dorsum ; Pertz, *Mon., Scr.* iv 64, 10 ; Gidel, 198 f ; Bursian, i 42 ; Specht, 205 ; Ker's *Dark Ages*, 178.

[4] *Poëtae Lat. Medii Aevi*, iv 354 f ; Ugo Balzani's *Chroniclers*, 119 f ; and Manitius, 632 f.

[5] E. Sackur, *Die Cluniacenser*, 1891–4 ; Wattenbach, i[7] 472–4.

[6] Heeren, i 201.        [7] Migne, cxxxiii 49 A.

He afterwards complained about 'the mere logicians who had
more belief in Boëthius than in the Bible '[1].   His writings prove,
however, that he had studied Virgil and Priscian[2], St Augustine's
*Dialectic* and Martianus Capella, besides showing some knowledge
of Greek[3]; while his contemporary and namesake, Odo, archbishop
of Canterbury (d. 958), was taught Greek as well as Latin[4].   Both
of these languages were also known to Bruno, archbishop of
Cologne (d. 965), a younger brother of Otho the Great[5].   Bruno,
who had himself learnt Greek from certain eastern
monks at the imperial court, called an Irish bishop
from Trier to teach Greek at Aachen, and also encouraged the
transcription of the works of Latin authors, which became models
of style to historians such as Widukind of Corvey (d. 1004), whose
*Res Gestae Saxonicae* gives proof of his study of Sallust and Livy[6].
Greek and Latin were also known to Sergius, bishop of Naples[7].
Another Italian, Gunzo of Novara (d. 967), when
accused by the monks of St Gallen of using an
accusative instead of an ablative, justified himself in a long letter
to the monks of Reichenau, in the course of which he quotes a
score of Latin authors, his favourite poets being apparently Persius
and Juvenal[8].   The hundred MSS, which he carried with him into
Germany, included the *De Interpretatione* and the *Topics* of
Aristotle, and the *Timaeus* of Plato, doubtless in the Latin
translations of Boëthius and Chalcidius respectively[9].   He
discussed the controversy between the Platonists and the
Aristotelians as to the nature of 'universals'[10]; and he is credited
with combining the study of Greek with an interest in science;
but, as he uses Latin characters in quoting half a line of Homer

*Marginal note:* Bruno

*Marginal note:* Gunzo

[1] Pez, *Thesaur.* III ii 144 (Cramer ii 41).

[2] Migne, *l. c.* 'immensum Prisciani transiit transnatando pelagus'.

[3] Cp. Hauréau, *Singularités Historiques,* 129 f; Ebert, iii 170–3.   His
*Occupatio* has been edited by Swoboda (1900).

[4] Cramer, ii 38; Tougard, 40.

[5] Cramer, ii 35; Tougard, 42; Bursian, i 41, 43 f; Norden, *Kunstprosa,*
711 n; Poole's *Medieval Thought,* 86–8; Wattenbach, *GQ,* i[7] 358, 401–3.

[6] ed. Waitz, 1882 (Pertz, *Scriptores*); Ebert, iii 428; Bursian, i 44 f;
Wattenbach, i[7] 365 n. 2; Ker's *Dark Ages,* 186 f; Manitius, 714–8.

[7] Gidel, 196.                              [8] Migne, cxxxvi 1283 (960 A.D.).

[9] Wattenbach, i[7] 352.                    [10] Migne, *l. c.*

(which he clearly borrows from Servius)[1], it is probable that the above texts were only Latin translations[2]. In this century the catalogue of Lorsch displays a goodly array of Latin classics[3].

In the same century the monastery of Gandersheim, founded

Hroswitha

to the S. of Hanover in 856, was famous as the retreat of the learned nun, Hroswitha[4] (*fl.* 984), who celebrated in 'Leonine' hexameters (inspired by Virgil, Prudentius and Sedulius) the acts of Otho down to 968. Further, with a view to providing the age with a purer literature than that of Latin Comedy, she composed six moral and religious plays, in which she imitates Boëthius as well as Terence. But, as the mediaeval copyists of Terence were unconscious that his plays were written in verse, the plays of Hroswitha are written in actual prose. They survive in a single MS at Munich, the discovery of which was welcomed with enthusiasm by the early humanists in Germany, the first to print them being Conrad Celtes (1501). It is true that the scenes in these plays are apt to be indecorous, but virtue always triumphs in the end, and the close of all the plays is invariably beyond reproach. Whether they were meant to be acted by the nuns or not, is a matter of dispute, and does not appear to admit of decision. The writer's simplicity of character is certainly extraordinary, and there is a charming candour in the unaffected phrases of her preface:—*si enim alicui placet mea devotio, gaudebo. Si autem vel pro mea abiectione vel pro vitiosi sermonis rusticitate nulli placet, memet ipsam iuvat quod feci.* An exceptional number of recent editions attests her enduring popularity[5].

Another learned lady of the tenth century is Hedwig, daughter

Hedwig and
Ekkehard II

of Henry of Bavaria, the brother of Otho I. A close parallel to the story of the daughter of Charles the Great, the princess who learned Greek in view

---

[1] Cramer, ii 41 f; Tougard, 42 f; Ebert, iii 370 f; Bursian, i 42 f.

[2] Bursian, i 34; Manitius, 531–6.

[3] Wilmanns, in *Rhein. Mus.* xxiii (1868) 385.

[4] *clamor validus* is her own rendering of her name.

[5] ed. Magnin (1843; 1857); Barack (1858); Bendixen (1862); Winterfeld (1902). Cp. Milman, *Lat. Christ.* ix 181 f; R. Köpke (1869); Ebert, iii 314 f; Bursian, i 45 f; Wattenbach, i[7] 369—372; Ker's *Dark Ages*, 179 f; and Manitius, 619—632.

of her proposed marriage to Constantine VI[1], may be found in
the story of the betrothal of the niece of Otho I to a 'Byzantine
prince named Constantine'. Hedwig learnt Greek, but she broke
off the match, and was learning Latin, when she transferred her
affections from the Byzantine prince to a wealthy countryman of
her own. Soon afterwards, in the years of her widowhood (973)
in the Black Forest, she devoted herself to the study of Virgil under
the guidance of Ekkehard II, a monk of the neighbouring monastery
of St Gallen; and, from the school of that monastery, her tutor
once brought with him a promising pupil, who, on coming into
her presence, modestly expressed his longing to learn Greek in
the Latin line:—*esse velim Graecus, cum sim vix, Domna, Latinus.*
Hedwig, in her delight, kissed the blushing boy, and placed him
on her foot-stool, where he went on confusedly improvising Latin
verses, while she taught him her own Greek rendering of the
antiphon *Maria et Flumina*:—

> *Thalassi, ke potami, eulogiton Kyrion.*
> *Ymnite pigonton Kyrion, alleluja*[2].

She often sent for him afterwards and listened to his Latin verses
and taught him Greek; and, when he finally left her, gave him a
copy of Horace and certain other books which were still preserved
in the library of St Gallen at the time of the writer of the continuation of the chronicle of Ekkehard IV[3]. The boy had in the
meantime risen to be abbot of the monastery (1001–22), while
the monk who read Virgil with Hedwig became provost of Mainz
(d. 990). His uncle, Ekkehard I, was the author of the great
epic on the exploits of Walter of Aquitaine, which includes many
reminiscences of Virgil and Prudentius[4]. Ekkehard I died in

---

[1] p. 478 *supra*.

[2] *i.e.* θάλασσαι καὶ ποταμοί, εὐλογεῖτε τὸν Κύριον, ὑμνεῖτε πηγαὶ τὸν Κύριον,
ἀλληλούϊα.

[3] Ekkehardi IV *Casus S. Galli*, c. 10 (Pertz, *Mon., Scr.* ii 122 f, esp. 125;
also ed. Meyer von Knonau in *St Galler Geschichtsquellen*, iii, 1877).
Ekkehard IV did not go beyond 971 (Wattenbach, i[7] 443). Cp. Wattenbach,
i[7] 356; Scheffel's *Ekkehard*, 309 f; Ker's *Dark Ages*, 191–7.

[4] Grimm u. Schmeller, *Lat. Gedichte, x—xi Jahrh.* (1838); also Peiper's
*Ekkehardi Primi Waltharius* (1873); Scheffel and Holder (1874); and
Althof's *Waltharii Poësis* (1899—1905); cp. Ebert, iii 265–76; Graf's *Roma*,

973, and his poem was revised by the fourth of that name (d. *c.* 1060)[1].

Ten years after the death of Ekkehard I, Walther, a school-master of Speier (983), names (among the authorities for Greek and Roman mythology etc.) Homer, Terence, Virgil, Horace, Lucan, Persius, Juvenal, Boëthius and others. His chief model is Virgil, while he also shows his acquaintance with Ovid, Statius, Sedulius, and Martianus Capella, and with the translation of Porphyry by Boëthius[2].

Walther of Speier

While Walther is a scholar of purely local interest, France, Germany and Italy alike claim a part in the career of one of the most prominent personages of the century, Gerbert of Aurillac in the Auvergne. Born about 950, he studied at Aurillac under Raimund[3], a pupil of Odo of Cluni, and his studies carried him even as far as Barcelona, near the Arab frontier of Spain. He afterwards taught at Tours, Fleury, Sens and Rheims, was successively abbot of Bobbio and archbishop of Rheims, withdrew from France to the court of the emperor in Germany, and became archbishop of Ravenna, and finally pope of Rome (as Silvester II) at the close of the century (d. 1003). In an age described by himself as *dira et miseranda tempora*[4], he was deemed a prodigy of science and learning, the range of his studies having included mathematics, music and medicine, and having even involved him in the imputation of being addicted to magic arts. The papal legate, who protested against his appointment as archbishop of Rheims, passionately declared that the Vicars of St Peter (and his disciples) declined to have as their master a Plato, a Terence, or other *pecudes philoso- phorum*[5]. Gerbert probably owed all his knowledge of Plato to the Latin translation of part of the *Timaeus*, though he quotes

Gerbert (Silvester II)

ii 174; Strecker's *Ekk. u. Vergil* in *Zeitschr. f. deutsches Alt.* 1898, 339–65; and Ker's *Dark Ages*, 222–6; Germ. trans. Althof, 1902; ed. Strecker, 1907; cp. Manitius, 609–14.

[1] For the death of Ekkehard IV the date *c.* 1060 (instead of *c.* 1036) is proposed by Dümmler in Haupt's *Zeitschrift*, 1869, p. 2. On Ekkehard I, II, IV, cp. Specht, III, 323–8.

[2] Cp. W. Harster, 1877 (Bursian, i 52).　　　　[3] *Ep.* 16.

[4] *Ep.* 130.　　　[5] Pertz, *Mon., Scr.* iii 687; Milman, *Lat. Christ.* iii 342.

Greek words in his *Geometry* and elsewhere[1]. His pupil and friend, the historian Richer of Rheims[2] (d. 1010), describes him as expounding Porphyry's *Introduction* in the translation of Victorinus and with the commentary of Boëthius, as well as the (Latin version of the) *Categories* and *De Interpretatione* of Aristotle, together with Boëthius on the *Topics* of Cicero[3]. Apparently, the old version of the *Categories* by Boëthius, which had been lost for a while, had now been recovered[4]. He also asks a friend to send him an extract from Boëthius, *De Interpretatione*[5]. Among the authors which he expounded at Rheims were Terence, Virgil, Horace, Lucan, Persius, Juvenal and Statius. He is familiar with Sallust, Caesar, Suetonius, and (above all) with Cicero. He urges one of his friends to collect MSS on his behalf in Italy, and to send him transcripts of Boëthius and Victorinus, with the *Ophthalmicus* of Demosthenes[6]; and he advises another to bring with him on his journey Cicero's *Speeches* and the *De Republica*, probably meaning by the latter the *Somnium Scipionis*, the sole surviving portion of the Sixth Book[7]. He also writes for a complete copy of Cicero *pro rege Deiotaro*[8]. It has even been surmised that the preservation of Cicero's *Speeches*, which he frequently quotes, may have been largely due to Gerbert. He is eager to obtain MSS of Caesar, Pliny, Suetonius, Symmachus and the *Achilleis* of Statius. He tells a friend that he is forming a library with the aid of MSS from Germany and Belgium, and from Rome and other parts of Italy, and asks for transcripts from France[9]. He quotes Terence, Virgil, the *Odes* as well as the *Epistles* of Horace, the *Letters* of Seneca, and the *Catilina* of Sallust[10]. Besides these, he mentions Eugraphius[11] on Terence, and Cassiodorus, but no Greek author whatsoever. He was once, however, abbot of Bobbio, the library of which included, in the tenth century, a Greek text of the

---

[1] Tougard, 45.

[2] ed. Waitz 1877 (Pertz, *Scriptores*); cp. Ker's *Dark Ages*, 188—191.

[3] Migne, cxxxviii, *Hist.* iii c. 46 (Cramer, ii 51; Gidel, 201); cp. Mullinger's *Cambridge*, i 44.

[4] Hauréau, i 213.                                [5] *Ep.* 123.

[6] *Ep.* 130. Demosthenes Philalethes (who lived under Nero) was an Alexandrian physician of the school of Herophilus.

[7] *Ep.* 86; Norden, 706 n.                    [8] *Ep.* 9.

[9] *Ep.* 44.                            [10] *Ep.* 123.                    [11] *Ep.* 7.

*Categories*[1], and we have a short treatise from his pen, in which he reconciles an apparent contradiction between the *Categories* and Porphyry's *Introduction*[2].  A knowledge of Greek has been sometimes inferred from his correspondence with Otho III, but it will be observed that the latter (who inherited his Greek from his Byzantine mother) only asks Gerbert to recommend him a manual

Fulbert
of arithmetic[3].  Among Gerbert's pupils was Fulbert, who included medicine in the wide range of his studies, and became bishop of Chartres and founder of its famous school (990, d. 1029).  We shall find pupils of Fulbert prominent

Richer
as teachers in many parts of France in the following century[4].  Another of Gerbert's pupils, Richer (who has been already mentioned), was also a student at Chartres, which, at the end of this century, had a flourishing school of medicine, and, under Fulbert and his successors, became an important school of learning.  Among the authors there studied by Richer (in and after 991) were Hippocrates[5], Galen and Soranus, obviously in Latin translations and abridgements of the Greek text[6].

The most original hellenist of this age is doubtless Luitprand

Luitprand
or Liudprand (*c.* 920—972), bishop of Cremona.
A Lombard by birth, he repeatedly represented Berengar II and Otho I as envoy at Constantinople, where he acquired a remarkably varied but far from accurate knowledge of Greek, and where he apparently died in 972.  His reports on his missions of 950[7] and 968[8] supply us with a vivid description of

---

[1] Hauréau, i 217 n.            [2] *ib.* 213 f.

[3] 'Deposcimus ut Graecorum vivax ingenium suscitetis, et nos arithmeticae librum edoceatis' (with Gerbert's reply, *Ep.* 187).  On Gerbert, see *Opera* in Migne, cxxxix, and ed. Olleris (1867); *Epistolae* ed. Havet (1889); and cp. Muratori, *Antiq.* iii 872–4; Maitland's *Dark Ages*, 55 n; Ebert, iii 384–92; Wattenbach, i[7] 460; Werner, *Gerbert von Aurillac* (1878); Hock, *Hist. du Pape Sylvestre II* (1837); Poole's *Medieval Thought*, 88 f; Norden, 705–10; Ker's *Dark Ages*, 198.

[4] *Opera* in Migne, cxli; Léon Maître, *Écoles*, 102 f; Clerval, *Écoles de Chartres* (1895), 31—91; p. 517 *infra*.

[5] See esp. iv c. 50 (translated in Ker's *Dark Ages*, 188 f).

[6] ed. Waitz, 1877 (Pertz, *Scr.*); cp. Cramer, ii 50–5, Gidel, 202; Ebert, iii 434 f; Wattenbach, i[7] 462–6; and Ker's *Dark Ages*, 188—191.

[7] *Antapodosis*, vi 5—10.

[8] *Relatio*, pp. 136—166 of *Liudprandi Opera*, ed. Dümmler, 1877[2].

the many differences between Italy and the new Rome in manners
and opinions[1]. They abound in Greek words, phrases and idioms,
and snatches of odd stories, which attain a new interest owing to
the fact that the author always takes pains to set down the Latin
pronunciation of the Greek, *e.g.* ἄθεοι καὶ ἀσεβεῖς, *athei ke asevis*[2].
It was once supposed that in the MS all the Greek words were
inserted by the author himself[3]. He quotes from the *Iliad* and
from Lucian's *Somnium*, and is familiar with Plato's celebrated
saying, αἰτία ἑλομένου, θεὸς ἀναίτιος[4]. He also cites Terence,
Plautus, Virgil, Horace and Juvenal, and even knows when they
wrote[5]. The embassies of Luitprand and others were concerned
with certain proposals for a marriage between Otho II and
Theophanu, daughter of Nicephorus II[6]. They were ultimately
successful, and Theophanu's knowledge of Greek descended to
her son, Otho III, whose father owed his life to the remarkable
skill with which he personated the speech and action of a Greek
soldier, when he was defeated and captured in Calabria in 982.
Otho III was educated under Bernward, who became bishop of
Hildesheim in 993, and lived to see its large library of sacred and
philosophical literature fall a prey to the flames in 1013[7]. Other
German monasteries, at Corvey and Herford, suffered a similar
fate at the hands of the Hungarians[8].

Meanwhile, in England, in the second half of the tenth
century, Oswald, archbishop of York (d. 992), who
had himself been educated at Fleury on the Loire,     Abbo of
invited Abbo of Fleury[9] (d. 1004) to become the      Fleury

---

[1] Finlay's *Hist. of Greece*, ii 329.                    [2] *Antap.* ii 3.

[3] Pertz, *Mon.* iii 270; refuted by F. Koehler (Wattenbach, i[7] 480).

[4] *Rep.* 617 E.

[5] On Luitprand, cp. Migne, cxxxvi; Cramer, ii 47 f; Gidel, 204–25;
Ebert, iii 414–27; Wattenbach, i[7] 474—480; Balzani's *Chroniclers*, 123—142;
Preface to Dümmler's ed. (1877); J. Becker, *Textgeschichte* (1908).

[6] Uhlirz in *Byz. Zeitschr.* iv 467 f, and in *Alg. D. Biogr.*

[7] *Ann. Hild.* in Pertz, *Mon.* iii 94, 'sed hoc ah! ah! nobis restat lugendum,
quia in eodem incendio…inexplicabilis et inrecuperabilis copia periit librorum'.

[8] Both of these were restored by bp Rotho (*c.* 1043), *Vita Meinwerci*, c. 49
§ 150 (*Mon.*, *Scr.* xi 40).

[9] The *Life* by the monk Aimoin, in Migne, cxxxix 390, states that he
studied grammar, arithmetic and dialectic at Fleury (near Orleans), astronomy
at Paris and Rheims, and music on his return to Orleans, besides attending to

instructor of the monks of the abbey which the archbishop had
caused to be founded in 969 at Ramsey near Huntingdon.
Besides composing (*c.* 985), with the aid of Dunstan, a Life of St
Edmund, king of the East Angles, Abbo wrote for his pupils at
Ramsey a scholarly work known as the *Quaestiones Grammaticales.*
He here deals with their difficulties in matters of prosody and
pronunciation, showing in his treatment of the same an accurate
knowledge of Virgil and Horace, and even an interest in textual
criticism[1]. In the same age, the early *Lives of Dunstan* (d. 988),
and the *Letters* bearing on his times, are (like other writings of
the same period across the Channel) not unfrequently interspersed
with Greek words. These may have been derived from Greek
hymns or versicles, or from Greek glossaries[2]. In the same half-
century, Ælfric (*c.* 955—*c.* 1030), the abbot of

*Ælfric*

Eynsham in Oxfordshire, who must be distinguished
from both of his eminent namesakes, the archbishops of Canterbury (d. 1006) and York (d. 1051), was the chief helper of bishop
Ethelwold (d. 984) in making Winchester famous as a place of
education. It was there that he began, and it was at Eynsham
that he continued and completed, the preparation of those school-
books which did so much for the early study of the Latin language
in England. They included a *Latin Grammar*[3], with extracts
translated from Priscian, followed by a *Glossary* of some 3000
words in Latin and English, arranged (more or less) in order of
subjects. This *Glossary* is the oldest Latin-English Dictionary in
existence[4]. The third of these educational works was the *Col-*

---

geometry, and to rhetoric (in the text-book of Victorinus). Cp. *Hist. Litt.* vii
and Cuissard-Gaucheron in *Mém. de la Soc. archéol....de l'Orléanais*, xiv (1875),
579—715; and Wattenbach, i[7] 466 f.

[1] ed. Mai, *Cl. Auct. Vat.* v (1833) 329–49, esp. 334, 346 f; Migne, cxxxix
375 f; Léon Maître, *Écoles*, 76 f; Ebert, iii 392–9. Cp. Haase, *De Medii
Aevi Stud. Philol.* 27. The 600 MSS of Ramsey Abbey (at a later date)
included Terence, Virgil, Ovid, Lucan, Martial and three copies of Horace ;
also the 'Sompnum Cypionis' (Macray's ed. of *Chronicon*, p. xliii, in *Rolls
Series*) ; while the Graeco-Latin Psalter of prior Gregory (*fl.* 1290) has been
found among the MSS at Corpus (M. R. James, *Parker MSS*, p. 10).

[2] See end of Pref. and Index, ed. Stubbs in *Rolls Series*.

[3] *Facsimile* from Cambridge Univ. MS, Hh. 1, 10, on p. 515 *infra.* There
are also MSS in C.C.C. and Trin. Coll. Cambridge, and St John's, Oxford.

[4] Printed at Oxford (1659) ; ed. Zupitza (1880) ; both include the *Grammar.*

*loquium,* in which Latin, being still a living language, is taught in a conversational manner; the Latin words of the dialogue are explained by an interlinear translation; the pupil is made to answer questions as to his own occupations and those of his companions; and the use of the rod is not forgotten[1]. Ælfric is still better known as the author of three courses of *Homilies* (990–6) partly translated from Augustine, Jerome, Gregory and Bede, the Saxon preface of which includes an impressive reference to the expected end of the world[2]. The same topic was the theme of a discourse described in 990 as having been heard at Paris (long before) by Abbo, who became abbot of Fleury after his return from England.

The approach of the year 1000 is said to have filled Christian Europe with an awestruck apprehension that the end of all things was at hand. It is sometimes supposed that the ensuing panic led to a general pause in the pursuits of public life, and that even the tranquil routine of the cloister was paralysed by an imminent expectation of the day of doom. It is further said that, at this crisis, the fear of the future stimulated the generosity of many benefactors of the Church; but, if so, it must (no less inevitably) have arrested the efforts of the student in the monastic school and the copyist in the *scriptorium.* At such a time the latter might well ask himself what avail was there in continuing to transcribe the classic page, if the original and the copy were so soon to perish in the world-wide conflagration of a *Dies Irae,*

> 'When, shriveling like a parched scroll,
> The flaming heavens together roll'.

But, when the fatal hour was past, we are told that monasteries, which had been falling into decay, were rebuilt; 'the earth arrayed herself anew with a white robe of churches'[3]; a great

*The year 1000*

---

[1] M. 'Vultis flagellari in discendo?' D. 'Carius est nobis flagellari pro doctrina quam nescire'. Ed. Thorpe, *Analecta Anglo-Saxonica* (1834) 101 f; and Wright and Wülker's *Vocabularies* (1884) i[2] 79 f. *Facsimile* in *Social England,* i 189[2].

[2] On Ælfric, cp. esp. Dietrich in *Zeitschr. f. hist. Theol.* 1855–6; Ebert, iii 509–16; J. E. B. Mayor in *Journ. of Cl. and S. Philol.* iv 2—5; and Skeat, *Introd.* to *Ælfric's Lives of Saints,* i (1881); also Caroline Louisa White in *Yale Studies in English,* ii (1898) 218 pp.

[3] Rodulfus Glaber, *Hist.* iii 4 (1003 A.D.), 'erat enim instar ac si

architectural movement was begun ; and, in the monastic schools, letters and arts were awakened to a new life[1].   It would doubtless be an exaggeration to assume that this new life was suddenly aroused by no other cause than the passing away of a temporary terror[2].   But, in any case, the millenary year marks the transition from one of the darkest centuries of the Middle Ages to one that was in the main a period of progress culminating in the intellectual revival of the twelfth century.

mundus ipse excutiendo semet, rejecta vetustate, passim candidam ecclesiarum vestem indueret'.

[1] Léon Maître, *Écoles*, 96, and Olleris, *Vie de Gilbert*, 21 (quoted in Mullinger's *Cambridge*, i 45 f) ; also Milman, *Lat. Christ.* iii 329, and Bartoli, *Precursori del Rinascimento*, 18 f.   The approach of the end of the world had been announced in 909, and at least eight deeds of gift between 944 and 1048 begin with the formula, *appropinquante mundi termino* (De Vic et Vaisette, *Hist. de Languedoc*, 1733, ii, *Preuves* pp. 86—215) ; but a similar phrase is to be found in the *Formulae* collected in 660 by an aged monk of Paris named Marculf (see quarto series of *Mon. Germ. Hist., Legum Sectio* v, 1886, p. 74). Cp. Rodulfus Glaber, *Hist.* iv, *Praef.* and cc. 4—5.

[2] Eicken, in *Forschungen zur deutschen Gesch.*, 1883 ; Chr. Pfister, *Études sur le règne de Robert le Pieux* (1885), 322–5 ; Jules Roy, *L'An Mille*, 1885 ; Orsi, in *Rivista Storica Italiana*, 1887, 1—56 ; also G. L. Burr in *Amer. Hist. Rev.* vi no. 3 (April 1901) ; and Rashdall's *Universities*, i 31.

mancipium loquitur min þeal. spptð. mei mancipii filius.
mineþ þealar sunu. meo mancipio fabrico domus. minum
þeale ictimbȳre hus. meum mancipiū ǫecuso. minne þeal
ic beladige. Omeū mancipium sere bene. tala þu minn þeal
sag þel. ameo mancipio multa bona accepi. ɲɲam minū þeale
ic undeþ ɲenᵹ ɲela goda. Et þtr mea mancipia amnt:nine
þealar ᴇiuad. meox mancipiox seᵹttes. ninᵹia beop manna
æceþaᵹ. meis mancipiis diuido denarios. minū beop mannū
ic dæle peneᵹaᵹ. mea mancipia arguo. mine beopan menn
ic þþreaᵹe. Omea mancipia estote fideles. tala ᵹe mine beopan bᴇoð ᵹeþreope. ameis mancipiis adiutus. sum. ɲɲam
minum beopum mannum ic tom ᵹepultumoð. Seþoþma
had. eᵹo. ic. macað hiᵹ metiᵹþealde ᵹetel. nos. þe. ꝼoꝼ
hiᵹ᷄ genitiuum. nꝛi. cumað þa. diriuatiua. nꝛ. ꝺnius.
nꝛ. fꝛ. uþe bþodoþ. nꝛmi ꝼætᴇ. uþne bþoboþ. onꝛ fꝛ. tala
þu uþe bþoboþ. aniŏ ꝼiᴇ. ɲɲam uþᷤ bþtꝺeþ. Eoptꝛ. nꝛi
fꝛi. uþe ᵹebþoþta. nꝛox fꝛm obedientia. uþᷤ ᵹebþoðta
ᵹe hyþsumneᵹs. nꝛis fꝛilᵹ ministro. uþū ᵹebþoþṗm ie beme.
nꝛos fꝛi amo. uþe ᵹebþoþta icluþie. anꝛis fꝛib: ɲɲam uþū
ᵹebþoþṗū. Generis femimini. nꝛ soror. uþe sþu stᴇþ. nꝛe
sororis. ꝺspa poþd spa þe æþ declinodon. mea ancilla.
Generis neutri. nꝛum consilium. uþe pað. nꝛi consilii.
uþeᵹ paðeþ. ꝺspa poþd æþᴇ neutri ᵹeneris. hic & haec
nꝛes. & hoc nꝛ te. uþeᵹ landeᵹ mann oððe elleᵹ hþæt.
nꝛtus. ꝺspa poþd æþᴇ. bæþe bþudan declimnᵹᵹ. Eall
spa ᵹað. hic & haec uꝛi & hoc uꝛ te. toþþeᵹ landeᵹ
mann. Seᴇᴇþeþ had isci. þa. ꝺhiᵹ᷄ ᵹenꝛꝛꝰ us. bᴇŏ cu.

FROM CAMBRIDGE UNIVERSITY MS (Cent. xi) OF ÆLFRIC'S LATIN GRAMMAR,
folio 33 (=p. 18 Zupitza); see p. 512 *supra*.

# Conspectus of History of Scholarship, &c., in the West, 1000—1200 A.D.

| Italy | Spain | France | Germany | British Isles |
|---|---|---|---|---|
| **1000** | | | | |
| 1005 b. Lanfranc | | 1004 d. Abbo of Fleury | 1004 d. Widukind of Corvey | |
| | | | 1017 f. Bamberg | |
| | | 1010 d. Richer of Rheims | 1022 d. Notker Labeo | _c._ 1030 d. Ælfric |
| 1033 b. Anselm | | 1029 d. Fulbert of Char-tres | 1022 d. Bernward of Hildesheim | Eynsham |
| | | 1034 f. Bec | 1036 d. Meinwerk of Paderborn | |
| | | 1045–66 Lanfranc prior of Bec | | |
| _c._ 1050 _fl._ Salerno | | 1050 d. Rodulfus Glaber | 1054 d. Hermannus Contractus | |
| 1053 Papias | | 1066 Lanfranc abbot of Caen | 1060 d. Ekkehard IV | |
| 1056 Anselm of Bi-sate | | 1066–78 Anselm prior of Bec | 1058–77 _fl._ Lambert of Hersfeld | 1070–89 Lanfran abp of Canterbu |
| 1007–72 Petrus Da-miani | 1020–70 Avice-bron | | | |
| 1075 _fl._ Leo Marsi-canus | | 1084 f. Carthusians | 1075 Adam of Bremen | 1075 b. Orderic Vitalis |
| 1050–80 Constanti-nus Afer | | | 1076 d. Immed of Paderborn | |
| 1058–85 Alfanus abp of Salerno | | 1088 d. Berengarius of Tours | | 1077–93 f. _scrip-rium_ at St Alba under abbot Pa |
| 1086–7 Victor III (Desiderius of Monte Cassino) | | 1078–93 Anselm abbot of Bec | | 1093–1109 Ansel abp of Canterbu |
| | | 1098 f. Cistercians | | |
| **1100** | | | | |
| | | | 1100 Conrad of Hir-schau | |
| 1111 William of Apulia | | 1106 d. Roscellinus | | 1109 d. Anselm |
| | | 1112 d. Sigebert of Gem-bloux | | |
| 1113 Irnerius of Bo-logna | | 1115 d. Ivo of Chartres | | |
| 1116 d. Leo Marsi-canus | | 1115 Radulfus Tortarius | | 1118 d. Florence Worcester |
| | | 1120 Honorius of Autun | | |
| 1117 d. Grossolano abp of Milan | | 1121 d. William of Cham-peaux | | |
| | | 1124 d. Guibert of No-gent | | |
| | | 1119–24 _fl._ Bernard of Chartres | | |
| 1128 Jacobus de Ve-netia | | 1125 d. Marbod of Rennes | Metellus of Tegern-see | |
| | | 1134 d. Hildebert of Tours | | 1130 Adelard of Ba |
| | 1138 d. Avem-pace | 1137 f. _Schol. Med._ Montpellier | 1137–58 Otto bp of Freising | |
| | 1130–50 Ray-mond abp of Toledo; trans-lations from Arabic by Joannes His-palensis and Gondisalvi | 1140 Bernard of Cluni | | |
| | | 1079–1142 Abelard | | 1142 d. William Malmesbury |
| | | 1142 d. Hugo of St Victor | | 1147 b. Giraldus Cambrensis |
| | | 1142 d. Ordericus Vi-talis | 1146–58 Wibald abbot of Corvey | 1154 d. Geoffrey Monmouth |
| | | 1142 _fl._ Petrus Helias | | 1155 d. Henry Huntingdon |
| | 1143 Robertus Retinensis | 1146 d. Macarius of Fleury | | 1160 Serlo Gramm ticus |
| | | 1153 d. Bernard of Clair-vaux | 1152–90 Emp. Fred-eric Barbarossa | 1170 Robert of Cri lade |
| 1150 Alberico of Bo-logna | | 1145–53 _fl._ Bernard Sil-vester of Tours | | 1110–80 John of Salisbury |
| | | 1154 d. William of Conches | | 1175 Peter of Bl settles in Englar |
| | | 1154 d. Gilbert de la Porrée | | 1175? b. Michael S |
| | | 1156 d. Petrus Venera-bilis | | 1167–83 Simon abl of St Albans |
| | | 1167 William of Gap | | |
| | | _c._ 1160–70 f. Univ. Paris | 1185 Saxo Gram-maticus | 1154–89 Henry I |
| 1187 d. Gerard of Cremona | 1175 Gerard of Cremona | 1173 d. Richard of St Victor | 1187 Gunther's _Li-gurinus_ | 1196 Walter Ma archdeacon of O ford |
| 1190 Godfrey of Vi-terbo | | 1174 Matthew of Ven-dôme | 1165–95 Herrad of Landsberg | 1198 d. William Newburgh |
| 1191 Henricus Septi-mellensis | 1126–98 Aver-roës | 1184 Jean de Hauteville | | Daniel de Morlai |
| 1194 Burgundio of Pisa | 1135–1204 Mai-monides | 1192 d. Adam of St Victor | | 1200 d. Nigellus V recker |
| **1200** | | | | |

_Continued from page_ 442.

# CHAPTER XXVII.

## THE ELEVENTH CENTURY.

IN France the most notable teacher in the first quarter of the eleventh century is Fulbert, bishop of Chartres (d. 1029). One of his admirers describes the influence of his teaching as passing through many channels:

School of Chartres

'Gurges altus ut minores solvitur in alveos,...
Sic insignes propagasti per diversa plurimos,...
Quorum quisque prae se tulit quod te usus fuerit'[1].

Among the many pupils, who were proud to acknowledge their indebtedness to his teaching, were Lambert and Adelmann at Liège, Berengarius at Tours, Olbert at Gembloux, Angelrann at Saint-Riquier, Reginald at Angers, and Domnus at Montmajour-lez-Arles[2]. In the middle of the century, Saint-Évroult, S. of Lisieux in Normandy, was celebrated as a school of copyists, which sent skilful transcribers to give instruction in the art to inmates of other monasteries in France[3]. The Norman monastery of Bec flourished under the rule of Lanfranc[4] (1045) and Anselm (1066), both of whom came from Northern Italy to Normandy, and were thence called to England to become archbishops of Canterbury.

St Évroult

Bec

In England the incursions of the Danes, which ended in the

---

[1] Mabillon, *Analecta*, i 422 (Léon Maître, *Écoles*, 103); Clerval, *Écoles de Chartres*, 59 f.

[2] See Index to Léon Maître; Clerval, 62 f, 72—91.

[3] Ordericus Vitalis, iii 483, v 582.

[4] *ib.* ii 246.

conquest of the island by Canute (1016), had left no leisure for the pursuits of learning; and the influence of the Norman Conquest of 1066–71 on the intellectual life of the country did not take effect until after the close of this century.  In the story of the many ruthless devastations recorded in the Anglo-Saxon Chronicle, books are mentioned only in connexion with the plundering of Peterborough by Hereward in 1070:—

> 'They took there so much gold and silver, and so many treasures in money and in raiment, and in books, as no man may tell to another, saying they did it from affection to the monastery'[1].

In Germany, the eleventh century saw the foundation of the

Schools of Bamberg and Paderborn

bishopric, library and school of Bamberg (1017), and a revival of learning in the school of Paderborn. This revival was due in part to the influence of Meinwerk, bishop in 1009–36, and still more to that of his nephew, Immed, bishop in 1052–76, in whose time the authors studied included Sallust, Virgil, Horace and Statius[2].  Latin verse on historic and other themes was being written with some success; but, towards the end of the century, the interest in the Classics began to abate.  This was partly due to the influence of the monks of Cluni, who insisted on a stricter monastic discipline and a more complete subservience to the will of the Church, while, in the absorbing struggle for supremacy between Hildebrand and the German emperor, the claims of learning fell into abeyance[3]. About the middle of the century, the styles of Sallust and Livy

Lambert of Hersfeld; Adam of Bremen

were admirably combined in the *Annals* of Lambert of Hersfeld (d. 1077), who was familiar with Terence, Virgil and Horace[4], while Sallust and Lucan were well known to Adam of Bremen, the author of the *Ecclesiastical History of Hamburg* (c. 1075), which is an important authority for the early history of Northern Europe[5].

Early in the century we find a distinguished teacher at

---

[1] Included in plate iii of Skeat's *XII Facsimiles*.

[2] *Vita Meinwerci* in *Mon. Germ. Hist.* xi 140 (Bursian i 55; incompletely quoted in Heeren, i 196).  Cp. Wattenbach, *GQ*, ii⁶ 35 f.

[3] Bursian, i 58—62.          [4] *ib.* i 57; Norden, *Kunstprosa*, 750 f.

[5] Bursian, i 58.  On Adam and Lambert cp. Wattenbach, *GQ*, ii⁶ 79 f, 97 f.

St Gallen in the person of Notker Labeo (d. 1022), also known as
Notker 'the German' from his having translated    Notker Labeo
(or taken part in translating) into that language, not
only the psalms of David, but also the *Andria* of Terence, the
*Eclogues* of Virgil, and the *Distichs* of 'Cato', together with
Martianus Capella, several treatises of Boëthius, and the Latin
version of Aristotle's *Categories* and *De Interpretatione*[1]. He writes
to the bishop of Sion, on the upper Rhone, to tell him that the
abbot of Reichenau has borrowed the bishop's copy of Cicero's
*First Philippic* and the commentary on the *Topica*, depositing as
security for their return the *Rhetoric* of Cicero and of Victorinus;
and he adds that, if the bishop wants certain books, he must send
more parchment and money for the copyists[2]. In the same
century a monk of Reichenau, Hermannus 'Con-
tractus' (the 'cripple', 1013—1054), composed a    Hermannus
                                  'Contractus'
Chronicle founded on the Latin translation of
Eusebius and on Cassiodorus and Bede[3]. The tenth and eleventh
centuries, the golden age of St Gallen, were succeeded by an iron
age in the twelfth century.

Meanwhile, in Italy, where the study of 'grammar' and poetry
seems never to have entirely died out, young nobles and students
preparing for the priesthood were not unfrequently learning Latin
literature together in private grammar-schools[4] conducted either
by lay 'philosophers' or by like-minded clerics, who were regarded
with suspicion by their stricter brethren. One of these liberal
clerics, Anselm of Bisate (*c.* 1047–56), describes
the Saints and the Muses as struggling for his    Anselm
possession, while he was utterly perplexed as to    of Bisate
which he should prefer:—'so noble, so sweet, were both companies
that I could not choose either of them; so that, were it possible,

---

[1] Jourdain, 285 f; Cramer, ii 43; Bursian, i 56. The translations of
Capella, Boëthius and Aristotle were published by Graff in 1837, and also by
Hattemer, *Denkm. d. Mittelalters*, iii 263—372 (Prantl, *Logik*, ii² 61 f);
Specht, 325 f; Manitius, 29 f, 33 f.

[2] J. Grimm, *kl. Schriften*, v 190; P. Piper, *Die Schriften Notkers u. seiner
Schule*, i 861 (Norden, 708).

[3] Bursian, i 56 f; Wattenbach, *GQ*, ii⁶ 42—47.

[4] Giesebrecht, *De Litt. Studiis apud Italos*, p. 15 (=29 of Ital. trans.);
Ozanam, *Documents Inédits* (1850), 1—79.

I had rather choose both than either"[1]. In the same century,
Desiderius, the abbot of Monte Cassino, who became
pope as Victor III (1086–7), was causing his monks
to make copies of Horace, and Ovid's *Fasti*, as well as Seneca and
several treatises of Cicero[2]; Cicero, Sallust and Virgil were
familiar to Leo Marsicanus, the Chronicler of Monte Cassino[3];
and the composition of Latin hexameters and elegiacs, and of
lyrics after the model of Horace and Boëthius, was successfully
cultivated by Alfanus, a monk of the same monastery, who was
archbishop of Salerno from 1058 to 1085[4]. The strict disci-
plinarian, Petrus Damiani (d. 1072), protests in a narrow-minded
way against the 'grammatical' studies of the monks of his time,
who 'cared little for the Rule of Benedict in comparison with the
rules of Donatus'[5]. He admits, however, that ' to study poets and
philosophers with a view to making the wit more keen and better
fitted to penetrate the mysteries of the Divine Word, is to spoil
the Egyptians of their treasures in order to build the Tabernacle
of God'[6]. In sacred verse he is best represented by the hymn on
'the joys and the glory of Paradise', beginning with the words :—
*Ad perennis vitae fontem*[7].

Most of our evidence as to the knowledge of Greek in this
century is derived from certain points of contact
between the West and Constantinople. Early in
the century, Greek artists came to the Old Rome
from the New to cast the bronze doors of the ancient basilica of
' St Paul's outside the Walls ', and Greek characters were used to
inscribe the names of the prophets adorning those doors[8]. Greek,

*Desiderius*

*Greek in
century xi*

---

[1] *Rhetorimachia*, ii ; Dümmler, *Anselm der Peripatetiker* (1872) p. 39
(Poole's *Medieval Thought*, 82).

[2] *Chron. Cassin.* iii c. 63 in Muratori iv 474 ; Giesebrecht, 34 (59 f Ital.
trans.) ; Balzani's *Chroniclers*, 160 f.

[3] d. c. 1116 ; Pertz, *Mon.* vii ; Balzani, 164—173 (*Leo Ostiensis*) ; Wattenbach, *GQ*, ii[6] 234.

[4] Giesebrecht, 54, 66—95 (in Ital. ed. only) ; Ozanam, *l. c.*, 255—270 ;
Shipa, *Alfano I, Arcivescovo di Salerno*, p. 45 (Salerno, 1880).

[5] *Opusc.* xiii c. 11 ; Migne, cxlv 306.

[6] *Opusc.* xxxii c. 9 ; Migne, cxlv 560.

[7] Trench, *Sacred Latin Poetry*, 315 ; J. M. Neale, *Hymns* (1865), 2—15.

[8] Gradenigo, *Letteratura Greco-Italiana* (Brescia, 1759), p. 29.

as well as Latin, was in use in the services at St Peter's[1].   A
patriarch of Venice, Dominico Marengo, who was sent to Constantinople to promote the reunion of the Churches, addressed
the bishop of Antioch in a Greek letter (1053), which is still
extant[2].  Thirteen years later, an Italian known as John Italus
was lecturing at Constantinople on Plato and Aristotle, and on
Proclus and Porphyry[3].  Meanwhile, in the literature of text-
books, we find Papias the Lombard[4] compiling, in          Papias
1053–63, a dictionary of Latin, in which he marks
the quantity and gives the gender and the inflexions of the words,
but draws no distinction between the ancient classical forms and
the barbarous forms in modern use, and cares little for matters of
etymology.   But he invariably gives the Latin rendering of any
Greek word which he has occasion to quote ; he even transcribes
five lines of Hesiod[5], and translates them into Latin hexameters[6].
It has, however, been suspected that this is an interpolation due
to the editor of the Venice edition (1485)[7].  The work includes
definitions of legal terms, with excerpts from earlier glossaries and
from manuals of the liberal arts, including the current text-books
on logic[8].  It was still in use in the sixteenth century.  About
1061 Benzo, bishop of Alba, in his panegyric on          Benzo
the emperor Henry IV[9], makes a display of his
Greek and Latin learning by naming Pindar and Homer, as well
as Terence, Virgil, Lucan, Statius, Horace (*Horatius noster*), and
Quintilian[10] ; but it is probable that his acquaintance with Greek
was solely due to his South-Italian origin[11].  Evidence of Italian
interest in Greek literature is traced by the Laurentian librarian,

---

[1] Gradenigo, *Letteratura Greco-Italiana* (Brescia, 1759), p. 31.

[2] *ib.* 40.                    [3] p. 413 *supra*; Prantl's *Logik*, ii² 301.

[4] Tiraboschi, iii 339 f; Hallam, *Lit.* i 72⁴; Littré on *Glossaires* in *Hist.
Litt. de la France*, xxii (1852) 5—8; *Rhein. Mus.* xxiv (1869) 378, 390;
Teuffel, § 42, 6—9, and § 472, 7.  The principal source of Papias is the
anonymous *Liber glossarum*, partly derived from Placidus (cent. v ?), and
assigned to the early part of cent. viii by Goetz (*Abhandl. sächs. Ges.* xiii 287).

[5] *Theog.* 907–11.                          [6] Gradenigo, 38.

[7] Haase, *De Medii Aevi Studiis Philologicis*, 32 n.

[8] Loewe, *Prodromus Corporis Glossariorum Latinorum*, 235–8; Prantl,
*Logik*, ii² 70.                          [9] Pertz, *Mon.* xi 592.

[10] Graf, *Roma*, ii 172 ; Wattenbach, *GQ*, ii⁶ 228.

[11] Dresdner, *Kultur- u. Sittengeschichte*, 195.

Bandini, in the Greek MSS of the tenth and eleventh centuries belonging to the library of the Benedictine monks in Florence[1]. Italy claims two students of Greek in the persons of Lanfranc and Anselm, both of whom were of Lombard race.

Lanfranc and Anselm

Lanfranc of Pavia (b. *c.* 1005), who studied the liberal arts and law in Italy, spent many years at Bec in Normandy, and was abbot of Caen (1066) and archbishop of Canterbury (1070–89). He is said to have studied Greek[2]. Bec was also (1060–93) the monastic retreat of another future archbishop of Canterbury, Anselm of Aosta (d. 1109), who shows an interest in Greek by quoting the opinions of the Greeks[3], by inquiring for copies of their writings[4], and by selecting Greek names for the titles of two of his works, *monologion* and *proslogion*[5]. He recommends his pupils to study Virgil and other profane authors with due reserve[6].

Before turning to the history of Scholasticism in connexion with the name of Anselm, we may briefly notice that, early in the eleventh century, a Greek Lectionary was copied at Cologne for the Abbey of St Denis (1021)[7]; also that, among the authorities for Norman history, Dudo of St Quentin uses not a few Greek words in the midst of the strange medley of prose and verse in which he panegyrises the early dukes of Normandy, while a more important writer, William of Poitiers, is familiar with Sallust and Caesar[8]. In the same age, the monastery of Hildesheim rose to distinction under Bernward, while that of Fulda was on the decline in 1066. In the second half of the century, St Gallen and Hirschau were continuing to flourish, Hirschau becoming specially

---

[1] *Specimen litt. Florentinae s. xv*, i (1748), p. xxvi.

[2] Migne, cl 30 B; on Lanfranc's studies, cp. Crozals (1877), c. 1, 2. His influence may be traced in a 'prickly' style of writing probably derived from the 'Lombard' hand which he apparently introduced at Bec and Caen, and afterwards at Canterbury (M. R. James, *Sandars Lecture*, 29 May, 1903, and *Ancient Libraries of Canterbury*, p. xxviii). See *facsimile* on p. 523.

[3] Migne, clviii 1144 C.        [4] *ib.* 1120 C.        [5] Tougard, p. 55.

[6] *Ep.* i 55, exceptis his in quibus aliqua turpitudo sonat. Cp. Migne, clvi 852 f.

[7] *Lectionary of Epistles and Gospels*, now in Paris Library (Omont, *MSS Grecs Datés*, pl. xiv).

[8] Migne, cxli; Körting, *Litt. Ital.* III i 85–7; Wattenbach, i[7] 471.

famous as a school of copyists[1].   The latter part of the century
saw the foundation of two new religious Orders, or new branches
of the great Benedictine Order, the Carthusians (1084) and the
Cistercians (1098).   The Rule of the Carthusians enjoins the
duty of keeping useful books and diligently transcribing them.
Guigo (d. 1137), the fifth abbot of the Grande
Chartreuse near Grenoble, who is described by   **Carthusians
and Cistercians**
Trithemius as a man of learning in secular as well
as sacred literature[2], insists on special diligence in the work of
a copyist[3].   The Cistercians distinguished themselves in the
following century by their skill in calligraphy[4]; but neither of
these Orders made any provision for schools open to pupils
unconnected with their monasteries[5].

[1] Heeren, i 234 f.                    [2] *Chron. Hirsaug.* a. 1133.

[3] Heeren, i 254 ; cp. J. W. Clark, *Care of Books*, 69.

[4] *ib.* 232 ; cp. *Hist. Litt. de la France*, vii 11 ; J. W. Clark, 70, 84–9.

[5] On education in cent. x—xi, cp. Schmid's *Gesch. der Erziehung*, II i
232–58 (where Ælfric is strangely omitted).

---

Hunc libru̅ dato precio emptu̅ ego LANFRANCUS archieps de bececu̅li cenobio in
anglica̅ ti̅ram deferri feci & eccl̅e xpi dedi. Siqs eu̅ de iure pꝛfatꜹ ecclesiꜹ
abstulerit· anathema sit·

Clemens epi̅s seruus seruoꝝ d̅i Lanfraa̅co cantuarbieriensi archiepo· salutm̅ & aplica̅m beneddicꞇioꞇe̅.
trinitatis tue latas dilecꞇionis chrigmi̅· quia famꜹ & bone opinionis tue fragrantia̅ sepius odoramefcr̅
pꝛximu̅ d̅o moribus & scientia estimam̅. Bene g̅ certu̅ tene quia te munscerib· nr̅s diligim̅· aplecam̅·
& magis magisq̅ dede indie tui pꝛsentia̅ cꝛoptam̅· cu̅ q̅a tibi ac salutu tue boni· tu̅ etia̅ quia ecclie
d̅i uniuerse· cu̅ haceti̅· maxime in hoc tpore necessarius· Quid q̅ apta acuigilantib· oculis de
nia admiratione refe rem̅ꞇ trinitatis tua pura minati oportet· te aut neglegentia̅ tua̅ emenda
re non deletet. Debuit eni scias & pdentia tue gubernationis ecclie d̅i te uentoꝝ tunstionib· agi
ta̅ꞇ· te aquarum mundationib· pressꜹ· te ruinis & quassationib· lessꜹ· ut me̅ ipsas pcellas maris sub
ueniste· aduto̅rio ei freta q̅ ar· & potar inseri n̅ pꝛ uulebum aduerfuse̅· Visita g̅ fr̅ & adiuua ma
tre̅ tua̅· respice penitu· uide petra̅ supꝛ qua̅ fundaute dicecla̅m sui̅· Honno͞sppe̅ peccatanti̅ despicꜹ
ad̅· si admerita mi inte̅ntione retorqueat· Spꝛ us eni meruint ruina̅ quia cathedra̅· quia teste d̅o
minti suscepti̅· mulesq̅ modisf utriatur uoliunt̅· Ad q̅o rande fr̅ trinatatie tua̅ dilectionis nr̅e pꝛsentib̅
latis co̅monent̅· ad q̅o cu̅ memo itta̅ & amoris affectu mutatamut̅· habito pꝛ oculis amore & timore d̅
expguscere· simulq̅ quo pote serrore ac supbia̅ quꜹ contra scia̅m romana̅ ecca̅m pullulaunt euellere con
tende· omisq̅ coepos fr̅ti nr̅os eunta parte salima· & adhonore & utilitatꜹ scꝉ romanꜹ eccꝉe studio scia̅is̅
siueriu̅ hortare·

SPECIMENS OF CHRIST CHURCH, CANTERBURY, HAND (*c.* 1070–84), from
the last few leaves of a beautifully written xi century MS of *Decretals*
(in a Christ Church hand) and *Canons* (apparently in an Italian hand),
given by Lanfranc to Christ Church, Canterbury, and by Whitgift to
Trinity College, Cambridge; MS B 16. 44 (M. R. James, *Catalogue of
Western MSS*, i 540 f). Size rather larger than ¼ of the original. See
further in *List of Illustrations*.

# CHAPTER XXVIII.

## THE TWELFTH CENTURY.—THE SCHOOLMEN AND THE CLASSICS.

WHILE John the Scot was a precursor of Scholasticism, an important place in the first period of its history

**The early Schoolmen and the Classics**

is occupied by Anselm. It may therefore be convenient, at this stage of our survey, to glance at that history, so far as it has points of contact with the study of Greek or Latin texts, and to endeavour to indicate, in the case of the leading Schoolmen, the extent of their acquaintance with the Classics[1].

The term σχολαστικός is first found, in the sense of 'devoting one's leisure to learning', in a letter addressed by Theophrastus to his pupil Phanias[2]; *scholasticus* is applied to a Scholar by Gregory the Great[3]; and the title of *doctores scholastici* was given

---

[1] Among the books consulted in this connexion are Ueberweg's *Grundriss der Gesch. der Philosophie* (ed. 8 Heinze, 1894), E.T. 1875; Hauréau, *La Philosophie Scolastique*, ed. 2 (1872); Prantl, *Gesch. der Logik im Abendlande* (1855–70); Maurice, *Mediaeval Philosophy* (1857; new ed. 1870); Milman's *Lat. Christ.* ix 100–161; also Tables vi, vii in F. Schultze's *Stammbaum der Philosophie* (1890), and Prof. Seth in *Enc. Brit.* xxi 417—431 (where the Histories by Kaulich and Stöckl are quoted). Among the monographs on portions of the subject are Jourdain's *Recherches* (ed. 1843); Rousselot's *Études* (1840-2); Cousin's Introd. to *Abélard* (1836), reprinted in *Frag. Phil.* ii; Hauréau's *Singularités Hist. et Litt.* (1861), and *Notices et Extraits*, 6 vols. (1891-3); R. L. Poole's *Illustrations of the History of Medieval Thought* (1884); and, among more general works, Erdmann's *Grundriss der Gesch. der Philosophie*, ed. 3, 1878, E.T. 1898³, i §§ 149—225; and Schmid's *Gesch. der Erziehung*, II i 282—308; also Gröber's *Grundriss*, II i 239—247. Cp. *Enc. Brit.* ed. 1911, xxiv 346—356.

[2] Diog. Laërt. v 35.                    [3] *Epp.* ix 26 in *Mon. Germ. Hist.*

to the teachers of theology and the liberal arts, and particularly
to the teachers of dialectic, in the Caroline age. Scholasticism
may be described as a reproduction of ancient philosophy under
the control of ecclesiastical doctrine[1]. Its history (including that
of its precursors) falls into two main divisions, (1) the accommodation of Aristotelian logic and Neo-Platonic philosophy to the
doctrine of the Church, from the time of Joannes Scotus (d. 875)
to that of Amalrich (d. 1207) and his followers, *i.e.* from century
ix to the beginning of century xiii ; (2) the accommodation of the
Aristotelian philosophy, *which had now become fully known*, to the
dogmas of the Church, from the time of Alexander of Hales
(d. 1245) to the end of the Middle Ages.

John the Scot had affirmed the identity of true religion with
true philosophy[2], but he interpreted the teaching of the Church
in the light of ' Dionysius the Areopagite ', whose doctrines he
wrongly supposed to be those of the early Christians, whereas
they were really those of the Neo-Platonists of the latter part of
the fifth century[3]. Believing that the ' general ' existed before the
' particular ', he practically held the Platonic doctrine of ideas in
the form afterwards expressed by the phrase, *universalia ante rem.*
On the other hand, those whom he describes as *dialectici* held
that individual objects were substances in a primary sense, while
*species* and *genera* were substances only in a secondary way. This
doctrine was derived partly from the dialectical works of Aristotle,
and from Porphyry's *Introduction*, as translated and expounded by
Boëthius ; and partly from works attributed to St Augustine.
Porphyry's *Introduction*, as translated by Boëthius, mentions the
five predicables, *i.e.* the notions of genus, species, difference,
property, and accident. It also touches on the question whether
*genera* and *species* have a substantial existence, or whether they
exist merely as mental conceptions. This question, and others

---

[1] ' The scholastic philosophy was an attempt to codify all existing knowledge
under laws or formulae analogous to the general principles of justice. It was
no attempt...to bind all knowledge with chains to the rock of S. Peter, or even
to the rock of Aristotle...Truth is one and indivisible, and the medieval
philosophy found its work in reconciling all existing knowledge logically with
the One Truth which it believed itself to possess '. Stubbs, *Lectures on
Medieval...History*, Lect. xi, 211[1].

[2] p. 493 *supra.*                    [3] p. 376 *supra.*

arising out of it, had been suggested to Porphyry by the *Metaphysics* of Aristotle, by the *Parmenides* of Plato, and by the teaching of his own master, Plotinus. Porphyry, however, declined to discuss them, but this passage of Porphyry, as translated by Boëthius[1], gave the first impulse to the long controversy between Realism and Nominalism, which continued until the revival of learning. ' A single ray borrowed from the literature of the ancient world called Scholasticism into being; the complete revelation of that literature extinguished it'[2].

Plato's doctrine (as stated by Aristotle) that ' universals ' have an independent existence and are ' before ' individual objects (whether in point of rank alone, or in point of time as well) is extreme Realism. Its formula is *universalia sunt realia ante rem*. The Aristotelian view that ' universals ', while possessing a real existence, exist only *in* individual objects, is moderate Realism. Its formula is *universalia sunt realia in re*. Nominalism, on the other hand, implies that individuals alone have a real existence, that *genera* and *species* are only subjective combinations of similar elements, united by the aid of the same concept, which we express by one and the same word (*vox* or *nomen*). Nominalism has two varieties, stress being laid in (1) on the subjective nature of the concept, and in (2) on the identity of the word employed to denote the objects comprehended under the concept. (1) is Conceptualism, and (2) is extreme Nominalism; and the formula of both is *universalia sunt nomina post rem*. All these views appear in different degrees of developement in the ninth and tenth centuries.

The first period of Scholasticism began in Platonic Realism and ended in Conceptualism; while the second began in Aristotelian Realism and ended in Nominalism. Thus, in the first period, the Realism of Joannes Scotus (d. 875), and that of Anselm (d. 1109), which stands in contrast with the early Nominalism of Roscellinus (d. 1106), are followed by the Realism of William of Champeaux (d. 1121) and the Conceptualism of Abelard (d. 1142). In the second, the Aristotelian Realism of the Franciscans, Alexander of Hales (d. 1245) and Bonaventura

---

[1] p. 253 *supra*.

[2] Cousin quoted on p. 441 (cp. Mullinger's *Cambridge*, i 50).

(d. 1274), and of the Dominicans, Albertus Magnus (d. 1280) and
Thomas Aquinas (d. 1274), is criticised by Roger Bacon (d. 1294)
and Duns Scotus (d. 1308), who are succeeded by the great
Nominalist, William of Ockham (d. 1347).

Until the fourth decade of the twelfth century, the only logical
writings of the ancients known in the Middle Ages
were Aristotle's *Categories* and *De Interpretatione*          Aristotle
(in the translation of Boëthius); Porphyry's *Introduction to the
Categories*, as translated by Victorinus and Boëthius; the
Augustinian *Principia Dialecticae*, and the Pseudo-Augustinian
*Categoriae Decem*; Martianus Capella, and Cassiodorus *On
Dialectic*; and the following works of Boëthius:—his com-
mentaries on the above translations of Porphyry and on Aristotle
*De Interpretatione* and Cicero's *Topica*, with certain minor works
on syllogisms etc. Besides these there was Isidore. Thus of the
five parts of Aristotle's *Organon*, the *Categories* and *De Inter-
pretatione* alone were known, while the *Analytics*, *Topics* and
*Sophistici Elenchi* remained (for the time being) unknown. The
*Analytics* and *Topics* (as translated by Boëthius) were unknown to
Sigebert of Gembloux (d. 1112)[1]; they came into notice after
1128 (the date of the Venice translation by Jacobus Clericus)[2], the
*Prior Analytics* being discussed in 1132[3] by Adam du Petit-Pont
(afterwards bishop of St Asaph), and cited by Gilbert de la Porrée
(d. 1154)[4]. The whole of the *Organon* was known to John of
Salisbury (in 1159), while the *Physics* and *Metaphysics* came into
notice about 1200[5]. Meanwhile, Plato was represented by the
Latin rendering of part of the *Timaeus* executed by Chalcidius
(cent. iv), which included some account of the theory of Ideas[6];
by the statement of Plato's opinions in Aristotle; by the passages
quoted in Cicero, Augustine and Macrobius; and by the account

---

[1] Prantl, *Logik*, ii[2] 77, 212 f.                          [2] p. 557 *infra*.

[3] Cousin, *Frag. Phil*. ii 333 f; Prantl, ii[2] 104.

[4] Prantl, ii[2] 105, 217 f.

[5] Amable Jourdain, *Recherches critiques sur l'âge et l'origine des traductions
latines d'Aristote, et sur les commentaires grecs ou arabes employés par les
docteurs scolastiques* (1819), ed. 2 (Charles Jourdain, 1843). Cousin, *Frag.
Phil*. ii 55—62; Hauréau, i 90—121; Prantl, *Logik*, ii c. 13 and 14; Summary
in Ueberweg, i 367 E.T., and by C. H. Haskins, *Am. Hist. Rev*. 1920, 612.

[6] 28 A, 48 E (trans. ends with 53 C). Cp. p. 374 *supra*.

of his tenets given by Apuleius *De Dogmate Platonis*. The
*Phaedo* and the *Meno* had been translated about 1160[1], but were
little known.

Late in the tenth and early in the eleventh century, Logic was
eagerly studied at Fulda and Würzburg, and at St Gallen under
Notker Labeo[2]; also, in France, in the eleventh century, by
Gerbert and his pupil, Fulbert of Chartres (d. 1029), and by the
latter's pupil, Berengarius of Tours (d. 1088). Berengarius cast
contempt on the traditional authority of Priscian,
Donatus and Boëthius[3], and preferred the study of
the *arts* of Grammar and Logic to that of the
ancient *authors*, thus anticipating a conflict which will attract our
attention in the sequel[4]. He also anticipates one of the great
scholastic debates of the future in his attack on the doctrine
afterwards known as that of transubstantiation, which was defended
by Lanfranc (d. 1089). But, in this controversy, both the contending parties (unlike the Schoolmen of the future) appealed to
authority, and not to reason[5]. Reason *subordinated* to authority
was the guiding principle of Lanfranc's great successor, Anselm
(d. 1109), the champion of Realism and also of
the normal tenets of the Church against that early
Nominalist, Roscellinus (d. 1106)[6], whose Nominalism led him to tritheism. 'The Platonically conceived proof of
the being of God contained in the *Monologium* shows that Anselm's
doctrine of the universals as substances in things (*universalia in
re*) was closely connected in his mind with the thought of the
*universalia ante rem*, the exemplars of perfect goodness and truth
and justice, by participation in which all earthly things are judged
to possess those qualities. In this way he rises like Plato to the
absolute Goodness, Justice and Truth, and then proceeds in

*Berengarius
and Lanfranc*

*Roscellinus
and Anselm*

---

[1] By 'Euericus' Aristippus, archdeacon of Catania (Rashdall's *Universities*,
ii 744). The trans. of the *Phaedo* is found in Paris catalogues of 1250 and
1290 (V. Le Clerc, *Hist. Litt. de la France au 14ᵉ s.*, 425, cp. Cousin, *Frag.
Phil.* ii 466). The translator is identified by Rose (*Hermes*, i, 1866, 373–89)
with Henricus Aristippus, possibly the 'learned Greek' with whom John of
Salisbury studied the *Organon*, probably at Beneventum (p. 540 *infra*). See,
however, Haskins and Lockwood in *Harvard Studies* XXI (1910), 86–9.

[2] p. 519 *supra*.          [3] Prantl, *Logik*, ii² 73 n.          [4] End of c. xxxii.
[5] Cp. Poole's *Medieval Thought*, 102 f.          [6] Prantl, *Logik*, ii² 78—96.

Neo-platonic fashion to a deduction of the Trinity as involved in the idea of the Divine Word'[1].

Nominalism made its first prominent appearance in the latter part of the eleventh century[2], when certain Schoolmen ascribed to Aristotle the doctrine that Logic was concerned only with the right use of words and that *genera* and *species* were only subjective, and disputed the real existence of 'universals'. These Schoolmen were sometimes called the '*modern* dialecticians', because they opposed the traditional realistic interpretation of Aristotle. The extreme Nominalism of Roscellinus and the Realism of William of Champeaux (d. 1121)[3] were impartially opposed by a celebrated pupil of both, Abelard (d. 1142), who maintained the moderate form of Nominalism since known as Conceptualism[4]. Abelard went further than his predecessors in the application of dialectic to theology. In dialectic he regards Aristotle as the highest authority :—'if we suppose Aristotle, the leader of the Peripatetics, to have been in fault, what other authority shall we receive in matters of this kind?' The only thing that Abelard cannot tolerate in Aristotle is his polemic against Plato. Abelard prefers, by a favourable interpretation of Plato, to pronounce both to be in the right[5]. His voluminous writings include glosses on Porphyry's *Introduction*, on Aristotle's *Categories* and *De Interpretatione*, and also on the *Topica* of Boëthius[6]. He was acquainted with no Greek works except in Latin translations, but he advises the nuns of 'the Paraclete' to study Greek and Hebrew, as well as Latin, and points to the example set by their mother superior, Heloïssa[7]. Plato[8] he knew only through the quotations in Aristotle, Cicero, Macrobius, Augustine and Boëthius. He definitely states that he could not learn Plato's dialectic from Plato's own writings, because the latter had not been translated[9]. He certainly used the translation of the *Timaeus*

---

[1] Seth in *Enc. Brit.* xxi 422.

[2] On 'precursors of Nominalism', cp. Poole, 336 f.

[3] Michaud (1867) ; Prantl, ii 130[2] f.

[4] Poole, 140 f.

[5] *Dial.* pp. 204–6 (Ueberweg, i 391 E.T.).

[6] Ueberweg, i 388.                    [7] Cousin, *Frag. Phil.* ii 51.

[8] *Inst. Theol.* i 17 ; ii 17 etc.

[9] *Dial.* 205 f ; Cousin, *Frag. Phil.* ii 50—56.

by Chalcidius[1]; he is familiar with the 'pattern-forms, which Plato calls the ideas', and he knows that 'Plato conceived of God as an artificer who planned and ordered everything before he made it'[2]. He is also inclined to accept Plato's exclusion of poets from his commonwealth, holding that their study, however necessary, should not be too long continued[3]. He states that Aristotle's *Physics* and *Metaphysics* had not been translated[4]. His knowledge of Aristotle was confined to the *Categories* and *De Interpretatione*, and the *Analytica Priora* in some other translation than that of Boëthius[5]. Besides these, his text-books include Porphyry's *Introduction*, four treatises of Boëthius[6], and the writings ascribed to 'Hermes Trismegistus'. But before composing his *Dialectica*, which is his most permanent contribution to the advancement of learning (and must be earlier than 1132), he certainly had an indirect knowledge of three of the logical treatises of Aristotle, which gradually became known after 1128[7]. The anonymous treatise *De Intellectibus*, once ascribed to Abelard, implies an acquaintance with a translation of the *Analytica Posteriora*[8] different from that of Boëthius. While his strictly orthodox opponent, Bernard of Clairvaux, looked with suspicion on all human learning, Abelard maintained the importance of secular literature as an indispensable aid to sacred studies[9]. When he foresaw the likelihood of his own condemnation for heresy, he gave proof of his familiarity with the Latin Classics by turning to Gilbert de la Porrée (who apparently lay under similar suspicions), and applying to Gilbert the line of Horace :—

'nam tua res agitur, paries cum proximus ardet'[10].

Even so strong an opponent of secular learning as Peter the

---

[1] *Intr. ad Theol.* clxxviii 1007, 1013 Migne (*Tim.* 27 C, 34 C).

[2] *Intr. ad Theol.* ii 109 (Poole, 172).

[3] *Theol. Chr.* ii 445 (Poole, 169).

[4] *Dialect.* p. 200 Cousin.

[5] Prantl, ii[2] 100 f.

[6] *Dial.* 140 f, libros Divisionum cum Syllogismis tam categoricis quam hypotheticis (Ueberweg, i 390).

[7] p. 527 *supra*; Prantl, ii[3] 102 f.

[8] Prantl, ii[2] 104 n. 19, and 206 f.   Ueberweg, i 396.

[9] Poole, 169.

[10] i *Ep.* 18, 84; *ib.* 134.

Venerable, in breaking to Heloïssa the news of the death of Abelard, charitably describes him as 'ever to be named with honour as the servant of Christ and verily Christ's philosopher'[1]. He has also left his mark on the history of European education. The great popularity of the lectures given in Paris by this eloquent, brilliant, vain, impulsive and self-confident disputant, has led to his being regarded as the precursor of the time when Paris became the School of Europe[2].

Bernard of Chartres (d. *c.* 1126), William of Conches (d. 1154) and Adelard of Bath (*fl.* 1130) held a Platonism modified by Christianity, while they maintained the authority of Aristotle with regard to our knowledge **Bernard of Chartres** of the world of sense. 'In comparison with the ancients, we stand (says Bernard, of himself and his contemporaries) like dwarfs on the shoulders of giants'[3]. Bernard, 'the most perfect Platonist of his age'[4], was a believer in the essential harmony of Plato and Aristotle. He looked on learning as the fruit of humble and patient research, pursued through a tranquil life of poverty and seclusion from public affairs[5]. The fame of his School of Classical Scholarship, and the story of his method, still live in the pages of John of Salisbury[6]. Next to Bernard of Chartres, his pupil William of Conches (d. 1154), who **William of Conches** taught at Chartres and Paris, is regarded by John of Salisbury as the most accomplished scholar of his time[7]. He produced a commentary on the *Timaeus* of Plato and on the *Consolatio* of Boëthius, with a comprehensive but incomplete work

[1] Poole, 166.

[2] On Abelard, cp. (besides Hauréau and Ueberweg) Rémusat (1845); Prantl, ii[2] 162—205; Milman, *Lat. Christ.* iv 326—368; Poole's *Medieval Thought*, 136—176, and the literature there quoted (p. 137); also Compayré (1893), J. McCabe (1901), and Rashdall's *Universities*, i 48—57.

[3] Quoted by John of Salisbury, *Met.* iii 4, and (without name) by Peter of Blois, *Ep.* 92.

[4] *Met.* iv 35.

[5] 'mens humilis, studium quaerendi, vita quieta, | scrutinium tacitum, paupertas, terra aliena, | haec reserare solent multis obscura legendo'; quoted and expounded by John of Salisbury, *Policraticus*, vii 13, and by Hugo of St Victor (d. 1141).

[6] *Met.* i 24; Clerval, *Écoles de Chartres*, 158 f, 180 f, 248 f; *infra* p. 539.

[7] *ib.* i 5, 'grammaticus opulentissimus'.

on *Philosophy*, in which Galen is quoted, while words borrowed
from Greek are not rare[1]. This work was reduced to a more
orthodox form in his *Dragmaticon*, where, in regard to his
relations towards Plato, he says of himself, 'Christianus sum,
non Academicus'[2]. In the same age the great
Adelard of<br>Bath traveller, Adelard of Bath (*c.* 1130), visited Spain,
Greece, Asia Minor and Egypt. He was one of the
earliest translators of Euclid from Arabic into Latin[3]; he also
endeavoured to reconcile the opinions of Plato and Aristotle on
the question of 'universals'[4]. A contemporary pupil of Bernard,
Gilbert de la Porrée (*c.* 1075—1154), the foremost
Gilbert de la<br>Porrée logician among the Realists of this century, was the
author of a commentary on Boëthius *De Trinitate*,
and of a work on the last six of the Categories which was printed
in the earliest Latin editions of Aristotle. He was the first writer
after Boëthius and Isidore, who was recognised in the Middle Ages
as an authority on Logic[5]. He cites the *Analytics* as already
generally known[6]. His pupil, Otto of Freising
Otto of<br>Freising (d. 1158), was one of the first to introduce into
Germany the *Topica, Analytica* and *Sophistici
Elenchi*, possibly in the translation by Boëthius[7]; but he is far
more famous as the faithful counsellor and as the sagacious
historian of the earlier exploits of his distinguished nephew,
Frederic Barbarossa[8].

Bernard of Chartres, the chancellor of 1119 to 1126, was
succeeded by Gilbert de la Porrée, who held that office from
about 1126 to 1141, and was afterwards bishop of Poitiers from

---

[1] *Hist. Litt. de la France*, xii 466.

[2] vi 306; Hauréau, i 430 f; Prantl, ii[2] 127 f; Poole, 124—131; Clerval,
181 f, 264 f.

[3] An earlier translation of cent. x—xi, at Munich, is mentioned by
M. Curtze, in Bursian's *Jahresb.* xl (1884) 19.

[4] *De Eodem et Diverso* (*c.* 1105–16); Jourdain, *Recherches critiques*, 258;
Hauréau, i 352 f; Wüstenfeld, *Göttingen Abhandl.* 1877, pp. 20—23; Steinschneider, *Hebr. Uebersetz.* 463, 507.

[5] Poole, 132–5; 179—200; Berthaud (Poitiers, 1892); Clerval, 163 f, 261 f.

[6] *Liber Sex Principiorum*, ed. 1552 (Jourdain, p. 29).

[7] Ragevinus, *Gesta Frid.* iv 11, Pertz, *Mon.* xx 451 (Prantl, ii[2] 105, 229).

[8] Balzani's *Chroniclers*, 249–56; Wattenbach, *GQ*, ii[6] 271–9.

1142 to his death in 1154. In the breadth of his intellectual
interests, and in his power of bringing all of them to bear on
any subject he had in hand, Gilbert was true to the traditions of
Bernard[1]. His successor as chancellor was Bernard's younger
brother Theodoric, who was appointed in 1141 and
died *c.* 1150–5. He is known as the author of the      Theodoric of
                                                        Chartres
following works:—(1) a philosophic treatise *de sex*
*dierum operibus*, being an attempt to reconcile the Biblical account
of the Creation with the views of Plato in the *Timaeus*[2]; (2) a
commentary on the *Ad Herennium*[3]; (3) a survey of the Seven
Liberal Arts in two vast volumes filling in all 1190 pages, which
he bequeathed to the Chapter of Chartres, where it is still to be
seen in the public library[4]. In this work, probably written about
1141, he deals (under the head of *Dialectic*) with all the treatises
in the *Organon* except the *Later Analytics*, and is among the first
of the mediaeval writers to attempt to popularise their contents[5].
John of Salisbury, who tells us that he attended his lectures on
Rhetoric[6] without much profit, describes him as *artium studiosis-*
*simus investigator*[7]. He has been identified as the keen disputant
mentioned in the *Metamorphosis Goliae* (1141):—the 'doctor
Carnotensis, | cujus lingua vehemens truncat velut ensis'[8]. In
1144 Rodolphus of Bruges, a pupil of Theodoric, and of Hermann
the Dalmatian (one of the early translators from Arabic into
Latin), sent him from Toulouse a rendering of Ptolemy's *Plani-*
*sphere* with a flattering dedication[9]; and, between 1145 and 1153,

---

[1] John of Salisbury, *Hist. Pontificalis*, xii p. 526 (Poole, 121).

[2] Paris MS 3584; Hauréau, *Notices et Extraits*, xxii (2) 167; Clerval,
*Écoles de Chartres*, 254–9.

[3] Wattenbach in *S. Ber. bayr. Akad.* 1872, p. 581; P. Thomas in
*Mélanges Graux*, 42.

[4] Clerval, *L'Enseignement des Arts Libéraux à Chartres et à Paris...d'après*
*l'Eptateuchon de Thierry* (1893), and *Écoles* (1895), 220—240. First identified
in 1888 by the Abbé Clerval, who showed me the MS at Chartres in April,
1903. It is written in double columns, in a bold and clear hand; but the
Greek words (borrowed from Priscian) are somewhat inaccurately spelt.

[5] Clerval, *Écoles*, 244 f.          [6] *Met.* ii 10.          [7] *Met.* i 5.

[8] *Metamorphosis Goliae*, 189 (p. 28 ed. Wright); Hauréau, *Mém. de l'Acad.*
*des Inscr.* xxviii (2), 1876, 226.

[9] Wüstenfeld, *Göttingen Abhandl.* 1877, 52; Clerval, *Écoles*, 171; Steinschneider, *Hebr. Uebersetz.* 534 f.

Bernard Silvester of Tours dedicated his celebrated treatise *De Mundi Universitate* to Theodoric in the following terms:— 'Terrico, veris scientiarum titulis Doctori famosissimo, Bernardus Silvestris opus suum'. The perusal of the rest of the dedication[1] is hardly needed to convince us that Bernard Silvester is not the same as Bernard of Chartres, the brother of Theodoric. Theodoric was succeeded as chancellor by a third Bernard, Bernard of Moélan, who, like the brothers Bernard and Theodoric of Chartres, was of Breton birth, and ended his days in his native land as bishop of Quimper (1159—1167)[2].

Bernard Silvester (or Silvestris) is definitely connected with Tours in the following couplet written by his pupil Matthew of Vendôme:—

Bernard Silvester of Tours

'me docuit dictare decus Turonense magistri
      Silvestris, studii gemma, scolaris honor'[3];

and, in his *Poëtria*, the same pupil quotes as *in libro Cosmographiae Turonensis*, a couplet which is found in the *De Mundi Universitate* of Bernard Silvester, the date of which is determined by its reference to the pontificate of another Bernard, Eugenius III (1145–53). Bernard Silvester is described as follows by Henri d'Andely in the *Bataille des Sept Arts*[4]:—

> 'Bernardin li Sauvages,
> Qui connoissoit toz les langages
> Des esciences et des arts'.

---

[1] Reprinted from Barach's text by Clerval, 220, who draws no inference from the terms of the dedication. The tone is clearly not that of a *brother*.

[2] Bernard of Chartres was formerly identified with Bernard Silvester (*Hist. Litt.* xii 261), and both of them with Bernard of Moélan, bishop of Quimper (Hauréau, *Comptes Rendus, Acad. des Inscr.* 1873, 75, and Poole, 114 f). But it has since been made clear by Clerval (*Lettres Chrétiennes*, v 393) and admitted by Hauréau (*Mém. Acad. Inscr.* xxxi (2) 1884, 77—104), that there were three different persons:—(1) Bernard of Chartres (d. *c.* 1126–30); (2) B. Silvester of Tours (*fl.* 1145–53); and (3) B. of Moélan, bp of Quimper (d. 1167). C. V. Langlois, *Bibl. de l'école des chartes*, 1893, 237–50, still identifies (1) and (2). Hauréau's date for the death of (1), 'soon after 1141', is corrected by Clerval, *Écoles*, 1895, 158 f.

[3] Hauréau, *Mém.* 1884, 99. Bernard's *Summa Dictaminum*, a manual of instruction in writing Latin letters, was composed in verse, probably at Tours, in or after 1153. It was abridged in prose by a canon of Meung (Langlois, *l. c.* 225–37).          [4] 328 f.

Bernard was a scholar of a musing, meditative type, who, in his two short books *On the Universe* (entitled the *Megacosmus* and the *Microcosmus* respectively)[1] supplies us with a work on philosophical Mythology, mainly founded on the *Timaeus*, and written in a somewhat pagan spirit. Like the *Consolatio* of Boëthius, it consists of prose varied with verse. The prose is concise and obscure, while the verse is vigorous, and is suggestive of a wide knowledge of the classical poets. Most of the nine poems are in elegiacs, and only one in hexameters. Notwithstanding an able writer's opinion that the model of the author of these poems was Lucretius[2], they supply no certain proof of any knowledge of that poet; the rhythm of the hexameters is clearly that of Lucan, while the vocabulary is mainly that of Ovid[3]. The work was ranked by Eberhard of Bethune[4] next to the *Consolatio* of Boëthius and the *Satyricon* of Martianus Capella. Its author is characterised by Gervase of Tilbury as *egregius*, both as a 'versifier' and as a 'philosopher'[5]. Bernard also wrote an allegorical commentary on the first half of the *Aeneid*[6], as well as an exposition of the *Eclogues* of Theodulus[7], and a prose and verse rendering of

---

[1] *De Mundi Universitate*, ed. Barach and Wrobel (Innsbruck, 1876).

[2] Poole, 118, 219 n. (after Schaarschmidt, *Johannes Saresberiensis*, 75).

[3] My opinion is confirmed by that of Mr J. D. Duff, who, after examining the whole work at my request, has noted reminiscences of Ovid, *Met.* i 85 (p. 55, l. 30) and *Am.* i 5, 21 f (p. 69, l. 3); also of Juvenal, iii 203 f (p. 16, l. 41) and v 23 (p. 17, l. 68). In the *verse*, he finds no certain trace of Lucretius, but he notices an apparent parallel to Lucr. iii 19 f in the following passage of the *prose* (p. 36 f) :—' Anastros in caelo regio est...indefecto lumine, serenitate perpetua...Ea igitur...non densatur pluviis, non procellis incutitur nec nubilo turbidatur'. Here, however, I have no doubt that, while *Anastros* comes from Mart. Capella, viii § 814, the rest is derived from Apuleius, *De Mundo*, c. 33 (translated from the Pseudo-Aristotelian *De Mundo*, c. vi p. 400) : —(Ὄλυμπος) 'neque caliginem nubium recipit vel pruinas et nives sustinet; nec pulsatur ventis nec imbribus caeditur'. Then follows in Apuleius, as in 'Aristotle', a quotation of Homer, *Od.* vi 42–5, the original source of Lucr. iii 19 f.

[4] *Lab.* iii 85 p. 830 Leyser.

[5] *Otia imp.* in Leibnitz, *Scr. Rer. Brunsw.* (1707) i 888, 975.

[6] Specimens of this, and the *Megacosmus* and *Microcosmus* in Cousin, *Frag. Phil.* ii 265—291, cp. 134—142, ed. 1855 etc. Cp. Hauréau, i 407 f; Prantl, ii 162²; Gröber, 384. The *Megacosmus*, c. iii ll. 37—48, is imitated by Chaucer, *Cant. Tales*, 4617.

[7] Cp. G. L. Hamilton, *Theodulus, a mediaeval textbook*, and *Th. in France*, in *Modern Philology*, Oct. 1909, and Apr. 1911.

an Arabic treatise on astrology, probably translated for him by Hermann the Dalmatian[1]. A treatise on the astrolabe in the library at Chartres is dedicated by Hermann to one B., who is probably Bernard Silvester[2], sometimes erroneously identified with his earlier contemporary Bernard of Chartres.

[1] *Experimentarius Bernardi, sive Bernardini, Silvestris*; Bodl. MSS, Digby 46 and Ashmole 304 (Langlois, *l. c.* 248 f). On examining the Pepys MS 911, *De Virtute Planetarum*, in Magdalene Coll., Cambridge, I find that this is another copy of the *Experimentarius*.

[2] Clerval, *Hermann le Dalmate*, 1891, p. 11.

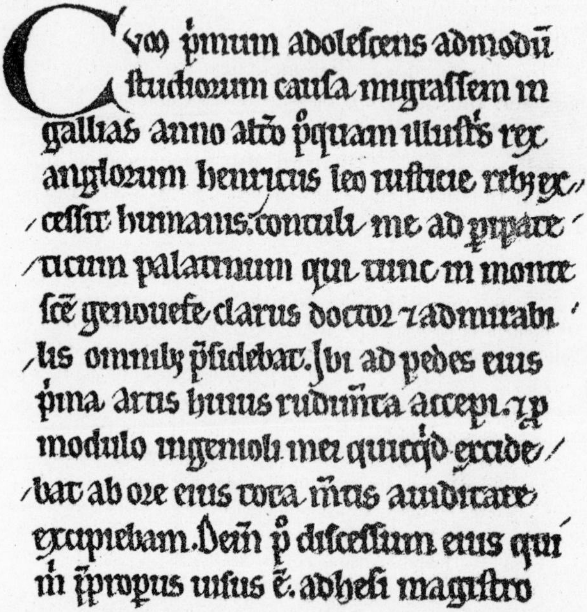

Cum primum adolescens admodum
studiorum causa migrassem in
gallias anno altero postquam illustris rex
anglorum henricus leo iustitie rebus ex-
cessit humanis. contuli me ad peripate-
ticum palatinum qui tunc in monte
sancte genouefe clarus doctor et admirabi-
lis omnibus presidebat. Ibi ad pedes eius
prima artis huius rudimenta accepi. et pro
modulo ingenioli mei quicquid excide-
bat ab ore eius tota mentis auiditate
excipiebam. Deinde post discessum eius qui
mihi preproperus uisus est. adhesi magistro

FROM THE MS OF JOHN OF SALISBURY'S METALOGICUS ETC. in the Library of Corpus Christi College, Cambridge. This copy once belonged to Becket, *Sancti Thome archiepiscopi* having been erased on the flyleaf (see M. R. James, quoted on p. 538 n. 3 *infra*). In the above extract from *Met.* ii 10, the *Leo Justitiae* is Henry I (d. 1135), and the *Peripateticus Palatinus*, Abelard (b. at *Palatium*, Le Pallet, near Nantes).

# CHAPTER XXIX.

## THE TWELFTH CENTURY CONTINUED.

THE narrow scholastic study of Logic found an able critic in John of Salisbury (1110—1180). In 1136 he went to Paris, where he attended Abelard's lectures on Logic, as well as those of the orthodox Realists, Alberic of Rheims and Robert of Melun (afterwards bishop of Hereford). Both of these last would, in his opinion, have distinguished themselves in physical studies, 'if they had relied on the great foundation of literature and had followed the footsteps of the ancients'[1]. After two years thus spent on Logic in Paris, he studied 'Grammar' for three years at Chartres[2], under the celebrated 'grammarian', William of Conches. At Chartres he also studied the *Quadrivium* and (at a later date) Logic and Theology under Gilbert de la Porrée[3]. He subsequently returned to Paris for a course on Theology, thus traversing the main subjects of mediaeval study in a wide and comprehensive manner very different to the mechanical routine prescribed in the following century[4]. After spending ten or twelve years abroad, he returned to England, became secretary to three successive archbishops of Canterbury, Theobald, Thomas Becket and Richard, was often sent to France and Italy on diplomatic missions, was for 30 years the central figure of English learning[5], and, for the last four years

[1] *Met.* ii 10 (cxcix 867 D, Migne). See *facsimile* on p. 536.

[2] The place has been determined by Schaarschmidt, *Joh. Saresberiensis*, 1862, p. 22. See also Poole in *Eng. Hist. Rev.* July 1920, pp. 321—342.

[3] Among his other teachers he names Richard 'l'Évêque', Hartwin the German, Petrus Elias and Theodoric.

[4] Rashdall, i 64.    [5] Stubbs, *Lectures*, Lect. vii, 139[1].

of his life, bishop of Chartres. His principal works are his
*Entheticus*, in 1852 lines of elegiac verse ; his *Policraticus*[1] (with
an introduction in 306 elegiacs, called by the same name as his
earlier poem) ; his *Metalogicus*; and his *Letters*[2]. The *Policraticus*
and *Metalogicus* were dedicated to Becket[3]. Both of them were
finished in 1159, while Henry II (attended by his chancellor,
Becket) was engaged in the siege of Toulouse. In the *Policraticus*,
which is 'to some extent an encyclopaedia of the cultivated
thought of the middle of the twelfth century'[4], we have an interesting chapter on Aristotle[5], and a satirical account of the
scholastic controversies of the age. When the writer went to
Paris to study Canon law, he found the Schoolmen busy with
their wordy warfare, ever producing some new opinion on *genera*
and *species*, unknown to Plato or Boëthius, which they had been
fortunate enough to extract from the mine of Aristotle[6]. The
scholastic treatment of Logic is also abundantly illustrated in his
*Metalogicus*[7], where he vindicates the claims of 'Grammar', or a
scholarly knowledge of ancient literature, while, in defending an
intelligent study of Logic, he insists that it is useless in itself,
being only important when associated with the other arts[8]. He
considers Aristotle more convincing in his arguments against the
opinions of others than in the proof of his own, and regards him
as far from infallible or *sacrosanctus*[9]. He meets the attacks of a
critic, whom he calls *Cornificius*[10] (after the opponent of Virgil
mentioned by Donatus in his life of that poet), and, under the

[1] *De nugis curialium* (i—vi) *et de vestigiis philosophorum* (vii, viii).

[2] The *Historia Pontificalis* (1161–3) was not printed until 1868 (*Mon.* xx
515–45), and not identified as his work until 1873.

[3] A copy of both, belonging to Becket, is among the Parker MSS at
Corpus Christi Coll., Cambridge (No. xlvi ; M. R. James, *Abp Parker's MSS*,
pp. 5, 22). See p. 536.

[4] Poole, 218 ; Hardy's *Descr. Cat.* (in *Rolls Series*), II xxxiii f.

[5] vii c. 6 ; Schaarschmidt, p. 176.

[6] vii 12 ; Migne, cxcix 664 c (Mullinger, i 56 f).

[7] ii 9 ; iv 27.

[8] ii 10, sicut dialectica alias expedit disciplinas, sic si sola fuerit, jacet ex-
sanguis et sterilis; cp. iv 28, tunc demum eminet, cum adjunctarum virtute
splendescit.

[9] iii 8 ; iv 27.

[10] Identified as Reginaldus by Prantl, ii[2] 232–4.

title of *Cornificiani*, satirises the narrow-minded specialists in Logic who despised literature, and describes by way of contrast the system of literary instruction which prevailed in the School of Chartres. Early in the eleventh century the cathedral school of that city had been famous under Fulbert (d. 1029), as a home of sacred learning; and learning continued to be represented there in the person of Lanfranc's pupil, the great lawyer, bishop Ivo (d. 1115). Soon after the death of Ivo the School rose once more into fame under Bernard (1119–26) and his brother Theodoric (1141 f), canons and chancellors of Chartres. In John of Salisbury's day (1138), William of Conches and Richard l'Évêque continued to perpetuate the teaching of Bernard, and thus carried on a sound and healthy tradition[1]. In that School the study of 'figures of speech' was treated as merely introductory to that of the classical texts, which were explained not only on grammatical but also on general principles, the different excellences of prose and verse being pointed out, and emphasis laid on the sense as well as the style of the author studied. The pupils wrote daily exercises in prose and verse, founded on the best models only[2], and corrected one another's compositions, besides learning passages by heart and holding discussions on a set subject. The general method of the School was founded on the scheme of education laid down by Quintilian[3].

John of Salisbury, the ripest product of this School, stands out as the most learned man of his time. He gives an analysis of the whole series of Aristotle's treatises on Logic[4]. His *Metalogicus* (1159) is, in fact, the first work of the Middle Ages, in which the whole of the *Organon* is turned to account[5], and Aristotle's own criticisms on Plato's doctrine of Ideas applied to

---

[1] Bernard belongs to a former generation, having probably died before 1130; *Met.* i 24, *Sequebatur* hunc morem Bernardus Carnotensis...Ad hujus magistri formam praeceptores mei etc.; *Pol.* vii 13 *senex* Carnotensis.

[2] *Met.* i 24, ea sufficere quae a claris auctoribus scripta sunt.

[3] *Met. l. c.*; cp. Schaarschmidt, 65 f, 73 f, 82 f; Norden, *Kunstprosa*, 715–9; Poole, 113—124; Rashdall, i 65 f; Clerval, 223—232.

[4] *Met.* iii—iv.

[5] The same ground is apparently traversed less completely in the *Eptateuchon* of Theodoric (*c.* 1141), where the *Later Analytics* is omitted; p. 533 *supra*. Cp. C. H. Haskins, *Med. Versions of Post. Analytics*, in *Harvard Studies*, xxv (1914), 90.

the scholastic controversy on universals[1]. He is familiar not only with the Boëthian translations but also with certain new renderings[2]. He laments the obscurity of the translation of the *Later Analytics*[3], and the long neglect of the *Topics*[4]. He has studied certain parts of the *Organon* with a learned Greek[5] (possibly during his stay of three months with Hadrian IV at Beneventum[6]); but he never professes to have read any Greek work without such assistance ; he derives *Analytica* from ἀνὰ and λέξις[7]; and he never quotes from any Greek author unless that author exists in a Latin translation. In the *Metalogicus* he mentions Boëthius as often as Aristotle, and borrows from Boëthius the explanations of all the Greek terms of Grammar or Logic that he uses[8]. He asks his former teacher, Richard 'l'Évêque', now archdeacon of Coutances, for transcripts of any of Aristotle's works (to be executed at his own expense), and for explanations of difficult passages[9]; and his correspondence with John the Saracen shows that he was ignorant of Greek[10]. And yet, though he is opposed to Plato's teaching, and is only acquainted with the incomplete translation of the *Timaeus* by Chalcidius and a few traditional passages from the *Republic*, he is so conscious of Plato's greatness as to declare that, on the day when Plato, the first of philosophers, passed away, it seemed as though the sun itself had vanished from the heavens[11]. He repeatedly supports the Scriptures by citations from Latin authors, but he warns us not to allow *authority* (as represented by the Classics) to do prejudice to *reason* (or the mental faculty enlightened by Christianity)[12]. He praises the method of instruction pursued (as we have seen) by Bernard of Chartres, whom he describes as 'in modern times, the

---

[1] *Met.* ii 20.

[2] *Ep.* 211 and *Met.* ii 20 (the *nova translatio* has the more literal *cicadationes* instead of *monstra* in the rendering of τερετίσματα in *Anal. Post.* i 22, 4). See also Prantl, ii[2] 108 n. 34, and Rose in *Hermes*, i 383.

[3] *Met.* iv 6.          [4] *Met.* iii 5 ; Prantl, ii[2] 106.

[5] *Met.* i 15 ; iii 5 ; p. 528 n. 1 *supra*.          [6] *Pol.* vi 24.

[7] *Met.* iv 2 ; *Analetica* in text, and *Analectica* in summary, of Corpus MS.

[8] Jourdain, *Recherches*, 254 f ; cp. Schaarschmidt, 113.

[9] *Ep.* 211 (Schaarschmidt, 264).

[10] *Epp.* 149, 169.          [11] *Pol.* vii 6 (init.); Hauréau, i 540.

[12] *Pol.* vii 10 (Poole, 219), sic ergo legantur ut auctoritas non praeiudicet rationi.

most abounding spring of letters in Gaul'[1]. That method began with Donatus and Priscian, and included Cicero and Quintilian, and the poets and historians of Rome. He himself quotes, in varying degrees of frequency, poets such as Terence, Virgil, Horace, Ovid, Lucan, Statius, Persius, Martial, Juvenal and Claudian, as well as the apocryphal play called the *Querolus*[2], but he knows nothing of the genuine plays of Plautus, or of Lucretius; and he cites Catullus only once[3]. He quotes the historians Sallust, Suetonius, Justin and Valerius Maximus, but he makes the strange mistake of implying that Suetonius and Tranquillus were two different persons[4]. He has only one reference to Livy[5]; Caesar and Tacitus he knows by name alone, but he is familiar with Seneca and Petronius, Quintilian and the elder Pliny, and he even quotes the younger Pliny's *Panegyric*[6]. He owes much of his classical lore to Gellius and Macrobius and the Latin Grammarians, and he has an extensive knowledge of Apuleius. But his favourite Latin author is Cicero. Though he only quotes the *Speeches* once[7], he knows the *Epistolae ad Familiares*, and is thoroughly acquainted with the philosophical works. He is supposed to have possessed the *De Republica*[8], but all his references to that lost work are to passages already quoted by St Augustine. He says of Cicero: *orbis nil habuit maius Cicerone Latinus*[9], and the purity of his own Latin prose has been justly praised by modern critics[10]. Among the MSS that he bequeathed to the Library at Chartres were the *De Officiis* and *De Oratore* of Cicero, and the *Quaestiones Naturales* of Seneca[11]. The only Latin work known to him, which has since been lost, is that of an interlocutor in Macrobius,—Virius Nicomachus

---

[1] *Met.* i 24.

[2] Probably written in Gaul in cent. iv—v; Teuffel, § 421[a]; Schaarschmidt, 101; Norden's *Kunstprosa*, 630. On the late Latin plays of Vitalis Bles < ens > is, bearing the Plautine names *Aulularia* and *Amphitryon* (or *Geta*), cp. Gröber's *Grundriss*, II i 412; **Manitius**, 379.

[3] xiv 9 in *Met.* i 24.   [4] *Pol.* viii 18 ad fin.

[5] *Pol.* iii 10, scriptor belli Punici.   [6] *Pol.* iii 14, 'Caecilius Balbus'.

[7] *Pol.* viii 7 (*pro Ligario*, 12).   [8] Heeren, i 251.

[9] *Enth.* 1215.

[10] Ap. Hallam *Lit.* i 74[4]; cp. Poole, 123; Rashdall, i 67.

[11] Migne, cxcix col. xii.

Flavianus (d. 394), *de vestigiis sive dogmate philosophorum*, and he borrows the first part of this description in the full title of his *Policraticus*, and the second in that of his *Entheticus*[1]. In all the Latin literature that was accessible to him, he is obviously the best-read scholar of his age[2].

Peter of Blois (*c.* 1140—1212) settled in England about 1175, as secretary to Richard of Dover, archbishop of Canterbury, and was successively archdeacon of Bath (*c.* 1177—1204) and of London (*c.* 1204). He was sent as an envoy to the papal court in 1178[3] and 1187[4], and was in attendance on Queen Eleanor in 1193. His name is often found in charters, and he was probably the author of a small volume on some points of Canon Law[5].

Peter of Blois

A careful investigation of the *Letters* bearing his name has led to their being held unworthy of credit[6]. They purport to have been originally collected at the request of Henry II[7] (d. 1189), but some of them could not possibly have been written during the life-time of the king, or during that of the historical Peter of Blois[8]. Many of them are enriched with quotations from the Classics[9]. Their author quotes from Terence, Virgil, Horace, Ovid, Lucan, Persius, Juvenal, and Martial, but most of these quotations are borrowed from John of Salisbury, and the same is true of his citations from Macrobius, Frontinus, Suetonius, Justin, and

---

[1] Schaarschmidt, 103–7.

[2] Stubbs, *Lectures*, Lect. vii, 153[1]. *Opera* in Migne, cxcix; *Entheticus*, ed. Petersen, Hamburg, 1843; *Policraticus*, ed. C. C. J. Webb, Oxford. Cp., in general, Schaarschmidt in *Rheinisches Museum*, xix (1859) 200 ff, and esp. *Johannes Saresberiensis, nach Leben u. Studien, Schriften u. Philosophie* (1862); Jourdain, *Recherches*, 247—256; Prantl, *Logik*, ii[2] 234—260; Hauréau, i 533 f; R. L. Poole, *Medieval Thought*, 201—225; Wattenbach, *GQ*, ii[6] 483; and the literature quoted in these works; also Schrader, in *Rhein. Mus.* 67, 1 (1912).

[3] *Chron. W. Thorn.* in Twysden, *Hist. Angl. Scr. Decem* (1652), col. 1820 f.

[4] Twysden, col. 1491 f.          [5] ed. Reimar (Hamburg, 1837).

[6] By the Rev. W. G. Searle, late Fellow of Queens', Cambridge, whose unpublished work on this subject I have had the privilege of consulting.

[7] *Ep.* 1.

[8] *e.g.* 200 and 201, on the capture of Damietta, 1219.

[9] Esp. 72, 74, 80, 91, 92.

Valerius Maximus[1]. In a letter to the archdeacon of Nantes on his two nephews[2], we have a list of grammarians[3], and a list of historians[4]. Both of these are borrowed from John of Salisbury, and the borrower pretends to have 'frequently looked into' Tacitus—an author never mentioned by such well-informed contemporaries as Giraldus Cambrensis and Radulphus de Diceto. 'Many of these epistles relate to transactions connected with England; but they are frequently very bare of facts. After the opening paragraph, they run into scriptural or classical quotation or allusion, and have more the appearance of rhetorical effusions than letters of business, though many of them are written on public affairs in the name of persons of the highest consequence'[5]. The writer urges the importance of a literary training for a future king, and assures the archbishop of Palermo[6] that 'with the king of England there is school every day, constant conversation of the best scholars'[7].

His younger contemporary, the keen and active Norman-Welshman, Giraldus Cambrensis (1147—c. 1222), born at Manorbeer Castle in Pembrokeshire, studied from time to time in Paris until 1180, attended Prince John on his expedition to Ireland in 1185, and described its conquest by Henry II in a historical work, in which he aims at a style that is simple and easy, and absolutely free from all pedantry. 'Is it not better (as Seneca says) to be dumb than to speak so as not to be understood?'[8] To the Irish chiefs

Giraldus
Cambrensis

---

[1] *Epp.* 59, 65, 79, 85, are largely composed of passages derived from John of Salisbury; cp. *Ep.* 94 and *Policr.* v 10.

[2] *Ep.* 101.

[3] Donatus, Servius, Priscianus, Isidorus, Bede, Cassiodorus (cp. *Metal.* i 19).

[4] Profuit mihi frequenter inspicere Trogum Pompeium, Josephum, Suetonium, Hegesippum, Q. Curtium, Corn. Tacitum, Titum Livium (cp. *Policr.* viii 18, introduced by 'Quae si quis deligentius recenseri voluerit, legat ea quae' etc.).

[5] Hardy, *Descriptive Catalogue*, ii 556. [6] *Ep.* 66 (Stubbs, *Lectures*, 119[1]).

[7] *Petri Blesensis Opera*, ed. Giles, 4 vols. (1846–7); Migne, ccvii (1855); seven *Letters* in Denifle's *Chartularium Univ. Paris.* nos. 24—30; cp. Norden, 717–9, and Clerval, *Écoles de Chartres*, 293 f.

[8] Vol. v 208 (in *Rolls Series*); H. Morley, *English Writers*, iii 76.

he here assigns Greek patronymics, and makes them deliver set
speeches garnished with quotations from Caesar and Ovid.    He
also wrote works of the highest interest on the topography of
Ireland and Wales[1], reviving an ancient classical custom by
reciting the first of these during three memorable days of public
entertainment at Oxford (1187)[2].   He was an ardent reformer of
ecclesiastical abuses in his native land, and his great disappointment in life was that he never became (like his uncle) bishop of
St David's.    But his studies were never intermitted[3], and he
dwells with special interest on a description of his book-case[4].
His later writings teem with classical quotations.    In his work *De
Principis Instructione* (finished about 1217), with the exception of
Lucretius and Tacitus, there is hardly any notable author between
Terence and Boëthius whom he does not cite.    In the preface he
gives us extracts from Cicero and Pliny in praise of a quiet and
studious life[5]; while, in the body of the book, he illustrates the
virtue of patience by nine quotations[6], and the modesty of princes
by seventeen[7].    In the prologue to one of his latest works, the
*Speculum Ecclesiae* (*c.* 1220), he speaks of the neglect of the Latin
poets and philosophers, which had led to barbarism of style and
to ignorance of prosody[8].    He also regrets the recent importation
from Toledo of certain logical and physical treatises attributed to
Aristotle, which he describes as having been lately prohibited in
France on the ground of their heretical tendency[9].    The anecdotes
in his *Gemma Ecclesiastica* illustrate the ignorance of Latin which
prevailed among the clergy in Wales[10].

The Latin prose of the twelfth century is grammatically
correct, and, even in the next two centuries, it
has not ceased to be a living language.    In fact,
during the Middle Ages in general, Latin prose never dies out[11].

Latin Prose

---

[1] Vol. v and vi.              [2] i 410.              [3] iii 336.

[4] i 369.                      [5] viii p. lxiii.      [6] *ib.* 17.

[7] *ib.* 47 f.                 [8] iv 3, 7 f (note).

[9] iv 9 f.   See p. 561 *infra*.

[10] On Giraldus, cp. H. Morley, iii 64—82; Hardy, *Descr. Cat.* (in
*Rolls Series*), II xxxii, and the Prefaces to his works by Brewer (vol. iv) and
G. F. Warner (vol. viii), in the same *Series*; also H. Owen, *Gerald the
Welshman*, new ed. 1904.

[11] Stubbs, *Lectures*, Lect. vii, 152–5[1]; Norden, *Kunstprosa*, 748–63;
Traube, *Vorlesungen*, ii 31—101.

Among natives of England alone, the writers of historical prose
include Florence of Worcester (d. 1118), Ordericus Vitalis, born
near Wroxeter to become at Saint-Évroult the ecclesiastical
historian of England and Normandy, and to die in the same year
as William of Malmesbury (*c.* 1142); also Geoffrey of Monmouth
(d. 1154)[1], Henry of Huntingdon (d. *c.* 1155), William of Newburgh
(d. *c.* 1198), Roger of Hoveden and Ralph de Diceto (d. *c.* 1201),
Gervase of Tilbury (*fl.* 1211)[2], Matthew Paris (d. 1259) and Ralph
Higden (d. 1364)[3]. An unnamed Englishman was probably the
first collector of the *Gesta Romanorum*, with its many citations
from Ovid, Seneca, Pliny, Valerius Maximus, Macrobius, Gellius
and Boëthius[4]; the earliest MS belongs to 1342[5].

Meanwhile, in Italy, Latin verse had been successfully applied
to historic themes by William of Apulia, a native of
France who imitated Virgil in composing (between
1099 and 1111) his epic poem on the Norman
conquest of Southern Italy and the victorious career
of Robert Guiscard (d. 1085)[6]; and by other poets
of Como, Bergamo, Pisa, Eboli and Parma between 1088 and
1247[7]. The Tale of Troy was the theme of the
prose epic of Guido delle Colonne of Messina (end
of cent. xiii)[8]. The moralising type of verse, which was so dear

*Latin Verse
in centuries
xii, xiii*

*William of
Apulia*

*(Guido)*

---

[1] Cp. Gaston Paris, *Litt. Fr. au MA*, § 54, with H. L. D. Ward's
*Catalogue of Romances*, i (1883) 203—278.

[2] Wattenbach, *GQ*, ii[6] 484.

[3] H. Morley, iii, and the Prefaces to the editions in the *Rolls Series*, with
Sir Thomas Hardy's *Descriptive Catalogue*, and Gardiner and Mullinger's
*Introduction to English History*, 239—273, 285; also Gröber's *Grundriss*,
II i 288, 312.

[4] Swan's trans. ed. 1905, pp. x, 19 f, 69, 401 f, 404 f, 439.

[5] 1326 in Oesterley's ed., 1872; E. T. Swan, 1824, 1895; cp. H. Morley,
iii 367 f, and Gröber, 321.

[6] Text in Muratori, *Scr. Rer. Ital.* v 245—278; extracts in Gibbon c. 56
(vi 176—208, 522 Bury).

[7] Wiese u. Pèrcopo, *It. Litt.* (1899), 7 f; Gröber, 404 f; Ronca, *Cultura
medioevale e poesia Latina d'Italia nei Sec.* xi *e* xii, 2 vols., 1892.

[8] Strassburg, 1477; plagiarised from the French poem of Benoît de
Sainte-More (1165). Cp. Ward's *Catalogue of Romances*, i 35, 40; Bartoli,
*Precursori del Rinascimento*, 85; Gröber, 321 n. 1. Chaucer's 'debt to
Guido' has been discussed anew by Prof. G. L. Hamilton (1903).

to the Middle Ages, had, in the meantime, been represented in
Italy by Henricus Septimellensis (*fl.* 1191), who
imitates Boëthius in his allegorical poem *De diversitate Fortunae et Philosophiae consolatione*[1], and by
Henricus Mediolanensis who dedicates to Clement IV (1265-8)
his *Controversia Hominis et Fortunae*[2].

*Henry of Septimello, and of Milan*

In the twelfth century England claims at least seven Latin
poets. Serlo Grammaticus, canon of York and abbot of Fountains
(*fl.* 1160), wrote a poem in 70 accentual trochaic lines 'on the war
between the king of Scotland and the barons of England' (1138)[3].

Nigellus Wirecker of Canterbury (d. 1200) is known
as the witty author of a long elegiac poem on the
adventures of the donkey 'Burnellus', the typical
monk, who spends some time at the university of
Paris[4]. Jean de Hauteville (*fl.* 1184), who was born near Rouen
and passed part of his life in England, being sometimes called a
Norman monk of St Albans, was the composer of a poem in nine
books on the miseries of humanity, 'a learned, ingenious and very
entertaining performance'[5], describing modern students living a
hard life in Paris and ancient philosophers declaiming in distant
Thule against the vices of mankind[6]. Far better known is Walter
Map, the versatile archdeacon of Oxford (in 1197),
the author of an entertaining work in Latin prose,
*De Nugis Curialium*, on the gossip of the court[7]. He is credited,
in the MSS, with the authorship of the original Latin form of the
great prose Romance of *Lancelot du Lac*[8], including the Quest of

*Serlo. Nigellus. Jean de Hauteville*

*Walter Map*

---

[1] ed. Leyser, *Hist. Poëtarum Medii Aevi* (1741), 453 f; Migne, cciv;
Gröber, 374.

[2] ed. Popma (Cologne, 1570).

[3] Battle of the Standard; MS in Library of C. C. C., Cambridge; cp.
Leyser, 427 f; ed. Twysden in *Decem Scriptores*, i 331; his date is 1109—
1207?.

[4] *Anglo-Latin Satirical Poets*, i 11—145, ed. T. Wright (1872); cp. Chaucer,
*Cant. Tales* 15318; H. Morley, *English Writers*, iii 175; and Gröber, 378.

[5] Warton, *Eng. Poet.*, *Diss.* II cliv (1824).

[6] *Johannis de Altavilla Architrenius*, ed. T. Wright, *l. c.*, i pp. xxv f,
240—392; cp. Wright's *Hist. of Caricature*, 160.

[7] ed. T. Wright (1850); M. R. James (1914).

[8] H. L. D. Ward's *Catalogue of Romances*, i 345—354, and esp. 734—741.

the Holy Grail[1] and the Death of Arthur; but no such Latin
original by Walter Map has yet been found.   He is also credited
with the celebrated satirical poems called the Apocalypse and the
Confession of bishop Golias[2].   The following lines, naming several
of the leading teachers of the age, may be quoted as a specimen of
the Latin rhymes ascribed to him :—

> 'Celebrem theologum vidimus Lumbardum;
> Cum Ivone, Helyam Petrum, et Bernardum,
> Quorum opobalsamum spirat os et nardum;
> Et professi plurimi sunt Abaiëlardum'[3].

These satirical poems are the comparatively innocent counterpart
of the Latin rhymes of the wandering students of Western Europe
known from 1227 onwards by the name of *Goliardi*[4], who sing of
love and wine and the joys of springtime, and indulge in profane
parodies and in bitter satire of all classes secular or sacred[5].
Joseph of Exeter (d. *c.* 1210), who accompanied
Baldwin, archbishop of Canterbury, on his journey to   Joseph of
Exeter
Palestine (1188), is the only Latin epic poet claimed
by England.   He is described as 'a miracle of this age in classical
composition'[6].   He produced (with the aid of Dares, and in the

---

[1] ed. Furnivall (1864), '*La Queste de Saint-Graal in the French poem of
(as is supposed) Gaulters Map, or Walter Map*'.

[2] ed. T. Wright (1841); Hardy, *Descr. Cat.* II xxxv; H. Morley, iii
120—144, 164—174; Gröber, 362, 378.   The *Apocalypse* includes a curious
passage on the Seven Arts (H. Morley, iii. 168).   It is first ascribed to Map in
a Bodl. MS of cent. xiv, 'Apocalipsis Magistri Galteri Mahap'.

[3] p. 28 Wright, *Metamorphosis Goliae*; discussed in *Mém. Acad. Inscr.*
xxviii (2) by Hauréau, who regards the authorship as doubtful; the dramatic
date of the poem is 1141.   'Clerici ribaldi, maxime qui vulgo dicuntur de
familia Goliae', are condemned as early as the time of Gautier, abp of Sens
(d. 923); cp. T. Wright, p. x f; Léon Gautier, *Epopées Françaises*, ii 43.
The fact that Giraldus did not regard his contemporary as the author, is
against the ascription (Wright, p. xvi).

[4] Wright's *Hist. of Caricature*, etc., 162—73; J. Grimm, *Gedichte des Mittelalters* (1844); *Carmina Burana* (from Benedictbeuern, S. of Munich), (1847;
ed. 2, Schmeller, 1883); Hubatsch, *Vagantenlieder* (1870); translations in
J. A. Symonds, *Wine, Women and Song* (1884).   Cp. Gröber, 351 f, 365 f,
416 f, 421 f; Karl Breul, *The Cambridge Songs*, ed. 1915.

[5] Burckhardt's *Renaissance*, Part III c. 1, p. 173 f, Eng. ed. 1898, and
Bartoli's *Precursori*, 35—72.   Cp. Wattenbach, *GQ*, ii[6] 472-6.

[6] Warton, *l.c.*, p. clxii.

style of Ovid, Statius and Claudian) a poem *De Bello Trojano*, which is still extant[1], while his *Antiocheis* on the exploits of Richard I is now represented by a solitary fragment of twelve lines on *Flos Regum Arthurus*[2]. One of the best known

Geoffrey de Vinsauf

Latin poets of the time, Geoffrey de Vinsauf (*Galfridus de Vino Salvo*), educated at St Frideswide's, Oxford, and in the universities of France and Italy, dedicated to Innocent III (d. 1216) his *Poëtria Nova*, an Art of Poetry in more than 2000 lines founded partially on that of Horace and recommending the use of the ancient metres instead of the modern

Alexander Neckam

'Leonines' and rhyming verses, with examples of various kinds of poetic composition[3]. Alexander Neckam (1157—1217), born at St Albans, distinguished himself in Paris in 1180, and was abbot of Circencester in 1213–7[4]. He wrote in prose as well as in verse. In the course of his amusing treatise *De Naturis Rerum*, with its many anecdotes of animals, he borrows much from Aristotle, Pliny, Solinus and Cassiodorus, and also quotes Virgil, Horace, Ovid, Lucan, Juvenal, Martial and Claudian. In a long chapter on the Seven Arts he shows grave mistrust of scholastic learning, and attacks the teaching of Logic in the university of Paris[5], which he describes as the home of Theology and the Arts[6]. His vast elegiac poem *De Laudibus Divinae Sapientiae* traverses much of the same ground. It also describes the chief seats of learning in his day, summing up in a single couplet the four faculties of Arts, Theology, Law and Medicine recognised in the university of Paris, the 'paradisus deliciarum':—

---

[1] 'Long current under the names of Dares Phrygius and Cornelius Nepos, first published as his own at Frankfort, 1620, and edited by Jusserand, 1877' (*D. N. B.* ed. 1903).

[2] Quoted in Camden's *Britannia*, end of notes to Book iii; cp. H. Morley, iii 183.

[3] Leyser, 862—978; cp. Warton, *l.c.*, p. clxxi; Tyrwhitt on Chaucer, *Cant. Tales* 15353; H. Morley, iii 189; K. Francke, *Lat. Schulpoesie* (München, 1879); Gröber, 389; Saintsbury, i 412 f.

[4] H. Morley, iii 196; cp. Warton, *l.c.*, p. clx.

[5] c. 173 p. 283, ed. T. Wright in *Rolls Series* (1863).

[6] c. 174 p. 311.

> 'hic florent artes; coelestis pagina regnat;
> stant leges; lucet jus; medicina viget'[1].

His Latin fables, which have been printed[2], are praised for their vigorous style[3]. His lexicographical works, entitled *Vocabularium biblicum* and *Repertorium vocabulorum*, remain unpublished. In the *De utensilibus*[4] the Latin names of different articles are taught by means of a connected narrative with interlinear glosses in French. The author's own name, which was apparently pronounced like *nequam*, was the theme of repeated pleasantries. Once, when he played on the name of Phi-lippus (abbot of Leicester), the latter retorted with the couplet:

> 'Es niger et nequam dictus cognomine *Necham*:
> Nigrior esse potes, nequior esse nequis'[5].

Joannes de Garlandia, who studied at Oxford and Paris (1204), was an Englishman by birth, but regarded France as the land of his adoption[6]. He was present at the siege of Toulouse (1218), where he saw the catapult by which Simon de Montfort (the elder) was then slain[7]. He also assisted at the founding of the university (1229). In the course of one of his two principal poems, *De Mysteriis Ecclesiae*[8], he commemorated the death of Alexander of Hales (1245); he completed the other, *De Triumphis Ecclesiae* (on the crusade against the Albigenses), before 1252. The language of the latter abounds in grammatical conceits and fantastic devices of metre.

Joannes de Garlandia

---

[1] p. 453. His elegiac poem *De Vita Monachorum* is printed in another vol. of the *Rolls Series,—Anglo-Latin Satirical Poets*, ii 175—200. Aristotle there appears as a logician alone (p. 193).

[2] Du Méril, *Poésies Inédites du Moyen Age* (1854).

[3] Bernhardy, *Röm. Litt.* 672[6].

[4] ed. Scheler, 1867.

[5] Leland's *Itinerary* (1744) vi 48 (=54), quoted by J. E. B. Mayor, *Journ. of Cl. and S. Philol.*, iv 10.

[6] *De Triumphis Ecclesiae*, p. 59 (ed. T. Wright, Roxburghe Club, 1856), Anglia cui mater fuerat, cui Gallia nutrix, Matri nutricem praefero Marte meam.

[7] Gonv. and Caius MS 385 (605), MS of *Dictionarius*, § 47 p. 146 v.

[8] Same MS, part 5; cp. Leyser, 339.

The metrical models here named are Virgil, Ovid, Statius, Lucan[1];
and the following is a favourable specimen of its style :—

> 'Est caeli sine nocte dies, plausus sine planctu,
>   Absque fame saties, absque labore quies.
> Est ibi verus amor sine luxu, pax sine pugna,
>   Et sine sorde decor et sine lite favor'[2].

He was also the author of an *Ars Rhythmica*, in which whole
poems are given as examples of the rules of rhythm[3]. His prose
works included three Latin *Dictionarii*, or rather vocabularies, 'one
of common and another of obscure words, and a third of things'.
The last of these was clearly written for use at the University
of Paris[4]. In another work[5] he gives a list of authors which the
student should read in Latin literature[6], Grammar[7], Dialectic[8],
Rhetoric[9], Arithmetic, Geometry, Astronomy, Medicine, Law,
Theology, adding the names of the appliances required by a
*notarius* and a *librarius*[10]. Roger Bacon[11] heard Joannes de

---

[1] p. 125 Wright.                            [2] p. 129.

[3] ed. G. Mari, *I Trattati Medievali di Ritmica Latina* (1899), 35—80;
Saintsbury, i 408.

[4] Part 3 of above MS, f. 143; J. E. B. Mayor, *Journ. of Cl. and S. Phil.*
iv 7; and Hauréau, quoted in n. 10 below; T. Wright's *Vocabularies* (1857),
120—138; Scheler, *Lexicographie Latine du xii et du xiii s.* (1867), 18—83.

[5] Part 1 of above MS.

[6] Donatus, Cato, Theodulus, Statii *Thebais*, Virgilii *Aeneis*, Juvenal,
Horace, Ovid (esp. *Met.* and *De Remed. Am.* and possibly the *Fasti*), Statii
*Achilleis*, Virgilii *Bucol.* and *Georg.*; Sallust, Cic. *De Or.*, *Tusc. Disp.*, *De Am.*,
*De Sen.*, *De Fato*, *Paradoxa*, *De Nat. Deor.* (?), *De Off.*; parts of Martial and
Petronius; Symmachus, Solinus, Sidonius, Suetonius, Q. Curtius, Trogus
Pompeius, Hegesippus, Livy, Seneca (*Epp.*, *Quaest.*, *Ben.*, *Trag.* and *Declam.*!);
p. 47 f.                            [7] Donatus, Priscian.

[8] Boëthius, *De Categ. Syllog.*, *Topica*, *De Divisione*, *Porphyrii eisagoge*,
*Aristotelis Categ.*, *De Interpr.*, *Soph. El.*, *Anal. Pr.*, *Apodoxium* (= *Anal. Post.*,
probably a corruption of *Apodeixeon*); Cicero, *Topica*; Apuleius, *De Interpr.*;
Aristotle, *Met.*, *De Gen. et Corr.*, *De Anima*; p. 52 v.

[9] Cic. *De Inv.*, *ad Herenn.*, *De Or.*; Quintilian, '*Causae*' (i.e. *Decl.*), and
*De Or. Inst.*

[10] The same MS includes an *Accentuarius*, a *Compendium Gramm.*, and a
*Morale Scholarium* by the same author. He also wrote an *Opus Synonymorum*
(Leyser, 312 f; Migne, cl 1577) and *Aequivocorum* (Leyser, 338). See esp.
Hauréau in *Notices et Extraits*, xxvii 2 (1879), 1—86, where 31 of his works
are discriminated; also Gröber's *Grundriss*, II i 253, 390.

[11] *Op. Minus*, c. 7.

Garlandia discourse in Paris on the orthography of *orichalcum*, and his *Dictionarii* were still in use during the boyhood of Erasmus[1].

Latin verse was well represented in France by Radulfus Tortarius of Fleury (*fl.* 1115), who versified Valerius    Radulfus Maximus, and described his journey to Blois, Caen    Tortarius. and Bayeux in the style of Horace[2]; by Marbod,    Marbod. Hildebert bishop of Rennes (d. 1123), the author of the poem *De Gemmis*[3]; and by Hildebert, bishop of Mans and archbishop of Tours (d. 1134)[4], whose *Letters* were studied, and even learnt by heart, as patterns of epistolary composition[5]. Taking Virgil, Horace, the elegiac poets and Martial as his models, he wrote no less than 10,000 lines of verse, his principal poems being on the *Creation of the World*[6] and the *Ruins of Rome*. The last of these, which is quoted in full by William of Malmesbury[7], was inspired by a visit to Rome in 1106. It is a striking poem, beginning with the couplet:—

> 'par tibi, Roma, nihil, cum sis prope tota ruina;
>     quam magni fueras integra, fracta doces'.

As a writer of Sacred Verse he is more classical than Bernard of Cluni (*fl.* 1140), the author of the famous poem    Writers of of nearly 3000 lines *De Contemptu Mundi*[8], or    Church hymns Bernard of Clairvaux (d. 1153), with his strains

---

[1] Mayor, *l. c.*, p. 6 note.

[2] De Certain in *Bibl. de l'école des chartes*, t. xvi; Léon Maître, *Écoles*, 101 f; Barth, *Adv.* l. lii c. 7; *Hist. Litt.* x 88; Migne, clx.

[3] ed. Beckmann (1799); Migne, clxxi 1758; cp. Steinschneider, *Hebr. Uebersetz.* 956.

[4] ed. Beaugendre (1708); Migne, clxxi; Hauréau, in *Notices et Extraits*, xxviii 2 (1887), 289 f; cp. Neckam, *De Laudibus*, p. 454 Wright; Gröber, 323.

[5] Hildebert, *Epp.* (Migne, clxxi 141—312); cp. Peter of Blois, Migne, ccvii 314; Rashdall, i 65 n.

[6] Leyser, 391 f. The poem on the *Fall of Troy*, conjecturally ascribed to him by Leyser, 398 f, was not written by him, but was the work of Simon Capra Aurea, abbot of St Victor; partly printed in *Hist. Litt.* xii 487 f. Cp. Dunger, *Die Sage vom trojanischen Kriege*, p. 22 n.; Ward's *Catal. of Romances*, i 27.

[7] ii 403 Stubbs; Burman's *Anth. Vet. Lat. Epigr.* i 457; extract in Trench, *Sacred Latin Poetry*, 108, and in Norden, *Kunstprosa*, 723.

[8] *Latin Satirical Poets*, ii 7—102 (*Rolls Series*); extracts in Trench, 304 f, partly translated by J. M. Neale (1858 etc.); *Hymns A. and M.*, Nos. 225-8.

of deepest feeling, or other hymn-writers, for example Peter the
Venerable (d. 1156), Adam of St Victor (d. *c.* 1192), and, among
the Italians, Thomas Aquinas (d. 1274), and the authors of the
*Dies Irae* and the *Stabat Mater* respectively,—Thomas of Celano
(*fl.* 1226) and Jacobus de Benedictis (d. 1306)[1].  In the hymns of
authors such as these, the Latin Verse of the Middle Ages held its
own against the vernacular languages of Europe; it was only when
it was consecrated to the service of the Church that that Verse
became immortal.   The sacred lyrics of the twelfth and thirteenth
centuries attain a far higher level of literary interest than the

Petrus Riga. Matthew of Vendôme

*Aurora* of Petrus Riga, canon of Rheims (d. 1209)[2],
whose vast poem of 15,050 lines supplies a
paraphrase of a large part of the historical books of
the Bible[3].   The story of Tobit is the theme of
Matthew of Vendôme, a pupil of Bernard Silvester and an imitator
of Tibullus and Propertius[4].   Epic poetry was meanwhile

Brito. Gautier de Lille

represented by the *Philippis* of Guilielmus Brito of
St Pol de Léon (1150—1226), chaplain to king
Philip Augustus, and an imitator of Ovid, Statius
and Virgil.   The ten books of the *Alexandreis*[5] of Gautier de
Châtillon or de Lille (*Gualterus ab Insulis*, d. 1201) were founded
on Curtius, and modelled mainly on Lucan;—*lucet Alexander
Lucani luce*[6].   In 1330[7] his epic poem was regarded as a Classic

[1] Trench, *l. c.*; Neale, *Eccl. Lat. Poetry* in *Enc. Metrop.*, *Roman Lit.*
211—66 (1852[3]); Moorsom, *Hist. Companion*, 117—149[2]; also Daniel's
*Thesaurus*, and Julian's *Dictionary*.

[2] Grässe, *Handbuch*, ii 306; in the prologue to his *Aurora*, he says 'Petrus
Riga vocor'.  Migne, clxxi 1381; Hauréau, *Mélanges*, 1 f; *Notices et Extraits*,
xxxi (1) 89 f (Gröber, 370).

[3] Leyser, 692 f.

[4] Wright and Halliwell, *Reliquiae Antiquae*, ii 257 f.  *Fl.* at Tours after
1174.  His poetic epistles in *S. Ber. bayr. Akad.* 1872, 561—631.

[5] ed. princeps Pynson; ed. Müldener (1863); cp. R. Peiper (Breslau,
1869); Ivančić, *Wie hat Walterus Virgil nachgeahmt?* (1878).

[6] Eberhard, *Labyrinthus*, iii 39; cp. K. Francke, *Schulpoësie* (1879), p. 89 f
(in the same work Geoffrey de Vinsauf, Eberhard, Henricus of Septimello
and of Milan, Bernhard of Gest (near Münster) and Nigellus are discussed).
Cp. also H. Christensen, *Das Alexanderlied Walters von Chatillon*, Halle,
1905.

[7] Warton, *l. c.*, p. clxix.

in Flanders, the land of his birth, but all that is now remembered
is the single line:—*incidis in Scyllam cupiens vitare Charybdim*[1].
His prose work, the *Moralium Dogma* (which has led to his being
regarded as a precursor of the Renaissance), is a purely pagan
treatise founded mainly on Cicero and Seneca and abounding in
quotations from Terence, Sallust, Virgil, Horace, Lucan, Statius,
Persius and Juvenal[2]. The rising reputation of his *Alexandreis*
was attacked by the poet's countryman, Alain de
Lille (*Alanus ab Insulis*), the 'Universal Doctor',      Alain
who died as a monk at Clairvaux (*c.* 1203). He is      de Lille
best known as the author of the remarkable poem called the *Anti-
Claudianus*[3]. Here[4], as in Claudian's first poem *In Rufinum*[5],
Alecto summons her infernal crew to attack the hero of the epic,
—Rufinus in the earlier poem, and the newly-created Man in the
later; but, while in Claudian the attack is triumphant, in Alanus
the Vices are vanquished by the Virtues. In the *Anti-Claudianus*
the Palace of Nature is adorned with portraits of Plato, Aristotle,
Cicero, Virgil, Seneca and Ptolemy[6], while Aristotle, Zeno,
Porphyry and Boëthius are singled out in connexion with
Dialectic[7]. The long and elaborate descriptions of the Seven
Liberal Arts that conspire in making the several parts of the chariot
of Wisdom[8], and also in bestowing their varied gifts on the perfect
Man[9], point to the influence of Martianus Capella. That of
Boëthius is no less clearly marked in the mingled prose and verse
of the *De Planctu Naturae*[10], where the character of 'Genius'
excommunicating all who abuse the laws of Nature has found an
imitator in the 'Roman de la Rose' of Jean de Meung (*c.* 1270)[11],

---

[1] v 301; Migne, ccix 514.

[2] p. 33 ed. Sundby (1869); Bartoli's *Precursori*, 27–9.

[3] *Satirical Poets*, ii 268—428 T. Wright, beginning *Incipit prologus in
Anticlaudianum de Antirufino.* Cp. O. Leist, *Der Anticlaudianus* (Seehausen,
1878 f); Gröber, 385.

[4] p. 404.                              [5] l. 25 f.

[6] p. 277 f.                            [7] p. 313 f.

[8] pp. 304—332.                         [9] pp. 390-3.

[10] ed. Wright, ii 429—522.

[11] H. Morley, iv 15 f; Gaston Paris, *Litt. Fr. au MA*, § 114, p. 170. Jean
de Meung cites not a few classical authors, and mentions more (*Rev. Critique*
1884, i 391).

while Chaucer[1] knows this poem as well as the 'Anticlaudian'[2].
In the latter, the allegory of the journey of Wisdom to the throne
of God may have had its influence on Dante[3], and the following
lines seem not entirely unworthy of comparison with part of
Milton's sublime invocation of 'celestial Light'[4]:—

> 'Tu mihi praeradia divina luce, meamque
> Plenius irrorans divino nectare mentem
> Complue, terge notas animi, tenebrasque recidens
> Discute, meque tuae lucis splendore serena'[5].

The poem includes a singularly elegant description of the
island-home of Fortune[6], besides repeated references to Plato's
theory of Ideas[7]; and its last two pages are remarkably fine. As
a poet, the author is even regarded by Joannes de Garlandia as
*Virgilio major, et Homero certior*[8]. In his prose works he borrows
moral sentiments from Cicero[9] and Seneca[10], besides showing
his familiarity with the Latin translation of the *Timaeus*[11] and the
Neo-Platonic *Liber de Causis*. Eberhard of Bethune (*fl.* 1212)

Eberhard    and Alexander of Ville-Dieu (d. 1240) write their
Grammars[12] in Latin verse, but have no pretensions
to being poets. But the former is also the reputed author of the
*Labyrinthus*[13], a poem on the miseries of teachers of rhetoric and

---

[1] *Parlement of Foules*, 316, 'Alayne, in the Pleynt of Kynde'.

[2] *House of Fame*, ii 478. He also imitates in *Cant. Tales*, 16430 f, a couplet
from the *Parabolae*:—'Non teneas aurum totum quod splendet ut aurum, | Nec
pulchrum pomum quodlibet esse bonum' (Leyser, 1074).

[3] Ten Brink, and Rambeau (H. Morley, v 231).

[4] *P. L.* iii 51 f.          [5] p. 356.          [6] p. 396-9.

[7] pp. 290, 372, 379, 449, 518 (all suggested by the *Timaeus* alone). Like
Abelard and Bernard Silvester, he personifies νοῦς as Noÿs.

[8] *De Triumphis Ecclesiae*, p. 74.

[9] Migne, ccx, *De arte praedicatoria*, c. 1, where *nihil citius arescit lacryma*,
quoted as from Lucretius, really comes from *ad Herenn.* ii 31 § 50, or Cic. *de
Inv.* i 56 § 109.

[10] *ib.* cc. 3, 21, 23-5, 29, 36 (Hauréau, i 523).

[11] Hauréau, i 528.          [12] p. 667 *infra*.

[13] Leyser, 796—854. Eberhardus is named as the author in Part iii 689;
cp. Saintsbury, i 408 f. Gröber, 389, distinguishes between Evrardus Bethune
(*c.* 1200), the author of the *Graecismus*, and a German grammarian Eberhard
(cent. xiii), who supplements it in the *Labyrinthus* (Hauréau, *Notices et
Extraits*, iv 281). Cp. Traube, *Vorlesungen*, ii 109, n. 1.

poetry, the third and last part of which supplies us with a critical estimate of the poets in vogue, more than 30 in number.   By the side of Virgil and Ovid, Persius and Juvenal, Statius and Claudian, we here find later poets such as Petrus Riga and Alanus ab Insulis, and the authors of the *Architrenius*, the *Alexandreis*, the *Physiologus* (Theobaldus[1]), and the *Solimarius*[2] (Gunther).  The writer of this last, a Cistercian monk, who was probably of German origin and lived in the Vosges Gunther until after 1210, is far better known as the author of the *Ligurinus* (1187), a famous epic in ten books on the exploits of Frederic Barbarossa, where the facts are derived from Otto of Freising and the style from Lucan[3].   Justin and Valerius Maximus, with Martianus Capella, are the models followed in the blended prose and verse of the Danish History of Saxo Grammaticus (ending with 1185)[4].   In the following century the only Latin poems of note in Germany are the Ovidian *Lippiflorium*[5] of Justinus of Lippstadt (before 1264) on the varied career of Bernard of Lippe as knight, monk and bishop; and the *Herlingsberga*[6] of Heinrich Rosla of Nienburg (near Hanover) on certain heroïc exploits of a duke of Braunschweig-Lüneberg in 1287.   These exploits were fortunate in being celebrated by a *vates sacer*, but the *vates* himself has attained little more than local fame.   Late in century xii the *Hortus Deliciarum* gives proof of a prejudice against poetry, and a preference for philosophy and the Liberal Arts[7].

Before turning to the second period in the history of Scholasticism, we may here notice a few of the indications of the study of Greek in the twelfth century.   Greek in<br>France Guibert, abbot of Nogent (d. 1124), notes the rise

---

[1] His description of the Sirens was known to Chaucer, *Cant. Tales*, 15277 Tyrwhitt.

[2] A poem of the Crusades; Warton, *Eng. Poet.*, *Diss.* II clxx; 240 lines published by Wattenbach, 1881 (Bursian, *Cl. Philol.*, i 73).

[3] Migne, ccxii 327—476 (with *Prooemia* 255 f and *eruditorum testimonia*, 280 f); Pannenborg in *Forschungen zur deutschen Gesch.*, 1871–3; Norden, *Kunstprosa*, 875–9; Bursian, i 72; Gröber, 403; and esp. Wattenbach, *GQ*, ii⁶ 286—290.    [4] Bursian, i 73 f.

[5] ed. Meibom, in *Scr. Rer. Germ.* i 575; ed. Laubmann (1872); Wattenbach, *GQ*, ii⁶ 362.

[6] ed. Meibom, i 775 (Bursian, i 85 f).    [7] See plate on p. 559.

in his own lifetime of a new interest in literary studies[1], but he supplies no proof of any interest in Greek. While Abelard knew no Greek, the mystic Hugo of St Victor, who died in the same year (1142), produced a new translation of 'Dionysius the Areopagite'[2]. His pupil, Richard of St Victor (d. 1173), 'who was in contemplation more than man'[3], so far from studying Greek, prompted men to leave in the plain Aristotle and Plato and all the herd of philosophers, and to ascend the mount of contemplation that looks down on all the sciences and on all philosophy[4]. Macarius, abbot of Fleury (d. 1146), has the credit of having compiled a Greek lexicon (printed in the fifth volume of Stephens' *Thesaurus*[5]), but this 'lexicon' is merely an abstract from Suïdas, and is probably the work of a Byzantine monk[6]. The Greek books which Guillaume de Gap, abbot of St Denis from 1172–3 to 1186, brought to St Denis from Constantinople in 1167[7], included a panegyric on Dionysius by Michael, 'patriarch' of Jerusalem, which is still extant[8], and a life of the philosopher Secundus, which Guillaume himself translated into Latin, while the panegyric was translated by another Guillaume of St Denis, the correspondent of another translator of Dionysius, John the Saracen[9]. Pierre le Chantre, bishop of Paris (d. 1197), mentions, among Greek authorities, Aristippus, Aristotle, Demosthenes, Diogenes, Epicurus, Josephus, Plato and Porphyry[10], and borrows a quotation from the *Phoenissae*[11]. About the same time the sub-prior of Ste-Barbe-en-Auge reminds a monk at Caen that 'a cloister without books is like a castle without an armoury'[12]. But, in the catalogue of the neighbouring monastery at Bec (*c.* 1164), not a single Greek book is to be found[13]. About the year 1100, Hélinand, a monk of Froidmont, near Beauvais, writes

---

[1] Migne, clvi 844 (Rashdall's *Universities*, i 32).

[2] Migne, clxxviii 1080 D, 1704 B—C.      [3] Dante, *Par.* x 132.

[4] Migne, cxcvi 54; *Benjamin Minor*, c. 75.      [5] Tougard, 64.

[6] *Macarii hieromonachi ecloge e lexico Suïdae* (Krumbacher, p. 563[2]).

[7] p. 425 *supra*.          [8] Paris Library, *fonds grec*, no. 933.

[9] Delisle in *Journal des Savants* (1900), 725—739.

[10] Migne, ccv 19 (Tougard, 61).

[11] *ib.* 30 D, borrowed from Seneca, *Ep.* 49.

[12] *ib.* 845 A (quoted on p. 441).

[13] Migne, cl 769—792; Mullinger's *Cambridge*, i 100 f.

for γνῶθι σεαυτόν *nothiselitos* and *nothiselito*[1].  It was only through
the Fathers that some of the Latin scholars of France caught a
far-off echo of Greek learning[2].  Meanwhile, in Germany, we find
David the 'Scot' writing at Würzburg on the *De
Interpretatione* (1137)[3], Otto of Freising (d. 1158)

Germany

promoting the study of Aristotle[4], and Wibald, abbot of Corvey
(d. 1158), reading Greek and Latin poets, orators and philosophers.  When he borrows certain works of Cicero from the
library at Hildesheim, he deposits as pledge 'the commentaries
of Origen' and a Greek book on *Tactics*[5].  The Italian hellenists
of this century include Grossolano, archbishop of

Italy

Milan (d. 1117), who was sent by Pascal II to
Constantinople, and whose Greek argument on the Procession of
the Holy Ghost is still extant[6]; Jacobus Clericus of Venice, who
translated and expounded the *Topics*, *Analytics* and *Sophistici
Elenchi* of Aristotle (1128)[7]; Alberico of Bologna (*c.* 1150), who
translated the aphorisms of Hippocrates[8]; the Tuscan brothers,
Hugo and Leo (*c.* 1170–77), both of whom took part in Greek
discussions at Constantinople, and the latter of whom produced
a rendering of the *Oneirocritici Graeci*[9]; and Godfrey of Viterbo
(d. 1190), who is supposed to have known Greek, Hebrew,
Chaldee and other languages[10].  About 1192 Pisa is represented
by Hugutio, bishop of Ferrara (1191—1212), who compiled an
etymological dictionary in which Greek words are quoted[11]; and

---

[1] Gidel, 274 n.

[2] Philip de Harveng, abbot of Bonne-Espérance (Migne, cciii 154), etsi
(lingua) Hebraea et Graeca eo datae sunt ordine patribus ab antiquo, tamen
quia non usu sed *fama sola ad nos veniunt de longinquo*, eisdem valefacto ad
Latinam praesentem noster utcunque se applicat intellectus (Denifle, in *Archiv
für...MA*, iv 595).

[3] Heeren, i 257 f.                    [4] Bursian, i 68, 75 f; p. 532 *supra*.

[5] 'quem Graece *stratagematon* vocant, quod militare est'; Migne, clxxxix
1298 f (Tougard, 59); pp. 619, 649 *infra*.          [6] Gradenigo, 50 f.

[7] Robertus de Monte, abbot of Mont S. Michel (Pertz, *Mon.* viii, *Scr.* vi,
489 n.); cp. Jourdain, 58; Prantl, ii 99²; Ueberweg, i 391.

[8] Gradenigo, 70.                      [9] *ib.* 71–5.

[10] *ib.* 76—83; depreciated by Muratori, in Pref. to *Scr. Rerum Ital.*, i p. vii;
his *Gesta Friderici* in Pertz, *Mon.* xxii 307; cp. Wattenbach, *GQ*, ii⁶ 291–8;
and Gröber, 404.

[11] Du Cange, *Praef.* § 46; Gradenigo, 83 f.  Hugutio is not really founded
on Papias (as stated in the Nonantola chronicle, quoted by Du Cange), but he

by the famous jurist Joannes Burgundio (d. 1194), an envoy of
Barbarossa in the East, who translated certain of the works of
'Gregory of Nyssa' (*i.e.* Nemesius, *On the Nature of Man*)[1],
Chrysostom, and John of Damascus (*On the Orthodox Faith*),
together with the Greek passages in the Pandects, the rendering
of which is ascribed to another by Accursius[2]. It was Burgundio
who pointed out to John of Salisbury the importance of the
*Posterior Analytics*[3]. The state of Greek learning in England

England        may be inferred from the fact that, in the catalogue
of Christ Church, Canterbury (end of cent. xii),
while there are 18 MSS connected with Priscian, the only Greek
book is a grammar (*Donatus Graece*), and Aristotle is represented
solely by Latin renderings of the *Topica* and *Sophistici Elenchi* and
of Porphyry's *Introduction*, with the commentaries by Boëthius[4].
'Master Thomas Brown', who enjoyed the confidence of king
Roger of Sicily (d. 1154), is the first Englishman whose name was
written in Greek, Thomas Brounos appearing among the attestations
of the Greek charters of king Roger[5]. The Greek studies of
John of Salisbury (d. 1180) have already been noticed[6]
Alexander Neckam of St Albans (d. 1217)[7], who learnt and
taught in Paris (1180), quotes the *Analytica Posteriora*[8], the
*Topica* and *De Anima*[9]. His younger fellow-countryman, Alfred
de Sereshel, in his work *De Motu Cordis*, dedicated to Neckam,
names nearly all the works of Aristotle which had lately been
translated from Arabic into Latin[10]. He has been identified
with 'Alfred the Englishman', the translator of the *De Plantis*,
whom we shall shortly meet again among the translators from the
Arabic, who gave a new extension to the knowledge of Aristotle in
the West of Europe[11].

borrows from the same sources as Osbernus (Loewe, *Prodromus Corp. Gloss.
Lat.*, 244—6).

[1] ed. C. J. Burkhard (Wien, 1902).

[2] Gradenigo, 86—94. Cp. C. H. Haskins in *Am. Hist. Rev.* 1920, 607—610.

[3] *Met.* iv 7 (Prantl, ii² 106); omitted in Theodoric's *Eptateuchon* (1141),
Clerval, *Écoles de Chartres*, 245.

[4] Mullinger, i 100 f; *facsimile* in M. R. James, *Canterbury Libraries*.

[5] Stubbs, *Lectures*, 133[1]; Freeman, *Hist. Essays*, iii 472. Neither gives
the original text: Cusa, *Diplomi*, Palermo, 1868, i 313, μάς ρο θωμᾶ τοῦ βρούνου.

[6] p. 540 *supra*.        [7] p. 548 f *supra*.

[8] *De Naturis Rerum*, pp. 57, 142, 291, 293, 299. He calls it *Analectica*.

[9] Hauréau, II i 63.        [10] *ib.* 65 f.        [11] p. 569 *infra*.

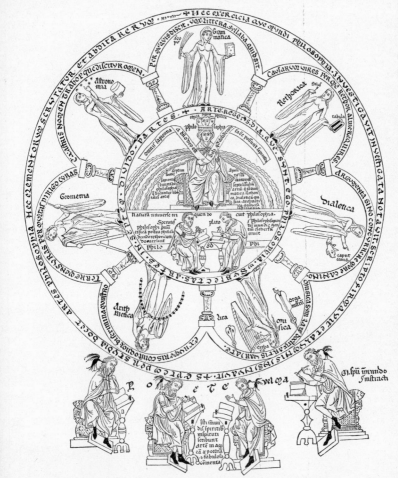

PHILOSOPHY AND THE LIBERAL ARTS, VERSUS THE POETS.

From the *Hortus Deliciarum* of Herrad von Landsberg (d. 1195), reduced
from plate xi *bis* of Straub and Keller's folio ed. (Strassburg, 1899).
See p. 618 f *infra*, and *List of Illustrations*.

| 1200 Italy | Spain | France | Germany | British Isles |
|---|---|---|---|---|
| | | 1201 d. Gautier de Lille | | 1200 d. Nigellus Wirecker |
| | | 1203 d. Alain de Lille | | |
| | | 1135-1204 Peter of Blois | | 1200 Geoffrey Vinsauf |
| | | 1207 d. Amalrich | | 1201 d. Roger Hoveden |
| | | 1209 d. Petrus Riga | | 1202 d. Ralph de Diceto |
| 1210 f. Franciscans | | 1210 Aristotle's *Physics* proscribed in Paris | 1210 Albrecht v. Halberstadt | |
| 1212 d. Hugutio bp of Ferrara | | 1212 Eberhard of Bethune | | 1210 d. Joseph of Exeter |
| | | | | 1211 Gervase of Tilbury |
| 1220 Frederic II crowned at Rome | 1209?-1217 Michael Scot at Toledo | 1215 Aristotle's *Physics* and *Metaphysics* proscribed | 1215 Frederic II crowned at Aachen | |
| 1221 Michael Scot at Bologna | | 1215 f. Dominicans | | |
| 1220 or 1232 Frederic II sends translations of Aristotle to Bologna and Paris | | 1217 Dominicans in Paris | | 1217 d. Alexander Neckam |
| | | 1226 d. Guilielmus Brito | | 1147-1222 Giraldus Cambrensis |
| 1222 f. Univ. Padua | | 1228-48 *fl.* William of Auvergne | | |
| 1224 f. Univ. Naples | | | | |
| 1226 Thomas of Celano | | 1230 Franciscans in Paris, joined 1231 by Alexander of Hales (d. 1245) | | |
| 1230 Bonaccursius | | 1231 Aristotle's *Physics* conditionally allowed | | 1234? d. Michael Scot |
| | 1240 & 1256 Hermann the German at Toledo | 1240 d. Alexander of Villedieu | | 1240 d. Edmund Rich abp of Canterbury |
| | | | | 1245 d. Alexander Hales (Paris) |
| | | | 1193-1280 Albertus Magnus | 1230-50 *fl.* Bartholomaeus Anglicus |
| 1249 d. Petrus de Vinea | 1243 f. Univ. Salamanca | 1204-52 *fl.* Joannes de Garlandia | | 1249 f. Univ. Coll. Ox. |
| 1250-64 *fl.* Bartholomew of Messina | | | | 1252 d. John of Basingstoke |
| | | 1253 d. John of Rochelle | | 1175-1253 Grosseteste |
| | | 1255 Aristotle's *Physics* and *Metaphys.* studied in Paris | | 1258 d. Adam Marsh |
| | | | | 1259 d. Matthew Paris |
| | | | | 1260 William Shirwood |
| 1260 d. Accursius | | 1261 The new Orders recognised in Univ. of Paris | | 1260-9 f. Balliol Coll. Ox |
| 1266 Henricus Mediolanensis | | 1264 d. Vincent of Beauvais | | 1264 f. Merton Coll. Ox. |
| 1271 Gerard of Sabbionetta | | | | 1215-70 *fl.* Alfred de Sereshel |
| 1221-74 Bonaventura | | 1272 Siger of Brabant leaves Paris | 1280 Hugo von Trimberg | |
| 1225-74 Thomas Aquinas | 1277 d. Petrus Hispanus | | 1281 Conrad von Mure | 1279 d. Kilwardby abp of Canterbury |
| (1268-81 *fl.* William of Moerbeke) | | | 1281-3 Nicolaus de Bibera | 1284 f. Peterhouse, Camb. |
| 1283-4 Siger of Brabant d. at Orvieto | | 1283 Gilles de Paris, *De Regimine Principum* | | 1214-94 Roger Bacon |
| 1286 Balbi | | | 1284 H. Kosbein of Lübeck | |
| 1294 d. Brunetto Latini | | | | |
| Guido delle Colonne | | | | |
| **1300** | | | | |
| Marchesini of Reggio | | | | 1300 Geoffrey of Waterford |
| 1306 d. Jacobus de Benedictis | | 1311 Council of Vienne | | 1308 d. Duns Scotus (Cologne) |
| 1309 d. Lovato | | 1315 d. Raymund Lull | | 1316 f. Exeter Coll. Ox. |
| 1250-1315 Petrus Aponensis | | 1294-1316 Gilles de Paris (*Egidio da Roma*) bp of Bourges | | 1326 f. Oriel and Clare |
| | | | | 1340 f. Queen's Coll. Ox. |
| 1265-1321 Dante | | 1322 Jean de Jandun | | 1345 d. Richard of Bury |
| 1261-1329 Mussato | | 1327 Buridan, rector Univ. Paris, d. 1350 | | 1345? d. Walter Burley |
| 1319-27 *fl.* Del Virgilio | | 1344 Levi ben Gerson | | 1346 d. John of Baconthorpe |
| 1337 Ferreto | | | | |
| 1343 f. Univ. Pisa | | | 1347-8 f. Univ. Prague | 1347 d. William of Ockham |
| | | | 1365 f. Univ. Vienna | 1347 f. Pembroke Coll. Camb. |
| 1349 f. Univ. Florence | | 1348 Nicolas d'Autrecour | 1383 Deventer school f. by Gerardus Magnus, and 1396 Florentius Radewyns | 1348 f. Gonville Hall, C. |
| | | | | 1349 d. Thomas Bradwardine abp of Canterbury |
| | | | | 1350 f. Trinity Hall, C. |
| | | | | 1352 f. Corp. Chr. Coll. Camb. |
| 1304-74 Petrarch | | 1362 d. Pierre Bersuire | 1386 f. Univ. Heidelberg | |
| 1313-75 Boccaccio | | 1366 Study of Aristotle recognised in Paris | 1388 f. Univ. Cologne | 1373 f. Winchester School |
| 1330-1406 Coluccio Salutato | | | | 1380 f. New Coll. Ox. |
| 1396-1400 Chrysoloras at Florence | | 1382 d. Nicole Oresme | 1392 f. Univ. Erfurt | 1324-84 Wycliffe |
| **1400** | | | | 1328-1400 Chaucer |

*Continued from page* 516.

# CHAPTER XXX.

## THE THIRTEENTH CENTURY. THE NEW ARISTOTLE.

THE Schoolmen had apparently become acquainted with the whole of Aristotle's *Organon* after 1128[1], and there is definite proof of such acquaintance on the part of John of Salisbury in 1159[2]. Much of the mediaeval knowledge of Greek literature in Western Europe came through Latin translations of Arabic renderings of the original Greek[3]. Works of Hippocrates and Galen were translated from the Arabic, at Monte Cassino, by the monk Constantine (*c.* 1050–80), who was born in Northern Africa and who studied in distant Babylon[4]; and the first acquaintance of Western Europe with any of the Aristotelian writings other than the *Organon* was due to the Arabs of Spain. In the middle of the twelfth century, and again, during the first half of the thirteenth, the great centre of activity in the production of Latin renderings from the Arabic was Toledo on the Tagus, which had been under Arab rule from 714 to 1085, when it was added by Alphonso the Brave to the dominion of Castile. Before 1150 Avicenna's commentary on the *De Anima*,

The new Aristotle

---

[1] pp. 527, 557.  [2] p. 539.

[3] Cp. Steinschneider, *Oriental. Uebersetzungen griech. Autoren*, in *Lit. Beiblatt zum Virchow's Archiv* (1888) no. 5 ; and *Centralblatt für Bibliotheks-wesen*, Beiheft v (1889) §§ 1—23 ; also Traube, *Vorlesungen*, ii 87–9.

[4] Jourdain, *Recherches*, 96. Cp. Rashdall's *Universities*, i 81 ; and Steinschneider in *Virchow's Archiv*, xxxvii 351—410, xxxix 333, *Constantinus Africanus u. seine arabischen Quellen*, and *Hebr. Uebersetzungen*, 789 f ; also F. Wüstenfeld in *Göttingen Abhandl.* xxii 2, 1877 (*Die Uebersetzungen arabischer Werke in das Lateinische*, 133 pp.), 10–20. On mediaeval medicine, cp. Gröber's *Grundriss*, II i 258—261. 'Constantyn' is named with 'old Ypocras' and 'Galien' in Chaucer's *Prologue*, 433.

and other physical and metaphysical writings of Arabian philosophers, were there translated from Arabic through

Gondisalvi
Castilian into Latin by Dominic Gondisalvi with
the aid of the Jewish interpreter, Joannes Avendeath (ben David),
and by the command of Raymund, archbishop of Toledo (c. 1130—
1150)[1].  Gerard of Cremona, the elder (d. 1187),
Gerard of
Cremona
was attracted to Toledo by his interest in Ptolemy's
*Almagest,* which he translated from the Arabic in
1175[2].  Among the more than 70 other works, which he rendered
from Arabic into Latin, were Aristotle's *Analytica Posteriora,*
*Physics, De Caelo et Mundo, De Generatione et Corruptione* and
*Meteorologica,* as well as the Pseudo-Aristotelian *De Causis*[3].

The thirteenth century witnessed a still further and far more
important extension in the knowledge of the works of Aristotle.
For this extension the Schoolmen were indebted, on the one hand,
to the Arabs and Jews in the West, and on the other, either
directly or indirectly, to the Greeks in the East.    Aristotle had
long been studied in Syria and Arabia[4]; and the knowledge of

---

[1] Jourdain, 112 f.  In the preface to the Latin version of Avicenna's Arabic
treatise *De Anima,* 'Joannes Avendehut' (i.e. *Joannes Hispalensis*), writing to
the abp of Toledo, describes it as 'hunc librum vobis praecipientibus, et me
singula verba *vulgariter* proferente, et Dominico Archidiacono singula in
Latinum convertente, ex Arabico translatum', *ib.* 449; cp. 151, 217.
Gondisalvi also translated the *De Caelo, Physics* and *Metaphysics* of Avicenna
(Brown, *Michael Scot,* pp. 236, 238), and the 'Logic and Philosophy' of
Algazel (Ueberweg, i 407).  Joannes Hispalensis was the translator of the *De
differentia spiritus et animae* of Costa ben Luca, a Christian philosopher and
physician of Baalbek (864—923), who brought Greek MSS into Syria and
translated Greek works at Bagdad (Barach, *Bibl. Philos. Med. Aet.* ii 118).
Cp. Wüstenfeld, *Göttingen Abhandl.* 25—39, and Steinschneider, *Hebr. Uebersetzungen,* 281 f, 981 f.  The translation of the Koran promoted by Peter the
Venerable (d. 1156) was executed in Spain in 1141–3 by Robertus Retinensis,
an Englishman who ended his days as archdeacon of Pampeluna.  He was
probably aided by Hermann the Dalmatian and 'Master Peter of Toledo'
(Brown, 119; cp. Migne, clxxxix 14, 659; Wüstenfeld, 44—50).  Rodolfus
Brugensis, who translated Ptolemy's *Planisphere* at Toulouse in 1144, was a
pupil of Hermann, and Robertus Retinensis was a younger friend of the latter
(Wüstenfeld, 48—53).

[2] Cp. Steinschneider, 522, n. 158; already translated from the Greek in
Sicily *c.* 1160 (*Harvard Studies,* xxi 78).

[3] Wüstenfeld, *Göttingen Abhandl.* 58, 66 f.  Cp. Steinschneider, 792.

[4] p. 394 *supra.*

his writings, which had passed from Constantinople to the East, had subsequently followed the course of Arab conquest along the Northern coast of Africa, till it reached the West in Spain, and thence found its way into France; but the Arabic translations executed at Bagdad in the first half of the ninth century did not reach Paris in their Latin form until after the middle of the twelfth.

The Arabian philosophy was a form of Aristotelianism blended with Neo-Platonism.  In the twelfth century its principal representatives in Spain were Avempace (d. 1138) and Averroës (d. 1198).  Avempace, who wrote a number of logical treatises at Seville (c. 1118), and afterwards lived at Granada and in Africa, left behind him commentaries on the *Physics*, the *Meteorologica* and other physical works of Aristotle.  Averroës, who was born at Cordova (1126), became a judge at Seville and Cordova, and (in 1163) was recommended to the Calif as the fittest person to expound the works of Aristotle and make them accessible to all[1].  He was physician to the Calif and to his successor, Almansur, by whom he was banished in 1195, the study of Greek philosophy having already been forbidden in the Moorish dominions in Spain.  In 1198 he died, and, not long after, the Moors were defeated on the uplands of Tolosa (1212), subsequently losing Cordova in 1236 and Seville in 1244.  The Arabian philosophy was soon extinguished in Spain and elsewhere, and the interest in Aristotelianism transferred from the Moslems to the Christians.  Averroës, whose reverence for Aristotle exceeded even that of his Eastern exponent, Avicenna, regarded the Greek philosopher as 'the only man whom God had permitted to attain the highest summit of perfection', and as 'the founder and perfecter of scientific knowledge'[2].  His services to Aristotle were threefold.  He prepared (1) short abstracts reproducing Aristotle's own opinions in strictly systematic order; (2) intermediate commentaries; and (3) complete expositions (these last being of later date than the others).  All these three types are extant in the case of the *Analytica Posteriora*, the *Physics*, the *De Caelo*, *De Anima* and *Metaphysics*; (1) and (2) alone in that of Porphyry's *Introduction*, the *Categories*, *De Interpretatione*,

*Avempace*

*Averroës*

[1] Abd-el-Wahid ap. Renan, *Averroës*, 17[4].        [2] Renan, *l.c.*, 54[4] f.

*Analytica Priora, Topica, Sophistici Elenchi, Rhetoric, Poetic, De Generatione et Corruptione*, and *Meteorologica* ; (1) alone in that of the *Parva Naturalia*, the *De Partibus Animalium* and *De Generatione Animalium* ; while only (2) was ever written on the *Ethics*. We have no comments of his on the *Historia Animalium* or the *Politics*. The former had already been abridged by Avicenna, and it is doubtful whether the latter was ever translated into Arabic at all. Averroës knew neither Greek nor Syriac, but he studied Aristotle in Arabic translations of Syriac versions of the original Greek, and the printed editions of his commentaries reach us in a Latin rendering of a Hebrew version of his own Arabic[1]. His later reputation was twofold. He was the great *Commentator*, who was imitated by Thomas Aquinas ; and the great *heretic*, who was refuted by him[2].

The Jewish philosophy of the Middle Ages included Alexandrian and Neo-Platonic elements. Neo-Platonic as well as Aristotelian influence is represented by the Spanish Jew, Solomon Ibn Gebirol (*c.* 1020—1070), who wrote in Arabic and has been identified as the philosopher known to the Schoolmen as Avicebron. His arguments assume the Neo-Platonic theory of the real existence of all that is apprehended by means of universal concepts. He was not acquainted with Plotinus, but probably derived his Neo-Platonic views from Arabic translations of Proclus and of works erroneously ascribed to Empedocles, Pythagoras and Aristotle. The reconciliation of Aristotelian philosophy with Jewish theology was the aim of Abraham ben David of Toledo (*c.* 1150), and of Moses Maimonides of Cordova (1135—1204), who assigns to Aristotle an unlimited authority in all secular knowledge. The commentaries on Porphyry's *Introduction* and on Aristotle's *Categories* and *De Interpretatione* by Levi ben Gerson (1288—1344) are printed in a Latin rendering in the old Latin editions of Aristotle. Their author lived in the South of France.

The Arabs and the Jews did great service by inspiring the

---

[1] Renan, *l.c.*, 52[4]. On the Hebrew versions of the commentaries on Aristotle by Averroës and others, cp. Steinschneider, *Hebr. Uebersetz.* 54—275.
[2] See plate opp. p. 582.

students of the West with a new enthusiasm for learning.   It was
through learned Jews, acquainted with Latin as well as Arabic,
that Arabic renderings of Aristotle were translated into Latin
and thus came to the knowledge of the Schoolmen, and these
translations owed their popularity to the fact that they were not
only literal but were also accompanied by explanations of
obscurities in the original [1].

It will be remembered that the centre of attraction for all
translators from the Arabic in this age was Toledo [2].
Shortly before 1200, an Englishman named Daniel     Daniel
de Morlai (of Morley, near Norwich), discontented     de Morlai
with the dull traditional teaching of the doctors of Paris
(c. 1170—1190), went to study under the Arabs at Toledo and
came back to England 'with a number of precious MSS' [3],
being warmly welcomed on his return by John of Oxford,
bishop of Norwich, who was specially interested in astronomy.
He had at first hesitated to return on hearing that in England
' there was no liberal education, and that, to make way for Titius
and Seius, Aristotle and Plato were forgotten'; and he was
afraid lest he should be 'the only Greek among the Romans' [4].
His only extant work is on the teaching of the Arabians
as to the earth and as to the orbs of heaven.   Among the
translators from the Arabic in centuries xii and xiii     Translators
were Gerard of Cremona, Michael Scot, Hermann the     from the
                                                        Arabic
German, and Alfred the Englishman.   The earliest
of these, Gerard of Cremona [5], translated the Almagest of

---

[1] Jourdain, *Recherches*, 16.

[2] p. 561.          [3] cum pretiosa multitudine librorum.

[4] Pref. to *De Naturis Inferiorum et Superiorum*, Arundel MS 377 f, printed
by Prof. Holland in Oxford Hist. Soc., *Collectanea*, ii 171 f; cp. H. Morley's
*English Writers*, iii 187 ; Rashdall, i 323, ii 338 ; F. A. Gasquet, *Dublin Rev.*,
1898, 359.

[5] Roger Bacon, *Comp. Phil.* 471. Tiraboschi, iii 192, 381, and Boncompagni, *Vita di Gherardo Cremonense* (1851), distinguish between Gerard
the elder, who, according to the Chronicle of Francesco Pipino, died in 1187,
and Gerard the younger (*di Sabbionetta*, S.E. of Cremona), who lived to about
1255-60, and was an older contemporary of Hermann the German (Hermann
was still alive in 1271). Guido Bonatti, cent. xiii (Boncompagni, p. 65),
describes as his own contemporaries Michael Scotus, and 'Girardus de
Sabloneto Cremonensis'. But the difficulties as to the two Gerards are not

Ptolemy[1], and certain works of Galen, Hippocrates and Avicenna[2].

**Michael Scot**       His translations were executed at Toledo[3].  The next, Michael Scot, is said to have studied at Oxford[4], and is traditionally associated with Bologna[5].  He was certainly a student at Paris, and probably learned Arabic at Palermo before 1209[6].  He there lived at the brilliant court of Frederic II, the youthful King of Sicily, to whom he dedicated three of his earliest works.  On the marriage of Frederic to the elder daughter of the King of Aragon (1209), he apparently left for Toledo and there completed a rendering of two Arabic abstracts of Aristotle's *Historia Animalium*, (1) *De Animalibus ad Caesarem*[7], and (2) *Abbreviatio Avicennae*.  The latter was dedicated to Frederic as 'Emperor of the Romans and Lord of the World'. As Frederic was not crowned Emperor at Aachen until 1215, it is impossible to assign the second version to any earlier date[8]. In 1217 Michael produced a translation of Alpetraugi's Arabic

yet entirely removed.  In Boncompagni's work Gerard the elder is identified with the translator, and Gerard the younger is an astronomer, whereas the latter alone (whom Roger Bacon describes as a translator) could have been a contemporary of Hermann.  Possibly there is a mistake in Pipino's date for the death of Gerard the elder, but that date is repeated in several MSS of his *Life* and is consistent with the date of his translation of the *Almagest* (1175). Accordingly, it appears more probable that, in *Compend. Philos.* c. 10, Roger Bacon confounded the 'older contemporary of Hermann' with the translator of cent. xii.

[1] Charles, *Roger Bacon*, 331; p. 562 *supra*; Traube, *Vorlesungen*, ii 87, n. 2.

[2] Dr J. F. Payne, in Rashdall, ii 780-2.  For his translations from Arabic versions of Aristotle, see p. 562 *supra*.

[3] *e.g.* Vatican MS 2089, p. 307 v, incipit sextus de naturalibus auicenae translatus a magistro Girardo cremonensi de arabico in latinum in toleto (J. Wood Brown, *Michael Scot*, p. 238).

[4] Jourdain, *Recherches*, 125.

[5] Boccaccio, *Dec.* viii 9.

[6] J. Wood Brown, p. 24.

[7] Caius Coll. MS 109 (178) fol. 9—107.  Wüstenfeld, *Gött. Abhandl.* 102-6, holds that Michael Scot translated from a *Hebrew* rendering of Avicenna's Arabic abstract of the *Hist. An.*  He is refuted by Steinschneider, *Hebr. Uebersetz.* 478 f.

[8] Mr J. Wood Brown (p. 55) assigns it to 1210, and so reads the colophon of Vat. MS 4428, p. 158; but in his own facsimile (opposite p. 55) I notice a straggling v above the end of M°C°C°X.

treatise on the *Sphere*[1]. Between that date and his return to
the imperial court in 1223, he translated the commentaries of
Averroës on the *De Caelo* and the *De Anima* of Aristotle. The
versions of the other commentaries of Averroës contained in the
same MSS as the above were doubtless the work of the Toledo
School of translators, and the renderings of the commentaries on
the *Physics* and *Metaphysics* may well be assigned to Michael
Scot, who is attacked by Albertus Magnus[2] for a digression
on the part of Averroës stating the opinions of Nicholas the
Peripatetic[3]. Frederic II was crowned at Rome in 1220, and
Michael Scot was at Bologna on 21 Oct., 1221[4], and had
apparently returned to the imperial court at Palermo by 1223.
He was highly esteemed as an astrologer and a physician. He
was even recommended for ecclesiastical preferment in England
by Honorius III (1224[5]) and Gregory IX (1227[6]), the latter
attesting his proficiency in Arabic and Hebrew, but saying
nothing as to any knowledge of Greek. Roger Bacon who, on
the authority of Hermann the German, says that Scot was
ignorant of languages, and adds that he was largely aided by a

---

[1] Jourdain, 133; Renan, 208[4]; Brown, 99—105. The author flourished
*c.* 1190 and was a pupil of Abubacer. His name, which is spelt in several
different ways, is really Ibn el-Bitraugi (from Petroches, N. of Cordova).

[2] *Op.* ii 140.

[3] Hauréau, i 470; Renan, 209[4]; Brown, 127. The other commentaries of
Averroës in the Venice MS are those on the *Meteorologica*, *De Gen. et Corr.*,
*Parva Naturalia*, and the apocryphal *De Causis*; also the original work *De
Substantia Orbis* (Jourdain, 128—130; Brown, 132). In the St Victor MS the
*Parva Nat.* is ascribed to Gerard of Cremona. Rose (Aristot. *de lap.* 341)
holds that Scot translated the *Physics*, *De Caelo et Mundo*, and *Metaphysics* of
Averroës, and that his renderings from Aristotle were only a smoother version
of Gerard of Cremona's translation; while Danou believes that the translation
from Aristotle was confined to *Hist. An.*, the *De Caelo et Mundo* (with the
comm. of Averroës), and the *De Anima* (Steinschneider, *Hebr. Uebersetz.*
478).

[4] Caius Coll. MS 109 (178) fol. 102 *b* has a transcript of the translator's
note to the *De Animalibus ad Caesarem* :—'et iuro ego Michael Scotus qui
dedi hunc librum latinitati quod in anno M°CC°XX°I, xii Kal. Novembr. die
Mercurii accessit nobilior domina totius civitatis hononiensis (*sic*), quae erat
hospita mea etc.' (a new and definite date in Scot's career, communicated by
Dr M. R. James).

[5] *Chartul. Univ. Paris,* i 105.        [6] *ib.* 110.

learned Jew, named Andreas[1], describes him as introducing to the
scholars of the West certain of the physical and mathematical (?)
works of Aristotle, with the commentators on the same.   Translations from the Arabic are doubtless meant, and the date of
their introduction is 'after 1230'[2].   In 1232 the emperor
granted special permission for the transcription of Michael Scot's
*Abbreviatio Avicennae*, the second of the two works in which
Scot had dealt with Aristotle's *Historia Animalium*[3].   It was
apparently not long after 1232 that Frederic II sent to the
universities of Bologna and Paris the translations he had caused
to be made from the Greek and Arabic MSS of the 'works of
Aristotle and other philosophers relating to Mathematics and
Logic', which were contained in the imperial library[4].   Copies
of the emperor's letters addressed to Bologna[5] and Paris[6] have
come down to us, and it is possible that they were delivered by
Michael Scot himself, who may also have visited Oxford.   He
died before 1235[7], and tradition places his burial, as well as
his birth, in the lowlands of Scotland.   With his fame as an
alchemist, astrologer and necromancer we are not here concerned.
His reputed skill in magic has been celebrated by Dante[8],
Boccaccio[9] and Walter Scott[10].

[1]  *Comp. Phil.* 472.

[2]  *Op. Maj.* 36 f, tempore Michaelis Scoti, qui annis 1230 transactis apparuit
deferens librorum Aristotelis partes aliquas de naturalibus et mathematicis cum
expositoribus sapientioribus, magnificata est Aristotelis philosophia apud
Latinos.  Cp. Jourdain, 128 f.   Bridges, iii 66, has 'de Naturalibus et
Metaphysicis (Bodl. MS) cum expositionibus authenticis'.

[3]  Brown, 178.

[4]  Jourdain, 154 f, 163 f.   Prantl (*Logik*, iii 5) assigns this to 1220.   It is
contended that Frederic would more probably have communicated with Bologna and Paris *before* founding his own university at Naples (1224) than *after*.

[5]  Petrus de Vineis, *Epp.* iii 67 (vol. i p. 432 ed. Iselius, 1740).

[6]  *Chartul.* i 435 (in the name of Manfred) ; cp. Brown, 174.

[7]  Henri d'Avranches, quoted by Brown, p. 176.   The date of the treatise
' written for Manfred in 1256 ' may be that of the Spanish era, corresponding
to 1218, and may refer to a work written for Frederic II in 1218, and afterwards copied for Manfred (*Eng. Hist. Rev.*, 1898, p. 349).   Jourdain's opinion
that Scot died in Italy shortly after Frederic II (1250) is supported by
Steinschneider, *Hebr. Uebersetz.* 477.

[8]  *Inf.* xx 115–7.                                    [9]  *Dec.* viii 9.

[10]  Notes 2 C—E on *The Lay*.

Hermann the German completed at Toledo in 1240[1] his translation of the intermediate commentary of Averroës on the *Ethics*, and, at some other date, a translation of an Arabic abridgement of the *Ethics* (possibly the work of Averroës). His work on the *Rhetoric* consisted simply of the glosses of Alfarabi, while that on the *Poetic* was merely the abridgement by Averroës[2]. It was only in this form that Aristotle's treatise on Poetry was known to the Middle Ages. These slight works on the *Rhetoric* and *Poetic* bear the date of 'Toledo, 1256.' Frederic II had died in 1250, and the date of 1256 is in agreement with the fact that Roger Bacon, writing in 1267[3], describes Hermann as a translator in the service of 'Manfred, recently conquered by king Charles' of Anjou (1266)[4]. Some MSS of the above-mentioned Letter to the Universities bear the name of Manfred[5], who may have re-issued his father's Letter, with presentation copies of the translations made in his own time. A translation of the *Magna Moralia* was dedicated to Manfred by Bartholomew of Messina[6].

Hermann the German

The last of these translators from the Arabic is Alfred the Englishman (*fl.* 1215–70), chaplain to Cardinal Ottoboni in Rome and papal legate to England under Henry III[7]. He quotes Arabic writers and apparently knew no Greek[8]. He produced a Latin translation of the Arabic version of the Pseudo-Aristotelian *De Plantis*[9], with a short supplementary comment on the same, in the course of which he quotes the *De generatione et corruptione*, the *Meteorologica*,

Alfred the Englishman

[1] MS Laur. lxxix 18.

[2] Printed at Venice, 1481, and included in the Venice Aristotle of 1560; also reprinted by Fr. Heidenhain (1890). Cp. Roger Bacon, *Op. Maj.* 59, *Comp. Phil.* 473; Jourdain, 139—144; Charles, *Roger Bacon*, 122 note 1, and 329; Wüstenfeld, *Göttingen Abhandl.* 91–6.

[3] *Op. Tertium*, p. 91.     [4] Renan, *Av.* 211–5[4].

[5] Cp. Denifle on *Chartul. Univ. Paris.*, i 435 (Rashdall, i 359).

[6] Tiraboschi, iv 170.

[7] Bale, s.v. *Alphredus Anglicus*, p. 322, ed. 1557; Morley's *Eng. Writers*, iii 187.

[8] *Introd.* to Roger Bacon's *Gk Gr.* (1902), p. li, n. 5.

[9] p. 558 *supra*; quoted by Vincent of Beauvais (1250), *Spec. Nat.* ix pp. 91–2, ed. 1494 (Wüstenfeld, *l. c.*, 87 f.).

*De Anima* and *Analytica Posteriora*[1]. He also appears to have revised the first translation of the *Meteorologica* and to have interpolated that translation with additions of his own. This is stated by Roger Bacon[2], who had a very low opinion of all these translators from the Arabic, including 'William the Fleming', to whom we shall return at a later point[3].

While the knowledge of Aristotle had thus been reaching the scholars of the West through the circuitous route of translations from the Arabic, the Latin conquest of Constantinople in 1204 had opened to those scholars the prospect of a direct access to the stores of Greek learning. The conquerors themselves regarded that learning with contempt, but the natural result of their conquest was the dispersion of Greek MSS, some of which found their way to the West. The only evidence as to any MSS of Aristotle having been brought from Constantinople refers to the *Metaphysics*[4], but the *Physics* is probably meant. The Schoolmen, no longer satisfied with renderings from the Arabic versions of Aristotle, began to obtain translations taken directly from the Greek. Thus the *De Anima* was known to William of Auvergne (who became bishop of Paris in 1228 and was still alive in 1248) in a translation from the Greek, before the Schools of Paris had received Michael Scot's translation of the commentary by Averroës[5]. The *Rhetoric*, the *Politics*, the first four books of the *Nicomachean Ethics*, the *Magna Moralia*, part at least of the *Metaphysics*, and the *Parva Naturalia*, were known from the first in Latin translations from the original, but the earliest *complete* versions of the *Ethics* and *Metaphysics* (with those of the *Physics*, *Hist. Animalium*, *De Caelo* and *Meteorologica*) were from the Arabic[6]. The translations from the Arabic had been often disfigured with Arabic words merely transliterated into Latin, because their meaning was unknown. On the other hand, those from the Greek were, indeed, slavishly literal and not always

---

[1] Barach, *Bibl. Philos. Med. Aet.* ii 11—13, 113.

[2] ap. Charles, 372 f. The 'first translation' is presumably that of Gerard of Cremona.

[3] pp. 585, 591 f.                                                    [4] p. 427 *supra*.

[5] Jourdain, 170, implies that Michael Scot translated the *text*, but Mr J. Wood Brown assures me that he knows of no proof of this.

[6] Jourdain, 144, 177 ; cp. Rashdall, i 359 f.

accurate, but they had at least the advantage of bringing the
student one stage nearer to the original.   The studies of the
Schoolmen were greatly extended and transformed by their wider
acquaintance with Aristotle, as well as with the partly Neo-
Platonic and partly Aristotelian writings of Arabian and Jewish
philosophers.   The Neo-Platonic teaching of 'Dionysius the
Areopagite', as represented in the pantheistic doctrine of Joannes
Scotus, was revived by Amalrich (of Bena, near Chartres, d. 1207),
and his most distinguished follower[1], David of Dinant.   This
revival of pantheism was probably stimulated in part by the
Aristotelian commentary of Alexander of Aphrodisias (translated
by Gerard of Cremona[2]), and by the pseudo-Aristotelian *Liber de
Causis*[3].   Amalrich was already in his grave when the pantheistic
drift of his writings was discovered.   As the result of a Council
held in Paris in 1210, his doctrines were condemned, his bones
disinterred, and ten of his followers burnt alive[4].   At the same
time, it was ordered that 'neither the books of Aristotle on
natural philosophy, nor comments on the same, should be read,
either privately or publicly'[5].   It is uncertain whether the 'books
of Aristotle' were his own *Physics*, or one of the Arabic adaptations of the same, *e.g.* that of Avicenna or Averroës[6], or some
Pseudo-Aristotelian work, such as the *De Causis* or the *De
secretiore Aegyptiorum doctrina*[7].   Guillaume le Breton inaccurately
reports that it was the *metaphysical* (probably meaning the *physical*)
writings of Aristotle, recently brought from Constantinople and
translated from Greek into Latin, which were burnt and proscribed

---

[1]  See, however, Erdmann, i § 192.

[2]  Jourdain, *Recherches*, 123 f, and C. Jourdain, *Mém. de l'Acad. d'Inscr.*
26 (1867), 493, 497.

[3]  Hauréau, II i 103 f.

[4]  See the miniature in Lacroix, *Vie...Religieuse au Moyen Age*, p. 445.

[5]  Denifle and Chatelain, *Chartularium Univ. Paris.*, i 70, with Denifle's n.,
'Inter auctores ante concilium mortuos inveni citatos libros *De Metaphysica*...
Absque dubio erant etiam noti *libri Physicorum* et forsan *De Caelo et Mundo*'.
See Giraldus Cambr. on p. 544 *supra*.   Cp. Hauréau, II i 101 ; Ueberweg, i
431 ; and literature in Rashdall, i 356 n.

[6]  So Jourdain, Hauréau and Denifle.   *Ce qui reste indubitable* (says Renan,
221[4]), *c'est que le concile de* 1209 [1210] *frappa l'Aristote arabe, traduit de
l'arabe, expliqué par les Arabes.*

[7]  Cp. Charles, *Roger Bacon*, p. 313.

in 1209 (*sic*)[1].  In 1215 the Statutes drawn up for the university
of Paris by the papal legate order the study of the Aristotelian
books on Dialectic, while they forbid the study of the *Physics*
and *Metaphysics* (the latter being now mentioned for the first
time in a public document)[2].  Roger Bacon states that the
opponents of the study of Aristotle brought against that philosopher (in connexion with his belief in the eternity of the world)
a passage at the end of the *De generatione et corruptione*[3].  The
fact that this is *one* of Aristotle's works on 'natural philosophy'
may have led to *all* his works on that subject being condemned
at the same time as the *Metaphysics*[4].  In 1220 we vaguely hear
of a translation of Aristotle, partly from the Greek, partly from
the Arabic, by those who knew both[5].  From 1228 to 1231,
owing to a conflict between the university and the citizens of
Paris, the members of the former withdrew to other places.  On
their return in 1231, Gregory IX directed that 'the *libri naturales*
...should not be used until they had been examined and revised'[6].
This implied a considerable mitigation of the severe sentences
passed on the study of Aristotle in 1210 and 1215.  Between
1230 and 1240 his reputation was so much enhanced by the
introduction of his *philosophical* (as contrasted with his *dialectical*)
works, that he was recognised as the 'prince of philosophers'[7].
All his works began to be expounded in Paris by the most
eminent doctors of the Church, such as Albertus Magnus (1245)
and Thomas Aquinas (1257); and, in 1255, even the *Physics* and

[1] p. 427 *supra*.  Cp. Launoy, *De varia Aristotelis in acad. Paris. fortuna*
(1653), c. 1; Jourdain, 187; Luquet, *Aristote et l'Univ. de Paris pendant le
xiii s.* (1904).

[2] *Chartul.* i 78 f, 'non legantur libri Aristotelis *de methafisica et de naturali
philosophia*, nec summae de eisdem'.  Cp. Roger Bacon, *Opus Majus*, p. 14,
'temporibus nostris Parisius diu fuit contradictum naturali philosophiae Aristotelis per Avicennae et Averrois expositores, et ob densam ignorantiam
fuerunt libri eorum excommunicati'; *Op. Tert.* p. 28, and *Comp. Theol.*
(p. 592 *infra*).

[3] ap. Charles, *Roger Bacon*, 315, note 1.

[4] Charles, 315.  The eternity of the world is also maintained in *Physics*,
viii 1.                                    [5] Jourdain, 7.

[6] *Chartul.* i 138, '(magistri artium) libris illis naturalibus qui in concilio
provinciali ex certa causa prohibiti fuere, Parisius non utantur, quousque
examinati fuerint et ab omni errorum suspitione purgati'; cp. Hauréau, II i
108 f.                                    [7] Jourdain, 28.

*Metaphysics* were included among the subjects prescribed in the Faculty of Arts at the university of Paris [1].

Meanwhile, the monks had long ceased to be the sole educators of Europe, the line of great monastic teachers having ended with the name of Anselm, who ceased to be abbot of Bec in 1093. A generation later the monasteries began to close their doors against secular students [2]. Even the revival of monasticism and the reforms of the twelfth century were of no permanent avail for the promotion of learning. The control of education passed from the monks and the monastic schools to the secular clergy and the cathedral schools [3]; and the cathedral school of Notre-Dame, which was already famous under William of Champeaux (*c.* 1100), developed into the university of Paris (*c.* 1170) [4]. The Order of the Franciscans was founded at Assisi in 1210, and that of the Dominicans at Toulouse in 1215; and both of these Orders, whose centre of activity was in the towns, resolved on establishing themselves at the great seats of education. The Dominicans, who were characterised by a strictly conservative orthodoxy, fixed their head-quarters at Bologna and at Paris (1217), besides forming a settlement at Oxford (1221). The Franciscans, who were generally less highly intellectual than the Dominicans, and less strongly opposed to novel forms of opinion [5], settled at Oxford and Cambridge in 1224, and at Paris in 1230 [6]. A long struggle between both of these Orders and the university of Paris ended in their having certain restricted rights in connexion with that university in 1261 [7]. When once these Orders had been founded, all the great Schoolmen were either Franciscans or Dominicans [8].

---

[1] *Chartul.* i 278.    [2] Rashdall, i 42.

[3] Cp. Léon Maître, *Les Écoles Épiscopales et Monastiques* (768—1180), 1866, esp. p. 169.

[4] *ib.* p. 145; Compayré, *Abelard*, 6—8; Rashdall, i 277 f.

[5] Renan, *Averroès*, p. 259[4], En général, l'école franciscaine nous apparaît comme beaucoup moins orthodoxe que l'école dominicaine. Cp. V. Le Clerc, *Hist. Litt. de la France au 14e siècle*, pp. 97—144, esp. p. 129 f.

[6] Rashdall, i 346 f.    [7] *ib.* 369—392.

[8] The great work on the writers of the Franciscan Order is Wadding, *Annales Minorum*, 6 folio vols. (1625 f), ed. 2 in 25 vols. (1731—1886). That on the Dominicans is Quétif et Echard, *Scriptores Ordinis Praedicatorum*, 2 folio vols. (1719 f).

The first of the Schoolmen who was familiar with the whole
range of Aristotle's philosophy, and with his Arabic
commentators, and who employed the same in the
service of theology, was Alexander of Hales, who
derived his name from a place in the N. of Gloucestershire, now
known as Hailes, near Winchcombe. He joined the Franciscan
Order in Paris in 1231, on the return of the university from the
dispersion of ' 1229 '[1], and, after a distinguished scholastic career,
died in 1245[2]. He is a representative of Realism. His ponderous
*Summa Theologiae*, left unfinished at his death, was completed by
others in 1252. It shows the influence of the Eastern Arabs
Avicenna and Algazel far more than that of the Western Arab
Averroës[3]. The commentary on the *Metaphysics*, once ascribed
to him, is now recognised as the work of another Franciscan,
Alexander of Alexandria. In the University Library at Cambridge[4], a MS of Alexander of Hales' exposition of the Apocalypse,
certainly belonging to his time and possibly written by his own
hand, includes a portrait of the author represented kneeling in
the habit of a Franciscan friar[5].

*(margin: Alexander of Hales)*

Another Englishman, Edmund Rich, born in Berks, and
afterwards archbishop of Canterbury (1235-40),
canonised as St Edmund of Abingdon, was the
first to expound the *Sophistici Elenchi* at Oxford[6]. The ideology
and cosmology of Plato were taught in Paris by William of
Auvergne (d. 1249), who knew the *Phaedo* and
the *Timaeus* alone, and wrote works *De Universo*
and *De Anima* largely founded on Aristotle,
quoting the *Physics, Metaphysics, De Anima, Ethics* etc. in Latin
translations, though he had little confidence in Aristotle's *dicta*[7].
He denounces as heretical a number of propositions mainly taken
from the Pseudo-Aristotelian *De Causis*, and frequently attacks
Averroism under the name of Aristotle and his followers, but he
only mentions the name of Averroës once (when he calls him a

*(margin: Edmund Rich)*

*(margin: William of Auvergne)*

---

[1] Bacon, *Op. Minus,* 326 Brewer, where his *Summa* is bitterly attacked.

[2] He is lamented by Joannes de Garlandia, *De Myst. Eccl.*, as the 'flos
philosophiae' etc.

[3] Renan, *Averroès,* 224[4].        [4] Mm. V 31.

[5] J. R. Green's *Short History*, illustr. ed., p. 287.        [6] pp. 589, 592.

[7] Hauréau, II i 145; cp. N. Valois (1880).

'most noble philosopher'[1]), while he has many quotations from
Aristotle himself[2]. John of Rochelle, who, as the
pupil and successor of Alexander of Hales, taught   John of Rochelle
at Paris from 1245 to 1253, shows his familiarity
with the *De Anima* of Aristotle, and its Greek and Arabic
expositors, in a treatise bearing the same name and exemplifying
a new interest in the study of psychology[3].

Platonic and Aristotelian doctrines were combined by
the eminent Franciscan, Robert Grosseteste
(*c.* 1175—1253), bishop of Lincoln, and the   Grosseteste
earliest recorded chancellor of Oxford, who was born at
Stradbroke in Suffolk, and educated at Oxford and (possibly)
at Paris. About 1199 Giraldus Cambrensis[4] commends him
as one whose education had been ' built on the foundation of the
liberal arts and on an abundant knowledge of literature '. He
was appointed lecturer to the Franciscans shortly after their
establishment in Oxford in 1224[5]. His contemporary, Matthew
Paris, writing at St Albans, then the centre of classical learning
in England, describes him as *vir in Latino et Graeco peritissimus*[6],
and states that in his Greek studies he was assisted by a Greek
monk of St Albans named Nicholas[7]. His great admirer, Roger
Bacon, while he states much to his credit, assures us that, until
the latter part of his life[8], his knowledge of Greek was not
sufficient to enable him to translate from that language, and that
he could never translate from either Greek or Hebrew without
assistance[9]. He also tells us that Grosseteste entirely neglected
the works of Aristotle[10]; but the context seems to show that this
statement should be limited to the current translations of Arabic
versions of certain of the *physical* treatises alone[11]. It was
probably during his life at Oxford that he prepared his commentaries on the *Categories, Analytics*[12] and *Sophistici Elenchi.*

---

[1] *De Univ.* i 851 ; Renan, *Av.*, 225–7[4].    [2] Jourdain, 31, 288–99.

[3] Hauréau, II i 192.    [4] i 249 Brewer.

[5] *Mon. Franc.* i 37.    [6] *Hist. Angl.* ii 467 Madden.

[7] *Chron. Maj.* iv 233 Luard.    [8] *Op. Tert.* 91.

[9] *Comp. Phil.* 472.    [10] *ib.* 469.

[11] Cp. F. S. Stevenson's *Robert Grosseteste*, p. 41.

[12] That on the *Anal. Post.*, which was tacitly utilised by Albertus Magnus
(Stevenson, p. 55), was printed six times between 1494 and 1552.

He had access to translations of the *Posterior Analytics* besides
that of Boëthius, and he was also acquainted with the commentary
of Themistius[1].  He drew up a summary of the *Physics*, with a
commentary on the same[2], and a few notes on the *Consolatio* of
Boëthius.  Further, he supplied the Western Church with 'translations' from 'Dionysius the Areopagite' and John of Damascus[3].
It was under his direction that in 1242 Nicholas of St Albans
translated the *Testaments of the Twelve Patriarchs* from a MS
lately brought from Athens by the bishop's own archdeacon, John
of Basingstoke[4], which has been identified with a MS of the tenth
century in the Cambridge University Library[5].  No less than
31 copies of the Latin version of this apocryphal work are in
existence, one of them transcribed for the abbey of St Albans
by Matthew Paris[6], who has further transcribed for us the Greek
numerals introduced by John of Basingstoke[7].  The name of Grosseteste has also been connected with the Greek romance of Asenath,
the patriarch Joseph's Egyptian wife, the Latin version of which
has been preserved by Vincent of Beauvais[8].  In the *Compendium
Scientiarum* Grosseteste classified all the departments of knowledge
recognised in his day, and a MS of his *Summa Philosophiae* in
the Cambridge Library contains twenty chapters identical with
the encyclopaedia in question[9].  All the above works probably
belong to the time between 1239 and 1244.  At the latter date,
Grosseteste quotes from the *Nicomachean Ethics*[10], and not (as
before) from the *Eudemian*[11].  It is uncertain whether he actually
translated the former; a translation and exposition of the same,

---

[1] i 10, littera *aliarum* translationum et sententia *Themistii* neutri praedict-
arum sententiarum videtur concordari (Prantl, *Logik*, iii 85).

[2] Printed at Venice, 1498.

[3] Bacon, *Comp. Phil.* 474.  Grosseteste's *commentary* on Dionysius is
printed in the *Opera Dion. Areop.* 264—271, Argent. 1503.  His 'translation'
of John of Damascus is apparently a commentary on Burgundio's version of
the *De Fide Orthodoxa*.

[4] p. 423 *supra*.              [5] Ff. 1 24.

[6] British Museum, Royal MSS 4 D vii ; *facsimile* in Hardy's *Descriptive Cat.*
iii, plate 9.

[7] *Chron. Maj.* v 285.

[8] *Spec. Hist.* i c. 118—122 ; M. R. James, in *Camb. Mod. Hist.* i 586.

[9] Ii. III 19.          [10] *Ep.* 106.          [11] *Epp.* 94, 101.

ascribed to Grosseteste, was once in the Library of the Jacobins
in the Rue St Honoré, Paris[1].   M. Charles, however, refuses to
believe that the translation was executed by Grosseteste[2].   But it
may be pointed out that he certainly caused a copy of the *Ethics*
(doubtless in the form of a Latin translation) to be transcribed
for him, and that he was asked to lend this copy to a Franciscan
in London in 1251[3]; also that Hermann the German, who
finished his translation of the Arabic commentary of Averroës
on the *Ethics* in 1240, states, in the preface to his rendering of
Alfarabi's comments on the *Rhetoric* in 1256, that his work on the
*Ethics* had been rendered useless by Grosseteste's translations of
the latter from the original Greek[4].   It may therefore be inferred
that a Latin translation of the Greek text of the *Ethics* was known
under the name of Grosseteste, having probably been executed
under his direction between 1240 and 1244 by one of the Greeks
whom he had invited to England.   A Latin rendering of the
important 'middle recension' of the Epistles of Ignatius, conjecturally attributed to Grosseteste by Ussher (1644), is definitely
assigned to him in a MS at Tours[5].   This translation betrays
some acquaintance with the Lexicon of Suïdas[6], renderings from
which are ascribed to Grosseteste by John Boston of Bury.
These renderings consisted of only a few of the biographical
articles, but even the fact that he possessed such a work is worthy
of notice.   The translations drawn up for his use by others were
apparently extremely literal, while in those executed by himself
he was content to give the general sense of the original[7].   He
was not strong in verbal scholarship; he had strange ideas on the
etymology of *monachus* and the meaning of *Therapeutae*[8]; but, on

---

[1] Jourdain, *Recherches*, 59.                    [2] *Roger Bacon*, 328.

[3] Adam Marsh's *Ep.* in Brewer's *Mon. Franc.* i 114, librum ethicorum
Aristotelis quem scribi fecistis vestra gratia etc.

[4] Reverendus pater, magister Robertus, Lincolniensis episcopus, ex primo
fonte unde emanaverat, Graeco videlicet, ipsum librum est completius inter-
pretatus, et Graecorum commentis praecipuas annexens notulas commentatus
(Jourdain, 140; cp. Renan, *Av.* 212[4]).

[5] Lightfoot, *Apostolic Fathers*, II i 76[2] f.

[6] Val. Rose in *Hermes*, v 155 ; Brit. Mus. Royal 8 B i (M. R. James, *Bibl.
Buriensis*, p. 76).

[7] *Ep.* 57 (Stevenson, p. 225).                    [8] *Epp.* p. 173 Luard.

his death-bed, he showed that he held orthodox views on the
derivation of 'heresy', and, even in his last hours, he could
aptly apply to the Mendicant Orders the line of Juvenal, *cantabit
vacuus coram latrone viator*[1]. In his *Letters* he frequently quotes
Horace[2], Ovid[3] and Seneca[4]. 'Probably no one' (in the language
of their editor, Dr Luard) 'has had a greater influence upon
English thought and English literature for the two centuries that
followed his age'. Wycliffe actually ranks Democritus, Plato,
Augustine and Grosseteste above Aristotle[5]; and Gower calls him
'the grete clerc Grossteste'[6]. Apart from his important services
as a reformer and a statesman, he fully deserves the credit of
having given 'a powerful impulse to almost every department of
intellectual activity, revived the study of neglected languages, and
grasped the central idea of the unity of knowledge'[7]. He also
deserves to be remembered as one of the earliest leaders of
thought at Oxford, as a promoter of Greek learning, and as an
interpreter of Aristotle, who went far beyond his master in the
*experimental* knowledge of physical science[8]. The MSS which he
bequeathed to the Franciscans at Oxford have almost entirely
vanished, but his copy of St Augustine *De Civitate Dei* is still
carefully preserved in the Bodleian[9].

When Walter de Merton, the founder of the College bearing

**Adam Marsh**  his name at Oxford (1264), applied to Grosseteste
for subdeacon's orders, he presented a letter of
introduction from Grosseteste's friend Adam de Marisco[10], or
Adam Marsh (d. 1258), who entered the Franciscan order shortly
after 1226, and was unsuccessfully nominated bishop of Ely in
opposition to Hugh Balsham, the future founder of Peterhouse,

[1] Matth. Paris, *Chron. Maj.* v 400 f.

[2] *Sat.* i 7, 3; *Ep.* i 1, 60; *A. P.* 25.

[3] *Ars Am.* i 655; *Rem. Am.* 91; *Her.* v 7; *Ex Ponto* ii 6, 38 (twice).

[4] *Epp.* 23, 35, 67 (all on p. 23).

[5] *Trial*, iv c. 3 (Stevenson, p. 335).

[6] *Conf. Am.* iv 234.

[7] Stevenson, p. 337.

[8] Roger Bacon, *Op. Tert.* 469 (Rashdall, i 521). Cp. Mullinger, i 84 f,
153 f, and (in general) F. S. Stevenson's *Robert Grosseteste* (1899), and the
literature there quoted.

[9] No. 198.

[10] *Mon. Franc.* i, *Ep.* 242.

the earliest of the Colleges of Cambridge (1284). Adam Marsh was the first Franciscan who lectured at Oxford. His *Letters* (in the course of which he writes to Cambridge for parchment to supply the needs of the Franciscans at Oxford[1]) contain only one verbal reminiscence of the Classics[2], and his style is far less classical than that of his friend Grosseteste. But the attainments of both of these early Franciscans are warmly eulogised by a younger member of the same Order, their pupil Roger Bacon[3], Among their contemporaries abroad, the teaching of Plato (as represented by the Neo-Platonists and Augustine) was followed in preference to that of Aristotle by the pupil of Alexander of Hales and the immediate successor (in 1253) of John of Rochelle, the mystical Franciscan, Bonaventura (1221—1274).

Bonaventura

In the Dominican Order the most learned scholar of this age was Vincent of Beauvais (d. 1264), tutor to the sons of Louis IX, who took pleasure in reading Vincent's works and in collecting, in the Library at the Sainte Chapelle, all the MSS needed for their composition. Vincent is best known in connexion with the *Speculum Mundi*, a vast encyclopaedia divided into four parts distinguished by the epithets *Naturale, Doctrinale* (*c.* 1250), *Historiale* (*c.* 1254) and *Morale* (doubtless by a later writer, *c.* 1310–20)[4]. The spirit in which he prepared his colossal work may be discerned in the opening words of his preface :—

Vincent of Beauvais

'Quoniam multitudo librorum et temporis brevitas, memoriae labilitas, non patitur cuncta, quae scripta sunt, pariter animo comprehendi, mihi, omnium fratrum minimo, plurimorum libros assidue revolventi, ac longo tempore studiose legenti, visum est tandem (accedente etiam majorum meorum consilio) quosdam flores pro modulo ingenii mei electos, ex omnibus fere quos legere potui, sive nostrorum, id est, Catholicorum Doctorum, sive gentilium, scilicet Philosophorum et Poëtarum et ex utrimque Historiarum, in unum corpus voluminis quodam compendio et ordine summatim redigere'.

[1] *Mon. Franc.* i 391.

[2] *ib.* 274, propter causam vivendi, vivendi finem facere (Juv. viii 84).

[3] *Op. Tert.* 75, perfecti in sapientia divina et humana, and 70. Cp. (on both) Pauli's *Abhandlung* (Tübingen, 1864); also (on Marsh) Little's *Grey Friars at Oxford*, 134–9, and Stevenson's *Grosseteste*, 76 f.

[4] Printed at Strassburg, 1473– , Nuremberg, 1483–6, Venice, 1494; also at Douai, 1624. Separate ed. of *Spec. Hist.* Augsburg (and Paris), 1474.

In compiling the *Speculum Naturale*, he had the assistance of many members of his Order, who made the extracts required for his purpose. In reference to his omnivorous reading he is justly described as a *librorum helluo*. The number of authors cited by him in the *Speculum Naturale* alone is as many as 350, with 100 more in the *Speculum Doctrinale* and *Historiale*; but, his knowledge of these authors being far from profound, he is sometimes landed in curious mistakes. Thus he supposes that there were two authors bearing the name of Sophocles and only one of the name of Seneca, while he actually describes Cicero as a Roman general[1]. He knew no Greek : he calls the emperor Isaac Angelus *Conrezach* (ed. 1474) or *Corezas* (ed. 1624), obviously a corruption of Κύρ' Ἰσαάκ[2]. He supplies us, however, with valuable evidence as to the successive stages which marked the translation of the 'Aristotelian' writings into the Latin language. Thus, for the *Organon*, he uses the old rendering from the Greek, by Boëthius; that from the Arabic in the *Historia Animalium*, *De Plantis*, *De Caelo et Mundo*, and in all except Book IV of the *Meteorologica*; the recent rendering from the Greek in the *Parva Naturalia*, the *Physics*, *Metaphysics*, *De Anima* and *Ethics*, while he never quotes the *Politics*[3]. In the case of Tibullus, he derives his quotations from certain excerpts earlier in date than any complete MS of that author now in existence[4].

In this age the great exponents of Aristotle among the Schoolmen were the two Dominicans, Albertus Magnus (1193—1280) and his famous pupil Thomas Aquinas (1225-7—1274). The former,

**Albertus Magnus**

---

[1] Graf, *Roma*, ii 178 ; cp. *Hist. Litt. de la France*, xviii 482 f, and Bartoli's *Precursori*, 29—31.

[2] *Spec. Hist.* xxix 64; Gidel, 274. Cp. Hallam, *Lit.* i 117[4]; Boutaric, *Vincent de B. et la connaissance de l'antiquité classique au xiii^e s.* (1875) in *Rev. des quest. hist.* xvii.

[3] Jourdain, 33, 360-72.

[4] O. Richter, *De Vincentii Bellovacensis excerptis Tibullianis* (1865). On the later literature, see Bursian's *Jahresb.* li 318. The influence of the mediaeval encyclopaedias of Vincent de Beauvais, Brunetto Latini and Bartholomaeus Anglicus on western literature, and especially on German poetry in cent. xiv—xv, is indicated in Liliencron's *Festrede* (München, 1876). Cp. *Hist. Litt. de la France*, xviii 449—519, F. C. Schlosser (1819); and Gröber, ii i 248—250.

a Suabian by birth, was a student at Padua and Bologna, and taught at Paris (near the narrow street still called the *Rue de Maître-Albert*), and also at the great school of the German Dominicans at Cologne. He was the first of his Order to teach philosophy and the first of the Schoolmen to state the philosophy of Aristotle in a systematic form, with constant reference to the Arabic commentators. Without neglecting the Platonic and Neo-Platonic writings (so far as they were known to him), he paid special attention to Aristotle, all of whose works were accessible to him in Latin translations either from the Arabic or the Greek or both. Thus, in the case of the *De Anima* and the *Physics*, he is able to quote a rendering from the Greek which is purer in its Latinity than that of the Arabic-Latin version of the fourth book *De Caelo*, where the Latin is largely interspersed with transliterations from the Arabic. In interpreting the several works of Aristotle, he mainly follows Avicenna, continuing Avicenna's plan of freely paraphrasing the text[1]. These paraphrases, in which he adapts the teaching of Aristotle to the requirements of the Church, are invariably followed by a 'digression', in which he states and discusses the views of his predecessors. The only case in which we find a regular commentary, instead of a paraphrase, is that of the *Politics*, which probably belongs to the latter part of his life[2]. His works, as printed at Lyons in 1651, fill 21 folio volumes, forming an encyclopaedia of all the learning and the polemics of his time. He is somewhat severely criticised by Prantl[3] as merely an indefatigable compiler; but he may perhaps be regarded with greater justice as a man of rich and varied endowments, who in astronomy and chemistry sought for truth in nature, and who deserves full credit as the restorer of the study of Aristotle[4]. As 'provincial' of his Order in Germany, he visited many monasteries, and, whenever he heard of any ancient MSS, he

[1] Cp. Jourdain, 38; Renan, *Av.* 231, 236[4]; and list in Bursian, i 78 n.

[2] Charles, *Roger Bacon*, 316 note 2. He here follows the method of his pupil Thomas Aquinas. But the authorship is disputed (Erdmann, i § 200, 8).

[3] *Logik*, iii 189. It is possibly Albertus who is attacked by Roger Bacon in *Op. Tertium*, p. 30 f and *Op. Minus*, p. 327 f (Charles, pp. 108, 355, '*ignorat linguas*'); see, however, Brewer's *Pref.* p. xxxiv.

[4] Cp. T. Clifford Allbutt, *Science and Medieval Thought*, p. 74 note.

either copied them himself or caused them to be copied by his companions[1]. But the influence of that Order, during the first century of its existence, was, in general, detrimental to classical learning. The Dominicans studied the Classics not for their own sake but for the purposes of preaching, and their own Latin style, which was doubtless debased by the low standard of Latinity attained in the current translations and comments on Aristotle, was apt to be exceedingly barbarous[2].

Thomas Aquinas

The great pupil of Albertus Magnus, Thomas Aquinas, the son of a count of Aquino, was born (*c.* 1225–7) at a castle near the ancient Aquinum; he received his first education at the neighbouring monastery of Monte Cassino, and continued his studies for six years at the *studium generale* lately founded by Frederic II at Naples, where he entered the Dominican Order. He next studied at Cologne under Albertus Magnus (who took his favourite pupil with him to Paris and brought him back to Cologne), taught philosophy at Cologne, Paris, Bologna, Naples and elsewhere; lived at the papal court in Rome from 1260 to 1269, and was less than 50 years of age when he died in 1274, on his way to the Council of Lyons. In his teaching he brought Scholasticism to its highest development by harmonising Aristotelianism with the doctrines of the Church. Certain dogmas were, however, excluded from comparison by being regarded as mysteries to be received as matters of faith alone. With Aquinas, the logical and metaphysical basis is that of Aristotle, with elements derived from Platonism and from Christian theology[3]. While Albertus had composed *paraphrases* of Aristotle after the manner of his eastern exponent Avicenna, Aquinas produced *commentaries* after that of his western interpreter Averroës. He thus comments on the *De Interpretatione, Analytica Posteriora, Physics, Parva Naturalia, Metaphysics, De Anima, Ethics, Politics, Meteorologica, De Caelo et Mundo* and *De Generatione et Corruptione.* These com-

[1] Hauréau, II i 218. On Albertus Magnus, cp. Pouchet, *Albert le Grand et son époque* (1853); Sighart, *Albertus Magnus* (1857); D'Assailly, *Albert le Grand* (1870).

[2] Bursian, i 77. Cp. Hallam, *Lit.* i 77[4] note *y*.

[3] All these sources of illumination are indicated by the convergent rays in the upper five-eighths of Traini's celebrated picture. See opposite page.

St Luke  St Matthew  St Paul     *Christ in Glory*     Moses   St John   St Mark

*St Thomas Aquinas*

*Aristotle*          *Plato*

*Averroes*

ALTAR-PIECE BY TRAINI (1345), IN THE CHURCH OF S. CATERINA, PISA.

Reduced from Rosini's *Pittura Italiana*, tav. xx.

*To face p.* 582.

mentaries were composed in Italy (*c.* 1260–9). His three greatest works are his Exposition of the Sentences of Peter Lombard, his *De Veritate Fidei Catholicae* (1261–4), and his celebrated *Summa Theologiae* (which was left unfinished).    In this last his teaching on the subject of Angels is naturally founded on 'Dionysius the Areopagite'; one of his favourite phrases is *ut docet Dionysius*; and he has no suspicion of the true date of that author.    In the domain of theology the *Summa* is an embodiment of the *scientific* spirit of the thirteenth century, a spirit which, as represented by Alexander of Hales, Albertus Magnus and Thomas Aquinas, stands in sharp contrast with the *literary and classical* spirit of the twelfth century, as exemplified in John of Salisbury and Peter of Blois[1].    As a commentator on Aristotle, Thomas Aquinas does not indulge in 'digressions', like those of Albertus Magnus, and in this respect he is followed by his Dominican pupil Robert Kilwardby (archbishop of Canterbury, d. 1279), who left behind him 39 treatises in philosophy alone[2]. On the question of 'universals' Thomas Aquinas is a Realist in the moderate Aristotelian sense, while he opposes the Platonic theory of ideas, as represented by Aristotle, though he accepts it, so far as it is supported by St Augustine[3].    The question how far he was familiar with Greek has been often discussed.    He has been described as ignorant of Greek by Oudin[4] and others[5], who are vaguely opposed by Gradenigo[6] on the ground of his frequent citations from Aristotle and the Greek fathers, and the wide prevalence of a study of Greek in the Dominican Order. The dissertations by Bernardo de Rubeis (1750), reprinted in the first volume of the papal edition of Thomas Aquinas (1882), tend to show that, though he was not a consummate hellenist, he was

---

[1] F. A. Gasquet, in *Dublin Review*, 1898, 373.

[2] Hauréau, II ii 29.        [3] Ueberweg, i 444 f.

[4] *Comm. de Scriptoribus Eccl.* (1722), iii 256, 'nesciebat...linguas quas appellant exoticas ;...ut Graeca nec tantisper intelligeret'.

[5] Brucker, *Hist. Crit. Phil.* iii 803 f; Gidel, p. 232.    Erasmus on *Ep. Rom.* i described him as 'dignus plane cui linguarum quoque peritia...contingeret'.    L. Schütz, in *Philosophisches Jahrbuch*, viii (1895) 273—283, maintains that he was ignorant of Greek, and E. Rolfes, in *Jahrb. f. phil. u spek. Theol.* x (1896) 408—414, has little to urge on the other side.

[6] *Lett. Greco-Italiana* (1759), 62.

not an entire stranger to the Greek language. He had doubtless some original Greek texts at his disposal, and obtained fresh versions taken directly from the Greek, as his biographer expressly states[1]. In a single work, the *Catena Aurea*, he cites the opinions of 60 Greek writers; in his *Summa*, he refers to a score of ecclesiastical and about the same number of secular Greek authors (including Heraclitus and Aristophanes), and Greek etymologies present themselves on the opening pages of that work[2]. He compares the Latin renderings of the Greek texts of the *Ethics* and *Politics*, and records variants which are copied from him by his master Albert. In his Commentary on the *Ethics*[3] (as observed by Dr Jackson) 'the presentation of the right reading misspelt, and of a ludicrous etymology side by side with one which is very nearly right, seems to show that, whilst Aquinas had about him people who knew Greek, he himself had no substantial knowledge of it'[4]. His Commentary on the *De Interpretatione* offers some criticisms on the Greek text, and implies the use of two Latin versions. He also refers to the Greek in commenting on the *Analytica Posteriora*. In the *Physics*[5] he explains the Greek words *spathesis* and *cercisis*, which are retained in the Latin versions. In the *De Caelo et Mundo* he notices that the words *De Caelo* alone represent the Greek title[6], and he also gives the meaning of a number of Greek terms. The same is true of the *Meteorologica*, where he apparently used three versions, all derived directly from the Greek[7]. In quoting Aristotle he uses translations from the Greek alone and not from the Arabic[8]. It was at his own instance that 'William of Brabant' is said to have produced in 1273 (doubtless with the help of others) a literal Latin translation of the Greek text of 'all the works of Aristotle',

---

[1] Tocco, in *Acta Sanct.*, Antwerp, i 665, 'scripsit etiam super philosophiam naturalem et moralem, et super metaphysicam, quorum librorum procuravit ut fieret *nova translatio* quae sententiae Aristotelis contineret clarius veritatem'. Cp. Jourdain, 40, 392.

[2] Tougard, 63 f.

[3] n 1, (νόμος) ἀπεσχεδιασμένος (p. 1129 *b* 15).

[4] Clifford Allbutt, *l. c.*, p. 76 f.                    [5] vii 2, 4.

[6] apud Graecos intitulatur *De Caelo*.

[7] Jourdain, 396—400.                    [8] *ib.* 40.

which superseded the old renderings from the Arabic[1]. 'William of Brabant', Roger Bacon's 'William the Fleming'[2], is none other than William of Moerbeke, or Meerbecke, a small town S. of Ghent and on the borders of Flanders and Brabant.

He was educated at Louvain and was probably one of the young Dominicans annually sent to Greece to learn the language. After his return (*c.* 1268) he was chaplain to Clement IV and Gregory X, and acted as Greek secretary at the Council of Lyons (1274), where he was one of those who chanted the Nicene Creed in Greek, thrice repeating the words contested by the Greek Church[3]. Roger Bacon, who does not mention him in 1267 among the translators of Aristotle[4], describes him as well known in 1272[5]. Towards the close of his life he became archbishop of Corinth (1277—1281) and continued the work of executing (and possibly superintending) translations from Greek into Latin. His translations included Simplicius on Aristotle *De Caelo et Mundo*, and probably Simplicius on the *Categories* (1266) and Ammonius *De Interpretatione*, possibly the *Organon*, *Physics* and *Historia Animalium*, certainly the 'Theological Elements' of Proclus (at Viterbo 1268)[6], the *Prognostics* of Hippocrates, and Galen *De Alimentis* (1277), and (above all) the

William of Moerbeke

---

[1] 1273: *Wilhelmus de Brabantia*, ordinis Praedicatorum, transtulit omnes libros Aristotelis de graeco in latinum, verbum ex verbo, qua translatione scholares adhuc hodierna die utuntur in scholis, ad instantiam domini *Thomae de Aquino* (Slav. Chron. in Lindenbrog's *Scriptores rerum Germ. septent.*, 1706, p. 206; cp. Jourdain, 67). 'Henri de Hervordia' adds: nam temporibus domini *Alberti* translatione veteri omnes communiter utebantur (*ib.* 68). Cp. Tocco on p. 584; also MS of *De Caelo et Mundo* in Trin. Coll. Library (no. 1498, late in c. xiii) 'hec est noua translacio'.

[2] *Comp. Phil.* 471; *infra* pp. 591 f.

[3] *Hist. Litt. de la France*, xxi 144.

[4] *Op. Tertium*, 91.

[5] *Comp. Phil.* 471.

[6] Specimen quoted by Cousin, ed. 1820–7; MS in Peterhouse Library, after 1268, part 4 of no. 121 in M. R. James' *Catalogue*; p. 588 *infra*. Thomas Aquinas (xxi 718, ed. 1866) notices that the Pseudo-Aristotelian *Liber De Causis* is an Arabic abstract of the 'Theological Elements' of Proclus (Wüstenfeld, *Gött. Abhandl.* 110 f); the *De Causis* is ascribed to Alfarabius (d. at Damascus, 950). The *Decem Dubitationes*, *De Providentia* and *De Malorum Subsistentia* of Proclus were all translated by William at Corinth in 1280=1281 N.S. (Quétif, i 390).

*Rhetoric* (1281) and *Politics* of Aristotle[1]. The value of the last two translations has been fully appreciated by Spengel and Susemihl respectively. Though this translator's knowledge of Greek is imperfect[2], the very baldness and literalness of his rendering, which has been denounced by Roger Bacon and by Sepulveda[3], add to its value as evidence of the text of the lost MS from which it was translated, a MS better than the best of those that have survived.

The Greek text of the *Ethics* is said to have been translated by Henry Kosbein of Brabant[4], who may possibly be identified with one of that name who was bishop of Lübeck from 1270 to

Siger<br>of Brabant 1284. Siger of Brabant is described by Dante as lecturing at Paris in the Rue du Fouarre[5]; and it was once supposed that Dante might have listened to his lectures in Paris. But it is now known that Dante was only seven when Siger left Paris (1272) and under eighteen when Siger died in prison at Orvieto, in 1283–4[6]. It is therefore clear that he is introduced by Dante, not as the poet's teacher, but as 'the typical representative of the faculty of *Arts*, to balance the Theologians and the representatives of the other Faculties', mentioned in the same canto. It has also been ascertained that 'Siger was an Averroist, *i.e.* a pure Aristotelian who taught the doctrine of Aristotle as to the eternity of the world, the unity of intellect, the mortality of the individual soul, without the compromises, accommodations, and corrections adopted by the orthodox Aristotelians like St Thomas'[7]. He wrote several works

---

[1] Jourdain, 67 f. The *Rhetoric* of Aristotle and of Cicero, and the *Summa* of Aquinas, are among the MSS received at Avignon by Adam bp of Hereford in 1319, for Laurence Bruton de Chepyn Norton, nephew of the abbot of Hayles (Gasquet, *Essays*, 37). William's transl. of the *Politics* was finished before the death of Thomas Aquinas (1274), who quotes it twice in the *Summa contra Gentiles*, c. 1261–5 (*Rhein. Mus.* xxxix 457). A *Nova Translatio* of the *Ethics*, bearing in the MS the date 1281 (probably by Henry Kosbein of Brabant, printed in 1497), was used by Thomas before 1262 (Quétif, *u. s.*).

[2] See Newman's *Politics*, vol. II p. xliv f, where examples of the translator's ignorance are cited. Cp. Busse (1881) in Susemihl-Hicks, 71–3.

[3] *Pol.* trans. 1548.

[4] Quétif, i 469; *Hist. Litt. de la France*, xxi 141 ; Gidel, 264 f.

[5] *Par.* x 136.

[6] Mandonnet, *Siger de Brabant* (Fribourg, 1899, Louvain, 1911).

[7] Rashdall on Mandonnet in *Eng. Hist. Rev.* 1902, 347 f.

on Logic, including a commentary on the *Prior Analytics*[1]. He is further said to have publicly expounded the *Politics*[2], and the same is reported of Nicolas d'Autrecour (*c.* 1348) and the Carmelite Pierre la Casa and the Benedictine Gui de Strasbourg. Meanwhile, about the date of Siger's death, the Augustinian monk Egidio (Colonna) da Roma, better known as Gilles de Rome, or Gilles de Paris, who became bishop of Bourges in 1294, and died at Avignon in 1316, had founded **Gilles de Paris** on the *Politics* a work *De Regimine Principum*, written (*c.* 1283) for the benefit of the future king, Philip le Bel[3]. In 1295 Durand d'Auvergne, and two Greek bishops, translated the *Oeconomics*[4]. About the same time, an Irish Dominican, Geoffrey of Waterford (d. 1300), translated the Pseudo-Aristotelian treatise called the *Secretum Secretorum* (including the *Physiognomica*[5]), and, in the preface to his rendering of that treatise, recorded the legend that, at the death of Aristotle, his spirit passed into the heavens in the semblance of flame[6]. The Saracenic interest in Aristotle is embodied in the belief that the bones of that philosopher were preserved in the principal Mosque of Palermo[7].

We have now seen that, in the course of about 130 years, *i.e.* in the interval between the early translations at Toledo in 1150 and the death of William of Moerbeke in 1281, the knowledge of Aristotle's philosophy had passed in Europe from a phase of almost total darkness to one of nearly perfect light. The whole of the *Organon* had become known. The *Physics*, *Metaphysics*, and *Ethics* had reached Europe through translations from the

---

[1] Cp. *Hist. Litt. de la France*, xxi 96—127.     [2] *ib.* 106.

[3] Le Clerc, *Hist. Litt.* 505 f; Steinschneider, *Hebr. Uebers.* 464, 491 f; Lajard in *Hist. Litt.* xxx 421—566; Tiraboschi, iv 147—51. He repeatedly quotes the *Politics* and *Ethics* in his *De Regimine Principum*, which was printed 11 times in Latin (1473—1617) and translated into French soon after 1286 (ed. Molenaer, 1899). It is one of the sources of Hoccleve's *Regiment of Princes* (H. Morley, *Eng. Writers*, vi 131).

[4] *Hist. Litt. de la France*, xix 58; *Notices et Extraits*, xxxiii (1) 230.

[5] *Hist. Litt. de la France*, xxi 216, 839; Gidel, 263; Gaston Paris, *Litt. Fr. au MA*, § 101. On the *Secretum Secretorum*, or Pseudo-Politics, cp. Steinschneider, 245—255. G. L. Hamilton, *Romanic Review*, I 3 (1910) 261, shows that Geoffrey 'only used one Latin version of the Arabic work '.

[6] Gidel, 353.     [7] Baddeley's *Charles III of Naples*, 123.

Arabic, and the *De Anima*, the *Magna Moralia, Politics* and *Rhetoric* through translations from the Greek[1]. The treatise on Poetry had already been translated into Arabic from a Syriac version founded on a Greek MS far older than any text of the treatise now extant, but this translation, which was probably little known, has only recently been made available for the purposes of textual criticism[2].

[1] Cp. p. 570 *supra*.

[2] Margoliouth, *Anecdota Orientalia* (1887) ; Butcher's ed. 2, p. 4. Cp. Egger, *Hist. de la Critique*, 554–60[3] ; Immisch in *Philol.* lv (1896) 20—38 ; J. Tkač in *Wiener Studien*, xxiv (1902) 70—98. The date of the Arabic version is *c*. 935. The intermediate commentary of Averroës on *Rhet.* and *Poet.* was translated from the Arabic into Hebrew by Todros (Theodoros) of Arles in 1337. This translation of the commentary on the *Rhet.* was published by Goldenthal (Leipzig, 1842) and Lasinio (Pisa, 1875–7) ; and the latter has also edited the commentary on the *Poet.* (1872).

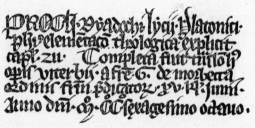

COLOPHON OF THE 'THEOLOGICAL ELEMENTS' OF PROCLUS.

From a xiii cent. MS in the Library of Peterhouse, Cambridge,
    copied from the translation finished at Viterbo by William
    of Moerbeke, 18 May, 1268 (p. 585 *supra*).

Part iv of MS I. 2. 6 (M. R. James, *Catalogue of the MSS in the
    Library of Peterhouse, Cambridge*, no. 121, p. 142).

# CHAPTER XXXI.

## THE THIRTEENTH CENTURY AND AFTER.

## ROGER BACON (1214-94) TO DANTE (1265—1321).

AMONG the keenest critics of the Schoolmen, and also of the recent translators of Aristotle, was Roger Bacon (*c.* 1214—1294). Born near Ilchester and educated at Oxford and Paris, he included among his teachers at Oxford men such as Robert Grosseteste, Adam Marsh and Thomas Wallensis (afterwards bishop of St David's). All of these are said to have been pupils of Edmund Rich (archbishop of Canterbury, 1234-40), who, according to a biography ascribed to the Dominican Robert Bacon, studied as though he were to live for ever, and lived as though he were to die on the morrow[1]. It was probably under the influence of Grosseteste, the first lecturer to the Franciscans at Oxford[2], that he entered the Franciscan Order. After pursuing his studies in Paris, he returned to England about 1250. Some seven years later, he fell under the suspicions of his Order, and, by the authority of its recently appointed general, afterwards known as the 'seraphic' Bonaventura, was for ten years (1257-67) kept in close confinement in Paris. He probably owed his partial release to the goodwill of Clement IV (d. 1268), for whom he now wrote, in the wonderfully brief space of 15 months, his three great works, the *Opus Majus*, the *Opus Minus* and the *Opus Tertium* (1267). These were followed

Roger Bacon

---

[1] St John's Coll. MS, fol. iii v, col. 2, (studebat) discere, quasi semper victurus; vivere, quasi cras moriturus (printed in *Life* by W. Wallace, 1893).

[2] Grosseteste, *Epp.* p. 179 Luard.

by his *Compendium Studii Philosophiae* (1271–2). He was once more placed under restraint in 1278; but he had again been released before writing his *Compendium Studii Theologiae* (1292), and he probably died at Oxford in 1294. His earlier reputation as an alchemist and a necromancer was greatly transformed by the publication (by Dr Samuel Jebb) of his *Opus Majus* (1733), which has been recognised as at once the Encyclopaedia and the Organon of the thirteenth century[1]. He here discusses the hindrances to the progress of true science, and broadly sketches the outlines of grammar, logic, mathematics, physics (especially optics), experimental research and moral philosophy; but in the text, as first published, the part on grammar was imperfect and that on moral philosophy[2] was wanting. Extracts from a MS of the *Opus Tertium* were published by Cousin in 1848[3]; fragments of the *Opus Minus*, with the *Opus Tertium* and the *Compendium Studii Philosophiae*, were first edited by Professor J. S. Brewer in the *Opera Inedita* of 1859; and an excellent monograph on their author was produced by M. Émile Charles in 1861. The following is the general purport of the passages in the above works of Roger Bacon which bear on our present subject:—

'Ignorance of the truths set forth by the ancients is due to the little care that is spent on the study of the ancient languages. It is vain to object that some of the Fathers neglected that study and misunderstood its advantages. Worthy as they are of respect in many ways, they cannot serve as our models in everything. They knew and appreciated Plato, but were almost entirely ignorant of Aristotle. The first to translate and explain the *Categories* was Augustine, who praises Aristotle more for that one small work than we for all (*Opus Majus*, p. 18). The next to translate Aristotle was Boëthius, who rendered parts of the Logic and a few other works...The Fathers often follow Aristotle's teaching on Grammar, Logic and Rhetoric, and the common axioms of his *Metaphysics*; but they neglect the rest and even bid us neglect it (p. 19). Philosophy is also neglected by modern doctors, who use inferior text-books (p. 21). It is impossible to obtain a perfect knowledge of the Scriptures,

---

[1] Whewell's *Phil. of the Inductive Sciences*, xii c. 7.

[2] Its omission in Dr Samuel Jebb's ed. was first noticed by J. K. Ingram, 'On the *Opus Majus* of Bacon' (Dublin, 1858). Cp. E. Charles, *Roger Bacon*, pp. 339—348. The Preface was first printed by F. A. Gasquet in *Eng. Hist. Rev.* 1897 p. 516 f. The *Op. Majus* has been edited by Bridges (1897—1900), where the part on moral philosophy appears for the first time in print. (For Life and Works, and Bibliography, cp. *Essays*, ed. A. G. Little, 1914.)        [3] *Journal des Savants* (1848), Mars—Juin.

without knowing Hebrew and Greek, or of philosophy without knowing Arabic as well (p. 44). A translator ought to be thoroughly familiar with the science of which he is treating, and with the language of his original and that of his own rendering. Boëthius alone has known the meaning of the languages[1]; Grosseteste alone, the meaning of the science. All the other translators are ignorant of both. Their translations of Aristotle in particular are impossible to understand (p. 45). The Latin translations of Josephus, Dionysius, Basil, John of Damascus and others, are inferior to those executed by Grosseteste' (p. 46).

'There are not four men in Latin Christendom who are acquainted with the Hebrew, Greek and Arabic Grammar...There are many among the Latins who can *speak* Greek, Arabic, and Hebrew ; very few, who understand the *grammar* of these languages, or know how to teach them...So it is now with nearly all the Jews, and even with the native Greeks...Even when they *do* understand the languages, they know nothing of the sciences...We must have the original texts of the separate parts of philosophy, that the falsities and defects in the Latin copies may be discovered' (*Opus Tertium*, p. 33). 'The scientific works of Aristotle, Avicenna, Seneca, Cicero, and other ancients, cannot be had except at a great cost; their principal works have not been translated into Latin...The admirable books of Cicero *De Republica* are not to be found anywhere...I could never find the works of Seneca...although I made diligent search for them during twenty years and more' (p. 55)[2].

'Though we have numerous translations of all the sciences by Gerard of Cremona, Michael Scot, Alfred the Englishman, Hermann the German, and William <the> Fleming, there is such an utter falsity in all their writings that none can sufficiently wonder at it...Certainly none of the above-named had any true knowledge of the tongues or the sciences, as is clear, not from their translations only, but also from their condition of life. All were alive in my time ; some, in their youth, contemporaries with Gerard of Cremona, who was somewhat more advanced in years among them. Hermann the German, who was very intimate with Gerard, is still alive (1272) and a bishop. When I questioned him about certain books of Logic[3], which he had to translate from the Arabic, he roundly told me he knew nothing of Logic, and therefore did not dare to translate them...Nor did he understand Arabic, as he confessed ; in fact, he was rather an assistant in the translations, than the real translator. For he kept Saracens about him in Spain, who had a principal hand in his translations. In the same way Michael the Scot claimed the merit of numerous translations. But it is certain that Andrew, a Jew, laboured at them more than he did. And even Michael, as Hermann reported, did not understand

---

[1] Cp. *Op. Tert.* 33 ; *Gk Gr.* 29.

[2] Brewer's *Preface*, pp. lxi—lxiii.

[3] The *Rhet.* and *Poet.* are meant ; cp. *Comp. Stud. Philos.* p. 473. Hermann the German (ap. Wüstenfeld, *Gött. Abhandl.* 93) himself describes them as *logici negocii Aristotelis complementum.* Cp. Charles, p. 122 n. 1, and Immisch, in *Philol.* lv 20 ; p. 569 *supra.*

either the sciences or the tongues. And so of the rest ; especially the notorious William <the> Fleming, who is now in such reputation (1272); whereas it is well known to all men of letters in Paris, that he is ignorant of the sciences in the original Greek, to which he makes such pretensions ; and therefore he translates falsely and corrupts the philosophy of the Latins' (*Compendium Studii Philosophiae*, p. 471)[1]. 'If I had any authority over the translations of Aristotle, I should have all of them burnt to save men from wasting their time in studying them and thus multiplying the sources of error and ignorance' (p. 469).

'Slowly has any portion of the philosophy of Aristotle come into use among the Latins. His *Natural Philosophy*, and his *Metaphysics*, with the commentaries of Averroës and others, were translated in my time (*temporibus nostris*), and interdicted at Paris before the year A.D. 1237, because of the eternity of the world and of time, and because of the book of the *Divination by Dreams*, which is the third book *De Somno et Vigilia*, and because of many passages erroneously translated. Even his Logic was slowly received and lectured on. For St Edmund, the archbishop of Canterbury [Edmund Rich], was the first who in my time read the *Elenchi*[2] at Oxford. And I have seen Master Hugo, who first read the book of *Posterior* (*Analytics*), and have also seen his writing (*verbum*). So there have been few, considering the multitude of the Latins, who are of any account in the philosophy of Aristotle ; nay, very few indeed, and scarcely any up to this year of grace 1292...The *Ethics* has but slowly become known[3], having been only lately, and that seldom, expounded by our masters[4]...Thus far, there have only been three persons who could form a true judgement of the small portion of the whole of Aristotle that has been translated'[5].

In the *Opus Majus* Roger Bacon protests against the inordinate amount of time spent on the metaphysical controversy as to Universals[6]; notices the expansion in the knowledge of Aristotle's

[1] Brewer's *Preface*, p. lix.

[2] *librum Elenchorum* (Univ. Coll. Oxf. MS, Rashdall ii 754); *librum Elemętorum* (Brit. Mus. MS Royal 7 F vii, folio 155).

[3] *coïtata* (*communicata* ?) Brit. Mus. MS.

[4] *a magistris* (*ib.*), not *Parisiis* (as printed by Charles).

[5] *Compendium Studii Theologiae*, p. lv of Brewer's *Preface*, corrected and supplemented from text in Charles, p. 412, and Rashdall, ii 754, and from MS in Brit. Mus.

[6] p. 28. His own position may be inferred from the fact that he criticises the 'Unity of Form' held by Thomas Aquinas, thus anticipating Scotus; while, in his doctrine of Universals, he anticipates Ockham, but avoids the mistake of supposing that the particular alone is real. Cp. Extracts in Charles, p. 383, 'Universale non est nisi convenientia plurium individuorum'...'Individuum est prius secundum naturam' etc. ; also the full discussion, *ib.* pp. 164—244, and the brief summary in Rashdall, ii 525.

writings dating from the time of Michael Scot, *i.e.* from after 1230[1];
and denounces the inadequacy of the current translations, and
especially the ignorance which had led the translator to leave
foreign words standing in their text[2]. Three times over he
expresses his annoyance at the use of the word *belenum* in the
Latin translation of the (Pseudo-Aristotelian) *De Plantis*. Once,
while lecturing on Aristotle, he had hesitated and stumbled over
this unwonted word, whereupon his Spanish pupils laughed out-
right and told him that it was only the Spanish for 'henbane'
(*hyoscyamus*)[3]. Curiously enough, the late Greek translator of
this Spanish equivalent for the Arabic rendering of the lost
original of Nicolaus Damascenus, although he uses the word
ὑοσκύαμος elsewhere[4], has actually borrowed, from the Spanish-
Latin rendering, the word βελένιον, which has no real authority
whatsoever.

In the fragmentary *Opus Minus* Roger Bacon points out
errors of translation in the Vulgate, as well as mistakes due to
modern correctors of the text :—'everyone presumes to change
anything he does not understand,—a thing he would not dare to
do for the books of the classical poets'[5]. Here and elsewhere
he lays the foundations for the textual criticism of the Scriptures[6].
He also protests against the implicit trust placed in the works of
an earlier Franciscan, Alexander of Hales, even suggesting that
his ponderous *Summa Theologiae* ('plusquam pondus unius equi')
was not composed by himself[7]. In the *Opus Tertium* he boldly

[1] p. 36.                    [2] p. 45.

[3] *Opus Majus*, p. 45 ; *Op. Tertium*, p. 91 ; *Comp. Phil.* p. 467. Cp. *De
Plantis* i 7, 2 (p. 821 *a* 32 = iv 28, 39 Didot). The Latin translator of the
Arabic was 'Alfred the Englishman'. Bacon has the delicacy not to mention
this fact, but he ascertains the right rendering from 'Hermann the German'
(p. 467).

[4] 820 *b* 5 (*Ar.* iv 27, 13 Didot).

[5] p. 330 f. The unnamed scholar, who had spent 40 years in cautiously
correcting and expounding the Vulgate, has been identified as the Oxford
Franciscan, William de Mara, or de la Mare. Cp. Denifle, *Archiv f. Litt.
etc. des MAs*, 1888, 545. (See F. A. Gasquet in *Dublin Rev.* 1898, p. 21.)

[6] Charles, p. 263 ; cp. J. P. P. Martin, *La Vulgate latine au xiii s. d'après
Roger Bacon* (1888), and esp. F. A. Gasquet on 'English Biblical Criticism in
the 13th cent.', in *Dublin Rev.* Jan. 1898, 1—21 and in *Essays*, ed. Little, 1914.

[7] p. 326. Cp. p. 574 *supra*.

challenges a comparison of his own work with that of Albertus Magnus and William Shirwood[1], while he is never weary of extolling the merits of Grosseteste[2], or of descanting on the mistakes in the current renderings of Aristotle[3]. He also discourses on textual corruptions, on accents, on aspirates, and on punctuation and prosody[4]. Lastly, in the *Compendium Studii Philosophiae*, he tells us that, in many parts of Italy, the clergy and the people were Greek[5], and that teachers of that language, who had been brought from Italy by Grosseteste, were still to be found in England[6]. In urging the study of Greek as well as Hebrew, he adds:—'we are the heirs of the scholars of the past, and (even in our own interests) are bound to maintain the traditions of learning, on pain of being charged with infinite folly'[7]. He next gives a long list of Latin words derived from Greek[8], attacks the etymological works of Papias, Hugutio and Brito[9]; quotes with approval the criticism on *auricalcum* (a mistake for *orichalcum*[10]) which he had himself heard from Joannes de Garlandia in Paris[11]; and adds a number of common errors in spelling, scansion and etymology[12]. He urges many further reasons for studying Greek[13], insists that Aristotle should be read in the original[14], and assures us that he had seen the Greek text of the 50 books of Aristotle on Natural History[15], mentioned by Pliny[16]. Towards the close, he sets forth the Greek alphabet, with the name and sound and numerical value of each letter[17], classifies all the letters, and discourses at length on accentuation and prosody[18].

[1] p. 14.

[2] pp. 33, 70, 75, 88, 91 ; cp. *Op. Maj.* 45, 64 ; *Comp. Phil.* 469, 472, 474 ; *Gk Gr.* 118.

[3] pp. 75, 77, 124 ; cp. *Op. Maj.* 262, 420, 460.         [4] pp. 234—256 f.

[5] Cp. *Op. Tert.* 33 ; and *Gk Gr.* 31, in regno Siciliae (*meaning S. Italy*) multae ecclesiae Graecorum et populi multi sunt qui veri Graeci sunt etc.

[6] p. 434.                                    [7] p. 435.

[8] p. 441. Cp. *Gk Gr.* 68 and *Introd.* xxxv f.

[9] pp. 447—452. Cp. *Gk Gr.* 37, 92, 98 ; Charles, pp. 330, 359, and *infra*, p. 666 f.

[10] Cp. p. 386, *Op. Min.* c. 7, and *Gk Gr.* p. 92.

[11] p. 453.              [12] pp. 454—462.              [13] p. 464 f.

[14] p. 469.              [15] p. 473.              [16] viii 17.

[17] p. 495 f. *Facs.* in Brewer's *Opera Inedita* ad fin. Cp. frontispiece to *Opus Majus*, vol. iii, ed. Bridges.

[18] pp. 508—519.

The desirability of the study of Greek is sufficiently shown by the copyist of the above treatise, who clumsily tries to represent Greek words in Latin characters.　On the other hand, the Greek is beautifully written in the MS of Roger Bacon's *Greek Grammar* preserved in the Library of Corpus Christi College, Oxford, which includes a short Greek Accidence and ends with the paradigm of τύπτω[1]　This Grammar has now been published, together with a fragment, ascribed to the same work, in the Cambridge Library[2]. The author holds that 'the Grammar of all languages is *substantially* the same, though there may be *accidental* variations in each'[3].　Greek Grammars had already been collected for Grosseteste in Greece itself[4], and one of his friends had actually brought such a work from Athens and had translated it into Latin[5].　Bacon's own knowledge of Greek was mainly derived from the Greeks of his day, and it is their pronunciation that he invariably adopts[6].　In his Grammar he naturally followed the Byzantine tradition, which was also followed subsequently by Constantine Lascaris and Chrysoloras[7].　He may have had some direct knowledge of Theodosius[8]; but it seems more probable that, like Theodorus Prodromus[9], he used a Greek Catechism resembling that preserved in the Wolfenbüttel *Erotemata*[10]. Besides the Grammar, there is a Greek lexicon which may be attributed to Roger Bacon[11].　But these are isolated works; in the library of Christ Church, Canterbury (*c.* 1300), not a single Greek text was to be found[12].

In the *Opus Majus*[13] Roger Bacon refers to the translation of

[1] Brewer's Pref. to *Op. Inedita*, p. lxiv; cp. Charles, 66.

[2] E. Nolan (Cambridge Univ. Press, 1902).

[3] p. 27.　　　　　　　　　　　　[4] *Op. Tert.* 91.

[5] p. 423 *supra*.

[6] *Gk Gr.* p. xx of *Introd.*, and pp. 32, 48 and *passim* in the transliterations there given.

[7] Heiberg in *Byz. Zeitschr.* 1900, 472 f; and S. A. Hirsch in *Introd.* to *Gk Gr.* p. lx and (on *R. B. and Philology*) in *Essays*, ed. Little, 101—151.

[8] p. 361 *supra*.　　　　　　　　[9] p. 361.

[10] S. A. Hirsch, *u. s.*, p. lxii.

[11] M. R. James in *Camb. Mod. Hist.* i 587.

[12] *ib.* 589; p. 558 *supra*.

[13] p. 44, si cuiquam videatur linguae gratiam interpretatione non mutari, Homerum exprimat in Latinum ad verbum.

Homer in a way which, at first sight, seems to imply a personal familiarity with the charm of the original; but this impression is unhappily dispelled when we find two parallel passages, from both of which it is certain that he is here quoting Jerome[1]. In the preface to his *Compendium Theologiae* he justifies certain quotations from Cicero, Pliny and Seneca by adding:—'etiam causa specialis me monet ut *excitem lectorem ad quaerendum libros auctorum dignos*, in quibus magna pulchritudo et dignitas sapientiae reperitur, qui nunc temporis sicut a multitudine studentium, sic a doctoribus eius penitus ignorantur'[2]. In philosophy his greatest names are Aristotle[3] and his Arabian exponents, Avicenna and Averroës. He refers to the *Phaedo* and *Timaeus* of Plato, which were probably known to him only in Latin translations[4]. In Latin his favourite authors are Cicero, whose appeal to Caesar he aptly applies to the pope:—*noli nostro periculo esse sapiens*[5], and Seneca[6], who helps him to denounce the blind following of authority:—*vivimus ad exempla*[7]. In history he knows Sallust, Livy and 'Trogus Pompeius'; he is also familiar with Pliny and Solinus, and with Donatus, Servius, Apuleius, Gellius, Censorinus, Boëthius, Cassiodorus and Priscian[8].

---

[1] *Op. Tert.* 90; *Comp. Phil.* 466.            [2] ap. Charles, p. 411.

[3] He knew the whole of the *Organon*, the *Physics*, *De Caelo* (of which he had two translations, one of them taken from the Greek), *De Anima*, *De Generatione et Corruptione*, *Parva Naturalia*, the 'nineteen' books of the *Hist. An.*, ten books of the *Metaphysics* (*Comp. Phil.* 473), and the *Ethics* (in three translations). He had some slight knowledge of the *Rhet.* and *Poët.* (Charles, p. 325), and the *Politics*, but called it the 'Book of Laws' (*ib.* 397, and *Comp. Phil.* 422 f). He also knew the Pseudo-Aristotelian *De Plantis*, *De Causis* and *Liber Secretorum*. The *Problems* had only been partially and inadequately translated (Charles, 376). Cp., in general, Charles, 315-7.

[4] Charles, 323.

[5] *Pro Marc.* 25 (*Op. Tert.* p. 87). He also knew the *Verrines, Phil., Paradoxa, De Part. Orat., De Div., De Am., De Sen., De Nat. D., De Off.*, and the then 'little known' *Tusc. Disp.* He mentions 'five' books of the *Academica* (*Op. Tert.* p. 50, and Brit. Mus. MS, Royal 7. F. vii, folio 154 v), probably meaning the *De Finibus*; he cites fragments of the *Hortensius* and *Timaeus* and searches in vain for the *De Republica*. Cp. Charles, 323.

[6] He knows the *Letters, De Benef., Ira, Clem.*, and *Quaest. Nat.* (besides certain apocryphal works). Charles, 322.

[7] *Ep.* 123 § 6 (ap. *Op. Tert.* 50).

[8] Charles, 330, 333 f.

He describes Bede as *literatissimus in grammatica*[1], and even as *antiquior Prisciano*[2]! but he mainly relies on Priscian, without slavishly following him[3]. In verse he quotes freely from Terence, Virgil, Juvenal, Lucan, Statius and the later poets. He urges that boys should not be taught the 'foolish fables' of poets such as Ovid[4]; but, when he needs a new argument for the study of Greek, he tacitly borrows a line from the *Epistolae ex Ponto*:— 'gratius ex ipso fonte bibuntur aquae'[5]. He knew Arabic and Hebrew, as well as Greek, and the same keenness of spirit, that prompted him to insist on the importance of the study of Greek, impelled him to extend the bounds of science. In science he was at least a century in advance of his time, and, in spite of the long and bitter persecutions that he endured, he was full of hope for the future. The spirit in which he looked forward to an age of wider knowledge was like that expressed in one of his own citations from Seneca[6]:—' veniet tempus quo ista quae nunc latent, in lucem dies extrahat et longioris aevi diligentia '[7].

In Roger Bacon's day, notwithstanding his eagerness for promoting the study of Aristotle in the original Greek, it was the *Latin* Aristotle alone that was studied in the schools. In the very year in which he was writing his three great works in Paris (1267), Oxford was prescribing for the course in Arts the whole of the Latin *Organon*, and, as an alternative, the *De Anima* and the *Physics*[8]. The study of the *Physics* in England during this century may be illustrated by the MS of the Latin translation of that work, written in England and illuminated with a representation of a mediaeval lecture-room, in which a closely packed group of

[1] *Op. Min.* 332. [2] *Gk Gr.* 41.
[3] *Op. Tert.* 245, and *Gk Gr.* 131. [4] *Op. Tert.* 55.
[5] iii 5, 18. Printed as prose in *Comp. Phil.* 465 (with *dulcius*).
[6] *N. Q.* vii 25, 4.
[7] Extr. in Charles, p. 393. See, in general, *Hist. Litt. de la France*, xvi 138–41; E. Charles, *Roger Bacon, sa vie, ses ouvrages, ses doctrines* (1861); A. Parrot, *R. B., sa personne, son génie, ses œuvres et ses contemporains* (1894); Brewer's Pref. to *Opera Inedita* (1859); and Adamson in *Dict. Nat. Biogr.*; and cp. Mullinger, i 154–9; Rashdall, ii 522–5; Gasquet in *Dublin Review*, 1898, 1—21; Clifford Allbutt, *Science and Medieval Thought*, pp. 72, 78 f; and Hirsch in *Introd.* to *The Greek Grammar of Roger Bacon* (1902); also *Essays*, ed. A. G. Little, 1914; J. H. Bridges, *Life and Work of R. B.*, 1914; J. E. Sandys, in British Academy Proc. 27 May 1914, and in *Essays*, 359; Picavet, *ib.* 55. [8] Rashdall, ii 455.

nine tonsured students, with their books resting on their knees, is listening to a scholar, who is lecturing with uplifted hand, robed in an academic gown and enthroned on a professorial chair[1].

Roger Bacon's interest in Greek and Arabic was shared by a slightly later Franciscan, the unwearied traveller, Raymundus Lullius (1234—1315), who urged the pope and the authorities of the university of Paris to establish a college in which Greek and Arabic and the language of the Tartar races could be taught with a view to the refutation of the doctrines of Mahomet and Averroës[2].

*Raymundus Lullius*

While, among the Franciscans, the extreme Realist, Alexander of Hales, and the mystic Bonaventura had, in their philosophic opinions, agreed in adhering to the Augustinian tradition as to the teaching of Plato, the Dominicans Albertus Magnus and Thomas Aquinas had introduced Aristotelianism into theology. The views of these Dominicans were opposed at Paris and Oxford (1277), and this opposition was followed by further developments of Franciscan philosophy[3]. A new form of Realism culminated in the teaching of the Franciscan Joannes Duns Scotus, who was possibly born at Dunstan (near Dunstanburgh Castle) in Northumberland, and who opposed the teaching of Thomas Aquinas at Oxford, Paris (1304) and Cologne, where he died in 1308[4]. While the system of Thomas Aquinas implies the harmony of faith and reason, Duns Scotus has less confidence in the power of reason and enlarges the number of the doctrines already recognised as capable of being apprehended by faith alone. He has also a less high regard than Thomas for the teaching of Aristotle, and he adopts many Platonic and Neo-Platonic opinions. His works include *Quaestiones* on Aristotle *De Anima* and *Meteorologica*, and an exposition and summaries and conclusions, as well as *Quaestiones*, on the *Metaphysics*. The

*Duns Scotus*

[1] British Museum, Royal 12. G. v. (reproduced in *Social England*, ill. ed., i 623). The double columns of the text of this MS have two narrow columns of glosses on each side.

[2] Renan, *Averroès*, 255[2] f; Rashdall, ii 96; F. A. Gasquet in *Dublin Review*, 1898, 365; *Hist. Litt. de la France*, xxix 1—386; Erdmann, i § 206.

[3] Rashdall, ii 527 f.

[4] The tombstone in the *Minoritenkirche* bears the inscription :—'Scotia me genuit, Anglia me suscepit, Gallia me docuit, Colonia me tenet'.

*Quaestiones* on the *Physics* are now acknowledged to be spurious. In the domain of pure Scholarship he is represented by the *Grammatica Speculativa*[1], which is also described as a treatise *De Modis Significandi*, and is sometimes attributed to Albert of Saxony[2], although Duns Scotus himself refers to it in his work on Logic, which he wrote early in his career. In his Grammar, he quotes Petrus Helias, as well as Donatus and Priscian.

Even in the ranks of the Realists, the extravagant Realism of Duns Scotus was followed by a reaction led by Wycliffe (1324–84), who (for England at least) is at once 'the last of the Schoolmen' and 'the first of the Reformers'. Humanists were agreed with later Reformers, such as Tyndale (1530), in opposing the subtleties of Scotus. In 1535 (a date which marks the close of the influence of Scholasticism in England) the idol of the Schools was dragged from his pedestal at Oxford and Cambridge; and one of Thomas Cromwell's commissioners at Oxford writes :—'We have set Dunce in *Bocardo*, and have utterly banished him Oxford for ever, with all his blynd glosses ... (At New College) wee fownd all the great Quadrant Court full of the Leaves of Dunce, the wind blowing them into every corner'[3]. But, a little more than a century later, a magnificent edition of his works, excluding the biblical commentaries, and including the philosophical and dogmatic writings alone, was published in 13 folio volumes by the Irish Franciscans at Lyons (1639). In the first volume of this edition he is called 'amplissimae scholae nobilis antesignanus', and is even described as 'ita Aristotelis discipulus, ut doceri ab eo Aristoteles vellet, si viveret'. He also survives, as a typical Schoolman, in Butler's *Hudibras* (1664), where the hero of the poem is compared to Duns Scotus (as well as to Thomas Aquinas and 'the irrefragable Doctor', Alexander of Hales) :—

> 'In school-divinity as able
> As he that hight Irrefragable ;
> A second Thomas, or, at once
> To name them all, another Dunce'.

By a strange caprice of fortune the name of one who was celebrated

---

[1] i 39—76 (ed. 1639). Cp. Bäbler's *Beiträge* (1885), 84–8.

[2] Title of Venice ed. of 1519. Albert taught in Paris, *c.* 1350–60.

[3] Layton in Strype's *Eccl. Memorials*, i 324.

as 'the subtle Doctor', and was regarded by Hooker as 'the wittiest of school divines'[1], and by Coleridge as the only Englishman possessed of 'high metaphysical subtlety'[2], has become synonymous with stupidity[3].

Duns Scotus is distinguished from all the other Schoolmen by what Prantl[4] has described as 'a peculiarly copious infusion of Byzantine Logic'. The first six sections of the *Summulae Logicales* of Petrus Hispanus of Lisbon, who died as Pope John XX (XXI) in 1277, contain the substance of the Logic of Aristotle, derived from Arabic sources, while the seventh section was translated into Greek by Georgios Scholarios (1400—1464)[5]. A *Synopsis* of Aristotle's Logic was also produced by William Shirwood, who was a prebendary of Lincoln Cathedral in 1245, and treasurer in 1258 and 1267[6].

The teaching of the Dominican Thomas Aquinas was opposed not only by the Realist Duns Scotus, but also by another Franciscan, the great Nominalist William of Ockham (d. 1347). The date of his birth is unknown, but, in his boyhood, he must often have gazed on the seven lancet-windows of the thirteenth century, which make the church of his birthplace in Surrey unique in the annals of architecture. He studied at Oxford and graduated in Paris. Realism, which had been shaken more than two centuries before by Roscellinus, was to all appearance shattered by William of Ockham, who is the last of the greater Schoolmen. He opposes the real existence of universals, pointing out that,

*William of Ockham*

---

[1] *Eccl. Pol.* I xi 5.

[2] *Literary Remains*, iii 21.

[3] Trench, *Study of Words*, 83 f; early exx. (1577) in Murray, *Oxf. Dict.* s.v.

[4] *Logik*, iii 203.

[5] Val. Rose and Thurot (as well as Mansel and Hamilton) held that the Latin was the original form. An entry in a single MS at Munich led Prantl, *Logik* ii[2] 263—301 (followed by Ueberweg, i 404, 459 E.T., and by Mullinger, i 175—186), to ascribe the Greek to Psellus and to regard it as the original. But several MSS ascribe the Greek to Scholarios (Stapper in *Festschrift*, Freiburg in B., 1896, 130-8), whom Krumbacher, in *Byz. Zeitschr.* vi 443, identifies with Georgios Scholarios. The mnemonic words *Barbara, celarent, darii, ferio* are represented in Greek by γράμματα, ἔγραψε, γραφίδι, τεχνικός; and similarly in the other figures.

[6] Confused by Leland with William of Durham, *Dict. Nat. Biogr.* lii 146.

if (with Plato) an independent existence is ascribed to the
universal, the latter practically becomes an individual object.
He also regards Aristotle's doctrine of Categories as resting on
a division, not of things, but of words, and as primarily having
a grammatical reference[1].  His chief service to philosophy is that
'he brought again to light . . . the true value of the inductive
method, as auxiliary to the deductive,—the great truth which
Aristotle had indicated and the Schoolmen had shut out'[2].

As an opponent of Ockham at Oxford we have Walter
Burley (1275—1345 ?), whose ignorance of Greek
did not debar him from writing commentaries on
the *Ethics* and *Politics*, which he dedicated to Richard of Bury.
His *liber de vita ac moribus philosophorum*, extending from Thales
to Seneca (and not excluding poets), was the first attempt in
modern times at writing a history of ancient philosophy ; but
it is marred by strange mistakes in matters of literary history,
the two Plinies and the two Senecas being treated as one,
Statius Caecilius confounded with Papinius Statius, and Livy
with Livius Andronicus[3].  The doctrines of Averroës were
accepted by Burley and by the 'prince of the Averroists',
the English Carmelite, John of Baconthorpe (d. 1346), but the
influence of these two Englishmen was stronger in Italy than
in England[4].

Though the pretensions of Scholasticism had been reduced
by William of Ockham, its methods survived in
works such as that of Thomas Bradwardine, who
was archbishop of Canterbury at his death in 1349.  He is the
author of a scholastic treatise *De Causa Dei*, founded mainly
on Augustine ; it is in company with Augustine and Boëthius
that he is respectfully mentioned by Chaucer[5], and, in the view
of his editor, Sir Henry Savile (1618), 'solidam ex Aristotelis

---

[1] Ueberweg, i 462 f and 154.

[2] Mullinger, i 189; cp. Rashdall, ii 535 f; Clifford Allbutt, p. 89 f;
H. Morley, *Eng. Writers*, iii 326 f, v 12—14 ; and Hauréau, II ii 356—430.

[3] Haase, *De Med. Aevi stud. Philol.* 13 f. MS in Trinity Coll. Library,
O. 2. 50 (no. 1154 M. R. James), first ed. 1467 ; latest ed., Tübingen, 1886.
Burley is said to have written 130 treatises on Aristotle alone.

[4] Renan, *Av.* 318[4] f.

[5] *Cant. Tales* 15248.

et Platonis fontibus hausit philosophiam'.   It is true that his
pages abound in citations from Seneca, Ptolemy, Boëthius and
Cassiodorus, as well as the Fathers and the Schoolmen, but we
have reason to know that all this erudition is derived from the
library of his friend Richard of Bury (1287—1345)[1].

Richard
of Bury

Richard, the son of Sir Richard Aungerville, was
educated at Oxford, and was appointed bishop of
Durham in recognition of his success as envoy (in 1330) to the
pope at Avignon, where he made the acquaintance of Petrarch.
The latter describes him as 'a man of ardent temperament, not
ignorant of literature, and with a strong natural curiosity for obscure
and recondite lore', but the Italian attempted in vain to enlist the
Englishman's aid in determining the topography of the ancient
Thule[2].   As the author of the *Philobiblon*, Richard is more of a
bibliophile than a scholar, and the few Greek words that occur in
its pages do not warrant our inferring that he had any extensive
knowledge of the language.   He is fully conscious of the great
debt of Latin literature to that of Greece[3].   He proposes to remedy
the prevailing ignorance by providing a Greek as well as a Hebrew
grammar for the use of students[4], whom he describes as at
present getting 'a smattering of the rules of Priscian and Donatus,
and as chattering childishly concerning the *Categories* and
*Perihermenias*, in the composition of which Aristotle spent his
whole soul'[5].   He agrees with Bradwardine and Holkot (who is
sometimes supposed to have been the real writer of the *Philobiblon*[6]) in quoting 'Hermes Trismegistus' and 'Dionysius the
Areopagite'.   His weakness for books is indicated by the fact
that Richard II, abbot of St Albans (1326–35), once bribed the
future bishop of Durham by presenting him with four volumes

---

[1] Mullinger, i 198 f; H. Morley, iv 61–4.

[2] *De Rebus Fam.* iii 1 p. 137 Fracassetti; cp. Voigt, *Humanismus*,
ii 248[3]; Mullinger, i 201.

[3] c. x § 162 f.

[4] c. x § 167.

[5] c. ix § 154, in cuius scriptura...calamum in corde tinxisse confingitur.
The phrase is found in Isidore, *Et.* ii 27, and also earlier, in Cassiodorus, *De
Dialectica* (see *supra*, p. 268).

[6] Holkot *inter alia* 'moralised' the *Metamorphoses*; cp. *Philobiblon*, c. 13
§ 178, 'veritas indagatur sub eloquio typicae fictionis'.

from the monastic library, viz. Terence, Virgil, Quintilian, and
Hieronymus against Rufinus, besides selling him for £50
thirty-two other volumes from the same collection, including a
large folio MS of the works of John of Salisbury[1].

One of the best known of the supporters of the revived
Nominalism of William of Ockham was Buridan,
rector of the university of Paris in 1327 (d. after
1350), who wrote *Quaestiones* on Aristotle's *Physics, De Anima,
Parva Naturalia, Ethics* and *Politics*[2]. His text-book of Logic
taught the student how to find the middle term of a syllogism ;
and, as Aristotle[3] holds that the quick discovery of the middle
term shows acuteness of intellect, this aid towards enabling
dullards to gain credit for acumen became famous as a *pons
asinorum*. Buridan's proverbial ass, which stands unmoved
between two bundles of hay, because it is attracted equally in
both directions, has not been found in any of his works. In
his commentary on the *Ethics*[4], however, he declares it impossible
to decide whether the will, when under the influence of two
evenly-balanced motives, can with equal facility decide for or
against any given action ; and the popular illustration of the
'ass' may have been suggested by a passage in Aristotle, *De Caelo*[5].

> Buridan

Among the most active exponents of Aristotle was Jean de
Jandun, who nevertheless (*c.* 1322) showed himself
fully conscious of the futility of the contemporary
passion for argumentation which was only interested
in the process of discussion and indifferent to its result[6].
Benedictines, Dominicans and Franciscans were at one in their
keenness for expounding Aristotle. The catalogues of the
Sorbonne for 1290 and 1338 show how vast a literature had

> Jean de
> Jandun

---

[1] *Chron. Mon. S. Albani*, ii 200 (quoted by E. C. Thomas, ed. *Philobiblon*,
p. xxxix f) ; cp. H. Morley's *Eng. Writers*, iv 38—61.

[2] The last two, printed in Paris in 1500, were reprinted at Oxford,
1637-40.

[3] *Anal. Post.* i 34.        [4] *In Eth. Nic.* iii, *Qu.* 1.

[5] ii 13, τῶν ἐδωδίμων καὶ ποτῶν ἴσον ἀπέχοντος (καὶ γὰρ τοῦτον ἠρεμεῖν
ἀναγκαῖον). Ueberweg, i 466 E. T.

[6] Le Clerc, *Hist. Litt. de la France au* 14$^e$ *s.*, i 502 f. This enthusiastic
admirer of Averroës wrote *Quaestiones in Ar. libros Phys., Metaph., De Anima,
De Caelo* (printed in cent. xv, xvi). Cp. Renan, *Av.* 339-42[4].

gathered round Aristotle in the form of translations and comments by his Arabic and his Latin expositors.

In the thirteenth century the extension of the knowledge of Aristotle beyond the narrow limits of the *Organon* widened the intellectual horizon by stimulating the study of Psychology and Metaphysics. Aristotle was now recognised as the supreme and infallible authority, not in Logic alone, but also in Metaphysics, in Morals, and (unhappily) in Physiology and Natural Science in general. He was associated in Northern Europe with the study of speculative philosophy and theology, and in Italy with that of medicine, thus incidentally leading to an alliance between the Faculties of Medicine and Arts in the Italian universities[1]. Under the wing of Aristotle, room was found even for Averroës. About the middle of the fourteenth century the Inceptor in Arts at the university of Paris was compelled to swear that he would teach nothing that was inconsistent with 'Aristotle and his commentator Averroës'[2]. But the mediaeval dependence on the authority of Aristotle gradually gave way. The change was in part occasioned by the recovery of some of the lost works of ancient literature, and the transition from the Middle Ages to the Renaissance was attended by a general widening of the range of classical studies, and by a renewed interest in Plato.

Early in the twelfth century the study of Roman Law had been revived at Bologna by Irnerius (*c.* 1113), who, besides expounding the Roman code in lectures, introduced the custom of explaining verbal difficulties by means of brief annotations known as 'glosses'. But Bologna was far from being a School of Law alone. It was also famous as a School of Rhetoric and the Liberal Arts, where composition in prose and verse was practised under the name of *Dictamen*, especially in the early part of the thirteenth century, when Buoncompagno was the great master of Rhetoric and Composition[3]. In the same century the example of Irnerius was

Bologna

---

[1] Rashdall, i 235.

[2] *Chartul.* ii 680 (Rashdall, i 368), with the important addition, *nisi in casibus qui sunt contra fidem.*

[3] Tiraboschi, iv 464—500; Rashdall, i 111. He produced a work in six books on the art of writing letters (1215). Cp. Gröber's *Grundriss*, II i 252.

followed by Accursius of Florence, who also taught at Bologna
(d. 1260). Whenever in his public lectures he came upon a line
of Homer quoted by Justinian, tradition describes him as saying:
*Graecum est, nec potest legi*[1]. The phrase would naturally occur
in his oral teaching only, and its alternative form, *non legitur*,
need mean nothing more than, 'This is Greek, and is not
lectured upon'. It has not been found in the published Glosses
of Accursius, who, in his translation of the Pandects, as was
shown by Albericus Gentilis[2] (d. 1611), correctly explains the
large number of Greek words occurring in the text. It has been
suggested, however, that if the phrase was used at all by Accursius,
it was not due to any ignorance of Greek on the part of this
learned lawyer, but to the fact that the public assumption of a
knowledge of that language would have laid him open to an
imputation of heresy which he deemed it prudent to avoid[3].
In the first half of the sixteenth century, his 'barbarism' and
his 'ignorance' are attacked by humanists such as Vives and
Brassicanus, Budaeus and Alciatus[4], but none of these deal with
his knowledge of Greek.

Bologna's early fame as a school of Law was due (1) to the
study of the Digest, (2) to a closer and more technical study of
texts, and (3) to the fuller organisation of legal study. In the
interpretation of Civil Law, the work of that school has been
described as representing, in many respects, 'the most brilliant
achievement of the intellect of mediaeval Europe'[5]. It certainly
promoted textual criticism in its own department of study. The
jurists of Bologna repeatedly made pilgrimages to Pisa to consult
the famous MS of the Pandects, which was removed to Florence

---

[1] W. Burton, *Gr. Ling. Hist.* (1657), 49, notum est illud Francisci Accursi,
quoties ad Homeri versus a Justiniano citatos pervenit, *Graecum est*, inquit,
*nec potest legi*. Cp. Tiraboschi, iv 356 ; Gidel, 236 f. On the omission of the
*Greek* Constitutions of Justinian in the Western MSS, cp. Windscheid, *Lehrbuch
des Pandektenrechts*, ed. 1900, § 3.

[2] *Dial.* (1721), 188 ; cp. E. Otto, *Vita Papiniani* (1743), 67.

[3] Gidel, 236 f.                    [4] Bayle, s.v. *Accurse*.

[5] Rashdall, i 122 f; Gebhart, *Les Origines de la Renaissance en Italie*
(1879), 59 f, *Le droit romain...est la grande originalité doctrinale de l'Italie au
moyen âge...A Paris, on dispute sur Aristote dont le texte original manque ; à
Bologne, à Rome, on commente les monuments authentiques du droit écrit.*

in 1406, and by the collation of this and other MSS formed the ordinary text of the Civil Law[1].

While Accursius of Florence was lecturing at Bologna, Bologna counted among her native scholars the Dominican Bonaccursius, whose knowledge of Greek led to his being sent to the East in 1230 to discuss the points at issue between the Greek and Latin Churches[2]. In the same century Cremona claims four hellenists[3]; while Genoa is the home of the learned

**Balbi of Genoa**

Dominican, Balbi (1286)[4], whose *Catholicon* (a Latin Grammar, followed by a Dictionary founded on Papias and Hugutio) was placed, as a book of reference, in the churches of France[5]. It was printed by Gutenberg at Mainz in 1460[6], and was translated into French and used in the schools of Paris as late as 1759. France also adopted a Latin Grammar of the thirteenth century compiled by a Lombard named Caesar, in which the examples are selected from Sallust,

**Petrus of Padua**

Virgil, Horace, Ovid, Lucan and Juvenal[7]. Pietro d' Abano (*Petrus Aponensis, c.* 1250—1315) studied in Greece and at Paris, where he began the translation of the *Problems* of Aristotle, which he completed at Padua[8]. He also translated portions of the Greek text of Galen, and of the problems ascribed to Alexander of Aphrodisias, having been engaged on the latter during his stay in Constantinople[6].

---

[1] Rashdall, i 254 f. Cp. Bartoli's *Precursori*, 26 f.

[2] Gradenigo, 99; Tiraboschi, iv 160; Krumbacher, p. 98[2].

[3] Gradenigo, 102.

[4] *ib.* 103 f. The small extent of his knowledge of Greek is indicated in the words: 'hoc difficile est scire, et maxime mihi non bene scienti linguam Graecam'. Cp. Tiraboschi, iv 356, 481, 526; Loewe, *Prodromus Corp. Gloss. Lat.* 247.

[5] Le Clerc, *Hist. Litt.* 430[2]. The sacristan of Saint-Oyan had a *Catholicum*, with an iron chain attached to it (inventory of 1483 in *Bibl. de l'école des chartes*, 1 322). Cp. Ducange, § 47.

[6] Hallam, *Lit.* i 80[4]; *facsimile* of page in Steffen, *Lat. Pal.* 90, and of colophon in Bouchot, *Le Livre*, 33.

[7] ed. C. Fierville (1886).

[8] Jacobus Philippus Bergamas, *Suppl. Chron.*, p. 331 (Gradenigo, 107). The translation and exposition of the *Problems* of Aristotle, and of Alexander Aphrod., was printed at Venice in 1519. The latter are included in the Didot Aristotle, iv 291-8.        [6] Tiraboschi, v 204.

In 1311 the Council of Vienne, in discussing the reunion of the Churches, recommended the appointment of two teachers of Greek in each of the principal cities of Italy. Under Clement V (d. 1314) a Greek *Teaching of Greek* school was accordingly opened in Rome, and money collected for the founding of Greek and Hebrew professorships at Oxford[1]. In 1325 there were lectures on Greek, as well as Arabic, Chaldee and Hebrew, in the university of Paris, but the papal legate was instructed to take care that these strange tongues were not made the means of introducing outlandish doctrines. The suspicion of heresy clung to the Greek language in particular, and bishops gave up the traditional custom of signing their names in Greek. There were hardly any hellenists except among the Dominicans, who, as they had early secured complete control of the Inquisition, could with perfect impunity learn as much Greek as they pleased[2]. In the same age, a certain prejudice against the study of the Aristotelian Logic is implied in the story that, about 1330, a Bachelor of Arts of the university of Paris emerged from the tomb, robed in a cloak of parchment black with Latin characters scribbled over its folds, to warn his former instructor against the vanities of the world and to tell him of the torments he was enduring in consequence of his having studied Logic at Paris[3]. After many decrees to the contrary, the study of Aristotle was restored with hardly any restrictions by the Papal Legates of 1366. For the B.A. degree it was necessary to take up Grammar, Logic and Psychology, the first of these including the 'Doctrinale' of Alexander of Villedieu; the second, the *Organon* of Aristotle and the *Topics* of Boëthius; and the third, the *De Anima*. For the License in Arts, the subjects comprised the *Physics* and the *Parva Naturalia*, and, for the M.A. degree, the greater part of

---

[1] Rashdall, ii 459. Cp. Burton, *Ling. Gr. Hist.* 54. Clement V ordered in the Council of Vienne, *scholas in Parisiensi et Oxoniensi studiis erigendas Hebraicae, Graecae, Arabicae et Chaldaicae linguarum* (Friedberg, *Decretal. Collectio,* ii 1179). Cp. F. Liebermann in *Athenaeum*, 1904, 272.

[2] Le Clerc, *Hist. Litt. en 14ᵉ s.* 423-6²; *Hist. Litt. de la France*, xxi 143, 216; Gebhart, *Origines de la Renaissance*, 136, (*Les dominicains*) *ont brûlé beaucoup de livres, en qualité d'inquisiteurs, mais ils en lisaient aussi beaucoup.*

[3] Le Clerc, *l.c.*, 502.

the *Ethics* and at least three books of the *Meteorologica*[1]. But Aristotle was not studied in the original. The vast number of lucubrations on Aristotle included in the two oldest catalogues of the library of the Sorbonne (1290 and 1338) supply no proof of any direct acquaintance with the Greek text[2].

The university of Paris was too closely bound up with the study of Aristotle and too strictly subservient to his supreme authority, to be able to take the lead in that general revival of Classical interests which we associate with the age of the Renaissance. Yet the Western lands of Europe, France as well as England, had seen more than one revival of learning in the course of the early Middle Ages. The first two revivals are associated with the names of Aldhelm and Bede, and of Alcuin and Charles the Great. Among the Latin versifiers of the Caroline age, the Englishman[3] who assumes the classic name of Naso writes Virgilian Eclogues in which he borrows phrases from the poets of Rome to express his consciousness that he is himself living in the age of a *renascence*:—

*Earlier revivals of learning*

> 'rursus in antiquos mutataque saecula mores;
> aurea Roma iterum renovata *renascitur* orbi'[4].

Even under the successors of Charles the Great, Latin verse lived on in the lines of Ermoldus Nigellus and of Abbo Cernuus, while Greek prose found an interpreter in the person of Joannes Scotus. In the tenth century Gerbert had been conspicuous in the study of Cicero; in the twelfth, Cicero and Seneca had inspired the moral teaching of Gautier de Châtillon[5]; and, in the thirteenth, the composition of works in Latin prose had flourished in England under Henry II, while in France a wide acquaintance with Latin literature had been displayed in the vast encyclopaedia of Vincent of Beauvais[6]. In the province of education, the changes which began to pass over the schools of France in the eleventh century

---

[1] De Launoy, *De Var. Arist. fortuna*, p. 50. Cp. Rashdall, i 436 f.

[2] Le Clerc, *l. c.*, 503.

[3] Modoin, or Muadwin, bishop of Autun (815–40).

[4] *Ecl.* i 8 in *Poetae Lat. Aevi Car.* i 385 Dümmler; Ovid, *A. A.* iii 113, 'aurea Roma'; Calpurnius, *Ecl.* i 42, 'aurea secura cum pace renascitur aetas'; cp. Körting's *Litt. It.* iii 82.

[5] p. 553 *supra*.    [6] Cp. Bartoli's *Precursori*, 10—31.

had culminated in a great intellectual renaissance in the early part of the twelfth, during the age of Abelard[1]. Throughout the Middle Ages the region of France which lay north of the Loire had taken the lead in the education of Europe, but that region had been too completely permeated and possessed by the mediaeval spirit to become the native land of the Renaissance[2]. That honour was reserved for the classic soil of Italy, where the Renaissance was slowly called into life by a variety of causes[3], by the prevailing spirit of intellectual freedom, by the social and political condition of the country, by the continuous tradition of the Latin language, by the constant witness to the existence of Greek in the region once known as *Magna Graecia*, by the survival of the remains of antique sculpture, such as the marble reliefs which inspired the art of Niccola Pisano[4], and by the abiding presence of the ruins of ancient Rome, which aroused the enthusiasm, not only of unnamed pilgrims of the tenth and twelfth centuries, but also of men of mark such as Giovanni Villani[5], and Rienzi[6], and Petrarch, in the first third of the fourteenth[7]. 'During the gloomy and disastrous centuries which followed the downfall of the Roman Empire, Italy had preserved, in a far greater degree than any other part of Western Europe, the traces of ancient civilisation. The night which descended upon her was the night of an Arctic summer. The dawn began to reappear before the last reflection of the preceding sunset had faded from the horizon'[8].

*Causes of the Renaissance in Italy*

---

[1] Rashdall, i 30—71. John of Salisbury, *Met.* i 5, tells us that, under the influence of *amatores litterarum* (such as Abelard, William of Conches and Theodoric of Chartres), *redierunt artes et, quasi jure postliminii, honorem pristinum nactae sunt, et post exsilium gratiam et gloriam ampliorem.*

[2] Körting, *Litt. It.* iii 93.

[3] Cp. Gebhart's *Origines de la Renaissance en Italie* (1879), esp. pp. 51—146. Sicily and Apulia had already seen a temporary revival of learning under Frederic II (pp. 566-7 *supra*). See also Courajod, *Les véritables Origines de la Renaissance* (1888), and Novati, *L' influsso del pensiero Latino sopra la civiltà italiana del medio evo* (cent. xiii), 1899.

[4] Vasari, *Vita*, init.     [5] 1300; *Cron.* viii 6; Balzani's *Chroniclers*, 332.

[6] Voigt, *Humanismus*, i 53[3].

[7] Petrarch, *De Rebus Fam.* vi 2 p. 314 Fracassetti.

[8] Macaulay, *Machiavelli* (1827), p. 30 of *Essays* (1861). Harris, *Philological Inquiries* (1780), p. 251[5], compares the 'Middle Age' to 'the twilight

But, although the night was luminous, the sun was absent, and Petrarch was the morning-star of a new day; yet there were other stars in the sky before the star of Petrarch.

The Renaissance generally associated in its early stages with the name of Petrarch, was a gradual and protracted process, and not a single and sudden event with a fixed and definite date. One of the prominent characteristics of that Renaissance was Petrarch's enthusiasm for Cicero. But the Umbrian poet Jacopone da Todi, who died in 1306, two years after the birth of Petrarch, mentions the 'melody' of Cicero's writings on the laws of Rome as one of the vanities that he abandoned when he renounced the world[1].

Among the immediate precursors of the Renaissance in Italy we may here mention two prominent representatives of Latin poetry at Padua. One of these, the eloquent and learned Lovato (d. 1309), was the first to recognise the rules of metre followed by Seneca[2]. The other, his younger contemporary and the inheritor of his literary interests, was the eminent statesman, historian and poet, Albertino Mussato (1261—1329). Mussato was the author of poems abounding in reminiscences of Virgil, Ovid and Lucan, and of works in prose recalling Livy's eulogies of the old Roman heroes, Camillus and Scipio Africanus. Seneca is his model in the diction, and, to some extent, in the general framework of his celebrated tragedy, the *Eccerinis*, a work founded on the career of

*Precursors of the Renaissance; Lovato and Mussato*

of a summer's night, that auspicious gleam between the setting and the rising sun, which, though it cannot retain the lustre of the day, helps at least to save us from the totality of darkness'; and Ozanam, *Doc. Inédits* (1850), p. 28, has similarly described 'the night which intervened between the intellectual daylight of antiquity and the dawn of the Renaissance' as *une de ces nuits lumineuses où les dernières clartés du soir se prolongent jusqu'aux premières blancheurs du matin.*

[1] *Le poesie spirituali* (1617) p. 5, *Rinunzia del Mondo*, str. 20, *lassovi le scritture antiche,* | *che mi eran cotanto amiche,* | *et le Tulliane rubriche,* | *che mi fean tal melodia*; Gebhart, 157; Norden, 738.

[2] Cp. Muratori, *Script. Rer. Ital.* x 1, 'habuit...Padua civitas Lovatum, Bonatinum et Mussatum, qui delectarentur metris et amice versibus concertarent'; Körting, *Litt. It.* iii (1884) 355 f; Wiese u. Pèrcopo, *It. Litt.* 120; Novati, quoted in Wicksteed and Gardner's *Dante and Giovanni del Virgilio*, 36.

the brutal tyrant, Ezzelino, who became lord of Padua in 1237. In a literary controversy with a Dominican monk of Mantua, Mussato strangely contends that poetry is a branch of theology; and, although he imitates ancient models in all his works, whether in verse or prose, he has only a dim apprehension of the beauty of the old classical literature. He thus belongs to the early twilight rather than the actual dawn of the Renaissance[1].

A smoother and more flowing style in Latin prose was attained by the two historians, Giovanni da Cermenate of Milan (1312), who successfully imitated Livy and Sallust[2], and Ferrĕto of Vicenza (d. 1337), who made Virgil, Lucan, Statius and Claudian his models in an epic in honour of Can Grande of Verona[3]. It was the Latin epic on a modern heroic theme that Giovanni del Virgilio of Bologna suggested to Dante, when he had the audacity to send him (early in 1319) a set of Latin hexameters, criticising with a somewhat pedantic and superior air the poet's preference of Italian to Latin as the language of the *Divina Commedia*. Del Virgilio's claim to be regarded as a precursor of the Renaissance rests mainly on his admiration for Virgil, whose name was either assumed by himself or won from others by his success as an exponent or an imitator of the Roman poet[4]. He has no claim on the ground of any revival of the Virgilian Eclogue, for the credit of that rather unhappy innovation is clearly due to Mussato[5] and Dante. The only direct reminiscence of Virgil in Dante's first *Eclogue* is caught up by Del Virgilio, who adds seven more in his reply[6]; but, in a poem of 1327, six years after Dante's death, Virgilio himself describes the pastoral flute of Virgil as first breathed upon by Dante :—

*(margin: Cermenate. Ferreto. Del Virgilio)*

---

[1] Muratori, *Antiq. Ital.* 787; Körting, iii 302—55; Voigt, *Humanismus*, i 16—18³; Balzani's *Chroniclers*, 275—91, esp. 287 f; Cloetta, *Beiträge*, ii (1892) 5—76; Wicksteed and Gardner, 1—58. The diction and metre of Seneca are also imitated in the *Achilles* of Mussato or Loschi (R. Ellis, *Catullus in xiv cent.* 24—29). On Mussato and other Italian precursors of the Renaissance, cp. Sabbadini, *Scoperte*, ii (1914) 106—190.

[2] Tiraboschi, v 451; Voigt, i 19³.

[3] Muratori, ix 1197; cp. Körting, iii 358; Balzani's *Chroniclers*, 272—4; and M. Laue, *Ferreto von Vicenza* (1884).

[4] Wicksteed and Gardner, 121.     [5] Körting, iii 324, 365.

[6] Wicksteed and Gardner, 207 f.

'fistula non posthac nostris inflata poëtis
donec ea mecum certaret Tityrus olim,
Lydius Adriaco qui nunc in litore dormit'[1].

Since the time of Virgil, Eclogues had been written by Calpurnius
under Nero and by Alcuin under Charles the Great, and
Benedictine Bucolics on sacred themes had been attempted from
the ninth to the twelfth centuries[2], but their revival is here
ascribed to Dante. In the year of that poet's death (1321),
Del Virgilio was the only professor of poetry, the only interpreter
of Virgil, Lucan, Statius and the author of the *Metamorphoses*,
left in Bologna[3]. He had repeatedly sent his poetic greetings to
the exile at Ravenna, and he now wrote a brief poem in his
memory[4]. Six years later he sent a Virgilian *Eclogue* to one who
in his day was at least as famous a poet as Dante, Mussato, then
in exile at Chioggia. Virgilio was also the author of a treatise on
the *Metamorphoses*[5], which proves that the mediaeval passion for
'moralising' and allegorizing mythology was as strong as ever
towards the close of the Middle Ages.

A still earlier precursor of the Renaissance may be justly
recognised in the person of the eminent notary of
Florence, Brunetto Latini (d. 1290), who, during
his exile in France (1260–7), wrote his *Tesoretto*
and his *Tesoro* in Italian verse and French prose respectively.
The former is a didactic poem in an allegorical form; the latter,
an encyclopaedia of learning ranging over History, Astronomy,
Geography, Zoology, Ethics, Rhetoric and Politics. In treating
of Rhetoric, the author gives us a French translation of Caesar's
and Cato's speeches in the *Catiline* of Sallust. Italian translations
of the first seventeen chapters of the *De Inventione*, and of Cicero's
speeches in defence of Ligarius, Marcellus and Deiotarus, were
also executed by Brunetto; but the renderings of Cicero's
'Catilinarians' and of the speeches in Livy, which have been
ascribed to him, probably belong to the times of the Renaissance.
The general cast of both of his best-known works is mainly

**Brunetto Latini**

---

[1] Wicksteed and Gardner, 176.

[2] *ib.* 230 f; *e.g.* the 'egloga' ascribed to Paschasius Radbertus (d. after
856), in *Poet. Lat. Aevi Car.* iii 45.

[3] *ib.* 133.                                         [4] *ib.* 174.

[5] *ib.* 120, 314 21.

mediaeval, but he obviously takes a keen delight in quoting the
Classics in his *Tesoro*, the work in which he 'still lives'. Such is
the language which he is made to apply to his masterpiece in that
Canto in which Dante mysteriously confesses that he had learned
from its author 'how man becomes eternal'[1].

Dante (1265—1321) is a precursor of the Renaissance in a
limited sense alone,—in his breaking loose from
the mediaeval tradition by writing his great poem
not in the Latin but in the Tuscan tongue; in his delight in
minutely realistic descriptions, whether of the tortures of Hell or
of the course of his travels through all the three realms of the
spirit-world; in his proud self-consciousness as a poet; and in his
personal longing for immortal fame. His individualism is also
apparent in the autobiographical facts imbedded in the mediaeval
mysticism of the *Vita Nuova*. The *Convito*, begun as a commentary on that work, is written in a comparatively modern spirit.
The *De Monarchia*, again, combines the political principles of the
Middle Ages with a new enthusiasm for the traditions of the old
Roman Empire; while the *De Vulgari Eloquio* discriminates
between different varieties of Latin prose, and recognises the
claim of a modern language to a strictly scientific investigation.
It is a new thing to find such wide learning outside the clerical
order. Dante is true to the strictest theology of the Middle Ages,
but at the same time he is as learned a layman as any that we
shall meet in the coming age of the Renaissance[2].

The speculative basis of Dante's great poem is furnished
by the scholastic combination of Christian theology with the
Aristotelian philosophy. For Aristotle himself he has the highest
regard. In the Limbo of the unbaptized, in a green meadow
surrounded by the sevenfold walls of a noble castle, the poet sees
'the Master of them that know', with Plato and Socrates hard by;
and, amongst others, Tully and Livy and the 'moralist Seneca',
with Avicenna, and Averroës 'who the great Comment made'[3].

---

[1] *Inf.* xv; Körting, iii 370—401.

[2] Körting, iii 401-15; Gebhart, 282—308. Cp. Villani, *Cron.* ix 136,
(Dante) 'fu grande letterato quasi in ogni scienza, tutto fosse laico'. See also
Burckhardt, *Renaissance*, Part II c. 3, and Voigt, i 11—15[3]; also Vossler,
in *N. Heidelb. Jahrb.* xi, *Dante und die Renaissance*.

[3] *Inf.* iv 130—144.

In his works in general he frequently refers to the Latin Classics. He 'was born a student' (says Professor Norton), 'as he was born a poet, and had he never written a single poem, he would still have been famous as the most profound scholar of his times'[1]. His references to ancient literature have been collected and classified, and the following list shows approximately the number of times he quotes each of the works mentioned:—the Vulgate (500 +), Aristotle (300 +)[2], Virgil (*c.* 200), Ovid (*c.* 100), Cicero (*c.* 50)[3], Statius and Boëthius (30—40), Horace (7)[4], Livy and Orosius (10—20); the *Timaeus* of Plato in the translation by Chalcidius, with Homer, Juvenal, Seneca, Ptolemy, Aesop, Valerius Maximus and St Augustine (less than 10 each)[5]. The above list does not include the references to the Schoolmen, such as Peter Lombard, Bonaventura, Hugh and Richard of St Victor and (above all) Albertus Magnus, and Thomas Aquinas, whose greatest disciple is Dante[6]. Sometimes, when he appears to be quoting Aristotle, his real authority is Albertus Magnus. Thus, in the *Convito*[7], where he discusses the theories on the Origin of the Milky Way, his statement of the opinions of Anaxagoras and Democritus is derived, not from Aristotle's *Meteorologica*[8], but from the corresponding work of Albertus Magnus, who knew the *Meteorologica* in an Arabic translation alone. Dante here compares the Old translation with the New, meaning by the 'Old' one of the renderings from the Arabic, and by the 'New' one of those from the Greek[9]. Again, in the *Convito*[10], where he discusses the nature of vision, and refers to Aristotle, *di Senso*

---

[1] Norton's *New Life* of Dante, p. 102.

[2] Mainly the *Ethics, Physics, Metaphysics* and *De Anima.*

[3] *De Off., Sen., Am.*; also *De Finibus.*

[4] Six from *Ars Poetica*, and one from *Ep.* i 14, 43.

[5] E. Moore, *Studies*, i 4 f.

[6] *Contrapasso* (*Inf.* xxviii 142), Aristotle's ἀντιπεπονθός, comes from Aquinas, *Summa*, ii² qu. 61, art. 4. Cp., in general, Ozanam, *Dante et la Philosophie Catholique au xiii s.* (1839), and Hettinger, on Aquinas and Dante (*Die Theologie der Göttlichen Komödie*, 1879, E. T. 1887), with other works cited in Ueberweg, ii § 33, p. 290[8], esp. Berthier's *Comm.* (Turin, 1893 f).

[7] ii 15.               [8] i 8.

[9] Paget Toynbee, *Dante Studies*, 42 f; cp. Moore, i 305-18.          [10] iii 9.

*e Sensato*, his statement as to Aristotle's views apparently comes from the treatise by Albertus Magnus, which bears the corresponding title[1]. Dante's eight references to Pythagoras are, directly or indirectly, due in four cases to Aristotle, in one to Diogenes Laërtius, and in the rest to Cicero or St Augustine[2]. He follows Albertus and the Arabs in treating the *De Partibus* as a portion of the *Historia Animalium*[3]. Like Apollinaris Sidonius and Vincent of Beauvais, he apparently regards Seneca the moralist as different from the poet, and he wrongly describes the *De Quatuor Virtutibus* as the work of Seneca[4]. On the death of Beatrice, he finds consolation in Cicero's *Laelius* and in Boëthius[5]. On her first appearance in the *Purgatorio* he indulges his frequent fancy for interweaving the sacred and the secular by describing her as welcomed in the words of the Vulgate and of Virgil alike, *benedictus qui venis* being immediately followed by *manibus o date lilia plenis*[6]. His five great pagan poets are Homer, Virgil, Horace, Ovid, Lucan[7]. Statius is not found in the *Inferno*, his place, as a 'Christian', converted by Virgil's *Fourth Eclogue*, being in the *Purgatorio*[8]. Elsewhere, Dante names Virgil, Ovid, Lucan and Statius alone as the 'regular' Latin poets[9], his omission of Horace being possibly due to a mere accident[10], especially as he has previously quoted the *Ars Poëtica* with respect, as the work of *magister noster Horatius*[11]. His standard authors in Latin prose are Cicero, Livy, Pliny, Frontinus and Orosius[12].

His knowledge of Greek appears to have been practically *nil*[13]. The only four references to Homer are borrowed from others[14]. It is true that he quotes the Greek word *hormen*[15] and carefully

---

[1] Toynbee, 53.          [2] *ib.* 87—96.          [3] *ib.* 247 f.

[4] *De Mon.* ii 5 ; Toynbee, 155 f.     [5] *Conv.* ii 13, 14 ; Moore, i 282.

[6] *Purg.* xxx 19 ; Moore, i 26 f.     [7] *Inf.* iv 88.

[8] xxi f. Cp. Verrall in *Independent Review*, Nov. 1903.

[9] *De Vulgari Eloquio*, ii 6.

[10] Hora*tium* might easily have fallen out before S*tatium*.

[11] *De Vulg. El.* ii 4.          [12] *ib.* ii 6.

[13] Manetti (d. 1459), *Boccaccii Vita*, 'graecarum litterarum cognitione Dantes omnino caruit'; Gradenigo, 110.

[14] Moore, i 341 ; Toynbee, 204 f. In *Conv.* i 7 *ult.*, 'Homer cannot be rendered into Latin'.... Cp. p. 595 n. 13 *supra*.

[15] *Conv.* iv 21.

explains *filosofo* as *amatore di sapienza*[1]; but, on the other hand, he blindly follows Hugutio in deriving *autore* from *autentin* (αὐθέντην)[2], 'worthy of trust and obedience', adding on his own account that Aristotle is most 'worthy of' such 'trust', and that his teaching is of the 'highest authority'[3]. But Dante's Aristotle was only the Latin Aristotle, and of the treatise on Poetry he unfortunately knew nothing. Like the mediaeval scholars in general, he lay in bondage to the Latin versions of the *Timaeus* and of Aristotle, and it was high time for a revival of learning to restore a knowledge of the Greek texts, and to extend the range of study, and inspire it with a new interest, even in the case of Latin literature.

[1] *Conv.* iii 11.

[2] Priscian, v 20, '*auctor*, quando αὐθέντην significat, commune est; quando αὐξητὴν, *auctrix* facit femininum'. Eberhard, *Graecismus*, c. xi, distinguishes *auctor* 'ab augendo', from *autor* 'ab authentin, quod Grecum est'.

[3] *Conv.* iv 6. Dante's relation to Greek is discussed by Gradenigo, *Lett. Greco-Italiana*, 110 f, and Celestino Cavedone (Modena, 1860); cp. Moore's *Studies*, i 164 n; and, on Dante's Classical studies in general, Schück in *Neue Jahrb.* (1865), ii 253—281. A. J. Butler, *Dante, his Times and his Work*, pp. 198—201 (his 'use of classical literature'), mainly deals with mythological allusions.

# CHAPTER XXXII.

## THE SURVIVAL OF THE LATIN CLASSICS.

WHILE the Greek Classics owed their safe preservation to the libraries of Constantinople and to the monasteries of the East, it is primarily to the monasteries of the West that we are indebted for the survival of the Latin Classics[1]. A certain prejudice against pagan learning, and especially against pagan poetry, had doubtless been traditional in the Christian community. Tertullian[2] asked, what had Athens *Prejudice against the Classics* to do with Jerusalem, or the Academy with the Church; and Jerome[3], what concern had Horace with the Psalter, Virgil with the Gospel, and Cicero with the Apostles? But Jerome[4] agreed with Origen[5] in holding that it was as lawful for Christians, as for Jews, to 'spoil the Egyptians', and (after due precautions) to appropriate any prize they had captured from the hands of the enemy[6]. The prejudice, however, lived on among Churchmen

---

[1] Of 772 known Latin authors, there are only 144 whose works have survived; 64 of this number have lost most of their books on the way; 43 remain with the greater part of their writings; and only 37 with practically all. These last two groups include nearly all the best poets (A. F. West, in *Proc. Amer. Phil. Assoc.* 1902, xxii f). Cp. in general Traube, *Vorlesungen*, ii 121—137.

[2] *De Praescr.* 7 (Migne, ii 20). But elsewhere he declares that profane studies are 'necessary for the acquisition of the science of things divine,' *De Idol.* 10 (Migne, i 675).

[3] *Ep.* 22 § 29 (Migne, xxii 416); cp. St Augustine, *De Doctrina Christiana*, ii 40 (60), Migne, xxxiv 63; Maitland's *Dark Ages*, 173[3].

[4] *Ep.* 70 (Migne, xxii 665); cp. *Ep.* 21 (*ib.* 385).

[5] Migne, xi 87, xii 490. Cp. Norden's *Kunstprosa*, 675–80.

[6] Deut. xxi 10.

such as Gregory the Great, Alcuin of Tours and Odo of Cluni[1].
In a similar spirit, Honorius of Autun, in the preface to the
*Gemma Animae* (*c.* 1120), asks 'how is the soul profited by the
strife of Hector, the arguments of Plato, the poems of Virgil, or
the elegies of Ovid, who, with others like them, are now gnashing
their teeth in the prison of the infernal Babylon, under the cruel
tyranny of Pluto ?'[2]    Even Abelard (who quotes Jerome's opinion)
inquires 'why the bishops and doctors of the Christian religion do
not expel from the City of God those poets whom Plato forbade
to enter into his city of the world'[3] ; while Nicholas, the secretary
of Bernard of Clairvaux, (writing after 1153,) sighs over the charm
he had once found in Cicero and the poets, and in the golden
sayings of the philosophers and the 'songs of the Sirens'[4].    The
Benedictine chronicler, Rodulfus Glaber (d. 1050), tells the
story of one Vilgardus, a student of 'grammar' in the neighbourhood of Ravenna, who, in a dream, saw three demons who had
assumed the forms of Virgil, Horace and Juvenal, the study of
whose texts betrayed him into heretical opinions, for which he
was condemned by Peter, archbishop of Ravenna (in or before
971)[5].    Herbert de Losinga, the first bishop of Norwich (d. 1119),
had a dream that compelled him to renounce the reading and the
imitation of Virgil and Ovid[6].    Poets (unless their writings were
of highly moral purport, or capable of being 'moralised' by means
of allegorical interpretation) were in fact regarded with far less
favour than philosophers.    One of the celebrated illustrations in
the *Hortus Deliciarum*, the pictorial encyclopaedia composed, or
compiled, by the abbess Herrad of Landsberg for the nuns of
Mont St Odile in Alsace (1167-95), represents two large con-

---

[1] pp. 444, 476 f, 504 *supra*, and Norden, 531 ; also (on Alcuin and Virgil)
Schmid, *Gesch. der Erziehung*, 11 i 177, and (in general) Roger, 131—143.

[2] Migne, clxxii 543 ; Maitland, 185[3].

[3] *Theol. Christ.* ii, Migne, clxxxviii 1210 D ; Maitland, 186[3].

[4] 'Petri Damiani' *Sermo* 61, p. 296 E Caëtani (Migne, cxliv 852 D).

[5] *Hist.* ii c. 12 (Migne, cxlii, and ed. Prou, 1886) ; Tiraboschi, iii 192 ;
Giesebrecht, *De litt. studiis* (Ital. trans. p. 24). Cp. Wattenbach, *GQ*, ii[6] 213 ;
Gebhart in *Rev. des deux Mondes*, Oct. 1, 1891 ; and Ker's *Dark Ages*, 198 f.

[6] *Epp* p. 53-7, cp. pp. 63, 93.    Nevertheless he tells his pupils to take
Ovid as their model in Latin verse (p. 75), and himself quotes *Tristia*, i 9,
5—6 (Goulburn and Symonds, *Life and Letters of H. de L.*, i 249).

centric circles filled with the following figures.   In the upper half
of the inner circle, Philosophy, a queenly form whose crown is
parted into the semblance of three human heads identified as
'Ethics', 'Logic' and 'Physics', may be seen enthroned in majesty,
while, in the lower half of the same circle, we have Socrates and
Plato seated at desks with books open before them.   The outer
circle is filled with a series of seven arches, and, under each of
these, we have a personification of one of the Seven Liberal Arts,
with her emblems in her hands, Grammar with a book and a
birch, Rhetoric with a tablet and stylus, and similarly with the
rest.   Below and *outside* this outer circle are four 'poets or
magicians', each of them writing at a desk, with an evil spirit
prompting him, in the form of a raven hovering near his ear.
The whole design is further embellished with many mottoes in
appropriate places[1].

The philosophical works of Cicero had supplied a model for
the Latin prose of the Fathers and of their successors in the
Middle Ages ; but even Cicero, it was sometimes felt, might be
studied with an undue devotion.   In 1150 we find the prior
of Hildesheim writing to Wibald, abbot of Corvey, in the following
terms :—

'Though you desire to have the books of Tully, I know that you are a
Christian and not a Ciceronian[2].   You go over to the camp of the enemy, not
as a deserter, but as a spy[3].   I should therefore have sent you the books of
Tully which we have,—*De Re Agraria, Philippics* and *Epistles*, but that it is
not our custom that any books should be lent to any person without good
pledges.   Send us therefore the *Noctes Atticae* of Aulus Gellius and Origen *On
the Canticles*'.   The abbot replies in the same strain, assuring the prior that
Cicero is not the main staple of his repast, but only serves as dessert, and
sending him Origen and (in the absence of Gellius) a book on Tactics[4].

Lastly, the abbot of Cluni, Peter the Venerable (d. 1156),

---

[1] The MS perished in the flames during the bombardment of Strassburg
in 1870.   The illustrations have since been reproduced (from earlier copies)
in Straub and Keller's magnificent folio (1879–99); see Plate, p. 559 *supra*.
Cp. Engelhardt (1818) 31 f (with plate) ; Wattenbach, *GQ*, ii[6] 399 ; Bursian,
i 74 ; and Graf, *Roma*, ii 193 f.

[2] p. 232 *supra*.

[3] Seneca, *Ep.* 2 § 5.

[4] Maitland, 175[3] f.   Text in Jaffé, *Bibl. Rer. Germ.* i 326.

writing to Master Peter of Poitiers, thus urges the uselessness of
the study of the ancients :—

'See now, without the study of Plato, without the disputations of the
Academy, without the subtleties of Aristotle, without the teaching of philosophers, the place and the way of happiness are discovered...Why, vainly
studious, are you reciting with the comedians, lamenting with the tragedians,
trifling with the metricians, deceiving with the poets, and deceived with the
philosophers?'[1]

A more generous spirit had animated Cassiodorus when he
exhorted his monks to study the liberal arts and to follow the
example of Moses, who was 'learned in all the wisdom of the
Egyptians', and also that of the learned Fathers of the Church[2];
and, late in the twelfth century, the example of the Fathers is
pleaded by the Norman poet, Étienne de Rouen, in the abstract
of Quintilian, which he prepared for his pupils at Bec[3]. Doubtless
many of those who entered the monastery were drawn to it as a
place of peace and quietness, a home of learning and leisure,
where they could live apart from the 'strife of tongues' and the
tumult of war. The influence of such studious votaries of the
'religious' life must have done much to counteract the traditional
prejudice against the pagan Classics[4]; and intelligent learners of
Latin could hardly fail to be attracted by the perfection of form
attained by many of the old authors whose works they studied
with a view to mastering the language that had long been
traditional in the teaching and in the services of the Church, and
remained (for the present) the only medium of literary expression
in Western Europe. Thus an interest in the Latin Classics had
succeeded in surviving all the fulminations of the Fathers and the
censures of the Church. But, in the centuries with which we are
now concerned, the study of the Classics, wherever it actually
prevailed, was regarded not as an end in itself, but as a means
towards the better understanding of the Bible, and this is the

---

[1] Migne, clxxxix 77 D; Maitland, 445[3]. Cp., in general, Specht, *Gesch.
des Unterrichtswesens*, 40—57; and Wattenbach, *GQ*, i[7] 361.

[2] *Div. Lect.* c. 28.

[3] Comparetti, *Virgilio nel Medio Evo*, i 112, note 2; Léon Maître, *Écoles*,
159; Fierville, *Introd.* to Quintil. 1, p. xxviii f.

[4] Cp. Clifford Allbutt, *Science and Medieval Thought*, 79; Putnam, i 122.

main difference in the attitude assumed towards that study in the
Middle Ages and in the Renaissance.

While the reading of pagan authors was discouraged by writers
such as Isidore of Seville, and by the founders of the monastic
Orders, no restriction was placed on the copying of MSS. Jerome
had recommended that form of industry as one of the most
suitable occupations of the monastic life[1]; and Ephraem the
Syrian (d. 378) had mentioned the transcription of books, as
well as the dyeing of parchments, among the manual labours of
monks[2]. The copying of MSS was in fact the only manual
occupation recognised in the monasteries founded by St Martin
of Tours, where it was confined to younger members of the
house[3]. The Benedictine Rule is vague, but it assumes the
existence of a monastic library[4], naturally consisting of ecclesiastical books, while the work of the monastic schools would no
less naturally involve the acquisition of a number of classical
texts. Thus the celebrated MSS known as the Vatican Virgil
(cent. ii or iii) and the Carolingian Terence (cent. ix) once
belonged to the Benedictine abbey of St Denis, near Paris. The
devotion of the Benedictine Order to the cause of classical and
general literature has been fully and elaborately justified and
exemplified in the seventeenth and eighteenth centuries by
Mabillon[5] and Ziegelbauer[6], and has since been more succinctly
set forth by Montalembert[7] and Dantier[8]. The Rule of the
Cluniacs appoints a special officer to take charge of the books,
and provides for an annual audit of the volumes assigned to the

---

[1] *Ep.* 125, scribantur libri. Cp. Norden, in *Kultur der Gegenwart*,
I viii 381.

[2] Wattenbach, *Schriftwesen im MA*, 417[3]; Lecoy de la Marche, *Les
MSS*, 89.

[3] Sulp. Severus, *Vita Martini*, c. 7.

[4] c. 48.

[5] *Traité des études monastiques* (1691), and *Réflexions* (1693).

[6] *Observationes Literariae O.S.B.* four folio volumes (Augsburg, 1784)
Cp. C. Acheri's (*i.e.* Father Cahier's) 12 *Essais* in *Annales de philosophie
chrétienne*, xvii—xviii, Oct. 1838-9, esp. *Essais* 3—7 *bibliothèques*, 8 *calli-
graphie*, 9—10 *miniatures*, 11—12 *luxe bibliographique au moyen-âge*.

[7] *Monks of the West*, Bk xviii c. 41.

[8] *Les monastères bénédictins d'Italie*, 2 vols. (1866), on Monte Cassino,
Bobbio, etc.

several monks, and a similar provision is to be found in the
statutes of Oriel College, Oxford (1329)[1]. The Carthusian Rule
assumes that very few of the monks are incapable of being copyists
and punishes any monk who refuses to copy when he is able to
do so[2]. The Carthusian abbot Guigo (d. 1137) regards the labour
of the copyist as an 'immortal work'[3]. But the members of
this Order apparently confined their attention to ecclesiastical
literature. The Frisian brothers, Emo and Addo, were wider in
their interests. As students at Paris, Orleans and Oxford, they
divided the night between them, and spent it in copying all the
texts they could find, with the explanations given them by their
lecturers; and, as head of the Premonstratensian abbey of
Wittewierum in Groningen (d. 1237), Emo afterwards instructed
nuns as well as monks in the art of transcribing MSS[4]. At Cluni
all the requirements of the copyist were provided by the *armarius*
or librarian[5], and the rule of silence was strictly enjoined. If the
copyist wanted a book, he had to stretch out his hands and make
a movement as of turning over leaves. To distinguish different
kinds of books, various further signs were in use. If he required
a Psalter, he placed his hands over his head, in allusion to the
royal crown of David; if a pagan book, he scratched his ear after
the manner of a dog[6]. Sometimes, for lack of parchment, a
copyist effaces a pagan text to make room for a Christian work;
but the converse occasionally happens, and a case is known in
which the Epistles of St Paul have been superseded by the books
of the *Iliad*[7]. Occasionally, the copyist protests against or even
alters a text which, on moral grounds, he disapproves[8]; and the
heathen incantations, copied in a MS of Apuleius *de herbis* in a

---

[1] J. W. Clark, *Care of Books*, 67, 133. Cp. Gasquet's *Essays*, 20, 28.

[2] Lecoy de la Marche, 90.

[3] Migne, cliii 883.

[4] Wattenbach, *Schriftwesen im MA*, 444[3]; cp. Montalembert, v 136 f
(1896).

[5] *ib.* 441[5].

[6] Martène, *De Antiq. Monach. Ritibus*, lib. v, c. 18 § 4, pro signo libri
saecularis, praemisso generali signo libri, adde ut aurem tangat cum digito,
sicut canis cum pede pruriens solet.

[7] Comparetti, *Virgilio*, i 114.

[8] Comparetti, i 115; Friedländer's *Martial*, i p. 73 f.

hand of the ninth century, are marked for omission in a hand of the fifteenth[1].

The scene of the copyist's industry was the *scriptorium*[2]. This might be either a large room where twelve copyists could be at work at once, or a small cell for a single transcriber.   In the old plan of the monastery at St Gallen, the *scriptorium* is beside the church and below the library[3].   Under Alcuin, St Martin's at Tours became famous for a time as a school of copyists, and one of his epigrams had the *scriptorium* for its theme, an epigram borrowed in part by Alcuin's pupil, Rabanus Maurus, for the *scriptorium* at Fulda[4]. In the Benedictine monasteries in general, it became customary to institute, first the library, then the *scriptorium*, and finally the school.   At St Albans, the *scriptorium* founded by abbot Paul

The scriptorium

SIMON, ABBOT OF ST ALBANS,
SEATED AT HIS BOOK-CHEST.
British Museum, Cotton MS, Claudius E 4.
(From J. W. Clark, *Care of Books*, 293.)

[1] Haase, *De Med. Aevi Stud. Philol.* 19.
[2] Ducange, s.v. *Scriptores*; Hardy, *Descriptive Catalogue*, Pref. to vol. iii (*Rolls Series*); cp. Gasquet's *Essays*, 41 f; F. Madan, *Books in MS*, 34 f.
[3] North of the chancel; Pertz, *Mon.* ii 95; Wattenbach, 440[3].
[4] Browerus, *Antiquitates Fuldenses* (1612), p. 46, and p. 483 *supra*.

(1077–93) was above the chapter-house, while the MSS collected a century later by abbot Simon (1167–83) were kept 'in the painted aumbry in the church'[1]. In many cases the *scriptorium* was considerately placed in the immediate neighbourhood of the calefactory. Instead of a large room, there might be a number of small *scriptoria* ranged round a cloister, each of them opening on to the cloister-walk and lighted by a single window on the opposite side, like the 'carrels' of St Peter's abbey, now forming part of Gloucester cathedral. 'Over against the carrells' (in the great Benedictine House at Durham) 'did stande certaine great almeries of waynscott all full of bookes, wherein did lye as well the old auncyent written Doctors of the Church as other prophane authors with dyverse other holie men's wourks'[2]. Nicholas, the secretary of Bernard of Clairvaux, describes his *scriptoriolum* (with its door open to the apartment of the novices, and with the cloister to the right and the infirmary and place of exercise to the left) as 'a place to be desired, and pleasant to look upon'; as 'comfortable for retirement', and 'fitted with choice and divine books'[3]. The task of the copyist was often carried on in the open cloister[4]. No MS was copied in the monk's own cell, and, for fear of accidents, candle-light was (in general) not allowed; but we know of one at least who (in his own pathetic words) 'Dum scripsit, friguit, et quod cum lumine solis Scribere non potuit, perfecit lumine noctis'[5]. The scribe was expected to copy exactly what he saw before him, even when it was clearly wrong : and his work was afterwards revised by the *corrector*[6].

The extreme elaboration with which the copyists of Cluni executed their work was criticised by the Cistercians, who, however, ended by following their example, even exempting their

---

[1] *Gesta Abbatum*, i 184, 192 (Gasquet's *Essays*, 6).

[2] *Rites of Durham* p. 70 (J. W. Clark, *Care of Books*, 90).

[3] *Ep.* 35, Migne, cxcvi 1626 f; Maitland, 404³ f.

[4] Gasquet, 43 f; J. W. Clark, 80 f.

[5] Pez, *Thesaurus*, i p. xx.

[6] Wattenbach, *Schriftwesen im MA* 428³ f (cp. Bursian, i 31 f). On the mediaeval book-trade, cp. Albrecht Kirchhoff, *Die Handschriftenhändler des Mittelalters*, ed. 2, 1853, and, on the economic results of the custom of copying MSS, Levasseur, *Hist. des classes ouvrières en France avant* 1789, 182—196, ed. 1900.

copyists from all labour in the fields except at the time of harvest[1]. Among the most famous schools of copyists were those of Tours, Orleans, Metz, Rheims, Prüm and St Gallen. But in 1297 at St Gallen, and in 1291 at Murbach in the upper Vosges, few (if any) of the monks were competent copyists[2], and similarly at Corbie (near Amiens) the monks ceased to act as copyists themselves at the end of the thirteenth century[3]. The Lucretius, which was there c. 1200, has since been lost. Many of the other MSS have, however, survived, notably a MS of the elder Pliny (cent. ix) and two of the *Thebais* of Statius (cent. ix, x)[4]; and (although the copyist seldom signed his work) the names of 27 librarians, copyists or correctors of MSS at Corbie are still known[5]. At Cluni, the MSS included Livy, Sallust, Suetonius, Trogus Pompeius (*i.e.* Justin), Seneca, 'Aristotle', Cicero, Ovid, Virgil, Horace, Juvenal, Statius, Lucan, Terence, Claudian, Aesop, Pliny the elder, Festus, Priscian (besides the chief mediaeval authors), the catalogues of centuries xii and xiii containing nearly 1000 volumes[6]. The monks of centuries x, xi and xii are credited with having been keener copyists than their successors; but the love of learning, which had received its first impulse from Cassiodorus, never entirely died out. It left its results in the MSS of Monte Cassino and Bobbio; of Corbie and Cluni; of Moissac on the upper Garonne, and Tours[7] and Fleury on the Loire[8];

---

[1] Wattenbach, *Schriftwesen im MA*, 442[3].

[2] On Murbach, cp. H. Bloch, *Ein Karolingischer Bibliothekskatalog aus Kloster Murbach*.

[3] Wattenbach, 443[3]; cp. Gasquet's *Essays*, 52.

[4] *Facsimiles* in Chatelain, *Pal. des Cl. Lat.* Pl. 140 f, 161.

[5] Delisle, *Bibl. de Corbie* (1860), *Mém. de l'Acad. des Inscr.* xxiv 266—342 = *Bibl. de l'école des chartes*, xxxi 393—439, 498—515; *Cabinet des MSS*, ii 427.

[6] Found by Mabillon and Martène; Delisle, *Cabinet des MSS*, ii 458–87; *Inventaire* (1884), 337–79; Lecoy de la Marche, 92; cp. E. Sackur, *Die Cluniacenser* (Halle, 1892-4).

[7] *e.g.* the Bern Virgil, and the Leyden Nonius Marcellus.

[8] *e.g.* the Bern Horace and Statius, the Paris Lucan, the Vatican *Fasti* of Ovid. Cp. also Traube, *S. Ber. bayr. Akad.* 1891, 400–2; Delisle, *Cab. des MSS*, ii 364–6, and *Notices et Extraits*, xxxi (1) 357—439; Cuissard-Gaucheron, *MSS...d'Orléans, Fonds de Fleury* (Orleans, 1855).

of St Gallen and Reichenau; of Lorsch, Hersfeld[1] and Fulda[2]. The work accomplished at Monte Cassino under Desiderius has been already mentioned[3]. Among other Italian libraries were those at Novalesa, near Mont Cenis, which contained more than 6000 volumes in 906, when the monks removed them to Turin for fear of the Saracens[4]; and at Pomposa, near Ravenna, including copies of Seneca and Pliny[5]. In France the monastery of Moissac alone preserved a copy of 'Lactantius' *De Mortibus Persecutorum*[6]; that of Murbach, the only MS of Velleius Paterculus; that of Fleury, near Orleans, the longer version of the Commentary on Virgil by Servius[7]; Bobbio once possessed the only MS of Terentianus Maurus; and similarly in many other cases[8]. Thus it is that the monasteries of the Middle Ages may justly be regarded not only as ' repositories of the learning that then was', but also as 'well-springs of the learning which was to be'[9]. While the records of other literatures have perished, we are indebted to the monks for the fact that

> ' Classic lore glides on,
> By these Religious saved for all posterity'[10].

The survival of certain of the Latin Classics was due to their local interest. Catullus survived in his birthplace, Verona (possibly owing to Pacificus, the archdeacon of that city, who, before 846, presented 218 MSS to the local College of Canons[11]); Caesar's

---

[1] Cp. Holder-Egger's *Lambert* (1894), p. xii f.

[2] J. Gegenbaur (Fulda, 1871–4, 1878). On all the monasteries in this line, see Index to Wattenbach, *Geschichtsquellen*, and to Specht, *Unterrichtswesen*; on Lorsch and Fulda, Falk's *Beiträge zur Rekonstruktion der alten Bibliotheca Fuldensis und Bibliotheca Laureshamensis*, 1902.

[3] p. 520 *supra*.

[4] Muratori, *Script. Rer. Ital.* II ii 731; Tiraboschi, iii 194; Balzani's *Chroniclers*, 183 f; Cipolla, *Mon. Novaliciensia* (Rome, 1898).

[5] Montfaucon, *Diar. Ital.* c. 6.

[6] Now Par. Colbert. 1297.

[7] Now Par. 7929.

[8] Cp. Vadianus ap. Ziegelbauer, *Obs. Lit. O.S.B.* ii 520. For Rutilius Namatianus we depend entirely on a Vienna transcript of a unique MS formerly at Bobbio.

[9] Maitland's *Dark Ages*, Pref.

[10] Wordsworth, *Eccl. Sonnets*, xxv.

[11] Muratori, *Ant. Ital.* iii 838; Tiraboschi, iii 264.

*Gallic War*, in France; the *Germania* and the early books of the *Annals* of Tacitus, with all that remains of Ammianus Marcellinus[1], in Germany; and Frontinus, *On Aqueducts*, at Monte Cassino, S. E. of the Roman Campagna, where this unique MS is still preserved[2]. The interests of education prompted the preservation of authors on Grammar, with Terence and Virgil, and (in a less degree) Lucan and Statius, Persius and Juvenal. Sallust, Livy and Suetonius were retained as models for historical, Cicero's *Speeches* for rhetorical, and Ovid for poetical composition. The ethical interest prolonged the existence of the philosophical writings of Cicero and Seneca, and of the historical anecdotes of Valerius Maximus[3]. Germany seems to have been mainly interested in subject-matter; France, in style and form. Catullus was preserved in France, as well as in Italy; Horace, chiefly in France; Propertius, probably in France alone, being first mentioned by Richard de Fournival, chancellor of Amiens (xiii)[4]. The two earliest notices of Tibullus come from France[5], and his allusions to the local rivers may have added to his popularity in that country[6]. The *Cynegetica* of Nemesianus is mentioned by Hincmar of Rheims alone, as a book which he had studied as a boy (d. 882). Cicero's *Speeches* survived at Cluni, Langres and Liège, and the Ciceronian MSS at Hirschau were brought from France[7]. The first to translate any of the *Speeches* was an Italian, Brunetto Latini (d. 1294); the *Brutus* survived solely in Italy; the *De Oratore* and *Orator*, in Italy and France. As an authority on matters of diction, the grammarian Festus was known in France, and was also preserved in Italy[8], Paulus Diaconus,

---

[1] *Codex Fuldensis* (cent. x) now in Vatican. The corruptions of the text are due to the fact that the 'insular' script of the archetype had ceased to be familiar at Fulda (Traube in *S. Ber.* Munich Acad. Dec. 1900, 496).

[2] Complete *facsimile* in Clemens Herschel's ed. (Boston, 1899).

[3] On Valerius cp. Wibald of Corvey (*c.* 1150) in *Bibl. Rer. Germ.* i 280 Jaffé.

[4] Propercii Aurelii Nautae monobiblos (cp. Teuffel, § 246, 1), Manitius in *Rhein. Mus.* xlvii, Suppl. p. 31. List of Richard's books in Delisle, *Cab. des MSS*, ii 514.

[5] Norden, *Kunstprosa*, 718 n. 2, cp. 692, 724; and Schanz, § 284 *a*.

[6] i 7, 1—12. Cp. Postgate, in *Cl. Rev.* xvii (1903) 112-7.

[7] *Bibl. Rer. Germ.* i 327.    [8] Cp. Manitius, in *Philol.* xlix 384.

generally recognised as the author of the extant abridgement, having lived in both of these lands. The historians (with the exception of the author of the *Gallic War*) were diligently read and copied in Germany[1]; and Pliny the elder in Germany and England.

Richard of Bury looks back with regret on the ages when the monks used to copy MSS 'between the hours of prayer', giving all the time they could to the making of books, and contrasts the industry of the past with the idleness of his own day (1345)[2]. He also presents us with a vivid picture of his own eagerness in collecting MSS with the aid of the *stationarii* and *librarii* of France, Germany and Italy. For some of his books he sends to Rome; he also dwells with rapture on his visits to Paris, 'the paradise of the world', with its delightful libraries, its MSS of Aristotle and Plotinus, St Paul and Dionysius, and 'all the works in which the Latin Muse reproduces the lore of Greece'[3]. He adds that, in his own manors in England, he always employed a large number of copyists[4], scribes and correctors, besides binders and illuminators[5]; and he pays an eloquent and well-known tribute to his beloved books[6]. All the rooms in his house are said to have been crowded with them. They are even said to have encroached on his bedroom in such numbers that he could not get to bed without stepping over them. His library has unfortunately been lost, and even its catalogue has vanished[7].

From the Monasteries the copying of MSS passed to the Universities. During the 70 years preceding the date of the *Philobiblon*, authorised copyists for the production of text-books were licensed and controlled by the university of Paris (1275), numbering 24 in 1292 and 29 in 1323[8]. The library of the Sorbonne was instituted in 1289; its catalogue

---

[1] Manitius in *Rhein. Mus. l. c.*, with summary in Norden, 691 f.

[2] *Philobiblon*, c. 5.          [3] c. 8, §§ 126-8.

[4] *antiquarii* (§ 143=*transcriptores veterum*, § 207).

[5] § 143.          [6] c. 1 §§ 26—29.

[7] H. Morley's *Eng. Writers*, iv 56; Putnam, i 168; p. 602 *supra*.

[8] Paul Lacroix, quoted by Lecoy de la Marche, p. 110 f. On 'Books in the early Universities', see Schmid, *Gesch. d. Erziehung*, II i 490–5, and Putnam, i 178—224. On the mediaeval trade in MSS, see Albrecht Kirchhoff, *Die Handschriftenhändler des MAs*, 1853.

(which is still extant) numbers 1017 titles, and by the statutes
of 1321 one copy of every work in its best form was added to the
collection[1]. But, at least half a century before Paris became
famous as the home of Scholasticism (c. 1100) or Bologna as a
school of Law (c. 1113), and more than a century before Oxford
began to flourish, possibly owing to the withdrawal of certain
English students from Paris (1167), Salerno had been known
throughout Europe as a school of Medicine (c. 1050), and Latin
translations of Arabic renderings of the great Greek physicians
began to be in use in that 'city of Hippocrates' before the end of
the eleventh century[2]. Montpellier is first noticed as a school
of Medicine in 1137, and the text-books there used are chiefly
those of the Greek Galen, as translated from Arabic into Latin in
the twelfth century, mainly by Gerard of Cremona[3]. We hear of
students migrating from Oxford to Cambridge in 1209, and from
Bologna to Padua in 1222, and we find Salamanca and Toulouse
coming into being about the same date, while the only important
universities founded between that time and the middle of the
fourteenth century are those of Pisa (1343), Florence (1349), and
Prague (1347–8), this last being the earliest of German universities.
The traditions of study, which had been in a measure maintained
by the Monasteries down to about the end of the twelfth century,
passed in part to the Dominican and Franciscan Orders in the
thirteenth, while, before the close of the Middle Ages, they also
found a home in Universities such as those which have here been
briefly mentioned.

A few of the indications of the relative importance attached to
the principal Latin authors in the Middle Ages may here be
noticed[4], with some mention of the leading mediaeval MSS still

---

[1] A. Franklin, *Les Anciennes Bibl. de Paris* (1867), *La Sorbonne*, 221—318;
cp. Putnam, i 166.

[2] Rashdall, i 77 f.          [3] *ib.* ii 115, 780.

[4] Cp. Manitius in *Philologus*, xlvii—lii, and Suppl. vii, 1899 (for mediaeval
quotations), and *Rhein. Mus.* xlvii, Suppl. 152 pp. (for evidence from
mediaeval catalogues), with literature in Hübner, *Bibliographie*, §§ 34, 38; also
A. Graf, *Roma nella Memoria...del Medio Evo* (1883), ii 153—367; and the
very brief sketches in G. Meier's *Sieben Freien Künste* (Einsiedeln, 1886),
i 17—21, and Bursian's *Cl. Philol. in Deutschland*, i 27 f. See also Manitius,
in *Mitt. für Schulgeschichte*, 1906 (1) and (3); Sabbadini, *Scoperte*, ii 199 ff.

extant, and of the mediaeval libraries where they were formerly
preserved[1].   It will thus be seen how large a portion of the Latin
Classics owes its present existence to the industry of copyists
prior to the age of the Renaissance.  Plautus was little read[2];

Plautus          he is only quoted second-hand by Rabanus Maurus,
who clearly derives his knowledge from Priscian
and Isidore ; but many isolated lines are cited in the *Glossarium
Osberni*[3], a work of English origin.   In the mediaeval catalogues,
he is found at Bury[4] and at Bamberg[5] only, but he is mentioned
by Ratherius, bishop of Verona (965)[6], and Philip de Harveng
(cent. xii)[7], both of whom once belonged to the diocese of Cambrai.
The text of Plautus now depends (1) on the Ambrosian palimpsest
in Milan (cent. iv—v), containing the *Trinummus* and *Miles
Gloriosus* and portions of fifteen other plays, which almost certainly came from Bobbio[8], and (2) on five MSS of the 'Palatine'
recension, viz. one at Heidelberg[9], two in the Vatican, one in the
British Museum (xi), and a second Ambrosian MS (xii).   Until
1429, only the first eight of the twenty extant plays were really

Terence          known.  Terence was far more familiar.  A line from
his plays was even quoted in St Peter's by Liberius,
bishop of Rome (352–66), in an exhortation addressed to the
sister of Ambrose on her reception as a nun in the presence of

[1] Nearly all the MSS here mentioned are included in Chatelain's *Paléographie
des Classiques Latins*, containing more than 300 *facsimiles*, with descriptive
letterpress (1884—1900).   Further details as to the 'class-marks' etc. of MSS
in *modern* libraries may be found in Teuffel or Schanz, and the current critical
editions.  Cp. H. W. Johnston, *Latin MSS*, Chicago, 1897 ; F. W. Hall,
*Companion to Classical Texts*, Oxford, 1913.

[2] Peiper, *Archiv f. Lit. Gesch.* v 495; *Rhein. Mus.* xxxii 516 ; Manitius,
*Philol.* Suppl. vii 758 f.

[3] A column and a half of references in Index to Mai, *Auctores*, viii.   The
work was ascribed by Leland to Osbern, a monk of Gloucester (*c.* 1150);
W. Meyer in *Rhein. Mus.* xxix (1874) 179 f; Loewe, *Prodromus Corporis
Gloss. Lat.* 240–3.

[4] M. R. James, *Bibl. Buriensis*, p. 27.

[5] Manitius, *Rhein. Mus.* xlviii 101.

[6] Migne, cxxxvi 752, Catullum nunquam antea lectum, Plautum iam olim
lego [nec]lectum.

[7] Migne, cciii 872 (*Captivi*), 1008 (*Asinaria*).

[8] p. 454 *supra*.

[9] Complete *facsimile* (Leyden, 1900).

her brother[1].  He was closely imitated by Hroswitha, and not
unfrequently cited by others[2] ; but, although his metres had been
expounded by Priscian, he was regarded as a prose-author not
only by the learned abbess of Gandersheim, but also by the well-
informed schoolmaster of Bamberg, Hugo of Trimberg[3].  The
text depends on the Bembine MS in the Vatican (iv—v), so called
because it belonged to Cardinal Bembo's father, who describes it
as a *codex mihi carior auro*[4].  The later MSS (ix) belong to the
inferior recension by Calliopius (iii—iv)[5].

Lucretius, who, in the Roman Age, had been imitated by
Horace and Virgil[6], had been familiar to Arnobius,
Lactantius[7] and Jerome[8], and had been occasion-              Lucretius
ally copied by Commodianus and frequently quoted by Isidore,
was little read in the Middle Ages[9].  But he is mentioned by
Ratherius, and, through the medium of the grammarians, he
became known to Bede, one of whose quotations enabled
Lachmann to emend the poet's text (vi 868).  A few consecutive
lines are quoted by Ermenrich of Ellwangen[10].  Some at least of
the quotations in Rabanus Maurus are undoubtedly derived (as
in the case of Plautus) from Priscian and Isidore.  If any of them
are first-hand, they may have been taken from the ninth century
MS now at Leyden (A), which was formerly in the library of
St Martin's church at Mainz, the see of Rabanus.  The tenth

---

[1] *Hautontim.* 373 ; Ambrose in Migne, xvi 225 C.

[2] Manitius, *Philol.* lii 546–53 ; Cloetta, *Beiträge*, i ; *Komödie u. Tragödie
im MA*, 2 f (Halle, 1890) ; Magnin, *Bibl. de l'école des chartes*, i 524–31.
John of Salisbury, *Pol.* vii 9, calls him *Comicus qui prae ceteris placet* ; but the
only plays he quotes are the *Andria* and *Eunuchus*.

[3] *Registrum Multorum Auctorum* (1280), ed. Hümer, *Ein Quellenbuch zur
Lat. Literaturgeschichte des MAs*, Vienna *Akad. Sitzungsber*. 1888, (Sallust,
Cicero, Terence) 'non in numero ponuntur metricorum' (l. 282).

[4] Complete *facsimile* (Leyden, 1903).

[5] Dziatzko (*Comment. Woelfflin*, 221–6) notes that the term *recensui* first
appears *c.* 500, and would assign Calliopius to that date.

[6] Schanz, § 95.

[7] Philippe, *Rev. de l'Hist. des Religions*, 1896, 16—36.

[8] *Adv. Ruf.* iii c. 29.

[9] Manitius, in *Philol.* lii 536–8.  Jourdain, *Recherches*, 21, seems hardly
justified in saying that *à toutes les époques du moyen âge on a lu...le poème de
Lucrèce.*                          [10] ed. Dümmler, p. 20 (Lucr. i 150–8).

century MS at Leyden (B) was once in the abbey of St Bertin, near St Omer and not far from Corbie, and mediaeval catalogues show that Lucretius was not unknown at Corbie itself, as well as at Murbach and Bobbio. In Lachmann's opinion, our present authorities, A and B, are derived from a lost original of century iv—v, consisting of 302 pages written in *thin capitals*, which was formerly in some part of Frankland[1]; but it has since been shown by a French scholar that the original was written in *minuscules*, with abbreviations wrongly interpreted in the existing transcripts[2]. Marbod, bishop of Rennes (d. 1123), who opposed the Epicureanism of his day, has an obvious echo of Lucretius in the lines,

'Hanc (*sc.* mortem) indoctus homo summum putat esse malorum,
    Omnia cum vita tollentur commoda vitae'[3].

A single line of Lucretius[4] is inaccurately quoted in works bearing the names of Wilhelm of Hirschau[5] (d. 1091) and Honorius of Autun[6] (*c.* 1120), both of which are now generally ascribed to William of Conches[7]. The same line is quoted by Giraldus Cambrensis[8] (d. 1222); but, with William and Giraldus alike, the ultimate authority is Priscian (iv 27), as is proved by their agreeing with Priscian in making the last word of the line *nasci* instead of *gigni*[9]. Giraldus actually quotes it as a line of Plautus, thus revealing his ignorance of the text of Plautus and Lucretius, and of the metres of both. Richard of Bury[10] mentions Lucretius (with Homer and Theocritus) as a poet imitated by Virgil. This remark is described by Manitius[11] as a proof of very wide reading, but Richard may easily have found his authority (for Virgil's debt to Lucretius) in

---

[1] Lachmann, *Comm.* init.

[2] Louis Duvau, in *Rev. de Philol.* xii (1888) 30—37.

[3] *Liber decem Capitulorum*, ix; Lucr. iii 898—901, and iii 2, 'commoda vitae'.

[4] ii 888, ex insensilibus ne credas sensile gigni.

[5] *Philosophicae Institutiones*, i p. 24.

[6] *De Philos. Mundi*, i c. 21, Migne, clxxii 54.

[7] Poole's *Medieval Thought*, 339-46.          [8] vol. iv 1.

[9] The Vatican *Glossarium Osberni* (xii) in Mai, *Auctores*, viii 515, also quotes the line with *nasci*.

[10] *Philobiblon*, § 162.                    [11] *Philol.* lii 538.

one of his favourite authors, Gellius[1]; or (for the poet's debt to
Homer and Theocritus, as well as Lucretius) in Macrobius[2], whom
he mentions in the very next section[3]. The few quotations in
Petrarch and Boccaccio are borrowed from Macrobius[4]. It was
not until about 1417 that Lucretius was recovered by Poggio.

Verona's poet Catullus, who had been imitated in the Roman
Age[5], and partially known to Ausonius, Paulinus
and Apollinaris Sidonius in Gaul, and to Corippus          Catullus
in Africa[6], is quoted by Isidore of Seville in the seventh century,
but is not even named again until the time of Ratherius, bishop
of Verona (965)[7]. The MS at Verona, lost for a time but recovered
shortly before 1323, was known to Petrarch (1347) and Coluccio
Salutati (1374), but had vanished again before Traversari's visit
(July 1433)[8]. It is (directly or indirectly) the source of all the
extant MSS[9], the best of them being the Vatican MS, which once
belonged to Coluccio Salutati[10], the Paris MS from Saint-Germain-
des-Prés, transcribed from a copy made at Verona in 1375[11], the
Oxford MS from the collection of the Venetian Jesuit Canonici
(1817), copied about 1400, and the *codex Datanus* in Berlin
(1463). The *Epithalamium* alone is included in a Paris Anthology
of century ix.

Of all the poets by far the most popular in the Middle Ages
was Virgil. The allegorical interpretation of the
*Aeneid*, as an image of human life, as a story of          Virgil
the triumph of wisdom and virtue over folly and passion, first put

---

[1] i 21, 7.                    [2] (Theocr., Homer, v 2, 4—6); (Lucr.) vi 1—6.

[3] See, in general, Manitius, *l. c.*; Jessen in *Philol.* xxx 236–8; J. Philippe,
in *Rev. de l'Hist. des Religions*, xxxii (1895) 284—302, xxxiii (1896) 19—36,
125—162. Cp. Lambinus, *Lucr.* ed. 1583, p. vii; Barth on Statius *Silv.* ii 7,
76 (1664); and Munro, *Lucr.*, notes i p. 1; also Voigt, i³ 241 n. 2.

[4] De Nolhac, *Petrarque et l'humanisme*, 134. Cp. Hortis, *Studi*, 392.

[5] Magnus in Bursian's *Jahresb.* li 239; Schanz, § 106.

[6] *Philol.* xlviii 760; cp. Bährens, ii 65.

[7] p. 630 *supra*, n. 6; R. Ellis, *Prol.* vi f.

[8] *Hodoeporicon*, p. 34; Voigt, *Humanismus*, i 207, 439, ii 384³; Bährens,
i pp. v—xi; R. Ellis, *Prol.* x—xii; also *Catullus in xiv cent.* (1905).

[9] Disputed by L. Schwabe (1886) and B. Schmidt (1887).

[10] W. G. Hale, in *Proc. Amer. Phil. Assoc.* 1897; *Cl. Rev.* xii 447, xx 160.

[11] Chatelain, no. 15; complete *facsimile* (Paris, Leroux, 1890).

forward by Fulgentius[1], was accepted by Bernard Silvester and his contemporary John of Salisbury[2], as well as by Dante, and by scholars in the Renaissance, such as Alberti and Landini. Virgil was of course the constant model of the mediaeval epics. Benoît de Sainte-More founded on an annotated edition of the *Aeneid* his romance of *Énéas* (after 1160)[3]. Virgil's general popularity in the Christian community was partly due to his *Fourth Eclogue*, which had been regarded by Lactantius, Eusebius, St Augustine and Prudentius as a prophecy of the coming of Christ[4]. Vincent of Beauvais[5] ascribed the conversion of three pagans to the perusal of that poem. In the mystery-plays of the Middle Ages, Virgil, with the Sibyl and the Prophets, appeared as witnesses to the Incarnation. In a play of the eleventh century the *Praecentor*, addressing the poet, says :—

> 'Vates Maro gentilium,
> Da Christo testimonium';

and the poet replies :—

> ' Ecce polo demissa solo nova progenies est '[6].

It was also a pious belief in Italy that St Paul had visited the poet's tomb when he passed through Naples, and had shed tears of regret at the thought that the poet had not lived at a time when he might have been converted by the Apostle. A hymn in honour of St Paul, which continued to be sung at Mantua down to the fifteenth century, included the following stanza :—

> ' Ad Maronis mausoleum
> Ductus fudit super eum
> Piae rorem lacrymae ;
> Quem te, inquit, reddidissem,
> Si te vivum invenissem,
> Poëtarum maxime ! '[7]

---

[1] *Virgiliana continentia* (c. 520 A.D.), ed. Helm, 1898.

[2] Comparetti, *Virgilio*, Part I, c. 8; Schaarschmidt, 97 f; Poole's *Medieval Thought*, 119; Boissier, in *Rev. des Deux Mondes*, xix 522.

[3] Gaston Paris, *Litt. Fr. au MA*, § 46.

[4] Comparetti, *Virgilio*, i 132–5, and Schanz, § 224, p. 39². Jerome, *Ep.* 53 (Migne, xxii 545), describes such views as *puerilia*.

[5] *Spec. Hist.* xi 50.

[6] Du Meril, *Origines Latines du théâtre moderne*, p. 184 (Graf's *Roma*, ii 206).

[7] Daniel, *Thesaurus*, v 266 (Comparetti, *Virgilio*, i 131).

To Dante (as is well known) Virgil is 'the glory of the Latin race'[1], 'the honour of all science and all wit'[2], 'the sea of all wisdom'[3], 'the gentile sage, who all things knew'[4], the poet who, as the symbol of human wisdom and philosophy, is his 'leader, lord and master'[5] in his journey through the *Inferno* and the greater part of the *Purgatorio*[6].

The text of Virgil rests mainly on the *Medicean* MS (v), once at Bobbio; the *Palatine* (v ?), formerly at Heidelberg; and the *Vatican* MS (3867), with 16 illustrations (vi ?), from St Denis. Hardly a quarter of the text is preserved in an older *Vatican* MS (iv ?) including 50 pictures of Virgilian scenes[7]. There are seven leaves, from a St Denis MS (ii or iii ?), now in the Vatican and in Berlin, and fragments (iv ?) at St Gallen[8]; also a Paris palimpsest from Corbie, and a Verona palimpsest with scholia (both of cent. iv ?). Lastly, we have two important MSS from Tours and Fleury (ix), now in Bern[9] and Paris respectively; and, among the Paris MSS (ix—xii), one from the abbey of St Martial at Limoges.

The study of Horace in the Caroline age is represented mainly by Alcuin, who assumes the name of Flaccus, and displays a knowledge of the *Odes* and *Epodes* as well as the *Satires* and *Epistles*, which may also be traced in the

Horace

[1] *Purg.* vii 16.                          [2] *Inf.* iv 73.
[3] *Inf.* viii 7.                          [4] *Inf.* vii 3.
[5] *Inf.* ii 140.   *De Monarchia*, ii 3, divinus poëta noster Virgilius.
[6] Virgil leaves Dante in *Purg.* xxx 49 f.   Cp. H. M. Beatty, *Dante and Virgil*, 1905.—A long list of reminiscences of Virgil in the Latin poets of cent. v—xii is collected in Zappert, *Virgils Fortleben im MA* (Vienna *Akad.* 1851); see also Ribbeck's Index. The subject in general is fully treated in Comparetti's *Virgilio nel Medio Evo*, 2 vols. (1872 and 1896), E.T. 1895 (cp. *Quarterly Review*, vol. 137, 77 f), Graf's *Roma*, ii 196—258, Teuffel, § 231, 12; cp. J. S. Tunison's *Master Virgil*, ed. 2 (1890), and C. G. Leland, *Unpublished Legends of Virgil* (1899), also Du Méril in *Mélanges archéol. et lit.* (1850), 425–78, and Schanz, §§ 247, 249. On Virgil in mediaeval schools, cp. Specht, *Unterrichtswesen*, 97 f, and Manitius, *Zur Ueberlieferungsgeschichte, Sonderdruck aus Mitt. der Ges. f. deutsche...Schulgeschichte*, xvi 3 (1906), p. 16. See also Schanz, II i[2] § 249.
[7] Photographed in *Fragmenta et picturae Verg. cod. Vat.* 3225 (Rome, 1899); partly reproduced in G. F. Hill's *Illustrations of School Classics*, No. 221 f (1903). Cp. Nolhac in *Notices et Extraits*, xxxv 2, 1897.
[8] *Facsimile* on p. 197 *supra*.
[9] p. 476 *supra*.   *Facsimile* in Steffen's *Lat. Pal.* 102.

poems of Theodulfus, bishop of Orleans (d. 821). The oldest extant MS of Horace, the *codex Bernensis*, came from the neighbourhood of Orleans, and was probably originally at Bobbio. The famous description of Death[1] is cited as follows by Notker Balbulus of St Gallen (cent. ix):—

> 'ut cecinit sensu verax Horatius iste,
>     caetera vitandus lubricus atque vagus :
>   pallida Mors aequo pulsans pede sive tabernas
>     aut regum turres, vivite, ait, venio'.

In the Montpellier MS (cent. x) the *Ode to Phyllis* (iv 11) is set to the music of the lines ascribed to Paulus Diaconus, which supplied Guido of Arezzo with the names of the notes, *ut, re, mi, fa, sol, la, si*:—

> '*ut* quaent laxis *re*sonare fibris
>   *mi*ra gestorum *fa*muli tuorum,
>     *sol*ve polluti *la*bii reatum,
>       Sancte *I*ohannes'[2].

The *Satires* and *Epistles* supply, in 250 lines, an eighth part of the Epics of the 'Calf and Wolf', and the 'Fox and Lion', known as the *Ecbasis Captivi* (written by a monk of Toul shortly after 936)[3]. The poet is called *noster Horatius* by Benzo, the bishop of Alba (*fl.* 1061), who, in the *Panegyric* dedicated to the emperor Henry IV, also names Virgil, Lucan, Statius, 'Homer', and Quintilian[4]. The *Odes* and *Epodes* (as well as Virgil's *Eclogues*) are imitated by Metellus of Tegernsee (first half of cent. xii) in the poems written in many metres in honour of St Quirinus[5]. Horace is named by Abelard among the 'pagan philosophers' cited by the doctors of the Church. In 1280 his hexameter poems are regarded by Hugo of Trimberg[6] as more important than the lyrics : the former are the *libri principales*, the latter are

[1] *Odes*, i 4 13 f.

[2] Dümmler, *Poëtae Lat. Aevi Car.*, *Appendix Carminum Dubiorum*, i 83 ; Orelli's *Horace*, Appendix to vol. ii ed. 3.

[3] ed. Voigt (1875) ; Bursian, i 49 f, and in *S. Ber. bayr. Akad.* 1873, 460 f; Ebert, iii 276, 285—326 ; and Testimonia in Keller-Holder's *Horace*, ii (1869) ; also Manitius, 616-9.                      [4] Graf, *Roma*, ii 172.

[5] Canisius, *Lect. Ant.* i, appendix, p. 35 f. Cp. Bursian, i 71 ; *S. Ber. bayr. Akad.* 1873, Aufsatz 3 ; and *Jahresb.* i 9.

[6] *Registrum*, 68 f.

*minus usuales.* Thus the moral precepts embodied in the conversational style[1] of his hexameters were apparently recognised as
possessing a permanent value, while his elaborate and almost
inimitable lyrics were regarded as only the occasional poetry of a
by-gone age, and were probably all the less likely to be appreciated,
or imitated, owing to the perplexing variety of the metres employed.
The distinction drawn by Hugo is fully confirmed by statistics.
Out of 1289 scattered quotations from Horace in the Middle
Ages, exactly 250 (or less than $\frac{1}{5}$) are from the lyrics and as many
as 1039 from the hexameters[2]. The total number of quotations
from the lyrics in Italy is only 19, distributed over several centuries,
and gradually diminishing till they reach the age of Dante, when
they entirely disappear. Horace was, in fact, little known in Italy
before the Renaissance, while he was far more familiar in France
and Germany. Germany in century xiii claims the only two
mediaeval quotations from the *Carmen Saeculare*. It was in the
lands watered by the Rhine, the Mosel and the Meuse (within
the limits corresponding to the mediaeval Lotharingia), that
Horace was best appreciated; and the same is true of other
Latin poets. Thus it was apparently in the region immediately
surrounding the ancient court of Aachen, that the influence of
the revival of learning under Charles the Great lasted longest[3].

Most of the 250 extant MSS come from France. The oldest,
now known as the *codex Bernensis*, which belongs to the Mavortian
recension (527) and is written in an Irish hand (ix), came from
Fleury on the Loire. It has Celtic glosses here and there in the
margin, and is one of a group of MSS now ascribed to Irish
contemporaries of Sedulius of Liège[4]. Among other MSS, which
are interesting by reason of the places of their origin or their

---

[1] Sellar's *Horace etc.* (1892), 82 f.

[2] See tabular conspectus in Moore's *Studies in Dante*, i 201.

[3] The *Analecta ad carminum Horatianorum historiam*, carried by
M. Hertz (1876–82) down to Venantius Fortunatus, have been continued to
1300 in the *Analekten* of Manitius (1893); cp. Haupt, *Opusc.* iii 47, and
Campaux, *Histoire du texte d'Horace* (1891). Further reminiscences of Horace
are quoted by Torraca, *Nuove Rassegne* (1894), pp. 421–9; cp. also Graf's
*Roma*, ii 293–6; Schanz, § 265 *a*, and Manitius in *Mitt.* 12 f.

[4] Traube, *Abhandl.* Munich Acad. 1892, p. 348 f. Cp., in general, Schanz,
§ 263. Complete *facsimile* (Leyden, 1897), pp. 333–72.

preservation, we have the *Leidensis* (ix) from Beauvais, the *Bruxellensis* (xi) probably from Gembloux, Paris MSS (x) from Rheims and Autun, a Vatican MS (x) from Weissenburg in Alsace, and others at Einsiedeln (x) and St Gallen (xi). The ancient *codex Blandinius* perished in the fire which destroyed in 1566 the Benedictine monastery in Ghent, from which it had once been borrowed by Cruquius[1]. A similar fate befell a MS of century ix—x during the siege of Strassburg in 1870.

A popularity intermediate between that of Virgil and Horace

Ovid was attained by Ovid, especially in his *Meta-morphoses*, his *Fasti*, his *Ars Amatoria* and his *Remedia Amoris*[2]. He is named by Isidore of Seville in his treatise *De Summo Bono* as the particular pagan writer who is most to be avoided, but this does not debar the bishop from quoting about 20 passages from the poet. It is fair, however, to add that he only once quotes the *Ars Amatoria* (ii 24), and even this quotation (harmless in itself) may be regarded as neutralised by a reminiscence of the *Remedia Amoris* (140). Ovid was imitated by the scholars at the court of Charles the Great, one of whom assumed the name of Naso, while another, Theodulfus, believed that profound truths were contained in his poems, if properly (*i.e.* allegorically) understood[3]. The *Metamorphoses* was translated into German by Albrecht von Halberstadt (1210), and parts of that work, and of the *Heroides*, borrowed in the vast poem of Conrad of Würzburg on the Trojan War[4]. The *Tristia* inspired the laments of Ermoldus Nigellus (d. 834) in the days of his exile[5]. Ancient and mediaeval poems, which Ovid never wrote, were ascribed to his pen, and, in England, the spurious *De Vetula* was strangely accepted as genuine by Walter Burley, Richard de Bury and Thomas Bradwardine. All his genuine works were known and quoted,

---

[1] p. 197 *supra*.

[2] Manitius in *Philol.* Suppl. vii 721–58. Cp. Wattenbach, *GQ*, i[7] 361, and Specht, *Unterrichtswesen*, 99.

[3] p. 479 n. 2 *supra*.

[4] Bartsch, *Albrecht...u. Ovid im MA* (1861).

[5] Migne, cv 551—640 ; Dümmler's *Poëtae Lat. Aevi Car.* ii 1—93 (where Virgil is, however, imitated more than Ovid). On the *Tristia*, cp. Ehwald (Gotha, 1889).

and most of them imitated and translated, during the Middle
Ages[1]. He is often cited by the Troubadours and the
Minnesingers. Early in century xii his *Heroides* are imitated by
Baudri de Bourgueil, bishop of Dol (d. 1130). In the same
century we find the monks of Canterbury using his poems as a
treasury of stock quotations[2]; and even the *Art of Love* was
allegorised for the benefit of nuns[3]. The *Art of Love* was translated by Chrétien de Troies (*c.* 1155–88), whose rendering is lost;
and it was freely imitated by Jacques d'Amiens (xiii)[4]. It is only
the first book of the *Amores* that is much quoted in the Middle
Ages. There is no poet who is cited oftener by Vincent of
Beauvais (d. 1264). Early in the thirteenth century he is imitated
by André, the chaplain of the French court[5]; while his influence
may be traced in Guillaume de Lorris, the author of the first part
of the *Roman de la Rose* (*c.* 1237)[6]. In the middle of the same
century, all the works, except the spurious *Halieutica*, are named
by Richard de Fournival of Amiens, while Conrad von Mure of
Zürich (d. 1281) quotes from all, except the *Medicamina Faciei*.
Philip de Vitri translated and 'moralised' the *Metamorphoses* in
French verse, at the request of Jean de Bourgogne, wife of Philip V
(d. 1322)[7]. Dante regards the *Metamorphoses* as a model of

[1] Gaston Paris, in *Hist. Litt. de la France*, xxix (1885) 455—525; *Litt.
Fr. au MA* (1888) § 49 (a poem of *c.* 70,000 verses by the Franciscan
Crestien Legouais, cent. xiv); and *La Poésie du MA*, sér. 1 (1895); also
E. Stengel, in *Römanische Philol.* xlvii (1886). On the French imitations and
translations of the *Met.* cp. L. Sudre (1893). More than 2000 lines in the
*Roman de la Rose* are inspired by Ovid. See also Hortis, *Studi*, 399 f;
Gröber's *Grundriss*, II i 411; and Schanz, § 313.

[2] Stubbs, *Epp. Cantuarienses* (1187–99) in *Rolls Series*; and *Lectures*,
129[1]. The monks quote *Ex Ponto* i 10, 36; ii 6, 38; iv 16, 52; *Amores* i 15,
39; *Ars Am.* i 444; *Rem. Am.* 462.

[3] Wattenbach, *Sitzungsb. bayr. Akad.* 1873, 695.

[4] Gaston Paris, *Litt. Fr. au MA*, § 104.

[5] André le Chapelain, *De arte amandi et de reprobatione amoris*, ed. Trojel
(1892); cp. *Hist. Litt.* xxix 455—525; Gröber's *Grundriss*, II i 262, 592, 709,
744 f, 860, 1184; and Gaston Paris, *l. c.*, § 104.

[6] Gaston Paris, § 111.

[7] Le Clerc, *Hist. Litt.*, 406, 498. A similar work by the English
Benedictine, Thomas of Wales (*c.* 1340) was printed in 1484.

style[1], and as a work requiring allegorical interpretation[2], in which sense it was fully expounded by his younger contemporary Giovanni del Virgilio[3]. Chaucer's *Legend of Good Women* proves his familiarity with the *Metamorphoses* and *Heroides*; and there is no Latin poet that he cites more frequently[4]. The interest which he excited is proved by the mediaeval story of the two students who visited the tomb of Ovid, *eo quod sapiens fuerat*. One of them asked the poet which was (morally) the best line that he had ever written; a voice replied:—*virtus est licitis abstinuisse bonis*[5]. The other inquired which was the worst; the voice replied:—*omne juvans statuit Jupiter esse bonum*[6]. Thereupon both the students proposed to pray for the repose of the poet's soul, but the voice ungratefully sent them on their way with the words:—*nolo Pater Noster; carpe, viator, iter*[7].

The earliest extant MSS of any part of Ovid, those in Paris, Oxford and Vienna, belong to century ix. The Oxford MS, which includes (besides three other works) the first book of the *Ars Amatoria* with Latin and Celtic glosses, is written in a Welsh hand[8]. It was once in the possession of Dunstan, abbot of Glastonbury from 943, who has drawn a portrait of himself on its opening page[9]; and there is a certain piquancy at finding such a MS in the hands of one who, after falling in love with a lady of the court, was ultimately among the strictest of monastic disciplinarians. One of the best of all classical MSS is the *codex Puteaneus* of the *Heroides* (xi) in the Paris Library[10]. The MS of

---

[1] *De Vulg. El.* ii 6.

[2] *Conv.* ii 1; iv 25, 27, 28; cp. Szombathely, *Dante ed Ovidio* (Trieste, 1888).

[3] Wicksteed and Gardner, *Dante and Giovanni del Virgilio*, 314 f.

[4] See Index to Skeat's *Chaucer*.

[5] *Her.* xvii 98, *est virtus*.

[6] A paraphrase of *Her.* iv 133, *Juppiter esse pium statuit quodcumque iuvaret*.

[7] T. Wright, *Latin Stories from MSS of XIII—XIV cent.* (1842), c. 45. On Ovid in MA, cp., in general, Graf, *Roma* ii 296—315, and Manitius in *Philol.* Suppl. vii, 723–58, and in *Mitt.* 10 f.

[8] R. Ellis, *Hermes*, 1880, 425 f, and *XII Facs.* 1885, pl. 1.

[9] Illustr. ed. of Green's *History*, p. 105.

[10] *Facs.* in Palmer's ed.

the *Fasti* now in the Vatican (x) has been identified with one formerly at Fleury. The best MS of the *Metamorphoses* (x—xi) was once in the monastery of San Marco at Florence. A palimpsest of two leaves from the *Epistolæ ex Ponto*, now at Wolfenbüttel, belongs to the sixth century.

Lucan was one of the best known of the Classical poets. He owed his popularity largely to his learned allusions to matters of geography, mythology and natural     Lucan history, as well as to his rhetorical style and his pointed sayings. The anonymous author of a Life of archbishop Oswald (d. 992) in Latin verse (c. xiii?) names, as the three typical epic poets, Homer, Walter of Châtillon, and Lucan[1]. He was regarded as a historical authority, being the main source of the mediaeval romances on Julius Caesar. He was also the source of the prose work of Jean de Thuin in Hainau (c. 1240), which was turned into verse by Jacob de Forest[2]. He is quoted by Geoffrey of Monmouth and John of Salisbury, and is the principal model of Gunther's *Ligurinus* (1187). His poem was translated into Italian in 1310. He is mentioned by Dante as the last of the four great Latin poets in the fourth canto of the *Inferno*; and is placed by Chaucer on the summit of an iron column in the *House of Fame*;

> 'And by him stoden all these clerkes,
> That write of Romes mighty werkes'[3].

On certain other columns in the same building the poet places Homer, Virgil, Ovid and Statius[4].

The MSS of Lucan belong to two recensions. (1), that of Paulus Constantinopolitanus, identified by Usener[5] with the Papulus Const[s] Theyderich of a Paris MS of 674, is well represented by one of the two MSS at Montpellier (ix—x), which was formerly at Autun: (2) is best represented by a MS at Leyden written in a German hand (x). Of two Paris MSS of century ix,

---

[1] Warton's *English Poetry, Diss.* 3, i 231 (Hazlitt).

[2] Gaston Paris, *Litt. Fr. au MA*, § 48.

[3] iii 407–16.

[4] Cp., in general, Graf, *Roma*, ii 315–8, Manitius in *Philol.* li 704–19, and in *Mitt.* 17 f, and Schanz, § 392; also Creizenach, Frankfurt Progr. 1864.

[5] *Rhein. Mus.* xxiii (1868) 497; refuted by Lejay, in *Rev. de Philol.* xviii (1894) 53.

one came from Epternach and is possibly the source of the MS at
Bern; while another (xi) came from Fleury. There are also
two sets of fragmentary palimpsests, (1) at Rome, and (2) at
Naples and Vienna; the latter once belonged to Bobbio.

Statius was no less famous than Lucan. The *Thebais* was
**Statius**   imitated in the romance of *Thèbes* attributed to
Benoît de Sainte-More[1], and by Chaucer in his
*Troilus and Creseide* and elsewhere; the *Achilleis* by Joseph of
Exeter, and by Conrad of Würzburg[2]. Both of his great epic poems
are known to Conrad of Hirschau, and Conrad von Mure, and are
often quoted by others[3], while his *Silvae,* familiar to Ausonius,
Claudian, and Apollinaris Sidonius, but imitated only once in the
Caroline age by Paulus Diaconus[4], remained practically unknown[5]
till its discovery by Poggio at St Gallen (1417). In an ancient
Norman poem he is called *Estace le Grand,* though Virgil (in the
same line) has no epithet whatsoever[6]. In the *liber glossarum* it is
Statius (and not Virgil or Lucan) that is cited simply as *poëta*[7].
He was expounded by Gerbert (x), closely imitated in the same
century in the *Panegyricus Berengarii* (*c.* 920), and much quoted
in the *Glossarium Osberni* (xii) as well as by Vincent of Beauvais
and Conrad von Mure (xiii). Dante attributes the 'conversion'
of Statius to the perusal of Virgil's *Fourth Eclogue*[8]. It has
been suggested that Statius was possibly credited with an aversion
to idolatry, owing to the lines in the *Thebaid*:—

> 'nulla autem effigies, nulli commissa metallo
> forma dei, mentes habitare et pectora gaudet'[9].

Among the more than 70 MSS of the *Thebais*, the earliest are the
three at Paris, viz two from Corbie, *i.e.* the *codex Puteaneus* (ix)

[1] Gaston Paris, *Litt. Fr. au MA*, § 47.

[2] Dunger, *Die Sage vom trojanischen Kriege*, 46—48.

[3] Manitius in *Philol.* lii 538–45; and in *Mitt.* 8 f (on the *scholia* of 'Lactantius Placidus'); cp. Kohlmann's ed. of Statius, fasc. i 5 f.

[4] *Carmen* 35, *Curre per* Ausoniae *non segnis epistola campos* (*Silv.* iv 4); Manitius in *Philol.* Suppl. vii 762.

[5] O. Müller, *Rhein. Mus.* xviii 189.

[6] Cp. Graf, *Roma* ii 318–21, and Joly, *Benoît de Sainte-More*, ii 317 f.

[7] *Revue Critique*, 1894, i 424.

[8] *Purg.* xxii 66—73.

[9] *Theb.* xii 493, *v. l.* 'deae .

and another (x), and one from Epternach (x); also MSS at
Bamberg (x), Bern (xi) formerly at Fleury, and Leyden (xi)
once at Würzburg.  The MS belonging to St John's College,
Cambridge (x), from the Priory at Dover, and once the property
of the poet Crashaw's brother, is possibly identical with the *codex
Anglicanus* of N. Heinsius[1].  The far fewer MSS of the *Achilleis*
include the above-mentioned *codex Puteaneus* (ix), and those at
Eton (xi), Paris (xii) and Wolfenbüttel (xiv).

The quotations from Martial preserved by the grammarians
from the time of Victorinus, Charisius and Servius,
to that of Priscian and Isidore, prove that he was          **Martial**
well known from the fourth to the sixth centuries.   There are
many reminiscences of his epigrams in Ausonius and in
Apollinaris Sidonius; but it is the variety of his metres, rather
than his vocabulary, that finds an imitator in Luxorius (cent. vi)[2].
The epitaph of a bishop of Seville, who died in 641, ends with a
line from Martial (vii 76, 4) :—'non timet hostiles iam lapis iste
minas '.   The curious name of *Coquus* is given him in certain
ancient Glossaries[3]; also sometimes in John of Salisbury[4], Walter
Map, and Conrad von Mure, and always in Vincent of Beauvais,
who reserves the name of Martial for Gargilius Martialis[5].  Martial
is imitated by Godfrey, Prior of Winchester (d. 1107)[6], and, less
successfully, by Henry of Huntingdon (d. after 1154)[7].

The MSS of Martial fall into three families.   The first includes
MSS (ix—x) at Leyden, Paris (no. 8071) and Vienna, the last of
which was brought from France into Italy by Sannazaro (early in
xvi).   These MSS were copied from a lost MS of century viii—ix.
The second, including a Lucca MS now in Berlin (xii), and a
Heidelberg MS now in the Vatican (xv), also an Arundel MS in

---

[1] A conjecture due to Mr H. W. Garrod, C.C.C., Oxford, who collated it
in 1902; cp. *Cl. Rev.* xviii (1904), 38 f.

[2] Friedländer's *Martial*, p. 68 f.                    [3] *id.* on iii 77.

[4] iv 128, 230, 287 Giles; cp. Manitius, in *Philol.* xlix 560–4, esp. note
on 562.  'Marcialis coquus' is the old title of a MS in C.C.C. Cambridge.

[5] Cp., in general, Schanz, § 415.

[6] Godfrey's Epigrams were even ascribed to Martial.  Wright, *Satirical
Poets*, ii 103 (Gröber, 377, 344).

[7] Wright, ii 162 (Gröber, 378).

the British Museum, formerly in the possession of Pirckheimer
and Thomas Howard, Duke of Norfolk (xv), and a MS in
Florence (xv, Laur. 35, 39)[1], represents the recension made by
Torquatus Gennadius (401). The third (inferior to the first and
second), including a MS in the Advocates' Library at Edinburgh
(x) and a *codex Puteaneus* in Paris (x), is derived from a MS in
Lombard minuscules of century viii or ix. The *Excerpta
Frisingensia*, now in Munich, belong to century xi[2].

The moral earnestness of Juvenal led to his being highly
esteemed in the Middle Ages. According to the
monastic catalogues, his Satires were preserved in
three copies at Bobbio, St Bertin and Rouen, and in two at
Corbie, Bamberg and Durham. Abbot Marleberge (1218)
brought to the monastic library at Evesham a Juvenal, as well as
a Lucan and a Cicero[3]. He is often quoted by Geoffrey of
Monmouth, John of Salisbury, Vincent of Beauvais, and others[4].
The composers of the semi-pagan student-songs of the twelfth
and thirteenth centuries *magis credunt Juvenali, quam doctrinae
prophetali*[5]. His popularity is still further attested by the fact
that (apart from *scholia* of the fourth century) he is the theme of
mediaeval *scholia* bearing the name of Cornutus. A reminiscence
of the Tenth Satire may be noticed in Chaucer's *Troilus and
Creseide*[6] :—

> 'O Juvenal lord, true is thy sentence,
> That little wenen folk what is to yerne'.

The best MS, the *codex Pithoeanus* at Montpellier (cent. ix), which
includes Persius, formerly belonged to the abbey of Lorsch, and
may once have been in that of St Gallen, which still possesses an
important MS of the early *scholia* (ix), almost identical with those
in the margin of the Montpellier MS. There are also early MSS of
Juvenal in the British Museum (ix)[7], two in the library of

---

[1] W. M. Lindsay, *Cl. Rev.* 1901, 413 f; 1902, 315 f.

[2] See Friedländer's ed. pp. 67—108; also W. M. Lindsay's *Ancient
editions of Martial* (1902), and text, 1902. The 'Lucca MS' formerly belonged
to the monastery of S. Maria Corte-Orlandini (in Lucca).

[3] *Chron. Abb. de Evesham*, p. 267 Macray.

[4] Manitius in *Philol.* l 354–68. Cp. Schanz, 11 ii[2] § 420 *a*.

[5] *Anz. f. Kunde d. deutschen Vorzeit*, 1871, 232.          [6] iv 197.

[7] Add. 15,600 (one of 59 MSS); Winstedt, *Cl. Rev.* xvi 40.

Trinity College, Cambridge (x) from St Augustine's, Canterbury, besides those at St Gallen and Einsiedeln, Vienna, Leyden and Paris (x), the last of which once belonged to the abbey of St Furcy at Lagny-sur-Marne. Another Paris MS (xi) was formerly in the abbey of St Martial at Limoges. Two MSS of century xi at Leyden and Florence end with a subscription referring to a recension by Nicaeus, a pupil of Servius[1]. Either Nicaeus or some other grammarian composed the commentary from which our earlier *scholia* are derived ; and a further recension connected with the name of Epicarpius (v ?) is attested in a Paris MS (xi). From a copy of this recension, in which the last sheet was missing, came the revision connected with the later *scholia* bearing the name of 'Cornutus', and this in turn was the origin of the recension by Eric of Auxerre[2], which is the source of all our existing MSS, except the Oxford MS (xi), which has supplied us with additions to the Sixth Satire (1899)[3].

The popularity of Persius is attested by many quotations, especially in Rabanus Maurus, Ratherius of Verona, Gunzo of Novara, and John of Salisbury[4]. His name appears often in mediaeval catalogues of centuries ix—xii[5]. Among the three best MSS are two at Montpellier (ix and ix—x), the latter of which, like the MS in the library of the Canons of St Peter's at Rome (ix), belongs to a recension of 402 A.D. There are also good MSS in Paris (x and xi), and Leyden (x—xi), with two closely connected MSS, both written in England, one in Trinity College, Cambridge (x), and the other in the Bodleian (xi), which was given to the cathedral library of Exeter by bishop Leofric (1050–72).

The only MS of Propertius mentioned in the Middle Ages belonged to France[6]. The only complete MS earlier than century

*Persius*

---

[1] *Legi ego Niceus Romae apud Servium magistrum et emendavi.*

[2] *Heiricus magister* is quoted on ix 37. Cp. Manitius in *Mitt.* 13 f.

[3] S. G. Owen, *Cl. Rev.* xi 402, xix 218 ; Winstedt, *ib.* xiii 201 ; Lindsay, *ib.* xix 462–5 (on Housman's ed. 1905).

[4] Manitius in *Philol.* xlvii 710–20; and in *Mitt.* 14 f ; also *Rhein. Mus.* xlvii Suppl. 52.

[5] He is described as an *aureus auctor* (Gottlieb, *Mitt. Bibliotheken*, p. 12 n. 3, quoted by Schanz, § 384 p. 69[2]).

[6] Manitius in *Rhein. Mus. l.c.*, p. 31 (Schanz, § 290).

xv is that at Wolfenbüttel (xii), formerly at Naples, a MS known
to Politian[1]. Little more than the first book is
MSS of
Propertius,
Tibullus,
Val. Flaccus,
Silius Italicus,
Phaedrus
contained in a Leyden MS (xiv). The earliest
evidence for the text of Tibullus is contained in
certain *Excerpta Parisina* (ix—x) known to Vincent
of Beauvais[2]; later than these are the *Excerpta Frisingensia* (xi) now at Munich; the earliest complete MS, that at Milan
(xiv), was once in the possession of Coluccio Salutati[3]. The text of
Valerius Flaccus rests on the Vatican MS (ix—x) and the MS found
by Poggio at St Gallen (1416) and now known only through copies,
especially Poggio's copy in Madrid and an independent copy at
Queen's College, Oxford[4]. A MS of Silius Italicus is entered in a
catalogue of St Gallen in the ninth century, but otherwise he has
left no trace of his existence from the time of Apollinaris
Sidonius[5] to that of Poggio (1417). The only complete MS of
Phaedrus is the *codex Pithoeanus,* now at Du Mesnil near Mantes
(ix—x). We have to be content with secondary evidence of the
text of its twin-brother, the MS formerly at Rheims, which perished
by fire in 1774.

The fame of Boëthius, the 'last of the Romans', was per-
Boëthius
petuated throughout the whole of the Middle
Ages. He was known not only as the first inspirer
of the great scholastic problem and the translator of certain of
the logical treatises of Aristotle[6], but also as the author of
the *Consolatio,* which is preserved in many MSS (ix—x), was
translated by the Anglo-Norman, Simon de Fraisne (xiii), and by
Jean de Meung and others[7], and was specially familiar to Dante
and to Chaucer. The blended prose and poetry of that work was
not unfrequently imitated, as by Bernard Silvester and by Alain

---

[1] *Miscell.* 23, and 81.      [2] p. 580.

[3] On Tibullus in MA, cp. p. 627 *supra.*

[4] A. C. Clark, *Cl. Rev.* xiii 119—124. On Valerius Flaccus in MA,
cp. Schanz, § 401 p. 116². 'Manilius' similarly 'survived' at Gembloux and
elsewhere (x—xii), awaiting the Renaissance. Cp. H. W. Garrod, *Cl. Q.* iii 56 f.

[5] *Carm.* ix 260. Cp. Schanz, § 405 p. 125².

[6] p. 253 *supra.*

[7] Gaston Paris, *Litt. Fr. au MA,* § 103; *Hist. Litt.* xxviii 408; *Romania,*
ii 271 ; p. 257 *supra.*

de Lille[1]. Its author is named with Terence, Sallust, Cicero, Virgil and Statius, as well as Arator, Prudentius, Sedulius and Juvencus, in a poem combining wide reading with much ignorance of grammar, composed by Winric, master of the cathedral school of Trier in the twelfth century[2].

The principal ancient and 'modern' poets are briefly reviewed as models of style in the third part of Eberhard of Bethune's *Labyrinthus* (1212)[3], where Horace is strangely omitted. A typical list of the authors studied in the schools of the Middle Ages may be found in the rhyming lines of Hugo of Trimberg's *Registrum* (1280)[4], while, in a satire by a monk of Erfurt (1281–3)[5], we have a shorter list, including the grammarians Donatus and Priscian, and the poets Ovid, Juvenal, Terence, Horace, Persius, Plautus, Virgil, Lucan, Maximianus and Boëthius[6]. The library of the abbey of St Edmund at Bury included Plautus, Terence, Horace, Juvenal, Persius, Virgil and Statius[7]. In the absence of all knowledge of the Greek Homer, who 'apud Graecos remanens nondum est translatus'[8], mediaeval students read of the Trojan War in the poem of 'Pindarus Thebanus'[9] and the prose narratives of Dictys and Dares[10]; and the Tale of Troy was the theme of many Latin and vernacular poems in the Middle Ages[11].

[1] This kind of composition was called *prosimetrum* in cent. xii—xiii (Norden, 756).

[2] ed. Kraus (Bursian i 70). On Boëthius, cp. Graf, ii 322—367, and Manitius in *Mitt.* 39 f.

[3] p. 554 *supra*, and Manitius in *Mitt.* xvi 3 (1906), pp. 1—44.

[4] ed. Hümer; cp. Bursian, i 82.

[5] *Nicolai de Bibera Occulti Erfordensis carmen satiricum*, ed. T. Fischer (1870); *c.* 1307, according to Gröber, 403.

[6] Bursian, i 83; Gottlieb, *Mitt. Bibliotheken*, 446. Cp. Joannes de Garlandia's list on p. 550 n. 6.

[7] M. R. James, *Bibl. Buriensis*, 103.            [8] Hugo's *Registrum*, 162.

[9] Quoted by Ermenrich (850) and in the *Gesta Berengarii* (920), and often in later works (Manitius in *Philol.* l 368—72). Cp. Lucian Müller, in *Philol.* xv 475—507; Teuffel, § 320, 7; Schanz, § 394.

[10] Teuffel, §§ 423, 471; and Collilieux, *Dictys et Darès*, and *Deux Éditeurs de Virgile* (Grenoble, 1886–7); also N. E. Griffin (*Dares and Dictys*, 1907).

[11] A. Joly, *Benoît de Sainte-More et le Roman de Troie, ou les métamorphoses d'Homère de l'épopée Gréco-Latine au MA* (*Mém. de la soc. des Ant. de Norm.*

Turning from verse to prose, we find Cicero revered throughout the Middle Ages as the great representative of
the 'liberal art' of Rhetoric. His famous sayings
were collected by Bede; his *De Inventione* was the source of a
short treatise on rhetoric by Alcuin; the *Tusculan Disputations*
were quoted, and the *pro Milone*, the first *Catilinarian* and the
second *Verrine* imitated, by Einhard; while the text of his
*Epistles*, which was not unknown to the Irish monk, Sedulius[1],
was carefully studied by Servatus Lupus[2]. He is 'the king of
eloquence' to Paschasius Radbertus in the ninth century, and to
William of Malmesbury in the twelfth. In the former century
Almannus[3] declares that to celebrate St Helena adequately
would call for an eloquence greater even than that of Cicero.
The knowledge of Cicero exhibited by all the above writers, and
b Rabanus Maurus and Joannes Scotus[4], is far exceeded by that
shown by the presbyter Hadoardus, the *custos* of an unidentified
library in Western Frankland, whose excerpts in a Vatican MS of
century ix include many passages from the *De Oratore*, and
more than 600 from the philosophical works[5]. In the tenth
century Gerbert is specially interested not only in the rhetorical
and philosophical works but also in the speeches, and the
preservation of these last in France is possibly due to his
influence[6]. In the same century the *Letters* existed in the library
at Lorsch, and they were known to Luitprand[7]. Honorius of
Autun (d. 1136), in his treatise *De Animae Exsilio*[8], says that
those who dwell in the 'City of Rhetoric' are taught by Tully to
speak with grace, and are trained by him in the virtues of

xxvii; also printed separately, 1870-1). Benoît was plagiarised by Guido
delle Colonne (p. 545 *supra*), and either or both may have been the source of
Chaucer's *Troilus*. Cp. also Dunger (Dresden, 1869), Körting (Halle, 1874),
Gorra (Turin, 1887), Greif, *die mittelalt. Bearbeitungen der Trojanersage*
(1886); Gaston Paris, *Litt. Fr. au MA*, § 45 ; Ward's *Catalogue of Romances*,
i 1—86; H. Morley, *English Writers*, iii 207-31 ; Morf in *Romania*, 1892 ;
and Gröber, II i 407 f.

[1] Mommsen, *Hermes*, xiii 298.                    [2] p. 488 *supra*.

[3] *Acta SS. Bolland.*, August iii 581 *a*.

[4] P. Schwenke, *Philol.* Suppl. v (1889) 404-9.

[5] Schwenke, *ib.* 397—588 ; Manitius, 478-83.          [6] p. 509 *supra*.

[7] Cic. *Epp.* ed. Mendelssohn, p. vi f.                [8] c. 3, Migne clxxii 1244.

prudence, fortitude, justice and temperance. In the same
century Abelard cites only four of his works, the *De Inventione*
and *Topica*, and the *De Officiis* and *Paradoxa*. Abelard's pupil,
John of Salisbury, knew many more, and (besides being acquainted
with the *Letters*[1]) was specially familiar with the philosophical
treatises, which are also quoted by his friend, Peter of Blois
(d. *c.* 1212). Vincent of Beauvais (d. 1264) and Walter Burley
(d. 1357) give long lists of his works, but there is nothing to
show that the former really knew the *Letters* included in his list.
The latter does not even name them[2]. Meanwhile, in Germany,
Lambert of Hersfeld[3] (*fl.* 1058–77) is familiar with the
*Catilinarians*; Conrad of Hirschau (*c.* 1100), who knew the
*Laelius* and *Cato* alone, is eloquent in praise of their author[4];
and Wibald, abbot of Corvey (1146), whose Letters show an
extensive knowledge of Latin literature, is eager to make a
collection of all the works of Cicero in a single volume[5]. Herbord
of Michelsberg, near Bamberg (d. 1168), quotes whole chapters
of the *De Officiis*[6], and Ethelred of Rievaulx (d. 1166) wrote a
Ciceronian dialogue on Christian friendship. In century xii the
library of Cluni possessed three MSS of the *Letters* and of the
*Speeches*, five of the philosophical and seven of the rhetorical
works[7]. Of the MSS of the *Speeches* one has been identified with a
ninth century MS containing the greater part of the *Catilinarian*

---

[1] Mendelssohn, p. ix.

[2] Orelli's *Cicero*, III[2] x—xi. The *Letters* are there described as unknown
in cent. x—middle of cent. xiv; but we shall see shortly that there were 3 MSS
at Cluni in cent. xii.

[3] ed. Holder-Egger (Norden, *Kunstprosa*, 708).

[4] *Dial. sup. auctores*, 51 (ed. Schepps, 1889), Tullius nobilissimus auctor
iste libros plurimos philosophicos studiosis philosophiae pernecessarios edidit
et vix similem in prosa vel praecedentem vel subsequentem habuit (Norden, *l.c.*).

[5] Jaffé, *Bibl. Rer. Germ.* i 326 (after asking the abbot of Hildesheim for
*Tullii libros* he adds) 'nec pati possumus, quod illud nobile ingenium, illa splen-
dida inventa, illa tanta rerum et verborum ornamenta oblivione et negligentia
depereant; set ipsius opera universa, quantacunque inveniri poterunt, in unum
volumen confici volumus'; and he receives from Hildesheim the *Philippics*,
the *De Lege Agraria* and the *Letters* (Norden, 709; Bursian, i 75).

[6] ii 15, 16, in *Vita Ottonis Episcopi Babenbergensis* (*Mon. Hist. Germ.* xx
706–7).

[7] *Rhet.* (*ad Herennium*, and *de Inventione*), transl. by Jean d'Antioche,
1282 (Delisle, *Notices et Extraits*, xxxvi, 1899).

*Speeches*, and of the *pro rege Deiotaro*, with a portion of the *pro
Ligario* and *Second Verrine*, now in Lord Leicester's collection at
Holkham[1]; another, with the MS discovered by Poggio at Cluni
in 1415[2]. The library of the Sorbonne (1338) has 24 MSS of
the rhetorical and philosophical works, as well as the *Letters*.
The *Speeches* best known in the Middle Ages were those against
Verres, Catiline and Antonius. The rhetoric of attack was
apparently more popular than that of defence. But the latter
was also appreciated. Philip Harcourt, bishop of Bayeux,
bequeathed to Corbie a collection of books including the *pro
Ligario*, *Marcello* and *Deiotaro*, the *De Divinatione*, *Natura
Deorum*, *Legibus* and *Fato*, the *Tusculan Disputations* and '*ad
Hortensium liber I*'[3], probably meaning thereby not the lost
*Hortensius* but the second book of the *Prior Academics*, described
by Vincent of Beauvais[4] as the *Dialogus ad Hortensium*. It may
be remembered that the three speeches above mentioned were
translated by Brunetto Latini (d. 1294)[5]. Dante's references to
Cicero are primarily to the *De Officiis* and *Cato*, secondarily to
the *Laelius* and *De Finibus*, with one or two notices of the *De
Inventione* and *Paradoxa*. The *Laelius* is one of the two books
in which he finds consolation on the death of Beatrice[6].

Among the earlier MSS of Cicero, the most important of the
*codices mutili* of the *De Oratore* and *Orator* is the MS now at
Avranches (ix) formerly in the abbey of Mont-St-Michel. The
*codex mutilis* of the *De Oratore* in the British Museum (ix)
came from the abbey of Cormery, S.E. of Tours; and the
corresponding MS at Erlangen (x) was copied for Gerbert at

---

[1] W. Peterson, *Anecd. Oxon.* ix; *Cl. Rev.* xvi (1902) 322, 401; doubted
by R. Ellis, *ib.* 460; *ib.* xvii (1903) 162 f; xviii (1904) 23 n. Prof. Ellis'
doubts as to the erased library-mark, *de conventu Clun.*, have since been
removed (A. C. Clark, *Anecd. Oxon.* x (1905) p. vii n.).

[2] A. C. Clark, *Anecd. Oxon.* x, p. iii.

[3] Ravaisson, *Les Bibl. de l'Ouest*, p. xi.

[4] *Spec. Doctr.* v 12 (Kayser's *Cic.* xi 56).                    [5] p. 612 *supra*.

[6] E. Moore, *Studies in Dante*, i 258—273. Cp., in general, P. Deschamps,
*Essai Bibliographique sur Cicéron* (1863); de Nolhac, *Pétrarque et l'humanisme*
(1892) 179, n. 4; Graf, *Roma*, ii 259—267; Norden, 708-10 n.; Zielinski,
*Cicero im Wandel der Jahrhunderte*, 1897; J. E. Sandys, *Harvard Lectures*
(1905) 145 f.

Aurillac. The complete text of the above works, and of the *Brutus*, was unknown until 1422. The *Topica* is included in MSS at Einsiedeln (ix) and St Gallen (x). There are important MSS of certain of the *Speeches* in Rome (viii), Milan (ix), Paris (ix), and Munich, viz two from Tegernsee (x, xi) and one from St Peter's, Salzburg (xi); also a MS from Reichenau at Zürich (xi), and a MS from Cluni at Holkham Hall, Norfolk (ix)[1]. The fragmentary palimpsests of Turin (iii? and iv?)[2], Milan and Rome (v?) once belonged to Bobbio; another in the Vatican (iv?) was for a short time at S. Andrea della Valle, near Pompey's theatre[3]. The fragments of the *pro Fonteio* and *in Pisonem*, included in a MS at Cues, have been traced to Sedulius of Liège[4]. The Brussels MS of the *pro Archia* (xi) came from the abbey of Gembloux. For the *Epp. ad Atticum* we have no longer to rely entirely on the transcript in Florence (*Laur.* 49, 18) made for Coluccio Salutati at Milan in 1392, from the MS found by Petrarch at Verona in 1345; there is independent evidence in a few leaves of a MS at Würzburg (xi); also in 6 Italian MSS and two in Paris (xiv—xv)[5]. For the *Epp. ad Familiares* our main authority is another MS (ix—x) in Florence (*Laur.* 49, 9), which was taken from Vercelli to Milan, where it was first heard of in 1389; a transcript of this was made for Salutati (*Laur.* 49, 7)[6], and there is an independent transcript of the two halves of the same original in the British Museum (xii, *Harl.* 2773; and xi, *Harl.* 2682; the latter from Cologne[7]). The first half alone is preserved in a

---

[1] p. 650 *supra*.

[2] Destroyed in the fire of 26 Jan. 1904.

[3] This palimpsest (of the *Verrines*) *possibly* came from Bobbio, but it has not been traced to any earlier owner than Pius II (d. 1464), on the later fortunes of whose MSS cp. E. Piccolomini in *Bolletino Storico Senese*, 1899, fasc. iii (*Cl. Rev.* xvii, 1903, 460). Text first published by Mai (1828), *Cl. Auctores*, ii 390 f, *in Verrem*.

[4] Traube, *Abhandl.* Munich Acad. 1891, p. 367 f. The fragments were published by J. Klein, *Ueber eine HS des Nicolaus von Cues, nebst unge-druckten Fragmenten Ciceronischer Reden* (1866).

[5] C. A. Lehmann (Weidmann, 1892); cp. S. B. Platner, in *A. J. P.* 1899, 290 f; 1900, 420 f; and A. C. Clark, in *Philol.* 1901, 195 f.

[6] Cp. R. F. Leighton in *Trans. Amer. Phil. Assoc.* xxi (1890) 59—87.

[7] The same MS is specially important for the Speeches *pro Milone, Marcello, Ligario* and *Rege Deiotaro* (ed. A. C. Clark, 1900).

Paris MS (xii), formerly in the library of Notre-Dame. The two MSS of the first half had a common origin. The Harleian MS of the second half (xi), together with an Erfurt MS (xii—xiii), and a Palatine MS in the Vatican, formerly at Heidelberg (xv—xvi), form an independent German group, the last at least of the three having probably been copied *c.* 1500 from a lost MS from Lorsch[1]. Among the numerous MSS of the philosophical works are those in Florence (ix?), Rome (ix, x), Vienna (ix), Leyden (ix—xi) and Paris (ix—xii). The Paris MS of the *De Amicitia* (xi) came from the abbey of St Martial at Limoges. There are also MSS of the *De Officiis* at Bern (ix), and in the British Museum (x), and a MS of the *De Senectute* at Zürich (xii); the latter once belonged to Reichenau, but there are earlier MSS in Paris (ix) and Leyden (ix and x). One of the former (ix) came from Tours; one of the latter, from Fleury. Considerable portions of the *De Republica* were published by Mai from a Vatican palimpsest formerly at Bobbio (v)[2].

The best MS of Varro, *De lingua Latina,* is in Florence (xi),
Varro          but an extract from that work is included in a much
earlier miscellaneous MS, now in Paris, which was copied at Monte Cassino about 800 A.D. The text of Varro *De re rustica* (like that of the corresponding work by Cato) depends on a lost MS formerly in the library of San Marco, Florence.

Cato enjoyed the reputation of being the writer of the
'Cato.'          widely popular *Distichs*[3], which, with 'Aesop'
'Aesop'          and Avianus[4], were studied by beginners in the mediaeval schools. The *Distichs* were translated by 'Elie de Winchester', and Everard de Kirkham (xii), and by Adam de Suel (xiii)[5]. Avianus, and a prose version of Phaedrus called *Romulus*, were the sources of many mediaeval fables[6].

---

[1] Mendelssohn, ed. 1893, pp. vi, xxiv; cp. Gurlitt (1896).

[2] For further details as to the MSS of the several speeches and philosophical works, see Teuffel, §§ 179, 183—5, and the current critical editions.

[3] Manitius in *Philol.* li 164—71; and in *Mitt.* 1 f; Graf, *Roma,* ii 268—78; p. 230 n. 7 *supra.*                    [4] Manitius in *Mitt.* 4 f.

[5] Stengel's *Ausg. u. Abhandl.* xlvii (1886); Gaston Paris, *Litt. Fr. au MA,* § 103.

[6] *ib.* §§ 79, 80; also O. Keller, *Gr. Fabel,* in *Jahrb. f. cl. Phil.* Suppl. iv (3) 307—418; and Hervieux, *Les Fabulistes Latins,* 2 vols (1884).

The principal MSS of the elder Seneca are those of century x
in the Vatican, and at Antwerp and Brussels, with
the excerpts at Montpellier, the last of which     Seneca
    the elder
belonged in century xiv to the Benedictine abbey
of St Thierry near Rheims. The best MS of the unabridged text,
that in Brussels, formerly belonged to Nicolas Cusanus, and may
have had a common origin with the MS of the poems of Sedulius;
it has hence been inferred that the preservation of the elder
Seneca's Greek quotations, however inaccurately they have been
transcribed, is probably due to the influence of the Irish monk
of Liège[1].

Seneca the younger was famous as the author of the *Naturales
Quaestiones* and still more as a moralist. He is
called *Seneca morale* by Dante[2], and is quoted by     Seneca the
    younger
writers such as Otto of Freising, Giraldus Cambrensis
and Roger Bacon, oftener than either Cicero or 'Cato'. He was
believed to be a Christian, his 'correspondence with St Paul'[3]
being first mentioned by Jerome, who accepts it as genuine and
includes its supposed author among his *scriptores ecclesiastici*.
Jerome's opinion was followed by John of Salisbury, Vincent of
Beauvais and many others[4]. The 'Palatine' MS of Seneca *De
Beneficiis* and *De Clementia* (ix) came from Lorsch. Of the MSS
of the *Letters*, that at Bamberg (ix) is now the sole authority for
Letters 89—124. The earliest of the MSS of the *Letters* in Paris
(ix, x, xi) probably came from Corbie; there are also MSS in
Florence, Leyden and Oxford (x). The MS of the *Dialogues* in
Milan (xi) was probably copied at Monte Cassino. The *Naturales
Quaestiones* are preserved in MSS at Bamberg, Leyden and
Geneva (xii) and at Montpellier (xiii). The MS of the *Tragedies*
(xi) in the Laurentian Library came from the Convent of San
Marco.

Pliny the elder, whose 'Natural History' exactly suited the
encyclopaedic tastes of the Middle Ages, was widely read in

---

[1] Traube, *Abhandl.* Munich Acad. 1891, p. 356.

[2] *Inf.* iv 141.          [3] Haase's *Seneca*, iii 476—481.

[4] Graf, ii 278—293. Bernard of Clairvaux (*Ep.* 256) borrows a spirited
sentence from Seneca (*Ep.* 20, 7) in urging the reluctant pope, Eugenius III,
to proclaim a new Crusade (1146); Schanz, § 471.

the original, and also in the excerpts of Solinus. In the

mediaeval catalogues he is named nine times in France and in Germany, and only twice in Italy and England. But this gives a very imperfect impression of the care with which he was studied in England. A more convincing proof of the thoroughness of that study may be found in the Northumbrian excerpts now in Bern (viii)[1], and in the fact that Robert of Cricklade, prior of St Frideswide at Oxford, dedicated to Henry II (1154–89) a *Defloratio* consisting of nine books of selections taken from one of the older class of MSS, which has been recently recognised as sometimes supplying us with the only evidence for the true text[2]. The more important of the 200 MSS of Pliny are divided into (1) the incomplete *vetustiores* and (2) the complete *recentiores*. The best of the former is a MS of books xxxii–vii, now at Bamberg (x). Further, there is a palimpsest of parts of books xi—xv, formerly at Reichenau, and now in the Benedictine abbey of St Paul in the E. of Carinthia; a MS of books ii—vi in Leyden (ix) and two in Paris (ix—x). One of the latter (G), and the Vatican MS (D), and a Leyden MS (V), are separate parts of a single MS formerly at Corbie. Even before the Corbie MS had been revised and corrected, it was copied early in century x in another of the MSS now at Leyden (F)[3].

The younger Pliny was little known, being mentioned only

twice in the mediaeval catalogues of Germany, and only thrice in those of France, but his *Letters* are quoted once by Ratherius of Verona[4], and his

---

[1] K. Rück, *Auszüge* (München, 1888); Welzhofer on Bede's quotations, in *Christ-Abhandl.* 1891, 25—41. King John lent a MS of Pliny to the abbot of Reading (Pauli, *Gesch. v. Engl.* iii 486).

[2] K. Rück in *S. Ber.* Munich Acad. 3 Mai 1902, p. 195 f. On quotations from Pliny, see Manitius in *Philol.* xlix 380-4, and *Rhein. Mus.* xlvii, Suppl. 59; on those from Solinus, *ib.* xlvii 562-5. Cp. Detlefsen, *ib.* xxviii 296 f, and Rück, *S. Ber.* Munich Acad. 1898, 203—318; also Schanz, § 494, p. 382[2]. Robert of Cricklade became prior in 1130 or 1141, and visited Italy and Sicily in 1158-9. In his dedication he addresses Henry II in the words : *es in liberali scientia studiosus.*

[3] *Facsimiles* of G, V, F in Chatelain, *Pal.* pl. 140-2.

[4] Migne, cxxxvi 391 (*Ep.* i 5, 16); Manitius, *Philol.* xlvii 566 f.

*Panegyric* by John of Salisbury[1], while Walter Map even knows
of Pliny's wife, Calpurnia[2]. For the *Letters* we have to depend
mainly on the Medicean MS (ix) consisting of the first 17 quires
of the sole MS of the early books of Tacitus' *Annals*. This MS
of the *Letters* was transcribed (probably before it left Germany) in
a MS now at Prague (xiv). The Vatican MS of books i—iv (x)
was copied from the same original as the Medicean. For the
latter part of book ix we depend partly on a Dresden MS (xv),
one of a class containing eight books in all, but omitting book viii;
the date of the oldest of this class, now at Monte Cassino, is 1429.
There is also a third class of MSS including only 100 Letters.
This is represented by Florence MSS from the Riccardi palace
(ix—x) and from San Marco (x—xi). It was MSS of this class
alone that were known to Vincent of Beauvais[3] and to Coluccio
Salutati, the first Italian who mentions the *Letters*[4]. For most of
the *Correspondence with Trajan* we have now no MSS[5]. The
*Panegyricus* is preserved only in MSS of the ' Panegyrici ' copied
from a lost MS formerly at Mainz (xv), and in three leaves of a
palimpsest from Bobbio (vii—viii).

The *Declamations* (or Causae) ascribed to Quintilian are alone
mentioned by Trebellius Pollio and by Lactantius.      Quintilian
There is evidence of a recension *c.* 500 A.D.   They
were abridged by Adelard of Bath (1130)[6], and their study lasted
through the Middle Ages down to the time of Petrarch (1350)[7].
His genuine *Institutio Oratoria* is described by Jerome as the
model followed by Hilary of Poitiers (d. 367), and it was also
studied by Rufinus and Cassiodorus, by Julius Victor and Isidore
of Seville. It was known to Lupus of Ferrières and Wibald of
Corvey[8]; to Bernard of Chartres, to John of Salisbury and to
Peter of Blois (xii), and, in the next century, to Vincent of

---

[1] Schaarschmidt, 95.

[2] p. 28 l. 182 Wright.   ' Plinium Calpurniae succendit scintilla '.

[3] *Spec. Hist.* x c. 67.   The MS from the Riccardi palace was formerly in
the chapter library at Beauvais.

[4] Plin. *Epp.*, ed. Keil, p. xvi.

[5] The MS discovered in Paris by Fra Giocondo, *c.* 1500, is lost.   Cp.
E. G. Hardy in *Journal of Philology*, xvii (1888) 95—108 ; and ed. 1889.

[6] *Catal. Bibl. Leiden* (1716), p. 383.

[7] *Ep. Fam.* xxiv 7.              [8] *Ep.* 167 Jaffé, *Mon. Corb.*

Beauvais[1]. Meanwhile, among the books bequeathed to the abbey of Bec by Philip Harcourt, bishop of Bayeux (1164), there was a MS of the *Institutio Oratoria*. This MS was copied in the same century by the poet Étienne de Rouen in an abstract extending to about a third of the ten books therein condensed. This abstract passed from Bec to the abbey of Saint-Germain-des-Prés, and, under the name of the *codex Pratensis* (xii), it is now in the Paris Library[2]. Harcourt's MS, which is now lost, was also copied in the *codex Puteaneus* (xiii) in the same collection. The principal MSS fall into three classes:—(1) represented only by the *First Ambrosian* at Milan (x—xi), consisting of three-fourths of a transcript of a complete MS which has disappeared[3]; (2) the MS at Bern, formerly at Fleury[4], which has been copied in the *Second Ambrosian*[5], and an independent Paris MS of the same class, formerly in Notre-Dame[6], all three belonging to century x, and all marked by many *lacunae* small or great; (3) the mixed MSS, primarily represented by that at Bamberg, which consists of two parts, the first (x) having been copied from the defective MS at Bern, and the second from a complete MS of class (1) now lost. Early in century xi, while this second part was being added to the Bamberg MS, the latter was itself copied in an exceptionally important MS, which was taken to Cologne[7] and afterwards to Düsseldorf, and is now in the British Museum (*Harl.* 2664)[8]. Of this Harleian MS there are two transcripts of special interest, both belonging to century xi. The earlier of these is now at Florence, the later at Zürich. The former owner of the first, Werner (*Werinharius*), bishop of Strassburg (1001–29), attended the Council of Frankfort in 1006 and interested himself in the

---

[1] Orelli-Baiter, *Cic.* III[2] viii f; Quintil. I, ed. Fierville (1890) xiv—xvi. Cp. Schanz, § 486 *a*.

[2] Fierville, xxviii f, and *facsimile* ad fin.

[3] *Facsimile* in Chatelain, *Pal.* pl. 174–5.        [4] *ib.* 179 (1).

[5] *ib.* 179 (2).

[6] Akin to this is a MS in the library of St John's Coll. Camb. (xiii). Petrarch's copy (xiv), now in Paris (7720), is a direct or indirect transcript of the *cod. Bernensis*.

[7] A. C. Clark, in *Neue Heidelb. Jahrb.* 1891, p. 238 f.

[8] L. C. Purser in *Hermathena*, 1886, p. 39; Peterson, on Quintil. x, p. lxiv, with *facsimile*; also in Chatelain, pl. 176.

erection of the cathedral at Bamberg[1]. He may thus have been
led to acquire a transcript of the Cologne copy of the Bamberg
MS. He certainly gave to the library of Strassburg Cathedral in
or before 1029 a MS of Quintilian, which has been identified as a
transcript of the Cologne MS. In 1372 this copy was one of the
chained books in the monastic dormitory at Strassburg; afterwards
(with a Strassburg MS of Cicero's philosophical works[2]) it found its
way into the Medicean Library in Florence, where it is still to be
seen[3]. It was supposed by Raphaël Regius (1491)[4] to be the
MS found by Poggio at St Gallen (1416). But, although Poggio
made a hasty copy of the MS at Constance[5], there is nothing to
prove that he did not return the original to St Gallen[6]. That
original is probably the slightly later copy of the Cologne
manuscript, a copy which was certainly once at St Gallen and
has been at Zürich since the early part of cent. xviii[7]. Some of
the quires show Italian memoranda giving the number of lines
(*rige*) contained in the page[8].

Cornelius Nepos, Caesar, Sallust, Livy, Suetonius, Justin and
Florus were much studied in the Middle Ages,        Historians.
and a special popularity attended the historical     Cornelius
anecdotes of Valerius Maximus. The history of       Nepos
the text of Cornelius Nepos goes back to the time of Theodosius

---

[1] *Gallia Christiana*, v 792–4, ed. 1731.

[2] San Marco 257 (in Laur.); Ebeling, in *Philol.* xliii 705 f; Chatelain,
pl. 37.

[3] *Laur.* 46, 7 (examined at Florence). *Facsimile* on p. 215; Chatelain,
pl. 177.

[4] ap. Bandini, *Cat.* ii 382.

[5] Poggio to Guarino, 16 Dec. 1416, haec mea manu transcripsi.

[6] Cp. Reifferscheid, *Rhein. Mus.* 1868, 145.

[7] It was regarded by Mabillon (1673), *It. Germ.* 36, as the MS found by
Poggio. Sabbadini, *Riv. di Filol.* xx, 1892, 307 f, cites a letter of Guarino
to Poggio (early in 1418) mentioning a *second* complete MS as in Poggio's
possession, which Sabbadini regards as identical with the Florence MS
formerly at Strassburg, while he does not admit that the *first* MS found by
Poggio is that at Zürich. The controversy might be settled by examining
*codex Urbinas* 327 (577), which purports to be a copy of Poggio's transcript of
the original.

[8] Letter-press to Chatelain's pl. 178. See, in general, Peterson's *Introd.* to
Quint. X, pp. lviii—lxxv, and lit. there quoted.

II (d. 450)[1]. One of the best MSS, the *liber Danielis* (now lost),
came from a library at or near Orleans. The extant MSS include
the *codex Gudianus* (xii—xiii) at Wolfenbüttel, and the sole
survivor of a better class of MSS, the MS at Louvain (xv),
formerly in the neighbouring Premonstratensian abbey of Parc[2].

Caesar is often quoted in the *Gesta Treverorum*. Like Livy
and Eutropius, he is known to Flodoard[3]. A life of
Caesar, mainly founded on Sallust, Caesar, Lucan,
and Suetonius, was included, under the title of the *Faits des
Romains*, in many MSS of the *Livre des Histoires* (*c.* 1225)[4].
During the Middle Ages, and even in the pages of Petrarch, the
author of the *Gallic War* is constantly called Julius Celsus, the
name of a reviser of the text mentioned in the *subscriptiones* to
the MSS of that work. In the mediaeval catalogues (except in
those of France) he is one of the rarer authors[5]. Among the best
MSS now extant are an Amsterdam MS (ix—x); two Paris MSS,
from Fleury (ix—x) and Moissac (xi—xii), which are better than
the interpolated *codex Thuaneus* (xi—xii); and a Vatican MS (x)
corresponding to that from Fleury. Besides these there are MSS
in the British Museum and at Leyden (xi), the latter from
Beauvais, which is probably the former home of one of the two
Florence MSS (xi); there are also MSS in the Vatican and in
Vienna (xii).

The writer of a Pelagian letter (*c.* 410–30) protests against the
study of Virgil, Sallust, Terence and Cicero, *et caeteros stultitiae et
perditionis auctores*[6]; and a school-book belonging to the latter
part of the previous century contains quotations from each of these
four writers in the above-mentioned order[7]. Sallust
was imitated by Sulpicius Severus, and (together
with Virgil and Cicero) by Ambrose; and the *Bellum Catilinae*[8]

**Caesar**

**Sallust**

---

[1] Traube, *S. Ber.* Munich Acad. 1891, 409–25; Hülsen, in *Hermes*, xxviii.
[2] On mediaeval quotations, see Manitius, *Philol.* xlvii 567 f.
[3] *Hist. Rem.* i 1 (Gröber, 121).
[4] Gaston Paris, *Litt. Fr. au MA*, p. 139.
[5] Manitius, *Rhein. Mus.* xlviii; *Philol.* xlviii 567 f.
[6] Caspari, *Briefe &c.* (1890), p. 17.
[7] Keil, *Gr. Lat.* vii 449.
[8] 37, 5, sicut in sentinam confluxerant.

was even quoted by Leo the Great[1]. The last to study the *Histories* at first-hand was Augustine (d. 425)[2]; later writers borrowed their quotations from Priscian and Isidore; but a new interest in Sallust was awakened in century viii[3]. His *Jugurtha* was known to the compiler of the Annals of Fulda (875)[4]. In the latter half of century x his phraseology is reproduced by Richer of Rheims, and also by Ragevinus, in his continuation (1160) of Otto of Freising's history of Barbarossa[5]. Among the many MSS of the *Bella* are three in Paris (two of cent. ix, and one of xi). A *lacuna* in these has to be supplied from later MSS, including several at Munich (xi etc.), and a Paris MS (xi) from Epternach. There is also a MS at St Gallen (xi), and one in Brussels (xi) from the church at Egmont[6]. The Speeches in the *Bella* and in the *Histories* are contained in the Vatican excerpts from Corbie (x), and fragments of the *Histories*[7] in four leaves of a MS divided between the Vatican, Berlin and Orleans (iv—v), which probably came from Fleury.

The great work of Livy was originally in 142 books, of which only 35 (viz. books 1—10 and 21—45) have survived. An abridgement is mentioned by Martial[8]. Part of an abstract of books 48—55 has been found at Oxyrhynchus[9]. An epitome was the source of the collection of prodigies made by Julius Obsequens (vii). A summary of the contents of the lost books is preserved in the *Periochae*, best represented by a MS at Heidelberg (ix), and we have direct quotations from or vague references to the lost books in Asconius, Tacitus, Frontinus; in Plutarch and Dion Cassius; in Servius and Censorinus; and in Priscian and Cassiodorus; also in the Bernese *scholia* on Lucan. Thus the whole of Livy appears to

*Livy.*
*Florus*

---

[1] *Sermo*, xvi 4 (Weyman, in *Philol.* lv 471-3).

[2] Sallust was a favourite model with African writers of cent. ii—v (Monceau, *Les Africains*, 1894, 86—90); also with 'Dictys', 'Hegesippus', Sulpicius Severus, and Julius Exuperantius (Schanz, § 133).

[3] Vogel, *Quaest. Sall.* Erlangen, 1881, pp. 426-32.

[4] Gröber, II i 121.

[5] Bursian, i 76. He is also imitated by Widukind and Adam of Bremen.

[6] Cp., in general, Maurenbrecher, in Bursian's *Jahresb.* ci 189—206.

[7] Hauler, in *Wiener Studien*, 1887, 25 f; ed. Maurenbrecher, 1891-3.

[8] xiv 190.　　　　　　[9] *Oxyr. Papyri*, iv (1904) 90—116.

have survived to the end of the Roman Age, but the books
known to the Middle Ages[1] were the same as those known to
ourselves, and the rumours of the survival of a complete Livy at
some place in the diocese of Lübeck, which were rife in the times
of the Renaissance[2], remained unconfirmed.    The style of Livy
was imitated by Einhard[3], and, with greater freedom, by Lambert
of Hersfeld[4].   His work was first translated into French by the
Dominican Pierre Bersuire at the request of king John III
(d. 1341)[5].

For books of the *first decade* the earliest authority, and the
only representative of the earlier of the two recensions, is the
Verona palimpsest of books 3—6 (v).   All the ten books were
included in the later recension by Victorianus, and books 3—8
were further revised by one or other of the two Nicomachi[6], both
of whom held office at Rome in 431.   This recension is best
represented by the Medicean MS (x—xi)[7], next to which comes a
MS from the Colbert collection in Paris (x), besides one from
Fleury (ix—x), and others at Einsiedeln, and in the British
Museum and the Vatican (x), and also in Florence and Leyden
(xi)[8]   Similarly we have two recensions of the *third decade*, one
of which is best represented by the Paris MS, *codex Puteaneus* (v)
from Corbie, and its Vatican copy, *codex Reginensis* (ix, c. 804–34)
from Tours[9], and by a Florence MS (x); the other, by a Turin
palimpsest (v)[10] and by MSS nearly related to the lost MS of Speier.
The text of the *fourth decade* depends on a Bamberg MS (xi) and
on the recorded readings of the lost MS of Mainz; and that of the
first five books of the *fifth decade*, on a Vienna MS (v) from Lorsch,
which in century viii belonged to the bishop of a place near

---

[1] Manitius, *Philol.* xlviii 570-2.           [2] Voigt, *Humanismus*, i 247³ f

[3] Manitius, in *Neues Archiv*, 1882, 523, and 1886, 67.

[4] *Ann.* p. 71 f, cp. Liv. ii 6; Manitius, in *Neues Archiv*, 1886, 376
(Schanz, § 327, p. 269²).

[5] Le Clerc, *Hist. Litt.* 431, 499.

[6] p. 228 *supra*.                       [7] *Facsimile* on p. 250 *supra*.

[8] On the Medicean MS, and the Leyden MS L, see *Proc. Camb. Philol. Soc*
30.Oct. 1902.

[9] Châtelain, in *Rev. de Philol.* xiv (1890) 78 f; *Paléographie*, pl. cxvi f
Traube, *S. Ber.* Munich Acad. 1891, 425 f.

[10] Destroyed by fire in 1904.

Utrecht.  The epitome of Livy by Florus is preserved in an uninterpolated form in a MS at Bamberg (ix).  Suetonius was successfully imitated by Einhard (830), who was educated at Fulda[1].  Servatus Lupus, who could find no MS of Suetonius in France, borrowed the Fulda MS (*c.* 850), and at the close of the same century a MS of Suetonius was copied at Tours.  This copy still exists in Paris under the name of the *codex Memmianus* (ix), the best that has come down to us[2].  While Eric of Auxerre made extracts from Suetonius and Valerius Maximus at the suggestion of Servatus Lupus, Sedulius of Liège had already been culling excerpts from Valerius and Vegetius[3].  Valerius is represented by MSS at Bern (ix) and Florence (x), the former from Fleury, the latter from the abbey of Malmédy-Stavelot near Liège[4]; also by the Vatican MS (ix) of the abridgement by Julius Paris (late iv).  This MS of the abridgement, which came from Fleury, and the Bern MS of the original belong to a Ravenna recension by Domnulus (v)[5].

Suetonius.
Val. Maximus

Vegetius, *De Re Militari*, was much studied during the wars of the ninth century.  An abridged excerpt of part of the work was made by Rabanus Maurus[6], and a set of elegiacs was written by Sedulius to accompany the gift of a MS from bishop Hartgarius to Eberhardus[7].  The prose translation by Jean de Meung (1284) was rendered in verse by Jean Priorat of Besançon (1290)[8].  The extant MSS fall into two classes, best represented by a MS in Paris and a Palatine MS in the Vatican (x), the former belonging to the recension of Eutropius (450).  The MSS of Justin, who was a favourite model for historical

Vegetius.
Justin.
Q. Curtius

[1] See also Schanz, § 536, p. 66[2].

[2] *ib.* § 530, p. 52[2]; and Traube, in *Neues Archiv*, 1902, 266.

[3] MS C 14 at Cues on the Mosel (including fragments of Cic. *in Pisonem* and *pro Fonteio*).  Cp. Traube, *Abhandl.* Munich Acad. 1891, 366—72.

[4] Cp. Wibald (of Stavelot and Corvey), c. 1150, in *Bibl. Rer. Germ.* i 280.

[5] Brandes, *Wiener Studien*, 1890, 297 f; Traube, *S. Ber.* Munich Acad. 1891, 387—400.

[6] *Mon. Germ.*, *Epp.* v 515, 619; *Zeitschr. für deutsches Altertum*, xv (1872) 443.

[7] *Poëtae Lat. Aevi Car.* iii 212 Traube.

[8] *Hist. Litt.* xxviii 398; Gaston Paris, *Litt. Fr. au MA*, § 102.

composition[1], similarly fall into two groups, the first represented
only by a MS in Florence (xi), the second including a MS at
St Gallen (ix—x), a St Denis MS in Paris (ix), and a Fleury MS
at Leyden (ix—x). Quintus Curtius, the imitator of Livy and
Seneca, was studied by Einhard and Servatus Lupus and others
in the Middle Ages[2]. The earlier MSS (ix—xi) include those
in Leyden (ix, x), Paris and Bern (ix) and fragments at
Einsiedeln (x).

In the mediaeval catalogues there is no certain trace of Tacitus.

Tacitus
Reminiscences of the *Germania* and the *Histories*
have been detected in Einhard, and of the *Annals*
in a single passage of Rudolf's annals of Fulda (852)[3], while the
*Germania* is the source of the same writer's description of the
Saxons[4], and of the epigram in Guibert of Nogent (d. 1124):—
*modernum hoc saeculum corrumpitur et corrumpit*[5]. William of
Malmesbury supplies a remarkably close parallel to a passage in
the *Histories*[6], and Peter of Blois professes to have frequently
referred to that work[7]. Books i—vi of the *Annals* have survived
only in the Medicean MS (ix), found in 1509[8] and supposed to
have come from one of the monasteries of Northern Germany,

---

[1] F. Rühl, *Die Verbreitung des Justinus im MA* (1871); known to Regino
(892).

[2] Eussner, in *Philologus*, xxxii (1873) 162; Manitius, in *Neues Archiv*, 1882,
527; Dosson, *Étude*, 360 (Schanz, § 426, p. 209 f).

[3] Pertz, *Mon.* i 368, super amnem quem Cornelius Tacitus [*Ann.* ii 9—17]
scriptor rerum a Romanis in ea gente gestarum Visurgim, moderni vero
Wisahara vocant.

[4] *Mon.* ii 675 f [*Germ.* 4, 5, 10, 11].

[5] Migne, clvi 858 (G. Meier's *Sieben Freien Künste*, i 19); Tac. *Germ.* 19,
nec corrumpere et corrumpi saeculum vocatur.

[6] ii 73, vix credibile memoratu est quantum...adoleverit; cp. *Gesta Regum
Angl.* c. 68, incredibile quantum brevi adoleverit (Manitius, *Philol.* xlvii 566).
Apart, however, from *adoleverit*, both historians may have been imitating
Sallust, *Cat.* 7, incredibile memoratu est...quantum brevi creverit; and even
*brevi adoleverit* may have been suggested to the English historian by Sallust,
who has *brevi adolevit* in *Jug.* 11 and 63.

[7] *Ep.* 101, quoted *supra*, p. 543 n. 4. Cp., in general, E. Cornelius, *Quomodo
Tacitus...in hominum memoria versatus sit usque ad renascentes litteras* (1888),
where Widukind and the author of the Life of Henry IV are credited with a
knowledge of Tacitus; also Manitius, *Philol.* xlvii 565 i.

[8] Soderini *Ep.*, quoted by Urlichs, *Eos*, i 244.

most probably Corvey[1] ; *Annals* xi—xvi and *Histories* i—v, solely
in another Medicean MS (xi), 'found' in 1427, which is written in
'Lombard' characters and was possibly copied at Monte Cassino[2].
The extant MSS of the *Dialogus, Germania,* and *Agricola* are all of
century xv, with the exception of a MS of the *Agricola* and
*Germania* discovered in 1902 in a private library at Jesi near
Ancona, which includes eight leaves of the *Agricola* from the
Hersfeld MS (x) first discovered in 1455[3].

The poem on the Civil War contained in the *Satires* of
Petronius[4] was known to Eric of Auxerre[5]. It is
possibly Eric's MS of excerpts from the *Satires* that        Petronius
was once at Auxerre[6] and is now at Bern (ix—x). Two leaves
at Leyden belong to the same MS. There are also two MSS in
Paris (xii, xv), the second of which (the only authority for the
*Cena Trimalchionis*) was found at Trau in Dalmatia. Fuller
excerpts than those in the Bern MS were copied by Scaliger,
Tornaesius and Pithoeus from MSS which have since vanished.

A favourable impression of the extent to which the ancient
historians were sometimes studied is conveyed by Radulfus de
Diceto, dean of St Paul's (d. 1202)[7], who gives a dated list of the
historical authorities followed in his *Abbreviationes Chronicorum*,
beginning with 'Trogus Pompeius' and Valerius Maximus, while
he quotes, in his own work, authors such as Caesar, Suetonius,

---

[1] *Ep. Leonis X*, 1 Dec. 1517; Tac., ed. Beatus Rhenanus 1533; *Philol.*
xlv 376–80; Hüffer, *Korveier Studien*, 1898, 14. The MS was ascribed to
Fulda in Ritter's Tacitus, p. xxxvii f (refuted by Urlichs, *Eos*, i 243 f, ii 224 f);
and to Lübeck by Voigt, *Humanismus*, i 253[3] (corrected in *Neue Jahrb.* 1881,
423, 805, and in *Curtius-Aufsätze*, 333). Cp. Sabbadini, *Scoperte*, ii 254.

[2] *Chron. Cass.* iii 63 ; possibly copied *c.* 1053–87 in the time of Desiderius.
The MS was known to Boccaccio in 1370 (d. 1375), cp. *Rhein. Mus.* 1848, 145,
and Voigt, i 250[3]; complete *facsimile* of both MSS, Leyden, 1902.

[3] Sabbadini, *Scoperte*, 142; cp. F. Ramorino, in *Atti del congresso inter-
nazionale di scienze storiche*, Roma, 1905, ii 230–2, with *facsimile* of one of
the eight leaves; paper by Cesare Annibaldi, 1907, and ed. of *Germ.* and *Agr.*
Turin, 1916.                                          [4] §§ 119—124.

[5] *Vita S. Germani*, i 109—113, v 207, 229; cp. Traube's *Poetae Latini*,
iii 424.

[6] Usener, in *Rhein. Mus.* xxii (1867) 413 f; not in Eric's hand, says
Traube, iii 822. See also Schanz, § 398 p. 110.

[7] ed. Stubbs (1876).

Solinus, Florus, Apuleius, Virgil, Lucan, Martial, Statius, Claudian
and Vegetius[1]. But, in the Middle Ages as a whole, we find an
ignorance of ancient history in general, and even of the history of
philosophy and literature[2]. Geoffrey of Waterford (d. 1300)
translated not only the history of Eutropius, but also the fabulous
narrative of Dares, which was rendered in French by Jean de
Flixicourt (*c.* 1250)[3]. Historical studies were entangled with
strange versions of the tale of Troy[4] and fabulous stories of
Alexander the Great[5], while the wildest legends gathered round
the names of Aristotle[6] and of Virgil[7]. The fables of mythology,
again, were either denounced as diabolical inventions or forced
to minister to edification with the aid of allegory. The direct
study of classical authors was largely superseded by the use of
encyclopaedic compilations[8], such as those of Isidore and
Rabanus, of William de Conches and Honorius d'Autun, the
*Floridum* of Lambert (*c.* 1120), the *Image du Monde* of Gautier
de Metz (1245)[9], the versified *Mappemonde* of Pierre (cent. xiii),
founded on Solinus[10], the *Specula* of Vincent of Beauvais (d. 1264),
and the nineteen books *De proprietatibus rerum* of the English
Franciscan, Bartholomew (*fl.* 1230—50), whose knowledge of
Geography is derived solely from the Bible and from Pliny,
Orosius and Isidore, with the commentaries on the same. His
quotations from Aristotle are always taken from the Latin trans-

---

[1] Gottlieb, *Mitt. Bibl.*, p. 447 f.

[2] Cp., in general, B. Lasch, *Das Erwachen u. das Entwickelung der hist.
Kritik im MA* (1887).

[3] Gaston Paris, *Litt. Fr. au MA*, § 95.

[4] p. 647 *supra*, n. 11.

[5] P. Meyer, *Bibl. franç. du MA*, t. iv—v (1886); Gaston Paris, *Litt. Fr.
au MA*, § 44; Steinschneider, *Hebr. Uebersetz.* 894 n. 261; H. Morley,
*English Writers*, iii 286—303; Krumbacher, 849; Ausfeld, *Der gr. Alexander-
roman*, 1907; Manitius, 529—31.

[6] Gidel, *Nouvelles Études*, 331—384; Hertz, *Abhandl.* Munich Acad.
1892, 1—104.          [7] Comparetti, *Virgilio*, ii.

[8] Haase, *De Medii Aevi Studiis Philol.* (1856), pp. 4—6; Liliencron's
*Festrede* (1876); and Norden, 740 note 1.

[9] In French verse, *Notices et Extraits*, v 243—66; *Hist. Litt.* xxiii 221;
*Romania*, xv 314, 643.

[10] *Notices et Extraits*, xxxiii (1) 9—48; Gaston Paris, *Litt. Fr. au MA*,
§ 101.

lations of the *Arabic* versions[1]. The *Reductorium Morale* of Pierre Bersuire (d. 1362) was of the same encyclopaedic type as the above productions[2].

The classical learning of the Middle Ages was largely derived second-hand, not only from comprehensive en- cyclopaedias, but also from books of elegant extracts or *florilegia*; and, even if the student never attained to the reading of the authors themselves, he at least went through a protracted course of Latin Grammar. Early in the Middle Ages the vast compilation of Priscian was succeeded by the minor manuals of Cassiodorus and Isidore, of Aldhelm and Bede. All of these treated Grammar in a sober and serious spirit; it was reserved for the eccentric sciolist, who called himself 'Virgilius Maro' (cent. vi—vii), to invent new words at his own caprice[3] and to justify their existence by fabricating quotations which imposed upon his successors. After the eighth century the history of Grammar falls into two periods, (1) from the age of Alcuin to that of Abelard (centuries ix—xi), and (2) from the age of Abelard to the Renaissance (centuries xii—xiv). In the first period the authorities mainly followed are Donatus and Priscian. The few examples of texts quoted in illustration of grammatical rules are all borrowed from earlier grammars. Little of Greek is known except the letters; but, in the MSS of writers on grammar, while the orthography of Greek words is in general correct (the words being written in capitals, and without accents), there is no knowledge of Greek Accidence. Donatus has in the meantime been converted into a catechism (*Donatus minor*), and the most popular text-book is the commentary on that catechism by Remigius of Auxerre (d. 908)[4]. A superstitious respect for a standard grammatical text, an ignorance of Greek and of classical

---

[1] *Hist. An., Meteor., De Caelo et Mundo*; Jourdain, 359. The original Latin of Bartholomew was printed in 1470-2, and Trevisa's English version (of 1398) in 1495 &c. Extracts are given in Steele's *Mediaeval Lore* (1893; also in the 'King's Classics', 1905). On similar treatises, cp. *Hist. Litt.* xxx 334—388.

[2] Hallam, *Lit.* i 117-9[4]; *Bibl. de l'école des chartes*, xxxii 325 f; Hauréau, *Mém. de l'Acad. des Inscr.* xxx (2) 45—55.

[3] Cp. p. 450 *supra*.                                    [4] p. 496 n. 4 *supra*.

antiquity in general, a disposition to reason *about* grammatical
facts instead of studying the facts themselves, a preference for
ecclesiastical as compared with classical usage, are among the
main characteristics of the first period. All these reappear in an
exaggerated form in the second ; but, in the latter, we find Logic
intruding into the sphere of Grammar, asserting itself first in the
early part of the twelfth century and still more strongly in the
thirteenth[1]. Although the study of Logic spread over all Europe,
the general trend of grammatical studies in Italy and in France,
south of the Loire, is different from that north of that river
and in lands under the educational influence of Northern France,
such as England, Flanders and Germany. In Italy and in
Southern France the study of Logic, combined with that of
Grammar, is subordinate to that of Law ; and Grammar is
cultivated solely for the practical purpose of enabling the student
to speak and write Latin with correctness. The most popular
lexicons of the Middle Ages were produced by Italians. Papias[2]
(1053) is a Lombard ; Hugutio[3] (*fl.* 1192, d. 1212) and Balbi[4]

---

[1] 'Cupio per auxilium dialecticae grammaticam adiuvare', the student's
reply to Buoncompagno's warning against the neglect of Grammar (cent. xii),
cp. Thurot, *Notices et Extraits*, xxii (2) 90. The following comparison is
ascribed to Albertus Magnus (cent. xiii) : ' sicut se habet stultus ad sapientem,
sic se habet grammaticus ignorans logicam ad peritum in logica '. The *glosa
notabilis* on Alexander of Villedieu by Gerhard of Zutphen (Cologne, 1488)
applies all the precision of Scholasticism to points of Syntax (Alexander, ed.
Reichling, pp. xii, lxiv f).

[2] p. 521 *supra*.

[3] Of Papias and Hugutio Roger Bacon said, *nesciverunt Graecum* (p. 557
*supra*) ; Ducange, *Praef.* §§ 44, 46 ; Haase, *De Medii Aevi Studiis Philologicis*,
31–3 ; Charles, *Roger Bacon*, 330, 359. Cp. A. Scheler, *Lexicogr. Lat.* (1867);
S. Berger, *De glossariis...medii aevi* (Paris, 1879) ; Salvioli in *Rivista Europea*,
xiv (1880) 745 f; G. Meier, *Die Sieben Freien Künste*, i 17 ; and Eckstein, *Lat.
u. Gr. Unterricht* (1887) 53 f. Hugutio, s.v. *cera*, after showing that the
second syllable of *sincerus* is long, severely adds that, if in any verse that
syllable is made short, *abradatur cum suo auctore de libro vitae et cum justis
non scribatur*. For *sincēris*, cp. Charisius in Keil's *Gr. Lat.* i 81, 218 ;
Hagen, *Anecd. Helv.* ccl ; and Eberhard, *Graecismus* (c. xiii), 71–4.

[4] On Balbi (*Joannes Januensis*), see p. 606 *supra* ; Ducange, § 47 ; and
Haase, 34 f. He explains *laicus* 'i.e. *popularis*, et dicitur a *laos*, quod est
*populus*, vel potius a *laos*, quod est *lapis*; inde *laicus* est *lapideus*, quia durus
et extraneus est a scientia literarum '. Hugutio and Balbi are among the

(1286) are of Pisa and Genoa respectively. The biblical glossary
called the *Mammotrectus* (μαμμόθρεπτος) is ascribed to Marchesini
of Reggio (*c.* 1300).

In the second period the chief authorities on Grammar are
men of Northern Europe who have studied in Paris. Petrus
Helias, the author of a commentary on Priscian, is a Frenchman
who taught in Paris (*c.* 1142). Alexander of Villedieu, the
composer of a hexameter poem, in 2645 lines, on (1) Accidence,
(2) Syntax, and (3) Prosody, Accentuation and Figures of Speech,
compiled from Priscian, Donatus, Petrus Riga, and possibly also
from unknown grammarians of the twelfth century, is a native of
Normandy (1200)[1]. Flanders is the native land of his contemporary, Eberhard of Bethune (1212), the author of a poem on
Grammar, written in hexameters interspersed with elegiacs, which
owes its name of *Graecismus* to the fact that it includes a chapter
on derivations from the Greek[2]. Flanders also claims Michael
' Modista ' of Marbais (cent. xiii), the writer of a treatise *De Modis
Significandi*, who actually invokes the authority of Aristotle for the
simple statement that one cannot give to another that which one
has not got oneself[3]. Lastly, we find two Englishmen, the first
of whom is Joannes de Garlandia (*fl.* 1204–52), who was known
to Roger Bacon[4], and left behind him about fourteen works on

sources of the *Promptorium Parvulorum* (1440), ascribed to the Dominican
Geoffrey of Lynn. Mai, *Class. Auct.* viii, prints a French *thesaurus novus
latinitatis* (cent. xii). Cp. Gröber, II i 251.

[1] ed. Reichling in *Mon. Germ. Paed.* XII (1893), date, p. xxxvi f; authorities,
pp. lxxvi—ix ; 250 MSS (1259—1526), and *c.* 300 printed editions (1470—1588).
Cp. Haase, 17, 45 (where the clearness of his Syntax is commended); Bäbler,
*Beiträge zu einer Gesch. d. Lat. Gr. im MA*, 116 f; Neudecker, *Das Doctrinale*
(Pirna, 1885); and Gröber, II i 390. Alexander is mentioned in the *Epp.
Obscurorum Virorum*, i *Epp.* 7, 25, ii *Ep.* 35.

[2] ed. Wrobel (1887); cp. Bäbler, 95 f; Norden, *Kunstprosa*, 741 n.;
Manitius in *Mitt.* 35 f; Gröber, II i 389 f. His date (1212 Leyser, Ducange,
Reichling) rests on the somewhat ambiguous lines : ' anno milleno centeno
bis duodeno | condidit Ebrardus Graecismum Bethuniensis '. Haase (45)
incorrectly interpreted this as 1124. On his ignorance of Greek, cp. *ib.* 15.
He fills 60 folios of the ' Canterbury lesson-book ' (*c.* 1480) described in
Gasquet's *Essays*, 279. Conrad von Mure produced a *Novus Graecismus* at
Zürich (1281), cp. Bursian, i 84 f.

[3] Thurot, 118 n. 2.        [4] *Comp. Phil.* 453 ; p. 594 *supra.*

Latin Grammar and cognate subjects[1]. The second is Robert
Kilwardby, archbishop of Canterbury (1272–9), who was a Master
of Arts of Paris and famous as a commentator on Priscian[2]. In
the thirteenth century Priscian was compelled to share the place
of honour with his commentators Helias and Kilwardby, while
in the fourteenth he was practically superseded by the modern
compilations of Alexander of Villedieu and Eberhard of Bethune[3].
These last owed much of their popularity to the fact that they
were written in Latin verse. Verse was also the medium used
by a Canon of Hildesheim, Ludolf of Luchow, for his treatise on
Syntax known as *Florista*, beginning with 'Flores grammaticae
propono scribere', which was widely used in Germany, Flanders
and France[4]. Even in the prose grammars of the previous
century the principal rules had always been given in verse, as
an aid to the memory. In this second period any Greek words
that occur in the MSS of the grammarians are mechanically copied,
and are often wrongly read and erroneously explained. Latin
Grammar ceases to be cultivated as the art of speaking and
writing Latin with correctness. It has now become a purely
speculative science.

Modern Syntax owes much to the grammarians of the Middle
Ages. In the thirteenth century a complete system of philosophical grammar was composed, which was destined to hold its
ground in the schools for two centuries. The work in which
this philosophy of grammar was first laid down was entitled
*De Modis Significandi*, and its teachers were called *Modistae*.
It has been variously attributed to Thomas Aquinas or Thomas
of Erfurt or Duns Scotus in century xiii[5], and even to Albert
the Saxon in the following century. It was the theme of
several commentaries, and of manuals such as that of Michael

---

[1] p. 550 n. 10 *supra*; and Bäbler, 172, 175–8.

[2] Comm. on Books i—xv in Camb. Univ. Library, MS Kk. 3. 20.

[3] *Chartul. Univ. Paris.* iii 145.

[4] Florista, Papias, Hugutio, Michael Modista, and Joannes de Garlandia
are all satirised by Erasmus in his *Conflictus Thaliae*, Act ii, *Opera* i 892;
cp. Rabelais i 14 (*Journ. of Cl. and S. Phil.* iv 6 note); also Erasmus, *Epp.*
2, 79, 507, 810, and 394 (Gudanus to Battus), ed. Leyden.

[5] p. 599 *supra*.

de Marbais already mentioned. These manuals were denounced
by the early humanists because of the barbarous character of
their Latinity, the inordinate number of their definitions, and
the extreme subtlety of their distinctions[1]; but much that was
useful in them was incorporated in the new text-books[2].

The grammarians of the Middle Ages dealt with Latin as
the living language of the Church and the Schools, and it was
precisely because it was a living language that it departed
further and further from the classical standard. Founded on
the Vulgate and the Fathers, it enlarged its vocabulary by
incorporating names of things unknown to the ancients, together
with technical terms of the Schools, whether invented by the
Schoolmen or the Grammarians. We owe 'instance' to the
former[3], and 'substantive' (in the ordinary sense, different from
that of Priscian[4]) to the latter. It is open to Seneca[5] to complain
that he cannot translate τὸ ὄν except by *quod est*, but Thomas
Aquinas and Duns Scotus would have felt no such difficulty,
and Quintilian[6] would not have condemned them for using *ens*
or *essentia.* 'If fear' (says Priscian[7]) 'had prevented authors from
using any new words, which were necessarily demanded either by
the nature of things or by the desire of expressing a certain
meaning, *perpetuis Latinitas angustiis damnata mansisset*'. Among
changes of Syntax, the commonest are the use of *quod* or *quia*,
instead of the Accusative with the Infinitive; *fore*, for *esse*, with
the Future Participle; the Accusative for the Ablative Absolute;
and *quatenus* in the 'final' sense of *ut*. Even Grammarians
gravely endeavour to maintain the legitimacy of the constructions
*legitur Virgilium*[8] and *sillogizantem ponendum est terminos*[9]. The

---

[1] *e.g.* Erasmus, in his *Antibarbarus*, calls Michael an *autor insulsissimus.*

[2] Haase, 38—42, 44 f; Reichling's ed. of Alexander, pp. cvi—cx.

[3] *instantia* used for ἔνστασις in Buridan, *in Metaph. Arist. Quaestiones*
(Prantl, iv 35); in the secondary sense of 'example', not found in English
earlier than 1586.

[4] *verbum* (not nomen) *substantivum* is normal in Priscian.

[5] *Ep.* 58 § 7.                                [6] viii 3, 33.

[7] viii 92; cp. Paulsen, *Gesch. des gelehrten Unterrichts*, i 42[2]; Reichling,
*l. c.* iv—vi.

[8] 'There-is-a-reading-of Virgil'. Thurot, 302 f.

[9] *ib.* 307 f.

scholastic Latin of the twelfth and thirteenth centuries degenerates in the fourteenth; and this degeneracy was doubtless accelerated by the uncouth style of the renderings of Aristotle which began to be common in the thirteenth century[1].

Grammar was the portal of all the Liberal Arts; the latter could only be approached through the study of the 'parts of speech':—*qui nescit partes, in vanum tendit ad artes*[2]. But it was only one of the Seven Arts constituting the normal course of mediaeval study. Combined with Logic and Rhetoric, it formed the *trivium*, with which ordinary students were generally content. In the case of the more advanced, the study of these three Arts was followed by that of the *quadrivium*, consisting of Music, Arithmetic, Geometry and Astronomy[3]. The late Latin couplet summing up the Seven Arts in two memorial lines corresponding to these divisions is well known to many who may not have heard the name of its author, or rather its earliest recorder[4]:—

*The conflict between the Arts and the Authors*

'GRAM loquitur; DIA vera docet; RHET verba colorat;
MUS canit; AR numerat; GE ponderat; AST colit astra'.

---

[1] Cp. C. Thurot, *Doctrines Grammaticales au Moyen Age*, in *Notices et Extraits*, xxii 2 (1868) pp. 591, esp. 60—121, 500–6; and V. Le Clerc, *Hist. Litt. de la France au 14ᵉ s.* (1865), 420 f, 426 f; also F. Haase, *De Medii Aevi Studiis Philologicis* (Breslau, 1856), and *Vorlesungen* (1874), i 12—14; Paulsen, *Gesch. des gelehrten Unterrichts* (1884; ed. 2, 1896), i 40—48²; Specht, *Gesch. des Unterrichtswesens* (1885), 86—96; Eckstein, *Lat. u. Gr. Unterricht* (1887), 54 f; Schmid, *Gesch. der Erziehung*, ii i (1892) 299, 439; Salvioli, in *Rivista Europea*, xiv 732 f; and Gröber's *Grundriss*, ii i 251. The study and use of Latin in Germany is treated by Jakob Burckhard, *De linguae latinae in Germania...fatis* (2 vols, 1713, Suppl. 1721). On mediaeval Grammar, cp. Bäbler's *Beiträge* (1885).

[2] 'Metrista' (Haase, 44); Buoncompagno (ap. Thurot, 90), qui partes ignorat, se ad artes transferre non debet. A woodcut in Reisch, *Margarita Philosophica* (1504), copied in Geiger's *Renaissance*, 499, and in Reicke, *Der Gelehrte* (1900), Abb. 43, exhibits Grammar opening the gate of a tower with representatives of the Arts looking out of the windows in the successive storeys, and with that of Theology on the summit.

[3] See esp. G. Meier, *Die Sieben Freien Künste im MA*, Einsiedeln, 1886–7; also Schmid, *l.c.* ii i 439—448; and Specht, *l.c.* 81—139.

[4] The Franciscan Scotist, Nicolaus de Orbellis (*Dorbellus*), d. 1455; born and died at Angers; lived chiefly at Poitiers. *Logica*, f. 3; Prantl, iv 175.

The Middle Ages were the battle-ground of a struggle between the study of the Liberal Arts, as represented in meagre manuals like that of Martianus Capella, and the study of the classical authors themselves. The study of the Arts was regarded as subservient not only to the study of the Scriptures[1], but also to that of theoretic Theology ; and, in a work of art belonging to the close of the Middle Ages, a fresco of the Spanish Chapel in Florence (c. 1355), we may see Thomas Aquinas enthroned among the Prophets and Evangelists, while, in a lower row, a subordinate position is assigned to the personifications and the representatives of the Liberal Arts[2]. But the study of the Arts, though subordinate to that of the Scriptures, was deemed far more important than that of the Authors. In comparison with the latter, the text-books of the Arts in general, and of Logic in particular, were considered safer reading : a syllogism might possibly involve a fallacy, but it was at any rate free from the taint of paganism[3]. From the first part of the eleventh century, the influence of the Schoolmen made the *schools* of Paris the stronghold of the study of Logic ; and, at the beginning of the thirteenth, we find the earliest statute of the *university* of Paris insisting on the study of Plato and Aristotle alone, to the neglect of a general classical education[4]. Meanwhile, in the twelfth, an interest in the Classics still survived at Chartres during the three years (1137–40) in which John of Salisbury was studying there, under one of Bernard's pupils, William of Conches, and Richard l'Évêque[5]. Bernard had been succeeded as chancellor by Gilbert de la Porrée (1126) and ultimately by Bernard's brother Theodoric (1141—c. 1150–5), who composed (c. 1141) a great work on the Seven Liberal Arts, treating each of them in

---

[1] Alcuin, ci 853 Migne ; Abelard, ii 67 Cousin ; John of Salisbury, *Enth.* 373 f, 441–5, etc. (Norden, *Kunstprosa*, 680–4).

[2] Woltmann and Woermann, *History of Painting*, i fig. 128 (p. 461 E.T.).

[3] Cp. Rashdall, i 36. The mystic Hugo of St Victor (d. 1141) regards the *Authors* as a mere 'appendix' to the *Arts*, describing the former as *ludicra*, and the latter as *seria*, Migne clxxvi 768 (Norden, 688 f).

[4] *ib.* i 71 f.

[5] p. 537 *supra.*

connexion with ancient or modern text-books.   For Grammar he quotes Donatus and Priscian; for Dialectic, Aristotle and Boëthius; for Rhetoric, Cicero; for Music and Arithmetic, Boëthius; for Geometry, Adelard of Bath (the translator of Euclid), with Frontinus and Isidore; for Astronomy, Hyginus and Ptolemy[1]. In this connexion it is interesting to point out that it was between 1134 and 1150[2], at a time when the influence of Bernard was still strong in Chartres, when his immediate pupils were actually teaching in its famous school, and while his brother Theodoric was successively 'master of the school' and 'chancellor', that the right-hand door-way of the West Front of the cathedral was adorned with figures of the Seven Arts, each of them associated with an ancient personage, Grammar with Priscian, Dialectic with Aristotle, Rhetoric with Cicero, Music with Pythagoras, Arithmetic with Nicomachus, Geometry with Euclid, and Astronomy with Ptolemy[3].

GRAMMAR AND PRISCIAN
from Chartres Cathedral.

(Viollet-le-Duc, *Dict. Archit.* ii 2.)

We may here notice a certain preference for Greek authorities, even in cases where the text-books in current use were Latin; and it will be observed that Boëthius, who fills a large part of the *Eptateuchon* of

---

[1] Abbé Clerval, *Les Écoles de Chartres au Moyen-Age* (1895), p. 222 f (synopsis of the *Eptateuchon*).  Cp. p. 533 n. 4.

[2] The dates given by Abbé Clerval, *Guide Chartrain*, 7 f.

[3] Cuts in Viollet-le-Duc, *Dict. Archit.* s.v. *Arts Libéraux*, and E. Mâle, *L'Art Religieux du xiiie s.* (1898), 117.   The idea was borrowed from Martianus Capella (p. 243 *supra*).   Among other cathedrals, where the Seven Liberal Arts were represented (at a later date than at Chartres, and unaccompanied by classical personages) are those of Laon and Sens (xii), Auxerre (end

Theodoric, is absent from the sculptures. These are approximately assigned to 1145[1]; it may therefore be conjectured that the absence of any public recognition of Boëthius among the external sculptures of the cathedral may have been possibly due to the suspicions of heresy, which in 1146–8[2] gathered round the name of Gilbert de la Porrée, chancellor of Chartres, in connexion with his commentary on the four books *On the Trinity*, ascribed to Boëthius. But the names of the above representatives of the Arts, though probably correct, are only conjectural; and, after all, it is from Boëthius that the designations of the Greek authorities on Music, Arithmetic and Geometry are derived. Apart from the cathedral of Clermont, that of Chartres stands alone in according, among its works of art, a place of honour to representatives of the old classical world[3]; and this is true not only of the sculptures of the West Front (1145), but also of those of the North Porch (1275), where Medicine is represented by Hippocrates, Geometry by Archimedes, Painting by Apelles, and Philosophy by Aristotle[4].

To the school of Chartres (as we have already seen)[5] John of Salisbury owes his excellent Latin style and his general interest in Classics. He regretfully remarks that, since the days that he spent under the pupils of Bernard, 'less time and less care have been bestowed on *grammar*, and persons who profess all arts, liberal and mechanical, are ignorant of the *primary art*, without which a man proceeds in vain to the rest; for, albeit the other studies assist literature, yet this has the sole privilege of making one lettered'[6]. The results of the classical education

of xiii), Rouen and Soissons. At Clermont Aristotle, Cicero and Pythagoras are represented with the attributes of the corresponding Arts, but the Arts themselves are absent. The statues of Philosophy at Laon and at Sens are modelled on the description in Boëthius, *Cons.* i 1 (Mâle, pp. 122–5, and, in general, 102—121). For the representations of the Seven Arts in the *Hortus Deliciarum*, see plate on p. 559 *supra*.

[1] W. Vöge, *Die Anfänge des monumentalen Stils im MA* (1894), pp. 118—123, 156; E. Mâle, 119.

[2] Poole, 179—191.          [3] Mâle, 121, 426 f.

[4] Cuts in Viollet-le-Duc, ii 8—9.

[5] pp. 517—522.

[6] *Met.* i 27 (Poole, 122 f).

initiated by Bernard are also clearly seen in the author of the letters ascribed to Peter of Blois (*c.* 1140—1212)[1]. The writer of those letters was probably educated at Tours[2], studied theology in Paris under John of Salisbury[3], and resided in later life at Chartres[4]. In one of these letters the writer expresses his doubts about a pupil who, neglecting a knowledge of Grammar and classical authors, has betaken himself to the subtleties of Logic, 'which supply no proper foundation for literary learning'[5]. Similarly, Giraldus Cambrensis, writing in his old age (*c.* 1220), requires of all who desire to speak, not only *recte*, but also *lepide* and *ornate*, an education, not in the *trivium* alone, but also in the authors[6].

From the twelfth century onwards, a marked improvement in Latin versification is manifest in France. A careful study of models such as Statius, Lucan and Ovid, as well as Tibullus and Propertius, may be noted in the poems of Matthew of Vendôme[7]. Virgil, Horace, the elegiac poets and Martial are imitated by the best of the mediaeval Latin poets, Hildebert, archbishop of Tours[8].

In the history of classical studies in the Middle Ages an
Orleans     important place must be assigned to the struggle
between the schools of Paris and Orleans[9]. The latter had been founded in the age of Charles the Great by the bishop of Orleans, Theodulfus, whose familiarity with classical literature is proved by his poem *de libris quos legere solebam*[10].

---

[1] p. 542 *supra*.                                  [2] *Ep.* 12.

[3] *Epp.* 26; cp. 1, 22, and *Comm. in Job*, iii 26 ult. Giles.          [4] *Ep.* 49.

[5] *Ep.* 101, as printed in *Chartularium Univ. Paris.* i 27 f, grammaticae et auctorum scientia praetermissa volavit ad versutias logicorum...non est in talibus fundamentum scientiae litteralis, multisque perniciosa est ista subtilitas.

[6] *Prooem.* of *Speculum Eccl.*, preserved by Ant. Wood, quoted in Brewer's ed. iv 7. Cp. p. 544 *supra*.

[7] p. 552 *supra*.

[8] p. 551 *supra*. His *Moralis Philosophia* (clxxi Migne) abounds in quotations from the Classics.

[9] Delisle in *Annuaire Bulletin de la Soc. de l'Histoire de France*, vii (1869), 139—154; Mlle A. de Foulques de Villaret, *Mém. de la Soc. archéologique de l'Orléanais*, xiv (1875) 299—440; Norden, 724 f; Rashdall, ii 136–8.

[10] i 543 Dümmler.

The classical tradition was maintained at Orleans, and was further strengthened by the proximity of the schools of Fleury[1] and Chartres. The school of Orleans sent forth a series of men of learning in the eleventh and twelfth centuries. During the twelfth and thirteenth centuries in particular, the art of writing Latin letters flourished at Orleans and in its immediate neighbourhood. That art became, indeed, so widely popular in the thirteenth century, that it even ceased to retain the distinction, which it had won in the hands of men of mark in the previous century[2]. The success with which classical composition was cultivated at Orleans is proved by the fact that the three papal secretaries of 1159 to 1185 (besides several Latin poets, and commentators on Ovid and Lucan[3]) were produced by that school. A Latin versifier, who wrote in England about the year 1200, places Orleans as a school of Literature (literally 'Authors') on a level with Salerno, Bologna and Paris as schools of Medicine, Law and Logic respectively[4]. While the school of Orleans was attacked by Alexander of Villedieu[5], the Latin poets produced by that school were lauded by two poets of English birth, Alexander Neckam[6] and Joannes de Garlandia[7]. Even when the school of Chartres, overshadowed by Paris, began to decline, the classical tradition lived on at Orleans till at least the middle of the

---

[1] Cuissard-Gaucheron in *Mém. de la Soc. archéol. de l'Orléanais*, xiv (1875) 551—715. The great abbey church of St Benoît-sur-Loire is all that now survives of the buildings of the famous school of Fleury. Its MSS were dispersed in 1562.

[2] N. Valois, *De Arte Scribendi Epistolas apud Gallicos Medii Aevi Scriptores* (1880), 24, 28 f, 39 f, 43. Cp. Gröber's *Grundriss*, II i 252. On Bernard Silvester's *Summa Dictaminum* (*c.* 1153) see p. 534 *supra*. On mediaeval *formulae* for letter-writing, cp. Langlois, in *Notices et Extraits*, xxxiv–v, and C. H. Haskins, in *Amer. Hist. Rev.* iii 203 f.

[3] In one of the models of the art of letter-writing the student asks for commentaries on Virgil and Lucan. There were glosses on Ovid by Arnoul le Roux of Orleans (c. xii).

[4] Galfridus de Vino Salvo, *Poëtria Nova*, 1009 f, with other passages quoted by Delisle, Reichling (*Mon. Germ. Paed.* XII p. xxxvii f), and Norden, 727 f. Cp. p. 548 *supra*.

[5] *Ecclesiale*, prolog.

[6] *De Naturis Rerum*, p. 454 Wright.

[7] *Ars Lectoria* (1234), Delisle *l. c.* p. 145.

thirteenth century[1]. In that century the school acquired a new
interest through its struggle with the Sorbonne. Orleans had
neglected the study of philosophy and had insisted solely on the
attainment of purity of style through the direct study of classical
authors, especially Virgil and Lucan. The *Authors* were supreme
at Orleans, the *Arts* in Paris[2]. This contrast is clearly shown in
certain Latin poems of the twelfth and thirteenth centuries[3]. It is
still more vividly represented in the contemporary poem of Henri
d'Andely on the *Battle of the Seven Arts*[4], the author of which was
a *magister* and a *clericus* of Rouen in 1259[5]. The conflict between
the study of philosophy in Paris and the cultivation of literature,
especially poetic literature, at Orleans, is here represented as a
battle between the forces of Logic and of Grammar. The piece
is not without interest as a precursor of a far better known
production, Swift's *Battle of the Books* (1697). The following
may serve as a brief summary:—

Grammar unfurls her banner before the walls of Orleans, and summons all
her forces to the fray. Around that banner gather 'Homer' and Claudian,
Persius, Donatus and Priscian, with many another knight and squire. They
are soon reinforced by the chieftains of Orleans itself, when they all combine in
a march on Paris. Logic trembles at their approach ; she summons aid from
Tournai and elsewhere, and places in a chariot three of her champions who
are skilled in all the Liberal Arts. Rhetoric has meanwhile taken up her
stand with the Lombard knights[6] at a fort six leagues distant from Paris[7],
where her forces are joined by those of certain other Arts :—Physic, Surgery,
Music, Astronomy, Arithmetic and Geometry, while Theology remains apart
in Paris. Among the champions of that city are Plato and Aristotle. Donatus
begins the battle by attacking Plato; Aristotle meanwhile attacks Priscian,

---

[1] Rashdall, ii 138.

[2] The Statute of 1254 prescribes certain parts of Aristotle, with Donatus,
Boëthius and Priscian, but none of the Latin Classics.

[3] Quoted by Delisle, *l.c.*; others add a passage from the discourse delivered
at Toulouse by the learned monk, Hélinand, in 1229 : 'ecce quaerunt clerici
*Parisiis artes liberales*, *Aurelianis auctores*, Bononiae codices, Salerni pyxides,
Toleti daemones, et nusquam mores' (*Sermo* 2, *In Asc. Domini*).

[4] Gröber's *Grundriss*, II i 820. Gaston Paris places it 'vers le tiers du xiii[e]
siècle' (*Litt. Fr. au MA* § 110), or after 1236 (*Romania*, xi 141).

[5] *Registrum Visitationum* of abp of Rouen, Eude Rigaud, p. 334, quoted
by Héron, ed. 1880.

[6] See n. 3, p. 677 *infra*.          [7] Mont-l'Héri.

but is thrown from his steed and continues to fight on foot against Grammar,
*i.e.* Priscian (who is aided by his modern 'nephews', Alexander and Eberhard),
when he is himself attacked, not by Priscian only, but by Virgil and Horace,
Lucan and Statius, Persius and Juvenal, Propertius, Sedulius, Arator, Terence
and 'Homer'; and would certainly have surrendered, but for the aid of Logic
and the several impersonations of the *Organon*, *Physics* and *Ethics*, with
Porphyry, Macrobius and Boëthius.    Dan Barbarime, though a vassal of
Grammar, takes up arms against her, because he also holds lands in the
domain of Logic.    While the battle goes on raging, the Authors find it hard
to hold their own, although Ovid and Seneca hasten to their aid, together with
certain modern poets, including Jean de Hauteville and Alain de Lille[1].
Logic, however, is obliged to withdraw to the fort held by Rhetoric and
Astronomy, and is there beleaguered by the forces of Grammar, till she sends
down an envoy who unfortunately knows so little of the rules of speech that
he cannot even deliver his message clearly and is accordingly compelled to
return without result.    Meanwhile Astronomy flings her lightning on her foes,
burns their tents and scatters their forces; and, since that day, the Muse of
Poetry has buried herself out of sight, somewhere between Orleans and Blois,
never daring to show herself in the land where her rival, Logic, is holding
sway.    But she is honoured still by the Britons and the Germans[2], although
the Lombards hate her[3].    'This will last' (adds the poet) 'for thirty years;
but the next generation will once more give heed to Grammar.    Meanwhile,
I declare that any scholar who cannot construe his text is a contemptible
person, since, in every science, whoever is not perfect in his parts of speech,
must be deemed the merest boy'[4].

[1] Only indicated by the names of their poems, *Architrenius* and *Anti-
claudianus* respectively (pp. 546, 553 *supra*).    Similarly, Gautier de Châtillon
is clearly meant by 'geta ducis Macidum', which an editor of the text has
twice refrained from correcting into *Gesta ducis Macedum*, the first words of
the *Alexandreis* (p. 552 *supra*).

[2] *Li Breton et li Alemant.*    'Les Anglais', says d'Aussy in his paraphrase,
implying that Bretons are not meant.    In l. 404 the poet uses the unambiguous
*l'Englois* in allusion to Adam du Petit-Pont.

[3] A reference to the Lombard usurers in France, who are represented as
hating the Muse of Poetry, only because they dun poets for their dues.

[4]
> *Quar en toute Science est gars,*
> *Mestres, qui n'entent bien ses pars.*

Text in Appendix to Jubinal's ed. of Rutebeuf ii (1839) 415—435 and in iii
(1875) 325—347; also in *Œuvres de Henri d'Andeli*, limited ed. by A. Héron,
Rouen, 1880 (reviewed in *Romania*, xi 137—144); abstract by Legrand
d'Aussy in *Notices et Extraits*, v (1800) 496—512, and in Norden, 728-31.
Cp. Augustin, *Untersuchungen über die Werke Henris d'Andeli*, Marburg,
1886, and esp. L. J. Paetow, *The Battle of the Seven Arts*, ed. and trans., with
facsimiles of the two MSS, in *Memoirs of the Univ. of California*, Berkeley, 1914.

Before the year 1300 the literary school of Orleans had been
thrown into the shade by the schools of the Seven Arts in Paris,
and the study of Law alone survived[1].    But the fourteenth century
saw the fulfilment of the poet's prophecy of a revival of learning,
which began, not in France or Germany or England, but in
Northern Italy, where, in the early years of that century, the
morning-star of the Renaissance arose in the person of Petrarch.

[1] V. Le Clerc, *Hist. Litt.* 278[2] ; Rashdall, ii 138 f ; and, in general, L. J.
Paetow, *The Arts Course at Medieval Universities with special reference to
Grammar and Rhetoric*, Champaign, Illinois (1910), 134 pp., showing 'how
and why the study of language and literature was neglected especially during
the century before Petrarch'.

# INDEX.

# GREEK INDEX.

CAMBRIDGE: PRINTED BY J. B. PEACE, M.A., AT THE UNIVERSITY PRESS.